CRIME
IN THE
UNITED STATES

2012

SIXTH EDITION

CRIME
IN THE
UNITED STATES

2012

SIXTH EDITION

 Bernan Press

Published in the United States of America
by Bernan Press, a wholly owned subsidiary of
The Rowman & Littlefield Publishing Group, Inc.
4501 Forbes Boulevard, Suite 200
Lanham, Maryland 20706

Bernan Press
800-865-3457
info@bernan.com
www.bernan.com

ISBN: 978-1-59888-521-7
eISBN: 978-1-59888-522-4

∞™ The paper used in this publication meets the minimum requirements of
American National Standard for Information Sciences—Permanence of
Paper for Printed Library Materials, ANSI/NISO Z39.48-1992.
Manufactured in the United States of America.

CONTENTS

SECTION I:
SUMMARY OF THE UNIFORM CRIME REPORTING (UCR) PROGRAM

SUMMARY OF THE UNIFORM CRIME REPORTING (UCR) PROGRAM

Bernan Press is proud to present its sixth edition of *Crime in the United States*. This title was formerly published by the Federal Bureau of Investigation (FBI), but is no longer available in printed form from the government. This edition contains final data from 2010, the latest data that are currently available.

This section describes the history of the UCR Program, which collects the data used in *Crime in the United States,* and it examines the best way to use the data in this publication.

About the UCR Program

The UCR Program's primary objective is to generate reliable information for use in law enforcement administration, operation, and management; however, over the course of the program, its data have become one of the country's leading social indicators.

The UCR Program is a nationwide, cooperative statistical effort of more than 18,000 city, university and college, county, state, tribal, and federal law enforcement agencies voluntarily reporting data on crimes brought to their attention. Since 1930, the FBI has administered the UCR Program and continued to assess and monitor the nature and type of crime in the Nation. Criminologists, sociologists, legislators, municipal planners, the media, and other students of criminal justice use the data for varied research and planning purposes. In 2010, law enforcement agencies active in the UCR Program represented more than 300 million United States inhabitants—97.4 percent of the total population. The coverage amounted to 98.4 percent of the population in Metropolitan Statistical Areas, 92.3 percent of the population in cities outside metropolitan areas, and 92.7 percent of the population in nonmetropolitan counties.

Note for Users

It is important for UCR data users to remember that the FBI's primary objective is to generate a reliable set of crime statistics for use in law enforcement administration, operation, and management. The FBI does not provide a ranking of agencies; instead, it provides alphabetical tabulations of states, metropolitan statistical areas, cities with over 10,000 inhabitants, suburban and rural counties, and colleges and universities. Law enforcement officials use these data for their designed purposes. Additionally, the public relies on these data for information about the fluctuations in levels of crime from year to year, while criminologists, sociologists, legislators, city planners, media outlets, and other students of criminal justice use them for a variety of research and planning purposes. Since crime is a sociological phenomenon influenced by a variety of factors, the FBI discourages data users from ranking agencies and using the data as a measurement of the effectiveness of law enforcement.

To ensure that data are uniformly reported, the FBI provides contributing law enforcement agencies with a handbook that explains how to classify and score offenses and provides uniform crime offense definitions. Acknowledging that offense definitions may vary from state to state, the FBI cautions agencies to report offenses according to the guidelines provided in the handbook, rather than by local or state statutes. Most agencies make a good faith effort to comply with established guidelines.

The UCR Program publishes the statistics most commonly requested by data users. More information regarding the availability of UCR Program data is available by telephone at (304) 625-4995, by fax at (304) 625-5394, or by e-mail at cjis_comm@leo.gov. E-mail data requests cannot be processed without the requester's full name, mailing address, and contact telephone number.

Variables Affecting Crime: Caution against Ranking

Until data users examine all the variables that affect crime in a town, city, county, state, region, or college or university, they can make no meaningful comparisons. In each edition of *Crime in the United States*, many entities—including news media, tourism agencies, and other organizations with an interest in crime in the nation—use reported figures to compile rankings of cities and counties. However, these rankings are merely a quick choice made by that data user; they provide no insight into the many variables that mold the crime in a particular town, city, county, state, or region. Consequently, these rankings may lead to simplistic and/or incomplete analyses, which can create misleading perceptions and thus adversely affect cities and counties, along with their residents.

Considering Other Characteristics of a Jurisdiction

To assess criminality and law enforcement's response from jurisdiction to jurisdiction, data users must consider many variables, some of which (despite having significant impact on crime) are not readily measurable or applicable among all locales. Geographic and demographic factors specific to each jurisdiction must be considered and applied in order to make an accurate and complete assessment of crime in that jurisdiction. Several sources of information are available to help the researcher explore the variables that affect crime in a particular locale. U.S. Census Bureau data, for example, can help the user better understand the makeup of a locale's population. The transience of the population, its racial and ethnic makeup, and its composition by age and gender, educational levels, and prevalent family structures are all key factors in assessing and understanding crime.

Local chambers of commerce, planning offices, and similar entities provide information regarding the economic and cultural makeup of cities and counties. Understanding a jurisdiction's industrial/economic base, its dependence upon neighboring jurisdictions, its transportation system, its economic dependence on nonresidents (such as tourists and convention attendees), and its proximity to military installations, correctional institutions, and other types of facilities all contribute to accurately gauging and interpreting the crime known to and reported by law enforcement.

The strength (including personnel and other resources) and aggressiveness of a jurisdiction's law enforcement agency are also key factors in understanding the nature and extent of crime occurring in that area. Although information pertaining to the number of sworn and civilian employees can be found in this publication, it cannot be used alone as an assessment of the emphasis that a community places on enforcing the law. For example, one city may report more crime than another comparable city because its law enforcement agency identifies more offenses. Attitudes of citizens toward crime and their crime reporting practices—especially for minor offenses—also have an impact on the volume of crimes known to police.

Make Valid Assessments of Crime

It is essential for all data users to become as well educated as possible about understanding and quantifying the nature and extent of crime in the United States and in the more than 18,000 jurisdictions represented by law enforcement contributors to the UCR Program. Valid assessments are possible only with careful study and analysis of the various unique conditions that affect each local law enforcement jurisdiction.

Some factors that are known to affect the volume and type of crime occurring from place to place are:

- Population density and degree of urbanization

- Variations in composition of population, particularly in the concentration of youth

- Stability of the population with respect to residents' mobility, commuting patterns, and transient factors

- Modes of transportation and highway systems

- Economic conditions, including median income, poverty level, and job availability

- Cultural factors and educational, recreational, and religious characteristics

- Family conditions, with respect to divorce and family cohesiveness

- Climate

- Effective strength of law enforcement agencies

- Administrative and investigative emphases of law enforcement

- Policies of other components of the criminal justice system (that is, prosecutorial, judicial, correctional, and probational policies)

- Residents' attitudes toward crime

- Crime reporting practices of residents

Although many of the listed factors equally affect the crime of a particular area, the UCR Program makes no attempt to relate them to the data presented. **The data user is therefore cautioned against comparing statistical data of individual reporting units from cities, counties, metropolitan areas, states, or colleges or universities solely on the basis on their population coverage or student enrollment.** Until data users examine all the variables that affect crime in a town, city, county, state, region, or college or university, they can make no meaningful comparisons.

Historical Background

Since 1930, the FBI has administered the UCR Program; the agency continues to assess and monitor the nature and type of crime in the nation. Data users look to the UCR Program for various research and planning purposes.

Recognizing a need for national crime statistics, the IACP formed the Committee on Uniform Crime Records in the 1920s to develop a system of uniform crime statistics. After studying state criminal codes and making an evaluation of the recordkeeping practices in use, the Committee completed a plan for crime reporting that became the foundation of the UCR Program in 1929. The plan included standardized offense definitions for seven main offense classifications known as Part I crimes to gauge fluctuations in the overall volume and rate of crime. Developers also instituted the Hierarchy Rule as the main reporting procedure for what is now known as the Summary Reporting System of the UCR Program.

Seven main offense classifications, known as Part I crimes, were chosen to gauge the state of crime in the nation. These seven offense classifications included the violent crimes of murder and nonnegligent manslaughter, forcible rape, robbery, and aggravated assault; also included were the property crimes of burglary, larceny-theft, and motor vehicle theft. By congressional mandate, arson was added as the eighth Part I offense category. Data collection for arson began in 1979.

During the early planning of the program, it was recognized that the differences among criminal codes precluded a mere aggregation of state statistics to arrive at a national total. Also, because of the variances in punishment for the same offenses in different states, no distinction between felony and misdemeanor crimes was possible. To avoid these problems and provide nationwide uniformity in crime reporting, standardized offense definitions were developed. Law enforcement agencies use these to submit data without regard for local statutes. UCR Program offense definitions can be found in Appendix II.

In January 1930, 400 cities (representing 20 million inhabitants in 43 states) began participating in the UCR Program. Congress enacted Title 28, Section 534, of the United States Code that same year, which authorized the attorney general to gather crime information. The attorney general, in turn, designated the FBI to serve as the national clearinghouse for the collected crime data. Since then, data based on uniform classifications and procedures for reporting have been obtained annually from the nation's law enforcement agencies.

Advisory Groups

Providing vital links between local law enforcement and the FBI for the UCR Program are the Criminal Justice Information Systems Committees of the IACP and the National Sheriffs' Association (NSA). The IACP represents the thousands of police departments nationwide, as it has since the program began. The NSA encourages sheriffs throughout the country to participate fully in the program. Both committees serve the program in advisory capacities.

In 1988, a Data Providers' Advisory Policy Board was established. This board operated until 1993, when it combined with the National Crime Information Center Advisory Policy Board to form a single Advisory Policy Board (APB) to address all FBI criminal justice information services. The current APB works to ensure continuing emphasis on UCR-related issues. The Association of State Uniform Crime Reporting Programs (ASUCRP) focuses on UCR issues within individual state law enforcement associations and also promotes interest in the UCR Program. These organizations foster widespread and responsible use of uniform crime statistics and lend assistance to data contributors.

Redesign of UCR

Although UCR data collection was originally conceived as a tool for law enforcement administration, the data were widely used by other entities involved in various forms of social planning by the 1980s. Recognizing the need for more detailed crime statistics, law enforcement called for a thorough evaluative study to modernize the UCR Program. The FBI formulated a comprehensive three-phase redesign effort. The Bureau of Justice Statistics (BJS) an agency in the Department of Justice responsible for funding criminal justice information projects, agreed to underwrite the first two phases. These phases were conducted by an independent contractor and structured to determine what, if any, changes should be made to the current program. The third phase would involve implementation of the changes identified.

The final report, the *Blueprint for the Future of the Uniform Crime Reporting Program,* was released in the summer of 1985. It specifically outlined recommendations for an expanded, improved UCR Program to meet future informational needs. Three areas of enhancement were recommended for the UCR Program:

- Offenses and arrests would be reported using an incident-based system.

- Data would be collected on two levels. Agencies in level one would report important details about those offenses comprising the Part I crimes, their victims, and arrestees. Level two would consist of law enforcement agencies covering populations of more than 100,000 and a sampling of smaller agencies that would collect expanded detail on all significant offenses.

- A quality assurance program would be introduced.

In January 1986, phase III of the redesign effort began, guided by the general recommendations set forth in the *Blueprint.* The FBI selected an experimental site to implement the redesigned program, while contractors developed new data guidelines and system specifications. Upon selecting the South Carolina Law Enforcement Division (SLED), which enlisted the cooperation of nine local law enforcement agencies, the FBI developed automated data capture specifications to adapt the SLED's state system to the national UCR Program's standards, and the BJS funded the revisions. The pilot demonstration ran from March 1 through September 30, 1987, and resulted in further refinement of the guidelines and specifications.

March 1–3, 1988, the FBI held a National UCR Conference to present the new system to law enforcement and to obtain feedback on its acceptability. Attendees of the Conference passed three overall recommendations without dissent: first, that there be established a new, incident-based national crime reporting system; second, that the FBI manage this program, and third, that an Advisory Policy Board composed of law enforcement executives be formed to assist in directing and implementing the new program. Furthermore, attendees recommended that the implementation of national incident-based reporting proceed at a pace commensurate with the resources and limitations of contributing law enforcement agencies.

Establishing the NIBRS

From March 1988 through January 1989, the FBI developed and assumed management of the UCR Program's National Incident-Based Reporting System (NIBRS), and by April 1989, the first test of NIBRS data was submitted to the national UCR Program. Over the next few years, the national IUCR Program published information about the rdesigned program in five documents:

- *Uniform Crime Reporting Handbook,* NIBRS Edition (1992) provides a nontechnical program overview focusing on definitions, policies, and procedures of the IBRS.

- *Data Submission Specifications* (May 1992) is used by local and state systems personnel, who are responsible for preparing magnetic media for submission to the FBI.

- Approaches to Implementing an Incident-Based System (July 1992) is a guide for system designers.

- *Error Message Manual* (revised December 1999) contains designations of mandatory and optional data elements, data element edits, and error messages.

- *Data Collection Guidelines* (revised August 2000) contains a system overview and descriptions of the offense codes, reports, data elements, and data values used in the system.

As more agencies inquired about the NIBRS, the FBI, in May 2002, made the *Handbook for Acquiring a Records Management System (RMS) that is Compatible with the NIBRS* available to agencies considering or developing automated incident-based records management systems. The handbook, developed under the sponsorship of the FBI and the BJS, provides instructions for planning and conducting a system acquisition and offers guidelines on preparing an agency for conversion to the new system and to the NIBRS.

Originally designed with 52 data elements, the redesigned NIBRS captures up to 57 data elements via 6 types of data segments: administrative, offense, victim property, offender, and arrestee. Although, in the late 1980s, the FBI committed to hold all changes to the NIBRS in abeyance until a substantial amount of contributors implemented the system, modifications have been necessary. The system's flexibility has allowed the collection of four additional pieces of information to be captured within an incident: bias-motivated offenses (1990), the presence of gang activity (1997), data for law enforcement officers killed and assaulted (2003), and data on cargo theft (2005).

The FBI began accepting NIBRS data from a handful of agencies in January 1989. As more contributing law enforcement agencies become educated about the rich data available through incident-based reporting and as resources permit, more agencies are implementing the NIBRS. Based on 2010 data submissions, approximately 43 percent of reporting agencies are certified for NIBRS participation. These agencies include one individual agency in each of the following: Alabama, Illinois, Mississippi, and the District of Columbia; as well as the state UCR Programs of the following 32 states: Arizona, Arkansas, Colorado, Connecticut, Delaware, Idaho, Iowa, Kansas, Kentucky, Louisiana, Maine, Massachusetts, Michigan, Missouri, Montana, Nebraska, New Hampshire, North Dakota, Ohio, Oklahoma, Oregon, Rhode Island, South Carolina, South Dakota, Tennessee, Texas, Utah, Vermont, Virginia, Washington, West Virginia, and Wisconsin. Among those that submit NIBRS data, 15 states (Arkansas, Delaware, Idaho, Iowa, Michigan, Montana, New Hampshire, North Dakota, Rhode Island, South Carolina, South Dakota, Tennessee, Vermont, Virginia, and West Virginia) submit all their data via the NIBRS. Eight state UCR Programs have tested the NIBRS. Five other programs are planning and developing the NIBRS, including four state agencies and Washington, D.C.

Suspension of the Crime Index and Modified Crime Index

In June 2004, the CJIS APB approved discontinuing the use of the Crime Index in the UCR Program and its publications and directed the FBI to publish a violent crime total and a property crime total. The Crime Index, first published in *Crime in the United States* in 1960, was the title used for a simple aggregation of the seven main offense classifications (Part I offenses) in the Summary Reporting System. The Modified Crime Index was the number of Crime Index offenses plus arson.

For several years the CJIS Division studied the appropriateness and usefulness of these indices and brought the matter before many advisory groups including the UCR Subcommittee of the CJIS APB, the ASUCRP, and a meeting of leading criminologists and sociologists hosted by the BJS. In short, the Crime Index and the Modified Crime Index were not true indicators of the degrees of criminality because they were always driven upward by the offense with the highest number, typically larceny-theft. The sheer volume of those offenses overshadowed more serious but less frequently committed offenses, creating a bias against a jurisdiction with a high number of larceny-thefts but a low number of other serious crimes such as murder and forcible rape.

Recent Development in UCR Program

In response to federal legislation outlined in the USA Patriot Improvement and Reauthorization Act of 2005, the UCR Program began accepting cargo theft data from local, state, tribal, and federal agencies on January 1, 2010. Congress commissioned the FBI to begin capturing crime data on human trafficking in the William Wilberforce Trafficking Victims Protection Reauthorization Act of 2008. The Matthew Shepard and James Byrd, Jr. Hate Crime Prevention Act of 2009 requires the collection of data on crimes motivated by "gender and gender identity" bias, as well as "crimes committed by, and crimes directed against, juveniles." The national UCR Program staff is developing collection strategies to meet both of these most recent mandates.

In addition, to meet a directive of the U.S. Government's Office of Management and Budget, the national UCR Program will expand race categories from four (White, Black, American Indian or Alaska Native, and Asian or Other Pacific Islander) to five (White, Black, American Indian or Alaska Native, Asian, and Native Hawaiian or Other Pacific Islander). The ethnicity categories will change from "Hispanic" to "Hispanic or Latino Origin" and from "Non-Hispanic" to "Not of Hispanic or Latino Origin."

UCR Redevelopment Project Update

To streamline the program's database management and quality control activities, the FBI created the UCR Redevelopment Project (UCRRP). The UCRRP's goal is to improve the efficiency, usability, and maintainability of the UCR Program while increasing the value to users. The redevelopment project will:

- decrease the time it takes to analyze data,

- reduce, to the point of elimination, the exchange of printed materials between agencies and the FBI,

- provide an enhanced external data query tool so that the public can view and analyze published UCR data from the Internet, and

- decrease the time needed to release and publish crime data.

To reach this goal, an effort is underway to transition all submissions to an electronic format on or before January 2013. After January 2013, the UCR Program will no longer accept paper or the electronic submissions of documents (for example, Portable Document Format files). The UCRRP is working with agencies to collect information and identify ways to assist in the transition, including the adoption of an electronic submission via the NIBRS, electronic Summary Reporting System, or Extensible Markup Language.

Expanded Offense Tables

Expanded offense data are the details of the various offenses that the Uniform Crime Reporting Program collects beyond the count of how many crimes law enforcement agencies report. These details may include the type of weapon used in a crime, the type or value of items stolen, and so forth. Expanded homicide data provide supplemen-tal details about murders such as the age, sex, and race of both the victim and the offender, the weapon used in the homicide, the circumstances surrounding the offense, and the relationship of the victim to the offender. In addition, expanded data includes trends (for example, 2-year comparisons) and rates per 100,000 inhabitants.

Expanded offense data, including expanded homicide data, are information collected beyond the reports of the number of crimes known. As a result, law enforcement agencies can report an offense without providing the supplemental data about that offense. These additional tables can be found at www.fbi.gov/about-us/cjis/ucr/crime-in-the-u.s/2010/crime-in-the-u.s.-2010/offenses-known-to-law-enforcement/expanded/expandedoffensemain .

About the Editor

Gwenavere W. Dunn is a research editor with Bernan Press. She holds a Master of Science degree in Human Resource Management from Trinity Washington University and is a former senior editor with the Board of Governors of the Federal Reserve System and managing editor of the *Federal Reserve Bulletin*. She has also served as assistant editor of *The Who, What, and Where of America*, also published by Bernan Press.

SECTION II:
OFFENSES KNOWN TO POLICE

VIOLENT CRIME

- Murder
- Forcible Rape
- Robbery
- Aggravated Assault

PROPERTY CRIME

- Burglary
- Larceny-Theft
- Motor Vehicle Theft
- Arson

VIOLENT CRIME

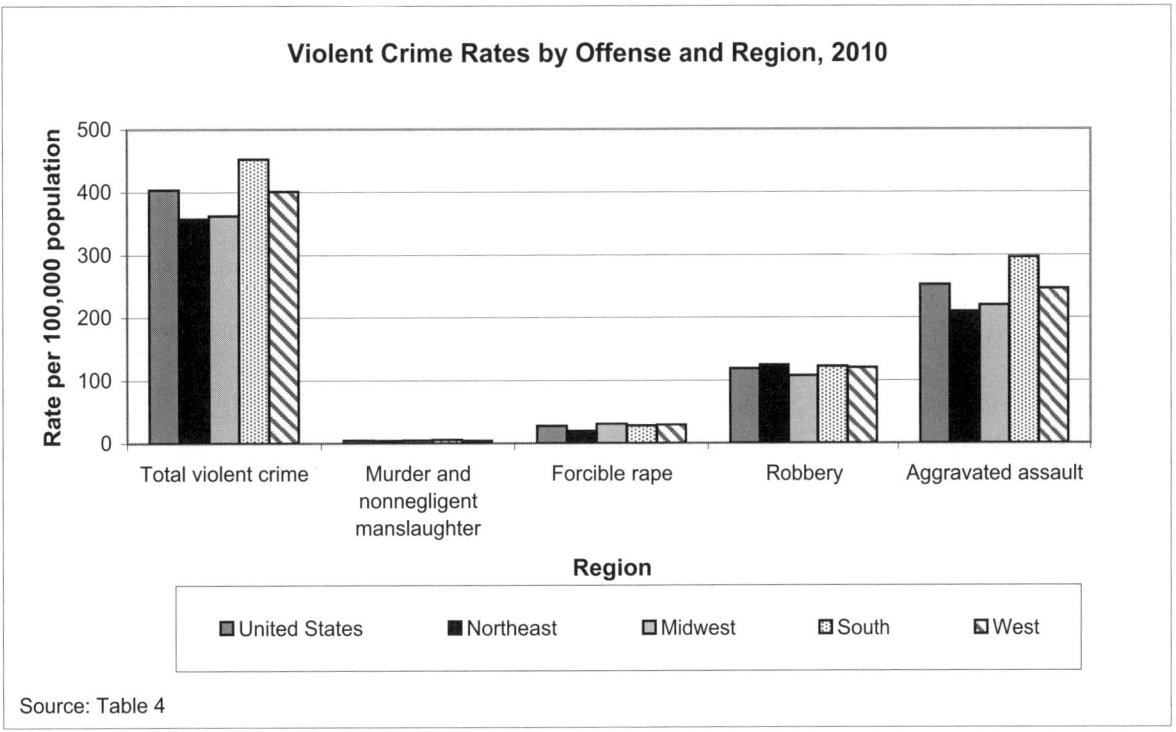

Violent Crime Rates by Offense and Region, 2010

Rate per 100,000 population

Region

■ United States   ■ Northeast   ▨ Midwest   ▨ South   ▨ West

Source: Table 4

Definition

Violent crime consists of four offenses: murder and non-negligent manslaughter, forcible rape, robbery, and aggravated assault. According to the Uniform Crime Reporting (UCR) Program, run by the Federal Bureau of Investigation (FBI), violent crimes involve either the use of force or the threat of force.

Data Collection

The data presented in *Crime in the United States* reflect the Hierarchy Rule, which counts only the most serious offense in a multiple-offense criminal incident. In descending order of severity, the violent crimes are murder and nonnegligent manslaughter, forcible rape, robbery, and aggravated assault; these are followed by the property crimes of burglary, larceny-theft, and motor vehicle theft. More information on the expanded violent crime tables (which are available online but not included in this publication) can be found in Section I.

National Volume, Trends, and Rate

In 2010, an estimated 1,246,248 violent crimes occurred in the United States, showing a decrease of 6.0 percent from the 2009 estimate. An estimated 403.6 violent crimes were committed per 100,000 inhabitants in 2010. Aggravated assaults accounted for 62.5 percent of violent crimes, the highest number of violent crimes reported to law enforce-

ment. Robbery made up 29.5 percent of violent crimes (a decrease of 1.5 percentage points), forcible rape accounted for 6.8 percent, and murder accounted for 1.2 percent (no change from 2009) of estimated violent crimes in 2010. (Table 1)

All violent crimes decreased in 2010, a continuation of the trend in 2009. Murder decreased 4.2 percent; forcible rape fell 5.1 percent; aggravated assault declined 4.1 percent; and robbery dropped 10.0 percent. The 2010 murder rate, 4.8 offenses per 100,000 inhabitants, was also a decrease of 4.8 percent when compared with the rate for 2009. (Tables 1 and 1A)

The UCR Program reports data in 2-year, 5-year, and 10-year increments to formulate trend information. The 2010 estimated violent crime total was 13.2 percent below the 2006 level and 13.4 percent below the 2001 level. The 5-year and 10-year trend data showed that the violent crime rate decreased 15.8 percent between 2006 and 2010 and decreased 20.0 percent between 2001 and 2010. The rate of violent crime declined in 2010 to 403.6 per 100,000, a decrease of 6.5 percent when compared with 2009 data. (Tables 1 and 1A)

In 2010, offenders used firearms in 67.5 percent of the nation's murders, 41.4 percent of robberies, and 20.6 percent of aggravated assaults. Although the largest percent of murders and robberies were committed with firearms, weapons such as clubs and blunt objects accounted for the majority

(33.1 percent) of aggravated assaults. (Weapon data are not collected for forcible rape offenses.) (Expanded Homicide Table 7, Expanded Offense Robbery Table 3, and Expanded Aggravated Assault Table, www.fbi.gov/about-us/cjis/ucr/crime-in-the-u.s/2010/crime-in-the-u.s.-2010/tables/10aggvtbl.xls)

Regional Offense Trends and Rate

The UCR Program divides the United States into four regions: the Northeast, the South, the Midwest, and the West. (More details concerning geographic regions are provided in Appendix III.) The population distribution of the regions can be found in Table 3, and the estimated volume and rate of violent crime by region are provided in Table 4.

The Northeast

The Northeast accounted for an estimated 17.9 percent of the nation's population in 2010 and an estimated 15.8 percent of its violent crimes. (Table 3) The estimated number of violent crimes remained relatively unchanged in 2010 when compared with the estimate from 2009. Murder decreased 8.9 percent in the Northeast, which was the largest decrease in all the regions. Forcible rapes decreased 1.0 percent and the aggravated assaults decreased 0.5 percent again in 2010, the same as it did in 2009. In 2010, there were an estimated 357.0 violent crimes per 100,000 inhabitants. (Table 4)

The Midwest

With an estimated 21.7 percent of the total population of the United States, the Midwest accounted for 19.5 percent of the nation's estimated number of violent crimes in 2010. (Table 3) The region had a 6.5 percent decrease in violent crime from 2009 to 2010. The estimated number of aggravated assaults declined 4.3 percent, the estimated number of robberies fell 10.7 percent, the number of murders declined 4.9 percent, and the estimated number of forcible rapes decreased 6.0 percent from 2009 to 2010. The rate of violent crime per 100,000 inhabitants in the Midwest declined 6.6 percent from 2009 to 2010. (Table 4)

The South

The South, the nation's most populous region, accounted for 37.1 percent of the nation's population in 2010. Almost 42 percent (41.5) of violent crimes in 2010 occurred in the South. (Table 3) While the estimated number of violent crimes decreased in all four regions, the largest decrease (7.9 percent) occurred in the South. The estimated number of forcible rapes fell 6.4 percent in the South. Robberies had the largest decline (13.0 percent) of the four offenses, followed by murders (6.4 percent) and aggravated assaults (5.8 percent). While all four regions experienced declines in the estimated number of aggravated assaults, the greatest decrease was in the South. The estimated rate of violent crime in the South was 452.0 incidents per 100,000 inhabitants in 2010. (Table 4)

The West

Again maintaining 23.3 percent of the nation's population in 2010, the West accounted for an estimated 23.1 percent of the nation's violent crime. (Table 3) Violent crime in the West decreased 5.6 percent from 2009 to 2010. All four violent offense categories decreased in number from 2009 to 2010: murder declined another 7.6 percent, aggravated assault decreased 3.6 percent, robbery fell 10.0 percent, and forcible rape dropped 3.8 percent. The region's violent crime rate in 2010 was 400.8 per 100,000 population, a 6.1 percent decrease from the 2009 rate. (Table 4)

Community Types

The UCR Program aggregates crime data into three community types: metropolitan statistical areas (MSAs), cities outside MSAs, and nonmetropolitan counties outside MSAs. Appendix III provides additional information regarding community types. In 2010, 83.7 percent of the nation's population lived in MSAs. Residents of cities outside MSAs continued to account for 6.5 percent of the country's population, and residents living in nonmetropolitan counties continued to account for 9.8 percent of the population. (Table 2)

Approximately 88 percent of the areas actually reporting violent crimes in the United States occurred in MSAs, 5.9 percent occurred in cities outside MSAs, and 4.4 percent occurred in nonmetropolitan counties. By community type, the violent crime rates were estimated at 428.3 incidents per 100,000 inhabitants in MSAs, 399.7 incidents per 100,000 inhabitants in cities outside MSAs, and 195.1 incidents per 100,000 inhabitants in nonmetropolitan counties. (Table 2)

Population Groups: Trends and Rates

In the UCR Program, data are also aggregated into population groups; these groups are described in more detail in Appendix III. The nation's cities had an overall decrease of another 5.5 percent in the estimated number of violent crimes from 2009 to 2010. By city population group, cities with 250,000 to 499,999 inhabitants had the largest percentage decline in the estimated number of violent crimes (6.7 percent). (Table 12)

The law enforcement agencies in the nation's cities collectively reported a rate of 481.7 violent crimes per 100,000 inhabitants in 2010. Law enforcement agencies in cities subset of 500,000 to 999,999 inhabitants reported the highest violent crime rate, with 806.6 violent crimes per 100,000 inhabitants; the violent crime rate for all cities with 250,000 or more inhabitants was 751.4 per 100,000 inhabitants. Agencies in cities with 10,000 to 24,999 inhabitants reported the lowest violent crime rate (285.4 incidents per 100,000 inhabitants). Law enforcement agencies in the nation's metropolitan counties reported a collective violent crime rate of 284.1 per 100,000 inhabitants, while agencies in nonmetropolitan counties reported a collective rate of 199.3 violent crimes per 100,000 inhabitants. (Table 16)

MURDER

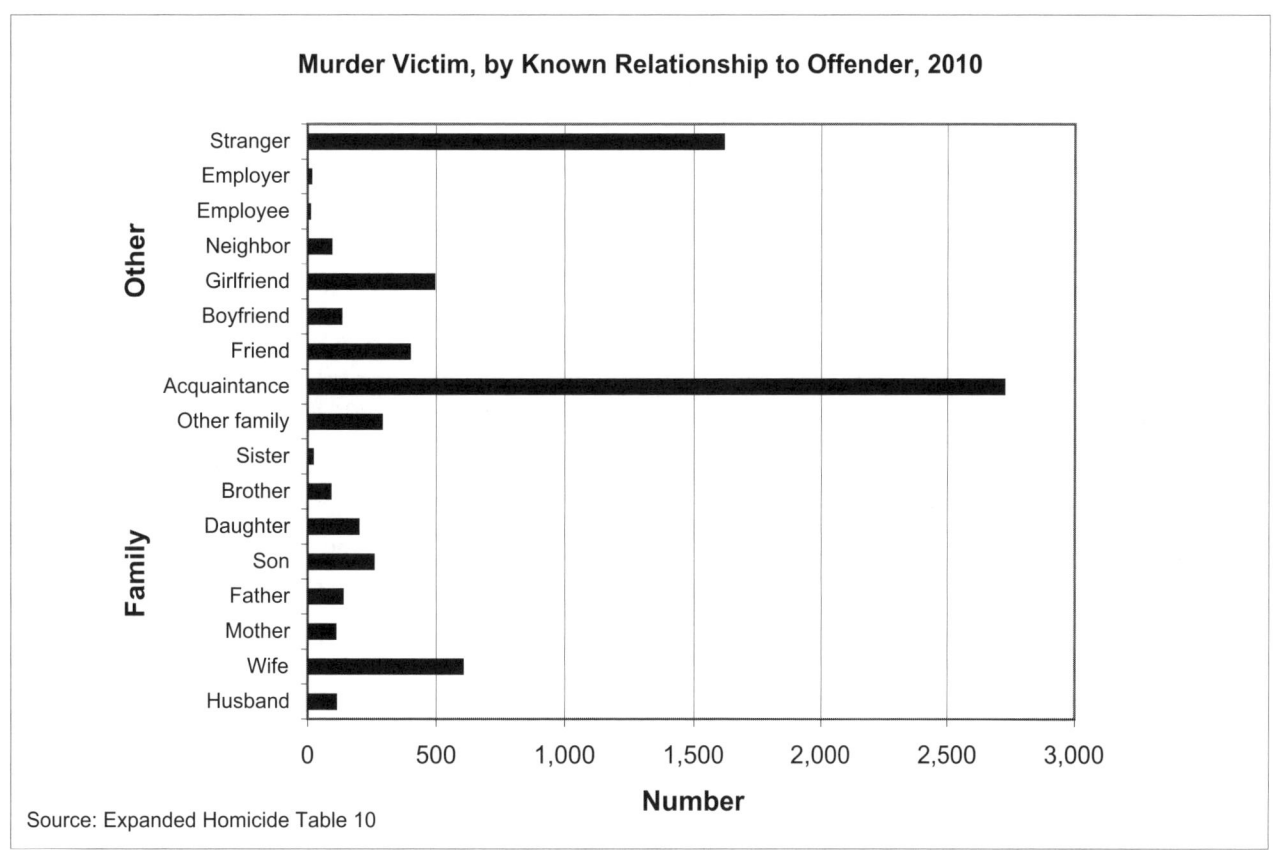

Murder Victim, by Known Relationship to Offender, 2010

Source: Expanded Homicide Table 10

Definition

The UCR Program defines murder and non-negligent manslaughter as the willful (non-negligent) killing of one human being by another. The classification of this offense is based solely on police investigation, rather than on the determination of a court, medical examiner, coroner, jury, or other judicial body. The UCR Program does not include the following situations under this offense classification: deaths caused by negligence, suicide, or accident; justifiable homicides; and attempts to murder or assaults to murder, which are considered aggravated assaults.

Data Collection/Supplementary Homicide Reports (SHR)

The UCR Program's *Supplementary Homicide Report* (SHR) provides information about murder victims and offenders by age, sex, and race; the types of weapons used in the murders; the relationships of the victims to the offenders; and the circumstances surrounding the incident. Law enforcement agencies are asked to complete an SHR for each murder reported to the UCR Program. Data from SHRs can be viewed in the Expanded Homicide Data section, found on the FBI web site: www.fbi.gov/about-us/cjis/ucr/crime-in-the-u.s/2010/crime-in-the-u.s.-2010/offen ses-known-to-law-enforcement/expanded/expandhomicidemain . Of the estimated 14,748 murders that were committed in the United States in 2010, law enforcement agencies contributed data to the UCR Program through SHRs for 12,996 murders. More information on these reports and the expanded homicide tables can be found in Section I. Highlights from these tables have been included below.

National Volume, Trends, and Rates

An estimated 14,748 persons were murdered nationwide in 2010. This number was a 4.2 percent decrease from the 2009 estimate, a 14.8 percent decrease from the 2006 figure, and an 8.0 percent decrease from the 2001 estimate. The 2010 murder rate, 4.8 offenses per 100,000 inhabitants, was a 4.8 percent decrease when compared with the rate for 2009. For a second year, murder accounted for 1.2 percent of the overall estimated number of violent crimes in 2010. (Tables 1 and 1A)

Regional Offense Trends and Rates

The UCR Program divides the United States into four regions: the Northeast, the South, the Midwest, and the West. (More details concerning geographic regions are provided in

Appendix III.) In 2010, nearly 44 percent of murders were reported in the South, the most populous region. The West reported 20.6 percent of murders, 19.9 percent were reported in the Midwest, and 15.6 percent were reported in the Northeast. In 2010, the estimated number of murders decreased in three of the four regions, with the largest decrease, 7.6 percent, occurring in the West. The Northeast reported an increase of 9 percent.

The Northeast

In 2010, the Northeast accounted for an estimated 17.9 percent of the nation's population and 15.6 percent of its estimated number of murders. With an estimated 2,307 murders, the Northeast saw a 9.0 percent increase compared with the 2009 figure. The offense rate for the Northeast was 4.2 murders per 100,000 inhabitants, up from 3.8 murders per 100,000 inhabitants in 2009. (Tables 3 and 4)

The Midwest

The Midwest accounted for an estimated 21.7 percent of the nation's total population and 19.9 percent of the country's estimated number of murders in 2010. The Midwest reported an estimated 2,938 murders in 2010, a 4.9 percent decrease from the estimated figure for 2009. The region experienced a rate of 4.4 murders per 100,000 inhabitants in 2010, slightly lower than in 2009. (Tables 3 and 4)

The South

The South accounted for an estimated 37.1 percent of the nation's population in 2010 and 43.8 percent of the nation's murders, the highest proportion among the four regions. The region's population grew 1.1 percent from 2009 to 2010. The estimated 6,459 murders represented a 6.4 percent decrease in the estimated number of murders from 2009 to 2010. The region's estimated rate of 5.6 murders per 100,000 inhabitants represented a decrease of 7.4 percent from the estimated rate for 2009. (Tables 3 and 4)

The West

The West again accounted for an estimated 23.3 percent of the nation's population and 20.6 percent of the estimated number of murders in 2010. The West experienced an estimated 3,044 murders, a 7.6 percent decrease from the 2009 estimate. The region's murder rate was 4.2 per 100,000 inhabitants, an 8.1 percent decrease from the 2009 rate. (Tables 3 and 4)

Community Types

The UCR Program aggregates data for three community types: metropolitan statistical areas (MSAs), cities outside MSAs, and nonmetropolitan counties outside MSAs. (See Appendix III for definitions.) In 2010, MSAs accounted for 83.7 percent of the nation's population and 88.5 percent of the estimated total number of murders. With 13,050 estimated homicides, MSAs experienced a rate of 5.0 murders per 100,000 inhabitants in 2010. Cities outside MSAs accounted for 6.5 percent of the U.S. population and (with an estimated 728 murders) accounted for 4.9 percent of the estimated murders in the nation. The murder rate for cities outside MSAs was 3.6 per 100,000 inhabitants. In 2010, 9.8 percent of the nation's population lived in nonmetropolitan counties outside MSAs. An estimated 970 murders took place in these counties, accounting for 6.6 percent of the nation's estimated total. (Table 2)

Population Groups: Trends and Rates

The UCR Program uses the following population group designations in its data presentations: cities (grouped according to population size) and counties (classified as either metropolitan or nonmetropolitan). A breakdown of these classifications is provided in Appendix III.

From 2009 to 2010, the nation's cities experienced a 4.0 percent decrease in homicides. The only city group to experience an increase (4.3 percent) was those with populations between 250,000 and 499,999. The city group with the largest decrease (23.1 percent) was those with fewer than 10,000 inhabitants. Metropolitan counties experienced a decrease in homicides of 1.6 percent from 2009 to 2010, while nonmetropolitan counties experienced a decrease of 10.2 percent. (Table 12)

In 2010, cities collectively had a rate of 5.5 murders per 100,000 inhabitants. Cities with 250,000 to 499,999 inhabitants had the highest murder rate (11.3 murders per 100,000 inhabitants). Cities with fewer than 10,000 inhabitants had the lowest murder rates, with 2.4 murders per 100,000 inhabitants. The homicide rate for metropolitan counties was 3.6 (the same that it had been in 2009, and for nonmetropolitan counties it was 3.3 (slightly lower than in 2009) per 100,000 inhabitants. Suburban areas had a homicide rate of 3.0 per 100,000 inhabitants, the same rate that it had in 2009. (Table 16)

Supplementary Homicide Reports Data

Victims/Offenders

Based on 2010 supplemental homicide data (where the ages, sexes, or races of the murder victims were *known*), 89.0 percent of victims were over 18 years of age, 24.4 percent were under age 22, 9.8 percent were under 18 years of age, and the age of 1.2 percent of the victims was unknown. Of the 12,996 murder victims in 2010 for whom gender was known, 77.4 percent were male. Concerning murder victims for whom race was known, 46.5 percent were white, 49.8 percent were black, and 2.5 percent were from other races. Race was unknown for 152 victims. (Expanded Homicide Tables 1 and 2) For murders where the gender of the offender was known, 66.1 percent were males. Of the offenders for whom race was known, 38.2 percent were Black, 32.1 percent were White, and 1.7 percent were other races; 28.0 percent were of unknown race. (Based on Expanded Homicide Data Table 3)

Victim-Offender Relationships

For incidents in which the victim-offender relationship was known, 24.8 percent of victims were slain by family members, 22.2 percent were murdered by strangers, and 53.0 percent were killed by acquaintances (neighbor, friend, boyfriend, etc.). Among female victims for whom relationships with their offenders were known, 37.5 percent were murdered by their husbands or boyfriends. (Based on Expanded Homicide Data Tables 2 and 10)

Circumstances/Weapons

Concerning the known circumstances surrounding murders, 41.7 percent of victims were murdered during arguments (including romantic triangles) in 2010. Felony circumstances (rape, robbery, burglary, etc.) accounted for 23.1 percent of murders. Circumstances were unknown for 35.8 percent of reported homicides. (Based on Expanded Homicide Data Table 12) Of the homicides for which the type of weapon was specified, 67.5 percent involved the use of firearms. Of the identified firearms used, handguns comprised 68.5 percent. (Based on Expanded Homicide Data Table 8)

Justifiable Homicide

Certain willful killings must be reported as justifiable, or excusable, homicide. In the UCR Program, justifiable homicide is defined as, and is limited to, the following:

- The killing of a felon by a peace officer in the line of duty.

- The killing of a felon, during the commission of a felony, by a private citizen.

Because these killings are determined by law enforcement investigation to be justifiable, they are tabulated separately from murder and nonnegligent manslaughter. Law enforcement reported 665 justifiable homicides in 2010. Of those, law enforcement officers justifiably killed 387 individuals, and private citizens justifiably killed 278 individuals. (Based on Expanded Homicide Data Tables 14 and 15)

FORCIBLE RAPE

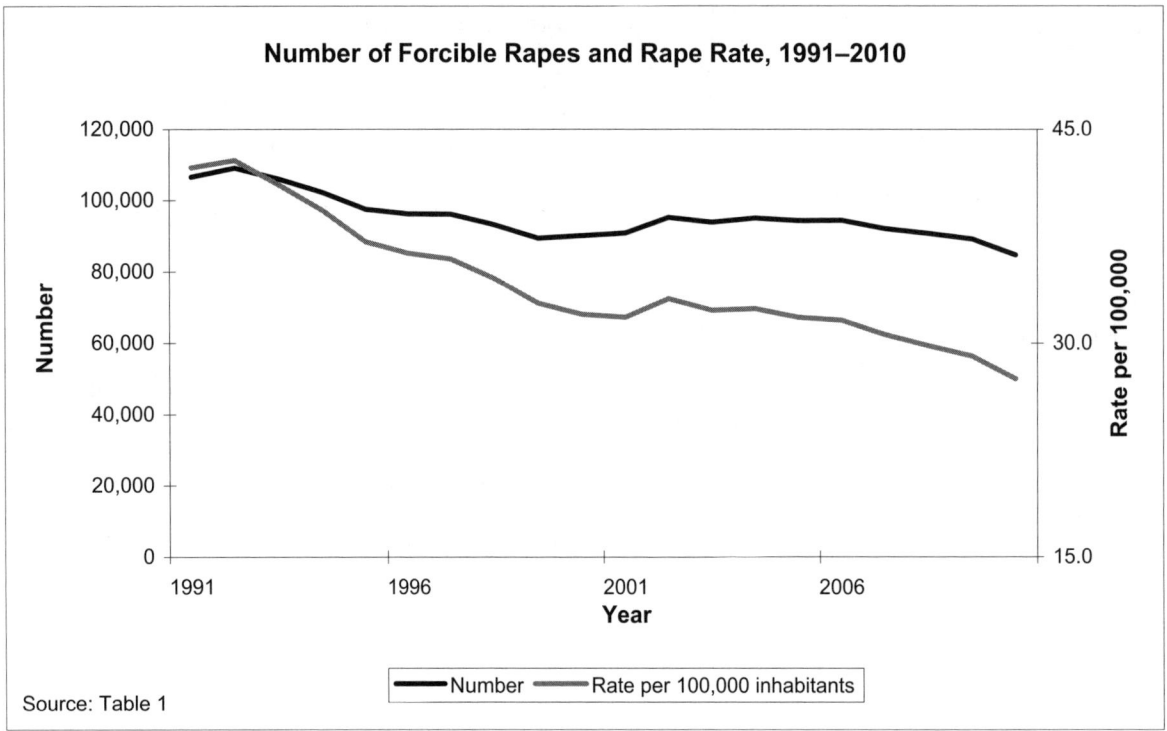

Number of Forcible Rapes and Rape Rate, 1991–2010

Source: Table 1

— Number — Rate per 100,000 inhabitants

Definition

Forcible rape is the carnal knowledge of a female forcibly and against her will. Assaults and attempts to commit rape by force or threat of force are included; however, statutory rape (without force) and other sex offenses are excluded.

Data Collection

The UCR Program counts one offense for each female victim of a forcible rape, attempted forcible rape, or assault with intent to rape, regardless of the victim's age. A rape by force involving a female victim and a familial offender is counted as a forcible rape not an act of incest. The Program collects only arrest statistics concerning all other crimes of a sexual nature. The offense of statutory rape, in which no force is used but the female victim is under the age of consent, is included in the arrest total for the sex offenses category. Sexual attacks on males are counted as aggravated assaults or sex offenses, depending on the circumstances and the extent of any injuries.

For this overview only, the FBI deviated from standard procedure and manually calculated the 2009 and 2010 rates of females raped based on the national female population provided by the U.S. Census Bureau.

National Volume, Trends, and Rates

In 2010, the estimated number of forcible rapes (84,767)—the lowest figure in the last 21 years—decreased 5.0 percent from the 2009 estimate. The estimated volume of rapes in

2010 was 10.3 percent lower than in 2006 and was 6.7 percent below the 2001 level. (Tables 1 and 1A)

Of the forcible rapes known to law enforcement agencies in 2010, rapes by force made up 93 percent of reported rape offenses, and assaults to rape attempts accounted for 7.0 percent of reported rape offenses. (Tables 1 and 19)

Regional Offense Trends and Rates

The UCR Program divides the United States into four regions: the Northeast, the South, the Midwest, and the West. (More details concerning geographic regions are provided in Appendix III.) Regional analysis offers estimates of the volume of female rapes, the percent change from the previous year's estimate, and the rate of rape per 100,000 female inhabitants in each region.

The Northeast

The Northeast made up 17.9 percent of the U.S. population in 2010 and experienced a slight increase in population from 2009 to 2010 (0.06 percent). In 2010, an estimated 10,724 forcible rapes of females—12.7 percent of the national total—occurred in the Northeast. This was a decrease of 1.0 percent from the 2009 estimated figure. (Tables 3 and 4)

The Midwest

The Midwest, which accounted for 21.7 percent of the U.S. population in 2010, experienced a 0.1 percent increase in population from 2009 to 2010. Almost one-quarter (24.6

percent) of all forcible rapes in the nation occurred in the Midwest in 2010. The 2010 estimate (20,825 forcible rapes) represented a decline of 6.0 percent from the 2009 estimate. (Tables 3 and 4)

The South

The South, the nation's most populous region, accounted for an estimated 37.1 percent of the nation's population in 2010 (and experienced a population growth of 1.1 percent from 2009 to 2010); the region also accounted for an estimated 37.7 percent of the nation's estimated number of forcible rapes. An estimated 31,969 female victims reported forcible rape in the South in 2010, down 6.4 percent from 34,156 in 2009. (Tables 3 and 4)

The West

The West, which experienced a population growth of .5 percent from 2009 to 2010, again accounted for 23.3 percent of the nation's population in 2010. The region also accounted for 25.1 percent of the nation's total number of estimated forcible rapes with an estimated 21,249 offenses. The West saw a 3.8 percent decline in forcible rapes from 2009 to 2010. (Tables 3 and 4)

Community Types

Using the U.S. Office of Management and Budget's designations, the UCR Program aggregates crime data by type of community in which the offenses occur: metropolitan statistical areas (MSAs), cities outside MSAs, and nonmetropolitan counties outside MSAs. (Appendix III provides more detailed information about community types.)

MSAs

In 2010, MSAs accounted for 83.7 percent of the nation's population and 79.3 percent of the nation's estimated number of forcible rapes. An estimated 69,746 females were forcibly raped in metropolitan areas. (Table 2)

Cities Outside MSAs

Cities outside MSAs are mostly incorporated areas served by city law enforcement agencies. Although accounting for only 6.5 percent of the U.S. population as it did in 2010, cities outside MSAs accounted for 9.9 percent of the nation's estimated forcible rapes (8,259 offenses). (Table 2)

Nonmetropolitan Counties

As in 2009, in 2010, approximately 9.8 percent of the nation's population lived in nonmetropolitan counties outside MSAs (counties made up of mostly non-incorporated areas served by noncity law enforcement agencies). Collectively, these areas had an estimated 6,654 forcible rapes, representing 7.8 percent of the nation's estimated total. (Table 2)

ROBBERY

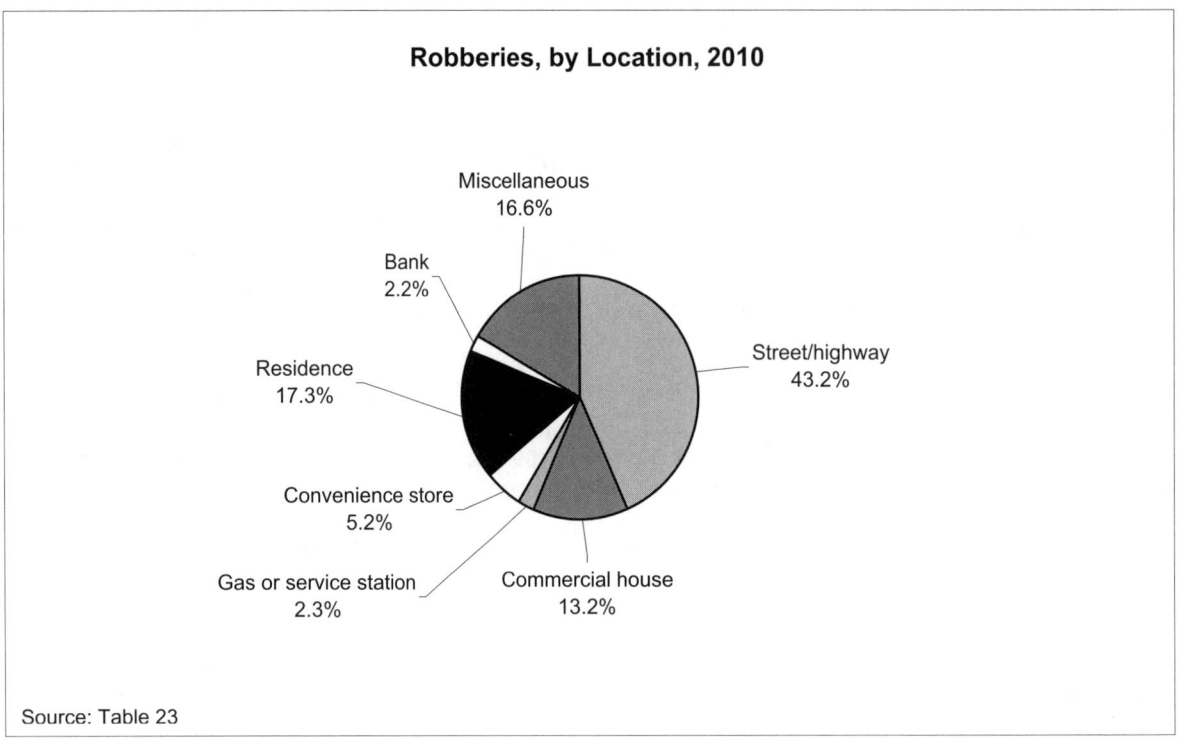

Robberies, by Location, 2010

Miscellaneous
16.6%

Bank
2.2%

Residence
17.3%

Convenience store
5.2%

Gas or service station
2.3%

Commercial house
13.2%

Street/highway
43.2%

Source: Table 23

Definition

The UCR Program defines robbery as the taking or the attempt to take anything of value from the care, custody, or control of a person or persons by force or threat of force or violence and/or by putting the victim in fear.

National Volume, Trends, and Rates

In 2010, the estimated robbery total (367,832) decreased 10.0 percent from the 2009 estimate. The 5-year robbery trend (2006 data compared with 2010 data) showed an decrease of 13.1 percent. The 2010 estimated robbery rate (119.1 per 100,000 inhabitants) showed a decrease of 10.5 percent when compared with the 2009 rate. (Tables 1 and 1A)

Regional Offense Trends and Rates

The UCR Program divides the United States into four regions: the Northeast, the South, the Midwest, and the West. (More details concerning geographic regions are provided in Appendix III.)

The Northeast

The Northeast, with an estimated 17.9 percent of the nation's population in 2010, accounted for 18.7 percent of its estimated number of robberies. (Table 3) The estimated number of robberies decreased 2.0 percent from 2009. The rate for this region was 124.4 robberies per 100,000 inhabi-

tants, down from 127.5 robberies per 100,000 inhabitants in 2009. (Table 4)

The Midwest

The Midwest accounted for 21.7 percent of the total population of the United States, and 19.6 percent of its estimated number of robberies, in 2010. (Table 3) An estimated 72,093 robberies occurred in the Midwest in 2010, a 10.7 percent decrease from the estimated figure from 2009. The region's robbery rate was 107.7 robberies per 100,000 inhabitants in 2010, the lowest rate among the four regions. (Table 4)

The South

The South, the nation's most highly populated region, experienced a 1.1 percent growth in population from 2009 to 2010; in 2010, it accounted for an estimated 37.1 percent of the nation's population and 38.1 percent of the nation's estimated number of robberies. (Table 3) Robberies accounted for an estimated 140,161 violent crimes in this region in 2010, representing a 13.0 percent decrease from the 2009 figure, and the greatest decline in all four regions. Of the four regions, the South experienced the second highest rate of robberies per 100,000 inhabitants (122.4), however this rate was 13.9 percent lower than its 2009 rate. (Table 4)

The West

The West was again home to an estimated 23.3 percent of the nation's population and accounted for 23.6 percent of the nation's estimated number of robberies in 2010. (Table 3) The estimated number of robberies (86,779) in the region in 2010 represented a 10.0 percent decrease from the 2009 figure. The rate of robberies per 100,000 inhabitants in the West was 120.6, a 10.4 percent decrease from the 2009 rate. This was the second lowest rate among the four regions. (Table 4)

Community Types

The UCR Program aggregates data for three community types: metropolitan statistical areas (MSAs), cities outside MSAs, and nonmetropolitan counties outside MSAs. MSAs include a central city or urbanized area with at least 50,000 inhabitants, as well as the county that contains the principal city and other adjacent counties that have, as defined by the U.S. Office of Management and Budget, a high degree of social and economic integration as measured through commuting. Cities outside MSAs are mostly incorporated areas, and nonmetropolitan counties are made up of mostly unincorporated areas served by noncity law enforcement.

In 2010, MSAs were home to an estimated 83.7 percent of the nation's population, and 95.6 percent of the nation's estimated number of robberies took place in these areas. Robberies in MSAs occurred at a rate of 136.0 per 100,000 inhabitants. Cities outside MSAs accounted for 6.5 percent of the U.S. population and accounted for 3.1 percent of the estimated number of robberies in the nation. The robbery rate for cities outside MSAs was 57.1 per 100,000 inhabitants. Nonmetropolitan counties made up 9.8 percent of the nation's estimated population and 1.3 percent of the nation's estimated robberies, at a rate of 15.9 robberies per 100,000 inhabitants. (Table 2)

Population Groups: Trends and Rates

The national UCR Program aggregates data by various population groups, which include cities, metropolitan counties, and nonmetropolitan counties. A definition of these groups can be found in Appendix III. The number of robberies in cities as a whole decreased 9.6 percent. Among the population groups labeled *city*, those cities with 25,000 to 49,999 inhabitants had the greatest decrease in the number of robberies (11.0 percent). Nonmetropolitan counties had a 6.8 percent decrease in the estimated number of robberies, and metropolitan counties showed an 11.0 percent decrease. The number of robberies in suburban areas fell 10.8 percent. (Table 12)

Among the population groups, the nation's cities collectively had a rate of 157.5 robberies per 100,000 inhabitants. Of the population groups and subsets designated *city*, those with 1,000,000 or more inhabitants had the highest rate

(303.2 per 100,000 inhabitants), while those with fewer than 10,000 inhabitants had the lowest rate (47.4 per 100,000 inhabitants) of robberies. Of the two county groups, metropolitan counties had a rate of 61.3 robberies per 100,000 inhabitants, while nonmetropolitan counties had a rate of 16.0 robberies per 100,000 inhabitants. Suburban areas had a robbery rate of 62.9 (Table 16)

Offense Analysis

The UCR Program collects supplemental data about robberies to document the use of weapons, the dollar loss associated with the offense, and the location types.

Robbery by Weapon

Firearms were used in 41.4 percent of robberies in 2010. Strong-arm robberies accounted for 42.0 percent of the total. Offenders used knives or cutting instruments in 7.9 percent of these crimes. In the remainder of the robberies (8.8 percent), the offenders used other types of weapons. (Table 19)

Loss by Dollar Value

Based on the supplemental reports from law enforcement agencies, robberies cost victims, collectively, an estimated $456 million in 2010. (Tables 1 and 23) The average loss per robbery was $1,239. Average dollar losses were the highest for banks, which suffered an average loss of $4,410 per offense. Gas and service stations lost an average of $939 per offense. Commercial houses, which include supermarkets, department stores, and restaurants, had average losses of $1,858. An average of $1,491 was taken from residences. An average of $782 was lost in each offense against convenience stores. (Table 23)

Robbery Trends by Location

Among the location types, gas or service station robberies had the greatest percentage decrease from 2009 to 2010, declining 14.6 percent. Robberies that occurred at residences decreased 8.8 percent. The number of robberies that occurred at convenience stores fell 14.3 percent, robberies on streets and highways decreased 9.6 percent, robberies at commercial houses decreased 13.4 percent, and robberies at banks decreased 8.8 percent. (Table 23)

By location type, the greatest proportion of robberies in 2010 occurred on streets and highways (43.2 percent). Robbers targeted commercial houses in 13.2 percent of offenses and residences in 17.3 percent of offenses. Convenience stores accounted for 5.2 percent of robberies, followed by gas and service stations (2.3 percent) and banks (2.2 percent). (Table 23)

AGGRAVATED ASSAULT

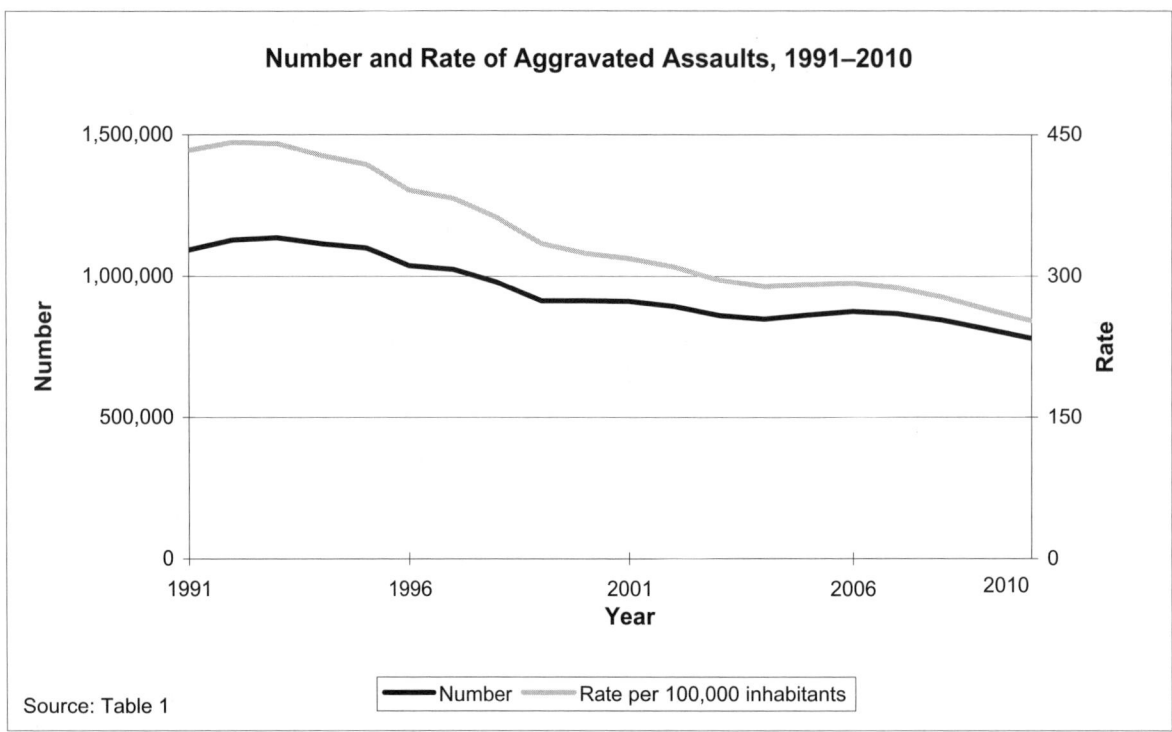

Number and Rate of Aggravated Assaults, 1991–2010

Source: Table 1

Legend: Number — Rate per 100,000 inhabitants

Definition

The UCR Program defines aggravated assault as an unlawful attack by one person upon another for the purpose of inflicting severe or aggravated bodily injury. This type of assault is usually accompanied by the use of a weapon or by other means likely to produce death or great bodily harm. Attempted aggravated assaults that involve the display or threat of a gun, knife, or other weapon are included in this crime category because serious personal injury would likely result if these assaults were completed. When aggravated assault and larceny-theft occur together, the offense falls under the category of robbery.

National Volume, Trends, and Rates

In 2010, estimated occurrences of aggravated assaults totaled 778,901, a 4.1 percent decrease from the 2009 figure, and a 14.3 percent decline when compared with the estimates for 2001. The 2010 data also show a decrease for the fifth consecutive year in the rate of aggravated assaults per 100,000 U.S. inhabitants. This rate, estimated at 252.3, represents a 4.7 percent decrease from the 2009 rate. However, it also represents a 13.6 percent decrease from the 2006 (5-year trend) rate and a 20.8 percent decrease from the 2001 (10-year trend) rate. (Tables 1 and 1A)

Among the four types of violent crime offenses (murder, forcible rape, robbery, and aggravated assault), aggravated assault typically has the highest rate of occurrence. This

trend continued in 2010 with aggravated assault accounting for 62.4 percent of all violent crime. (Table 1)

Regional Offense Trends and Rates

The UCR Program divides the United States into four regions: the Northeast, the South, the Midwest, and the West. (More details concerning geographic regions are provided in Appendix III.) Three of the four regions experienced decreases in the number of aggravated assaults from 2009 to 2010. (Table 4)

The Northeast

The region with the smallest proportion of the nation's population (an estimated 17.9 percent in 2010) also accounted for the smallest proportion of the nation's estimated number of aggravated assaults (14.8 percent). (Table 3) Occurrences of aggravated assault increased slightly from 2009 to 2010, up to an estimated 115,661. However, the region continued to have the lowest aggravated assault rate in the nation, at 209.1 incidents per 100,000 inhabitants. (Table 4)

The Midwest

With 21.7 percent of the nation's total population in 2010—and with a 0.5 percent growth in population from 2009 to 2010—the Midwest accounted for approximately 18.8 percent of the nation's estimated number of aggravated assaults. (Table 3) Occurrences of this offense decreased 4.3

percent from the estimated total for 2009, declining to an estimated 146,770 incidents. The region's aggravated assault rate, at 219.3 incidents per 100,000 inhabitants, represented a 4.5 percent decrease from the 2009 rate. (Table 4)

The South

The South, the nation's most highly populated region, accounted for an estimated 37.1 percent of the nation's population in 2010 and the largest amount of the nation's estimated number of aggravated assaults (43.6 percent). (Table 3) From 2009 to 2010, the estimated number of aggravated assaults decreased 5.8 percent, falling to a total of 339,216 incidents. The rate of aggravated assaults declined to 296.1 per 100,000 inhabitants. (Table 4)

The West

In 2010, the West was home to an estimated 23.3 percent of the nation's population, and had experienced 0.5 percent growth in population from 2009 to 2010. The region accounted for 22.8 percent of the nation's estimated number of aggravated assaults. (Table 3) From 2009 to 2010, the estimated number of offenses decreased 3.6 percent to 177,254 incidents. The rate, estimated at 246.4 offenses per 100,000 inhabitants, fell 4.1 percent from 2009. (Table 4)

Community Types

The UCR Program aggregates data for three community types: metropolitan statistical areas (MSAs), cities outside MSAs, and nonmetropolitan counties outside MSAs. MSAs include a central city or urbanized area with at least 50,000 inhabitants, as well as the county that contains the principal city and other adjacent counties that have a high degree of social and economic integration as measured through commuting. Cities outside MSAs are mostly incorporated areas, and nonmetropolitan counties are made up of mostly unincorporated areas. (For additional information about community types, see Appendix III.)

In 2010, 83.7 percent of the nation's population lived in MSAs, where the rate of aggravated assault was an estimated 260.3 per 100,000 inhabitants. Cities outside MSAs (with 6.5 percent of the U.S. population) had the highest rate of aggravated assault at 297.3 offenses per 100,000 inhabitants. Nonmetropolitan counties accounted for 9.8 percent of the U.S. population and had an offense rate of 154.0 aggravated assaults per 100,000 inhabitants. (Table 2)

From 2009 to 2010, the number of aggravated assaults fell for all cities. Cities with 250,000 to 499,999 inhabitants experienced the greatest decrease (5.3 percent), followed by cities with 50,000 to 99,999, which fell 4.8 percent. In metropolitan counties, the number of aggravated assaults declined 5.5 percent; in nonmetropolitan counties, this number also decreased 5.5 percent. Aggravated assaults in suburban areas declined 4.9 percent from 2009 to 2010. (Table 12)

Based on reports from agencies submitting 12 months of complete data for 2010, aggravated assault occurred at an estimated rate of 255.5 offenses per 100,000 inhabitants nationwide. The collective rate for cities was 288.2 aggravated assaults per 100,000 inhabitants. Among city population groups, rates ranged from a high of 468.5 offenses per 100,000 inhabitants (in cities with 250,000 to 499,999 inhabitants) to a low of 191.7 offenses per 100,000 inhabitants (in cities with 10,000 to 24,999 inhabitants). The aggravated assault rate was 197.5 in metropolitan counties and 156.6 in nonmetropolitan counties. (Table 16)

Offense Analysis

Aggravated Assault by Weapon

Of the aggravated assault offenses for which law enforcement agencies provided expanded data in 2010, 33.1 percent were committed with blunt objects or other dangerous weapons; 27.4 percent involved personal weapons such as hands, fists, and feet; 20.6 percent were committed with firearms; and 19.0 percent involved knives or other cutting instruments. (Table 19)

PROPERTY CRIME

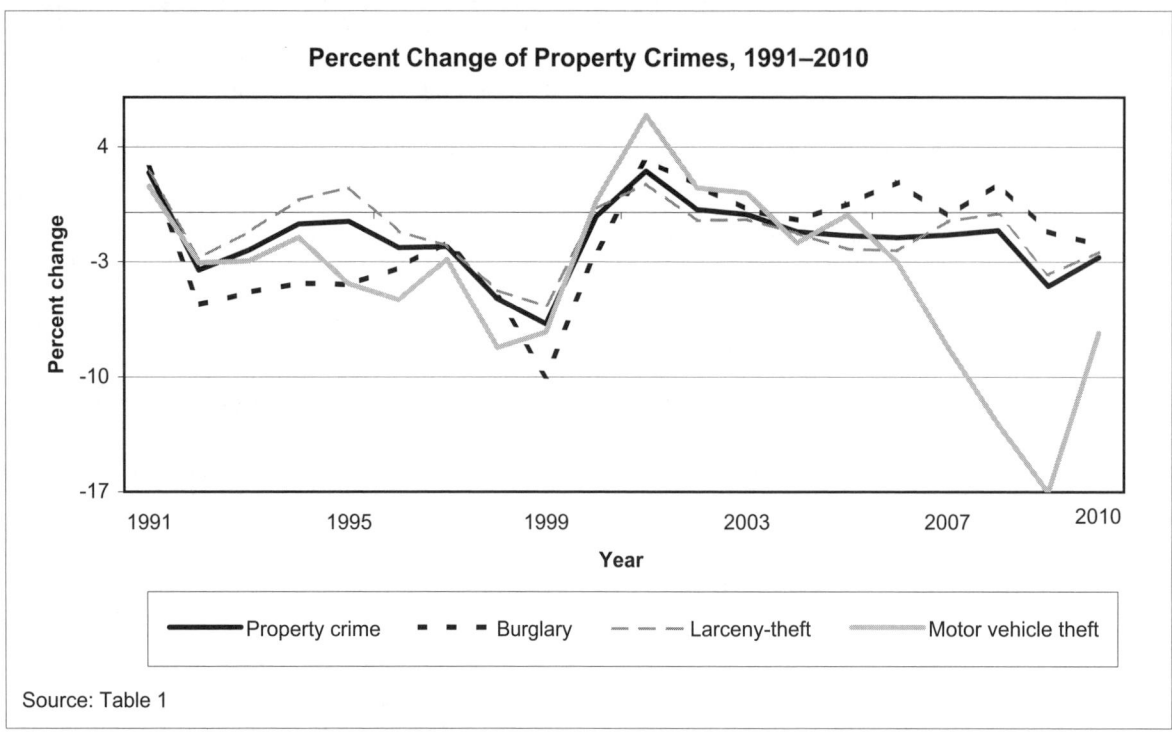

Percent Change of Property Crimes, 1991–2010

Source: Table 1

Definition

The Uniform Crime Reporting (UCR) Program's definition of property crime includes the offenses of burglary, larceny-theft, motor vehicle theft, and arson. The object of theft-type offenses is the taking of money or property without the use of force or threat of force against the victims. Property crime includes arson because the offense involves the destruction of property; however, arson victims may be subjected to force. Because of limited participation and the varying collection procedures conducted by local law enforcement agencies, only limited data are available for arson. Arson statistics are included in the trend, clearance, and arrest tables in *Crime in the United States*, but they are not included in any estimated volume data. More information on the expanded arson tables (which are available online but not included in this publication) can be found in Section I.

Data Collection

The data presented in *Crime in the United States* reflect the Hierarchy Rule, which counts only the most serious offense in a multiple-offense criminal incident. In descending order of severity, the violent crimes are murder and nonnegligent manslaughter, forcible rape, robbery, aggravated assault; these are followed by the property crimes of burglary, larceny-theft, and motor vehicle theft. The Hierarchy Rule does not apply to the offense of arson.

National Volume, Trends, and Rates

An estimated 9,082,887 property crimes were committed in the United States in 2010, representing a 2.7 percent decrease from the 2009 (2-year trend) estimate, a 9.3 percent decrease from the 2006 (5-year trend) estimate, and a 13.0 percent decrease from the 2001 (10-year trend) estimate. (Tables 1 and 1A)

From 2009 to 2010, motor vehicle theft fell 7.4 percent. Larceny-theft (2.4 percent) and burglary (2.0 percent) both showed decreases from their 2009 estimates as well as from both the 2006 and 2001 estimates. (Tables 1 and 1A)

The estimated property crime rate per 100,000 inhabitants in 2010 was 2,941.9, a 3.3 percent decrease from the 2009 rate, a 12.1 percent decrease from the 2006 rate, and a 19.6 percent decrease from the 2001 rate. The number of burglaries grew 2.0 percent from 2001 to 2010, but the burglary rate per 100,000 inhabitants fell 5.7 percent. The motor vehicle theft rates per 100,000 residents fell from 430.5 in 2001 to 238.8 in 2010. (Tables 1 and 1A)

Regional Offense Trends and Rates

The UCR Program separates the United States into four regions: the Northeast, the Midwest, the South, and the West. (Geographic breakdowns can be found in Appendix III.) Property crime data collected by the UCR Program and aggregated by region reflected the following results.

The Northeast

The Northeast region accounted for 17.9 percent of the nation's population and experienced a slight increase in population from 2009 to 2010 (0.06 percent). The region also accounted for 12.9 percent of the nation's estimated number of property crimes in 2010. (Table 3) Law enforcement in the Northeast saw a slight decrease in the estimated number of property crimes from 2009 to 2010. The property crime rate for the Northeast, estimated at 2,115.8 incidents per 100,000 inhabitants, was 0.4 percent lower than the 2009 rate. (Table 4)

The Midwest

The Midwest, with 21.7 percent of the U.S. population in 2010 and a 0.1 percent growth in population from 2009 to 2010, accounted for 20.9 percent of the nation's estimated number of property crimes. (Table 3) Law enforcement in the Midwest saw a 2.3 percent decrease in the estimated number of property crimes from 2009 to 2010. The rate of property crime in the Midwest in 2010, estimated at 2,833.6 incidents per 100,000 inhabitants, represented a 2.4 percent decrease from the 2009 rate. (Table 4)

The South

The South, the nation's most populous region, accounted for 37.1 percent of the U.S. population in 2010 and experienced a 1.1 percent growth in population from 2009 to 2010. The region also accounted for an estimated 43.4 percent of the nation's property crimes. (Table 3) The South experienced a 3.8 percent decrease in its estimated number of property crimes from 2009 to 2010. The 2010 property crime rate, an estimated 3,438.8 incidents per 100,000 inhabitants, was 4.9 percent lower than the 2009 rate. (Table 4)

The West

In 2010, the West again accounted for 23.3 percent of the nation's population; the region experienced a 0.5 percent growth in population from 2009 to 2010. The West also accounted for 22.9 percent of the nation's estimated number of property crimes. (Table 3) From 2009 to 2010, the estimated number of property crimes in this region decreased 2.3 percent. The estimated property crime rate in the West in 2010, 2,886.55 incidents per 100,000 inhabitants, was 2.8 percent lower than the 2009 rate. (Table 4)

Community Types

The UCR Program aggregates data by three community types: metropolitan statistical areas (MSAs), cities outside metropolitan areas, and nonmetropolitan counties. (Addi-

tional in-depth information regarding community types can be found in Appendix III.) In 2010, 83.7 percent of the U.S. population lived in MSAs. The property crime rate for MSAs was 3,046.5 per 100,000 inhabitants. Cities outside metropolitan areas, which accounted for 6.5 percent of the total population in 2010, had a property crime rate of 3,602.3 per 100,000 inhabitants. Nonmetropolitan counties, with 9.8 percent of the nation's population in 2010, had a property crime rate of 1,605.8 per 100,000 inhabitants. (Table 2)

Population Groups: Trends and Rates

The UCR Program organizes the agencies that contribute data into population groups, which include cities, metropolitan counties, and nonmetropolitan counties. (Appendix III provides further details about these groups.) From 2009 to 2010, law enforcement in the nation's cities collectively reported a 3.0 percent decrease in the number of property crimes. All city groups experienced decreases in the number of property crimes; cities with 500,000 to 999,999 inhabitants had the largest declines at 3.9 percent. Metropolitan counties experienced a decrease of 2.7 percent from 2009 to 2010 and property crime decreased in nonmetropolitan counties 2.2 percent. (Table 12)

The nation's cities collectively had a property crime rate of 3,413.3 incidents per 100,000 inhabitants in 2010. Nonmetropolitan counties had a rate of 1,645.7 incidents per 100,000 inhabitants, and metropolitan counties had a rate of 2,190.2 incidents per 100,000 inhabitants. (Table 16)

Offense Analysis

The estimated dollar loss attributing to property crimes, not including arson, in 2010 was again $15.2 billion. Among the individual property crime categories, the dollar losses were an estimated $4.6 billion for burglary, $6.1 billion for larceny-theft, and $4.5 billion for motor vehicle theft. (Tables 1 and 23) Arson had an average dollar loss of $17,612. Arsons of industrial/manufacturing structures resulted in the highest average dollar losses ($133,717), followed by Other Commercial structures, with average losses of $113,186. (Expanded Arson Table 2) In 2010, the average dollar value per motor vehicle stolen in the United States was $6,152. The average dollar value of property taken during burglaries was $2,119; during robberies, $1,239; and during larceny-thefts, $988.

BURGLARY

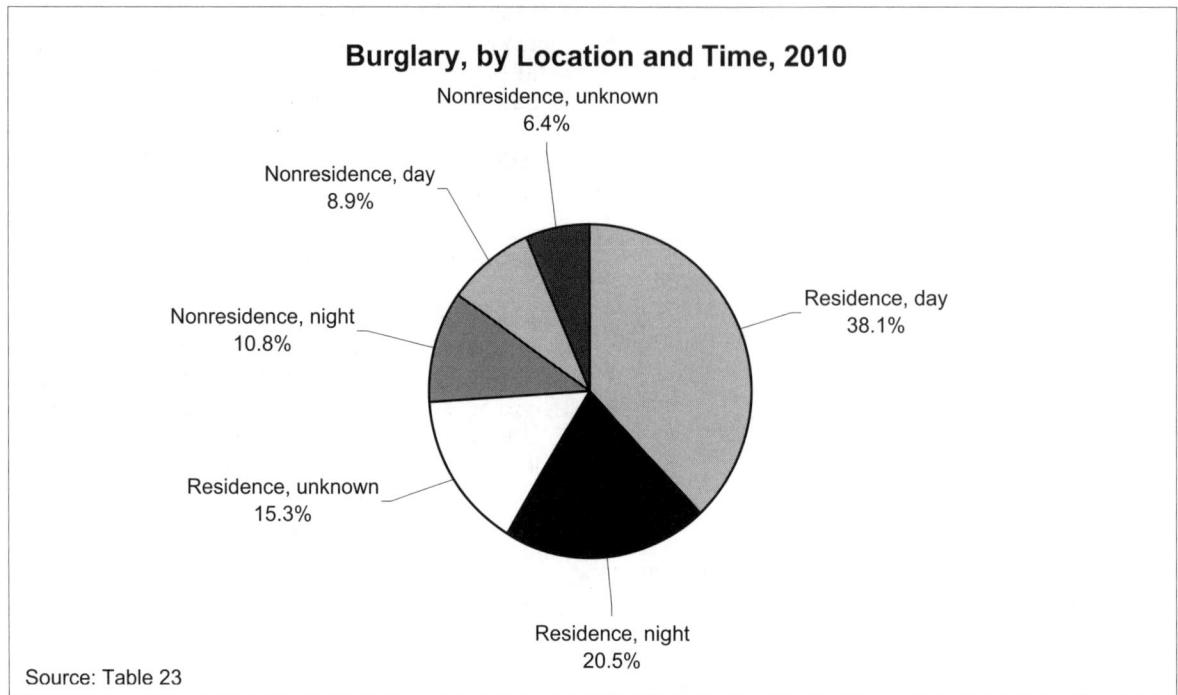

Burglary, by Location and Time, 2010

Residence, day 38.1%

Nonresidence, unknown 6.4%

Nonresidence, day 8.9%

Nonresidence, night 10.8%

Residence, unknown 15.3%

Residence, night 20.5%

Source: Table 23

Definition

The UCR Program defines burglary as the unlawful entry of a structure to commit a felony or theft. To classify an offense as a burglary, the use of force to gain entry need not have occurred. The program has three subclassifications for burglary: forcible entry, unlawful entry where no force is used, and attempted forcible entry. The UCR definition of "structure" includes, but is not limited to, apartments, barns, house trailers or houseboats (when used as permanent dwellings), offices, railroad cars (but not automobiles), stables, and vessels (that is, ships).

National Volume, Trends, and Rate

In 2010, there were an estimated 2,159,878 burglaries—a decrease of 2.0 percent when compared with 2009 data. There was a decrease of 1.6 percent in the number of burglaries in 2010 when compared with the 2006 estimate and an increase of 2.0 percent when compared with the 2001 estimate. Burglary accounted for 23.8 percent of the estimated number of property crimes committed in 2010. The burglary rate for the United States in 2010 was 699.6 incidents per 100,000 inhabitants, a 2.5 percent decrease from the 2009 rate. (Tables 1 and 1A)

Regional Offense Trends and Rates

The UCR Program divides the United States into four regions: the Northeast, the Midwest, the South, and the West. (Details regarding these regions can be found in Appendix III.) An analysis of burglary data by region showed the following details.

The Northeast

In 2010, 17.9 percent of the nation's population lived in the Northeast, which experienced a slight increase in population from 2009 to 2010 (0.06 percent). This region accounted for 10.8 percent of the estimated total number of burglary offenses in the nation in 2010. The region's burglary rate, an estimated 423.2 offenses per 100,000 inhabitants, represented a increase of 4.0 percent from the 2009 rate. The Northeast had the lowest burglary rate of the four regions. (Tables 3 and 4)

The Midwest

The Midwest accounted for 21.7 percent of the nation's population in 2010 and experienced a 0.1 percent growth in population from 2009 to 2010. This region accounted for 20.7 percent of the nation's estimated number of burglaries. The estimated number of burglaries in this region decreased 1.1 percent from 2009 to 2010. The Midwest had a burglary rate of 668.6 offenses per 100,000 inhabitants, a 1.2 percent decrease from the 2009 rate. (Tables 3 and 4)

The South

The South, the nation's most highly populated region, had the most burglaries in 2010 (an estimated 1,015,404). With 37.1 percent of the nation's population (and having experienced a 1.1 percent growth in population from 2009 to 2010), this region accounted for 47.0 percent of all burglaries in the United States. The estimated rate of burglary in the South was 886.4 incidents per 100,000 inhabitants, a 5.0 percent decrease from the 2009 rate. (Tables 3 and 4)

The West

The West again accounted for 23.3 percent of the nation's population in 2010 and experienced a 0.5 percent growth in population from 2009 to 2010. In 2010, this region accounted for an estimated 21.4 percent of the nation's burglaries. The region's burglary rate was 643.4, a 1.7 percent decrease from the 2009 rate. The total number of burglaries (462,912) represented a 1.2 percent decrease from the 2009 figure. (Tables 3 and 4)

Community Types

The UCR Program aggregates data by three community types: metropolitan statistical areas (MSAs), cities outside MSAs, and nonmetropolitan counties. (See Appendix III for more information regarding community types.) In 2010, 83.7 percent of the U.S. population lived in MSAs, and an estimated 84.5 percent of all burglaries occurred in this type of community. Inhabitants of cities outside MSAs accounted for 6.5 percent of the total population in 2010 and 7.6 percent of the estimated number of burglaries; nonmetropolitan counties, with 9.8 percent of the U.S. population, accounted for 7.8 percent of all burglaries. The burglary rates per 100,000 inhabitants were 706.5 in MSAs, 819.9 in cities outside MSAs, and 559.7 in nonmetropolitan counties. (Table 2)

Population Groups: Trends and Rates

In addition to analyzing data by region and community type, the UCR Program aggregates crime statistics by population groups. Cities are categorized into six groups based on the number of inhabitants; counties are categorized into two groups, metropolitan and nonmetropolitan. (Appendix III offers further details regarding these population groups.)

An examination of data from law enforcement agencies that provided statistics for at least six common months in 2009 and 2010 showed that the nation's cities again experienced a collective 1.7 percent decrease in burglaries from 2009 to 2010. Burglaries decreased the most in cities with a population of 500,000 to 999,999, a decrease of 3.6 percent

(the same percentage experienced from 2008 to 2009). The volume of burglaries decreased 2.3 percent in metropolitan counties, and 1.9 percent in suburban areas, but increased 0.9 percent in nonmetropolitan counties. (Table 12)

The UCR Program calculates burglary rates for population groups from the information provided by participating agencies that submitted all 12 months of offense data for the year. In 2010, the nation's cities had 756.9 offenses per 100,000 inhabitants. Cities with 500,000 to 999,999 population had the highest burglary rate at 1,078.7 incidents per 100,000 inhabitants. Cities with 10,000 to 24,999 inhabitants had the lowest burglary rate—600.0 incidents per 100,000 inhabitants. Metropolitan counties had a rate of 602.0 per 100,000 inhabitants, and nonmetropolitan counties had a rate of 574.4 per 100,000 inhabitants. (Table 16)

Offense Analysis

The UCR Program requests that participating law enforcement agencies provide details regarding the nature of burglaries in their jurisdictions, such as type of entry, type of structure, time of day, and dollar loss associated with each offense.

Of all burglaries, 60.5 percent involved forcible entry, 33.2 percent were unlawful entries (without force), and the remainder (6.3 percent) were forcible entry attempts. (Table 19)

Victims of burglary offenses suffered an estimated $4.6 billion in lost property in 2010; overall, the average dollar loss per burglary offense was $2,119. (Tables 1 and 23)

As in the past, burglars targeted residences more often than nonresidential structures. In 2010, burglaries of residential properties accounted for 73.8 percent of all burglary offenses. Law enforcement agencies were unable to determine the time of day for 21.7 percent of all reported burglaries. However, of the burglaries for which time of day could be established, most burglaries of residences (64.9 percent) occurred during the day, while most burglaries of nonresidential structures (54.8 percent) occurred at night. (Table 23)

LARCENY-THEFT

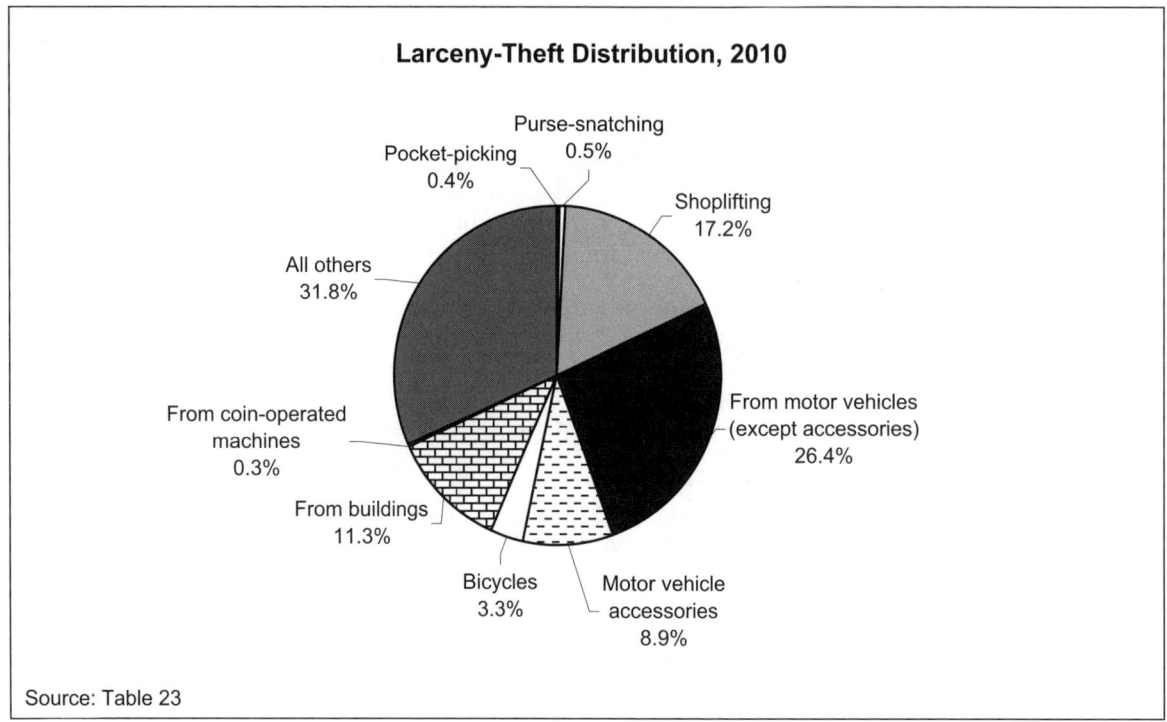

Larceny-Theft Distribution, 2010

- Purse-snatching 0.5%
- Pocket-picking 0.4%
- Shoplifting 17.2%
- All others 31.8%
- From motor vehicles (except accessories) 26.4%
- From coin-operated machines 0.3%
- From buildings 11.3%
- Bicycles 3.3%
- Motor vehicle accessories 8.9%

Source: Table 23

Definition

The UCR Program defines larceny-theft as the unlawful taking, carrying, leading, or riding away of property from the possession or constructive possession of another. Examples are thefts of bicycles, motor vehicle parts and accessories, shoplifting, pocket picking, or the stealing of any property or article not taken by force and violence or by fraud. Attempted larcenies are included. Embezzlement, confidence games, forgery, check fraud, and so on, are excluded from this category.

National Volume, Trends, and Rates

Larceny-thefts accounted for an estimated 68.1 percent of property crimes in 2010—an estimated 6 million (6,185,867) larceny-thefts nationwide. The estimated number of larceny-thefts dropped 2.4 percent in 2010 compared with the 2009 estimate. The 2010 figure showed a 12.8 percent decline compared with the 2001 estimate. The trend data also showed decreases in the larceny-theft rates per 100,000 inhabitants during these periods. The rate of larceny-thefts declined 3.0 percent from 2009 to 2010, and the rate declined 19.4 percent from 2001 to 2010. (Tables 1 and 1A)

Regional Offense Trends and Rates

The UCR Program defines four regions within the United States: the Northeast, the Midwest, the South, and the West. (See Appendix III for a geographical description of each region.) Larceny-theft decreased in all four regions; the South and the Midwest saw the largest declines, 3.1 percent and 2.6 percent, respectively, while the West and Northeast

dropped 1.6 and 1.0 percent, respectively. (Tables 3 and 4) The following paragraphs provide a region overview of larceny-theft.

The Northeast

The Northeast was the region with the smallest proportion (17.9 percent) of the U.S. population in 2010. The region's population increased slightly from 2009 to 2010 (0.06 percent). The region also experienced the fewest larceny-thefts in the country, accounting for only 13.9 percent of all larceny-thefts. (Table 3) The estimated number of offenses in 2009 (860,706) represented a 1.0 percent decline from 2009, and the estimated rate—1,555.9 incidents per 100,000 inhabitants—represented a 1.1 percent decline. (Table 4)

The Midwest

With 21.7 percent of the U.S. population in 2010, and a 0.1 percent growth in population from 2009 to 2010, the Midwest accounted for an estimated 21.2 percent of the nation's larceny-thefts, the same as it had in 2009). (Table 3) The estimated number of offenses (1,310,742) declined 2.6 percent compared with the 2009 data, and the estimated rate of occurrences (1,958.5 incidents per 100,000 inhabitants) declined 2.7 percent. (Table 4)

The South

With more than one-third of the U.S. population in 2010 (37.1 percent), the South experienced a 1.1 percent growth in population from 2009 to 2010. The region had the nation's highest proportion of larceny-theft offenses: an estimated 42.9 percent. (Table 3) Estimated offenses in this region totaled 2,653,060, a 3.1 percent decrease from the 2009 estimate. The South's larceny-theft rate—estimated at 2,315.1 offenses per 100,000 inhabitants—decreased 4.2 percent from the 2009 estimate. (Table 4)

The West

In 2010, an estimated 23.3 percent of the U.S. population lived in the West, which experienced a 0.5 percent growth in population from 2009 to 2010. This region was also where 22.0 percent of the nation's estimated number of larceny-thefts took place. (Table 3) Occurrences of larceny-theft declined 1.6 percent from 2009 to 2010, dropping to an estimated total of 1,362,359 offenses. The region's larceny-theft rate, estimated at 1,893.6 offenses per 100,000 inhabitants, declined 2.1 percent from the 2009 rate. (Table 4)

Community Types

The UCR Program aggregates data for three community types: metropolitan statistical areas (MSAs), cities outside MSAs, and nonmetropolitan counties outside MSAs. MSAs include a central city or urbanized area with at least 50,000 inhabitants, as well as the county that contains the principal city and other adjacent counties that share a high degree of social and economic integration as measured through commuting. Cities outside MSAs are mostly incorporated areas, and nonmetropolitan counties are composed of unincorporated areas. (See Appendix III for more information regarding community types.)

In 2010, MSAs were home to an estimated 83.7 percent of the nation's population and again experienced 87.1 percent of the nation's larceny-theft incidents. Cities outside MSAs accounted for 6.5 percent of the U.S. population and 8.6 percent of larceny-theft offenses. Nonmetropolitan counties, which were home to 9.8 percent of the nation's population, accounted for 4.6 percent of the estimated number of larceny-theft offenses. (Table 2)

Population Groups: Trends and Rates

In cities, collectively, occurrences of larceny-theft declined 2.9 percent between 2009 and 2010. Cities with 100,000 to 249,999 inhabitants experienced the greatest decrease (3.7 percent), followed by 2 city groups, 500,000 to 999,999 and 1,000,000 or more inhabitants, both showing decreases of

3.6 percent. In metropolitan and suburban areas, larceny-theft decreased 2.0 percent and 2.1 percent, respectively. Nonmetropolitan counties experienced an increase of 3.8 percent. (Table 12)

Based on reports of larceny-theft offenses from U.S. law enforcement agencies that submitted 12 months of complete data for 2010, this offense occurred at a rate of 2,023.3 offenses per 100,000 inhabitants. The collective rate for cities was 2,370.5 offenses per 100,000 inhabitants. Among city population groups, cities with 500,000 to 999,000 inhabitants had the highest larceny-theft rate, 2,972.9 incidents per 100,000 inhabitants. Cities with more than 1,000,000 inhabitants had the lowest rate, at 2,074.2. In metropolitan counties, the rate was 1,408.4 incidents per 100,000 inhabitants; in nonmetropolitan counties, the rate was 967.3 incidents per 100,000 inhabitants. (Table 16)

Offense Analysis

Distribution

Thefts from motor vehicles accounted for the majority of larceny-theft offenses in 2010 (35.3 percent). Table 23 provides a further breakdown of larceny-theft offenses, including shoplifting, thefts from buildings, thefts of motor vehicle accessories, thefts of bicycles, thefts from coin-operated machines, purse snatching, and pocket picking. The "all other" category, which includes the less-defined types of larceny-theft, accounted for 31.8 percent of all offenses.

Loss by Dollar Value

Larceny-theft offenses cost victims an estimated $6.1 billion dollars in 2010, up from $5.5 billion in 2009. (Tables 1 and 23) The average value of property stolen was $988 per offense. Larceny-theft from buildings had the highest average dollar loss per offense at $1,406. Thefts from motor vehicles had an average dollar loss of $704 per offense; thefts of motor vehicle accessories, $681; purse snatching, $400; pocket picking, $526; thefts from coin-operated machines, $365; thefts of bicycles, $351; and shoplifting, $174. (Table 23)

Offenses in which the stolen property was valued at more than $200 accounted for 45.3 percent of all larceny-thefts. Table 23 provides further analysis, including the average dollar value per offense, of all offenses in the overall category of property crime.

MOTOR VEHICLE THEFT

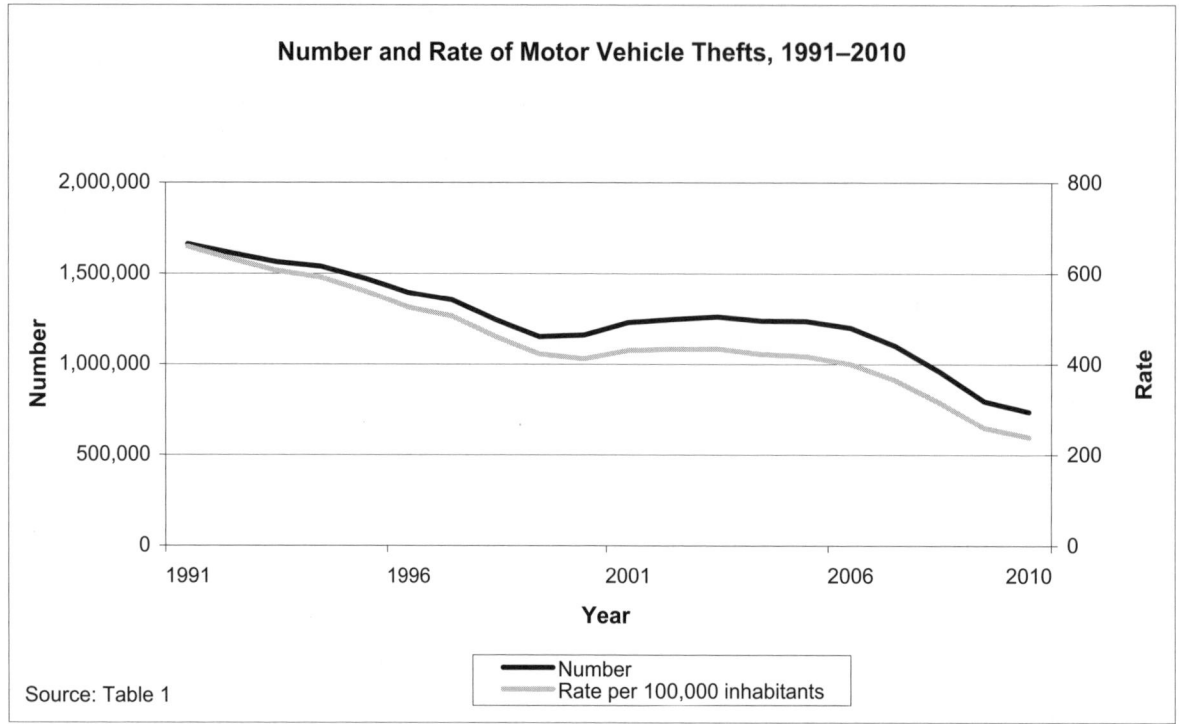

Source: Table 1

Definition

The UCR Program defines motor vehicle theft as the theft or attempted theft of a motor vehicle. The offense includes the stealing of automobiles, trucks, buses, motorcycles, snowmobiles, etc. The taking of a motor vehicle for temporary use by a person or persons with lawful access is excluded.

National Volume, Trends, and Rates

In 2010, an estimated 737,142 motor vehicle thefts took place in the United States. The estimated number of motor vehicle thefts declined 7.4 percent when compared with data from 2009, 38.5 percent when compared with 2006 figures, and 40.0 percent when compared with 2001 figures. (Tables 1 and 1A)

The estimated rate of motor vehicle theft in 2010 was 238.8 incidents per 100,000 inhabitants. In the 2-year, 5-year, and 10-year trend data, this rate showed decline: the 2010 rate was 7.9 percent lower than the 2009 rate, 40.3 percent lower than the 2006 rate, and 44.5 percent lower than the 2001 rate. (Tables 1 and 1A)

Regional Offense Trends and Rates

In order to analyze crime by geographic area, the UCR Program divides the United States into four regions: the Northeast, the Midwest, the South, and the West. (Appendix III provides a map delineating the regions.) This section provides a regional overview of motor vehicle theft.

The Northeast

The Northeast accounted for an estimated 17.9 percent of the nation's population in 2010 and experienced a 0.06 percent increase in population from 2009 to 2010. The region also accounted for an estimated 10.3 percent of its motor vehicle thefts. (Table 3) An estimated 75,616 motor vehicle thefts occurred in the Northeast in 2010, representing a 5.0 percent decrease from the 2009 estimate. The estimated rate of 136.7 motor vehicle thefts per 100,000 inhabitants in the Northeast in 2010 represented a 5.0 percent decline from the 2009 rate. (Table 4)

The Midwest

An estimated 21.7 percent of the country's population resided in the Midwest in 2010, and the region experienced a 0.1 growth in population from 2009 to 2010. The region accounted for 18.7 percent of the nation's motor vehicle thefts. (Table 3) The Midwest had an estimated 138,214 motor vehicle thefts in 2010, a 3.1 percent decrease from the previous year's total. This was the largest decline among the regions. The motor vehicle theft rate was estimated at 206.5 motor vehicles stolen per 100,000 inhabitants, a 3.2 percent decrease from the 2009 rate. (Table 4)

The South

The South, the nation's most populous region, was home to an estimated 37.1 percent of the U.S. population in 2010 and experienced a 1.1 percent growth in population from 2009 to 2010. This region accounted for 36.9 percent of the nation's motor vehicle thefts. (Table 3) The estimated 271,853 motor vehicle thefts in the South decreased 9.6 percent from the 2009 estimate. Motor vehicles in the South were stolen at an estimated rate of 237.3 per 100,000 inhabitants in 2010, a rate that was 10.6 percent lower than the 2009 rate. (Table 4)

The West

With approximately 23.3 percent of the U.S. population in 2010, the West experienced a 0.5 percent growth in population from 2009 to 2010. This region accounted for 34.1 percent of all motor vehicle thefts in the nation in 2010. (Table 3) An estimated 251,459 motor vehicle thefts occurred in this region. This number represented a 7.8 percent decrease from the previous year's estimate. The motor vehicle theft rate for the West was also lower in 2010 than in 2009; the 2010 rate of 349.5 motor vehicles stolen per 100,000 inhabitants was 8.3 percent lower than the 2009 rate. (Table 4)

Community Types

The UCR Program aggregates data by three community types: metropolitan statistical areas (MSAs), cities outside MSAs, and nonmetropolitan counties. MSAs are areas that include a principal city or urbanized area with at least 50,000 inhabitants and the county that contains the principal city and other adjacent counties that have, as defined by the U.S. Office of Management and Budget, a high degree of economic and social integration.

In 2010, the vast majority (83.7 percent) of the U.S. population resided in MSAs, where approximately 92.0 percent of motor vehicle thefts occurred. For 2010, the UCR Program estimated an overall rate of 262.5 motor vehicles stolen per 100,000 MSA inhabitants. Cities outside MSAs accounted for 3.8 percent of motor vehicle thefts, and nonmetropolitan counties accounted for 4.2 percent of motor vehicle thefts. The UCR Program estimated a 2010 rate of 138.9 motor vehicles stolen for every 100,000 inhabitants in cities outside MSAs and a rate of 101.7 motor vehicles stolen per 100,000 inhabitants in nonmetropolitan counties. (Table 2)

Population Groups: Trends and Rates

The UCR Program aggregates data by various population groups, which include cities, metropolitan counties, and

nonmetropolitan counties. (A definition of these groups can be found in Appendix III.)

In cities, collectively, the number of motor vehicle thefts decreased 7.3 percent from 2009 to 2010. The number of motor vehicle thefts decreased for all city groups. Two city groups, those with 100,000 to 249,999 inhabitants, and those with 10,000 to 24,999 inhabitants experienced the greatest decline—both at 9.3 percent. Suburban areas experienced a decrease of 9.0 percent; while metropolitan counties experienced a decrease of 8.7 percent, and nonmetropolitan counties experienced a decrease of 4.2 percent. (Table 12)

In 2010, cities had a collective motor vehicle theft rate of 285.9 per 100,000 inhabitants. Among the population groups, cities with 500,000 to 999,999 inhabitants experienced the highest rate of motor vehicle thefts with 537.0 motor vehicle thefts per 100,000 inhabitants. Conversely, the nation's smallest cities, those with populations under 10,000, had the lowest rate of motor vehicle theft with 132.2 incidents per 100,000 in population. Within the county groups, metropolitan counties had a rate of 140.0 motor vehicles stolen per 100,000 inhabitants, while nonmetropolitan counties had a rate of 104.0 incidents per 100,000 inhabitants. (Table 16)

Offense Analysis

Based on the reports of law enforcement agencies, the UCR Program estimated the combined value of motor vehicles stolen nationwide in 2010 at approximately $4.5 billion. (Tables 1 and 23) In 2010, the average dollar value per motor vehicle stolen in the United States was $6,152. Automobiles were, by far, the most frequently stolen vehicle, accounting for 72.9 percent of all vehicles stolen. Trucks and buses accounted for 16.5 percent of stolen vehicles, and other vehicles accounted for 10.6 percent of stolen vehicles. (Expanded Motor Vehicle Theft Table)

By type of vehicle, automobiles were stolen at a rate of 180.3 cars per 100,000 inhabitants in 2010. Trucks and buses were stolen at a rate of 40.9 vehicles per 100,000 in population, and other types of vehicles were stolen at a rate of 26.1 vehicles per 100,000 inhabitants. (Table 19)

ARSON

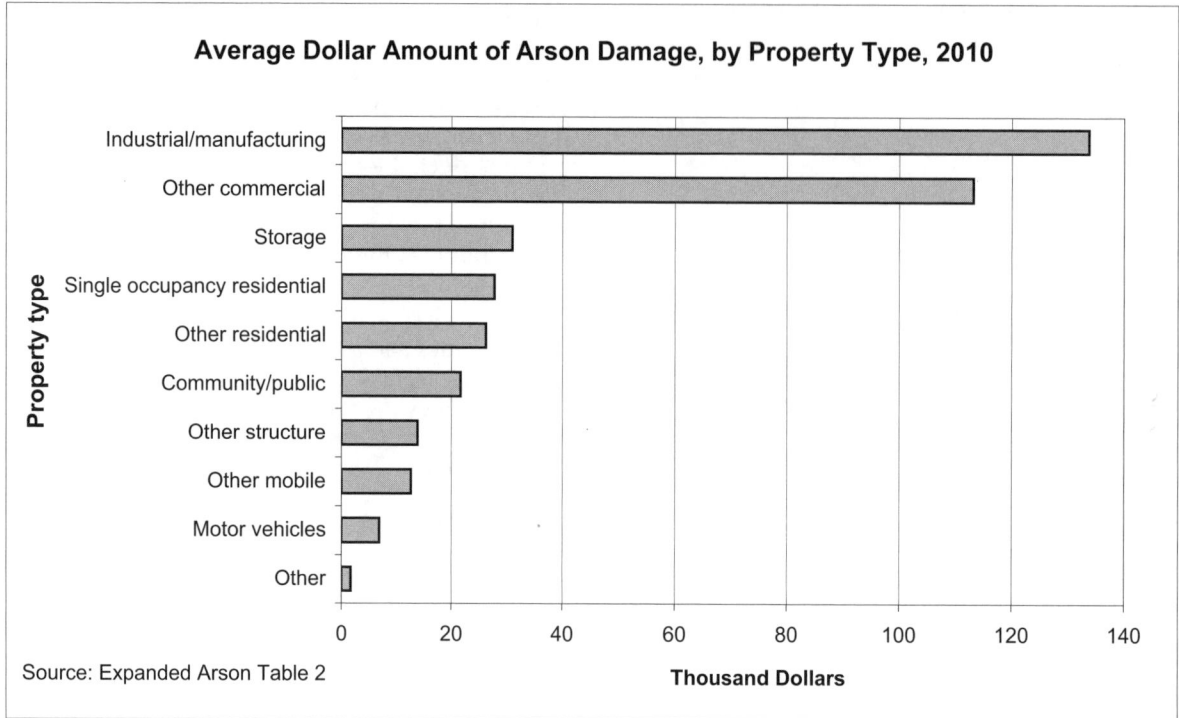

Average Dollar Amount of Arson Damage, by Property Type, 2010

Source: Expanded Arson Table 2

Thousand Dollars

Definition

The UCR Program defines arson as any willful or malicious burning or attempt to burn (with or without intent to defraud) a dwelling house, public building, motor vehicle, aircraft, or personal property of another, and so on.

Data Collection

Only fires that investigators determined were willfully set (not fires labeled as "suspicious" or "of unknown origin") are included in this arson data collection. Points to consider regarding arson statistics include:

National offense rates per 100,000 inhabitants (found in Tables 1, 2, and 4) do not include arson data; the FBI presents rates for arson separately. Arson rates are calculated based upon data received from all law enforcement agencies that provide the UCR Program with data for 12 complete months.

Arson data collection does not include estimates for arson, because the degree of reporting arson offenses varies from agency to agency. Because of this unevenness of reporting, arson offenses are excluded from Tables 1 through 7, all of which contain offense estimations.

The number of arsons reported by individual law enforcement agencies is available in Tables 8 through 11. Arson trend data (which indicate year-to-year changes) can be found in Tables 12 through 15, and arson clearance data (crimes solved) can be found in Table 2, and Tables 25 through 28.

National Coverage

In 2010, 15,475 agencies (providing 1 to 12 months of data) reported 56,825 arson offenses. Of those agencies, 14,747 provided expanded offense data about 48,619 arsons. (Unpublished Expanded Arson Table 1; see Section I for more information)

Population Groups: Trends and Rates

The number of arsons reported in 2010 decreased 7.6 percent from the 2009 figure. Law enforcement agencies in the nation's cities collectively reported a 6.5 percent decline in the number of arsons from the 2009 figure. The number of arsons declined for all population groups. Among the population groups labeled *city,* the subset with 1,000,000 or more inhabitants had the largest year-to-year decrease in reported arsons, 15.2 percent. Agencies in the nation's metropolitan counties reported a 11.8 percent decrease in the number of arsons, and those in nonmetropolitan counties reported an 7.0 percent decline. Those in suburban areas reported a 10.8 percent decline. (Table 12)

Arson rates were based on information received from 12,821 agencies that provided 12 months of complete arson data to the UCR Program. An examination of data indicated that in 2010, the highest rate among city groups—32.4 arsons per 100,000 inhabitants—was reported in cities with 250,000 or more inhabitants. Among cities with 250,000 or more inhabitants, those with a population of 250,000 to 499,999 had the highest rate at 35.7 per 100,000 inhabitants. Cities with 10,000 to 24,999 inhabitants had the lowest rate of arson at 14.1 per 100,000 inhabitants. Metropolitan counties had 15.1 arsons per 100,000 inhabitants, and non-metropolitan counties had 13.9 arsons per 100,000 inhabitants, the lowest of all the population groups. (Expanded Arson Table 1)

Offense Analysis

The UCR Program breaks down arson offenses into three property categories: structural, mobile, and other. In addition, the structural property type is broken down into seven types of structures, and the mobile property type consists of two subgroupings. The program also collects information on the estimated dollar value of the damaged property.

Property Type

The total number of arsons decreased in 2010. Arsons for the structural property type decreased 5.2 percent, mobile property type dropped 15.5 percent, and other arsons fell 4.9 percent from 2009 to 2010. (Table 15)

Distribution by Property Type

Arsons involving structures (residential, storage, public, etc.) accounted for 45.5 percent of the total number of arson offenses; arsons involving mobile property accounted for 26.0 percent; and other types of property (such as crops, timber, fences, etc.) accounted for 28.5 percent of reported arsons. Of the arsons involving structures, 63.9 percent involved residential properties. Of the residential arsons, 75.3 percent were single-occupancy residences. Approximately 18 percent of structures were not in use when the arson occurred. Mobile arsons accounted for 25.5 percent of all arsons. Within this category, 91.8 percent of offenses involved the burning of motor vehicles. (Expanded Arson Table 2)

Dollar Loss

In monetary terms, the average dollar loss in 2010 for arson was $17,612. The average dollar loss for a structural arson was $33,658. Within the structural arson category, the industrial/manufacturing subcategory had the highest average dollar loss at $133,717. Within that same category, single-occupancy dwellings had an average dollar loss of $27,671. Mobile property had an average dollar loss of $7,084. Other property types had an average dollar loss of $1,647. (Expanded Arson Table 2)

Table 1.   Crime in the United States, by Volume and Rate per 100,000 Inhabitants, 1991–2010

(Number, rate per 100,000 population, percent.)

Year	Population[1]	Violent crime		Murder and nonnegligent manslaughter		Forcible rape		Robbery		Aggravated assault	
		Number	Rate	Number	Rate	Number	Rate	Number	Rate	Number	Rate
1991	252,153,092	1,911,767	758.2	24,703	9.8	106,593	42.3	687,732	272.7	1,092,739	433.4
1992	255,029,699	1,932,274	757.7	23,760	9.3	109,062	42.8	672,478	263.7	1,126,974	441.9
1993	257,782,608	1,926,017	747.1	24,526	9.5	106,014	41.1	659,870	256.0	1,135,607	440.5
1994	260,327,021	1,857,670	713.6	23,326	9.0	102,216	39.3	618,949	237.8	1,113,179	427.6
1995	262,803,276	1,798,792	684.5	21,606	8.2	97,470	37.1	580,509	220.9	1,099,207	418.3
1996	265,228,572	1,688,540	636.6	19,645	7.4	96,252	36.3	535,594	201.9	1,037,049	391.0
1997	267,783,607	1,636,096	611.0	18,208	6.8	96,153	35.9	498,534	186.2	1,023,201	382.1
1998	270,248,003	1,533,887	567.6	16,974	6.3	93,144	34.5	447,186	165.5	976,583	361.4
1999	272,690,813	1,426,044	523.0	15,522	5.7	89,411	32.8	409,371	150.1	911,740	334.3
2000	281,421,906	1,425,486	506.5	15,586	5.5	90,178	32.0	408,016	145.0	911,706	324.0
2001[2]	285,317,559	1,439,480	504.5	16,037	5.6	90,863	31.8	423,557	148.5	909,023	318.6
2002	287,973,924	1,423,677	494.4	16,229	5.6	95,235	33.1	420,806	146.1	891,407	309.5
2003	290,788,976	1,383,676	475.8	16,528	5.7	93,883	32.3	414,235	142.5	859,030	295.4
2004	293,656,842	1,360,088	463.2	16,148	5.5	95,089	32.4	401,470	136.7	847,381	288.6
2005	296,507,061	1,390,745	469.0	16,740	5.6	94,347	31.8	417,438	140.8	862,220	290.8
2006[3]	299,398,484	1,435,123	479.3	17,309	5.8	94,472	31.6	449,246	150.0	874,096	292.0
2007[3]	301,621,157	1,422,970	471.8	17,128	5.7	92,160	30.6	447,324	148.3	866,358	287.2
2008[3]	304,059,724	1,394,461	458.6	16,465	5.4	90,750	29.8	443,563	145.9	843,683	277.5
2009[3]	307,006,550	1,325,896	431.9	15,399	5.0	89,241	29.1	408,742	133.1	812,514	264.7
2010	308,745,538	1,246,248	403.6	14,748	4.8	84,767	27.5	367,832	119.1	778,901	252.3

Year	Property crime		Burglary		Larceny-theft		Motor vehicle theft	
	Number	Rate	Number	Rate	Number	Rate	Number	Rate
1991	12,961,116	5,140.2	3,157,150	1,252.1	8,142,228	3,229.1	1,661,738	659.0
1992	12,505,917	4,903.7	2,979,884	1,168.4	7,915,199	3,103.6	1,610,834	631.6
1993	12,218,777	4,740.0	2,834,808	1,099.7	7,820,909	3,033.9	1,563,060	606.3
1994	12,131,873	4,660.2	2,712,774	1,042.1	7,879,812	3,026.9	1,539,287	591.3
1995	12,063,935	4,590.5	2,593,784	987.0	7,997,710	3,043.2	1,472,441	560.3
1996	11,805,323	4,451.0	2,506,400	945.0	7,904,685	2,980.3	1,394,238	525.7
1997	11,558,475	4,316.3	2,460,526	918.8	7,743,760	2,891.8	1,354,189	505.7
1998	10,951,827	4,052.5	2,332,735	863.2	7,376,311	2,729.5	1,242,781	459.9
1999	10,208,334	3,743.6	2,100,739	770.4	6,955,520	2,550.7	1,152,075	422.5
2000	10,182,584	3,618.3	2,050,992	728.8	6,971,590	2,477.3	1,160,002	412.2
2001[2]	10,437,189	3,658.1	2,116,531	741.8	7,092,267	2,485.7	1,228,391	430.5
2002	10,455,277	3,630.6	2,151,252	747.0	7,057,379	2,450.7	1,246,646	432.9
2003	10,442,862	3,591.2	2,154,834	741.0	7,026,802	2,416.5	1,261,226	433.7
2004	10,319,386	3,514.1	2,144,446	730.3	6,937,089	2,362.3	1,237,851	421.5
2005	10,174,754	3,431.5	2,155,448	726.9	6,783,447	2,287.8	1,235,859	416.8
2006[3]	10,019,601	3,346.6	2,194,993	733.1	6,626,363	2,213.2	1,198,245	400.2
2007[3]	9,882,212	3,276.4	2,190,198	726.1	6,591,542	2,185.4	1,100,472	364.9
2008[3]	9,774,152	3,214.6	2,228,887	733.0	6,586,206	2,166.1	959,059	315.4
2009[3]	9,337,060	3,041.3	2,203,313	717.7	6,338,095	2,064.5	795,652	259.2
2010	9,082,887	2,941.9	2,159,878	699.6	6,185,867	2,003.5	737,142	238.8

[1] Populations are U.S. Census Bureau provisional estimates as of July 1 for each year except 2000, which is decennial census counts.
[2] The murder and nonnegligent homicides that occurred as a result of the events of September 11, 2001, are not included in this table.
[3] The crime figures have been adjusted.

Table 1A.   Crime in the United States, Percent Change in Volume and Rate per 100,000 Inhabitants for 2 Years, 5 Years, and 10 Years

(Percent change)

Year	Violent crime		Murder and nonnegligent manslaughter		Forcible rape		Robbery		Aggravated assault	
	Number	Rate	Number	Rate	Number	Rate	Number	Rate	Number	Rate
2009–2010	-6.0	-6.5	-4.2	-4.8	-5.0	-5.5	-10.0	-10.5	-4.1	-4.7
2006–2010	-13.2	-15.8	-14.8	-17.4	-10.3	-13.0	-18.1	-20.6	-10.9	-13.6
2001–2010	-13.4	-20.0	-8.0	-15.0	-6.7	-13.8	-13.2	-19.7	-14.3	-20.8

Year	Property crime		Burglary		Larceny-theft		Motor vehicle theft	
	Number	Rate	Number	Rate	Number	Rate	Number	Rate
2009–2010	-2.7	-3.3	-2.0	-2.5	-2.4	-3.0	-7.4	-7.9
2006–2010	-9.3	-12.1	-1.6	-4.6	-6.6	-9.5	-38.5	-40.3
2001–2010	-13.0	-19.6	2.0	-5.7	-12.8	-19.4	-40.0	-44.5

Table 2.   Crime in the United States, by Community Type, 2010

(Number, percent, rate per 100,000 population)

Area	Population[1]	Violent crime	Murder and non-negligent manslaughter	Forcible rape	Robbery	Aggravated assault	Property crime	Burglary	Larceny-theft	Motor vehicle theft
United States Total	308,745,538	1,246,248	14,748	84,767	367,832	778,901	9,082,887	2,159,878	6,185,867	737,142
Rate per 100,000 inhabitants		403.6	4.8	27.5	119.1	252.3	2,941.9	699.6	2,003.5	238.8
Metropolitan Statistical Areas....................	258,465,216									
Area actually reporting[2]............................	98.4%	1,096,842	12,972	67,204	349,702	666,964	7,781,587	1,805,180	5,302,840	673,567
Estimated total..............................	100.0%	1,107,026	13,050	69,746	351,558	672,672	7,874,193	1,826,166	5,369,510	678,517
Rate per 100,000 inhabitants		428.3	5.0	27.0	136.0	260.3	3,046.5	706.5	2,077.5	262.5
Cities Outside Metropolitan Areas..............	20,099,952									
Area actually reporting[2]............................	92.3%	74,175	670	7,570	10,575	55,360	668,260	151,836	490,490	25,934
Estimated total..............................	100.00%	80,340	728	8,367	11,485	59,760	724,070	164,796	531,347	27,927
Rate per 100,000 inhabitants		399.7	3.6	41.6	57.1	297.3	3,602.3	819.9	2,643.5	138.9
Nonmetropolitan Counties	30,180,370									
Area actually reporting[2]............................	92.7%	55,422	902	6,136	4,492	43,892	454,658	158,126	267,599	28,933
Estimated total..............................	100.00%	58,882	970	6,654	4,789	46,469	484,624	168,916	285,010	30,698
Rate per 100,000 inhabitants		195.1	3.2	22.0	15.9	154.0	1,605.8	559.7	944.4	101.7

[1] Population figures are U.S. Census Bureau provisional estimates as of July 1, 2010.

[2] The percentage reported under "Area actually reporting" is based on the population covered by agencies providing 3 months or more of crime reports to the FBI.

Table 3.   Crime in the United States, Population and Offense Distribution, by Region, 2010

(Percent distribution)

Region	Population	Violent crime	Murder and non-negligent manslaughter	Forcible rape	Robbery	Aggravated assault	Property crime	Burglary	Larceny-theft	Motor vehicle theft
United States Total[1]........................	100.0	100.0	100.0	100.0	100.0	100.0	100.0	100.0	100.0	100.0
Northeast..	17.9	15.8	15.6	12.7	18.7	14.8	12.9	10.8	13.9	10.3
Midwest..	21.7	19.5	19.9	24.6	19.6	18.8	20.9	20.7	21.2	18.7
South..	37.1	41.5	43.8	37.7	38.1	43.6	43.4	47.0	42.9	36.9
West...	23.3	23.1	20.6	25.1	23.6	22.8	22.9	21.4	22.0	34.1

[1] Because of rounding, the percentages may not add to 100.0.

Table 4.   Crime, by Region, Geographic Division, and State, 2009–2010

(Number, rate per 100,000 population, percent)

Area	Population[1]	Violent crime		Murder and non-negligent manslaughter		Forcible rape		Robbery	
		Number	Rate	Number	Rate	Number	Rate	Number	Rate
UNITED STATES TOTAL[2,3,4]									
2009	307,006,550	1,325,896	431.9	15,399	5.0	89,241	29.1	408,742	133.1
2010	308,745,538	1,246,248	403.6	14,748	4.8	84,767	27.5	367,832	119.1
Percent change		-6.0	-6.5	-4.2	-4.8	-5.0	-5.5	-10.0	-10.5
Northeast									
2009	55,283,679	198,722	359.5	2,120	3.8	10,842	19.6	70,501	127.5
2010	55,317,240	197,491	357.0	2,307	4.2	10,724	19.4	68,799	124.4
Percent change		-1	-0.7	9	8.8	-1	-1.1	-2	-2.5
New England									
2009	14,429,720	48,311	334.8	356	2.5	3,593	24.9	13,217	91.6
2010	14,444,865	47,945.0	331.9	413.0	2.9	3,557.0	24.6	12,146.0	84.1
Percent change		-0.8	-0.9	16.0	15.9	-1.0	-1.1	-8.1	-8.2
Connecticut									
2009	3,518,288	10,588	300.9	106	3.0	657	18.7	4,001	113.7
2010	3,574,097	10,057	281.4	130	3.6	583	16.3	3,553	99.4
Percent change		-5.0	-6.5	22.6	20.7	-11.3	-12.6	-11.2	-12.6
Maine									
2009	1,318,301	1,580	119.9	26	2.0	375	28.4	399	30.3
2010	1,328,361	1,621	122.0	24	1.8	389	29.3	414	31.2
Percent change		2.6	1.8	-7.7	-8.4	3.7	2.9	3.8	3.0
Massachusetts									
2009	6,593,587	30,503	462.6	173	2.6	1,734	26.3	7,467	113.2
2010	6,547,629	30,553	466.6	210	3.2	1,745	26.7	6,874	105.0
Percent change		0	0.9	21	22.2	1	1.3	-7.9	-7.3
New Hampshire									
2009	1,324,575	2,125	160.4	11	0.8	399	30.1	454	34.3
2010	1,316,470	2,198	167.0	13	1.0	412	31.3	451	34.3
Percent change		3.4	4.1	18.2	18.9	3.3	3.9	-0.7	0.0
Rhode Island									
2009	1,053,209	2,678	254.3	32	3.0	296	28.1	785	74.5
2010	1,052,567	2,701	256.6	29	2.8	296	28.1	780	74.1
Percent change		0.9	0.9	-9.4	-9.3	0.0	0.1	-0.6	-0.6
Vermont									
2009	621,760	837	134.6	8	1.3	132	21.2	111	17.9
2010	625,741	815	130.2	7	1.1	132	21.1	74	11.8
Percent change		-2.6	-3.2	-12.5	-13.1	0.0	-0.6	-33.3	-33.8
Middle Atlantic									
2009	40,853,959	150,411	368.2	1,764	4.3	7,249	17.7	57,284	140.2
2010	40,872,375	149,546	365.9	1,894	4.6	7,167	17.5	56,653	138.6
Percent change		-0.6	-0.6	7.4	7.3	-1.1	-1.2	-1.1	-1.1
New Jersey									
2009	8,707,739	27,113	311.4	319	3.7	1,041	12.0	11,639	133.7
2010	8,791,894	27,055	307.7	371	4.2	981	11.2	11,818	134.4
Percent change		-0.2	-1.2	16.3	15.2	-5.8	-6.7	1.5	0.6
New York									
2009	19,541,453	75,110	384.4	781	4.0	2,582	13.2	28,141	144.0
2010	19,378,102	75,977	392.1	866	4.5	2,771	14.3	28,473	146.9
Percent change		1.2	2.0	10.9	11.8	7.3	8.2	1.2	2.0
Pennsylvania									
2009	12,604,767	48,188	382.3	664	5.3	3,626	28.8	17,504	138.9
2010	12,702,379	46,514	366.2	657	5.2	3,415	26.9	16,362	128.8
Percent change		-3.5	-4.2	-1.1	-1.8	-5.8	-6.5	-6.5	-7.2
Midwest[2,3]									
2009	66,836,911	259,451	388.2	3,088	4.6	22,161	33.2	80,758	120.8
2010	66,927,001	242,626	362.5	2,938	4.4	20,825	31.1	72,093	107.7
Percent change		-6.5	-6.6	-4.9	-5.0	-6.0	-6.2	-10.7	-10.8
East North Central[2]									
2009	46,500,668	188,420	405.2	2,381	5.1	15,283	32.9	65,271	140.4
2010	46,421,564	175,192	377.4	2,196	4.7	14,353	30.9	58,749	126.6
Percent change		-7.0	-6.9	-7.8	-7.6	-6.1	-5.9	-10.0	-9.8
Illinois[2]									
2009	12,910,409	64,185	497.2	773	6.0	3,901	30.2	22,923	177.6
2010	12,830,632	55,835	435.2	706	5.5	3,033	23.6	20,054	156.3
Percent change		-13.0	-12.5	-8.7	-8.1	-22.3	-21.8	-12.5	-12.0
Indiana									
2009	6,423,113	21,455	334.0	312	4.9	1,621	25.2	7,347	114.4
2010	6,483,802	20,389	314.5	292	4.5	1,761	27.2	6,219	95.9
Percent change		-5.0	-5.9	-6.4	-7.3	8.6	7.6	-15.4	-16.1

[1] Populations are U.S. Census Bureau provisional estimates as of July 1, 2010, and July 1, 2009.

[2] Because of changes in the state's reporting practices, figures are not comparable to previous years' data.

[3] The data collection methodology for the offense of forcible rape used by the Minnesota state Uniform Crime Reporting (UCR) Program (with the exception of Minneapolis and St. Paul, Minnesota) does not comply with national UCR Program guidelines. Consequently, its figures for forcible rape and violent crime (of which forcible rape is a part) are not published in this table.

[4] Includes offenses reported by the Zoological Police and the Metro Transit Police.

* Less than one-tenth of 1 percent.

Table 4.   Crime, by Region, Geographic Division, and State, 2009–2010—*Continued*

(Number, rate per 100,000 population, percent)

Area	Aggravated assault		Property crime		Burglary		Larceny-theft		Motor vehicle theft	
	Number	Rate	Number	Rate	Number	Rate	Number	Rate	Number	Rate
UNITED STATES TOTAL[2,3,4]										
2009	812,514	264.7	9,337,060	3,041.3	2,203,313	717.7	6,338,095	2,064.5	795,652	259.2
2010	778,901	252.3	9,082,887	2,941.9	2,159,878	699.6	6,185,867	2,003.5	737,142	238.8
Percent change	-4.1	-4.7	-2.7	-3.3	-2.0	-2.5	-2.4	-3.0	-7.4	-7.9
Northeast										
2009	115,259	208.5	1,174,338	2,124.2	225,041	407.1	869,775	1,573.3	79,522	143.8
2010	115,661	209.1	1,170,424	2,115.8	234,102	423.2	860,706	1,555.9	75,616	136.7
Percent change	0	0.3	0	-0.4	4	4.0	-1	-1.1	-5	-5.0
New England										
2009	31,145	215.8	338,867	2,348.4	70,555	489.0	243,987	1,690.9	24,325	168.6
2010	31,829.0	220.3	335,198.0	2,320.5	75,226.0	520.8	237,014.0	1,640.8	22,958.0	158.9
Percent change	2.2	2.1	-1.1	-1.2	6.6	6.5	-2.9	-3.0	-5.6	-5.7
Connecticut										
2009	5,824	165.5	82,625	2,348.4	15,172	431.2	59,992	1,705.1	7,461	212.1
2010	5,791	162.0	78,386	2,193.2	15,172	424.5	56,507	1,581.0	6,707	187.7
Percent change	-0.6	-2.1	-5.1	-6.6	0.0	-1.6	-5.8	-7.3	-10.1	-11.5
Maine										
2009	780	59.2	31,706	2,405.1	6,729	510.4	23,955	1,817.1	1,022	77.5
2010	794	59.8	32,934	2,479.3	7,359	554.0	24,585	1,850.8	990	74.5
Percent change	1.8	1.0	3.9	3.1	9.4	8.5	2.6	1.9	-3.1	-3.9
Massachusetts										
2009	21,129	320.4	153,178	2,323.1	34,515	523.5	106,799	1,619.7	11,864	179.9
2010	21,724	331.8	153,905	2,350.5	37,767	576.8	104,685	1,598.8	11,453	174.9
Percent change	3	3.5	0.5	1.2	9.4	10.2	-2.0	-1.3	-3.5	-2.8
New Hampshire										
2009	1,261	95.2	28,790	2,173.5	4,915	371.1	22,748	1,717.4	1,127	85.1
2010	1,322	100.4	28,782	2,186.3	5,441	413.3	22,373	1,699.5	968	73.5
Percent change	4.8	5.5	*	0.6	10.7	11.4	-1.6	-1.0	-14.1	-13.6
Rhode Island										
2009	1,565	148.6	27,558	2,616.6	5,753	546.2	19,403	1,842.3	2,402	228.1
2010	1,596	151.6	26,910	2,556.6	6,121	581.5	18,390	1,747.2	2,399	227.9
Percent change	2.0	2.0	-2.4	-2.3	6.4	6.5	-5.2	-5.2	-0.1	-0.1
Vermont										
2009	586	+94.2	15,010	2,414.1	3,471	558.3	11,090	1,783.6	449	72.2
2010	602	96.2	14,281	2,282.3	3,366	537.9	10,474	1,673.9	441	70.5
Percent change	2.7	2.1	-4.9	-5.5	-3.0	-3.6	-5.6	-6.2	-1.8	-2.4
Middle Atlantic										
2009	84,114	205.9	835,471	2,045.0	154,486	378.1	625,788	1,531.8	55,197	135.1
2010	83,832	205.1	835,226	2,043.5	158,876	388.7	623,692	1,525.9	52,658	128.8
Percent change	-0.3	-0.4	*	-0.1	2.8	2.8	-0.3	-0.4	-4.6	-4.6
New Jersey										
2009	14,114	162.1	180,752	2,075.8	36,945	424.3	128,303	1,473.4	15,504	178.0
2010	13,885	157.9	183,042	2,081.9	38,732	440.5	128,754	1,464.5	15,556	176.9
Percent change	-1.6	-2.6	1.3	0.3	4.8	3.8	0.4	-0.6	0.3	-0.6
New York										
2009	43,606	223.1	377,537	1,932.0	62,769	321.2	292,897	1,498.8	21,871	111.9
2010	43,867	226.4	376,161	1,941.2	64,973	335.3	290,755	1,500.4	20,433	105.4
Percent change	0.6	1.4	-0.4	0.5	3.5	4.4	-0.7	0.1	-6.6	-5.8
Pennsylvania										
2009	26,394	209.4	277,182	2,199.0	54,772	434.5	204,588	1,623.1	17,822	141.4
2010	26,080	205.3	276,023	2,173.0	55,171	434.3	204,183	1,607.4	16,669	131.2
Percent change	-1.2	-1.9	-0.4	-1.2	0.7	*	-0.2	-1.0	-6.5	-7.2
Midwest[2,3]										
2009	153,444	229.6	1,940,412	2,903.2	452,434	676.9	1,345,404	2,013.0	142,574	213.3
2010	146,770	219.3	1,896,416	2,833.6	447,460	668.6	1,310,742	1,958.5	138,214	206.5
Percent change	-4.3	-4.5	-2.3	-2.4	-1.1	-1.2	-2.6	-2.7	-3.1	-3.2
East North Central[2]										
2009	105,485	226.8	1,361,411	2,927.7	333,598	717.4	926,363	1,992.1	101,450	218.2
2010	99,894	215.2	1,326,443	2,857.4	329,469	709.7	898,451	1,935.4	98,523	212.2
Percent change	-5.3	-5.1	-2.6	-2.4	-1.2	-1.1	-3.0	-2.8	-2.9	-2.7
Illinois[2]										
2009	36,588	283.4	353,347	2,736.9	77,850	603.0	248,821	1,927.3	26,676	206.6
2010	32,042	249.7	343,989	2,681.0	75,399	587.6	239,794	1,868.9	28,796	224.4
Percent change	-12.4	-11.9	-2.6	-2.0	-3.1	-2.5	-3.6	-3.0	7.9	8.6
Indiana										
2009	12,175	189.5	199,907	3,112.3	48,880	761.0	137,190	2,135.9	13,837	215.4
2010	12,117	186.9	197,260	3,042.4	47,115	726.7	137,027	2,113.4	13,118	202.3
Percent change	-0.5	-1.4	-1.3	-2.2	-3.6	-4.5	-0.1	-1.1	-5.2	-6.1

[1] Populations are U.S. Census Bureau provisional estimates as of July 1, 2010, and July 1, 2009.
[2] Because of changes in the state's reporting practices, figures are not comparable to previous years' data.
[3] The data collection methodology for the offense of forcible rape used by the Minnesota state Uniform Crime Reporting (UCR) Program (with the exception of Minneapolis and St. Paul, Minnesota) does not comply with national UCR Program guidelines. Consequently, its figures for forcible rape and violent crime (of which forcible rape is a part) are not published in this table.
[4] Includes offenses reported by the Zoological Police and the Metro Transit Police.
* Less than one-tenth of 1 percent.

Table 4. Crime, by Region, Geographic Division, and State, 2009–2010—*Continued*

(Number, rate per 100,000 population, percent)

Area	Population[1]	Violent crime		Murder and non-negligent manslaughter		Forcible rape		Robbery	
		Number	Rate	Number	Rate	Number	Rate	Number	Rate
Michigan									
2009	9,969,727	49,825	499.8	623	6.2	4,524	45.4	12,427	124.6
2010	9,883,640	48,460	490.3	567	5.7	4,673	47.3	11,493	116.3
Percent change		-2.7	-1.9	-9.0	-8.2	3.3	4.2	-7.5	-6.7
Ohio									
2009	11,542,645	38,305	331.9	527	4.6	4,119	35.7	17,670	153.1
2010	11,536,504	36,366	315.2	476	4.1	3,699	32.1	16,479	142.8
Percent change		-5.1	-5.0	-9.7	-9.6	-10.2	-10.1	-6.7	-6.7
Wisconsin									
2009	5,654,774	14,650	259.1	146	2.6	1,118	19.8	4,904	86.7
2010	5,686,986	14,142	248.7	155	2.7	1,187	20.9	4,504	79.2
Percent change		-3.5	-4.0	6.2	5.6	6.2	5.6	-8.2	-8.7
West North Central[3]									
2009	20,336,243	71,031	349.3	707	3.5	6,878	33.8	15,487	76.2
2010	20,505,437	67,434	328.9	742	3.6	6,472	31.6	13,344	65.1
Percent change		-5.1	-5.8	5.0	4.1	-5.9	-6.7	-13.8	-14.5
Iowa									
2009	3,007,856	8,485	282.1	38	1.3	890	29.6	1,201	39.9
2010	3,046,355	8,333	273.5	39	1.3	836	27.4	1,011	33.2
Percent change		-1.8	-3.0	2.6	1.3	-6.1	-7.3	-15.8	-16.9
Kansas									
2009	2,818,747	11,460	406.6	125	4.4	1,179	41.8	1,786	63.4
2010	2,853,118	10,531	369.1	100	3.5	1,107	38.8	1,544	54.1
Percent change		-8.1	-9.2	-20.0	-21.0	-6.1	-7.2	-13.5	-14.6
Minnesota[3]									
2009	5,266,214	12,874	244.5	74	1.4	1,789	34.0	3,619	68.7
2010	5,303,925	12,515	236.0	96	1.8	1,798	33.9	3,388	63.9
Percent change		-2.8	-3.5	29.7	28.8	0.5	-0.2	-6.4	-7.0
Missouri									
2009	5,987,580	29,513	492.9	387	6.5	1,606	26.8	7,437	124.2
2010	5,988,927	27,252	455.0	420	7.0	1,432	23.9	6,132	102.4
Percent change		-7.7	-7.7	8.5	8.5	-10.8	-10.9	-17.5	-17.6
Nebraska									
2009	1,796,619	5,199	289.4	41	2.3	617	34.3	1,220	67.9
2010	1,826,341	5,104	279.5	54	3.0	672	36.8	1,025	56.1
Percent change		-1.8	-3.4	31.7	29.6	8.9	7.1	-16.0	-17.4
North Dakota									
2009	646,844	1,723	266.4	12	1.9	296	45.8	107	16.5
2010	672,591	1,513	225.0	10	1.5	237	35.2	90	13.4
Percent change		-12.2	-15.5	-16.7	-19.9	-19.9	-23.0	-15.9	-19.1
South Dakota									
2009	812,383	1,777	218.7	30	3.7	501	61.7	117	14.4
2010	814,180	2,186	268.5	23	2.8	390	47.9	154	18.9
Percent change		23.0	22.7	-23.3	-23.5	-22.2	-22.3	31.6	31.3
South[4]									
2009	113,317,879	562,140	496.1	6,897	6.1	34,156	30.1	161,102	142.2
2010	114,555,744	517,805	452.0	6,459	5.6	31,969	27.9	140,161	122.4
Percent change		-7.9	-8.9	-6.4	-7.4	-6.4	-7.4	-13.0	-13.9
South Atlantic[4]									
2009	59,195,930	295,535	499.2	3,457	5.8	15,536	26.2	88,467	149.4
2010	59,777,037	271,458	454.1	3,342	5.6	14,557	24.4	76,744	128.4
Percent change		-8.1	-9.0	-3.3	-4.3	-6.3	-7.2	-13.3	-14.1
Delaware									
2009	885,122	5,713	645.4	41	4.6	395	44.6	1,680	189.8
2010	897,934	5,575	620.9	48	5.3	312	34.7	1,829	203.7
Percent change		-2.4	-3.8	17.1	15.4	-21.0	-22.1	8.9	7.3
District of Columbia[4]									
2009	599,657	8,089	1,348.9	145	24.2	150	25.0	4,404	734.4
2010	601,723	8,004	1,330.2	132	21.9	187	31.1	4,325	718.8
Percent change		-1.1	-1.4	-9.0	-9.3	24.7	24.2	-1.8	-2.1
Florida									
2009	18,537,969	113,541	612.5	1,017	5.5	5,501	29.7	30,911	166.7
2010	18,801,310	101,969	542.4	987	5.2	5,373	28.6	26,086	138.7
Percent change		-10.2	-11.4	-2.9	-4.3	-2.3	-3.7	-15.6	-16.8
Georgia									
2009	9,829,211	42,073	428.0	566	5.8	2,323	23.6	14,631	148.9
2010	9,687,653	39,072	403.3	558	5.8	2,093	21.6	12,373	127.7
Percent change		-7.1	-5.8	-1.4	0.0	-9.9	-8.6	-15.4	-14.2

[1] Populations are U.S. Census Bureau provisional estimates as of July 1, 2010, and July 1, 2009.

[3] The data collection methodology for the offense of forcible rape used by the Minnesota state Uniform Crime Reporting (UCR) Program (with the exception of Minneapolis and St. Paul, Minnesota) does not comply with national UCR Program guidelines. Consequently, its figures for forcible rape and violent crime (of which forcible rape is a part) are not published in this table.

[4] Includes offenses reported by the Zoological Police and the Metro Transit Police.

Table 4.   Crime, by Region, Geographic Division, and State, 2009–2010—*Continued*

(Number, rate per 100,000 population, percent)

Area	Aggravated assault		Property crime		Burglary		Larceny-theft		Motor vehicle theft	
	Number	Rate	Number	Rate	Number	Rate	Number	Rate	Number	Rate
Michigan										
2009	32,251	323.5	284,019	2,848.8	76,046	762.8	178,628	1,791.7	29,345	294.3
2010	31,727	321.0	268,201	2,713.6	73,868	747.4	166,980	1,689.5	27,353	276.8
Percent change	-1.6	-0.8	-5.6	-4.7	-2.9	-2.0	-6.5	-5.7	-6.8	-6.0
Ohio										
2009	15,989	138.5	376,446	3,261.3	104,009	901.1	249,777	2,163.9	22,660	196.3
2010	15,712	136.2	374,381	3,245.2	106,521	923.3	246,742	2,138.8	21,118	183.1
Percent change	-1.7	-1.7	-0.5	-0.5	2.4	2.5	-1.2	-1.2	-6.8	-6.8
Wisconsin										
2009	8,482	150.0	147,692	2,611.8	26,813	474.2	111,947	1,979.7	8,932	158.0
2010	8,296	145.9	142,612	2,507.7	26,566	467.1	107,908	1,897.5	8,138	143.1
Percent change	-2.2	-2.7	-3.4	-4.0	-0.9	-1.5	-3.6	-4.2	-8.9	-9.4
West North Central[3]										
2009	47,959	235.8	579,001	2,847.1	118,836	584.4	419,041	2,060.6	41,124	202.2
2010	46,876	228.6	569,973	2,779.6	117,991	575.4	412,291	2,010.6	39,691	193.6
Percent change	-2.3	-3.1	-1.6	-2.4	-0.7	-1.5	-1.6	-2.4	-3.5	-4.3
Iowa										
2009	6,356	211.3	70,080	2,329.9	16,419	545.9	49,757	1,654.2	3,904	129.8
2010	6,447	211.6	68,315	2,242.5	16,656	546.8	47,883	1,571.8	3,776	124.0
Percent change	1.4	0.1	-2.5	-3.8	1.4	0.2	-3.8	-5.0	-3.3	-4.5
Kansas										
2009	8,370	296.9	90,930	3,225.9	19,473	690.8	65,499	2,323.7	5,958	211.4
2010	7,780	272.7	89,015	3,119.9	19,404	680.1	63,602	2,229.2	6,009	210.6
Percent change	-7.0	-8.2	-2.1	-3.3	-0.4	-1.6	-2.9	-4.1	0.9	-0.4
Minnesota[3]										
2009	7,392	140.4	139,286	2,644.9	25,580	485.7	105,160	1,996.9	8,546	162.3
2010	7,233	136.4	136,431	2,572.3	24,415	460.3	103,429	1,950.0	8,587	161.9
Percent change	-2.2	-2.8	-2.0	-2.7	-4.6	-5.2	-1.6	-2.3	0.5	-0.2
Missouri										
2009	20,083	335.4	201,783	3,370.0	43,591	728.0	140,764	2,350.9	17,428	291.1
2010	19,268	321.7	200,414	3,346.4	44,043	735.4	140,320	2,343.0	16,051	268.0
Percent change	-4.1	-4.1	-0.7	-0.7	1.0	1.0	-0.3	-0.3	-7.9	-7.9
Nebraska										
2009	3,321	184.8	49,731	2,768.0	8,726	485.7	37,496	2,087.0	3,509	195.3
2010	3,353	183.6	48,821	2,673.2	8,326	455.9	36,881	2,019.4	3,614	197.9
Percent change	1.0	-0.7	-1.8	-3.4	-4.6	-6.1	-1.6	-3.2	3.0	1.3
North Dakota										
2009	1,308	202.2	12,813	1,980.8	2,426	375.1	9,474	1,464.6	913	141.1
2010	1,176	174.8	11,895	1,768.5	1,966	292.3	9,070	1,348.5	859	127.7
Percent change	-10.1	-13.5	-7.2	-10.7	-19.0	-22.1	-4.3	-7.9	-5.9	-9.5
South Dakota										
2009	1,129	139.0	14,378	1,769.9	2,621	322.6	10,891	1,340.6	866	106.6
2010	1,619	198.9	15,082	1,852.4	3,181	390.7	11,106	1,364.1	795	97.6
Percent change	43.4	43.1	4.9	4.7	21.4	21.1	2.0	1.7	-8.2	-8.4
South[4]										
2009	359,985	317.7	4,096,256	3,614.8	1,057,193	932.9	2,738,203	2,416.4	300,860	265.5
2010	339,216	296.1	3,939,317	3,438.8	1,015,404	886.4	2,652,060	2,315.1	271,853	237.3
Percent change	-5.8	-6.8	-3.8	-4.9	-4.0	-5.0	-3.1	-4.2	-9.6	-10.6
South Atlantic[4]										
2009	188,075	317.7	2,075,722	3,506.5	525,268	887.3	1,391,957	2,351.4	158,497	267.7
2010	176,815	295.8	1,991,306	3,331.2	504,361	843.7	1,345,746	2,251.3	141,199	236.2
Percent change	-6.0	-6.9	-4.1	-5.0	-4.0	-4.9	-3.3	-4.3	-10.9	-11.8
Delaware										
2009	3,597	406.4	29,685	3,353.8	6,943	784.4	20,836	2,354.0	1,906	215.3
2010	3,386	377.1	30,963	3,448.2	7,515	836.9	21,519	2,396.5	1,929	214.8
Percent change	-5.9	-7.2	4.3	2.8	8.2	6.7	3.3	1.8	1.2	-0.2
District of Columbia[4]										
2009	3,390	565.3	28,495	4,751.9	3,696	616.4	19,267	3,213.0	5,532	922.5
2010	3,360	558.4	28,756	4,778.9	4,231	703.1	19,489	3,238.9	5,036	836.9
Percent change	-0.9	-1.2	0.9	0.6	14.5	14.1	1.2	0.8	-9.0	-9.3
Florida										
2009	76,112	410.6	712,010	3,840.8	181,884	981.1	479,867	2,588.6	50,259	271.1
2010	69,523	369.8	669,035	3,558.4	169,119	899.5	458,454	2,438.4	41,462	220.5
Percent change	-8.7	-9.9	-6.0	-7.4	-7.0	-8.3	-4.5	-5.8	-17.5	-18.7
Georgia										
2009	24,553	249.8	360,985	3,672.6	98,606	1,003.2	229,216	2,332.0	33,163	337.4
2010	24,048	248.2	352,679	3,640.5	96,723	998.4	225,651	2,329.3	30,305	312.8
Percent change	-2.1	-0.6	-2.3	-0.9	-1.9	-0.5	-1.6	-0.1	-8.6	-7.3

[3] The data collection methodology for the offense of forcible rape used by the Minnesota state Uniform Crime Reporting (UCR) Program (with the exception of Minneapolis and St. Paul, Minnesota) does not comply with national UCR Program guidelines. Consequently, its figures for forcible rape and violent crime (of which forcible rape is a part) are not published in this table.

[4] Includes offenses reported by the Zoological Police and the Metro Transit Police.

Table 4.   Crime, by Region, Geographic Division, and State, 2009–2010—*Continued*

(Number, rate per 100,000 population, percent)

Area	Population[1]	Violent crime		Murder and non-negligent manslaughter		Forcible rape		Robbery	
		Number	Rate	Number	Rate	Number	Rate	Number	Rate
Maryland									
2009	5,699,478	33,625	590.0	440	7.7	1,156	20.3	12,007	210.7
2010	5,773,552	31,620	547.7	430	7.4	1,227	21.3	11,054	191.5
Percent change		-6.0	-7.2	-2.3	-3.5	6.1	4.8	-7.9	-9.1
North Carolina									
2009	9,380,884	37,946	404.5	489	5.2	2,306	24.6	11,825	126.1
2010	9,535,483	34,653	363.4	476	5.0	2,013	21.1	9,610	100.8
Percent change		-8.7	-10.2	-2.7	-4.2	-12.7	-14.1	-18.7	-20.0
South Carolina									
2009	4,561,242	30,799	675.2	305	6.7	1,663	36.5	5,753	126.1
2010	4,625,364	27,648	597.7	280	6.1	1,466	31.7	4,982	107.7
Percent change		-10.2	-11.5	-8.2	-9.5	-11.8	-13.1	-13.4	-14.6
Virginia									
2009	7,882,590	18,195	230.8	370	4.7	1,572	19.9	6,342	80.5
2010	8,001,024	17,087	213.6	369	4.6	1,532	19.1	5,657	70.7
Percent change		-6.1	-7.5	-0.3	-1.7	-2.5	-4.0	-10.8	-12.1
West Virginia									
2009	1,819,777	5,554	305.2	84	4.6	470	25.8	914	50.2
2010	1,852,994	5,830	314.6	62	3.3	354	19.1	828	44.7
Percent change		5.0	3.1	-26.2	-27.5	-24.7	-26.0	-9.4	-11.0
East South Central									
2009	18,271,071	82,578	452.0	1,168	6.4	6,045	33.1	22,529	123.3
2010	18,432,505	75,508	409.6	1,025	5.6	5,795	31.4	19,654	106.6
Percent change		-8.6	-9.4	-12.2	-13.0	-4.1	-5.0	-12.8	-13.5
Alabama									
2009	4,708,708	21,194	450.1	322	6.8	1,504	31.9	6,265	133.1
2010	4,779,736	18,056	377.8	273	5.7	1,349	28.2	4,761	99.6
Percent change		-14.8	-16.1	-15.2	-16.5	10.3	-11.6	-24.0	-25.1
Kentucky									
2009	4,314,113	11,000	255.0	184	4.3	1,531	35.5	3,642	84.4
2010	4,339,367	10,528	242.6	187	4.3	1,381	31.8	3,748	86.4
Percent change		-4.3	-4.8	1.6	1.0	-9.8	-10.3	2.9	2.3
Mississippi									
2009	2,951,996	8,451	286.3	194	6.6	991	33.6	2,969	100.6
2010	2,967,297	8,003	269.7	208	7.0	927	31.2	2,779	93.7
Percent change		-5.3	-5.8	7.2	6.7	-6.5	-6.9	-6.4	-6.9
Tennessee									
2009	6,296,254	41,933	666.0	468	7.4	2,019	32.1	9,653	153.3
2010	6,346,105	38,921	613.3	357	5.6	2,138	33.7	8,366	131.8
Percent change		-7.2	-7.9	-23.7	-24.3	5.9	5.1	-13.3	-14.0
West South Central									
2009	35,850,878	184,027	513.3	2,272	6.3	12,575	35.1	50,106	139.8
2010	36,346,202	170,839	470.0	2,092	5.8	11,617	32.0	43,763	120.4
Percent change		-7.2	-8.4	-7.9	-9.2	-7.6	-8.9	-12.7	-13.8
Arkansas									
2009	2,889,450	14,905	515.8	179	6.2	1,378	47.7	2,576	89.2
2010	2,915,918	14,735	505.3	138	4.7	1,312	45.0	2,372	81.3
Percent change		-1.1	-2.0	-22.9	-23.6	-4.8	-5.7	-7.9	-8.8
Louisiana									
2009	4,492,076	28,878	642.9	529	11.8	1,351	30.1	6,150	136.9
2010	4,533,372	24,886	549.0	510	11.2	1,233	27.2	5,211	114.9
Percent change		-13.8	-14.6	-3.6	-4.5	-8.7	-9.6	-15.3	-16.0
Oklahoma									
2009	3,687,050	18,560	503.4	234	6.3	1,535	41.6	3,358	91.1
2010	3,751,351	17,987	479.5	195	5.2	1,450	38.7	3,337	89.0
Percent change		-3.1	-4.7	-16.7	-18.1	-5.5	-7.2	-0.6	-2.3
Texas									
2009	24,782,302	121,684	491.0	1,330	5.4	8,311	33.5	38,022	153.4
2010	25,145,561	113,231	450.3	1,249	5.0	7,622	30.3	32,843	130.6
Percent change		-6.9	-8.3	-6.1	-7.4	-8.3	-9.6	-13.6	-14.9
West[2]									
2009	71,568,081	305,583	427.0	3,294	4.6	22,082	30.9	96,381	134.7
2010	71,945,553	288,326	400.8	3,044	4.2	21,249	29.5	86,779	120.6
Percent change		-5.6	-6.1	-7.6	-8.1	-3.8	-4.3	-10.0	-10.4
Mountain									
2009	22,122,914	90,295	408.2	999	4.5	8,686	39.3	21,394	96.7
2010	22,065,451	85,326	386.7	937	4.2	8,244	37.4	18,696	84.7
Percent change		-5.5	-5.3	-6.2	-6.0	-5.1	-4.8	-12.6	-12.4
Arizona									
2009	6,595,778	28,128	426.5	380	5.8	2,279	34.6	8,199	124.3
2010	6,392,017	26,085	408.1	409	6.4	2,165	33.9	6,937	108.5
Percent change		-7.3	-4.3	7.6	11.1	-5.0	-2.0	-15.4	-12.7

[1] Populations are U.S. Census Bureau provisional estimates as of July 1, 2010, and July 1, 2009.
[2] Because of changes in the state's reporting practices, figures are not comparable to previous years' data.

Table 4.   Crime, by Region, Geographic Division, and State, 2009–2010—*Continued*

(Number, rate per 100,000 population, percent)

Area	Aggravated assault		Property crime		Burglary		Larceny-theft		Motor vehicle theft	
	Number	Rate	Number	Rate	Number	Rate	Number	Rate	Number	Rate
Maryland										
2009	20,022	351.3	182,295	3,198.5	36,905	647.5	125,771	2,206.7	19,619	344.2
2010	18,909	327.5	173,051	2,997.3	36,542	632.9	118,458	2,051.7	18,051	312.6
Percent change	-5.6	-6.8	-5.1	-6.3	-1.0	-2.3	-5.8	-7.0	-8.0	-9.2
North Carolina										
2009	23,326	248.7	343,707	3,663.9	107,830	1,149.5	215,923	2,301.7	19,954	212.7
2010	22,554	236.5	328,719	3,447.3	102,690	1,076.9	207,719	2,178.4	18,310	192.0
Percent change	-3.3	-4.9	-4.4	-5.9	-4.8	-6.3	-3.8	-5.4	-8.2	-9.7
South Carolina										
2009	23,078	506.0	178,310	3,909.2	45,443	996.3	119,250	2,614.4	13,617	298.5
2010	20,920	452.3	180,407	3,900.4	46,156	997.9	121,054	2,617.2	13,197	285.3
Percent change	-9.4	-10.6	1.2	-0.2	1.6	0.2	1.5	0.1	-3.1	-4.4
Virginia										
2009	9,911	125.7	194,020	2,461.4	31,956	405.4	150,374	1,907.7	11,690	148.3
2010	9,529	119.1	186,196	2,327.2	30,629	382.8	145,019	1,812.5	10,548	131.8
Percent change	-3.9	-5.3	-4.0	-5.5	-4.2	-5.6	-3.6	-5.0	-9.8	-11.1
West Virginia										
2009	4,086	224.5	46,215	2,539.6	12,005	659.7	31,453	1,728.4	2,757	151.5
2010	4,586	247.5	41,500	2,239.6	10,756	580.5	28,383	1,531.7	2,361	127.4
Percent change	12.2	10.2	-10.2	-11.8	-10.4	-12.0	-9.8	-11.4	-14.4	-15.9
East South Central										
2009	52,836	289.2	611,405	3,346.3	172,115	942.0	401,648	2,198.3	37,642	206.0
2010	49,034	266.0	599,507	3,252.4	167,024	906.1	395,479	2,145.6	37,004	200.8
Percent change	-7.2	-8.0	-1.9	-2.8	-3.0	-3.8	-1.5	-2.4	-1.7	-2.6
Alabama										
2009	13,103	278.3	178,007	3,780.4	48,844	1,037.3	118,072	2,507.5	11,091	235.5
2010	11,673	244.2	168,092	3,516.8	42,034	879.4	115,458	2,415.6	10,600	221.8
Percent change	-10.9	-12.2	-5.6	-7.0	-13.9	-15.2	-2.2	-3.7	-4.4	-5.8
Kentucky										
2009	5,643	130.8	108,914	2,524.6	29,880	692.6	72,938	1,690.7	6,096	141.3
2010	5,212	120.1	110,709	2,551.3	30,311	698.5	74,189	1,709.7	6,209	143.1
Percent change	-7.6	-8.2	1.6	1.1	1.4	0.9	1.7	1.1	1.9	1.3
Mississippi										
2009	4,297	145.6	87,327	2,958.2	29,559	1,001.3	52,329	1,772.7	5,439	184.2
2010	4,089	137.8	88,574	2,985.0	30,444	1,026.0	52,770	1,778.4	5,360	180.6
Percent change	-4.8	-5.3	1.4	0.9	3.0	2.5	0.8	0.3	-1.5	-2.0
Tennessee										
2009	29,793	473.2	237,157	3,766.6	63,832	1,013.8	158,309	2,514.3	15,016	238.5
2010	28,060	442.2	232,132	3,657.9	64,235	1,012.2	153,062	2,411.9	14,835	233.8
Percent change	-5.8	-6.6	-2.1	-2.9	0.6	-0.2	-3.3	-4.1	-1.2	-2.0
West South Central										
2009	119,074	332.1	1,409,129	3,930.5	359,810	1,003.6	944,598	2,634.8	104,721	292.1
2010	113,367	311.9	1,348,504	3,710.2	344,019	946.5	910,835	2,506.0	93,650	257.7
Percent change	-4.8	-6.1	-4.3	-5.6	-4.4	-5.7	-3.6	-4.9	-10.6	-11.8
Arkansas										
2009	10,772	372.8	109,078	3,775.0	34,753	1,202.8	68,228	2,361.3	6,097	211.0
2010	10,913	374.3	103,775	3,558.9	32,511	1,114.9	65,720	2,253.8	5,544	190.1
Percent change	1.3	0.4	-4.9	-5.7	-6.5	-7.3	-3.7	-4.6	-9.1	-9.9
Louisiana										
2009	20,848	464.1	172,619	3,842.7	46,928	1,044.7	114,102	2,540.1	11,589	258.0
2010	17,932	395.6	165,357	3,647.5	45,435	1,002.2	110,029	2,427.1	9,893	218.2
Percent change	-14.0	-14.8	-4.2	-5.1	-3.2	-4.1	-3.6	-4.4	-14.6	-15.4
Oklahoma										
2009	13,433	364.3	132,350	3,589.6	38,071	1,032.6	83,813	2,273.2	10,466	283.9
2010	13,005	346.7	128,126	3,415.5	37,476	999.0	80,460	2,144.8	10,190	271.6
Percent change	-3.2	-4.8	-3.2	-4.9	-1.6	-3.3	-4.0	-5.6	-2.6	-4.3
Texas										
2009	74,021	298.7	995,082	4,015.3	240,058	968.7	678,455	2,737.7	76,569	309.0
2010	71,517	284.4	951,246	3,783.0	228,597	909.1	654,626	2,603.3	68,023	270.5
Percent change	-3.4	-4.8	-4.4	-5.8	-4.8	-6.1	-3.5	-4.9	-11.2	-12.4
West[2]										
2009	183,826	256.9	2,126,054	2,970.7	468,645	654.8	1,384,713	1,934.8	272,696	381.0
2010	177,254	246.4	2,076,730	2,886.5	462,912	643.4	1,362,359	1,893.6	251,459	349.5
Percent change	-3.6	-4.1	-2.3	-2.8	-1.2	-1.7	-1.6	-2.1	-7.8	-8.3
Mountain										
2009	59,216	267.7	688,572	3,112.5	152,817	690.8	467,160	2,111.7	68,595	310.1
2010	57,449	260.4	664,768	3,012.7	147,486	668.4	459,707	2,083.4	57,575	260.9
Percent change	-3.0	-2.7	-3.5	-3.2	-3.5	-3.2	-1.6	-1.3	-16.1	-15.8
Arizona										
2009	17,270	261.8	236,721	3,589.0	54,308	823.4	155,976	2,364.8	26,437	400.8
2010	16,574	259.3	225,893	3,534.0	50,771	794.3	153,614	2,403.2	21,508	336.5
Percent change	-4.0	-1.0	-4.6	-1.5	-6.5	-3.5	-1.5	1.6	-18.6	-16.1

[2] Because of changes in the state's reporting practices, figures are not comparable to previous years' data.

Table 4. Crime, by Region, Geographic Division, and State, 2009–2010—*Continued*

(Number, rate per 100,000 population, percent)

Area	Population[1]	Violent crime		Murder and non-negligent manslaughter		Forcible rape		Robbery	
		Number	Rate	Number	Rate	Number	Rate	Number	Rate
Colorado									
2009	5,024,748	17,022	338.8	159	3.2	2,269	45.2	3,371	67.1
2010	5,029,196	16,133	320.8	120	2.4	2,198	43.7	3,132	62.3
Percent change		-5.2	-5.3	-24.5	-24.6	-3.1	-3.2	-7.1	-7.2
Idaho									
2009	1,545,801	3,805	246.2	24	1.6	575	37.2	254	16.4
2010	1,567,582	3,465	221.0	21	1.3	525	33.5	214	13.7
Percent change		-8.9	-10.2	-12.5	-13.7	-8.7	-10.0	-15.7	-16.9
Montana									
2009	974,989	2,798	287.0	32	3.3	357	36.6	228	23.4
2010	989,415	2,693	272.2	26	2.6	321	32.4	157	15.9
Percent change		-3.8	-5.2	-18.8	-19.9	-10.1	-11.4	-31.1	-32.1
Nevada									
2009	2,643,085	18,639	705.2	156	5.9	1,024	38.7	6,028	228.1
2010	2,700,551	17,841	660.6	158	5.9	965	35.7	5,298	196.2
Percent change		-4.3	-6.3	1.3	-0.9	-5.8	-7.8	-12.1	-14.0
New Mexico									
2009	2,009,671	12,709	632.4	198	9.9	1,069	53.2	1,932	96.1
2010	2,059,179	12,126	588.9	142	6.9	958	46.5	1,614	78.4
Percent change		-4.6	-6.9	-28.3	-30.0	-10.4	-12.5	-16.5	-18.5
Utah									
2009	2,784,572	5,998	215.4	39	1.4	941	33.8	1,304	46.8
2010	2,763,885	5,879	212.7	53	1.9	948	34.3	1,268	45.9
Percent change		-2.0	-1.3	35.9	36.9	0.7	1.5	-2.8	-2.0
Wyoming									
2009	544,270	1,196	219.7	11	2.0	172	31.6	78	14.3
2010	563,626	1,104	195.9	8	1.4	164	29.1	76	13.5
Percent change		-7.7	-10.9	-27.3	-29.8	4.7	-7.9	-2.6	-5.9
Pacific[2]									
2009	49,445,167	215,288	435.4	2,295	4.6	13,396	27.1	74,987	151.7
2010	49,880,102	203,000	407.0	2,107	4.2	13,005	26.1	68,083	136.5
Percent change		-5.7	-6.5	-8.2	-9.0	-2.9	-3.8	-9.2	-10.0
Alaska									
2009	698,473	4,424	633.4	22	3.1	513	73.4	654	93.6
2010	710,231	4,537	638.8	31	4.4	533	75.0	594	83.6
Percent change		2.6	0.9	40.9	38.6	3.9	2.2	-9.2	-10.7
California									
2009	36,961,664	174,934	473.3	1,972	5.3	8,713	23.6	64,093	173.4
2010	37,253,956	164,133	440.6	1,809	4.9	8,331	22.4	58,116	156.0
Percent change		-6.2	-6.9	-8.3	-9.0	-4.4	-5.1	-9.3	-10.0
Hawaii									
2009	1,295,178	3,550	274.1	23	1.8	385	29.7	1,030	79.5
2010	1,360,301	3,574	262.7	24	1.8	365	26.8	1,054	77.5
Percent change		0.7	-4.1	4.3	-0.6	-5.2	-9.7	2.3	-2.6
Oregon[2]									
2009	3,825,657	9,968	260.6	88	2.3	1,202	31.4	2,499	65.3
2010	3,831,074	9,655	252.0	91	2.4	1,214	31.7	2,390	62.4
Percent change		-3.1	-3.3	3.4	3.3	1.0	0.9	-4.4	-4.5
Washington									
2009	6,664,195	22,412	336.3	190	2.9	2,583	38.8	6,711	100.7
2010	6,724,540	21,101	313.8	152	2.3	2,562	38.1	5,929	88.2
Percent change		-5.8	-6.7	-20.0	-20.7	-0.8	-1.7	-11.7	-12.4

[1] Populations are U.S. Census Bureau provisional estimates as of July 1, 2010, and July 1, 2009.
[2] Because of changes in the state's reporting practices, figures are not comparable to previous years' data.

Table 4.   Crime, by Region, Geographic Division, and State, 2009–2010—*Continued*

(Number, rate per 100,000 population, percent)

Area	Aggravated assault		Property crime		Burglary		Larceny-theft		Motor vehicle theft	
	Number	Rate	Number	Rate	Number	Rate	Number	Rate	Number	Rate
Colorado										
2009	11,223	223.4	134,196	2,670.7	26,637	530.1	95,079	1,892.2	12,480	248.4
2010	10,683	212.4	134,992	2,684.2	26,153	520.0	97,592	1,940.5	11,247	223.6
Percent change	-4.8	-4.9	0.6	0.5	-1.8	-1.9	2.6	2.6	-9.9	-10.0
Idaho										
2009	2,952	191.0	31,220	2,019.7	6,682	432.3	23,066	1,492.2	1,472	95.2
2010	2,705	172.6	31,286	1,995.8	6,502	414.8	23,462	1,496.7	1,322	84.3
Percent change	-8.4	-9.6	0.2	-1.2	-2.7	-4.0	1.7	0.3	-10.2	-11.4
Montana										
2009	2,181	223.7	24,826	2,546.3	3,686	378.1	19,528	2,002.9	1,612	165.3
2010	2,189	221.2	25,169	2,543.8	3,654	369.3	19,989	2,020.3	1,526	154.2
Percent change	0.4	-1.1	1.4	-0.1	-0.9	-2.3	2.4	0.9	-5.3	-6.7
Nevada										
2009	11,431	432.5	80,976	3,063.7	22,115	836.7	46,463	1,757.9	12,398	469.1
2010	11,420	422.9	74,932	2,774.7	22,226	823.0	42,521	1,574.5	10,185	377.1
Percent change	-0.1	-2.2	-7.5	-9.4	0.5	-1.6	-8.5	-10.4	-17.8	-19.6
New Mexico										
2009	9,510	473.2	74,639	3,714.0	21,955	1,092.5	46,182	2,298.0	6,502	323.5
2010	9,412	457.1	70,742	3,435.4	21,014	1,020.5	44,481	2,160.1	5,247	254.8
Percent change	-1.0	-3.4	-5.2	-7.5	-4.3	-6.6	-3.7	-6.0	-19.3	-21.2
Utah										
2009	3,714	133.4	91,751	3,295.0	15,258	547.9	69,556	2,497.9	6,937	249.1
2010	3,610	130.6	87,880	3,179.6	15,017	543.3	66,914	2,421.0	5,949	215.2
Percent change	-2.8	-2.1	-4.2	-3.5	-1.6	-0.8	-3.8	-3.1	-14.2	-13.6
Wyoming										
2009	935	171.8	14,243	2,616.9	2,176	399.8	11,310	2,078.0	757	139.1
2010	856	151.9	13,874	2,461.6	2,149	381.3	11,134	1,975.4	591	104.9
Percent change	-8.4	-11.6	-2.6	-5.9	-1.2	-4.6	-1.6	-4.9	-21.9	-24.6
Pacific[2]										
2009	124,610	252.0	1,437,482	2,907.2	315,828	638.7	917,553	1,855.7	204,101	412.8
2010	119,805	240.2	1,411,962	2,830.7	315,426	632.4	902,652	1,809.6	193,884	388.7
Percent change	-3.9	-4.7	-1.8	-2.6	-0.1	-1.0	-1.6	-2.5	-5.0	-5.8
Alaska										
2009	3,235	463.2	20,538	2,940.4	3,600	515.4	15,251	2,183.5	1,687	241.5
2010	3,379	475.8	20,259	2,852.5	3,105	437.2	15,535	2,187.3	1,619	228.0
Percent change	4.5	2.7	-1.4	-3.0	-13.8	-15.2	1.9	0.2	-4.0	-5.6
California										
2009	100,156	271.0	1,009,433	2,731.0	230,198	622.8	615,402	1,665.0	163,833	443.3
2010	95,877	257.4	981,939	2,635.8	228,857	614.3	600,558	1,612.1	152,524	409.4
Percent change	-4.3	-5.0	-2.7	-3.5	-0.6	-1.4	-2.4	-3.2	-6.9	-7.6
Hawaii										
2009	2,112	163.1	47,516	3,668.7	9,244	713.7	33,415	2,580.0	4,857	375.0
2010	2,131	156.7	45,083	3,314.2	8,663	636.8	31,320	2,302.4	5,100	374.9
Percent change	0.9	-3.9	-5.1	-9.7	-6.3	-10.8	-6.3	-10.8	5.0	*
Oregon[2]										
2009	6,179	161.5	114,780	3,000.3	19,739	516.0	85,064	2,223.5	9,977	260.8
2010	5,960	155.6	115,428	3,012.9	19,637	512.6	86,879	2,267.7	8,912	232.6
Percent change	-3.5	-3.7	0.6	0.4	-0.5	-0.7	2.1	2.0	-10.7	-10.8
Washington										
2009	12,928	194.0	245,215	3,679.6	53,047	796.0	168,421	2,527.3	23,747	356.3
2010	12,458	185.3	249,253	3,706.6	55,164	820.3	168,360	2,503.7	25,729	382.6
Percent change	-3.6	-4.5	1.6	0.7	4.0	3.1	*	-0.9	8.3	7.4

[2] Because of changes in the state's reporting practices, figures are not comparable to previous years' data.

* Less than one-tenth of 1 percent.

Table 5.   Crime, by State and Area, 2010

(Number, percent, rate per 100,000 population)

Area	Population	Violent crime	Murder and non-negligent man-slaughter	Forcible rape	Robbery	Aggravated assault	Property crime	Burglary	Larceny-theft	Motor vehicle theft
ALABAMA										
Metropolitan statistical area	3,424,852									
Area actually reporting	89.8%	13,207	215	949	4,243	7,800	124,845	32,759	83,928	8,158
Estimated total	100.0%	14,072	224	1,027	4,403	8,418	133,796	35,225	89,830	8,741
Cities outside metropolitan areas	622,679									
Area actually reporting	84.5%	2,300	23	163	256	1,858	21,402	3,730	16,606	1,066
Estimated total	100.0%	2,704	26	193	299	2,186	25,061	4,364	19,447	1,250
Nonmetropolitan counties	732,205									
Area actually reporting	69.6%	891	16	90	41	744	6,428	1,702	4,302	424
Estimated total	100.0%	1,280	23	129	59	1,069	9,235	2,445	6,181	609
State total	4,779,736	18,056	273	1,349	4,761	11,673	168,092	42,034	115,458	10,600
Rate per 100,000 inhabitants		377.8	5.7	28.2	99.6	244.2	3,516.8	879.4	2,415.6	221.8
ALASKA										
Metropolitan statistical area	351,488									
Area actually reporting	100.0%	2,846	13	343	499	1,991	12,534	1,472	10,087	975
Cities outside metropolitan areas	123,081									
Area actually reporting	96.5%	672	3	124	53	492	4,211	557	3,351	303
Estimated total	100.0%	697	3	129	55	510	4,364	577	3,473	314
Nonmetropolitan counties	235,662									
Area actually reporting	100.0%	994	15	61	40	878	3,361	1,056	1,975	330
State total	710,231	4,537	31	533	594	3,379	20,259	3,105	15,535	1,619
Rate per 100,000 inhabitants		638.8	4.4	75.0	83.6	475.8	2,852.5	437.2	2,187.3	228.0
ARIZONA										
Metropolitan statistical area	5,932,512									
Area actually reporting	99.5%	22,116	347	1,511	6,784	13,474	210,393	46,069	144,476	19,848
Estimated total	100.0%	22,185	348	1,517	6,799	13,521	211,304	46,260	145,139	19,905
Cities outside metropolitan areas	197,445									
Area actually reporting	89.9%	2,891	47	561	98	2,185	10,314	2,854	6,331	1,129
Estimated total	100.0%	3,217	52	624	109	2,432	11,479	3,176	7,046	1,257
Nonmetropolitan counties	262,060									
Area actually reporting	98.0%	669	9	24	28	608	3,047	1,308	1,400	339
Estimated total	100.0%	683	9	24	29	621	3,110	1,335	1,429	346
State total	6,392,017	26,085.0	409.0	2,165.0	6,937.0	16,574.0	225,893.0	50,771.0	153,614.0	21,508.0
Rate per 100,000 inhabitants		408.1	6.4	33.9	108.5	259.3	3,534.0	794.3	2,403.2	336.5
ARKANSAS										
Metropolitan statistical area	1,771,078									
Area actually reporting	95.5%	10,571	83	898	1,971	7,619	69,693	20,533	45,220	3,940
Estimated total	100.0%	10,883	84	928	1,991	7,880	71,561	21,289	46,214	4,058
Cities outside metropolitan areas	502,369									
Area actually reporting	93.5%	2,315	25	213	307	1,770	20,207	6,787	12,692	728
Estimated total	100.0%	2,476	27	228	328	1,893	21,606	7,257	13,571	778
Nonmetropolitan counties	642,471									
Area actually reporting	86.6%	1,191	23	135	46	987	9,187	3,434	5,140	613
Estimated total	100.0%	1,376	27	156	53	1,140	10,608	3,965	5,935	708
State total	2,915,918	14,735	138	1,312	2,372	10,913	103,775	32,511	65,720	5,544
Rate per 100,000 inhabitants		505.3	4.7	45.0	81.3	374.3	3,558.9	1,114.9	2,253.8	190.1
CALIFORNIA										
Metropolitan statistical area	36,417,786									
Area actually reporting	100.0%	160,871	1,784	8,001	57,748	93,338	963,339	222,573	589,966	150,800
Cities outside metropolitan areas	266,745									
Area actually reporting	100.0%	1,475	3	135	220	1,117	9,716	2,946	6,121	649
Nonmetropolitan counties	569,425									
Area actually reporting	100.0%	1,787	22	195	148	1,422	8,884	3,338	4,471	1,075
State total	37,253,956	164,133	1,809	8,331	58,116	95,877	981,939	228,857	600,558	152,524
Rate per 100,000 inhabitants		440.6	4.9	22.4	156.0	257.4	2,635.8	614.3	1,612.1	409.4
COLORADO										
Metropolitan statistical area	4,346,239									
Area actually reporting	99.2%	14,735	105	1,986	3,043	9,601	121,162	23,765	86,725	10,672
Estimated total	100.0%	14,817	105	2,000	3,052	9,660	121,865	23,899	87,238	10,728
Cities outside metropolitan areas	316,138									
Area actually reporting	91.9%	827	5	145	68	609	9,477	1,459	7,706	312
Estimated total	100.0%	900	5	158	74	663	10,316	1,588	8,388	340
Nonmetropolitan counties	366,819									
Area actually reporting	79.4%	331	8	32	5	286	2,233	529	1,562	142
Estimated total	100.0%	416	10	40	6	360	2,811	666	1,966	179
State total	5,029,196	16,133	120	2,198	3,132	10,683	134,992	26,153	97,592	11,247
Rate per 100,000 inhabitants		320.8	2.4	43.7	62.3	212.4	2,684.2	520.0	1,940.5	223.6

Table 5. Crime, by State and Area, 2010—*Continued*

(Number, percent, rate per 100,000 population)

Area	Population	Violent crime	Murder and non-negligent man-slaughter	Forcible rape	Robbery	Aggravated assault	Property crime	Burglary	Larceny-theft	Motor vehicle theft
CONNECTICUT										
Metropolitan statistical area	2,867,895									
Area actually reporting	100.0%	9,527	125	499	3,455	5,448	70,438	13,047	51,135	6,256
Cities outside metropolitan areas	160,274									
Area actually reporting	100.0%	227	0	44	43	140	3,024	542	2,349	133
Nonmetropolitan counties	545,928									
Area actually reporting	100.0%	303	5	40	55	203	4,924	1,583	3,023	318
State total	3,574,097	10,057	130	583	3,553	5,791	78,386	15,172	56,507	6,707
Rate per 100,000 inhabitants		281.4	3.6	16.3	99.4	162.0	2,193.2	424.5	1,581.0	187.7
DELAWARE										
Metropolitan statistical area	700,791									
Area actually reporting	100.0%	4,560	44	208	1,628	2,680	24,072	5,365	17,022	1,685
Cities outside metropolitan areas	44,036									
Area actually reporting	100.0%	386	1	28	102	255	2,536	565	1,918	53
Nonmetropolitan counties	153,107									
Area actually reporting	100.0%	629	3	76	99	451	4,355	1,585	2,579	191
State total	897,934	5,575	48	312	1,829	3,386	30,963	7,515	21,519	1,929
Rate per 100,000 inhabitants		620.9	5.3	34.7	203.7	377.1	3,448.2	836.9	2,396.5	214.8
DISTRICT OF COLUMBIA[1]										
Metropolitan statistical area	601,723									
Area actually reporting	100.0%	8,004	132	187	4,325	3,360	28,756	4,231	19,489	5,036
Cities outside metropolitan areas	None									
Nonmetropolitan counties	None									
Total	601,723	8,004	132	187	4,325	3,360	28,756	4,231	19,489	5,036
Rate per 100,000 inhabitants		1,330.2	21.9	31.1	718.8	558.4	4,778.9	703.1	3,238.9	836.9
FLORIDA										
Metropolitan statistical area	17,701,972									
Area actually reporting	99.9%	96,825	931	5,000	25,426	65,468	638,732	158,911	439,639	40,182
Estimated total	100.0%	96,858	931	5,002	25,436	65,489	638,989	158,970	439,821	40,198
Cities outside metropolitan areas	192,844									
Area actually reporting	98.2%	1,528	10	109	300	1,109	8,661	2,295	5,997	369
Estimated total	100.0%	1,555	10	111	305	1,129	8,819	2,337	6,106	376
Nonmetropolitan counties	906,494									
Area actually reporting	100.0%	3,556	46	260	345	2,905	21,227	7,812	12,527	888
State total	18,801,310	101,969	987	5,373	26,086	69,523	669,035	169,119	458,454	41,462
Rate per 100,000 inhabitants		542.4	5.2	28.6	138.7	369.8	3,558.4	899.5	2,438.4	220.5
GEORGIA										
Metropolitan statistical area	7,922,112									
Area actually reporting	98.9%	32,080	503	1,727	11,189	18,661	291,234	79,704	184,177	27,353
Estimated total	100.0%	32,383	507	1,744	11,287	18,845	294,205	80,456	186,146	27,603
Cities outside metropolitan areas	659,535									
Area actually reporting	87.2%	3,575	21	170	754	2,630	29,276	7,062	21,159	1,055
Estimated total	100.0%	4,098	24	195	864	3,015	33,555	8,095	24,251	1,209
Nonmetropolitan counties	1,106,006									
Area actually reporting	91.8%	2,379	25	141	204	2,009	22,877	7,502	14,004	1,371
Estimated total	100.0%	2,591	27	154	222	2,188	24,919	8,172	15,254	1,493
State total	9,687,653	39,072	558	2,093	12,373	24,048	352,679	96,723	225,651	30,305
Rate per 100,000 inhabitants		403.3	5.8	21.6	127.7	248.2	3,640.5	998.4	2,329.3	312.8
HAWAII										
Metropolitan statistical area	950,268									
Area actually reporting	100.0%	2,548	19	218	891	1,420	31,668	5,760	22,007	3,901
Cities outside metropolitan areas	None									
Nonmetropolitan counties	410,033									
Area actually reporting	100.0%	1,026	5	147	163	711	13,415	2,903	9,313	1,199
State total	1,360,301	3,574	24	365	1,054	2,131	45,083	8,663	31,320	5,100
Rate per 100,000 inhabitants		262.7	1.8	26.8	77.5	156.7	3,314.2	636.8	2,302.4	374.9
IDAHO										
Metropolitan statistical area	1,032,982									
Area actually reporting	99.3%	2,301	18	349	169	1,765	22,823	4,517	17,413	893
Estimated total	100.0%	2,310	18	350	169	1,773	22,917	4,543	17,477	897
Cities outside metropolitan areas	242,324									
Area actually reporting	98.9%	753	1	95	38	619	5,430	1,088	4,126	216
Estimated total	100.0%	761	1	96	38	626	5,488	1,100	4,170	218
Nonmetropolitan counties	292,276									
Area actually reporting	98.9%	390	2	78	7	303	2,849	849	1,795	205
Estimated total	100.0%	394	2	79	7	306	2,881	859	1,815	207
State total	1,567,582	3,465	21	525	214	2,705	31,286	6,502	23,462	1,322
Rate per 100,000 inhabitants		221.0	1.3	33.5	13.7	172.6	1,995.8	414.8	1,496.7	84.3

[1] Includes offenses reported by the Zoological Police and the Metro Transit Police.

Table 5.   Crime, by State and Area, 2010—*Continued*

(Number, percent, rate per 100,000 population)

Area	Population	Violent crime	Murder and non-negligent man-slaughter	Forcible rape	Robbery	Aggravated assault	Property crime	Burglary	Larceny-theft	Motor vehicle theft
ILLINOIS[2]										
Metropolitan statistical area	11,201,035									
Area actually reporting	87.1%	48,565	646	2,059	19,114	26,746	282,971	61,212	195,250	26,509
Estimated total	100.0%	51,529	676	2,444	19,773	28,636	311,473	66,965	216,650	27,858
Cities outside metropolitan areas	878,599									
Area actually reporting	66.6%	2,152	15	312	170	1,655	16,265	3,803	12,053	409
Estimated total	100.0%	3,230	23	468	255	2,484	24,409	5,707	18,088	614
Nonmetropolitan counties	750,998									
Area actually reporting	77.7%	836	5	94	20	717	6,302	2,120	3,930	252
Estimated total	100.0%	1,076	7	121	26	922	8,107	2,727	5,056	324
State total	12,830,632	55,835	706	3,033	20,054	32,042	343,989	75,399	239,794	28,796
Rate per 100,000 inhabitants		435.2	5.5	23.6	156.3	249.7	2,681.0	587.6	1,868.9	224.4
INDIANA										
Metropolitan statistical area	5,091,659									
Area actually reporting	89.5%	17,931	266	1,374	5,788	10,503	157,572	37,922	108,540	11,110
Estimated total	100.0%	18,612	275	1,447	5,911	10,979	167,230	40,069	115,460	11,701
Cities outside metropolitan areas	507,282									
Area actually reporting	91.5%	930	8	157	223	542	17,531	3,530	13,227	774
Estimated total	100.0%	1,017	9	172	244	592	19,159	3,858	14,455	846
Nonmetropolitan counties	884,861									
Area actually reporting	76.9%	584	6	109	49	420	8,364	2,453	5,472	439
Estimated total	100.0%	760	8	142	64	546	10,881	3,188	7,112	571
State total	6,483,802	20,389	292	1,761	6,219	12,117	197,260	47,115	137,027	13,118
Rate per 100,000 inhabitants		314.5	4.5	27.2	95.9	186.9	3,042.4	726.7	2,113.4	202.3
IOWA										
Metropolitan statistical area	1,738,525									
Area actually reporting	98.7%	5,766	21	590	891	4,264	47,077	10,678	33,663	2,736
Estimated total	100.0%	5,801	21	595	892	4,293	47,405	10,758	33,894	2,753
Cities outside metropolitan areas	591,878									
Area actually reporting	92.3%	1,640	7	170	104	1,359	14,707	3,604	10,471	632
Estimated total	100.0%	1,777	8	184	113	1,472	15,934	3,905	11,344	685
Nonmetropolitan counties	715,952									
Area actually reporting	88.7%	670	9	51	5	605	4,416	1,769	2,347	300
Estimated total	100.0%	755	10	57	6	682	4,976	1,993	2,645	338
State total	3,046,355	8,333	39	836	1,011	6,447	68,315	16,656	47,883	3,776
Rate per 100,000 inhabitants		273.5	1.3	27.4	33.2	211.6	2,242.5	546.8	1,571.8	124.0
KANSAS										
Metropolitan statistical area	1,962,752									
Area actually reporting	99.5%	7,750	75	749	1,334	5,592	64,217	13,616	45,682	4,919
Estimated total	100.0%	7,773	75	752	1,337	5,609	64,436	13,654	45,850	4,932
Cities outside metropolitan areas	562,915									
Area actually reporting	95.6%	1,924	10	252	183	1,479	18,954	3,867	14,361	726
Estimated total	100.0%	2,010	10	263	191	1,546	19,818	4,043	15,016	759
Nonmetropolitan counties	327,451									
Area actually reporting	94.9%	709	14	87	15	593	4,518	1,620	2,596	302
Estimated total	100.0%	748	15	92	16	625	4,761	1,707	2,736	318
State total	2,853,118	10,531	100	1,107	1,544	7,780	89,015	19,404	63,602	6,009
Rate per 100,000 inhabitants		369.1	3.5	38.8	54.1	272.7	3,119.9	680.1	2,229.2	210.6
KENTUCKY										
Metropolitan statistical area	2,512,952									
Area actually reporting	99.1%	7,866	93	701	3,089	3,983	77,341	19,078	53,942	4,321
Estimated total	100.0%	7,926	93	709	3,114	4,010	78,133	19,250	54,525	4,358
Cities outside metropolitan areas	527,128									
Area actually reporting	96.4%	1,057	17	183	406	451	16,178	3,765	11,836	577
Estimated total	100.0%	1,097	18	190	421	468	16,788	3,907	12,282	599
Nonmetropolitan counties	1,299,287									
Area actually reporting	91.9%	1,384	70	443	196	675	14,515	6,577	6,787	1,151
Estimated total	100.0%	1,505	76	482	213	734	15,788	7,154	7,382	1,252
State total	4,339,367	10,528	187	1,381	3,748	5,212	110,709	30,311	74,189	6,209
Rate per 100,000 inhabitants		242.6	4.3	31.8	86.4	120.1	2,551.3	698.5	1,709.7	143.1

[2] Because of changes in the state's reporting practices, figures are not comparable to previous years' data.

Table 5. Crime, by State and Area, 2010—*Continued*

(Number, percent, rate per 100,000 population)

Area	Population	Violent crime	Murder and non-negligent man-slaughter	Forcible rape	Robbery	Aggravated assault	Property crime	Burglary	Larceny-theft	Motor vehicle theft
LOUISIANA										
Metropolitan statistical area	3,392,596									
Area actually reporting	97.9%	17,520	460	882	4,318	11,860	123,646	32,645	82,758	8,243
Estimated total	100.0%	17,866	463	901	4,367	12,135	126,541	33,258	84,924	8,359
Cities outside metropolitan areas	394,908									
Area actually reporting	83.1%	3,127	21	126	455	2,525	17,319	5,364	11,397	558
Estimated total	100.0%	3,762	25	152	547	3,038	20,837	6,454	13,712	671
Nonmetropolitan counties	745,868									
Area actually reporting	95.8%	3,119	21	172	284	2,642	17,218	5,481	10,911	826
Estimated total	100.0%	3,258	22	180	297	2,759	17,979	5,723	11,393	863
State total	4,533,372	24,886	510	1,233	5,211	17,932	165,357	45,435	110,029	9,893
Rate per 100,000 inhabitants		549.0	11.2	27.2	114.9	395.6	3,647.5	1,002.2	2,427.1	218.2
MAINE										
Metropolitan statistical area	779,766									
Area actually reporting	100.0%	971	16	209	336	410	20,151	4,066	15,473	612
Cities outside metropolitan areas	273,009									
Area actually reporting	100.0%	421	2	118	53	248	8,263	1,580	6,519	164
Nonmetropolitan counties	275,586									
Area actually reporting	100.0%	229	6	62	25	136	4,520	1,713	2,593	214
State total	1,328,361	1,621	24	389	414	794	32,934	7,359	24,585	990
Rate per 100,000 inhabitants		122.0	1.8	29.3	31.2	59.8	2,479.3	554.0	1,850.8	74.5
MARYLAND										
Metropolitan statistical area	5,465,306									
Area actually reporting	100.0%	30,535	417	1,179	10,857	18,082	164,703	34,509	112,457	17,737
Cities outside metropolitan areas	80,827									
Area actually reporting	100.0%	498	3	24	121	350	4,034	846	3,092	96
Nonmetropolitan counties	227,419									
Area actually reporting	100.0%	587	10	24	76	477	4,314	1,187	2,909	218
State total	5,773,552	31,620	430	1,227	11,054	18,909	173,051	36,542	118,458	18,051
Rate per 100,000 inhabitants		547.7	7.4	21.3	191.5	327.5	2,997.3	632.9	2,051.7	312.6
MASSACHUSETTS										
Metropolitan statistical area	6,520,338									
Area actually reporting	99.1%	30,236	208	1,720	6,832	21,476	151,787	37,290	103,166	11,331
Estimated total	100.0%	30,439	208	1,733	6,868	21,630	153,055	37,606	104,035	11,414
Cities outside metropolitan areas	27,205									
Area actually reporting	100.0%	113	2	12	6	93	848	160	649	39
Nonmetropolitan counties	86									
Area actually reporting	100.0%	1	0	0	0	1	2	1	1	0
State total	6,547,629	30,553	210	1,745	6,874	21,724	153,905	37,767	104,685	11,453
Rate per 100,000 inhabitants		466.6	3.2	26.7	105.0	331.8	2,350.5	576.8	1,598.8	174.9
MICHIGAN										
Metropolitan statistical area	8,066,088									
Area actually reporting	98.5%	44,042	533	3,515	11,202	28,792	228,343	64,196	138,346	25,801
Estimated total	100.0%	44,410	535	3,557	11,284	29,034	231,532	64,890	140,589	26,053
Cities outside metropolitan areas	620,812									
Area actually reporting	82.7%	1,405	9	340	126	930	15,419	2,380	12,628	411
Estimated total	100.0%	1,659	11	402	148	1,098	18,378	2,826	15,061	491
Nonmetropolitan counties	1,196,740									
Area actually reporting	94.6%	2,263	20	676	58	1,509	17,310	5,822	10,722	766
Estimated total	100.0%	2,391	21	714	61	1,595	18,291	6,152	11,330	809
State total	9,883,640	48,460	567	4,673	11,493	31,727	268,201	73,868	166,980	27,353
Rate per 100,000 inhabitants		490.3	5.7	47.3	116.3	321.0	2,713.6	747.4	1,689.5	276.8
MINNESOTA[3]										
Metropolitan statistical area	3,989,141									
Area actually reporting	99.6%		89		3,288	5,816	112,030	19,286	85,447	7,297
Estimated total	100.0%		89		3,294	5,830	112,526	19,352	85,856	7,318
Cities outside metropolitan areas	494,530									
Area actually reporting	99.6%		3		70	842	13,670	2,076	11,009	585
Estimated total	100.0%		3		70	845	13,724	2,084	11,053	587
Nonmetropolitan counties	820,254									
Area actually reporting	98.2%		4		24	548	9,997	2,925	6,402	670
Estimated total	100.0%		4		24	558	10,181	2,979	6,520	682
State total	5,303,925	12,515	96	1,798	3,388	7,233	136,431	24,415	103,429	8,587
Rate per 100,000 inhabitants		236.0	1.8	33.9	63.9	136.4	2,572.3	460.3	1,950.0	161.9

[3] The data collection methodology for the offense of forcible rape used by the Minnesota state Uniform Crime Reporting (UCR) Program (with the exception of Minneapolis and St. Paul, Minnesota) does not comply with national UCR Program guidelines. Consequently, its figures for forcible rape and violent crime (of which forcible rape is a part) are not published in this table.

Table 5.   Crime, by State and Area, 2010—*Continued*

(Number, percent, rate per 100,000 population)

Area	Population	Violent crime	Murder and non-negligent man-slaughter	Forcible rape	Robbery	Aggravated assault	Property crime	Burglary	Larceny-theft	Motor vehicle theft
MISSISSIPPI										
Metropolitan statistical area	1,326,220									
Area actually reporting	89.8%	3,693	83	428	1,665	1,517	43,229	13,289	26,685	3,255
Estimated total	100.0%	3,898	89	466	1,706	1,637	46,144	14,194	28,488	3,462
Cities outside metropolitan areas	600,833									
Area actually reporting	85.7%	1,977	50	205	649	1,073	23,184	8,073	14,229	882
Estimated total	100.0%	2,308	58	239	758	1,253	27,065	9,424	16,611	1,030
Nonmetropolitan counties	1,040,244									
Area actually reporting	60.7%	1,091	37	135	191	728	9,326	4,143	4,656	527
Estimated total	100.0%	1,797	61	222	315	1,199	15,365	6,826	7,671	868
State total	2,967,297	8,003	208	927	2,779	4,089	88,574	30,444	52,770	5,360
Rate per 100,000 inhabitants		269.7	7.0	31.2	93.7	137.8	2,985.0	1,026.0	1,778.4	180.6
MISSOURI										
Metropolitan statistical area	4,517,557									
Area actually reporting	99.9%	22,830	353	1,189	5,837	15,451	164,192	35,093	114,672	14,427
Estimated total	100.0%	22,835	353	1,189	5,838	15,455	164,263	35,106	114,725	14,432
Cities outside metropolitan areas	638,289									
Area actually reporting	98.4%	2,475	22	139	245	2,069	24,153	4,594	18,743	816
Estimated total	100.0%	2,515	22	141	249	2,103	24,554	4,670	19,054	830
Nonmetropolitan counties	833,081									
Area actually reporting	99.2%	1,887	45	101	45	1,696	11,505	4,233	6,489	783
Estimated total	100.0%	1,902	45	102	45	1,710	11,597	4,267	6,541	789
State total	5,988,927	27,252	420	1,432	6,132	19,268	200,414	44,043	140,320	16,051
Rate per 100,000 inhabitants		455.0	7.0	23.9	102.4	321.7	3,346.4	735.4	2,343.0	268.0
MONTANA										
Metropolitan statistical area	350,785									
Area actually reporting	100.0%	787	8	66	97	616	12,170	1,711	9,758	701
Cities outside metropolitan areas	217,382									
Area actually reporting	98.5%	945	8	151	41	745	7,107	955	5,731	421
Estimated total	100.0%	959	8	153	42	756	7,213	969	5,817	427
Nonmetropolitan counties	421,248									
Area actually reporting	98.2%	930	10	100	18	802	5,683	957	4,335	391
Estimated total	100.0%	947	10	102	18	817	5,786	974	4,414	398
State total	989,415	2,693	26	321	157	2,189	25,169	3,654	19,989	1,526
Rate per 100,000 inhabitants		272.2	2.6	32.4	15.9	221.2	2,543.8	369.3	2,020.3	154.2
NEBRASKA										
Metropolitan statistical area	1,077,532									
Area actually reporting	98.1%	3,920	40	413	945	2,522	33,263	5,491	24,844	2,928
Estimated total	100.0%	3,944	40	415	946	2,543	33,561	5,560	25,052	2,949
Cities outside metropolitan areas	391,292									
Area actually reporting	94.2%	837	9	196	67	565	11,230	1,784	9,002	444
Estimated total	100.0%	889	10	208	71	600	11,924	1,894	9,559	471
Nonmetropolitan counties	357,517									
Area actually reporting	79.9%	216	3	39	6	168	2,666	697	1,814	155
Estimated total	100.0%	271	4	49	8	210	3,336	872	2,270	194
State total	1,826,341	5,104	54	672	1,025	3,353	48,821	8,326	36,881	3,614
Rate per 100,000 inhabitants		279.5	3.0	36.8	56.1	183.6	2,673.2	455.9	2,019.4	197.9
NEVADA										
Metropolitan statistical area	2,431,751									
Area actually reporting	100.0%	16,860	149	884	5,215	10,612	69,956	20,645	39,512	9,799
Cities outside metropolitan areas	47,206									
Area actually reporting	100.0%	250	0	28	27	195	1,512	448	974	90
Nonmetropolitan counties	221,594									
Area actually reporting	100.0%	731	9	53	56	613	3,464	1,133	2,035	296
State total	2,700,551	17,841	158	965	5,298	11,420	74,932	22,226	42,521	10,185
Rate per 100,000 inhabitants		660.6	5.9	35.7	196.2	422.9	2,774.7	823.0	1,574.5	377.1
NEW HAMPSHIRE										
Metropolitan statistical area	823,922									
Area actually reporting	91.7%	1,426	9	226	327	864	16,408	3,144	12,660	604
Estimated total	100.0%	1,490	9	238	339	904	17,349	3,309	13,402	638
Cities outside metropolitan areas	442,399									
Area actually reporting	89.7%	592	4	144	99	345	9,966	1,791	7,891	284
Estimated total	100.0%	660	4	161	110	385	11,111	1,997	8,797	317
Nonmetropolitan counties	50,149									
Area actually reporting	3.0%	15	0	3	1	11	91	9	80	2
Estimated total	100.0%	48	0	13	2	33	322	135	174	13
State total	1,316,470	2,198	13	412	451	1,322	28,782	5,441	22,373	968
Rate per 100,000 inhabitants		167.0	1.0	31.3	34.3	100.4	2,186.3	413.3	1,699.5	73.5

Table 5.   Crime, by State and Area, 2010—*Continued*

(Number, percent, rate per 100,000 population)

Area	Population	Violent crime	Murder and non-negligent man-slaughter	Forcible rape	Robbery	Aggravated assault	Property crime	Burglary	Larceny-theft	Motor vehicle theft
NEW JERSEY										
Metropolitan statistical area	8,791,894									
Area actually reporting	100.0%	27,055	371	981	11,818	13,885	183,042	38,732	128,754	15,556
Cities outside metropolitan areas	None									
Nonmetropolitan counties	None									
State total	8,791,894	27,055	371	981	11,818	13,885	183,042	38,732	128,754	15,556
Rate per 100,000 inhabitants		307.7	4.2	11.2	134.4	157.9	2,081.9	440.5	1,464.5	176.9
NEW MEXICO										
Metropolitan statistical area	1,375,520									
Area actually reporting	99.7%	8,012	74	600	1,303	6,035	49,468	13,823	31,439	4,206
Estimated total	100.0%	8,034	74	601	1,304	6,055	49,602	13,855	31,532	4,215
Cities outside metropolitan areas	391,114									
Area actually reporting	97.6%	3,150	49	251	262	2,588	16,592	4,931	10,962	699
Estimated total	100.0%	3,226	50	257	268	2,651	16,993	5,050	11,227	716
Nonmetropolitan counties	292,545									
Area actually reporting	94.6%	820	17	95	40	668	3,924	1,996	1,629	299
Estimated total	100.0%	866	18	100	42	706	4,147	2,109	1,722	316
State total	2,059,179	12,126	142	958	1,614	9,412	70,742	21,014	44,481	5,247
Rate per 100,000 inhabitants		588.9	6.9	46.5	78.4	457.1	3,435.4	1,020.5	2,160.1	254.8
NEW YORK										
Metropolitan statistical area	17,857,493									
Area actually reporting	99.6%	73,208	842	2,412	28,113	41,841	343,968	57,773	266,598	19,597
Estimated total	100.0%	73,319	843	2,417	28,153	41,906	345,218	57,967	267,615	19,636
Cities outside metropolitan areas	558,102									
Area actually reporting	97.6%	1,527	15	169	232	1,111	16,774	3,143	13,294	337
Estimated total	100.0%	1,564	15	173	238	1,138	17,185	3,220	13,620	345
Nonmetropolitan counties	962,507									
Area actually reporting	100.0%	1,094	8	181	82	823	13,758	3,786	9,520	452
State total	19,378,102	75,977	866	2,771	28,473	43,867	376,161	64,973	290,755	20,433
Rate per 100,000 inhabitants		392.1	4.5	14.3	146.9	226.4	1,941.2	335.3	1,500.4	105.4
NORTH CAROLINA										
Metropolitan statistical area	6,758,596									
Area actually reporting	97.6%	24,673	314	1,441	7,575	15,343	232,547	68,270	150,510	13,767
Estimated total	100.0%	25,045	319	1,467	7,648	15,611	237,265	69,684	153,567	14,014
Cities outside metropolitan areas	852,780									
Area actually reporting	90.2%	4,523	64	213	1,201	3,045	41,005	11,567	27,920	1,518
Estimated total	100.0%	5,002	71	236	1,327	3,368	45,356	12,796	30,882	1,678
Nonmetropolitan counties	1,924,107									
Area actually reporting	94.1%	4,337	81	292	598	3,366	43,400	19,027	21,908	2,465
Estimated total	100.0%	4,606	86	310	635	3,575	46,098	20,210	23,270	2,618
State total	9,535,483	34,653	476	2,013	9,610	22,554	328,719	102,690	207,719	18,310
Rate per 100,000 inhabitants		363.4	5.0	21.1	100.8	236.5	3,447.3	1,076.9	2,178.4	192.0
NORTH DAKOTA										
Metropolitan statistical area	331,649									
Area actually reporting	100.0%	746	3	127	64	552	7,191	1,117	5,657	417
Cities outside metropolitan areas	148,656									
Area actually reporting	94.2%	642	4	82	23	533	3,365	553	2,511	301
Estimated total	100.0%	681	4	87	24	566	3,573	587	2,666	320
Nonmetropolitan counties	192,286									
Area actually reporting	97.3%	83	3	22	2	56	1,101	255	727	119
Estimated total	100.0%	86	3	23	2	58	1,131	262	747	122
State total	672,591	1,513	10	237	90	1,176	11,895	1,966	9,070	859
Rate per 100,000 inhabitants		225.0	1.5	35.2	13.4	174.8	1,768.5	292.3	1,348.5	127.7
OHIO										
Metropolitan statistical area	9,328,810									
Area actually reporting	95.3%	32,775	443	3,115	15,572	13,645	309,593	90,562	200,027	19,004
Estimated total	100.0%	33,470	445	3,217	15,835	13,973	321,443	93,031	208,990	19,422
Cities outside metropolitan areas	930,069									
Area actually reporting	81.2%	1,376	14	256	415	691	28,006	5,777	21,569	660
Estimated total	100.0%	1,694	17	315	511	851	34,497	7,116	26,568	813
Nonmetropolitan counties	1,277,625									
Area actually reporting	91.2%	1,096	13	152	121	810	16,821	5,814	10,202	805
Estimated total	100.0%	1,202	14	167	133	888	18,441	6,374	11,184	883
State total	11,536,504	36,366	476	3,699	16,479	15,712	374,381	106,521	246,742	21,118
Rate per 100,000 inhabitants		315.2	4.1	32.1	142.8	136.2	3,245.2	923.3	2,138.8	183.1

Table 5.   Crime, by State and Area, 2010—*Continued*

(Number, percent, rate per 100,000 population)

Area	Population	Violent crime	Murder and non-negligent man-slaughter	Forcible rape	Robbery	Aggravated assault	Property crime	Burglary	Larceny-theft	Motor vehicle theft
OKLAHOMA										
Metropolitan statistical area	2,407,430									
Area actually reporting	100.0%	13,598	145	1,034	2,964	9,455	92,843	27,301	57,313	8,229
Cities outside metropolitan areas	725,417									
Area actually reporting	99.3%	3,235	32	282	341	2,580	27,021	7,010	18,743	1,268
Estimated total	100.0%	3,259	32	284	344	2,599	27,225	7,063	18,884	1,278
Nonmetropolitan counties	618,504									
Area actually reporting	100.0%	1,130	18	132	29	951	8,058	3,112	4,263	683
State total	3,751,351	17,987	195	1,450	3,337	13,005	128,126	37,476	80,460	10,190
Rate per 100,000 inhabitants		479.5	5.2	38.7	89.0	346.7	3,415.5	999.0	2,144.8	271.6
OREGON[2]										
Metropolitan statistical area	2,998,714									
Area actually reporting	96.4%	7,960	59	944	2,127	4,830	91,148	14,508	68,989	7,651
Estimated total	100.0%	8,138	61	970	2,157	4,950	93,185	14,920	70,469	7,796
Cities outside metropolitan areas	390,919									
Area actually reporting	86.7%	891	11	146	167	567	13,419	2,389	10,497	533
Estimated total	100.0%	1,028	13	168	193	654	15,481	2,756	12,110	615
Nonmetropolitan counties	441,441									
Area actually reporting	75.0%	367	13	57	30	267	5,072	1,471	3,225	376
Estimated total	100.0%	489	17	76	40	356	6,762	1,961	4,300	501
State total	3,831,074	9,655	91	1,214	2,390	5,960	115,428	19,637	86,879	8,912
Rate per 100,000 inhabitants		252.0	2.4	31.7	62.4	155.6	3,012.9	512.6	2,267.7	232.6
PENNSYLVANIA										
Metropolitan statistical area	10,710,034									
Area actually reporting	99.3%	42,240	601	2,768	15,878	22,993	241,670	46,958	179,314	15,398
Estimated total	100.0%	42,396	601	2,777	15,919	23,099	243,093	47,187	180,455	15,451
Cities outside metropolitan areas	931,295									
Area actually reporting	96.7%	2,294	20	198	285	1,791	18,609	3,536	14,520	553
Estimated total	100.0%	2,373	21	205	295	1,852	19,241	3,656	15,013	572
Nonmetropolitan counties	1,061,050									
Area actually reporting	100.0%	1,745	35	433	148	1,129	13,689	4,328	8,715	646
State total	12,702,379	46,514	657	3,415	16,362	26,080	276,023	55,171	204,183	16,669
Rate per 100,000 inhabitants		366.2	5.2	26.9	128.8	205.3	2,173.0	434.3	1,607.4	131.2
RHODE ISLAND										
Metropolitan statistical area	1,052,567									
Area actually reporting	100.0%	2,696	28	296	780	1,592	26,831	6,121	18,367	2,343
Cities outside metropolitan areas	None									
Nonmetropolitan counties	None									
Area actually reporting	100.0%	5	1	0	0	4	79	0	23	56
State total	1,052,567	2,701	29	296	780	1,596	26,910	6,121	18,390	2,399
Rate per 100,000 inhabitants		256.6	2.8	28.1	74.1	151.6	2,556.6	581.5	1,747.2	227.9
SOUTH CAROLINA										
Metropolitan statistical area	3,549,779									
Area actually reporting	99.9%	20,477	197	1,155	3,920	15,205	137,670	33,747	93,517	10,406
Estimated total	100.0%	20,503	197	1,156	3,924	15,226	137,869	33,784	93,669	10,416
Cities outside metropolitan areas	282,845									
Area actually reporting	97.7%	2,868	20	118	527	2,203	15,111	3,738	10,766	607
Estimated total	100.0%	2,934	20	121	539	2,254	15,463	3,825	11,017	621
Nonmetropolitan counties	792,740									
Area actually reporting	100.0%	4,211	63	189	519	3,440	27,075	8,547	16,368	2,160
State total	4,625,364	27,648	280	1,466	4,982	20,920	180,407	46,156	121,054	13,197
Rate per 100,000 inhabitants		597.7	6.1	31.7	107.7	452.3	3,900.4	997.9	2,617.2	285.3
SOUTH DAKOTA										
Metropolitan statistical area	382,490									
Area actually reporting	96.9%	1,071	7	222	120	722	9,286	1,953	6,904	429
Estimated total	100.0%	1,086	7	225	120	734	9,443	1,988	7,019	436
Cities outside metropolitan areas	205,213									
Area actually reporting	89.7%	840	7	122	25	686	4,076	746	3,068	262
Estimated total	100.0%	936	8	136	28	764	4,542	831	3,419	292
Nonmetropolitan counties	226,477									
Area actually reporting	79.1%	130	6	23	5	96	867	286	528	53
Estimated total	100.0%	164	8	29	6	121	1,097	362	668	67
State total	814,180	2,186	23	390	154	1,619	15,082	3,181	11,106	795
Rate per 100,000 inhabitants		268.5	2.8	47.9	18.9	198.9	1,852.4	390.7	1,364.1	97.6

[2] Because of changes in the state's reporting practices, figures are not comparable to previous years' data.

Table 5.   Crime, by State and Area, 2010—*Continued*

(Number, percent, rate per 100,000 population)

Area	Population	Violent crime	Murder and non-negligent man-slaughter	Forcible rape	Robbery	Aggravated assault	Property crime	Burglary	Larceny-theft	Motor vehicle theft
TENNESSEE										
Metropolitan statistical area	4,671,121									
Area actually reporting	100.0%	32,181	286	1,763	7,715	22,417	180,615	48,939	119,713	11,963
Cities outside metropolitan areas	614,285									
Area actually reporting	100.0%	3,681	27	203	486	2,965	27,889	6,527	20,222	1,140
Nonmetropolitan counties	1,060,699									
Area actually reporting	100.0%	3,059	44	172	165	2,678	23,628	8,769	13,127	1,732
State total	6,346,105	38,921	357	2,138	8,366	28,060	232,132	64,235	153,062	14,835
Rate per 100,000 inhabitants		613.3	5.6	33.7	131.8	442.2	3,657.9	1,012.2	2,411.9	233.8
TEXAS										
Metropolitan statistical area	22,153,872									
Area actually reporting	99.8%	103,798	1,148	6,687	31,949	64,014	877,796	206,229	606,955	64,612
Estimated total	100.0%	103,914	1,149	6,698	31,976	64,091	879,209	206,519	607,994	64,696
Cities outside metropolitan areas	1,394,578									
Area actually reporting	99.4%	6,040	35	515	694	4,796	47,412	12,370	33,335	1,707
Estimated total	100.0%	6,060	35	517	695	4,813	47,559	12,415	33,436	1,708
Nonmetropolitan counties	1,597,111									
Area actually reporting	99.8%	3,250	65	406	172	2,607	24,421	9,641	13,165	1,615
Estimated total	100.0%	3,257	65	407	172	2,613	24,478	9,663	13,196	1,619
State total	25,145,561	113,231	1,249	7,622	32,843	71,517	951,246	228,597	654,626	68,023
Rate per 100,000 inhabitants		450.3	5.0	30.3	130.6	284.4	3,783.0	909.1	2,603.3	270.5
UTAH										
Metropolitan statistical area	2,463,884									
Area actually reporting	99.9%	5,438	46	857	1,246	3,289	81,528	13,644	62,207	5,677
Estimated total	100.0%	5,438	46	857	1,246	3,289	81,540	13,646	62,216	5,678
Cities outside metropolitan areas	148,476									
Area actually reporting	88.2%	246	5	55	17	169	3,746	672	2,927	147
Estimated total	100.0%	279	6	62	19	192	4,247	762	3,318	167
Nonmetropolitan counties	151,525									
Area actually reporting	88.3%	144	1	26	3	114	1,849	538	1,219	92
Estimated total	100.0%	162	1	29	3	129	2,093	609	1,380	104
State total	2,763,885	5,879	53	948	1,268	3,610	87,880	15,017	66,914	5,949
Rate per 100,000 inhabitants		212.7	1.9	34.3	45.9	130.6	3,179.6	543.3	2,421.0	215.2
VERMONT	209,845									
Metropolitan statistical area	100.0%	312	2	49	39	222	5,926	1,055	4,696	175
Area actually reporting	205,894									
Cities outside metropolitan areas	96.7%	338	0	44	32	262	4,902	951	3,836	115
Area actually reporting	100.0%	349	0	45	33	271	5,067	983	3,965	119
Nonmetropolitan counties	210,002									
Area actually reporting	98.1%	151	5	37	2	107	3,224	1,302	1,778	144
Estimated total	100.0%	154	5	38	2	109	3,288	1,328	1,813	147
State total	625,741	815	7	132	74	602	14,281	3,366	10,474	441
Rate per 100,000 inhabitants		130.2	1.1	21.1	11.8	96.2	2,282.3	537.9	1,673.9	70.5
VIRGINIA										
Metropolitan statistical area	6,881,309									
Area actually reporting	100.0%	15,474	315	1,299	5,395	8,465	167,152	26,536	131,063	9,553
Cities outside metropolitan areas	273,315									
Area actually reporting	100.0%	624	14	83	144	383	8,018	1,155	6,624	239
Nonmetropolitan counties	846,400									
Area actually reporting	100.0%	989	40	150	118	681	11,026	2,938	7,332	756
State total	8,001,024	17,087	369	1,532	5,657	9,529	186,196	30,629	145,019	10,548
Rate per 100,000 inhabitants		213.6	4.6	19.1	70.7	119.1	2,327.2	382.8	1,812.5	131.8
WASHINGTON										
Metropolitan statistical area	5,904,442									
Area actually reporting	99.9%	19,171	134	2,223	5,626	11,188	221,822	47,788	150,317	23,717
Estimated total	100.0%	19,173	134	2,223	5,627	11,189	221,862	47,795	150,346	23,721
Cities outside metropolitan areas	335,901									
Area actually reporting	98.2%	1,247	4	217	215	811	16,829	3,625	12,113	1,091
Estimated total	100.0%	1,270	4	221	219	826	17,139	3,692	12,336	1,111
Nonmetropolitan counties	484,197									
Area actually reporting	100.0%	658	14	118	83	443	10,252	3,677	5,678	897
State total	6,724,540	21,101	152	2,562	5,929	12,458	249,253	55,164	168,360	25,729
Rate per 100,000 inhabitants		313.8	2.3	38.1	88.2	185.3	3,706.6	820.3	2,503.7	382.6

Table 5. Crime, by State and Area, 2010—*Continued*

(Number, percent, rate per 100,000 population)

Area	Population	Violent crime	Murder and non-negligent man-slaughter	Forcible rape	Robbery	Aggravated assault	Property crime	Burglary	Larceny-theft	Motor vehicle theft
WEST VIRGINIA										
Metropolitan statistical area.........	1,034,548									
Area actually reporting............	92.5%	3,342	30	213	556	2,543	24,407	6,275	16,713	1,419
Estimated total....................	100.0%	3,566	32	227	581	2,726	26,450	6,725	18,203	1,522
Cities outside metropolitan areas............	223,928									
Area actually reporting............	78.0%	727	9	39	114	565	5,497	1,125	4,203	169
Estimated total....................	100.0%	932	12	50	146	724	7,043	1,441	5,385	217
Nonmetropolitan counties....................	594,518									
Area actually reporting............	92.7%	1,235	17	71	94	1,053	7,419	2,400	4,443	576
Estimated total....................	100.0%	1,332	18	77	101	1,136	8,007	2,590	4,795	622
State total.........	1,852,994	5,830	62	354	828	4,586	41,500	10,756	28,383	2,361
Rate per 100,000 inhabitants..............		314.6	3.3	19.1	44.7	247.5	2,239.6	580.5	1,531.7	127.4
WISCONSIN										
Metropolitan statistical area.........	4,162,487									
Area actually reporting............	99.9%	12,205	139	907	4,389	6,770	112,702	20,423	85,114	7,165
Estimated total....................	100.0%	12,205	139	907	4,389	6,770	112,705	20,423	85,117	7,165
Cities outside metropolitan areas............	625,718									
Area actually reporting............	97.4%	1,141	7	146	91	897	18,939	2,621	15,890	428
Estimated total....................	100.0%	1,171	7	150	93	921	19,436	2,690	16,307	439
Nonmetropolitan counties....................	898,781									
Area actually reporting............	98.8%	757	9	128	22	598	10,341	3,410	6,404	527
Estimated total....................	100.0%	766	9	130	22	605	10,471	3,453	6,484	534
State total.........	5,686,986	14,142	155	1,187	4,504	8,296	142,612	26,566	107,908	8,138
Rate per 100,000 inhabitants..............		248.7	2.7	20.9	79.2	145.9	2,507.7	467.1	1,897.5	143.1
WYOMING										
Metropolitan statistical area.........	169,109									
Area actually reporting............	100.0%	328	3	51	47	227	5,637	849	4,534	254
Cities outside metropolitan areas............	237,483									
Area actually reporting............	98.1%	578	4	87	20	467	6,456	895	5,322	239
Estimated total....................	100.0%	589	4	89	20	476	6,581	912	5,425	244
Nonmetropolitan counties....................	157,034									
Area actually reporting............	100.0%	187	1	24	9	153	1,656	388	1,175	93
State total.........	563,626	1,104	8	164	76	856	13,874	2,149	11,134	591
Rate per 100,000 inhabitants..............		195.9	1.4	29.1	13.5	151.9	2,461.6	381.3	1,975.4	104.9

Table 6.   Crime, by Metropolitan Statistical Area, 2010

(Number, percent, rate per 100,000 population)

Area	Population	Violent crime	Murder and non-negligent man-slaughter	Forcible rape	Robbery	Aggravated assault	Property crime	Burglary	Larceny-theft	Motor vehicle theft
Abilene, TX M.S.A...............................	**159,566**									
Includes Callahan, Jones, and Taylor Counties										
City of Abilene	116,938	578	4	68	112	394	4,897	1,340	3,375	182
Total area actually reporting	100.0%	675	5	78	116	476	5,772	1,610	3,925	237
Rate per 100,000 inhabitants		423.0	3.1	48.9	72.7	298.3	3,617.3	1,009.0	2,459.8	148.5
Akron, OH M.S.A................................	**698,613**									
Includes Portage and Summit Counties										
City of Akron	205,760	1,665	22	159	602	882	10,851	4,247	5,855	749
Total area actually reporting	94.2%	2,063	26	276	709	1,052	21,127	6,389	13,637	1,101
Estimated total	100.0%	2,129	26	286	734	1,083	22,255	6,621	14,493	1,141
Rate per 100,000 inhabitants		304.7	3.7	40.9	105.1	155.0	3,185.6	947.7	2,074.5	163.3
Albany, GA M.S.A...............................	**160,950**									
Includes Baker, Dougherty, Lee, Terrell, and Worth Counties										
City of Albany	73,034	722	11	28	203	480	5,037	1,629	3,108	300
Total area actually reporting	86.9%	845	13	36	219	577	6,624	2,093	4,125	406
Estimated total	100.0%	911	14	40	242	615	7,263	2,282	4,512	469
Rate per 100,000 inhabitants		566.0	8.7	24.9	150.4	382.1	4,512.6	1,417.8	2,803.4	291.4
Albany-Schenectady-Troy, NY M.S.A.	**851,078**									
Includes Albany, Rensselaer, Saratoga, Schenectady, and Schoharie Counties										
City of Albany	92,713	981	2	42	316	621	4,643	926	3,488	229
City of Schenectady	60,751	679	8	53	256	362	3,387	856	2,347	184
City of Troy	46,861	423	2	22	137	262	2,352	656	1,551	145
Total area actually reporting	100.0%	2,642	13	179	838	1,612	22,925	4,358	17,670	897
Rate per 100,000 inhabitants		310.4	1.5	21.0	98.5	189.4	2,693.6	512.1	2,076.2	105.4
Albuquerque, NM M.S.A.	**884,210**									
Includes Bernalillo, Sandoval, Torrance, and Valencia Counties										
City of Albuquerque	545,389	4,291	42	338	940	2,971	26,372	5,465	18,134	2,773
Total area actually reporting	100.0%	5,928	51	396	1,099	4,382	34,450	8,140	22,867	3,443
Rate per 100,000 inhabitants		670.4	5.8	44.8	124.3	495.6	3,896.1	920.6	2,586.2	389.4
Alexandria, LA M.S.A.	**155,654**									
Includes Grant and Rapides Parishes										
City of Alexandria	49,283	592	4	11	184	393	3,787	943	2,714	130
Total area actually reporting	94.4%	948	9	34	200	705	6,766	1,795	4,653	318
Estimated total	100.0%	993	9	36	206	742	7,149	1,873	4,944	332
Rate per 100,000 inhabitants		638.0	5.8	23.1	132.3	476.7	4,592.9	1,203.3	3,176.3	213.3
Allentown-Bethlehem-Easton, PA-NJ M.S.A.	**828,068**									
Includes Warren County, NJ and Carbon, Lehigh, and Northampton Counties, PA										
City of Allentown, PA	108,473	732	9	67	460	196	5,089	1,327	3,345	417
City of Bethlehem, PA	73,634	234	0	18	110	106	2,069	445	1,522	102
Total area actually reporting	99.6%	1,883	29	168	773	913	18,967	3,569	14,508	890
Estimated total	100.0%	1,890	29	168	775	918	19,029	3,579	14,558	892
Rate per 100,000 inhabitants		228.2	3.5	20.3	93.6	110.9	2,298.0	432.2	1,758.1	107.7
Altoona, PA M.S.A.	**126,459**									
Includes Blair County										
City of Altoona	46,213	167	0	29	51	87	947	294	616	37
Total area actually reporting	100.0%	308	1	48	63	196	2,291	538	1,667	86
Rate per 100,000 inhabitants		243.6	0.8	38.0	49.8	155.0	1,811.7	425.4	1,318.2	68.0
Amarillo, TX M.S.A.	**247,721**									
Includes Armstrong, Carson, Potter, and Randall Counties										
City of Amarillo	190,393	1,184	10	91	238	845	11,064	2,590	7,827	647
Total area actually reporting	100.0%	1,271	14	101	245	911	11,922	2,817	8,399	706
Rate per 100,000 inhabitants		513.1	5.7	40.8	98.9	367.8	4,812.7	1,137.2	3,390.5	285.0
Ames, IA M.S.A.	**88,803**									
Includes Story County										
City of Ames	57,817	177	1	24	10	142	1,556	289	1,217	50
Total area actually reporting	100.0%	266	1	37	11	217	2,245	425	1,746	74
Rate per 100,000 inhabitants		299.5	1.1	41.7	12.4	244.4	2,528.1	478.6	1,966.1	83.3

Table 6. Crime, by Metropolitan Statistical Area, 2010—*Continued*

(Number, percent, rate per 100,000 population)

Area	Population	Violent crime	Murder and non-negligent man-slaughter	Forcible rape	Robbery	Aggravated assault	Property crime	Burglary	Larceny-theft	Motor vehicle theft
Anchorage, AK M.S.A.	313,181									
Includes Anchorage Municipality and Matanuska-Susitna Borough										
City of Anchorage	290,334	2,432	13	264	454	1,701	10,214	1,223	8,178	813
Total area actually reporting	100.0%	2,546	13	269	465	1,799	10,981	1,303	8,811	867
Rate per 100,000 inhabitants		812.9	4.2	85.9	148.5	574.4	3,506.3	416.1	2,813.4	276.8
Anderson, IN M.S.A.	131,703									
Includes Madison County										
City of Anderson	57,156	199	3	32	85	79	3,072	753	2,095	224
Total area actually reporting	100.0%	271	3	44	93	131	4,417	1,117	3,022	278
Rate per 100,000 inhabitants		205.8	2.3	33.4	70.6	99.5	3,353.8	848.1	2,294.6	211.1
Anderson, SC M.S.A.	187,031									
Includes Anderson County										
City of Anderson	27,325	200	6	15	36	143	1,924	466	1,342	116
Total area actually reporting	100.0%	1,096	10	68	142	876	8,805	2,427	5,689	689
Rate per 100,000 inhabitants		586.0	5.3	36.4	75.9	468.4	4,707.8	1,297.6	3,041.7	368.4
Ann Arbor, MI M.S.A.	346,839									
Includes Washtenaw County										
City of Ann Arbor	111,745	284	0	43	76	165	2,937	524	2,284	129
Total area actually reporting	100.0%	1,174	5	150	242	777	9,412	2,288	6,519	605
Rate per 100,000 inhabitants		338.5	1.4	43.2	69.8	224.0	2,713.7	659.7	1,879.5	174.4
Anniston-Oxford, AL M.S.A.[1]	115,376									
Includes Calhoun County										
City of Anniston[1]	23,703		3	23	76		2,038	831	1,107	100
City of Oxford[1]	18,397		3	1		49	1,079	162	867	50
Total area actually reporting	100.0%		6	40			4,616	1,437	2,995	184
Rate per 100,000 inhabitants			5.2	34.7			4,000.8	1,245.5	2,595.9	159.5
Appleton, WI M.S.A.	224,034									
Includes Calumet and Outagamie Counties										
City of Appleton	70,975	202	0	17	13	172	1,716	305	1,379	32
Total area actually reporting	100.0%	349	0	48	31	270	4,787	848	3,827	112
Rate per 100,000 inhabitants		155.8	0.0	21.4	13.8	120.5	2,136.7	378.5	1,708.2	50.0
Asheville, NC M.S.A.	417,415									
Includes Buncombe, Haywood, Henderson, and Madison Counties										
City of Asheville	77,067	432	2	31	165	234	3,671	743	2,638	290
Total area actually reporting	99.5%	952	8	91	248	605	10,158	3,108	6,343	707
Estimated total	100.0%	959	8	91	250	610	10,247	3,129	6,407	711
Rate per 100,000 inhabitants		229.7	1.9	21.8	59.9	146.1	2,454.9	749.6	1,534.9	170.3
Athens-Clarke County, GA M.S.A.	188,596									
Includes Clarke, Madison, Oconee, and Oglethorpe Counties										
City of Athens-Clarke County	112,851	371	5	29	110	227	4,931	1,334	3,299	298
Total area actually reporting	99.3%	701	8	37	131	525	7,193	1,909	4,840	444
Estimated total	100.0%	707	8	37	133	529	7,249	1,920	4,881	448
Rate per 100,000 inhabitants		374.9	4.2	19.6	70.5	280.5	3,843.7	1,018.0	2,588.1	237.5
Atlanta-Sandy Springs-Marietta, GA M.S.A.	5,432,336									
Includes Barrow, Bartow, Butts, Carroll, Cherokee, Clayton, Cobb, Coweta, Dawson, DeKalb, Douglas, Fayette, Forsyth, Fulton, Gwinnett, Haralson, Heard, Henry, Jasper, Lamar, Meriwether, Newton, Paulding, Pickens, Pike, Rockdale, Spalding, and Walton Counties										
City of Atlanta	536,472	5,749	93	89	2,162	3,405	30,800	8,016	17,741	5,043
City of Sandy Springs	82,898	189	7	18	115	49	2,666	718	1,756	192
City of Marietta	65,308	462	2	10	136	314	2,857	723	1,968	166
Total area actually reporting	99.6%	22,390	333	1,128	8,107	12,822	187,204	51,803	115,363	20,038
Estimated total	100.0%	22,481	334	1,133	8,134	12,880	188,099	51,985	116,017	20,097
Rate per 100,000 inhabitants		413.8	6.1	20.9	149.7	237.1	3,462.6	957.0	2,135.7	370.0
Atlantic City-Hammonton, NJ M.S.A.	275,382									
Includes Atlantic County										
City of Atlantic City	39,787	783	11	27	434	311	2,969	492	2,344	133
City of Hammonton	13,603	20	1	2	4	13	254	72	175	7
Total area actually reporting	100.0%	1,459	22	52	676	709	9,777	2,042	7,396	339
Rate per 100,000 inhabitants		529.8	8.0	18.9	245.5	257.5	3,550.3	741.5	2,685.7	123.1

[1] The FBI determined that the agency's data were underreported. Consequently, those data are not included in this table.

Table 6.   Crime, by Metropolitan Statistical Area, 2010—*Continued*

(Number, percent, rate per 100,000 population)

Area	Population	Violent crime	Murder and non-negligent man-slaughter	Forcible rape	Robbery	Aggravated assault	Property crime	Burglary	Larceny-theft	Motor vehicle theft
Augusta-Richmond County, GA-SC M.S.A......................	**531,786**									
Includes Burke, Columbia, McDuffie, and Richmond Counties, GA and Aiken and Edgefield Counties, SC										
Total area actually reporting	99.8%	2,192	54	199	832	1,107	25,559	7,196	16,119	2,244
Estimated total...............................	100.0%	2,196	54	199	833	1,110	25,607	7,206	16,154	2,247
Rate per 100,000 inhabitants.................		412.9	10.2	37.4	156.6	208.7	4,815.3	1,355.1	3,037.7	422.5
Austin-Round Rock-San Marcos, TX M.S.A.....................	**1,752,518**									
Includes Bastrop, Caldwell, Hays, Travis, and Williamson Counties										
City of Austin	796,310	3,790	38	265	1,231	2,256	45,826	8,749	34,827	2,250
City of Round Rock	111,099	116	0	26	35	55	3,016	464	2,452	100
City of San Marcos	55,100	152	1	13	34	104	1,726	263	1,390	73
Total area actually reporting	100.0%	5,746	60	432	1,472	3,782	66,456	13,219	50,243	2,994
Rate per 100,000 inhabitants.................		327.9	3.4	24.7	84.0	215.8	3,792.0	754.3	2,866.9	170.8
Bakersfield-Delano, CA M.S.A.	**822,752**									
Includes Kern County										
City of Bakersfield...........................	333,458	2,104	33	34	641	1,396	15,197	4,235	8,507	2,455
City of Delano...............................	54,298	247	0	6	55	186	1,651	773	446	432
Total area actually reporting	100.0%	4,879	74	164	1,221	3,420	30,550	9,445	15,892	5,213
Rate per 100,000 inhabitants.................		593.0	9.0	19.9	148.4	415.7	3,713.1	1,148.0	1,931.6	633.6
Baltimore-Towson, MD M.S.A.	**2,720,381**									
Includes Anne Arundel, Baltimore, Carroll, Harford, Howard, and Queen Anne's Counties and Baltimore City										
City of Baltimore	639,929	9,316	223	265	3,336	5,492	28,280	7,573	16,298	4,409
Total area actually reporting	100.0%	18,642	279	641	5,833	11,889	84,079	17,669	58,094	8,316
Rate per 100,000 inhabitants.................		685.3	10.3	23.6	214.4	437.0	3,090.7	649.5	2,135.5	305.7
Bangor, ME M.S.A.	**150,537**									
Includes Penobscot County										
City of Bangor................................	31,587	52	3	4	30	15	1,730	198	1,485	47
Total area actually reporting	100.0%	103	3	19	41	40	4,664	863	3,657	144
Rate per 100,000 inhabitants.................		68.4	2.0	12.6	27.2	26.6	3,098.2	573.3	2,429.3	95.7
Barnstable Town, MA M.S.A.	**218,615**									
Includes Barnstable County										
City of Barnstable	45,599	355	0	29	46	280	1,325	428	833	64
Total area actually reporting	100.0%	950	1	79	126	744	6,499	2,441	3,858	200
Rate per 100,000 inhabitants.................		434.6	0.5	36.1	57.6	340.3	2,972.8	1,116.6	1,764.7	91.5
Battle Creek, MI M.S.A.	**134,169**									
Includes Calhoun County										
City of Battle Creek	60,386	702	5	63	120	514	3,134	1,075	1,910	149
Total area actually reporting	98.7%	930	6	100	146	678	4,922	1,527	3,202	193
Estimated total...............................	100.0%	936	6	101	147	682	4,969	1,537	3,235	197
Rate per 100,000 inhabitants.................		697.6	4.5	75.3	109.6	508.3	3,703.5	1,145.6	2,411.1	146.8
Bay City, MI M.S.A.	**106,214**									
Includes Bay County										
City of Bay City	33,200	250	1	53	45	151	1,056	340	681	35
Total area actually reporting	98.1%	350	1	82	53	214	2,572	636	1,849	87
Estimated total...............................	100.0%	356	1	83	54	218	2,626	648	1,887	91
Rate per 100,000 inhabitants.................		335.2	0.9	78.1	50.8	205.2	2,472.4	610.1	1,776.6	85.7
Beaumont-Port Arthur, TX M.S.A.	**376,711**									
Includes Hardin, Jefferson, and Orange Counties										
City of Beaumont	109,430	900	10	65	312	513	5,941	1,611	4,041	289
City of Port Arthur	56,424	419	6	26	169	218	2,752	1,020	1,567	165
Total area actually reporting	100.0%	1,877	21	142	595	1,119	14,561	4,358	9,374	829
Rate per 100,000 inhabitants.................		498.3	5.6	37.7	157.9	297.0	3,865.3	1,156.9	2,488.4	220.1
Bellingham, WA M.S.A...............................	**203,393**									
Includes Whatcom County										
City of Bellingham...........................	81,139	282	2	37	73	170	3,653	589	2,931	133
Total area actually reporting	100.0%	543	5	91	103	344	6,504	1,412	4,826	266
Rate per 100,000 inhabitants.................		267.0	2.5	44.7	50.6	169.1	3,197.8	694.2	2,372.7	130.8
Bend, OR M.S.A.[2]	**162,019**									
Includes Deschutes County[2]										
City of Bend[2]	79,556	247	5	14	31	197	2,410	387	1,951	72
Total area actually reporting	100.0%	494	7	47	50	390	4,818	806	3,824	188
Rate per 100,000 inhabitants.................		304.9	4.3	29.0	30.9	240.7	2,973.7	497.5	2,360.2	116.0

[2] Because of changes in the state/local agency's reporting practices, figures are not comparable to previous years' data.

Table 6.   Crime, by Metropolitan Statistical Area, 2010—*Continued*

(Number, percent, rate per 100,000 population)

Area	Population	Violent crime	Murder and non-negligent man-slaughter	Forcible rape	Robbery	Aggravated assault	Property crime	Burglary	Larceny-theft	Motor vehicle theft
Billings, MT M.S.A.	**157,205**									
Includes Carbon and Yellowstone Counties										
City of Billings	108,039	280	2	25	42	211	5,021	848	3,811	362
Total area actually reporting	100.0%	343	3	31	45	264	5,978	1,026	4,517	435
Rate per 100,000 inhabitants		218.2	1.9	19.7	28.6	167.9	3,802.7	652.7	2,873.3	276.7
Binghamton, NY M.S.A.	**241,233**									
Includes Broome and Tioga Counties										
City of Binghamton	43,628	266	4	18	70	174	2,085	423	1,644	18
Total area actually reporting	100.0%	534	6	49	123	356	6,047	1,094	4,855	98
Rate per 100,000 inhabitants		221.4	2.5	20.3	51.0	147.6	2,506.7	453.5	2,012.6	40.6
Bismarck, ND M.S.A.	**111,613**									
Includes Burleigh and Morton Counties										
City of Bismarck	64,142	197	1	21	17	158	1,508	182	1,250	76
Total area actually reporting	100.0%	255	2	37	19	197	1,981	245	1,622	114
Rate per 100,000 inhabitants		228.5	1.8	33.2	17.0	176.5	1,774.9	219.5	1,453.2	102.1
Blacksburg-Christiansburg-Radford, VA M.S.A.	**161,019**									
Includes Giles, Montgomery, and Pulaski Counties and Radford City										
City of Blacksburg	43,355	38	0	14	9	15	687	117	547	23
City of Christiansburg	19,997	38	1	9	9	19	677	76	581	20
City of Radford	16,277	64	1	6	6	51	458	103	340	15
Total area actually reporting	100.0%	278	5	46	41	186	4,082	804	3,144	134
Rate per 100,000 inhabitants		172.7	3.1	28.6	25.5	115.5	2,535.1	499.3	1,952.6	83.2
Bloomington, IN M.S.A.	**187,290**									
Includes Greene, Monroe, and Owen Counties										
City of Bloomington	72,286	306	1	31	72	202	3,143	815	2,203	125
Total area actually reporting	86.7%	451	4	52	86	309	5,230	1,294	3,708	228
Estimated total	100.0%	478	4	55	91	328	5,627	1,390	3,984	253
Rate per 100,000 inhabitants		255.2	2.1	29.4	48.6	175.1	3,004.4	742.2	2,127.2	135.1
Bloomington-Normal, IL M.S.A.[2]	**167,701**									
Includes McLean County[2]										
City of Bloomington[2]	74,304	385	1	43	75	266	1,960	493	1,414	53
City of Normal[2]	53,014	146	0	11	38	97	1,497	350	1,109	38
Total area actually reporting	95.8%	606	1	74	121	410	3,894	965	2,819	110
Estimated total	100.0%	622	1	76	125	420	4,047	993	2,937	117
Rate per 100,000 inhabitants		370.9	0.6	45.3	74.5	250.4	2,413.2	592.1	1,751.3	69.8
Boise City-Nampa, ID M.S.A.	**619,814**									
Includes Ada, Boise, Canyon, Gem, and Owyhee Counties										
City of Boise	205,902	539	3	89	58	389	5,707	888	4,660	159
City of Nampa	84,179	275	2	51	17	205	2,299	450	1,721	128
Total area actually reporting	98.8%	1,332	10	208	113	1,001	12,717	2,456	9,774	487
Estimated total	100.0%	1,341	10	209	113	1,009	12,811	2,482	9,838	491
Rate per 100,000 inhabitants		216.4	1.6	33.7	18.2	162.8	2,066.9	400.4	1,587.3	79.2
Boston-Cambridge-Quincy, MA-NH M.S.A.	**4,558,433**									
Includes the Metropolitan Divisions of Boston-Quincy, MA; Cambridge-Newton-Framingham, MA; and Peabody, MA and Rockingham County-Strafford County, NH										
City of Boston, MA	644,064	5,819	73	256	1,926	3,564	20,628	3,587	15,004	2,037
City of Cambridge, MA	108,356	476	0	22	171	283	3,232	483	2,569	180
City of Quincy, MA	90,304	414	11	22	112	269	1,782	505	1,152	125
City of Newton, MA	83,781	86	0	6	15	65	1,212	170	1,016	26
City of Framingham, MA	66,493	189	0	5	25	159	1,409	313	1,025	71
City of Waltham, MA	60,106	151	2	13	24	112	1,032	200	759	73
City of Peabody, MA	51,517	111	0	15	15	81	1,216	136	1,025	55
Total area actually reporting	98.5%	18,382	158	1,016	4,648	12,560	98,607	20,653	70,596	7,358
Estimated total	100.0%	18,508	158	1,030	4,671	12,649	99,807	20,899	71,492	7,416
Rate per 100,000 inhabitants		406.0	3.5	22.6	102.5	277.5	2,189.5	458.5	1,568.3	162.7
Boston-Quincy, MA M.D.	***1,908,436***									
Includes Norfolk, Plymouth, and Suffolk Counties										
Total area actually reporting	99.6%	10,760	111	511	3,106	7,032	45,800	9,425	32,663	3,712
Estimated total	100.0%	10,787	111	513	3,111	7,052	45,964	9,466	32,775	3,723
Rate per 100,000 inhabitants		565.2	5.8	26.9	163.0	369.5	2,408.5	496.0	1,717.4	195.1

[2] Because of changes in the state/local agency's reporting practices, figures are not comparable to previous years' data.

Table 6.   Crime, by Metropolitan Statistical Area, 2010—*Continued*

(Number, percent, rate per 100,000 population)

Area	Population	Violent crime	Murder and non-negligent man-slaughter	Forcible rape	Robbery	Aggravated assault	Property crime	Burglary	Larceny-theft	Motor vehicle theft
Cambridge-Newton-Framingham, MA M.D.	*1,492,762*									
Includes Middlesex County										
Total area actually reporting	99.4%	4,393	20	254	914	3,205	29,038	6,135	21,197	1,706
Estimated total	100.0%	4,421	20	256	919	3,226	29,215	6,179	21,318	1,718
Rate per 100,000 inhabitants		296.2	1.3	17.1	61.6	216.1	1,957.1	413.9	1,428.1	115.1
Peabody, MA M.D.	*736,478*									
Includes Essex County										
Total area actually reporting	99.1%	2,669	21	156	525	1,967	16,056	3,781	10,594	1,681
Estimated total	100.0%	2,691	21	157	529	1,984	16,192	3,815	10,687	1,690
Rate per 100,000 inhabitants		365.4	2.9	21.3	71.8	269.4	2,198.6	518.0	1,451.1	229.5
Rockingham County-Strafford County, NH M.D.	*420,757*									
Includes Rockingham and Strafford Counties										
Total area actually reporting	89.3%	560	6	95	103	356	7,713	1,312	6,142	259
Estimated total	100.0%	609	6	104	112	387	8,436	1,439	6,712	285
Rate per 100,000 inhabitants		144.7	1.4	24.7	26.6	92.0	2,005.0	342.0	1,595.2	67.7
Boulder, CO M.S.A.	*302,365*									
Includes Boulder County										
City of Boulder	99,255	210	4	33	29	144	2,722	478	2,155	89
Total area actually reporting	100.0%	598	7	57	71	463	6,903	1,172	5,448	283
Rate per 100,000 inhabitants		197.8	2.3	18.9	23.5	153.1	2,283.0	387.6	1,801.8	93.6
Bowling Green, KY M.S.A.	*122,243*									
Includes Edmonson and Warren Counties										
City of Bowling Green	57,308	152	0	39	55	58	2,662	512	2,022	128
Total area actually reporting	99.3%	185	0	48	59	78	3,402	788	2,450	164
Estimated total	100.0%	187	0	48	60	79	3,430	794	2,471	165
Rate per 100,000 inhabitants		153.0	0.0	39.3	49.1	64.6	2,805.9	649.5	2,021.4	135.0
Bremerton-Silverdale, WA M.S.A.	*240,976*									
Includes Kitsap County										
City of Bremerton	34,897	263	0	52	50	161	1,786	414	1,263	109
Total area actually reporting	100.0%	1,019	1	165	116	737	6,618	1,707	4,532	379
Rate per 100,000 inhabitants		422.9	0.4	68.5	48.1	305.8	2,746.3	708.4	1,880.7	157.3
Bridgeport-Stamford-Norwalk, CT M.S.A.	*895,941*									
Includes Fairfield County										
City of Bridgeport	138,810	1,412	22	57	561	772	4,683	1,448	2,377	858
City of Stamford	122,933	351	2	19	152	178	1,969	348	1,429	192
City of Norwalk	84,944	343	6	12	129	196	1,878	323	1,379	176
City of Danbury	81,242	116	2	21	46	47	1,515	258	1,177	80
City of Stratford	49,469	148	1	15	43	89	1,312	188	1,004	120
Total area actually reporting	100.0%	2,531	34	143	991	1,363	15,971	3,323	10,986	1,662
Rate per 100,000 inhabitants		282.5	3.8	16.0	110.6	152.1	1,782.6	370.9	1,226.2	185.5
Brownsville-Harlingen, TX M.S.A.	*401,641*									
Includes Cameron County										
City of Brownsville	180,040	563	7	31	165	360	9,316	1,286	7,784	246
City of Harlingen	65,765	399	3	34	87	275	4,405	850	3,375	180
Total area actually reporting	100.0%	1,344	11	101	316	916	18,479	3,572	14,254	653
Rate per 100,000 inhabitants		334.6	2.7	25.1	78.7	228.1	4,600.9	889.4	3,548.9	162.6
Brunswick, GA M.S.A.	*101,534*									
Includes Brantley, Glynn, and McIntosh Counties										
City of Brunswick	15,871	238	2	8	76	152	1,418	406	960	52
Total area actually reporting	100.0%	577	6	26	152	393	5,384	1,553	3,652	179
Rate per 100,000 inhabitants		568.3	5.9	25.6	149.7	387.1	5,302.7	1,529.5	3,596.8	176.3
Buffalo-Niagara Falls, NY M.S.A.	*1,106,808*									
Includes Erie and Niagara Counties										
City of Buffalo	265,128	3,599	55	157	1,466	1,921	14,753	4,296	9,027	1,430
City of Cheektowaga Town	76,671	155	1	17	52	85	2,748	431	2,221	96
City of Tonawanda	14,475	21	0	1	2	18	312	32	271	9
City of Niagara Falls	50,321	610	5	23	185	397	2,924	956	1,834	134
Total area actually reporting	100.0%	5,354	67	287	1,929	3,071	34,306	8,227	24,000	2,079
Rate per 100,000 inhabitants		483.7	6.1	25.9	174.3	277.5	3,099.5	743.3	2,168.4	187.8
Burlington, NC M.S.A.	*152,475*									
Includes Alamance County										
City of Burlington	52,210	395	3	11	69	312	3,519	794	2,599	126
Total area actually reporting	100.0%	620	9	23	96	492	5,840	1,590	4,014	236
Rate per 100,000 inhabitants		406.6	5.9	15.1	63.0	322.7	3,830.1	1,042.8	2,632.6	154.8

Table 6.   Crime, by Metropolitan Statistical Area, 2010—*Continued*

(Number, percent, rate per 100,000 population)

Area	Population	Violent crime	Murder and non-negligent man-slaughter	Forcible rape	Robbery	Aggravated assault	Property crime	Burglary	Larceny-theft	Motor vehicle theft
Canton-Massillon, OH M.S.A.	407,101									
Includes Carroll and Stark Counties										
City of Canton	77,938	652	2	54	324	272	4,129	1,523	2,337	269
City of Massillon	32,768	39	3	4	21	11	833	210	601	22
Total area actually reporting	98.6%	996	10	124	435	427	10,242	3,054	6,700	488
Estimated total	100.0%	1,005	10	125	439	431	10,399	3,086	6,819	494
Rate per 100,000 inhabitants		246.9	2.5	30.7	107.8	105.9	2,554.4	758.0	1,675.0	121.3
Cape Coral-Fort Myers, FL M.S.A.	603,092									
Includes Lee County										
City of Cape Coral	160,432	276	3	23	64	186	3,787	1,083	2,595	109
City of Fort Myers	66,053	698	7	29	152	510	2,699	628	1,877	194
Total area actually reporting	100.0%	2,327	27	136	604	1,560	16,208	4,949	10,348	911
Rate per 100,000 inhabitants		385.8	4.5	22.6	100.2	258.7	2,687.5	820.6	1,715.8	151.1
Cape Girardeau-Jackson, MO-IL M.S.A.[2]	93,412									
Includes Alexander County, IL[2] and Bollinger and										
Cape Girardeau Counties, MO										
City of Cape Girardeau, MO	37,627	238	1	13	54	170	2,463	414	1,985	64
City of Jackson, MO	14,043	17	0	2	1	14	358	50	298	10
Total area actually reporting	94.9%	499	1	28	66	404	3,405	689	2,606	110
Estimated total	100.0%	506	1	29	67	409	3,474	709	2,652	113
Rate per 100,000 inhabitants		541.7	1.1	31.0	71.7	437.8	3,719.0	759.0	2,839.0	121.0
Carson City, NV M.S.A.	55,119									
Includes Carson City										
Total area actually reporting	100.0%	162	0	1	20	141	1,133	281	768	84
Rate per 100,000 inhabitants		293.9	0.0	1.8	36.3	255.8	2,055.6	509.8	1,393.3	152.4
Casper, WY M.S.A.	77,252									
Includes Natrona County										
City of Casper	56,813	108	2	6	20	80	2,405	382	1,934	89
Total area actually reporting	100.0%	145	3	10	24	108	2,848	512	2,201	135
Rate per 100,000 inhabitants		187.7	3.9	12.9	31.1	139.8	3,686.6	662.8	2,849.1	174.8
Cedar Rapids, IA M.S.A.	260,733									
Includes Benton, Jones, and Linn Counties										
City of Cedar Rapids	129,605	379	1	33	123	222	4,966	1,026	3,701	239
Total area actually reporting	98.9%	498	2	57	130	309	6,569	1,486	4,745	338
Estimated total	100.0%	503	2	58	130	313	6,621	1,496	4,785	340
Rate per 100,000 inhabitants		192.9	0.8	22.2	49.9	120.0	2,539.4	573.8	1,835.2	130.4
Charleston-North Charleston-Summerville, SC M.S.A.	671,885									
Includes Berkeley, Charleston, and Dorchester Counties										
City of Charleston	117,551	429	10	18	151	250	3,980	601	3,150	229
City of North Charleston	99,447	851	12	51	293	495	5,960	966	4,469	525
City of Summerville	47,479	157	1	8	45	103	1,611	240	1,291	80
Total area actually reporting	99.5%	3,434	40	173	823	2,398	23,907	5,031	17,029	1,847
Estimated total	100.0%	3,452	40	174	826	2,412	24,046	5,057	17,135	1,854
Rate per 100,000 inhabitants		513.8	6.0	25.9	122.9	359.0	3,578.9	752.7	2,550.3	275.9
Charlottesville, VA M.S.A.	199,881									
Includes Albemarle, Fluvanna, Greene, and Nelson										
Counties and Charlottesville City										
City of Charlottesville	42,590	195	3	29	51	112	1,693	163	1,443	87
Total area actually reporting	100.0%	407	6	62	80	259	4,548	666	3,664	218
Rate per 100,000 inhabitants		203.6	3.0	31.0	40.0	129.6	2,275.4	333.2	1,833.1	109.1
Chattanooga, TN-GA M.S.A.	523,569									
Includes Catoosa, Dade, and Walker Counties, GA and										
Hamilton, Marion, and Sequatchie Counties, TN										
City of Chattanooga, TN	172,460	1,557	18	78	512	949	10,866	2,691	7,350	825
Total area actually reporting	100.0%	2,736	24	137	626	1,949	19,851	4,915	13,509	1,427
Rate per 100,000 inhabitants		522.6	4.6	26.2	119.6	372.3	3,791.5	938.7	2,580.2	272.6
Cheyenne, WY M.S.A.	91,857									
Includes Laramie County										
City of Cheyenne	59,361	131	0	27	21	83	2,269	236	1,948	85
Total area actually reporting	100.0%	183	0	41	23	119	2,789	337	2,333	119
Rate per 100,000 inhabitants		199.2	0.0	44.6	25.0	129.5	3,036.2	366.9	2,539.8	129.5

[2] Because of changes in the state/local agency's reporting practices, figures are not comparable to previous years' data.

Table 6.　Crime, by Metropolitan Statistical Area, 2010—*Continued*

(Number, percent, rate per 100,000 population)

Area	Population	Violent crime	Murder and non-negligent man-slaughter	Forcible rape	Robbery	Aggravated assault	Property crime	Burglary	Larceny-theft	Motor vehicle theft
Chico, CA M.S.A.	**222,130**									
Includes Butte County										
City of Chico	85,630	245	1	47	88	109	2,347	710	1,416	221
Total area actually reporting	100.0%	762	7	92	157	506	5,940	1,849	3,515	576
Rate per 100,000 inhabitants		343.0	3.2	41.4	70.7	227.8	2,674.1	832.4	1,582.4	259.3
Cincinnati-Middletown, OH-KY-IN M.S.A.	**2,185,076**									
Includes Dearborn, Franklin, and Ohio Counties, IN; Boone, Bracken, Campbell, Gallatin, Grant, Kenton, and Pendleton Counties, KY; and Brown, Butler, Clermont, Hamilton, and Warren Counties, OH										
City of Cincinnati, OH	332,365	3,608	68	233	2,116	1,191	20,513	6,490	12,408	1,615
City of Middletown, OH	51,464	344	2	23	98	221	3,999	1,142	2,712	145
Total area actually reporting	96.8%	6,777	90	694	3,430	2,563	71,646	17,422	50,868	3,356
Estimated total	100.0%	6,863	91	707	3,452	2,613	72,997	17,737	51,839	3,421
Rate per 100,000 inhabitants		314.1	4.2	32.4	158.0	119.6	3,340.7	811.7	2,372.4	156.6
Clarksville, TN-KY M.S.A.	**271,954**									
Includes Christian and Trigg Counties, KY and Montgomery and Stewart Counties, TN										
City of Clarksville, TN	126,548	802	9	55	121	617	4,102	1,373	2,525	204
Total area actually reporting	99.3%	1,103	16	102	184	801	7,240	2,291	4,582	367
Estimated total	100.0%	1,108	16	103	186	803	7,309	2,306	4,633	370
Rate per 100,000 inhabitants		407.4	5.9	37.9	68.4	295.3	2,687.6	847.9	1,703.6	136.1
Cleveland, TN M.S.A.	**114,041**									
Includes Bradley and Polk Counties										
City of Cleveland	40,452	351	0	19	29	303	1,983	439	1,470	74
Total area actually reporting	100.0%	631	0	25	40	566	3,179	791	2,222	166
Rate per 100,000 inhabitants		553.3	0.0	21.9	35.1	496.3	2,787.6	693.6	1,948.4	145.6
Cleveland-Elyria-Mentor, OH M.S.A.	**2,081,340**									
Includes Cuyahoga, Geauga, Lake, Lorain, and Medina Counties										
City of Cleveland	426,042	5,525	81	341	3,181	1,922	23,436	9,854	10,079	3,503
City of Elyria	54,701	221	1	28	100	92	2,139	590	1,446	103
City of Mentor	51,924	40	0	5	21	14	1,200	125	1,010	65
Total area actually reporting	88.7%	8,283	100	614	4,137	3,432	52,733	17,324	30,508	4,901
Estimated total	100.0%	8,653	102	668	4,276	3,607	59,018	18,648	35,246	5,124
Rate per 100,000 inhabitants		415.7	4.9	32.1	205.4	173.3	2,835.6	896.0	1,693.4	246.2
Coeur d'Alene, ID M.S.A.	**142,212**									
Includes Kootenai County										
City of Coeur d'Alene	44,626	254	0	21	17	216	1,579	284	1,244	51
Total area actually reporting	100.0%	408	4	47	25	332	3,529	789	2,609	131
Rate per 100,000 inhabitants		286.9	2.8	33.0	17.6	233.5	2,481.5	554.8	1,834.6	92.1
College Station-Bryan, TX M.S.A.	**214,518**									
Includes Brazos, Burleson, and Robertson Counties										
City of College Station	88,416	220	3	37	44	136	2,655	475	2,091	89
City of Bryan	75,350	410	4	34	90	282	3,647	890	2,632	125
Total area actually reporting	100.0%	767	8	93	141	525	7,830	1,725	5,826	279
Rate per 100,000 inhabitants		357.5	3.7	43.4	65.7	244.7	3,650.0	804.1	2,715.9	130.1
Colorado Springs, CO M.S.A.	**626,259**									
Includes El Paso and Teller Counties										
City of Colorado Springs	397,886	1,957	20	319	526	1,092	16,794	3,452	12,054	1,288
Total area actually reporting	99.5%	2,889	23	405	569	1,892	20,167	4,300	14,269	1,598
Estimated total	100.0%	2,896	23	406	570	1,897	20,260	4,314	14,341	1,605
Rate per 100,000 inhabitants		462.4	3.7	64.8	91.0	302.9	3,235.1	688.9	2,289.9	256.3
Columbia, MO M.S.A.	**167,279**									
Includes Boone and Howard Counties										
City of Columbia	103,417	530	3	37	131	359	3,816	552	3,129	135
Total area actually reporting	100.0%	683	4	47	138	494	4,995	761	4,053	181
Rate per 100,000 inhabitants		408.3	2.4	28.1	82.5	295.3	2,986.0	454.9	2,422.9	108.2
Columbia, SC M.S.A.	**755,777**									
Includes Calhoun, Fairfield, Kershaw, Lexington, Richland, and Saluda Counties										
City of Columbia	130,498	1,306	16	74	345	871	7,898	1,699	5,528	671
Total area actually reporting	99.9%	5,416	40	274	918	4,184	29,559	7,303	19,711	2,545
Estimated total	100.0%	5,418	40	274	918	4,186	29,576	7,306	19,724	2,546
Rate per 100,000 inhabitants		716.9	5.3	36.3	121.5	553.9	3,913.3	966.7	2,609.8	336.9

Table 6. Crime, by Metropolitan Statistical Area, 2010—*Continued*

(Number, percent, rate per 100,000 population)

Area	Population	Violent crime	Murder and non-negligent man-slaughter	Forcible rape	Robbery	Aggravated assault	Property crime	Burglary	Larceny-theft	Motor vehicle theft
Columbus, GA-AL M.S.A..............................	**286,528**									
Includes Russell County, AL and Chattahoochee,										
Harris, Marion, and Muscogee Counties, GA										
City of Columbus, GA..	184,576	1,005	15	38	477	475	13,442	3,454	8,981	1,007
Total area actually reporting	92.9%	1,307	19	58	540	690	16,076	4,211	10,684	1,181
Estimated total..	100.0%	1,369	20	62	561	726	16,689	4,393	11,054	1,242
Rate per 100,000 inhabitants.............................		477.8	7.0	21.6	195.8	253.4	5,824.6	1,533.2	3,857.9	433.5
Columbus, IN M.S.A........................................	**76,785**									
Includes Bartholomew County										
City of Columbus	40,554	78	0	17	21	40	2,269	282	1,834	153
Total area actually reporting	99.5%	108	0	27	22	59	2,782	421	2,171	190
Estimated total..	100.0%	109	0	27	22	60	2,795	423	2,181	191
Rate per 100,000 inhabitants.............................		142.0	0.0	35.2	28.7	78.1	3,640.0	550.9	2,840.4	248.7
Columbus, OH M.S.A.[2]....................................	**1,817,671**									
Includes Delaware, Fairfield, Franklin, Licking,[2]										
Madison, Morrow, Pickaway, and Union Counties										
City of Columbus	772,974	5,451	94	566	3,359	1,432	50,168	15,234	30,784	4,150
Total area actually reporting	98.4%	6,661	106	779	3,865	1,911	76,622	21,060	50,602	4,960
Estimated total..	100.0%	6,708	106	786	3,883	1,933	77,427	21,226	51,213	4,988
Rate per 100,000 inhabitants.............................		369.0	5.8	43.2	213.6	106.3	4,259.7	1,167.8	2,817.5	274.4
Corpus Christi, TX M.S.A.	**416,086**									
Includes Aransas, Nueces, and San Patricio Counties										
City of Corpus Christi	287,315	2,067	16	191	389	1,471	15,086	2,623	12,015	448
Total area actually reporting	100.0%	2,521	21	222	457	1,821	19,361	3,778	14,998	585
Rate per 100,000 inhabitants.............................		605.9	5.0	53.4	109.8	437.6	4,653.1	908.0	3,604.5	140.6
Corvallis, OR M.S.A.[2]	**82,256**									
Includes Benton County[2]										
City of Corvallis[2]	51,276	57	0	9	12	36	1,377	209	1,132	36
Total area actually reporting	100.0%	96	0	17	16	63	1,804	312	1,433	59
Rate per 100,000 inhabitants.............................		116.7	0.0	20.7	19.5	76.6	2,193.2	379.3	1,742.1	71.7
Crestview-Fort Walton Beach-Destin, FL M.S.A.	**179,091**									
Includes Okaloosa County										
City of Crestview	20,424	87	1	8	16	62	644	155	460	29
City of Fort Walton Beach	18,432	98	1	11	17	69	929	186	681	62
Total area actually reporting	100.0%	663	3	53	114	493	5,244	1,168	3,832	244
Rate per 100,000 inhabitants.............................		370.2	1.7	29.6	63.7	275.3	2,928.1	652.2	2,139.7	136.2
Cumberland, MD-WV M.S.A.	**100,405**									
Includes Allegany County, MD and Mineral County, WV										
City of Cumberland, MD	20,449	196	1	17	40	138	1,442	370	1,049	23
Total area actually reporting	98.4%	389	5	33	54	297	3,028	764	2,202	62
Estimated total..	100.0%	394	5	33	55	301	3,084	774	2,246	64
Rate per 100,000 inhabitants.............................		392.4	5.0	32.9	54.8	299.8	3,071.6	770.9	2,236.9	63.7
Dallas-Fort Worth-Arlington, TX M.S.A.............................	**6,574,246**									
Includes the Metropolitan Divisions of Dallas-Plano-Irving and Fort Worth-Arlington										
City of Dallas...	1,306,775	9,161	148	505	4,487	4,021	64,125	19,594	36,147	8,384
City of Fort Worth	746,433	4,293	63	318	1,330	2,582	35,090	9,352	23,274	2,464
City of Arlington	383,715	1,925	16	119	532	1,258	19,350	4,763	13,342	1,245
City of Plano	278,244	503	4	53	152	294	6,716	1,237	5,093	386
City of Irving	206,308	529	6	36	170	317	7,744	1,632	5,488	624
City of Carrollton	130,862	184	4	4	63	113	3,510	897	2,256	357
City of Denton	127,251	326	3	67	65	191	3,256	564	2,535	157
City of McKinney...	138,306	222	1	31	40	150	3,103	643	2,322	138
City of Richardson..	104,051	193	0	13	90	90	2,999	608	2,192	199
Total area actually reporting	99.4%	24,391	311	1,841	8,590	13,649	235,912	60,656	154,828	20,428
Estimated total..	100.0%	24,493	312	1,851	8,614	13,716	237,152	60,910	155,740	20,502
Rate per 100,000 inhabitants.............................		372.6	4.7	28.2	131.0	208.6	3,607.3	926.5	2,368.9	311.9
Dallas-Plano-Irving, TX M.D.	*4,415,040*									
Includes Collin, Dallas, Delta, Denton, Ellis, Hunt, Kaufman, and Rockwall Counties										
Total area actually reporting	99.2%	15,660	207	1,150	6,241	8,062	151,599	39,801	96,765	15,033
Estimated total..	100.0%	15,762	208	1,160	6,265	8,129	152,839	40,055	97,677	15,107
Rate per 100,000 inhabitants.............................		357.0	4.7	26.3	141.9	184.1	3,461.8	907.2	2,212.4	342.2
Fort Worth-Arlington, TX M.D.	*2,159,206*									
Includes Johnson, Parker, Tarrant, and Wise Counties										
Total area actually reporting	100.0%	8,731	104	691	2,349	5,587	84,313	20,855	58,063	5,395
Rate per 100,000 inhabitants.............................		404.4	4.8	32.0	108.8	258.8	3,904.8	965.9	2,689.1	249.9

[2] Because of changes in the state/local agency's reporting practices, figures are not comparable to previous years' data.

Table 6.   Crime, by Metropolitan Statistical Area, 2010—*Continued*

(Number, percent, rate per 100,000 population)

Area	Population	Violent crime	Murder and non-negligent man-slaughter	Forcible rape	Robbery	Aggravated assault	Property crime	Burglary	Larceny-theft	Motor vehicle theft
Dalton, GA M.S.A...........................	**131,302**									
Includes Murray and Whitfield Counties										
City of Dalton................................	33,064	76	0	4	27	45	1,182	285	838	59
Total area actually reporting..............	98.4%	320	5	32	40	243	3,918	954	2,718	246
Estimated total...............................	100.0%	329	5	32	43	249	4,008	972	2,784	252
Rate per 100,000 inhabitants.............		250.6	3.8	24.4	32.7	189.6	3,052.5	740.3	2,120.3	191.9
Danville, IL M.S.A.[2]......................	**78,867**									
Includes Vermilion County[2]										
City of Danville[2].............................	31,942	348	1	35	86	226	2,178	826	1,295	57
Total area actually reporting..............	98.6%	475	1	63	98	313	3,076	1,124	1,866	86
Estimated total...............................	100.0%	478	1	63	99	315	3,100	1,128	1,885	87
Rate per 100,000 inhabitants.............		606.1	1.3	79.9	125.5	399.4	3,930.7	1,430.3	2,390.1	110.3
Danville, VA M.S.A........................	**105,798**									
Includes Pittsylvania County and Danville City										
City of Danville..............................	44,192	168	8	20	60	80	2,182	540	1,577	65
Total area actually reporting..............	100.0%	219	12	27	68	112	2,965	800	2,028	137
Rate per 100,000 inhabitants.............		207.0	11.3	25.5	64.3	105.9	2,802.5	756.2	1,916.9	129.5
Davenport-Moline-Rock Island, IA-IL M.S.A.[2]..................	**378,802**									
Includes Henry, Mercer, and Rock Island Counties, IL[2] and Scott County, IA										
City of Davenport, IA	102,628	865	2	59	209	595	4,894	1,148	3,521	225
City of Moline, IL[2]	42,510	216	1	26	22	167	1,487	302	1,140	45
City of Rock Island, IL[2]	37,534	307	3	21	51	232	1,306	356	872	78
Total area actually reporting..............	96.8%	1,722	7	169	307	1,239	10,831	2,484	7,889	458
Estimated total...............................	100.0%	1,747	7	172	312	1,256	11,082	2,530	8,083	469
Rate per 100,000 inhabitants.............		461.2	1.8	45.4	82.4	331.6	2,925.5	667.9	2,133.8	123.8
Dayton, OH M.S.A.........................	**831,823**									
Includes Greene, Miami, Montgomery, and Preble Counties										
City of Dayton...............................	152,319	1,509	34	92	782	601	8,891	3,380	4,840	671
Total area actually reporting..............	96.2%	2,564	41	256	1,169	1,098	27,070	7,614	17,983	1,473
Estimated total...............................	100.0%	2,616	41	264	1,189	1,122	27,954	7,796	18,654	1,504
Rate per 100,000 inhabitants.............		314.5	4.9	31.7	142.9	134.9	3,360.6	937.2	2,242.5	180.8
Decatur, AL M.S.A.........................	**153,306**									
Includes Lawrence and Morgan Counties										
City of Decatur	57,153	212	4	17	74	117	2,751	682	1,920	149
Total area actually reporting..............	100.0%	292	4	27	86	175	4,033	1,047	2,786	200
Rate per 100,000 inhabitants.............		190.5	2.6	17.6	56.1	114.2	2,630.7	682.9	1,817.3	130.5
Decatur, IL M.S.A.[2].......................	**106,467**									
Includes Macon County[2]										
City of Decatur[2].............................	74,857	468	4	20	136	308	3,121	1,514	1,481	126
Total area actually reporting..............	100.0%	549	4	30	137	378	3,654	1,686	1,828	140
Rate per 100,000 inhabitants.............		515.7	3.8	28.2	128.7	355.0	3,432.0	1,583.6	1,717.0	131.5
Deltona-Daytona Beach-Ormond Beach, FL M.S.A...........	**500,849**									
Includes Volusia County										
City of Daytona Beach.......................	63,736	811	3	31	229	548	4,635	1,083	3,089	463
City of Ormond Beach.......................	37,923	251	0	13	14	224	1,385	277	1,050	58
Total area actually reporting..............	100.0%	2,723	17	145	492	2,069	18,392	4,813	12,265	1,314
Rate per 100,000 inhabitants.............		543.7	3.4	29.0	98.2	413.1	3,672.2	961.0	2,448.8	262.4
Denver-Aurora-Broomfield, CO M.S.A.[2]...........................	**2,555,601**									
Includes Adams, Arapahoe, Broomfield, Clear Creek, Denver, Douglas, Elbert, Gilpin, Jefferson,[2] and Park Counties										
City of Denver................................	607,051	3,291	22	367	926	1,976	20,671	4,501	12,944	3,226
City of Aurora................................	323,483	1,443	23	183	505	732	10,051	2,290	6,873	888
City of Broomfield...........................	57,126	41	3	10	12	16	1,161	118	995	48
Total area actually reporting..............	99.1%	8,562	65	1,240	2,036	5,221	70,472	13,427	49,628	7,417
Estimated total...............................	100.0%	8,616	65	1,250	2,041	5,260	70,827	13,508	49,872	7,447
Rate per 100,000 inhabitants.............		337.1	2.5	48.9	79.9	205.8	2,771.4	528.6	1,951.5	291.4
Des Moines-West Des Moines, IA M.S.A...........................	**577,321**									
Includes Dallas, Guthrie, Madison, Polk, and Warren Counties										
City of Des Moines...........................	202,564	1,072	6	105	224	737	9,795	2,248	6,808	739
City of West Des Moines	58,600	109	0	22	11	76	1,736	173	1,516	47
Total area actually reporting..............	98.1%	1,654	9	195	272	1,178	16,345	3,533	11,769	1,043
Estimated total...............................	100.0%	1,668	9	197	272	1,190	16,446	3,568	11,826	1,052
Rate per 100,000 inhabitants.............		288.9	1.6	34.1	47.1	206.1	2,848.7	618.0	2,048.4	182.2

[2] Because of changes in the state/local agency's reporting practices, figures are not comparable to previous years' data.

Table 6. Crime, by Metropolitan Statistical Area, 2010—*Continued*

(Number, percent, rate per 100,000 population)

Area	Population	Violent crime	Murder and non-negligent man-slaughter	Forcible rape	Robbery	Aggravated assault	Property crime	Burglary	Larceny-theft	Motor vehicle theft
Detroit-Warren-Livonia, MI M.S.A.	**4,359,587**									
Includes the Metropolitan Divisions of Detroit-Livonia-Dearborn and Warren-Troy-Farmington Hills										
City of Detroit	899,447	16,976	310	405	5,538	10,723	47,787	17,090	18,095	12,602
City of Warren	132,266	770	5	69	171	525	3,703	953	2,035	715
City of Livonia	87,434	152	2	14	36	100	2,039	315	1,503	221
City of Dearborn	82,612	373	3	30	128	212	3,718	488	2,759	471
City of Troy	79,794	59	1	9	9	40	1,728	292	1,327	109
City of Farmington Hills	77,646	118	1	16	13	88	1,381	292	959	130
City of Southfield	74,587	396	5	27	111	253	2,760	660	1,690	410
City of Pontiac	65,517	1,113	9	67	239	798	2,055	1,074	765	216
City of Taylor	58,158	348	2	29	78	239	2,500	629	1,640	231
City of Novi	54,857	36	1	4	3	28	1,000	96	856	48
Total area actually reporting	99.9%	27,683	395	1,513	7,875	17,900	128,453	35,104	72,627	20,722
Estimated total	100.0%	27,702	395	1,515	7,879	17,913	128,619	35,140	72,744	20,735
Rate per 100,000 inhabitants		635.4	9.1	34.8	180.7	410.9	2,950.3	806.0	1,668.6	475.6
Detroit-Livonia-Dearborn, MI M.D.	*1,895,974*									
Includes Wayne County										
Total area actually reporting	100.0%	21,069	345	794	6,600	13,330	78,729	24,023	38,216	16,490
Rate per 100,000 inhabitants		1,111.2	18.2	41.9	348.1	703.1	4,152.4	1,267.1	2,015.6	869.7
Warren-Troy-Farmington Hills, MI M.D.	*2,463,613*									
Includes Lapeer, Livingston, Macomb, Oakland, and St. Clair Counties										
Total area actually reporting	99.7%	6,614	50	719	1,275	4,570	49,724	11,081	34,411	4,232
Estimated total	100.0%	6,633	50	721	1,279	4,583	49,890	11,117	34,528	4,245
Rate per 100,000 inhabitants		269.2	2.0	29.3	51.9	186.0	2,025.1	451.2	1,401.5	172.3
Dothan, AL M.S.A.	**145,215**									
Includes Geneva, Henry, and Houston Counties										
City of Dothan	68,041	405	1	29	116	259	3,086	995	2,001	90
Total area actually reporting	92.7%	610	5	59	131	415	4,490	1,387	2,935	168
Estimated total	100.0%	645	5	62	140	438	4,886	1,459	3,237	190
Rate per 100,000 inhabitants		444.2	3.4	42.7	96.4	301.6	3,364.7	1,004.7	2,229.1	130.8
Dover, DE M.S.A.	**161,556**									
Includes Kent County										
City of Dover	37,113	239	1	10	52	176	2,122	151	1,858	113
Total area actually reporting	100.0%	902	6	71	183	642	5,509	1,126	4,103	280
Rate per 100,000 inhabitants		558.3	3.7	43.9	113.3	397.4	3,410.0	697.0	2,539.7	173.3
Dubuque, IA M.S.A.	**94,362**									
Includes Dubuque County										
City of Dubuque	57,744	333	0	18	36	279	1,771	463	1,257	51
Total area actually reporting	100.0%	399	0	23	36	340	2,024	555	1,397	72
Rate per 100,000 inhabitants		422.8	0.0	24.4	38.2	360.3	2,144.9	588.2	1,480.5	76.3
Duluth, MN-WI M.S.A.[4]	**276,508**									
Includes Carlton and St. Louis Counties, MN[3] and Douglas County, WI										
City of Duluth, MN[1,3]	84,249		1		90	165		605	3,301	
Total area actually reporting	100.0%		4		124	345		1,670	7,300	
Rate per 100,000 inhabitants			1.4		44.8	124.8		604.0	2,640.1	
Durham-Chapel Hill, NC M.S.A.	**509,834**									
Includes Chatham, Durham, Orange, and Person Counties										
City of Durham	233,790	1,614	23	60	659	872	11,357	3,652	6,987	718
City of Chapel Hill	54,164	88	0	11	32	45	1,666	508	1,108	50
Total area actually reporting	100.0%	2,177	36	121	776	1,244	19,330	6,285	12,011	1,034
Rate per 100,000 inhabitants		427.0	7.1	23.7	152.2	244.0	3,791.4	1,232.8	2,355.9	202.8
Eau Claire, WI M.S.A.	**161,272**									
Includes Chippewa and Eau Claire Counties										
City of Eau Claire	66,737	139	2	21	23	93	1,906	406	1,446	54
Total area actually reporting	100.0%	245	7	44	28	166	3,293	738	2,443	112
Rate per 100,000 inhabitants		151.9	4.3	27.3	17.4	102.9	2,041.9	457.6	1,514.8	69.4
El Centro, CA M.S.A.	**169,405**									
Includes Imperial County										
City of El Centro	41,535	197	1	7	45	144	2,408	672	1,546	190
Total area actually reporting	100.0%	618	3	26	105	484	5,772	1,887	3,119	766
Rate per 100,000 inhabitants		364.8	1.8	15.3	62.0	285.7	3,407.2	1,113.9	1,841.1	452.2

[1] The FBI determined that the agency's data were underreported. Consequently, those data are not included in this table.

[3] The data collection methodology for the offense of forcible rape used by the Minnesota state UCR Program (with the exception of Minneapolis and St. Paul, Minnesota) does not comply with national UCR Program guidelines. Consequently, its figures for forcible rape and violent crime (of which forcible rape is a part) are not published in this table.

[4] The FBI determined that the agency did not follow national Uniform Crime Reporting (UCR) Program guidelines for reporting an offense. Consequently, this figure is not included in this table.

Table 6.   Crime, by Metropolitan Statistical Area, 2010—*Continued*

(Number, percent, rate per 100,000 population)

Area	Population	Violent crime	Murder and non-negligent man-slaughter	Forcible rape	Robbery	Aggravated assault	Property crime	Burglary	Larceny-theft	Motor vehicle theft
Elizabethtown, KY M.S.A...................	**113,924**									
Includes Hardin and Larue Counties										
City of Elizabethtown	24,712	48	0	13	22	13	956	139	784	33
Total area actually reporting	100.0%	227	0	24	38	165	1,893	394	1,427	72
Rate per 100,000 inhabitants...............		199.3	0.0	21.1	33.4	144.8	1,661.6	345.8	1,252.6	63.2
Elkhart-Goshen, IN M.S.A.	**203,013**									
Includes Elkhart County										
City of Elkhart	53,296	156	1	35	116	4	2,330	709	1,507	114
City of Goshen	32,812	33	0	11	15	7	1,040	242	764	34
Total area actually reporting	100.0%	234	2	55	157	20	5,198	1,504	3,410	284
Rate per 100,000 inhabitants...............		115.3	1.0	27.1	77.3	9.9	2,560.4	740.8	1,679.7	139.9
Elmira, NY M.S.A.	**87,073**									
Includes Chemung County										
City of Elmira	28,823	108	4	5	29	70	1,057	259	773	25
Total area actually reporting	100.0%	203	4	11	39	149	1,877	399	1,431	47
Rate per 100,000 inhabitants...............		233.1	4.6	12.6	44.8	171.1	2,155.7	458.2	1,643.4	54.0
El Paso, TX M.S.A..............................	**756,304**									
Includes El Paso County										
City of El Paso	624,322	2,861	5	179	479	2,198	17,404	1,953	13,899	1,552
Total area actually reporting	100.0%	3,419	7	222	530	2,660	20,779	2,701	16,277	1,801
Rate per 100,000 inhabitants...............		452.1	0.9	29.4	70.1	351.7	2,747.4	357.1	2,152.2	238.1
Erie, PA M.S.A.	**281,637**									
Includes Erie County										
City of Erie	104,077	491	12	78	173	228	3,490	1,106	2,245	139
Total area actually reporting	100.0%	762	13	133	218	398	6,999	1,798	4,975	226
Rate per 100,000 inhabitants...............		270.6	4.6	47.2	77.4	141.3	2,485.1	638.4	1,766.5	80.2
Evansville, IN-KY M.S.A.[4]	**353,847**									
Includes Gibson, Posey, Vanderburgh,[4] and Warrick Counties, IN and Henderson and Webster Counties, KY										
City of Evansville, IN	116,541	493	5	63	143	282	5,544	1,086	4,248	210
Total area actually reporting	94.2%		8	90	168		9,395	1,761	7,270	364
Estimated total......................................	100.0%		8	93	172		9,713	1,843	7,487	383
Rate per 100,000 inhabitants...............			2.3	26.3	48.6		2,745.0	520.8	2,115.9	108.2
Fairbanks, AK M.S.A.[2]	**38,307**									
Includes Fairbanks North Star Borough										
City of Fairbanks[2]	35,989	284	0	70	33	181	1,367	149	1,117	101
Total area actually reporting	100.0%	300	0	74	34	192	1,553	169	1,276	108
Rate per 100,000 inhabitants...............		783.1	0.0	193.2	88.8	501.2	4,054.1	441.2	3,331.0	281.9
Fargo, ND-MN M.S.A.[4]	**208,388**									
Includes Clay County, MN[3] and Cass County, ND										
City of Fargo, ND.................................	99,694	302	0	44	35	223	2,764	392	2,205	167
Total area actually reporting	100.0%		2		46	307	4,637	746	3,650	241
Rate per 100,000 inhabitants...............			1.0		22.1	147.3	2,225.2	358.0	1,751.5	115.6
Farmington, NM M.S.A.	**126,955**									
Includes San Juan County										
City of Farmington	44,563	477	3	63	25	386	1,678	319	1,270	89
Total area actually reporting	100.0%	820	4	95	35	686	2,784	642	1,972	170
Rate per 100,000 inhabitants...............		645.9	3.2	74.8	27.6	540.3	2,192.9	505.7	1,553.3	133.9
Fayetteville, NC M.S.A.	**363,142**									
Includes Cumberland and Hoke Counties										
City of Fayetteville	208,263	1,101	17	57	461	566	12,566	3,928	7,916	722
Total area actually reporting	100.0%	1,739	23	77	613	1,026	18,961	6,353	11,558	1,050
Rate per 100,000 inhabitants...............		478.9	6.3	21.2	168.8	282.5	5,221.4	1,749.5	3,182.8	289.1
Fayetteville-Springdale-Rogers, AR-MO M.S.A.[5].............	**478,404**									
Includes Benton, Madison, and Washington Counties, AR and McDonald County, MO										
City of Fayetteville, AR.......................	79,237	328	1	55	37	235	2,746	465	2,168	113
City of Springdale, AR.........................	71,047	325	0	68	18	239	2,129	373	1,631	125
City of Rogers, AR[5].............................	61,417	219	2	50	11	156			1,629	44
City of Bentonville, AR........................	39,161	63	0	15	4	44	705	142	537	26
Total area actually reporting	99.3%	1,537	4	277	81	1,175			7,665	480
Estimated total......................................	100.0%	1,551	4	278	83	1,186			7,733	484
Rate per 100,000 inhabitants...............		324.2	0.8	58.1	17.3	247.9			1,616.4	101.2

[2] Because of changes in the state/local agency's reporting practices, figures are not comparable to previous years' data.

[3] The data collection methodology for the offense of forcible rape used by the Minnesota state UCR Program (with the exception of Minneapolis and St. Paul, Minnesota) does not comply with national UCR Program guidelines. Consequently, its figures for forcible rape and violent crime (of which forcible rape is a part) are not published in this table.

[4] The FBI determined that the agency did not follow national Uniform Crime Reporting (UCR) Program guidelines for reporting an offense. Consequently, this figure is not included in this table.

[5] The FBI determined that the agency's data were overreported. Consequently, those data are not included in this table.

Table 6. Crime, by Metropolitan Statistical Area, 2010—*Continued*

(Number, percent, rate per 100,000 population)

Area	Population	Violent crime	Murder and non-negligent man-slaughter	Forcible rape	Robbery	Aggravated assault	Property crime	Burglary	Larceny-theft	Motor vehicle theft
Flagstaff, AZ M.S.A.	**125,838**									
Includes Coconino County										
City of Flagstaff	58,739	267	5	37	49	176	2,955	226	2,666	63
Total area actually reporting	100.0%	507	6	61	59	381	4,418	520	3,794	104
Rate per 100,000 inhabitants		402.9	4.8	48.5	46.9	302.8	3,510.9	413.2	3,015.0	82.6
Flint, MI M.S.A.	**419,008**									
Includes Genesee County										
City of Flint	109,245	2,412	53	92	670	1,597	6,237	3,648	1,936	653
Total area actually reporting	96.3%	3,418	58	220	917	2,223	15,034	6,238	7,605	1,191
Estimated total	100.0%	3,465	58	225	928	2,254	15,448	6,328	7,896	1,224
Rate per 100,000 inhabitants		827.0	13.8	53.7	221.5	537.9	3,686.8	1,510.2	1,884.5	292.1
Florence, SC M.S.A.	**201,596**									
Includes Darlington and Florence Counties										
City of Florence	32,273	354	2	8	108	236	2,891	546	2,215	130
Total area actually reporting	100.0%	1,390	21	61	306	1,002	9,724	2,551	6,646	527
Rate per 100,000 inhabitants		689.5	10.4	30.3	151.8	497.0	4,823.5	1,265.4	3,296.7	261.4
Fond du Lac, WI M.S.A.	**100,387**									
Includes Fond du Lac County										
City of Fond du Lac	42,369	131	0	21	13	97	1,130	194	908	28
Total area actually reporting	100.0%	175	1	31	13	130	1,750	367	1,324	59
Rate per 100,000 inhabitants		174.3	1.0	30.9	12.9	129.5	1,743.3	365.6	1,318.9	58.8
Fort Collins-Loveland, CO M.S.A.	**298,883**									
Includes Larimer County										
City of Fort Collins	138,689	438	0	64	50	324	4,551	643	3,706	202
City of Loveland	66,857	128	0	21	15	92	1,592	199	1,325	68
Total area actually reporting	100.0%	713	0	113	83	517	7,709	1,136	6,234	339
Rate per 100,000 inhabitants		238.6	0.0	37.8	27.8	173.0	2,579.3	380.1	2,085.8	113.4
Fort Smith, AR-OK M.S.A.	**296,159**									
Includes Crawford, Franklin, and Sebastian Counties, AR and Le Flore and Sequoyah Counties, OK										
City of Fort Smith, AR	86,096	667	6	74	124	463	4,815	1,073	3,530	212
Total area actually reporting	99.8%	1,238	14	123	151	950	8,898	2,312	6,189	397
Estimated total	100.0%	1,241	14	123	151	953	8,923	2,320	6,205	398
Rate per 100,000 inhabitants		419.0	4.7	41.5	51.0	321.8	3,012.9	783.4	2,095.2	134.4
Fort Wayne, IN M.S.A.[2]	**418,216**									
Includes Allen, Wells, and Whitley Counties										
City of Fort Wayne[2]	257,009	746	23	96	314	313	8,860	2,140	6,433	287
Total area actually reporting	94.5%	862	25	117	337	383	10,930	2,542	8,010	378
Estimated total	100.0%	883	25	120	340	398	11,247	2,626	8,223	398
Rate per 100,000 inhabitants		211.1	6.0	28.7	81.3	95.2	2,689.3	627.9	1,966.2	95.2
Fresno, CA M.S.A.	**926,736**									
Includes Fresno County										
City of Fresno	484,734	3,034	45	70	1,021	1,898	24,460	5,262	14,645	4,553
Total area actually reporting	100.0%	4,976	63	181	1,368	3,364	39,398	9,082	23,296	7,020
Rate per 100,000 inhabitants		536.9	6.8	19.5	147.6	363.0	4,251.3	980.0	2,513.8	757.5
Gadsden, AL M.S.A.	**104,600**									
Includes Etowah County										
City of Gadsden	36,835	318	5	30	110	173	2,620	681	1,797	142
Total area actually reporting	100.0%	481	7	44	116	314	4,087	933	2,953	201
Rate per 100,000 inhabitants		459.8	6.7	42.1	110.9	300.2	3,907.3	892.0	2,823.1	192.2
Gainesville, FL M.S.A.	**263,388**									
Includes Alachua and Gilchrist Counties										
City of Gainesville	116,880	906	4	86	199	617	5,404	1,213	3,859	332
Total area actually reporting	99.0%	1,629	13	131	298	1,187	9,311	2,356	6,451	504
Estimated total	100.0%	1,642	13	132	302	1,195	9,416	2,380	6,525	511
Rate per 100,000 inhabitants		623.4	4.9	50.1	114.7	453.7	3,575.0	903.6	2,477.3	194.0
Gainesville, GA M.S.A.	**186,894**									
Includes Hall County										
City of Gainesville	35,657	119	1	17	39	62	1,623	278	1,283	62
Total area actually reporting	100.0%	326	4	36	87	199	4,515	1,101	3,111	303
Rate per 100,000 inhabitants		174.4	2.1	19.3	46.6	106.5	2,415.8	589.1	1,664.6	162.1

[2] Because of changes in the state/local agency's reporting practices, figures are not comparable to previous years' data.

Table 6.   Crime, by Metropolitan Statistical Area, 2010—*Continued*

(Number, percent, rate per 100,000 population)

Area	Population	Violent crime	Murder and non-negligent man-slaughter	Forcible rape	Robbery	Aggravated assault	Property crime	Burglary	Larceny-theft	Motor vehicle theft
Glens Falls, NY M.S.A.	**127,776**									
Includes Warren and Washington Counties										
City of Glens Falls	13,650	42	0	2	3	37	209	29	177	3
Total area actually reporting	100.0%	187	0	34	14	139	1,978	414	1,519	45
Rate per 100,000 inhabitants		146.3	0.0	26.6	11.0	108.8	1,548.0	324.0	1,188.8	35.2
Goldsboro, NC M.S.A.	**113,929**									
Includes Wayne County										
City of Goldsboro	38,179	386	5	3	105	273	2,525	734	1,663	128
Total area actually reporting	97.4%	584	8	6	151	419	5,018	1,880	2,886	252
Estimated total	100.0%	593	8	7	153	425	5,140	1,909	2,973	258
Rate per 100,000 inhabitants		520.5	7.0	6.1	134.3	373.0	4,511.6	1,675.6	2,609.5	226.5
Grand Forks, ND-MN M.S.A.[3]	**99,717**									
Includes Polk County, MN[3] and Grand Forks County, ND										
City of Grand Forks, ND	53,382	119	0	33	7	79	1,424	252	1,095	77
Total area actually reporting	100.0%		1		9	119	2,190	418	1,665	107
Rate per 100,000 inhabitants			1.0		9.0	119.3	2,196.2	419.2	1,669.7	107.3
Grand Junction, CO M.S.A.	**147,126**									
Includes Mesa County										
City of Grand Junction	59,029	206	2	42	28	134	2,167	333	1,734	100
Total area actually reporting	97.7%	383	3	72	44	264	3,697	649	2,866	182
Estimated total	100.0%	391	3	73	45	270	3,794	664	2,941	189
Rate per 100,000 inhabitants		265.8	2.0	49.6	30.6	183.5	2,578.7	451.3	1,999.0	128.5
Grand Rapids-Wyoming, MI M.S.A.	**774,621**									
Includes Barry, Ionia, Kent, and Newaygo Counties										
City of Grand Rapids	191,566	1,645	9	90	521	1,025	7,760	2,771	4,609	380
City of Wyoming	70,160	230	1	39	46	144	1,586	515	911	160
Total area actually reporting	96.4%	2,930	16	352	690	1,872	18,704	5,682	12,084	938
Estimated total	100.0%	3,019	17	362	710	1,930	19,465	5,848	12,619	998
Rate per 100,000 inhabitants		389.7	2.2	46.7	91.7	249.2	2,512.8	754.9	1,629.1	128.8
Great Falls, MT M.S.A.	**82,913**									
Includes Cascade County										
City of Great Falls	59,984	124	4	6	21	93	2,776	308	2,343	125
Total area actually reporting	100.0%	162	4	6	23	129	2,994	340	2,509	145
Rate per 100,000 inhabitants		195.4	4.8	7.2	27.7	155.6	3,611.0	410.1	3,026.1	174.9
Greeley, CO M.S.A.	**259,483**									
Includes Weld County										
City of Greeley	92,804	425	1	41	56	327	2,970	537	2,285	148
Total area actually reporting	97.9%	674	3	69	76	526	5,556	1,114	4,110	332
Estimated total	100.0%	687	3	71	78	535	5,714	1,138	4,232	344
Rate per 100,000 inhabitants		264.8	1.2	27.4	30.1	206.2	2,202.1	438.6	1,630.9	132.6
Green Bay, WI M.S.A.[2]	**307,162**									
Includes Brown, Kewaunee, and Oconto Counties										
City of Green Bay[2]	101,320	370	2	54	67	247	2,595	568	1,917	110
Total area actually reporting	100.0%	483	3	94	75	311	5,641	1,146	4,302	193
Rate per 100,000 inhabitants		157.2	1.0	30.6	24.4	101.2	1,836.5	373.1	1,400.6	62.8
Greensboro-High Point, NC M.S.A.	**722,587**									
Includes Guilford, Randolph, and Rockingham Counties										
City of Greensboro	257,237	1,512	20	56	626	810	13,776	4,221	8,755	800
City of High Point	103,473	598	2	28	216	352	4,796	1,291	3,289	216
Total area actually reporting	99.9%	2,772	31	121	992	1,628	28,992	8,673	18,817	1,502
Estimated total	100.0%	2,773	31	121	992	1,629	29,004	8,676	18,825	1,503
Rate per 100,000 inhabitants		383.8	4.3	16.7	137.3	225.4	4,013.9	1,200.7	2,605.2	208.0
Greenville-Mauldin-Easley, SC M.S.A.	**648,658**									
Includes Greenville, Laurens, and Pickens Counties										
City of Greenville	62,368	468	3	20	132	313	3,265	597	2,499	169
City of Mauldin	23,218	75	0	2	17	56	548	83	428	37
City of Easley	20,818	70	2	4	10	54	1,034	161	826	47
Total area actually reporting	100.0%	3,364	30	213	593	2,528	22,296	5,494	15,257	1,545
Rate per 100,000 inhabitants		518.6	4.6	32.8	91.4	389.7	3,437.3	847.0	2,352.1	238.2

[2] Because of changes in the state/local agency's reporting practices, figures are not comparable to previous years' data.

[3] The data collection methodology for the offense of forcible rape used by the Minnesota state UCR Program (with the exception of Minneapolis and St. Paul, Minnesota) does not comply with national UCR Program guidelines. Consequently, its figures for forcible rape and violent crime (of which forcible rape is a part) are not published in this table.

Table 6.   Crime, by Metropolitan Statistical Area, 2010—*Continued*

(Number, percent, rate per 100,000 population)

Area	Population	Violent crime	Murder and non-negligent man-slaughter	Forcible rape	Robbery	Aggravated assault	Property crime	Burglary	Larceny-theft	Motor vehicle theft
Gulfport-Biloxi, MS M.S.A.	**238,426**									
Includes Hancock, Harrison, and Stone Counties										
City of Gulfport	70,806	161	6	23	67	65	3,715	920	2,642	153
City of Biloxi	45,350	211	1	33	118	59	2,516	943	1,442	131
Total area actually reporting	83.7%	483	10	75	209	189	9,606	2,641	6,481	484
Estimated total	100.0%	529	12	84	217	216	10,277	2,874	6,862	541
Rate per 100,000 inhabitants		221.9	5.0	35.2	91.0	90.6	4,310.4	1,205.4	2,878.0	226.9
Hagerstown-Martinsburg, MD-WV M.S.A.	**273,944**									
Includes Washington County, MD and Berkeley and Morgan Counties, WV										
City of Hagerstown, MD	40,564	177	0	10	97	70	1,436	303	1,013	120
City of Martinsburg, WV	17,654	65	0	2	17	46	969	115	815	39
Total area actually reporting	99.6%	669	2	48	161	458	5,594	1,291	3,943	360
Estimated total	100.0%	673	2	48	162	461	5,635	1,298	3,975	362
Rate per 100,000 inhabitants		245.7	0.7	17.5	59.1	168.3	2,057.0	473.8	1,451.0	132.1
Hanford-Corcoran, CA M.S.A.	**150,689**									
Includes Kings County										
City of Hanford	50,903	181	0	6	43	132	1,159	252	707	200
City of Corcoran	25,112	42	0	1	4	37	289	119	135	35
Total area actually reporting	100.0%	533	3	29	85	416	2,956	791	1,731	434
Rate per 100,000 inhabitants		353.7	2.0	19.2	56.4	276.1	1,961.7	524.9	1,148.7	288.0
Harrisburg-Carlisle, PA M.S.A.	**542,444**									
Includes Cumberland, Dauphin, and Perry Counties										
City of Harrisburg	47,509	780	14	63	446	257	2,235	666	1,377	192
City of Carlisle	18,708	54	0	10	27	17	557	72	482	3
Total area actually reporting	99.7%	1,646	19	186	647	794	11,484	2,162	8,881	441
Estimated total	100.0%	1,649	19	186	648	796	11,509	2,166	8,901	442
Rate per 100,000 inhabitants		304.0	3.5	34.3	119.5	146.7	2,121.7	399.3	1,640.9	81.5
Harrisonburg, VA M.S.A.	**121,985**									
Includes Rockingham County and Harrisonburg City										
City of Harrisonburg	45,804	91	1	11	13	66	1,072	135	901	36
Total area actually reporting	100.0%	142	1	28	15	98	1,721	303	1,350	68
Rate per 100,000 inhabitants		116.4	0.8	23.0	12.3	80.3	1,410.8	248.4	1,106.7	55.7
Hartford-West Hartford-East Hartford, CT M.S.A.	**1,023,921**									
Includes Hartford, Middlesex, and Tolland Counties										
City of Hartford	125,626	1,624	26	46	570	982	5,495	1,019	3,639	837
City of West Hartford	61,603	61	1	2	44	14	1,464	210	1,190	64
City of East Hartford	49,156	186	6	20	74	86	1,545	345	1,042	158
City of Middletown	49,281	59	0	4	20	35	1,130	157	914	59
Total area actually reporting	100.0%	3,045	46	181	1,094	1,724	25,933	4,731	19,086	2,116
Rate per 100,000 inhabitants		297.4	4.5	17.7	106.8	168.4	2,532.7	462.0	1,864.0	206.7
Hattiesburg, MS M.S.A.	**145,273**									
Includes Forrest, Lamar, and Perry Counties										
City of Hattiesburg	53,678	115	4	9	62	40	2,317	434	1,809	74
Total area actually reporting	91.7%	189	5	35	72	77	3,506	920	2,467	119
Estimated total	100.0%	204	6	38	75	85	3,714	992	2,585	137
Rate per 100,000 inhabitants		140.4	4.1	26.2	51.6	58.5	2,556.6	682.9	1,779.4	94.3
Hickory-Lenoir-Morganton, NC M.S.A.	**367,927**									
Includes Alexander, Burke, Caldwell, and Catawba Counties										
City of Hickory	41,892	217	1	22	76	118	2,573	616	1,836	121
City of Lenoir	17,840	55	0	3	26	26	864	178	641	45
City of Morganton	17,001	40	0	4	11	25	494	121	355	18
Total area actually reporting	99.6%	786	13	64	190	519	11,637	3,659	7,415	563
Estimated total	100.0%	790	13	64	191	522	11,699	3,674	7,459	566
Rate per 100,000 inhabitants		214.7	3.5	17.4	51.9	141.9	3,179.7	998.6	2,027.3	153.8
Hinesville-Fort Stewart, GA M.S.A.	**72,276**									
Includes Liberty and Long Counties										
City of Hinesville	29,764	149	5	9	45	90	1,660	448	1,148	64
Total area actually reporting	85.5%	242	6	14	61	161	2,207	662	1,446	99
Estimated total	100.0%	274	7	16	72	179	2,518	757	1,630	131
Rate per 100,000 inhabitants		379.1	9.7	22.1	99.6	247.7	3,483.9	1,047.4	2,255.2	181.2

Table 6.   Crime, by Metropolitan Statistical Area, 2010—*Continued*

(Number, percent, rate per 100,000 population)

Area	Population	Violent crime	Murder and non-negligent man-slaughter	Forcible rape	Robbery	Aggravated assault	Property crime	Burglary	Larceny-theft	Motor vehicle theft
Holland-Grand Haven, MI M.S.A.	**261,957**									
Includes Ottawa County										
City of Holland	26,443	115	0	25	12	78	813	153	641	19
City of Grand Haven	10,574	27	0	6	1	20	359	40	314	5
Total area actually reporting	100.0%	471	0	152	29	290	4,636	986	3,561	89
Rate per 100,000 inhabitants		179.8	0.0	58.0	11.1	110.7	1,769.8	376.4	1,359.4	34.0
Honolulu, HI M.S.A.	**950,268**									
Includes Honolulu County										
City of Honolulu	950,268	2,548	19	218	891	1,420	31,668	5,760	22,007	3,901
Total area actually reporting	100.0%	2,548	19	218	891	1,420	31,668	5,760	22,007	3,901
Rate per 100,000 inhabitants		268.1	2.0	22.9	93.8	149.4	3,332.5	606.1	2,315.9	410.5
Hot Springs, AR M.S.A.	**99,611**									
Includes Garland County										
City of Hot Springs	40,081	402	7	22	72	301	3,124	793	2,161	170
Total area actually reporting	100.0%	560	9	53	92	406	5,517	1,955	3,234	328
Rate per 100,000 inhabitants		562.2	9.0	53.2	92.4	407.6	5,538.5	1,962.6	3,246.6	329.3
Houma-Bayou Cane-Thibodaux, LA M.S.A.	**204,653**									
Includes Lafourche and Terrebonne Parishes										
City of Houma	32,688	254	4	12	86	152	1,576	358	1,131	87
City of Thibodaux	14,487	69	0	4	16	49	796	119	653	24
Total area actually reporting	100.0%	787	12	46	164	565	7,084	1,394	5,324	366
Rate per 100,000 inhabitants		384.6	5.9	22.5	80.1	276.1	3,461.5	681.2	2,601.5	178.8
Houston-Sugar Land-Baytown, TX M.S.A.	**5,978,213**									
Includes Austin, Brazoria, Chambers, Fort Bend,										
Galveston, Harris, Liberty, Montgomery, San Jacinto,										
and Waller Counties										
City of Houston	2,280,859	22,491	269	712	9,449	12,061	115,323	27,924	74,582	12,817
City of Sugar Land	83,368	142	0	7	60	75	1,879	235	1,556	88
City of Baytown	71,082	301	6	21	148	126	3,849	822	2,707	320
City of Galveston	55,835	373	1	77	128	167	3,181	787	2,144	250
City of Conroe	60,677	248	5	22	80	141	2,815	601	2,079	135
Total area actually reporting	99.9%	37,103	435	1,543	14,174	20,951	235,759	58,274	155,376	22,109
Estimated total	100.0%	37,104	435	1,543	14,174	20,952	235,777	58,278	155,389	22,110
Rate per 100,000 inhabitants		620.7	7.3	25.8	237.1	350.5	3,943.9	974.8	2,599.3	369.8
Huntsville, AL M.S.A.	**416,848**									
Includes Limestone and Madison Counties										
City of Huntsville	183,357	1,182	12	76	463	631	9,768	2,677	6,230	861
Total area actually reporting	99.2%	1,648	22	115	562	949	14,595	4,023	9,419	1,153
Estimated total	100.0%	1,659	22	116	565	956	14,722	4,046	9,516	1,160
Rate per 100,000 inhabitants		398.0	5.3	27.8	135.5	229.3	3,531.7	970.6	2,282.8	278.3
Idaho Falls, ID M.S.A.	**128,311**									
Includes Bonneville and Jefferson Counties										
City of Idaho Falls	55,524	182	3	23	14	142	1,582	327	1,194	61
Total area actually reporting	100.0%	289	3	36	15	235	2,564	582	1,873	109
Rate per 100,000 inhabitants		225.2	2.3	28.1	11.7	183.1	1,998.3	453.6	1,459.7	84.9
Iowa City, IA M.S.A.	**155,935**									
Includes Johnson and Washington Counties										
City of Iowa City	70,411	183	0	32	31	120	1,533	283	1,176	74
Total area actually reporting	100.0%	362	2	62	41	257	2,661	508	2,031	122
Rate per 100,000 inhabitants		232.1	1.3	39.8	26.3	164.8	1,706.5	325.8	1,302.5	78.2
Ithaca, NY M.S.A.	**101,158**									
Includes Tompkins County										
City of Ithaca	29,791	60	0	4	23	33	1,143	152	963	28
Total area actually reporting	100.0%	119	2	16	27	74	2,371	311	2,017	43
Rate per 100,000 inhabitants		117.6	2.0	15.8	26.7	73.2	2,343.9	307.4	1,993.9	42.5
Jackson, MI M.S.A.	**158,512**									
Includes Jackson County										
City of Jackson	32,741	319	5	42	54	218	1,586	406	1,127	53
Total area actually reporting	98.6%	602	11	84	76	431	3,430	785	2,511	134
Estimated total	100.0%	609	11	85	78	435	3,489	798	2,552	139
Rate per 100,000 inhabitants		384.2	6.9	53.6	49.2	274.4	2,201.1	503.4	1,610.0	87.7

Table 6.   Crime, by Metropolitan Statistical Area, 2010—*Continued*

(Number, percent, rate per 100,000 population)

Area	Population	Violent crime	Murder and non-negligent man-slaughter	Forcible rape	Robbery	Aggravated assault	Property crime	Burglary	Larceny-theft	Motor vehicle theft
Jackson, MS M.S.A.............................	**546,069**									
Includes Copiah, Hinds, Madison, Rankin, and Simpson Counties										
City of Jackson...............................	174,153	1,718	41	101	1,086	490	13,250	4,818	6,877	1,555
Total area actually reporting...................	89.9%	2,151	55	157	1,170	769	19,088	6,309	10,815	1,964
Estimated total..............................	100.0%	2,258	57	175	1,193	833	20,589	6,728	11,809	2,052
Rate per 100,000 inhabitants...................		413.5	10.4	32.0	218.5	152.5	3,770.4	1,232.1	2,162.5	375.8
Jackson, TN M.S.A.............................	**113,975**									
Includes Chester and Madison Counties										
City of Jackson...............................	63,969	541	2	25	145	369	4,044	1,096	2,704	244
Total area actually reporting...................	100.0%	747	5	43	157	542	5,334	1,501	3,476	357
Rate per 100,000 inhabitants...................		655.4	4.4	37.7	137.7	475.5	4,680.0	1,317.0	3,049.8	313.2
Jacksonville, FL M.S.A.........................	**1,350,025**									
Includes Baker, Clay, Duval, Nassau, and St. Johns Counties										
City of Jacksonville..........................	822,414	5,469	80	316	1,693	3,380	37,424	9,588	25,863	1,973
Total area actually reporting...................	100.0%	7,519	97	417	1,998	5,007	50,928	12,410	36,023	2,495
Rate per 100,000 inhabitants...................		557.0	7.2	30.9	148.0	370.9	3,772.4	919.2	2,668.3	184.8
Janesville, WI M.S.A...........................	**161,013**									
Includes Rock County										
City of Janesville............................	63,651	170	1	30	39	100	2,411	383	1,980	48
Total area actually reporting...................	100.0%	398	4	53	109	232	4,743	977	3,617	149
Rate per 100,000 inhabitants...................		247.2	2.5	32.9	67.7	144.1	2,945.7	606.8	2,246.4	92.5
Jefferson City, MO M.S.A.......................	**147,169**									
Includes Callaway, Cole, Moniteau, and Osage Counties										
City of Jefferson City.........................	41,092	197	1	6	40	150	1,668	284	1,348	36
Total area actually reporting...................	100.0%	431	4	24	60	343	3,680	775	2,751	154
Rate per 100,000 inhabitants...................		292.9	2.7	16.3	40.8	233.1	2,500.5	526.6	1,869.3	104.6
Johnson City, TN M.S.A........................	**198,527**									
Includes Carter, Unicoi, and Washington Counties										
City of Johnson City..........................	63,750	278	1	25	59	193	3,010	574	2,346	90
Total area actually reporting...................	100.0%	691	5	45	82	559	5,920	1,519	4,184	217
Rate per 100,000 inhabitants...................		348.1	2.5	22.7	41.3	281.6	2,982.0	765.1	2,107.5	109.3
Johnstown, PA M.S.A...........................	**143,909**									
Includes Cambria County										
City of Johnstown............................	22,900	105	3	6	43	53	786	256	502	28
Total area actually reporting...................	93.1%	281	4	23	59	195	2,496	564	1,851	81
Estimated total..............................	100.0%	301	4	24	64	209	2,682	594	2,000	88
Rate per 100,000 inhabitants...................		209.2	2.8	16.7	44.5	145.2	1,863.7	412.8	1,389.8	61.1
Jonesboro, AR M.S.A...........................	**121,519**									
Includes Craighead and Poinsett Counties										
City of Jonesboro............................	67,382	295	2	22	56	215	2,901	1,213	1,619	69
Total area actually reporting...................	98.8%	471	5	50	60	356	4,187	1,660	2,428	99
Estimated total..............................	100.0%	478	5	51	61	361	4,235	1,676	2,458	101
Rate per 100,000 inhabitants...................		393.4	4.1	42.0	50.2	297.1	3,485.1	1,379.2	2,022.7	83.1
Joplin, MO M.S.A..............................	**174,867**									
Includes Jasper and Newton Counties										
City of Joplin................................	50,346	288	1	39	64	184	3,404	558	2,612	234
Total area actually reporting...................	100.0%	658	3	77	84	494	6,489	1,205	4,816	468
Rate per 100,000 inhabitants...................		376.3	1.7	44.0	48.0	282.5	3,710.8	689.1	2,754.1	267.6
Kalamazoo-Portage, MI M.S.A..................	**324,853**									
Includes Kalamazoo and Van Buren Counties										
City of Kalamazoo............................	71,775	721	9	81	185	446	3,534	1,039	2,320	175
City of Portage..............................	46,192	102	1	19	16	66	1,815	235	1,534	46
Total area actually reporting...................	99.4%	1,346	14	207	262	863	9,934	2,468	7,025	441
Estimated total..............................	100.0%	1,352	14	208	263	867	9,986	2,479	7,062	445
Rate per 100,000 inhabitants...................		416.2	4.3	64.0	81.0	266.9	3,074.0	763.1	2,173.9	137.0

Table 6. Crime, by Metropolitan Statistical Area, 2010—*Continued*

(Number, percent, rate per 100,000 population)

Area	Population	Violent crime	Murder and non-negligent man-slaughter	Forcible rape	Robbery	Aggravated assault	Property crime	Burglary	Larceny-theft	Motor vehicle theft
Kansas City, MO-KS M.S.A.[2]	2,089,752									
Includes Franklin, Johnson, Leavenworth, Linn, Miami, and Wyandotte Counties, KS and Bates, Caldwell, Cass, Clay, Clinton, Jackson, Lafayette, Platte, and Ray Counties, MO										
City of Kansas City, MO[2]	483,191	5,506	102	234	1,626	3,544	26,919	7,124	16,625	3,170
City of Overland Park, KS	178,669	289	0	40	36	213	4,185	491	3,389	305
City of Kansas City, KS	143,867	823	25	62	289	447	7,735	1,922	4,684	1,129
Total area actually reporting	99.9%	9,637	172	666	2,502	6,297	72,612	16,297	49,139	7,176
Estimated total	100.0%	9,639	172	666	2,502	6,299	72,641	16,302	49,161	7,178
Rate per 100,000 inhabitants		461.3	8.2	31.9	119.7	301.4	3,476.1	780.1	2,352.5	343.5
Kennewick-Pasco-Richland, WA M.S.A.	251,139									
Includes Benton and Franklin Counties										
City of Kennewick	68,501	239	0	25	39	175	2,517	388	2,003	126
City of Pasco	61,747	183	3	22	38	120	1,448	324	1,006	118
City of Richland	48,335	66	0	12	8	46	956	146	751	59
Total area actually reporting	100.0%	593	5	76	95	417	6,024	1,163	4,475	386
Rate per 100,000 inhabitants		236.1	2.0	30.3	37.8	166.0	2,398.7	463.1	1,781.9	153.7
Killeen-Temple-Fort Hood, TX M.S.A.	383,261									
Includes Bell, Coryell, and Lampasas Counties										
City of Killeen	122,557	993	11	91	259	632	5,837	2,062	3,536	239
City of Temple	60,444	209	1	23	71	114	2,079	537	1,462	80
Total area actually reporting	100.0%	1,595	17	161	377	1,040	12,466	3,824	8,206	436
Rate per 100,000 inhabitants		416.2	4.4	42.0	98.4	271.4	3,252.6	997.8	2,141.1	113.8
Kingsport-Bristol-Bristol, TN-VA M.S.A.	306,196									
Includes Hawkins and Sullivan Counties, TN and Scott and Washington Counties and Bristol City, VA										
City of Kingsport, TN	44,587	377	1	26	52	298	2,864	509	2,257	98
City of Bristol, TN	25,799	140	0	12	9	119	1,003	182	778	43
City of Bristol, VA	17,794	60	1	11	10	38	601	90	490	21
Total area actually reporting	100.0%	1,088	14	107	115	852	9,840	2,424	6,991	425
Rate per 100,000 inhabitants		355.3	4.6	34.9	37.6	278.3	3,213.6	791.6	2,283.2	138.8
Kingston, NY M.S.A.	179,764									
Includes Ulster County										
City of Kingston	22,012	81	1	5	29	46	611	142	451	18
Total area actually reporting	100.0%	408	2	31	63	312	3,445	712	2,625	108
Rate per 100,000 inhabitants		227.0	1.1	17.2	35.0	173.6	1,916.4	396.1	1,460.2	60.1
Knoxville, TN M.S.A.	706,304									
Includes Anderson, Blount, Knox, Loudon, and Union Counties										
City of Knoxville	185,554	1,755	15	122	625	993	12,322	2,723	8,789	810
Total area actually reporting	100.0%	3,292	35	203	893	2,161	26,658	6,973	18,040	1,645
Rate per 100,000 inhabitants		466.1	5.0	28.7	126.4	306.0	3,774.3	987.3	2,554.1	232.9
Kokomo, IN M.S.A.	98,871									
Includes Howard and Tipton Counties										
City of Kokomo	45,412	152	3	20	63	66	2,380	475	1,862	43
Total area actually reporting	100.0%	205	3	28	68	106	3,074	743	2,266	65
Rate per 100,000 inhabitants		207.3	3.0	28.3	68.8	107.2	3,109.1	751.5	2,291.9	65.7
La Crosse, WI-MN M.S.A.[3]	133,588									
Includes Houston County, MN[3] and La Crosse County, WI										
City of La Crosse, WI	51,184	155	1	23	34	97	1,723	336	1,309	78
Total area actually reporting	97.9%		3		37	149	2,987	570	2,304	113
Estimated total	100.0%		3		38	151	3,064	580	2,368	116
Rate per 100,000 inhabitants			2.2		28.4	113.0	2,293.6	434.2	1,772.6	86.8
Lafayette, IN M.S.A.	198,921									
Includes Benton, Carroll, and Tippecanoe Counties										
City of Lafayette	66,388	264	2	30	49	183	2,704	524	2,000	180
Total area actually reporting	96.8%	383	2	51	63	267	4,902	980	3,646	276
Estimated total	100.0%	389	2	52	64	271	4,992	1,004	3,706	282
Rate per 100,000 inhabitants		195.6	1.0	26.1	32.2	136.2	2,509.5	504.7	1,863.1	141.8
Lafayette, LA M.S.A.	266,765									
Includes Lafayette and St. Martin Parishes										
City of Lafayette	115,378	940	12	20	240	668	6,989	1,432	5,267	290
Total area actually reporting	94.5%	1,577	19	44	319	1,195	10,469	2,391	7,651	427
Estimated total	100.0%	1,654	20	48	329	1,257	11,116	2,522	8,144	450
Rate per 100,000 inhabitants		620.0	7.5	18.0	123.3	471.2	4,167.0	945.4	3,052.9	168.7

[2] Because of changes in the state/local agency's reporting practices, figures are not comparable to previous years' data.

[3] The data collection methodology for the offense of forcible rape used by the Minnesota state UCR Program (with the exception of Minneapolis and St. Paul, Minnesota) does not comply with national UCR Program guidelines. Consequently, its figures for forcible rape and violent crime (of which forcible rape is a part) are not published in this table.

Table 6.   Crime, by Metropolitan Statistical Area, 2010—*Continued*

(Number, percent, rate per 100,000 population)

Area	Population	Violent crime	Murder and non-negligent man-slaughter	Forcible rape	Robbery	Aggravated assault	Property crime	Burglary	Larceny-theft	Motor vehicle theft
Lake Charles, LA M.S.A.	**195,066**									
Includes Calcasieu and Cameron Parishes										
City of Lake Charles	71,795	488	7	27	148	306	3,047	1,826	1,088	133
Total area actually reporting	96.0%	1,231	16	109	210	896	8,303	3,112	4,750	441
Estimated total	100.0%	1,272	16	111	216	929	8,651	3,183	5,015	453
Rate per 100,000 inhabitants		652.1	8.2	56.9	110.7	476.2	4,434.9	1,631.8	2,570.9	232.2
Lakeland-Winter Haven, FL M.S.A.	**593,733**									
Includes Polk County										
City of Lakeland	94,569	459	12	20	140	287	5,099	1,104	3,754	241
City of Winter Haven	33,981	244	2	10	68	164	1,915	368	1,462	85
Total area actually reporting	99.4%	2,392	30	128	525	1,709	20,826	5,758	14,080	988
Estimated total	100.0%	2,409	30	129	530	1,720	20,956	5,788	14,172	996
Rate per 100,000 inhabitants		405.7	5.1	21.7	89.3	289.7	3,529.5	974.8	2,386.9	167.8
Lancaster, PA M.S.A.	**514,044**									
Includes Lancaster County										
City of Lancaster	55,582	511	5	55	214	237	2,857	583	2,160	114
Total area actually reporting	98.4%	940	9	119	330	482	9,534	1,706	7,514	314
Estimated total	100.0%	956	9	120	334	493	9,684	1,730	7,634	320
Rate per 100,000 inhabitants		186.0	1.8	23.3	65.0	95.9	1,883.9	336.5	1,485.1	62.3
Lansing-East Lansing, MI M.S.A.	**450,078**									
Includes Clinton, Eaton, and Ingham Counties										
City of Lansing	112,254	1,236	10	97	262	867	4,193	1,410	2,544	239
City of East Lansing	45,058	166	1	7	26	132	1,089	272	771	46
Total area actually reporting	98.3%	1,849	12	213	356	1,268	11,253	2,855	7,937	461
Estimated total	100.0%	1,873	12	216	361	1,284	11,464	2,901	8,085	478
Rate per 100,000 inhabitants		416.2	2.7	48.0	80.2	285.3	2,547.1	644.6	1,796.4	106.2
Laredo, TX M.S.A.	**245,929**									
Includes Webb County										
City of Laredo	230,674	1,142	9	78	209	846	11,464	1,821	8,740	903
Total area actually reporting	100.0%	1,273	11	82	211	969	11,944	1,957	9,041	946
Rate per 100,000 inhabitants		517.6	4.5	33.3	85.8	394.0	4,856.7	795.8	3,676.3	384.7
Las Cruces, NM M.S.A.	**212,820**									
Includes Dona Ana County										
City of Las Cruces	97,065	408	3	11	62	332	4,326	1,110	3,026	190
Total area actually reporting	98.0%	723	9	63	75	576	6,290	1,739	4,205	346
Estimated total	100.0%	745	9	64	76	596	6,424	1,771	4,298	355
Rate per 100,000 inhabitants		350.1	4.2	30.1	35.7	280.0	3,018.5	832.2	2,019.5	166.8
Las Vegas-Paradise, NV M.S.A.	**1,951,609**									
Includes Clark County										
City of Las Vegas Metropolitan Police Department	1,416,401	12,648	107	652	4,003	7,886	43,219	13,824	22,231	7,164
Total area actually reporting	100.0%	14,899	131	776	4,696	9,296	57,024	17,571	30,835	8,618
Rate per 100,000 inhabitants		763.4	6.7	39.8	240.6	476.3	2,921.9	900.3	1,580.0	441.6
Lawrence, KS M.S.A.	**118,966**									
Includes Douglas County										
City of Lawrence	93,945	413	0	40	61	312	3,841	522	3,163	156
Total area actually reporting	100.0%	460	0	46	62	352	4,572	659	3,737	176
Rate per 100,000 inhabitants		386.7	0.0	38.7	52.1	295.9	3,843.1	553.9	3,141.2	147.9
Lawton, OK M.S.A.	**114,290**									
Includes Comanche County										
City of Lawton	92,025	831	3	60	113	655	5,254	1,757	3,279	218
Total area actually reporting	100.0%	882	5	65	114	698	5,674	1,884	3,535	255
Rate per 100,000 inhabitants		771.7	4.4	56.9	99.7	610.7	4,964.6	1,648.4	3,093.0	223.1
Lebanon, PA M.S.A.	**132,213**									
Includes Lebanon County										
City of Lebanon	24,357	98	4	10	31	53	678	169	473	36
Total area actually reporting	97.5%	243	5	24	42	172	2,126	453	1,601	72
Estimated total	100.0%	250	5	24	44	177	2,188	463	1,651	74
Rate per 100,000 inhabitants		189.1	3.8	18.2	33.3	133.9	1,654.9	350.2	1,248.7	56.0
Lewiston, ID-WA M.S.A.	**60,690**									
Includes Nez Perce County, ID and Asotin County, WA										
City of Lewiston, ID	31,860	53	0	20	2	31	1,332	277	992	63
Total area actually reporting	100.0%	102	1	30	4	67	2,022	391	1,550	81
Rate per 100,000 inhabitants		168.1	1.6	49.4	6.6	110.4	3,331.7	644.3	2,554.0	133.5

Table 6.   Crime, by Metropolitan Statistical Area, 2010—*Continued*

(Number, percent, rate per 100,000 population)

Area	Population	Violent crime	Murder and non-negligent man-slaughter	Forcible rape	Robbery	Aggravated assault	Property crime	Burglary	Larceny-theft	Motor vehicle theft
Lewiston-Auburn, ME M.S.A.	107,282									
Includes Androscoggin County										
City of Lewiston	35,153	93	2	16	42	33	1,056	179	862	15
City of Auburn	22,953	41	0	9	19	13	895	134	742	19
Total area actually reporting	100.0%	171	3	40	64	64	2,579	485	2,035	59
Rate per 100,000 inhabitants		159.4	2.8	37.3	59.7	59.7	2,403.9	452.1	1,896.9	55.0
Lexington-Fayette, KY M.S.A.	477,150									
Includes Bourbon, Clark, Fayette, Jessamine, Scott, and Woodford Counties										
City of Lexington	300,069	1,724	18	87	593	1,026	11,024	2,679	7,704	641
Total area actually reporting	99.9%	2,070	22	122	692	1,234	16,770	3,880	12,072	818
Estimated total	100.0%	2,072	22	122	693	1,235	16,789	3,884	12,086	819
Rate per 100,000 inhabitants		434.2	4.6	25.6	145.2	258.8	3,518.6	814.0	2,533.0	171.6
Lima, OH M.S.A.	103,688									
Includes Allen County										
City of Lima	37,182	336	3	37	88	208	2,222	792	1,328	102
Total area actually reporting	96.7%	418	4	55	111	248	3,863	1,154	2,557	152
Estimated total	100.0%	424	4	56	113	251	3,957	1,173	2,629	155
Rate per 100,000 inhabitants		408.9	3.9	54.0	109.0	242.1	3,816.3	1,131.3	2,535.5	149.5
Lincoln, NE M.S.A.	304,589									
Includes Lancaster and Seward Counties										
City of Lincoln	259,672	1,258	2	143	182	931	10,218	1,464	8,406	348
Total area actually reporting	97.5%	1,291	2	148	183	958	10,895	1,566	8,967	362
Estimated total	100.0%	1,300	2	149	183	966	11,004	1,592	9,042	370
Rate per 100,000 inhabitants		426.8	0.7	48.9	60.1	317.1	3,612.7	522.7	2,968.6	121.5
Little Rock-North Little Rock-Conway, AR M.S.A.	693,930									
Includes Faulkner, Grant, Lonoke, Perry, Pulaski, and Saline Counties										
City of Little Rock	192,922	2,938	25	149	859	1,905	14,796	4,241	9,440	1,115
City of North Little Rock	60,129	562	6	14	184	358	5,088	1,136	3,618	334
City of Conway	61,425	257	4	21	49	183	2,603	444	2,068	91
Total area actually reporting	91.5%	5,018	43	307	1,221	3,447	32,913	9,238	21,560	2,115
Estimated total	100.0%	5,245	44	329	1,234	3,638	34,241	9,788	22,250	2,203
Rate per 100,000 inhabitants		755.8	6.3	47.4	177.8	524.3	4,934.4	1,410.5	3,206.4	317.5
Logan, UT-ID M.S.A.	127,228									
Includes Franklin County, ID and Cache County, UT										
City of Logan, UT	48,819	22	0	5	2	15	616	111	486	19
Total area actually reporting	100.0%	81	0	30	5	46	1,428	217	1,167	44
Rate per 100,000 inhabitants		63.7	0.0	23.6	3.9	36.2	1,122.4	170.6	917.3	34.6
Longview, TX M.S.A.	207,545									
Includes Gregg, Rusk, and Upshur Counties										
City of Longview	76,523	568	10	40	131	387	4,191	837	3,002	352
Total area actually reporting	99.4%	979	20	95	168	696	7,811	1,779	5,367	665
Estimated total	100.0%	982	20	95	169	698	7,849	1,787	5,395	667
Rate per 100,000 inhabitants		473.2	9.6	45.8	81.4	336.3	3,781.8	861.0	2,599.4	321.4
Longview, WA M.S.A.	102,585									
Includes Cowlitz County										
City of Longview	36,550	132	2	22	22	86	1,944	414	1,372	158
Total area actually reporting	100.0%	321	2	98	48	173	3,579	794	2,512	273
Rate per 100,000 inhabitants		312.9	1.9	95.5	46.8	168.6	3,488.8	774.0	2,448.7	266.1
Los Angeles-Long Beach-Santa Ana, CA M.S.A.	12,912,749									
Includes the Metropolitan Divisions of Los Angeles-Long Beach-Glendale and Santa Ana-Anaheim-Irvine										
City of Los Angeles	3,841,707	21,484	293	923	10,924	9,344	89,704	17,410	55,248	17,046
City of Long Beach	462,267	2,720	32	134	1,202	1,352	11,642	2,929	6,524	2,189
City of Santa Ana	340,240	1,510	28	88	719	675	6,580	1,116	4,189	1,275
City of Anaheim	338,492	1,161	7	88	492	574	8,473	1,594	5,869	1,010
City of Irvine	217,193	120	0	24	40	56	2,798	480	2,197	121
City of Glendale	196,877	277	0	17	119	141	3,717	642	2,747	328
City of Pomona	152,673	877	16	37	323	501	4,504	867	2,406	1,231
City of Pasadena	144,496	554	3	21	189	341	4,074	832	2,864	378
City of Torrance	140,411	290	4	19	152	115	2,859	516	2,008	335
City of Orange	137,606	150	3	3	56	88	2,569	404	1,944	221
City of Fullerton	133,139	425	3	26	145	251	3,847	680	2,825	342
City of Costa Mesa	110,424	240	1	34	93	112	3,194	458	2,454	282
City of Burbank	103,304	221	0	13	98	110	2,687	478	1,933	276
City of Compton	93,916	1,327	25	25	477	800	2,784	847	1,223	714

Table 6. Crime, by Metropolitan Statistical Area, 2010—*Continued*

(Number, percent, rate per 100,000 population)

Area	Population	Violent crime	Murder and non-negligent man-slaughter	Forcible rape	Robbery	Aggravated assault	Property crime	Burglary	Larceny-theft	Motor vehicle theft
Los Angeles-Long Beach-Santa Ana, CA M.S.A.—*Continued*										
City of Carson	92,409	499	6	12	130	351	2,326	441	1,421	464
City of Santa Monica	87,817	392	1	12	167	212	3,120	413	2,541	166
City of Newport Beach	81,882	117	0	4	42	71	2,176	425	1,617	134
City of Tustin	72,982	128	1	9	56	62	1,567	237	1,186	144
City of Montebello	61,570	214	3	10	92	109	1,941	737	724	480
City of Monterey Park	61,662	96	3	0	57	36	860	219	415	226
City of Gardena	58,358	347	2	9	202	134	1,446	271	835	340
City of Arcadia	56,465	88	1	5	36	46	1,737	364	1,267	106
City of Paramount	54,914	343	4	12	185	142	1,554	297	770	487
City of Fountain Valley	55,879	103	3	5	28	67	1,292	266	951	75
City of Cerritos	51,025	93	0	3	49	41	1,696	301	1,167	228
Total area actually reporting	100.0%	57,146	684	2,520	24,470	29,472	294,026	60,107	184,435	49,484
Rate per 100,000 inhabitants		442.6	5.3	19.5	189.5	228.2	2,277.0	465.5	1,428.3	383.2
Los Angeles-Long Beach-Glendale, CA M.D.	**9,870,891**									
Includes Los Angeles County										
Total area actually reporting	100.0%	50,239	617	2,071	21,896	25,655	233,179	49,188	140,573	43,418
Rate per 100,000 inhabitants		509.0	6.3	21.0	221.8	259.9	2,362.3	498.3	1,424.1	439.9
Santa Ana-Anaheim-Irvine, CA M.D.	**3,041,858**									
Includes Orange County										
Total area actually reporting	100.0%	6,907	67	449	2,574	3,817	60,847	10,919	43,862	6,066
Rate per 100,000 inhabitants		227.1	2.2	14.8	84.6	125.5	2,000.3	359.0	1,441.9	199.4
Louisville/Jefferson County, KY-IN M.S.A.	**1,268,689**									
Includes Clark, Floyd, Harrison, and Washington Counties, IN and Bullitt, Henry, Jefferson, Meade, Nelson, Oldham, Shelby, Spencer, and Trimble Counties, KY										
City of Louisville Metro, KY	637,428	3,734	52	229	1,603	1,850	29,551	7,571	20,005	1,975
Total area actually reporting	95.8%	4,911	61	331	1,923	2,596	43,264	11,116	29,344	2,804
Estimated total	100.0%	5,014	62	342	1,953	2,657	44,651	11,397	30,373	2,881
Rate per 100,000 inhabitants		395.2	4.9	27.0	153.9	209.4	3,519.5	898.3	2,394.0	227.1
Lubbock, TX M.S.A.	**278,595**									
Includes Crosby and Lubbock Counties										
City of Lubbock	227,867	2,001	10	91	328	1,572	12,391	3,083	8,802	506
Total area actually reporting	100.0%	2,252	10	133	339	1,770	13,754	3,425	9,736	593
Rate per 100,000 inhabitants		808.3	3.6	47.7	121.7	635.3	4,936.9	1,229.4	3,494.7	212.9
Lynchburg, VA M.S.A.	**250,323**									
Includes Amherst, Appomattox, Bedford, and Campbell Counties and Bedford and Lynchburg Cities										
City of Lynchburg	75,137	323	4	26	75	218	2,594	433	2,067	94
Total area actually reporting	100.0%	719	16	55	99	549	5,020	888	3,909	223
Rate per 100,000 inhabitants		287.2	6.4	22.0	39.5	219.3	2,005.4	354.7	1,561.6	89.1
Macon, GA M.S.A.	**224,947**									
Includes Bibb, Crawford, Jones, Monroe, and Twiggs Counties										
City of Macon	89,125	708	22	34	284	368	7,277	2,136	4,516	625
Total area actually reporting	98.5%	1,076	27	56	346	647	11,854	3,341	7,435	1,078
Estimated total	100.0%	1,090	27	57	350	656	11,999	3,370	7,541	1,088
Rate per 100,000 inhabitants		484.6	12.0	25.3	155.6	291.6	5,334.1	1,498.1	3,352.3	483.7
Madera-Chowchilla, CA M.S.A.	**151,283**									
Includes Madera County										
City of Madera	58,147	357	8	22	100	227	1,319	460	552	307
City of Chowchilla	19,795	64	0	5	5	54	344	153	168	23
Total area actually reporting	100.0%	654	10	49	129	466	3,317	1,198	1,529	590
Rate per 100,000 inhabitants		432.3	6.6	32.4	85.3	308.0	2,192.6	791.9	1,010.7	390.0
Madison, WI M.S.A.[2]	**577,374**									
Includes Columbia, Dane, and Iowa Counties										
City of Madison[2]	238,224	933	2	87	326	518	8,037	1,647	6,025	365
Total area actually reporting	99.9%	1,377	5	139	423	810	15,135	2,688	11,856	591
Estimated total	100.0%	1,377	5	139	423	810	15,138	2,688	11,859	591
Rate per 100,000 inhabitants		238.5	0.9	24.1	73.3	140.3	2,621.9	465.6	2,054.0	102.4
Manchester-Nashua, NH M.S.A.	**403,165**									
Includes Hillsborough County										
City of Manchester	108,101	544	1	62	154	327	3,754	907	2,687	160
City of Nashua	86,523	173	1	39	47	86	2,209	398	1,744	67
Total area actually reporting	94.2%	866	3	131	224	508	8,695	1,832	6,518	345
Estimated total	100.0%	881	3	134	227	517	8,913	1,870	6,690	353
Rate per 100,000 inhabitants		218.5	0.7	33.2	56.3	128.2	2,210.8	463.8	1,659.4	87.6

[2] Because of changes in the state/local agency's reporting practices, figures are not comparable to previous years' data.

Table 6.   Crime, by Metropolitan Statistical Area, 2010—*Continued*

(Number, percent, rate per 100,000 population)

Area	Population	Violent crime	Murder and non-negligent man-slaughter	Forcible rape	Robbery	Aggravated assault	Property crime	Burglary	Larceny-theft	Motor vehicle theft
Manhattan, KS M.S.A.	**125,477**									
Includes Geary, Pottawatomie, and Riley Counties										
Total area actually reporting	100.0%	413	6	48	44	315	2,602	565	1,985	52
Rate per 100,000 inhabitants		329.1	4.8	38.3	35.1	251.0	2,073.7	450.3	1,582.0	41.4
Mankato-North Mankato, MN M.S.A.[3]	**94,016**									
Includes Blue Earth and Nicollet Counties[3]										
City of Mankato[3]	36,921		1		14	59	1,527	248	1,231	48
City of North Mankato[3]	12,748		1		4	5	232	22	207	3
Total area actually reporting	100.0%		3		18	96	2,336	393	1,871	72
Rate per 100,000 inhabitants			3.2		19.1	102.1	2,484.7	418.0	1,990.1	76.6
Mansfield, OH M.S.A.	**123,762**									
Includes Richland County										
City of Mansfield	49,069	159	3	35	73	48	2,933	905	1,966	62
Total area actually reporting	98.5%	218	4	47	94	73	5,083	1,490	3,469	124
Estimated total	100.0%	220	4	47	95	74	5,133	1,500	3,507	126
Rate per 100,000 inhabitants		177.8	3.2	38.0	76.8	59.8	4,147.5	1,212.0	2,833.7	101.8
McAllen-Edinburg-Mission, TX M.S.A.	**758,016**									
Includes Hidalgo County										
City of McAllen	134,623	299	5	14	115	165	7,398	711	6,283	404
City of Edinburg	75,091	232	2	23	44	163	4,599	1,011	3,294	294
City of Mission	71,556	92	2	7	37	46	3,243	482	2,454	307
City of Pharr	68,274	251	6	13	55	177	3,692	698	2,697	297
Total area actually reporting	100.0%	2,434	35	220	546	1,633	36,366	7,699	26,119	2,548
Rate per 100,000 inhabitants		321.1	4.6	29.0	72.0	215.4	4,797.5	1,015.7	3,445.7	336.1
Medford, OR M.S.A.[2]	**201,375**									
Includes Jackson County[2]										
City of Medford[2]	73,525	300	3	46	40	211	3,219	379	2,678	162
Total area actually reporting	100.0%	533	3	75	63	392	5,774	823	4,655	296
Rate per 100,000 inhabitants		264.7	1.5	37.2	31.3	194.7	2,867.3	408.7	2,311.6	147.0
Memphis, TN-MS-AR M.S.A.	**1,313,722**									
Includes Crittenden County, AR; DeSoto, Marshall, Tate, and Tunica Counties; MS, and Fayette, Shelby, and Tipton Counties, TN										
City of Memphis	673,650	10,384	89	422	3,236	6,637	42,138	13,094	25,114	3,930
Total area actually reporting	97.8%	13,185	112	598	3,647	8,828	60,222	18,576	36,582	5,064
Estimated total	100.0%	13,222	113	606	3,654	8,849	60,757	18,757	36,892	5,108
Rate per 100,000 inhabitants		1,006.5	8.6	46.1	278.1	673.6	4,624.8	1,427.8	2,808.2	388.8
Merced, CA M.S.A.	**248,716**									
Includes Merced County										
City of Merced	77,484	549	7	33	141	368	2,808	633	1,934	241
Total area actually reporting	100.0%	1,448	26	72	269	1,081	8,244	2,347	4,944	953
Rate per 100,000 inhabitants		582.2	10.5	28.9	108.2	434.6	3,314.6	943.6	1,987.8	383.2
Miami-Fort Lauderdale-Pompano Beach, FL M.S.A.	**5,597,226**									
Includes the Metropolitan Divisions of Fort Lauderdale-Pompano Beach-Deerfield Beach, Miami-Miami Beach-Kendall, and West Palm Beach-Boca Raton-Boynton Beach										
City of Miami	440,482	4,879	68	46	1,856	2,909	21,218	4,604	14,165	2,449
City of Fort Lauderdale	186,170	1,356	7	73	627	649	9,914	2,841	6,437	636
City of Pompano Beach	102,749	992	7	50	364	571	4,997	1,101	3,529	367
City of West Palm Beach	101,267	789	19	49	264	457	5,052	1,246	3,415	391
City of Miami Beach	87,990	864	8	39	352	465	8,743	1,192	6,957	594
City of Boca Raton	86,707	176	1	13	49	113	2,507	459	1,940	108
City of Deerfield Beach	75,195	429	1	24	156	248	2,509	581	1,752	176
City of Boynton Beach	70,574	585	4	6	143	432	3,195	727	2,361	107
City of Delray Beach	65,087	590	3	22	198	367	3,340	724	2,423	193
City of Homestead	63,761	857	3	25	298	531	3,012	896	1,983	133
Total area actually reporting	100.0%	34,096	370	1,321	11,113	21,292	232,565	51,999	162,131	18,435
Rate per 100,000 inhabitants		609.2	6.6	23.6	198.5	380.4	4,155.0	929.0	2,896.6	329.4
Fort Lauderdale-Pompano Beach-Deerfield Beach, FL M.D.	*1,779,016*									
Includes Broward County										
Total area actually reporting	100.0%	8,597	63	439	3,137	4,958	68,314	17,354	46,243	4,717
Rate per 100,000 inhabitants		483.2	3.5	24.7	176.3	278.7	3,840.0	975.5	2,599.4	265.1

[2] Because of changes in the state/local agency's reporting practices, figures are not comparable to previous years' data.

[3] The data collection methodology for the offense of forcible rape used by the Minnesota state UCR Program (with the exception of Minneapolis and St. Paul, Minnesota) does not comply with national UCR Program guidelines. Consequently, its figures for forcible rape and violent crime (of which forcible rape is a part) are not published in this table.

Table 6.   Crime, by Metropolitan Statistical Area, 2010—*Continued*

(Number, percent, rate per 100,000 population)

Area	Population	Violent crime	Murder and non-negligent man-slaughter	Forcible rape	Robbery	Aggravated assault	Property crime	Burglary	Larceny-theft	Motor vehicle theft
Miami-Miami Beach-Kendall, FL M.D.	**2,523,928**									
Includes Miami-Dade County										
Total area actually reporting	100.0%	18,507	224	537	5,958	11,788	118,078	23,111	84,061	10,906
Rate per 100,000 inhabitants		733.3	8.9	21.3	236.1	467.0	4,678.3	915.7	3,330.6	432.1
West Palm Beach-Boca Raton-Boynton Beach, FL M.D.	**1,294,282**									
Includes Palm Beach County										
Total area actually reporting	100.0%	6,992	83	345	2,018	4,546	46,173	11,534	31,827	2,812
Rate per 100,000 inhabitants		540.2	6.4	26.7	155.9	351.2	3,567.5	891.2	2,459.0	217.3
Michigan City-La Porte, IN M.S.A.	**111,553**									
Includes La Porte County										
City of Michigan City	32,482	147	2	23	61	61	2,016	412	1,469	135
City of La Porte	21,282	36	0	5	18	13	1,111	186	895	30
Total area actually reporting	96.8%	228	5	36	91	96	4,130	942	2,963	225
Estimated total	100.0%	237	5	37	93	102	4,252	961	3,059	232
Rate per 100,000 inhabitants		212.5	4.5	33.2	83.4	91.4	3,811.6	861.5	2,742.2	208.0
Midland, TX M.S.A.[2]	**133,704**									
Includes Midland County										
City of Midland[2]	109,356	406	2	44	65	295	3,584	889	2,548	147
Total area actually reporting	100.0%	448	3	45	70	330	4,226	1,098	2,946	182
Rate per 100,000 inhabitants		335.1	2.2	33.7	52.4	246.8	3,160.7	821.2	2,203.4	136.1
Milwaukee-Waukesha-West Allis, WI M.S.A.	**1,566,270**									
Includes Milwaukee, Ozaukee, Washington, and Waukesha Counties										
City of Milwaukee	605,921	6,329	94	197	2,932	3,106	31,720	6,181	21,212	4,327
City of Waukesha	68,680	93	1	16	18	58	1,075	176	854	45
City of West Allis	60,502	190	1	13	90	86	2,975	481	2,319	175
Total area actually reporting	100.0%	7,269	100	281	3,262	3,626	52,631	8,772	38,803	5,056
Rate per 100,000 inhabitants		464.1	6.4	17.9	208.3	231.5	3,360.3	560.1	2,477.4	322.8
Minneapolis-St. Paul-Bloomington, MN-WI M.S.A.[3]	**3,302,492**									
Includes Anoka, Carver, Chisago, Dakota, Hennepin, Isanti, Ramsey, Scott, Sherburne, Washington, and Wright Counties, MN[3] and Pierce and St. Croix Counties, WI										
City of Minneapolis, MN	385,704	4,064	37	438	1,596	1,993	18,299	4,787	11,609	1,903
City of St. Paul, MN	281,166	2,112	16	183	665	1,248	11,756	2,883	6,820	2,053
City of Bloomington, MN[3]	82,715		0		46	45	3,175	226	2,860	89
City of Plymouth, MN[3]	73,579		0		15	30	1,226	232	970	24
City of Eagan, MN[3]	64,239		2		13	18	1,625	176	1,396	53
City of Eden Prairie, MN[3]	63,159		1		5	21	1,020	135	866	19
City of Minnetonka, MN[3]	50,753		1		7	13	983	184	772	27
Total area actually reporting	99.6%		78		3,045	5,038	95,254	16,520	72,028	6,706
Estimated total	100.0%		78		3,049	5,047	95,582	16,564	72,298	6,720
Rate per 100,000 inhabitants			2.4		92.3	152.8	2,894.2	501.6	2,189.2	203.5
Mobile, AL M.S.A.[2,6]	**416,582**									
Includes Mobile County										
City of Mobile[2,6]	255,178	1,702	25	59	653	965	14,179	3,873	9,279	1,027
Total area actually reporting	91.9%	2,115	30	98	708	1,279	18,006	5,044	11,648	1,314
Estimated total	100.0%	2,225	31	106	735	1,353	19,270	5,272	12,613	1,385
Rate per 100,000 inhabitants		534.1	7.4	25.4	176.4	324.8	4,625.7	1,265.5	3,027.7	332.5
Modesto, CA M.S.A.	**516,479**									
Includes Stanislaus County										
City of Modesto	203,890	1,398	10	62	427	899	9,383	2,171	5,786	1,426
Total area actually reporting	100.0%	2,672	29	135	767	1,741	20,778	5,400	11,782	3,596
Rate per 100,000 inhabitants		517.3	5.6	26.1	148.5	337.1	4,023.0	1,045.5	2,281.2	696.3
Monroe, LA M.S.A.	**175,187**									
Includes Ouachita and Union Parishes										
City of Monroe	51,709	408	6	19	86	297	4,577	1,577	2,884	116
Total area actually reporting	98.8%	741	16	40	117	568	8,497	2,776	5,476	245
Estimated total	100.0%	752	16	41	118	577	8,589	2,795	5,546	248
Rate per 100,000 inhabitants		429.3	9.1	23.4	67.4	329.4	4,902.8	1,595.4	3,165.8	141.6
Monroe, MI M.S.A.	**151,998**									
Includes Monroe County										
City of Monroe	21,062	115	0	16	33	66	869	190	586	93
Total area actually reporting	94.2%	396	2	83	82	229	3,620	924	2,425	271
Estimated total	100.0%	423	2	86	88	247	3,860	976	2,594	290
Rate per 100,000 inhabitants		278.3	1.3	56.6	57.9	162.5	2,539.5	642.1	1,706.6	190.8

[2] Because of changes in the state/local agency's reporting practices, figures are not comparable to previous years' data.

[3] The data collection methodology for the offense of forcible rape used by the Minnesota state UCR Program (with the exception of Minneapolis and St. Paul, Minnesota) does not comply with national UCR Program guidelines. Consequently, its figures for forcible rape and violent crime (of which forcible rape is a part) are not published in this table.

[6] The population for the city of Mobile, Alabama, includes 55,995 inhabitants from the jurisdiction of the Mobile County Sheriff's Department.

Table 6. Crime, by Metropolitan Statistical Area, 2010—*Continued*

(Number, percent, rate per 100,000 population)

Area	Population	Violent crime	Murder and non-negligent man-slaughter	Forcible rape	Robbery	Aggravated assault	Property crime	Burglary	Larceny-theft	Motor vehicle theft
Montgomery, AL M.S.A.	**371,821**									
Includes Autauga, Elmore, Lowndes, and Montgomery Counties										
City of Montgomery	203,966	797	25	55	401	316	11,260	3,279	7,200	781
Total area actually reporting	85.1%	1,142	25	81	451	585	14,132	3,743	9,479	910
Rate per 100,000 inhabitants	100.0%	1,269	26	93	472	678	15,404	4,136	10,271	997
		341.3	7.0	25.0	126.9	182.3	4,142.9	1,112.4	2,762.4	268.1
Morgantown, WV M.S.A.[1,5]	**123,352**									
Includes Monongalia[5] and Preston[5] Counties										
City of Morgantown[1]	31,247	100	1	9	22	68		187		22
Total area actually reporting	92.2%		3	21	42			704		109
Estimated total	100.0%		3	23	46			764		122
Rate per 100,000 inhabitants			2.4	18.6	37.3			619.4		98.9
Morristown, TN M.S.A.	**138,774**									
Includes Grainger, Hamblen, and Jefferson Counties										
City of Morristown	28,147	243	1	16	43	183	2,099	178	1,838	83
Total area actually reporting	100.0%	533	6	33	95	399	5,131	1,191	3,705	235
Rate per 100,000 inhabitants		384.1	4.3	23.8	68.5	287.5	3,697.4	858.2	2,669.8	169.3
Mount Vernon-Anacortes, WA M.S.A.	**120,890**									
Includes Skagit County										
City of Mount Vernon	32,630	89	0	15	23	51	2,109	290	1,756	63
City of Anacortes	17,132	14	0	3	1	10	561	81	461	19
Total area actually reporting	100.0%	252	0	50	54	148	5,964	1,144	4,605	215
Rate per 100,000 inhabitants		208.5	0.0	41.4	44.7	122.4	4,933.4	946.3	3,809.2	177.8
Muncie, IN M.S.A.	**115,258**									
Includes Delaware County										
City of Muncie	67,736	244	0	22	101	121	2,084	476	1,432	176
Total area actually reporting	100.0%	290	0	32	109	149	3,019	639	2,135	245
Rate per 100,000 inhabitants		251.6	0.0	27.8	94.6	129.3	2,619.3	554.4	1,852.4	212.6
Muskegon-Norton Shores, MI M.S.A.	**172,745**									
Includes Muskegon County										
City of Muskegon	38,829	371	1	46	90	234	2,234	528	1,609	97
City of Norton Shores	23,127	50	1	9	6	34	723	96	609	18
Total area actually reporting	100.0%	813	4	121	180	508	7,193	1,712	5,228	253
Rate per 100,000 inhabitants		470.6	2.3	70.0	104.2	294.1	4,163.9	991.1	3,026.4	146.5
Myrtle Beach-North Myrtle Beach-Conway, SC M.S.A.	**271,797**									
Includes Horry County										
City of Myrtle Beach	32,907	483	1	39	189	254	4,155	793	3,061	301
City of North Myrtle Beach	16,832	101	0	11	31	59	1,813	476	1,183	154
City of Conway	16,742	159	1	6	34	118	956	263	647	46
Total area actually reporting	99.8%	1,752	16	116	417	1,203	15,291	3,614	10,303	1,374
Estimated total	100.0%	1,754	16	116	417	1,205	15,308	3,617	10,316	1,375
Rate per 100,000 inhabitants		645.3	5.9	42.7	153.4	443.3	5,632.1	1,330.8	3,795.5	505.9
Napa, CA M.S.A.	**135,593**									
Includes Napa County										
City of Napa	75,482	245	1	21	44	179	1,557	328	1,102	127
Total area actually reporting	100.0%	651	2	29	71	549	2,824	641	1,966	217
Rate per 100,000 inhabitants		480.1	1.5	21.4	52.4	404.9	2,082.7	472.7	1,449.9	160.0
Naples-Marco Island, FL M.S.A.	**325,568**									
Includes Collier County										
City of Naples	22,239	25	1	1	8	15	630	88	533	9
City of Marco Island	15,820	18	0	3	1	14	161	21	135	5
Total area actually reporting	100.0%	1,021	11	54	204	752	5,739	1,199	4,344	196
Rate per 100,000 inhabitants		313.6	3.4	16.6	62.7	231.0	1,762.8	368.3	1,334.3	60.2
Nashville-Davidson Murfreesboro Franklin, TN M.S.A.	**1,608,441**									
Includes Cannon, Cheatham, Davidson, Dickson, Hickman, Macon, Robertson, Rutherford, Smith, Sumner, Trousdale, Williamson, and Wilson Counties										
City of Nashville	616,366	6,995	55	367	1,817	4,756	30,517	7,731	20,881	1,905
City of Murfreesboro	109,199	603	5	37	151	410	4,610	1,310	3,144	156
City of Franklin	62,127	104	2	14	9	79	1,066	115	921	30
Total area actually reporting	100.0%	10,345	100	660	2,234	7,351	54,509	13,618	37,843	3,048
Rate per 100,000 inhabitants		643.2	6.2	41.0	138.9	457.0	3,388.9	846.7	2,352.8	189.5

[1] The FBI determined that the agency's data were underreported. Consequently, those data are not included in this table.

[5] The FBI determined that the agency's data were overreported. Consequently, those data are not included in this table.

Table 6. Crime, by Metropolitan Statistical Area, 2010—*Continued*

(Number, percent, rate per 100,000 population)

Area	Population	Violent crime	Murder and non-negligent man-slaughter	Forcible rape	Robbery	Aggravated assault	Property crime	Burglary	Larceny-theft	Motor vehicle theft
New Haven-Milford, CT M.S.A.	**806,354**									
Includes New Haven County										
City of New Haven	124,856	1,992	23	70	787	1,112	7,227	1,399	4,815	1,013
City of Milford	57,565	55	1	3	19	32	1,628	183	1,365	80
Total area actually reporting	100.0%	3,392	40	124	1,247	1,981	25,124	4,246	18,548	2,330
Rate per 100,000 inhabitants		420.7	5.0	15.4	154.6	245.7	3,115.8	526.6	2,300.2	289.0
New Orleans-Metairie-Kenner, LA M.S.A.[1]	**1,201,385**									
Includes Jefferson, Orleans, Plaquemines, St. Bernard,[1]										
St. Charles, St. John the Baptist, and St. Tammany Parishes										
City of New Orleans	356,317	2,593	175	144	953	1,321	12,645	3,695	6,540	2,410
City of Kenner	67,889	209	8	22	80	99	2,352	386	1,809	157
Total area actually reporting	100.0%	5,604	250	307	1,620	3,427		9,055	24,669	
Rate per 100,000 inhabitants		466.5	20.8	25.6	134.8	285.3		753.7	2,053.4	
New York-Northern New Jersey-Long Island,										
NY-NJ-PA M.S.A.	**19,042,526**									
Includes the Metropolitan Divisions of Edison-										
New Brunswick, NJ; Nassau-Suffolk, NY; Newark-										
Union, NJ-PA; and New York-White Plains-Wayne,										
NY-NJ										
City of New York, NY	8,336,002	48,489	536	1,036	19,608	27,309	139,615	17,926	111,370	10,319
City of Newark, NJ	280,379	2,885	90	79	1,604	1,112	9,209	1,928	3,661	3,620
City of Edison Township, NJ	100,395	141	2	5	52	82	1,709	334	1,220	155
City of White Plains, NY	57,254	110	2	2	40	66	1,094	48	1,017	29
City of Wayne Township, NJ	54,234	32	0	4	15	13	1,321	113	1,147	61
City of Union Township, NJ	53,945	104	1	2	64	37	1,023	130	777	116
City of New Brunswick, NJ	52,245	361	3	16	164	178	1,372	410	842	120
Total area actually reporting	99.9%	74,629	899	1,925	31,266	40,539	327,283	53,183	247,609	26,491
Estimated total	100.0%	74,635	899	1,925	31,268	40,543	327,353	53,194	247,666	26,493
Rate per 100,000 inhabitants		391.9	4.7	10.1	164.2	212.9	1,719.1	279.3	1,300.6	139.1
Edison-New Brunswick, NJ M.D.	**2,366,214**									
Includes Middlesex, Monmouth, Ocean, and										
Somerset Counties										
Total area actually reporting	100.0%	3,689	40	189	1,414	2,046	43,659	8,248	33,599	1,812
Rate per 100,000 inhabitants		155.9	1.7	8.0	59.8	86.5	1,845.1	348.6	1,419.9	76.6
Nassau-Suffolk, NY M.D.	**2,855,486**									
Includes Nassau and Suffolk Counties										
Total area actually reporting	99.9%	4,673	80	147	1,933	2,513	47,998	7,482	37,772	2,744
Estimated total	100.0%	4,676	80	147	1,934	2,515	48,029	7,487	37,797	2,745
Rate per 100,000 inhabitants		163.8	2.8	5.1	67.7	88.1	1,682.0	262.2	1,323.7	96.1
Newark-Union, NJ-PA M.D.	**2,142,518**									
Includes Essex, Hunterdon, Morris, Sussex, and										
Union Counties, NJ and Pike County, PA										
Total area actually reporting	100.0%	8,345	148	294	4,152	3,751	41,971	9,207	25,272	7,492
Rate per 100,000 inhabitants		389.5	6.9	13.7	193.8	175.1	1,959.0	429.7	1,179.5	349.7
New York-White Plains-Wayne, NY-NJ M.D.	**11,678,308**									
Includes Bergen, Hudson, and Passaic Counties, NJ										
and Bronx, Kings, New York, Putnam, Queens,										
Richmond, Rockland, and Westchester Counties, NY										
Total area actually reporting	99.9%	57,922	631	1,295	23,767	32,229	193,655	28,246	150,966	14,443
Estimated total	100.0%	57,925	631	1,295	23,768	32,231	193,694	28,252	150,998	14,444
Rate per 100,000 inhabitants		496.0	5.4	11.1	203.5	276.0	1,658.6	241.9	1,293.0	123.7
North Port-Bradenton-Sarasota, FL M.S.A.	**697,913**									
Includes Manatee and Sarasota Counties										
City of North Port	59,076	194	1	11	26	156	1,386	320	1,035	31
City of Bradenton	54,337	383	0	28	114	241	2,064	530	1,435	99
City of Sarasota	51,928	510	6	16	165	323	3,188	825	2,229	134
City of Venice	20,997	36	2	0	4	30	567	87	466	14
Total area actually reporting	100.0%	3,570	25	177	864	2,504	25,784	7,028	17,801	955
Rate per 100,000 inhabitants		511.5	3.6	25.4	123.8	358.8	3,694.4	1,007.0	2,550.6	136.8
Norwich-New London, CT M.S.A.	**141,679**									
Includes New London County										
City of Norwich	37,157	144	2	21	46	75	971	266	656	49
City of New London	26,517	286	2	14	50	220	912	257	585	70
Total area actually reporting	100.0%	559	5	51	123	380	3,410	747	2,515	148
Rate per 100,000 inhabitants		394.6	3.5	36.0	86.8	268.2	2,406.8	527.2	1,775.1	104.5

[1] The FBI determined that the agency's data were underreported. Consequently, those data are not included in this table.

Table 6.   Crime, by Metropolitan Statistical Area, 2010—*Continued*

(Number, percent, rate per 100,000 population)

Area	Population	Violent crime	Murder and non-negligent man-slaughter	Forcible rape	Robbery	Aggravated assault	Property crime	Burglary	Larceny-theft	Motor vehicle theft
Ocala, FL M.S.A.	**336,017**									
Includes Marion County										
City of Ocala	56,396	461	3	34	155	269	3,171	712	2,372	87
Total area actually reporting	100.0%	1,794	9	144	240	1,401	8,296	2,371	5,611	314
Rate per 100,000 inhabitants		533.9	2.7	42.9	71.4	416.9	2,468.9	705.6	1,669.9	93.4
Ocean City, NJ M.S.A.	**96,094**									
Includes Cape May County										
City of Ocean City	14,725	27	0	4	9	14	894	189	700	5
Total area actually reporting	100.0%	244	2	17	61	164	4,549	1,103	3,369	77
Rate per 100,000 inhabitants		253.9	2.1	17.7	63.5	170.7	4,733.9	1,147.8	3,505.9	80.1
Odessa, TX M.S.A.	**135,675**									
Includes Ector County										
City of Odessa	101,580	726	3	36	96	591	3,523	824	2,508	191
Total area actually reporting	100.0%	893	7	35	110	741	4,822	1,188	3,383	251
Rate per 100,000 inhabitants		658.2	5.2	25.8	81.1	546.2	3,554.1	875.6	2,493.5	185.0
Ogden-Clearfield, UT M.S.A.	**536,184**									
Includes Davis, Morgan, and Weber Counties										
City of Ogden	81,431	327	1	24	110	192	4,655	867	3,479	309
City of Clearfield	27,788	41	0	12	14	15	846	125	685	36
Total area actually reporting	100.0%	802	8	168	191	435	16,113	2,753	12,580	780
Rate per 100,000 inhabitants		149.6	1.5	31.3	35.6	81.1	3,005.1	513.4	2,346.2	145.5
Oklahoma City, OK M.S.A.[5]	**1,254,299**									
Includes Canadian,[5] Cleveland, Grady, Lincoln, Logan,										
McClain, and Oklahoma Counties										
City of Oklahoma City	571,865	5,304	54	340	1,112	3,798	33,263	9,901	19,760	3,602
Total area actually reporting	100.0%		72	550	1,349		52,789	14,938	33,157	4,694
Rate per 100,000 inhabitants			5.7	43.8	107.6		4,208.6	1,190.9	2,643.5	374.2
Olympia, WA M.S.A.	**254,900**									
Includes Thurston County										
City of Olympia	46,264	150	0	37	29	84	2,562	425	1,987	150
Total area actually reporting	100.0%	631	4	86	86	455	8,132	2,051	5,653	428
Rate per 100,000 inhabitants		247.5	1.6	33.7	33.7	178.5	3,190.3	804.6	2,217.7	167.9
Omaha-Council Bluffs, NE-IA M.S.A.	**867,616**									
Includes Harrison, Mills, and Pottawattamie										
Counties, IA and Cass, Douglas, Sarpy, Saunders,										
and Washington Counties, NE										
City of Omaha, NE	464,628	2,263	34	194	723	1,312	17,334	3,046	12,091	2,197
City of Council Bluffs, IA	61,181	636	1	60	77	498	3,646	801	2,412	433
Total area actually reporting	97.8%	3,330	39	335	840	2,116	26,486	4,993	18,437	3,056
Estimated total	100.0%	3,355	39	337	842	2,137	26,784	5,058	18,653	3,073
Rate per 100,000 inhabitants		386.7	4.5	38.8	97.0	246.3	3,087.1	583.0	2,149.9	354.2
Orlando-Kissimmee-Sanford, FL M.S.A.	**2,130,297**									
Includes Lake, Orange, Osceola, and Seminole Counties										
City of Orlando	240,222	2,574	18	113	672	1,771	15,565	4,015	10,357	1,193
City of Kissimmee	64,122	599	1	19	122	457	3,218	856	2,192	170
City of Sanford	52,325	356	3	38	174	141	3,367	871	2,286	210
Total area actually reporting	100.0%	13,074	103	703	3,069	9,199	76,573	21,383	50,019	5,171
Rate per 100,000 inhabitants		613.7	4.8	33.0	144.1	431.8	3,594.5	1,003.8	2,348.0	242.7
Owensboro, KY M.S.A.	**113,908**									
Includes Daviess, Hancock, and McLean Counties										
City of Owensboro	55,848	115	2	36	28	49	2,255	399	1,772	84
Total area actually reporting	100.0%	132	2	44	29	57	2,730	522	2,093	115
Rate per 100,000 inhabitants		115.9	1.8	38.6	25.5	50.0	2,396.7	458.3	1,837.4	101.0
Oxnard-Thousand Oaks-Ventura, CA M.S.A. ...	**807,132**									
Includes Ventura County										
City of Oxnard	189,051	691	8	19	329	335	4,018	785	2,760	473
City of Thousand Oaks	124,042	139	1	16	50	72	2,036	358	1,606	72
City of Ventura	104,661	263	3	16	108	136	3,458	652	2,654	152
City of Camarillo	64,577	54	0	3	12	39	972	167	763	42
Total area actually reporting	100.0%	1,748	18	105	628	997	16,025	3,047	11,852	1,126
Rate per 100,000 inhabitants		216.6	2.2	13.0	77.8	123.5	1,985.4	377.5	1,468.4	139.5

[5] The FBI determined that the agency's data were overreported. Consequently, those data are not included in this table.

Table 6.   Crime, by Metropolitan Statistical Area, 2010—*Continued*

(Number, percent, rate per 100,000 population)

Area	Population	Violent crime	Murder and non-negligent man-slaughter	Forcible rape	Robbery	Aggravated assault	Property crime	Burglary	Larceny-theft	Motor vehicle theft
Palm Bay-Melbourne-Titusville, FL M.S.A.	**542,130**									
Includes Brevard County										
City of Palm Bay	103,350	521	4	19	60	438	2,460	740	1,622	98
City of Melbourne	77,861	685	7	28	144	506	3,672	771	2,769	132
City of Titusville	44,839	350	1	19	80	250	1,486	361	1,030	95
Total area actually reporting	100.0%	3,195	20	172	531	2,472	17,155	4,273	12,187	695
Rate per 100,000 inhabitants		589.3	3.7	31.7	97.9	456.0	3,164.4	788.2	2,248.0	128.2
Palm Coast, FL M.S.A.	**97,199**									
Includes Flagler County										
Total area actually reporting	100.0%	229	0	16	36	177	2,249	555	1,590	104
Rate per 100,000 inhabitants		235.6	0.0	16.5	37.0	182.1	2,313.8	571.0	1,635.8	107.0
Panama City-Lynn Haven-Panama City Beach, FL M.S.A.	**166,372**									
Includes Bay County										
City of Panama City	36,593	277	5	5	78	189	2,423	508	1,785	130
City of Lynn Haven	15,678	58	0	1	9	48	592	67	512	13
City of Panama City Beach	15,482	94	0	14	21	59	1,069	156	911	2
Total area actually reporting	100.0%	866	12	61	158	635	7,554	1,646	5,566	342
Rate per 100,000 inhabitants		520.5	7.2	36.7	95.0	381.7	4,540.4	989.3	3,345.5	205.6
Pascagoula, MS M.S.A.	**156,225**									
Includes George and Jackson Counties										
City of Pascagoula	23,479	87	2	20	38	27	1,409	300	1,050	59
Total area actually reporting	100.0%	424	6	91	111	216	5,255	1,888	3,057	310
Rate per 100,000 inhabitants		271.4	3.8	58.2	71.1	138.3	3,363.7	1,208.5	1,956.8	198.4
Pensacola-Ferry Pass-Brent, FL M.S.A.	**459,393**									
Includes Escambia and Santa Rosa Counties										
City of Pensacola	53,476	420	3	36	112	269	2,545	519	1,939	87
Total area actually reporting	100.0%	2,618	35	253	601	1,729	15,141	3,798	10,659	684
Rate per 100,000 inhabitants		569.9	7.6	55.1	130.8	376.4	3,295.9	826.7	2,320.2	148.9
Peoria, IL M.S.A.[2]	**372,866**									
Includes Marshall, Peoria, Stark, Tazewell, and Woodford Counties[2]										
City of Peoria[2]	114,557	878	22	31	306	519	5,163	1,460	3,436	267
Total area actually reporting	87.7%	1,415	27	127	345	916	8,765	2,304	6,014	447
Estimated total	100.0%	1,516	28	138	371	979	9,764	2,484	6,784	496
Rate per 100,000 inhabitants		406.6	7.5	37.0	99.5	262.6	2,618.6	666.2	1,819.4	133.0
Philadelphia-Camden-Wilmington, PA-NJ-DE-MD M.S.A.	**6,027,122**									
Includes the Metropolitan Divisions of Camden, NJ; Philadelphia, PA; and Wilmington, DE-MD-NJ										
City of Philadelphia, PA	1,558,378	18,535	306	945	8,363	8,921	57,788	10,796	39,924	7,068
City of Camden, NJ	79,081	1,841	37	73	712	1,019	3,500	1,015	1,966	519
City of Wilmington, DE	73,270	1,399	28	27	633	711	4,147	1,176	2,428	543
Total area actually reporting	99.8%	33,230	470	1,716	13,404	17,640	160,260	30,884	116,889	12,487
Estimated total	100.0%	33,256	470	1,718	13,411	17,657	160,485	30,920	117,070	12,495
Rate per 100,000 inhabitants		551.8	7.8	28.5	222.5	293.0	2,662.7	513.0	1,942.4	207.3
Camden, NJ M.D.	*1,268,710*									
Includes Burlington, Camden, and Gloucester Counties										
Total area actually reporting	100.0%	4,220	52	223	1,587	2,358	31,932	6,973	23,299	1,660
Rate per 100,000 inhabitants		332.6	4.1	17.6	125.1	185.9	2,516.9	549.6	1,836.4	130.8
Philadelphia, PA M.D.	*4,049,258*									
Includes Bucks, Chester, Delaware, Montgomery, and Philadelphia Counties										
Total area actually reporting	99.7%	24,508	370	1,307	10,163	12,668	104,703	18,246	77,293	9,164
Estimated total	100.0%	24,534	370	1,309	10,170	12,685	104,928	18,282	77,474	9,172
Rate per 100,000 inhabitants		605.9	9.1	32.3	251.2	313.3	2,591.3	451.5	1,913.3	226.5
Wilmington, DE-MD-NJ M.D.	*709,154*									
Includes New Castle County, DE; Cecil County, MD; and Salem County, NJ										
Total area actually reporting	100.0%	4,502	48	186	1,654	2,614	23,625	5,665	16,297	1,663
Rate per 100,000 inhabitants		634.8	6.8	26.2	233.2	368.6	3,331.4	798.8	2,298.1	234.5

[2] Because of changes in the state/local agency's reporting practices, figures are not comparable to previous years' data.

Table 6.   Crime, by Metropolitan Statistical Area, 2010—*Continued*

(Number, percent, rate per 100,000 population)

Area	Population	Violent crime	Murder and non-negligent man-slaughter	Forcible rape	Robbery	Aggravated assault	Property crime	Burglary	Larceny-theft	Motor vehicle theft
Phoenix-Mesa-Glendale, AZ M.S.A.	**4,229,275**									
Includes Maricopa and Pinal Counties										
City of Phoenix	1,544,427	8,002	117	522	3,250	4,113	61,362	15,626	38,012	7,724
City of Mesa	452,725	1,790	15	124	511	1,140	14,876	2,711	11,158	1,007
City of Glendale	245,387	963	12	46	385	520	13,529	2,264	9,936	1,329
City of Scottsdale	230,496	353	4	33	100	216	6,563	1,281	5,014	268
City of Tempe	173,004	779	11	43	268	457	8,472	1,416	6,412	644
Total area actually reporting	99.9%	15,672	231	1,095	5,246	9,100	149,378	33,623	101,519	14,236
Estimated total	100.0%	15,681	231	1,096	5,248	9,106	149,488	33,646	101,599	14,243
Rate per 100,000 inhabitants		370.8	5.5	25.9	124.1	215.3	3,534.6	795.6	2,402.3	336.8
Pine Bluff, AR M.S.A.	**100,121**									
Includes Cleveland, Jefferson, and Lincoln Counties										
City of Pine Bluff	49,971	687	7	40	165	475	3,748	1,371	2,074	303
Total area actually reporting	97.8%	784	9	55	172	548	4,542	1,721	2,456	365
Estimated total	100.0%	794	9	56	173	556	4,617	1,746	2,503	368
Rate per 100,000 inhabitants		793.0	9.0	55.9	172.8	555.3	4,611.4	1,743.9	2,500.0	367.6
Pittsburgh, PA M.S.A.	**2,359,460**									
Includes Allegheny, Armstrong, Beaver, Butler, Fayette, Washington, and Westmoreland Counties										
City of Pittsburgh	312,737	2,810	55	66	1,190	1,499	11,284	2,949	7,678	657
Total area actually reporting	99.0%	7,492	111	395	2,266	4,720	46,188	10,102	34,039	2,047
Estimated total	100.0%	7,538	111	398	2,278	4,751	46,614	10,171	34,380	2,063
Rate per 100,000 inhabitants		319.5	4.7	16.9	96.5	201.4	1,975.6	431.1	1,457.1	87.4
Pittsfield, MA M.S.A.	**127,393**									
Includes Berkshire County										
City of Pittsfield	41,666	281	1	26	17	237	1,183	375	749	59
Total area actually reporting	95.7%	560	1	47	33	479	3,075	918	2,041	116
Estimated total	100.0%	578	1	48	36	493	3,188	946	2,119	123
Rate per 100,000 inhabitants		453.7	0.8	37.7	28.3	387.0	2,502.5	742.6	1,663.4	96.6
Pocatello, ID M.S.A.	**90,644**									
Includes Bannock and Power Counties										
City of Pocatello	55,215	132	1	24	6	101	1,726	296	1,360	70
Total area actually reporting	100.0%	197	1	33	14	149	2,512	382	2,034	96
Rate per 100,000 inhabitants		217.3	1.1	36.4	15.4	164.4	2,771.3	421.4	2,243.9	105.9
Portland-South Portland-Biddeford, ME M.S.A.	**521,947**									
Includes Cumberland, Sagadahoc, and York Counties										
City of Portland	63,166	242	6	33	129	74	2,921	599	2,246	76
City of South Portland	24,144	49	0	2	11	36	902	92	788	22
City of Biddeford	21,511	66	0	17	18	31	1,029	157	850	22
Total area actually reporting	100.0%	697	10	150	231	306	12,908	2,718	9,781	409
Rate per 100,000 inhabitants		133.5	1.9	28.7	44.3	58.6	2,473.0	520.7	1,873.9	78.4
Port St. Lucie, FL M.S.A.	**415,985**									
Includes Martin and St. Lucie Counties										
City of Port St. Lucie	163,089	386	3	45	49	289	3,212	909	2,224	79
Total area actually reporting	100.0%	1,542	20	116	346	1,060	10,855	2,964	7,515	376
Rate per 100,000 inhabitants		370.7	4.8	27.9	83.2	254.8	2,609.5	712.5	1,806.6	90.4
Poughkeepsie-Newburgh-Middletown, NY M.S.A.	**675,016**									
Includes Dutchess and Orange Counties										
City of Poughkeepsie	29,175	398	7	21	142	228	1,055	273	729	53
City of Newburgh	27,836	522	11	7	195	309	1,132	342	724	66
City of Middletown	25,701	150	1	7	63	79	1,171	194	949	28
Total area actually reporting	93.3%	1,701	30	92	547	1,032	13,102	2,199	10,531	372
Estimated total	100.0%	1,782	31	96	576	1,079	13,996	2,338	11,258	400
Rate per 100,000 inhabitants		264.0	4.6	14.2	85.3	159.8	2,073.4	346.4	1,667.8	59.3
Prescott, AZ M.S.A.	**209,023**									
Includes Yavapai County										
City of Prescott	41,428	135	0	11	13	111	1,251	221	979	51
Total area actually reporting	100.0%	684	7	49	23	605	4,538	1,063	3,261	214
Rate per 100,000 inhabitants		327.2	3.3	23.4	11.0	289.4	2,171.1	508.6	1,560.1	102.4

Table 6. Crime, by Metropolitan Statistical Area, 2010—*Continued*

(Number, percent, rate per 100,000 population)

Area	Population	Violent crime	Murder and non-negligent man-slaughter	Forcible rape	Robbery	Aggravated assault	Property crime	Burglary	Larceny-theft	Motor vehicle theft
Providence-New Bedford-Fall River, RI-MA M.S.A.............	**1,595,372**									
Includes Bristol County, MA and Bristol, Kent, Newport, Providence, and Washington Counties, RI										
City of Providence, RI.................	171,565	1,214	15	74	405	720	8,229	2,034	5,078	1,117
City of New Bedford, MA	89,613	1,160	3	69	272	816	3,599	1,237	1,974	388
City of Fall River, MA.................	89,741	1,087	5	52	252	778	3,297	940	2,006	351
City of Warwick, RI.................	84,568	85	0	14	24	47	2,119	381	1,628	110
City of Cranston, RI.................	80,125	115	1	17	24	73	1,901	382	1,339	180
Total area actually reporting	100.0%	5,925	42	482	1,464	3,937	40,392	9,982	27,006	3,404
Rate per 100,000 inhabitants..............		371.4	2.6	30.2	91.8	246.8	2,531.8	625.7	1,692.8	213.4
Provo-Orem, UT M.S.A.	**560,264**									
Includes Juab and Utah Counties										
City of Provo	117,734	194	2	46	27	119	2,739	370	2,266	103
City of Orem	93,580	68	1	19	17	31	2,553	240	2,204	109
Total area actually reporting	100.0%	456	6	124	79	247	11,766	1,753	9,606	407
Rate per 100,000 inhabitants..............		81.4	1.1	22.1	14.1	44.1	2,100.1	312.9	1,714.5	72.6
Pueblo, CO M.S.A.[2]	**156,522**									
Includes Pueblo County										
City of Pueblo[2].................	103,612	885	1	30	157	697	4,972	1,622	2,899	451
Total area actually reporting	100.0%	916	4	30	164	718	6,658	1,967	4,170	521
Rate per 100,000 inhabitants..............		585.2	2.6	19.2	104.8	458.7	4,253.7	1,256.7	2,664.2	332.9
Punta Gorda, FL M.S.A.	**158,377**									
Includes Charlotte County										
City of Punta Gorda	17,389	27	0	1	2	24	376	176	198	2
Total area actually reporting	100.0%	381	1	23	47	310	4,199	1,153	2,934	112
Rate per 100,000 inhabitants..............		240.6	0.6	14.5	29.7	195.7	2,651.3	728.0	1,852.5	70.7
Racine, WI M.S.A..................	**201,891**									
Includes Racine County										
City of Racine	82,059	387	8	19	201	159	3,406	971	2,279	156
Total area actually reporting	100.0%	511	8	32	221	250	5,411	1,253	3,909	249
Rate per 100,000 inhabitants..............		253.1	4.0	15.9	109.5	123.8	2,680.2	620.6	1,936.2	123.3
Raleigh-Cary, NC M.S.A.	**1,165,131**									
Includes Franklin, Johnston, and Wake Counties										
City of Raleigh	419,700	1,740	14	99	643	984	12,995	3,021	9,104	870
City of Cary	141,461	120	1	14	35	70	2,179	535	1,580	64
Total area actually reporting	99.4%	2,806	40	187	872	1,707	28,165	7,248	18,791	2,126
Estimated total.................	100.0%	2,827	40	188	877	1,722	28,459	7,318	19,001	2,140
Rate per 100,000 inhabitants..............		242.6	3.4	16.1	75.3	147.8	2,442.6	628.1	1,630.8	183.7
Rapid City, SD M.S.A.	**125,249**									
Includes Meade and Pennington Counties										
City of Rapid City	67,436	404	2	91	59	252	2,823	518	2,178	127
Total area actually reporting	100.0%	516	4	117	62	333	3,567	678	2,735	154
Rate per 100,000 inhabitants..............		412.0	3.2	93.4	49.5	265.9	2,847.9	541.3	2,183.7	123.0
Reading, PA M.S.A..................	**412,575**									
Includes Berks County										
City of Reading	81,370	767	10	21	384	352	3,662	1,425	1,582	655
Total area actually reporting	100.0%	1,360	13	64	444	839	8,980	2,165	5,897	918
Rate per 100,000 inhabitants..............		329.6	3.2	15.5	107.6	203.4	2,176.6	524.8	1,429.3	222.5
Redding, CA M.S.A.	**182,780**									
Includes Shasta County										
City of Redding	91,414	793	2	61	105	625	3,037	849	1,946	242
Total area actually reporting	100.0%	1,457	3	120	138	1,196	4,782	1,508	2,849	425
Rate per 100,000 inhabitants..............		797.1	1.6	65.7	75.5	654.3	2,616.3	825.0	1,558.7	232.5
Reno-Sparks, NV M.S.A..................	**425,023**									
Includes Storey and Washoe Counties										
City of Reno	222,242	1,168	9	46	385	728	7,468	1,638	5,101	729
City of Sparks.................	91,433	357	8	35	103	211	2,761	699	1,829	233
Total area actually reporting	100.0%	1,799	18	107	499	1,175	11,799	2,793	7,909	1,097
Rate per 100,000 inhabitants..............		423.3	4.2	25.2	117.4	276.5	2,776.1	657.1	1,860.8	258.1

[2] Because of changes in the state/local agency's reporting practices, figures are not comparable to previous years' data.

Table 6.   Crime, by Metropolitan Statistical Area, 2010—*Continued*

(Number, percent, rate per 100,000 population)

Area	Population	Violent crime	Murder and non-negligent man-slaughter	Forcible rape	Robbery	Aggravated assault	Property crime	Burglary	Larceny-theft	Motor vehicle theft
Richmond, VA M.S.A.	**1,257,811**									
Includes Amelia, Caroline, Charles City, Chesterfield, Cumberland, Dinwiddie, Goochland, Hanover, Henrico, King and Queen, King William, Louisa, New Kent, Powhatan, Prince George, and Sussex Counties and Colonial Heights, Hopewell, Petersburg, and Richmond Cities										
City of Richmond	205,883	1,506	41	40	735	690	8,567	1,783	5,918	866
Total area actually reporting	100.0%	3,387	90	199	1,406	1,692	31,985	6,236	23,610	2,139
Rate per 100,000 inhabitants		269.3	7.2	15.8	111.8	134.5	2,542.9	495.8	1,877.1	170.1
Riverside-San Bernardino-Ontario, CA M.S.A.	**4,239,406**									
Includes Riverside and San Bernardino Counties										
City of Riverside	301,859	1,448	9	78	502	859	9,963	2,068	6,434	1,461
City of San Bernardino	199,214	1,624	31	66	632	895	8,967	2,318	4,928	1,721
City of Ontario	172,814	630	3	48	237	342	4,918	850	3,170	898
City of Victorville	117,057	681	6	38	256	381	3,674	1,274	1,964	436
City of Temecula	102,474	74	2	3	42	27	2,351	535	1,642	174
City of Chino	84,170	264	0	13	76	175	2,009	479	1,314	216
City of Hemet	73,111	369	8	17	129	215	2,887	875	1,682	330
City of Redlands	70,552	243	2	25	104	112	2,536	587	1,706	243
City of Colton	50,706	170	6	14	79	71	1,579	406	890	283
City of Palm Desert	52,625	48	0	6	30	12	1,911	638	1,150	123
Total area actually reporting	100.0%	15,622	191	864	4,903	9,664	114,236	31,647	65,738	16,851
Rate per 100,000 inhabitants		368.5	4.5	20.4	115.7	228.0	2,694.6	746.5	1,550.6	397.5
Roanoke, VA M.S.A.	**302,738**									
Includes Botetourt, Craig, Franklin, and Roanoke Counties and Roanoke and Salem Cities										
City of Roanoke	94,795	677	9	27	176	465	4,735	883	3,608	244
Total area actually reporting	100.0%	917	19	69	206	623	8,059	1,496	6,182	381
Rate per 100,000 inhabitants		302.9	6.3	22.8	68.0	205.8	2,662.0	494.2	2,042.0	125.9
Rochester, MN M.S.A.[3]	**187,922**									
Includes Dodge, Olmsted, and Wabasha Counties[3]										
City of Rochester[3]	105,027		1		58	123	2,429	399	1,925	105
Total area actually reporting	98.3%		1		64	190	3,314	559	2,601	154
Estimated total	100.0%		1		65	193	3,405	571	2,676	158
Rate per 100,000 inhabitants			0.5		34.6	102.7	1,811.9	303.8	1,424.0	84.1
Rochester, NY M.S.A.	**1,023,376**									
Includes Livingston, Monroe, Ontario, Orleans, and Wayne Counties										
City of Rochester	203,802	2,229	41	99	816	1,273	11,820	3,448	7,620	752
Total area actually reporting	99.8%	3,242	50	226	1,014	1,952	28,886	6,416	21,304	1,166
Estimated total	100.0%	3,245	50	226	1,015	1,954	28,927	6,422	21,338	1,167
Rate per 100,000 inhabitants		317.1	4.9	22.1	99.2	190.9	2,826.6	627.5	2,085.1	114.0
Rockford, IL M.S.A.[2]	**353,502**									
Includes Boone and Winnebago Counties[2]										
City of Rockford	156,180	2,272	21	110	495	1,646	7,805	2,375	4,992	438
Total area actually reporting	93.7%	2,638	22	182	552	1,882	11,496	3,305	7,595	596
Estimated total	100.0%	2,688	23	188	565	1,912	11,980	3,392	7,968	620
Rate per 100,000 inhabitants		760.4	6.5	53.2	159.8	540.9	3,388.9	959.5	2,254.0	175.4
Rocky Mount, NC M.S.A.	**147,080**									
Includes Edgecombe and Nash Counties										
City of Rocky Mount	59,688	688	11	14	210	453	3,566	1,057	2,339	170
Total area actually reporting	100.0%	901	15	35	252	599	5,344	1,747	3,315	282
Rate per 100,000 inhabitants		612.6	10.2	23.8	171.3	407.3	3,633.4	1,187.8	2,253.9	191.7
Rome, GA M.S.A.	**93,639**									
Includes Floyd County										
City of Rome	34,896	233	1	17	90	125	1,990	447	1,439	104
Total area actually reporting	100.0%	451	3	22	100	326	3,387	839	2,353	195
Rate per 100,000 inhabitants		481.6	3.2	23.5	106.8	348.1	3,617.1	896.0	2,512.8	208.2

[2] Because of changes in the state/local agency's reporting practices, figures are not comparable to previous years' data.

[3] The data collection methodology for the offense of forcible rape used by the Minnesota state UCR Program (with the exception of Minneapolis and St. Paul, Minnesota) does not comply with national UCR Program guidelines. Consequently, its figures for forcible rape and violent crime (of which forcible rape is a part) are not published in this table.

Table 6.   Crime, by Metropolitan Statistical Area, 2010—*Continued*

(Number, percent, rate per 100,000 population)

Area	Population	Violent crime	Murder and non-negligent man-slaughter	Forcible rape	Robbery	Aggravated assault	Property crime	Burglary	Larceny-theft	Motor vehicle theft
Sacramento Arden-Arcade Roseville, CA M.S.A.	**2,161,081**									
Includes El Dorado, Placer, Sacramento, and Yolo Counties										
City of Sacramento	472,469	4,112	33	165	1,491	2,423	20,200	5,027	11,179	3,994
City of Roseville	119,755	334	1	17	87	229	3,802	542	3,029	231
City of Folsom	69,497	105	0	9	32	64	1,484	262	1,159	63
City of Woodland	55,814	161	1	17	39	104	1,513	352	993	168
Total area actually reporting	100.0%	10,333	90	564	3,466	6,213	67,137	16,626	40,804	9,707
Rate per 100,000 inhabitants.....................		478.1	4.2	26.1	160.4	287.5	3,106.6	769.3	1,888.1	449.2
Saginaw-Saginaw Township North, MI M.S.A.[1].................	**197,310**									
Includes Saginaw County[1]										
City of Saginaw[1]	54,155	1,209	4	61	192	952	2,195	1,310	763	122
Total area actually reporting	100.0%	1,718	7	150	255	1,306	5,579	2,161	3,165	253
Rate per 100,000 inhabitants.....................		870.7	3.5	76.0	129.2	661.9	2,827.5	1,095.2	1,604.1	128.2
Salem, OR M.S.A.[2].................	**397,398**									
Includes Marion and Polk Counties[2]										
City of Salem[2]....................	155,820	483	1	48	118	316	6,056	868	4,761	427
Total area actually reporting	76.6%	806	3	79	156	568	9,284	1,420	7,224	640
Estimated total....................	100.0%	957	5	101	179	672	10,924	1,771	8,397	756
Rate per 100,000 inhabitants.....................		240.8	1.3	25.4	45.0	169.1	2,748.9	445.6	2,113.0	190.2
Salinas, CA M.S.A.	**410,773**									
Includes Monterey County										
City of Salinas	144,242	1,162	19	23	365	755	4,648	1,358	2,437	853
Total area actually reporting	100.0%	2,037	44	82	574	1,337	10,405	2,973	6,054	1,378
Rate per 100,000 inhabitants.....................		495.9	10.7	20.0	139.7	325.5	2,533.0	723.8	1,473.8	335.5
Salisbury, MD M.S.A......................	**121,993**									
Includes Somerset and Wicomico Counties										
City of Salisbury.....................	29,046	450	7	22	143	278	2,238	575	1,598	65
Total area actually reporting	100.0%	817	11	35	200	571	4,436	1,287	2,991	158
Rate per 100,000 inhabitants.....................		669.7	9.0	28.7	163.9	468.1	3,636.3	1,055.0	2,451.8	129.5
Salt Lake City, UT M.S.A.	**1,113,915**									
Includes Salt Lake, Summit, and Tooele Counties										
City of Salt Lake City.....................	177,873	1,289	8	146	359	776	13,839	2,177	10,173	1,489
Total area actually reporting	99.9%	3,960	32	515	957	2,456	49,641	8,376	36,950	4,315
Estimated total.....................	100.0%	3,960	32	515	957	2,456	49,653	8,378	36,959	4,316
Rate per 100,000 inhabitants.....................		355.5	2.9	46.2	85.9	220.5	4,457.5	752.1	3,317.9	387.5
San Angelo, TX M.S.A......................	**110,207**									
Includes Irion and Tom Green Counties										
City of San Angelo	92,234	276	1	48	50	177	4,169	1,035	2,976	158
Total area actually reporting	100.0%	303	2	58	54	189	4,558	1,125	3,267	166
Rate per 100,000 inhabitants.....................		274.9	1.8	52.6	49.0	171.5	4,135.9	1,020.8	2,964.4	150.6
San Antonio-New Braunfels, TX M.S.A......................	**2,104,901**									
Includes Atascosa, Bandera, Bexar, Comal, Guadalupe, Kendall, Medina, and Wilson Counties										
City of San Antonio.....................	1,392,198	8,434	79	467	2,360	5,528	88,353	17,301	65,395	5,657
City of New Braunfels.....................	57,796	121	0	10	25	86	1,966	373	1,530	63
Total area actually reporting	99.9%	10,184	98	686	2,677	6,723	110,104	22,539	80,924	6,641
Estimated total.....................	100.0%	10,188	98	686	2,678	6,726	110,152	22,549	80,959	6,644
Rate per 100,000 inhabitants.....................		484.0	4.7	32.6	127.2	319.5	5,233.1	1,071.3	3,846.2	315.6
San Diego-Carlsbad-San Marcos, CA M.S.A......................	**3,075,127**									
Includes San Diego County										
City of San Diego.....................	1,313,433	5,616	29	300	1,636	3,651	30,753	6,387	17,977	6,389
City of Carlsbad	100,461	195	0	20	41	134	1,820	399	1,313	108
City of San Marcos	83,671	237	1	16	70	150	1,642	350	1,054	238
City of National City	56,270	428	4	11	148	265	1,849	310	1,033	506
Total area actually reporting	100.0%	11,639	67	675	3,350	7,547	67,850	14,071	41,222	12,557
Rate per 100,000 inhabitants.....................		378.5	2.2	22.0	108.9	245.4	2,206.4	457.6	1,340.5	408.3

[1] The FBI determined that the agency's data were underreported. Consequently, those data are not included in this table.

[2] Because of changes in the state/local agency's reporting practices, figures are not comparable to previous years' data.

Table 6.   Crime, by Metropolitan Statistical Area, 2010—*Continued*

(Number, percent, rate per 100,000 population)

Area	Population	Violent crime	Murder and non-negligent man-slaughter	Forcible rape	Robbery	Aggravated assault	Property crime	Burglary	Larceny-theft	Motor vehicle theft
Sandusky, OH M.S.A.	**76,515**									
Includes Erie County										
City of Sandusky	25,380	150	0	7	20	123	1,273	310	960	3
Total area actually reporting	98.7%	226	0	13	26	187	2,108	478	1,621	9
Estimated total	100.0%	228	0	13	27	188	2,136	484	1642	10
Rate per 100,000 inhabitants		298.0	0.0	17.0	35.3	245.7	2,791.6	632.6	2,146.0	13.1
San Francisco-Oakland-Fremont, CA M.S.A.	**4,333,063**									
Includes the Metropolitan Divisions of Oakland-Fremont-Hayward and San Francisco-San Mateo-Redwood City										
City of San Francisco	818,594	5,747	48	133	3,180	2,386	32,365	4,557	23,905	3,903
City of Oakland	409,723	6,267	90	318	2,917	2,942	17,325	4,961	7,720	4,644
City of Fremont	205,477	488	3	40	189	256	4,414	1,167	2,757	490
City of Hayward	144,509	652	13	48	391	200	3,753	1,097	1,649	1,007
City of Berkeley	102,700	533	5	23	365	140	5,943	1,088	4,240	615
City of San Mateo	92,724	292	1	24	82	185	1,905	242	1,464	199
City of San Leandro	78,447	347	4	10	209	124	3,137	634	1,911	592
City of Redwood City	74,355	174	3	16	69	86	1,641	461	988	192
City of Pleasanton	67,823	78	0	4	24	50	1,294	210	1,002	82
City of Walnut Creek	63,897	115	1	5	38	71	2,372	436	1,783	153
City of South San Francisco	63,006	152	5	13	54	80	1,479	458	808	213
City of San Rafael	55,832	236	3	34	82	117	1,603	312	1,030	261
Total area actually reporting	100.0%	22,922	269	1,026	10,405	11,222	134,662	28,406	83,973	22,283
Rate per 100,000 inhabitants		529	6.2	23.7	240.1	259.0	3,107.8	655.6	1,938.0	514.3
Oakland-Fremont-Hayward, CA M.D.	*2,544,121*									
Includes Alameda and Contra Costa Counties										
Total area actually reporting	100.0%	14,794	197	713	6,436	7,448	81,003	19,492	45,603	15,908
Rate per 100,000 inhabitants		581.5	7.7	28.0	253.0	292.8	3,183.9	766.2	1,792.5	625.3
San Francisco-San Mateo-Redwood City, CA M.D.	*1,788,942*									
Includes Marin, San Francisco, and San Mateo Counties										
Total area actually reporting	100.0%	8,128	72	313	3,969	3,774	53,659	8,914	38,370	6,375
Rate per 100,000 inhabitants		454.3	4.0	17.5	221.9	211.0	2,999.5	498.3	2,144.8	356.4
San Jose-Sunnyvale-Santa Clara, CA M.S.A.	**1,848,534**									
Includes San Benito and Santa Clara Counties										
City of San Jose	970,252	3,215	20	253	976	1,966	22,081	3,940	12,730	5,411
City of Sunnyvale	134,073	169	0	26	59	84	2,227	407	1,574	246
City of Santa Clara	112,917	182	2	7	62	111	3,016	481	2,210	325
City of Mountain View	72,321	168	1	4	46	117	1,458	177	1,179	102
City of Milpitas	68,371	91	0	9	53	29	1,981	264	1,461	256
City of Palo Alto	60,288	58	0	4	39	15	1,346	217	1,080	49
City of Cupertino	54,403	60	0	6	17	37	981	216	728	37
Total area actually reporting	100.0%	4,890	26	401	1,481	2,982	41,710	7,781	26,669	7,260
Rate per 100,000 inhabitants		264.5	1.4	21.7	80.1	161.3	2,256.4	420.9	1,442.7	392.7
San Luis Obispo-Paso Robles, CA M.S.A.	**268,735**									
Includes San Luis Obispo County										
City of San Luis Obispo	44,008	126	0	27	35	64	1,686	372	1,260	54
City of Paso Robles	29,089	95	0	13	15	67	1,006	268	688	50
Total area actually reporting	100.0%	717	6	82	93	536	6,180	1,533	4,329	318
Rate per 100,000 inhabitants		266.8	2.2	30.5	34.6	199.5	2,299.7	570.5	1,610.9	118.3
Santa Barbara-Santa Maria-Goleta, CA M.S.A.	**407,452**									
Includes Santa Barbara County										
City of Santa Barbara	85,967	341	3	28	92	218	2,528	487	1,939	102
City of Santa Maria	87,803	771	3	32	152	584	2,319	506	1,496	317
City of Goleta	29,605	57	0	5	11	41	407	121	277	9
Total area actually reporting	100.0%	1,841	11	131	313	1,386	8,703	1,975	6,131	597
Rate per 100,000 inhabitants		451.8	2.7	32.2	76.8	340.2	2,136.0	484.7	1,504.7	146.5
Santa Cruz-Watsonville, CA M.S.A.	**256,048**									
Includes Santa Cruz County										
City of Santa Cruz	56,860	553	6	31	120	396	2,936	495	2,262	179
City of Watsonville	51,488	327	1	13	98	215	1,539	271	1,091	177
Total area actually reporting	100.0%	1,313	14	68	269	962	8,267	1,737	5,874	656
Rate per 100,000 inhabitants		512.8	5.5	26.6	105.1	375.7	3,228.7	678.4	2,294.1	256.2

Table 6.   Crime, by Metropolitan Statistical Area, 2010—*Continued*

(Number, percent, rate per 100,000 population)

Area	Population	Violent crime	Murder and non-negligent man-slaughter	Forcible rape	Robbery	Aggravated assault	Property crime	Burglary	Larceny-theft	Motor vehicle theft
Santa Fe, NM M.S.A.	**151,535**									
Includes Santa Fe County										
City of Santa Fe	76,442	367	8	39	81	239	4,349	2,392	1,781	176
Total area actually reporting	100.0%	541	10	46	94	391	5,944	3,302	2,395	247
Rate per 100,000 inhabitants		357.0	6.6	30.4	62.0	258.0	3,922.5	2,179.0	1,580.5	163.0
Santa Rosa-Petaluma, CA M.S.A.	**472,897**									
Includes Sonoma County										
City of Santa Rosa	158,182	767	2	56	166	543	4,096	757	3,041	298
City of Petaluma	55,168	197	1	13	19	164	778	117	604	57
Total area actually reporting	100.0%	1,876	6	126	279	1,465	8,828	1,902	6,273	653
Rate per 100,000 inhabitants		396.7	1.3	26.6	59.0	309.8	1,866.8	402.2	1,326.5	138.1
Savannah, GA M.S.A.	**337,256**									
Includes Bryan, Chatham, and Effingham Counties										
City of Savannah-Chatham Metropolitan	210,744	843	20	30	454	339	9,202	2,552	6,026	624
Total area actually reporting	100.0%	1,155	22	69	522	542	12,479	3,368	8,284	827
Rate per 100,000 inhabitants		342.5	6.5	20.5	154.8	160.7	3,700.2	998.6	2,456.3	245.2
Scranton Wilkes-Barre, PA M.S.A.	**551,176**									
Includes Lackawanna, Luzerne, and Wyoming Counties										
City of Scranton	71,920	234	1	23	103	107	2,422	675	1,631	116
City of Wilkes-Barre	40,970	196	2	13	1	11	70	1,814	352	1,373 89
Total area actually reporting	97.2%	1,286	12	118	332	824	12,050	2,503	9,006	541
Estimated total	100.0%	1,317	12	120	340	845	12,337	2,549	9,236	552
Rate per 100,000 inhabitants		238.9	2.2	21.8	61.7	153.3	2,238.3	462.5	1,675.7	100.1
Seattle-Tacoma-Bellevue, WA M.S.A.	**3,434,812**									
Includes the Metropolitan Divisions of Seattle-Bellevue-Everett and Tacoma										
City of Seattle	620,195	3,515	19	96	1,429	1,971	33,186	6,449	23,284	3,453
City of Tacoma	199,595	1,700	14	141	535	1,010	12,670	2,893	7,741	2,036
City of Bellevue	127,735	138	0	10	59	69	3,769	657	2,905	207
City of Everett	99,387	535	5	76	181	273	7,672	994	5,536	1,142
City of Kent	85,768	501	2	67	157	275	4,464	1,018	2,665	781
City of Renton	62,968	280	0	38	112	130	4,114	847	2,673	594
City of Auburn	64,139	235	3	15	79	138	3,828	725	2,533	570
Total area actually reporting	100.0%	12,128	79	1,152	4,098	6,799	134,157	28,407	89,667	16,083
Rate per 100,000 inhabitants		353	2.3	33.5	119.3	197.9	3,905.8	827.0	2,610.5	468.2
Seattle-Bellevue-Everett, WA M.D.	*2,630,578*									
Includes King and Snohomish Counties										
Total area actually reporting	100.0%	8,331	52	819	3,014	4,446	102,112	20,355	69,850	11,907
Rate per 100,000 inhabitants		316.7	2.0	31.1	114.6	169.0	3,881.7	773.8	2,655.3	452.6
Tacoma, WA M.D.	*804,234*									
Includes Pierce County										
Total area actually reporting	100.0%	3,797	27	333	1,084	2,353	32,045	8,052	19,817	4,176
Rate per 100,000 inhabitants		472.1	3.4	41.4	134.8	292.6	3,984.5	1,001.2	2,464.1	519.3
Sebastian-Vero Beach, FL M.S.A.	**137,445**									
Includes Indian River County										
City of Sebastian	21,063	50	0	6	8	36	553	163	378	12
City of Vero Beach	17,254	72	0	4	22	46	628	179	425	24
Total area actually reporting	100.0%	448	0	27	90	331	4,248	1,193	2,898	157
Rate per 100,000 inhabitants		325.9	0.0	19.6	65.5	240.8	3,090.7	868.0	2,108.5	114.2
Sherman-Denison, TX M.S.A.	**120,587**									
Includes Grayson County										
City of Sherman	38,623	180	5	4	34	137	1,456	311	1,109	36
City of Denison	24,196	77	1	2	13	61	1,109	215	858	36
Total area actually reporting	100.0%	338	11	21	58	248	3,600	854	2,606	140
Rate per 100,000 inhabitants		280.3	9.1	17.4	48.1	205.7	2,985.4	708.2	2,161.1	116.1
Shreveport-Bossier City, LA M.S.A.	**394,702**									
Includes Bossier, Caddo, and De Soto Parishes										
City of Shreveport	199,900	1,533	26	121	355	1,031	9,459	2,616	6,317	526
City of Bossier City	64,232	397	1	27	71	298	2,663	480	2,036	147
Total area actually reporting	98.3%	2,440	33	168	443	1,796	14,352	3,691	9,852	809
Estimated total	100.0%	2,476	33	170	448	1,825	14,656	3,753	10,083	820
Rate per 100,000 inhabitants		627.3	8.4	43.1	113.5	462.4	3,713.2	950.8	2,554.6	207.8

Table 6.   Crime, by Metropolitan Statistical Area, 2010—*Continued*

(Number, percent, rate per 100,000 population)

Area	Population	Violent crime	Murder and non-negligent man-slaughter	Forcible rape	Robbery	Aggravated assault	Property crime	Burglary	Larceny-theft	Motor vehicle theft
Sioux City, IA-NE-SD M.S.A.	**145,711**									
Includes Woodbury County, IA; Dakota and Dixon Counties, NE; and Union County, SD										
City of Sioux City, IA	83,494	285	0	22	32	231	3,103	618	2,333	152
Total area actually reporting	96.8%	343	0	26	35	282	3,753	736	2,834	183
Estimated total	100.0%	348	0	27	35	286	3,827	748	2,893	186
Rate per 100,000 inhabitants		238.8	0.0	18.5	24.0	196.3	2,626.4	513.3	1,985.4	127.6
Sioux Falls, SD M.S.A.	**242,527**									
Includes Lincoln, McCook, Minnehaha, and Turner Counties										
City of Sioux Falls	160,679	482	3	96	55	328	4,854	989	3,637	228
Total area actually reporting	96.9%	552	3	103	58	388	5,654	1,271	4,110	273
Estimated total	100.0%	562	3	105	58	396	5,737	1,294	4,166	277
Rate per 100,000 inhabitants		231.7	1.2	43.3	23.9	163.3	2,365.5	533.5	1,717.7	114.2
South Bend-Mishawaka, IN-MI M.S.A.	**318,113**									
Includes St. Joseph County, IN and Cass County, MI										
City of South Bend, IN	104,182	746	6	52	339	349	5,929	2,216	3,411	302
City of Mishawaka, IN	50,632	142	0	15	52	75	3,065	523	2,386	156
Total area actually reporting	96.2%	1,073	8	104	419	542	12,053	3,624	7,859	570
Estimated total	100.0%	1,109	8	108	427	566	12,382	3,694	8,093	595
Rate per 100,000 inhabitants		348.6	2.5	34.0	134.2	177.9	3,892.3	1,161.2	2,544.1	187.0
Spartanburg, SC M.S.A.	**290,534**									
Includes Spartanburg County										
City of Spartanburg	40,448	646	6	18	129	493	3,087	679	2,207	201
Total area actually reporting	99.8%	1,428	15	84	254	1,075	10,190	2,549	6,913	728
Estimated total	100.0%	1,432	15	84	255	1,078	10,216	2,554	6,933	729
Rate per 100,000 inhabitants		492.9	5.2	28.9	87.8	371.0	3,516.3	879.1	2,386.3	250.9
Spokane, WA M.S.A.	**472,494**									
Includes Spokane County										
City of Spokane	203,272	1,270	6	80	432	752	15,042	2,859	10,174	2,009
Total area actually reporting	100.0%	1,635	12	147	526	950	23,810	5,024	15,968	2,818
Rate per 100,000 inhabitants		346.0	2.5	31.1	111.3	201.1	5,039.2	1,063.3	3,379.5	596.4
Springfield, IL M.S.A.²	**206,661**									
Includes Menard and Sangamon Counties²										
City of Springfield²	117,383	1,452	7	104	338	1,003	7,567	2,167	5,160	240
Total area actually reporting	89.8%	1,728	9	139	367	1,213	9,102	2,693	6,112	297
Estimated total	100.0%	1,768	9	145	375	1,239	9,495	2,777	6,403	315
Rate per 100,000 inhabitants		855.5	4.4	70.2	181.5	599.5	4,594.5	1,343.7	3,098.3	152.4
Springfield, MA M.S.A.	**693,388**									
Includes Franklin, Hampden, and Hampshire Counties										
City of Springfield	154,314	2,090	16	129	587	1,358	7,547	2,660	4,015	872
Total area actually reporting	98.0%	3,969	26	295	870	2,778	20,934	6,071	13,149	1,714
Estimated total	100.0%	4,014	26	298	878	2,812	21,214	6,141	13,341	1,732
Rate per 100,000 inhabitants		578.9	3.7	43.0	126.6	405.5	3,059.5	885.7	1,924.0	249.8
Springfield, MO M.S.A.	**434,773**									
Includes Christian, Dallas, Greene, Polk, and Webster Counties										
City of Springfield	157,110	1,328	11	120	310	887	15,216	2,188	12,024	1,004
Total area actually reporting	100.0%	1,952	13	148	352	1,439	20,753	3,643	15,834	1,276
Rate per 100,000 inhabitants		449.0	3.0	34.0	81.0	331.0	4,773.3	837.9	3,641.9	293.5
Springfield, OH M.S.A.	**138,838**									
Includes Clark County										
City of Springfield	61,540	480	4	37	216	223	4,494	1,501	2,723	270
Total area actually reporting	99.8%	500	4	40	220	236	5,664	1,764	3,596	304
Estimated total	100.0%	500	4	40	220	236	5,672	1,766	3,602	304
Rate per 100,000 inhabitants		360.1	2.9	28.8	158.5	170.0	4,085.3	1,272.0	2,594.4	219.0
State College, PA M.S.A.	**148,015**									
Includes Centre County										
City of State College	54,649	74	0	9	16	49	892	111	769	12
Total area actually reporting	100.0%	158	0	24	34	100	2,455	360	2,048	47
Rate per 100,000 inhabitants		106.7	0.0	16.2	23.0	67.6	1,658.6	243.2	1,383.6	31.8

² Because of changes in the state/local agency's reporting practices, figures are not comparable to previous years' data.

Table 6.   Crime, by Metropolitan Statistical Area, 2010—*Continued*

(Number, percent, rate per 100,000 population)

Area	Population	Violent crime	Murder and non-negligent man-slaughter	Forcible rape	Robbery	Aggravated assault	Property crime	Burglary	Larceny-theft	Motor vehicle theft
St. Cloud, MN M.S.A.[3]	**191,426**									
Includes Benton and Stearns Counties[3]										
City of St. Cloud[3]	67,942		3		43	134	2,542	347	2,102	93
Total area actually reporting	100.0%		3		48	189	4,226	559	3,527	140
Rate per 100,000 inhabitants			1.6		25.1	98.7	2,207.6	292.0	1,842.5	73.1
Steubenville-Weirton, OH-WV M.S.A.	**120,642**									
Includes Jefferson County, OH and Brooke and Hancock Counties, WV										
City of Steubenville, OH	18,522	75	2	5	34	34	1,098	190	872	36
City of Weirton, WV	18,717	18	1	1	5	11	196	46	143	7
Total area actually reporting	90.3%	169	6	14	45	104	1,961	461	1,411	89
Estimated total	100.0%	196	6	17	52	121	2,314	530	1,682	102
Rate per 100,000 inhabitants		162.5	5.0	14.1	43.1	100.3	1,918.1	439.3	1,394.2	84.5
St. George, UT M.S.A.	**139,058**									
Includes Washington County										
City of St. George	73,086	68	0	12	10	46	1,616	315	1,224	77
Total area actually reporting	100.0%	151	0	23	14	114	2,630	551	1,946	133
Rate per 100,000 inhabitants		108.6	0.0	16.5	10.1	82.0	1,891.3	396.2	1,399.4	95.6
St. Joseph, MO-KS M.S.A.	**126,176**									
Includes Doniphan County, KS and Andrew, Buchanan, and De Kalb Counties, MO										
City of St. Joseph, MO	75,922	305	5	20	70	210	3,605	870	2,547	188
Total area actually reporting	100.0%	376	7	28	75	266	4,411	1,136	3,043	232
Rate per 100,000 inhabitants		298.0	5.5	22.2	59.4	210.8	3,495.9	900.3	2,411.7	183.9
St. Louis, MO-IL M.S.A.[2]	**2,822,879**									
Includes Bond, Calhoun, Clinton, Jersey, Macoupin, Madison, Monroe, and St. Clair Counties, IL[2] and Franklin, Jefferson, Lincoln, St. Charles, St. Louis, Warren, and Washington Counties and St. Louis City, MO										
City of St. Louis, MO	355,151	6,205	144	188	2,125	3,748	27,324	6,705	16,356	4,263
City of St. Charles, MO	65,729	126	2	8	35	81	1,891	323	1,517	51
Total area actually reporting	95.3%	13,754	216	699	3,513	9,326	86,392	19,083	59,196	8,113
Estimated total	100.0%	14,040	219	733	3,582	9,506	89,188	19,612	61,327	8,249
Rate per 100,000 inhabitants		497.4	7.8	26.0	126.9	336.7	3,159.5	694.8	2,172.5	292.2
Stockton, CA M.S.A.	**686,072**									
Includes San Joaquin County										
City of Stockton	292,047	4,033	49	107	1,413	2,464	16,177	4,482	9,654	2,041
Total area actually reporting	100.0%	5,524	63	163	1,849	3,449	28,296	7,666	17,303	3,327
Rate per 100,000 inhabitants		805.2	9.2	23.8	269.5	502.7	4,124.3	1,117.4	2,522.0	484.9
Sumter, SC M.S.A.	**104,569**									
Includes Sumter County										
City of Sumter	38,228	459	4	15	88	352	2,747	879	1,760	108
Total area actually reporting	100.0%	741	6	34	177	524	4,955	1,370	3,290	295
Rate per 100,000 inhabitants		708.6	5.7	32.5	169.3	501.1	4,738.5	1,310.1	3,146.2	282.1
Syracuse, NY M.S.A.	**638,467**									
Includes Madison, Onondaga, and Oswego Counties										
City of Syracuse	136,284	1,291	15	68	377	831	5,708	2,174	3,167	367
Total area actually reporting	98.7%	1,855	22	144	505	1,184	15,923	4,013	11,245	665
Estimated total	100.0%	1,869	22	145	510	1,192	16,082	4,038	11,374	670
Rate per 100,000 inhabitants		292.7	3.4	22.7	79.9	186.7	2,518.8	632.5	1,781.5	104.9
Tallahassee, FL M.S.A.	**363,918**									
Includes Gadsden, Jefferson, Leon, and Wakulla Counties										
City of Tallahassee	174,516	1,802	13	130	492	1,167	8,579	2,920	5,310	349
Total area actually reporting	99.8%	2,817	19	183	590	2,025	13,168	4,293	8,322	553
Estimated total	100.0%	2,820	19	183	591	2,027	13,190	4,298	8,338	554
Rate per 100,000 inhabitants		774.9	5.2	50.3	162.4	557.0	3,624.4	1,181.0	2,291.2	152.2
Tampa-St. Petersburg-Clearwater, FL M.S.A.	**2,783,954**									
Includes Hernando, Hillsborough, Pasco, and Pinellas Counties										
City of Tampa	347,830	2,170	27	47	684	1,412	11,453	3,131	7,484	838
City of St. Petersburg	243,666	2,758	13	105	752	1,888	13,815	3,564	9,015	1,236
City of Clearwater	105,647	775	5	35	245	490	4,338	777	3,360	201
City of Largo	73,019	506	3	39	131	333	3,347	527	2,668	152
Total area actually reporting	100.0%	13,921	119	740	3,506	9,556	94,297	23,602	65,063	5,632
Rate per 100,000 inhabitants		500.0	4.3	26.6	125.9	343.3	3,387.2	847.8	2,337.1	202.3

[2] Because of changes in the state/local agency's reporting practices, figures are not comparable to previous years' data.

[3] The data collection methodology for the offense of forcible rape used by the Minnesota state UCR Program (with the exception of Minneapolis and St. Paul, Minnesota) does not comply with national UCR Program guidelines. Consequently, its figures for forcible rape and violent crime (of which forcible rape is a part) are not published in this table.

Table 6. Crime, by Metropolitan Statistical Area, 2010—*Continued*

(Number, percent, rate per 100,000 population)

Area	Population	Violent crime	Murder and non-negligent man-slaughter	Forcible rape	Robbery	Aggravated assault	Property crime	Burglary	Larceny-theft	Motor vehicle theft
Texarkana, TX-Texarkana, AR M.S.A.	**138,018**									
Includes Miller County, AR and Bowie County, TX										
City of Texarkana, TX	37,220	527	3	26	98	400	2,350	647	1,592	111
City of Texarkana, AR	30,488	298	0	19	51	228	1,935	425	1,389	121
Total area actually reporting	90.3%	969	4	54	159	752	5,445	1,476	3,647	322
Estimated total	100.0%	1,020	4	59	162	795	5,730	1,598	3,790	342
Rate per 100,000 inhabitants		739.0	2.9	42.7	117.4	576.0	4,151.6	1,157.8	2,746.0	247.8
Toledo, OH M.S.A.[4]	**671,876**									
Includes Fulton, Lucas, Ottawa, and Wood Counties										
City of Toledo[4]	315,647	2,854	23	140	1,097	1,594		7,287		1,197
Total area actually reporting	94.9%	3,191	27	182	1,184	1,798		8,855		1,463
Estimated total	100.0%	3,246	27	190	1,205	1,824		9,050		1,496
Rate per 100,000 inhabitants		483.1	4.0	28.3	179.3	271.5		1,347.0		222.7
Topeka, KS M.S.A.	**233,079**									
Includes Jackson, Jefferson, Osage, Shawnee, and Wabaunsee Counties										
City of Topeka	125,306	697	14	51	222	410	7,506	1,598	5,404	504
Total area actually reporting	97.8%	900	14	64	230	592	9,769	2,168	6,962	639
Estimated total	100.0%	913	14	66	232	601	9,889	2,189	7,054	646
Rate per 100,000 inhabitants		391.7	6.0	28.3	99.5	257.9	4,242.8	939.2	3,026.4	277.2
Trenton-Ewing, NJ M.S.A.	**370,040**									
Includes Mercer County										
City of Trenton	83,552	1,198	15	13	500	670	2,516	865	1,289	362
City of Ewing Township	36,612	121	2	1	31	87	710	182	466	62
Total area actually reporting	100.0%	1,655	20	24	684	927	7,699	1,871	5,253	575
Rate per 100,000 inhabitants		447.2	5.4	6.5	184.8	250.5	2,080.6	505.6	1,419.6	155.4
Tucson, AZ M.S.A.[4]	**988,683**									
Includes Pima County										
City of Tucson[4]	527,107	3,331	51	158	1,088	2,034		5,002		3,433
Total area actually reporting	100.0%	4,208	79	231	1,331	2,567		7,787		4,600
Rate per 100,000 inhabitants		425.6	8.0	23.4	134.6	259.6		787.6		465.3
Tulsa, OK M.S.A.	**946,096**									
Includes Creek, Okmulgee, Osage, Pawnee, Rogers, Tulsa, and Wagoner Counties										
City of Tulsa	393,412	4,304	54	252	1,381	2,617	21,355	7,146	11,857	2,352
Total area actually reporting	100.0%	5,660	61	400	1,495	3,704	32,634	9,975	19,482	3,177
Rate per 100,000 inhabitants		598.2	6.4	42.3	158.0	391.5	3,449.3	1,054.3	2,059.2	335.8
Tuscaloosa, AL M.S.A.	**214,600**									
Includes Greene, Hale, and Tuscaloosa Counties										
City of Tuscaloosa	95,570	449	7	31	190	221	4,828	1,462	3,188	178
Total area actually reporting	96.0%	904	11	63	262	568	8,394	2,590	5,405	399
Estimated total	100.0%	927	11	65	267	584	8,621	2,650	5,557	414
Rate per 100,000 inhabitants		432.0	5.1	30.3	124.4	272.1	4,017.2	1,234.9	2,589.5	192.9
Tyler, TX M.S.A.	**207,175**									
Includes Smith County										
City of Tyler	100,125	644	6	44	99	495	5,091	1,040	3,828	223
Total area actually reporting	99.0%	857	13	112	128	604	7,605	1,748	5,459	398
Estimated total	100.0%	863	13	113	129	608	7,674	1,762	5,510	402
Rate per 100,000 inhabitants		416.6	6.3	54.5	62.3	293.5	3,704.1	850.5	2,659.6	194.0
Utica-Rome, NY M.S.A.	**289,389**									
Includes Herkimer and Oneida Counties										
City of Utica	57,153	416	2	25	146	243	2,717	577	2,059	81
City of Rome	32,930	40	1	5	8	26	648	158	464	26
Total area actually reporting	98.5%	747	7	60	180	500	6,820	1,469	5,163	188
Estimated total	100.0%	754	7	60	183	504	6,906	1,482	5,233	191
Rate per 100,000 inhabitants		260.5	2.4	20.7	63.2	174.2	2,386.4	512.1	1,808.3	66.0
Valdosta, GA M.S.A.	**133,042**									
Includes Brooks, Echols, Lanier, and Lowndes Counties										
City of Valdosta	51,089	270	3	17	81	169	2,633	856	1,665	112
Total area actually reporting	96.5%	458	5	33	99	321	4,619	1,433	2,940	246
Estimated total	100.0%	478	5	34	105	334	4,814	1,473	3,082	259
Rate per 100,000 inhabitants		359.3	3.8	25.6	78.9	251.0	3,618.4	1,107.2	2,316.6	194.7

[4] The FBI determined that the agency did not follow national Uniform Crime Reporting (UCR) Program guidelines for reporting an offense. Consequently, this figure is not included in this table.

Table 6. Crime, by Metropolitan Statistical Area, 2010—*Continued*

(Number, percent, rate per 100,000 population)

Area	Population	Violent crime	Murder and non-negligent man-slaughter	Forcible rape	Robbery	Aggravated assault	Property crime	Burglary	Larceny-theft	Motor vehicle theft
Vallejo-Fairfield, CA M.S.A.[2]	**407,939**									
Includes Solano County										
City of Vallejo[2]	114,258	822	17	59	458	288	5,101	2,249	1,675	1,177
City of Fairfield	104,202	502	8	18	185	291	3,395	757	2,169	469
Total area actually reporting	100.0%	1,929	33	143	806	947	12,522	3,884	6,494	2,144
Rate per 100,000 inhabitants		472.9	8.1	35.1	197.6	232.1	3,069.6	952.1	1,591.9	525.6
Victoria, TX M.S.A.	**115,411**									
Includes Calhoun, Goliad, and Victoria Counties										
City of Victoria	63,215	388	7	37	75	269	3,320	788	2,426	106
Total area actually reporting	100.0%	654	8	63	86	497	4,447	1,108	3,184	155
Rate per 100,000 inhabitants		566.7	6.9	54.6	74.5	430.6	3,853.2	960.0	2,758.8	134.3
Vineland-Millville-Bridgeton, NJ M.S.A.	**159,934**									
Includes Cumberland County										
City of Vineland	59,924	223	3	6	83	131	2,127	515	1,536	76
City of Millville	29,497	169	1	7	58	103	1,216	265	919	32
City of Bridgeton	25,243	320	4	1	126	189	1,047	360	637	50
Total area actually reporting	100.0%	791	10	15	280	486	5,273	1,430	3,652	191
Rate per 100,000 inhabitants		494.6	6.3	9.4	175.1	303.9	3,297.0	894.1	2,283.4	119.4
Virginia Beach-Norfolk-Newport News, VA-NC M.S.A.	**1,690,968**									
Includes Currituck County, NC and Gloucester, Isle of Wight, James City, Mathews, Surry, and York Counties and Chesapeake, Hampton, Newport News, Norfolk, Poquoson, Portsmouth, Suffolk, Virginia Beach, and Williamsburg Cities, VA										
City of Virginia Beach, VA	435,873	820	14	55	422	329	13,232	2,151	10,431	650
City of Norfolk, VA	234,100	1,445	34	90	596	725	13,159	2,158	10,079	922
City of Newport News, VA	195,225	953	20	83	366	484	6,558	1,247	4,877	434
City of Hampton, VA	144,545	395	14	29	175	177	5,334	759	4,230	345
City of Portsmouth, VA	99,576	609	14	17	265	313	5,474	1,318	3,885	271
Total area actually reporting	100.0%	5,697	112	345	2,250	2,990	58,889	10,249	45,302	3,338
Rate per 100,000 inhabitants		336.9	6.6	20.4	133.1	176.8	3,482.6	606.1	2,679.1	197.4
Visalia-Porterville, CA M.S.A.	**435,945**									
Includes Tulare County										
City of Visalia	125,036	578	6	26	176	370	5,334	1,237	3,497	600
City of Porterville	52,777	222	4	11	59	148	1,852	449	1,154	249
Total area actually reporting	100.0%	2,075	35	100	444	1,496	15,757	3,934	9,649	2,174
Rate per 100,000 inhabitants		476.0	8.0	22.9	101.8	343.2	3,614.4	902.4	2,213.4	498.7
Waco, TX M.S.A.	**234,649**									
Includes McLennan County										
City of Waco	127,039	838	5	51	195	587	6,439	1,856	4,373	210
Total area actually reporting	100.0%	1,274	9	119	241	905	9,613	2,533	6,715	365
Rate per 100,000 inhabitants		542.9	3.8	50.7	102.7	385.7	4,096.8	1,079.5	2,861.7	155.6
Warner Robins, GA M.S.A.	**133,908**									
Includes Houston County										
City of Warner Robins	60,825	338	4	19	94	221	3,547	804	2,568	175
Total area actually reporting	100.0%	474	8	30	119	317	5,036	1,155	3,628	253
Rate per 100,000 inhabitants		354.0	6.0	22.4	88.9	236.7	3,760.8	862.5	2,709.3	188.9
Washington-Arlington-Alexandria, DC-VA-MD-WV M.S.A.	**5,573,842**									
Includes the Metropolitan Divisions of Bethesda-Rockville-Frederick, MD and Washington-Arlington-Alexandria, DC-VA-MD-WV										
City of Washington, D.C.	601,723	7,468	132	184	3,914	3,238	27,138	4,224	18,050	4,864
City of Alexandria, VA	152,801	276	2	21	125	128	3,242	317	2,639	286
City of Frederick, MD	60,686	454	2	16	162	274	1,712	262	1,363	87
Total area actually reporting	100.0%	21,179	294	993	10,012	9,880	142,169	21,961	103,545	16,663
Rate per 100,000 inhabitants		380.0	5.3	17.8	179.6	177.3	2,550.6	394.0	1,857.7	298.9
Bethesda-Rockville-Frederick, MD M.D.	***1,219,883***									
Includes Frederick and Montgomery Counties										
Total area actually reporting	100.0%	2,535	23	155	1,178	1,179	24,551	4,016	18,809	1,726
Rate per 100,000 inhabitants		207.8	1.9	12.7	96.6	96.6	2,012.6	329.2	1,541.9	141.5

Table 6. Crime, by Metropolitan Statistical Area, 2010—*Continued*

(Number, percent, rate per 100,000 population)

Area	Population	Violent crime	Murder and non-negligent man-slaughter	Forcible rape	Robbery	Aggravated assault	Property crime	Burglary	Larceny-theft	Motor vehicle theft
Washington-Arlington-Alexandria, DC-VA-MD-WV M.D.	*4,353,959*									
Includes District of Columbia; Calvert, Charles, and Prince George's Counties, MD; Arlington, Clarke, Fairfax, Fauquier, Loudoun, Prince William, Spotsylvania, Stafford, and Warren Counties and Alexandria, Fairfax, Falls Church, Fredericksburg, Manassas, and Manassas Park Cities, VA; and Jefferson County, WV										
Total area actually reporting	100.0%	18,644	271	838	8,834	8,701	117,618	17,945	84,736	14,937
Rate per 100,000 inhabitants		428.2	6.2	19.2	202.9	199.8	2,701.4	412.2	1,946.2	343.1
Waterloo-Cedar Falls, IA M.S.A.	**166,624**									
Includes Black Hawk, Bremer, and Grundy Counties										
City of Waterloo	67,203	435	3	33	70	329	2,558	812	1,635	111
City of Cedar Falls	39,350	71	1	10	3	57	684	113	552	19
Total area actually reporting	100.0%	629	4	62	74	489	3,859	1,103	2,593	163
Rate per 100,000 inhabitants		377.5	2.4	37.2	44.4	293.5	2,316.0	662.0	1,556.2	97.8
Wausau, WI M.S.A.	**132,256**									
Includes Marathon County										
City of Wausau	38,429	102	0	19	14	69	1,187	267	894	26
Total area actually reporting	100.0%	171	0	27	20	124	2,369	506	1,802	61
Rate per 100,000 inhabitants		129.3	0.0	20.4	15.1	93.8	1,791.2	382.6	1,362.5	46.1
Wenatchee-East Wenatchee, WA M.S.A.	**110,709**									
Includes Chelan and Douglas Counties										
City of Wenatchee	30,287	80	1	16	10	53	1,181	150	971	60
City of East Wenatchee	12,620	29	0	5	8	16	536	63	446	27
Total area actually reporting	100.0%	185	1	48	25	111	2,986	520	2,309	157
Rate per 100,000 inhabitants		167.1	0.9	43.4	22.6	100.3	2,697.2	469.7	2,085.6	141.8
Wichita, KS M.S.A.	**621,313**									
Includes Butler, Harvey, Sedgwick, and Sumner Counties										
City of Wichita	376,880	3,026	16	246	481	2,283	18,241	4,241	12,472	1,528
Total area actually reporting	99.5%	3,605	18	328	510	2,749	23,536	5,375	16,357	1,804
Estimated total	100.0%	3,613	18	329	511	2,755	23,606	5,387	16,411	1,808
Rate per 100,000 inhabitants		581.5	2.9	53.0	82.2	443.4	3,799.4	867.0	2,641.3	291.0
Wichita Falls, TX M.S.A.	**146,544**									
Includes Archer, Clay, and Wichita Counties										
City of Wichita Falls	100,716	463	7	44	133	279	5,314	1,317	3,710	287
Total area actually reporting	100.0%	529	7	47	140	335	6,139	1,591	4,244	304
Rate per 100,000 inhabitants		361.0	4.8	32.1	95.5	228.6	4,189.2	1,085.7	2,896.1	207.4
Williamsport, PA M.S.A.	**117,110**									
Includes Lycoming County										
City of Williamsport	29,320	102	2	12	55	33	1,220	232	954	34
Total area actually reporting	100.0%	197	2	28	67	100	2,329	462	1,796	71
Rate per 100,000 inhabitants		168.2	1.7	23.9	57.2	85.4	1,988.7	394.5	1,533.6	60.6
Wilmington, NC M.S.A.	**363,901**									
Includes Brunswick, New Hanover, and Pender Counties										
City of Wilmington	102,649	724	5	47	282	390	5,706	1,447	3,781	478
Total area actually reporting	98.2%	1,304	11	101	370	822	13,348	4,036	8,511	801
Estimated total	100.0%	1,324	11	102	375	836	13,623	4,101	8,707	815
Rate per 100,000 inhabitants		363.8	3.0	28.0	103.1	229.7	3,743.6	1,127.0	2,392.7	224.0
Winchester, VA-WV M.S.A.	**127,037**									
Includes Frederick County and Winchester City, VA and Hampshire County, WV										
City of Winchester, VA	26,698	56	0	8	20	28	1,125	146	956	23
Total area actually reporting	99.8%	210	2	58	44	106	2,924	623	2,167	134
Estimated total	100.0%	211	2	58	44	107	2,934	625	2,175	134
Rate per 100,000 inhabitants		166.1	1.6	45.7	34.6	84.2	2,309.6	492.0	1,712.1	105.5
Winston-Salem, NC M.S.A.	**491,903**									
Includes Davie, Forsyth, Stokes, and Yadkin Counties										
City of Winston-Salem	232,928	1,517	11	96	449	961	13,349	4,482	8,225	642
Total area actually reporting	99.4%	2,239	17	149	505	1,568	20,481	6,517	13,010	954
Estimated total	100.0%	2,248	17	150	507	1,574	20,594	6,544	13,090	960
Rate per 100,000 inhabitants		457.0	3.5	30.5	103.1	320.0	4,186.6	1,330.3	2,661.1	195.2

Table 6. Crime, by Metropolitan Statistical Area, 2010—*Continued*

(Number, percent, rate per 100,000 population)

Area	Population	Violent crime	Murder and non-negligent man-slaughter	Forcible rape	Robbery	Aggravated assault	Property crime	Burglary	Larceny-theft	Motor vehicle theft
Worcester, MA M.S.A...	**800,461**									
Includes Worcester County										
City of Worcester	181,908	1,744	7	19	368	1,350	6,190	1,910	3,687	593
Total area actually reporting	97.6%	3,706	14	192	574	2,926	16,824	4,658	11,025	1,141
Estimated total...	100.0%	3,769	14	196	585	2,974	17,222	4,757	11,298	1,167
Rate per 100,000 inhabitants...................................		470.9	1.7	24.5	73.1	371.5	2,151.5	594.3	1,411.4	145.8
Yakima, WA M.S.A...	**239,998**									
Includes Yakima County										
City of Yakima	85,802	490	12	46	144	288	5,555	1,464	3,501	590
Total area actually reporting	100.0%	826	24	105	233	464	11,139	3,357	6,563	1,219
Rate per 100,000 inhabitants...................................		344.2	10.0	43.8	97.1	193.3	4,641.3	1,398.8	2,734.6	507.9
York-Hanover, PA M.S.A....	**436,009**									
Includes York County										
City of York	40,553	421	5	37	248	131	2,071	555	1,330	186
City of Hanover	15,234	32	0	3	10	19	484	34	439	11
Total area actually reporting	100.0%	909	11	100	388	410	9,125	1,425	7,257	443
Rate per 100,000 inhabitants...................................		208.5	2.5	22.9	89.0	94.0	2,092.8	326.8	1,664.4	101.6
Youngstown-Warren-Boardman, OH-PA M.S.A...............	**558,674**									
Includes Mahoning and Trumbull Counties, OH and										
Mercer County, PA										
City of Youngstown, OH..	71,380	694	25	28	235	406	4,431	2,101	1,806	524
City of Warren, OH	42,850	262	4	22	123	113	2,313	1,068	1,099	146
City of Boardman, OH	38,524	63	0	6	44	13	1,886	340	1,466	80
Total area actually reporting	97.9%	1,669	33	134	548	954	18,355	6,214	10,992	1,149
Estimated total...	100.0%	1,688	33	137	555	963	18,675	6,280	11,235	1,160
Rate per 100,000 inhabitants...................................		302.1	5.9	24.5	99.3	172.4	3,342.7	1,124.1	2,011.0	207.6
Yuba City, CA M.S.A....	**168,270**									
Includes Sutter and Yuba Counties										
City of Yuba City	62,694	216	2	22	51	141	1,783	409	1,222	152
Total area actually reporting	100.0%	609	7	54	108	440	4,174	1,136	2,543	495
Rate per 100,000 inhabitants...................................		361.9	4.2	32.1	64.2	261.5	2,480.5	675.1	1,511.3	294.2
Yuma, AZ M.S.A...	**190,887**									
Includes Yuma County										
City of Yuma	88,291	550	3	24	56	467	3,060	815	2,058	187
Total area actually reporting	87.0%	650	8	32	65	545	4,228	1,280	2,659	289
Estimated total...	100.0%	710	9	37	78	586	5,029	1,448	3,242	339
Rate per 100,000 inhabitants...................................		371.9	4.7	19.4	40.9	307.0	2,634.5	758.6	1,698.4	177.6

Table 7.   Offense Analysis, 2006–2010

(Number)

Classification	2006[1]	2007[1]	2008[1]	2009[1]	2010
Murder...	**17,309**	**17,128**	**16,465**	**15,399**	**14,748**
Forcible rape..	**94,472**	**92,160**	**90,750**	**89,241**	**84,767**
Robbery[2]..	**449,246**	**447,324**	**443,563**	**408,742**	**367,832**
By location:					
Street/highway..	200,062	195,734	191,050	174,886	158,765
Commercial house	61,266	62,333	61,207	55,980	48,638
Gas or service station	12,125	11,825	11,468	9,881	8,520
Convenience store	25,023	25,056	24,394	21,983	19,216
Residence..	64,288	67,841	72,217	69,280	63,562
Bank	9,631	9,298	8,996	8,829	8,007
Miscellaneous...	76,852	75,238	74,231	67,903	61,124
Burglary[2]...	**2,194,993**	**2,190,198**	**2,228,887**	**2,203,313**	**2,159,878**
By location:					
Residence (dwelling):	1,453,002	1,486,405	1,567,682	1,599,047	1,595,717
Residence Night..	413,678	423,995	438,323	445,983	443,717
Residence Day...	708,807	742,403	807,617	819,725	821,897
Residence Unknown	330,517	320,007	321,742	333,339	330,102
Nonresidence (store, office, etc.):	741,991	703,793	661,205	604,266	564,161
Nonresidence Night	308,658	294,958	276,743	255,147	232,840
Nonresidence Day	235,666	228,244	223,303	200,924	192,222
Nonresidence Unknown	197,668	180,591	161,159	148,195	139,100
Larceny-theft (except motor vehicle theft)[2].....	**6,626,363**	**6,591,542**	**6,586,206**	**6,338,095**	**6,185,867**
By type:					
Pocket-picking..	28,854	27,504	27,140	26,631	24,158
Purse-snatching	40,114	38,191	33,314	30,493	28,052
Shoplifting..	875,191	982,402	1,067,655	1,149,406	1,061,394
From motor vehicles (except accessories)	1,757,565	1,712,949	1,714,745	1,727,583	1,633,723
Motor vehicle accessories	640,549	601,158	642,964	573,270	548,245
Bicycles..	231,915	225,130	221,846	212,362	206,053
From buildings..	832,186	791,882	753,450	704,184	697,487
From coin-operated machines............................	35,367	31,145	26,899	26,085	20,248
All others..	2,184,623	2,181,182	2,098,192	1,888,080	1,966,509
By value:					
Over $200..	2,813,554	2,894,212	2,965,832	2,833,851	2,803,066
$50 to $200..	1,479,012	1,476,222	1,465,002	1,443,919	1,417,050
Under $50	2,333,797	2,221,108	2,155,372	2,060,325	1,965,751
Motor vehicle theft..	**1,198,245**	**1,100,472**	**959,059**	**795,652**	**737,142**

[1] The crime figures have been adjusted.

[2] Because of rounding, the number of offenses may not add to the total.

Table 8.   Offenses Known to Law Enforcement, by State and City, 2010

(Number)

State/city	Population	Violent crime	Murder and non-negligent man-slaughter	Forcible rape	Robbery	Aggravated assault	Property crime	Burglary	Larceny-theft	Motor vehicle theft	Arson[1]
ALABAMA											
Abbeville	2,950	21	1	0	0	20	67	19	45	3	
Adamsville	4,796	10	0	3	2	5	294	21	250	23	
Addison	714	0	0	0	0	0	33	3	26	4	
Alabaster	30,781	33	0	0	7	26	515	22	458	35	
Albertville	20,588	81	0	6	13	62	1,112	346	710	56	
Alexander City	15,229	59	1	8	9	41	646	113	522	11	
Aliceville	2,423	12	0	1	0	11	51	10	35	6	
Andalusia[2]	8,946	24	0	3	0	21				11	
Anderson	358	1	0	0	0	1	8	4	4	0	
Anniston[2]	23,703		3	23	76		2,038	831	1,107	100	
Ardmore	1,328	2	0	0	1	1	49	12	30	7	
Argo	2,005	3	0	1	0	2	21	10	8	3	
Ariton	750	2	0	0	0	2	11	2	9	0	
Arley	320	0	0	0	0	0	17	1	14	2	
Ashford	2,146	3	0	1	0	2	88	39	41	8	
Ashland	1,900	3	0	0	0	3	43	4	37	2	
Ashville	2,708	8	0	0	2	6	32	13	19	0	
Athens	24,989	34	0	4	12	18	717	129	564	24	
Atmore	10,182	49	0	2	5	42	335	62	252	21	
Attalla	6,621	60	0	4	4	52	297	65	226	6	0
Auburn	59,651	83	3	4	13	63	1,818	206	1,559	53	
Bayou La Batre	3,253	23	0	1	0	22	172	62	90	20	
Bear Creek	993	7	0	0	0	7	11	0	10	1	
Bessemer	28,881	289	5	18	83	183	2,189	273	1,753	163	
Blountsville	2,042	4	0	0	0	4	96	18	74	4	
Boaz	8,656	10	0	2	1	7	496	69	403	24	
Brantley	912	0	0	0	0	0	0	0	0	0	
Brent	4,361	19	0	1	2	16	106	9	93	4	
Brewton	5,262	95	0	0	1	94	239	24	210	5	
Bridgeport	2,616	1	0	0	0	1	76	7	61	8	
Brilliant	943	3	0	1	1	1	30	1	26	3	
Brookside	1,343	0	0	0	0	0	1	0	0	1	
Brundidge	2,271	9	0	0	1	8	59	23	34	2	
Butler	1,681	14	0	0	2	12	49	25	21	3	
Calera	12,424	24	0	4	4	16	322	23	293	6	
Camden	2,153	2	0	0	0	2	8	1	4	3	
Camp Hill	1,219	15	0	0	0	15	24	1	23	0	
Carbon Hill	2,040	5	0	0	1	4	35	6	25	4	
Carrollton	911	2	0	0	0	2	22	1	19	2	
Cedar Bluff	1,666	11	0	0	1	10	135	21	93	21	
Centre	3,515	3	0	2	0	1	114	18	86	10	
Centreville	2,646	7	0	2	1	4	20	1	15	4	
Chatom	1,153	5	0	0	1	4	19	2	15	2	
Chickasaw	5,948	36	0	4	10	22	345	104	219	22	
Citronelle	3,791	24	0	0	4	20	122	33	81	8	
Clanton2	9,109	47	0	3	8	36			388	11	
Clayhatchee	496	0	0	0	0	0	7	0	5	2	
Clayton	1,396	4	0	0	0	4	6	1	5	0	
Cleveland	1,460	0	0	0	0	0	13	2	11	0	
Clio	2,391	0	0	0	0	0	1	0	0	1	
Coffeeville	340	1	0	0	0	1	4	2	2	0	
Collinsville	2,026	4	0	0	1	3	83	23	54	6	
Columbia	866	1	0	0	0	1	8	0	7	1	
Columbiana	4,210	3	0	0	0	3	108	7	99	2	
Coosada	1,731	1	0	0	0	1	20	1	17	2	
Cottonwood	1,231	3	0	0	0	3	27	7	19	1	
Courtland	767	3	0	0	0	3	9	1	7	1	
Creola	2,100	4	0	1	0	3	79	18	55	6	
Crossville	1,535	0	0	0	0	0	7	0	3	4	
Cullman	15,540	23	0	3	3	17	675	78	571	26	
Dadeville	3,265	37	0	1	0	36	192	8	171	13	
Daleville2	4,561	17	0	3	2	12			174	15	
Daphne	20,018	31	0	0	5	26	453	77	368	8	
Dauphin Island	1,640	3	0	0	0	3	57	27	28	2	
Decatur	57,153	212	4	17	74	117	2,751	682	1,920	149	
Demopolis	7,312	58	0	7	7	44	392	67	313	12	
Dora	2,431	5	0	0	0	5	57	7	47	3	
Dothan	69,134	411	1	29	118	263	3,136	1,011	2,034	91	
Douglas	643	9	0	1	0	8	54	2	49	3	
Eclectic	1,183	6	0	0	1	5	39	11	28	0	
Elba	4,254	21	1	3	2	15	125	30	84	11	
Elberta	1,527	9	0	0	0	9	80	8	64	8	
Enterprise[3]	26,649	124	4	8	23	89				46	

[1] The FBI does not publish arson data unless it receives data from either the agency or the state for all 12 months of the calendar year.

[2] The FBI determined that the agency's data were underreported. Consequently, those data are not included in this table.

[3] The FBI determined that the agency's data were overreported. Consequently, those data are not included in this table.

Table 8. Offenses Known to Law Enforcement, by State and City, 2010—*Continued*

(Number)

State/city	Population	Violent crime	Murder and non-negligent man-slaughter	Forcible rape	Robbery	Aggravated assault	Property crime	Burglary	Larceny-theft	Motor vehicle theft	Arson[1]
ALABAMA—*Continued*											
Eufaula[2]	14,709	19	1	5	6	7			411	8	
Eutaw	2,833	34	0	1	2	31	75	26	45	4	3
Evergreen	3,468	36	0	0	6	30	188	60	124	4	
Excel	609	4	0	0	0	4	8	1	7	0	
Fairfield	11,344	105	4	5	36	60	1,352	396	869	87	
Falkville	1,229	3	0	1	0	2	45	13	27	5	
Fayette	4,676	14	0	0	2	12	105	10	87	8	
Flomaton	1,547	2	0	0	0	2	31	4	26	1	
Florala	1,878	9	0	0	0	9	65	2	56	7	
Florence[2]	38,643		1	12		58			1,475	30	11
Foley	15,044	45	0	4	4	37	501	63	408	30	
Fort Deposit	1,154	14	0	0	0	14	52	2	45	5	
Fultondale	7,095	3	0	1	1	1	231	18	202	11	
Gadsden	36,835	318	5	30	110	173	2,620	681	1,797	142	22
Gantt	239	1	0	0	0	1	2	0	2	0	
Gardendale	14,048	30	2	1	14	13	516	91	405	20	
Georgiana	1,548	7	0	0	1	6	39	6	32	1	
Geraldine	857	2	0	0	0	2	20	2	13	5	
Glencoe	5,393	18	0	4	0	14	139	39	97	3	
Gordo	1,520	4	0	0	0	4	16	3	13	0	
Grant	732	3	0	0	0	3	24	5	16	3	
Graysville	2,394	0	0	0	0	0	3	0	3	0	
Greenville	6,961	31	0	0	7	24	362	74	270	18	
Grove Hill	1,320	10	0	0	2	8	24	12	10	2	
Guin	2,146	7	0	0	0	7	28	0	23	5	
Gulf Shores	10,999	24	1	9	4	10	469	28	428	13	
Guntersville[2]	8,775	34	0	7	8	19			556	29	1
Gurley	885	1	0	0	0	1	3	2	0	1	
Hackleburg	1,432	4	0	0	0	4	35	3	27	5	
Haleyville	4,080	10	0	2	0	8	196	8	178	10	
Hamilton	6,324	6	0	0	0	6	171	10	152	9	
Hammondville	556	0	0	0	0	0	5	0	5	0	
Hanceville	3,531	12	0	2	2	8	94	8	78	8	
Harpersville	1,869	3	0	0	0	3	7	1	5	1	
Hartford	2,447	12	0	2	0	10	112	9	98	5	0
Hartselle	14,258	8	0	2	0	6	560	80	457	23	
Heflin	3,592	12	0	1	0	11	67	13	50	4	
Helena	15,845	8	0	1	0	7	102	12	85	5	
Henagar	2,654	5	0	0	0	5	63	19	44	0	
Highland Lake	522	0	0	0	0	0	2	0	2	0	
Hillsboro	593	3	0	1	0	2	1	0	0	1	
Hokes Bluff	4,531	3	0	0	1	2	44	2	40	2	
Hollywood	923	2	0	0	0	2	9	0	9	0	
Homewood	24,101	114	0	3	69	42	1,540	298	1,156	86	
Hoover	74,687	75	1	3	47	24	2,172	397	1,670	105	2
Hueytown	15,942	24	0	1	8	15	674	35	615	24	
Huntsville	183,357	1,182	12	76	463	631	9,768	2,677	6,230	861	21
Ider	733	4	0	0	0	4	20	6	14	0	
Irondale	9,865	51	1	1	11	38	627	179	378	70	
Jacksons Gap	773	4	0	0	0	4	28	0	27	1	
Jasper[2]	14,138	72	0	7	13	52			920	79	
Jemison	3,077	7	0	0	0	7	114	7	96	11	
Killen	1,154	6	0	0	0	6	48	3	43	2	
Kimberly	3,027	0	0	0	0	0	19	4	15	0	
Kinston	630	4	0	0	1	3	15	10	4	1	
Lafayette	2,875	27	0	1	0	26	120	11	103	6	
Lake View	2,630	1	0	0	0	1	42	5	33	4	
Lanett	7,026	38	0	6	3	29	715	50	639	26	
Leeds	11,679	63	2	2	33	26	514	105	379	30	
Leesburg	827	4	0	0	1	3	39	6	30	3	
Leighton	832	0	0	0	0	0	7	4	3	0	
Level Plains	1,537	12	0	0	0	12	32	9	22	1	0
Lexington	852	0	0	0	0	0	9	3	6	0	
Lincoln	6,279	27	1	5	1	20	317	80	208	29	
Linden	2,225	8	0	0	0	8	49	15	30	4	
Lineville	2,333	21	0	0	0	21	28	2	26	0	
Lipscomb	2,036	9	1	0	4	4	94	32	50	12	
Littleville	1,056	6	0	0	0	6	32	5	27	0	
Livingston	2,869	15	1	1	1	12	111	25	81	5	
Lockhart	542	1	0	0	0	1	1	0	0	1	
Louisville	573	1	0	0	0	1	6	3	3	0	
Loxley	2,063	25	0	3	14	8	156	17	135	4	
Lynn	718	0	0	0	0	0	4	1	2	1	
Madison	41,426	82	1	12	26	43	925	166	712	47	
Margaret	1,313	4	0	1	0	3	42	1	35	6	

[1] The FBI does not publish arson data unless it receives data from either the agency or the state for all 12 months of the calendar year.
[2] The FBI determined that the agency's data were underreported. Consequently, those data are not included in this table.

Table 8. Offenses Known to Law Enforcement, by State and City, 2010—*Continued*

(Number)

State/city	Population	Violent crime	Murder and non-negligent man-slaughter	Forcible rape	Robbery	Aggravated assault	Property crime	Burglary	Larceny-theft	Motor vehicle theft	Arson[1]
ALABAMA—*Continued*											
McIntosh	231	11	0	2	1	8	16	5	9	2	
Mentone	492	0	0	0	0	0	2	0	2	0	
Midfield	5,215	34	2	4	17	11	348	10	311	27	
Midland City	1,927	9	0	0	1	8	70	14	47	9	
Millbrook	17,750	33	0	3	15	15	445	106	336	3	
Millry	588	1	0	0	0	1	3	0	3	0	
Mobile[4,5]	255,178	1,702	25	59	653	965	14,179	3,873	9,279	1,027	77
Monroeville	6,285	80	0	5	2	73	425	75	328	22	
Montevallo[2]	6,657	15	0	1	3	11			187	11	
Montgomery	203,966	797	25	55	401	316	11,260	3,279	7,200	781	50
Moody[2]	14,726	2	0	0	0	2				28	
Morris	1,927	4	0	0	0	4	44	1	38	5	
Mosses	1,006	7	0	0	0	7	8	3	4	1	
Moulton	3,259	10	0	0	4	6	80	5	70	5	
Moundville	2,660	16	0	2	0	14	72	16	48	8	
Mount Vernon	819	10	0	0	0	10	79	31	43	5	
Muscle Shoals	13,277	50	0	5	7	38	614	134	460	20	
Napier Field	398	3	0	0	0	3	12	5	6	1	
New Brockton	1,258	12	0	0	2	10	28	14	12	2	
New Site	843	0	0	0	0	0	0	0	0	0	
Newville	547	0	0	0	0	0	5	5	0	0	
Northport	24,019	171	2	8	41	120	970	273	649	48	
Notasulga	825	3	0	0	0	3	59	3	53	3	
Oakman	921	0	0	0	0	0	8	0	8	0	
Odenville	2,968	11	0	2	0	9	80	13	55	12	
Ohatchee	1,285	1	0	0	0	1	10	2	6	2	
Oneonta	7,317	12	0	2	0	10	161	8	145	8	0
Opelika	28,815	156	2	17	31	106	1,492	430	1,044	18	
Opp	6,552	14	1	1	0	12	193	17	168	8	
Orange Beach[2]	6,575	6	0	0	0	6			224	4	
Owens Crossroads	1,814	1	0	0	0	1	26	1	21	4	
Oxford[2]	21,171		4	1		56	1,242	186	998	58	
Ozark	14,669	72	1	5	7	59	452	5	426	21	
Parrish	1,252	5	0	0	0	5	28	2	25	1	
Pelham	22,777	32	1	2	7	22	457	65	374	18	
Pell City	13,637	41	0	5	4	32	477	63	392	22	
Phenix City	31,662	157	4	12	55	86	1,628	561	944	123	
Phil Campbell	1,061	1	0	0	1	0	21	0	20	1	
Piedmont	4,994	19	0	3	2	14	193	53	128	12	
Pine Hill	878	7	0	1	0	6	36	6	27	3	
Pisgah	693	0	0	0	0	0	8	0	8	0	
Pleasant Grove	10,407	11	0	1	2	8	164	26	130	8	
Powell	1,002	0	0	0	0	0	13	9	4	0	
Prattville	33,738	90	0	10	25	55	1,296	203	1,045	48	
Priceville	3,072	0	0	0	0	0	53	1	47	5	
Ragland	2,232	7	0	0	0	7	53	7	42	4	
Rainbow City	9,569	11	0	2	1	8	253	52	195	6	
Rainsville	5,141	2	0	0	0	2	108	7	91	10	
Ranburne	488	3	0	0	0	3	13	7	5	1	
Red Bay	3,338	7	0	1	0	6	57	1	52	4	
Red Level	549	0	0	0	0	0	1	0	1	0	
Reform[2]	1,751	13	0	2	1	10			35	3	
River Falls	611	0	0	0	0	0		0	1	0	
Riverside[3]	2,146	4	0	0	0	4		7		5	
Roanoke	6,716	19	1	0	5	13	105	8	92	5	
Robertsdale	5,320	17	1	3	2	11	220	28	185	7	
Rockford	386	0	0	0	0	0	3	0	3	0	
Rogersville	1,219	4	0	0	0	4	34	3	27	4	
Samson	2,039	7	0	0	0	7	42	6	35	1	
Saraland	13,238	53	0	4	8	41	547	86	439	22	
Sardis City	2,227	1	0	0	0	1	64	5	53	6	
Section	757	0	0	0	0	0	6	0	6	0	
Sheffield	9,053	17	0	5	6	6	256	99	147	10	
Silas	472	0	0	0	0	0	2	1	1	0	
Silverhill	719	1	0	0	0	1	30	4	26	0	
Skyline	883	0	0	0	0	0	14	2	12	0	
Slocomb	2,065	9	0	0	1	8	23	1	20	2	

[1] The FBI does not publish arson data unless it receives data from either the agency or the state for all 12 months of the calendar year.
[2] The FBI determined that the agency's data were underreported. Consequently, those data are not included in this table.
[3] The FBI determined that the agency's data were overreported. Consequently, those data are not included in this table.
[4] The population for the city of Mobile, Alabama, includes 55,995 inhabitants from the jurisdiction of the Mobile County Sheriff's Department.
[5] Because of changes in the state/local agency's reporting practices, figures are not comparable to previous years' data.

Table 8.   Offenses Known to Law Enforcement, by State and City, 2010—Continued

(Number)

State/city	Population	Violent crime	Murder and non-negligent man-slaughter	Forcible rape	Robbery	Aggravated assault	Property crime	Burglary	Larceny-theft	Motor vehicle theft	Arson[1]
ALABAMA—*Continued*											
Snead	879	8	0	1	0	7	33	10	17	6	
Somerville	662	0	0	0	0	0	9	1	7	1	
Southside	8,731	7	1	0	0	6	143	10	128	5	
Spanish Fort	7,873	13	0	0	2	11	367	28	338	1	
Springville	3,906	8	0	0	1	7	114	22	91	1	0
Steele	1,273	0	0	0	0	0	7	0	7	0	
St. Florian	538	4	0	0	0	4	18	3	12	3	
Sulligent	1,949	4	0	1	0	3	44	5	34	5	
Sumiton	2,566	7	0	1	1	5	207	13	182	12	
Summerdale	787	6	0	1	0	5	73	9	63	1	
Sylacauga	13,159	46	1	8	10	27	669	154	494	21	1
Sylvania	1,425	1	0	0	0	1	29	3	26	0	
Talladega	16,826	91	0	3	9	79	1,138	361	707	70	
Tarrant	6,529	61	3	4	17	37	621	227	355	39	1
Taylor	2,059	1	0	0	0	1	9	2	7	0	
Thomasville	4,433	43	1	3	1	38	189	58	119	12	
Thorsby	2,148	3	0	0	0	3	13	0	12	1	
Town Creek	1,213	6	0	0	0	6	29	3	24	2	
Trafford	500	0	0	0	0	0	0	0	0	0	
Trinity	2,079	4	0	0	0	4	55	2	49	4	
Troy[3]	15,395		0	10	15			337	625		3
Tuscaloosa	95,570	449	7	31	190	221	4,828	1,462	3,188	178	6
Tuscumbia[3]	8,490		0	3	6			54	276		
Valley	9,966	42	0	1	4	37	505	25	459	21	
Valley Head	667	2	0	0	0	2	5	2	3	0	
Vance	1,307	8	0	0	0	8	43	18	22	3	0
Vernon	1,863	2	0	1	0	1	21	1	19	1	
Vestavia Hills	31,420	18	1	2	5	10	531	48	444	39	
Warrior	3,171	0	0	0	0	0	31	5	24	2	
Weaver	2,972	7	0	1	0	6	72	23	48	1	0
Webb	1,417	0	0	0	0	0	5	0	5	0	
Wedowee	823	10	0	0	0	10	19	0	18	1	
West Blocton	1,422	0	0	0	0	0	3	1	1	1	
Winfield[2]	4,573	13	1	3	0	9			119	9	
Woodstock	1,099	14	0	0	1	13	123	10	102	11	
York	2,466	14	0	0	0	14	79	22	53	4	
ALASKA											
Anchorage	290,334	2,432	13	264	454	1,701	10,214	1,223	8,178	813	86
Bethel	6,667	63	2	14	6	41	149	44	73	32	7
Bristol Bay Borough	856	1	0	0	0	1	52	9	23	20	0
Cordova	2,231	5	0	0	0	5	6	0	5	1	0
Craig	1,184	11	0	0	0	11	14	3	10	1	0
Dillingham	2,496	55	0	31	0	24	69	5	56	8	0
Fairbanks[5]	35,989	284	0	70	33	181	1,367	149	1,117	101	4
Haines	2,412	7	0	0	0	7	21	3	17	1	0
Homer	6,158	40	0	1	5	34	265	40	219	6	1
Houston[5]	2,412	18	0	2	0	16	53	18	27	8	0
Juneau[5]	30,966	133	1	20	23	89	1,523	181	1,279	63	6
Kenai	8,094	30	0	7	3	20	279	37	226	16	0
Ketchikan	7,479	29	0	8	3	18	405	31	350	24	1
Kodiak[5]	6,387	80	0	8	5	67	209	22	168	19	6
Kotzebue	3,173	27	0	10	4	13	103	22	52	29	3
Nome	3,688	17	0	8	0	9	79	14	55	10	2
North Pole	2,318	10	0	2	1	7	97	12	78	7	1
North Slope Borough	6,728	69	0	10	0	59	109	36	51	22	1
Palmer	8,964	34	0	3	3	28	207	25	170	12	4
Petersburg	2,797	12	0	0	0	12	74	11	62	1	1
Seward	3,224	3	0	0	0	3	102	10	91	1	0
Sitka	8,783	33	0	3	2	28	222	19	182	21	1
Skagway	930	2	0	0	0	2	27	5	21	1	0
Soldotna	4,621	20	0	0	2	18	249	26	217	6	0
St. Paul	431	6	0	0	0	6	1	0	1	0	0
Unalaska	3,539	9	0	2	0	7	87	16	57	14	0
Valdez	3,786	20	0	2	0	18	119	14	99	6	2
Wasilla[6]	11,471		0	0	8		326	32	263	31	3
Wrangell	2,130	0	0	0	0	0	43	7	36	0	0
ARIZONA											
Apache Junction	33,225	108	3	15	14	76	1,043	266	697	80	3
Avondale	82,580	199	0	18	78	103	3,732	802	2,559	371	
Buckeye	50,008	43	1	0	13	29	1,245	344	815	86	11
Bullhead City	39,488	59	3	0	17	39	1,540	336	1,107	97	6
Camp Verde	10,535	18	0	0	1	17	240	60	166	14	2

[1] The FBI does not publish arson data unless it receives data from either the agency or the state for all 12 months of the calendar year.

[2] The FBI determined that the agency's data were underreported. Consequently, those data are not included in this table.

[3] The FBI determined that the agency's data were overreported. Consequently, those data are not included in this table.

[5] Because of changes in the state/local agency's reporting practices, figures are not comparable to previous years' data.

[6] The FBI determined that the agency did not follow national Uniform Crime Reporting Program guidelines for reporting an offense. Consequently, this figure is not included in this table.

Table 8.   Offenses Known to Law Enforcement, by State and City, 2010—*Continued*

(Number)

State/city	Population	Violent crime	Murder and non-negligent man-slaughter	Forcible rape	Robbery	Aggravated assault	Property crime	Burglary	Larceny-theft	Motor vehicle theft	Arson[1]
ARIZONA—*Continued*											
Casa Grande	42,522	250	1	6	52	191	2,847	599	2,075	173	12
Chandler	241,826	691	6	61	195	429	7,516	1,373	5,766	377	50
Chino Valley	10,837	48	0	4	0	44	220	44	165	11	2
Clarkdale	4,121	11	0	0	0	11	82	52	27	3	0
Clifton	2,490	12	0	0	0	12	27	12	13	2	0
Colorado City	4,524	4	0	0	0	4	25	4	19	2	0
Coolidge	10,737	80	0	8	10	62	564	133	401	30	7
Cottonwood	11,010	58	0	2	3	53	376	51	318	7	3
Eagar	4,376	11	0	0	2	9	125	39	83	3	0
El Mirage	24,047	83	1	9	25	48	846	225	540	81	6
Eloy	12,897	88	4	3	8	73	675	270	341	64	9
Flagstaff	58,739	267	5	37	49	176	2,955	226	2,666	63	21
Florence	21,096	39	0	1	1	37	247	106	126	15	4
Fredonia	1,110	2	0	0	0	2	11	6	4	1	1
Gilbert	215,215	205	5	26	61	113	4,080	791	3,135	154	38
Glendale	245,387	963	12	46	385	520	13,529	2,264	9,936	1,329	
Globe	6,936	38	0	2	2	34	285	77	203	5	2
Goodyear	61,721	134	0	11	26	97	1,991	883	907	201	11
Holbrook	4,926	62	0	0	1	61	333	68	250	15	3
Huachuca City	1,896	6	0	0	0	6	21	7	10	4	0
Jerome	366	2	0	0	0	2	27	3	23	1	0
Kingman	26,671	83	1	15	22	45	1,574	358	1,142	74	2
Mammoth	2,618	2	0	0	1	1	40	19	19	2	0
Marana	34,039	28	0	3	12	13	1,095	125	900	70	3
Mesa	452,725	1,790	15	124	511	1,140	14,876	2,711	11,158	1,007	59
Miami	1,710	24	0	0	3	21	66	36	28	2	14
Nogales	19,399	51	0	0	5	46	766	114	556	96	0
Oro Valley	42,644	30	0	4	10	16	774	94	654	26	4
Page	6,854	118	0	1	3	114	428	43	368	17	1
Paradise Valley	14,715	11	0	0	4	7	279	172	99	8	0
Parker	3,024	5	0	0	0	5	124	28	89	7	2
Payson	15,067	122	0	3	3	116	405	89	302	14	1
Peoria	158,184	282	6	38	66	172	4,630	867	3,380	383	14
Phoenix	1,544,427	8,002	117	522	3,250	4,113	61,362	15,626	38,012	7,724	320
Pinetop-Lakeside	4,382	56	1	0	7	48	231	65	164	2	1
Prescott	41,428	135	0	11	13	111	1,251	221	979	51	8
Prescott Valley	37,275	109	1	8	4	96	670	105	552	13	3
Quartzsite	3,359	8	0	0	0	8	89	7	69	13	0
Sahuarita	24,067	14	0	3	0	11	369	55	292	22	7
Scottsdale	230,496	353	4	33	100	216	6,563	1,281	5,014	268	12
Sedona	11,240	17	0	6	0	11	210	50	155	5	1
Sierra Vista	41,892	121	1	21	13	86	1,395	212	1,129	54	7
Snowflake-Taylor	9,563	47	2	0	0	45	192	66	110	16	2
Somerton	12,360	5	0	0	3	2	225	41	160	24	1
South Tucson	5,855	149	0	4	51	94	854	83	725	46	1
Springerville	1,943	11	0	3	0	8	61	13	47	1	0
Surprise	92,294	106	0	13	35	58	1,977	440	1,438	99	27
Tempe	173,004	779	11	43	268	457	8,472	1,416	6,412	644	42
Thatcher	4,913	3	0	0	0	3	126	38	88	0	0
Tolleson	7,103	49	0	2	16	31	723	204	471	48	2
Tombstone	1,514	12	0	1	1	10	70	6	61	3	0
Tucson[6]	527,107	3,331	51	158	1,088	2,034		5,002		3,433	153
Wellton	1,891	3	0	2	0	1	13	9	4	0	0
Willcox	3,704	9	0	2	2	5	216	57	151	8	5
Williams	3,233	11	0	2	1	8	137	21	116	0	0
Youngtown	4,759	18	0	1	3	14	84	33	39	12	2
Yuma	88,291	550	3	24	56	467	3,060	815	2,058	187	27
ARKANSAS											
Alma	5,318	9	0	1	3	5	273	85	183	5	0
Arkadelphia	11,213	50	1	10	5	34	387	168	206	13	2
Atkins	2,992	0	0	0	0	0	51	18	28	5	0
Bald Knob	3,456	9	0	2	1	6	131	43	82	6	1
Barling	4,587	20	0	0	0	20	51	7	37	7	0
Beebe	7,173	56	0	6	2	48	302	114	177	11	1
Bella Vista	26,745	18	0	2	0	16	155	74	77	4	0
Benton	30,692	145	1	8	32	104	1,359	260	1,036	63	3
Bentonville	39,161	63	0	15	4	44	705	142	537	26	4
Berryville	5,391	12	0	0	2	10	222	61	157	4	1
Blytheville	15,787	175	10	14	35	116	1,192	454	664	74	8
Booneville	4,024	21	0	2	0	19	136	51	82	3	2
Bradford	973	0	0	0	0	0	22	9	11	2	2
Bryant	16,740	9	0	4	5	0	742	191	520	31	1

[1] The FBI does not publish arson data unless it receives data from either the agency or the state for all 12 months of the calendar year.

[6] The FBI determined that the agency did not follow national Uniform Crime Reporting Program guidelines for reporting an offense. Consequently, this figure is not included in this table.

Table 8.   Offenses Known to Law Enforcement, by State and City, 2010—*Continued*

(Number)

State/city	Population	Violent crime	Murder and non-negligent man-slaughter	Forcible rape	Robbery	Aggravated assault	Property crime	Burglary	Larceny-theft	Motor vehicle theft	Arson[1]
ARKANSAS—*Continued*											
Bull Shoals	2,138	1	0	1	0	0	31	10	21	0	0
Cabot	24,900	72	0	12	8	52	1,048	493	535	20	1
Camden	11,163	83	2	4	23	54	580	170	393	17	5
Carlisle	2,470	4	0	0	0	4	37	15	21	1	0
Cave City	2,028	2	0	0	0	2	29	4	25	0	1
Cave Springs	1,892	0	0	0	0	0	20	9	11	0	0
Centerton	9,788	18	0	4	0	14	100	53	46	1	0
Charleston	2,999	1	0	0	0	1	11	3	7	1	0
Cherokee Village	4,710	4	0	1	0	3	121	29	89	3	3
Clarksville	8,843	28	0	5	1	22	404	66	328	10	0
Clinton	2,609	2	0	0	0	2	57	7	45	5	0
Conway	61,425	257	4	21	49	183	2,603	444	2,068	91	9
Crossett	5,349	26	1	0	4	21	265	98	161	6	1
Danville	2,529	5	0	2	0	3	7	4	3	0	0
Dardanelle	4,548	26	0	2	0	24	225	108	108	9	3
Decatur	2,143	4	0	1	0	3	34	23	11	0	0
De Queen	6,251	29	0	6	4	19	179	63	105	11	1
De Witt	3,175	13	0	1	4	8	146	57	84	5	1
Dumas	4,496	18	0	2	0	16	115	25	84	6	1
Earle	2,732	14	0	1	6	7	137	59	78	0	1
El Dorado	19,441	157	1	3	39	114	1,123	526	559	38	2
Eureka Springs	2,402	7	3	1	0	3	128	41	85	2	0
Fairfield Bay	2,460	2	0	0	0	2	31	17	13	1	0
Farmington	4,795	12	0	2	1	9	126	35	89	2	1
Fayetteville	79,237	328	1	55	37	235	2,746	465	2,168	113	9
Flippin	1,357	2	0	0	0	2	33	13	20	0	0
Fordyce	4,087	25	0	1	2	22	111	40	63	8	0
Forrest City	13,052	101	2	5	31	63	1,188	236	921	31	4
Fort Smith	86,096	667	6	74	124	463	4,815	1,073	3,530	212	14
Gassville	2,210	2	0	0	0	2	29	8	21	0	0
Gentry	3,200	6	0	3	1	2	19	6	13	0	1
Glenwood	1,986	10	0	2	1	7	36	21	15	0	0
Gosnell	3,541	21	0	1	1	19	91	45	44	2	0
Gravette	2,756	5	0	1	0	4	29	17	12	0	0
Greenbrier	4,746	0	0	0	0	0	1	0	1	0	0
Green Forest	3,106	8	0	2	0	6	90	61	26	3	0
Greenland	1,278	3	0	0	0	3	17	7	10	0	0
Greenwood	8,937	20	0	2	1	17	115	48	64	3	1
Gurdon	2,251	14	0	1	2	11	60	24	34	2	0
Hamburg	2,644	28	0	0	3	25	40	15	25	0	1
Hampton	1,392	3	0	1	1	1	20	8	11	1	0
Hardy	799	1	0	0	0	1	65	15	46	4	0
Harrison	13,285	86	0	12	3	71	576	180	378	18	1
Hazen	1,441	3	0	0	1	2	24	9	15	0	0
Heber Springs	7,392	15	0	4	0	11	334	104	224	6	0
Helena-West Helena	11,502	93	0	6	20	67	739	422	294	23	7
Highland	1,099	0	0	0	0	0	9	2	7	0	0
Hope	10,368	106	0	4	8	94	649	194	427	28	2
Horseshoe Bend	2,226	3	0	3	0	0	18	7	11	0	0
Hot Springs	40,081	402	7	22	72	301	3,124	793	2,161	170	4
Jacksonville	31,833	190	1	27	30	132	1,333	364	903	66	5
Jonesboro	67,382	295	2	22	56	215	2,901	1,213	1,619	69	9
Judsonia	2,207	3	0	0	0	3	38	18	18	2	0
Kensett	1,874	3	0	0	0	3	25	7	13	5	1
Lakeview	849	0	0	0	0	0	9	2	7	0	0
Lake Village	2,301	62	0	1	1	60	74	31	42	1	0
Lepanto	2,001	1	0	0	0	1	30	13	17	0	0
Little Flock	3,328	4	0	4	0	0	6	0	5	1	0
Little Rock	192,922	2,938	25	149	859	1,905	14,796	4,241	9,440	1,115	100
Lonoke	4,721	35	0	2	2	31	188	42	145	1	1
Lowell	7,660	10	0	3	0	7	135	49	77	9	0
Luxora	1,210	4	0	0	1	3	9	5	4	0	0
Magnolia	10,882	37	0	5	7	25	427	229	182	16	2
Marianna	4,079	32	0	0	3	29	174	70	104	0	4
Marion	12,769	60	0	3	13	44	409	155	235	19	1
Marked Tree	2,601	1	0	0	1	0	68	4	64	0	1
Marmaduke	1,177	1	0	0	0	1	35	4	31	0	0
Maumelle	17,331	19	0	1	1	17	307	190	106	11	0
McCrory	1,509	0	0	0	0	0	18	14	4	0	0
McGehee	3,821	95	1	4	1	89	175	70	94	11	1
Mena	5,605	13	0	2	1	10	288	105	178	5	1
Mineral Springs	1,287	11	0	1	1	9	22	15	7	0	0
Monette	1,255	0	0	0	0	0	16	7	9	0	0

[1] The FBI does not publish arson data unless it receives data from either the agency or the state for all 12 months of the calendar year.

Table 8. Offenses Known to Law Enforcement, by State and City, 2010—*Continued*

(Number)

State/city	Population	Violent crime	Murder and non-negligent man-slaughter	Forcible rape	Robbery	Aggravated assault	Property crime	Burglary	Larceny-theft	Motor vehicle theft	Arson[1]
ARKANSAS—*Continued*											
Monticello	9,207	54	0	7	8	39	360	125	220	15	0
Morrilton	6,571	24	0	4	2	18	444	62	369	13	1
Mountain Home	12,642	3	0	0	0	3	406	31	368	7	1
Mountain View	3,121	11	0	1	0	10	57	15	41	1	0
Murfreesboro	1,625	2	0	1	0	1	15	4	11	0	0
Nashville	4,855	12	0	5	0	7	250	66	182	2	0
Newport	7,303	72	1	9	5	57	458	124	320	14	0
North Little Rock	60,129	562	6	14	184	358	5,088	1,136	3,618	334	21
Ola	1,272	2	0	0	0	2	7	6	1	0	0
Osceola	7,807	144	0	11	10	123	383	110	255	18	5
Ozark	3,532	20	0	3	0	17	119	25	90	4	1
Paragould	25,350	86	0	15	8	63	1,754	526	1,164	64	5
Paris	3,553	17	0	1	2	14	115	51	60	4	2
Pea Ridge	5,098	8	0	2	0	6	35	17	17	1	0
Piggott	3,372	11	0	0	3	8	93	65	27	1	0
Pine Bluff	49,971	687	7	40	165	475	3,748	1,371	2,074	303	38
Plainview	799	1	0	0	0	1	15	6	9	0	0
Plummerville	867	5	0	2	1	2	7	0	6	1	1
Pocahontas	6,631	2	0	0	0	2	80	7	68	5	0
Pottsville	2,941	12	0	1	0	11	39	22	16	1	0
Prairie Grove	3,986	11	0	0	1	10	112	42	69	1	0
Prescott	4,406	18	0	1	3	14	139	38	96	5	1
Quitman	742	1	0	0	0	1	13	2	11	0	0
Redfield	1,191	1	0	0	0	1	19	9	10	0	0
Rogers[3]	61,417	219	2	50	11	156			1,629	44	7
Rose Bud	460	1	0	0	0	1	10	1	7	2	0
Russellville	27,992	97	0	13	15	69	1,242	273	887	82	11
Salem	1,591	1	0	0	0	1	28	6	22	0	0
Searcy	23,791	74	0	4	16	54	1,216	413	771	32	5
Sheridan	4,670	19	1	4	0	14	125	30	92	3	2
Sherwood	29,370	130	1	6	6	117	965	205	708	52	6
Siloam Springs	15,337	31	0	5	0	26	323	100	205	18	4
Springdale	71,047	325	0	68	18	239	2,129	373	1,631	125	7
Stamps	1,835	6	0	0	1	5	48	24	24	0	0
Stuttgart	8,750	47	3	2	8	34	480	166	298	16	3
Texarkana	30,488	298	0	19	51	228	1,935	425	1,389	121	3
Trumann	6,766	31	0	3	3	25	452	121	325	6	1
Van Buren	23,072	74	0	9	8	57	654	167	479	8	1
Vilonia	3,753	10	0	2	1	7	63	18	43	2	0
Waldron	3,523	9	0	1	0	8	172	84	83	5	1
Ward	4,311	20	0	4	0	16	128	38	88	2	0
Warren	6,015	26	0	5	2	19	135	90	36	9	0
West Fork	2,365	7	0	1	0	6	40	21	17	2	0
West Memphis	27,196	685	6	26	124	529	2,271	1,049	1,075	147	17
White Hall	5,216	6	0	1	1	4	89	4	80	5	0
Wynne	8,317	29	0	5	9	15	297	125	167	5	1
CALIFORNIA											
Adelanto	29,697	242	4	9	39	190	726	359	273	94	13
Agoura Hills	22,318	18	0	2	1	15	240	59	173	8	0
Alameda	71,016	173	1	15	74	83	1,964	389	1,360	215	10
Albany	16,096	37	0	5	24	8	582	95	392	95	4
Alhambra	84,987	185	3	8	82	92	2,075	345	1,460	270	18
Aliso Viejo	41,989	37	0	4	8	25	439	87	324	28	3
Alturas	2,733	5	0	2	0	3	63	28	30	5	1
American Canyon	17,507	38	0	2	20	16	515	100	375	40	1
Anaheim	338,492	1,161	7	88	492	574	8,473	1,594	5,869	1,010	47
Anderson	10,851	77	0	5	10	62	510	90	394	26	2
Antioch	102,125	864	13	32	313	506	3,096	1,087	1,049	960	36
Apple Valley	71,834	188	2	22	58	106	1,889	592	1,107	190	14
Arcadia	56,465	88	1	5	36	46	1,737	364	1,267	106	3
Arcata	17,172	40	0	6	14	20	648	172	444	32	15
Arroyo Grande	17,358	25	0	3	5	17	317	76	224	17	2
Artesia	16,146	64	0	3	33	28	265	81	140	44	1
Arvin	15,410	187	0	1	19	167	500	186	232	82	14
Atascadero	28,468	79	0	10	8	61	620	152	435	33	5
Atherton	7,527	21	0	3	4	14	136	28	107	1	0
Atwater	26,495	114	4	6	23	81	1,128	322	700	106	14
Auburn	13,432	59	0	7	14	38	291	60	189	42	5
Avalon	3,087	24	0	0	0	24	75	21	38	16	0
Avenal	16,523	57	2	2	8	45	143	63	66	14	10
Azusa	46,824	226	2	11	63	150	1,136	276	731	129	1
Bakersfield	333,458	2,104	33	34	641	1,396	15,197	4,235	8,507	2,455	103

[1] The FBI does not publish arson data unless it receives data from either the agency or the state for all 12 months of the calendar year.

[3] The FBI determined that the agency's data were overreported. Consequently, those data are not included in this table.

Table 8. Offenses Known to Law Enforcement, by State and City, 2010—*Continued*

(Number)

State/city	Population	Violent crime	Murder and non-negligent man-slaughter	Forcible rape	Robbery	Aggravated assault	Property crime	Burglary	Larceny-theft	Motor vehicle theft	Arson[1]
CALIFORNIA—*Continued*											
Baldwin Park	77,127	253	2	8	102	141	1,752	306	940	506	11
Banning	29,563	155	3	7	32	113	546	278	205	63	0
Barstow	24,704	190	6	8	45	131	777	263	371	143	13
Bear Valley	4,655	1	0	1	0	0	72	9	60	3	0
Beaumont	37,399	87	0	6	16	65	781	173	543	65	6
Bell	36,506	241	1	12	90	138	601	176	285	140	0
Bellflower	72,790	415	1	24	176	214	1,776	413	906	457	7
Bell Gardens	44,591	210	5	5	112	88	940	150	391	399	4
Belmont	24,881	26	0	0	8	18	367	69	268	30	1
Belvedere	2,050	0	0	0	0	0	25	1	21	3	0
Benicia	26,082	50	1	7	15	27	471	136	268	67	4
Berkeley	102,700	533	5	23	365	140	5,943	1,088	4,240	615	25
Beverly Hills	34,329	75	3	4	35	33	985	263	677	45	3
Big Bear Lake	6,209	28	0	1	5	22	253	58	190	5	0
Biggs	1,815	3	0	0	1	2	28	11	15	2	0
Bishop	3,412	22	0	2	3	17	84	19	62	3	0
Blythe	21,365	77	0	3	13	61	605	256	332	17	28
Bradbury	1,092	0	0	0	0	0	11	6	5	0	0
Brawley	23,464	53	0	5	10	38	1,102	354	622	126	11
Brea	38,725	71	1	3	28	39	1,471	197	1,200	74	4
Brentwood	53,312	112	0	6	41	65	1,117	214	796	107	21
Brisbane	3,712	5	0	0	1	4	68	13	47	8	0
Broadmoor	4,428	14	0	1	2	11	79	25	45	9	0
Buellton	4,348	11	1	0	1	9	78	13	62	3	0
Buena Park	79,929	241	0	13	82	146	2,007	355	1,270	382	10
Burbank	103,304	221	0	13	98	110	2,687	478	1,933	276	8
Burlingame	27,838	59	0	5	20	34	702	108	520	74	1
Calabasas	22,223	13	0	1	3	9	321	83	220	18	2
Calexico	40,186	77	0	5	34	38	1,429	518	584	327	5
California City	15,573	56	3	4	2	47	475	184	257	34	0
Calimesa	7,594	18	0	2	6	10	166	65	81	20	2
Calipatria	7,715	15	0	0	0	15	19	12	7	0	0
Calistoga	5,252	8	0	2	2	4	126	25	97	4	0
Camarillo	64,577	54	0	3	12	39	972	167	763	42	13
Campbell	38,854	83	0	10	32	41	1,451	319	1,017	115	18
Canyon Lake	11,335	10	0	0	3	7	223	45	146	32	1
Capitola	9,747	113	0	3	11	99	708	78	608	22	3
Carlsbad	100,461	195	0	20	41	134	1,820	399	1,313	108	9
Carmel	3,882	13	0	3	3	7	106	31	74	1	0
Carpinteria	13,708	39	0	3	3	33	184	26	149	9	0
Carson	92,409	499	6	12	130	351	2,326	441	1,421	464	12
Cathedral City	53,449	249	3	17	49	180	1,505	556	660	289	9
Ceres	43,505	168	3	7	57	101	1,946	360	1,134	452	9
Cerritos	51,025	93	0	3	49	41	1,696	301	1,167	228	6
Chico	85,630	245	1	47	88	109	2,347	710	1,416	221	33
Chino	84,170	264	0	13	76	175	2,009	479	1,314	216	14
Chino Hills	74,520	80	1	5	16	58	978	239	657	82	7
Chowchilla	19,795	64	0	5	5	54	344	153	168	23	5
Chula Vista	229,060	663	2	54	254	353	5,124	760	3,255	1,109	24
Citrus Heights	84,476	385	4	25	155	201	3,931	756	2,675	500	17
City of Angels	3,774	11	0	1	2	8	67	24	38	5	0
Claremont	35,527	49	0	5	26	18	877	231	595	51	5
Clayton	11,487	15	0	0	9	6	142	38	96	8	2
Clearlake	15,352	73	0	9	20	44	584	188	310	86	2
Cloverdale	8,357	19	0	5	2	12	174	39	123	12	5
Clovis	95,901	165	2	31	55	77	3,569	755	2,428	386	22
Coachella	42,480	193	2	3	74	114	1,623	551	667	405	11
Coalinga	18,833	124	0	6	12	106	539	173	343	23	6
Colma	1,456	8	0	0	5	3	259	6	236	17	0
Colton	50,706	170	6	14	79	71	1,579	406	890	283	4
Colusa	5,952	11	0	2	1	8	124	37	77	10	0
Commerce	13,466	142	2	4	54	82	1,000	157	511	332	5
Compton	93,916	1,327	25	25	477	800	2,784	847	1,223	714	41
Concord	122,119	551	4	28	167	352	3,799	922	2,128	749	6
Corcoran	25,112	42	0	1	4	37	289	119	135	35	1
Corning	7,323	46	0	5	6	35	314	63	228	23	8
Corona	153,311	199	2	15	90	92	3,536	650	2,453	433	14
Coronado	22,033	25	0	0	3	22	442	69	336	37	1
Costa Mesa	110,424	240	1	34	93	112	3,194	458	2,454	282	10
Cotati	7,306	35	0	0	6	29	86	28	55	3	0
Covina	46,728	171	1	7	77	86	1,643	377	1,072	194	6
Crescent City	7,809	28	0	8	2	18	287	87	190	10	0
Cudahy	24,256	161	4	6	65	86	475	68	289	118	2

[1] The FBI does not publish arson data unless it receives data from either the agency or the state for all 12 months of the calendar year.

Table 8. **Offenses Known to Law Enforcement, by State and City, 2010**—*Continued*

(Number)

State/city	Population	Violent crime	Murder and non-negligent man-slaughter	Forcible rape	Robbery	Aggravated assault	Property crime	Burglary	Larceny-theft	Motor vehicle theft	Arson[1]
CALIFORNIA—*Continued*											
Culver City	38,342	149	0	4	94	51	1,638	177	1,337	124	2
Cupertino	54,403	60	0	6	17	37	981	216	728	37	9
Cypress	47,320	63	0	2	37	24	787	121	584	82	5
Daly City	101,939	250	2	9	105	134	1,804	332	1,152	320	17
Dana Point	35,888	66	0	2	13	51	595	129	438	28	4
Danville	41,500	32	0	2	10	20	531	91	406	34	3
Davis	63,292	99	0	18	30	51	1,738	415	1,220	103	15
Delano	54,298	247	0	6	55	186	1,651	773	446	432	59
Del Mar	4,554	19	0	1	2	16	129	24	100	5	0
Del Rey Oaks	1,529	1	0	0	0	1	57	6	50	1	0
Desert Hot Springs	25,309	374	3	8	67	296	1,380	573	630	177	5
Diamond Bar	57,130	48	0	4	14	30	808	250	480	78	2
Dinuba	21,094	177	1	2	25	149	825	301	402	122	8
Dixon	17,518	69	0	11	18	40	481	71	358	52	7
Dorris	833	3	0	0	0	3	17	6	10	1	2
Dos Palos	4,951	48	1	3	5	39	171	58	105	8	6
Downey	106,992	394	6	17	199	172	3,956	656	2,372	928	4
Duarte	21,789	72	0	4	24	44	440	115	249	76	2
Dublin	46,209	69	0	5	20	44	720	122	526	72	2
Dunsmuir	1,779	5	0	1	1	3	63	14	47	2	0
East Palo Alto	34,294	271	4	18	103	146	846	364	248	234	0
El Cajon	94,311	387	0	15	169	203	2,766	552	1,678	536	12
El Centro	41,535	197	1	7	45	144	2,408	672	1,546	190	13
El Cerrito	22,263	134	0	2	75	57	947	208	590	149	4
Elk Grove	142,330	529	2	14	108	405	3,204	653	2,208	343	15
El Monte	121,884	600	3	27	265	305	2,598	607	1,194	797	13
El Segundo	16,181	34	0	5	17	12	541	141	360	40	2
Emeryville	10,207	128	0	2	58	68	981	113	777	91	0
Encinitas	61,898	146	1	9	37	99	947	216	639	92	5
Escalon	7,463	15	0	3	1	11	179	54	110	15	0
Escondido	140,662	597	3	37	212	345	4,033	743	2,460	830	19
Etna	764	0	0	0	0	0	2	0	2	0	0
Eureka	25,143	184	1	17	57	109	1,576	651	771	154	24
Exeter	10,048	22	0	3	5	14	247	79	142	26	3
Fairfax	7,071	14	0	1	2	11	129	32	83	14	3
Fairfield	104,202	502	8	18	185	291	3,395	757	2,169	469	17
Farmersville	10,211	68	3	1	7	57	207	54	129	24	1
Ferndale	1,383	1	0	0	0	1	13	3	10	0	0
Fillmore	15,363	38	2	2	5	29	277	51	206	20	4
Firebaugh	7,079	21	0	0	2	19	176	53	88	35	1
Folsom	69,497	105	0	9	32	64	1,484	262	1,159	63	22
Fontana	192,595	759	6	37	240	476	3,681	804	2,130	747	13
Fort Bragg	6,550	44	1	4	4	35	232	65	156	11	2
Fort Jones	646	1	0	0	0	1	16	6	10	0	1
Fortuna	11,434	40	0	4	4	32	438	87	324	27	7
Foster City	29,283	24	0	1	2	21	416	103	273	40	1
Fountain Valley	55,879	103	3	5	28	67	1,292	266	951	75	9
Fowler	5,769	25	0	1	4	20	130	25	71	34	0
Fremont	205,477	488	3	40	189	256	4,414	1,167	2,757	490	22
Fresno	484,734	3,034	45	70	1,021	1,898	24,460	5,262	14,645	4,553	147
Fullerton	133,139	425	3	26	145	251	3,847	680	2,825	342	22
Galt	24,517	50	0	5	7	38	467	131	300	36	6
Gardena	58,358	347	2	9	202	134	1,446	271	835	340	9
Garden Grove	166,287	539	3	22	184	330	3,590	810	2,318	462	13
Gilroy	51,108	205	1	14	78	112	1,555	237	1,126	192	21
Glendale	196,877	277	0	17	119	141	3,717	642	2,747	328	12
Glendora	49,720	62	0	9	24	29	1,249	228	946	75	9
Goleta	29,605	57	0	5	11	41	407	121	277	9	1
Gonzales	8,830	35	1	0	6	28	153	44	93	16	0
Grand Terrace	12,233	20	0	1	6	13	278	83	157	38	2
Grass Valley	12,330	111	0	8	15	88	500	111	370	19	3
Greenfield	15,626	104	3	3	41	57	344	85	229	30	7
Gridley	6,528	48	0	3	3	42	236	76	141	19	1
Grover Beach	13,199	32	0	6	5	21	317	82	213	22	5
Guadalupe	6,692	12	0	2	0	10	67	18	45	4	1
Gustine	5,130	8	0	0	1	7	175	69	85	21	1
Half Moon Bay	12,648	11	0	1	5	5	248	45	193	10	0
Hanford	50,903	181	0	6	43	132	1,159	252	707	200	5
Hawaiian Gardens	15,211	83	3	5	32	43	237	53	131	53	4
Hawthorne	83,849	653	9	33	281	330	2,200	653	1,112	435	21
Hayward	144,509	652	13	48	391	200	3,753	1,097	1,649	1,007	55
Healdsburg	11,146	16	0	1	2	13	283	50	226	7	0
Hemet	73,111	369	8	17	129	215	2,887	875	1,682	330	13

[1] The FBI does not publish arson data unless it receives data from either the agency or the state for all 12 months of the calendar year.

Table 8.   Offenses Known to Law Enforcement, by State and City, 2010—*Continued*

(Number)

State/city	Population	Violent crime	Murder and non-negligent man-slaughter	Forcible rape	Robbery	Aggravated assault	Property crime	Burglary	Larceny-theft	Motor vehicle theft	Arson[1]
CALIFORNIA—*Continued*											
Hercules	25,192	46	2	3	12	29	356	74	201	81	4
Hermosa Beach	19,408	40	0	6	19	15	553	107	423	23	1
Hesperia	88,876	287	2	27	67	191	1,919	626	1,025	268	13
Hidden Hills	2,031	3	0	0	0	3	18	10	8	0	0
Highland	51,622	242	4	8	96	134	1,492	504	738	250	15
Hillsborough	10,951	4	1	1	0	2	95	26	69	0	0
Hollister	35,056	159	1	9	30	119	889	421	374	94	4
Hughson	6,617	9	0	0	1	8	92	31	50	11	1
Huntington Beach	193,545	449	2	32	109	306	4,673	767	3,621	285	28
Huntington Park	60,514	559	6	4	394	155	2,095	234	1,217	644	12
Huron	8,220	70	0	1	13	56	129	32	81	16	4
Imperial	14,727	5	0	0	2	3	84	21	44	19	0
Imperial Beach	26,978	145	0	9	23	113	453	115	207	131	1
Indian Wells	5,331	4	0	1	1	2	177	67	105	5	0
Indio	89,621	453	10	32	113	298	2,729	878	1,336	515	10
Industry	930	77	0	0	38	39	1,183	118	852	213	8
Inglewood	112,100	843	20	32	381	410	2,672	627	1,342	703	16
Ione	7,744	24	0	2	0	22	114	28	82	4	0
Irvine	217,193	120	0	24	40	56	2,798	480	2,197	121	23
Irwindale	1,431	19	1	0	5	13	136	37	77	22	4
Isleton	843	5	0	0	1	4	8	0	7	1	2
Jackson	4,258	22	0	1	4	17	136	45	84	7	2
Kensington	5,430	2	0	0	0	2	110	37	61	12	0
Kerman	13,293	49	1	0	11	37	681	172	371	138	1
King City	11,704	56	4	7	9	36	205	102	80	23	3
Kingsburg	11,461	26	1	1	2	22	458	128	253	77	3
La Canada Flintridge	20,567	21	0	2	7	12	346	95	238	13	4
Lafayette	25,527	20	0	4	7	9	447	116	293	38	1
Laguna Beach	24,147	78	0	5	8	65	474	82	379	13	1
Laguna Hills	31,909	43	0	4	14	25	510	78	404	28	4
Laguna Niguel	64,812	40	2	0	10	28	641	107	504	30	1
Laguna Woods	18,286	15	2	0	7	6	104	14	82	8	0
La Habra	59,355	169	0	18	60	91	1,236	258	846	132	1
La Habra Heights	5,876	7	0	1	0	6	81	32	42	7	0
Lake Elsinore	54,018	108	0	15	38	55	1,571	398	959	214	2
Lake Forest	75,780	92	0	8	32	52	959	161	736	62	5
Lakeport	5,256	20	0	2	5	13	282	63	210	9	0
Lake Shastina	2,409	3	0	0	0	3	1	1	0	0	0
Lakewood	77,901	296	0	15	128	153	1,876	307	1,249	320	2
La Mesa	55,580	184	0	12	68	104	2,025	427	1,328	270	12
La Mirada	50,002	74	0	3	31	40	726	113	502	111	4
Lancaster	148,632	900	7	60	255	578	3,411	1,033	1,939	439	44
La Palma	15,733	9	0	0	5	4	218	65	141	12	2
La Puente	40,367	162	2	4	49	107	581	134	306	141	2
La Quinta	47,441	137	1	9	25	102	1,288	447	777	64	12
La Verne	34,066	56	0	4	18	34	643	130	477	36	3
Lawndale	31,132	228	4	10	67	147	513	152	223	138	2
Lemon Grove	24,543	156	1	5	53	97	531	180	231	120	5
Lemoore	24,766	110	0	11	18	81	689	114	508	67	0
Lincoln	50,936	28	1	8	4	15	447	117	273	57	7
Lindsay	10,725	69	0	2	3	64	333	82	191	60	4
Livermore	81,769	323	0	16	53	254	1,770	369	1,250	151	19
Livingston	13,679	103	0	4	13	86	346	163	151	32	6
Lodi	61,812	243	1	12	112	118	2,002	531	1,272	199	8
Loma Linda	21,896	28	0	3	7	18	554	173	298	83	1
Lomita	20,106	86	0	4	21	61	330	99	195	36	3
Lompoc	41,049	311	1	22	26	262	932	154	727	51	16
Long Beach	462,267	2,720	32	134	1,202	1,352	11,642	2,929	6,524	2,189	79
Los Alamitos	11,698	14	0	1	7	6	279	74	179	26	1
Los Altos	28,652	8	0	4	3	1	233	67	163	3	6
Los Altos Hills	8,740	1	0	0	0	1	45	19	26	0	0
Los Angeles	3,841,707	21,484	293	923	10,924	9,344	89,704	17,410	55,248	17,046	1,341
Los Banos	36,124	139	2	4	36	97	1,050	323	637	90	3
Los Gatos	29,558	34	0	8	10	16	576	114	434	28	12
Lynwood	69,677	615	4	14	271	326	1,328	392	442	494	20
Madera	58,147	357	8	22	100	227	1,319	460	552	307	0
Malibu	13,078	26	1	1	6	18	350	73	260	17	0
Mammoth Lakes	7,413	46	0	8	2	36	230	68	156	6	2
Manhattan Beach	36,803	48	1	6	21	20	839	162	627	50	1
Manteca	67,344	241	1	10	71	159	1,883	344	1,304	235	9
Marina	17,921	53	2	2	17	32	531	115	390	26	4
Martinez	35,344	73	1	6	25	41	847	196	521	130	0
Marysville	11,548	83	1	9	17	56	405	125	213	67	2

[1] The FBI does not publish arson data unless it receives data from either the agency or the state for all 12 months of the calendar year.

Table 8. Offenses Known to Law Enforcement, by State and City, 2010—*Continued*

(Number)

State/city	Population	Violent crime	Murder and non-negligent man-slaughter	Forcible rape	Robbery	Aggravated assault	Property crime	Burglary	Larceny-theft	Motor vehicle theft	Arson[1]
CALIFORNIA—*Continued*											
McFarland	12,452	64	1	2	8	53	263	95	105	63	20
Mendota	10,690	71	0	3	22	46	411	62	289	60	8
Menifee	45,933	64	0	3	22	39	1,339	378	745	216	4
Menlo Park	30,202	41	0	3	20	18	645	139	467	39	5
Merced	77,484	549	7	33	141	368	2,808	633	1,934	241	23
Millbrae	21,295	33	1	0	5	27	388	95	265	28	3
Mill Valley	13,372	6	0	0	1	5	225	64	151	10	0
Milpitas	68,371	91	0	9	53	29	1,981	264	1,461	256	15
Mission Viejo	94,679	70	0	5	19	46	1,135	168	917	50	9
Modesto	203,890	1,398	10	62	427	899	9,383	2,171	5,786	1,426	56
Monrovia	37,544	72	0	3	26	43	1,080	158	797	125	0
Montague	1,454	3	0	0	0	3	20	4	15	1	1
Montclair	36,508	173	1	6	84	82	1,752	197	1,208	347	16
Montebello	61,570	214	3	10	92	109	1,941	737	724	480	15
Monterey	27,619	154	1	7	33	113	1,183	211	913	59	5
Monterey Park	61,662	96	3	0	57	36	860	219	415	226	0
Monte Sereno	3,672	1	0	0	1	0	37	13	24	0	0
Moorpark	37,193	48	0	8	16	24	383	61	301	21	10
Moraga	17,334	11	0	0	3	8	222	39	173	10	1
Moreno Valley	197,294	724	15	33	373	303	5,222	1,843	2,595	784	10
Morgan Hill	38,986	54	0	9	9	36	642	146	430	66	16
Morro Bay	10,382	29	0	1	1	27	171	37	120	14	0
Mountain View	72,321	168	1	4	46	117	1,458	177	1,179	102	7
Mount Shasta	3,509	7	0	1	0	6	85	39	44	2	0
Murrieta	104,343	99	1	10	33	55	1,407	429	852	126	6
Napa	75,482	245	1	21	44	179	1,557	328	1,102	127	11
National City	56,270	428	4	11	148	265	1,849	310	1,033	506	3
Needles	5,338	19	0	0	3	16	253	89	125	39	5
Nevada City	2,936	36	0	1	1	34	98	27	63	8	0
Newark	42,099	187	4	7	66	110	1,428	327	974	127	9
Newman	10,544	25	0	1	6	18	270	91	133	46	0
Newport Beach	81,882	117	0	4	42	71	2,176	425	1,617	134	12
Norco	26,699	41	2	3	10	26	669	174	420	75	4
Norwalk	102,221	449	4	14	159	272	2,072	438	1,040	594	13
Novato	54,009	99	0	3	29	67	1,035	204	722	109	11
Oakdale	21,023	41	0	3	9	29	796	218	504	74	2
Oakland	409,723	6,267	90	318	2,917	2,942	17,325	4,961	7,720	4,644	163
Oakley	33,556	49	2	6	13	28	483	162	265	56	4
Oceanside	173,901	650	4	47	177	422	3,909	765	2,799	345	25
Ojai	7,794	19	0	0	1	18	163	31	128	4	1
Ontario	172,814	630	3	48	237	342	4,918	850	3,170	898	32
Orange	137,606	150	3	3	56	88	2,569	404	1,944	221	13
Orinda	18,778	5	0	1	3	1	169	39	121	9	0
Orland	7,326	36	0	1	9	26	223	68	111	44	2
Oroville	14,718	218	1	10	26	181	1,011	291	632	88	16
Oxnard	189,051	691	8	19	329	335	4,018	785	2,760	473	21
Pacifica	37,917	69	0	7	17	45	760	114	580	66	6
Pacific Grove	14,537	17	1	2	2	12	401	123	270	8	2
Palmdale	146,819	832	8	41	261	522	3,334	959	1,890	485	35
Palm Desert	52,625	48	0	6	30	12	1,911	638	1,150	123	3
Palm Springs	48,696	282	1	22	69	190	1,973	607	1,188	178	18
Palo Alto	60,288	58	0	4	39	15	1,346	217	1,080	49	22
Palos Verdes Estates	13,553	5	0	0	1	4	116	44	69	3	2
Paradise	26,424	104	1	11	11	81	546	174	340	32	2
Paramount	54,914	343	4	12	185	142	1,554	297	770	487	7
Parlier	13,532	155	0	9	20	126	465	128	231	106	4
Pasadena	144,496	554	3	21	189	341	4,074	832	2,864	378	13
Paso Robles	29,089	95	0	13	15	67	1,006	268	688	50	10
Patterson	19,938	72	1	5	22	44	796	239	408	149	6
Perris	58,622	160	2	10	89	59	1,735	502	875	358	3
Petaluma	55,168	197	1	13	19	164	778	117	604	57	13
Pico Rivera	62,783	247	2	15	97	133	1,553	235	989	329	9
Piedmont	10,519	4	0	0	4	0	214	49	139	26	0
Pinole	18,899	79	0	1	33	45	670	137	392	141	1
Pismo Beach	8,639	24	0	3	5	16	347	75	267	5	0
Pittsburg	65,930	154	6	4	83	61	2,055	501	1,046	508	2
Placentia	50,237	85	0	5	23	57	844	158	614	72	5
Placerville	10,124	65	0	5	6	54	247	77	156	14	0
Pleasant Hill	33,048	94	1	2	43	48	1,407	206	1,085	116	13
Pleasanton	67,823	78	0	4	24	50	1,294	210	1,002	82	6
Pomona	152,673	877	16	37	323	501	4,504	867	2,406	1,231	16
Porterville	52,777	222	4	11	59	148	1,852	449	1,154	249	0
Port Hueneme	21,510	65	1	6	11	47	375	103	229	43	4

[1] The FBI does not publish arson data unless it receives data from either the agency or the state for all 12 months of the calendar year.

Table 8. Offenses Known to Law Enforcement, by State and City, 2010—*Continued*

(Number)

State/city	Population	Violent crime	Murder and non-negligent man-slaughter	Forcible rape	Robbery	Aggravated assault	Property crime	Burglary	Larceny-theft	Motor vehicle theft	Arson[1]
CALIFORNIA—*Continued*											
Poway	50,010	90	2	5	18	65	525	157	328	40	4
Rancho Cordova	63,895	387	4	13	159	211	2,293	657	1,349	287	7
Rancho Cucamonga	176,686	340	2	14	111	213	3,703	879	2,505	319	13
Rancho Mirage	17,175	17	0	3	7	7	555	197	332	26	1
Rancho Palos Verdes	40,905	42	0	8	5	29	422	160	244	18	0
Rancho Santa Margarit	49,665	26	3	4	5	14	364	83	272	9	3
Red Bluff	13,836	142	0	14	14	114	900	292	578	30	5
Redding	91,414	793	2	61	105	625	3,037	849	1,946	242	11
Redlands	70,552	243	2	25	104	112	2,536	587	1,706	243	18
Redondo Beach	66,985	210	1	1	68	140	1,557	216	1,238	103	2
Redwood City	74,355	174	3	16	69	86	1,641	461	988	192	3
Reedley	23,893	138	2	9	15	112	522	162	250	110	3
Rialto	99,232	497	7	32	193	265	2,565	721	1,338	506	10
Richmond	103,442	1,176	21	44	405	706	4,623	1,521	1,506	1,596	51
Ridgecrest	25,973	130	3	12	12	103	611	210	348	53	21
Rio Dell	3,181	12	0	1	1	10	78	20	48	10	1
Rio Vista	8,340	27	0	1	3	23	138	55	74	9	0
Ripon	15,271	22	0	3	4	15	251	33	198	20	3
Riverbank	21,241	36	1	1	9	25	644	218	348	78	4
Riverside	301,859	1,448	9	78	502	859	9,963	2,068	6,434	1,461	49
Rocklin	55,524	59	0	7	24	28	1,032	215	750	67	19
Rohnert Park	40,843	164	1	9	22	132	836	143	639	54	10
Rolling Hills	1,904	4	0	0	0	4	8	5	3	0	0
Rolling Hills Estates	7,841	15	0	0	3	12	137	30	101	6	0
Rosemead	54,294	167	5	10	79	73	1,118	221	695	202	2
Roseville	119,755	334	1	17	87	229	3,802	542	3,029	231	6
Ross	2,281	1	0	0	0	1	35	10	25	0	0
Sacramento	472,469	4,112	33	165	1,491	2,423	20,200	5,027	11,179	3,994	202
Salinas	144,242	1,162	19	23	365	755	4,648	1,358	2,437	853	23
San Anselmo	12,016	8	0	0	1	7	260	73	176	11	1
San Bernardino	199,214	1,624	31	66	632	895	8,967	2,318	4,928	1,721	61
San Bruno	41,517	81	1	5	30	45	909	127	641	141	2
San Clemente	62,796	61	3	1	24	33	782	199	526	57	4
Sand City	372	3	0	0	2	1	125	7	116	2	0
San Diego	1,313,433	5,616	29	300	1,636	3,651	30,753	6,387	17,977	6,389	155
San Dimas	35,008	80	0	4	28	48	663	165	435	63	4
San Fernando	23,719	63	0	0	24	39	379	79	213	87	3
San Francisco	818,594	5,747	48	133	3,180	2,386	32,365	4,557	23,905	3,903	156
San Gabriel	40,281	85	0	2	37	46	566	164	342	60	1
Sanger	26,246	158	2	14	24	118	1,105	271	665	169	4
San Jacinto	39,703	108	2	6	50	50	1,371	489	670	212	0
San Jose	970,252	3,215	20	253	976	1,966	22,081	3,940	12,730	5,411	181
San Juan Capistrano	35,241	41	0	3	15	23	503	116	348	39	5
San Leandro	78,447	347	4	10	209	124	3,137	634	1,911	592	15
San Luis Obispo	44,008	126	0	27	35	64	1,686	372	1,260	54	22
San Marcos	83,671	237	1	16	70	150	1,642	350	1,054	238	5
San Marino	12,725	13	0	0	1	12	224	69	153	2	0
San Mateo	92,724	292	1	24	82	185	1,905	242	1,464	199	19
San Pablo	31,122	241	2	7	109	123	1,369	296	560	513	6
San Rafael	55,832	236	3	34	82	117	1,603	312	1,030	261	12
San Ramon	50,006	35	0	6	17	12	975	215	693	67	7
Santa Ana	340,240	1,510	28	88	719	675	6,580	1,116	4,189	1,275	139
Santa Barbara	85,967	341	3	28	92	218	2,528	487	1,939	102	12
Santa Clara	112,917	182	2	7	62	111	3,016	481	2,210	325	16
Santa Clarita	170,458	375	1	21	123	230	2,670	574	1,853	243	18
Santa Cruz	56,860	553	6	31	120	396	2,936	495	2,262	179	20
Santa Fe Springs	17,120	73	2	1	38	32	1,206	186	842	178	2
Santa Maria	87,803	771	3	32	152	584	2,319	506	1,496	317	8
Santa Monica	87,817	392	1	12	167	212	3,120	413	2,541	166	26
Santa Paula	28,810	101	1	3	26	71	517	100	376	41	2
Santa Rosa	158,182	767	2	56	166	543	4,096	757	3,041	298	9
Santee	55,533	153	0	9	22	122	959	172	628	159	7
Saratoga	30,692	22	0	1	9	12	265	92	164	9	6
Sausalito	7,180	9	0	1	0	8	195	43	141	11	0
Scotts Valley	11,243	13	0	3	2	8	247	46	195	6	4
Seal Beach	24,225	47	1	4	5	37	524	122	374	28	5
Seaside	34,057	129	1	10	21	97	592	139	402	51	8
Sebastopol	7,574	17	0	0	5	12	221	77	134	10	0
Selma	23,169	141	0	3	41	97	1,355	293	735	327	13
Shafter	16,247	43	0	7	11	25	549	178	285	86	16
Sierra Madre	10,796	14	0	0	4	10	186	58	126	2	0
Signal Hill	10,981	40	0	3	17	20	428	86	275	67	0
Simi Valley	121,755	129	1	14	37	77	2,209	388	1,687	134	6

[1] The FBI does not publish arson data unless it receives data from either the agency or the state for all 12 months of the calendar year.

Table 8.   Offenses Known to Law Enforcement, by State and City, 2010—*Continued*

(Number)

State/city	Population	Violent crime	Murder and non-negligent man-slaughter	Forcible rape	Robbery	Aggravated assault	Property crime	Burglary	Larceny-theft	Motor vehicle theft	Arson[1]
CALIFORNIA—*Continued*											
Solana Beach	13,055	43	1	4	13	25	248	65	162	21	0
Soledad	28,655	75	1	4	24	46	331	163	133	35	1
Solvang	5,153	8	0	1	1	6	55	16	37	2	0
Sonoma	10,068	33	2	3	1	27	225	61	159	5	5
Sonora	4,627	24	0	2	6	16	381	78	290	13	5
South El Monte	21,705	134	3	4	45	82	477	93	247	137	5
South Gate	96,182	598	7	13	326	252	2,603	484	1,295	824	14
South Lake Tahoe	23,540	164	0	14	26	124	377	171	190	16	5
South Pasadena	24,320	25	0	8	13	4	423	107	262	54	1
South San Francisco	63,006	152	5	13	54	80	1,479	458	808	213	30
Stallion Springs	1,674	7	0	0	0	7	17	4	8	5	0
Stanton	37,912	156	2	1	63	90	643	151	405	87	4
St. Helena	5,908	12	0	0	2	10	127	18	102	7	0
Stockton	292,047	4,033	49	107	1,413	2,464	16,177	4,482	9,654	2,041	62
Suisun City	27,053	81	2	14	33	32	665	158	426	81	0
Sunnyvale	134,073	169	0	26	59	84	2,227	407	1,574	246	51
Susanville	17,067	82	1	6	11	64	359	134	208	17	0
Sutter Creek	2,690	4	0	0	0	4	76	14	54	8	1
Taft	9,046	37	0	1	7	29	343	87	219	37	2
Tehachapi	12,137	23	0	1	3	19	304	100	188	16	0
Temecula	102,474	74	2	3	42	27	2,351	535	1,642	174	5
Temple City	38,648	61	0	8	17	36	430	140	254	36	0
Thousand Oaks	124,042	139	1	16	50	72	2,036	358	1,606	72	9
Tiburon	8,728	4	0	1	1	2	89	10	74	5	1
Torrance	140,411	290	4	19	152	115	2,859	516	2,008	335	21
Tracy	81,712	135	4	9	57	65	2,105	334	1,526	245	15
Truckee	16,491	25	0	0	2	23	209	50	151	8	1
Tulare	58,790	390	5	21	75	289	2,613	527	1,645	441	8
Tulelake	949	4	0	0	0	4	15	8	7	0	0
Turlock	69,961	466	1	21	124	320	2,881	686	1,730	465	37
Tustin	72,982	128	1	9	56	62	1,567	237	1,186	144	14
Twentynine Palms	34,165	119	1	15	18	85	517	135	337	45	12
Twin Cities	21,067	26	0	1	9	16	680	196	419	65	1
Ukiah	14,781	92	0	12	10	70	466	156	291	19	6
Union City	73,356	324	4	8	138	174	1,810	465	1,084	261	11
Upland	73,341	208	2	9	86	111	2,358	495	1,509	354	2
Vacaville	92,177	272	3	27	71	171	1,866	322	1,370	174	30
Vallejo[5]	114,258	822	17	59	458	288	5,101	2,249	1,675	1,177	35
Ventura	104,661	263	3	16	108	136	3,458	652	2,654	152	7
Vernon	89	26	0	1	18	7	316	43	191	82	7
Victorville	117,057	681	6	38	256	381	3,674	1,274	1,964	436	26
Villa Park	5,991	6	0	0	1	5	69	20	48	1	0
Visalia	125,036	578	6	26	176	370	5,334	1,237	3,497	600	8
Vista	92,765	405	5	21	112	267	2,110	463	1,260	387	22
Walnut	30,636	29	0	3	4	22	447	159	248	40	2
Walnut Creek	63,897	115	1	5	38	71	2,372	436	1,783	153	5
Waterford	9,127	40	2	1	6	31	265	52	173	40	0
Watsonville	51,488	327	1	13	98	215	1,539	271	1,091	177	14
Weed	3,023	21	0	4	3	14	99	32	57	10	0
West Covina	105,395	318	0	19	120	179	2,979	531	1,854	594	2
West Hollywood	35,885	389	6	12	154	217	1,545	288	1,124	133	8
Westlake Village	8,460	6	1	0	2	3	143	48	92	3	0
Westminster	89,604	259	2	17	102	138	2,539	419	1,848	272	10
Westmorland	2,231	6	0	0	1	5	17	7	8	2	0
West Sacramento	49,816	172	1	27	65	79	1,345	304	863	178	19
Wheatland	3,715	5	0	1	0	4	48	9	34	5	0
Whittier	81,611	343	2	20	96	225	2,433	413	1,734	286	9
Wildomar	22,816	59	0	11	15	33	703	188	365	150	2
Williams	4,896	15	0	0	2	13	93	22	58	13	2
Willits	4,931	41	0	3	12	26	112	30	62	20	4
Willows	6,234	21	0	4	6	11	176	36	134	6	0
Windsor	25,870	38	0	2	5	31	320	66	240	14	1
Winters	7,096	6	0	3	0	3	169	58	99	12	0
Woodlake	7,791	18	1	2	3	12	195	35	144	16	1
Woodland	55,814	161	1	17	39	104	1,513	352	993	168	19
Yorba Linda	66,813	58	0	3	9	46	804	150	621	33	2
Yountville	3,293	5	0	1	1	3	57	9	47	1	1
Yreka	7,345	54	0	2	2	50	263	69	176	18	2
Yuba City	62,694	216	2	22	51	141	1,783	409	1,222	152	11
Yucaipa	50,939	139	0	10	31	98	805	233	464	108	9
Yucca Valley	20,746	104	2	11	13	78	528	157	306	65	6

[1] The FBI does not publish arson data unless it receives data from either the agency or the state for all 12 months of the calendar year.

Table 8.   Offenses Known to Law Enforcement, by State and City, 2010—*Continued*

(Number)

State/city	Population	Violent crime	Murder and non-negligent man-slaughter	Forcible rape	Robbery	Aggravated assault	Property crime	Burglary	Larceny-theft	Motor vehicle theft	Arson[1]
COLORADO											
Alamosa	8,660	64	0	9	18	37	514	76	428	10	2
Arvada	107,227	135	1	30	28	76	2,716	386	2,123	207	14
Aspen	6,012	14	0	3	0	11	359	32	321	6	1
Ault	1,449	8	0	1	0	7	40	14	22	4	0
Aurora	323,483	1,443	23	183	505	732	10,051	2,290	6,873	888	68
Avon	6,737	4	0	2	0	2	143	23	117	3	0
Basalt	3,347	5	0	0	1	4	61	8	50	3	0
Bayfield	2,114	0	0	0	0	0	11	1	8	2	0
Black Hawk	112	1	0	0	0	1	171	1	168	2	0
Boulder	99,255	210	4	33	29	144	2,722	478	2,155	89	56
Brighton	33,166	64	0	10	6	48	1,184	161	938	85	16
Broomfield	57,126	41	3	10	12	16	1,161	118	995	48	14
Brush	5,338	3	0	0	3	0	107	15	90	2	0
Buena Vista	2,107	1	0	1	0	0	24	1	23	0	0
Burlington	4,414	9	0	3	0	6	80	13	66	1	1
Canon City	15,706	66	0	17	1	48	446	70	363	13	2
Castle Rock	48,715	26	0	9	3	14	480	71	389	20	1
Cedaredge	2,284	2	0	2	0	0	31	6	22	3	0
Centennial	98,902	159	0	18	26	115	1,455	274	1,121	60	9
Center	2,347	5	0	0	1	4	54	11	43	0	0
Central City	650	4	0	0	1	3	34	1	33	0	0
Cherry Hills Village	6,389	1	0	0	0	1	75	18	53	4	0
Colorado Springs	397,886	1,957	20	319	526	1,092	16,794	3,452	12,054	1,288	100
Commerce City	46,771	118	0	20	12	86	1,337	229	953	155	7
Cortez	8,570	19	0	0	2	17	345	18	316	11	1
Craig	9,178	14	0	7	0	7	277	49	222	6	2
Crested Butte	1,663	0	0	0	0	0	5	0	5	0	0
Cripple Creek	1,002	6	0	0	2	4	79	7	70	2	0
Dacono	4,237	6	0	1	0	5	55	13	37	5	0
Del Norte	1,543	0	0	0	0	0	24	6	17	1	0
Delta	9,270	32	0	7	3	22	381	61	306	14	5
Denver	607,051	3,291	22	367	926	1,976	20,671	4,501	12,944	3,226	128
Durango	16,608	74	0	18	8	48	800	107	657	36	1
Eagle	6,367	4	0	1	0	3	82	21	55	6	3
Edgewater	5,055	20	0	5	8	7	330	37	269	24	1
Elizabeth	1,443	2	0	0	0	2	40	10	28	2	0
Empire	311	0	0	0	0	0	11	6	5	0	0
Englewood	32,494	145	1	16	27	101	1,968	254	1,520	194	8
Erie	18,772	1	0	0	0	1	42	12	26	4	0
Estes Park	6,553	1	0	0	1	0	99	16	81	2	0
Evans	20,440	35	2	3	8	22	414	89	294	31	11
Fairplay	640	2	0	0	0	2	12	3	5	4	1
Federal Heights	12,114	58	1	14	10	33	476	70	370	36	7
Firestone	9,436	8	0	1	1	6	207	23	167	17	0
Florence	3,533	4	0	0	0	4	40	5	32	3	0
Fort Collins	138,689	438	0	64	50	324	4,551	643	3,706	202	36
Fort Lupton	7,677	11	0	1	4	6	165	32	123	10	1
Fort Morgan	10,262	24	1	1	7	15	281	47	225	9	1
Fraser/Winter Park	1,825	12	0	0	0	12	41	9	27	5	1
Frederick	9,196	0	0	0	0	0	116	27	84	5	0
Fruita	12,848	12	1	5	1	5	275	52	215	8	9
Glendale	4,790	29	1	1	8	19	447	33	377	37	2
Glenwood Springs	9,105	30	0	6	2	22	396	40	351	5	2
Golden	17,226	20	0	2	3	15	403	60	332	11	4
Granby	1,636	9	1	2	0	6	43	7	36	0	0
Grand Junction	59,029	206	2	42	28	134	2,167	333	1,734	100	9
Greeley	92,804	425	1	41	56	327	2,970	537	2,285	148	36
Greenwood Village	14,430	34	0	6	9	19	565	96	438	31	4
Gunnison	5,451	24	0	2	0	22	366	53	307	6	3
Hayden	1,623	7	0	2	1	4	37	7	30	0	1
Holyoke	2,190	3	0	1	0	2	21	1	20	0	0
Idaho Springs	1,648	15	0	1	1	13	94	8	78	8	1
Ignacio	781	1	0	0	0	1	3	1	2	0	0
Johnstown	10,277	20	0	1	1	18	153	43	99	11	2
Kersey	1,472	7	0	1	0	6	25	5	18	2	0
Kiowa	607	6	0	1	0	5	16	3	13	0	1
Kremmling	1,451	6	0	0	0	6	20	3	15	2	0
Lafayette	26,055	40	1	7	4	28	485	97	379	9	6
Lakeside	19	1	0	0	1	0	10	2	8	0	0
Lakewood	139,615	618	1	95	137	385	5,970	949	4,500	521	18
La Salle	2,000	7	0	0	0	7	31	10	19	2	0
Leadville	2,693	20	0	1	0	19	39	13	24	2	0
Limon	1,644	1	0	0	0	1	7	3	4	0	0

[1] The FBI does not publish arson data unless it receives data from either the agency or the state for all 12 months of the calendar year.

Table 8.   Offenses Known to Law Enforcement, by State and City, 2010—*Continued*

(Number)

State/city	Population	Violent crime	Murder and non-negligent man-slaughter	Forcible rape	Robbery	Aggravated assault	Property crime	Burglary	Larceny-theft	Motor vehicle theft	Arson[1]
COLORADO—*Continued*											
Littleton	40,544	53	1	3	22	27	1,185	238	851	96	3
Lone Tree	9,718	22	0	5	5	12	494	19	468	7	0
Longmont	88,913	277	1	5	36	235	2,205	329	1,736	140	54
Louisville	19,429	8	0	0	0	8	239	36	196	7	1
Loveland	66,857	128	0	21	15	92	1,592	199	1,325	68	13
Mancos	1,256	9	0	1	0	8	18	6	11	1	2
Manitou Springs	5,169	12	0	2	2	8	200	28	166	6	1
Meeker	2,457	14	0	0	0	14	32	6	25	1	1
Milliken	6,593	4	0	1	0	3	59	20	38	1	0
Monte Vista	3,879	9	0	1	2	6	98	39	58	1	0
Montrose	18,758	42	2	5	5	30	697	94	586	17	15
Monument	5,257	1	0	1	0	0	105	15	86	4	1
Morrison	409	6	0	0	0	6	7	1	6	0	0
Mount Crested Butte	866	2	0	1	0	1	14	4	9	1	0
Nederland	1,381	0	0	0	0	0	14	4	10	0	0
Northglenn	34,467	88	1	13	7	67	1,047	150	785	112	6
Olathe	1,755	0	0	0	0	0	21	8	12	1	0
Pagosa Springs	1,814	9	0	1	1	7	101	15	82	4	0
Parachute	1,301	1	0	1	0	0	14	6	6	2	0
Parker	46,794	31	0	8	7	16	512	96	393	23	3
Platteville	2,685	2	0	0	0	2	27	2	21	4	0
Pueblo5	103,612	885	1	30	157	697	4,972	1,622	2,899	451	51
Rangely	2,166	3	0	0	0	3	21	1	20	0	0
Rocky Ford	3,830	15	0	0	0	15	115	44	69	2	0
Salida	5,337	9	0	2	0	7	154	13	137	4	1
Sheridan	6,150	40	1	10	7	22	374	58	268	48	2
Silt	2,767	2	0	1	0	1	35	5	25	5	0
Silverthorne	4,094	9	1	2	1	5	132	17	112	3	2
Snowmass Village	2,009	0	0	0	0	0	52	2	48	2	1
Springfield	1,221	7	0	1	0	6	7	1	4	2	0
Steamboat Springs	12,426	34	0	6	1	27	308	41	254	13	1
Sterling	12,517	61	0	16	0	45	429	120	290	19	2
Telluride	2,380	6	0	1	1	4	170	22	144	4	0
Thornton6	119,989		5	42	55		3,625	555	2,766	304	18
Timnath	683	0	0	0	0	0	21	0	19	2	0
Vail	4,794	13	0	1	0	12	346	42	301	3	0
Westminster	108,383	231	1	34	48	148	3,250	529	2,395	326	12
Wheat Ridge	30,400	172	0	22	30	120	1,306	241	932	133	6
Windsor	18,088	18	0	5	0	13	251	47	198	6	4
Woodland Park	6,540	3	0	0	0	3	64	5	59	0	0
Yuma	3,240	1	0	0	0	1	38	10	27	1	1
CONNECTICUT											
Ansonia	18,743	27	0	2	18	7	324	36	249	39	2
Avon5	17,734	5	0	1	1	3	186	38	147	1	1
Berlin	20,963	15	0	2	2	11	340	69	260	11	3
Bethel	18,814	5	0	1	3	1	195	31	158	6	1
Bloomfield	21,086	32	1	3	9	19	490	76	394	20	2
Branford	29,415	37	1	0	6	30	804	101	653	50	1
Bridgeport	138,810	1,412	22	57	561	772	4,683	1,448	2,377	858	20
Bristol	61,879	200	1	27	32	140	1,335	290	974	71	0
Brookfield	16,994	5	0	0	2	3	142	39	102	1	0
Canton	10,392	5	0	0	1	4	114	14	98	2	0
Cheshire	29,569	12	0	0	2	10	303	62	230	11	1
Clinton	13,832	17	0	7	2	8	388	134	248	6	4
Coventry	12,546	7	0	1	4	2	165	45	109	11	1
Cromwell	13,919	17	0	1	12	4	354	48	290	16	1
Danbury	81,242	116	2	21	46	47	1,515	258	1,177	80	5
Darien	20,617	1	0	0	1	0	142	39	97	6	0
Derby	12,542	36	0	2	9	25	380	69	280	31	0
East Hampton	13,122	9	0	0	3	6	160	54	97	9	0
East Hartford	49,156	186	6	20	74	86	1,545	345	1,042	158	10
East Haven	28,973	43	0	3	20	20	944	119	744	81	1
Easton	7,483	0	0	0	0	0	35	15	20	0	0
East Windsor	11,310	13	0	2	4	7	309	53	235	21	8
Fairfield	58,331	35	0	2	15	18	1,044	118	849	77	0
Farmington	25,615	11	0	6	4	1	698	40	634	24	4
Glastonbury	33,921	29	0	1	11	17	349	85	258	6	0
Granby	11,451	4	0	1	0	3	109	22	83	4	2
Greenwich	63,281	22	0	1	9	12	553	94	421	38	4
Groton	9,492	26	0	4	6	16	157	27	124	6	0
Groton Long Point	703	0	0	0	0	0	7	1	6	0	0
Groton Town	29,842	29	1	6	8	14	509	95	403	11	3
Guilford	22,861	20	0	2	1	17	435	70	352	13	0

[1] The FBI does not publish arson data unless it receives data from either the agency or the state for all 12 months of the calendar year.

[5] Because of changes in the state/local agency's reporting practices, figures are not comparable to previous years' data.

Table 8. Offenses Known to Law Enforcement, by State and City, 2010—*Continued*

(Number)

State/city	Population	Violent crime	Murder and non-negligent man-slaughter	Forcible rape	Robbery	Aggravated assault	Property crime	Burglary	Larceny-theft	Motor vehicle theft	Arson[1]
CONNECTICUT—*Continued*											
Hartford	125,626	1,624	26	46	570	982	5,495	1,019	3,639	837	95
Madison	19,155	18	1	3	1	13	211	58	150	3	1
Manchester	57,271	131	8	11	36	76	1,847	253	1,510	84	5
Meriden	60,032	144	0	6	70	68	1,837	416	1,289	132	6
Middlebury	7,588	2	0	1	0	1	97	25	70	2	0
Middletown	49,281	59	0	4	20	35	1,130	157	914	59	3
Milford	57,565	55	1	3	19	32	1,628	183	1,365	80	4
Monroe	19,696	4	0	0	0	4	132	34	92	6	1
Naugatuck	32,529	30	0	9	9	12	623	75	503	45	2
New Britain	71,344	308	2	6	157	143	3,052	762	1,886	404	2
New Canaan	20,312	1	0	0	0	1	134	32	100	2	0
New Haven	124,856	1,992	23	70	787	1,112	7,227	1,399	4,815	1,013	17
Newington	30,246	32	0	5	17	10	814	104	668	42	0
New London	26,517	286	2	14	50	220	912	257	585	70	8
New Milford	29,006	18	0	3	1	14	356	18	325	13	3
Newtown	27,366	16	1	3	2	10	204	48	154	2	0
North Branford	14,619	8	0	1	0	7	277	48	206	23	0
North Haven	24,306	17	2	0	8	7	583	74	493	16	0
Norwalk	84,944	343	6	12	129	196	1,878	323	1,379	176	12
Norwich	37,157	144	2	21	46	75	971	266	656	49	19
Plainfield	15,720	6	0	2	1	3	53	27	24	2	0
Plainville	17,511	54	0	0	11	43	596	59	512	25	0
Plymouth	12,202	12	0	1	4	7	270	58	197	15	1
Portland	9,785	12	0	0	1	11	71	22	38	11	0
Putnam	9,458	30	0	3	3	24	176	32	139	5	6
Redding	9,003	0	0	0	0	0	75	15	59	1	0
Ridgefield	24,591	3	0	0	0	3	84	6	77	1	0
Rocky Hill	19,152	10	0	4	4	2	289	34	238	17	2
Seymour	16,616	20	0	3	3	14	189	46	124	19	2
Shelton	41,037	28	0	5	11	12	488	115	333	40	2
Simsbury	23,988	6	0	1	3	2	180	20	154	6	0
Southington	43,354	26	0	5	12	9	733	124	558	51	6
South Windsor	26,781	4	0	1	1	2	408	56	337	15	0
Stamford	122,933	351	2	19	152	178	1,969	348	1,429	192	10
Stonington	18,807	8	0	1	5	2	267	41	222	4	0
Stratford	49,469	148	1	15	43	89	1,312	188	1,004	120	8
Suffield	15,524	2	0	0	0	2	121	50	66	5	0
Thomaston	7,928	1	0	0	0	1	127	27	95	5	1
Torrington	35,876	51	0	20	10	21	862	140	703	19	2
Trumbull	35,425	21	0	3	8	10	695	51	609	35	0
Vernon	30,785	28	0	5	11	12	274	66	190	18	12
Wallingford	45,636	31	0	4	15	12	776	101	646	29	2
Waterbury	108,489	366	5	6	176	179	4,646	781	3,441	424	3
Waterford	19,161	48	0	4	5	39	496	57	435	4	3
Watertown	22,552	29	0	3	3	23	399	71	313	15	0
West Hartford	61,603	61	1	2	44	14	1,464	210	1,190	64	0
West Haven	53,746	428	4	1	56	367	1,400	208	995	197	9
Weston	10,344	1	0	1	0	0	68	7	58	3	1
Westport	27,242	14	0	2	5	7	393	78	299	16	0
Wethersfield	26,042	24	0	1	10	13	479	81	378	20	7
Willimantic	16,605	51	0	9	17	25	470	93	331	46	0
Wilton	18,007	0	0	0	0	0	96	20	76	0	0
Winchester	10,927	22	0	3	3	16	219	68	138	13	2
Windsor	29,447	23	1	3	8	11	500	69	406	25	6
Wolcott	16,799	4	1	1	1	1	269	55	206	8	1
Woodbridge	9,324	1	0	0	0	1	156	27	114	15	0
DELAWARE											
Bethany Beach	988	4	0	0	2	2	168	13	153	2	0
Blades	1,206	7	0	1	1	5	27	11	15	1	0
Bridgeville	1,724	16	0	0	5	11	80	10	67	3	0
Camden	2,642	14	0	2	5	7	227	10	211	6	0
Cheswold	526	3	0	2	0	1	16	0	16	0	0
Clayton	1,520	8	0	0	0	8	29	7	21	1	0
Dagsboro	596	1	0	0	0	1	23	4	19	0	0
Delaware City	1,542	2	0	0	0	2	34	10	21	3	1
Delmar	1,597	9	0	1	0	8	37	9	28	0	0
Dewey Beach	325	13	0	1	2	10	73	12	58	3	0
Dover	37,113	239	1	10	52	176	2,122	151	1,858	113	11
Ellendale	371	0	0	0	0	0	5	0	5	0	0
Elsmere	5,726	43	0	3	6	34	193	46	130	17	0
Felton	922	0	0	0	0	0	19	4	15	0	0
Fenwick Island	375	0	0	0	0	0	10	2	8	0	0
Frankford	800	0	0	0	0	0	2	2	0	0	0

[1] The FBI does not publish arson data unless it receives data from either the agency or the state for all 12 months of the calendar year.

Table 8. Offenses Known to Law Enforcement, by State and City, 2010—*Continued*

(Number)

State/city	Population	Violent crime	Murder and non-negligent man-slaughter	Forcible rape	Robbery	Aggravated assault	Property crime	Burglary	Larceny-theft	Motor vehicle theft	Arson[1]
DELAWARE—*Continued*											
Georgetown	5,313	46	0	6	16	24	279	75	199	5	0
Greenwood	931	2	0	0	0	2	42	17	25	0	0
Harrington	3,580	24	0	1	8	15	147	40	101	6	0
Laurel	4,087	69	0	5	18	46	254	74	174	6	2
Lewes	3,222	8	0	2	2	4	82	16	65	1	0
Middletown	13,710	66	0	4	18	44	406	75	317	14	2
Milford	8,792	133	0	9	42	82	649	90	543	16	0
Millsboro	2,831	24	0	3	1	20	142	26	110	6	0
Milton	1,882	26	0	1	2	23	133	79	51	3	0
Newark	30,543	139	1	10	39	89	947	185	733	29	11
New Castle	5,049	24	0	2	7	15	254	35	213	6	0
Newport	1,138	5	0	0	0	5	50	14	33	3	0
Ocean View	1,178	1	0	0	0	1	39	18	21	0	0
Rehoboth Beach	1,624	13	0	0	8	5	227	27	198	2	0
Seaford	7,403	56	1	3	19	33	419	78	331	10	0
Selbyville	1,935	14	0	0	2	12	94	34	58	2	1
Smyrna	9,322	54	0	8	14	32	273	65	203	5	0
South Bethany	538	0	0	0	0	0	24	6	18	0	0
Wilmington	73,270	1,399	28	27	633	711	4,147	1,176	2,428	543	2
Wyoming	1,468	1	0	1	0	0	33	14	17	2	0
DISTRICT OF COLUMBIA											
Washington	601,723	7,468	132	184	3,914	3,238	27,138	4,224	18,050	4,864	49
FLORIDA											
Alachua	9,757	42	0	3	12	27	278	76	193	9	0
Altamonte Springs	39,774	165	0	11	45	109	1,364	283	1,005	76	5
Altha	514	1	0	0	0	1	11	2	9	0	0
Apalachicola	2,192	0	0	0	0	0	12	2	9	1	0
Apopka	40,095	244	2	9	106	127	1,411	406	929	76	4
Arcadia	6,926	96	0	7	21	68	247	86	147	14	3
Astatula	1,908	2	0	0	0	2	8	4	4	0	0
Atlantic Beach	13,139	72	0	5	18	49	416	98	298	20	0
Atlantis	2,088	11	0	0	3	8	8	7	0	1	0
Auburndale	14,204	64	1	2	18	43	797	199	575	23	0
Aventura	30,874	55	1	0	22	32	2,216	117	2,054	45	0
Avon Park	8,850	56	0	2	15	39	337	85	243	9	3
Bal Harbour Village	3,230	1	0	0	0	1	84	4	76	4	0
Bartow	17,072	112	3	6	34	69	1,050	247	767	36	1
Bay Harbor Islands	5,126	1	0	1	0	0	64	28	30	6	0
Belleair	4,052	1	0	0	0	1	51	10	39	2	0
Belleair Beach	1,572	4	0	1	0	3	29	6	22	1	0
Belleair Bluffs	2,141	3	0	0	2	1	43	10	32	1	0
Belle Glade	16,992	353	4	11	71	267	1,229	400	769	60	7
Belle Isle	6,603	12	0	0	2	10	149	60	72	17	0
Belleview	4,538	21	0	7	6	8	235	85	145	5	0
Biscayne Park	3,054	4	0	0	0	4	104	63	36	5	0
Blountstown	2,475	6	0	0	0	6	32	3	27	2	0
Boca Raton	86,707	176	1	13	49	113	2,507	459	1,940	108	1
Bonifay	2,696	4	0	1	0	3	29	6	22	1	1
Bowling Green	2,986	8	1	1	0	6	71	28	42	1	0
Boynton Beach	70,574	585	4	6	143	432	3,195	727	2,361	107	5
Bradenton	54,337	383	0	28	114	241	2,064	530	1,435	99	14
Bradenton Beach	1,585	2	0	0	1	1	33	6	26	1	0
Brooksville	8,333	69	0	3	11	55	317	61	243	13	0
Bunnell	3,096	48	0	1	6	41	157	27	97	33	0
Bushnell	2,279	9	0	0	3	6	93	20	71	2	0
Cape Coral	160,432	276	3	23	64	186	3,787	1,083	2,595	109	9
Carrabelle	1,222	5	0	0	1	4	25	11	9	5	0
Casselberry	24,802	213	0	16	45	152	869	191	645	33	1
Cedar Key	970	0	0	0	0	0	21	5	15	1	0
Center Hill	1,117	4	0	1	0	3	6	3	3	0	0
Chattahoochee	3,661	39	0	0	3	36	44	14	28	2	0
Chiefland	2,193	4	0	0	0	4	276	115	120	41	0
Chipley	3,780	26	0	1	0	25	84	25	53	6	0
Clearwater	105,647	775	5	35	245	490	4,338	777	3,360	201	12
Clermont	13,802	93	1	12	27	53	932	194	697	41	4
Clewiston	7,168	48	0	1	11	36	239	61	164	14	1
Cocoa	16,469	442	2	20	75	345	1,431	474	892	65	4
Cocoa Beach	11,790	95	0	8	14	73	890	81	786	23	2
Coconut Creek	51,184	89	0	7	29	53	1,433	283	1,038	112	0
Cooper City	29,679	50	0	5	10	35	624	156	452	16	7
Coral Gables	44,559	93	2	3	35	53	1,953	376	1,512	65	1
Coral Springs	127,113	261	1	8	78	174	2,884	517	2,192	175	4
Crescent City	1,779	15	0	0	6	9	108	47	56	5	0

[1] The FBI does not publish arson data unless it receives data from either the agency or the state for all 12 months of the calendar year.

Table 8.   Offenses Known to Law Enforcement, by State and City, 2010—*Continued*

(Number)

State/city	Population	Violent crime	Murder and non-negligent man-slaughter	Forcible rape	Robbery	Aggravated assault	Property crime	Burglary	Larceny-theft	Motor vehicle theft	Arson[1]
FLORIDA—*Continued*											
Crestview	20,424	87	1	8	16	62	644	155	460	29	3
Cross City	1,776	3	0	0	3	0	30	5	24	1	0
Crystal River	3,497	33	0	1	5	27	227	32	191	4	0
Cutler Bay	30,221	207	0	5	64	138	1,862	297	1,464	101	0
Dade City	7,268	51	0	3	8	40	300	109	183	8	2
Dania	28,533	227	0	14	76	137	1,477	366	984	127	3
Davenport	3,002	6	0	3	3	0	50	23	18	9	0
Davie	92,661	367	3	21	92	251	3,643	799	2,586	258	17
Daytona Beach	63,736	811	3	31	229	548	4,635	1,083	3,089	463	16
Daytona Beach Shores	5,137	31	0	4	2	25	228	100	110	18	0
Deerfield Beach	75,195	429	1	24	156	248	2,509	581	1,752	176	5
De Funiak Springs	5,122	72	0	5	1	66	193	69	118	6	1
Deland	27,926	153	0	4	36	113	1,366	359	948	59	9
Delray Beach	65,087	590	3	22	198	367	3,340	724	2,423	193	7
Doral	32,645	88	0	3	24	61	2,737	319	2,257	161	0
Dunedin	35,854	108	0	15	19	74	1,160	208	915	37	6
Dunnellon	1,941	6	0	0	1	5	30	20	10	0	0
Eatonville	2,359	30	1	1	2	26	122	39	72	11	0
Edgewater	21,456	50	0	3	10	37	633	199	399	35	4
Edgewood	2,116	3	0	0	2	1	90	29	56	5	0
El Portal	2,393	7	0	0	3	4	84	21	41	22	0
Eustis	19,455	41	1	5	12	23	642	138	476	28	2
Fellsmere	5,194	13	0	0	5	8	94	26	52	16	0
Fernandina Beach	11,721	43	0	2	15	26	351	73	274	4	1
Flagler Beach	5,467	8	0	0	1	7	141	40	94	7	0
Florida City	10,883	305	0	0	95	210	1,213	244	917	52	0
Fort Lauderdale	186,170	1,356	7	73	627	649	9,914	2,841	6,437	636	44
Fort Myers	66,053	698	7	29	152	510	2,699	628	1,877	194	7
Fort Pierce	42,797	482	9	27	142	304	2,396	689	1,615	92	15
Fort Walton Beach	18,432	98	1	11	17	69	929	186	681	62	1
Fruitland Park	4,914	18	0	1	1	16	113	28	76	9	0
Gainesville	116,880	906	4	86	199	617	5,404	1,213	3,859	332	22
Golden Beach	909	1	0	0	0	1	29	6	20	3	0
Graceville	2,411	2	0	0	1	1	80	23	54	3	0
Greenacres City	33,244	179	2	15	60	102	1,057	342	651	64	2
Green Cove Springs	6,731	70	0	9	11	50	239	48	174	17	0
Gretna	1,749	20	0	0	1	19	29	17	11	1	0
Groveland	8,353	21	0	1	0	20	163	35	111	17	0
Gulf Breeze	6,704	5	0	1	1	3	82	13	66	3	0
Gulfport	12,212	41	0	2	15	24	466	103	330	33	6
Gulf Stream	744	1	0	0	0	1	12	4	8	0	0
Haines City	19,411	127	0	5	40	82	832	239	560	33	2
Hallandale	39,359	346	0	7	108	231	1,786	478	1,183	125	2
Hampton	460	2	0	0	0	2	5	3	1	1	0
Havana	1,668	6	0	0	2	4	71	27	43	1	0
Hialeah	217,995	951	12	40	256	643	7,858	1,098	5,693	1,067	14
Hialeah Gardens	20,554	52	0	3	17	32	989	119	792	78	4
Highland Beach	4,016	3	0	1	0	2	39	7	31	1	0
High Springs	4,775	23	0	2	2	19	133	37	91	5	2
Hillsboro Beach	2,279	3	0	0	2	1	38	6	31	1	0
Holly Hill	13,204	123	0	6	34	83	670	163	416	91	1
Hollywood	142,793	596	7	40	237	312	7,265	1,833	4,797	635	8
Holmes Beach	5,130	5	0	0	2	3	149	53	95	1	0
Homestead	63,761	857	3	25	298	531	3,012	896	1,983	133	11
Howey-in-the-Hills	1,270	0	0	0	0	0	13	5	7	1	0
Hypoluxo	2,606	2	0	0	1	1	49	8	41	0	0
Indialantic	2,905	4	0	1	0	3	88	21	67	0	0
Indian Creek Village	40	0	0	0	0	0	0	0	0	0	0
Indian Harbour Beach	8,253	9	0	0	3	6	167	34	125	8	2
Indian River Shores	3,449	0	0	0	0	0	19	7	12	0	0
Indian Rocks Beach	5,108	22	0	6	1	15	107	22	81	4	0
Indian Shores	4,213	2	0	1	0	1	64	13	49	2	0
Inglis	1,630	8	0	1	0	7	72	23	48	1	0
Interlachen	1,497	12	0	0	3	9	89	27	56	6	0
Jacksonville	822,414	5,469	80	316	1,693	3,380	37,424	9,588	25,863	1,973	99
Jacksonville Beach	22,140	201	0	9	39	153	1,127	128	949	50	3
Jasper	2,063	15	0	0	3	12	61	31	30	0	0
Jennings	861	8	0	0	2	6	25	10	13	2	0
Juno Beach	3,369	3	0	0	1	2	89	13	70	6	0
Jupiter	51,785	122	2	10	37	73	1,068	203	818	47	1
Jupiter Inlet Colony	392	0	0	0	0	0	4	1	3	0	0
Jupiter Island	684	0	0	0	0	0	5	3	2	0	0
Kenneth City	4,257	33	0	2	5	26	203	31	161	11	0

[1] The FBI does not publish arson data unless it receives data from either the agency or the state for all 12 months of the calendar year.

Table 8.   Offenses Known to Law Enforcement, by State and City, 2010—*Continued*

(Number)

State/city	Population	Violent crime	Murder and non-negligent man-slaughter	Forcible rape	Robbery	Aggravated assault	Property crime	Burglary	Larceny-theft	Motor vehicle theft	Arson[1]
FLORIDA—*Continued*											
Key Biscayne	10,097	2	0	0	0	2	191	8	170	13	0
Key Colony Beach	760	1	0	0	0	1	23	5	17	1	0
Key West	22,167	186	1	21	63	101	1,709	363	1,224	122	2
Kissimmee	64,122	599	1	19	122	457	3,218	856	2,192	170	17
Lady Lake	15,487	50	0	7	2	41	341	61	250	30	1
Lake Alfred	4,652	14	0	0	2	12	99	26	69	4	0
Lake City	12,850	188	3	6	27	152	777	175	581	21	2
Lake Clarke Shores	3,341	9	0	0	1	8	76	19	50	7	0
Lake Hamilton	1,494	5	0	0	3	2	53	14	32	7	1
Lake Helen	2,767	6	0	1	0	5	64	18	43	3	0
Lakeland	94,569	459	12	20	140	287	5,099	1,104	3,754	241	6
Lake Mary	15,641	24	0	1	1	22	326	67	251	8	0
Lake Park	8,727	73	0	1	25	47	624	116	478	30	0
Lake Placid	1,996	10	0	0	4	6	97	28	67	2	0
Lake Wales	14,593	52	0	0	15	37	861	161	684	16	0
Lake Worth	35,977	449	3	12	202	232	1,677	507	1,051	119	7
Lantana	10,229	75	0	12	31	32	465	102	348	15	1
Largo	73,019	506	3	39	131	333	3,347	527	2,668	152	14
Lauderdale-by-the-Sea	5,874	16	0	1	6	9	177	48	120	9	0
Lauderdale Lakes	32,139	329	5	10	90	224	1,602	532	975	95	6
Lauderhill	67,442	538	2	33	205	298	2,582	1,021	1,368	193	10
Lawtey	698	0	0	0	0	0	8	5	3	0	0
Leesburg	22,949	198	1	14	58	125	1,095	207	856	32	2
Lighthouse Point	11,232	14	0	0	5	9	339	54	273	12	1
Live Oak	7,232	73	0	3	18	52	344	150	182	12	0
Longboat Key	7,223	1	0	0	0	1	119	24	94	1	0
Longwood	13,443	75	1	2	15	57	544	170	364	10	0
Lynn Haven	15,678	58	0	1	9	48	592	67	512	13	1
Madeira Beach	4,292	34	0	4	6	24	268	56	208	4	4
Madison	2,992	40	0	2	4	34	218	72	142	4	0
Maitland	15,489	35	0	1	12	22	456	136	293	27	0
Manalapan	345	1	0	1	0	0	16	3	13	0	0
Mangonia Park	1,240	65	0	4	22	39	241	72	145	24	1
Marco Island	15,820	18	0	3	1	14	161	21	135	5	0
Margate	54,478	151	1	3	44	103	1,141	337	725	79	4
Marianna	6,170	78	2	12	14	50	288	57	215	16	1
Mascotte	6,042	18	0	2	0	16	80	23	52	5	0
Medley	1,077	16	1	0	3	12	339	30	263	46	0
Melbourne	77,861	685	7	28	144	506	3,672	771	2,769	132	13
Melbourne Beach	3,107	3	0	0	0	3	37	2	34	1	0
Melbourne Village	666	0	0	0	0	0	10	2	8	0	0
Mexico Beach	1,304	4	0	0	0	4	64	28	35	1	0
Miami	440,482	4,879	68	46	1,856	2,909	21,218	4,604	14,165	2,449	104
Miami Beach	87,990	864	8	39	352	465	8,743	1,192	6,957	594	9
Miami Gardens	110,130	1,061	22	25	351	663	5,410	1,321	3,515	574	12
Miami Lakes	22,578	55	2	2	17	34	672	121	490	61	0
Miami Shores	10,132	46	0	0	30	16	631	146	454	31	0
Miami Springs	12,924	45	1	3	21	20	503	105	352	46	1
Milton	8,805	32	0	4	10	18	345	88	252	5	0
Minneola	9,599	37	0	2	1	34	156	42	105	9	1
Miramar	113,385	540	9	34	170	327	3,651	1,262	2,099	290	13
Monticello	2,426	37	0	0	3	34	52	44	7	1	0
Mount Dora	14,053	71	0	10	18	43	510	90	384	36	2
Naples	22,239	25	1	1	8	15	630	88	533	9	0
Neptune Beach	6,707	22	1	1	3	17	313	44	257	12	1
New Port Richey	17,634	166	0	10	42	114	891	353	501	37	3
New Smyrna Beach	23,656	117	1	3	22	91	1,151	290	821	40	3
Niceville	12,145	17	0	3	1	13	235	49	171	15	0
North Bay Village	8,316	9	0	0	0	9	181	59	103	19	0
North Lauderdale	42,998	198	0	13	75	110	1,097	459	563	75	2
North Miami	57,796	616	6	23	278	309	3,371	931	2,110	330	18
North Miami Beach	41,170	346	2	29	136	179	2,109	743	1,189	177	7
North Palm Beach	12,255	24	0	0	9	15	296	80	194	22	0
North Port	59,076	194	1	11	26	156	1,386	320	1,035	31	9
North Redington Beach	1,464	6	0	0	0	6	42	7	35	0	0
Oak Hill	1,654	12	0	6	1	5	75	23	45	7	1
Oakland	1,228	6	0	1	1	4	41	13	23	5	0
Oakland Park	42,572	300	3	17	133	147	2,121	611	1,387	123	2
Ocala	56,396	461	3	34	155	269	3,171	712	2,372	87	4
Ocean Ridge	1,654	3	0	0	0	3	44	14	30	0	0
Ocoee	33,650	159	0	9	48	102	1,255	257	929	69	7
Okeechobee	5,924	33	0	1	17	15	380	74	296	10	0
Oldsmar	13,561	36	0	6	7	23	475	78	376	21	0

[1] The FBI does not publish arson data unless it receives data from either the agency or the state for all 12 months of the calendar year.

Table 8. Offenses Known to Law Enforcement, by State and City, 2010—*Continued*

(Number)

State/city	Population	Violent crime	Murder and non-negligent man-slaughter	Forcible rape	Robbery	Aggravated assault	Property crime	Burglary	Larceny-theft	Motor vehicle theft	Arson[1]
FLORIDA—*Continued*											
Opa Locka	16,762	413	5	8	113	287	1,150	422	583	145	3
Orange City	10,149	38	0	0	11	27	551	83	451	17	0
Orange Park	9,066	36	0	2	7	27	231	65	155	11	0
Orlando	240,222	2,574	18	113	672	1,771	15,565	4,015	10,357	1,193	42
Ormond Beach	37,923	251	0	13	14	224	1,385	277	1,050	58	1
Oviedo	33,670	78	3	8	9	58	564	106	438	20	2
Pahokee	6,797	67	0	2	13	52	155	54	95	6	2
Palatka	10,726	158	1	16	29	112	833	189	634	10	6
Palm Bay	103,350	521	4	19	60	438	2,460	740	1,622	98	10
Palm Beach	9,607	7	0	1	1	5	132	22	107	3	0
Palm Beach Gardens	51,458	72	1	3	35	33	1,614	265	1,286	63	5
Palm Beach Shores	1,576	0	0	0	0	0	43	14	24	5	0
Palmetto	14,554	201	2	2	59	138	661	249	390	22	2
Palmetto Bay	23,525	70	0	3	25	42	916	158	703	55	0
Palm Springs	17,223	122	2	6	40	74	874	231	582	61	1
Panama City	36,593	277	5	5	78	189	2,423	508	1,785	130	6
Panama City Beach	15,482	94	0	14	21	59	1,069	156	911	2	4
Parker	4,557	15	1	4	1	9	206	73	116	17	0
Parkland	25,432	17	0	1	1	15	268	56	195	17	5
Pembroke Park	4,904	39	0	0	19	20	361	74	241	46	1
Pembroke Pines	147,343	276	4	12	92	168	5,026	1,102	3,619	305	5
Pensacola	53,476	420	3	36	112	269	2,545	519	1,939	87	4
Perry	6,647	111	1	16	8	86	249	92	156	1	3
Pinellas Park	47,180	263	2	24	68	169	2,820	471	2,207	142	10
Plantation	85,000	291	2	14	124	151	3,755	779	2,732	244	5
Plant City	33,421	184	2	6	40	136	1,623	299	1,184	140	8
Pompano Beach	102,749	992	7	50	364	571	4,997	1,101	3,529	367	10
Ponce Inlet	3,165	1	0	0	1	0	37	9	28	0	0
Port Orange	55,381	102	2	2	19	79	1,411	262	1,072	77	1
Port Richey	3,426	22	1	0	14	7	142	29	111	2	0
Port St. Joe	3,479	15	0	0	4	11	23	9	13	1	0
Port St. Lucie	163,089	386	3	45	49	289	3,212	909	2,224	79	9
Punta Gorda	17,389	27	0	1	2	24	376	176	198	2	2
Quincy	6,736	110	1	8	18	83	380	106	266	8	3
Redington Beaches	1,467	3	0	0	0	3	30	7	20	3	0
Riviera Beach	37,637	584	14	13	125	432	1,851	638	1,050	163	7
Rockledge	25,230	72	0	0	14	58	742	159	553	30	0
Royal Palm Beach	31,800	111	0	14	22	75	1,062	174	826	62	4
Safety Harbor	17,010	29	0	3	4	22	406	80	319	7	2
Sanford	52,325	356	3	38	174	141	3,367	871	2,286	210	2
Sanibel	5,526	3	0	0	1	2	108	18	89	1	1
Sarasota	51,928	510	6	16	165	323	3,188	825	2,229	134	8
Satellite Beach	11,792	41	1	3	5	32	172	49	121	2	0
Sea Ranch Lakes	741	0	0	0	0	0	24	2	22	0	0
Sebastian	21,063	50	0	6	8	36	553	163	378	12	0
Sebring	10,518	59	1	4	15	39	462	129	323	10	3
Seminole	19,055	71	0	3	12	56	592	80	497	15	1
Sewall's Point	2,019	1	0	1	0	0	17	5	12	0	0
Shalimar	687	1	0	0	1	0	12	8	4	0	0
Sneads	1,944	5	0	2	0	3	98	3	94	1	3
South Bay	4,606	43	0	1	6	36	149	72	74	3	2
South Daytona	13,513	83	0	0	11	72	626	179	395	52	0
South Miami	11,154	88	3	2	33	50	820	126	668	26	1
South Palm Beach	1,474	0	0	0	0	0	17	5	12	0	0
South Pasadena	5,496	7	0	0	1	6	154	14	132	8	0
Southwest Ranches	7,298	13	0	2	3	8	185	44	127	14	1
Springfield	8,858	59	1	5	10	43	353	126	208	19	1
Starke	5,928	19	0	0	5	14	243	23	215	5	0
St. Augustine	12,794	93	0	7	19	67	741	127	587	27	1
St. Augustine Beach	6,522	7	0	0	1	6	190	26	157	7	0
St. Cloud	30,245	133	1	9	18	105	949	283	642	24	5
St. Pete Beach	9,855	35	0	6	5	24	532	152	364	16	3
St. Petersburg	243,666	2,758	13	105	752	1,888	13,815	3,564	9,015	1,236	90
Stuart	15,986	52	0	4	10	38	687	108	560	19	1
Sunny Isles Beach	17,052	33	0	7	6	20	464	79	359	26	0
Sunrise	90,016	338	2	13	124	199	3,972	832	2,957	183	4
Surfside	4,684	13	0	1	2	10	154	19	131	4	0
Sweetwater	13,563	40	0	3	11	26	248	43	178	27	4
Tallahassee	174,516	1,802	13	130	492	1,167	8,579	2,920	5,310	349	21
Tamarac	59,989	186	1	12	57	116	1,269	364	810	95	0
Tampa	347,830	2,170	27	47	684	1,412	11,453	3,131	7,484	838	107
Tarpon Springs	23,695	158	1	4	40	113	646	146	473	27	0
Tavares	14,353	35	0	3	7	25	210	42	146	22	0

[1] The FBI does not publish arson data unless it receives data from either the agency or the state for all 12 months of the calendar year.

Table 8.   Offenses Known to Law Enforcement, by State and City, 2010—*Continued*

(Number)

State/city	Population	Violent crime	Murder and non-negligent man-slaughter	Forcible rape	Robbery	Aggravated assault	Property crime	Burglary	Larceny-theft	Motor vehicle theft	Arson[1]
FLORIDA—*Continued*											
Temple Terrace	22,760	111	0	5	36	70	843	277	535	31	3
Tequesta	5,799	12	0	3	0	9	91	23	68	0	0
Titusville	44,839	350	1	19	80	250	1,486	361	1,030	95	7
Treasure Island	7,399	12	0	2	3	7	283	37	242	4	0
Umatilla	3,564	12	0	1	0	11	103	3	95	5	0
Valparaiso	5,783	6	0	1	2	3	58	14	43	1	0
Venice	20,997	36	2	0	4	30	567	87	466	14	1
Vero Beach	17,254	72	0	4	22	46	628	179	425	24	1
Village of Pinecrest	19,367	22	0	5	7	10	574	81	474	19	0
Virginia Gardens	2,241	2	0	0	0	2	25	6	13	6	0
Wauchula	4,640	33	0	3	9	21	225	115	101	9	1
Webster	922	4	0	0	0	4	23	6	15	2	0
Welaka	800	0	0	0	0	0	5	1	4	0	0
Wellington	56,532	125	4	8	17	96	1,590	301	1,191	98	5
West Melbourne	15,969	47	1	2	11	33	648	268	360	20	1
West Miami	5,739	11	0	0	1	10	181	67	103	11	0
Weston	65,406	38	0	3	5	30	756	135	585	36	1
West Palm Beach	101,267	789	19	49	264	457	5,052	1,246	3,415	391	17
West Park	14,516	83	2	2	34	45	606	232	321	53	1
White Springs	843	6	0	0	1	5	23	4	15	4	0
Wildwood	12,797	43	0	2	3	38	138	46	86	6	0
Williston	2,919	29	0	0	4	25	122	27	89	6	2
Wilton Manors	12,873	65	4	0	39	22	590	160	396	34	0
Windermere	2,689	0	0	0	0	0	10	2	8	0	0
Winter Garden	32,096	160	0	6	30	124	1,074	197	821	56	8
Winter Haven	33,981	244	2	10	68	164	1,915	368	1,462	85	6
Winter Park	28,069	69	0	2	26	41	879	272	565	42	4
Winter Springs	32,862	56	0	5	9	42	412	112	278	22	1
Zephyrhills	13,360	65	1	4	23	37	943	232	688	23	0
GEORGIA											
Acworth	19,939	14	0	0	5	9	426	35	366	25	0
Adairsville	3,358	17	0	1	6	10	148	38	107	3	0
Adel	5,236	10	0	2	2	6	269	105	158	6	0
Alamo	2,671	1	0	0	0	1	32	11	20	1	0
Albany	73,034	722	11	28	203	480	5,037	1,629	3,108	300	15
Alma	3,435	29	1	4	6	18	127	34	89	4	1
Alpharetta	50,392	49	0	2	24	23	1,467	189	1,253	25	1
Alto	911	2	0	0	0	2	12	3	8	1	0
Americus	15,694	271	0	1	36	234	1,176	471	666	39	
Aragon	1,051	0	0	0	0	0	23	0	23	0	0
Arcade	1,908	3	0	0	0	3	22	12	10	0	0
Athens-Clarke County	112,861	371	5	29	110	227	4,931	1,334	3,299	298	15
Atlanta	536,472	5,749	93	89	2,162	3,405	30,800	8,016	17,741	5,043	95
Attapulgus	433	0	0	0	0	0	0	0	0	0	0
Auburn	7,600	4	0	0	1	3	70	25	32	13	
Austell	7,024	42	0	1	3	38	267	55	188	24	
Avondale Estates	2,788	4	1	0	3	0	98	8	82	8	0
Bainbridge	11,641	99	1	3	21	74	654	178	462	14	
Ball Ground	1,003	2	0	0	1	1	30	10	18	2	0
Barnesville	6,159	57	1	3	6	47	181	35	133	13	0
Baxley	4,377	28	0	2	6	20	262	62	194	6	1
Berlin	602	0	0	0	0	0	2	1	1	0	0
Blackshear	3,461	24	0	6	4	14	198	55	133	10	0
Blairsville	697	0	0	0	0	0	0	0	0	0	0
Blakely	4,960	34	0	1	0	33	129	41	86	2	
Bloomingdale	2,591	0	0	0	0	0	69	20	45	4	
Blythe	814	0	0	0	0	0	9	1	8	0	0
Bowdon	2,008	23	0	0	0	23	65	18	44	3	0
Braselton	6,538	10	0	4	5	1	106	9	84	13	0
Brooklet	1,329	0	0	0	0	0	18	3	15	0	0
Brunswick	15,871	238	2	8	76	152	1,418	406	960	52	8
Buchanan	982	2	0	0	0	2	70	20	47	3	0
Buena Vista	1,584	18	0	0	4	14	61	13	46	2	0
Butler	1,705	10	0	0	1	9	16	5	8	3	0
Cairo	9,607	22	0	6	8	8	269	61	191	17	
Calhoun	14,710	38	0	3	9	26	685	149	513	23	9
Camilla	5,149	67	0	2	6	59	210	55	151	4	0
Canton	24,697	17	0	3	5	9	471	51	394	26	1
Carrollton	23,014	318	2	13	27	276	1,400	253	1,107	40	10
Cartersville	18,646	58	0	7	16	35	904	161	692	51	2
Cave Spring	1,020	4	0	0	0	4	25	5	15	5	
Cedartown	9,900	56	0	7	5	44	313	68	224	21	0
Centerville	7,332	19	0	5	6	8	267	44	219	4	2

[1] The FBI does not publish arson data unless it receives data from either the agency or the state for all 12 months of the calendar year.

Table 8. Offenses Known to Law Enforcement, by State and City, 2010—*Continued*

(Number)

State/city	Population	Violent crime	Murder and non-negligent man-slaughter	Forcible rape	Robbery	Aggravated assault	Property crime	Burglary	Larceny-theft	Motor vehicle theft	Arson[1]
GEORGIA—*Continued*											
Chamblee	10,990	91	2	2	60	27	677	80	540	57	
Chatsworth	4,086	14	0	0	0	14	146	19	124	3	1
Chattahoochee Hills	2,315	14	1	0	0	13	35	10	19	6	0
Chickamauga	2,554	10	0	0	0	10	82	21	61	0	0
Clarkesville	1,708	13	0	0	0	13	43	5	37	1	0
Claxton	2,289	10	0	0	1	9	138	32	99	7	
Cleveland	2,856	37	0	0	1	36	226	84	137	5	0
Climax	269	0	0	0	0	0	0	0	0	0	0
Cochran	5,087	15	0	2	3	10	210	60	148	2	1
College Park	19,917	293	10	21	154	108	2,237	592	1,348	297	6
Colquitt	1,871	6	0	3	0	3	40	16	23	1	0
Columbus	184,576	1,005	15	38	477	475	13,442	3,454	8,981	1,007	65
Commerce	6,477	24	0	2	2	20	180	27	145	8	1
Conyers	13,738	74	4	2	34	34	1,020	205	757	58	2
Coolidge	545	2	0	0	1	1	12	6	2	4	0
Cordele	11,110	85	1	7	31	46	874	222	619	33	1
Cornelia	3,725	12	0	4	3	5	181	28	148	5	0
Cumming	5,891	17	2	2	2	11	368	51	309	8	0
Cuthbert	3,286	5	0	0	4	1	63	15	47	1	
Dallas	11,260	41	1	1	5	34	348	83	236	29	0
Dalton	33,064	76	0	4	27	45	1,182	285	838	59	4
Danielsville	423	6	0	0	0	6	25	5	19	1	0
Dawson	4,470	31	0	0	4	27	97	97	0	0	0
Decatur	18,391	35	1	2	21	11	577	100	431	46	0
Dillard	228	0	0	0	0	0	0	0	0	0	0
Donalsonville	2,589	5	0	0	1	4	61	15	44	2	0
Doraville	9,965	83	0	1	26	56	376	68	285	23	0
Douglasville	32,033	209	1	9	36	163	2,173	221	1,863	89	4
Dublin	17,200	145	0	3	42	100	1,400	314	1,046	40	2
Duluth	26,199	42	1	3	15	23	643	140	469	34	0
Dunwoody	32,815	103	3	8	50	42	1,691	240	1,334	117	
East Dublin	2,748	24	0	0	2	22	97	25	70	2	0
East Ellijay	700	3	0	0	0	3	70	2	67	1	0
Eastman	5,334	52	0	3	8	41	488	79	401	8	0
East Point	42,311	359	7	15	205	132	3,644	1,228	1,955	461	6
Edison	1,167	6	0	0	3	3	17	9	6	2	
Elberton	4,471	37	0	2	6	29	489	134	347	8	
Ellaville	1,820	2	0	0	0	2	20	7	13	0	
Ellijay	1,569	0	0	0	0	0	0	0	0	0	0
Emerson	1,513	6	0	1	1	4	34	3	28	3	1
Enigma	855	8	0	0	0	8	28	4	24	0	0
Ephesus	374	0	0	0	0	0	0	0	0	0	0
Eton	470	2	0	0	0	2	14	6	8	0	0
Fairburn	11,644	39	0	2	14	23	500	144	302	54	0
Fairmount	790	1	0	0	0	1	19	7	11	1	0
Fayetteville	15,019	39	1	3	13	22	414	58	332	24	
Flowery Branch	4,287	0	0	0	0	0	50	16	34	0	
Folkston	3,076	14	0	1	1	12	90	23	61	6	0
Forest Park	21,132	183	2	10	95	76	1,033	247	688	98	7
Forsyth	5,111	21	0	2	6	13	190	17	164	9	0
Fort Gaines	922	0	0	0	0	0	0	0	0	0	0
Fort Oglethorpe	9,863	30	0	2	10	18	528	62	459	7	0
Fort Valley	7,785	111	0	2	14	95	502	147	342	13	0
Franklin	912	7	0	1	0	6	40	3	35	2	
Franklin Springs	708	0	0	0	0	0	12	1	11	0	0
Gainesville	35,657	119	1	17	39	62	1,623	278	1,283	62	3
Garden City	9,134	142	0	1	20	121	545	142	337	66	4
Glennville	5,515	11	0	0	7	4	120	34	82	4	0
Gordon	2,028	0	0	0	0	0	29	6	22	1	0
Grantville	2,840	11	0	1	0	10	48	19	20	9	
Greensboro	3,136	32	0	1	0	31	167	41	120	6	
Greenville	884	11	0	0	1	10	50	10	38	2	0
Griffin	23,186	152	6	7	48	91	1,632	285	1,285	62	6
Grovetown	9,970	66	0	0	6	60	218	51	155	12	0
Guyton	1,969	5	0	3	0	2	24	11	9	4	1
Hahira	2,340	5	0	2	0	3	34	4	27	3	0
Hampton	5,342	18	0	1	5	12	142	36	98	8	0
Hapeville	6,624	34	1	2	20	11	392	96	230	66	0
Harlem	2,119	13	0	3	2	8	41	14	27	0	0
Harrison	452	0	0	0	0	0	0	0	0	0	0
Hartwell	4,152	20	0	0	7	13	336	32	290	14	0
Hazlehurst	3,780	7	0	0	2	5	248	52	195	1	0
Helen	879	9	0	0	0	9	80	6	72	2	0

[1] The FBI does not publish arson data unless it receives data from either the agency or the state for all 12 months of the calendar year.

Table 8.   Offenses Known to Law Enforcement, by State and City, 2010—*Continued*

(Number)

State/city	Population	Violent crime	Murder and non-negligent man-slaughter	Forcible rape	Robbery	Aggravated assault	Property crime	Burglary	Larceny-theft	Motor vehicle theft	Arson[1]
GEORGIA—*Continued*											
Helena	2,268	3	0	0	0	3	14	13	1	0	
Hephzibah	4,531	15	0	0	0	15	139	46	79	14	0
Hiawassee	828	5	0	1	0	4	21	1	20	0	0
Hinesville	29,764	149	5	9	45	90	1,660	448	1,148	64	5
Hiram	2,102	23	0	2	10	11	283	23	255	5	0
Hoboken	511	0	0	0	0	0	4	1	2	1	0
Hogansville	2,841	30	0	2	1	27	93	28	59	6	0
Holly Springs	9,708	6	0	0	0	6	91	19	69	3	0
Homeland	759	0	0	0	0	0	4	1	3	0	0
Homerville	2,583	30	1	1	7	21	122	29	87	6	0
Irwinton	566	0	0	0	0	0	0	0	0	0	0
Jackson	4,481	10	0	1	3	6	118	23	89	6	
Jefferson	8,232	13	0	2	4	7	160	42	103	15	1
Jesup	10,175	62	0	6	22	34	673	127	510	36	1
Johns Creek	59,893	50	0	5	13	32	644	159	471	14	0
Jonesboro	4,082	25	0	4	3	18	140	32	93	15	
Kennesaw	33,398	20	0	2	5	13	526	110	394	22	0
Keysville	225	0	0	0	0	0	0	0	0	0	0
Kingsland	14,033	70	0	2	6	62	516	112	391	13	3
Lafayette	7,366	35	0	0	0	35	441	64	373	4	13
LaGrange	27,712	132	0	6	60	66	1,686	376	1,234	76	
Lake City	2,586	11	0	0	10	1	176	23	126	27	3
Lavonia	2,009	10	0	1	5	4	113	24	86	3	
Lawrenceville	29,625	98	4	5	54	35	1,251	263	907	81	5
Leary	582	0	0	0	0	0	0	0	0	0	0
Leesburg	2,932	16	0	3	2	11	101	14	82	5	0
Lilburn	11,645	47	0	2	24	21	577	108	441	28	0
Locust Grove	5,136	10	0	2	5	3	258	47	199	12	0
Loganville	11,256	13	0	3	3	7	320	55	241	24	0
Lookout Mountain	1,459	0	0	0	0	0	10	2	8	0	0
Ludowici	1,578	5	0	1	2	2	47	20	25	2	
Lumber City	1,114	8	0	0	1	7	26	10	16	0	0
Lumpkin	1,136	10	0	0	4	6	17	10	4	3	2
Macon	89,125	708	22	34	284	368	7,277	2,136	4,516	625	72
Madison	3,839	16	1	2	3	10	182	49	119	14	0
Manchester	3,609	19	0	0	1	18	273	115	144	14	1
Marietta	65,318	462	2	10	136	314	2,857	723	1,968	166	6
Maysville	1,681	3	0	0	0	3	29	7	22	0	0
McCaysville[3]	957	2	0	0	0	2			10	1	0
McDonough	21,010	101	0	8	13	80	843	139	638	66	0
McIntyre	693	2	0	0	1	1	37	10	24	3	0
McRae	4,385	19	0	0	1	18	90	19	66	5	0
Meigs	1,053	8	0	0	1	7	18	7	11	0	0
Midville	434	0	0	0	0	0	0	0	0	0	0
Midway	1,514	14	0	2	3	9	69	23	43	3	0
Milledgeville	20,543	59	3	7	19	30	984	290	661	33	3
Milton	15,747	13	0	4	2	7	314	53	252	9	0
Monroe	13,305	37	2	2	8	25	665	200	430	35	1
Montezuma	3,547	56	1	0	3	52	168	42	116	10	0
Morrow	5,423	26	0	0	19	7	955	70	819	66	1
Moultrie	15,093	114	4	8	44	58	1,311	322	925	64	3
Mountain City	718	0	0	0	0	0	1	0	1	0	0
Mount Airy	1,285	2	0	0	0	2	7	5	2	0	0
Mount Zion	1,574	0	0	0	0	0	13	0	9	4	0
Nahunta	968	6	0	0	0	6	38	19	19	0	
Nashville	4,671	34	0	3	7	24	235	94	136	5	4
Newington	288	4	0	0	0	4	9	3	6	0	0
Newnan	32,623	131	2	1	32	96	1,216	302	859	55	
Newton	729	1	0	0	1	0	3	0	3	0	0
Nicholls	2,787	5	0	0	1	4	45	13	32	0	0
Norcross	10,870	54	0	7	28	19	354	94	228	32	2
Oakwood	5,414	19	0	0	2	17	214	33	168	13	
Omega	1,367	0	0	0	0	0	0	0	0	0	0
Oxford	2,548	3	0	0	0	3	36	11	24	1	0
Palmetto	5,178	26	1	1	2	22	87	29	48	10	0
Patterson	675	4	0	1	1	2	20	3	16	1	0
Pavo	664	2	0	0	1	1	4	1	3	0	0
Peachtree City	33,956	12	0	2	3	7	475	44	365	66	8
Pembroke	2,575	3	0	0	0	3	67	16	48	3	
Pine Lake	636	0	0	0	0	0	15	5	10	0	0
Pine Mountain	1,301	8	0	1	2	5	84	23	59	2	0
Plains	576	1	0	0	0	1	10	2	8	0	0
Pooler	17,306	15	0	0	7	8	632	123	468	41	

[1] The FBI does not publish arson data unless it receives data from either the agency or the state for all 12 months of the calendar year.

[3] The FBI determined that the agency's data were overreported. Consequently, those data are not included in this table.

Table 8.   Offenses Known to Law Enforcement, by State and City, 2010—*Continued*

(Number)

State/city	Population	Violent crime	Murder and non-negligent man-slaughter	Forcible rape	Robbery	Aggravated assault	Property crime	Burglary	Larceny-theft	Motor vehicle theft	Arson[1]
GEORGIA—*Continued*											
Porterdale	1,835	4	0	0	0	4	54	22	28	4	1
Port Wentworth	4,928	17	0	1	3	13	131	26	90	15	0
Poulan	843	3	0	0	0	3	22	5	17	0	
Powder Springs	15,768	36	1	1	7	27	355	137	191	27	0
Quitman	4,173	83	1	4	7	71	263	80	165	18	
Reidsville	2,412	15	0	0	3	12	131	26	101	4	2
Reynolds	994	0	0	0	0	0	0	0	0	0	0
Richmond Hill	11,455	15	0	1	7	7	188	27	155	6	
Rincon	8,354	4	1	0	3	0	184	22	157	5	
Ringgold	2,777	24	0	3	0	21	196	24	167	5	0
Riverdale	15,112	125	1	3	59	62	1,017	338	606	73	
Rockmart	4,489	33	0	7	3	23	166	52	105	9	0
Rome	34,896	233	1	17	90	125	1,990	447	1,439	104	7
Rossville	3,268	38	0	1	5	32	195	58	119	18	1
Roswell	85,461	131	0	16	65	50	1,862	429	1,334	99	5
Royston	2,640	1	0	0	0	1	56	0	56	0	0
Sandersville	5,890	29	0	3	8	18	322	99	214	9	
Sandy Springs	82,898	189	7	18	115	49	2,666	718	1,756	192	
Savannah-Chatham Metropolitan	210,744	843	20	30	454	339	9,202	2,552	6,026	624	43
Screven	770	2	0	0	0	2	10	5	5	0	1
Senoia	3,866	4	0	1	0	3	63	15	45	3	0
Shiloh	432	0	0	0	0	0	3	0	3	0	0
Sky Valley	208	0	0	0	0	0	5	0	5	0	0
Snellville	20,323	61	0	1	19	41	749	75	652	22	0
Social Circle	4,858	3	0	0	0	3	74	22	47	5	
Sparta	1,193	11	0	1	1	9	75	41	34	0	0
Springfield	2,353	4	0	1	0	3	68	16	47	5	0
Statesboro	26,413	251	0	6	47	198	1,457	288	1,118	51	1
Statham	3,041	16	0	1	4	11	85	33	45	7	0
St. Marys	16,424	59	0	2	9	48	519	133	377	9	
Suwanee	17,028	21	3	0	3	15	388	51	320	17	1
Sylvania	2,610	12	0	0	3	9	150	37	109	4	1
Sylvester	5,540	17	0	1	2	14	332	79	240	13	0
Tallapoosa	3,006	1	0	1	0	0	142	29	99	14	1
Tallulah Falls	158	0	0	0	0	0	2	1	1	0	0
Temple	4,620	27	0	0	5	22	136	28	102	6	0
Tennille	1,386	17	0	1	2	14	44	11	32	1	0
Thomaston	8,804	57	0	2	16	39	455	120	312	23	1
Thunderbolt	2,575	4	0	0	3	1	105	30	66	9	0
Tifton	17,012	185	1	5	64	115	1,285	328	916	41	4
Tignall	591	1	0	0	0	1	5	1	4	0	0
Toomsboro	598	0	0	0	0	0	0	0	0	0	0
Trenton	2,325	3	0	0	0	3	35	4	25	6	1
Tunnel Hill	1,199	10	0	0	2	8	46	12	30	4	0
Tybee Island	3,817	6	0	0	1	5	107	12	94	1	0
Tyrone	6,653	2	0	0	1	1	93	29	55	9	0
Union City	17,584	347	2	6	43	296	1,404	329	879	196	
Union Point	1,467	1	0	1	0	0	63	17	42	4	0
Valdosta	51,089	270	3	17	81	169	2,633	856	1,665	112	9
Vidalia	10,973	108	1	5	35	67	819	200	568	51	3
Villa Rica	13,906	109	0	5	6	98	514	88	380	46	2
Warner Robins	61,332	341	4	19	95	223	3,575	810	2,589	176	23
Washington	3,851	42	0	2	3	37	96	20	74	2	
Watkinsville	2,941	3	0	0	1	2	72	16	55	1	1
Waverly Hall	773	4	0	0	0	4	7	0	7	0	0
Waycross	14,182	58	1	5	26	26	1,084	177	880	27	5
Waynesboro	5,602	41	3	1	13	24	314	76	211	27	4
West Point	3,368	35	0	3	6	26	286	62	204	20	2
Whigham	561	3	0	0	0	3	0	0	0	0	0
Winder	14,658	116	0	4	8	104	705	162	527	16	2
Winterville	1,177	3	0	0	0	3	18	4	14	0	0
Woodbury	1,023	0	0	0	0	0	55	19	32	4	0
Woodstock	24,370	48	0	7	8	33	518	77	432	9	
Wrens	2,111	13	0	0	2	11	139	24	109	6	0
Zebulon	1,192	3	0	0	0	3	36	4	30	2	
HAWAII											
Honolulu	950,268	2,548	19	218	891	1,420	31,668	5,760	22,007	3,901	349
IDAHO											
Aberdeen	1,762	2	0	0	0	2	9	7	2	0	0
American Falls	4,075	7	0	3	0	4	61	3	58	0	1
Bellevue	2,259	4	0	0	0	4	32	14	17	1	0
Blackfoot	11,176	39	0	11	1	27	437	91	337	9	1
Boise	205,902	539	3	89	58	389	5,707	888	4,660	159	50

[1] The FBI does not publish arson data unless it receives data from either the agency or the state for all 12 months of the calendar year.

Table 8.   Offenses Known to Law Enforcement, by State and City, 2010—*Continued*

(Number)

State/city	Population	Violent crime	Murder and non-negligent man-slaughter	Forcible rape	Robbery	Aggravated assault	Property crime	Burglary	Larceny-theft	Motor vehicle theft	Arson[1]
IDAHO—*Continued*											
Bonners Ferry	2,550	4	0	1	1	2	21	6	14	1	0
Buhl	4,105	15	0	0	0	15	95	24	70	1	5
Caldwell	45,089	150	0	14	14	122	1,167	274	837	56	7
Cascade	964	0	0	0	0	0	3	0	3	0	0
Chubbuck	12,745	46	0	4	8	34	511	44	448	19	1
Coeur d'Alene	44,626	254	0	21	17	216	1,579	284	1,244	51	17
Cottonwood	1,039	2	0	1	0	1	4	2	2	0	0
Emmett	6,329	8	0	1	0	7	94	15	78	1	0
Filer	2,268	1	0	0	0	1	11	3	7	1	0
Fruitland	4,853	9	0	1	0	8	105	27	73	5	0
Garden City	11,969	35	0	6	7	22	360	72	268	20	3
Gooding	3,179	5	0	0	1	4	42	13	27	2	0
Grangeville	3,099	3	0	1	0	2	74	14	58	2	0
Hagerman	825	0	0	0	0	0	9	3	6	0	0
Hailey	8,242	36	0	2	0	34	100	64	30	6	2
Heyburn	2,747	4	0	0	0	4	24	11	12	1	0
Idaho Falls	55,524	182	3	23	14	142	1,582	327	1,194	61	8
Jerome	9,714	31	0	3	2	26	214	58	149	7	1
Kamiah	1,123	2	0	0	0	2	12	1	11	0	0
Kellogg	2,146	9	0	1	0	8	66	19	43	4	1
Ketchum	3,401	13	0	1	0	12	105	15	87	3	0
Kimberly	3,302	5	0	1	1	3	35	10	21	4	4
Lewiston	31,860	53	0	20	2	31	1,332	277	992	63	4
McCall	2,595	12	0	4	1	7	142	18	121	3	0
Meridian	72,688	108	3	17	11	77	1,185	197	952	36	6
Montpelier	2,302	8	0	2	0	6	60	19	39	2	0
Moscow	24,550	20	0	5	2	13	557	81	457	19	5
Mountain Home	12,301	64	0	8	6	50	336	51	276	9	13
Nampa	84,179	275	2	51	17	205	2,299	450	1,721	128	23
Orofino	2,951	12	0	2	1	9	53	12	40	1	1
Osburn	1,341	2	0	0	0	2	16	7	9	0	0
Parma	1,884	4	0	1	1	2	22	7	14	1	0
Payette	7,688	37	0	7	0	30	215	66	147	2	2
Pinehurst	1,541	0	0	0	0	0	23	7	14	2	0
Pocatello	55,215	132	1	24	6	101	1,726	296	1,360	70	5
Ponderay	733	2	0	0	0	2	85	7	76	2	0
Post Falls	27,882	39	2	11	2	24	640	114	501	25	4
Preston	5,133	3	0	2	0	1	21	0	21	0	0
Priest River	1,978	2	0	2	0	0	34	11	22	1	0
Rathdrum	7,174	15	0	2	2	11	168	57	105	6	0
Rexburg	30,200	10	0	2	1	7	243	17	221	5	1
Rigby	3,568	6	0	3	0	3	97	15	78	4	0
Rupert	5,166	15	0	1	3	11	111	20	88	3	1
Salmon	3,120	10	0	0	0	10	50	12	35	3	0
Sandpoint	8,503	12	0	3	1	8	228	34	185	9	2
Shelley	4,403	4	0	1	1	2	52	5	46	1	0
Soda Springs	3,062	1	0	0	0	1	23	3	20	0	0
Spirit Lake	1,788	3	0	0	0	3	20	3	15	2	0
St. Anthony	3,443	3	0	1	0	2	32	2	28	2	0
St. Maries	2,593	5	0	1	0	4	13	7	5	1	0
Sun Valley	1,483	3	0	0	0	3	14	4	10	0	0
Twin Falls	43,434	145	1	21	13	110	1,374	219	1,107	48	6
Weiser	5,181	7	0	1	0	6	40	4	30	6	0
Wendell	2,426	3	0	1	0	2	33	4	26	3	1
Wilder	1,482	2	0	0	0	2	22	5	17	0	0
ILLINOIS[5]											
Addison	36,581	67	0	16	17	34	827	109	662	56	12
Albany	917	0	0	0	0	0	24	14	9	1	0
Aledo	3,466	11	0	0	0	11	91	23	63	5	0
Algonquin	30,848	79	0	2	2	75	529	50	476	3	2
Alton	28,841	174	4	16	27	127	1,265	292	913	60	12
Antioch	14,266	5	0	1	0	4	296	26	264	6	1
Arcola	2,685	3	0	0	0	3	11	4	7	0	0
Arlington Heights	72,061	41	0	5	12	24	1,154	153	978	23	4
Arthur	2,084	0	0	0	0	0	43	10	31	2	0
Ashland	1,299	0	0	0	0	0	6	0	5	1	1
Ashton	1,143	0	0	0	0	0	18	5	13	0	0
Atwood	1,194	1	0	0	0	1	10	4	6	0	0
Aurora	174,255	634	4	64	113	453	3,767	820	2,809	138	31
Aviston	1,754	0	0	0	0	0	3	0	3	0	0
Bannockburn	1,919	0	0	0	0	0	28	6	22	0	0
Barrington	10,240	0	0	0	0	0	127	15	107	5	0
Barrington Hills	4,373	2	0	0	1	1	46	4	42	0	5

[1] The FBI does not publish arson data unless it receives data from either the agency or the state for all 12 months of the calendar year.

[5] Because of changes in the state/local agency's reporting practices, figures are not comparable to previous years' data.

Table 8.   Offenses Known to Law Enforcement, by State and City, 2010—*Continued*

(Number)

State/city	Population	Violent crime	Murder and non-negligent man-slaughter	Forcible rape	Robbery	Aggravated assault	Property crime	Burglary	Larceny-theft	Motor vehicle theft	Arson[1]
ILLINOIS—*Continued*											
Bartlett	42,962	21	0	4	3	14	373	34	328	11	10
Bartonville	6,142	27	0	0	2	25	216	36	173	7	1
Batavia	27,759	40	0	3	3	34	509	56	447	6	8
Beckemeyer	1,049	0	0	0	0	0	8	6	2	0	0
Beecher	3,159	2	0	1	0	1	41	5	36	0	1
Belgium	453	0	0	0	0	0	0	0	0	0	0
Bellwood	18,500	73	2	0	22	49	369	87	228	54	3
Belvidere	26,712	67	0	21	7	39	515	88	408	19	6
Benton	6,836	46	0	0	1	45	330	77	244	9	0
Berkeley	4,800	16	0	4	3	9	104	15	88	1	0
Berwyn	48,737	205	1	15	74	115	1,257	397	753	107	11
Bethalto	9,896	10	0	3	0	7	28	7	20	1	0
Blandinsville	679	0	0	0	0	0	5	3	2	0	0
Bloomingdale	21,638	11	1	3	3	4	849	42	802	5	1
Bloomington	74,304	385	1	43	75	266	1,960	493	1,414	53	11
Blue Mound	996	4	0	0	0	4	17	10	7	0	0
Bourbonnais	19,340	24	0	8	0	16	333	49	276	8	0
Bradley	15,131	47	1	7	6	33	798	66	724	8	2
Braidwood	6,886	8	0	0	0	8	121	17	101	3	0
Bridgeview	14,816	36	0	6	7	23	459	58	368	33	1
Broadview	7,432	36	0	0	26	10	362	79	261	22	1
Brooklyn	611	34	0	4	10	20	60	21	21	18	10
Buda	553	0	0	0	0	0	1	0	1	0	0
Buffalo Grove	42,361	8	0	3	4	1	392	46	341	5	2
Bull Valley	1,129	0	0	0	0	0	8	3	5	0	0
Bunker Hill	1,706	15	0	0	0	15	27	10	17	0	0
Burbank	27,135	67	0	4	17	46	611	87	488	36	0
Burr Ridge	11,359	1	0	0	0	1	156	26	129	1	0
Byron	3,903	5	1	2	0	2	70	3	64	3	0
Cahokia	14,826	58	1	3	27	27	864	253	611	0	4
Cairo	2,909	93	0	8	5	80	212	84	118	10	2
Calumet City	36,004	247	4	31	160	52	2,694	688	1,688	318	4
Cambridge	2,054	0	0	0	0	0	10	3	7	0	0
Campton Hills	9,739	2	0	0	0	2	63	12	50	1	0
Canton	14,269	47	1	16	2	28	368	71	291	6	4
Carbondale	25,959	244	1	33	47	163	1,155	302	821	32	14
Carlinville	5,837	14	0	0	3	11	173	23	148	2	1
Carlyle	3,292	8	0	1	1	6	90	1	82	7	0
Carol Stream	39,577	44	0	7	9	28	577	75	476	26	13
Carpentersville	38,387	43	1	1	13	28	579	113	463	3	4
Carrier Mills	1,796	14	0	0	1	13	30	11	19	0	0
Carrollton	2,395	7	0	0	0	7	37	4	32	1	0
Carthage	2,404	4	0	0	0	4	53	9	44	0	0
Caseyville	4,159	17	0	4	11	2	102	24	73	5	2
Catlin	2,063	1	0	0	1	0	11	1	10	0	0
Central City	1,285	0	0	0	0	0	33	6	23	4	0
Centralia	13,237	101	0	13	13	75	805	212	569	24	1
Cerro Gordo	1,321	9	0	0	0	9	15	3	12	0	0
Charleston	21,538	60	0	15	2	43	329	116	204	9	2
Chatham	10,950	14	0	2	0	12	134	25	104	5	1
Chester	7,677	29	0	7	1	21	103	31	62	10	0
Chicago[7]	2,833,649		432		14,213	13,757	120,045	26,203	74,764	19,078	
Clarendon Hills	8,581	0	0	0	0	0	76	15	60	1	0
Clayton	814	0	0	0	0	0	7	1	6	0	0
Coal City	5,817	6	0	1	0	5	158	19	139	0	0
Coal Valley	4,026	1	0	0	0	1	50	5	45	0	0
Cobden	1,071	1	0	0	0	1	7	0	7	0	0
Colfax	1,003	0	0	0	0	0	14	5	9	0	0
Collinsville	25,851	55	1	4	12	38	729	98	606	25	2
Colona	5,150	23	0	11	1	11	82	23	58	1	0
Columbia	9,520	6	0	1	0	5	136	20	111	5	2
Cortland	4,501	5	0	0	0	5	54	3	51	0	2
Country Club Hills	16,472	64	0	10	23	31	572	150	406	16	6
Countryside	5,698	6	0	2	3	1	211	9	193	9	0
Crestwood	10,845	15	0	1	7	7	478	55	370	53	0
Crete	9,154	10	0	0	1	9	184	39	137	8	4
Crystal Lake	42,137	54	1	3	3	47	827	97	717	13	9
Danville	31,942	348	1	35	86	226	2,178	826	1,295	57	9
Darien	22,097	12	3	0	6	3	277	40	221	16	2
Decatur	74,857	468	4	20	136	308	3,121	1,514	1,481	126	27
Deerfield	19,543	8	0	2	1	5	172	14	158	0	0
Deer Park	3,339	0	0	0	0	0	47	7	39	1	0
De Kalb	45,959	162	2	28	25	107	1,246	205	1,021	20	15

[1] The FBI does not publish arson data unless it receives data from either the agency or the state for all 12 months of the calendar year.

[7] The data collection methodology for the offense of forcible rape used by Chicago, Illinois, and the Minnesota state UCR Program (with the exception of Minneapolis and St. Paul, Minnesota) does not comply with national UCR Program guidelines. Consequently, its figures for forcible rape and violent crime (of which forcible rape is a part) are not published in this table.

Table 8. Offenses Known to Law Enforcement, by State and City, 2010—*Continued*

(Number)

State/city	Population	Violent crime	Murder and non-negligent man-slaughter	Forcible rape	Robbery	Aggravated assault	Property crime	Burglary	Larceny-theft	Motor vehicle theft	Arson[1]
ILLINOIS—*Continued*											
Delavan	1,738	4	0	0	0	4	37	10	25	2	0
De Pue	1,707	2	0	1	0	1	36	4	32	0	0
De Soto	1,517	4	0	0	0	4	19	8	11	0	0
Des Plaines	56,188	57	0	10	7	40	729	141	551	37	4
Divernon	1,112	1	0	0	0	1	29	6	23	0	0
Dixon	14,696	31	0	16	2	13	503	60	437	6	0
Downers Grove	48,574	41	0	2	13	26	946	127	801	18	16
Du Quoin	6,222	10	0	0	2	8	117	19	94	4	1
Durand	1,070	3	0	0	0	3	18	1	17	0	0
Dwight	4,223	3	0	0	1	2	30	8	20	2	0
East Alton	6,450	15	1	3	2	9	328	48	264	16	0
East Dubuque	1,870	13	0	0	0	13	32	4	25	3	0
East Hazel Crest	1,503	1	0	0	1	0	78	31	43	4	0
East Moline	20,589	74	1	13	8	52	563	174	357	32	4
Easton	338	0	0	0	0	0	1	0	0	1	0
East Peoria	22,638	118	0	32	9	77	754	175	542	37	7
East St. Louis	28,188	1,642	21	74	276	1,271	2,516	1,091	781	644	58
Edinburg	1,085	1	0	0	0	1	9	4	4	1	0
Edwardsville	24,437	20	0	2	1	17	432	42	380	10	1
Effingham	12,442	25	1	9	2	13	360	53	300	7	3
Elgin	107,731	355	4	86	99	166	2,186	425	1,653	108	7
Elizabeth	633	0	0	0	0	0	13	9	3	1	0
Elk Grove Village	32,620	38	0	10	6	22	752	97	595	60	2
Elmhurst	46,160	22	0	5	7	10	655	85	545	25	0
Elmwood	1,862	6	0	0	0	6	25	8	17	0	0
Elmwood Park	23,536	29	1	1	10	17	376	85	263	28	1
El Paso	2,853	3	0	3	0	0	20	5	15	0	1
Energy	1,197	2	0	0	0	2	18	6	12	0	0
Eureka	5,421	10	0	2	0	8	94	17	76	1	0
Evanston	77,418	213	6	8	73	126	2,101	429	1,606	66	14
Evergreen Park	18,888	33	0	7	18	8	689	48	620	21	0
Fairfield	4,996	11	0	4	0	7	93	25	67	1	1
Fairmont City	2,216	1	0	1	0	0	65	17	44	4	0
Fairmount	617	0	0	0	0	0	1	0	1	0	0
Fairview	472	0	0	0	0	0	1	1	0	0	0
Fairview Heights	16,712	37	0	3	6	28	954	60	864	30	9
Fithian	538	0	0	0	0	0	0	0	0	0	0
Flora	4,595	4	0	0	0	4	137	6	126	5	0
Flossmoor	9,152	7	0	0	3	4	177	50	125	2	0
Forest Park	14,926	34	0	0	21	13	713	89	582	42	2
Forest View	700	1	0	0	0	1	33	2	18	13	0
Fox Lake	11,125	28	0	6	4	18	300	46	245	9	2
Fox River Grove	5,168	5	1	0	0	4	87	15	71	1	1
Frankfort	19,115	15	0	2	2	11	303	17	279	7	1
Franklin Grove	988	3	0	2	0	1	17	4	13	0	0
Freeport	24,277	49	0	5	15	29	880	238	633	9	6
Fulton	3,775	6	0	1	0	5	54	14	37	3	0
Geneseo	6,322	7	0	0	0	7	104	15	88	1	0
Geneva	24,648	9	0	0	0	9	313	25	285	3	1
Genoa	5,190	5	0	4	0	1	43	3	36	4	0
Georgetown	3,356	8	0	2	0	6	72	28	42	2	0
Germantown	1,126	0	0	0	0	0	1	0	1	0	0
Gibson City	3,221	7	0	0	0	7	61	21	39	1	0
Gifford	998	1	0	0	1	0	3	0	3	0	0
Gilberts	7,297	6	1	2	0	3	49	11	37	1	0
Gillespie	3,088	13	0	1	0	12	67	14	50	3	1
Gilman	1,649	1	0	0	0	1	5	2	3	0	0
Girard	2,120	8	0	0	0	8	18	8	9	1	0
Glasford	1,029	2	0	0	0	2	3	1	2	0	0
Glendale Heights	31,532	39	0	9	12	18	582	60	505	17	4
Glen Ellyn	26,950	10	0	2	1	7	389	58	325	6	5
Glenwood	8,310	19	0	2	9	8	204	84	77	43	0
Grafton	678	1	0	0	0	1	25	7	17	1	0
Grand Tower	564	0	0	0	0	0	9	3	6	0	3
Grandview	1,381	10	0	0	0	10	34	17	15	2	0
Granite City	30,254	158	0	31	22	105	777	281	490	6	13
Grantfork	345	0	0	0	0	0	2	1	0	1	0
Grant Park	1,717	5	0	0	2	3	12	2	10	0	0
Granville	1,320	0	0	0	0	0	3	1	2	0	0
Grayslake	21,790	24	0	4	2	18	469	61	399	9	4
Grayville	1,554	15	0	0	1	14	24	4	18	2	1
Greenville	7,233	2	0	0	0	2	126	22	103	1	0
Gurnee	30,415	28	0	5	5	18	1,365	79	1,263	23	0

[1] The FBI does not publish arson data unless it receives data from either the agency or the state for all 12 months of the calendar year.

Table 8.   Offenses Known to Law Enforcement, by State and City, 2010—*Continued*

(Number)

State/city	Population	Violent crime	Murder and non-negligent man-slaughter	Forcible rape	Robbery	Aggravated assault	Property crime	Burglary	Larceny-theft	Motor vehicle theft	Arson[1]
ILLINOIS—*Continued*											
Hampshire	6,006	2	0	0	1	1	64	18	45	1	0
Hanover	768	24	0	0	0	24	20	3	17	0	0
Hanover Park	36,166	49	0	10	15	24	536	81	436	19	0
Harvard	10,063	4	0	1	1	2	89	16	72	1	0
Harvey	27,461	401	12	20	239	130	1,766	755	753	258	9
Harwood Heights	7,896	1	0	0	0	1	157	34	115	8	0
Hawthorn Woods	8,205	1	0	0	0	1	34	0	29	5	0
Hazel Crest	13,771	40	2	7	24	7	529	167	315	47	2
Henning	225	0	0	0	0	0	0	0	0	0	0
Henry	2,385	9	0	1	0	8	51	12	38	1	0
Herrin	12,421	174	1	5	1	167	467	243	205	19	4
Hickory Hills	13,050	20	0	2	4	14	297	31	252	14	0
Highland	9,841	9	0	0	1	8	192	26	163	3	0
Highland Park	31,306	17	0	2	0	15	364	60	296	8	1
Highwood	5,317	9	1	2	0	6	46	5	39	2	0
Hillsboro	6,017	21	0	2	0	19	46	5	41	0	0
Hinckley	2,079	3	0	0	0	3	25	10	14	1	0
Hinsdale	18,362	3	0	0	1	2	237	23	212	2	1
Hodgkins	2,010	4	0	0	0	4	252	2	244	6	1
Hoffman Estates	53,500	58	0	8	18	32	749	118	610	21	4
Homer	1,111	6	0	0	0	6	6	2	4	0	0
Hometown	4,004	0	0	0	0	0	54	7	46	1	0
Homewood	18,062	32	0	0	23	9	738	104	613	21	0
Hoopeston	5,507	23	0	9	1	13	208	64	137	7	0
Huntley	26,256	7	0	0	2	5	206	22	181	3	1
Indianola	217	0	0	0	0	0	0	0	0	0	0
Irving	468	1	0	0	0	1	7	4	3	0	0
Itasca	8,573	4	0	0	0	4	126	14	109	3	0
Jacksonville	18,937	75	0	14	5	56	514	165	343	6	11
Jerseyville	8,285	37	0	10	0	27	235	21	205	9	0
Johnsburg	6,887	1	0	0	0	1	128	18	108	2	0
Joliet	150,723	543	11	31	126	375	4,190	957	3,058	175	25
Kankakee	26,481	245	4	42	99	100	1,132	339	746	47	12
Kenilworth	2,354	0	0	0	0	0	38	5	33	0	0
Kewanee	12,042	50	0	12	4	34	538	76	455	7	2
Kildeer	4,131	1	0	0	0	1	40	5	35	0	0
Kincaid	1,430	5	0	0	0	5	11	4	6	1	8
Kingston	1,067	0	0	0	0	0	6	2	4	0	0
Knoxville	2,860	1	0	0	0	1	58	16	39	3	0
Lacon	1,797	1	0	0	0	1	18	5	12	1	0
La Grange	14,987	11	0	0	8	3	202	46	150	6	0
La Grange Park	12,119	7	0	0	3	4	119	5	111	3	0
Lake Bluff	6,173	0	0	0	0	0	31	11	19	1	0
Lake in the Hills	30,023	32	0	0	3	29	238	41	189	8	5
Lakemoor	6,129	12	0	0	1	11	79	37	41	1	0
Lake Villa	8,922	13	0	1	2	10	97	7	87	3	0
Lake Zurich	20,408	8	0	2	2	4	301	25	271	5	3
La Salle	9,359	17	0	1	2	14	160	38	118	4	1
Lawrenceville	4,201	15	0	1	0	14	60	23	31	6	3
Leland Grove	1,408	0	0	0	0	0	22	7	14	1	0
Lemont	16,379	5	0	0	0	5	170	18	148	4	2
Le Roy	3,551	6	0	1	0	5	74	27	46	1	3
Libertyville	21,709	17	0	10	2	5	360	40	312	8	0
Lincoln	14,291	68	0	1	1	66	667	141	511	15	6
Lincolnshire	8,080	3	0	0	2	1	108	9	99	0	1
Lincolnwood	11,560	13	0	3	3	7	484	71	398	15	1
Lindenhurst	14,743	4	0	3	0	1	76	10	66	0	0
Lisle	22,976	16	0	0	8	8	314	34	264	16	1
Litchfield	6,482	21	0	1	1	19	229	33	193	3	0
Loami	777	0	0	0	0	0	4	1	3	0	0
Lockport	25,986	35	1	4	4	26	312	31	275	6	3
Lombard	42,394	53	0	5	12	36	1,187	94	1,069	24	1
Loves Park	24,660	86	0	17	29	40	864	175	650	39	4
Lyons	10,075	21	1	0	8	12	261	61	192	8	4
Machesney Park	22,686	59	0	7	5	47	706	155	532	19	1
Macomb	19,674	26	0	5	1	20	412	55	352	5	0
Mahomet	6,784	11	0	1	1	9	74	16	56	2	0
Manhattan	7,858	6	0	0	0	6	36	3	33	0	0
Maple Park	1,352	0	0	0	0	0	5	0	5	0	0
Marissa	1,965	6	0	0	2	4	51	18	31	2	2
Maroa	1,538	6	0	0	0	6	18	4	13	1	0
Martinsville	1,178	2	0	0	1	1	35	15	20	0	0
Mascoutah	6,838	4	0	1	2	1	95	6	89	0	0

[1] The FBI does not publish arson data unless it receives data from either the agency or the state for all 12 months of the calendar year.

Table 8.   Offenses Known to Law Enforcement, by State and City, 2010—*Continued*

(Number)

State/city	Population	Violent crime	Murder and non-negligent man-slaughter	Forcible rape	Robbery	Aggravated assault	Property crime	Burglary	Larceny-theft	Motor vehicle theft	Arson[1]
ILLINOIS—*Continued*											
Mattoon	16,834	91	2	21	5	63	486	141	323	22	10
Maywood	24,448	221	3	9	98	111	962	297	562	103	3
McCook	232	11	0	0	0	11	32	4	16	12	0
McHenry	27,477	37	1	9	2	25	542	55	480	7	3
McLean	790	0	0	0	0	0	5	0	5	0	0
Melrose Park	21,405	57	0	10	15	32	628	93	439	96	2
Mendota	6,908	3	0	1	1	1	177	24	152	1	0
Meredosia	942	0	0	0	0	0	6	2	4	0	0
Metropolis	6,414	45	0	7	6	32	278	50	226	2	4
Midlothian	13,361	42	0	2	29	11	345	104	226	15	5
Milan	5,124	11	0	4	1	6	130	23	98	9	0
Milledgeville	903	1	0	0	0	1	29	7	22	0	8
Millstadt	3,413	8	0	1	0	7	39	19	19	1	1
Minooka	11,652	7	0	0	1	6	173	20	153	0	0
Mokena	19,567	12	1	4	1	6	214	20	184	10	5
Moline	42,510	216	1	26	22	167	1,487	302	1,140	45	3
Momence	3,022	31	0	0	1	30	49	14	35	0	0
Monmouth	9,092	56	1	6	5	44	473	78	380	15	4
Montgomery	16,835	23	0	4	6	13	348	61	281	6	2
Monticello	5,341	12	0	0	2	10	58	8	48	2	1
Morris	14,035	33	0	5	5	23	505	65	432	8	6
Morrison	4,245	5	0	1	0	4	76	19	57	0	0
Morton	16,115	8	0	0	2	6	168	44	116	8	1
Morton Grove	22,177	11	0	3	3	5	396	75	306	15	0
Mount Carmel	7,227	21	0	7	0	14	114	24	83	7	2
Mount Carroll	1,615	1	0	0	0	1	44	7	35	2	0
Mount Morris	3,065	1	0	0	0	1	51	8	42	1	0
Mount Prospect	52,190	35	1	5	4	25	666	72	567	27	0
Mount Pulaski	1,549	2	0	0	0	2	13	1	12	0	0
Mount Zion	5,214	4	0	1	1	2	54	10	43	1	1
Moweaqua	1,798	0	0	0	0	0	3	2	1	0	0
Mundelein	33,921	12	0	3	3	6	421	57	358	6	2
New Athens	1,979	0	0	0	0	0	18	4	14	0	0
New Lenox	24,716	10	0	1	2	7	266	18	244	4	2
Normal	53,014	146	0	11	38	97	1,497	350	1,109	38	2
Norridge	13,664	14	0	2	6	6	539	50	479	10	2
North Aurora	16,276	35	0	6	3	26	283	28	253	2	0
Northbrook	33,432	8	0	3	2	3	450	63	379	8	2
Northfield	5,396	0	0	0	0	0	112	18	92	2	0
Northlake	11,213	11	1	0	5	5	395	42	340	13	2
North Riverside	6,092	16	0	2	7	7	541	20	506	15	0
Oak Brook	8,753	3	1	0	0	2	609	13	591	5	0
Oakbrook Terrace	2,371	3	0	0	1	2	121	8	111	2	0
Oak Forest	27,339	39	0	3	15	21	459	88	356	15	5
Oak Lawn	52,172	89	1	5	40	43	1,117	166	885	66	5
Oak Park	52,629	192	1	5	138	48	1,725	380	1,274	71	2
Oakwood	1,405	0	0	0	0	0	15	7	8	0	0
Oakwood Hills	2,390	1	0	0	0	1	19	8	11	0	0
Oblong	1,491	14	0	0	0	14	20	12	8	0	1
O'Fallon	28,102	33	0	12	11	10	704	114	572	18	1
Ogden	712	0	0	0	0	0	0	0	0	0	0
Oglesby	3,644	5	0	0	0	5	46	3	41	2	2
Old Shawneetown	245	1	0	0	0	1	4	1	3	0	0
Olney	8,267	26	0	10	0	16	311	52	245	14	3
Olympia Fields	4,665	10	0	3	4	3	204	23	171	10	1
Orion	1,654	0	0	0	0	0	25	1	24	0	0
Orland Park	55,051	23	1	1	7	14	1,159	38	1,106	15	3
Oswego	31,336	32	0	11	2	19	473	36	434	3	11
Palatine	66,024	34	0	9	10	15	893	39	840	14	3
Palestine	1,296	1	0	0	0	1	9	1	8	0	0
Palos Heights	12,369	3	0	0	3	0	220	9	210	1	1
Palos Hills	16,571	4	0	0	2	2	188	23	158	7	1
Palos Park	5,007	1	0	0	1	0	32	5	26	1	0
Pana	5,601	3	0	0	0	3	110	29	76	5	1
Paris	8,446	45	0	0	0	45	108	25	71	12	0
Park City	6,644	9	0	3	3	3	142	34	97	11	1
Park Forest	22,125	50	4	3	18	25	433	186	240	7	4
Park Ridge	36,324	15	0	1	4	10	571	134	424	13	6
Pawnee	2,514	4	1	0	0	3	31	4	26	1	0
Pekin	33,196	116	3	15	6	92	843	170	634	39	4
Peoria	114,557	878	22	31	306	519	5,163	1,460	3,436	267	61
Peotone	4,374	2	0	1	0	1	49	7	42	0	0
Peru	9,683	10	0	4	0	6	259	31	224	4	0

[1] The FBI does not publish arson data unless it receives data from either the agency or the state for all 12 months of the calendar year.

Table 8.   Offenses Known to Law Enforcement, by State and City, 2010—*Continued*

(Number)

State/city	Population	Violent crime	Murder and non-negligent man-slaughter	Forcible rape	Robbery	Aggravated assault	Property crime	Burglary	Larceny-theft	Motor vehicle theft	Arson[1]
ILLINOIS—*Continued*											
Pinckneyville	5,303	7	1	0	0	6	26	5	20	1	1
Pittsfield	4,328	0	0	0	0	0	6	0	6	0	0
Plainfield	40,084	21	0	4	4	13	510	65	436	9	4
Plano	13,645	19	0	11	3	5	198	44	146	8	1
Plymouth	502	1	0	0	0	1	9	0	9	0	0
Pontiac	11,076	53	0	6	2	45	360	57	300	3	0
Pontoon Beach	6,094	6	0	2	3	1	114	31	79	4	0
Posen	4,838	13	0	0	7	6	240	48	173	19	0
Potomac	644	0	0	0	0	0	4	1	3	0	0
Prairie du Rocher	557	0	0	0	0	0	0	0	0	0	0
Prospect Heights	15,688	8	0	3	2	3	163	48	104	11	2
Quincy	39,579	186	1	37	16	132	1,339	263	1,039	37	5
Rankin	572	1	0	0	0	1	0	0	0	0	0
Rantoul	12,053	129	0	20	6	103	318	123	181	14	3
Raymond	874	0	0	0	0	0	1	1	0	0	0
Red Bud	3,600	27	0	1	0	26	38	14	23	1	0
Richmond	2,467	2	0	0	1	1	28	3	22	3	0
Richton Park	12,694	35	0	7	17	11	385	135	205	45	0
Ridge Farm	836	0	0	0	0	0	3	0	3	0	0
River Forest	10,964	17	0	1	10	6	274	43	228	3	0
River Grove	9,758	11	0	5	0	6	226	36	169	21	0
Riverside	8,086	8	0	0	0	8	188	15	169	4	0
Riverwoods	4,051	1	0	0	0	1	28	4	24	0	0
Rochester	3,250	0	0	0	0	0	47	14	32	1	0
Rock Falls	9,139	21	0	7	1	13	380	91	283	6	0
Rockford	156,180	2,272	21	110	495	1,646	7,805	2,375	4,992	438	89
Rock Island	37,534	307	3	21	51	232	1,306	356	872	78	6
Romeoville	39,759	32	1	5	10	16	776	112	648	16	5
Roodhouse	1,881	2	1	0	0	1	18	8	10	0	0
Roselle	22,945	24	0	8	9	7	267	48	214	5	1
Rosemont	3,836	4	0	0	0	4	231	12	206	13	1
Round Lake	18,435	34	0	2	7	25	173	23	146	4	3
Round Lake Beach	27,668	64	0	15	12	37	650	91	552	7	7
Round Lake Heights	2,988	2	0	0	1	1	47	3	43	1	1
Roxana	1,530	1	0	0	0	1	52	11	36	5	1
Royalton	1,145	4	0	0	0	4	16	3	13	0	0
Ruma	302	0	0	0	0	0	4	0	4	0	0
Rushville	2,959	2	0	0	0	2	43	8	34	1	0
Salem	7,180	16	0	2	1	13	357	69	284	4	3
Sauget	236	17	1	3	1	12	58	2	51	5	0
Schaumburg	70,170	85	1	18	35	31	2,282	243	1,974	65	4
Schiller Park	11,279	21	0	4	10	7	241	49	177	15	2
Shawneetown	1,219	2	0	0	0	2	12	0	12	0	0
Sherman	3,945	5	0	0	0	5	39	7	31	1	0
Shiloh	11,750	21	0	7	4	10	220	51	158	11	1
Shorewood	16,666	15	0	3	2	10	172	38	131	3	2
Sidell	580	0	0	0	0	0	0	0	0	0	0
Silvis	7,728	28	0	3	2	23	319	44	268	7	1
Skokie	66,088	157	0	9	61	87	1,800	368	1,356	76	13
Sleepy Hollow	3,688	0	0	0	0	0	13	3	10	0	0
Smithton	3,550	0	0	0	0	0	25	0	24	1	0
Somonauk	1,847	1	0	1	0	0	30	3	27	0	0
South Chicago Heights	3,701	20	0	0	8	12	149	22	117	10	0
South Elgin	21,632	18	0	3	1	14	230	13	212	5	1
Southern View	1,609	3	0	0	0	3	48	5	41	2	0
South Holland	20,710	50	0	3	36	11	483	141	304	38	2
South Jacksonville	3,145	5	0	3	0	2	40	3	37	0	0
South Pekin	1,191	8	0	1	0	7	18	5	11	2	0
Sparta	4,247	10	0	3	1	6	99	21	78	0	1
Springfield	117,383	1,452	7	104	338	1,003	7,567	2,167	5,160	240	57
Spring Grove	5,966	2	0	0	0	2	70	8	62	0	0
St. Anne	1,238	2	0	1	0	1	33	8	25	0	6
Staunton	5,025	9	0	1	2	6	107	15	89	3	0
Steger	10,387	28	0	2	11	15	334	72	242	20	2
Sterling	14,823	42	0	12	2	28	645	119	515	11	3
Stockton	1,747	5	0	3	0	2	74	15	57	2	0
Stone Park	4,774	14	0	0	1	13	97	42	51	4	0
Streamwood	36,621	35	0	5	4	26	698	112	566	20	2
Sugar Grove	10,523	6	0	3	1	2	73	13	56	4	0
Summit	10,018	72	2	1	25	44	332	94	172	66	2
Swansea	13,142	13	0	2	4	7	241	44	187	10	0
Sycamore	18,283	7	0	2	1	4	286	22	257	7	1
Thornton	2,331	3	0	1	1	1	50	11	34	5	0

[1] The FBI does not publish arson data unless it receives data from either the agency or the state for all 12 months of the calendar year.

Table 8.   Offenses Known to Law Enforcement, by State and City, 2010—*Continued*

(Number)

State/city	Population	Violent crime	Murder and non-negligent man-slaughter	Forcible rape	Robbery	Aggravated assault	Property crime	Burglary	Larceny-theft	Motor vehicle theft	Arson[1]
ILLINOIS—*Continued*											
Tilton	3,008	11	0	2	4	5	51	16	34	1	5
Tinley Park	59,607	49	0	8	16	25	975	108	845	22	1
Trenton	2,600	2	0	1	0	1	22	0	22	0	0
Troy	9,891	12	0	6	0	6	97	13	81	3	1
Tuscola	4,531	3	0	0	0	3	53	7	46	0	2
Urbana	39,784	292	0	23	64	205	1,253	341	889	23	8
Vermont	739	0	0	0	0	0	0	0	0	0	0
Vernon Hills	24,585	6	1	0	0	5	673	53	617	3	0
Villa Park	21,984	30	1	2	12	15	492	65	401	26	4
Warrensburg	1,136	1	0	0	0	1	12	1	11	0	0
Warrenville	12,882	14	0	7	4	3	144	31	106	7	3
Washburn	1,095	0	0	0	0	0	4	1	3	0	1
Waterloo	10,073	3	0	0	0	3	81	7	74	0	0
Watseka	5,290	13	0	0	1	12	166	45	118	3	0
Wauconda	12,456	10	0	1	3	6	165	27	137	1	0
Wayne	2,407	0	0	0	0	0	12	3	7	2	0
Westchester	15,331	15	0	0	5	10	282	63	205	14	1
West Chicago	26,470	29	0	7	3	19	361	82	267	12	4
West City	761	10	0	1	0	9	46	11	35	0	0
West Dundee	8,220	8	0	1	2	5	240	11	227	2	2
Western Springs	12,520	1	0	0	0	1	104	22	81	1	2
West Frankfort	8,029	27	0	1	5	21	177	80	81	16	6
Westmont	24,745	29	3	5	10	11	342	74	251	17	2
Westville	2,922	14	0	2	2	10	46	13	29	4	0
Wheaton	53,898	24	0	6	3	15	786	94	679	13	164
Wheeling	35,500	62	1	9	8	44	637	99	512	26	1
White Hall	2,397	1	0	1	0	0	29	6	23	0	0
Willowbrook	8,674	9	0	1	0	8	167	22	141	4	0
Willow Springs	5,872	1	0	0	1	0	48	7	39	2	0
Wilmington	6,253	3	0	0	0	3	117	9	95	13	1
Winfield	10,005	2	0	0	0	2	59	6	52	1	0
Winnebago	3,228	1	0	0	0	1	56	24	31	1	1
Winnetka	12,242	7	0	0	1	6	148	19	127	2	2
Winthrop Harbor	7,171	10	0	4	1	5	96	22	69	5	2
Witt	935	0	0	0	0	0	8	5	3	0	0
Wood Dale	13,765	8	0	0	2	6	205	21	170	14	0
Woodridge	34,137	48	0	8	13	27	429	42	366	21	3
Wood River	10,787	44	0	11	8	25	541	66	455	20	3
Woodstock	24,517	25	0	4	4	17	391	36	350	5	2
Worth	10,210	9	0	0	2	7	157	31	117	9	1
Yorkville	18,182	18	0	3	1	14	214	50	162	2	3
INDIANA											
Albion	2,366	1	0	0	0	1	1	0	1	0	0
Alexandria	5,609	4	0	1	0	3	255	40	208	7	0
Anderson	57,156	199	3	32	85	79	3,072	753	2,095	224	21
Angola	8,347	8	0	2	1	5	432	31	398	3	2
Attica	3,239	6	0	2	2	2	66	15	44	7	1
Auburn	13,229	14	0	5	3	6	361	76	276	9	0
Aurora	4,120	19	0	1	1	17	134	24	110	0	0
Austin	4,590	24	0	1	9	14	153	41	100	12	1
Avon	13,259	51	0	0	5	46	548	47	487	14	0
Bargersville	3,644	7	0	0	0	7	2	1	0	1	0
Batesville	6,474	22	0	1	1	20	113	19	93	1	0
Bedford	13,438	14	1	4	1	8	425	46	352	27	0
Beech Grove	14,487	46	1	6	24	15	456	71	348	37	1
Berne	4,451	5	0	1	0	4	31	7	22	2	0
Bloomington	72,286	306	1	31	72	202	3,143	815	2,203	125	17
Bluffton	9,160	0	0	0	0	0	386	71	314	1	0
Boonville	6,863	11	0	0	0	11	178	7	160	11	
Brazil	8,266	50	0	4	0	46	198	23	167	8	0
Bremen	4,682	1	0	0	0	1	81	11	67	3	0
Brownsburg	21,380	32	0	2	1	29	276	57	210	9	2
Burns Harbor	1,231	2	0	0	0	2	23	4	16	3	0
Carmel	71,647	42	0	8	1	33	897	114	748	35	5
Cedar Lake	11,411	7	0	3	4	0	417	57	341	19	1
Charlestown	7,548	7	0	1	3	3	367	71	292	4	0
Chesterfield	2,786	11	0	1	1	9	67	5	57	5	0
Chesterton	13,140	14	0	3	3	8	281	46	226	9	2
Clarksville	22,347	135	0	10	40	85	1,471	213	1,176	82	0
Columbia City	8,501	10	0	5	1	4	181	26	145	10	0
Columbus	40,554	78	0	17	21	40	2,269	282	1,834	153	9
Corydon	2,819	1	0	0	0	1	45	12	31	2	0
Crawfordsville	15,139	29	1	4	3	21	640	149	475	16	1

[1] The FBI does not publish arson data unless it receives data from either the agency or the state for all 12 months of the calendar year.

Table 8. Offenses Known to Law Enforcement, by State and City, 2010—*Continued*

(Number)

State/city	Population	Violent crime	Murder and non-negligent man-slaughter	Forcible rape	Robbery	Aggravated assault	Property crime	Burglary	Larceny-theft	Motor vehicle theft	Arson[1]
INDIANA—*Continued*											
Crown Point	25,011	19	0	2	8	9	522	36	460	26	1
Culver	1,515	0	0	0	0	0	47	4	40	3	0
Danville	8,652	4	0	2	0	2	109	13	91	5	0
Decatur	9,682	3	0	0	1	2	66	18	46	2	0
Delphi	2,828	3	0	1	0	2	88	11	74	3	0
Dyer	16,198	10	1	0	4	5	353	25	292	36	0
East Chicago	29,773	210	12	11	109	78	1,959	571	1,112	276	11
Elkhart	53,296	156	1	35	116	4	2,330	709	1,507	114	25
Ellettsville	6,169	43	0	1	1	41	85	26	57	2	0
Elwood	9,042	13	0	5	4	4	536	117	411	8	1
Evansville	116,541	493	5	63	143	282	5,544	1,086	4,248	210	68
Fairmount	2,712	7	0	2	0	5	47	14	32	1	0
Fishers	75,734	18	0	2	12	4	730	82	623	25	1
Fort Wayne[5]	257,009	746	23	96	314	313	8,860	2,140	6,433	287	50
Fowler	2,141	1	0	0	0	1	6	1	3	2	0
Frankfort	16,533	43	0	4	9	30	716	144	541	31	3
Franklin	24,118	51	0	6	3	42	903	96	799	8	3
Gas City	5,661	42	0	5	2	35	247	63	179	5	0
Goshen	32,812	33	0	11	15	7	1,040	242	764	34	10
Greendale	4,427	8	0	1	2	5	33	13	20	0	0
Greenfield	19,972	15	0	1	4	10	383	39	327	17	0
Greenwood	49,847	179	0	3	21	155	1,772	113	1,602	57	8
Griffith	16,252	36	1	6	10	19	621	93	470	58	1
Hagerstown	1,618	1	0	1	0	0	59	19	39	1	0
Hammond	76,216	663	10	27	209	417	3,881	1,070	2,317	494	36
Hartford City	6,273	7	0	0	5	2	204	60	137	7	0
Highland	22,583	17	0	1	6	10	821	81	683	57	1
Hobart	28,136	78	0	2	19	57	1,467	158	1,225	84	11
Huntingburg	6,113	0	0	0	0	0	88	10	73	5	0
Huntington	16,803	21	0	2	1	18	366	76	277	13	7
Jasper	14,292	4	0	2	0	2	173	29	136	8	0
Jeffersonville	33,421	323	1	0	34	288	1,354	370	869	115	2
Kokomo	45,412	152	3	20	63	66	2,380	475	1,862	43	0
Lafayette	66,388	264	2	30	49	183	2,704	524	2,000	180	25
Lake Station	13,253	27	1	5	8	13	541	85	428	28	4
La Porte	21,282	36	0	5	18	13	1,111	186	895	30	5
Lawrenceburg	4,856	10	0	4	5	1	210	15	191	4	0
Ligonier	4,600	2	0	0	1	1	34	7	19	8	0
Linton	5,679	2	0	1	0	1	208	0	207	1	0
Logansport	18,544	21	0	7	3	11	872	96	724	52	8
Long Beach	1,561	0	0	0	0	0	19	18	0	1	0
Lowell	8,599	15	0	1	1	13	158	16	138	4	1
Marion	30,342	90	0	21	53	16	1,435	268	1,079	88	14
Martinsville	12,054	18	0	3	2	13	954	110	809	35	2
Merrillville	33,839	95	3	4	35	53	1,273	110	1,038	125	0
Michigan City	32,482	147	2	23	61	61	2,016	412	1,469	135	16
Mishawaka	50,632	142	0	15	52	75	3,065	523	2,386	156	15
Monticello	5,162	4	0	0	2	2	144	15	121	8	1
Mooresville	11,970	7	0	1	1	5	331	51	261	19	0
Mount Vernon	6,917	39	0	5	4	30	454	123	322	9	2
Muncie	67,736	244	0	22	101	121	2,084	476	1,432	176	28
Munster	22,188	29	0	0	8	21	453	43	400	10	0
Nappanee	7,249	1	0	0	1	0	153	21	127	5	0
New Albany	37,619	109	1	8	44	56	2,238	478	1,620	140	19
New Castle	18,093	14	1	4	7	2	1,075	241	820	14	1
New Haven	13,914	24	0	1	9	14	379	69	294	16	0
New Whiteland	6,031	18	0	0	0	18	98	15	77	6	0
Noblesville	44,661	31	1	7	3	20	872	119	720	33	7
North Liberty	1,404	8	0	0	1	7	21	9	11	1	1
North Vernon	6,274	5	0	3	0	2	255	43	198	14	0
Oakland City	2,516	4	0	0	0	4	51	8	43	0	1
Peru	12,184	16	0	1	2	13	220	69	137	14	4
Plainfield	29,592	36	0	3	9	24	684	97	560	27	1
Plymouth	11,294	11	0	4	2	5	417	54	345	18	2
Portage	37,852	98	0	5	17	76	1,222	181	974	67	4
Porter	5,475	4	0	0	0	4	82	11	67	4	1
Portland	6,050	4	0	4	0	0	212	19	188	5	1
Princeton	8,477	12	0	3	1	8	272	22	249	1	0
Rensselaer	6,372	17	0	2	1	14	235	44	190	1	0
Richmond	36,455	170	0	33	76	61	1,620	557	948	115	48
Rushville	5,979	13	0	2	2	9	334	69	257	8	0
Schererville	29,332	15	0	2	7	6	766	47	672	47	0
Scottsburg	5,935	42	0	4	1	37	343	60	275	8	0

[1] The FBI does not publish arson data unless it receives data from either the agency or the state for all 12 months of the calendar year.

[5] Because of changes in the state/local agency's reporting practices, figures are not comparable to previous years' data.

Table 8.   Offenses Known to Law Enforcement, by State and City, 2010—*Continued*

(Number)

State/city	Population	Violent crime	Murder and non-negligent man-slaughter	Forcible rape	Robbery	Aggravated assault	Property crime	Burglary	Larceny-theft	Motor vehicle theft	Arson[1]
INDIANA—*Continued*											
Seymour	19,507	82	1	9	9	63	1,089	165	873	51	3
Shelbyville[2]	18,797	8	0	2	0	6			934	22	0
South Bend	104,182	746	6	52	339	349	5,929	2,216	3,411	302	51
South Whitley	1,856	1	0	0	0	1	21	3	18	0	0
Speedway	12,770	31	2	2	20	7	608	92	477	39	1
St. John	13,874	1	0	0	1	0	171	10	156	5	0
Tell City	7,465	9	0	4	1	4	214	46	162	6	1
Terre Haute	60,156	146	2	33	68	43	4,202	1,086	2,760	356	47
Tipton	4,982	3	0	1	1	1	148	31	116	1	0
Valparaiso	30,981	46	0	5	14	27	811	112	668	31	3
Vincennes	17,883	19	0	0	6	13	1,146	223	857	66	0
Walkerton	2,175	2	0	0	0	2	30	9	18	3	1
Warsaw	13,844	6	0	3	3	0	633	64	556	13	3
Washington	11,706	21	0	1	0	20	559	156	369	34	0
Waterloo	2,177	12	0	0	0	12	91	20	69	2	0
Westfield	23,334	17	0	4	3	10	431	47	376	8	2
West Lafayette	31,945	48	0	4	6	38	486	79	382	25	1
Westville	5,034	2	0	1	0	1	58	12	44	2	1
Whitestown	1,462	4	3	0	0	1	40	1	34	5	0
Whiting	4,740	3	0	0	2	1	235	49	171	15	0
Winchester	4,554	2	0	1	0	1	272	31	240	1	1
Winona Lake	4,334	8	0	0	1	7	28	3	22	3	0
Zionsville	14,472	3	0	0	0	3	194	36	157	1	3
IOWA											
Adel	4,462	12	0	2	0	10	76	28	44	4	1
Albia	3,541	4	0	1	0	3	69	13	55	1	0
Algona	5,229	10	1	1	0	8	36	7	26	3	2
Altoona	15,012	21	1	5	1	14	426	84	327	15	0
Ames	57,817	177	1	24	10	142	1,556	289	1,217	50	3
Anamosa	5,825	6	0	1	1	4	121	58	61	2	1
Ankeny	44,995	47	1	12	8	26	704	105	578	21	4
Atlantic	6,742	8	0	2	0	6	153	27	125	1	1
Audubon	2,115	0	0	0	0	0	36	17	19	0	0
Bettendorf	33,690	25	0	1	4	20	479	79	385	15	1
Boone	12,565	37	0	3	0	34	298	99	191	8	2
Burlington	25,650	164	1	16	19	128	1,002	255	711	36	5
Camanche	4,315	7	0	0	0	7	60	16	40	4	0
Carlisle	3,776	0	0	0	0	0	24	7	17	0	0
Carroll	9,953	6	0	1	0	5	145	22	111	12	0
Cedar Falls	39,350	71	1	10	3	57	684	113	552	19	3
Cedar Rapids	129,605	379	1	33	123	222	4,966	1,026	3,701	239	11
Centerville	5,367	24	0	3	0	21	190	43	133	14	7
Chariton	4,366	12	0	1	0	11	100	29	63	8	3
Charles City	7,373	9	0	0	0	9	134	22	110	2	0
Cherokee	4,654	47	0	3	1	43	88	34	50	4	1
Clarinda	5,316	19	0	3	0	16	168	31	127	10	0
Clarion	2,669	1	0	0	0	1	32	4	24	4	2
Clinton	26,591	148	1	13	20	114	1,166	246	875	45	13
Clive	15,894	33	0	3	3	27	282	47	219	16	7
Coralville	19,419	26	0	5	9	12	471	55	402	14	1
Council Bluffs	61,181	636	1	60	77	498	3,646	801	2,412	433	31
Cresco	3,714	3	0	0	1	2	101	41	56	4	3
Creston	7,627	18	0	0	1	17	193	41	138	14	1
Davenport	102,628	865	2	59	209	595	4,894	1,148	3,521	225	24
Decorah	7,800	5	0	1	0	4	60	7	47	6	0
Denison	7,241	7	0	1	0	6	77	15	59	3	0
Des Moines	202,564	1,072	6	105	224	737	9,795	2,248	6,808	739	43
De Witt	5,313	8	0	1	0	7	84	21	57	6	0
Dubuque	57,744	333	0	18	36	279	1,771	463	1,257	51	24
Dyersville	4,236	3	0	2	0	1	46	6	39	1	0
Eldora	2,706	12	0	3	0	9	36	13	19	4	0
Eldridge	5,078	3	0	0	1	2	67	8	55	4	1
Emmetsburg	3,581	3	0	0	0	3	11	0	10	1	0
Estherville	6,211	15	0	0	0	15	77	22	55	0	0
Evansdale	5,177	7	0	3	0	4	134	45	79	10	1
Fairfield	9,251	15	0	2	2	11	263	80	175	8	4
Forest City	3,961	14	0	0	0	14	32	15	15	2	1
Fort Dodge	25,204	79	0	3	23	53	1,270	380	835	55	17
Fort Madison	10,901	63	0	17	1	45	357	88	244	25	1
Glenwood	5,737	17	0	0	0	17	120	54	61	5	1
Grinnell	9,147	20	0	3	1	16	172	26	144	2	1
Hampton	4,187	1	0	0	0	1	23	1	22	0	0
Hawarden	2,380	4	0	0	0	4	19	8	10	1	0

[1] The FBI does not publish arson data unless it receives data from either the agency or the state for all 12 months of the calendar year.

[2] The FBI determined that the agency's data were underreported. Consequently, those data are not included in this table.

Table 8. Offenses Known to Law Enforcement, by State and City, 2010—*Continued*

(Number)

State/city	Population	Violent crime	Murder and non-negligent man-slaughter	Forcible rape	Robbery	Aggravated assault	Property crime	Burglary	Larceny-theft	Motor vehicle theft	Arson[1]
IOWA—*Continued*											
Hiawatha	6,779	3	1	1	1	0	135	25	107	3	2
Humboldt	4,205	1	0	0	0	1	21	9	10	2	0
Independence	6,133	4	0	0	0	4	83	18	61	4	2
Indianola	14,785	26	1	7	2	16	290	53	216	21	2
Iowa City	70,411	183	0	32	31	120	1,533	283	1,176	74	8
Iowa Falls	4,911	1	0	0	0	1	126	15	106	5	1
Jefferson	4,109	4	0	0	0	4	54	17	35	2	0
Johnston	17,024	19	0	1	3	15	193	28	154	11	0
Keokuk	10,413	117	0	6	2	109	502	89	384	29	0
Le Mars	9,199	17	0	5	0	12	261	39	204	18	2
Lisbon	2,048	0	0	0	0	0	42	5	37	0	0
Manchester	4,880	20	0	3	0	17	73	15	55	3	1
Maquoketa	5,823	22	0	4	1	17	239	100	129	10	1
Marion	34,562	53	0	10	5	38	581	132	418	31	7
Marshalltown	26,041	107	0	1	3	103	1,061	293	718	50	4
Mason City	27,344	47	0	11	1	35	1,058	203	807	48	6
Monticello	3,742	2	0	0	0	2	35	8	23	4	1
Mount Pleasant	8,751	40	0	4	0	36	247	71	169	7	1
Mount Vernon	4,263	8	0	2	0	6	52	4	46	2	0
Muscatine[2]	22,866	114	1	19	4	90		163		20	6
Nevada	6,806	55	0	6	0	49	174	26	142	6	3
New Hampton	3,401	2	0	0	0	2	28	5	21	2	1
Newton	14,909	19	1	0	0	18	473	70	385	18	0
North Liberty	13,609	21	0	3	0	18	94	24	67	3	1
Norwalk	9,331	7	0	1	0	6	104	15	85	4	0
Oelwein	5,985	27	0	4	0	23	155	38	104	13	0
Ogden	1,945	5	0	0	0	5	21	6	15	0	1
Orange City	5,889	6	0	2	0	4	70	21	43	6	0
Osage	3,461	3	0	0	0	3	33	7	25	1	0
Osceola	4,814	3	0	1	0	2	101	15	82	4	1
Oskaloosa	10,990	38	0	9	1	28	219	45	166	8	2
Ottumwa	24,501	101	2	13	12	74	913	202	677	34	19
Pella	10,332	31	0	1	0	30	126	23	95	8	3
Perry	9,568	36	0	1	1	34	124	19	101	4	1
Pleasant Hill	8,922	12	0	1	0	11	165	73	77	15	3
Prairie City	1,446	3	0	0	0	3	16	10	5	1	0
Red Oak	5,623	13	0	0	0	13	152	46	99	7	1
Sac City	2,073	1	0	0	0	1	29	9	20	0	0
Sergeant Bluff	4,142	9	0	0	0	9	66	8	57	1	2
Sheldon	4,866	5	0	0	2	3	65	20	42	3	0
Shenandoah	4,814	2	0	1	0	1	76	6	65	5	1
Sioux City	83,494	285	0	22	32	231	3,103	618	2,333	152	16
Spirit Lake	4,672	3	0	0	1	2	125	16	108	1	0
St. Ansgar	1,036	0	0	0	0	0	3	0	3	0	0
State Center	1,348	1	0	0	0	1	14	3	11	0	0
Storm Lake	9,582	45	0	1	2	42	276	87	181	8	8
Story City	3,438	1	0	0	0	1	45	21	23	1	0
Tipton	3,028	5	0	0	0	5	42	9	32	1	0
Urbandale	40,124	58	0	12	4	42	718	122	576	20	3
Vinton	5,144	10	0	3	0	7	67	11	54	2	1
Washington	7,280	38	1	1	0	36	92	24	60	8	0
Waterloo	67,203	435	3	33	70	329	2,558	812	1,635	111	33
Waukee	14,091	15	0	2	0	13	207	61	142	4	0
Webster City	7,664	32	0	4	0	28	263	71	181	11	2
West Burlington	3,383	6	0	1	4	1	120	27	88	5	0
West Des Moines	58,600	109	0	22	11	76	1,736	173	1,516	47	26
West Liberty	3,725	2	0	0	0	2	59	26	31	2	0
West Union	2,405	1	0	0	0	1	19	5	13	1	1
Williamsburg	2,865	4	0	0	1	3	34	12	21	1	0
Wilton	2,867	8	0	1	0	7	39	14	23	2	0
Windsor Heights	4,657	13	0	3	4	6	182	16	160	6	0
Winterset	4,883	6	0	1	0	5	174	85	86	3	0
KANSAS											
Abilene	6,284	14	0	2	2	10	266	30	230	6	2
Andover	11,091	14	0	4	0	10	361	34	315	12	0
Anthony	2,130	1	0	0	0	1	42	12	25	5	1
Arkansas City	10,960	53	0	9	2	42	495	89	388	18	6
Arma	1,519	4	0	0	0	4	29	5	23	1	0
Atchison	10,483	18	0	3	2	13	337	87	238	12	3
Atwood	1,021	1	0	0	0	1	10	1	8	1	0
Auburn	1,178	0	0	0	0	0	0	0	0	0	0
Augusta	8,830	18	0	1	2	15	286	30	248	8	3
Baldwin City	4,533	10	0	2	0	8	95	7	86	2	0

[1] The FBI does not publish arson data unless it receives data from either the agency or the state for all 12 months of the calendar year.

[2] The FBI determined that the agency's data were underreported. Consequently, those data are not included in this table.

Table 8.   Offenses Known to Law Enforcement, by State and City, 2010—*Continued*

(Number)

State/city	Population	Violent crime	Murder and non-negligent man-slaughter	Forcible rape	Robbery	Aggravated assault	Property crime	Burglary	Larceny-theft	Motor vehicle theft	Arson[1]
KANSAS—*Continued*											
Basehor	4,713	3	0	0	1	2	71	12	53	6	1
Baxter Springs	4,132	6	0	2	0	4	60	20	36	4	3
Bel Aire	7,009	3	0	0	1	2	53	9	42	2	1
Beloit	3,659	12	0	1	0	11	44	14	29	1	0
Bonner Springs	7,349	14	0	2	3	9	249	57	169	23	2
Bucklin	794	0	0	0	0	0	0	0	0	0	0
Burlington	2,685	2	0	0	0	2	16	4	12	0	0
Bushton	284	0	0	0	0	0	0	0	0	0	0
Caldwell	1,128	4	0	1	0	3	13	4	8	1	0
Chanute	8,736	28	0	7	3	18	321	89	217	15	4
Chase	447	0	0	0	0	0	0	0	0	0	0
Chetopa	1,234	2	0	0	0	2	22	11	7	4	0
Clay Center	4,378	6	0	1	0	5	116	32	78	6	0
Clearwater	2,477	1	0	0	0	1	40	13	25	2	0
Coffeyville	10,241	82	0	6	12	64	506	134	359	13	4
Colby	4,811	10	0	0	0	10	141	28	109	4	1
Columbus	3,179	5	0	1	1	3	51	10	37	4	1
Concordia	5,091	14	0	7	0	7	154	32	113	9	3
Council Grove	2,274	0	0	0	0	0	43	16	24	3	1
Derby	23,607	46	0	5	0	41	574	83	470	21	1
Dodge City	26,213	129	0	20	14	95	883	141	682	60	2
Eastborough	815	1	0	0	0	1	0	0	0	0	0
Edwardsville	4,595	10	0	1	1	8	90	30	49	11	0
El Dorado	12,712	45	0	10	4	31	434	90	311	33	1
Ellinwood	1,974	3	0	0	0	3	50	18	30	2	0
Ellis	1,952	0	0	0	0	0	11	2	7	2	0
Ellsworth	2,823	6	0	0	0	6	52	8	40	4	0
Elwood	1,119	7	0	1	1	5	29	12	14	3	0
Emporia	24,856	83	0	19	4	60	1,004	149	832	23	5
Eskridge	563	0	0	0	0	0	4	3	1	0	0
Eudora	6,540	9	0	0	0	9	143	20	116	7	1
Fairway	3,912	3	0	0	1	2	26	6	19	1	0
Fort Scott	7,959	24	0	2	2	20	399	94	289	16	3
Frontenac	3,244	7	0	0	0	7	87	40	43	4	0
Galena	3,126	14	0	0	0	14	90	25	55	10	2
Garden City	28,736	116	0	22	13	81	1,019	144	840	35	6
Gardner	19,112	30	0	4	3	23	378	49	321	8	7
Garnett	3,166	22	0	1	0	21	61	20	36	5	0
Geneseo	261	0	0	0	0	0	0	0	0	0	0
Girard	2,719	7	0	1	0	6	101	18	81	2	0
Goddard	4,352	6	0	1	0	5	74	13	58	3	0
Grandview Plaza	1,432	11	0	2	0	9	36	11	25	0	0
Great Bend	15,794	95	1	18	4	72	868	161	669	38	5
Hays	20,537	62	0	7	2	53	630	73	542	15	6
Haysville	10,765	41	0	14	4	23	269	35	223	11	7
Herington	2,396	9	0	3	0	6	73	17	56	0	0
Hesston	3,881	1	0	0	0	1	67	16	50	1	0
Hiawatha	3,178	1	0	0	0	1	43	6	35	2	0
Highland	936	0	0	0	0	0	33	12	19	2	0
Hill City	1,292	5	0	0	0	5	32	5	26	1	0
Hillsboro	2,607	4	0	3	0	1	52	9	41	2	1
Hoisington	2,802	6	0	1	0	5	49	16	28	5	1
Holcomb	2,176	0	0	0	0	0	30	18	12	0	0
Holton	3,306	9	0	1	0	8	85	23	58	4	1
Hoxie	1,076	0	0	0	0	0	11	0	10	1	0
Hugoton	3,456	0	0	0	0	0	15	0	15	0	0
Humboldt	1,812	2	0	1	0	1	21	4	16	1	0
Hutchinson	40,981	244	2	23	35	184	2,870	588	2,177	105	22
Iola	5,704	20	0	8	0	12	230	42	175	13	0
Junction City	21,298	157	4	11	25	117	529	102	416	11	4
Kansas City	143,867	823	25	62	289	447	7,735	1,922	4,684	1,129	
Lansing	11,003	34	0	2	0	32	197	67	124	6	0
Larned	3,504	21	0	0	2	19	89	23	63	3	0
Lawrence	93,945	413	0	40	61	312	3,841	522	3,163	156	21
Leavenworth	35,290	257	2	15	47	193	1,225	391	762	72	10
Leawood	32,422	13	0	2	1	10	479	66	389	24	0
Lebo	912	1	0	0	0	1	7	2	5	0	0
Lenexa	49,282	66	1	9	12	44	995	159	752	84	4
Liberal	20,226	91	2	6	11	72	612	160	436	16	3
Lindsborg	3,237	3	0	1	0	2	60	18	40	2	0
Louisburg	4,093	0	0	0	0	0	50	10	39	1	0
Lyons	3,394	2	0	1	0	1	3	0	3	0	0
Macksville	477	0	0	0	0	0	5	3	2	0	0

[1] The FBI does not publish arson data unless it receives data from either the agency or the state for all 12 months of the calendar year.

Table 8. Offenses Known to Law Enforcement, by State and City, 2010—*Continued*

(Number)

State/city	Population	Violent crime	Murder and non-negligent man-slaughter	Forcible rape	Robbery	Aggravated assault	Property crime	Burglary	Larceny-theft	Motor vehicle theft	Arson[1]
KANSAS—*Continued*											
Maize	3,477	12	0	0	0	12	95	25	70	0	0
Marion	1,849	4	0	1	0	3	35	10	22	3	0
Marysville	3,103	6	0	2	0	4	65	15	49	1	0
Mayetta	363	0	0	0	0	0	0	0	0	0	0
McLouth	822	7	0	0	0	7	19	2	16	1	0
McPherson	13,371	29	0	5	0	24	282	60	211	11	1
Meriden	752	0	0	0	0	0	0	0	0	0	0
Minneapolis	1,956	3	0	2	0	1	53	14	36	3	1
Mission	9,920	36	0	4	16	16	403	36	302	65	0
Moran	521	0	0	0	0	0	0	0	0	0	0
Moundridge	1,635	2	0	2	0	0	16	3	13	0	0
Mulvane	6,033	9	0	1	2	6	102	22	77	3	0
Neodesha	2,559	8	1	1	0	6	33	6	27	0	1
Newton	18,637	92	0	15	5	72	430	83	329	18	5
Norton	2,643	2	0	1	0	1	30	4	24	2	0
Oakley	1,794	3	0	0	0	3	17	3	14	0	0
Oberlin	1,600	2	0	0	0	2	14	6	8	0	1
Olathe	126,090	216	4	41	28	143	2,307	243	1,922	142	19
Osage City	2,766	12	0	0	0	12	69	11	56	2	0
Osawatomie	4,554	23	0	1	0	22	110	20	87	3	0
Ottawa	13,073	37	1	7	1	28	366	62	289	15	4
Overland Park	178,669	289	0	40	36	213	4,185	491	3,389	305	38
Paola	5,415	13	0	3	3	7	127	27	94	6	1
Park City	8,295	24	0	5	1	18	158	32	116	10	1
Parsons	11,026	132	0	6	18	108	735	249	469	17	4
Pittsburg	19,817	72	2	8	10	52	1,140	209	884	47	15
Prairie Village	21,821	51	0	5	1	45	331	75	239	17	5
Pratt	6,336	18	0	0	1	17	156	36	117	3	2
Roeland Park	7,059	17	0	5	9	3	265	27	220	18	0
Rose Hill	4,187	3	0	1	0	2	53	7	44	2	0
Russell	4,167	18	0	1	1	16	63	15	42	6	0
Sabetha	2,454	7	0	0	1	6	34	10	21	3	0
Salina	46,547	189	1	27	29	132	2,269	393	1,787	89	39
Scott City	3,475	14	1	5	1	7	57	13	36	8	0
Shawnee	63,652	119	4	22	22	71	1,215	223	868	124	11
South Hutchinson	2,559	2	0	0	0	2	107	16	88	3	0
Spring Hill	5,644	14	0	3	0	11	101	17	80	4	0
Sterling	2,541	3	0	1	0	2	43	12	31	0	0
St. Marys	2,326	1	0	1	0	0	19	1	17	1	1
Tonganoxie	4,657	11	0	1	1	9	111	22	86	3	4
Topeka	125,306	697	14	51	222	410	7,506	1,598	5,404	504	14
Ulysses	5,512	14	0	0	2	12	84	19	62	3	0
Valley Center	6,799	13	0	3	0	10	126	24	95	7	0
Wa Keeney	1,730	2	0	0	0	2	13	3	9	1	0
Wakefield	907	0	0	0	0	0	0	0	0	0	0
Wamego	4,414	1	0	0	0	1	73	7	63	3	0
Wathena	1,280	3	0	0	1	2	35	7	25	3	0
Wellington	7,639	31	0	2	1	28	328	83	230	15	2
Wellsville	1,729	5	0	0	1	4	55	14	40	1	1
Westwood	1,879	1	0	0	0	1	43	8	33	2	0
Wichita	376,880	3,026	16	246	481	2,283	18,241	4,241	12,472	1,528	129
Winchester	562	0	0	0	0	0	4	0	4	0	0
Winfield	11,126	41	0	4	4	33	409	69	323	17	0
KENTUCKY											
Alexandria	8,509	2	0	1	1	0	182	21	158	3	0
Anchorage	3,414	0	0	0	0	0	23	11	12	0	0
Ashland	21,209	76	0	9	46	21	1,408	408	953	47	1
Auburn	1,508	1	0	0	0	1	8	5	2	1	0
Audubon Park	1,680	3	0	0	0	3	55	20	31	4	0
Barbourville	3,625	0	0	0	0	0	50	15	32	3	0
Bardstown	11,339	22	0	3	6	13	323	84	223	16	0
Bardwell	826	0	0	0	0	0	2	0	2	0	0
Beattyville	1,096	2	0	0	2	0	10	5	5	0	0
Beaver Dam	3,120	6	0	1	0	5	15	2	11	2	0
Bellefonte	855	0	0	0	0	0	6	1	5	0	0
Bellevue	5,822	7	0	0	4	3	299	47	242	10	1
Benham	524	0	0	0	0	0	1	1	0	0	0
Benton	4,346	0	0	0	0	0	92	18	68	6	1
Berea	15,130	17	0	1	7	9	486	117	344	25	2
Bowling Green	57,308	152	0	39	55	58	2,662	512	2,022	128	2
Brandenburg	2,155	4	0	0	2	2	43	15	27	1	0
Brownsville	995	2	0	0	0	2	6	4	0	2	1
Burnside	995	1	0	0	0	1	42	11	30	1	1

[1] The FBI does not publish arson data unless it receives data from either the agency or the state for all 12 months of the calendar year.

SECTION II: OFFENSES KNOWN TO POLICE   127

Table 8.   Offenses Known to Law Enforcement, by State and City, 2010—*Continued*

(Number)

State/city	Population	Violent crime	Murder and non-negligent man-slaughter	Forcible rape	Robbery	Aggravated assault	Property crime	Burglary	Larceny-theft	Motor vehicle theft	Arson[1]
KENTUCKY—*Continued*											
Cadiz	2,602	7	0	0	5	2	80	22	55	3	0
Calhoun	774	0	0	0	0	0	1	1	0	0	0
Calvert City	2,753	1	0	1	0	0	26	7	14	5	0
Campbellsville	11,340	23	0	4	9	10	392	97	288	7	0
Carrollton	3,933	6	0	0	0	6	82	21	56	5	0
Catlettsburg	1,824	4	0	1	0	3	84	25	57	2	1
Cave City	2,009	2	0	0	0	2	44	10	26	8	0
Central City	5,655	9	1	3	1	4	57	8	47	2	0
Clarkson	841	0	0	0	0	0	6	3	3	0	0
Clay City	1,328	7	0	0	1	6	27	14	13	0	0
Cloverport	1,222	1	0	1	0	0	2	2	0	0	0
Coal Run Village	626	1	0	0	1	0	7	4	3	0	0
Cold Spring	6,172	7	0	0	5	2	179	13	155	11	0
Columbia	4,644	1	0	1	0	0	29	12	15	2	1
Corbin	8,335	32	1	3	17	11	334	89	235	10	4
Covington	43,054	321	1	39	186	95	2,330	695	1,454	181	12
Cumberland	2,329	2	0	0	0	2	26	10	14	2	0
Cynthiana	6,281	15	0	3	4	8	313	57	246	10	0
Danville	15,646	48	1	8	19	20	582	139	427	16	1
Dawson Springs	2,872	6	0	1	0	5	36	10	22	4	0
Dayton	5,418	7	0	1	2	4	131	35	88	8	1
Dry Ridge	2,222	1	0	0	1	0	7	1	4	2	0
Earlington	1,550	1	0	1	0	0	4	1	2	1	0
Eddyville	2,409	0	0	0	0	0	31	4	25	2	0
Edgewood	8,885	3	0	1	2	0	148	24	121	3	0
Edmonton	1,606	0	0	0	0	0	6	3	2	1	0
Elizabethtown	24,712	48	0	13	22	13	956	139	784	33	8
Elkton	1,988	1	0	0	0	1	30	11	15	4	0
Elsmere	7,999	16	0	2	9	5	122	43	68	11	0
Eminence	2,245	6	0	0	0	6	25	8	15	2	1
Erlanger	21,384	36	0	13	14	9	678	114	535	29	2
Falmouth	2,028	3	0	0	0	3	72	21	50	1	0
Ferguson	940	0	0	0	0	0	4	4	0	0	0
Flatwoods	7,678	6	0	0	6	0	104	57	42	5	1
Flemingsburg	2,654	0	0	0	0	0	38	15	23	0	0
Florence	28,869	63	0	18	27	18	1,586	206	1,317	63	3
Fort Mitchell	7,539	3	0	0	2	1	173	23	135	15	0
Fort Thomas	15,141	6	0	4	1	1	226	43	176	7	0
Fort Wright	5,436	14	0	0	11	3	404	40	355	9	1
Frankfort	27,319	76	5	6	42	23	951	188	745	18	3
Franklin	7,944	17	0	4	7	6	329	72	240	17	1
Fulton	2,388	9	0	4	1	4	95	22	63	10	2
Georgetown	22,441	126	2	7	18	99	1,008	123	849	36	
Glasgow	14,381	22	0	3	6	13	301	62	221	18	3
Graymoor-Devondale	3,156	2	0	0	2	0	81	23	55	3	0
Grayson	3,871	5	0	2	3	0	99	36	57	6	0
Greensburg	2,389	2	0	0	1	1	19	5	14	0	0
Greenville	4,286	3	0	2	1	0	20	9	10	1	0
Guthrie	1,455	6	0	1	2	3	13	4	9	0	0
Hardinsburg	2,420	0	0	0	0	0	5	2	2	1	0
Harlan	1,838	9	0	2	2	5	88	10	76	2	0
Harrodsburg	8,154	18	0	6	3	9	121	54	62	5	2
Hartford	2,632	1	0	0	1	0	7	1	4	2	0
Hazard	4,736	15	0	3	4	8	316	93	211	12	0
Henderson	27,978	23	0	3	8	12	1,045	174	828	43	0
Highland Heights Southgate	10,660	65	0	2	4	59	145	46	93	6	0
Hillview	7,601	10	0	1	4	5	201	56	136	9	0
Hodgenville	2,732	1	0	0	0	1	18	8	10	0	0
Hopkinsville	32,265	129	4	26	42	57	1,253	335	868	50	10
Horse Cave	2,292	1	0	0	1	0	7	4	3	0	0
Independence	22,935	14	0	7	2	5	319	66	240	13	2
Indian Hills	3,555	3	0	0	1	2	34	18	15	1	0
Inez	419	0	0	0	0	0	5	0	3	2	0
Irvine	2,616	4	0	1	1	2	66	24	39	3	0
Irvington	1,398	0	0	0	0	0	0	0	0	0	0
Jackson	2,361	1	0	0	0	1	35	15	18	2	1
Jamestown	1,755	2	0	0	0	2	17	7	9	1	1
Jeffersontown	26,411	47	0	8	33	6	570	121	402	47	0
Jenkins	2,190	2	0	0	1	1	9	5	4	0	0
Junction City	2,211	1	0	0	1	0	11	6	5	0	0
La Grange	6,638	10	0	2	6	2	123	30	91	2	1
Lakeside Park-Crestview Hills	6,458	7	0	1	2	4	141	14	124	3	0
Lancaster	4,459	3	0	1	0	2	82	23	56	3	0

[1] The FBI does not publish arson data unless it receives data from either the agency or the state for all 12 months of the calendar year.

Table 8. Offenses Known to Law Enforcement, by State and City, 2010—*Continued*

(Number)

State/city	Population	Violent crime	Murder and non-negligent man-slaughter	Forcible rape	Robbery	Aggravated assault	Property crime	Burglary	Larceny-theft	Motor vehicle theft	Arson[1]
KENTUCKY—*Continued*											
Lawrenceburg	10,225	17	0	7	4	6	60	15	39	6	0
Lebanon	6,371	9	1	2	4	2	175	71	98	6	1
Leitchfield	6,562	8	0	2	0	6	182	47	125	10	0
Lewisburg	912	0	0	0	0	0	6	1	5	0	0
Lexington	300,069	1,724	18	87	593	1,026	11,024	2,679	7,704	641	39
Liberty	1,914	3	0	0	1	2	8	6	1	1	0
London	7,958	16	1	5	3	7	390	60	305	25	0
Louisa	2,091	3	0	1	1	1	83	23	59	1	0
Louisville Metro	637,428	3,734	52	229	1,603	1,850	29,551	7,571	20,005	1,975	223
Loyall	697	0	0	0	0	0	24	12	12	0	0
Ludlow	4,845	16	0	5	9	2	227	57	161	9	0
Lynch	812	1	0	0	0	1	2	2	0	0	0
Manchester	1,962	2	0	0	0	2	59	16	41	2	0
Marion	3,031	2	0	1	0	1	51	13	36	2	0
Mayfield	10,149	34	0	6	8	20	280	101	169	10	2
Maysville	9,207	17	0	6	6	5	540	188	341	11	1
Meadow Vale	861	1	0	0	0	1	10	1	7	2	0
Middlesboro	9,775	31	1	3	15	12	599	96	490	13	1
Monticello	6,152	13	0	0	6	7	175	71	101	3	4
Morehead	7,714	14	2	2	3	7	202	42	149	11	1
Morganfield	3,240	0	0	0	0	0	25	5	20	0	0
Morgantown	2,558	1	0	0	0	1	9	3	5	1	0
Mount Sterling	7,145	31	0	2	15	14	435	100	318	17	0
Mount Vernon	2,555	12	0	1	7	4	52	20	28	4	1
Mount Washington	12,414	8	0	2	1	5	185	50	124	11	1
Munfordville	1,588	2	0	1	0	1	15	4	9	2	0
Murray	16,677	24	1	8	6	9	670	164	493	13	0
Newport	15,738	62	3	5	42	12	1,222	240	917	65	4
Nicholasville	27,686	52	0	8	25	19	1,186	297	845	44	6
Nortonville	1,223	0	0	0	0	0	10	2	7	1	0
Oak Grove	9,673	27	0	7	9	11	273	111	141	21	4
Olive Hill	1,758	0	0	0	0	0	21	5	15	1	0
Owensboro	55,848	115	2	36	28	49	2,255	399	1,772	84	12
Owenton	1,467	0	0	0	0	0	7	0	6	1	0
Owingsville	1,645	3	0	1	0	2	38	8	30	0	0
Paducah	25,643	92	0	14	50	28	1,232	183	1,005	44	7
Paintsville	4,152	9	0	2	4	3	125	22	93	10	1
Paris	9,189	22	0	4	9	9	250	80	155	15	0
Park Hills	2,770	1	0	0	0	1	35	6	27	2	0
Pikeville	6,407	11	0	1	4	6	389	28	352	9	1
Pineville	2,041	1	0	1	0	0	50	14	34	2	0
Pioneer Village	2,733	3	1	1	1	0	4	1	3	0	0
Prestonsburg	3,825	12	0	1	4	7	100	26	68	6	1
Princeton	6,366	19	1	1	11	6	192	50	133	9	7
Providence	3,399	2	0	0	1	1	44	12	32	0	0
Raceland	2,857	1	0	0	0	1	25	6	18	1	0
Radcliff	22,251	171	0	10	13	148	710	164	521	25	4
Richmond	34,068	126	2	8	66	50	1,923	461	1,405	57	4
Russell	3,632	4	0	0	3	1	90	20	70	0	0
Russell Springs	2,335	2	0	0	1	1	51	16	34	1	0
Russellville	7,254	22	0	9	6	7	292	64	213	15	3
Sadieville	333	0	0	0	0	0	1	1	0	0	0
Science Hill	667	1	0	0	0	1	4	2	2	0	0
Scottsville	4,558	0	0	0	0	0	0	0	0	0	0
Shelbyville	11,637	37	0	6	18	13	302	103	191	8	0
Shepherdsville	9,424	16	1	6	3	6	280	66	200	14	1
Shively	16,609	92	1	5	64	22	690	197	408	85	1
Silver Grove	1,150	0	0	0	0	0	26	9	16	1	0
Simpsonville	1,500	0	0	0	0	0	16	4	11	1	0
Somerset	12,266	33	0	8	20	5	686	112	558	16	1
South Shore	1,277	1	0	0	1	0	3	2	1	0	0
Springfield	2,785	0	0	0	0	0	15	4	11	0	0
Stamping Ground	709	0	0	0	0	0	4	1	3	0	0
Stanford	3,379	2	0	0	1	1	24	10	13	1	0
Stanton	3,070	1	0	0	0	1	54	9	44	1	0
St. Matthews	18,885	27	0	1	15	11	744	124	595	25	0
Strathmoor Village	738	0	0	0	0	0	9	7	1	1	0
Sturgis	1,889	1	0	0	0	1	5	0	5	0	1
Taylor Mill	7,123	3	0	1	1	1	88	28	57	3	1
Taylorsville	1,300	1	0	0	1	0	15	3	12	0	0
Tompkinsville	2,603	3	0	1	1	1	3	2	1	0	0
Uniontown	1,017	0	0	0	0	0	8	4	3	1	0
Vanceburg	1,681	1	0	0	0	1	13	3	10	0	1

[1] The FBI does not publish arson data unless it receives data from either the agency or the state for all 12 months of the calendar year.

Table 8.   Offenses Known to Law Enforcement, by State and City, 2010—*Continued*

(Number)

State/city	Population	Violent crime	Murder and non-negligent man-slaughter	Forcible rape	Robbery	Aggravated assault	Property crime	Burglary	Larceny-theft	Motor vehicle theft	Arson[1]
KENTUCKY—*Continued*											
Versailles	7,924	20	0	6	6	8	666	137	508	21	2
Villa Hills	7,704	0	0	0	0	0	33	8	24	1	0
Vine Grove	4,558	4	0	0	2	2	80	21	52	7	0
Warsaw	1,798	0	0	0	0	0	18	5	10	3	0
West Liberty	3,356	1	0	0	1	0	47	10	33	4	0
West Point	968	0	0	0	0	0	5	1	4	0	1
Whitesburg	1,452	2	0	0	1	1	17	1	15	1	0
Wilder	2,956	3	0	0	2	1	77	8	66	3	0
Williamsburg	5,176	9	0	3	0	6	141	49	87	5	2
Williamstown	3,533	3	0	0	0	3	97	28	62	7	1
Wilmore	6,028	0	0	0	0	0	85	11	73	1	1
Winchester	16,754	76	2	4	21	49	841	200	622	19	6
Worthington	1,700	0	0	0	0	0	9	8	1	0	0
LOUISIANA											
Abbeville	12,310	123	1	5	14	103	428	160	259	9	0
Addis	4,043	6	0	0	0	6	1	0	1	0	0
Alexandria	49,283	592	4	11	184	393	3,787	943	2,714	130	
Amite	4,386	71	0	5	11	55	467	131	324	12	3
Baker	13,460	23	0	2	12	9	503	132	347	24	1
Basile	2,357	3	0	0	0	3	9	1	8	0	0
Bastrop	11,542	118	0	3	26	89	1,349	454	832	63	5
Berwick	4,266	5	0	0	1	4	66	25	39	2	0
Blanchard	2,734	1	0	0	0	1	51	14	35	2	0
Bogalusa	12,581	182	0	12	40	130	838	301	486	51	8
Bossier City	64,232	397	1	27	71	298	2,663	480	2,036	147	3
Broussard	8,227	43	2	5	9	27	665	349	316	0	0
Brusly	2,129	0	0	0	0	0	2	1	1	0	0
Carencro	6,897	71	0	1	11	59	260	65	183	12	0
Church Point	4,664	34	0	2	3	29	67	39	25	3	
Clarence	501	0	0	0	0	0	0	0	0	0	0
Clinton	1,867	11	0	0	1	10	40	11	27	2	1
Coushatta	2,030	23	0	0	1	22	56	15	41	0	0
Covington	9,325	34	0	2	4	28	272	49	213	10	2
Crowley	13,878	112	1	4	15	92	526	129	382	15	0
Cullen	1,345	18	0	0	1	17	12	5	7	0	0
Denham Springs	10,504	53	0	5	16	32	817	135	665	17	0
De Ridder	10,250	70	0	0	0	70	261	59	201	1	
Epps	1,090	9	0	0	0	9	2	2	0	0	0
Erath	2,160	15	0	0	4	11	11	1	10	0	0
Eunice	11,492	125	0	8	15	102	764	253	497	14	1
Farmerville	3,574	39	0	3	2	34	194	55	132	7	0
Ferriday	3,529	33	1	0	2	30	52	49	0	3	0
Franklin	7,538	76	2	0	11	63	468	85	368	15	0
Franklinton	3,771	25	0	1	1	23	219	46	166	7	0
French Settlement	1,081	3	0	0	1	2	33	2	30	1	0
Georgetown	320	1	0	0	0	1	1	1	0	0	0
Golden Meadow	2,095	12	0	0	4	8	50	19	31	0	0
Gonzales[6]	9,738	9	0	0	1	8			378	17	0
Grambling	4,931	15	0	0	1	14	137	127	8	2	
Gramercy	3,266	27	0	0	0	27	79	8	63	8	0
Greenwood	2,808	11	0	1	2	8	57	27	26	4	0
Gretna	17,901	89	2	6	17	64	644	146	440	58	2
Hammond	20,386	335	0	10	97	228	2,326	964	1,253	109	0
Harahan	9,431	14	0	1	2	11	124	31	89	4	0
Houma	32,688	254	4	12	86	152	1,576	358	1,131	87	
Independence	1,806	20	0	0	1	19	75	26	49	0	0
Iowa	2,634	8	0	0	2	6	111	33	77	1	0
Jeanerette	5,848	47	0	0	5	42	129	48	74	7	0
Jena	2,845	3	0	0	1	2	2	1	0	1	0
Jennings	10,418	58	2	2	7	47	312	85	222	5	0
Kaplan	4,996	217	0	4	7	206	409	117	287	5	0
Kenner	67,889	209	8	22	80	99	2,352	386	1,809	157	31
Kentwood	2,315	22	1	0	5	16	209	78	128	3	0
Kinder	2,403	11	0	1	0	10	82	0	80	2	
Lafayette	115,378	940	12	20	240	668	6,989	1,432	5,267	290	26
Lake Arthur	2,857	4	0	1	0	3	95	18	76	1	0
Lake Charles	71,795	488	7	27	148	306	3,047	1,826	1,088	133	0
Lake Providence	4,128	37	0	0	2	35	27	19	8	0	2
Leesville	5,817	69	0	8	21	40	355	27	324	4	
Lutcher	3,407	31	0	1	0	30	47	34	12	1	1
Mamou	3,372	5	0	0	0	5	121	7	110	4	0
Mandeville	12,825	32	0	0	2	30	339	32	304	3	1
Mansfield	5,339	144	0	1	1	142	347	117	222	8	0

[1] The FBI does not publish arson data unless it receives data from either the agency or the state for all 12 months of the calendar year.

[6] The FBI determined that the agency did not follow national Uniform Crime Reporting Program guidelines for reporting an offense. Consequently, this figure is not included in this table.

Table 8.   Offenses Known to Law Enforcement, by State and City, 2010—*Continued*

(Number)

State/city	Population	Violent crime	Murder and non-negligent man-slaughter	Forcible rape	Robbery	Aggravated assault	Property crime	Burglary	Larceny-theft	Motor vehicle theft	Arson[1]
LOUISIANA—*Continued*											
Many	2,698	26	0	0	3	23	164	35	127	2	2
Marion	753	8	0	0	0	8	15	7	8	0	
Minden	12,799	27	1	1	6	19	252	60	179	13	2
Monroe	51,709	408	6	19	86	297	4,577	1,577	2,884	116	
Moreauville	931	4	0	0	0	4	6	0	5	1	
Morgan City	11,367	89	0	10	22	57	567	139	410	18	
Napoleonville	646	1	0	0	0	1	0	0	0	0	0
Natchitoches	17,667	144	4	5	16	119	1,018	420	590	8	1
New Orleans	356,317	2,593	175	144	953	1,321	12,645	3,695	6,540	2,410	
Norwood	327	0	0	0	0	0	1	1	0	0	0
Oak Grove	1,918	15	0	1	0	14	70	36	28	6	0
Oil City	1,212	2	0	0	0	2	15	4	10	1	0
Olla	1,328	4	0	2	0	2	34	5	28	1	0
Opelousas	23,268	248	6	15	41	186	1,364	370	931	63	
Pearl River	2,256	11	0	2	0	9	88	17	66	5	0
Pineville	15,064	47	1	0	7	39	693	119	552	22	
Plaquemine	6,646	56	2	0	3	51	295	33	250	12	0
Pollock	385	3	0	0	0	3	12	5	7	0	0
Ponchatoula	6,524	74	0	5	8	61	350	117	218	15	0
Port Allen	4,892	21	0	1	4	16	221	63	143	15	0
Port Vincent	541	8	0	0	1	7	40	19	19	2	0
Rayville	3,988	25	0	1	5	19	259	40	211	8	0
Ruston	21,391	111	0	7	20	84	1,013	368	620	25	1
Scott	9,335	27	1	1	2	23	204	37	156	11	
Shreveport	199,900	1,533	26	121	355	1,031	9,459	2,616	6,317	526	99
Slidell	27,772	106	0	16	21	69	1,549	177	1,295	77	0
Springhill	5,064	6	0	0	3	3	142	31	111	0	0
Sterlington	1,447	4	0	1	0	3	6	4	2	0	0
Stonewall	1,930	1	0	0	0	1	7	1	6	0	
Sulphur	19,632	269	0	3	19	247	999	220	753	26	3
Tallulah	7,218	62	1	2	6	53	257	83	169	5	0
Thibodaux	14,487	69	0	4	16	49	796	119	653	24	1
Tickfaw	703	4	1	0	3	0	27	0	25	2	0
Vidalia	4,070	39	0	2	3	34	176	38	137	1	0
Vinton	3,385	11	0	1	0	10	105	28	71	6	0
Walker	6,567	45	0	4	13	28	368	77	285	6	3
West Monroe	12,930	71	2	7	11	51	949	205	709	35	
Westwego	10,226	15	0	0	3	12	196	45	138	13	1
Winnfield	4,995	140	0	3	13	124	264	89	160	15	1
Zachary	15,696	44	2	1	8	33	219	22	189	8	0
Zwolle	1,737	13	0	1	2	10	40	39	1	0	
MAINE											
Ashland	1,457	1	0	0	0	1	16	13	3	0	0
Auburn	22,953	41	0	9	19	13	895	134	742	19	6
Augusta	18,514	57	0	13	12	32	1,208	222	965	21	12
Baileyville	1,524	2	0	1	0	1	42	10	29	3	0
Bangor	31,587	52	3	4	30	15	1,730	198	1,485	47	9
Bar Harbor	5,243	1	0	1	0	0	55	5	49	1	2
Bath	8,879	8	0	4	3	1	251	25	220	6	0
Belfast	6,748	12	0	7	2	3	254	39	206	9	3
Berwick	7,707	9	0	3	0	6	146	34	108	4	2
Biddeford	21,511	66	0	17	18	31	1,029	157	850	22	16
Boothbay Harbor	2,252	4	0	2	0	2	96	11	84	1	0
Brewer	9,097	7	0	2	0	5	314	37	273	4	1
Bridgton	5,608	5	0	3	0	2	107	16	90	1	0
Brownville	1,288	0	0	0	0	0	53	17	36	0	0
Brunswick	22,171	16	0	6	6	4	422	55	355	12	3
Bucksport	4,951	13	0	1	0	12	116	32	81	3	1
Buxton	8,179	7	0	2	3	2	97	22	67	8	0
Calais	3,145	43	0	2	1	40	192	45	146	1	6
Camden	5,279	1	0	1	0	0	85	12	71	2	0
Cape Elizabeth	8,825	1	0	0	0	1	119	14	104	1	1
Caribou	8,063	7	0	0	1	6	182	32	149	1	1
Carrabassett Valley	474	1	0	1	0	0	55	1	53	1	0
Clinton	3,328	11	0	4	1	6	62	29	31	2	0
Cumberland	7,744	3	0	1	0	2	36	14	22	0	0
Damariscotta	1,905	7	0	3	0	4	57	12	45	0	0
Dexter	3,687	3	0	1	0	2	109	35	72	2	1
Dixfield	2,532	2	0	1	0	1	46	8	38	0	0
Dover-Foxcroft	4,165	5	0	1	0	4	145	34	105	6	0
East Millinocket	3,177	1	0	1	0	0	41	6	33	2	0
Eastport	1,509	0	0	0	0	0	10	3	7	0	0
Eliot	6,358	2	0	2	0	0	24	9	15	0	0

[1] The FBI does not publish arson data unless it receives data from either the agency or the state for all 12 months of the calendar year.

Table 8.   Offenses Known to Law Enforcement, by State and City, 2010—*Continued*

(Number)

State/city	Population	Violent crime	Murder and non-negligent man-slaughter	Forcible rape	Robbery	Aggravated assault	Property crime	Burglary	Larceny-theft	Motor vehicle theft	Arson[1]
MAINE—*Continued*											
Ellsworth	7,243	15	0	1	4	10	263	36	219	8	0
Fairfield	6,695	5	0	2	1	2	245	45	192	8	3
Falmouth	10,921	3	0	0	2	1	146	26	116	4	1
Farmington	7,602	10	0	7	1	2	224	19	203	2	1
Fort Fairfield	3,443	7	0	0	0	7	31	4	25	2	0
Fort Kent	4,212	5	0	0	0	5	24	4	20	0	0
Freeport	8,392	2	0	1	1	0	181	31	149	1	0
Fryeburg	3,313	7	0	1	0	6	69	25	43	1	0
Gardiner	6,103	11	0	6	1	4	193	46	144	3	2
Gorham	15,940	15	0	4	5	6	174	63	98	13	2
Gouldsboro	2,011	0	0	0	0	0	15	9	6	0	1
Greenville	1,721	6	0	0	0	6	39	14	25	0	1
Hallowell	2,434	1	1	0	0	0	66	13	51	2	1
Hampden	7,052	0	0	0	0	0	122	13	106	3	0
Holden	3,048	1	0	0	1	0	50	15	35	0	0
Houlton	6,105	7	0	1	0	6	145	19	126	0	0
Jay	4,739	4	0	3	0	1	76	19	55	2	1
Kennebunk	11,577	4	0	3	0	1	141	38	102	1	1
Kennebunkport	4,031	0	0	0	0	0	52	4	47	1	0
Kittery	10,632	6	0	4	2	0	183	35	144	4	2
Lewiston	35,153	93	2	16	42	33	1,056	179	862	15	16
Limestone	2,252	3	0	0	0	3	59	17	39	3	1
Lincoln	5,318	5	0	2	0	3	217	67	144	6	1
Lincolnville	2,205	2	0	0	0	2	41	13	28	0	1
Lisbon	9,355	6	0	2	1	3	107	24	80	3	0
Livermore Falls	3,134	5	0	4	0	1	82	23	56	3	1
Machias	2,124	9	0	3	0	6	39	9	30	0	0
Madawaska	4,319	0	0	0	0	0	40	13	25	2	0
Madison	4,578	2	0	1	0	1	186	38	145	3	2
Mechanic Falls	3,254	1	0	1	0	0	27	5	22	0	1
Mexico	2,828	2	0	0	1	1	108	25	83	0	0
Milbridge	1,289	0	0	0	0	0	8	1	7	0	0
Millinocket	4,891	3	0	0	0	3	102	22	76	4	0
Milo	2,313	1	0	1	0	0	94	31	60	3	1
Monmouth	3,959	2	0	2	0	0	66	18	48	0	0
Mount Desert	2,188	0	0	0	0	0	44	19	25	0	0
Newport	3,151	4	0	1	2	1	163	37	121	5	0
North Berwick	4,921	3	0	0	1	2	57	25	30	2	1
Norway	4,755	5	0	2	1	2	127	31	93	3	1
Oakland	6,236	3	0	1	0	2	154	22	130	2	0
Ogunquit	1,264	0	0	0	0	0	37	4	33	0	0
Old Orchard Beach	9,494	27	0	5	6	16	317	64	238	15	0
Old Town	7,731	3	0	0	1	2	303	34	265	4	0
Orono	10,290	2	0	0	1	1	165	19	144	2	2
Oxford	3,935	2	0	0	1	1	103	16	85	2	2
Paris	4,942	6	0	3	2	1	82	15	65	2	0
Phippsburg	2,185	0	0	0	0	0	13	3	8	2	0
Pittsfield	4,186	4	0	2	0	2	90	14	72	4	0
Portland	63,166	242	6	33	129	74	2,921	599	2,246	76	7
Presque Isle	9,050	12	0	2	5	5	424	60	361	3	3
Rangeley	1,183	1	0	0	0	1	15	4	11	0	1
Richmond	3,457	1	0	0	0	1	43	19	20	4	0
Rockland	7,458	5	1	1	0	3	408	45	357	6	5
Rockport	3,563	0	0	0	0	0	34	9	25	0	0
Rumford	6,236	10	0	9	0	1	171	41	125	5	1
Sabattus	4,744	3	0	2	0	1	88	26	58	4	0
Saco	18,417	21	0	1	6	14	570	110	439	21	2
Sanford	21,216	42	0	15	7	20	831	158	635	38	3
Scarborough	19,549	10	0	4	2	4	485	73	403	9	1
Searsport	2,588	3	0	1	0	2	61	18	42	1	0
Skowhegan	8,611	15	0	6	4	5	349	58	282	9	1
South Berwick	7,221	1	0	1	0	0	70	13	57	0	5
South Portland	24,144	49	0	2	11	36	902	92	788	22	1
Southwest Harbor	1,962	1	0	0	0	1	43	6	36	1	0
Swan's Island	302	0	0	0	0	0	0	0	0	0	0
Thomaston	3,652	0	0	0	0	0	56	10	45	1	0
Topsham	9,953	2	0	1	0	1	122	20	94	8	2
Van Buren	2,464	1	0	0	0	1	13	4	8	1	0
Veazie	1,910	2	0	1	1	0	17	2	13	2	0
Waldoboro	5,007	7	0	0	2	5	80	20	55	5	0
Washburn	1,572	0	0	0	0	0	43	9	33	1	0
Waterville	16,076	30	0	11	11	8	664	84	566	14	2
Wells	10,005	1	0	0	1	0	143	31	108	4	0

[1] The FBI does not publish arson data unless it receives data from either the agency or the state for all 12 months of the calendar year.

Table 8. Offenses Known to Law Enforcement, by State and City, 2010—*Continued*

(Number)

State/city	Population	Violent crime	Murder and non-negligent man-slaughter	Forcible rape	Robbery	Aggravated assault	Property crime	Burglary	Larceny-theft	Motor vehicle theft	Arson[1]
MAINE—*Continued*											
Westbrook	16,762	39	0	12	15	12	657	95	541	21	9
Wilton	4,167	8	0	7	0	1	81	18	61	2	1
Windham	17,187	18	1	5	2	10	411	90	306	15	1
Winslow	7,825	6	0	4	0	2	168	58	104	6	1
Winter Harbor	969	0	0	0	0	0	7	3	4	0	0
Winthrop	6,419	2	0	2	0	0	128	29	97	2	1
Wiscasset	3,798	2	0	0	2	0	77	9	68	0	0
Yarmouth	8,157	5	0	2	2	1	91	12	76	3	4
York	14,201	3	0	2	0	1	239	48	186	5	1
MARYLAND											
Aberdeen	14,198	86	0	5	35	46	627	69	527	31	3
Annapolis	37,180	226	4	7	91	124	1,101	197	800	104	9
Baltimore	639,929	9,316	223	265	3,336	5,492	28,280	7,573	16,298	4,409	321
Baltimore City Sheriff	0	0	0	0	0	0	0	0	0	0	0
Bel Air	9,894	45	1	0	11	33	453	34	407	12	3
Berlin	4,125	3	0	1	1	1	110	28	82	0	1
Berwyn Heights	2,997	9	0	0	7	2	128	34	85	9	0
Bladensburg	7,732	93	1	2	44	46	521	123	271	127	0
Boonsboro	3,417	0	0	0	0	0	18	3	14	1	0
Bowie	53,840	106	1	2	57	46	1,044	212	715	117	2
Brentwood	2,853	0	0	0	0	0	4	1	1	2	0
Brunswick	5,338	2	0	0	0	2	86	16	70	0	0
Cambridge	12,167	140	1	7	47	85	566	107	442	17	4
Capitol Heights	4,188	11	0	0	8	3	73	16	35	22	0
Centreville	3,766	7	0	0	1	6	59	9	49	1	0
Chestertown	5,101	30	0	2	8	20	175	54	112	9	1
Cheverly	6,510	43	0	0	18	25	184	61	103	20	
Chevy Chase Village	2,180	1	0	0	1	0	42	7	34	1	0
Colmar Manor	1,286	12	0	0	6	6	41	10	26	5	0
Cottage City	1,147	7	0	0	0	7	60	9	39	12	0
Crisfield	2,734	16	0	0	3	13	77	12	65	0	1
Cumberland	20,449	196	1	17	40	138	1,442	370	1,049	23	6
Delmar	3,524	12	0	3	2	7	78	27	48	3	1
Denton	4,189	5	0	0	3	2	233	56	167	10	1
District Heights	6,164	25	0	0	8	17	231	55	131	45	0
Easton	15,252	58	0	5	15	38	503	74	416	13	2
Edmonston	1,359	5	0	0	2	3	62	13	42	7	0
Elkton	15,144	341	1	16	100	224	1,172	240	867	65	12
Fairmount Heights	1,529	2	0	0	1	1	2	1	1	0	0
Federalsburg	2,660	29	0	1	4	24	86	27	56	3	0
Forest Heights	2,608	9	0	0	2	7	83	44	31	8	0
Frederick	60,686	454	2	16	162	274	1,712	262	1,363	87	8
Frostburg	7,831	18	1	2	3	12	234	37	193	4	1
Fruitland	4,606	50	0	1	2	47	263	43	214	6	3
Glenarden	6,451	13	0	0	5	8	106	35	56	15	0
Greenbelt	21,585	172	2	11	106	53	1,115	221	761	133	0
Greensboro	2,053	3	0	0	0	3	73	19	51	3	1
Hagerstown	40,564	177	0	10	97	70	1,436	303	1,013	120	27
Hampstead	5,510	7	1	1	1	4	108	13	92	3	2
Hancock	1,763	6	0	1	1	4	55	7	47	1	0
Havre de Grace	13,585	78	0	4	14	60	481	62	398	21	2
Hurlock	2,043	16	0	1	4	11	105	42	56	7	1
Hyattsville	15,688	128	0	1	88	39	1,496	166	1,233	97	0
Landover Hills	1,545	6	0	0	3	3	34	17	14	3	1
La Plata	9,266	51	0	0	15	36	341	44	287	10	0
Laurel	22,960	148	0	5	69	74	1,084	163	768	153	1
Lonaconing	1,121	1	0	0	0	1	4	0	4	0	0
Luke	72	0	0	0	0	0	0	0	0	0	0
Manchester	3,511	6	0	0	1	5	60	8	47	5	1
Morningside	1,284	10	0	0	7	3	43	9	25	9	0
Mount Rainier	8,497	86	0	1	58	27	314	58	192	64	2
New Carrollton	12,734	78	0	5	42	31	453	92	296	65	0
North East	2,898	10	0	0	5	5	136	23	102	11	2
Oakland	2,002	0	0	0	0	0	50	10	40	0	0
Ocean City	7,020	123	0	2	27	94	1,439	292	1,133	14	6
Ocean Pines	11,442	4	0	2	1	1	126	22	101	3	0
Oxford	696	0	0	0	0	0	2	0	2	0	0
Perryville	3,852	10	0	0	4	6	125	18	100	7	4
Pocomoke City	3,880	29	2	3	9	15	261	44	207	10	3
Port Deposit	713	0	0	0	0	0	21	6	14	1	0
Preston	685	2	0	0	1	1	6	3	3	0	0
Princess Anne	3,079	28	0	1	6	21	128	40	85	3	0
Ridgely	1,550	41	0	0	1	40	126	37	86	3	1

[1] The FBI does not publish arson data unless it receives data from either the agency or the state for all 12 months of the calendar year.

Table 8. Offenses Known to Law Enforcement, by State and City, 2010—*Continued*

(Number)

State/city	Population	Violent crime	Murder and non-negligent man-slaughter	Forcible rape	Robbery	Aggravated assault	Property crime	Burglary	Larceny-theft	Motor vehicle theft	Arson[1]
MARYLAND—*Continued*											
Rising Sun	1,835	3	0	0	0	3	88	10	78	0	0
Riverdale Park	6,484	77	2	0	46	29	270	58	151	61	0
Rock Hall	1,493	1	0	0	0	1	24	9	15	0	1
Salisbury	29,046	450	7	22	143	278	2,238	575	1,598	65	11
Seat Pleasant	4,932	31	1	0	14	16	195	67	98	30	0
Smithsburg	3,011	3	0	0	0	3	33	8	25	0	0
Snow Hill	2,280	9	0	0	0	9	27	5	20	2	0
St. Michaels	1,047	5	0	0	0	5	54	12	41	1	1
Sykesville	4,489	2	0	0	0	2	49	2	44	3	2
Takoma Park	18,200	76	0	2	48	26	577	149	364	64	2
Taneytown	5,496	7	0	1	1	5	98	12	85	1	1
Thurmont	6,179	5	0	2	0	3	108	36	70	2	4
Trappe	1,142	0	0	0	0	0	7	1	5	1	0
University Park	2,330	3	0	0	3	0	103	30	71	2	
Upper Marlboro	673	1	1	0	0	0	29	3	21	5	0
Westminster	18,196	101	1	0	15	85	674	77	586	11	5
MASSACHUSETTS											
Abington	16,836	46	0	2	9	35	346	112	213	21	3
Acton	21,090	24	1	2	1	20	217	43	167	7	0
Acushnet	10,275	21	0	2	2	17	146	61	75	10	0
Adams	8,120	35	0	4	1	30	249	65	175	9	2
Agawam	28,215	47	0	6	5	36	260	75	155	30	7
Amesbury	16,549	44	0	5	0	39	266	52	201	13	2
Amherst	36,004	81	0	20	2	59	560	274	257	29	1
Andover	33,505	15	0	2	4	9	331	75	239	17	3
Arlington	41,212	96	0	0	9	87	635	154	460	21	8
Ashburnham	6,050	13	0	2	0	11	83	23	56	4	1
Ashby	3,115	5	0	2	0	3	15	15	0	0	0
Ashland	15,279	27	0	2	0	25	181	50	119	12	0
Athol	11,773	65	1	9	5	50	250	75	171	4	3
Attleboro	43,385	152	1	8	27	116	823	188	579	56	7
Auburn	16,335	59	0	2	11	46	644	93	525	26	3
Avon	4,323	8	0	0	1	7	139	26	106	7	0
Ayer	7,828	40	0	3	7	30	151	67	71	13	4
Barnstable	45,599	355	0	29	46	280	1,325	428	833	64	12
Barre	5,599	19	0	0	1	18	84	30	45	9	3
Becket	1,788	2	0	0	0	2	63	32	29	2	0
Bedford	13,794	11	0	1	3	7	130	30	98	2	0
Belchertown	14,252	24	0	3	2	19	171	46	117	8	1
Bellingham	15,728	21	0	1	4	16	280	43	227	10	2
Belmont	23,430	31	0	4	6	21	330	151	168	11	1
Berkley	6,526	6	0	0	1	5	83	36	44	3	1
Berlin	2,978	0	0	0	0	0	48	7	38	3	0
Beverly	39,064	114	2	8	9	95	657	131	502	24	2
Billerica6	39,519		0	10	9		592	105	462	25	3
Blackstone	9,725	22	0	2	1	19	94	17	74	3	0
Bolton	4,595	6	0	2	0	4	54	25	27	2	0
Boston	644,064	5,819	73	256	1,926	3,564	20,628	3,587	15,004	2,037	
Bourne	19,239	77	0	3	6	68	659	240	382	37	7
Boylston	4,384	2	0	0	0	2	133	10	116	7	0
Braintree	35,298	60	1	2	10	47	936	119	769	48	2
Brewster	9,854	21	0	0	2	19	224	53	166	5	1
Brockton	92,383	1,086	9	61	243	773	2,870	750	1,675	445	21
Brookline	55,751	161	0	3	30	128	828	149	656	23	2
Burlington	25,782	47	0	0	12	35	689	71	600	18	2
Cambridge	108,356	476	0	22	171	283	3,232	483	2,569	180	8
Canton	22,291	52	0	3	4	45	230	67	150	13	0
Carver	11,999	24	0	3	4	17	196	75	111	10	2
Charlton	12,626	21	0	5	3	13	145	48	88	9	2
Chatham	6,689	18	0	0	1	17	167	26	136	5	0
Chelmsford	33,785	67	0	3	4	60	536	61	456	19	3
Chelsea	37,335	620	8	34	186	392	1,370	447	745	178	6
Cheshire	3,258	0	0	0	0	0	15	6	8	1	
Chicopee	55,444	274	1	12	56	205	1,689	533	1,016	140	2
Chilmark	892	0	0	0	0	0	28	6	21	1	0
Clinton	14,101	20	0	1	3	16	58	16	31	11	0
Cohasset	7,347	10	0	0	1	9	94	33	57	4	0
Concord	17,457	7	0	1	2	4	171	53	117	1	1
Cummington	957	0	0	0	0	0	6	3	3	0	0
Dalton	6,449	24	0	3	0	21	74	17	49	8	3
Danvers	27,165	46	0	6	8	32	964	108	822	34	1
Dartmouth	34,450	67	0	6	13	48	995	142	819	34	2
Dedham	24,687	38	1	3	6	28	631	71	546	14	0

[1] The FBI does not publish arson data unless it receives data from either the agency or the state for all 12 months of the calendar year.

Table 8.   Offenses Known to Law Enforcement, by State and City, 2010—*Continued*

(Number)

State/city	Population	Violent crime	Murder and non-negligent man-slaughter	Forcible rape	Robbery	Aggravated assault	Property crime	Burglary	Larceny-theft	Motor vehicle theft	Arson[1]
MASSACHUSETTS—*Continued*											
Deerfield	4,627	9	0	0	1	8	113	40	68	5	0
Dennis	15,212	74	0	10	6	58	636	231	392	13	2
Dighton	6,760	20	0	0	2	18	59	29	28	2	0
Douglas	8,109	10	0	3	0	7	69	39	26	4	0
Dover	5,685	2	0	0	0	2	28	6	22	0	0
Dracut	29,179	5	0	1	3	1	315	26	269	20	0
Dudley	11,227	37	0	3	1	33	74	36	37	1	4
Duxbury	14,222	12	0	1	2	9	108	27	78	3	1
East Bridgewater	14,060	30	0	2	2	26	184	40	138	6	3
East Brookfield	2,062	5	0	0	1	4	36	7	25	4	1
Eastham	5,402	6	0	2	0	4	73	7	66	0	1
Easthampton	16,116	27	0	3	3	21	178	47	123	8	5
East Longmeadow	15,916	34	0	4	8	22	348	65	269	14	2
Easton	22,807	41	0	4	10	27	235	67	153	15	0
Edgartown	4,049	13	0	2	1	10	166	45	115	6	1
Egremont	1,329	0	0	0	0	0	26	6	20	0	0
Erving	1,538	6	0	1	0	5	38	18	18	2	0
Essex	3,310	1	0	0	0	1	41	12	29	0	0
Everett	37,897	220	3	13	70	134	1,196	320	767	109	2
Fairhaven	15,916	61	1	6	10	44	415	99	303	13	0
Fall River	89,741	1,087	5	52	252	778	3,297	940	2,006	351	35
Falmouth	32,471	125	0	4	25	96	1,168	640	498	30	1
Fitchburg	42,046	314	1	22	53	238	1,119	355	684	80	4
Foxborough	17,023	47	0	7	3	37	207	75	122	10	0
Framingham	66,493	189	0	5	25	159	1,409	313	1,025	71	
Franklin	31,979	12	0	3	5	4	127	24	99	4	0
Freetown	9,027	33	0	1	4	28	121	33	73	15	1
Gardner	20,743	94	0	10	13	71	621	212	380	29	3
Georgetown	8,772	14	0	1	1	12	71	23	47	1	0
Gill	1,381	1	0	0	0	1	24	9	15	0	1
Gloucester	30,226	32	0	0	4	28	647	86	557	4	3
Goshen	971	0	0	0	0	0	8	3	4	1	0
Grafton	17,897	27	0	4	4	19	96	38	49	9	0
Granby	6,228	10	1	1	1	7	83	20	57	6	2
Granville	1,639	1	0	0	0	1	7	5	2	0	0
Great Barrington	7,263	27	0	3	1	23	153	41	111	1	3
Greenfield	17,625	124	1	10	8	105	533	226	295	12	3
Groton	10,793	0	0	0	0	0	37	15	19	3	0
Groveland	7,533	6	0	0	0	6	40	6	32	2	0
Hadley	4,674	15	0	0	1	14	212	38	170	4	1
Halifax	7,745	11	0	1	1	9	97	29	62	6	0
Hamilton	8,155	5	0	1	0	4	51	16	33	2	0
Hampden	5,346	1	0	1	0	0	57	18	36	3	0
Hanover	14,051	5	0	0	2	3	320	35	280	5	0
Hanson[6]	10,091		0	3	0		134	27	99	8	0
Hardwick	2,648	12	0	0	0	12	36	11	25	0	2
Harvard	6,100	3	0	0	0	3	66	27	38	1	0
Harwich	12,104	34	0	5	5	24	271	148	118	5	0
Hatfield	3,212	0	0	0	0	0	3	2	1	0	0
Haverhill	61,179	350	2	24	26	298	1,625	822	682	121	17
Hingham	23,433	7	0	0	1	6	307	43	256	8	0
Hinsdale	1,890	5	0	0	0	5	2	2	0	0	0
Holbrook	10,615	59	0	4	6	49	244	75	149	20	0
Holden	17,657	13	0	1	0	12	96	18	71	7	2
Holliston	14,076	8	0	1	0	7	67	18	44	5	2
Holyoke	40,026	477	4	38	97	338	2,697	535	1,951	211	17
Hopedale	6,215	19	0	2	0	17	64	31	32	1	1
Hopkinton	14,627	2	0	1	0	1	98	0	97	1	0
Hubbardston	4,483	22	0	1	1	20	42	16	22	4	0
Hudson	19,985	24	2	1	5	16	251	51	186	14	0
Hull	11,008	58	0	3	1	54	170	47	112	11	0
Ipswich	13,307	4	0	0	0	4	133	57	69	7	4
Kingston	12,419	38	0	3	6	29	319	54	255	10	3
Lakeville	10,587	16	0	0	1	15	219	96	118	5	1
Lancaster	7,013	8	0	3	1	4	71	22	45	4	1
Lawrence	69,679	631	10	12	161	448	2,387	662	956	769	
Lee	5,654	6	0	0	0	6	135	27	106	2	0
Leicester	11,072	27	0	5	0	22	205	26	168	11	2
Lenox	5,027	8	0	1	2	5	108	30	76	2	0
Leominster	41,884	284	1	22	29	232	1,324	238	1,015	71	7
Lexington	30,649	19	0	0	3	16	300	58	237	5	0
Lincoln	8,622	7	0	0	0	7	57	11	46	0	0
Littleton	8,959	5	0	1	0	4	94	29	60	5	2

[1] The FBI does not publish arson data unless it receives data from either the agency or the state for all 12 months of the calendar year.

[6] The FBI determined that the agency did not follow national Uniform Crime Reporting Program guidelines for reporting an offense. Consequently, this figure is not included in this table.

Table 8.   Offenses Known to Law Enforcement, by State and City, 2010—*Continued*

(Number)

State/city	Population	Violent crime	Murder and non-negligent man-slaughter	Forcible rape	Robbery	Aggravated assault	Property crime	Burglary	Larceny-theft	Motor vehicle theft	Arson[1]
MASSACHUSETTS—*Continued*											
Longmeadow	15,324	5	0	0	3	2	271	45	220	6	0
Lowell	103,065	1,191	1	51	190	949	3,584	893	2,285	406	27
Ludlow	22,028	28	0	2	9	17	324	66	230	28	0
Lunenburg	10,111	17	0	0	2	15	255	86	161	8	0
Lynn	86,340	764	3	41	208	512	2,496	595	1,595	306	3
Lynnfield	11,954	11	2	0	3	6	185	36	142	7	0
Malden	55,540	282	2	11	85	184	1,487	405	961	121	1
Manchester-by-the-Sea	5,144	4	0	0	0	4	16	6	9	1	0
Mansfield	23,749	47	0	6	5	36	389	126	246	17	3
Marblehead	19,705	26	0	2	2	22	186	42	131	13	0
Marion	5,131	10	0	0	1	9	78	18	56	4	0
Marlborough	38,250	162	0	14	8	140	745	111	599	35	3
Marshfield	24,675	38	0	4	1	33	307	73	226	8	6
Mashpee	14,347	71	0	5	8	58	367	92	265	10	0
Mattapoisett	6,474	9	0	0	1	8	88	17	65	6	1
Maynard	10,534	36	0	3	2	31	83	11	71	1	0
Medfield	12,134	5	0	0	0	5	64	16	45	3	2
Melrose	26,796	35	0	3	8	24	291	92	184	15	1
Mendon	5,676	9	0	2	1	6	55	18	33	4	1
Methuen	43,938	105	1	5	21	78	992	178	723	91	3
Middleboro	21,286	96	0	8	14	74	457	117	309	31	4
Middleton	9,284	7	0	0	0	7	81	6	75	0	0
Milford	27,375	101	0	5	17	79	487	98	359	30	2
Millbury	13,483	36	0	7	2	27	296	54	237	5	2
Milton	25,922	30	0	0	9	21	299	65	219	15	
Monson	9,031	15	0	1	0	14	121	61	56	4	1
Montague	8,045	33	0	10	1	22	138	47	84	7	7
Monterey	952	0	0	0	0	0	2	1	1	0	0
Nahant	3,590	7	0	0	0	7	38	13	22	3	0
Nantucket	11,393	66	0	3	3	60	355	46	296	13	1
Natick	32,017	63	0	5	10	48	766	76	665	25	1
Needham	28,765	9	0	2	3	4	269	28	236	5	0
New Bedford	89,613	1,160	3	69	272	816	3,599	1,237	1,974	388	29
Newbury	6,865	5	0	0	0	5	53	11	37	5	0
Newburyport	17,447	21	0	1	5	15	232	25	198	9	2
Newton	83,781	86	0	6	15	65	1,212	170	1,016	26	1
Norfolk	11,136	1	0	0	0	1	69	28	40	1	0
North Adams	13,590	128	0	7	9	112	616	174	421	21	4
Northampton	28,184	107	2	5	7	93	836	189	604	43	2
North Andover	27,581	7	0	0	2	5	338	48	277	13	0
North Attleboro	27,559	10	0	2	2	6	476	44	419	13	0
Northborough	14,774	10	0	0	1	9	115	24	86	5	0
Northbridge	14,705	30	1	4	4	21	351	97	240	14	4
North Brookfield[6]	5,034		0	2	0		55	13	40	2	0
Northfield	3,003	3	0	0	0	3	45	12	33	0	1
North Reading	14,417	21	0	2	1	18	128	41	84	3	0
Norton	19,217	3	0	0	1	2	98	35	59	4	0
Norwell	10,279	14	1	3	2	8	115	44	67	4	0
Norwood	28,130	29	0	7	5	17	493	110	346	37	4
Oak Bluffs	3,948	17	1	3	2	11	145	28	112	5	0
Orleans	6,177	10	0	2	1	7	222	51	164	7	0
Oxford	13,690	40	0	3	8	29	198	27	146	25	2
Palmer	13,021	51	0	2	4	45	190	53	121	16	2
Paxton	4,820	5	0	0	1	4	22	12	10	0	1
Peabody	51,517	111	0	15	15	81	1,216	136	1,025	55	1
Pelham	1,377	0	0	0	0	0	9	3	6	0	0
Pembroke	18,843	31	0	2	2	27	281	86	184	11	2
Pepperell	11,418	36	0	1	3	32	122	38	75	9	1
Pittsfield	41,666	281	1	26	17	237	1,183	375	749	59	10
Plainville	8,271	9	0	1	2	6	105	34	68	3	1
Plymouth[6]	56,751		1	3	22		1,115	283	810	22	2
Plympton	2,787	4	0	0	0	4	37	11	21	5	1
Princeton	3,504	1	0	0	0	1	38	24	13	1	1
Provincetown	3,378	21	0	0	0	21	215	19	196	0	1
Quincy	90,304	414	11	22	112	269	1,782	505	1,152	125	8
Randolph	30,701	113	1	8	16	88	605	106	462	37	1
Raynham	13,601	26	0	0	4	22	333	62	262	9	2
Reading	23,233	13	0	0	8	5	256	90	156	10	0
Rehoboth	11,516	14	2	2	0	10	159	57	88	14	4
Revere	51,597	308	0	10	86	212	1,599	361	1,048	190	3
Rochester	5,304	1	0	0	0	1	54	22	32	0	3
Rockland	17,932	52	1	1	13	37	442	101	322	19	
Rockport	7,580	5	0	2	0	3	13	5	7	1	0

[1] The FBI does not publish arson data unless it receives data from either the agency or the state for all 12 months of the calendar year.

[6] The FBI determined that the agency did not follow national Uniform Crime Reporting Program guidelines for reporting an offense. Consequently, this figure is not included in this table.

Table 8.   Offenses Known to Law Enforcement, by State and City, 2010—*Continued*

(Number)

State/city	Population	Violent crime	Murder and non-negligent man-slaughter	Forcible rape	Robbery	Aggravated assault	Property crime	Burglary	Larceny-theft	Motor vehicle theft	Arson[1]
MASSACHUSETTS—*Continued*											
Rowley	5,795	7	0	1	0	6	30	6	20	4	0
Rutland	8,189	21	0	2	0	19	52	22	26	4	0
Salem	41,017	188	1	15	26	146	1,015	213	729	73	
Salisbury	8,612	36	0	7	4	25	189	79	98	12	2
Sandwich	19,721	41	0	7	2	32	273	76	190	7	3
Saugus	27,830	57	0	5	18	34	1,124	229	832	63	1
Scituate	18,143	32	0	2	0	30	223	49	158	16	0
Seekonk	13,635	35	0	0	9	26	401	65	320	16	2
Sharon	17,903	4	0	0	1	3	115	36	77	2	0
Sherborn	4,251	0	0	0	0	0	37	17	17	3	0
Shirley	8,073	15	1	1	2	11	73	28	37	8	0
Shrewsbury[6]	33,796		1	2	3		316	84	216	16	0
Somerset	18,364	42	0	4	5	33	217	47	156	14	2
Somerville	75,585	238	0	12	71	155	1,925	486	1,274	165	5
Southampton	5,957	7	0	3	0	4	57	17	39	1	3
Southbridge	17,305	102	0	10	9	83	362	118	231	13	4
South Hadley	17,138	37	0	1	6	30	288	73	198	17	4
Southwick	9,673	24	0	2	3	19	166	58	97	11	3
Spencer	11,909	40	1	1	2	36	213	49	157	7	1
Springfield	154,314	2,090	16	129	587	1,358	7,547	2,660	4,015	872	66
Sterling	7,745	11	0	3	0	8	89	44	41	4	2
Stockbridge	2,164	7	0	1	1	5	116	58	56	2	0
Stoneham	21,285	35	0	2	17	16	358	134	204	20	1
Stoughton	26,866	111	2	5	21	83	601	179	388	34	1
Stow	6,678	3	0	0	1	2	33	10	23	0	0
Sturbridge	8,865	26	0	2	2	22	165	45	110	10	2
Sudbury	17,552	4	0	1	0	3	89	13	75	1	0
Sutton	9,161	11	0	2	0	9	110	60	43	7	3
Swampscott	13,883	19	0	0	4	15	269	44	216	9	1
Swansea	16,012	37	0	4	2	31	301	45	244	12	1
Taunton	55,156	304	2	13	60	229	940	410	487	43	5
Tewksbury	30,447	88	0	8	16	64	625	127	466	32	5
Tisbury	3,901	9	0	2	0	7	120	21	89	10	1
Townsend	9,630	11	0	4	0	7	93	54	35	4	0
Truro	2,104	0	0	0	0	0	24	6	17	1	0
Tyngsboro	11,952	19	0	1	2	16	170	35	127	8	3
Upton	6,745	5	0	0	0	5	74	22	49	3	0
Uxbridge	12,909	16	0	2	1	13	185	70	108	7	2
Wakefield	24,973	61	0	3	9	49	301	76	209	16	4
Walpole	23,257	18	0	3	4	11	454	43	401	10	0
Waltham	60,106	151	2	13	24	112	1,032	200	759	73	2
Ware	9,748	44	0	4	11	29	191	53	132	6	3
Wareham	21,218	165	0	7	20	138	729	174	515	40	6
Warren	5,279	18	0	2	0	16	81	27	46	8	0
Watertown	32,780	64	0	4	13	47	534	69	436	29	0
Wayland	13,396	4	0	0	1	3	37	16	21	0	0
Webster	16,721	96	0	7	19	70	436	93	317	26	7
Wellesley	27,143	21	0	1	3	17	210	40	164	6	3
Wellfleet	2,820	8	0	0	1	7	62	16	45	1	0
Wenham	4,705	4	0	0	0	4	33	3	27	3	0
Westborough	18,214	16	1	3	1	11	261	42	207	12	1
West Boylston	8,085	10	0	3	1	6	156	32	116	8	1
Westfield	41,899	95	1	11	8	75	809	194	576	39	4
Westford	22,582	24	2	2	4	16	167	42	121	4	5
Westhampton	1,581	0	0	0	0	0	6	2	4	0	0
Westminster	7,447	8	0	0	1	7	101	35	62	4	0
West Newbury	4,393	6	0	0	0	6	32	4	26	2	0
Weston	11,815	5	1	0	0	4	56	12	42	2	1
Westport	15,496	24	0	4	0	20	235	92	126	17	2
West Springfield	27,861	154	0	12	34	108	1,337	269	947	121	9
West Tisbury	2,652	8	1	2	0	5	29	14	12	3	0
Westwood	14,190	15	0	1	1	13	170	34	128	8	1
Weymouth	53,400	180	0	7	47	126	1,032	277	698	57	3
Whately	1,554	2	0	0	0	2	17	4	11	2	0
Whitman	14,062	51	0	3	13	35	247	67	170	10	3
Wilbraham	14,070	12	0	0	2	10	249	47	178	24	3
Williamstown	7,902	3	0	1	0	2	202	40	159	3	1
Wilmington	22,230	35	0	4	6	25	334	105	213	16	1
Winchendon	10,261	52	0	5	2	45	245	24	205	16	1
Winchester	21,331	10	4	0	0	6	329	62	257	10	0
Woburn	38,731	86	1	9	22	54	754	105	602	47	1
Worcester	181,908	1,744	7	19	368	1,350	6,190	1,910	3,687	593	10
Wrentham	11,166	5	0	0	0	5	225	48	173	4	0
Yarmouth[6]	23,498		1	12	22		813	408	390	15	5

[1] The FBI does not publish arson data unless it receives data from either the agency or the state for all 12 months of the calendar year.

[6] The FBI determined that the agency did not follow national Uniform Crime Reporting Program guidelines for reporting an offense. Consequently, this figure is not included in this table.

Table 8. Offenses Known to Law Enforcement, by State and City, 2010—*Continued*

(Number)

State/city	Population	Violent crime	Murder and non-negligent man-slaughter	Forcible rape	Robbery	Aggravated assault	Property crime	Burglary	Larceny-theft	Motor vehicle theft	Arson[1]
MICHIGAN											
Albion	9,021	43	0	1	7	35	273	69	204	0	4
Algonac	4,445	6	0	0	0	6	46	10	35	1	0
Allegan	4,770	67	0	1	3	63	47	9	35	3	1
Allen Park	24,833	47	0	2	10	35	605	110	424	71	3
Alma	9,107	5	0	1	0	4	33	10	22	1	0
Almont	2,691	9	0	2	0	7	60	19	39	2	0
Alpena	10,184	22	1	6	1	14	368	52	312	4	3
Ann Arbor	111,745	284	0	43	76	165	2,937	524	2,284	129	22
Armada	1,644	0	0	0	0	0	18	1	16	1	0
Auburn Hills	20,870	80	0	8	26	46	884	141	697	46	3
Bad Axe	2,942	6	0	1	0	5	97	14	83	0	1
Bangor	1,814	10	0	1	0	9	66	13	52	1	0
Baroda Lake Township	870	3	0	1	0	2	48	13	31	4	0
Barry Township	3,457	5	0	1	0	4	29	9	19	1	0
Bath Township	11,955	12	0	1	5	6	114	39	70	5	1
Battle Creek	60,386	702	5	63	120	514	3,134	1,075	1,910	149	19
Bay City	33,200	250	1	53	45	151	1,056	340	681	35	9
Beaverton	1,036	0	0	0	0	0	28	4	24	0	1
Belding	5,599	16	0	11	1	4	171	26	141	4	1
Bellaire	1,093	0	0	0	0	0	12	0	11	1	0
Belleville	3,392	15	0	3	6	6	122	29	89	4	0
Bellevue	1,329	0	0	0	0	0	11	1	9	1	0
Berkley	14,609	13	0	1	1	11	203	31	164	8	1
Beverly Hills	9,739	16	0	2	0	14	148	22	121	5	4
Big Rapids	10,170	32	0	19	1	12	317	61	244	12	2
Birch Run	1,624	9	0	4	2	3	138	11	122	5	0
Birmingham	18,823	26	0	2	6	18	367	44	314	9	5
Blackman Township	37,751	51	1	9	13	28	655	89	541	25	1
Bloomfield Hills	3,731	1	0	0	0	1	68	23	45	0	0
Bloomfield Township	40,490	19	0	4	6	9	552	139	392	21	2
Boyne City	3,049	0	0	0	0	0	109	11	97	1	1
Breckenridge	1,257	1	0	0	0	1	23	10	13	0	0
Bridgeport Township	10,570	51	1	7	4	39	315	111	186	18	1
Brighton	7,238	14	0	1	4	9	216	20	193	3	0
Bronson	2,216	6	0	1	0	5	37	9	28	0	0
Brownstown Township	28,102	43	1	7	6	29	490	152	288	50	2
Buena Vista Township	9,156	115	0	6	16	93	370	194	154	22	5
Burr Oak	730	6	0	1	0	5	25	5	19	1	1
Cadillac	10,101	66	0	10	5	51	577	99	466	12	0
Cambridge Township	5,737	0	0	0	0	0	38	4	32	2	0
Canton Township	80,039	134	0	31	21	82	1,398	239	1,059	100	7
Capac	2,052	3	0	0	1	2	59	10	49	0	0
Carleton	2,537	5	0	1	1	3	39	8	28	3	2
Caro	3,889	13	0	1	0	12	115	23	91	1	5
Carrollton Township	5,810	22	0	4	2	16	141	37	100	4	0
Caseville	805	1	0	0	0	1	30	5	25	0	0
Cassopolis	1,872	3	0	1	0	2	16	3	11	2	0
Cedar Springs	3,254	26	0	1	2	23	100	17	82	1	2
Center Line	8,017	38	0	2	15	21	259	38	166	55	0
Central Lake	941	0	0	0	0	0	8	0	8	0	0
Charlevoix	2,570	7	0	1	1	5	96	9	86	1	1
Charlotte	8,839	25	0	10	0	15	270	36	227	7	2
Cheboygan	4,806	13	0	8	0	5	158	22	136	0	1
Chelsea	5,051	6	0	1	0	5	115	16	94	5	0
Chesaning	2,290	2	0	1	0	1	30	10	18	2	0
Chesterfield Township	45,027	145	1	7	15	122	1,056	179	818	59	10
Chikaming Township	3,641	3	0	0	1	2	56	11	44	1	1
Chocolay Township	5,993	0	0	0	0	0	44	0	44	0	0
Clare	3,021	17	0	6	0	11	131	16	108	7	0
Clawson	12,025	16	0	5	1	10	108	24	74	10	0
Clay Township	9,280	4	0	1	0	3	83	12	68	3	2
Clinton Township	95,167	351	6	26	65	254	2,333	538	1,590	205	9
Clio	2,434	9	0	2	1	6	83	17	61	5	0
Coldwater	10,335	29	0	5	4	20	395	34	355	6	1
Coleman	1,211	3	0	0	0	3	26	3	23	0	0
Colon	1,137	0	0	0	0	0	34	2	30	2	0
Columbia Township	7,431	7	0	0	2	5	128	19	107	2	2
Corunna	3,218	6	0	2	0	4	93	10	79	4	1
Covert Township	3,047	19	0	4	2	13	86	26	55	5	0
Crystal Falls	1,513	1	0	0	0	1	28	4	23	1	0
Dearborn	82,612	373	3	30	128	212	3,718	488	2,759	471	34
Dearborn Heights	49,674	191	0	21	45	125	1,465	443	836	186	5
Decatur	1,806	8	0	2	0	6	109	7	101	1	0

[1] The FBI does not publish arson data unless it receives data from either the agency or the state for all 12 months of the calendar year.

Table 8. Offenses Known to Law Enforcement, by State and City, 2010—*Continued*

(Number)

State/city	Population	Violent crime	Murder and non-negligent man-slaughter	Forcible rape	Robbery	Aggravated assault	Property crime	Burglary	Larceny-theft	Motor vehicle theft	Arson[1]
MICHIGAN—*Continued*											
Denton Township	5,247	3	0	2	0	1	81	12	61	8	0
Detroit	899,447	16,976	310	405	5,538	10,723	47,787	17,090	18,095	12,602	1,082
Dewitt	4,355	4	1	2	0	1	23	4	16	3	0
Dewitt Township	13,074	18	0	2	3	13	151	47	99	5	1
Dryden Township	4,490	1	0	0	0	1	50	11	37	2	1
East Grand Rapids	10,423	7	0	3	1	3	123	29	92	2	0
East Jordan	2,168	5	0	2	0	3	56	9	46	1	1
East Lansing	45,058	166	1	7	26	132	1,089	272	771	46	22
Eastpointe	32,016	238	2	17	61	158	1,036	261	556	219	9
East Tawas	2,657	11	0	4	3	4	104	15	89	0	1
Eaton Rapids	5,146	11	0	2	0	9	94	9	83	2	0
Ecorse	9,399	120	2	7	19	92	411	137	187	87	8
Elk Rapids	1,630	3	0	0	0	3	77	8	68	1	2
Elsie	962	0	0	0	0	0	17	8	9	0	0
Emmett Township	11,684	47	1	7	9	30	463	63	395	5	0
Escanaba	11,918	34	0	4	2	28	730	108	600	22	0
Essexville	3,421	6	0	0	0	6	68	5	61	2	0
Evart	1,622	5	0	3	0	2	75	13	61	1	2
Farmington	9,713	19	0	2	1	16	192	28	147	17	2
Farmington Hills	77,646	118	1	16	13	88	1,381	292	959	130	8
Fenton	11,542	15	0	1	2	12	325	38	268	19	0
Ferndale	20,847	75	0	3	31	41	674	201	379	94	5
Flint	109,245	2,412	53	92	670	1,597	6,237	3,648	1,936	653	343
Flint Township	30,778	260	2	23	101	134	1,898	494	1,288	116	14
Flushing Township	9,880	12	0	4	0	8	128	59	65	4	0
Fowlerville	3,083	6	0	2	1	3	82	8	73	1	2
Frankenmuth	4,556	10	0	2	1	7	115	21	91	3	0
Frankfort	1,414	2	0	0	0	2	33	5	28	0	0
Franklin	2,898	1	0	0	0	1	38	4	33	1	0
Fraser	14,770	35	0	4	3	28	411	50	343	18	2
Fruitport	1,058	13	0	3	3	7	768	51	703	14	0
Garden City	25,549	85	0	4	26	55	729	153	483	93	3
Gaylord	3,484	9	1	5	3	0	266	20	235	11	0
Genesee Township	22,571	88	1	6	14	67	633	252	318	63	8
Gerrish Township	2,996	1	0	1	0	0	41	9	28	4	0
Gibraltar	4,731	10	0	0	0	10	124	19	100	5	1
Gladstone	4,976	1	0	0	0	1	114	9	103	2	0
Gladwin	2,813	14	0	2	1	11	122	28	92	2	0
Grand Blanc	7,312	16	0	3	3	10	210	51	145	14	0
Grand Blanc Township	34,634	85	0	12	17	56	765	209	512	44	7
Grand Haven	10,574	27	0	6	1	20	359	40	314	5	1
Grand Ledge	7,530	4	0	1	0	3	198	31	162	5	3
Grand Rapids	191,566	1,645	9	90	521	1,025	7,760	2,771	4,609	380	100
Grandville	16,653	29	0	1	9	19	772	81	682	9	4
Grant	839	0	0	0	0	0	0	0	0	0	0
Grayling	1,768	1	0	1	0	0	71	9	61	1	0
Green Oak Township	17,817	20	0	1	2	17	287	51	223	13	0
Greenville	7,957	38	0	10	7	21	412	62	339	11	0
Grosse Ile Township	9,470	4	0	0	1	3	60	5	51	4	0
Grosse Pointe	4,765	9	0	0	5	4	93	5	81	7	1
Grosse Pointe Farms	8,218	8	0	1	3	4	117	17	89	11	0
Grosse Pointe Park	10,498	10	0	0	2	8	238	25	176	37	0
Grosse Pointe Shores	2,400	0	0	0	0	0	0	0	0	0	0
Grosse Pointe Woods	14,470	23	0	1	3	19	261	31	206	24	0
Hamburg Township	21,608	13	0	4	1	8	141	24	115	2	1
Hampton Township	9,583	19	0	2	2	15	296	33	259	4	0
Hamtramck	19,615	351	1	12	152	186	1,134	395	439	300	20
Harbor Beach	1,550	0	0	0	0	0	53	17	36	0	1
Harbor Springs	1,535	1	0	0	0	1	42	6	36	0	0
Harper Woods	12,012	126	2	4	42	78	1,100	135	794	171	3
Hart	1,885	1	0	0	0	1	113	9	103	1	0
Hartford	2,437	8	0	3	3	2	62	16	41	5	0
Hastings	6,685	16	0	5	1	10	246	39	201	6	0
Hazel Park	17,715	71	0	9	19	43	611	159	318	134	4
Hillsdale	7,574	8	0	2	0	6	178	39	130	9	2
Holland	33,652	146	0	32	15	99	1,035	195	816	24	6
Holly	6,226	13	0	4	3	6	120	25	94	1	0
Howell	9,636	25	0	6	2	17	282	54	220	8	4
Huntington Woods	5,732	0	0	0	0	0	64	9	53	2	0
Huron Township	15,652	31	0	5	2	24	284	72	192	20	1
Imlay City	3,600	8	0	3	0	5	93	11	80	2	0
Inkster	25,428	449	11	33	87	318	944	449	390	105	22
Ionia	11,342	26	0	10	4	12	204	25	171	8	0

[1] The FBI does not publish arson data unless it receives data from either the agency or the state for all 12 months of the calendar year.

Table 8.   Offenses Known to Law Enforcement, by State and City, 2010—*Continued*

(Number)

State/city	Population	Violent crime	Murder and non-negligent man-slaughter	Forcible rape	Robbery	Aggravated assault	Property crime	Burglary	Larceny-theft	Motor vehicle theft	Arson[1]
MICHIGAN—*Continued*											
Iron River	2,845	5	0	2	0	3	74	28	42	4	0
Ishpeming	6,402	10	1	0	1	8	123	7	104	12	2
Ishpeming Township	3,594	0	0	0	0	0	13	3	10	0	0
Jackson	32,741	319	5	42	54	218	1,586	406	1,127	53	14
Jonesville	2,164	13	0	0	0	13	81	6	71	4	0
Kalamazoo	71,775	721	9	81	185	446	3,534	1,039	2,320	175	36
Kalamazoo Township	21,977	71	1	10	12	48	507	176	299	32	1
Kalkaska	2,115	1	0	0	1	0	71	3	64	4	0
Keego Harbor	2,828	5	0	0	0	5	44	12	32	0	0
Kentwood	47,441	208	1	18	47	142	1,559	336	1,135	88	10
Kingston	408	0	0	0	0	0	9	1	8	0	0
Kinross Township	8,656	3	0	0	0	3	34	6	27	1	0
Laingsburg	1,220	6	0	2	0	4	19	4	15	0	0
Lake Odessa	2,180	10	0	1	0	9	12	2	10	0	0
Lake Orion	2,696	6	0	0	0	6	46	5	40	1	0
Lakeview	1,070	2	0	0	0	2	30	2	28	0	0
Lansing	112,254	1,236	10	97	262	867	4,193	1,410	2,544	239	34
Lapeer	8,947	35	0	11	4	20	332	26	295	11	2
Lapeer Township	4,864	0	0	0	0	0	19	2	16	1	0
Lathrup Village	4,012	11	1	1	4	5	82	20	55	7	1
Lawton	1,780	4	0	3	0	1	45	9	32	4	0
Leslie	2,280	2	0	1	0	1	22	1	21	0	0
Lexington	1,009	0	0	0	0	0	18	4	14	0	1
Lincoln Park	33,702	146	1	13	39	93	1,607	358	1,047	202	5
Linden	3,341	1	0	1	0	0	59	16	43	0	0
Litchfield	1,351	3	0	0	0	3	33	4	24	5	0
Livonia	87,434	152	2	14	36	100	2,039	315	1,503	221	10
Lowell	4,156	8	0	0	0	8	45	6	36	3	0
Luna Pier	1,507	9	0	1	1	7	61	10	49	2	0
Mackinac Island	449	4	0	2	1	1	251	4	246	1	0
Mackinaw City	830	5	0	3	0	2	46	3	43	0	0
Madison Heights	29,174	78	0	8	17	53	947	235	600	112	6
Mancelona	1,318	0	0	0	0	0	23	6	15	2	0
Manistee	5,985	9	0	3	2	4	151	25	124	2	0
Manistique	2,969	11	0	1	0	10	115	29	83	3	3
Manton	1,145	0	0	0	0	0	29	8	20	1	2
Marquette	20,849	21	0	11	2	8	377	39	330	8	0
Marshall	7,005	10	0	3	1	6	182	23	158	1	1
Mason	8,169	8	0	2	0	6	143	15	125	3	2
Mattawan	2,846	2	0	0	0	2	31	5	25	1	0
Mayville	952	2	0	0	0	2	53	1	52	0	3
Melvindale	9,443	53	0	9	19	25	343	74	226	43	3
Mendon	887	4	0	1	0	3	2	1	1	0	0
Meridian Township	38,105	83	0	9	22	52	922	155	753	14	9
Metamora Township	4,540	4	0	2	0	2	48	14	33	1	1
Midland	40,346	52	1	14	2	35	729	121	606	2	10
Milan	5,752	16	0	2	2	12	155	23	123	9	1
Milford	16,562	12	0	3	1	8	174	49	119	6	0
Monroe	21,062	115	0	16	33	66	869	190	586	93	7
Montague	2,251	1	0	1	0	0	41	7	34	0	0
Montrose Township	7,508	15	0	3	0	12	103	34	62	7	2
Mount Morris	3,091	11	0	0	4	7	99	28	65	6	0
Mount Morris Township	21,614	178	0	14	52	112	1,082	517	472	93	17
Mount Pleasant	26,580	63	1	18	8	36	519	99	407	13	3
Mundy Township	13,810	20	0	4	7	9	469	104	347	18	0
Munising	2,280	3	0	2	0	1	14	2	12	0	0
Muskegon	38,829	371	1	46	90	234	2,234	528	1,609	97	23
Muskegon Township	18,159	32	0	8	8	16	787	165	602	20	3
Napoleon Township	6,871	8	0	1	0	7	85	17	64	4	0
Nashville	1,620	9	0	0	0	9	49	3	45	1	0
Negaunee	4,405	1	0	0	0	1	109	29	76	4	1
Newaygo	1,668	6	0	0	0	6	84	11	73	0	0
New Baltimore	11,701	17	0	4	1	12	245	26	210	9	0
New Haven	5,368	6	0	1	0	5	16	3	13	0	0
Niles	11,084	52	0	17	5	30	370	72	281	17	2
North Branch	951	3	0	1	0	2	21	0	21	0	1
Northfield Township	8,484	30	0	4	1	25	172	60	101	11	1
North Muskegon	3,842	5	0	0	1	4	105	3	101	1	0
Northville	5,839	1	0	0	0	1	114	11	99	4	0
Northville Township	23,641	23	0	1	8	14	437	70	350	17	1
Norton Shores	23,127	50	1	9	6	34	723	96	609	18	3
Novi	54,857	36	1	4	3	28	1,000	96	856	48	0
Oak Park	30,131	182	0	22	52	108	969	282	553	134	5

[1] The FBI does not publish arson data unless it receives data from either the agency or the state for all 12 months of the calendar year.

Table 8. Offenses Known to Law Enforcement, by State and City, 2010—*Continued*

(Number)

State/city	Population	Violent crime	Murder and non-negligent man-slaughter	Forcible rape	Robbery	Aggravated assault	Property crime	Burglary	Larceny-theft	Motor vehicle theft	Arson[1]
MICHIGAN—*Continued*											
Olivet	1,819	3	0	0	1	2	30	7	21	2	0
Onaway	871	3	0	1	1	1	23	2	20	1	0
Orchard Lake	2,205	9	0	0	0	9	42	5	36	1	0
Oscoda Township	6,668	16	0	5	1	10	219	87	128	4	2
Otsego	3,762	7	0	3	1	3	70	11	55	4	0
Ovid	1,376	1	0	0	0	1	12	1	11	0	0
Owendale	256	0	0	0	0	0	2	1	1	0	0
Owosso	14,526	85	0	11	13	61	582	111	464	7	4
Oxford	3,498	2	0	1	0	1	55	10	44	1	0
Parchment	1,791	7	0	1	1	5	40	12	26	2	2
Paw Paw	3,179	7	0	2	1	4	140	27	111	2	0
Perry	1,966	0	0	0	0	0	16	2	14	0	0
Petoskey	5,971	5	0	1	0	4	104	9	93	2	2
Pinckney	2,429	3	0	2	0	1	65	13	50	2	4
Pinconning	1,295	0	0	0	0	0	17	4	12	1	0
Pittsfield Township	34,681	81	0	18	20	43	1,091	180	817	94	1
Plainwell	3,801	11	0	8	1	2	127	7	119	1	3
Pleasant Ridge	2,436	4	0	0	0	4	20	1	18	1	0
Plymouth	8,297	7	0	3	2	2	171	22	134	15	3
Plymouth Township	24,291	19	0	2	5	12	363	53	283	27	1
Pontiac	65,517	1,113	9	67	239	798	2,055	1,074	765	216	31
Portage	46,192	102	1	19	16	66	1,815	235	1,534	46	10
Port Huron	30,132	199	3	9	54	133	1,185	335	784	66	13
Potterville	2,121	5	0	1	0	4	51	7	44	0	0
Prairieville Township	3,438	1	0	0	0	1	21	2	19	0	0
Raisin Township	7,294	2	0	1	0	1	19	9	10	0	0
Reading	1,037	0	0	0	0	0	15	2	13	0	0
Redford Township	43,827	224	2	12	85	125	1,739	604	846	289	21
Reed City	2,266	11	0	7	1	3	83	13	69	1	0
Richfield Township, Genesee County	8,408	14	0	5	2	7	88	31	50	7	0
Richfield Township, Roscommon County	3,971	16	0	3	0	13	61	14	46	1	0
Richland	770	0	0	0	0	0	5	0	5	0	1
Richland Township, Saginaw County	4,190	4	0	0	0	4	42	19	23	0	0
Richmond	5,615	18	0	1	0	17	130	19	108	3	1
River Rouge	8,036	60	1	1	13	45	373	146	141	86	11
Riverview	11,306	10	0	0	3	7	204	14	147	43	0
Rochester	10,982	18	0	3	0	15	139	29	108	2	3
Rockford	5,525	9	0	0	1	8	113	24	83	6	1
Rockwood	3,026	2	0	0	0	2	34	3	29	2	0
Rogers City	2,921	3	0	3	0	0	42	11	30	1	0
Romulus	22,214	147	1	16	32	98	968	298	550	120	6
Roseville	46,221	210	1	19	46	144	1,931	293	1,415	223	7
Rothbury	430	2	0	1	1	0	21	2	19	0	0
Royal Oak	56,408	88	1	19	17	51	887	176	620	91	7
Saginaw	54,155	1,209	4	61	192	952	2,195	1,310	763	122	23
Saginaw Township	37,872	87	0	13	23	51	1,026	146	856	24	1
Saline	8,942	13	0	0	1	12	176	17	149	10	1
Sand Lake	514	0	0	0	0	0	8	1	7	0	1
Sault Ste. Marie	13,849	83	0	10	8	65	659	113	514	32	1
Shelby Township	71,589	89	2	17	9	61	945	182	691	72	2
Somerset Township	4,584	1	0	1	0	0	51	9	41	1	0
Southfield	74,587	396	5	27	111	253	2,760	660	1,690	410	11
Southgate	26,575	67	1	8	20	38	1,133	213	803	117	7
South Haven	5,112	19	0	4	3	12	247	36	208	3	2
South Lyon	10,983	15	1	2	2	10	139	17	121	1	0
South Rockwood	1,678	1	0	0	0	1	17	2	14	1	0
Sparta	4,021	4	0	0	0	4	97	14	82	1	0
Spaulding Township	2,132	1	0	0	0	1	10	2	8	0	0
Spring Arbor Township	8,397	2	0	0	0	2	66	12	51	3	1
Springfield	4,968	28	0	0	5	23	173	50	121	2	0
Spring Lake-Ferrysburg	5,419	6	0	4	1	1	85	22	62	1	0
Standish	1,774	0	0	0	0	0	6	0	6	0	0
St. Charles	1,967	10	0	2	0	8	44	12	32	0	1
St. Clair	5,646	8	0	4	0	4	163	32	127	4	1
St. Clair Shores	59,522	152	0	9	28	115	1,086	194	805	87	6
Sterling Heights	126,291	199	1	31	35	132	2,415	364	1,931	120	9
St. Ignace	2,270	0	0	0	0	0	77	9	62	6	0
St. Johns	7,191	4	0	2	0	2	132	20	109	3	1
St. Louis	6,895	5	0	3	0	2	63	3	57	3	0
Stockbridge	1,265	2	0	0	0	2	51	5	45	1	0
Sturgis	10,544	35	0	5	1	29	293	44	238	11	1
Sumpter Township	10,737	21	0	0	0	21	225	70	139	16	4
Swartz Creek	5,118	6	0	1	0	5	149	42	98	9	2

[1] The FBI does not publish arson data unless it receives data from either the agency or the state for all 12 months of the calendar year.

Table 8.   Offenses Known to Law Enforcement, by State and City, 2010—*Continued*

(Number)

State/city	Population	Violent crime	Murder and non-negligent manslaughter	Forcible rape	Robbery	Aggravated assault	Property crime	Burglary	Larceny-theft	Motor vehicle theft	Arson[1]
MICHIGAN—*Continued*											
Sylvan Lake	1,616	0	0	0	0	0	17	7	9	1	0
Taylor	58,158	348	2	29	78	239	2,500	629	1,640	231	27
Thetford Township	7,657	2	0	1	0	1	21	11	9	1	0
Thomas Township	12,096	17	0	2	0	15	216	28	178	10	1
Three Rivers	6,974	62	0	7	6	49	327	107	206	14	2
Tittabawassee Township	8,754	10	0	2	0	8	73	13	56	4	0
Traverse City	14,012	37	1	10	7	19	463	64	386	13	1
Trenton	17,217	41	0	1	3	37	256	48	185	23	1
Troy	79,794	59	1	9	9	40	1,728	292	1,327	109	1
Tuscarora Township	2,946	6	0	0	0	6	134	13	113	8	0
Unadilla Township	3,420	2	0	0	0	2	59	11	45	3	1
Union City	1,679	1	0	0	0	1	74	14	58	2	0
Utica	4,911	21	0	2	4	15	204	18	172	14	1
Van Buren Township	25,627	100	0	27	20	53	799	167	533	99	4
Vassar	2,578	7	0	0	0	7	32	6	25	1	0
Vicksburg	2,178	2	0	0	0	2	101	7	93	1	0
Walled Lake	6,833	15	0	1	1	13	161	27	126	8	1
Warren	132,266	770	5	69	171	525	3,703	953	2,035	715	35
Waterford Township	70,013	228	1	45	56	126	1,467	360	1,028	79	7
Waterloo Township	2,933	4	1	0	0	3	22	9	12	1	0
Watervliet	1,719	6	0	1	0	5	26	6	19	1	0
Wayne	16,454	120	1	17	33	69	537	119	368	50	7
West Bloomfield Township	63,345	33	1	8	1	23	778	146	604	28	8
West Branch	1,799	4	0	1	2	1	82	12	70	0	0
Westland	75,726	367	3	42	83	239	2,353	607	1,427	319	16
White Cloud	1,365	6	0	0	0	6	86	22	63	1	0
Whitehall	2,756	6	0	0	2	4	197	129	68	0	0
White Lake Township	29,890	23	0	3	3	17	531	90	419	22	1
Williamston	3,781	4	0	1	0	3	28	6	22	0	0
Wixom	13,344	18	0	2	4	12	297	54	227	16	0
Wolverine Lake	4,263	7	0	1	0	6	66	8	56	2	0
Woodhaven	12,239	12	0	2	7	3	240	20	197	23	0
Wyandotte	23,607	46	0	5	8	33	658	143	437	78	3
Wyoming	70,160	230	1	39	46	144	1,586	515	911	160	8
Ypsilanti	21,245	217	0	16	54	147	953	311	558	84	2
Zeeland	5,383	11	0	2	0	9	102	20	79	3	0
Zilwaukee	1,610	0	0	0	0	0	19	2	17	0	0
MINNESOTA											
Albany	2,239		0		0	4	26	7	17	2	0
Albert Lea	17,304		0		5	25	410	66	321	23	1
Alexandria	12,003		0		2	10	363	66	288	9	3
Annandale	3,212		0		0	2	125	10	114	1	0
Anoka	17,323		0		21	21	748	98	627	23	0
Appleton	2,971		0		0	7	49	13	34	2	0
Apple Valley	50,579		0		17	28	1,511	172	1,308	31	4
Arden Hills	9,860		0		0	1	151	18	122	11	0
Aurora	1,745		0		0	0	0	0	0	0	0
Austin	22,929		0		11	51	763	144	577	42	1
Avon	1,342		0		0	0	3	1	2	0	0
Babbitt	1,579		0		0	0	0	0	0	0	0
Baxter	8,748		0		0	5	297	9	285	3	0
Bayport	3,335		0		0	2	37	6	30	1	0
Becker	4,387		0		0	4	28	6	19	3	0
Belgrade	720		0		0	0	0	0	0	0	0
Belle Plaine	7,244		0		0	4	160	30	126	4	1
Bemidji	13,911		0		7	57	982	82	872	28	3
Benson	2,930		0		0	2	61	23	35	3	0
Big Lake	10,240		0		0	16	188	22	160	6	1
Blackduck	790		0		0	2	43	6	36	1	0
Blaine	57,561		0		11	35	1,953	203	1,708	42	6
Bloomington	82,715		0		46	45	3,175	226	2,860	89	15
Blue Earth	3,183		0		0	3	42	7	34	1	0
Brainerd	13,779		0		1	34	558	77	464	17	2
Breckenridge	3,151		0		0	1	49	5	41	3	0
Brooklyn Center	27,378		1		59	59	1,363	185	1,056	122	5
Browns Valley	579		0		0	0	0	0	0	0	0
Brownton	777		0		0	1	4	1	3	0	0
Buffalo	14,881		0		1	11	383	34	336	13	2
Burnsville	59,028		0		0	0	0	0	0	0	0
Cambridge	7,986		0		0	9	264	21	233	10	0
Cannon Falls	4,050		0		0	3	200	14	180	6	1
Centennial Lakes	11,423		0		1	6	136	12	119	5	0
Champlin	24,139		0		4	12	510	50	450	10	1

[1] The FBI does not publish arson data unless it receives data from either the agency or the state for all 12 months of the calendar year.

Table 8. Offenses Known to Law Enforcement, by State and City, 2010—*Continued*

(Number)

State/city	Population	Violent crime	Murder and non-negligent man-slaughter	Forcible rape	Robbery	Aggravated assault	Property crime	Burglary	Larceny-theft	Motor vehicle theft	Arson[1]
MINNESOTA—*Continued*											
Chaska	25,424		0		0	12	398	49	337	12	2
Chisholm	4,559		1		0	9	177	22	150	5	0
Cloquet	11,486		0		3	17	454	78	367	9	1
Cold Spring	5,108		0		0	3	66	5	60	1	1
Coon Rapids	62,419		0		38	65	2,709	186	2,467	56	11
Corcoran	5,749		0		0	4	38	6	32	0	0
Cottage Grove	34,276		0		5	10	566	94	460	12	12
Crookston	7,829		0		1	10	68	15	53	0	2
Crosby	2,245		0		0	1	23	2	19	2	0
Crystal	21,753		0		19	24	715	116	574	25	2
Dawson	1,323		0		0	0	18	6	12	0	0
Dayton	4,650		0		0	1	39	14	20	5	0
Deephaven-Woodland	4,339		0		0	1	17	4	13	0	0
Detroit Lakes	8,329		0		1	9	419	25	380	14	0
Dilworth	3,787		0		0	3	103	2	99	2	0
Duluth[2]	84,249		1		90	165		605	3,301		9
Eagan	64,239		2		13	18	1,625	176	1,396	53	13
Eagle Lake	2,416		0		0	1	14	6	7	1	0
East Grand Forks	7,878		0		0	11	235	33	197	5	0
Eden Prairie	63,159		1		5	21	1,020	135	866	19	6
Edina	46,503		0		5	12	899	124	756	19	0
Elk River	24,025		0		2	10	607	52	536	19	6
Elmore	642		0		0	0	12	6	5	1	0
Ely	3,459		0		0	1	76	9	64	3	0
Eveleth	3,559		0		4	10	119	29	84	6	0
Fairmont	10,029		0		2	6	279	36	243	0	1
Falcon Heights	5,661		0		2	2	107	15	85	7	0
Faribault	22,272		0		12	60	830	171	626	33	8
Farmington	20,229		0		1	10	177	24	145	8	1
Fergus Falls	13,531		0		2	19	350	35	309	6	2
Floodwood	499		0		0	6	29	3	25	1	0
Forest Lake	18,030		0		3	6	533	55	439	39	0
Fridley	25,857		0		19	50	1,329	142	1,114	73	0
Gilbert	1,748		0		0	0	0	0	0	0	0
Glencoe	5,517		0		0	0	113	18	92	3	0
Glenwood	2,467		0		0	1	8	1	6	1	0
Golden Valley	20,527		1		7	12	466	89	348	29	3
Goodview	3,737		0		0	4	91	24	58	9	1
Grand Rapids	9,457		0		0	21	359	32	321	6	0
Granite Falls	2,857		0		0	7	26	4	21	1	0
Hallock	981		0		0	0	0	0	0	0	0
Hastings	22,688		0		4	16	525	60	439	26	2
Hermantown	9,755		0		1	6	294	33	250	11	1
Hibbing	16,157		0		0	15	242	18	219	5	0
Hilltop	680		0		3	5	69	6	60	3	0
Hokah	553		0		0	1	16	5	11	0	0
Hopkins	17,020		0		11	9	495	100	374	21	4
Houston	943		0		0	2	16	3	13	0	0
Hoyt Lakes	1,953		0		0	0	0	0	0	0	0
Hutchinson	13,901		0		1	14	376	25	345	6	3
International Falls	5,763		0		1	10	204	45	146	13	0
Jackson	3,302		0		0	5	67	12	53	2	1
Janesville	2,259		0		0	0	25	3	22	0	0
Kasson	5,703		0		0	3	59	10	48	1	0
Kimball	718		0		0	3	4	0	4	0	0
La Crescent	4,897		0		0	1	89	5	82	2	0
Lake City	5,313		0		1	2	159	11	142	6	0
Lake Crystal	2,635		0		0	3	49	9	39	1	3
Lakefield	1,614		1		0	0	39	19	20	0	0
Lakes Area	8,654		0		0	11	222	32	183	7	0
Lakeville	57,470		0		6	9	830	140	671	19	7
Lauderdale	2,241		0		1	3	32	8	21	3	0
Lester Prairie	1,769		0		0	2	9	4	5	0	0
Lewiston	1,461		0		0	0	2	1	0	1	0
Lino Lakes	20,953		0		0	7	193	26	162	5	0
Litchfield	6,554		0		0	6	130	27	99	4	2
Little Canada	9,644		0		4	14	295	47	206	42	0
Little Falls	8,049		0		0	3	140	8	127	5	0
Long Prairie	2,757		0		0	0	66	5	60	1	0
Madison	1,527		0		0	3	17	4	12	1	0
Mankato	36,921		1		14	59	1,527	248	1,231	48	8
Maple Grove	64,861		0		9	25	1,241	132	1,087	22	2
Mapleton	1,672		0		0	0	29	4	25	0	0

[1] The FBI does not publish arson data unless it receives data from either the agency or the state for all 12 months of the calendar year.

[2] The FBI determined that the agency's data were underreported. Consequently, those data are not included in this table.

Table 8.   Offenses Known to Law Enforcement, by State and City, 2010—*Continued*

(Number)

State/city	Population	Violent crime	Murder and non-negligent man-slaughter	Forcible rape	Robbery	Aggravated assault	Property crime	Burglary	Larceny-theft	Motor vehicle theft	Arson[1]
MINNESOTA—*Continued*											
Maplewood	36,907		0		25	43	2,317	269	1,884	164	11
Medina	5,297		0		0	1	102	6	94	2	0
Melrose	3,261		0		0	0	30	9	21	0	0
Mendota Heights	11,697		0		1	10	221	36	179	6	0
Milaca	3,015		0		0	1	29	7	21	1	0
Minneapolis	385,704	4,064	37	438	1,596	1,993	18,299	4,787	11,609	1,903	116
Minnetonka	50,753		1		7	13	983	184	772	27	2
Minnetrista	8,796		0		0	4	82	10	70	2	0
Montevideo	5,148		0		0	6	125	26	98	1	0
Montgomery	3,305		0		0	8	57	14	41	2	0
Moorhead	37,274		2		8	29	938	135	777	26	5
Moose Lake	2,576		0		0	4	80	4	75	1	1
Morris	5,074		0		0	2	114	12	98	4	0
Mound	9,654		0		1	2	167	19	141	7	3
Mounds View	12,000		0		3	19	378	48	307	23	4
Mountain Iron	2,925		0		0	0	0	0	0	0	0
Mountain Lake	1,878		0		0	0	0	0	0	0	0
New Brighton	21,689		0		12	10	581	79	462	40	6
New Hope	20,644		0		17	16	677	93	559	25	3
Newport	3,495		0		2	5	134	21	103	10	1
New Prague	7,065		0		1	7	142	13	128	1	0
New Richland	1,148		0		0	1	0	0	0	0	0
New Ulm	12,843		0		1	6	232	69	156	7	0
North Branch	10,732		0		1	5	332	33	291	8	0
Northfield	19,918		0		1	9	404	75	319	10	4
North Mankato	12,748		1		4	5	232	22	207	3	1
North Oaks	4,883		0		0	1	46	9	37	0	0
North St. Paul	11,433		0		2	2	288	43	226	19	0
Oakdale	27,358		0		15	28	1,121	168	896	57	16
Oak Park Heights	4,839		0		0	2	201	7	186	8	0
Orono	12,294		0		0	5	111	17	92	2	0
Ortonville	1,911		0		0	1	15	0	14	1	0
Osakis	1,566		0		0	1	28	3	25	0	1
Osseo	2,597		0		1	0	3	0	2	1	0
Owatonna	25,210		0		4	28	482	76	386	20	3
Park Rapids	3,654		0		0	5	248	22	213	13	1
Paynesville	2,290		0		0	1	106	20	84	2	0
Plymouth	73,579		0		15	30	1,226	232	970	24	6
Princeton	4,839		0		0	2	146	10	131	5	0
Prior Lake	26,241		0		2	20	427	91	325	11	3
Proctor	2,840		0		1	3	107	11	88	8	0
Red Wing	15,641		0		2	16	472	102	357	13	2
Redwood Falls	5,050		0		0	17	166	29	132	5	0
Richfield	33,188		0		34	36	873	144	677	52	12
Robbinsdale	13,822		0		17	24	427	104	308	15	1
Rochester	105,027		1		58	123	2,429	399	1,925	105	24
Rogers	8,288		0		1	6	55	5	50	0	0
Roseau	2,752		0		0	0	26	3	23	0	0
Rosemount	22,870		1		5	6	316	48	262	6	4
Roseville	33,176		1		15	24	1,482	144	1,232	106	5
Sauk Centre	4,073		0		0	3	81	12	66	3	2
Sauk Rapids	12,130		0		0	3	75	17	54	4	0
Savage	29,151		0		4	26	686	114	548	24	7
Shakopee	36,290		2		7	60	1,028	105	891	32	1
Shoreview	25,419		0		3	4	299	33	251	15	3
Silver Bay	1,804		0		0	0	1	0	1	0	0
Silver Lake	794		0		0	3	13	4	7	2	0
Slayton	1,809		0		0	0	16	3	12	1	0
Sleepy Eye	3,363		0		0	1	0	0	0	0	0
South Lake Minnetonka	12,329		0		0	13	156	32	117	7	1
Springfield	2,103		0		0	0	0	0	0	0	0
Spring Grove	1,233		0		0	0	0	0	0	0	0
Spring Lake Park	6,577		0		6	10	366	41	301	24	0
St. Anthony	8,484		0		3	2	298	49	233	16	2
Staples	2,984		0		0	1	122	20	98	4	0
St. Charles	3,566		0		0	3	20	4	14	2	0
St. Cloud	67,942		3		43	134	2,542	347	2,102	93	18
St. Francis	7,644		0		0	4	134	16	113	5	1
Stillwater	18,208		0		0	12	603	92	496	15	4
St. James	4,271		0		0	3	77	5	70	2	1
St. Louis Park	45,690		2		27	21	1,473	188	1,227	58	6
St. Paul	281,166	2,112	16	183	665	1,248	11,756	2,883	6,820	2,053	131
St. Paul Park	5,262		0		0	5	134	23	106	5	0

[1] The FBI does not publish arson data unless it receives data from either the agency or the state for all 12 months of the calendar year.

Table 8. Offenses Known to Law Enforcement, by State and City, 2010—*Continued*

(Number)

State/city	Population	Violent crime	Murder and non-negligent man-slaughter	Forcible rape	Robbery	Aggravated assault	Property crime	Burglary	Larceny-theft	Motor vehicle theft	Arson[1]
MINNESOTA—*Continued*											
St. Peter	11,063		0		0	11	248	28	215	5	3
Thief River Falls	8,575		0		0	1	139	18	113	8	1
Tracy	2,063		0		0	0	0	0	0	0	0
Two Harbors	3,245		0		0	7	45	7	36	2	0
Vadnais Heights	12,733		0		1	6	289	35	213	41	1
Virginia	8,419		0		1	25	508	56	435	17	4
Wabasha	2,513		0		0	3	69	11	57	1	0
Wadena	3,920		0		0	8	114	12	98	4	0
Waite Park	6,873		0		7	13	683	29	648	6	1
Warroad	1,649		0		0	3	21	2	19	0	0
Waseca	8,668		0		0	13	183	20	153	10	0
Wayzata	3,953		0		1	6	89	13	69	7	0
Wells	2,299		0		0	0	5	3	2	0	0
West Hennepin	5,680		0		0	2	38	11	26	1	0
Wheaton	1,362		0		0	5	36	5	30	1	0
White Bear Lake	24,365		0		8	29	946	161	726	59	6
Willmar	17,854		0		2	44	576	54	502	20	5
Windom	4,101		0		0	10	94	17	70	7	0
Winnebago	1,308		0		0	2	27	12	13	2	1
Winona	26,447		0		7	18	489	87	377	25	2
Winsted	2,425		0		0	2	41	5	35	1	0
Woodbury	58,503		0		9	19	1,307	195	1,062	50	3
Worthington	11,114		0		3	17	232	59	156	17	0
Wyoming	8,148		0		0	2	174	12	155	7	0
Zumbrota	3,109		0		0	4	66	4	50	12	0
MISSISSIPPI											
Aberdeen	5,966	15	0	0	4	11	218	80	136	2	0
Amory	7,123	6	0	1	4	1	281	75	195	11	0
Bay St. Louis	8,190	8	0	4	1	3	352	92	241	19	0
Belzoni	2,315	11	1	0	0	10	7	2	5	0	0
Biloxi	45,350	211	1	33	118	59	2,516	943	1,442	131	5
Booneville	8,786	6	0	2	1	3	198	49	147	2	0
Brandon	22,877	15	0	1	6	8	239	74	156	9	2
Brookhaven	13,240	31	3	1	24	3	219	88	123	8	0
Byhalia	1,302	4	0	0	1	3	41	12	25	4	0
Carthage	4,904	4	0	0	1	3	99	49	45	5	0
Charleston	1,793	15	1	0	5	9	12	7	5	0	0
Clarksdale	17,484	104	3	10	28	63	1,152	681	415	56	5
Cleveland	11,874	43	4	3	13	23	836	197	615	24	2
Collins	2,881	9	0	1	3	5	219	55	153	11	0
Columbia	6,516	28	1	2	3	22	172	95	75	2	1
Columbus	23,638	83	2	1	34	46	945	192	730	23	2
Como	1,290	9	0	1	0	8	36	12	19	5	0
Crystal Springs	5,899	11	0	0	0	11	180	98	80	2	1
D'Iberville	9,082	28	1	3	9	15	675	57	586	32	2
Edwards	1,290	7	0	0	1	6	9	6	3	0	0
Eupora	2,175	8	0	0	1	7	47	17	29	1	0
Florence	3,869	3	0	0	1	2	29	10	19	0	0
Flowood	7,238	43	0	9	3	31	480	87	382	11	1
Fulton	4,049	12	0	1	4	7	75	14	60	1	0
Gautier	16,435	46	1	12	10	23	686	230	411	45	2
Gloster	996	1	0	0	0	1	7	7	0	0	0
Greenville	34,826	86	9	17	49	11	2,162	1,017	1,040	105	85
Greenwood	15,578	94	5	10	29	50	851	292	537	22	0
Gulfport	70,806	161	6	23	67	65	3,715	920	2,642	153	14
Hattiesburg	53,678	115	4	9	62	40	2,317	434	1,809	74	6
Heidelberg	795	0	0	0	0	0	24	3	20	1	0
Hernando	13,380	22	0	5	4	13	286	57	209	20	1
Holly Springs	7,868	72	1	3	15	53	309	119	164	26	1
Horn Lake	25,693	25	0	3	15	7	655	122	504	29	4
Indianola	10,370	58	1	5	14	38	581	130	438	13	0
Itta Bena	1,807	26	0	0	4	22	143	76	65	2	0
Iuka	2,926	13	0	2	2	9	108	59	45	4	0
Jackson	174,153	1,718	41	101	1,086	490	13,250	4,818	6,877	1,555	83
Kosciusko	7,351	24	1	1	7	15	203	91	112	0	1
Laurel	18,928	103	1	8	50	44	1,232	425	773	34	3
Leland	4,678	13	0	0	1	12	197	101	95	1	0
Long Beach	11,937	12	0	3	1	8	302	71	217	14	2
Louisville	6,557	22	0	1	6	15	103	76	22	5	0
Lucedale	3,154	8	0	0	4	4	70	15	51	4	0
Macon	2,651	30	0	0	2	28	145	24	121	0	
Madison	22,275	15	0	0	1	14	209	9	197	3	0
Magnolia	2,062	4	0	0	0	4	52	21	30	1	0

[1] The FBI does not publish arson data unless it receives data from either the agency or the state for all 12 months of the calendar year.

Table 8.   Offenses Known to Law Enforcement, by State and City, 2010—*Continued*

(Number)

State/city	Population	Violent crime	Murder and non-negligent man-slaughter	Forcible rape	Robbery	Aggravated assault	Property crime	Burglary	Larceny-theft	Motor vehicle theft	Arson[1]
MISSISSIPPI—*Continued*											
McComb	13,689	81	1	2	41	37	826	226	574	26	0
Meridian	39,566	202	7	27	106	62	2,398	1,056	1,195	147	16
Moss Point	13,788	118	0	16	31	71	792	411	311	70	0
Natchez	15,841	57	2	10	27	18	882	203	658	21	10
New Albany	8,206	3	0	0	1	2	126	27	92	7	0
Newton	3,690	0	0	0	0	0	8	2	5	1	0
Ocean Springs	17,388	19	1	4	9	5	583	256	312	15	1
Oxford	18,105	8	0	2	5	1	302	103	189	10	0
Pascagoula	23,479	87	2	20	38	27	1,409	300	1,050	59	7
Pass Christian	3,967	5	0	4	1	0	236	47	177	12	0
Pearl	25,078	68	1	12	10	45	601	213	367	21	5
Petal	10,906	2	0	0	1	1	117	71	39	7	0
Philadelphia	7,964	39	0	6	14	19	440	212	216	12	2
Picayune	12,194	31	0	4	11	16	456	104	333	19	2
Port Gibson	1,596	6	1	0	2	3	16	4	12	0	0
Purvis	2,757	2	0	0	0	2	16	5	11	0	0
Ridgeland	21,847	34	1	1	15	17	632	84	522	26	2
Ripley	5,773	7	0	0	0	7	91	27	60	4	0
Rosedale	2,275	11	0	1	1	9	33	21	12	0	3
Roxie	555	0	0	0	0	0	0	0	0	0	0
Southaven[5]	47,435	131	1	19	15	96	1,875	301	1,481	93	8
Starkville	24,588	57	1	3	18	35	626	128	471	27	1
Summit	1,606	1	0	0	1	0	39	16	23	0	0
Tupelo	36,574	81	2	26	30	23	1,729	361	1,270	98	1
Vicksburg	24,773	196	2	28	32	134	1,800	568	1,173	59	15
Waveland	5,592	15	0	3	5	7	385	72	303	10	0
West Point	11,082	54	0	10	16	28	318	77	241	0	1
Wiggins	5,162	23	0	1	1	21	226	93	133	0	0
Winona	4,350	9	0	0	0	9	35	16	19	0	0
Yazoo City	11,055	38	1	5	13	19	385	187	163	35	2
MISSOURI											
Adrian	1,863	9	0	0	1	8	36	5	30	1	2
Advance	1,180	0	0	0	0	0	13	5	8	0	0
Alma	355	1	0	0	0	1	0	0	0	0	0
Alton	630	0	0	0	0	0	4	1	2	1	0
Appleton City	1,246	5	0	1	0	4	20	7	12	1	0
Arbyrd	473	1	0	0	1	0	1	0	1	0	0
Archie	1,036	0	0	0	0	0	23	7	15	1	0
Arnold	20,535	49	0	1	5	43	888	49	819	20	1
Ashland	2,230	1	0	0	0	1	34	2	31	1	0
Aurora	7,430	61	0	4	3	54	381	83	285	13	1
Auxvasse	989	1	0	0	0	1	23	3	20	0	0
Ava	3,180	8	0	0	0	8	103	22	77	4	0
Ballwin	29,774	16	0	1	6	9	321	50	262	9	0
Bates City	261	1	0	0	0	1	2	0	1	1	0
Battlefield	4,534	1	0	0	0	1	60	9	49	2	0
Bella Villa	626	0	0	0	0	0	9	2	6	1	0
Bellefontaine Neighbors	10,103	71	0	3	16	52	483	183	209	91	2
Bellerive	250	0	0	0	0	0	0	0	0	0	0
Bellflower	380	0	0	0	0	0	2	1	1	0	0
Bel-Nor	1,457	2	0	0	0	2	22	4	16	2	0
Bel-Ridge	2,852	51	1	0	11	39	140	71	59	10	2
Belton	24,941	53	0	9	14	30	655	128	486	41	1
Berkeley	9,245	218	2	8	21	187	483	250	191	42	11
Bernie	1,740	7	1	0	1	5	15	4	9	2	0
Bethany	3,020	9	0	0	1	8	50	14	33	3	0
Beverly Hills	549	0	0	0	0	0	0	0	0	0	0
Billings	1,139	5	0	1	0	4	19	0	17	2	0
Birch Tree	613	0	0	0	0	0	3	1	2	0	0
Birmingham	233	0	0	0	0	0	3	1	2	0	0
Bismarck	1,541	0	0	0	0	0	9	5	1	3	0
Bloomfield	1,812	7	0	0	0	7	43	11	30	2	1
Blue Springs	56,226	99	0	16	25	58	1,701	268	1,272	161	3
Bolivar	11,308	22	0	0	2	20	355	67	277	11	1
Bonne Terre	7,456	12	3	1	1	7	36	14	17	5	1
Boonville	8,622	8	0	1	0	7	240	24	213	3	0
Bowling Green	5,268	0	0	0	0	0	123	14	108	1	0
Branson	8,621	131	1	7	19	104	1,062	142	897	23	0
Branson West	514	0	0	0	0	0	26	1	25	0	0
Braymer	931	1	0	0	0	1	5	1	4	0	0
Breckenridge Hills	4,413	26	0	0	8	18	206	69	127	10	1
Brentwood	7,086	11	0	1	6	4	320	26	284	10	1
Bridgeton	14,900	60	0	7	12	41	933	78	801	54	5

[1] The FBI does not publish arson data unless it receives data from either the agency or the state for all 12 months of the calendar year.

[5] Because of changes in the state/local agency's reporting practices, figures are not comparable to previous years' data.

Table 8.　Offenses Known to Law Enforcement, by State and City, 2010—*Continued*

(Number)

State/city	Population	Violent crime	Murder and non-negligent man-slaughter	Forcible rape	Robbery	Aggravated assault	Property crime	Burglary	Larceny-theft	Motor vehicle theft	Arson[1]
MISSOURI—*Continued*											
Brookfield	4,254	10	0	1	1	8	120	37	81	2	0
Brunswick	822	4	0	0	0	4	1	0	1	0	0
Bucklin	470	2	0	0	0	2	2	0	2	0	0
Buckner	2,900	10	0	0	1	9	71	24	42	5	0
Buffalo	3,250	13	0	0	2	11	143	35	108	0	3
Butler	4,178	4	2	0	0	2	147	25	118	4	1
Butterfield Village	414	1	0	0	0	1	8	3	5	0	0
Byrnes Mill	2,977	0	0	0	0	0	0	0	0	0	0
Cabool	2,118	3	0	0	1	2	41	6	32	3	0
California	4,123	4	0	0	3	1	72	9	58	5	1
Calverton Park	1,255	5	0	0	1	4	21	7	9	5	0
Camden Point	562	0	0	0	0	0	2	1	1	0	0
Camdenton	3,659	19	0	0	0	19	153	22	130	1	0
Cameron	8,946	27	2	2	1	22	218	45	168	5	2
Campbell	1,795	3	0	0	1	2	41	8	30	3	0
Canton	2,403	4	0	1	0	3	75	5	70	0	0
Cape Girardeau	37,627	238	1	13	54	170	2,463	414	1,985	64	7
Cardwell	701	2	0	1	0	1	4	1	3	0	0
Carl Junction	7,649	8	0	3	0	5	149	38	102	9	0
Carrollton	3,665	5	0	2	1	2	60	11	45	4	1
Carterville	1,994	1	0	1	0	0	10	1	7	2	0
Carthage	14,099	24	1	4	3	16	416	80	320	16	3
Caruthersville	5,912	49	2	2	5	40	293	120	166	7	3
Cassville	3,253	26	0	0	1	25	230	29	197	4	0
Centralia	3,672	9	0	0	0	9	97	17	75	5	0
Chaffee	2,928	3	0	0	0	3	69	28	36	5	0
Charlack	1,329	4	0	0	1	3	47	9	35	3	0
Charleston	5,008	45	2	0	3	40	131	44	84	3	1
Chesterfield	45,709	46	0	2	11	33	996	99	876	21	3
Chillicothe	8,622	22	0	0	1	21	232	48	175	9	6
Clarkton	1,206	1	0	0	0	1	20	5	13	2	1
Claycomo	1,376	4	0	1	1	2	45	11	33	1	0
Clayton	15,979	13	0	1	2	10	292	41	237	14	1
Cleveland	686	0	0	0	0	0	5	4	1	0	0
Clever	1,894	7	0	0	0	7	2	1	1	0	0
Clinton	9,316	50	0	3	6	41	447	128	298	21	2
Cole Camp	1,140	3	0	0	0	3	10	2	8	0	0
Columbia	103,417	530	3	37	131	359	3,816	552	3,129	135	7
Concordia	2,333	3	0	0	0	3	31	7	23	1	0
Conway	773	1	0	0	0	1	8	1	6	1	0
Cool Valley	990	18	0	0	0	18	78	23	45	10	2
Cooter	402	1	0	0	0	1	2	2	0	0	0
Corder	404	1	0	0	0	1	0	0	0	0	0
Cottleville	3,359	4	0	0	1	3	49	2	47	0	0
Country Club Hills	1,258	8	0	1	5	2	61	23	31	7	1
Country Club Village	2,437	6	0	1	1	4	15	4	9	2	0
Crane	1,353	8	0	0	1	7	27	11	14	2	1
Creighton	357	0	0	0	0	0	0	0	0	0	0
Crestwood	11,289	14	0	0	4	10	347	37	306	4	0
Creve Coeur	16,786	15	2	0	5	8	294	43	239	12	0
Crocker	1,042	5	0	0	0	5	23	3	20	0	0
Crystal City	4,517	19	0	2	1	16	157	20	134	3	1
Cuba	3,563	17	0	0	3	14	181	23	152	6	0
Deepwater	486	2	0	0	0	2	7	2	5	0	0
Dellwood	4,837	36	1	0	13	22	152	71	66	15	0
Delta	547	0	0	0	0	0	0	0	0	0	0
Desloge	5,213	12	0	1	1	10	260	25	231	4	1
De Soto	6,439	29	0	0	1	28	199	27	160	12	1
Des Peres	8,541	6	0	2	3	1	392	28	361	3	0
Dexter	7,493	12	0	1	1	10	320	70	239	11	1
Diamond	896	0	0	0	0	0	0	0	0	0	0
Dixon	1,624	0	0	0	0	0	58	8	48	2	0
Doniphan	1,845	2	0	0	0	2	139	13	122	4	0
Doolittle	664	0	0	0	0	0	2	2	0	0	0
Drexel	1,099	4	0	1	0	3	29	5	23	1	0
Duenweg	1,261	1	0	0	0	1	29	5	21	3	1
Duquesne	1,762	7	0	1	0	6	52	13	38	1	0
Edgerton	578	1	0	0	0	1	7	4	3	0	1
Edina	1,092	5	0	2	0	3	2	2	0	0	0
Edmundson	772	6	0	2	0	4	36	12	18	6	0
Eldon	4,905	24	0	5	2	17	200	36	158	6	0
El Dorado Springs	3,598	30	0	2	2	26	184	42	134	8	3
Ellington	935	3	0	0	0	3	9	0	9	0	0

[1] The FBI does not publish arson data unless it receives data from either the agency or the state for all 12 months of the calendar year.

Table 8.   Offenses Known to Law Enforcement, by State and City, 2010—*Continued*

(Number)

State/city	Population	Violent crime	Murder and non-negligent man-slaughter	Forcible rape	Robbery	Aggravated assault	Property crime	Burglary	Larceny-theft	Motor vehicle theft	Arson[1]
MISSOURI—*Continued*											
Ellisville	9,162	10	0	0	1	9	138	21	114	3	0
Elsberry	2,694	20	0	1	0	19	19	4	13	2	0
Eureka	9,472	14	0	1	2	11	231	17	206	8	0
Everton	297	0	0	0	0	0	1	1	0	0	0
Excelsior Springs	12,674	43	0	5	4	34	357	102	238	17	1
Exeter	736	0	0	0	0	0	0	0	0	0	0
Fair Grove	1,433	2	0	0	0	2	16	4	9	3	0
Fair Play	458	0	0	0	0	0	1	1	0	0	0
Farber	383	0	0	0	0	0	0	0	0	0	0
Farmington	16,461	20	1	2	1	16	547	38	498	11	0
Fayette	2,647	3	0	0	0	3	13	0	13	0	0
Ferguson	20,657	94	0	4	45	45	1,121	357	647	117	1
Ferrelview	601	3	0	1	0	2	11	5	6	0	0
Festus	11,457	37	0	2	3	32	243	51	185	7	2
Fleming	116	0	0	0	0	0	0	0	0	0	0
Flordell Hills	848	8	0	0	3	5	44	12	27	5	0
Florissant	49,886	96	0	2	47	47	1,350	294	887	169	2
Foley	215	1	0	0	0	1	2	0	2	0	0
Fordland	765	1	0	0	0	1	19	4	13	2	0
Foristell	374	1	0	0	0	1	36	4	30	2	0
Forsyth	1,703	7	0	2	1	4	86	11	73	2	0
Frankford	350	0	0	0	0	0	0	0	0	0	0
Fredericktown	4,152	3	0	0	0	3	78	12	63	3	0
Freeman	609	0	0	0	0	0	0	0	0	0	0
Frontenac	3,838	8	0	1	1	6	55	5	50	0	0
Fulton	12,796	41	0	4	1	36	516	71	413	32	1
Gallatin	1,745	2	0	0	0	2	16	6	7	3	0
Garden City	1,677	2	0	0	1	1	18	3	14	1	0
Gerald	1,255	6	0	1	0	5	33	8	24	1	0
Gideon	932	0	0	0	0	0	0	0	0	0	0
Glasgow	1,175	4	0	0	0	4	11	5	6	0	0
Glendale	5,421	2	0	0	0	2	43	7	36	0	0
Goodman	1,281	1	0	0	0	1	14	7	7	0	0
Gower	1,414	0	0	0	0	0	7	1	6	0	1
Grain Valley	11,384	16	0	1	2	13	260	41	185	34	1
Granby	2,224	0	0	0	0	0	7	1	5	1	0
Grandview	24,552	177	0	7	54	116	944	226	616	102	9
Greendale	681	1	0	0	0	1	13	7	6	0	0
Greenfield	1,199	3	0	0	0	3	20	8	11	1	0
Greenville	416	3	0	0	0	3	11	1	10	0	0
Greenwood	4,836	3	0	0	1	2	64	6	55	3	0
Hallsville	962	1	0	1	0	0	18	5	13	0	0
Hamilton	1,748	4	0	0	0	4	37	9	25	3	0
Hannibal	17,379	50	2	7	16	25	1,352	210	1,089	53	3
Hardin	543	0	0	0	0	0	3	0	3	0	0
Harrisonville	9,880	28	0	4	1	23	368	63	288	17	1
Hartville	580	2	0	0	0	2	6	2	4	0	0
Hawk Point	591	3	0	0	0	3	13	3	10	0	0
Hayti	2,870	6	0	2	1	3	175	36	133	6	1
Hazelwood	25,070	98	1	8	30	59	932	185	678	69	2
Henrietta	427	0	0	0	0	0	1	0	1	0	0
Herculaneum	3,728	3	0	1	1	1	88	4	81	3	0
Hermann	2,671	9	0	1	0	8	77	13	63	1	1
Higginsville	4,448	5	0	2	0	3	111	13	93	5	0
High Hill	207	0	0	0	0	0	2	1	1	0	0
Highlandville	973	1	0	0	0	1	3	0	3	0	0
Hillsboro	2,579	15	0	1	0	14	99	12	82	5	0
Hillsdale	1,392	25	1	2	4	18	46	29	14	3	1
Holcomb	657	0	0	0	0	0	0	0	0	0	0
Holden	2,556	14	0	0	1	13	100	9	85	6	1
Hollister	4,041	22	0	2	1	19	128	29	90	9	3
Holt	482	1	0	0	0	1	4	2	1	1	0
Holts Summit	3,882	14	0	1	1	12	76	31	42	3	0
Hornersville	639	2	0	0	0	2	1	0	1	0	0
Houston	2,015	7	0	0	0	7	74	13	58	3	0
Howardville	307	0	0	0	0	0	1	1	0	0	1
Humansville	1,021	0	0	0	0	0	12	6	5	1	0
Huntsville	1,620	0	0	0	0	0	12	1	10	1	0
Hurley	147	0	0	0	0	0	0	0	0	0	0
Iberia	657	2	0	0	0	2	3	2	0	1	0
Independence[5]	121,141	484	8	43	123	310	7,223	1,246	5,242	735	22
Indian Point	728	2	0	0	0	2	5	2	3	0	0
Ironton	1,297	2	0	0	0	2	35	10	25	0	0

[1] The FBI does not publish arson data unless it receives data from either the agency or the state for all 12 months of the calendar year.

[5] Because of changes in the state/local agency's reporting practices, figures are not comparable to previous years' data.

Table 8. Offenses Known to Law Enforcement, by State and City, 2010—*Continued*

(Number)

State/city	Population	Violent crime	Murder and non-negligent man-slaughter	Forcible rape	Robbery	Aggravated assault	Property crime	Burglary	Larceny-theft	Motor vehicle theft	Arson[1]
MISSOURI—*Continued*											
Jackson	14,043	17	0	2	1	14	358	50	298	10	0
Jasper	1,077	0	0	0	0	0	12	6	3	3	0
Jefferson City	41,092	197	1	6	40	150	1,668	284	1,348	36	19
Jennings	14,423	243	3	5	40	195	1,170	491	529	150	11
Joplin	50,346	288	1	39	64	184	3,404	558	2,612	234	29
Kahoka	2,143	9	0	1	0	8	16	7	8	1	0
Kansas City[5]	483,191	5,506	102	234	1,626	3,544	26,919	7,124	16,625	3,170	343
Kearney	9,442	3	0	0	0	3	144	17	126	1	0
Kennett	10,409	56	0	3	7	46	550	157	369	24	4
Kimberling City	2,408	3	0	1	0	2	34	11	22	1	0
Kimmswick	109	0	0	0	0	0	0	0	0	0	0
King City	860	2	0	0	0	2	3	2	1	0	0
Kinloch	420	11	1	1	3	6	11	6	5	0	7
Kirksville	17,406	90	0	0	2	88	527	76	441	10	0
Kirkwood	26,573	29	0	4	5	20	854	135	685	34	2
Knob Noster	3,359	4	0	0	0	4	86	15	71	0	0
Ladue	8,111	8	0	0	2	6	116	21	94	1	2
Lake Lafayette	366	1	0	0	0	1	4	1	2	1	0
Lake Lotawana	2,191	0	0	0	0	0	30	9	18	3	0
Lake Ozark	2,048	1	0	1	0	0	10	6	4	0	0
Lakeshire	1,266	0	0	0	0	0	33	16	17	0	0
Lake St. Louis	14,734	26	0	1	1	24	223	19	200	4	1
Lake Tapawingo	802	0	0	0	0	0	16	2	14	0	0
Lake Waukomis	926	0	0	0	0	0	8	1	7	0	0
Lake Winnebago	1,167	2	0	0	0	2	8	2	6	0	0
Lamar	4,385	10	0	1	2	7	91	22	68	1	1
La Monte	1,102	2	0	0	0	2	20	10	10	0	0
Lanagan	434	0	0	0	0	0	0	0	0	0	0
La Plata	1,434	3	0	0	0	3	2	0	1	1	0
Lathrop	2,319	4	0	0	0	4	54	19	31	4	0
Laurie	707	2	0	0	0	2	44	10	34	0	0
Lawson	2,316	2	1	0	0	1	63	20	42	1	0
Leadington	422	0	0	0	0	0	11	1	6	4	0
Leadwood	1,159	11	0	0	0	11	23	8	13	2	0
Lebanon	14,403	51	2	5	3	41	704	109	567	28	4
Lee's Summit	87,707	97	2	17	26	52	2,129	289	1,718	122	5
Leeton	629	1	0	0	0	1	15	3	12	0	0
Lexington	4,424	13	0	1	0	12	183	34	141	8	1
Liberal	759	2	0	0	0	2	13	9	4	0	0
Liberty	32,496	41	2	9	9	21	567	102	420	45	9
Licking	2,957	2	0	1	0	1	55	5	49	1	1
Lincoln	1,082	2	0	0	0	2	26	7	17	2	0
Linn Creek	310	2	0	0	0	2	7	3	3	1	0
Lockwood	887	0	0	0	0	0	8	3	4	1	0
Lone Jack	1,002	1	1	0	0	0	19	5	14	0	0
Lowry City	717	2	0	0	0	2	2	0	2	0	0
Macon	5,349	12	0	2	3	7	150	34	109	7	0
Malden	4,347	3	0	0	0	3	44	20	19	5	1
Manchester	18,396	2	0	0	1	1	349	23	323	3	1
Mansfield	1,303	2	0	0	0	2	50	10	40	0	0
Maplewood	8,510	35	1	1	9	24	397	40	340	17	0
Marble Hill	1,441	12	0	1	3	8	34	12	19	3	0
Marceline	2,270	3	0	0	0	3	41	6	27	8	1
Marionville	2,157	3	0	0	0	3	77	7	68	2	0
Marshall	12,127	26	0	2	1	23	305	67	232	6	0
Marshfield	7,368	2	0	1	0	1	137	21	110	6	0
Marthasville	857	1	0	1	0	0	0	0	0	0	0
Martinsburg	318	0	0	0	0	0	0	0	0	0	0
Maryland Heights	25,591	41	0	2	13	26	679	95	561	23	3
Maryville	10,782	28	0	0	1	27	182	23	145	14	0
Matthews	520	1	0	0	0	1	13	1	12	0	0
Maysville	1,120	0	0	0	0	0	0	0	0	0	0
Memphis	1,934	3	0	1	0	2	27	2	24	1	0
Mexico	10,736	34	0	5	3	26	210	40	161	9	1
Milan	1,799	6	0	0	0	6	17	4	11	2	0
Miner	1,335	14	0	0	1	13	30	9	19	2	0
Moberly	14,011	27	0	2	4	21	588	84	492	12	2
Moline Acres	2,487	29	0	1	8	20	110	32	73	5	2
Monett	8,884	8	0	2	2	4	310	65	224	21	2
Monroe City	2,413	28	0	0	0	28	41	7	30	4	0
Montgomery City	2,427	2	0	1	0	1	47	18	28	1	0
Morehouse	900	4	0	0	0	4	6	1	5	0	0
Mosby	255	1	0	0	0	1	10	0	10	0	0

[1] The FBI does not publish arson data unless it receives data from either the agency or the state for all 12 months of the calendar year.

[5] Because of changes in the state/local agency's reporting practices, figures are not comparable to previous years' data.

Table 8.   Offenses Known to Law Enforcement, by State and City, 2010—*Continued*

(Number)

State/city	Population	Violent crime	Murder and non-negligent man-slaughter	Forcible rape	Robbery	Aggravated assault	Property crime	Burglary	Larceny-theft	Motor vehicle theft	Arson[1]
MISSOURI—*Continued*											
Moscow Mills	2,749	18	0	1	0	17	67	9	57	1	2
Mound City	1,045	2	0	0	0	2	30	11	17	2	0
Mountain View	2,584	20	0	1	2	17	120	38	80	2	0
Mount Vernon	4,605	9	0	1	0	8	223	24	189	10	1
Napoleon	192	0	0	0	0	0	1	1	0	0	0
Naylor	586	0	0	0	0	0	2	0	1	1	0
Neosho	11,245	22	0	3	3	16	551	64	468	19	0
Nevada	8,287	66	0	4	4	58	499	108	370	21	2
New Bloomfield	740	1	0	1	0	0	5	2	3	0	0
Newburg	461	0	0	0	0	0	15	5	10	0	1
New Florence	737	3	0	0	0	3	14	3	11	0	0
New Franklin	1,093	0	0	0	0	0	8	0	7	1	0
New Haven	2,053	9	0	0	0	9	51	9	40	2	1
New London	986	1	0	0	0	1	25	6	19	0	0
New Madrid	2,945	0	0	0	0	0	21	2	19	0	0
New Melle	302	1	0	0	0	1	4	2	2	0	0
Niangua	496	1	0	0	0	1	6	6	0	0	0
Nixa	20,220	33	0	5	7	21	323	49	270	4	0
Noel	1,619	11	0	2	0	9	39	9	25	5	0
Norborne	722	2	0	0	0	2	0	0	0	0	0
Normandy	4,834	38	0	1	8	29	173	68	92	13	0
North Kansas City	6,116	31	0	2	14	15	343	48	266	29	0
Northmoor	415	1	0	0	0	1	11	1	5	5	0
Northwoods	4,244	30	0	1	9	20	193	84	86	23	1
Norwood	558	0	0	0	0	0	1	0	0	1	0
Oak Grove	7,154	9	0	2	0	7	237	37	179	21	2
Oakland	1,544	0	0	0	0	0	20	4	16	0	2
Oakview Village	414	1	0	0	0	1	4	0	4	0	0
Odessa	4,632	4	0	0	3	1	113	19	85	9	1
O'Fallon	81,851	72	0	2	9	61	1,273	135	1,101	37	0
Olivette	7,414	14	0	0	8	6	157	30	114	13	1
Oregon	852	2	0	0	0	2	9	3	4	2	0
Oronogo	2,963	4	0	0	0	4	40	12	26	2	1
Orrick	805	2	0	0	0	2	19	12	5	2	0
Osage Beach	4,787	15	1	1	0	13	336	39	286	11	1
Overland	15,400	42	0	0	13	29	664	123	514	27	1
Owensville	2,527	3	0	0	0	3	53	1	51	1	0
Ozark	19,449	23	0	2	4	17	544	79	447	18	1
Pacific	7,332	21	0	2	1	18	167	17	144	6	0
Pagedale	3,360	30	2	0	9	19	159	44	99	16	1
Palmyra	3,428	4	0	0	0	4	61	7	54	0	
Parkville	5,584	10	1	0	5	4	159	18	137	4	0
Parma	744	7	0	0	0	7	20	3	17	0	3
Pasadena Park	452	0	0	0	0	0	7	3	2	2	0
Peculiar	4,977	8	0	1	1	6	91	28	60	3	0
Perryville	8,185	39	0	2	4	33	250	42	199	9	0
Pevely	6,112	10	0	3	2	5	131	22	103	6	0
Piedmont	1,840	3	0	0	0	3	72	12	59	1	1
Pierce City	1,459	0	0	0	0	0	33	4	27	2	0
Pilot Grove	740	3	0	0	0	3	32	5	25	2	1
Pine Lawn	3,938	56	2	5	13	36	177	76	69	32	0
Platte City	5,034	6	0	1	0	5	133	13	116	4	0
Platte Woods	467	1	0	0	0	1	7	2	3	2	0
Plattsburg	2,390	9	0	1	0	8	25	8	17	0	0
Pleasant Hill	7,409	0	0	0	0	0	136	23	105	8	1
Pleasant Hope	605	0	0	0	0	0	6	2	4	0	0
Pleasant Valley	3,721	6	0	2	0	4	41	7	29	5	0
Polo	591	0	0	0	0	0	6	1	4	1	0
Poplar Bluff	16,938	108	0	1	28	79	1,415	257	1,106	52	8
Potosi	2,688	6	0	2	0	4	116	16	100	0	0
Purdy	1,135	6	0	2	0	4	22	8	14	0	0
Puxico	1,121	7	0	0	0	7	9	4	5	0	0
Queen City	611	0	0	0	0	0	0	0	0	0	0
Qulin	482	1	0	0	0	1	16	4	9	3	0
Randolph	54	1	0	0	0	1	7	0	6	1	0
Raymore	19,420	16	0	3	4	9	287	32	241	14	2
Raytown	28,616	117	5	4	61	47	1,088	301	679	108	5
Reeds Spring	810	0	0	0	0	0	4	1	3	0	0
Republic	14,880	84	1	1	5	77	573	79	475	19	1
Rich Hill	1,460	7	0	0	0	7	28	14	13	1	0
Richland	1,844	7	0	0	0	7	57	14	42	1	1
Richmond	5,787	17	0	0	0	17	214	33	176	5	4
Richmond Heights	8,985	20	0	1	10	9	760	23	709	28	0

[1] The FBI does not publish arson data unless it receives data from either the agency or the state for all 12 months of the calendar year.

Table 8.   Offenses Known to Law Enforcement, by State and City, 2010—*Continued*

(Number)

State/city	Population	Violent crime	Murder and non-negligent man-slaughter	Forcible rape	Robbery	Aggravated assault	Property crime	Burglary	Larceny-theft	Motor vehicle theft	Arson[1]
MISSOURI—*Continued*											
Riverside	3,075	10	2	4	1	3	217	19	176	22	0
Riverview	2,874	37	0	2	11	24	210	103	64	43	1
Rockaway Beach	586	0	0	0	0	0	13	2	11	0	0
Rock Hill	4,530	8	0	0	3	5	70	15	51	4	0
Rock Port	1,275	1	0	0	0	1	1	1	0	0	0
Rogersville	3,261	8	1	0	0	7	122	17	100	5	0
Rolla	18,575	97	0	8	22	67	874	145	699	30	3
Salem	4,898	8	1	0	0	7	198	18	174	6	0
Salisbury	1,513	1	0	0	0	1	23	8	14	1	0
Sarcoxie	1,382	14	0	0	1	13	44	9	32	3	2
Savannah	5,104	0	0	0	0	0	56	11	43	2	0
Scott City	4,525	5	0	0	0	5	79	22	54	3	2
Sedalia	21,091	152	2	3	20	127	1,301	280	968	53	7
Seligman	999	1	0	0	0	1	16	3	13	0	0
Seneca	2,248	2	0	0	2	0	79	21	55	3	1
Seymour	2,092	5	0	0	0	5	46	12	34	0	0
Shelbina	1,743	4	0	0	0	4	31	18	13	0	0
Shrewsbury	6,150	2	0	0	0	2	112	17	88	7	1
Sikeston	16,953	269	1	7	29	232	948	228	692	28	7
Slater	1,898	2	0	0	0	2	54	1	52	1	0
Smithville	8,800	8	0	1	0	7	103	14	86	3	0
Southwest City	939	6	1	0	0	5	12	2	8	2	0
Sparta	1,246	1	0	0	0	1	18	3	15	0	0
Springfield	157,110	1,328	11	120	310	887	15,216	2,188	12,024	1,004	59
St. Ann	12,475	60	0	0	6	54	384	65	296	23	0
St. Charles	65,729	126	2	8	35	81	1,891	323	1,517	51	16
St. Clair	4,445	34	0	1	1	32	293	48	227	18	1
Steele	2,017	21	2	0	1	18	95	40	53	2	0
Steelville	1,486	11	0	1	0	10	70	13	53	4	0
Stewartsville	734	0	0	0	0	0	1	0	1	0	0
St. James	3,994	22	0	0	3	19	195	38	147	10	1
St. John	6,283	29	0	1	2	26	226	41	175	10	0
St. Joseph	75,922	305	5	20	70	210	3,605	870	2,547	188	16
St. Louis	355,151	6,205	144	188	2,125	3,748	27,324	6,705	16,356	4,263	250
St. Marys	374	2	0	0	0	2	5	1	4	0	0
Stover	1,023	5	0	1	0	4	24	6	18	0	0
St. Peters	56,518	104	0	4	9	91	1,499	120	1,349	30	7
Strafford	2,232	7	0	0	1	6	126	14	105	7	7
Strasburg	137	0	0	0	0	0	0	0	0	0	0
St. Robert	3,702	32	1	4	2	25	398	68	324	6	0
Sugar Creek	3,606	20	0	1	4	15	186	47	121	18	0
Sullivan	6,757	9	0	0	3	6	401	53	325	23	0
Summersville	548	0	0	0	0	0	21	14	7	0	1
Sunset Hills	8,131	16	1	0	2	13	162	23	132	7	1
Sweet Springs	1,518	1	0	0	0	1	15	1	13	1	0
Tarkio	1,787	8	0	0	0	8	24	12	12	0	0
Thayer	2,143	2	0	0	0	2	20	1	18	1	0
Theodosia	251	1	0	0	0	1	6	2	4	0	0
Tipton	3,278	1	0	0	0	1	27	3	24	0	0
Town and Country	10,626	5	0	0	3	2	108	10	93	5	0
Tracy	218	0	0	0	0	0	14	3	10	1	0
Trenton	5,945	12	0	0	1	11	187	40	139	8	0
Trimble	469	0	0	0	0	0	0	0	0	0	0
Troy	13,056	3	0	0	0	3	353	43	298	12	1
Truesdale	700	3	0	0	0	3	8	5	3	0	0
Union	9,904	20	0	1	1	18	480	51	417	12	2
Unionville	1,788	4	0	0	0	4	16	8	8	0	0
Uplands Park	432	1	0	0	0	1	7	3	2	2	0
Urbana	427	0	0	0	0	0	0	0	0	0	0
Van Buren	801	0	0	0	0	0	8	5	3	0	0
Vandalia	4,344	4	0	0	0	4	85	14	65	6	0
Velda City	1,474	23	0	1	2	20	37	23	8	6	0
Verona	718	0	0	0	0	0	11	3	7	1	0
Versailles	2,654	3	0	0	0	3	93	13	76	4	0
Viburnum	777	1	0	0	0	1	10	8	2	0	1
Vienna	625	0	0	0	0	0	26	9	16	1	0
Vinita Park	1,760	15	0	0	6	9	73	29	38	6	0
Walnut Grove	666	3	0	0	0	3	3	1	1	1	0
Wardell	385	5	0	0	0	5	2	0	2	0	0
Warrensburg	19,376	23	0	1	8	14	627	115	501	11	7
Warrenton	7,714	24	0	1	1	22	387	50	326	11	5
Warsaw	2,226	6	0	0	0	6	126	35	83	8	0
Warson Woods	1,817	0	0	0	0	0	20	3	17	0	0

[1] The FBI does not publish arson data unless it receives data from either the agency or the state for all 12 months of the calendar year.

Table 8.   Offenses Known to Law Enforcement, by State and City, 2010—*Continued*

(Number)

State/city	Population	Violent crime	Murder and non-negligent man-slaughter	Forcible rape	Robbery	Aggravated assault	Property crime	Burglary	Larceny-theft	Motor vehicle theft	Arson[1]
MISSOURI—*Continued*											
Washburn	475	0	0	0	0	0	0	0	0	0	0
Washington	14,366	21	0	1	4	16	433	47	371	15	2
Waverly	771	0	0	0	0	0	13	3	10	0	0
Waynesville	4,337	26	0	4	3	19	145	37	104	4	1
Webb City	11,795	1	0	1	0	0	443	55	358	30	0
Webster Groves	22,106	21	0	2	6	13	297	74	207	16	0
Wellington	744	0	0	0	0	0	0	0	0	0	0
Wellsville	1,288	2	0	0	0	2	11	4	7	0	0
Wentzville	27,351	40	0	8	6	26	516	64	444	8	1
Weston	1,720	6	0	0	0	6	22	8	13	1	0
West Plains	12,034	50	0	2	5	43	880	176	676	28	0
Wheaton	744	0	0	0	0	0	7	2	4	1	1
Willard	3,368	7	0	2	0	5	91	14	75	2	0
Willow Springs	2,147	9	0	0	0	9	89	21	65	3	0
Winfield	1,180	3	0	0	1	2	14	6	5	3	0
Winona	1,309	8	0	0	0	8	66	23	39	4	0
Wood Heights	738	0	0	0	0	0	1	1	0	0	0
Woodson Terrace	3,963	12	0	1	3	8	131	35	66	30	0
Wright City	3,256	6	0	1	0	5	78	23	48	7	0
MONTANA											
Baker	1,647	2	0	0	0	2	20	3	16	1	0
Belgrade	8,518	24	0	4	1	19	220	21	190	9	1
Billings	108,039	280	2	25	42	211	5,021	848	3,811	362	14
Boulder	1,503	3	0	0	0	3	11	3	7	1	0
Bozeman	40,892	89	0	15	7	67	1,297	152	1,071	74	3
Bridger	740	4	1	0	0	3	6	0	6	0	0
Colstrip	2,395	11	0	0	0	11	25	1	22	2	1
Columbia Falls	5,569	6	0	2	0	4	219	8	207	4	0
Columbus	2,078	5	0	0	0	5	29	5	24	0	0
Conrad	2,481	8	0	0	0	8	37	5	30	2	0
Cut Bank	3,179	16	0	1	1	14	117	14	100	3	1
Dillon	4,250	14	0	0	0	14	47	4	39	4	0
East Helena	2,204	7	0	0	0	7	27	2	24	1	0
Ennis	1,077	0	0	0	0	0	9	4	5	0	0
Eureka	1,002	1	0	0	0	1	17	2	15	0	0
Fort Benton	1,438	4	0	0	0	4	25	2	22	1	0
Glasgow	2,854	7	0	0	1	6	63	10	52	1	0
Glendive	4,635	6	0	0	2	4	153	25	123	5	0
Great Falls	59,984	124	4	6	21	93	2,776	308	2,343	125	6
Hamilton	5,129	24	0	3	1	20	201	22	169	10	1
Havre	9,726	56	0	11	2	43	372	29	313	30	0
Helena	30,520	117	0	24	4	89	974	111	827	36	13
Hot Springs	590	7	0	1	0	6	6	0	6	0	0
Joliet	650	0	0	0	0	0	7	2	2	3	0
Kalispell	22,568	68	1	8	7	52	1,010	72	899	39	2
Laurel	6,841	8	0	0	0	8	169	22	141	6	0
Libby	2,898	14	0	1	0	13	102	10	90	2	1
Livingston	7,461	21	0	0	0	21	138	23	105	10	3
Manhattan	1,712	1	0	0	0	1	13	5	6	2	0
Miles City	8,141	16	1	2	0	13	205	10	180	15	1
Plains	1,268	1	0	0	1	0	18	3	13	2	1
Polson	5,383	42	1	6	0	35	203	30	162	11	0
Red Lodge	2,531	10	0	0	0	10	67	23	43	1	2
Ronan City	2,030	15	0	2	0	13	94	11	82	1	0
Sidney	4,855	4	0	2	0	2	61	4	48	9	0
Stevensville	2,087	10	0	2	0	8	43	4	37	2	1
St. Ignatius	814	4	0	0	0	4	29	2	26	1	0
Thompson Falls	1,450	5	0	0	0	5	23	5	16	2	0
Three Forks	2,004	1	0	0	0	1	10	2	7	1	0
Troy	969	6	0	0	0	6	40	2	36	2	0
West Yellowstone	1,549	2	0	0	1	1	4	0	3	1	0
Whitefish	8,776	10	0	3	0	7	196	22	168	6	3
Wolf Point	2,562	20	0	3	1	16	126	36	83	7	1
NEBRASKA											
Alliance	8,005	16	0	0	1	15	154	31	114	9	0
Ashland	2,728	3	0	0	1	2	8	1	7	0	1
Auburn	3,237	0	0	0	0	0	43	0	41	2	0
Aurora	4,240	1	0	1	0	0	33	14	13	6	0
Bayard	1,095	3	0	0	0	3	8	3	5	0	0
Beatrice	12,706	36	0	8	1	27	484	116	357	11	2
Bellevue	52,330	69	1	19	16	33	1,345	169	1,054	122	7
Bennington	1,029	0	0	0	0	0	11	0	11	0	0
Blair	7,805	9	0	7	0	2	125	19	101	5	4

[1] The FBI does not publish arson data unless it receives data from either the agency or the state for all 12 months of the calendar year.

Table 8. Offenses Known to Law Enforcement, by State and City, 2010—*Continued*

(Number)

State/city	Population	Violent crime	Murder and non-negligent man-slaughter	Forcible rape	Robbery	Aggravated assault	Property crime	Burglary	Larceny-theft	Motor vehicle theft	Arson[1]
NEBRASKA—*Continued*											
Bridgeport	1,431	0	0	0	0	0	27	5	22	0	0
Broken Bow	3,140	9	0	2	0	7	64	14	48	2	0
Central City	2,827	1	0	0	0	1	51	1	49	1	1
Chadron	5,480	14	0	3	0	11	161	11	140	10	2
Columbus	22,246	27	0	6	5	16	460	60	380	20	0
Cozad	4,355	5	0	2	2	1	44	12	28	4	1
Crete	6,380	8	0	2	1	5	161	30	127	4	1
Falls City	3,910	3	0	0	0	3	68	20	45	3	0
Fremont	25,262	49	0	13	5	31	801	113	662	26	6
Gering	7,825	8	0	0	0	8	198	50	141	7	2
Gothenburg	3,753	5	1	2	1	1	66	11	54	1	0
Grand Island	47,736	168	2	31	22	113	2,297	373	1,829	95	12
Hastings	25,705	33	0	15	2	16	746	84	631	31	4
Holdrege	5,128	4	0	1	0	3	112	18	93	1	1
Imperial	1,759	6	0	3	0	3	12	2	9	1	0
Kearney	31,436	62	0	10	3	49	872	112	734	26	13
La Vista	17,702	16	0	5	1	10	272	53	200	19	5
Lexington	10,415	31	2	8	3	18	305	68	221	16	1
Lincoln	259,672	1,258	2	143	182	931	10,218	1,464	8,406	348	
Lyons	841	2	0	0	0	2	5	2	2	1	0
Madison	2,218	4	0	2	0	2	26	3	20	3	0
McCook	7,437	8	0	5	0	3	195	29	161	5	0
Milford	2,069	1	0	1	0	0	21	2	19	0	1
Minden	2,800	2	0	0	0	2	66	13	53	0	2
Nebraska City	6,912	4	0	2	0	2	137	11	120	6	0
Norfolk	23,523	44	2	23	10	9	706	74	601	31	4
North Platte	24,429	55	0	20	3	32	1,131	162	918	51	10
Ogallala	4,373	7	0	4	0	3	141	9	126	6	0
Omaha	464,628	2,263	34	194	723	1,312	17,334	3,046	12,091	2,197	119
O'Neill	3,242	1	0	0	0	1	5	2	3	0	0
Papillion	25,213	27	0	8	3	16	322	23	283	16	0
Plainview	1,185	1	0	0	0	1	23	4	19	0	0
Plattsmouth	6,941	5	0	4	0	1	133	16	114	3	1
Ralston	6,178	3	0	0	2	1	138	14	115	9	1
Scottsbluff	15,053	35	0	8	5	22	874	138	719	17	2
Seward	6,842	1	0	0	0	1	80	14	64	2	0
Sidney	6,399	3	0	0	0	3	108	23	85	0	1
South Sioux City	12,374	19	0	0	2	17	283	23	246	14	0
Superior	1,729	0	0	0	0	0	8	3	5	0	0
Valentine	2,530	12	1	2	0	9	46	8	33	5	0
Valley	1,994	1	0	0	1	0	40	3	34	3	0
Wahoo	4,212	10	1	0	2	7	44	8	36	0	0
Wayne	5,386	8	0	6	0	2	114	24	88	2	0
West Point	3,291	0	0	0	0	0	6	3	3	0	0
Wilber	1,765	3	0	0	0	3	43	5	37	1	0
York	7,681	5	0	0	2	3	181	30	144	7	0
NEVADA											
Boulder City	14,794	14	0	1	1	12	120	49	53	18	2
Carlin	2,103	6	0	0	0	6	30	14	16	0	1
Elko	17,374	74	0	14	12	48	698	219	431	48	4
Fallon	8,552	29	0	2	8	19	314	54	256	4	2
Henderson	264,280	543	8	35	189	311	5,196	1,280	3,406	510	43
Las Vegas Metropolitan Police Department	1,416,401	12,648	107	652	4,003	7,886	43,219	13,824	22,231	7,164	240
Mesquite	18,130	29	0	1	7	21	254	47	189	18	0
Reno	222,242	1,168	9	46	385	728	7,468	1,638	5,101	729	29
Sparks	91,433	357	8	35	103	211	2,761	699	1,829	233	17
West Wendover	5,091	19	0	8	3	8	120	37	80	3	1
Winnemucca	8,361	12	0	0	2	10	122	29	81	12	1
Yerington	3,912	23	0	0	0	23	31	22	8	1	0
NEW HAMPSHIRE											
Alexandria	1,541	3	0	1	1	1	34	11	23	0	0
Alstead	2,090	1	0	1	0	0	28	14	11	3	0
Alton	5,114	2	0	0	0	2	80	26	52	2	2
Amherst	11,903	7	1	0	1	5	182	30	148	4	1
Antrim	2,630	3	0	3	0	0	55	11	39	5	1
Ashland	2,065	2	1	0	1	0	52	8	42	2	0
Auburn	5,177	2	2	0	0	0	81	31	49	1	0
Barnstead	4,619	6	0	3	0	3	103	36	62	5	1
Barrington	8,576	10	0	1	0	9	98	21	73	4	4
Bartlett	2,930	2	0	2	0	0	68	24	44	0	0
Bedford	21,304	11	0	5	1	5	324	32	286	6	3
Belmont	7,051	16	0	3	2	11	234	65	159	10	2
Bennington	1,469	2	0	0	0	2	37	0	35	2	0

[1] The FBI does not publish arson data unless it receives data from either the agency or the state for all 12 months of the calendar year.

Table 8.   Offenses Known to Law Enforcement, by State and City, 2010—*Continued*

(Number)

State/city	Population	Violent crime	Murder and non-negligent man-slaughter	Forcible rape	Robbery	Aggravated assault	Property crime	Burglary	Larceny-theft	Motor vehicle theft	Arson[1]
NEW HAMPSHIRE—*Continued*											
Berlin	9,155	19	0	8	1	10	148	54	94	0	3
Bethlehem	2,450	4	0	0	1	3	50	19	28	3	0
Boscawen	3,958	3	0	2	0	1	80	13	63	4	0
Bow	8,107	5	0	0	0	5	98	17	80	1	1
Bradford	1,524	0	0	0	0	0	17	4	12	1	1
Brentwood	3,998	0	0	0	0	0	58	13	41	4	0
Bristol	3,110	5	0	2	2	1	81	12	60	9	0
Campton	3,006	7	0	2	0	5	65	15	49	1	1
Candia	4,177	3	0	0	0	3	76	18	55	3	1
Canterbury	2,316	0	0	0	0	0	12	3	8	1	0
Carroll	726	1	0	1	0	0	77	7	68	2	0
Center Harbor	1,102	2	0	2	0	0	39	5	33	1	0
Charlestown	4,804	2	0	0	0	2	31	13	17	1	0
Chester	4,769	6	0	1	0	5	34	24	9	1	2
Claremont	12,788	19	0	3	4	12	433	54	364	15	1
Colebrook	2,282	4	0	0	1	3	51	21	29	1	0
Concord	42,190	96	0	17	27	52	1,225	167	1,039	19	12
Conway	9,195	24	0	9	3	12	504	92	393	19	4
Dalton	858	0	0	0	0	0	23	10	13	0	1
Danville	4,326	4	1	1	0	2	47	9	34	4	1
Deerfield	4,243	7	0	1	0	6	77	26	47	4	0
Deering	2,059	2	0	0	0	2	33	7	26	0	1
Derry	34,075	89	0	4	18	67	816	195	582	39	24
Dover	28,627	33	0	2	15	16	487	58	420	9	2
Dublin	1,574	1	0	1	0	0	19	7	10	2	0
Dunbarton	2,676	4	0	0	2	2	33	13	18	2	0
Durham	14,465	15	0	9	0	6	158	18	135	5	2
Enfield	4,811	3	0	1	1	1	74	31	43	0	3
Epping	6,435	9	0	2	0	7	193	30	162	1	2
Epsom	4,619	5	0	3	0	2	95	11	82	2	0
Exeter	14,924	4	1	1	0	2	130	22	107	1	1
Farmington	6,764	21	0	10	5	6	168	51	106	11	1
Fitzwilliam	2,296	2	0	1	0	1	42	16	22	4	1
Franconia	1,047	1	0	0	0	1	33	4	29	0	0
Freedom	1,443	0	0	0	0	0	16	6	10	0	0
Fremont	4,188	3	0	1	0	2	57	19	35	3	1
Gilford	7,427	15	1	0	1	13	218	24	186	8	0
Gilmanton	3,506	2	0	0	0	2	49	12	34	3	1
Goffstown	17,774	10	0	2	1	7	302	87	210	5	3
Gorham	2,718	1	0	0	0	1	34	2	32	0	0
Grantham	2,544	1	0	0	0	1	9	3	6	0	0
Greenland	3,435	2	0	0	0	2	47	3	41	3	0
Hampstead	8,981	5	0	1	1	3	92	26	63	3	0
Hampton	15,270	18	0	3	4	11	382	53	313	16	2
Hancock	1,807	4	0	0	0	4	12	2	10	0	0
Hanover	10,922	7	0	3	1	3	145	13	131	1	4
Haverhill	4,672	12	0	3	0	9	112	19	89	4	1
Henniker	5,021	4	1	3	0	0	101	15	85	1	3
Hill	1,106	0	0	0	0	0	0	0	0	0	0
Hillsborough	5,592	12	0	3	1	8	117	19	92	6	3
Hinsdale	4,124	8	0	2	1	5	79	10	63	6	0
Hooksett	14,075	13	0	4	5	4	401	79	313	9	2
Hopkinton	5,561	1	0	0	0	1	46	11	34	1	0
Hudson	24,901	29	0	4	2	23	408	76	302	30	9
Jaffrey	5,603	9	0	3	2	4	77	27	47	3	2
Keene	22,093	46	0	11	12	23	808	89	705	14	6
Kingston	6,199	5	0	3	1	1	73	18	49	6	1
Laconia	16,973	65	0	13	8	44	827	143	672	12	4
Lancaster	3,151	0	0	0	0	0	122	18	99	5	1
Lebanon	12,765	29	0	6	3	20	483	41	432	10	10
Lee	4,461	1	0	0	1	0	43	9	32	2	1
Lincoln	1,337	2	0	2	0	0	90	11	78	1	1
Lisbon	1,648	2	0	0	0	2	15	3	12	0	0
Litchfield	8,852	4	0	2	1	1	91	25	65	1	1
Littleton	6,111	10	0	1	0	9	137	27	106	4	1
Londonderry	25,014	29	1	5	3	20	338	78	246	14	6
Loudon	5,213	1	0	1	0	0	145	19	119	7	0
Madison	2,350	3	0	1	0	2	45	14	30	1	0
Manchester	108,101	544	1	62	154	327	3,754	907	2,687	160	59
Marlborough	2,052	3	0	0	1	2	36	6	29	1	1
Meredith	6,617	10	1	5	1	3	157	38	112	7	1
Merrimack	26,501	9	0	0	3	6	293	45	238	10	1
Middleton	1,861	0	0	0	0	0	14	7	7	0	0

[1] The FBI does not publish arson data unless it receives data from either the agency or the state for all 12 months of the calendar year.

Table 8. Offenses Known to Law Enforcement, by State and City, 2010—*Continued*

(Number)

State/city	Population	Violent crime	Murder and non-negligent man-slaughter	Forcible rape	Robbery	Aggravated assault	Property crime	Burglary	Larceny-theft	Motor vehicle theft	Arson[1]
NEW HAMPSHIRE—*Continued*											
Milford	15,089	25	0	4	9	12	301	52	235	14	6
Milton	4,633	14	0	4	0	10	113	43	64	6	1
Mont Vernon	2,378	4	0	0	0	4	17	3	12	2	0
Moultonborough	5,028	7	0	0	0	7	87	24	61	2	0
Nashua	86,523	173	1	39	47	86	2,209	398	1,744	67	29
New Boston	5,209	4	0	1	0	3	54	19	32	3	0
Newbury	2,120	2	0	1	0	1	19	1	17	1	0
New Durham	2,569	4	0	0	0	4	43	11	30	2	1
Newfields	1,625	1	0	1	0	0	20	5	15	0	0
New Hampton	2,256	4	0	0	0	4	64	21	42	1	0
Newington	797	2	0	0	1	1	255	2	253	0	1
New Ipswich	5,438	1	0	0	1	0	51	19	27	5	1
New London	4,402	0	0	0	0	0	44	10	34	0	0
Newmarket	9,497	9	0	1	0	8	33	9	23	1	1
Newport	6,474	10	0	4	2	4	201	31	169	1	2
Newton	4,587	5	0	2	0	3	51	13	37	1	1
Northfield	5,120	5	0	0	0	5	77	16	58	3	0
North Hampton	4,509	5	0	2	0	3	75	18	56	1	1
Northumberland	2,242	4	0	3	0	1	58	19	38	1	1
Northwood	4,164	2	0	0	1	1	91	19	67	5	0
Nottingham	4,601	2	0	1	0	1	55	9	44	2	0
Orford	1,039	0	0	0	0	0	8	0	8	0	0
Ossipee	4,706	5	0	0	1	4	108	15	84	9	1
Pelham	12,770	11	0	2	1	8	176	63	99	14	2
Pembroke	7,317	8	0	2	1	5	98	25	71	2	0
Peterborough	6,176	5	0	2	2	1	118	8	108	2	0
Pittsfield	4,348	5	0	1	1	3	84	11	63	10	0
Plaistow	7,522	4	0	0	3	1	217	13	183	21	0
Plymouth	6,647	12	0	3	2	7	252	43	205	4	6
Portsmouth	20,281	28	1	5	6	16	615	68	523	24	6
Raymond	10,260	10	0	5	2	3	216	31	176	9	0
Rindge	6,451	8	0	1	2	5	70	26	40	4	1
Rochester	30,827	102	0	15	25	62	978	163	794	21	10
Rollinsford	2,611	5	0	1	1	3	33	15	17	1	1
Rye	5,097	4	0	0	0	4	79	3	76	0	0
Sandown	5,907	3	0	2	0	1	53	18	32	3	0
Sandwich	1,318	0	0	0	0	0	50	13	35	2	0
Seabrook	8,471	15	0	2	1	12	301	21	271	9	3
Somersworth	11,940	50	0	5	12	33	546	61	480	5	6
South Hampton	871	0	0	0	0	0	2	1	1	0	0
Strafford	4,076	6	0	1	0	5	36	6	29	1	0
Stratham	7,328	3	0	0	2	1	76	8	66	2	1
Sunapee	3,365	1	0	1	0	0	7	1	5	1	0
Thornton	2,144	1	0	0	0	1	18	1	16	1	0
Tilton	3,542	12	0	0	3	9	177	17	152	8	1
Troy	2,045	1	0	1	0	0	30	9	20	1	0
Wakefield	5,455	5	0	2	0	3	128	25	93	10	0
Walpole	3,637	2	0	0	1	1	38	5	29	4	0
Warner	2,932	0	0	0	0	0	10	2	8	0	0
Washington	1,087	0	0	0	0	0	10	5	5	0	0
Waterville Valley	267	3	0	1	2	0	60	0	60	0	0
Weare	9,240	4	0	1	0	3	99	17	75	7	1
Webster	1,891	0	0	0	0	0	29	4	25	0	0
Wilton	3,938	2	0	1	0	1	62	12	48	2	2
Winchester	4,252	4	0	0	2	2	121	33	78	10	1
Windham	13,484	5	0	2	0	3	170	39	123	8	0
Wolfeboro	6,569	5	0	2	0	3	108	28	79	1	0
Woodstock	1,155	5	0	2	1	2	29	4	25	0	1
NEW JERSEY											
Aberdeen Township	18,575	21	0	3	10	8	272	56	208	8	1
Absecon	8,728	26	0	1	19	6	235	50	175	10	1
Allendale	6,641	3	0	1	0	2	60	9	50	1	1
Allenhurst	699	3	0	0	2	1	15	3	12	0	0
Allentown	1,847	0	0	0	0	0	18	2	16	0	0
Alpha	2,382	0	0	0	0	0	20	2	18	0	0
Alpine	2,552	1	0	0	0	1	8	4	4	0	0
Andover Township	6,623	2	0	0	1	1	37	9	27	1	0
Asbury Park	16,625	344	3	13	188	140	1,147	335	753	59	2
Atlantic City	39,787	783	11	27	434	311	2,969	492	2,344	133	13
Atlantic Highlands	4,609	5	0	0	1	4	79	12	67	0	0
Audubon	8,908	6	0	0	5	1	268	23	240	5	0
Audubon Park	1,057	5	1	0	0	4	16	4	12	0	0
Avalon	2,094	0	0	0	0	0	313	65	246	2	2

[1] The FBI does not publish arson data unless it receives data from either the agency or the state for all 12 months of the calendar year.

Table 8.   Offenses Known to Law Enforcement, by State and City, 2010—*Continued*

(Number)

State/city	Population	Violent crime	Murder and non-negligent man-slaughter	Forcible rape	Robbery	Aggravated assault	Property crime	Burglary	Larceny-theft	Motor vehicle theft	Arson[1]
NEW JERSEY—*Continued*											
Avon-by-the-Sea	2,252	2	0	0	0	2	73	8	64	1	1
Barnegat Light	859	1	0	0	0	1	9	1	8	0	0
Barnegat Township	23,692	33	0	0	5	28	244	77	163	4	5
Barrington	6,972	3	0	0	2	1	85	27	50	8	0
Bay Head	1,284	1	0	0	1	0	85	6	79	0	0
Bayonne	58,393	162	0	5	71	86	885	180	612	93	0
Beach Haven	1,425	3	0	0	0	3	136	18	117	1	0
Beachwood	11,001	9	0	0	4	5	284	45	230	9	1
Bedminster Township	8,456	3	0	2	0	1	45	10	33	2	0
Belleville	33,849	75	0	1	35	39	755	159	466	130	1
Bellmawr	11,275	18	0	0	8	10	315	54	243	18	1
Belmar	5,917	24	0	2	10	12	315	57	252	6	0
Belvidere	2,638	2	0	0	0	2	23	1	22	0	0
Bergenfield	25,680	30	0	1	9	20	107	29	76	2	1
Berkeley Heights Township	13,523	1	0	0	0	1	102	19	80	3	0
Berkeley Township	43,531	38	0	0	14	24	717	154	542	21	10
Berlin	8,194	12	0	0	3	9	207	26	173	8	2
Berlin Township	5,509	11	0	3	1	7	178	17	158	3	2
Bernards Township	26,990	3	0	0	2	1	146	36	102	8	1
Bernardsville	7,872	1	0	0	0	1	38	13	25	0	1
Beverly	2,580	9	0	1	2	6	51	25	25	1	1
Blairstown Township	5,985	3	0	0	0	3	50	17	31	2	0
Bloomfield	43,669	111	0	6	70	35	1,045	207	707	131	2
Bloomingdale	7,485	5	0	0	1	4	60	11	49	0	0
Bogota	7,933	12	0	1	2	9	72	21	48	3	0
Boonton	8,552	10	0	0	3	7	102	11	88	3	1
Boonton Township	4,539	3	0	1	0	2	23	4	18	1	0
Bordentown	3,830	1	0	1	0	0	72	7	61	4	0
Bordentown Township	10,300	8	0	0	3	5	138	34	99	5	0
Bound Brook	10,523	17	0	2	10	5	240	62	168	10	2
Bradley Beach	5,046	6	0	1	4	1	155	31	121	3	0
Branchburg Township	15,263	7	0	3	1	3	147	22	121	4	1
Brick Township	79,569	104	1	7	26	70	1,372	333	1,000	39	16
Bridgeton	25,243	320	4	1	126	189	1,047	360	637	50	4
Bridgewater Township	45,176	15	0	1	6	8	688	80	591	17	1
Brielle	4,925	1	0	0	0	1	56	16	39	1	0
Brigantine	12,729	11	0	0	3	8	263	69	187	7	1
Brooklawn	2,262	16	0	2	9	5	301	31	260	10	1
Buena	3,733	15	0	1	1	13	88	35	49	4	1
Burlington	9,423	44	1	3	27	13	198	49	137	12	0
Burlington Township	21,558	36	0	6	13	17	355	56	283	16	2
Butler	8,248	15	1	1	4	9	97	33	60	4	0
Byram Township	8,544	3	0	1	1	1	39	14	24	1	0
Caldwell	7,115	3	0	0	0	3	73	16	57	0	0
Califon	1,043	0	0	0	0	0	7	3	4	0	1
Camden	79,081	1,841	37	73	712	1,019	3,500	1,015	1,966	519	91
Cape May	3,691	2	0	0	0	2	185	29	156	0	0
Cape May Point	221	0	0	0	0	0	13	8	5	0	0
Carlstadt	6,111	19	0	0	5	14	154	16	104	34	0
Carney's Point Township	8,076	9	0	1	7	1	163	33	118	12	1
Carteret	24,246	52	1	3	16	32	399	72	296	31	0
Cedar Grove Township	12,774	9	0	3	3	3	128	30	97	1	2
Chatham	8,263	0	0	0	0	0	72	14	57	1	0
Chatham Township	10,302	0	0	0	0	0	46	15	31	0	0
Cherry Hill Township	71,338	79	0	0	34	45	2,210	307	1,833	70	0
Chesilhurst	1,997	5	0	0	3	2	41	22	14	5	1
Chester	1,700	1	0	0	1	0	21	6	15	0	0
Chesterfield Township	7,860	3	0	0	0	3	34	2	31	1	0
Chester Township	7,866	0	0	0	0	0	26	7	19	0	0
Cinnaminson Township	15,718	25	0	4	8	13	373	53	302	18	2
Clark Township	14,505	2	0	0	1	1	206	20	177	9	0
Clayton	7,682	12	0	3	4	5	138	30	103	5	4
Clementon	4,914	16	0	0	8	8	238	70	159	9	0
Cliffside Park	23,139	32	0	0	6	26	221	69	147	5	0
Clinton	2,576	2	0	0	1	1	37	12	25	0	1
Clinton Township	14,075	4	0	0	0	4	66	14	51	1	0
Closter	8,759	2	0	0	1	1	61	12	49	0	0
Collingswood	13,680	36	0	2	22	12	497	136	334	27	2
Colts Neck Township	10,180	4	0	0	1	3	73	26	47	0	1
Cranbury Township	4,023	3	0	0	0	3	39	6	31	2	0
Cranford Township	22,147	10	0	0	5	5	247	50	191	6	1
Cresskill	8,760	1	0	0	0	1	38	15	19	4	0
Deal	1,051	3	0	1	1	1	57	19	35	3	1

[1] The FBI does not publish arson data unless it receives data from either the agency or the state for all 12 months of the calendar year.

Table 8. Offenses Known to Law Enforcement, by State and City, 2010—*Continued*

(Number)

State/city	Population	Violent crime	Murder and non-negligent man-slaughter	Forcible rape	Robbery	Aggravated assault	Property crime	Burglary	Larceny-theft	Motor vehicle theft	Arson[1]
NEW JERSEY—*Continued*											
Delanco Township	5,000	7	1	2	1	3	125	37	87	1	0
Delaware Township	4,760	0	0	0	0	0	31	8	20	3	0
Delran Township	16,957	17	0	2	7	8	247	39	200	8	1
Demarest	5,216	0	0	0	0	0	36	10	26	0	0
Denville Township	16,708	7	1	0	2	4	157	36	117	4	2
Deptford Township	31,340	105	0	3	46	56	1,906	270	1,585	51	2
Dover	17,948	36	0	1	13	22	337	93	222	22	0
Dumont	17,022	11	1	0	2	8	115	14	101	0	0
Dunellen	7,150	12	0	4	4	4	190	51	137	2	1
Eastampton Township	6,597	6	0	0	3	3	109	24	80	5	0
East Brunswick Township	47,620	44	0	4	15	25	833	89	721	23	4
East Greenwich Township	8,733	4	0	0	2	2	154	33	115	6	2
East Hanover Township	11,500	6	0	0	0	6	172	18	148	6	0
East Newark	2,116	3	0	1	0	2	27	10	16	1	0
East Orange	65,118	487	6	31	178	272	1,367	351	656	360	19
East Rutherford	8,846	14	0	0	3	11	214	33	162	19	2
East Windsor Township	27,424	25	0	2	7	16	339	48	278	13	4
Eatontown	14,428	54	0	4	15	35	602	70	514	18	0
Edgewater	9,875	10	0	1	4	5	205	30	157	18	1
Edgewater Park Township	7,757	29	0	2	17	10	167	43	111	13	0
Edison Township	100,395	141	2	5	52	82	1,709	334	1,220	155	11
Egg Harbor City	4,391	20	1	0	6	13	148	51	92	5	0
Egg Harbor Township	41,573	116	1	2	30	83	1,007	217	758	32	14
Elizabeth	126,494	1,392	13	42	760	577	4,734	924	2,665	1,145	12
Elk Township	4,084	5	0	1	1	3	120	35	80	5	1
Elmer	1,346	0	0	0	0	0	7	3	4	0	0
Elmwood Park	18,736	21	0	0	13	8	382	87	278	17	2
Elsinboro Township	1,053	4	0	1	0	3	16	9	7	0	2
Emerson	7,504	3	0	0	0	3	72	5	67	0	0
Englewood	30,023	64	1	5	15	43	511	177	295	39	1
Englewood Cliffs	5,946	0	0	0	0	0	73	16	55	2	0
Englishtown	1,944	4	0	1	1	2	21	4	17	0	2
Essex Fells	2,149	2	1	0	0	1	7	2	4	1	0
Evesham Township	45,959	41	0	3	19	19	711	99	595	17	12
Ewing Township	36,612	121	2	1	31	87	710	182	466	62	4
Fairfield Township, Essex County	7,531	15	0	1	7	7	228	37	176	15	1
Fair Haven	5,984	3	0	1	2	0	51	6	45	0	0
Fair Lawn	30,607	27	0	1	9	17	360	58	289	13	9
Fairview	13,709	28	2	1	18	7	175	46	122	7	0
Fanwood	7,164	0	0	0	0	0	90	6	81	3	0
Far Hills	910	0	0	0	0	0	9	4	5	0	0
Fieldsboro	568	0	0	0	0	0	0	0	0	0	0
Flemington	4,452	7	0	0	1	6	86	12	72	2	0
Florence Township	11,663	17	0	2	4	11	110	39	66	5	0
Florham Park	12,669	2	0	1	1	0	65	7	56	2	0
Fort Lee	36,580	34	0	0	16	18	320	42	262	16	1
Franklin	5,115	6	0	0	1	5	143	11	130	2	0
Franklin Lakes	11,816	4	0	0	1	3	73	23	49	1	0
Franklin Township, Gloucester County	17,679	22	0	0	10	12	363	139	208	16	1
Franklin Township, Hunterdon County	3,289	0	0	0	0	0	32	5	26	1	0
Franklin Township, Somerset County	61,185	64	1	3	32	28	951	239	656	56	5
Freehold	11,548	49	2	2	18	27	275	48	213	14	0
Freehold Township	35,117	37	0	5	14	18	1,063	97	947	19	3
Frenchtown	1,474	0	0	0	0	0	32	2	28	2	0
Galloway Township	37,367	68	1	1	18	48	708	192	478	38	1
Garfield	29,068	49	1	1	14	33	444	98	303	43	2
Garwood	4,599	6	0	0	5	1	46	8	38	0	0
Gibbsboro	2,447	2	0	0	0	2	64	20	42	2	0
Glassboro	20,047	43	0	0	21	22	405	112	281	12	8
Glen Ridge	6,642	7	0	0	2	5	187	76	103	8	2
Glen Rock	11,158	5	0	0	2	3	102	9	93	0	0
Gloucester City	11,614	29	0	5	14	10	330	82	232	16	3
Gloucester Township	65,239	214	1	7	55	151	1,655	417	1,145	93	15
Green Brook Township	7,098	7	0	0	2	5	132	31	98	3	0
Greenwich Township, Gloucester County	5,040	2	0	0	1	1	111	14	95	2	0
Greenwich Township, Warren County	5,193	4	0	1	0	3	92	2	90	0	0
Guttenberg	10,643	38	0	0	12	26	96	29	62	5	3
Hackensack	43,111	107	0	6	31	70	1,073	89	910	74	4
Hackettstown	9,653	7	0	0	0	7	143	16	121	6	0
Haddonfield	11,499	11	0	1	6	4	307	73	230	4	2
Haddon Heights	7,736	6	0	0	1	5	154	35	115	4	1
Haddon Township	14,432	32	0	0	18	14	468	80	377	11	0
Haledon	8,806	17	0	0	13	4	220	86	118	16	0

[1] The FBI does not publish arson data unless it receives data from either the agency or the state for all 12 months of the calendar year.

Table 8.   Offenses Known to Law Enforcement, by State and City, 2010—*Continued*

(Number)

State/city	Population	Violent crime	Murder and non-negligent man-slaughter	Forcible rape	Robbery	Aggravated assault	Property crime	Burglary	Larceny-theft	Motor vehicle theft	Arson[1]
NEW JERSEY—*Continued*											
Hamburg	3,514	7	0	0	0	7	32	9	23	0	0
Hamilton Township, Atlantic County	24,892	71	4	8	21	38	1,074	154	888	32	7
Hamilton Township, Mercer County	91,439	189	2	3	101	83	1,845	434	1,315	96	9
Hammonton	13,603	20	1	2	4	13	254	72	175	7	1
Hanover Township	13,905	12	0	1	3	8	134	14	113	7	1
Harding Township	3,375	5	0	1	0	4	14	3	11	0	1
Hardyston Township	8,621	9	0	1	0	8	111	21	88	2	0
Harrington Park	4,914	0	0	0	0	0	8	2	6	0	0
Harrison	15,393	41	0	1	10	30	266	91	137	38	0
Harrison Township	13,122	9	0	2	6	1	184	22	160	2	1
Harvey Cedars	404	1	0	0	0	1	15	7	8	0	0
Hasbrouck Heights	11,497	1	0	0	1	0	72	11	60	1	0
Haworth	3,447	0	0	0	0	0	10	2	8	0	0
Hawthorne	18,083	9	0	0	4	5	200	50	135	15	0
Hazlet Township	21,013	10	0	1	4	5	305	27	272	6	1
Helmetta	2,039	2	0	0	0	2	15	5	9	1	0
High Bridge	3,712	10	0	5	0	5	47	13	33	1	0
Highland Park	14,455	17	1	2	6	8	168	35	131	2	0
Highlands	5,299	23	0	0	1	22	63	4	52	7	0
Hightstown	5,370	9	0	0	6	3	73	25	46	2	0
Hillsborough Township	40,011	14	0	2	2	10	270	61	203	6	6
Hillsdale	9,884	1	0	0	0	1	50	5	45	0	0
Hillside Township	21,346	110	0	10	63	37	609	147	322	140	0
Hi-Nella	1,003	1	0	0	0	1	34	9	21	4	0
Hoboken	41,515	131	0	4	35	92	927	166	674	87	1
Ho-Ho-Kus	4,024	0	0	0	0	0	16	4	11	1	0
Holland Township	5,314	1	0	0	0	1	27	2	24	1	0
Holmdel Township	17,066	9	1	0	2	6	274	27	240	7	2
Hopatcong	15,579	7	1	0	1	5	129	30	99	0	0
Hopewell	2,001	1	0	0	0	1	11	4	6	1	0
Hopewell Township	18,060	11	0	0	1	10	101	23	77	1	0
Howell Township	52,130	66	1	5	19	41	757	162	571	24	3
Independence Township	5,724	2	0	0	0	2	35	12	23	0	1
Interlaken	877	0	0	0	0	0	11	2	9	0	0
Irvington	56,019	900	14	29	374	483	2,159	625	852	682	9
Island Heights	1,917	1	0	0	0	1	14	1	13	0	0
Jackson Township	54,638	45	1	2	14	28	710	164	519	27	20
Jamesburg	6,437	8	0	2	3	3	62	17	41	4	1
Jefferson Township	21,997	22	0	2	3	17	202	53	146	3	2
Jersey City	244,201	1,829	25	44	943	817	5,992	1,523	3,662	807	51
Keansburg	10,579	42	0	0	10	32	301	62	228	11	6
Kearny	36,400	86	0	3	30	53	895	151	631	113	8
Kenilworth	7,711	7	0	2	2	3	108	16	85	7	0
Keyport	7,516	11	0	0	1	10	69	5	61	3	0
Kinnelon	9,703	1	0	0	0	1	81	17	64	0	0
Lacey Township	26,852	42	0	0	11	31	802	118	668	16	0
Lake Como	1,784	5	0	0	2	3	37	4	31	2	0
Lakehurst	2,743	2	0	0	0	2	42	7	34	1	0
Lakewood Township	72,960	113	4	5	51	53	1,048	247	746	55	6
Lambertville	3,802	8	0	0	0	8	50	4	44	2	0
Laurel Springs	1,912	4	0	1	3	0	48	9	38	1	0
Lavallette	2,802	3	0	0	0	3	71	26	45	0	0
Lawnside	2,870	23	1	0	11	11	67	9	56	2	0
Lawrence Township, Mercer County	32,104	41	0	3	19	19	823	93	715	15	9
Lebanon Township	6,291	0	0	0	0	0	31	5	23	3	0
Leonia	8,636	2	0	0	1	1	54	19	33	2	0
Lincoln Park	10,663	2	0	0	0	2	91	27	63	1	0
Linden	39,680	117	2	0	84	31	1,380	201	1,034	145	2
Lindenwold	17,875	140	2	6	55	77	657	225	400	32	5
Linwood	7,275	4	0	1	0	3	128	37	87	4	2
Little Egg Harbor Township	21,508	41	2	6	7	26	423	62	351	10	11
Little Falls Township	11,703	17	0	1	3	13	185	33	137	15	1
Little Ferry	10,510	7	0	0	1	6	118	31	74	13	0
Little Silver	6,175	0	0	0	0	0	79	22	57	0	0
Livingston Township	27,775	12	0	0	7	5	386	46	329	11	0
Loch Arbour	274	1	0	0	0	1	13	4	9	0	0
Lodi	23,895	30	0	0	11	19	320	69	227	24	0
Logan Township	6,352	13	0	1	5	7	154	32	117	5	0
Long Beach Township	3,628	5	0	0	0	5	124	18	106	0	0
Long Branch	33,368	112	1	5	47	59	820	224	565	31	1
Long Hill Township	8,676	3	0	0	2	1	67	15	50	2	1
Longport	1,104	0	0	0	0	0	21	1	20	0	0
Lopatcong Township	8,744	5	0	0	1	4	94	13	80	1	0

[1] The FBI does not publish arson data unless it receives data from either the agency or the state for all 12 months of the calendar year.

Table 8.   Offenses Known to Law Enforcement, by State and City, 2010—*Continued*

(Number)

State/city	Population	Violent crime	Murder and non-negligent man-slaughter	Forcible rape	Robbery	Aggravated assault	Property crime	Burglary	Larceny-theft	Motor vehicle theft	Arson[1]
NEW JERSEY—*Continued*											
Lower Alloways Creek Township	1,908	1	0	0	1	0	12	6	5	1	0
Lower Township	20,114	17	0	2	4	11	464	113	336	15	0
Lumberton Township	12,184	19	0	1	8	10	284	44	237	3	9
Lyndhurst Township	19,403	11	0	1	2	8	307	59	233	15	1
Madison	15,849	5	0	2	0	3	118	35	83	0	0
Magnolia	4,353	26	0	0	6	20	109	27	73	9	0
Mahwah Township	24,346	3	0	0	1	2	106	7	87	12	0
Manalapan Township	40,301	19	0	0	12	7	386	93	281	12	1
Manasquan	6,309	4	0	0	1	3	167	31	136	0	2
Manchester Township	42,400	24	0	1	2	21	459	140	310	9	7
Mansfield Township, Burlington County	8,405	2	0	1	1	0	119	13	105	1	1
Mansfield Township, Warren County	8,139	7	0	1	1	5	133	25	107	1	1
Mantoloking	461	0	0	0	0	0	36	3	33	0	0
Mantua Township	15,414	12	0	3	4	5	278	54	223	1	2
Manville	10,996	13	0	0	6	7	215	14	173	28	1
Maple Shade Township	19,297	27	0	2	10	15	424	102	287	35	2
Maplewood Township	21,944	58	2	1	32	23	443	106	300	37	2
Margate City	8,612	5	0	1	2	2	191	23	167	1	2
Marlboro Township	41,231	15	0	0	3	12	450	93	344	13	4
Matawan	9,175	5	0	0	4	1	96	28	64	4	0
Maywood	9,166	2	0	0	2	0	101	28	69	4	0
Medford Lakes	4,129	0	0	0	0	0	74	8	66	0	0
Medford Township	22,914	8	0	1	3	4	234	43	188	3	0
Mendham	5,110	1	0	0	0	1	25	4	21	0	0
Mendham Township	5,564	1	0	0	0	1	26	4	22	0	0
Merchantville	3,784	3	0	0	0	3	65	15	49	1	0
Metuchen	13,200	10	0	1	7	2	202	27	168	7	0
Middlesex	13,732	7	0	0	6	1	144	21	114	9	0
Middle Township	16,580	75	1	7	18	49	664	165	473	26	3
Middletown Township	66,915	42	0	4	11	27	830	151	656	23	0
Midland Park	6,783	6	0	0	0	6	71	9	62	0	0
Millburn Township	18,548	20	0	0	12	8	504	55	437	12	2
Milltown	7,007	4	0	1	1	2	102	12	87	3	0
Millville	29,497	169	1	7	58	103	1,216	265	919	32	6
Mine Hill Township	3,604	0	0	0	0	0	29	7	21	1	2
Monmouth Beach	3,590	1	0	1	0	0	51	12	37	2	1
Monroe Township, Gloucester County	33,950	41	0	4	11	26	797	211	560	26	4
Monroe Township, Middlesex County	38,777	21	2	0	8	11	283	39	231	13	3
Montclair	37,425	75	0	4	41	30	630	181	426	23	3
Montgomery Township	23,760	6	0	1	4	1	138	36	100	2	0
Montvale	7,746	2	0	0	1	1	54	2	51	1	0
Montville Township	21,253	6	0	0	2	4	128	28	96	4	1
Moonachie	2,770	5	0	0	1	4	58	15	35	8	0
Moorestown Township	19,653	25	0	5	14	6	520	67	445	8	3
Morris Plains	5,954	4	0	1	2	1	87	15	72	0	0
Morristown	19,085	78	0	0	29	49	456	95	347	14	1
Morris Township	21,418	19	0	1	3	15	114	50	60	4	0
Mountain Lakes	4,306	5	0	0	0	5	57	5	52	0	0
Mountainside	6,638	1	0	0	0	1	62	8	49	5	0
Mount Arlington	5,862	3	0	0	1	2	51	11	40	0	0
Mount Ephraim	4,443	13	0	0	9	4	156	20	122	14	0
Mount Holly Township	10,246	31	1	0	14	16	279	46	225	8	0
Mount Laurel Township	39,696	36	0	5	12	19	642	88	532	22	1
Mount Olive Township	26,431	12	0	5	1	6	272	46	222	4	5
Mullica Township	6,104	12	0	0	2	10	109	43	62	4	0
National Park	3,258	5	0	1	1	3	61	15	43	3	1
Neptune City	5,116	17	0	2	9	6	208	33	166	9	0
Neptune Township	28,586	132	1	7	59	65	1,673	358	1,256	59	6
Netcong	3,244	2	0	0	0	2	61	11	50	0	1
Newark	280,379	2,885	90	79	1,604	1,112	9,209	1,928	3,661	3,620	51
New Brunswick	52,245	361	3	16	164	178	1,372	410	842	120	10
Newfield	1,689	0	0	0	0	0	29	9	18	2	0
New Hanover Township	9,455	0	0	0	0	0	19	4	14	1	1
New Milford	16,005	5	0	1	4	0	100	13	82	5	0
New Providence	12,126	3	0	0	0	3	133	30	103	0	0
Newton	8,161	5	0	0	2	3	142	22	119	1	0
North Arlington	14,721	12	0	0	6	6	188	54	114	20	2
North Bergen Township	54,933	90	0	4	43	43	761	136	504	121	5
North Brunswick Township	40,123	57	1	2	16	38	747	137	547	63	1
North Caldwell	7,086	4	0	0	0	4	27	16	10	1	1
Northfield	7,965	2	0	0	2	0	91	26	64	1	0
North Haledon	9,058	4	0	0	0	4	30	7	20	3	0
North Hanover Township	7,421	8	0	0	0	8	72	30	41	1	3

[1] The FBI does not publish arson data unless it receives data from either the agency or the state for all 12 months of the calendar year.

Table 8. Offenses Known to Law Enforcement, by State and City, 2010—*Continued*

(Number)

State/city	Population	Violent crime	Murder and non-negligent man-slaughter	Forcible rape	Robbery	Aggravated assault	Property crime	Burglary	Larceny-theft	Motor vehicle theft	Arson[1]
NEW JERSEY—*Continued*											
North Plainfield	21,373	61	0	2	35	24	448	69	346	33	2
Northvale	4,874	1	0	0	1	0	16	0	16	0	0
North Wildwood	4,840	14	1	1	2	10	352	43	308	1	0
Norwood	6,290	3	0	0	0	3	21	4	16	1	0
Nutley Township	26,145	24	0	1	4	19	291	74	201	16	0
Oakland	13,454	4	0	0	1	3	137	16	120	1	1
Oaklyn	4,047	7	0	0	6	1	136	44	90	2	4
Ocean City	14,725	27	0	4	9	14	894	189	700	5	1
Ocean Gate	2,171	2	0	0	0	2	29	10	19	0	0
Oceanport	5,755	7	0	1	2	4	81	23	57	1	3
Ocean Township, Monmouth County	28,503	41	1	1	15	24	819	119	680	20	7
Ocean Township, Ocean County	9,501	5	0	1	0	4	130	19	108	3	0
Ogdensburg	2,565	0	0	0	0	0	34	9	25	0	0
Old Bridge Township	66,913	70	2	3	25	40	869	153	655	61	3
Old Tappan	6,151	4	0	0	0	4	36	6	30	0	0
Oradell	7,811	1	0	0	0	1	81	9	72	0	0
Orange	31,057	335	7	6	201	121	1,095	433	422	240	1
Oxford Township	2,612	1	0	0	0	1	9	2	7	0	0
Palisades Park	19,789	24	2	0	3	19	127	42	83	2	2
Palmyra	7,400	18	0	2	4	12	155	27	119	9	1
Paramus	26,340	92	0	0	31	61	1,757	80	1,631	46	4
Park Ridge	9,013	7	0	0	1	6	36	8	27	1	0
Parsippany-Troy Hills Township	50,760	19	0	2	9	8	566	212	327	27	0
Passaic	67,356	635	6	6	278	345	1,630	390	1,097	143	0
Paterson	146,356	1,566	18	44	769	735	4,521	1,491	2,329	701	15
Paulsboro	6,121	19	0	0	9	10	254	54	189	11	0
Peapack and Gladstone	2,600	1	0	1	0	0	17	4	11	2	0
Pemberton	1,634	8	0	0	2	6	28	6	17	5	0
Pemberton Township	28,107	54	0	9	14	31	572	176	366	30	4
Pennington	2,674	2	0	0	1	1	19	2	17	0	0
Pennsauken Township	35,105	131	4	9	60	58	1,257	301	869	87	4
Penns Grove	4,686	33	1	0	20	12	200	69	123	8	1
Pennsville Township	13,402	31	0	2	7	22	496	90	389	17	3
Pequannock Township	17,494	10	0	0	1	9	165	41	121	3	0
Perth Amboy	49,156	200	1	0	101	98	1,136	268	758	110	0
Phillipsburg	14,500	49	0	8	17	24	347	78	257	12	4
Pine Beach	2,110	1	0	0	0	1	29	2	27	0	0
Pine Hill	11,449	52	0	1	13	38	282	82	196	4	9
Pine Valley	24	0	0	0	0	0	4	4	0	0	0
Piscataway Township	52,897	60	1	4	18	37	620	102	465	53	2
Pitman	9,271	4	0	0	2	2	150	18	128	4	1
Plainfield	46,459	489	8	13	237	231	1,446	387	929	130	9
Plainsboro Township	21,407	17	0	1	3	13	179	29	145	5	1
Pleasantville	18,996	193	3	4	94	92	629	240	356	33	5
Plumsted Township	8,446	9	0	1	1	7	64	18	44	2	0
Pohatcong Township	3,331	7	0	0	2	5	109	5	103	1	0
Point Pleasant	20,569	19	0	0	5	14	352	59	288	5	0
Point Pleasant Beach	5,492	11	0	1	1	9	214	26	183	5	0
Pompton Lakes	11,150	10	0	0	2	8	101	19	82	0	0
Princeton	13,448	21	0	0	4	17	374	65	304	5	5
Princeton Township	17,581	14	1	0	3	10	170	40	128	2	0
Prospect Park	5,623	13	0	0	7	6	146	54	81	11	1
Rahway	29,443	97	0	1	45	51	473	104	331	38	2
Ramsey	14,846	10	0	0	0	10	156	13	136	7	2
Randolph Township	25,391	5	0	1	1	3	223	35	184	4	0
Raritan	7,487	11	0	0	2	9	164	18	144	2	1
Raritan Township	22,934	11	0	0	3	8	231	23	200	8	0
Readington Township	16,302	5	0	2	1	2	132	19	110	3	1
Red Bank	11,992	55	0	5	26	24	285	48	229	8	1
Ridgefield	10,953	9	0	0	6	3	59	17	31	11	0
Ridgefield Park	12,426	24	1	1	6	16	136	27	100	9	1
Ridgewood	24,260	7	0	0	0	7	215	50	165	0	1
Ringwood	12,822	3	2	0	0	1	79	11	67	1	1
Riverdale	3,590	5	0	0	0	5	105	9	93	3	0
River Edge	10,733	2	0	1	0	1	106	17	88	1	0
Riverside Township	7,703	13	0	3	5	5	112	24	81	7	0
Riverton	2,633	5	0	2	2	1	48	4	44	0	0
River Vale Township	9,730	0	0	0	0	0	15	5	10	0	0
Robbinsville Township	12,573	6	0	0	2	4	117	31	82	4	1
Rochelle Park Township	6,159	3	0	0	3	0	82	22	54	6	0
Rockaway	6,276	3	0	1	0	2	59	13	42	4	0
Rockaway Township	25,860	15	0	1	5	9	505	42	456	7	1
Rockleigh	390	0	0	0	0	0	1	1	0	0	0

[1] The FBI does not publish arson data unless it receives data from either the agency or the state for all 12 months of the calendar year.

Table 8.   Offenses Known to Law Enforcement, by State and City, 2010—*Continued*

(Number)

State/city	Population	Violent crime	Murder and non-negligent man-slaughter	Forcible rape	Robbery	Aggravated assault	Property crime	Burglary	Larceny-theft	Motor vehicle theft	Arson[1]
NEW JERSEY—*Continued*											
Roseland	5,390	5	0	1	1	3	46	11	33	2	0
Roselle	20,721	91	0	1	53	37	405	124	233	48	7
Roselle Park	12,899	17	0	0	8	9	109	28	75	6	0
Roxbury Township	23,485	8	0	0	3	5	253	22	225	6	0
Rumson	7,371	4	0	0	0	4	64	19	45	0	2
Runnemede	8,449	25	0	1	14	10	330	58	253	19	1
Rutherford	17,491	8	0	0	1	7	247	73	160	14	1
Saddle Brook Township	14,371	19	0	0	7	12	318	44	263	11	0
Saddle River	3,883	1	0	0	0	1	19	6	11	2	0
Salem	5,855	61	3	5	20	33	239	74	160	5	7
Sayreville	42,680	42	0	3	11	28	635	126	457	52	1
Scotch Plains Township	23,231	7	0	0	2	5	213	66	140	7	0
Sea Bright	1,818	2	0	0	0	2	33	2	31	0	0
Sea Girt	2,107	5	0	0	0	5	37	15	22	0	0
Sea Isle City	2,938	8	0	0	1	7	314	124	187	3	3
Seaside Heights	3,397	48	0	1	11	36	322	63	244	15	1
Seaside Park	2,351	4	0	0	3	1	88	15	71	2	0
Secaucus	15,852	30	0	0	17	13	480	46	412	22	0
Ship Bottom	1,479	0	0	0	0	0	59	6	53	0	0
Shrewsbury	3,815	6	0	0	3	3	101	11	87	3	0
Somerdale	5,116	7	0	0	4	3	176	40	125	11	0
Somers Point	11,401	48	0	2	11	35	425	92	330	3	1
Somerville	12,847	14	0	3	4	7	177	28	137	12	0
South Amboy	7,802	17	0	2	4	11	86	13	66	7	1
South Bound Brook	5,242	2	0	0	0	2	16	4	12	0	0
South Brunswick Township	41,861	31	0	2	9	20	466	99	343	24	0
South Hackensack Township	2,271	6	0	1	2	3	71	9	52	10	0
South Harrison Township	3,298	2	0	0	0	2	29	9	20	0	0
South Orange	16,024	58	0	0	41	17	414	135	248	31	1
South Plainfield	22,848	45	1	0	20	24	412	59	323	30	2
South River	15,809	32	0	3	4	25	228	31	191	6	2
South Toms River	3,759	9	0	0	4	5	92	21	66	5	1
Sparta Township	19,466	1	0	0	0	1	132	15	116	1	0
Spotswood	8,261	5	0	0	1	4	104	20	83	1	2
Springfield	15,353	9	0	0	4	5	211	34	162	15	2
Springfield Township	3,498	2	0	0	0	2	30	11	15	4	0
Spring Lake	3,561	1	0	0	0	1	115	22	92	1	0
Spring Lake Heights	5,164	1	0	0	0	1	35	10	25	0	0
Stafford Township	27,444	14	0	2	3	9	404	48	348	8	0
Stanhope	3,586	3	0	0	0	3	42	4	37	1	0
Stone Harbor	1,011	1	0	1	0	0	152	14	136	2	0
Stratford	7,067	13	0	0	3	10	143	37	100	6	2
Summit	20,783	19	1	1	2	15	219	39	176	4	0
Surf City	1,590	0	0	0	0	0	41	3	37	1	0
Swedesboro	2,422	3	0	0	0	3	14	3	9	2	0
Tavistock	33	0	0	0	0	0	0	0	0	0	1
Teaneck Township	38,666	78	3	2	36	37	599	127	448	24	9
Tenafly	14,864	3	0	0	0	3	101	21	74	6	0
Teterboro	17	0	0	0	0	0	18	2	12	4	0
Tewksbury Township	6,168	0	0	0	0	0	18	7	10	1	1
Tinton Falls	20,257	10	0	1	5	4	449	54	380	15	0
Toms River Township	98,282	101	3	5	52	41	2,849	547	2,274	28	7
Totowa	10,809	20	0	0	3	17	314	30	253	31	0
Trenton	83,552	1,198	15	13	500	670	2,516	865	1,289	362	45
Tuckerton	3,984	6	1	0	0	5	51	7	40	4	1
Union Beach	6,647	25	0	0	6	19	102	21	78	3	1
Union City	61,855	261	7	0	111	143	1,310	237	921	152	3
Union Township	53,945	104	1	2	64	37	1,023	130	777	116	3
Upper Saddle River	8,612	2	0	0	0	2	44	10	30	4	0
Ventnor City	12,177	25	0	1	11	13	367	119	245	3	1
Vernon Township	24,993	16	0	1	1	14	414	47	361	6	0
Verona	12,636	6	0	1	1	4	113	24	81	8	0
Vineland	59,924	223	3	6	83	131	2,127	515	1,536	76	7
Voorhees Township	32,441	37	0	5	14	18	807	139	646	22	3
Waldwick	9,643	4	0	0	1	3	70	6	64	0	0
Wallington	11,355	11	0	0	4	7	157	38	113	6	2
Wall Township	26,387	18	0	0	2	16	375	98	263	14	0
Wanaque	12,430	8	0	0	1	7	120	8	109	3	2
Warren Township	16,356	5	0	1	1	3	75	16	59	0	0
Washington	6,718	8	0	0	0	8	114	15	98	1	0
Washington Township, Bergen County	9,664	5	0	2	0	3	26	8	18	0	0
Washington Township, Glouchester County	52,251	87	0	1	34	52	1,218	189	985	44	10
Washington Township, Morris County	18,615	7	0	1	0	6	87	15	69	3	2

[1] The FBI does not publish arson data unless it receives data from either the agency or the state for all 12 months of the calendar year.

Table 8.   Offenses Known to Law Enforcement, by State and City, 2010—*Continued*

(Number)

State/city	Population	Violent crime	Murder and non-negligent man-slaughter	Forcible rape	Robbery	Aggravated assault	Property crime	Burglary	Larceny-theft	Motor vehicle theft	Arson[1]
NEW JERSEY—*Continued*											
Washington Township, Warren County	6,949	1	0	0	0	1	64	7	55	2	0
Watchung	6,752	4	0	1	2	1	333	21	309	3	0
Waterford Township	10,774	22	0	2	7	13	189	43	142	4	1
Wayne Township	54,234	32	0	4	15	13	1,321	113	1,147	61	0
Weehawken Township	12,351	22	0	0	19	3	264	34	201	29	1
Wenonah	2,376	0	0	0	0	0	32	13	17	2	1
Westampton Township	8,877	19	1	3	10	5	171	39	128	4	0
West Amwell Township	3,002	7	0	0	0	7	31	10	19	2	0
West Caldwell Township	10,392	4	0	0	1	3	81	15	63	3	1
West Cape May	981	0	0	0	0	0	34	5	27	2	0
West Deptford Township	22,482	28	0	2	12	14	495	117	353	25	2
Westfield	29,867	17	0	2	6	9	237	43	185	9	0
West Long Branch	8,482	12	0	0	5	7	230	38	189	3	0
West Milford Township	28,049	18	0	4	6	8	296	103	185	8	9
West New York	46,907	171	3	5	79	84	736	203	448	85	7
West Orange	42,590	87	0	5	35	47	581	131	402	48	3
Westville	4,490	25	1	0	3	21	180	46	124	10	1
West Wildwood	404	1	0	0	0	1	22	3	19	0	0
West Windsor Township	27,202	12	0	1	8	3	399	47	343	9	0
Westwood	10,739	6	0	0	0	6	73	12	49	12	0
Wharton	6,108	6	0	1	0	5	122	39	80	3	0
Wildwood	5,222	58	0	2	21	35	551	160	385	6	0
Wildwood Crest	4,058	6	0	0	1	5	178	40	137	1	0
Willingboro Township	36,888	108	0	15	41	52	652	216	401	35	7
Winfield Township	1,445	0	0	0	0	0	24	7	16	1	0
Winslow Township	40,393	186	0	4	24	158	772	255	468	49	7
Woodbridge Township	98,576	167	1	9	67	90	2,296	267	1,904	125	3
Woodbury	10,527	42	0	2	18	22	475	96	360	19	3
Woodbury Heights	3,079	4	0	0	3	1	126	19	106	1	1
Woodcliff Lake	6,020	1	0	0	1	0	43	4	38	1	0
Woodland Park	12,383	15	0	0	9	6	210	46	151	13	0
Woodlynne	2,693	21	0	1	8	12	115	43	61	11	1
Wood-Ridge	7,491	2	0	0	1	1	91	19	62	10	0
Woodstown	3,392	4	0	0	0	4	54	8	44	2	0
Woolwich Township	10,659	4	0	0	2	2	79	14	63	2	0
Wyckoff Township	17,056	9	0	0	0	9	94	19	73	2	1
NEW MEXICO											
Alamogordo	36,555	97	4	8	2	83	1,036	203	798	35	5
Albuquerque	545,389	4,291	42	338	940	2,971	26,372	5,465	18,134	2,773	121
Angel Fire	976	8	0	0	0	8	46	25	21	0	0
Aztec	7,135	43	0	2	3	38	174	28	141	5	7
Bayard	2,423	3	0	0	0	3	36	15	20	1	0
Belen	7,522	82	0	3	9	70	736	342	352	42	2
Bernalillo	9,878	124	1	2	5	116	330	91	221	18	0
Bloomfield	7,462	86	0	7	1	78	166	38	117	11	4
Bosque Farms	4,154	5	0	0	0	5	37	8	23	6	1
Carlsbad	26,801	197	0	29	20	148	1,376	382	936	58	10
Carrizozo	1,065	5	0	0	1	4	9	4	4	1	0
Cimarron	799	2	0	0	0	2	5	2	2	1	0
Clovis	33,359	226	2	34	30	160	1,892	706	1,124	62	25
Cuba	1,550	33	0	1	0	32	0	0	0	0	0
Deming	15,655	74	0	1	8	65	579	186	366	27	0
Edgewood	4,823	4	0	0	1	3	38	16	20	2	0
Espanola	9,846	229	2	2	19	206	846	325	494	27	13
Estancia	1,606	2	0	0	0	2	28	10	18	0	0
Eunice	2,905	5	0	0	0	5	49	23	25	1	0
Farmington	44,563	477	3	63	25	386	1,678	319	1,270	89	20
Gallup	19,825	364	2	29	56	277	1,546	250	1,178	118	6
Grants[6]	8,845		0	8	6		265	151	89	25	0
Hobbs	32,642	249	9	39	33	168	1,685	419	1,206	60	7
Hurley	1,427	0	0	0	0	0	19	10	9	0	0
Jal	2,133	6	0	0	1	5	27	10	13	4	4
Las Cruces	97,065	408	3	11	62	332	4,326	1,110	3,026	190	11
Las Vegas	13,797	175	1	9	9	156	542	173	342	27	7
Logan	1,002	3	0	0	0	3	70	43	25	2	0
Lordsburg	2,886	2	0	0	0	2	2	1	1	0	0
Los Alamos[6]	18,311		0	2	1		186	33	148	5	3
Los Lunas[6]	15,054		0	7	3		546	75	412	59	1
Lovington	10,422	46	0	6	1	39	369	193	159	17	0
Milan	2,566	20	1	0	0	19	74	37	31	6	0
Moriarty	2,014	5	0	0	0	5	91	41	41	9	0
Portales	12,468	69	1	7	3	58	374	108	256	10	0
Raton	6,330	36	0	0	2	34	181	83	83	15	1

[1] The FBI does not publish arson data unless it receives data from either the agency or the state for all 12 months of the calendar year.

[6] The FBI determined that the agency did not follow national Uniform Crime Reporting Program guidelines for reporting an offense. Consequently, this figure is not included in this table.

Table 8.   Offenses Known to Law Enforcement, by State and City, 2010—*Continued*

(Number)

State/city	Population	Violent crime	Murder and non-negligent man-slaughter	Forcible rape	Robbery	Aggravated assault	Property crime	Burglary	Larceny-theft	Motor vehicle theft	Arson[1]
NEW MEXICO—*Continued*											
Rio Rancho	87,608	160	0	7	18	135	1,476	344	1,023	109	12
Roswell	47,238	351	6	16	36	293	2,325	541	1,714	70	13
Ruidoso	9,504	30	1	4	2	23	240	92	142	6	1
Ruidoso Downs	2,740	39	0	4	0	35	89	20	64	5	0
Santa Clara	1,875	3	0	0	0	3	17	11	2	4	0
Santa Fe	76,442	367	8	39	81	239	4,349	2,392	1,781	176	9
Santa Rosa	2,593	17	0	0	0	17	66	32	31	3	0
Silver City	10,459	98	0	6	6	86	628	156	442	30	4
Socorro	9,056	77	0	0	4	73	336	93	229	14	2
Sunland Park	15,224	20	0	5	2	13	215	41	149	25	1
Taos	5,689	46	0	3	7	36	541	182	347	12	0
Taos Ski Valley	59	2	0	0	0	2	7	2	5	0	0
Tatum	793	0	0	0	0	0	39	0	38	1	0
Texico	997	0	0	0	0	0	8	4	4	0	0
Truth or Consequences	7,194	47	0	5	2	40	174	44	124	6	1
Tucumcari	5,255	45	0	5	2	38	282	136	142	4	0
Tularosa	3,078	24	0	3	0	21	83	23	60	0	0
NEW YORK											
Adams Village	1,664	1	0	0	0	1	17	7	10	0	0
Addison Town and Village	2,466	4	0	1	0	3	57	16	41	0	0
Akron Village	2,923	2	0	0	0	2	37	7	30	0	0
Albany	92,713	981	2	42	316	621	4,643	926	3,488	229	16
Alexandria Bay Village	1,114	1	0	0	0	1	21	7	14	0	0
Alfred Village	4,933	7	0	2	1	4	52	14	38	0	0
Allegany Village	1,715	2	0	1	0	1	17	2	15	0	0
Altamont Village	1,676	0	0	0	0	0	14	3	11	0	0
Amherst Town	109,138	119	2	8	33	76	2,066	218	1,801	47	7
Amity Town and Belmont Village	2,187	0	0	0	0	0	1	0	1	0	0
Amityville Village	9,962	10	0	0	4	6	153	16	130	7	0
Amsterdam5	17,187	45	1	1	9	34	566	138	416	12	7
Arcade Village	1,836	1	0	0	0	1	45	4	40	1	0
Ardsley Village	4,855	1	0	0	0	1	24	6	17	1	0
Asharoken Village	658	0	0	0	0	0	1	1	0	0	0
Attica Village	2,348	4	0	0	0	4	11	2	9	0	0
Auburn	26,448	96	0	8	12	76	976	172	790	14	4
Avon Village	2,850	4	0	0	1	3	30	2	28	0	0
Baldwinsville Village	7,201	5	0	1	1	3	140	20	114	6	0
Ballston Spa Village	5,444	8	0	0	2	6	144	39	103	2	0
Batavia	14,871	44	0	7	7	30	516	88	419	9	3
Bath Village	5,330	17	2	2	4	9	205	49	153	3	3
Beacon	14,342	63	1	3	11	48	320	74	231	15	3
Bedford Town	18,403	2	0	0	0	2	36	6	27	3	0
Bethlehem Town	32,862	20	0	6	1	13	495	87	399	9	1
Binghamton	43,628	266	4	18	70	174	2,085	423	1,644	18	2
Bolivar Village	1,069	0	0	0	0	0	7	1	6	0	1
Bolton Town	2,129	3	0	0	0	3	23	10	13	0	0
Boonville Village	1,996	0	0	0	0	0	7	2	5	0	0
Brant Town	1,801	1	0	0	0	1	34	10	24	0	0
Brewster	2,088	0	0	0	0	0	7	1	5	1	0
Briarcliff Manor Village	7,864	1	0	0	0	1	18	3	15	0	0
Brighton Town	33,701	45	0	6	13	26	1,051	150	877	24	0
Brockport Village	8,269	16	0	5	3	8	184	35	144	5	0
Bronxville Village	6,452	4	0	0	2	2	52	6	43	3	0
Brownville Village	1,052	0	0	0	0	0	9	1	8	0	0
Buchanan Village	2,223	1	0	0	1	0	11	6	4	1	0
Buffalo	265,128	3,599	55	157	1,466	1,921	14,753	4,296	9,027	1,430	90
Cairo Town	6,411	5	0	0	0	5	29	5	24	0	0
Cambridge Village	1,786	2	0	1	0	1	35	8	25	2	0
Camden Village	2,219	1	0	0	0	1	85	16	64	5	0
Camillus Town and Village	23,245	14	0	0	4	10	303	38	260	5	3
Canandaigua	11,054	20	0	3	3	14	362	57	298	7	1
Canisteo Village	2,175	3	0	0	0	3	43	6	37	0	0
Canton Village	6,065	2	0	1	1	0	88	9	78	1	0
Cape Vincent Village	785	0	0	0	0	0	7	0	7	0	0
Carmel Town	34,119	12	0	0	2	10	272	48	218	6	2
Carroll Town	3,410	2	0	0	0	2	8	5	3	0	0
Carthage Village	3,734	3	0	0	0	3	101	17	82	2	0
Catskill Village	4,128	12	0	1	3	8	130	12	118	0	1
Cayuga Heights Village5	3,626	1	0	0	1	0	49	3	46	0	0
Cazenovia Village	2,956	1	0	0	0	1	65	7	58	0	0
Central Square Village	1,749	0	0	0	0	0	35	2	31	2	0
Centre Island Village	441	0	0	0	0	0	4	0	4	0	0
Chatham Village	1,639	15	0	0	0	15	61	9	48	4	0

[1] The FBI does not publish arson data unless it receives data from either the agency or the state for all 12 months of the calendar year.

[5] Because of changes in the state/local agency's reporting practices, figures are not comparable to previous years' data.

Table 8.   Offenses Known to Law Enforcement, by State and City, 2010—*Continued*

(Number)

State/city	Population	Violent crime	Murder and non-negligent man-slaughter	Forcible rape	Robbery	Aggravated assault	Property crime	Burglary	Larceny-theft	Motor vehicle theft	Arson[1]
NEW YORK—*Continued*											
Cheektowaga Town	76,671	155	1	17	52	85	2,748	431	2,221	96	7
Chester Town[5]	9,972	0	0	0	0	0	61	10	50	1	0
Chester Village	3,548	4	0	0	3	1	148	5	142	1	0
Chittenango Village	4,811	3	0	1	1	1	72	15	54	3	0
Cicero Town	28,288	13	0	0	5	8	518	59	447	12	3
Clarkstown Town	78,365	92	0	4	35	53	1,700	156	1,512	32	2
Clifton Springs Village	2,117	0	0	0	0	0	16	2	14	0	0
Clyde Village	2,043	4	0	0	1	3	32	8	24	0	0
Cobleskill Village	4,486	4	0	1	2	1	162	19	140	3	0
Coeymans Town	7,939	15	0	0	1	14	48	11	35	2	1
Cohoes	14,884	40	0	1	11	28	302	92	195	15	1
Colchester Town	1,988	0	0	0	0	0	0	0	0	0	0
Colonie Town	77,078	54	0	3	31	20	2,259	228	1,988	43	9
Cooperstown Village	1,849	1	0	0	0	1	28	4	24	0	0
Copake Town	3,187	1	0	0	0	1	25	9	16	0	0
Corning	10,046	51	0	5	6	40	398	66	330	2	2
Cornwall Town[2]	9,724	0	0	0	0	0		6		0	0
Cortland[5]	17,930	45	0	6	10	29	357	112	228	17	2
Crawford Town[5]	9,492	11	0	0	0	11	67	10	52	5	0
Cuba Town	3,217	2	0	1	0	1	122	17	103	2	0
Dansville Village	4,363	11	0	4	2	5	114	4	110	0	0
Deerpark Town	8,495	8	0	0	3	5	142	60	81	1	0
Delhi Village	2,749	3	0	0	1	2	42	11	29	2	0
Depew Village	14,966	26	0	4	5	17	344	67	268	9	3
Deposit Village	1,547	0	0	0	0	0	20	1	19	0	0
Dewitt Town	21,202	37	1	1	14	21	592	81	492	19	6
Dexter Village	1,194	0	0	0	0	0	1	0	1	0	0
Dobbs Ferry Village	11,151	7	0	0	5	2	135	21	112	2	0
Dolgeville Village	1,973	3	0	0	0	3	59	6	52	1	0
Dryden Village	1,807	3	0	0	0	3	114	25	89	0	0
Dunkirk	11,801	45	0	7	16	22	353	59	285	9	1
Durham Town	2,664	0	0	0	0	0	10	5	5	0	0
East Aurora-Aurora Town	13,307	3	0	0	0	3	144	29	108	7	0
East Chester Town	18,612	8	0	0	5	3	203	23	174	6	0
East Greenbush Town	16,873	14	0	1	6	7	405	41	359	5	3
East Hampton Town	19,860	9	0	0	2	7	494	97	385	12	1
East Hampton Village	1,395	3	0	1	0	2	137	10	123	4	0
East Rochester Village	6,153	9	0	1	1	7	131	19	109	3	0
East Syracuse Village	2,924	9	0	0	4	5	165	25	132	8	1
Eden Town	7,604	3	0	2	1	0	42	11	31	0	0
Ellenville Village	3,851	33	0	0	4	29	95	30	62	3	0
Ellicott Town	5,162	12	0	0	1	11	224	61	159	4	0
Ellicottville	518	0	0	0	0	0	113	13	100	0	0
Elmira	28,823	108	4	5	29	70	1,057	259	773	25	3
Elmira Heights Village	3,849	7	0	0	3	4	88	19	67	2	0
Elmira Town	5,808	1	0	0	0	1	4	1	3	0	0
Elmsford Village	4,722	6	0	0	4	2	43	7	26	10	1
Endicott Village	12,103	43	0	4	11	28	604	117	475	12	0
Evans Town	16,561	25	0	3	3	19	328	75	242	11	4
Fairport Village	5,382	1	0	0	1	0	40	10	28	2	0
Fallsburg Town	12,285	30	2	2	1	25	207	63	135	9	1
Fishkill Town	19,772	5	0	0	0	5	269	32	234	3	1
Fishkill Village	1,666	0	0	0	0	0	30	1	28	1	0
Floral Park Village	15,699	16	0	0	11	5	79	16	52	11	1
Fort Plain Village	2,144	6	0	0	1	5	75	15	59	1	0
Frankfort Town	4,704	4	0	0	0	4	55	16	37	2	1
Franklinville Village	1,659	1	0	0	0	1	42	4	38	0	0
Fredonia Village	10,982	18	1	2	4	11	309	24	281	4	0
Freeport Village	43,458	213	1	3	103	106	1,026	153	772	101	4
Friendship Town	1,788	0	0	0	0	0	12	3	9	0	0
Fulton City	10,956	34	0	4	13	17	523	99	417	7	2
Garden City Village	22,314	9	0	0	3	6	354	39	305	10	0
Gates Town	28,357	44	0	1	20	23	938	89	828	21	1
Geddes Town	10,269	7	0	0	2	5	226	28	197	1	1
Geneseo Village	7,679	0	0	0	0	0	127	6	121	0	2
Geneva	13,090	33	0	4	8	21	324	63	253	8	1
Germantown Town	1,929	0	0	0	0	0	3	0	3	0	0
Glen Cove	26,661	23	0	1	10	12	227	25	196	6	0
Glen Park Village	501	0	0	0	0	0	5	1	4	0	0
Glens Falls	13,650	42	0	2	3	37	209	29	177	3	0
Glenville Town	21,844	15	0	1	5	9	372	65	303	4	0
Gloversville	14,713	82	1	6	14	61	636	116	495	25	1
Goshen Town	8,257	4	0	0	1	3	50	12	35	3	0

[1] The FBI does not publish arson data unless it receives data from either the agency or the state for all 12 months of the calendar year.

[2] The FBI determined that the agency's data were underreported. Consequently, those data are not included in this table.

[5] Because of changes in the state/local agency's reporting practices, figures are not comparable to previous years' data.

Table 8. Offenses Known to Law Enforcement, by State and City, 2010—*Continued*

(Number)

State/city	Population	Violent crime	Murder and non-negligent man-slaughter	Forcible rape	Robbery	Aggravated assault	Property crime	Burglary	Larceny-theft	Motor vehicle theft	Arson[1]
NEW YORK—*Continued*											
Goshen Village	5,553	3	0	0	0	3	78	11	66	1	0
Gouverneur Village	3,925	6	0	1	0	5	202	44	157	1	1
Granville Village	2,490	3	0	0	0	3	43	14	29	0	1
Great Neck Estates Village	2,760	0	0	0	0	0	5	4	1	0	0
Greece Town	92,282	119	5	12	26	76	2,552	384	2,108	60	3
Greenburgh Town	43,314	70	0	3	23	44	634	71	546	17	2
Greene Village	1,597	0	0	0	0	0	0	0	0	0	0
Green Island Village	2,529	6	0	0	0	6	59	11	43	5	0
Greenwich Village	1,791	4	0	0	0	4	31	8	22	1	0
Greenwood Lake Village	3,382	4	0	1	1	2	51	11	39	1	0
Groton Village	2,380	3	0	1	0	2	66	7	59	0	0
Guilderland Town	32,840	11	0	4	3	4	982	67	906	9	0
Hamburg Town	43,642	37	0	3	13	21	998	179	789	30	8
Hamburg Village	9,231	5	0	3	2	0	221	42	174	5	2
Hammondsport Village	717	0	0	0	0	0	17	3	14	0	0
Hancock Village	1,050	1	0	0	0	1	4	2	2	0	0
Harriman Village	2,312	1	0	0	1	0	12	3	9	0	0
Harrison Town	26,710	20	1	2	1	16	254	29	215	10	1
Hastings-on-Hudson Village	7,887	7	0	1	1	5	139	14	122	3	0
Haverstraw Town	37,489	65	0	6	27	32	438	106	312	20	3
Hempstead Village	53,443	452	12	3	218	219	1,051	304	613	134	8
Herkimer Village	6,824	74	0	2	6	66	354	49	305	0	1
Highland Falls Village	3,674	0	0	0	0	0	47	6	41	0	0
Holley Village	1,645	6	0	1	0	5	40	11	25	4	0
Homer Village	3,135	1	0	0	0	1	59	8	51	0	0
Hornell	8,441	19	0	1	0	18	157	22	132	3	0
Horseheads Village	6,193	12	0	1	1	10	145	16	123	6	0
Hudson	6,691	30	0	3	3	24	262	36	220	6	0
Hudson Falls Village	6,491	18	0	2	2	14	139	29	105	5	1
Hunter Town	2,650	3	0	0	1	2	6	4	2	0	0
Huntington Bay Village	1,504	0	0	0	0	0	14	2	12	0	0
Hyde Park Town	19,992	18	0	0	4	14	210	57	147	6	0
Ilion Village	7,844	14	0	5	1	8	232	33	193	6	1
Independence Town	1,009	0	0	0	0	0	4	1	3	0	0
Inlet Town	363	0	0	0	0	0	10	4	6	0	0
Irondequoit Town	49,101	93	0	2	32	59	1,482	251	1,181	50	1
Irvington Village	6,615	0	0	0	0	0	29	6	23	0	0
Ithaca	29,791	60	0	4	23	33	1,143	152	963	28	0
Jamestown	28,785	180	0	24	35	121	1,281	342	895	44	9
Johnson City Village	14,384	65	1	5	11	48	885	119	759	7	1
Johnstown	8,354	14	0	4	2	8	301	45	253	3	1
Jordan Village	1,297	0	0	0	0	0	3	1	2	0	0
Kenmore Village	14,652	27	0	4	11	12	339	49	279	11	0
Kensington Village	1,193	2	0	0	1	1	2	0	2	0	0
Kent Town	13,999	5	0	0	1	4	91	19	66	6	0
Kings Point Village	5,351	1	0	0	0	1	18	8	9	1	0
Kingston	22,012	81	1	5	29	46	611	142	451	18	4
Lackawanna	17,202	115	0	7	24	84	469	125	310	34	0
Lake Placid Village	2,700	0	0	0	0	0	71	18	51	2	0
Lake Success Village	2,869	3	0	0	1	2	42	8	31	3	0
Lakewood-Busti	7,273	5	0	1	3	1	275	22	248	5	0
Lancaster Town	23,380	21	0	3	4	14	507	73	430	4	5
Larchmont Village	6,517	2	0	0	2	0	81	7	72	2	0
Le Roy Village	4,057	12	0	1	5	6	110	25	85	0	0
Lewisboro Town	12,425	0	0	0	0	0	40	2	37	1	0
Lewiston Town and Village	16,604	4	0	0	2	2	204	43	142	19	3
Liberty Village	3,804	20	0	3	0	17	174	35	135	4	1
Little Falls	4,751	30	0	0	0	30	151	16	134	1	3
Liverpool Village	2,305	0	0	0	0	0	33	10	23	0	0
Lloyd Harbor Village	3,722	1	0	0	0	1	16	1	14	1	0
Lloyd Town	10,623	9	0	2	0	7	117	23	92	2	1
Lockport	20,175	61	0	3	15	43	761	151	587	23	6
Lowville Village	3,077	5	0	0	1	4	89	15	71	3	0
Lynbrook Village	19,656	26	0	1	11	14	164	16	141	7	1
Lyons Village	3,334	24	0	1	4	19	151	36	112	3	0
Macedon Town and Village	8,770	5	0	2	1	2	60	8	52	0	0
Malone Village	5,649	7	0	5	1	1	262	50	207	5	0
Malverne Village	8,785	2	0	0	1	1	47	6	41	0	0
Mamaroneck Town	11,466	8	0	0	5	3	144	21	121	2	0
Mamaroneck Village	18,309	15	1	1	1	12	135	30	101	4	0
Manchester Village	1,411	0	0	0	0	0	0	0	0	0	0
Manlius Town	24,597	16	0	1	6	9	444	67	369	8	0
Marcellus Village	1,792	0	0	0	0	0	11	3	8	0	0

[1] The FBI does not publish arson data unless it receives data from either the agency or the state for all 12 months of the calendar year.

Table 8. Offenses Known to Law Enforcement, by State and City, 2010—*Continued*

(Number)

State/city	Population	Violent crime	Murder and non-negligent man-slaughter	Forcible rape	Robbery	Aggravated assault	Property crime	Burglary	Larceny-theft	Motor vehicle theft	Arson[1]
NEW YORK—*Continued*											
Marlborough Town	8,178	17	0	0	0	17	142	29	110	3	0
Massena Village	10,286	19	0	3	7	9	397	64	328	5	3
Mechanicville	4,827	5	0	0	2	3	105	21	78	6	0
Medina Village	5,933	22	0	0	2	20	238	53	177	8	0
Menands Village	3,734	6	0	0	2	4	169	27	141	1	1
Middleport Village	1,746	0	0	0	0	0	36	2	34	0	0
Middletown	25,701	150	1	7	63	79	1,171	194	949	28	3
Monroe Village	8,172	19	0	6	7	6	348	37	303	8	0
Montgomery Village	4,977	0	0	0	0	0	11	0	11	0	0
Monticello Village	6,240	59	1	3	17	38	168	60	103	5	1
Moravia Village	1,263	1	0	0	0	1	12	2	8	2	0
Moriah Town	3,400	5	0	0	0	5	7	1	6	0	0
Mount Hope Town	7,540	2	0	0	0	2	29	4	23	2	0
Mount Kisco Village	10,314	27	0	1	6	20	164	25	134	5	4
Mount Morris Village	2,804	5	0	1	0	4	102	7	93	2	0
Mount Pleasant Town	26,257	9	0	1	4	4	186	29	155	2	0
Mount Vernon	68,081	678	2	12	330	334	1,584	354	1,052	178	5
Nassau Village	1,098	4	0	0	0	4	29	2	25	2	0
Newark Village	8,871	41	0	3	1	37	293	64	228	1	3
New Berlin Town	1,672	3	0	0	0	3	55	24	30	1	0
Newburgh	27,836	522	11	7	195	309	1,132	342	724	66	14
Newburgh Town	31,293	31	2	0	11	18	1,259	101	1,126	32	1
New Castle Town	17,598	3	0	0	2	1	107	29	75	3	0
New Hartford Town and Village	18,875	12	0	0	4	8	716	47	662	7	0
New Paltz Town and Village	14,279	55	0	4	7	44	244	41	197	6	0
New Rochelle	73,648	217	1	5	93	118	1,216	140	1,021	55	2
New Windsor Town	25,211	24	1	0	8	15	472	85	372	15	1
New York	8,336,002	48,489	536	1,036	19,608	27,309	139,615	17,926	111,370	10,319	
New York Mills Village	3,245	3	0	1	1	1	50	6	44	0	1
Niagara Falls	50,321	610	5	23	185	397	2,924	956	1,834	134	18
Niskayuna Town	21,735	13	0	1	5	7	394	56	332	6	0
Nissequogue Village	1,608	0	0	0	0	0	9	1	8	0	0
Norfolk Town	4,469	0	0	0	0	0	48	16	30	2	0
North Castle Town	12,173	1	0	0	0	1	71	16	51	4	0
North Greenbush Town	11,833	14	0	3	2	9	255	27	217	11	0
Northport Village	7,633	1	0	0	0	1	75	18	57	0	0
North Syracuse Village	6,477	6	0	0	0	6	79	10	64	5	1
North Tonawanda	30,564	54	0	8	12	34	583	147	422	14	2
Northville Village	1,146	0	0	0	0	0	11	0	11	0	0
Norwich	6,778	9	0	4	2	3	285	35	243	7	0
Nunda Town and Village	2,892	0	0	0	0	0	15	1	12	2	0
Ocean Beach Village	147	0	0	0	0	0	55	1	54	0	0
Ogdensburg	10,814	31	1	4	3	23	564	95	455	14	1
Ogden Town	19,177	18	0	2	2	14	380	42	331	7	1
Old Brookville Village	2,310	0	0	0	0	0	72	11	59	2	0
Old Westbury Village	5,329	2	0	0	0	2	25	4	21	0	0
Olean	13,778	73	1	5	4	63	556	92	460	4	1
Oneida	10,508	13	1	0	3	9	462	47	411	4	2
Oneonta City	12,785	75	0	3	5	67	353	84	259	10	4
Orangetown Town	36,021	43	0	0	18	25	472	68	386	18	0
Orchard Park Town	28,384	14	0	1	4	9	370	55	305	10	0
Oriskany Village	1,373	0	0	0	0	0	22	4	18	0	0
Ossining Town	5,678	0	0	0	0	0	15	2	12	1	0
Ossining Village	23,687	39	0	0	20	19	248	54	191	3	1
Oswego City	16,897	64	0	8	11	45	729	155	561	13	2
Oxford Village	1,493	0	0	0	0	0	4	0	4	0	0
Oyster Bay Cove Village	2,290	0	0	0	0	0	8	2	6	0	0
Painted Post Village	1,738	2	0	0	1	1	74	6	63	5	0
Peekskill	24,699	30	1	1	6	22	232	57	172	3	1
Pelham Village	6,418	20	0	0	10	10	100	19	79	2	0
Penn Yan Village	5,025	4	0	1	0	3	177	36	140	1	0
Perry Village	3,571	5	0	1	0	4	85	16	67	2	1
Phelps Village	1,879	0	0	0	0	0	1	0	1	0	0
Piermont Village	2,541	2	0	0	0	2	26	2	24	0	0
Pine Plains Town	2,676	0	0	0	0	0	14	4	10	0	0
Plattekill Town	10,755	17	0	0	1	16	120	38	77	5	1
Plattsburgh City	19,219	30	0	8	7	15	601	112	477	12	6
Pleasantville Village	7,069	2	0	0	1	1	3	0	3	0	0
Port Byron Village	1,207	0	0	0	0	0	0	0	0	0	0
Port Chester Village	27,939	51	0	2	28	21	678	92	558	28	0
Port Dickinson Village	1,557	3	0	0	1	2	13	1	12	0	0
Port Jervis	9,061	29	0	5	7	17	309	57	247	5	3
Portville Village	927	1	0	0	0	1	3	0	3	0	0

[1] The FBI does not publish arson data unless it receives data from either the agency or the state for all 12 months of the calendar year.

Table 8.   Offenses Known to Law Enforcement, by State and City, 2010—*Continued*

(Number)

State/city	Population	Violent crime	Murder and non-negligent man-slaughter	Forcible rape	Robbery	Aggravated assault	Property crime	Burglary	Larceny-theft	Motor vehicle theft	Arson[1]
NEW YORK—*Continued*											
Port Washington	18,808	2	0	0	1	1	121	9	109	3	0
Poughkeepsie	29,175	398	7	21	142	228	1,055	273	729	53	4
Poughkeepsie Town	42,538	39	1	0	25	13	1,330	120	1,202	8	3
Pound Ridge Town	4,915	0	0	0	0	0	97	7	90	0	0
Pulaski Village	2,244	0	0	0	0	0	66	10	56	0	0
Quogue Village	1,174	0	0	0	0	0	40	5	32	3	0
Ramapo Town	77,482	80	1	2	16	61	758	94	648	16	0
Red Hook Village	1,991	3	0	0	0	3	53	6	47	0	0
Rensselaer City	7,760	19	1	2	7	9	213	34	160	19	0
Rhinebeck Village	2,982	4	0	0	0	4	44	7	37	0	0
Riverhead Town	36,120	82	0	2	28	52	1,062	155	879	28	0
Rochester	203,802	2,229	41	99	816	1,273	11,820	3,448	7,620	752	176
Rockville Centre Village	24,188	31	0	0	23	8	291	56	221	14	0
Rome	32,930	40	1	5	8	26	648	158	464	26	5
Rosendale Town	6,138	1	0	0	0	1	55	9	46	0	0
Rotterdam Town	30,025	26	0	0	9	17	781	119	645	17	2
Rouses Point Village	2,265	0	0	0	0	0	10	0	10	0	0
Rye Brook Village	9,575	2	0	0	2	0	92	11	79	2	0
Sag Harbor Village	2,423	1	0	0	0	1	32	5	27	0	0
Salamanca	5,521	33	0	5	6	22	244	56	182	6	1
Sands Point Village	2,848	0	0	0	0	0	13	0	12	1	0
Saranac Lake Village	4,689	9	0	2	0	7	158	34	119	5	0
Saratoga Springs	29,080	31	0	2	9	20	599	92	498	9	0
Saugerties Town	19,375	4	0	2	1	1	278	71	203	4	5
Scarsdale Village	17,530	5	0	0	2	3	215	43	167	5	0
Schenectady	60,751	679	8	53	256	362	3,387	856	2,347	184	35
Schodack Town	11,453	9	0	0	2	7	91	24	64	3	0
Schoharie Village	957	2	0	0	0	2	8	0	8	0	0
Scotia Village	7,978	8	0	0	4	4	219	26	187	6	3
Seneca Falls Village	6,539	11	0	2	0	9	61	11	50	0	1
Shandaken Town	2,990	5	0	0	0	5	101	20	78	3	0
Shawangunk Town	12,570	12	0	0	0	12	121	26	93	2	1
Shelter Island Town	2,555	0	0	0	0	0	51	10	38	3	0
Sherburne Village	1,374	1	0	0	0	1	30	0	30	0	0
Sherrill	3,077	0	0	0	0	0	21	7	14	0	0
Shortsville Village	1,301	0	0	0	0	0	0	0	0	0	0
Sidney Village	3,541	13	0	2	0	11	181	23	155	3	1
Silver Creek Village	2,757	6	0	0	0	6	33	3	30	0	1
Skaneateles Village	2,544	2	0	0	0	2	3	0	3	0	0
Sleepy Hollow Village	10,212	11	0	0	3	8	102	20	80	2	10
Sodus Point Village	1,091	2	0	0	0	2	8	3	5	0	0
Sodus Village	1,572	1	0	0	0	1	47	9	37	1	0
Solvay Village	6,318	21	0	1	8	12	197	36	151	10	1
Southampton Town	52,425	55	0	4	10	41	1,140	248	837	55	3
Southampton Village	4,502	2	0	0	0	2	154	19	131	4	0
South Glens Falls Village	3,371	8	0	2	0	6	85	25	60	0	2
South Nyack Village	3,306	2	0	0	1	1	47	7	40	0	1
Southold Town	20,444	0	0	0	0	0	272	48	222	2	1
Spring Valley Village	24,965	139	1	4	43	91	623	106	491	26	0
Stillwater Town	6,556	0	0	0	0	0	27	2	25	0	0
St. Johnsville Village	1,574	0	0	0	0	0	7	1	6	0	0
Stockport Town	2,750	0	0	0	0	0	14	4	9	1	0
Stony Point Town	15,050	9	0	0	2	7	97	23	71	3	0
Suffern Village	10,917	4	0	0	1	3	56	5	45	6	0
Syracuse	136,284	1,291	15	68	377	831	5,708	2,174	3,167	367	54
Tarrytown Village	11,047	7	0	0	6	1	80	8	70	2	1
Ticonderoga Town	4,853	10	0	4	0	6	67	16	46	5	2
Tonawanda	14,475	21	0	1	2	18	312	32	271	9	0
Tonawanda Town	55,706	129	2	4	33	90	1,115	231	830	54	0
Troy	46,861	423	2	22	137	262	2,352	656	1,551	145	10
Tuckahoe Village	6,196	4	0	0	1	3	8	1	7	0	0
Tupper Lake Village	3,740	4	0	0	0	4	106	25	80	1	1
Tuxedo Park Village	713	0	0	0	0	0	0	0	0	0	0
Tuxedo Town	2,960	1	0	1	0	0	2	0	2	0	0
Ulster Town	12,469	8	0	0	7	1	482	29	443	10	0
Utica	57,153	416	2	25	146	243	2,717	577	2,059	81	10
Vernon Village	1,125	0	0	0	0	0	19	7	12	0	0
Vestal Town	27,146	14	0	0	8	6	546	41	500	5	2
Walden Village	6,991	29	0	3	1	25	51	7	42	2	0
Wallkill Town	27,941	27	0	0	15	12	858	100	745	13	2
Walton Village	2,739	5	1	1	0	3	53	14	37	2	0
Wappingers Falls Village	6,072	8	0	0	4	4	163	14	148	1	0
Warsaw Village	3,527	2	0	0	0	2	76	11	65	0	0

[1] The FBI does not publish arson data unless it receives data from either the agency or the state for all 12 months of the calendar year.

Table 8.   Offenses Known to Law Enforcement, by State and City, 2010—*Continued*

(Number)

State/city	Population	Violent crime	Murder and non-negligent man-slaughter	Forcible rape	Robbery	Aggravated assault	Property crime	Burglary	Larceny-theft	Motor vehicle theft	Arson[1]
NEW YORK—*Continued*											
Washingtonville Village	6,122	8	0	1	0	7	74	4	67	3	0
Waterford Town and Village	8,520	4	0	1	1	2	91	18	67	6	0
Waterloo Village	4,905	13	0	4	2	7	160	22	137	1	1
Watertown	27,267	118	3	14	20	81	1,166	171	972	23	10
Watervliet	9,320	23	0	0	2	21	259	42	200	17	1
Watkins Glen Village	1,951	0	0	0	0	0	95	12	82	1	0
Waverly Village	4,216	3	0	0	0	3	127	30	97	0	0
Wayland Village	1,746	0	0	0	0	0	27	3	24	0	0
Webster Town and Village	41,839	19	0	4	4	11	531	121	399	11	0
Weedsport Village	1,867	0	0	0	0	0	28	2	26	0	0
Wellsville Village	4,728	36	0	1	3	32	143	18	123	2	1
West Carthage Village	2,175	2	0	0	0	2	18	3	15	0	0
Westfield Village	3,303	5	0	0	0	5	43	8	34	1	0
Westhampton Beach Village	2,009	7	0	1	2	4	53	9	43	1	0
West Seneca Town	43,061	48	0	3	11	34	976	194	754	28	1
Whitehall Village	2,518	5	0	0	1	4	34	6	28	0	4
White Plains	57,254	110	2	2	40	66	1,094	48	1,017	29	0
Whitesboro Village	3,661	6	0	0	0	6	35	7	28	0	0
Whitestown Town	9,088	4	0	1	1	2	77	19	53	5	0
Windham Town	1,880	0	0	0	0	0	58	18	39	1	0
Woodbury Town	10,242	3	0	1	2	0	363	8	352	3	0
Woodstock Town	6,009	5	0	0	2	3	65	16	46	3	0
Yonkers	199,296	895	9	29	455	402	2,851	521	2,086	244	27
Yorktown Town	37,684	26	1	0	5	20	462	62	399	1	1
Yorkville Village	2,503	5	0	0	3	2	51	2	49	0	0
Youngstown Village	1,832	0	0	0	0	0	5	1	4	0	0
NORTH CAROLINA											
Aberdeen	6,116	20	0	2	13	5	311	60	243	8	2
Ahoskie	4,617	32	1	3	6	22	241	90	147	4	1
Albemarle	15,446	67	0	4	14	49	795	220	527	48	6
Archdale	9,344	10	0	0	4	6	368	82	265	21	4
Asheboro	25,017	52	0	11	24	17	1,662	423	1,175	64	2
Asheville	77,067	432	2	31	165	234	3,671	743	2,638	290	8
Atlantic Beach	1,855	19	0	2	6	11	190	59	129	2	0
Ayden	5,078	34	0	1	11	22	223	83	130	10	1
Bailey	691	0	0	0	0	0	21	10	11	0	1
Banner Elk	944	2	0	1	0	1	25	7	18	0	0
Beaufort	4,368	20	0	0	3	17	201	40	156	5	0
Belhaven	2,050	7	0	0	2	5	63	19	44	0	1
Belmont	9,601	41	0	4	8	29	461	69	372	20	2
Benson	3,632	47	0	0	14	33	243	76	148	19	0
Beulaville	1,133	6	1	0	1	4	43	7	33	3	0
Biscoe	1,685	0	0	0	0	0	112	25	85	2	0
Black Mountain	7,953	5	0	1	1	3	182	53	117	12	0
Boiling Spring Lakes	5,012	4	0	1	0	3	93	34	57	2	0
Boone	14,209	24	0	7	6	11	440	82	349	9	1
Brevard	6,722	21	0	4	3	14	207	52	149	6	1
Burgaw	4,478	20	0	0	1	19	110	19	87	4	0
Burlington	52,210	395	3	11	69	312	3,519	794	2,599	126	9
Canton	3,841	25	0	1	2	22	214	50	154	10	0
Cape Carteret	1,429	4	0	1	1	2	20	7	13	0	0
Carolina Beach	5,968	22	2	5	4	11	309	51	245	13	0
Carrboro	18,448	60	0	5	13	42	611	190	405	16	1
Carthage	2,080	7	1	0	3	3	70	34	35	1	3
Cary	141,461	120	1	14	35	70	2,179	535	1,580	64	2
Catawba	836	0	0	0	0	0	16	6	8	2	0
Chadbourn	2,043	21	2	0	1	18	168	73	93	2	0
Chapel Hill	54,164	88	0	11	32	45	1,666	508	1,108	50	4
Charlotte-Mecklenburg	797,733	4,891	61	239	1,795	2,796	34,701	9,325	22,711	2,665	247
Cherryville	5,862	29	0	2	2	25	197	28	160	9	0
China Grove	3,772	12	0	1	3	8	94	29	61	4	1
Claremont	1,163	2	0	0	1	1	48	16	29	3	0
Clayton	17,472	25	0	3	8	14	400	114	275	11	4
Cleveland	846	0	0	0	0	0	36	11	24	1	0
Clinton	8,753	33	0	0	13	20	479	127	339	13	0
Clyde	1,282	0	0	0	0	0	35	19	15	1	0
Columbus	1,056	3	0	1	0	2	51	5	45	1	1
Concord	68,461	139	3	11	57	68	2,842	354	2,321	167	22
Cornelius	26,180	34	0	2	7	25	618	148	452	18	4
Cramerton	3,184	3	0	1	0	2	127	34	90	3	0
Creedmoor	3,898	12	0	1	4	7	117	28	86	3	0
Dobson	1,452	3	0	0	0	3	45	18	24	3	0
Drexel	1,865	0	0	0	0	0	38	11	26	1	0

[1] The FBI does not publish arson data unless it receives data from either the agency or the state for all 12 months of the calendar year.

Table 8.   Offenses Known to Law Enforcement, by State and City, 2010—*Continued*

(Number)

State/city	Population	Violent crime	Murder and non-negligent man-slaughter	Forcible rape	Robbery	Aggravated assault	Property crime	Burglary	Larceny-theft	Motor vehicle theft	Arson[1]
NORTH CAROLINA—*Continued*											
Duck	504	1	0	0	0	1	81	52	29	0	0
Durham	233,790	1,614	23	60	659	872	11,357	3,652	6,987	718	28
Eden	15,310	92	0	5	19	68	834	232	556	46	0
Edenton	5,052	33	1	0	8	24	217	55	152	10	2
Elizabeth City	20,801	120	4	4	30	82	772	208	544	20	3
Elkin	4,117	22	0	1	1	20	302	69	227	6	0
Elon	7,198	20	0	1	3	16	137	41	90	6	0
Emerald Isle	3,719	6	0	0	2	4	249	142	104	3	1
Enfield	2,319	48	1	2	12	33	123	72	47	4	1
Erwin	4,954	20	0	0	4	16	185	3	176	6	2
Fairmont	2,625	26	0	0	7	19	162	47	112	3	0
Farmville	4,679	41	0	0	4	37	173	48	120	5	4
Fayetteville	208,263	1,101	17	57	461	566	12,566	3,928	7,916	722	53
Fletcher	4,819	8	0	2	3	3	151	43	102	6	0
Franklin	3,980	15	0	1	3	11	186	55	126	5	1
Franklinton	2,041	11	1	0	5	5	89	30	54	5	0
Garner	28,620	48	2	3	22	21	977	152	793	32	1
Garysburg	1,093	6	0	0	0	6	40	17	22	1	0
Gibsonville	4,905	4	0	1	0	3	90	25	59	6	0
Goldsboro	38,179	386	5	3	105	273	2,525	734	1,663	128	5
Graham	14,826	47	0	3	6	38	574	167	383	24	2
Granite Falls	4,571	11	0	2	1	8	307	56	243	8	0
Greensboro	257,237	1,512	20	56	626	810	13,776	4,221	8,755	800	87
Hamlet	5,725	53	0	2	13	38	508	191	302	15	15
Haw River	2,050	11	0	0	0	11	79	28	47	4	0
Henderson	15,730	175	3	6	50	116	1,807	522	1,241	44	7
Hendersonville	12,311	74	1	10	15	48	810	114	639	57	3
Hertford	2,170	4	0	0	1	3	69	26	43	0	0
Hickory	41,892	217	1	22	76	118	2,573	616	1,836	121	13
Highlands	964	0	0	0	0	0	35	14	21	0	0
High Point	105,278	608	2	28	220	358	4,879	1,313	3,346	220	36
Hillsborough	5,831	31	0	3	10	18	369	92	268	9	0
Holden Beach	859	3	0	0	0	3	54	22	32	0	0
Holly Ridge	1,000	3	0	0	1	2	48	32	12	4	0
Holly Springs	23,506	19	1	1	5	12	250	79	165	6	1
Hope Mills	14,008	63	0	1	23	39	945	416	494	35	7
Hudson	3,013	5	0	0	0	5	80	12	63	5	0
Huntersville	47,537	45	0	5	9	31	1,041	256	766	19	7
Indian Beach	95	0	0	0	0	0	6	0	6	0	0
Jonesville	2,233	6	0	0	1	5	131	41	86	4	0
Kannapolis	44,084	95	0	5	40	50	954	310	574	70	8
Kenansville	1,168	5	0	1	1	3	31	6	24	1	0
Kernersville	23,695	86	0	4	11	71	1,034	158	846	30	8
King	7,092	22	0	4	4	14	212	54	151	7	0
Kinston	21,900	223	2	10	50	161	1,231	379	807	45	12
Kitty Hawk	3,351	7	0	0	1	6	128	69	57	2	0
Knightdale	10,686	18	1	0	7	10	385	63	307	15	3
Lake Lure	1,001	0	0	0	0	0	40	15	24	1	0
Lake Royale		2	0	0	1	1	88	46	39	3	1
Laurinburg	15,325	119	3	6	31	79	896	395	460	41	10
Leland	6,165	23	0	2	1	20	392	133	246	13	0
Lenoir	17,840	55	0	3	26	26	864	178	641	45	2
Lexington	20,255	88	2	7	28	51	762	217	515	30	5
Liberty	2,738	7	0	0	1	6	37	11	24	2	0
Lincolnton	11,017	30	0	0	14	16	541	81	452	8	0
Long View	5,005	19	0	4	6	9	236	102	116	18	1
Louisburg	3,755	7	0	0	0	7	131	39	85	7	0
Lumberton	22,019	438	5	13	138	282	2,647	693	1,779	175	12
Madison	2,245	45	0	0	0	45	145	36	107	2	1
Maggie Valley	906	9	0	2	2	5	110	9	99	2	0
Magnolia	988	0	0	0	0	0	34	21	12	1	1
Maiden	3,521	10	0	0	1	9	134	37	89	8	1
Manteo	1,503	7	0	2	1	4	88	24	63	1	0
Marion	7,015	36	0	1	10	25	438	136	285	17	4
Marshville	3,389	15	0	0	2	13	106	40	60	6	1
Matthews	27,989	49	0	4	18	27	739	112	587	40	9
Maxton	2,727	21	1	0	10	10	112	54	51	7	2
Mayodan	2,625	22	0	1	4	17	239	24	212	3	0
Maysville	947	3	0	1	0	2	18	7	11	0	0
Middlesex	872	2	1	0	0	1	15	3	12	0	0
Mint Hill	21,032	53	0	5	16	32	451	132	294	25	12
Mocksville	4,683	17	0	4	3	10	249	38	205	6	0
Mooresville	22,430	84	0	7	22	55	1,451	262	1,143	46	9

[1] The FBI does not publish arson data unless it receives data from either the agency or the state for all 12 months of the calendar year.

Table 8.   Offenses Known to Law Enforcement, by State and City, 2010—*Continued*

(Number)

State/city	Population	Violent crime	Murder and non-negligent man-slaughter	Forcible rape	Robbery	Aggravated assault	Property crime	Burglary	Larceny-theft	Motor vehicle theft	Arson[1]
NORTH CAROLINA—*Continued*											
Morehead City	9,888	76	0	4	8	64	544	87	446	11	1
Morganton	17,001	40	0	4	11	25	494	121	355	18	4
Morrisville	15,446	12	0	1	5	6	401	66	321	14	1
Mount Airy	10,612	57	2	4	7	44	620	187	406	27	4
Mount Holly	10,228	52	0	4	7	41	407	122	267	18	1
Mount Olive	4,344	42	2	1	11	28	405	106	286	13	3
Murfreesboro	2,413	4	0	0	2	2	61	16	42	3	0
Murphy	1,526	17	0	1	1	15	95	9	83	3	1
Nags Head	3,097	16	0	6	1	9	334	141	190	3	4
New Bern	29,657	141	1	8	23	109	1,806	779	973	54	1
Newport	4,492	6	0	1	0	5	68	28	38	2	1
Oak Island	8,487	27	0	2	3	22	278	120	150	8	0
Old Fort	961	0	0	0	0	0	33	13	15	5	0
Oxford	8,699	110	1	1	23	85	674	264	382	28	5
Pinebluff	1,447	1	0	0	0	1	33	18	15	0	0
Pinehurst	12,749	5	0	1	1	3	131	2	124	5	0
Pinetops	1,228	10	0	0	1	9	53	25	27	1	0
Pineville	7,313	47	1	1	18	27	1,305	207	1,033	65	1
Pittsboro	2,820	8	0	1	1	6	75	8	65	2	0
Plymouth	3,768	64	0	0	5	59	175	57	115	3	2
Raeford	4,149	35	1	1	7	26	402	89	286	27	0
Raleigh	419,700	1,740	14	99	643	984	12,995	3,021	9,104	870	63
Ramseur	1,772	6	0	1	1	4	78	25	51	2	0
Randleman	3,692	9	0	0	3	6	264	51	208	5	0
Red Springs	3,503	49	0	0	16	33	349	147	179	23	1
Reidsville	14,739	57	2	0	19	36	884	279	579	26	5
Richlands	964	7	0	1	3	3	32	9	22	1	0
Roanoke Rapids	16,121	76	3	7	29	37	868	209	638	21	4
Robersonville	1,520	6	0	0	1	5	63	18	45	0	0
Rockingham	8,727	50	0	1	28	21	948	194	735	19	2
Rockwell	2,024	2	0	1	1	0	53	16	36	1	0
Rocky Mount	59,688	688	11	14	210	453	3,566	1,057	2,339	170	13
Rolesville	3,512	3	0	0	1	2	51	28	23	0	0
Rowland	1,154	10	0	0	4	6	57	29	26	2	0
Roxboro	8,683	68	0	5	12	51	504	140	349	15	4
Rutherfordton	4,050	3	0	0	3	0	161	29	127	5	0
Salisbury	31,106	211	6	9	78	118	1,667	361	1,210	96	7
Scotland Neck	2,122	30	0	1	5	24	132	58	73	1	0
Selma	7,172	51	0	4	16	31	437	201	214	22	0
Shallotte	2,260	18	0	3	3	12	271	77	179	15	3
Sharpsburg	2,412	17	0	1	4	12	69	30	36	3	2
Shelby	21,430	145	1	11	47	86	1,033	337	654	42	7
Siler City	8,938	40	1	1	11	27	354	100	240	14	2
Smithfield	13,448	84	2	2	18	62	794	191	586	17	13
Southern Pines	13,060	92	1	2	30	59	478	122	346	10	2
Sparta	1,760	7	0	2	0	5	59	14	42	3	0
Spencer	3,408	11	1	0	4	6	188	86	98	4	5
Spring Hope	1,310	11	0	1	2	8	40	14	22	4	0
Spruce Pine	1,947	7	0	2	3	2	62	4	54	4	0
Stallings	9,612	17	0	1	3	13	301	60	234	7	0
Stanley	3,228	58	0	2	1	55	110	48	62	0	2
Star	796	4	0	0	0	4	12	2	9	1	0
St. Pauls	2,036	12	1	0	5	6	107	34	73	0	1
Sunset Beach	2,721	0	0	0	0	0	56	36	19	1	0
Surf City	2,132	3	0	0	0	3	151	74	76	1	0
Swansboro	2,071	3	0	0	1	2	134	47	84	3	0
Tabor City	2,773	35	1	0	4	30	204	64	132	8	3
Tarboro	9,930	54	0	3	14	37	375	102	262	11	0
Taylorsville	1,815	3	0	0	0	3	137	33	102	2	1
Thomasville	26,850	120	0	2	19	99	1,138	298	805	35	6
Trent Woods	4,007	3	0	0	0	3	75	7	68	0	0
Troutman	2,024	4	0	0	0	4	106	37	69	0	1
Troy	3,458	13	0	1	1	11	123	25	92	6	0
Valdese	4,530	2	0	0	1	1	77	26	50	1	0
Vass	815	0	0	0	0	0	21	3	16	2	0
Walnut Cove	1,604	3	0	1	0	2	56	2	49	5	1
Warrenton	827	4	0	0	2	2	31	1	30	0	0
Warsaw	3,193	4	0	1	1	2	177	66	107	4	0
Washington	10,228	91	2	4	27	58	557	134	412	11	2
Waxhaw	4,355	11	0	1	2	8	155	29	122	4	1
Waynesville	10,261	27	0	4	4	19	432	165	256	11	3
Weaverville	3,118	6	0	0	1	5	127	6	121	0	1
Wendell	5,612	10	0	1	3	6	101	35	64	2	0

[1] The FBI does not publish arson data unless it receives data from either the agency or the state for all 12 months of the calendar year.

Table 8.   Offenses Known to Law Enforcement, by State and City, 2010—*Continued*

(Number)

State/city	Population	Violent crime	Murder and non-negligent man-slaughter	Forcible rape	Robbery	Aggravated assault	Property crime	Burglary	Larceny-theft	Motor vehicle theft	Arson[1]
NORTH CAROLINA—*Continued*											
Whispering Pines	2,180	0	0	0	0	0	21	10	10	1	0
Whitakers	766	3	0	0	0	3	12	5	6	1	0
Wilkesboro	3,123	16	2	2	4	8	322	38	277	7	1
Williamston	5,313	35	1	2	10	22	463	183	265	15	2
Wilmington	102,649	724	5	47	282	390	5,706	1,447	3,781	478	13
Wilson	49,134	282	4	9	80	189	2,151	642	1,413	96	4
Wilson's Mills	1,757	7	0	0	0	7	78	41	35	2	1
Winston-Salem	232,928	1,517	11	96	449	961	13,349	4,482	8,225	642	105
Winterville	4,886	16	2	2	4	8	186	44	139	3	1
Wrightsville Beach	2,660	10	0	1	3	6	137	20	115	2	1
Yadkinville	2,825	16	0	1	4	11	162	34	126	2	0
Youngsville	798	1	0	0	0	1	64	17	47	0	0
NORTH DAKOTA											
Belfield	844	1	0	0	0	1	5	2	2	1	0
Beulah	2,976	2	0	0	0	2	44	5	38	1	0
Bismarck	64,142	197	1	21	17	158	1,508	182	1,250	76	5
Burlington	1,043	0	0	0	0	0	3	0	3	0	0
Cando	1,033	0	0	0	0	0	20	2	18	0	0
Carrington	2,001	0	0	0	0	0	4	1	1	2	0
Cavalier	1,351	1	0	0	0	1	20	4	14	2	0
Devils Lake	6,917	26	0	5	3	18	306	34	252	20	1
Dickinson	16,917	42	0	0	5	37	420	63	336	21	5
Ellendale	1,500	1	0	0	0	1	13	4	9	0	2
Fargo	99,694	302	0	44	35	223	2,764	392	2,205	167	14
Fessenden	493	0	0	0	0	0	1	0	1	0	0
Grafton	4,052	8	0	2	1	5	97	15	73	9	0
Grand Forks	53,382	119	0	33	7	79	1,424	252	1,095	77	5
Harvey	1,604	4	0	0	0	4	33	3	29	1	0
Jamestown	15,164	43	0	10	1	32	333	59	246	28	4
Kenmare	1,125	0	0	0	0	0	1	1	0	0	0
Killdeer	704	0	0	0	0	0	0	0	0	0	0
Lincoln	3,140	0	0	0	0	0	9	0	8	1	0
Lisbon	2,185	5	0	0	0	5	41	18	20	3	0
Mandan	19,134	41	1	11	2	27	281	25	238	18	1
Medora	99	1	0	0	0	1	0	0	0	0	0
Minot	37,605	107	1	27	5	74	701	66	588	47	1
Napoleon	702	0	0	0	0	0	7	5	2	0	0
Northwood	944	1	0	0	0	1	23	6	16	1	0
Oakes	1,797	2	0	0	0	2	1	0	1	0	0
Rolla	1,483	0	0	0	0	0	25	5	19	1	0
Rugby	2,566	0	0	0	0	0	43	6	35	2	0
Sherwood	216	0	0	0	0	0	0	0	0	0	0
Steele	632	1	0	0	0	1	1	0	1	0	0
Thompson	985	0	0	0	0	0	2	1	1	0	0
Valley City	6,477	4	0	1	0	3	80	20	54	6	0
Wahpeton	7,592	10	0	3	0	7	149	16	127	6	0
Watford City	1,450	2	0	0	0	2	39	6	26	7	0
West Fargo	26,409	46	0	7	3	36	450	105	319	26	6
Williston	13,569	32	2	7	2	21	290	24	236	30	3
OHIO											
Ada	6,104	1	0	1	0	0	41	10	31	0	0
Akron	205,760	1,665	22	159	602	882	10,851	4,247	5,855	749	106
Alliance	22,467	69	1	21	15	32	918	219	675	24	22
Amberley Village	3,563	1	0	0	0	1	42	9	33	0	0
Amelia	3,644	6	0	4	2	0	106	18	88	0	0
Amherst	11,705	10	1	1	6	2	254	25	225	4	0
Archbold	4,430	1	0	1	0	0	67	6	61	0	0
Arlington Heights	836	0	0	0	0	0	20	5	13	2	0
Ashland	21,737	15	0	13	0	2	578	68	500	10	2
Ashville	3,294	0	0	0	0	0	83	20	60	3	0
Athens	22,161	21	0	3	7	11	475	88	375	12	1
Aurora	14,712	8	0	4	2	2	148	22	121	5	1
Austintown	34,548	23	0	0	22	1	1,381	263	1,043	75	0
Bainbridge Township	11,705	9	0	0	1	8	197	22	171	4	1
Barberton	26,332	51	1	18	19	13	1,183	264	890	29	9
Barnesville	3,987	2	0	0	0	2	15	3	11	1	1
Batavia	1,761	0	0	0	0	0	84	18	64	2	0
Beavercreek	42,247	28	1	5	13	9	1,104	124	948	32	3
Beaver Township	6,017	1	0	1	0	0	144	37	104	3	0
Bedford	12,694	30	0	1	8	21	475	47	399	29	1
Bedford Heights	10,328	26	1	2	14	9	224	50	122	52	0
Bellbrook	6,792	1	0	1	0	0	98	15	83	0	1
Bellefontaine	12,735	34	0	14	8	12	702	100	583	19	0

[1] The FBI does not publish arson data unless it receives data from either the agency or the state for all 12 months of the calendar year.

Table 8.   Offenses Known to Law Enforcement, by State and City, 2010—*Continued*

(Number)

State/city	Population	Violent crime	Murder and non-negligent man-slaughter	Forcible rape	Robbery	Aggravated assault	Property crime	Burglary	Larceny-theft	Motor vehicle theft	Arson[1]
OHIO—*Continued*											
Bellville	1,680	4	0	0	0	4	76	7	68	1	0
Belpre	6,437	4	0	4	0	0	73	14	58	1	0
Berea	17,858	8	0	1	0	7	323	38	280	5	2
Bethel	2,648	3	0	0	3	0	165	37	126	2	0
Beverly	1,320	0	0	0	0	0	28	6	22	0	0
Bexley[5]	12,632	11	0	0	8	3	298	86	196	16	2
Blanchester	4,284	1	0	1	0	0	77	12	63	2	1
Blue Ash	12,764	11	0	3	4	4	339	42	291	6	0
Bluffton	3,882	4	0	1	0	3	47	12	35	0	0
Boardman	38,524	63	0	6	44	13	1,886	340	1,466	80	11
Bowling Green	28,617	41	0	1	15	25	813	96	700	17	2
Brecksville	12,675	5	0	1	1	3	58	11	47	0	0
Bridgeport	2,031	1	0	1	0	0	8	1	6	1	0
Brimfield Township	7,959	16	0	5	8	3	298	47	241	10	0
Broadview Heights	17,249	10	0	1	1	8	26	10	15	1	0
Brookfield Township	9,310	37	0	2	4	31	261	96	154	11	0
Brooklyn	10,175	32	1	5	20	6	553	87	428	38	0
Brooklyn Heights	1,428	0	0	0	0	0	22	7	12	3	0
Brook Park	18,806	66	0	4	2	60	30	6	11	13	0
Brookville	5,455	2	0	2	0	0	90	8	82	0	2
Brunswick Hills Township	7,587	1	0	0	0	1	66	12	52	2	0
Burton	1,489	1	0	0	0	1	14	1	13	0	0
Butler Township	8,038	9	0	2	4	3	285	22	247	16	0
Cadiz	3,239	8	1	3	1	3	70	17	51	2	0
Cambridge	11,085	30	0	0	12	18	606	169	414	23	0
Canal Fulton	5,037	4	0	3	0	1	86	9	75	2	2
Canfield	6,754	2	0	1	0	1	71	10	60	1	1
Canton	77,938	652	2	54	324	272	4,129	1,523	2,337	269	46
Cardington	2,005	2	0	0	0	2	38	11	27	0	0
Carrollton	3,205	20	0	0	5	15	16	14	0	2	0
Celina	10,180	19	1	1	3	14	425	62	353	10	5
Centerville	22,745	22	0	2	3	17	488	77	390	21	2
Champion Township	9,059	6	0	1	0	5	193	61	129	3	1
Chardon	5,452	8	0	0	1	7	110	6	104	0	0
Cheviot	8,350	4	0	0	2	2	210	42	159	9	0
Chillicothe	22,143	240	1	7	43	189	2,199	435	1,722	42	8
Cincinnati	332,365	3,608	68	233	2,116	1,191	20,513	6,490	12,408	1,615	199
Circleville	13,686	38	0	7	21	10	996	209	770	17	7
Clayton	12,769	14	0	2	9	3	205	43	148	14	3
Clay Township, Ottawa County	2,724	4	0	0	1	3	28	8	19	1	0
Clearcreek Township	13,005	0	0	0	0	0	125	24	100	1	0
Cleveland	426,042	5,525	81	341	3,181	1,922	23,436	9,854	10,079	3,503	378
Cleveland Heights	44,799	73	0	1	68	4	670	166	417	87	0
Cleves	2,724	2	0	0	1	1	59	22	37	0	0
Clinton Township	4,075	38	0	0	29	9	375	83	264	28	1
Coitsville Township	1,614	4	0	1	2	1	42	26	16	0	0
Coldwater	4,374	0	0	0	0	0	20	3	17	0	0
Columbus	772,974	5,451	94	566	3,359	1,432	50,168	15,234	30,784	4,150	403
Conneaut	12,337	17	0	3	2	12	361	91	244	26	1
Copley Township	14,009	1	0	0	1	0	91	25	65	1	0
Cortland	6,257	7	0	1	2	4	87	19	67	1	1
Covington	2,623	0	0	0	0	0	73	19	54	0	0
Crestline	4,842	7	0	0	1	6	50	25	23	2	0
Creston	2,117	0	0	0	0	0	39	4	35	0	0
Cuyahoga Falls	51,140	68	0	20	11	37	1,217	234	935	48	4
Danville	1,074	1	0	0	0	1	16	1	13	2	1
Dayton	152,319	1,509	34	92	782	601	8,891	3,380	4,840	671	203
Deer Park	5,745	3	0	0	3	0	103	17	81	5	1
Defiance	15,912	20	0	8	6	6	656	76	575	5	3
Delaware	35,468	55	0	19	10	26	915	201	691	23	8
Delhi Township	31,310	21	0	5	4	12	501	98	394	9	1
Delphos	6,720	6	0	3	0	3	209	54	152	3	0
Delta	2,880	0	0	0	0	0	67	12	53	2	0
Dover	12,408	9	0	3	3	3	114	21	88	5	1
Dublin	40,073	12	0	1	8	3	758	118	621	19	8
Eastlake	19,635	13	1	0	7	5	420	38	375	7	2
Eaton	7,899	16	0	2	1	13	315	55	253	7	0
Edgerton	1,916	0	0	0	0	0	45	9	36	0	0
Elyria	54,701	221	1	28	100	92	2,139	590	1,446	103	13
Englewood	12,647	23	0	3	8	12	420	46	362	12	0
Evendale	3,007	19	0	0	4	15	222	11	206	5	0
Fairborn	31,731	50	0	10	26	14	742	196	521	25	5
Fairfield	42,494	125	0	6	28	91	1,308	205	1,050	53	2

[1] The FBI does not publish arson data unless it receives data from either the agency or the state for all 12 months of the calendar year.

[5] Because of changes in the state/local agency's reporting practices, figures are not comparable to previous years' data.

Table 8. Offenses Known to Law Enforcement, by State and City, 2010—*Continued*

(Number)

State/city	Population	Violent crime	Murder and non-negligent man-slaughter	Forcible rape	Robbery	Aggravated assault	Property crime	Burglary	Larceny-theft	Motor vehicle theft	Arson[1]
OHIO—*Continued*											
Fairlawn	6,961	12	0	0	3	9	331	10	311	10	0
Fairport Harbor	3,246	9	0	4	2	3	162	40	117	5	3
Findlay	36,324	75	1	17	16	41	1,381	265	1,087	29	3
Forest	1,441	0	0	0	0	0	19	5	13	1	0
Forest Park	18,476	34	0	3	30	1	422	105	304	13	3
Fort Shawnee	3,663	1	0	0	1	0	49	14	35	0	1
Frazeysburg	1,295	0	0	0	0	0	27	3	24	0	0
Fredericktown	2,500	1	0	1	0	0	72	13	54	5	0
Fremont	16,305	26	0	2	12	12	888	129	733	26	1
Gahanna	34,335	21	0	7	11	3	770	119	625	26	7
Gallipolis	4,087	8	0	2	5	1	403	47	351	5	2
Gates Mills	2,231	0	0	0	0	0	23	4	19	0	0
Geneva-on-the-Lake	1,479	1	0	0	0	1	23	7	15	1	0
Genoa	2,265	2	0	0	2	0	45	4	40	1	0
Germantown	4,990	3	0	1	0	2	86	14	71	1	1
German Township, Montgomery County	3,274	4	0	1	0	3	45	16	27	2	0
Gibsonburg	2,395	1	0	1	0	0	75	7	68	0	0
Girard	9,896	64	0	8	3	53	385	112	253	20	3
Glendale	2,224	0	0	0	0	0	54	19	33	2	1
Glouster	1,979	1	0	0	1	0	88	18	68	2	0
Goshen Township, Clermont County	16,559	4	0	0	0	4	317	65	241	11	3
Goshen Township, Mahoning County	3,407	12	0	0	0	12	93	28	62	3	2
Grandview Heights	6,342	1	0	1	0	0	85	20	63	2	1
Granville[5]	5,229	8	0	7	1	0	75	7	68	0	1
Greenhills	3,819	2	0	1	0	1	33	10	23	0	0
Greenville	12,713	38	0	5	9	24	482	118	341	23	6
Grove City	35,339	51	0	15	24	12	1,259	160	1,053	46	10
Groveport	5,501	8	0	0	3	5	145	32	110	3	0
Hamilton	62,805	414	2	64	205	143	3,866	1,000	2,661	205	52
Harrison	9,697	1	0	0	0	1	311	44	264	3	0
Hartville	2,596	2	0	0	1	1	41	8	32	1	0
Heath	8,950	14	0	2	3	9	517	55	448	14	6
Hebron	2,161	2	0	0	1	1	63	11	50	2	0
Hicksville	3,358	1	0	0	0	1	48	7	40	1	0
Highland Heights	8,665	0	0	0	0	0	73	17	54	2	0
Highland Hills	1,374	0	0	0	0	0	2	0	1	1	0
Hilliard	29,204	21	0	4	11	6	828	159	642	27	7
Hillsboro	6,674	2	0	0	1	1	374	31	342	1	2
Holland	1,323	4	0	0	2	2	173	11	160	2	0
Hubbard	7,549	19	0	2	6	11	203	63	133	7	1
Hubbard Township	5,612	7	0	0	0	7	220	95	120	5	0
Hudson	23,023	3	0	0	1	2	158	34	122	2	1
Independence	6,662	3	0	1	2	0	115	15	97	3	0
Indian Hill	6,095	0	0	0	0	0	57	6	51	0	0
Ironton	11,252	7	0	2	2	3	110	38	70	2	1
Jackson	6,145	8	0	2	3	3	405	55	345	5	0
Jackson Township, Mahoning County	2,246	1	0	0	0	1	80	43	36	1	1
Jackson Township, Montgomery County	3,826	0	0	0	0	0	45	24	19	2	0
Jackson Township, Stark County	40,877	55	0	10	17	28	1,256	179	1,040	37	2
Jamestown	1,804	2	0	0	0	2	56	13	40	3	0
Johnstown	4,100	0	0	0	0	0	73	6	65	2	1
Kent	27,823	39	1	8	9	21	631	156	451	24	19
Kenton	7,970	7	1	2	4	0	449	93	350	6	2
Kettering	52,931	61	0	16	25	20	1,300	362	887	51	11
Kirtland	7,524	1	0	0	0	1	56	17	39	0	0
Kirtland Hills	824	0	0	0	0	0	7	3	3	1	0
Lake Township	7,478	1	0	0	0	1	103	21	79	3	2
Lakewood	49,526	76	0	6	38	32	901	220	655	26	1
Lancaster	37,330	103	0	19	56	28	2,192	378	1,760	54	7
Lawrence Township	8,437	5	0	0	0	5	57	13	36	8	0
Lebanon	21,099	22	1	9	4	8	416	73	336	7	3
Lexington	4,057	4	0	3	1	0	90	17	71	2	0
Lima	37,182	336	3	37	88	208	2,222	792	1,328	102	32
Linndale	86	5	0	0	2	3	16	0	16	0	0
Liverpool Township	4,108	1	0	0	1	0	61	12	46	3	0
Lockland	3,463	24	0	1	11	12	170	50	105	15	2
Logan	7,418	3	0	0	2	1	511	182	319	10	0
London	9,692	16	0	4	7	5	308	45	255	8	0
Lorain	70,242	343	1	29	139	174	3,161	1,278	1,768	115	44
Lordstown	3,502	0	0	0	0	0	77	22	54	1	0
Loudonville	3,055	0	0	0	0	0	70	16	53	1	0
Louisville	9,481	7	0	0	2	5	217	40	174	3	2
Madison	3,159	3	0	2	0	1	32	3	26	3	1

[1] The FBI does not publish arson data unless it receives data from either the agency or the state for all 12 months of the calendar year.

[5] Because of changes in the state/local agency's reporting practices, figures are not comparable to previous years' data.

Table 8.   Offenses Known to Law Enforcement, by State and City, 2010—*Continued*

(Number)

State/city	Population	Violent crime	Murder and non-negligent man-slaughter	Forcible rape	Robbery	Aggravated assault	Property crime	Burglary	Larceny-theft	Motor vehicle theft	Arson[1]
OHIO—*Continued*											
Madison Township, Franklin County	18,751	11	0	1	3	7	141	45	84	12	1
Madison Township, Lake County	17,187	29	0	4	5	20	471	77	370	24	2
Mansfield	49,069	159	3	35	73	48	2,933	905	1,966	62	15
Mariemont	3,169	0	0	0	0	0	80	6	72	2	0
Marietta5	14,007	20	0	9	6	5	328	62	261	5	2
Marion	35,540	91	1	18	35	37	1,935	551	1,336	48	7
Marysville	18,580	14	0	9	2	3	398	46	341	11	3
Mason	30,805	7	0	2	2	3	463	64	394	5	0
Massillon	32,768	39	3	4	21	11	833	210	601	22	6
Mayfield Heights	17,396	19	0	0	8	11	300	35	250	15	1
McArthur	2,011	3	0	1	1	1	111	35	74	2	2
Medina Township	9,182	0	0	0	0	0	76	11	62	3	0
Mentor	51,924	40	0	5	21	14	1,200	125	1,010	65	5
Mentor-on-the-Lake	8,392	7	1	0	2	4	93	23	68	2	0
Miamisburg	19,679	35	0	4	15	16	561	156	376	29	3
Miami Township, Clermont County	40,101	22	0	4	11	7	876	144	723	9	5
Miami Township, Montgomery County	24,822	42	1	8	20	13	1,170	152	973	45	4
Middlefield	2,515	1	0	0	0	1	47	0	47	0	1
Middleport	2,448	3	0	0	1	2	11	6	5	0	0
Middletown	51,464	344	2	23	98	221	3,999	1,142	2,712	145	6
Milford	6,324	18	0	3	5	10	372	37	333	2	0
Millersburg	3,675	3	0	1	1	1	62	8	52	2	0
Minerva	3,900	0	0	0	0	0	75	19	55	1	1
Mingo Junction	3,233	34	0	0	0	34	71	30	38	3	0
Monroe	15,513	56	0	8	7	41	702	97	598	7	1
Montgomery	10,606	4	0	1	1	2	204	24	175	5	0
Montpelier	3,928	14	0	6	0	8	144	27	114	3	2
Moraine	6,376	22	1	5	9	7	864	90	760	14	3
Moreland Hills	3,010	1	0	1	0	0	10	2	7	1	0
Mount Gilead	3,558	2	0	2	0	0	164	32	131	1	0
Mount Healthy	6,062	28	1	4	15	8	277	89	174	14	0
Munroe Falls	5,119	0	0	0	0	0	41	10	31	0	0
Napoleon	8,664	14	0	6	5	3	374	76	292	6	1
Navarre	1,883	3	0	0	2	1	33	11	21	1	0
Nelsonville	5,717	9	0	4	3	2	260	96	158	6	1
New Albany	7,766	1	0	0	1	0	67	11	56	0	0
Newark	47,409	103	1	29	39	34	2,197	482	1,645	70	23
New Boston	2,131	10	0	3	5	2	223	68	144	11	0
New Franklin	14,976	2	0	2	0	0	122	43	76	3	1
New Lebanon	4,059	7	0	1	2	4	135	46	87	2	0
New Lexington	4,539	0	0	0	0	0	64	6	56	2	0
New Middletown	1,494	0	0	0	0	0	7	1	6	0	0
New Philadelphia	17,238	5	0	1	1	3	136	6	129	1	2
New Richmond	2,545	5	0	0	3	2	166	33	131	2	0
Newtown	4,153	1	0	0	0	1	22	6	16	0	1
New Washington	901	2	0	0	0	2	14	3	11	0	0
Niles	18,906	45	0	8	22	15	1,122	196	845	81	1
North Canton	16,737	10	0	2	7	1	312	72	234	6	3
North College Hill	9,515	39	1	1	28	9	409	93	295	21	1
Northfield	3,616	0	0	0	0	0	15	3	11	1	0
North Olmsted	30,689	23	0	3	8	12	397	94	293	10	1
North Ridgeville	29,437	26	1	5	2	18	226	46	170	10	2
Northwood	5,542	13	0	2	6	5	255	32	215	8	1
Norton	11,451	5	0	1	2	2	272	60	196	16	1
Norwood	20,240	112	0	12	83	17	1,284	292	953	39	0
Oberlin	8,447	13	0	5	5	3	213	30	180	3	3
Olmsted Falls	8,092	5	0	0	0	5	65	14	48	3	1
Ontario5	5,157	12	0	4	3	5	515	36	475	4	0
Orange Village	3,222	2	0	0	0	2	16	3	12	1	0
Oregon	18,912	25	0	2	10	13	877	125	726	26	5
Orrville	8,367	1	0	1	0	0	157	34	120	3	1
Ottawa Hills	4,578	5	0	0	0	5	52	10	37	5	1
Oxford	23,202	80	0	11	9	60	576	122	438	16	9
Painesville	19,084	35	0	13	11	11	364	100	252	12	9
Parma Heights	19,343	27	0	8	4	15	337	67	241	29	5
Pepper Pike	5,667	3	0	1	0	2	45	9	35	1	1
Perrysburg	17,658	14	0	2	2	10	405	56	340	9	0
Perry Township, Allen County	3,565	2	0	0	0	2	61	7	54	0	1
Perry Township, Franklin County	3,719	0	0	0	0	0	53	12	40	1	1
Perry Township, Montgomery County	3,812	1	0	1	0	0	48	19	26	3	0
Pickerington	18,801	17	0	3	9	5	342	38	300	4	0
Pierce Township	11,189	10	0	4	5	1	444	94	349	1	3
Piqua	20,478	18	0	8	10	0	1,120	232	862	26	3

[1] The FBI does not publish arson data unless it receives data from either the agency or the state for all 12 months of the calendar year.

Table 8. Offenses Known to Law Enforcement, by State and City, 2010—*Continued*

(Number)

State/city	Population	Violent crime	Murder and non-negligent man-slaughter	Forcible rape	Robbery	Aggravated assault	Property crime	Burglary	Larceny-theft	Motor vehicle theft	Arson[1]
OHIO—*Continued*											
Plain City	3,630	0	0	0	0	0	36	14	22	0	0
Poland Township	10,929	4	0	0	1	3	33	17	15	1	1
Poland Village	2,620	0	0	0	0	0	19	1	17	1	0
Pomeroy	1,940	3	0	0	0	3	9	0	6	3	0
Port Clinton	6,087	5	0	1	2	2	207	37	167	3	0
Portsmouth	20,254	117	3	12	78	24	2,340	642	1,642	56	2
Powell	14,121	0	0	0	0	0	87	22	65	0	0
Powhatan Point	1,642	4	0	0	0	4	19	7	12	0	0
Reading	10,469	24	0	7	11	6	412	80	313	19	1
Reminderville	2,864	0	0	0	0	0	11	4	7	0	0
Reynoldsburg	34,208	92	0	5	47	40	1,155	264	848	43	5
Richfield	3,611	1	0	0	0	1	32	6	21	5	1
Richmond Heights	10,048	12	0	0	7	5	234	31	198	5	0
Rio Grande	849	0	0	0	0	0	24	3	21	0	0
Rittman	6,257	5	0	0	4	1	195	47	146	2	1
Riverside	24,938	51	0	8	16	27	712	183	489	40	12
Russells Point	1,518	0	0	0	0	0	32	7	24	1	0
Russell Township	5,840	1	0	0	0	1	9	5	4	0	0
Sabina	2,764	1	0	1	0	0	44	9	34	1	0
Salem	11,676	3	0	2	0	1	315	30	282	3	1
Sandusky[5]	25,380	150	0	7	20	123	1,273	310	960	3	3
Sebring	4,451	2	0	1	0	1	89	21	67	1	1
Seville	2,438	3	0	0	1	2	55	10	41	4	0
Shaker Heights	25,852	35	0	0	26	9	592	199	350	43	0
Sharonville	13,337	21	0	6	15	0	562	100	445	17	0
Shawnee Township	8,742	7	0	1	2	4	113	37	71	5	0
Sheffield Lake	8,848	6	0	0	2	4	164	31	131	2	1
Shelby	9,195	3	0	0	1	2	378	87	282	9	2
Sidney	19,809	59	0	15	15	29	1,060	210	827	23	10
Silverton	5,134	6	0	2	1	3	118	29	80	9	2
Smith Township	4,774	3	0	1	0	2	73	13	55	5	2
Smithville	1,294	1	0	0	0	1	37	6	30	1	1
Solon	21,837	11	0	0	5	6	188	22	156	10	0
Somerset	1,558	2	0	0	0	2	61	3	58	0	0
South Bloomfield	1,682	0	0	0	0	0	38	5	31	2	0
South Charleston	1,762	0	0	0	0	0	12	0	11	1	0
South Euclid	20,750	36	0	5	24	7	491	147	315	29	2
South Point	4,058	8	0	0	0	8	52	52	0	0	0
South Russell	4,059	2	0	0	1	1	5	1	4	0	0
Spencerville	2,130	2	0	2	0	0	56	10	45	1	0
Springboro	18,460	9	0	2	3	4	228	41	177	10	0
Springdale	10,436	35	0	6	17	12	674	74	569	31	3
Springfield	61,540	480	4	37	216	223	4,494	1,501	2,723	270	28
Springfield Township, Hamilton County	39,931	61	1	6	36	18	723	220	466	37	3
Springfield Township, Mahoning County	5,985	5	0	0	0	5	111	52	58	1	1
Springfield Township, Summit County	18,150	28	0	4	11	13	1,022	147	857	18	6
St. Bernard	4,623	7	0	0	7	0	132	21	107	4	0
St. Clair Township	7,560	0	0	0	0	0	59	0	59	0	0
Steubenville	18,522	75	2	5	34	34	1,098	190	872	36	3
Stow	33,938	25	0	9	6	10	622	101	512	9	1
St. Paris	1,957	0	0	0	0	0	34	7	27	0	0
Strasburg	2,744	3	0	0	0	3	94	13	79	2	1
Streetsboro	14,937	3	0	0	1	2	46	2	44	0	0
Strongsville	42,134	11	0	2	6	3	767	76	670	21	1
Struthers	10,548	16	0	7	7	2	408	134	253	21	3
Sugarcreek Township	6,821	8	0	4	2	2	237	29	202	6	1
Swanton	3,639	11	0	2	0	9	94	15	74	5	1
Sycamore	862	0	0	0	0	0	2	0	2	0	0
Sylvania Township	25,964	29	0	1	12	16	737	113	607	17	2
Tallmadge	17,397	38	0	5	8	25	431	88	333	10	2
Tipp City	9,238	5	0	1	2	2	213	42	168	3	0
Toledo[6]	315,647	2,854	23	140	1,097	1,594		7,287		1,197	492
Trotwood	25,685	98	0	10	50	38	1,114	460	556	98	11
Twinsburg	17,325	5	0	2	2	3	138	25	105	8	2
Uhrichsville	5,437	5	0	1	1	3	181	48	125	8	1
Union	6,309	12	0	1	1	10	135	20	109	6	5
Union Township, Clermont County	44,619	20	0	6	13	1	1,682	233	1,427	22	13
University Heights	12,396	28	0	3	11	14	260	52	199	9	2
Upper Arlington	32,111	21	2	2	11	6	508	99	398	11	2
Upper Sandusky	6,327	0	0	0	0	0	16	0	16	0	0
Utica	2,103	2	0	1	0	1	66	8	51	7	0
Vandalia	14,015	13	0	4	3	6	422	102	294	26	3
Van Wert	10,022	30	1	6	4	19	454	97	349	8	4

[1] The FBI does not publish arson data unless it receives data from either the agency or the state for all 12 months of the calendar year.

[5] Because of changes in the state/local agency's reporting practices, figures are not comparable to previous years' data.

Table 8.   Offenses Known to Law Enforcement, by State and City, 2010—*Continued*

(Number)

State/city	Population	Violent crime	Murder and non-negligent man-slaughter	Forcible rape	Robbery	Aggravated assault	Property crime	Burglary	Larceny-theft	Motor vehicle theft	Arson[1]
OHIO—*Continued*											
Vermilion	10,708	21	0	1	6	14	269	73	185	11	3
Village of Leesburg	1,293	3	0	1	0	2	38	11	27	0	1
Wadsworth	21,212	11	0	7	1	3	492	85	398	9	1
Waite Hill	575	0	0	0	0	0	3	3	0	0	0
Walbridge	3,110	2	0	0	2	0	67	17	50	0	1
Walton Hills	2,244	0	0	0	0	0	22	8	11	3	0
Wapakoneta	9,433	4	0	0	1	3	137	21	115	1	0
Warren	42,850	262	4	22	123	113	2,313	1,068	1,099	146	4
Warrensville Heights	13,341	48	0	4	38	6	452	223	176	53	4
Warren Township	5,940	6	0	0	1	5	73	28	43	2	0
Washington Court House	13,468	17	0	3	4	10	465	109	348	8	1
Wauseon	7,209	8	0	3	2	3	245	21	222	2	4
Waverly	4,459	0	0	0	0	0	72	4	68	0	0
Wells Township	2,764	2	0	2	0	0	54	21	32	1	0
West Alexandria	1,275	1	0	1	0	0	17	2	15	0	1
West Carrollton	12,556	29	0	9	11	9	455	128	292	35	3
West Chester Township	56,305	71	0	21	21	29	1,520	334	1,160	26	11
Westerville	36,966	19	0	5	9	5	903	124	769	10	7
West Jefferson	4,255	4	0	2	0	2	139	37	98	4	0
West Lafayette	2,424	0	0	0	0	0	38	8	29	1	0
West Liberty	1,719	0	0	0	0	0	24	1	22	1	0
West Salem	1,471	1	0	1	0	0	30	3	27	0	0
West Union	3,076	3	1	0	0	2	175	53	120	2	0
Whitehall	18,332	146	1	15	97	33	1,433	272	1,092	69	0
Willard	6,553	7	0	3	2	2	210	25	167	18	4
Williamsburg	2,390	4	0	0	1	3	82	16	64	2	1
Willoughby	22,909	18	0	3	8	7	374	64	299	11	0
Willowick	13,802	12	1	5	4	2	149	31	112	6	1
Wilmington	12,578	15	0	0	8	7	623	71	548	4	1
Woodlawn	2,636	13	0	1	6	6	159	34	119	6	1
Woodsfield	2,362	0	0	0	0	0	14	0	12	2	0
Wooster	26,244	45	1	23	13	8	884	194	673	17	12
Worthington	13,401	15	0	2	8	5	355	72	275	8	4
Wyoming	8,331	0	0	0	0	0	132	25	106	1	0
Xenia	27,702	44	0	4	15	25	1,134	182	928	24	0
Yellow Springs	3,223	4	0	0	0	4	81	10	67	4	0
Youngstown	71,380	694	25	28	235	406	4,431	2,101	1,806	524	242
Zanesville	24,776	82	2	16	42	22	1,668	296	1,319	53	26
OKLAHOMA											
Achille	549	1	0	0	0	1	3	2	1	0	0
Ada	17,298	138	1	8	10	119	762	205	529	28	1
Allen	1,015	1	0	0	0	1	7	3	4	0	0
Altus	18,983	42	0	4	8	30	728	270	443	15	4
Alva	4,822	6	0	1	2	3	115	34	78	3	1
Anadarko	6,422	27	0	1	1	25	229	69	142	18	2
Antlers	2,547	7	0	0	1	6	86	28	51	7	0
Apache	1,540	6	0	0	1	5	16	8	7	1	0
Ardmore	25,238	295	2	11	30	252	1,363	394	923	46	6
Arkoma	2,194	1	0	0	0	1	19	7	11	1	0
Atoka	3,092	12	0	1	1	10	103	27	74	2	2
Bartlesville	36,586	146	3	11	27	105	1,226	273	894	59	13
Beggs	1,374	3	0	0	1	2	38	14	20	4	0
Bethany	19,923	55	0	7	15	33	572	197	317	58	0
Bixby	22,683	23	0	2	3	18	346	115	206	25	1
Blackwell	7,238	12	0	2	1	9	149	44	101	4	4
Blanchard	7,061	10	1	2	0	7	110	40	48	22	1
Boise City	1,207	4	0	0	0	4	15	11	3	1	0
Boley	1,097	6	0	0	0	6	4	1	3	0	0
Bristow	4,425	17	0	2	1	14	166	49	114	3	0
Broken Arrow	97,581	143	2	31	28	82	2,037	353	1,560	124	16
Broken Bow	4,135	30	0	4	2	24	199	59	119	21	4
Caddo	1,009	0	0	0	0	0	13	9	4	0	0
Calumet	553	1	0	0	0	1	3	0	3	0	0
Caney	212	0	0	0	0	0	4	2	2	0	1
Carnegie	1,619	5	0	0	0	5	25	14	10	1	0
Catoosa[3]	8,193		0	4	1		181	41	112	28	1
Chandler	2,874	10	0	2	0	8	63	12	50	1	0
Checotah	3,496	6	0	1	2	3	90	9	67	14	0
Chelsea	2,261	1	0	0	0	1	5	0	5	0	0
Cherokee	1,376	4	0	0	0	4	7	1	5	1	0
Chickasha	17,507	129	1	12	22	94	815	209	582	24	5
Choctaw	11,942	9	0	1	1	7	193	67	119	7	1
Chouteau	2,208	7	0	0	0	7	74	15	55	4	0

[1] The FBI does not publish arson data unless it receives data from either the agency or the state for all 12 months of the calendar year.

[3] The FBI determined that the agency's data were overreported. Consequently, those data are not included in this table.

Table 8. Offenses Known to Law Enforcement, by State and City, 2010—*Continued*

(Number)

State/city	Population	Violent crime	Murder and non-negligent man-slaughter	Forcible rape	Robbery	Aggravated assault	Property crime	Burglary	Larceny-theft	Motor vehicle theft	Arson[1]
OKLAHOMA—*Continued*											
Claremore	17,741	32	0	7	2	23	557	106	423	28	2
Cleveland	3,270	8	0	2	0	6	77	18	58	1	0
Clinton	8,948	23	0	6	3	14	136	43	84	9	2
Collinsville	5,380	14	0	6	1	7	113	38	64	11	3
Comanche	1,528	2	0	0	0	2	45	14	29	2	1
Cordell	2,983	15	0	1	0	14	28	0	26	2	0
Coweta	9,248	29	0	8	3	18	202	26	153	23	4
Crescent	1,463	8	0	0	0	8	11	5	6	0	0
Cushing	9,838	31	0	0	1	30	192	31	148	13	1
Davis	2,699	11	0	0	0	11	82	25	52	5	0
Del City	22,549	152	1	13	28	110	1,255	383	775	97	5
Dewey	3,367	16	0	2	2	12	113	24	89	0	0
Dibble	674	2	0	2	0	0	7	2	4	1	0
Drumright	2,908	10	0	1	1	8	100	20	75	5	0
Duncan	22,814	51	0	10	10	31	1,119	292	779	48	4
Durant	17,357	130	0	14	4	112	785	253	502	30	3
Edmond	83,337	74	1	9	19	45	1,691	372	1,274	45	3
Elk City	11,748	20	0	3	0	17	118	25	92	1	6
El Reno	17,262	89	2	12	4	71	440	144	281	15	7
Enid	48,581	226	2	28	25	171	2,173	466	1,642	65	7
Eufaula	2,808	10	1	1	0	8	84	24	55	5	0
Fairfax	1,429	2	0	0	0	2	23	11	8	4	0
Fairview	2,561	1	0	0	0	1	145	38	103	4	0
Forest Park	1,193	1	0	0	0	1	8	5	3	0	0
Fort Gibson	4,440	6	0	1	1	4	77	22	50	5	2
Frederick	3,778	17	0	2	1	14	111	48	60	3	1
Geary	1,243	2	1	0	0	1	40	17	18	5	0
Glenpool[3]	10,685		0	6	1		224	46	162	16	1
Goodwell	1,251	0	0	0	0	0	5	0	5	0	0
Grove	6,575	21	0	1	0	20	193	28	157	8	0
Guthrie	11,797	20	1	2	1	16	301	40	247	14	1
Guymon	11,294	25	0	1	7	17	332	84	235	13	1
Harrah	5,402	5	0	1	1	3	98	24	73	1	0
Hartshorne	2,088	2	0	0	0	2	63	19	29	15	1
Healdton	2,816	7	0	3	0	4	87	19	58	10	2
Heavener	3,254	6	0	0	1	5	67	20	43	4	1
Henryetta	6,053	6	0	3	0	3	156	49	89	18	1
Hinton	3,746	2	0	1	0	1	20	3	14	3	0
Hobart	3,512	4	0	0	1	3	103	48	53	2	0
Holdenville	5,638	14	0	0	0	14	159	70	82	7	2
Hollis	1,949	3	0	0	0	3	66	32	34	0	1
Hominy	3,588	4	0	0	0	4	19	6	9	4	0
Howe	728	0	0	0	0	0	0	0	0	0	0
Hugo[5]	5,434	4	0	1	0	3	67	19	47	1	0
Hulbert	544	2	0	0	0	2	9	4	3	2	0
Hydro	1,014	0	0	0	0	0	22	2	16	4	0
Idabel	6,829	37	1	8	3	25	260	67	184	9	0
Jay	3,051	8	0	1	0	7	62	13	48	1	0
Jenks	17,170	32	0	3	4	25	261	50	195	16	0
Jones	2,805	2	0	1	0	1	24	8	13	3	0
Kingfisher	4,418	5	0	1	0	4	48	7	40	1	1
Kingston	1,652	0	0	0	0	0	12	4	5	3	0
Krebs	2,164	5	0	1	0	4	78	22	52	4	0
Lawton	92,025	831	3	60	113	655	5,254	1,757	3,279	218	42
Lexington	2,185	10	0	0	0	10	41	12	26	3	2
Lindsay	2,916	8	0	0	0	8	69	11	54	4	0
Locust Grove	1,615	5	0	0	0	5	59	12	44	3	1
Lone Grove	5,496	11	0	3	2	6	109	24	77	8	1
Madill	3,855	6	0	2	0	4	105	38	66	1	0
Mangum	2,709	6	0	1	0	5	52	21	27	4	0
Mannford	2,938	2	0	0	0	2	44	13	28	3	0
Marietta	2,540	17	1	0	1	15	25	4	18	3	0
Marlow	4,639	15	0	1	0	14	171	46	122	3	0
Maysville	1,306	0	0	0	0	0	20	4	16	0	0
McAlester	18,675	38	1	3	10	24	773	164	583	26	0
McCurtain	491	1	0	0	0	1	6	3	3	0	0
McLoud[5]	4,784	12	0	1	1	10	120	26	80	14	0
Medicine Park	396	0	0	0	0	0	2	0	2	0	0
Meeker	983	2	0	0	0	2	31	11	19	1	0
Miami	12,967	74	0	11	7	56	570	105	448	17	4
Midwest City	58,095	265	2	24	52	187	2,737	817	1,752	168	19
Minco	1,850	0	0	0	0	0	8	1	6	1	0
Moore	55,788	58	1	13	19	25	2,145	423	1,578	144	1

[1] The FBI does not publish arson data unless it receives data from either the agency or the state for all 12 months of the calendar year.

[3] The FBI determined that the agency's data were overreported. Consequently, those data are not included in this table.

[5] Because of changes in the state/local agency's reporting practices, figures are not comparable to previous years' data.

Table 8. Offenses Known to Law Enforcement, by State and City, 2010—*Continued*

(Number)

State/city	Population	Violent crime	Murder and non-negligent man-slaughter	Forcible rape	Robbery	Aggravated assault	Property crime	Burglary	Larceny-theft	Motor vehicle theft	Arson[1]
OKLAHOMA—*Continued*											
Mooreland	1,270	1	0	1	0	0	22	9	12	1	0
Morris	1,325	0	0	0	0	0	5	0	3	2	0
Mountain View	758	1	0	0	0	1	4	1	3	0	1
Muldrow	3,201	12	0	2	0	10	53	16	34	3	1
Muskogee	40,499	373	6	18	57	292	1,689	578	1,026	85	29
Mustang	19,200	27	0	1	4	22	412	92	304	16	3
Newcastle	7,845	7	0	1	0	6	212	51	134	27	0
Newkirk	2,158	3	0	1	0	2	59	20	39	0	0
Nichols Hills	4,147	2	0	0	1	1	74	18	50	6	0
Nicoma Park	2,464	1	0	0	0	1	30	12	15	3	0
Noble	6,046	9	0	6	1	2	121	25	94	2	0
Norman	111,534	138	2	47	36	53	3,551	811	2,628	112	6
Nowata[3]	3,956		0	2	0		61	8	53	0	1
Oilton	1,141	1	0	0	0	1	16	9	7	0	1
Okemah	2,833	9	0	2	0	7	148	40	100	8	0
Oklahoma City	571,865	5,304	54	340	1,112	3,798	33,263	9,901	19,760	3,602	119
Okmulgee	12,648	101	1	7	13	80	584	159	400	25	9
Oologah	1,180	3	0	0	0	3	22	10	10	2	0
Owasso	30,431	42	0	2	11	29	826	108	680	38	5
Pauls Valley	6,112	34	0	3	5	26	362	89	262	11	1
Pawhuska	3,350	78	0	0	0	78	107	51	51	5	0
Pawnee	2,160	3	0	0	1	2	33	20	11	2	0
Perkins	2,680	1	0	0	0	1	15	1	12	2	0
Perry	4,972	8	0	1	0	7	99	25	68	6	0
Piedmont	6,079	1	0	0	0	1	48	24	22	2	0
Pocola	4,581	3	2	0	0	1	50	14	34	2	1
Ponca City	24,928	113	1	17	17	78	1,236	299	902	35	26
Porum	748	4	0	1	0	3	13	7	6	0	1
Poteau	8,408	35	0	3	1	31	271	46	192	33	3
Prague	2,153	8	0	2	0	6	44	12	27	5	0
Pryor[3]	9,400		1	8	4		310	93	202	15	1
Purcell	6,359	13	0	4	0	9	235	45	183	7	0
Ringling	1,065	5	0	0	0	5	18	6	11	1	0
Roland	3,605	7	0	0	0	7	57	14	39	4	0
Sallisaw	8,985	5	0	2	1	2	286	44	229	13	0
Sand Springs	19,204	33	1	3	11	18	636	98	481	57	1
Sapulpa	21,567	44	0	11	15	18	656	118	487	51	3
Sawyer	269	4	0	0	0	4	13	2	9	2	0
Sayre	4,137	12	0	0	1	11	37	13	24	0	0
Seminole	6,895	38	0	5	12	21	532	148	351	33	1
Shawnee[3]	31,002		2	10	19		1,757	528	1,091	138	0
Skiatook	7,118	106	0	9	0	97	276	75	184	17	1
Snyder	1,329	4	0	1	0	3	8	1	7	0	0
South Coffeyville	777	6	0	0	0	6	17	4	13	0	0
Spencer	4,150	11	0	0	1	10	83	33	39	11	3
Spiro	2,362	1	0	0	0	1	33	2	29	2	0
Stigler	2,979	3	0	1	0	2	58	10	46	2	0
Stillwater	47,414	100	1	16	16	67	1,548	269	1,191	88	11
Stilwell	3,530	7	0	2	1	4	77	16	58	3	0
Stratford[5]	1,497	5	0	1	0	4	15	3	9	3	0
Stroud	2,722	5	0	0	1	4	59	13	41	5	1
Sulphur	4,964	2	0	0	0	2	122	41	81	0	0
Tahlequah	17,067	33	0	7	6	20	694	103	577	14	2
Talihina	1,245	5	0	0	0	5	43	13	28	2	2
Tecumseh	6,857	16	0	0	3	13	206	63	128	15	0
The Village	9,923	49	0	2	3	44	324	73	232	19	2
Tishomingo	3,266	9	1	3	0	5	63	23	39	1	0
Tonkawa	3,194	8	0	2	0	6	103	25	74	4	0
Tryon	452	1	0	0	0	1	8	2	6	0	0
Tulsa	393,412	4,304	54	252	1,381	2,617	21,355	7,146	11,857	2,352	203
Tuttle	6,450	31	0	4	0	27	167	32	126	9	3
Valliant	743	6	0	0	0	6	17	7	10	0	0
Verdigris	3,245	1	0	1	0	0	29	11	18	0	0
Vian	1,562	3	0	0	0	3	25	7	17	1	0
Vinita	6,115	16	0	0	0	16	156	27	117	12	3
Wagoner	8,270	71	1	3	3	64	425	108	302	15	4
Walters	2,468	1	0	0	0	1	13	4	9	0	0
Warner[5]	1,560	4	0	0	0	4	32	17	11	4	0
Warr Acres	9,579	71	1	5	14	51	455	134	279	42	2
Washington	570	0	0	0	0	0	5	2	1	2	1
Watonga	5,833	15	0	1	2	12	50	15	30	5	0
Waynoka	906	0	0	0	0	0	13	5	8	0	0

[1] The FBI does not publish arson data unless it receives data from either the agency or the state for all 12 months of the calendar year.

[3] The FBI determined that the agency's data were overreported. Consequently, those data are not included in this table.

[5] Because of changes in the state/local agency's reporting practices, figures are not comparable to previous years' data.

Table 8.   Offenses Known to Law Enforcement, by State and City, 2010—*Continued*

(Number)

State/city	Population	Violent crime	Murder and non-negligent man-slaughter	Forcible rape	Robbery	Aggravated assault	Property crime	Burglary	Larceny-theft	Motor vehicle theft	Arson[1]
OKLAHOMA—*Continued*											
Weatherford[3]	10,551		0	4	1		311	88	215	8	0
Weleetka	903	6	0	0	1	5	51	18	31	2	0
Westville	1,658	7	0	1	0	6	43	15	24	4	2
Wetumka	1,416	1	0	0	0	1	35	15	18	2	0
Wewoka	3,320	10	0	1	1	8	177	64	103	10	0
Wilburton	2,928	13	0	0	1	12	65	20	44	1	1
Wilson	1,669	14	0	0	0	14	30	10	16	4	1
Woodward	12,535	17	0	10	1	6	446	165	265	16	1
Wright City	788	3	0	1	0	2	15	2	12	1	0
Wynnewood	2,286	2	1	0	0	1	37	2	33	2	0
Yale[5]	1,504	4	0	1	0	3	22	9	10	3	0
Yukon	24,023	12	0	1	0	11	381	74	291	16	2
OREGON[5]											
Adair Village	800	1	0	0	0	1	17	3	13	1	0
Albany	48,777	86	0	12	26	48	1,287	204	1,023	60	25
Amity	1,431	2	0	2	0	0	38	7	30	1	0
Ashland	20,942	25	0	7	8	10	550	81	445	24	9
Astoria	9,639	13	1	1	4	7	631	142	460	29	5
Aumsville	3,727	5	0	0	0	5	44	7	34	3	1
Aurora	1,056	6	0	0	0	6	11	3	7	1	0
Baker City	9,309	3	1	0	0	2	207	29	169	9	1
Bandon	3,222	0	0	0	0	0	93	12	78	3	0
Beaverton	93,993	239	0	31	45	163	1,773	198	1,439	136	24
Bend	79,556	247	5	14	31	197	2,410	387	1,951	72	19
Black Butte		0	0	0	0	0	10	2	8	0	0
Boardman	3,032	6	0	2	0	4	53	12	41	0	1
Burns	2,596	1	0	0	0	1	79	28	49	2	0
Canby	15,935	19	0	2	6	11	362	65	286	11	4
Cannon Beach	1,714	1	0	0	1	0	57	8	49	0	2
Carlton	1,720	2	0	0	0	2	19	7	11	1	0
Central Point	16,819	15	0	6	2	7	477	61	401	15	2
Clatskanie	1,615	1	0	0	0	1	41	6	35	0	0
Coburg	1,075	1	0	0	0	1	23	7	11	5	0
Condon	610	0	0	0	0	0	1	1	0	0	0
Coos Bay	15,227	64	0	9	10	45	832	156	652	24	3
Cornelius	11,703	24	0	2	5	17	318	87	209	22	9
Corvallis	51,276	57	0	9	12	36	1,377	209	1,132	36	23
Cottage Grove	9,173	44	0	0	3	41	440	52	348	40	7
Creswell	5,237	23	0	3	3	17	194	53	109	32	3
Dallas	16,416	30	0	3	4	23	290	46	238	6	4
Eagle Point	8,673	4	0	2	1	1	198	25	169	4	1
Enterprise	1,728	0	0	0	0	0	28	13	14	1	1
Estacada	2,712	5	0	1	0	4	133	24	106	3	1
Eugene	153,269	416	0	80	168	168	7,028	1,293	5,136	599	98
Florence	8,824	6	0	1	1	4	314	76	227	11	5
Forest Grove	21,600	53	0	8	4	41	700	129	548	23	6
Gearhart	1,196	0	0	0	0	0	14	4	10	0	0
Gervais	2,488	11	0	0	1	10	57	10	35	12	0
Gladstone	12,162	34	0	5	7	22	339	57	252	30	8
Gold Beach	1,878	3	0	0	0	3	26	3	23	0	0
Gresham	102,540	470	7	42	176	245	4,055	674	2,714	667	33
Hermiston	15,399	60	1	10	9	40	679	116	542	21	2
Hines	1,341	0	0	0	0	0	35	7	27	1	1
Hubbard	2,861	2	0	1	0	1	33	4	28	1	1
Independence	9,835	8	0	2	0	6	215	19	183	13	7
Jacksonville	2,182	0	0	0	0	0	28	2	26	0	0
John Day	1,440	0	0	0	0	0	17	2	13	2	2
Junction City	5,754	1	0	0	0	1	45	7	37	1	1
Keizer	36,191	64	0	5	11	48	870	128	699	43	6
King City	2,993	3	0	1	1	1	52	12	39	1	0
Klamath Falls	19,922	95	0	23	24	48	849	203	588	58	4
La Grande	12,600	18	0	5	3	10	328	60	258	10	3
Lake Oswego	37,349	30	0	5	5	20	495	79	400	16	12
Lakeview	2,319	25	0	2	0	23	41	14	26	1	0
Lebanon	16,084	24	0	2	9	13	619	104	506	9	2
Lincoln City	8,144	49	0	5	3	41	356	63	281	12	4
Madras	5,815	11	1	2	2	6	325	64	232	29	1
Manzanita	851	0	0	0	0	0	27	18	9	0	0
McMinnville	31,748	60	1	13	10	36	1,050	164	832	54	9
Medford	73,525	300	3	46	40	211	3,219	379	2,678	162	36
Milwaukie	20,674	21	0	7	11	3	517	99	389	29	1
Molalla	7,727	13	0	4	0	9	215	34	171	10	0

[1] The FBI does not publish arson data unless it receives data from either the agency or the state for all 12 months of the calendar year.

[3] The FBI determined that the agency's data were overreported. Consequently, those data are not included in this table.

[5] Because of changes in the state/local agency's reporting practices, figures are not comparable to previous years' data.

Table 8.   Offenses Known to Law Enforcement, by State and City, 2010—*Continued*

(Number)

State/city	Population	Violent crime	Murder and non-negligent man-slaughter	Forcible rape	Robbery	Aggravated assault	Property crime	Burglary	Larceny-theft	Motor vehicle theft	Arson[1]
OREGON—*Continued*											
Monmouth	9,851	16	0	4	2	10	145	25	117	3	2
Mount Angel	3,374	16	0	3	1	12	72	7	63	2	3
Myrtle Creek	3,401	3	0	2	0	1	29	5	23	1	1
Newberg-Dundee	26,738	30	1	8	4	17	458	44	383	31	13
Newport	9,877	38	0	11	5	22	380	64	300	16	1
Oakridge	3,195	10	0	1	0	9	85	29	53	3	0
Ontario	10,822	45	1	3	2	39	713	93	596	24	3
Oregon City	32,045	38	0	9	15	14	929	119	744	66	0
Pendleton	16,263	53	1	8	14	30	677	94	548	35	3
Philomath	4,542	1	0	1	0	0	58	22	34	2	0
Phoenix	4,387	2	0	1	1	0	107	22	77	8	0
Pilot Rock	1,487	1	0	1	0	0	25	6	18	1	0
Portland	564,392	3,051	22	230	1,005	1,794	28,391	4,120	21,026	3,245	214
Port Orford	1,073	6	0	1	0	5	39	5	34	0	0
Rainier	1,798	0	0	0	0	0	40	9	27	4	0
Redmond	25,480	89	0	17	12	60	1,360	187	1,120	53	30
Reedsport	4,093	1	0	1	0	0	116	8	106	2	0
Rockaway Beach	1,351	4	0	0	0	4	40	22	18	0	0
Rogue River	1,918	1	0	1	0	0	65	13	47	5	0
Roseburg	20,169	52	1	8	24	19	985	133	813	39	16
Salem	155,820	483	1	48	118	316	6,056	868	4,761	427	36
Sandy	9,426	8	0	3	3	2	268	38	208	22	1
Scappoose	6,480	13	0	5	0	8	123	13	102	8	0
Sherwood	18,483	9	0	5	1	3	199	25	170	4	1
Silverton	9,900	22	0	1	1	20	147	23	108	16	4
Stayton	7,369	28	0	3	1	24	375	51	299	25	4
St. Helens	12,708	11	0	4	2	5	258	41	203	14	14
Sunriver		2	0	1	0	1	55	15	40	0	0
Sutherlin	7,064	7	0	6	0	1	131	21	101	9	0
Sweet Home	8,950	17	0	3	2	12	452	74	369	9	1
Talent	6,242	9	0	0	5	4	141	12	126	3	0
The Dalles	12,186	12	0	2	7	3	697	103	563	31	2
Tigard	49,466	89	1	11	58	19	1,955	192	1,695	68	4
Tillamook	4,333	4	0	2	0	2	212	27	175	10	0
Toledo	3,239	26	0	2	6	18	172	41	127	4	1
Troutdale	15,692	25	0	8	7	10	488	87	361	40	4
Turner	1,782	4	0	0	0	4	43	16	26	1	3
Umatilla	6,387	8	0	0	1	7	76	8	61	7	0
Veneta	4,565	46	0	5	0	41	232	70	154	8	4
West Linn	25,614	9	0	1	6	2	295	45	241	9	1
Wilsonville	19,718	6	0	2	3	1	268	23	223	22	0
Winston	5,463	7	0	2	2	3	162	33	123	6	4
Woodburn	23,032	64	0	2	16	46	665	142	453	70	11
Yamhill	923	0	0	0	0	0	16	4	10	2	0
The Dalles	6,287	4	0	3	0	1	138	18	118	2	2
Tigard	11,874	14	0	3	3	8	610	151	431	28	0
Tillamook	49,422	63	0	12	37	14	1,684	173	1,454	57	8
Toledo	4,414	6	2	1	0	3	227	36	186	5	2
Troutdale	3,278	4	1	0	1	2	94	11	80	3	2
Tualatin	15,630	17	0	3	9	5	463	62	368	33	3
Turner	26,903	58	1	17	17	23	873	69	762	42	0
Umatilla	1,784	8	0	1	0	7	49	10	37	2	1
Veneta	6,443	12	0	1	0	11	69	8	51	10	1
Vernonia	4,489	41	0	4	2	35	212	58	132	22	5
Warrenton	2,280	0	0	0	0	0	33	13	19	1	1
West Linn	4,489	0	0	0	0	0	136	24	105	7	6
Weston	25,568	12	0	3	3	6	271	23	237	11	3
Wilsonville	690	1	0	0	0	1	20	4	14	2	0
Winston	19,666	14	0	2	6	6	587	55	489	43	5
Woodburn	5,622	6	0	1	1	4	110	26	77	7	15
Yamhill	23,103	59	0	6	24	29	997	139	702	156	6
PENNSYLVANIA											
Abington Township	54,235	96	0	1	43	52	1,258	189	1,037	32	6
Adamstown	1,597	0	0	0	0	0	20	5	15	0	0
Adams Township, Butler County	10,107	8	0	3	0	5	64	8	54	2	0
Adams Township, Cambria County	6,024	0	0	0	0	0	25	0	22	3	0
Akron	4,053	4	0	0	0	4	30	6	22	2	0
Alburtis	2,449	0	0	0	0	0	22	2	20	0	0
Aldan	4,284	9	0	0	2	7	119	9	110	0	1
Aleppo Township	1,220	0	0	0	0	0	9	2	7	0	0
Aliquippa	10,497	84	5	3	14	62	168	63	89	16	0
Allegheny Township, Westmoreland County	8,288	9	0	1	0	8	126	15	111	0	0
Allentown	108,473	732	9	67	460	196	5,089	1,327	3,345	417	29

[1] The FBI does not publish arson data unless it receives data from either the agency or the state for all 12 months of the calendar year.

Table 8. Offenses Known to Law Enforcement, by State and City, 2010—*Continued*

(Number)

State/city	Population	Violent crime	Murder and non-negligent man-slaughter	Forcible rape	Robbery	Aggravated assault	Property crime	Burglary	Larceny-theft	Motor vehicle theft	Arson[1]
PENNSYLVANIA—*Continued*											
Altoona	46,213	167	0	29	51	87	947	294	616	37	10
Ambler	6,228	13	0	2	2	9	155	14	136	5	0
Amity Township	12,299	7	2	1	0	4	159	30	121	8	5
Annville Township	4,808	1	0	0	0	1	62	19	43	0	2
Apollo	1,598	2	0	0	0	2	1	1	0	0	0
Archbald	6,584	25	0	0	1	24	92	19	73	0	0
Arnold	5,178	29	0	4	11	14	112	33	63	16	1
Ashland	3,088	4	0	0	0	4	59	15	42	2	1
Ashley	2,670	0	0	0	0	0	18	4	13	1	0
Aspinwall	2,692	1	0	0	1	0	46	13	33	0	0
Aston Township	17,100	24	0	2	9	13	354	43	303	8	0
Atglen	1,403	0	0	0	0	0	9	1	8	0	0
Athens	3,175	1	0	0	0	1	45	8	36	1	0
Athens Township	5,042	5	0	3	0	2	111	2	107	2	0
Avoca	2,659	1	0	1	0	0	43	12	30	1	0
Avondale	1,100	0	0	0	0	0	2	0	2	0	0
Avonmore Boro	761	0	0	0	0	0	0	0	0	0	0
Baden	3,965	2	0	0	0	2	55	6	46	3	0
Baldwin Borough	18,450	30	0	4	8	18	189	45	133	11	0
Baldwin Township	1,992	3	0	0	0	3	16	6	9	1	0
Bally	1,108	0	0	0	0	0	0	0	0	0	0
Bangor	5,343	23	0	2	1	20	153	18	133	2	1
Barrett Township	4,327	2	0	0	0	2	60	20	39	1	0
Beaver	4,321	6	0	0	0	6	104	18	82	4	0
Beaver Falls	8,926	77	3	6	18	50	342	29	295	18	1
Beaver Meadows	951	0	0	0	0	0	3	1	2	0	0
Bedford	2,967	6	3	0	0	3	28	4	24	0	1
Bedminster Township	6,480	2	0	1	1	0	45	2	43	0	0
Bell Acres	1,357	0	0	0	0	0	0	0	0	0	0
Bellefonte	6,179	5	0	0	0	5	75	7	68	0	0
Bellevue	7,969	20	1	2	11	6	257	60	186	11	1
Bellwood	1,871	0	0	0	0	0	4	1	3	0	0
Ben Avon	1,764	0	0	0	0	0	31	3	28	0	0
Ben Avon Heights	358	0	0	0	0	0	3	0	3	0	0
Bendersville	613	1	0	0	0	1	4	2	2	0	0
Bensalem Township	59,028	110	0	6	67	37	2,147	305	1,718	124	47
Berks-Lehigh Regional	31,334	15	0	0	5	10	279	56	210	13	3
Berlin	2,046	1	0	1	0	0	15	2	12	1	0
Bern Township	7,311	23	0	2	1	20	78	16	57	5	0
Bernville	888	0	0	0	0	0	0	0	0	0	0
Berwick	10,169	31	0	9	3	19	447	82	353	12	2
Bessemer	1,086	0	0	0	0	0	0	0	0	0	0
Bethel Park	31,514	35	0	4	5	26	292	50	237	5	2
Bethel Township, Armstrong County	1,188	0	0	0	0	0	0	0	0	0	0
Bethel Township, Berks County	4,572	0	0	0	0	0	22	0	21	1	0
Bethel Township, Delaware County	12,017	5	0	0	1	4	125	20	101	4	0
Bethlehem	73,634	234	0	18	110	106	2,069	445	1,522	102	12
Bethlehem Township	24,220	32	0	3	9	20	403	51	336	16	4
Biglerville	1,168	1	0	0	0	1	10	0	10	0	0
Birdsboro	5,237	6	0	0	0	6	81	15	61	5	1
Birmingham Township	4,366	5	0	0	0	5	28	4	24	0	0
Blacklick Township	2,063	0	0	0	0	0	4	0	4	0	0
Blair Township	4,781	0	0	0	0	0	47	8	38	1	1
Blairsville	3,333	18	0	0	7	11	106	16	84	6	0
Blakely	6,716	4	0	1	1	2	96	15	77	4	0
Blawnox	1,435	1	0	0	0	1	6	2	3	1	0
Bloomsburg Town	12,873	19	0	3	1	15	342	60	272	10	2
Blythe Township	916	0	0	0	0	0	0	0	0	0	0
Boswell	1,231	2	0	0	0	2	0	0	0	0	0
Boyertown	3,960	8	0	1	2	5	100	12	83	5	0
Brackenridge	3,234	12	0	0	2	10	81	12	69	0	0
Braddock	2,662	10	0	0	0	10	5	4	0	1	0
Braddock Hills	1,816	2	0	0	0	2	7	3	4	0	0
Bradford	8,271	49	2	3	3	41	355	37	306	12	4
Bradford Township	4,927	7	0	1	1	5	44	12	28	4	2
Brecknock Township, Berks County	5,008	0	0	0	0	0	24	11	12	1	0
Brentwood	9,470	21	0	1	7	13	230	38	180	12	0
Briar Creek Township	3,128	1	0	0	0	1	46	11	34	1	0
Bridgeport	4,425	7	0	0	3	4	139	16	109	14	2
Bridgeville	4,869	6	0	0	0	6	56	17	37	2	0
Bridgewater	871	2	0	0	1	1	57	11	44	2	0
Brighton Township	7,956	11	0	0	0	11	44	9	35	0	0
Bristol	9,699	24	0	1	15	8	342	33	288	21	2

[1] The FBI does not publish arson data unless it receives data from either the agency or the state for all 12 months of the calendar year.

Table 8.   Offenses Known to Law Enforcement, by State and City, 2010—*Continued*

(Number)

State/city	Population	Violent crime	Murder and non-negligent man-slaughter	Forcible rape	Robbery	Aggravated assault	Property crime	Burglary	Larceny-theft	Motor vehicle theft	Arson[1]
PENNSYLVANIA—*Continued*											
Bristol Township	54,171	127	1	12	74	40	1,474	261	1,088	125	14
Brockway	2,022	1	0	0	0	1	8	1	6	1	0
Brookhaven	8,024	16	0	0	5	11	233	38	189	6	4
Brookville	3,932	9	0	0	1	8	53	5	46	2	0
Brownsville	2,586	6	0	0	2	4	61	18	41	2	0
Bryn Athyn	1,346	0	0	0	0	0	22	2	18	2	1
Buckingham Township	20,119	1	0	0	0	1	167	24	138	5	0
Buffalo Township	7,411	8	0	0	0	8	53	16	36	1	1
Bushkill Township	8,546	19	1	0	0	18	74	18	52	4	0
Butler	13,916	82	0	0	35	47	602	111	481	10	2
Butler Township, Butler County	16,659	18	0	0	3	15	368	40	321	7	1
Butler Township, Luzerne County	9,568	48	0	6	1	41	112	29	75	8	2
Butler Township, Schuykill County	6,105	2	0	0	0	2	28	16	12	0	0
Caernarvon Township, Berks County	3,650	9	0	1	0	8	85	5	77	3	0
California	6,411	12	0	0	3	9	73	11	61	1	0
Caln Township	12,496	48	0	1	9	38	263	30	223	10	0
Cambria Township	6,168	10	0	0	3	7	124	22	98	4	0
Cambridge Springs	2,651	4	0	0	0	4	7	1	6	0	1
Camp Hill	7,454	12	0	2	4	6	122	8	113	1	0
Canonsburg	8,776	5	1	0	2	2	150	18	132	0	0
Canton	1,681	2	0	0	0	2	21	10	10	1	0
Carbondale	9,155	14	0	0	2	12	135	39	87	9	2
Carlisle	18,708	54	0	10	27	17	557	72	482	3	4
Carmichaels	516	0	0	0	0	0	1	1	0	0	0
Carnegie	7,929	12	0	0	3	9	225	30	185	10	0
Carrolltown	955	0	0	0	0	0	11	0	10	1	0
Carroll Township, Washington County	5,481	17	0	0	0	17	76	21	51	4	0
Carroll Township, York County	6,070	6	0	1	0	5	109	15	90	4	2
Carroll Valley	3,604	2	0	1	0	1	67	2	65	0	0
Cass Township	1,795	3	0	0	1	2	13	6	3	4	1
Castle Shannon	8,069	21	0	0	2	19	81	18	60	3	1
Catasauqua	6,628	10	0	0	3	7	153	17	132	4	0
Catawissa	1,532	2	0	1	0	1	44	5	38	1	0
Cecil Township	10,821	2	0	0	0	2	16	3	13	0	0
Center Township	11,649	18	1	4	2	11	454	51	401	2	0
Centerville	3,216	0	0	0	0	0	20	5	14	1	0
Central Berks Regional	9,487	10	0	1	4	5	184	32	132	20	1
Chalfont	4,221	0	0	0	0	0	37	2	34	1	0
Charleroi	5,692	30	0	4	11	15	187	29	150	8	1
Chartiers Township	7,507	4	0	1	0	3	65	12	52	1	0
Cheltenham Township	36,084	98	1	7	50	40	1,015	239	729	47	3
Cherry Tree	410	0	0	0	0	0	0	0	0	0	0
Chester	37,308	911	24	31	206	650	1,252	466	638	148	33
Chester Township	4,495	48	0	2	5	41	136	51	74	11	3
Chippewa Township	9,777	8	0	0	2	6	205	16	185	4	0
Christiana	1,118	1	0	0	0	1	16	5	11	0	0
Churchill	3,216	26	0	0	1	25	22	8	14	0	0
Clarion	5,177	3	0	0	2	1	86	7	71	8	0
Claysville	673	0	0	0	0	0	5	0	5	0	0
Clay Township	6,114	2	0	0	1	1	43	6	35	2	0
Clearfield	6,088	39	0	4	3	32	268	42	223	3	1
Cleona	2,150	1	0	0	0	1	21	10	11	0	0
Clifford Township	2,449	0	0	0	0	0	3	1	0	2	0
Coaldale	2,104	0	0	0	0	0	7	3	4	0	0
Coal Township	10,195	38	0	1	0	37	200	8	183	9	2
Coatesville	11,920	140	3	7	60	70	487	111	340	36	0
Cochranton	1,059	0	0	0	0	0	10	0	10	0	0
Colebrookdale District	6,483	3	0	1	0	2	107	2	101	4	0
Collegeville	5,117	4	0	0	3	1	74	6	67	1	0
Collier Township	6,588	7	0	1	2	4	156	17	136	3	0
Collingdale	8,436	97	0	4	11	82	208	33	157	18	1
Colonial Regional	20,560	10	0	4	5	1	483	65	409	9	2
Columbia	10,116	22	1	3	10	8	217	54	155	8	1
Conemaugh Township, Cambria County	2,441	3	0	0	0	3	10	2	8	0	0
Conemaugh Township, Somerset County	7,171	2	0	0	0	2	43	16	27	0	0
Conewago Township, Adams County	6,215	3	0	0	1	2	113	3	110	0	0
Conewango Township	3,542	9	0	4	1	4	146	18	128	0	1
Conneaut Lake Regional	3,501	1	0	0	0	1	45	17	28	0	0
Connellsville	8,313	21	0	3	9	9	309	54	243	12	0
Conoy Township	3,430	0	0	0	0	0	50	18	31	1	2
Conshohocken	8,593	22	0	3	2	17	205	23	177	5	0
Conway	2,112	6	0	0	0	6	11	2	9	0	0
Conyngham	1,840	0	0	0	0	0	0	0	0	0	0

[1] The FBI does not publish arson data unless it receives data from either the agency or the state for all 12 months of the calendar year.

Table 8. Offenses Known to Law Enforcement, by State and City, 2010—*Continued*

(Number)

State/city	Population	Violent crime	Murder and non-negligent man-slaughter	Forcible rape	Robbery	Aggravated assault	Property crime	Burglary	Larceny-theft	Motor vehicle theft	Arson[1]
PENNSYLVANIA—*Continued*											
Coopersburg	2,586	4	0	1	0	3	18	1	17	0	0
Coplay	3,401	1	0	0	0	1	75	12	62	1	0
Coraopolis	5,575	50	0	0	2	48	107	15	87	5	1
Cornwall	3,562	0	0	0	0	0	1	0	1	0	0
Corry	6,315	38	0	5	1	32	136	19	111	6	2
Coudersport	2,357	0	0	0	0	0	9	4	5	0	0
Covington Township	2,215	2	0	0	0	2	36	4	28	4	0
Cranberry Township	28,107	3	1	0	1	1	316	51	265	0	0
Crescent Township	2,778	12	0	0	1	11	44	13	29	2	1
Cresson	1,463	1	0	0	0	1	47	1	46	0	0
Cresson Township	4,533	10	0	0	0	10	17	0	17	0	1
Croyle Township	2,220	0	0	0	0	0	10	0	10	0	0
Cumberland Township, Adams County	6,469	2	0	1	0	1	43	25	18	0	0
Cumberland Township, Greene County	6,351	8	0	2	1	5	151	32	116	3	1
Cumru Township	15,163	11	1	1	6	3	321	35	274	12	0
Curwensville	2,431	2	0	0	0	2	39	12	27	0	1
Dale	1,342	0	0	0	0	0	5	2	3	0	3
Dallas	2,477	2	0	0	0	2	23	3	20	0	0
Dallas Township	9,187	7	1	3	0	3	61	14	47	0	1
Dalton	1,231	2	0	0	0	2	21	4	17	0	0
Danville	4,410	24	0	1	0	23	92	10	80	2	2
Darby	9,980	413	0	12	66	335	454	155	247	52	0
Darby Township	9,624	32	1	3	15	13	280	55	212	13	0
Darlington Township	2,023	0	0	0	0	0	0	0	0	0	0
Decatur Township	5,884	7	0	1	0	6	60	15	41	4	0
Delaware Water Gap	785	0	0	0	0	0	0	0	0	0	0
Delmont	2,449	1	0	0	0	1	43	12	31	0	0
Denver	3,714	5	0	1	0	4	63	14	48	1	1
Derry	2,763	9	0	0	0	9	12	0	12	0	0
Derry Township, Dauphin County	22,348	41	0	7	3	31	593	58	510	25	2
Dickson City	5,876	14	0	1	2	11	301	25	272	4	1
Donegal Township	2,923	2	0	0	0	2	6	2	4	0	0
Donora	5,242	14	0	3	0	11	72	18	50	4	4
Dormont	8,411	25	0	0	6	19	84	9	69	6	1
Douglass Township, Berks County	3,603	5	0	0	2	3	32	12	18	2	0
Douglass Township, Montgomery County	10,372	13	0	3	0	10	136	4	128	4	1
Downingtown	8,093	27	1	0	8	18	244	23	209	12	0
Doylestown	8,169	9	0	0	2	7	175	24	147	4	0
Doylestown Township	18,844	16	0	3	4	9	295	42	247	6	0
Dublin Borough	2,162	2	0	0	1	1	11	6	5	0	0
Du Bois	7,558	21	0	6	0	15	330	39	279	12	1
Duboistown	1,187	0	0	0	0	0	1	0	1	0	0
Duncannon	1,498	0	0	0	0	0	17	1	15	1	0
Duncansville	1,235	0	0	0	0	0	30	2	28	0	0
Dunmore	13,943	18	0	1	5	12	170	33	129	8	1
Dunnstable Township	983	0	0	0	0	0	4	0	4	0	0
Duquesne	6,678	94	3	7	30	54	314	124	164	26	21
Duryea	4,332	8	0	2	2	4	93	24	60	9	0
Earl Township	7,293	2	0	2	0	0	38	7	30	1	0
East Bangor	1,222	0	0	0	0	0	7	0	7	0	0
East Berlin	1,452	0	0	0	0	0	0	0	0	0	0
East Bethlehem Township	2,351	3	0	0	0	3	48	9	36	3	0
East Brandywine Township	7,133	12	1	0	2	9	61	8	53	0	0
East Buffalo Township	5,945	3	0	0	0	3	19	3	14	2	0
East Cocalico Township	10,642	1	0	0	0	1	119	18	91	10	1
East Conemaugh	1,150	5	0	0	0	5	5	2	3	0	0
East Coventry Township	7,177	4	0	0	0	4	34	5	29	0	0
East Deer Township	1,321	1	0	0	0	1	34	6	26	2	0
Eastern Adams Regional	10,116	7	1	3	2	1	99	6	85	8	0
Eastern Pike Regional	5,602	15	0	0	1	14	242	22	219	1	0
East Fallowfield Township	8,075	0	0	0	0	0	61	15	41	5	0
East Franklin Township	3,910	6	0	1	0	5	29	1	28	0	0
East Hempfield Township	24,035	33	0	6	17	10	435	61	368	6	3
East Lampeter Township	15,465	27	0	5	9	13	660	39	604	17	1
East Marlborough Township	8,316	0	0	0	0	0	16	1	13	2	1
East McKeesport	2,918	7	0	0	0	7	42	18	22	2	0
East Norriton Township	13,787	15	0	1	9	5	270	10	242	18	0
East Norwegian Township	832	0	0	0	0	0	0	0	0	0	0
Easton	26,506	127	3	9	63	52	793	108	641	44	6
East Pennsboro Township	20,147	13	0	4	6	3	324	33	286	5	0
East Penn Township	2,786	7	0	1	0	6	23	4	17	2	0
East Petersburg	4,374	1	0	0	0	1	34	7	26	1	2
East Pikeland Township	7,113	8	0	2	3	3	63	5	57	1	0

[1] The FBI does not publish arson data unless it receives data from either the agency or the state for all 12 months of the calendar year.

Table 8. Offenses Known to Law Enforcement, by State and City, 2010—*Continued*

(Number)

State/city	Population	Violent crime	Murder and non-negligent man-slaughter	Forcible rape	Robbery	Aggravated assault	Property crime	Burglary	Larceny-theft	Motor vehicle theft	Arson[1]
PENNSYLVANIA—*Continued*											
East Pittsburgh	1,937	50	0	2	7	41	95	25	68	2	0
East Taylor Township	2,514	3	0	0	1	2	19	8	10	1	0
Easttown Township	10,706	4	0	1	3	0	142	50	89	3	1
East Union Township	1,431	0	0	0	0	0	0	0	0	0	0
East Vincent Township	6,688	2	0	0	2	0	68	16	51	1	0
East Washington	1,859	8	0	1	0	7	55	11	44	0	0
East Whiteland Township	10,899	6	0	1	1	4	153	16	135	2	0
Ebensburg	2,898	16	0	0	0	16	68	16	50	2	0
Economy	9,150	1	0	0	1	0	42	4	36	2	0
Eddystone	2,360	17	0	0	2	15	226	9	212	5	1
Edgewood	3,116	8	0	0	5	3	199	15	181	3	0
Edgeworth	1,586	0	0	0	0	0	0	0	0	0	0
Edinboro	6,567	10	0	3	1	6	144	19	125	0	0
Edwardsville	4,651	37	0	2	2	33	141	10	125	6	1
Elizabethtown	12,186	13	0	2	3	8	167	25	137	5	0
Elizabeth Township	12,902	7	0	0	3	4	150	26	120	4	0
Ellwood City	7,887	24	0	2	8	14	281	75	203	3	3
Emelton Borough	726	0	0	0	0	0	7	1	6	0	0
Emmaus	11,485	13	1	1	8	3	216	39	174	3	1
Emsworth	2,381	8	0	0	0	8	31	4	27	0	0
Ephrata	13,247	31	1	2	10	18	249	43	201	5	2
Ephrata Township	9,982	12	1	3	1	7	172	17	151	4	1
Erie	104,077	491	12	78	173	228	3,490	1,106	2,245	139	46
Etna	3,612	15	0	0	2	13	130	17	107	6	0
Everett	1,838	6	0	0	0	6	19	8	11	0	0
Everson	774	0	0	0	0	0	0	0	0	0	0
Exeter	5,965	20	0	1	0	19	114	19	89	6	0
Exeter Township, Berks County	25,876	19	0	5	7	7	358	37	307	14	1
Exeter Township, Luzerne County	2,546	4	0	0	0	4	28	9	17	2	0
Fairfield	520	0	0	0	0	0	4	1	3	0	0
Fairview Township, Luzerne County	4,328	4	0	0	2	2	44	13	31	0	0
Fairview Township, York County	17,419	30	0	5	10	15	324	48	269	7	1
Fallowfield Township	4,200	1	0	0	0	1	25	5	18	2	0
Falls Township, Bucks County	33,850	52	0	3	33	16	775	108	627	40	3
Fawn Township	2,337	4	0	0	0	4	45	8	34	3	0
Fayette City	657	1	0	0	0	1	2	0	2	0	0
Ferguson Township	16,966	13	0	2	3	8	185	24	156	5	0
Ferndale	1,630	3	0	0	0	3	1	0	1	0	0
Findlay Township	5,090	6	0	0	0	6	44	12	31	1	0
Fleetwood	4,038	2	0	0	1	1	84	7	69	8	0
Folcroft	6,901	23	0	0	5	18	112	31	62	19	1
Ford City	3,108	2	0	0	1	1	59	12	47	0	0
Forest City	1,702	5	0	0	0	5	27	9	17	1	0
Forest Hills	6,459	3	0	1	1	1	82	16	64	2	0
Forks Township	15,331	4	0	2	0	2	139	11	126	2	0
Forty Fort	4,231	2	0	0	1	1	102	20	81	1	0
Forward Township	3,495	3	0	0	0	3	28	8	20	0	0
Foster Township	4,187	1	0	0	0	1	36	1	35	0	0
Fountain Hill	4,622	16	0	2	5	9	118	21	93	4	1
Fox Chapel	5,430	0	0	0	0	0	12	3	9	0	0
Frackville	4,106	2	0	0	0	2	5	3	0	2	0
Franconia Township	13,128	11	0	2	0	9	142	9	132	1	2
Franklin	6,590	13	0	1	3	9	167	32	132	3	3
Franklin Park	12,529	10	0	0	0	10	78	15	61	2	1
Frazer Township	1,195	1	0	0	0	1	75	4	69	2	0
Freedom	1,577	11	0	2	1	8	37	7	26	4	0
Freedom Township	3,334	4	0	1	0	3	42	8	33	1	0
Freemansburg	2,091	2	0	0	1	1	53	10	42	1	0
Freeport	1,771	3	0	0	0	3	12	4	8	0	0
Gaines Township	572	0	0	0	0	0	0	0	0	0	0
Galeton	1,200	1	0	0	0	1	6	1	5	0	0
Gallitzin Township	1,305	0	0	0	0	0	2	1	1	0	0
Gettysburg	8,172	33	0	13	7	13	182	26	155	1	3
Gilpin Township	2,480	0	0	0	0	0	2	1	1	0	0
Girard	2,932	5	0	1	1	3	71	7	64	0	0
Glassport	4,511	20	1	0	2	17	163	48	112	3	1
Glenolden	7,264	24	0	0	7	17	170	36	125	9	0
Granville Township	4,933	3	0	2	1	0	92	7	82	3	0
Greencastle	4,135	8	0	1	2	5	77	17	56	4	1
Greenfield Township, Blair County	3,775	3	0	1	0	2	129	22	107	0	1
Greensburg	15,271	35	1	1	5	28	444	72	365	7	4
Green Tree	4,407	8	0	0	5	3	57	12	45	0	0
Greenville	6,057	14	0	2	4	8	160	48	110	2	2

[1] The FBI does not publish arson data unless it receives data from either the agency or the state for all 12 months of the calendar year.

Table 8.   Offenses Known to Law Enforcement, by State and City, 2010—*Continued*

(Number)

State/city	Population	Violent crime	Murder and non-negligent man-slaughter	Forcible rape	Robbery	Aggravated assault	Property crime	Burglary	Larceny-theft	Motor vehicle theft	Arson[1]
PENNSYLVANIA—*Continued*											
Greenwood Township	2,083	0	0	0	0	0	0	0	0	0	0
Grove City	7,670	3	0	0	1	2	110	36	71	3	1
Halifax	840	0	0	0	0	0	4	3	1	0	0
Hamburg	4,260	12	0	0	2	10	77	10	62	5	0
Hamiltonban Township	2,834	3	0	0	0	3	5	0	5	0	0
Hampden Township	27,801	11	0	3	4	4	304	36	262	6	0
Hampton Township	17,361	14	0	1	0	13	148	13	132	3	0
Hanover	15,234	32	0	3	10	19	484	34	439	11	10
Hanover Township, Luzerne County	11,014	15	0	2	6	7	186	30	145	11	5
Hanover Township, Washington County	2,747	4	0	0	0	4	11	6	3	2	0
Harleton	263	0	0	0	0	0	6	4	2	0	0
Harmar Township	3,088	4	0	0	0	4	83	8	68	7	1
Harmony Township	3,016	5	0	0	1	4	94	10	77	7	0
Harrisburg	47,509	780	14	63	446	257	2,235	666	1,377	192	28
Harrisville	882	0	0	0	0	0	6	2	4	0	0
Harveys Lake	2,952	0	0	0	0	0	70	19	48	3	0
Hastings	1,285	13	0	0	0	13	41	8	31	2	2
Hatboro	7,166	9	0	0	0	9	96	20	72	4	0
Hatfield Township	20,276	23	0	5	4	14	282	30	243	9	6
Haverford Township	48,500	14	0	0	11	3	513	60	451	2	2
Hawley	1,301	0	0	0	0	0	14	1	13	0	0
Hazleton	21,705	90	1	9	26	54	509	130	325	54	0
Heidelberg Township, Berks County	1,787	1	0	0	1	0	9	2	7	0	0
Heidelberg Township, Lebanon County	4,274	0	0	0	0	0	17	4	13	0	0
Hellam Township	9,222	25	0	2	0	23	103	12	88	3	1
Hellertown	5,781	18	0	1	5	12	87	13	72	2	0
Hemlock Township	2,285	4	0	3	0	1	158	7	147	4	1
Hermitage	16,260	21	0	5	9	7	478	79	393	6	4
Highland Township	1,231	1	0	1	0	0	1	1	0	0	0
Highspire	2,630	18	0	0	2	16	77	15	58	4	4
Hilltown Township	13,752	9	1	0	3	5	259	31	222	6	2
Hollidaysburg	5,519	4	1	0	0	3	95	11	82	2	1
Homer City	1,690	2	0	0	0	2	10	2	8	0	0
Homestead	3,638	47	0	4	26	17	194	42	129	23	0
Honesdale	4,740	8	0	2	2	4	112	23	87	2	2
Honey Brook	1,636	0	0	0	0	0	1	0	1	0	0
Hooversville	695	0	0	0	0	0	6	1	5	0	0
Hop Bottom Borough	300	0	0	0	0	0	0	0	0	0	0
Hopewell Township	12,292	15	0	2	2	11	226	37	178	11	1
Horsham Township	24,983	15	1	0	2	12	259	32	211	16	2
Houston	1,242	2	0	0	0	2	2	1	1	0	0
Hughesville	2,034	1	0	0	0	1	66	6	58	2	0
Hulmeville	896	0	0	0	0	0	0	0	0	0	0
Hummelstown	4,476	11	0	0	1	10	81	9	68	4	0
Huntingdon	6,790	2	0	0	0	2	91	9	77	5	0
Independence Township, Beaver County	2,690	1	0	0	0	1	22	5	16	1	0
Indiana3	15,062		0	5	5		329	35	287	7	3
Indiana Township	7,036	4	0	0	0	4	54	15	37	2	0
Industry	1,770	0	0	0	0	0	22	5	17	0	0
Ingram	3,375	1	0	1	0	0	24	3	20	1	1
Irwin	4,031	3	0	0	0	3	5	0	5	0	0
Ivyland	852	0	0	0	0	0	12	1	11	0	0
Jackson Township, Butler County	3,782	5	0	0	0	5	50	14	35	1	0
Jackson Township, Luzerne County	4,742	1	0	0	0	1	13	2	11	0	0
Jamestown	628	0	0	0	0	0	13	1	12	0	0
Jeannette	9,824	11	0	0	1	10	97	23	74	0	1
Jefferson Hills Borough	9,862	14	0	0	1	13	91	25	62	4	0
Jefferson Township, Mercer County	2,315	0	0	0	0	0	7	6	1	0	0
Jenkins Township	4,949	4	0	0	1	3	108	18	84	6	1
Jenkintown	4,334	4	0	0	3	1	45	22	23	0	0
Jennerstown	685	0	0	0	0	0	2	1	1	0	0
Jermyn	2,227	23	0	0	0	23	46	17	27	2	0
Jim Thorpe	4,915	23	0	3	0	20	144	15	124	5	0
Johnsonburg	2,625	2	0	0	0	2	55	12	43	0	1
Johnstown	22,900	105	3	6	43	53	786	256	502	28	15
Juniata Valley Region	2,684	2	0	0	0	2	7	0	7	0	0
Kennett Square	5,339	15	0	0	7	8	120	20	93	7	2
Kidder Township	1,490	6	0	1	1	4	139	21	115	3	1
Kilbuck Township	626	0	0	0	0	0	14	0	14	0	0
Kingston	12,912	17	0	0	7	10	339	42	285	12	0
Kingston Township	7,086	6	0	0	1	5	63	4	56	3	2
Kiskiminetas Township	4,731	2	0	0	0	2	90	21	67	2	0
Kittanning	4,261	5	0	0	1	4	48	15	30	3	1

[1] The FBI does not publish arson data unless it receives data from either the agency or the state for all 12 months of the calendar year.

Table 8. Offenses Known to Law Enforcement, by State and City, 2010—*Continued*

(Number)

State/city	Population	Violent crime	Murder and non-negligent man-slaughter	Forcible rape	Robbery	Aggravated assault	Property crime	Burglary	Larceny-theft	Motor vehicle theft	Arson[1]
PENNSYLVANIA—*Continued*											
Kline Township	1,492	1	0	0	0	1	23	3	20	0	0
Knox	1,072	10	0	0	0	10	17	3	14	0	0
Kulpmont	2,752	2	0	0	0	2	56	11	45	0	0
Kutztown	5,159	7	0	2	3	2	118	17	96	5	0
Laflin Borough	1,493	3	0	1	0	2	14	3	11	0	0
Lake City	2,916	7	0	0	1	6	52	8	44	0	0
Lamar Township	2,388	0	0	0	0	0	15	2	13	0	0
Lancaster	55,582	511	5	55	214	237	2,857	583	2,160	114	35
Lancaster Township	14,950	20	0	1	12	7	578	66	496	16	2
Lanesboro	545	0	0	0	0	0	0	0	0	0	0
Langhorne Manor	1,068	0	0	0	0	0	7	0	7	0	0
Lansdale	15,622	33	0	8	9	16	249	39	200	10	1
Lansdowne	10,737	28	0	1	13	14	212	63	136	13	0
Lansford	4,152	2	0	0	0	2	72	24	47	1	1
Larksville	4,437	2	0	0	2	0	98	20	71	7	1
Latimore Township	2,915	4	0	0	1	3	32	4	27	1	0
Latrobe	8,307	45	1	5	3	36	225	29	192	4	1
Laureldale	3,772	0	0	0	0	0	21	5	12	4	0
Lawrence Park Township	3,690	3	0	0	1	2	56	5	51	0	0
Lawrence Township, Clearfield County	7,424	61	0	3	1	57	250	30	212	8	2
Lawrence Township, Tioga County	1,711	12	0	0	0	12	0	0	0	0	0
Lebanon	24,357	98	4	10	31	53	678	169	473	36	3
Leetsdale	1,111	5	0	0	0	5	26	5	19	2	0
Lehighton	5,450	14	0	2	4	8	186	36	141	9	2
Lehigh Township, Northampton County	11,215	13	2	0	0	11	121	26	90	5	1
Lewisburg	5,515	11	0	0	1	10	59	12	47	0	0
Liberty	2,413	2	0	0	0	2	11	0	10	1	0
Liberty Township, Adams County	1,331	2	0	0	0	2	24	2	13	9	0
Ligonier	1,598	4	0	0	0	4	10	1	9	0	1
Ligonier Township	6,763	7	0	0	0	7	54	10	43	1	0
Limerick Township	17,476	10	0	1	3	6	458	24	428	6	0
Lincoln	1,075	0	0	0	0	0	6	4	2	0	0
Linesville	1,086	2	0	0	0	2	5	0	5	0	0
Lititz	9,107	3	0	1	1	1	112	13	98	1	2
Littlestown	4,190	13	0	2	4	7	72	14	58	0	0
Lock Haven	8,484	14	1	3	3	7	236	35	200	1	4
Locust Township	2,563	2	0	1	0	1	47	13	34	0	0
Logan Township	12,341	45	0	5	5	35	352	46	301	5	1
Loretto	1,397	0	0	0	0	0	0	0	0	0	0
Lower Allen Township	18,025	4	0	0	2	2	199	20	176	3	3
Lower Burrell	12,078	10	0	2	0	8	128	23	97	8	0
Lower Frederick Township	4,859	0	0	0	0	0	13	2	10	1	0
Lower Gwynedd Township	11,627	19	1	0	2	16	186	13	168	5	0
Lower Heidelberg Township	5,620	4	0	0	0	4	30	5	25	0	0
Lower Makefield Township	32,410	16	0	0	5	11	321	64	251	6	0
Lower Merion Township	57,561	36	0	1	27	8	1,115	226	866	23	2
Lower Milford Township	3,973	1	0	1	0	0	6	2	3	1	1
Lower Moreland Township	12,940	8	1	1	2	4	197	63	127	7	1
Lower Paxton Township	46,144	93	2	16	27	48	1,216	208	977	31	6
Lower Pottsgrove Township	12,361	27	0	2	3	22	267	33	230	4	1
Lower Providence Township	26,475	53	0	0	3	50	278	57	202	19	2
Lower Salford Township	14,832	7	0	0	0	7	67	8	59	0	0
Lower Saucon Township	11,625	20	0	0	1	19	105	19	84	2	1
Lower Southampton Township	19,137	36	1	2	12	21	405	70	325	10	6
Lower Swatara Township	8,829	4	0	1	2	1	139	19	116	4	4
Lower Windsor Township	7,996	12	0	1	1	10	86	9	67	10	0
Luzerne Township	6,684	2	0	0	0	2	29	1	26	2	0
Lykens	1,867	0	0	0	0	0	12	1	11	0	0
Macungie	3,165	4	0	0	1	3	13	4	8	1	0
Mahanoy City	4,359	10	0	1	0	9	133	33	92	8	0
Mahanoy Township	3,502	0	0	0	0	0	0	0	0	0	0
Mahoning Township, Carbon County	4,493	32	0	0	0	32	142	15	127	0	0
Mahoning Township, Montour County	4,248	25	0	0	1	24	26	2	21	3	1
Main Township	1,293	0	0	0	0	0	0	0	0	0	0
Malvern	3,174	8	0	0	0	8	21	1	19	1	0
Manheim	4,680	10	0	1	2	7	101	16	83	2	0
Manheim Township	36,619	29	0	2	11	16	711	82	617	12	2
Manor	2,966	3	0	1	0	2	30	9	18	3	0
Manor Township, Armstrong County	3,881	0	0	0	0	0	0	0	0	0	0
Manor Township, Lancaster County	20,161	11	0	0	4	7	227	25	194	8	2
Mansfield	3,266	0	0	0	0	0	8	1	7	0	0
Marcus Hook	2,249	24	0	1	1	22	70	14	55	1	5
Marietta	2,629	1	0	0	0	1	53	7	46	0	1

[1] The FBI does not publish arson data unless it receives data from either the agency or the state for all 12 months of the calendar year.

Table 8.   Offenses Known to Law Enforcement, by State and City, 2010—*Continued*

(Number)

State/city	Population	Violent crime	Murder and non-negligent man-slaughter	Forcible rape	Robbery	Aggravated assault	Property crime	Burglary	Larceny-theft	Motor vehicle theft	Arson[1]
PENNSYLVANIA—*Continued*											
Marion Township, Beaver County	883	0	0	0	0	0	3	0	3	0	0
Marion Township, Berks County	1,827	2	0	0	0	2	5	2	3	0	0
Marlborough Township	3,337	4	1	2	0	1	28	8	18	2	0
Marple Township	23,682	12	0	2	7	3	351	15	328	8	0
Martinsburg	2,139	3	0	0	0	3	30	8	21	1	1
Marysville	2,456	2	0	0	1	1	14	5	9	0	0
Masontown	3,334	3	0	0	1	2	96	25	63	8	1
Mayfield	1,697	0	0	0	0	0	0	0	0	0	0
McAdoo	2,074	3	0	2	0	1	46	5	40	1	1
McCandless	27,188	6	0	2	1	3	277	33	242	2	0
McKeesport	22,009	293	6	8	60	219	787	278	469	40	16
McKees Rocks	6,038	82	0	3	43	36	322	115	186	21	1
McSherrystown	2,839	2	0	0	0	2	25	6	18	1	0
Meadville	13,229	19	0	0	7	12	339	57	282	0	2
Mechanicsburg	8,744	33	0	2	1	30	242	25	212	5	4
Media	5,448	26	0	0	8	18	88	7	78	3	0
Mercer	2,184	2	0	0	0	2	17	9	8	0	1
Mercersburg	1,593	1	0	0	1	0	33	6	26	1	0
Middleburg	1,333	3	0	1	0	2	50	8	40	2	1
Middlesex Township, Butler County	5,518	3	0	1	0	2	40	9	28	3	0
Middlesex Township, Cumberland County	7,124	9	0	1	3	5	196	17	169	10	0
Middletown	8,781	19	0	4	4	11	127	25	100	2	1
Middletown Township	47,432	46	0	4	23	19	1,356	194	1,106	56	2
Midland	2,809	10	0	1	2	7	379	29	344	6	1
Midway	924	0	0	0	0	0	1	1	0	0	0
Mifflin	600	0	0	0	0	0	1	1	0	0	0
Mifflinburg	3,514	3	0	1	1	1	54	10	44	0	2
Mifflin County Regional	30,294	40	0	7	3	30	592	83	480	29	1
Mifflin Township	2,272	0	0	0	0	0	0	0	0	0	0
Milford	2,930	3	0	0	3	0	40	9	30	1	0
Millbourne	914	7	0	0	1	6	13	3	10	0	0
Millcreek Township, Erie County	52,537	47	1	11	15	20	1,077	237	823	17	2
Millcreek Township, Lebanon County	3,274	3	0	0	0	3	49	10	38	1	1
Millersburg	2,479	11	0	0	0	11	42	8	33	1	5
Millersville	7,350	8	0	0	4	4	104	23	80	1	1
Mill Hall	1,456	0	0	0	0	0	0	0	0	0	0
Millvale	3,643	1	0	0	0	1	36	17	19	0	0
Milton	6,360	28	0	1	0	27	114	20	94	0	2
Minersville	4,187	11	0	0	2	9	64	10	50	4	5
Mohnton	3,110	6	0	0	1	5	18	4	14	0	0
Monaca	5,675	12	0	1	2	9	125	25	95	5	0
Monessen	7,977	51	2	2	13	34	244	68	170	6	3
Monongahela	4,409	22	0	1	7	14	133	22	107	4	1
Monroeville	27,622	86	0	3	11	72	389	94	276	19	1
Montgomery	5,379	5	0	0	0	5	29	5	24	0	0
Montgomery Township	24,720	6	0	0	5	1	443	22	410	11	2
Montoursville	4,600	0	0	0	0	0	40	2	38	0	0
Montrose	1,509	6	0	0	1	5	38	6	30	2	1
Moon Township	23,197	11	0	1	2	8	345	42	293	10	0
Moore Township	9,775	6	0	1	0	5	67	5	62	0	1
Moosic	5,811	31	0	0	5	26	240	37	197	6	2
Morris-Cooper Regional	5,623	6	0	0	0	6	16	7	8	1	0
Morrisville	9,639	26	0	2	4	20	252	49	181	22	0
Morton	2,658	9	0	0	3	6	121	23	98	0	0
Moscow	1,941	6	0	2	0	4	27	2	25	0	0
Mount Carmel	5,869	27	0	1	2	24	87	12	72	3	2
Mount Carmel Township	2,582	6	0	0	2	4	9	1	7	1	0
Mount Gretna Borough	237	0	0	0	0	0	0	0	0	0	0
Mount Holly Springs	1,923	6	0	1	0	5	32	6	26	0	0
Mount Jewett	983	2	0	0	0	2	4	3	1	0	0
Mount Joy	7,426	14	0	1	1	12	120	27	93	0	2
Mount Lebanon	30,380	15	0	0	5	10	250	36	203	11	0
Mount Oliver	3,644	54	2	3	32	17	155	51	75	29	0
Mount Pleasant	4,357	6	0	0	1	5	64	7	56	1	0
Mount Pleasant Township	3,667	7	0	0	1	6	22	5	16	1	0
Mount Union	2,313	10	0	0	2	8	89	16	68	5	1
Mountville	2,886	4	0	0	0	4	37	3	31	3	0
Muhlenberg Township	19,028	26	0	0	7	19	559	32	490	37	1
Muncy	2,444	0	0	0	0	0	0	0	0	0	0
Munhall	11,048	24	0	0	8	16	187	43	134	10	0
Murrysville	19,688	9	0	0	4	5	93	28	63	2	0
Myerstown	3,163	10	0	0	0	10	58	5	51	2	0
Nanticoke	10,183	58	0	9	11	38	425	110	293	22	2

[1] The FBI does not publish arson data unless it receives data from either the agency or the state for all 12 months of the calendar year.

Table 8.   Offenses Known to Law Enforcement, by State and City, 2010—*Continued*

(Number)

State/city	Population	Violent crime	Murder and non-negligent man-slaughter	Forcible rape	Robbery	Aggravated assault	Property crime	Burglary	Larceny-theft	Motor vehicle theft	Arson[1]
PENNSYLVANIA—*Continued*											
Nanty Glo	2,763	5	0	1	0	4	77	17	58	2	0
Narberth	4,063	2	0	0	0	2	51	11	39	1	0
Nazareth Area	6,118	16	0	1	1	14	107	14	91	2	2
Nelson Township	567	0	0	0	0	0	3	0	3	0	0
Nescopeck	1,426	0	0	0	0	0	4	0	2	2	0
Neshannock Township	9,282	6	0	1	0	5	135	17	110	8	1
Nether Providence Township	13,298	29	0	3	3	23	234	25	207	2	0
Neville Township	1,120	3	0	2	0	1	39	3	36	0	0
New Berlin	813	0	0	0	0	0	3	1	2	0	0
Newberry Township	15,825	19	1	2	1	15	383	57	315	11	1
New Brighton	9,246	77	0	0	17	60	462	72	386	4	1
New Britain	2,279	10	0	0	1	9	17	5	11	1	0
New Britain Township	11,109	3	0	1	1	1	100	17	77	6	0
New Castle	23,968	270	6	9	52	203	1,162	491	612	59	27
New Castle Township	396	2	0	0	0	2	19	0	19	0	0
New Cumberland	7,061	3	0	2	0	1	151	26	123	2	0
New Florence	724	0	0	0	0	0	2	1	1	0	0
New Garden Township	12,307	12	0	1	5	6	194	31	151	12	0
New Hanover Township	10,029	3	0	0	1	2	76	13	58	5	3
New Holland	5,223	7	0	0	1	6	74	13	56	5	0
New Hope	2,298	5	0	0	0	5	64	6	58	0	0
New Kensington	13,583	53	1	12	13	27	465	112	333	20	0
New Philadelphia	1,085	0	0	0	0	0	6	1	4	1	0
Newport	1,469	6	0	0	2	4	26	7	19	0	0
New Sewickley Township	7,651	17	0	1	1	15	129	33	92	4	0
Newton Township	2,812	2	0	0	0	2	10	3	7	0	0
Newtown	2,404	1	0	0	1	0	39	8	30	1	2
Newtown Township, Bucks County	19,713	8	0	0	0	8	205	32	168	5	3
Newtown Township, Delaware County	11,937	3	0	0	0	3	150	25	118	7	0
Newville	1,309	1	0	0	0	1	35	2	32	1	0
Norristown	32,217	394	6	23	172	193	1,048	229	688	131	8
Northampton	10,064	11	4	1	2	4	184	32	147	5	1
Northampton Township	41,145	11	0	1	2	8	285	63	218	4	0
North Belle Vernon	1,941	11	0	0	2	9	94	21	71	2	0
North Catasauqua	2,919	5	0	0	1	4	57	8	46	3	1
North Cornwall Township	6,683	13	0	2	0	11	129	16	104	9	0
North Coventry Township	7,924	11	0	2	1	8	194	14	176	4	1
North East, Erie County	4,186	8	0	0	1	7	137	11	125	1	0
Northeastern Regional	11,441	16	0	5	1	10	188	26	155	7	2
Northern Berks Regional	12,828	10	0	0	1	9	184	34	146	4	2
Northern Cambria Borough	3,875	2	0	2	0	0	111	35	71	5	0
Northern Regional	29,057	5	0	1	0	4	232	16	213	3	0
Northern York Regional	68,116	56	0	3	17	36	1,035	92	888	55	6
North Fayette Township	13,375	12	0	0	3	9	424	15	407	2	0
North Franklin Township	4,642	19	0	1	5	13	114	7	102	5	1
North Huntingdon Township	29,816	14	0	0	4	10	376	43	323	10	1
North Irwin	835	4	0	0	0	4	2	0	2	0	0
North Lebanon Township	11,141	5	0	0	4	1	274	37	230	7	1
North Londonderry Township	7,114	4	1	0	0	3	81	11	69	1	0
North Middleton Township	11,191	16	0	1	4	11	85	17	65	3	0
North Sewickley Township	5,628	4	0	2	0	2	124	26	97	1	1
North Strabane Township	12,876	7	0	0	0	7	154	23	126	5	0
Northumberland	3,505	6	0	1	0	5	68	11	55	2	0
North Union Township	1,264	1	0	0	0	1	1	1	0	0	0
North Versailles Township	12,051	81	1	4	10	66	248	51	191	6	4
North Wales	3,245	1	0	0	0	1	60	7	49	4	0
Northwest Lancaster County Regional	18,254	6	0	2	1	3	195	6	188	1	0
Norwood	5,825	14	0	1	1	12	105	15	88	2	0
Oakland	565	0	0	0	0	0	3	2	0	1	0
Oakmont	6,411	22	0	0	3	19	127	18	103	6	0
O'Hara Township	9,361	0	0	0	0	0	72	16	53	3	0
Ohio Township	4,397	0	0	0	0	0	91	1	89	1	0
Oil City	10,461	14	0	6	3	5	129	14	113	2	0
Old Forge	8,525	6	0	0	1	5	85	20	60	5	0
Old Lycoming Township	5,276	3	0	0	2	1	110	10	91	9	3
Oley Township	3,750	5	0	0	0	5	32	2	25	5	0
Olyphant	4,973	4	0	0	1	3	40	8	27	5	0
Orangeville Area	1,697	0	0	0	0	0	13	6	7	0	0
Orwigsburg	2,970	3	0	0	0	3	36	8	28	0	0
Osceola Township	709	0	0	0	0	0	0	0	0	0	0
Otto Eldred Regional	2,420	1	0	0	0	1	9	4	5	0	0
Oxford	4,776	27	0	0	10	17	111	9	99	3	0
Paint Township	3,156	13	0	0	0	13	11	3	8	0	1

[1] The FBI does not publish arson data unless it receives data from either the agency or the state for all 12 months of the calendar year.

Table 8.   Offenses Known to Law Enforcement, by State and City, 2010—*Continued*

(Number)

State/city	Population	Violent crime	Murder and non-negligent man-slaughter	Forcible rape	Robbery	Aggravated assault	Property crime	Burglary	Larceny-theft	Motor vehicle theft	Arson[1]
PENNSYLVANIA—*Continued*											
Palmerton	5,235	0	0	0	0	0	120	8	108	4	0
Palmer Township	21,029	16	0	1	6	9	462	45	402	15	2
Palmyra	7,099	7	0	0	1	6	148	17	127	4	0
Palo Alto	1,073	1	0	0	0	1	2	0	2	0	1
Parkesburg	3,514	12	1	4	0	7	51	12	32	7	0
Patterson Township	2,930	4	0	0	2	2	43	12	31	0	0
Patton	1,829	0	0	0	0	0	2	1	1	0	0
Patton Township	13,570	9	0	2	5	2	247	30	213	4	1
Paxtang	1,493	4	0	0	2	2	41	5	33	3	0
Pen Argyl	3,693	5	0	1	0	4	61	17	41	3	0
Penbrook	2,937	2	0	0	2	0	24	7	16	1	1
Penn Hills	44,001	177	5	15	64	93	939	388	502	49	4
Pennridge Regional	10,783	9	0	0	0	9	111	16	89	6	1
Penn Township, Butler County	5,212	2	0	0	0	2	37	15	20	2	1
Penn Township, Lancaster County	8,973	17	0	1	0	16	122	18	86	18	0
Penn Township, Perry County	3,284	3	0	0	0	3	33	8	24	1	0
Penn Township, Westmoreland County	20,387	8	0	0	1	7	111	21	88	2	1
Penn Township, York County	16,193	12	0	1	2	9	275	27	242	6	1
Pequea Township	4,581	9	0	1	1	7	61	17	41	3	1
Perkasie	8,695	13	0	1	2	10	197	27	167	3	0
Perryopolis	1,693	0	0	0	0	0	15	1	12	2	0
Peters Township	20,731	4	0	0	1	3	98	21	76	1	0
Philadelphia	1,558,378	18,535	306	945	8,363	8,921	57,788	10,796	39,924	7,068	
Phoenixville	16,923	49	0	6	3	40	416	19	394	3	2
Pine Creek Township	3,192	5	0	0	0	5	46	0	46	0	0
Pitcairn	3,308	26	0	2	7	17	165	43	117	5	0
Pittsburgh	312,737	2,810	55	66	1,190	1,499	11,284	2,949	7,678	657	154
Pittston	7,539	28	0	2	1	25	215	20	185	10	1
Plainfield Township	6,370	4	0	0	0	4	68	14	50	4	0
Plains Township	10,460	7	0	0	0	7	174	29	138	7	1
Pleasant Hills	7,959	3	0	0	3	0	80	15	63	2	0
Plum	26,311	39	0	1	5	33	156	63	93	0	0
Plumstead Township	11,937	6	0	1	1	4	145	22	115	8	0
Plymouth Township, Montgomery County	16,534	43	1	10	23	9	577	69	479	29	1
Pocono Mountain Regional	36,242	75	0	10	23	42	1,045	444	572	29	7
Pocono Township	11,430	9	1	1	4	3	388	85	292	11	0
Point Marion	1,225	13	0	1	0	12	22	6	16	0	0
Point Township	3,940	6	0	0	0	6	44	8	36	0	2
Polk	992	1	0	0	0	1	3	1	2	0	0
Portage	2,555	7	0	0	1	6	68	12	56	0	0
Port Allegany	2,160	4	0	0	1	3	8	4	4	0	0
Port Carbon	1,766	1	0	0	0	1	2	1	1	0	0
Port Vue	3,838	13	0	2	4	7	73	19	50	4	1
Pottstown	21,491	222	0	25	78	119	1,006	165	785	56	10
Prospect Park	6,545	30	0	0	8	22	171	26	139	6	0
Pulaski Township, Lawrence County	3,393	1	0	0	0	1	30	7	23	0	0
Punxsutawney	5,855	53	0	2	0	51	105	14	90	1	3
Pymatuning Township	3,555	4	0	0	1	3	119	28	85	6	0
Quakertown	8,690	40	0	2	6	32	241	29	209	3	8
Quarryville	2,184	7	0	1	3	3	55	7	48	0	0
Raccoon Township	3,218	1	0	1	0	0	13	6	7	0	0
Radnor Township	31,260	23	0	0	6	17	368	54	306	8	0
Ralpho Township	3,938	3	0	0	0	3	14	3	10	1	0
Rankin	2,101	10	0	0	0	10	3	3	0	0	0
Reading	81,370	767	10	21	384	352	3,662	1,425	1,582	655	29
Redstone Township	5,959	2	0	0	1	1	11	6	5	0	0
Resa Regional	2,558	2	0	0	0	2	10	4	5	1	0
Rice Township	3,098	5	0	0	1	4	7	3	3	1	0
Richland	1,514	0	0	0	0	0	0	0	0	0	0
Richland Township, Bucks County	13,124	5	0	0	4	1	250	29	215	6	1
Richland Township, Cambria County	12,562	13	0	1	2	10	549	27	519	3	1
Ridgway	4,013	8	0	3	1	4	196	38	153	5	1
Ridley Park	7,048	12	0	2	0	10	77	9	64	4	0
Ridley Township	30,135	63	1	5	21	36	568	99	438	31	2
Ringtown	759	0	0	0	0	0	3	0	3	0	0
Riverside	1,871	0	0	0	0	0	9	1	8	0	0
Roaring Brook Township	1,815	1	0	0	0	1	29	7	22	0	1
Roaring Spring	2,259	1	0	0	0	1	69	5	60	4	0
Robeson Township	7,807	6	0	0	1	5	75	12	52	11	1
Robinson Township, Allegheny County	13,742	21	0	1	5	15	320	19	294	7	1
Robinson Township, Washington County	2,144	0	0	0	0	0	30	3	26	1	0
Rochester Township	2,839	3	0	0	0	3	79	6	69	4	0
Rockledge	2,491	4	0	0	0	4	46	11	33	2	1

[1] The FBI does not publish arson data unless it receives data from either the agency or the state for all 12 months of the calendar year.

Table 8.   Offenses Known to Law Enforcement, by State and City, 2010—*Continued*

(Number)

State/city	Population	Violent crime	Murder and non-negligent man-slaughter	Forcible rape	Robbery	Aggravated assault	Property crime	Burglary	Larceny-theft	Motor vehicle theft	Arson[1]
PENNSYLVANIA—*Continued*											
Rosslyn Farms	421	0	0	0	0	0	0	0	0	0	0
Ross Township	30,615	33	0	1	12	20	802	101	687	14	0
Rostraver Township	11,729	12	0	2	8	2	429	66	353	10	0
Royalton	964	0	0	0	0	0	2	2	0	0	0
Royersford	4,763	16	0	1	1	14	80	16	62	2	1
Rush Township	3,756	8	0	1	0	7	115	6	108	1	0
Ryan Township	2,550	3	0	0	0	3	8	2	6	0	0
Sadsbury Township, Chester County	3,443	2	0	0	1	1	4	0	4	0	0
Salem Township, Luzerne County	4,121	5	0	0	0	5	36	7	29	0	0
Salisbury Township	14,197	7	0	0	3	4	263	54	201	8	0
Saltsburg	874	1	0	0	0	1	8	0	8	0	0
Sandy Lake	685	1	0	0	1	0	3	1	2	0	0
Sandy Township	11,527	9	0	0	0	9	272	40	219	13	2
Sankertown	649	1	0	0	1	0	6	1	5	0	0
Saxton	756	0	0	0	0	0	0	0	0	0	0
Scott Township, Allegheny County	15,778	13	0	1	4	8	248	44	197	7	0
Scott Township, Columbia County	5,049	1	0	1	0	0	84	2	82	0	0
Scott Township, Lackawanna County	4,911	4	0	0	0	4	14	12	2	0	0
Scranton	71,920	234	1	23	103	107	2,422	675	1,631	116	26
Selinsgrove	5,465	129	0	4	4	121	192	34	149	9	2
Seven Springs	99	0	0	0	0	0	5	0	5	0	0
Seward	451	0	0	0	0	0	1	1	0	0	0
Sewickley Heights	975	0	0	0	0	0	7	0	7	0	0
Shaler Township	27,862	20	1	1	5	13	259	43	213	3	2
Shamokin	7,337	4	0	0	0	4	29	6	22	1	1
Shamokin Dam	1,451	3	0	1	0	2	45	4	41	0	0
Sharon	14,672	104	1	12	29	62	618	246	357	15	9
Sharon Hill	5,367	51	0	2	11	38	159	18	131	10	0
Sharpsburg	3,281	17	0	0	1	16	98	24	64	10	0
Sharpsville	4,040	71	0	0	2	69	90	9	80	1	0
Shenandoah	5,121	20	0	1	10	9	137	23	110	4	1
Shenango Township, Lawrence County	7,652	8	0	2	2	4	211	42	159	10	0
Shillington	5,042	3	0	0	0	3	131	7	115	9	0
Shippensburg	5,609	6	0	1	2	3	80	14	61	5	0
Shiremanstown	1,466	2	0	0	0	2	3	1	2	0	0
Shohola Township	2,541	1	0	0	0	1	31	19	12	0	0
Silver Lake Township	1,719	3	0	0	0	3	16	3	11	2	0
Silver Spring Township	14,067	2	1	0	1	0	167	17	148	2	0
Sinking Spring	3,767	10	0	1	1	8	69	11	52	6	1
Slatington	4,452	9	0	0	0	9	82	9	70	3	0
Slippery Rock	2,957	4	0	2	0	2	15	3	12	0	0
Smethport	1,547	0	0	0	0	0	24	9	14	1	0
Smithfield	792	0	0	0	0	0	0	0	0	0	0
Smithton Borough	406	0	0	0	0	0	4	3	1	0	0
Smith Township	4,508	0	0	0	0	0	0	0	0	0	0
Solebury Township	8,957	0	0	0	0	0	78	18	56	4	0
Somerset	6,294	14	0	1	3	10	201	36	158	7	0
Souderton	6,601	11	1	0	2	8	61	5	53	3	0
South Abington Township	9,588	7	0	0	0	7	85	12	71	2	0
South Beaver Township	2,845	1	0	0	0	1	34	9	25	0	0
South Buffalo Township	2,771	0	0	0	0	0	20	4	16	0	1
South Centre Township	1,924	1	0	0	0	1	94	13	79	2	1
South Coatesville	1,185	15	0	1	0	14	20	4	11	5	0
South Connellsville Borough	2,121	1	0	0	0	1	9	0	9	0	0
Southern Regional Lancaster County	3,914	7	0	0	0	7	40	3	37	0	0
Southern Regional York County	10,136	8	0	1	5	2	168	25	141	2	7
South Fayette Township	13,359	5	1	1	1	2	70	12	58	0	1
South Fork	1,018	0	0	0	0	0	0	0	0	0	0
South Greensburg	2,216	3	0	0	0	3	27	7	20	0	0
South Heidelberg Township	7,542	9	0	1	0	8	70	6	63	1	1
South Heights	487	0	0	0	0	0	0	0	0	0	0
South Lebanon Township	8,867	3	0	0	0	3	110	24	86	0	0
South Londonderry Township	7,691	2	0	1	1	0	55	18	36	1	0
South Park Township	14,057	4	0	0	1	3	51	21	28	2	0
South Strabane Township	8,975	16	0	6	4	6	417	18	393	6	0
Southwestern Regional	18,477	17	1	6	0	10	120	18	100	2	1
Southwest Greensburg	2,187	15	1	2	0	12	56	11	45	0	0
Southwest Mercer County Regional	11,071	19	0	2	6	11	189	50	123	16	4
Southwest Regional	2,918	2	0	0	0	2	44	15	29	0	0
South Whitehall Township	20,110	37	0	3	9	25	629	80	544	5	1
Spring City	3,438	11	0	1	0	10	73	11	62	0	0
Springdale	3,474	3	0	0	0	3	52	3	49	0	0
Springdale Township	1,650	3	0	0	0	3	15	5	10	0	0

[1] The FBI does not publish arson data unless it receives data from either the agency or the state for all 12 months of the calendar year.

Table 8. Offenses Known to Law Enforcement, by State and City, 2010—*Continued*

(Number)

State/city	Population	Violent crime	Murder and non-negligent man-slaughter	Forcible rape	Robbery	Aggravated assault	Property crime	Burglary	Larceny-theft	Motor vehicle theft	Arson[1]
PENNSYLVANIA—*Continued*											
Springettsbury Township	25,205	39	0	2	20	17	911	64	832	15	1
Springfield Township, Delaware County	22,990	21	2	1	6	12	673	39	618	16	1
Springfield Township, Montgomery County	18,926	31	0	0	5	26	291	61	225	5	2
Spring Garden Township	12,218	25	0	1	13	11	494	60	422	12	0
Spring Township, Berks County	27,157	11	0	1	1	9	327	39	274	14	2
Spring Township, Centre County	7,243	0	0	0	0	0	25	1	22	2	0
Spring Township, Snyder County	1,569	0	0	0	0	0	4	1	3	0	0
State College	54,649	74	0	9	16	49	892	111	769	12	18
St. Clair Boro	2,962	2	0	0	2	0	111	2	109	0	0
St. Clair Township	1,338	0	0	0	0	0	0	0	0	0	0
Steelton	5,636	36	0	6	17	13	284	91	176	17	1
Stewartstown	2,036	3	0	0	1	2	49	10	37	2	1
St. Marys City	13,273	12	1	2	1	8	170	25	141	4	0
Stockertown	773	0	0	0	0	0	1	1	0	0	0
Stoneboro	1,007	0	0	0	0	0	7	0	6	1	0
Stowe Township	6,029	29	0	4	5	20	133	43	90	0	0
Strasburg	2,802	3	0	1	0	2	26	5	20	1	3
Stroud Area Regional	35,282	106	0	22	41	43	1,444	154	1,252	38	3
Sugarcreek	4,932	6	0	1	0	5	60	3	55	2	0
Sugarloaf Township, Luzerne County	4,112	0	0	0	0	0	21	1	20	0	0
Sugar Notch	957	0	0	0	0	0	15	2	13	0	0
Summerhill Township	2,554	1	0	0	0	1	34	4	29	1	0
Summit Hill	2,981	0	0	0	0	0	7	2	5	0	0
Summit Township	2,229	3	0	0	0	3	18	6	12	0	0
Sunbury	9,784	74	1	4	6	63	236	45	178	13	8
Susquehanna Depot	1,538	0	0	0	0	0	10	5	4	1	0
Susquehanna Regional	7,673	2	0	1	0	1	91	15	74	2	1
Susquehanna Township, Dauphin County	23,556	50	1	9	12	28	467	59	399	9	1
Sutersville	586	0	0	0	0	0	0	0	0	0	0
Swarthmore	6,161	1	0	1	0	0	83	21	61	1	0
Swatara Township	22,781	158	0	1	31	126	700	111	575	14	6
Sweden Township	711	0	0	0	0	0	0	0	0	0	0
Swissvale	8,721	109	0	0	25	84	272	82	177	13	1
Swoyersville	4,830	11	0	1	1	9	116	26	86	4	0
Sykesville	1,152	0	0	0	0	0	0	0	0	0	0
Tamaqua	6,525	9	0	3	2	4	220	31	182	7	2
Tarentum	4,501	20	0	2	4	14	149	28	118	3	0
Tatamy	1,112	0	0	0	0	0	14	0	14	0	0
Taylor	6,134	6	0	0	0	6	162	18	141	3	1
Telford	4,632	17	0	2	1	14	75	9	64	2	2
Throop	4,061	19	0	1	1	17	51	12	34	5	0
Tiadaghton Valley Regional	6,613	31	0	0	1	30	87	4	76	7	0
Tidioute	713	0	0	0	0	0	4	0	4	0	0
Tilden Township	3,895	3	0	0	1	2	53	1	49	3	0
Tinicum Township, Bucks County	4,259	3	0	2	0	1	26	5	21	0	0
Tinicum Township, Delaware County	4,237	22	0	0	2	20	223	17	183	23	0
Titusville	5,687	11	1	1	2	7	149	25	121	3	0
Towamencin Township	17,830	26	0	3	3	20	184	24	156	4	1
Towanda	2,796	10	0	4	0	6	51	12	38	1	0
Tower City	1,313	0	0	0	0	0	7	1	6	0	0
Trafford	3,080	17	0	2	3	12	19	10	9	0	0
Tredyffrin Township	29,336	10	0	0	2	8	249	26	220	3	0
Troy	1,445	3	0	0	0	3	30	7	23	0	0
Tulpehocken Township	3,611	2	0	0	0	2	17	5	11	1	0
Tunkhannock	1,760	5	0	0	0	5	29	5	20	4	1
Tunkhannock Township, Wyoming County	4,294	3	0	0	0	3	52	10	39	3	0
Turtle Creek	5,489	15	0	0	0	15	20	3	16	1	1
Tyrone	5,216	13	0	0	1	12	127	22	104	1	0
Union City	3,295	5	0	3	2	0	57	11	46	0	1
Union Dale	341	0	0	0	0	0	0	0	0	0	0
Uniontown	11,514	52	0	1	14	37	526	120	371	35	0
Union Township, Lawrence County	4,992	5	0	0	2	3	185	18	166	1	2
Union Township, Schuylkill County	1,348	0	0	0	0	0	0	0	0	0	0
Upland	2,889	58	0	1	6	51	116	39	71	6	0
Upper Allen Township	18,659	0	0	0	0	0	156	19	131	6	1
Upper Burrell Township	2,128	2	0	1	0	1	20	3	17	0	0
Upper Chichester Township	17,847	43	1	2	19	21	464	82	364	18	2
Upper Darby Township	79,046	439	4	17	240	178	2,084	317	1,637	130	8
Upper Dublin Township	26,118	22	0	3	3	16	332	44	285	3	1
Upper Gwynedd Township	16,481	17	1	2	2	12	142	11	129	2	1
Upper Leacock Township	8,785	13	0	0	2	11	99	29	66	4	0
Upper Makefield Township	8,691	5	0	0	0	5	107	24	82	1	0
Upper Merion Township	26,693	29	2	1	18	8	1,497	81	1,372	44	1

[1] The FBI does not publish arson data unless it receives data from either the agency or the state for all 12 months of the calendar year.

Table 8.   Offenses Known to Law Enforcement, by State and City, 2010—*Continued*
(Number)

State/city	Population	Violent crime	Murder and non-negligent man-slaughter	Forcible rape	Robbery	Aggravated assault	Property crime	Burglary	Larceny-theft	Motor vehicle theft	Arson[1]
PENNSYLVANIA—*Continued*											
Upper Moreland Township	24,291	13	0	1	7	5	477	53	410	14	1
Upper Perkiomen	6,422	8	0	3	1	4	121	19	98	4	3
Upper Pottsgrove Township	5,455	12	0	1	0	11	50	7	43	0	0
Upper Providence Township, Delaware County	11,280	5	0	0	0	5	58	14	41	3	0
Upper Providence Township, Montgomery County	20,416	9	0	1	1	7	329	32	289	8	0
Upper Saucon Township	15,514	5	0	2	1	2	151	41	109	1	0
Upper Southampton Township	15,349	9	1	2	4	2	178	49	123	6	0
Upper St. Clair Township	18,666	3	0	0	1	2	134	11	122	1	0
Upper Uwchlan Township	12,202	0	0	0	0	0	47	4	43	0	0
Upper Yoder Township	5,450	6	0	0	0	6	30	1	29	0	0
Uwchlan Township	19,079	14	0	1	2	11	193	22	168	3	1
Valley Township	7,223	10	0	0	1	9	82	11	70	1	0
Vandergrift	4,970	17	0	0	3	14	17	9	8	0	0
Vandling	697	1	0	0	0	1	2	0	2	0	0
Vernon Township	5,453	1	0	0	1	0	109	6	102	1	0
Verona	2,634	9	0	2	3	4	97	22	73	2	0
Vintondale	473	0	0	0	0	0	0	0	0	0	0
Walker Township	985	2	0	0	0	2	10	3	7	0	0
Wampum	620	1	0	0	0	1	6	0	5	1	0
Warminster Township	35,027	31	0	8	14	9	557	84	453	20	8
Warren	9,302	87	0	1	0	86	194	24	165	5	1
Warrington Township	23,663	17	0	1	6	10	237	36	198	3	0
Warwick Township, Bucks County	15,090	4	0	0	0	4	159	19	139	1	1
Warwick Township, Lancaster County	17,596	9	0	2	3	4	95	9	82	4	1
Washington, Washington County	14,745	72	0	10	26	36	526	110	366	50	1
Washington Township, Fayette County	4,095	5	0	0	0	5	56	12	44	0	1
Washington Township, Franklin County	12,440	9	1	2	2	4	264	48	202	14	1
Washington Township, Northampton County	5,022	2	0	1	1	0	58	17	39	2	0
Washington Township, Westmoreland County	7,409	4	0	1	0	3	59	15	43	1	0
Watsontown	2,107	20	0	0	0	20	21	3	18	0	0
Waymart	1,417	0	0	0	0	0	3	0	3	0	1
Waynesboro	10,259	13	0	2	3	8	240	43	192	5	0
Waynesburg	4,196	7	0	0	1	6	102	30	71	1	0
Weatherly	2,604	18	0	0	1	17	65	18	46	1	0
Wellsboro	3,254	0	0	0	0	0	36	2	31	3	1
Wesleyville	3,310	8	0	1	0	7	121	22	97	2	0
West Brandywine Township	8,049	11	0	0	1	10	86	23	55	8	1
West Brownsville	1,022	1	0	0	0	1	2	1	1	0	0
West Caln Township	8,657	14	0	0	0	14	96	35	61	0	0
West Carroll Township	1,339	5	0	0	0	5	15	5	8	2	0
West Chester	18,578	65	0	9	20	36	448	78	344	26	0
West Cocalico Township	7,265	2	1	0	0	1	70	28	41	1	3
West Conshohocken	1,513	6	0	1	0	5	20	2	16	2	0
West Cornwall Township	2,052	2	0	0	0	2	5	2	2	1	0
West Deer Township	12,079	4	0	0	0	4	89	25	59	5	0
West Earl Township	7,975	2	0	0	1	1	46	9	32	5	0
Western Berks Regional	4,569	3	0	0	2	1	83	12	69	2	0
West Fallowfield Township	2,621	0	0	0	0	0	17	1	16	0	0
Westfield	1,123	1	0	0	0	1	4	1	3	0	0
West Goshen Township	22,211	21	1	1	5	14	408	36	360	12	0
West Grove Borough	2,808	1	0	0	0	1	15	5	8	2	0
West Hazleton	3,295	19	2	0	6	11	162	35	121	6	0
West Hempfield Township	16,388	17	0	0	3	14	229	27	195	7	2
West Hills Regional	10,549	3	0	1	1	1	100	21	77	2	3
West Homestead	1,984	16	1	0	3	12	56	18	35	3	0
West Lampeter Township	15,972	11	0	1	8	2	147	15	126	6	1
West Lebanon Township	857	1	0	0	1	0	72	3	69	0	0
West Mahanoy Township	2,982	0	0	0	0	0	6	4	1	1	0
West Manchester Township	18,665	35	0	2	16	17	795	62	717	16	1
West Manheim Township	7,965	6	1	0	2	3	80	2	77	1	1
West Mayfield Borough	1,065	2	0	0	0	2	8	2	5	1	0
West Mead Township	5,051	0	0	0	0	0	0	0	0	0	0
West Mifflin	20,352	51	1	1	16	33	525	89	421	15	0
West Newton	2,840	19	0	1	2	16	72	8	63	1	0
West Norriton Township	14,593	34	0	4	13	17	324	16	293	15	1
West Nottingham Township	2,883	0	0	0	0	0	6	1	5	0	0
West Penn Township	4,389	2	0	1	0	1	15	6	8	1	0
West Pike Run	1,719	0	0	0	0	0	9	0	8	1	0
West Pittston	4,932	10	0	0	2	8	111	20	90	1	1
West Pottsgrove Township	3,789	13	0	2	4	7	147	11	132	4	2
West Reading	4,075	28	0	2	4	22	249	27	210	12	1
West Sadsbury Township	2,560	3	0	0	0	3	72	0	71	1	0
West Salem Township	3,329	5	0	0	1	4	32	17	14	1	0

[1] The FBI does not publish arson data unless it receives data from either the agency or the state for all 12 months of the calendar year.

Table 8.   Offenses Known to Law Enforcement, by State and City, 2010—*Continued*

(Number)

State/city	Population	Violent crime	Murder and non-negligent man-slaughter	Forcible rape	Robbery	Aggravated assault	Property crime	Burglary	Larceny-theft	Motor vehicle theft	Arson[1]
PENNSYLVANIA—*Continued*											
West Shore Regional	6,620	13	0	0	9	4	119	31	82	6	0
Westtown-East Goshen Regional	32,298	37	0	1	5	31	360	42	306	12	1
West View	6,628	14	0	1	2	11	169	8	154	7	0
West Vincent Township	5,164	3	0	0	1	2	29	7	20	2	0
West Whiteland Township	18,636	15	0	2	5	8	552	22	516	14	1
West Wyoming	2,687	5	0	1	0	4	25	7	17	1	0
West York	4,219	13	0	0	9	4	82	12	64	6	0
Whitaker Borough	1,208	1	0	0	1	0	33	13	19	1	0
Whitehall	13,364	10	0	1	2	7	51	10	41	0	1
Whitehall Township	27,352	35	1	4	21	9	1,386	104	1,253	29	6
White Haven Borough	1,143	2	0	0	1	1	10	1	8	1	0
Whitemarsh Township	17,991	7	0	0	1	6	247	36	203	8	0
White Oak	8,116	3	0	1	2	0	81	23	55	3	0
White Township	1,295	7	0	2	0	5	25	4	20	1	0
Whitpain Township	19,018	25	0	0	6	19	243	27	203	13	0
Wiconisco Township	1,114	1	0	0	0	1	2	0	2	0	0
Wilkes-Barre	40,970	196	2	13	111	70	1,814	352	1,373	89	8
Wilkes-Barre Township	3,081	7	0	2	4	1	679	19	654	6	2
Wilkinsburg	17,047	221	3	7	80	131	615	273	279	63	11
Wilkins Township	6,483	9	0	2	1	6	117	25	88	4	0
Williamsburg	1,250	0	0	0	0	0	11	0	11	0	0
Williamsport	29,320	102	2	12	55	33	1,220	232	954	34	19
Willistown Township	10,984	3	0	0	0	3	129	15	113	1	0
Wilson	7,760	60	0	4	15	41	319	64	245	10	2
Windber	3,953	19	0	0	1	18	46	5	35	6	1
Wind Gap	2,833	2	0	0	0	2	49	3	41	5	0
Womelsdorf	2,856	8	0	0	0	8	15	7	8	0	0
Woodward Township	2,252	0	0	0	0	0	31	4	27	0	0
Worthington	707	0	0	0	0	0	3	0	3	0	0
Wrightsville	2,255	1	0	0	0	1	32	7	25	0	0
Wright Township	5,945	0	0	0	0	0	84	11	73	0	0
Wyoming	2,988	7	0	0	0	7	97	10	86	1	0
Wyomissing	10,533	7	0	0	2	5	517	31	478	8	1
Yardley	2,524	1	0	0	0	1	22	2	20	0	0
Yeadon	11,462	75	0	2	47	26	313	53	225	35	1
York	40,553	421	5	37	248	131	2,071	555	1,330	186	3
York Area Regional	59,342	69	2	13	14	40	641	108	492	41	4
Youngsville	1,652	7	0	0	0	7	7	1	6	0	0
Zelienople	3,958	11	0	0	0	11	90	8	81	1	0
Zerbe Township	1,874	4	0	0	0	4	2	0	2	0	3
RHODE ISLAND											
Barrington	16,276	5	0	1	2	2	203	40	156	7	3
Bristol	22,266	22	0	4	5	13	279	31	240	8	0
Burrillville	16,637	9	0	1	1	7	185	55	120	10	2
Central Falls	18,676	101	0	16	30	55	512	153	289	70	7
Charlestown	8,093	11	0	5	1	5	120	20	97	3	2
Coventry	35,021	26	0	4	4	18	665	110	522	33	14
Cranston	80,125	115	1	17	24	73	1,901	382	1,339	180	12
Cumberland	34,589	27	1	1	8	17	550	94	429	27	3
East Greenwich	13,361	6	0	1	2	3	186	31	149	6	1
East Providence	48,507	64	1	12	17	34	732	146	529	57	14
Foster	4,561	0	0	0	0	0	33	20	11	2	0
Glocester	10,602	7	0	0	1	6	52	13	35	4	1
Hopkinton	8,021	5	0	0	0	5	86	18	63	5	1
Jamestown	5,451	5	0	2	0	3	74	12	61	1	2
Johnston	28,623	39	0	3	10	26	587	125	412	50	5
Lincoln	22,133	33	0	3	12	18	529	70	437	22	2
Little Compton	3,516	0	0	0	0	0	75	26	48	1	0
Middletown	15,895	7	0	2	1	4	266	45	215	6	3
Narragansett	16,485	15	0	2	4	9	281	52	220	9	0
Newport	23,173	138	0	11	18	109	1,011	213	755	43	18
New Shoreham	1,036	1	0	1	0	0	43	7	35	1	0
North Kingstown	26,656	21	0	5	4	12	449	67	369	13	6
North Providence	32,740	63	2	4	17	40	621	153	424	44	4
North Smithfield	11,629	13	0	1	2	10	141	25	110	6	0
Pawtucket	71,782	289	5	38	107	139	2,281	715	1,337	229	31
Portsmouth	16,845	12	0	2	1	9	306	105	190	11	7
Providence	171,565	1,214	15	74	405	720	8,229	2,034	5,078	1,117	36
Richmond	7,678	2	0	0	0	2	95	21	72	2	1
Scituate	10,894	5	0	0	0	5	114	31	78	5	2
Smithfield	21,242	8	0	1	2	5	286	34	234	18	4
South Kingstown	29,291	17	0	2	4	11	368	103	253	12	3
Tiverton	14,836	13	2	1	3	7	267	69	177	21	1

[1] The FBI does not publish arson data unless it receives data from either the agency or the state for all 12 months of the calendar year.

Table 8.   Offenses Known to Law Enforcement, by State and City, 2010—*Continued*

(Number)

State/city	Population	Violent crime	Murder and non-negligent man-slaughter	Forcible rape	Robbery	Aggravated assault	Property crime	Burglary	Larceny-theft	Motor vehicle theft	Arson[1]
RHODE ISLAND—*Continued*											
Warren	10,840	20	0	3	1	16	214	33	174	7	2
Warwick	84,568	85	0	14	24	47	2,119	381	1,628	110	21
Westerly	23,524	12	0	4	5	3	431	73	343	15	1
West Greenwich	6,531	2	0	0	1	1	115	32	79	4	0
West Warwick	29,251	66	0	17	13	36	628	154	434	40	14
Woonsocket	43,320	177	1	29	48	99	1,180	346	744	90	9
SOUTH CAROLINA											
Abbeville	5,443	53	0	4	4	45	225	44	169	12	1
Aiken	29,875	112	4	6	38	64	1,191	167	979	45	0
Allendale	3,510	78	1	0	7	70	171	70	93	8	0
Anderson	27,325	200	6	15	36	143	1,924	466	1,342	116	5
Andrews	2,965	21	0	3	3	15	173	42	123	8	1
Bamberg	3,303	21	0	0	5	16	122	23	94	5	2
Barnwell	4,714	27	0	2	11	14	351	130	218	3	1
Batesburg-Leesville	5,670	40	0	3	5	32	261	69	183	9	0
Beaufort	12,076	135	0	3	33	99	804	153	631	20	2
Belton	4,709	9	0	2	1	6	154	25	117	12	0
Bennettsville	8,941	120	4	2	18	96	456	90	353	13	3
Bishopville	3,773	26	0	0	6	20	251	67	175	9	0
Blacksburg	1,913	22	0	0	1	21	118	36	77	5	0
Blackville	2,807	20	0	0	5	15	101	25	69	7	0
Bluffton	14,899	31	1	2	6	22	416	72	323	21	4
Briarcliffe Acres	564	0	0	0	0	0	10	1	8	1	0
Burnettown	2,701	3	0	0	0	3	66	21	39	6	0
Calhoun Falls	2,151	13	0	1	1	11	32	6	25	1	0
Camden	7,152	55	0	2	6	47	418	106	291	21	1
Cayce	13,161	140	0	8	15	117	755	170	526	59	2
Central	4,127	17	0	0	3	14	245	55	182	8	1
Chapin	770	2	0	0	1	1	36	6	28	2	0
Charleston	117,551	429	10	18	151	250	3,980	601	3,150	229	3
Cheraw	5,372	43	0	3	8	32	292	44	236	12	0
Chesnee	1,115	4	0	0	1	3	63	15	44	4	0
Chester	5,915	102	0	8	23	71	322	108	201	13	3
Chesterfield	1,321	3	0	0	3	0	46	5	40	1	0
Clemson	13,134	27	0	3	6	18	431	78	327	26	0
Clinton	8,910	87	0	5	15	67	450	121	319	10	3
Clio	714	2	0	0	0	2	37	13	23	1	0
Clover	5,292	136	1	3	5	127	183	41	135	7	0
Columbia	130,498	1,306	16	74	345	871	7,898	1,699	5,528	671	11
Conway	16,742	159	1	6	34	118	956	263	647	46	2
Cottageville	674	6	0	0	0	6	19	3	16	0	0
Coward	691	2	0	0	0	2	15	6	9	0	0
Cowpens	2,480	29	0	1	1	27	109	31	71	7	1
Darlington	6,482	75	0	5	18	52	458	68	368	22	1
Denmark	2,900	31	0	1	7	23	169	66	92	11	0
Dillon	6,468	117	2	4	21	90	762	223	523	16	4
Due West	1,266	0	0	0	0	0	5	2	3	0	0
Duncan	3,258	5	0	1	1	3	90	11	68	11	0
Easley	20,818	70	2	4	10	54	1,034	161	826	47	3
Edgefield	4,357	3	0	0	0	3	62	12	48	2	0
Edisto Beach	724	4	0	0	0	4	62	21	41	0	1
Ehrhardt	530	5	0	0	1	4	25	9	15	1	0
Elgin	1,320	8	0	1	2	5	87	7	78	2	0
Elloree	674	2	0	0	0	2	10	4	6	0	0
Estill	2,306	41	0	0	4	37	100	33	63	4	1
Eutawville	294	2	0	0	2	0	20	5	14	1	0
Fairfax	3,081	30	0	0	0	30	108	43	65	0	1
Florence	32,273	354	2	8	108	236	2,891	546	2,215	130	5
Folly Beach	2,511	14	0	5	2	7	195	13	176	6	1
Forest Acres	9,871	77	1	0	26	50	569	156	387	26	0
Fort Lawn	801	3	0	0	1	2	36	11	23	2	2
Fort Mill	11,024	37	0	1	7	29	305	51	230	24	2
Fountain Inn	8,063	44	0	1	2	41	166	32	118	16	0
Gaffney	13,155	88	1	3	23	61	430	105	279	46	3
Georgetown	8,393	126	0	4	14	108	668	107	541	20	4
Great Falls	2,001	20	0	0	1	19	116	33	76	7	1
Greeleyville	369	4	0	0	0	4	19	9	8	2	0
Greenville	62,368	468	3	20	132	313	3,265	597	2,499	169	7
Greenwood	22,762	433	2	9	39	383	1,693	399	1,217	77	4
Greer	26,760	138	2	19	28	89	838	113	661	64	4
Hampton	2,730	21	0	1	6	14	130	22	105	3	0
Hanahan	16,639	70	2	4	16	48	419	99	291	29	3
Hardeeville	3,795	22	0	3	6	13	199	43	140	16	2

[1] The FBI does not publish arson data unless it receives data from either the agency or the state for all 12 months of the calendar year.

Table 8.   Offenses Known to Law Enforcement, by State and City, 2010—*Continued*

(Number)

State/city	Population	Violent crime	Murder and non-negligent man-slaughter	Forcible rape	Robbery	Aggravated assault	Property crime	Burglary	Larceny-theft	Motor vehicle theft	Arson[1]
SOUTH CAROLINA—*Continued*											
Harleyville	699	6	0	0	2	4	30	7	17	6	0
Hartsville	7,326	125	1	2	34	88	808	171	607	30	4
Hemingway	475	5	0	0	4	1	32	3	29	0	0
Holly Hill	1,308	9	0	0	4	5	78	19	55	4	0
Honea Path	3,734	78	0	3	3	72	244	77	148	19	0
Inman	2,154	7	0	0	3	4	76	22	48	6	1
Irmo	12,023	40	0	4	8	28	287	55	219	13	0
Isle of Palms	4,736	6	0	2	0	4	159	50	105	4	0
Jackson	1,669	6	0	0	2	4	53	15	27	11	0
Jamestown	108	0	0	0	0	0	2	0	2	0	0
Johnsonville	1,505	6	0	0	1	5	29	6	23	0	0
Johnston	2,334	23	0	1	4	18	64	27	33	4	0
Kingstree	3,139	48	0	6	16	26	259	45	203	11	1
Lake City	6,719	69	1	3	13	52	462	121	327	14	4
Lake View	782	2	0	0	1	1	38	16	21	1	0
Lamar	978	7	0	0	1	6	30	9	18	3	0
Lancaster	10,376	141	2	6	31	102	588	135	428	25	7
Landrum	2,693	15	0	1	1	13	95	17	74	4	2
Latta	1,483	16	0	1	0	15	98	12	80	6	3
Laurens	9,464	110	0	5	19	86	583	105	459	19	0
Lexington	17,046	59	0	2	8	49	548	41	488	19	0
Liberty	3,079	17	0	1	0	16	155	46	102	7	0
Loris	2,412	25	0	3	9	13	205	40	153	12	0
Lyman	3,065	4	0	1	1	2	114	15	95	4	0
Manning	3,855	44	0	4	14	26	273	57	209	7	0
Marion	6,649	108	0	3	25	80	585	148	416	21	6
Mauldin	23,218	75	0	2	17	56	548	83	428	37	2
McBee	734	4	0	0	2	2	21	6	15	0	1
McColl	2,284	32	0	1	5	26	125	31	92	2	1
McCormick	2,689	27	0	1	2	24	54	7	46	1	0
Moncks Corner	7,390	36	0	1	6	29	384	47	302	35	0
Mount Pleasant	68,555	155	2	4	24	125	1,277	192	1,040	45	0
Mullins	4,595	74	1	2	19	52	317	123	185	9	3
Myrtle Beach	32,907	483	1	39	189	254	4,155	793	3,061	301	5
Newberry	11,144	57	0	4	12	41	363	52	303	8	0
New Ellenton	2,252	18	0	0	0	18	79	24	53	2	0
Nichols	386	5	0	0	0	5	11	1	10	0	0
Ninety Six	1,951	10	0	1	0	9	58	14	38	6	0
North	788	8	0	0	1	7	29	7	21	1	0
North Augusta	21,242	53	0	2	24	27	1,050	192	795	63	2
North Charleston	99,447	851	12	51	293	495	5,960	966	4,469	525	20
North Myrtle Beach	16,832	101	0	11	31	59	1,813	476	1,183	154	3
Orangeburg	13,252	96	4	4	40	48	594	216	340	38	6
Pacolet	2,886	14	0	3	1	10	91	29	58	4	2
Pageland	2,508	53	1	1	2	49	214	49	161	4	1
Pamplico	1,164	1	0	0	0	1	6	1	4	1	0
Pelion	613	2	1	0	0	1	21	2	19	0	0
Pickens	3,039	14	1	2	4	7	149	20	119	10	2
Pine Ridge	2,025	0	0	0	0	0	27	5	21	1	0
Port Royal	11,663	20	0	3	8	9	269	73	180	16	1
Prosperity	1,063	8	0	0	0	8	29	7	22	0	0
Ridgeland	2,577	23	0	1	11	11	131	27	98	6	1
Rock Hill	71,456	537	6	28	80	423	2,512	453	1,914	145	9
Saluda	2,980	57	0	0	0	57	78	12	63	3	0
Santee	722	15	0	1	9	5	90	13	73	4	0
Scranton	1,093	2	0	0	0	2	16	7	9	0	0
Seneca	7,852	62	0	9	5	48	319	63	251	5	5
Simpsonville	18,119	82	1	5	10	66	668	133	512	23	2
South Congaree	2,458	7	0	0	0	7	53	7	38	8	0
Spartanburg	40,448	646	6	18	129	493	3,087	679	2,207	201	14
Springdale	2,819	6	0	1	3	2	69	8	55	6	0
St. George	2,156	23	0	1	9	13	128	32	94	2	0
St. Matthews	1,918	18	0	1	1	16	50	12	37	1	1
Sullivans Island	1,891	1	0	0	0	1	43	6	35	2	0
Summerton	1,009	13	0	0	1	12	53	12	39	2	1
Summerville	47,479	157	1	8	45	103	1,611	240	1,291	80	4
Sumter	38,228	459	4	15	88	352	2,747	879	1,760	108	10
Surfside Beach	4,884	19	0	2	4	13	362	90	230	42	1
Swansea	828	10	0	0	2	8	52	8	42	2	0
Tega Cay	5,293	3	0	0	1	2	109	16	91	2	0
Timmonsville	2,403	32	0	0	7	25	204	58	127	19	0
Travelers Rest	4,685	8	0	0	2	6	257	7	246	4	0
Turbeville	700	1	0	0	0	1	15	8	7	0	0

[1] The FBI does not publish arson data unless it receives data from either the agency or the state for all 12 months of the calendar year.

Table 8.   Offenses Known to Law Enforcement, by State and City, 2010—*Continued*

(Number)

State/city	Population	Violent crime	Murder and non-negligent man-slaughter	Forcible rape	Robbery	Aggravated assault	Property crime	Burglary	Larceny-theft	Motor vehicle theft	Arson[1]
SOUTH CAROLINA—*Continued*											
Union	7,832	120	0	5	17	98	444	109	318	17	4
Wagener	885	6	0	0	1	5	51	18	29	4	1
Walhalla	3,477	24	0	2	0	22	106	23	75	8	1
Walterboro	5,841	83	1	4	18	60	665	189	448	28	2
Ware Shoals	2,372	13	0	0	1	12	128	17	105	6	0
Wellford	2,618	6	0	0	3	3	40	10	25	5	3
West Columbia	14,145	153	3	8	42	100	933	122	750	61	1
Westminster	2,651	16	0	4	3	9	107	16	88	3	0
West Union	300	1	0	0	0	1	24	1	23	0	0
Whitmire	1,583	3	0	0	2	1	18	4	14	0	0
Williamston	4,015	13	0	1	1	11	148	24	112	12	3
Williston	3,121	17	0	0	1	16	139	43	92	4	1
Winnsboro	3,615	61	0	1	6	54	293	43	241	9	3
Woodruff	4,169	14	0	0	0	14	108	31	72	5	1
Yemassee	874	4	0	0	0	4	34	5	19	10	0
York	8,327	87	1	3	17	66	348	73	260	15	2
SOUTH DAKOTA											
Aberdeen	24,818	63	0	22	1	40	531	87	406	38	5
Avon	499	0	0	0	0	0	0	0	0	0	0
Belle Fourche	4,972	6	0	1	0	5	23	5	17	1	0
Box Elder	4,340	17	0	1	2	14	138	22	110	6	0
Brandon	8,330	2	0	2	0	0	57	2	51	4	0
Brookings	20,200	7	0	1	0	6	106	8	96	2	0
Burke	544	0	0	0	0	0	0	0	0	0	0
Canton	4,378	3	0	1	0	2	68	14	50	4	0
Centerville	818	0	0	0	0	0	1	1	0	0	0
Chamberlain	2,273	5	0	1	0	4	11	5	5	1	0
Deadwood	1,254	4	0	0	0	4	37	3	31	3	0
Delmont	208	0	0	0	0	0	0	0	0	0	0
Eagle Butte	928	0	0	0	0	0	3	1	2	0	0
Estelline	663	0	0	0	0	0	9	1	8	0	0
Eureka	904	0	0	0	0	0	0	0	0	0	0
Flandreau	2,171	5	0	1	0	4	35	2	27	6	0
Freeman	1,157	0	0	0	0	0	2	0	2	0	0
Gettysburg	987	1	0	0	0	1	4	0	4	0	0
Hermosa	353	0	0	0	0	0	0	0	0	0	0
Hot Springs	4,063	0	0	0	0	0	40	10	29	1	0
Hoven	367	0	0	0	0	0	0	0	0	0	0
Irene	391	0	0	0	0	0	0	0	0	0	0
Jefferson	617	0	0	0	0	0	0	0	0	0	0
Kadoka	611	2	0	0	0	2	16	13	3	0	0
Kimball	692	0	0	0	0	0	0	0	0	0	0
Lead	2,813	1	0	0	0	1	23	3	18	2	0
Lemmon	1,142	0	0	0	0	0	7	1	5	1	0
Lennox	2,920	0	0	0	0	0	5	1	4	0	0
Leola	374	0	0	0	0	0	0	0	0	0	0
Madison	6,573	3	0	0	0	3	119	11	106	2	0
Martin	966	2	0	0	0	2	3	1	2	0	0
McIntosh	201	0	0	0	0	0	0	0	0	0	0
Menno	633	0	0	0	0	0	1	1	0	0	0
Miller	1,296	1	0	0	0	1	5	0	5	0	0
Mitchell	14,669	17	1	5	2	9	519	75	425	19	0
Mobridge	3,085	8	0	0	0	8	53	5	47	1	0
North Sioux City	2,619	0	0	0	0	0	32	4	28	0	0
Pierre	14,003	26	0	5	2	19	449	81	345	23	1
Rapid City	67,436	404	2	91	59	252	2,823	518	2,178	127	8
Rosholt	425	0	0	0	0	0	0	0	0	0	0
Scotland	762	0	0	0	0	0	0	0	0	0	0
Selby	635	0	0	0	0	0	1	1	0	0	0
Sioux Falls	160,679	482	3	96	55	328	4,854	989	3,637	228	25
Sisseton	2,430	6	0	1	0	5	76	19	51	6	0
Spearfish	10,057	12	0	6	0	6	339	70	253	16	1
Springfield	1,456	0	0	0	0	0	0	0	0	0	0
Sturgis	5,897	5	0	0	0	5	154	21	128	5	1
Tea	5,058	10	0	0	1	9	121	33	84	4	0
Tripp	606	0	0	0	0	0	2	2	0	0	0
Tyndall	1,061	0	0	0	0	0	0	0	0	0	0
Vermillion	10,369	4	0	0	0	4	56	8	48	0	0
Viborg	747	0	0	0	0	0	4	0	4	0	0
Wagner	1,487	5	0	0	0	5	11	0	9	2	0
Watertown	20,232	60	0	19	1	40	596	88	472	36	1
Whitewood	852	2	0	1	0	1	3	1	2	0	0
Wilmot	515	0	0	0	0	0	0	0	0	0	0
Winner	2,614	4	0	0	0	4	24	5	17	2	0

[1] The FBI does not publish arson data unless it receives data from either the agency or the state for all 12 months of the calendar year.

Table 8.   Offenses Known to Law Enforcement, by State and City, 2010—*Continued*

(Number)

State/city	Population	Violent crime	Murder and non-negligent man-slaughter	Forcible rape	Robbery	Aggravated assault	Property crime	Burglary	Larceny-theft	Motor vehicle theft	Arson[1]
TENNESSEE											
Adamsville	2,134	2	0	0	0	2	61	16	31	14	0
Alamo	2,402	11	1	0	3	7	38	11	25	2	0
Alexandria	957	5	0	0	0	5	18	7	11	0	0
Algood	3,472	7	0	1	0	6	98	13	82	3	2
Ardmore	1,177	7	0	0	2	5	24	4	19	1	0
Ashland City	4,707	14	1	0	2	11	237	49	179	9	0
Athens	14,352	185	0	8	28	149	1,052	208	799	45	1
Atoka	7,978	16	0	0	1	15	148	32	109	7	0
Baileyton	492	0	0	0	0	0	32	5	23	4	0
Baneberry	489	0	0	0	0	0	3	1	2	0	0
Bartlett	48,358	103	1	7	9	86	839	197	589	53	1
Baxter	1,435	5	0	0	0	5	48	13	31	4	0
Bean Station	3,085	10	0	1	4	5	148	37	106	5	0
Belle Meade	3,572	0	0	0	0	0	38	9	29	0	1
Bells	2,283	17	0	1	3	13	47	19	25	3	1
Benton	1,182	3	0	0	0	3	51	21	29	1	0
Berry Hill	830	4	0	0	1	3	61	9	52	0	0
Bethel Springs	778	0	0	0	0	0	8	2	4	2	0
Big Sandy	502	6	0	0	0	6	16	8	8	0	2
Blaine	1,777	3	0	0	2	1	25	11	12	2	0
Bluff City	1,689	0	0	0	0	0	31	6	25	0	0
Bradford	1,061	1	0	0	0	1	18	6	11	1	0
Brentwood	38,371	29	2	2	8	17	440	85	341	14	2
Brighton	2,782	9	0	0	0	9	38	13	24	1	0
Bristol	25,799	140	0	12	9	119	1,003	182	778	43	5
Brownsville	10,138	164	1	8	20	135	539	200	318	21	1
Bruceton	1,418	1	0	0	0	1	20	5	13	2	0
Burns	1,461	1	0	0	0	1	25	7	17	1	0
Calhoun	525	0	0	0	0	0	5	0	5	0	0
Camden	3,545	8	0	1	1	6	173	30	136	7	1
Carthage	2,222	6	0	0	0	6	79	20	55	4	0
Caryville	2,373	12	0	0	0	12	118	20	88	10	1
Celina	1,342	4	0	0	0	4	18	5	13	0	0
Centerville	3,947	3	0	0	0	3	98	29	63	6	0
Chapel Hill	1,368	3	0	0	0	3	20	3	16	1	0
Charleston	674	1	0	0	0	1	13	2	9	2	0
Chattanooga	172,460	1,557	18	78	512	949	10,866	2,691	7,350	825	7
Church Hill	6,876	32	1	1	4	26	131	33	91	7	1
Clarksburg	368	0	0	0	0	0	1	0	1	0	0
Clarksville	126,548	802	9	55	121	617	4,102	1,373	2,525	204	24
Cleveland	40,452	351	0	19	29	303	1,983	439	1,470	74	5
Clifton	2,673	1	0	0	0	1	12	2	9	1	0
Clinton	9,715	44	0	1	5	38	470	90	360	20	1
Collegedale	8,343	5	0	0	2	3	155	29	119	7	0
Collierville	40,286	67	0	0	9	58	739	98	602	39	0
Collinwood	995	5	0	0	0	5	8	4	4	0	0
Columbia	35,364	282	4	13	31	234	1,397	305	1,043	49	7
Cookeville	30,179	98	1	8	21	68	1,764	426	1,270	68	5
Coopertown	3,520	2	0	0	0	2	26	9	15	2	0
Copperhill	428	1	0	0	1	0	10	5	5	0	0
Cornersville	986	0	0	0	0	0	10	1	8	1	0
Covington	9,396	69	0	4	21	44	514	124	378	12	0
Cowan	1,705	0	0	0	0	0	39	4	35	0	2
Cross Plains	1,728	5	0	0	0	5	36	9	26	1	0
Crossville	12,084	122	1	7	17	97	1,039	165	811	63	2
Crump	1,464	17	0	0	0	17	61	37	24	0	0
Cumberland City	329	1	1	0	0	0	11	3	8	0	0
Cumberland Gap	208	5	0	0	0	5	3	2	1	0	0
Dandridge	2,784	14	0	1	3	10	96	13	81	2	1
Dayton	6,945	18	0	5	6	7	258	33	215	10	1
Decatur	1,512	1	0	0	0	1	45	11	33	1	0
Decaturville	832	0	0	0	0	0	17	11	6	0	0
Decherd	2,113	12	0	1	0	11	70	17	48	5	2
Dickson	14,100	97	1	11	11	74	776	86	663	27	0
Dover	1,642	0	0	0	0	0	21	5	13	3	0
Dresden	2,810	6	0	0	0	6	91	15	74	2	0
Dunlap	5,672	25	0	1	2	22	183	62	109	12	1
Dyer	2,396	3	0	0	0	3	32	10	18	4	0
Dyersburg	17,104	167	0	5	26	136	1,490	371	1,071	48	3
Eagleville	533	0	0	0	0	0	6	5	1	0	0
East Ridge	19,882	175	0	5	39	131	1,066	279	725	62	2
Elizabethton	13,694	53	0	0	5	48	639	111	514	14	1
Elkton	591	0	0	0	0	0	10	3	6	1	0

[1] The FBI does not publish arson data unless it receives data from either the agency or the state for all 12 months of the calendar year.

Table 8. Offenses Known to Law Enforcement, by State and City, 2010—*Continued*

(Number)

State/city	Population	Violent crime	Murder and non-negligent man-slaughter	Forcible rape	Robbery	Aggravated assault	Property crime	Burglary	Larceny-theft	Motor vehicle theft	Arson[1]
TENNESSEE—*Continued*											
Englewood	1,815	5	0	0	0	5	44	8	35	1	0
Erin	1,448	12	0	1	2	9	34	12	21	1	0
Erwin	5,759	12	0	0	0	12	71	19	49	3	0
Estill Springs	2,232	13	0	0	0	13	32	13	17	2	0
Ethridge	560	1	0	0	0	1	9	5	4	0	0
Etowah	3,770	18	0	2	0	16	123	20	99	4	0
Fairview	8,324	11	0	0	0	11	118	23	93	2	1
Fayetteville	7,216	45	0	2	6	37	376	59	303	14	2
Franklin	62,127	104	2	14	9	79	1,066	115	921	30	8
Friendship	604	2	1	0	0	1	8	6	2	0	0
Gadsden	539	2	0	0	0	2	7	2	4	1	0
Gainesboro	835	3	0	0	0	3	9	3	6	0	0
Gallatin	31,229	115	2	6	20	87	535	79	442	14	2
Gallaway	760	1	0	0	1	0	11	2	9	0	0
Gates	836	3	0	1	0	2	10	0	7	3	0
Gatlinburg	6,104	20	0	2	7	11	479	188	281	10	5
Germantown	41,347	39	0	1	13	25	455	124	319	12	1
Gibson	415	0	0	0	0	0	17	3	12	2	0
Gleason	1,397	8	0	0	0	8	24	2	20	2	0
Goodlettsville	17,658	102	0	8	28	66	1,185	213	927	45	2
Gordonsville	1,311	6	0	0	0	6	39	8	28	3	0
Grand Junction	298	1	0	0	0	1	31	10	21	0	0
Graysville	1,468	8	0	0	0	8	17	1	15	1	0
Greenbrier	6,899	19	0	1	1	17	108	32	68	8	2
Greeneville	15,294	76	0	9	25	42	802	163	606	33	0
Greenfield	2,011	2	0	0	0	2	32	6	24	2	0
Halls	2,145	6	0	0	1	5	61	17	42	2	0
Harriman	6,612	48	0	2	11	35	326	82	228	16	5
Henderson	6,445	25	0	2	1	22	250	84	161	5	0
Hendersonville	49,010	143	1	7	15	120	1,257	193	1,019	45	11
Henning	1,251	10	2	0	1	7	30	10	20	0	0
Henry	551	0	0	0	0	0	10	4	6	0	0
Hohenwald	3,808	33	0	0	0	33	98	16	78	4	2
Hollow Rock	924	1	0	0	0	1	6	2	3	1	0
Hornbeak	410	1	0	0	0	1	2	0	2	0	0
Humboldt	9,114	121	0	3	17	101	470	131	322	17	2
Huntingdon	4,074	8	0	0	2	6	110	16	92	2	0
Huntland	862	0	0	0	0	0	9	1	7	1	0
Jacksboro	2,086	9	0	1	2	6	204	11	190	3	0
Jackson	63,969	541	2	25	145	369	4,044	1,096	2,704	244	11
Jamestown	1,916	5	0	0	1	4	99	9	88	2	1
Jasper	3,060	11	0	1	0	10	86	9	73	4	0
Jefferson City	8,232	20	0	3	9	8	401	74	311	16	2
Jellico	2,511	5	0	2	1	2	116	21	87	8	2
Johnson City	63,750	278	1	25	59	193	3,010	574	2,346	90	15
Jonesborough	5,583	23	0	1	2	20	96	22	70	4	0
Kenton	1,286	2	0	0	0	2	17	1	14	2	0
Kimball	1,390	0	0	0	0	0	82	5	74	3	0
Kingsport	44,587	377	1	26	52	298	2,864	509	2,257	98	15
Kingston	5,609	9	0	0	1	8	97	16	77	4	0
Kingston Springs	2,996	0	0	0	0	0	14	5	9	0	0
Knoxville	185,554	1,755	15	122	625	993	12,322	2,723	8,789	810	51
Lafayette	4,588	12	0	0	2	10	54	12	38	4	0
La Follette	8,082	77	0	3	20	54	752	255	460	37	2
Lake City	1,848	10	0	0	0	10	32	11	18	3	2
Lakewood	2,659	3	0	0	1	2	91	18	65	8	1
La Vergne	32,335	128	1	14	18	95	961	290	627	44	2
Lawrenceburg	10,877	109	2	13	3	91	655	154	463	38	4
Lebanon	25,446	215	0	5	37	173	1,239	233	945	61	4
Lenoir City	8,202	86	0	2	11	73	572	105	447	20	6
Lewisburg	11,126	49	0	4	4	41	277	68	197	12	2
Lexington	7,876	92	1	5	4	82	435	82	336	17	6
Livingston	3,552	23	0	1	1	21	67	10	54	3	0
Lookout Mountain	1,884	0	0	0	0	0	11	6	5	0	1
Loretto	1,800	6	0	0	0	6	30	10	17	3	0
Loudon	4,995	12	0	0	0	12	122	13	103	6	0
Lynnville	335	0	0	0	0	0	0	0	0	0	0
Madisonville	4,761	22	0	0	2	20	278	54	208	16	2
Manchester	10,210	65	3	2	1	59	541	98	427	16	0
Martin	10,145	53	0	3	4	46	367	79	283	5	0
Maryville	27,638	61	2	5	19	35	915	132	752	31	0
Mason	1,356	11	0	1	2	8	37	12	24	1	0
Maury City	702	1	0	0	0	1	16	4	11	1	0

[1] The FBI does not publish arson data unless it receives data from either the agency or the state for all 12 months of the calendar year.

Table 8. Offenses Known to Law Enforcement, by State and City, 2010—*Continued*

(Number)

State/city	Population	Violent crime	Murder and non-negligent man-slaughter	Forcible rape	Robbery	Aggravated assault	Property crime	Burglary	Larceny-theft	Motor vehicle theft	Arson[1]
TENNESSEE—*Continued*											
Maynardville	1,940	4	0	0	1	3	115	39	71	5	0
McEwen	1,678	5	0	0	1	4	14	2	12	0	1
McKenzie	5,283	18	0	3	2	13	124	38	83	3	0
McMinnville	13,647	88	0	6	8	74	539	120	386	33	0
Medina	2,465	3	0	0	0	3	37	13	23	1	1
Memphis	673,650	10,384	89	422	3,236	6,637	42,138	13,094	25,114	3,930	328
Middleton	605	1	0	0	0	1	14	5	9	0	0
Milan	7,913	67	1	3	10	53	256	69	176	11	0
Millersville	6,565	20	0	0	1	19	133	49	81	3	1
Millington	10,875	86	0	2	12	72	462	95	343	24	0
Minor Hill	446	0	0	0	0	0	2	1	1	0	0
Monteagle	1,204	1	0	0	1	0	16	4	9	3	0
Monterey	2,944	11	1	1	0	9	102	25	74	3	1
Morristown	28,147	243	1	16	43	183	2,099	178	1,838	83	7
Moscow	559	5	0	0	0	5	19	4	14	1	0
Mountain City	2,360	5	0	0	0	5	65	13	48	4	0
Mount Carmel	5,525	6	0	0	1	5	59	17	39	3	0
Mount Juliet	24,544	49	1	3	6	39	495	77	406	12	1
Mount Pleasant	4,532	27	0	1	2	24	167	49	106	12	0
Munford	6,880	9	0	1	0	8	122	27	90	5	0
Murfreesboro	109,199	603	5	37	151	410	4,610	1,310	3,144	156	15
Nashville	616,366	6,995	55	367	1,817	4,756	30,517	7,731	20,881	1,905	80
Newbern	3,173	17	0	2	1	14	87	25	59	3	1
New Hope	1,049	0	0	0	0	0	4	0	3	1	0
New Johnsonville	1,961	5	0	0	0	5	25	3	21	1	0
New Market	1,397	0	0	0	0	0	4	0	4	0	0
Newport	7,556	77	0	4	16	57	784	120	633	31	0
New Tazewell	2,845	3	0	0	1	2	63	15	48	0	0
Niota	811	1	0	0	0	1	8	5	2	1	0
Nolensville	3,178	1	0	0	0	1	50	12	36	2	0
Norris	1,490	0	0	0	0	0	16	10	6	0	0
Oakland	5,878	4	0	0	0	4	123	16	107	0	0
Oak Ridge	27,728	133	1	8	31	93	1,232	365	825	42	4
Obion	1,074	5	0	0	1	4	47	8	36	3	0
Oliver Springs	3,346	4	0	2	0	2	107	10	89	8	0
Oneida	3,812	12	0	0	0	12	251	50	194	7	0
Paris	9,946	56	1	2	8	45	490	107	377	6	0
Parsons	2,480	6	0	0	0	6	35	9	26	0	0
Petersburg	610	0	0	0	0	0	8	2	5	1	0
Pigeon Forge	6,532	72	1	6	15	50	598	150	410	38	3
Pikeville	1,863	3	0	0	0	3	32	7	22	3	0
Piperton	1,508	6	0	0	2	4	19	6	12	1	0
Pittman Center	716	0	0	0	0	0	14	8	6	0	0
Plainview	2,062	2	0	1	0	1	30	9	17	4	0
Pleasant View	4,304	3	0	0	0	3	57	13	42	2	0
Portland	11,682	73	0	3	2	68	267	75	182	10	1
Powells Crossroads	1,246	0	0	0	0	0	0	0	0	0	0
Pulaski	7,790	33	0	5	2	26	398	84	303	11	1
Puryear	676	2	0	0	0	2	13	1	10	2	1
Red Bank	11,680	59	0	4	14	41	544	149	366	29	8
Red Boiling Springs	1,114	3	0	0	1	2	30	11	19	0	0
Ridgely	1,486	7	0	2	0	5	34	20	14	0	0
Ridgetop	1,796	2	0	0	0	2	20	5	12	3	0
Ripley	7,473	120	0	5	18	97	508	209	286	13	0
Rockwood	5,536	38	0	2	2	34	334	69	251	14	2
Rogersville	4,340	29	0	0	9	20	375	65	299	11	2
Rossville	637	0	0	0	0	0	17	2	15	0	0
Rutherford	1,248	2	0	1	0	1	18	7	11	0	0
Rutledge	1,294	4	0	1	0	3	45	9	34	2	0
Samburg	249	0	0	0	0	0	3	0	3	0	0
Savannah	7,330	55	1	4	12	38	618	163	427	28	1
Scotts Hill	932	1	0	0	0	1	7	0	7	0	0
Selmer	4,699	19	0	0	4	15	241	59	179	3	0
Sevierville	17,854	78	1	7	17	53	966	186	711	69	0
Sewanee	2,634	0	0	0	0	0	53	14	38	1	1
Sharon	901	0	0	0	0	0	31	2	28	1	0
Shelbyville	20,527	123	1	13	11	98	662	143	487	32	4
Signal Mountain	7,217	3	0	1	1	1	58	9	49	0	0
Smithville	4,465	19	0	1	4	14	226	39	178	9	2
Smyrna	41,071	87	1	4	6	76	828	345	451	32	10
Sneedville	1,282	14	0	3	0	11	65	14	51	0	0
Soddy-Daisy	12,967	50	0	2	3	45	493	74	379	40	0
Somerville	2,970	40	0	1	2	37	107	17	86	4	0

[1] The FBI does not publish arson data unless it receives data from either the agency or the state for all 12 months of the calendar year.

Table 8.   Offenses Known to Law Enforcement, by State and City, 2010—*Continued*

(Number)

State/city	Population	Violent crime	Murder and non-negligent man-slaughter	Forcible rape	Robbery	Aggravated assault	Property crime	Burglary	Larceny-theft	Motor vehicle theft	Arson[1]
TENNESSEE—*Continued*											
South Carthage	1,355	7	0	0	0	7	40	9	31	0	0
South Fulton	2,373	14	0	1	2	11	79	25	49	5	0
South Pittsburg	3,079	16	0	0	2	14	72	10	58	4	0
Sparta	5,012	18	0	1	5	12	384	114	254	16	2
Spencer	1,687	1	0	0	0	1	25	10	14	1	0
Spring City	2,140	4	0	0	0	4	41	6	35	0	0
Springfield	17,903	208	1	22	40	145	606	88	485	33	8
Spring Hill	30,829	39	0	5	2	32	406	73	328	5	0
St. Joseph	864	0	0	0	0	0	17	2	13	2	1
Surgoinsville	1,834	1	0	0	0	1	16	3	12	1	0
Sweetwater	6,740	34	0	1	7	26	291	80	192	19	0
Tazewell	2,185	15	0	0	6	9	145	36	100	9	0
Tellico Plains	973	2	0	0	0	2	24	7	17	0	0
Tiptonville	3,959	5	0	0	0	5	24	9	15	0	0
Toone	344	3	0	1	0	2	6	3	3	0	0
Townsend	549	4	0	1	0	3	12	4	6	2	0
Tracy City	1,605	16	0	0	3	13	47	20	26	1	0
Trenton	4,480	54	0	0	2	52	250	36	208	6	3
Trezevant	868	4	0	0	0	4	19	9	9	1	0
Trimble	721	1	0	0	0	1	5	3	2	0	0
Troy	1,201	0	0	0	0	0	32	5	26	1	0
Tullahoma	18,535	127	3	2	20	102	784	181	582	21	3
Tusculum	2,317	1	0	0	1	0	19	2	16	1	0
Union City	10,486	60	0	2	9	49	606	125	464	17	7
Vonore	1,516	10	0	0	2	8	83	14	66	3	0
Wartburg	912	1	0	0	0	1	17	4	13	0	0
Wartrace	614	1	0	0	0	1	2	0	2	0	0
Watauga	428	0	0	0	0	0	1	0	1	0	0
Watertown	1,422	4	0	1	0	3	30	10	19	1	1
Waverly	4,192	2	0	0	0	2	73	14	57	2	0
Waynesboro	2,090	4	0	0	0	4	28	11	16	1	0
Westmoreland	2,243	5	0	1	1	3	40	5	31	4	0
White Bluff	2,570	12	0	1	3	8	41	5	34	2	0
White House	10,626	18	0	1	3	14	186	23	152	11	1
White Pine	2,202	9	1	0	2	6	125	20	101	4	0
Whiteville	4,480	11	0	0	1	10	65	18	44	3	0
Whitwell	1,572	11	0	1	1	9	66	17	44	5	1
Winchester	7,911	80	0	5	7	68	341	84	249	8	2
Winfield	994	3	0	0	0	3	41	27	13	1	2
Woodbury	2,619	13	0	2	0	11	80	21	53	6	0
TEXAS											
Abernathy	2,748	3	0	0	1	2	30	7	20	3	0
Abilene	116,938	578	4	68	112	394	4,897	1,340	3,375	182	26
Addison	15,862	97	1	7	20	69	862	105	651	106	0
Alamo	17,687	154	0	13	18	123	1,441	239	1,057	145	9
Alamo Heights	7,488	9	0	3	4	2	230	49	176	5	0
Alice	19,690	166	0	8	7	151	1,236	356	843	37	14
Allen	89,459	65	0	12	18	35	1,615	319	1,232	64	0
Alpine	6,490	6	0	1	0	5	55	16	39	0	1
Alto	1,157	3	0	0	1	2	63	23	39	1	0
Alton	12,349	27	0	1	7	19	482	116	324	42	4
Alvarado	4,379	13	2	1	2	8	112	25	81	6	0
Alvin	23,399	45	0	5	20	20	744	174	544	26	2
Amarillo	190,393	1,184	10	91	238	845	11,064	2,590	7,827	647	55
Andrews	10,508	49	0	9	0	40	242	75	159	8	2
Angleton	19,138	75	1	11	13	50	500	110	374	16	1
Anna	1,999	7	0	3	1	3	120	28	84	8	1
Anson	2,194	11	1	0	0	10	43	14	25	4	1
Anthony	4,550	21	0	1	4	16	216	19	195	2	2
Aransas Pass	8,787	42	2	7	12	21	611	184	414	13	3
Archer City	1,778	4	0	0	0	4	7	3	4	0	1
Arcola	1,252	1	0	0	0	1	35	17	13	5	1
Argyle	3,753	3	0	0	0	3	29	5	21	3	0
Arlington	383,715	1,925	16	119	532	1,258	19,350	4,763	13,342	1,245	48
Arp	981	1	0	0	0	1	4	0	4	0	0
Athens	12,173	62	0	9	16	37	535	152	347	36	3
Atlanta	5,380	26	0	4	5	17	256	67	174	15	0
Austin	796,310	3,790	38	265	1,231	2,256	45,826	8,749	34,827	2,250	122
Azle	11,689	30	1	1	6	22	371	101	250	20	2
Baird	1,644	1	0	0	0	1	17	6	10	1	0
Balch Springs	20,265	222	1	27	51	143	1,615	242	1,238	135	2
Balcones Heights	2,997	24	0	0	4	20	548	40	486	22	1
Ballinger	3,607	12	0	1	0	11	101	41	56	4	0

[1] The FBI does not publish arson data unless it receives data from either the agency or the state for all 12 months of the calendar year.

Table 8.   Offenses Known to Law Enforcement, by State and City, 2010—*Continued*

(Number)

State/city	Population	Violent crime	Murder and non-negligent man-slaughter	Forcible rape	Robbery	Aggravated assault	Property crime	Burglary	Larceny-theft	Motor vehicle theft	Arson[1]
TEXAS—*Continued*											
Bangs	1,532	2	0	0	0	2	22	4	16	2	0
Bastrop	8,790	24	0	1	9	14	565	47	507	11	2
Bay City	17,523	45	2	12	12	19	824	219	599	6	1
Bayou Vista	1,663	0	0	0	0	0	0	0	0	0	0
Baytown	71,082	301	6	21	148	126	3,849	822	2,707	320	7
Beaumont	109,430	900	10	65	312	513	5,941	1,611	4,041	289	48
Bedford	49,993	215	4	20	34	157	1,773	342	1,333	98	4
Bee Cave	3,435	3	0	0	0	3	122	15	105	2	0
Beeville	12,439	44	0	3	5	36	341	86	247	8	3
Bellaire	18,378	15	0	1	10	4	339	93	231	15	0
Bellmead	9,659	157	2	8	19	128	1,021	71	918	32	4
Bellville	4,552	13	0	6	1	6	92	28	60	4	0
Belton	17,955	79	0	0	10	69	766	171	586	9	4
Benbrook	23,589	37	1	4	11	21	448	105	319	24	4
Bertram	1,455	4	0	0	0	4	24	7	17	0	0
Beverly Hills	2,031	12	0	0	4	8	94	23	68	3	0
Big Sandy	1,348	3	0	0	2	1	6	5	1	0	0
Big Spring	24,357	178	0	17	9	152	1,401	353	1,001	47	1
Bishop	3,100	9	0	0	0	9	73	8	64	1	0
Blanco	1,673	7	0	0	0	7	32	12	19	1	0
Bloomburg	359	0	0	0	0	0	0	0	0	0	0
Blue Mound	2,385	2	0	0	0	2	51	26	20	5	0
Boerne	11,152	21	0	2	1	18	261	29	228	4	1
Bogata	1,209	3	0	0	0	3	31	11	18	2	0
Bonham	10,547	26	0	7	1	18	313	72	231	10	1
Borger	12,469	186	1	15	7	163	633	119	480	34	0
Bovina	1,697	1	0	0	0	1	23	11	12	0	1
Bowie	5,487	14	0	2	3	9	257	50	189	18	0
Brackettville	1,769	0	0	0	0	0	3	0	3	0	1
Brady	5,286	18	0	0	1	17	99	37	61	1	0
Brazoria	3,021	20	0	1	4	15	65	15	45	5	0
Breckenridge	5,606	10	0	2	1	7	75	23	52	0	3
Bremond	851	6	0	1	0	5	13	8	5	0	0
Brenham	16,267	62	0	2	9	51	521	113	386	22	1
Bridge City	8,421	17	0	10	1	6	167	44	117	6	0
Bridgeport	6,263	12	0	0	2	10	144	33	107	4	0
Brookshire	4,010	18	3	0	6	9	164	74	84	6	1
Brookside Village	1,823	4	0	0	0	4	23	14	8	1	0
Brownfield	8,863	21	0	0	7	14	183	55	117	11	0
Brownsville	180,040	563	7	31	165	360	9,316	1,286	7,784	246	26
Brownwood	18,725	123	0	10	12	101	738	163	564	11	2
Bruceville-Eddy	1,562	6	1	0	2	3	54	11	39	4	0
Bryan	75,350	410	4	34	90	282	3,647	890	2,632	125	59
Bullard	1,979	2	0	0	0	2	36	11	24	1	1
Bulverde	4,894	6	0	0	1	5	69	12	56	1	0
Burkburnett	10,424	5	0	0	1	4	229	102	125	2	0
Burleson	37,902	69	0	9	9	51	963	163	757	43	1
Burnet	6,114	16	0	1	0	15	163	28	126	9	1
Cactus	2,699	11	1	2	2	6	10	7	1	2	0
Caddo Mills	1,216	6	0	0	0	6	50	27	20	3	0
Caldwell	3,693	5	0	0	0	5	21	4	16	1	0
Calvert	1,340	12	1	2	1	8	43	13	29	1	1
Cameron	5,608	13	0	2	0	11	234	33	200	1	1
Canton	3,639	3	0	1	2	0	137	35	94	8	0
Canyon	14,634	13	1	1	2	9	119	15	102	2	0
Carrollton	130,862	184	4	4	63	113	3,510	897	2,256	357	13
Carthage	6,650	34	0	0	2	32	152	26	122	4	0
Castle Hills	4,227	4	0	0	2	2	319	65	245	9	0
Castroville	3,083	6	0	0	0	6	83	17	66	0	0
Cedar Hill	46,674	104	1	10	29	64	1,742	430	1,213	99	4
Cedar Park	70,363	58	2	8	12	36	796	147	622	27	4
Celina	6,115	6	0	3	0	3	77	22	53	2	0
Center	5,769	41	0	2	4	35	292	53	225	14	2
Childress	6,463	22	0	0	0	22	72	38	32	2	0
Chillicothe	655	4	0	1	0	3	30	13	14	3	0
Cibolo	18,403	17	0	4	1	12	194	36	153	5	1
Cisco	3,684	4	0	0	0	4	78	25	51	2	0
Clarksville	3,301	1	0	0	1	0	35	18	17	0	0
Cleburne	30,209	169	0	23	16	130	1,328	241	1,029	58	3
Cleveland	7,903	89	1	5	22	61	752	133	592	27	1
Clifton	3,488	0	0	0	0	0	30	6	24	0	0
Clint	972	3	0	0	1	2	12	1	10	1	0
Clute	10,930	54	1	3	6	44	361	107	244	10	3

[1] The FBI does not publish arson data unless it receives data from either the agency or the state for all 12 months of the calendar year.

Table 8.   Offenses Known to Law Enforcement, by State and City, 2010—*Continued*

(Number)

State/city	Population	Violent crime	Murder and non-negligent man-slaughter	Forcible rape	Robbery	Aggravated assault	Property crime	Burglary	Larceny-theft	Motor vehicle theft	Arson[1]
TEXAS—*Continued*											
Clyde	3,774	1	0	0	0	1	87	23	58	6	0
Cockrell Hill	4,287	22	0	3	7	12	130	34	83	13	2
Coffee City	208	0	0	0	0	0	9	2	7	0	0
Coleman	4,573	10	0	0	2	8	231	114	97	20	4
College Station	88,416	220	3	37	44	136	2,655	475	2,091	89	0
Colleyville	25,480	5	0	0	2	3	300	69	224	7	0
Collinsville	1,539	3	0	0	0	3	21	6	14	1	0
Colorado City	3,895	13	0	4	0	9	163	32	130	1	2
Columbus	3,854	25	1	2	2	20	142	50	89	3	4
Comanche	4,173	18	0	1	3	14	203	49	151	3	1
Combes	2,925	13	0	1	0	12	73	25	43	5	2
Commerce	9,187	38	0	7	12	19	374	112	249	13	1
Conroe	60,677	248	5	22	80	141	2,815	601	2,079	135	0
Converse	18,890	31	2	2	12	15	396	65	315	16	3
Coppell	39,870	66	1	7	11	47	626	153	424	49	1
Copperas Cove	30,791	149	2	1	15	131	1,075	258	803	14	14
Corinth	22,185	20	0	1	2	17	295	45	229	21	3
Corpus Christi	287,559	2,068	16	191	389	1,472	15,101	2,626	12,027	448	105
Corrigan	1,881	4	0	1	0	3	37	5	31	1	0
Corsicana	26,344	112	0	7	25	80	1,314	327	920	67	3
Cottonwood Shores	1,235	3	0	0	0	3	26	11	12	3	0
Crandall	4,036	14	0	2	1	11	56	23	29	4	0
Crane	3,318	5	0	2	0	3	35	3	31	1	5
Crockett	6,623	26	0	1	2	23	198	62	128	8	0
Crosbyton	1,561	5	0	0	0	5	24	11	13	0	0
Crowell	912	0	0	0	0	0	0	0	0	0	0
Crowley	13,600	29	0	1	3	25	290	66	214	10	1
Crystal City	7,052	22	0	0	0	22	70	21	49	0	1
Cuero	6,445	17	0	1	0	16	86	31	48	7	0
Daingerfield	2,354	8	0	3	1	4	91	32	56	3	1
Dalhart	7,101	26	0	3	0	23	129	32	90	7	1
Dallas	1,306,775	9,161	148	505	4,487	4,021	64,125	19,594	36,147	8,384	642
Dalworthington Gardens	2,473	5	0	1	2	2	45	13	28	4	0
Danbury	1,707	1	0	0	0	1	22	2	19	1	0
Dayton	7,828	15	0	6	5	4	182	44	121	17	0
Decatur	6,641	10	0	0	2	8	195	16	169	10	1
Deer Park	31,087	28	3	8	5	12	1,015	255	725	35	1
De Kalb	1,842	9	0	0	1	8	54	32	22	0	0
De Leon	2,329	8	0	1	0	7	35	16	19	0	0
Del Rio	36,840	73	0	2	16	55	731	148	558	25	6
Denison	24,196	77	1	2	13	61	1,109	215	858	36	3
Denton	127,251	326	3	67	65	191	3,256	564	2,535	157	21
Denver City	4,146	5	0	3	0	2	69	26	40	3	1
Desoto	49,328	135	1	11	46	77	1,659	538	996	125	6
Devine	4,610	1	0	0	0	1	122	29	88	5	0
Diboll	5,519	19	0	6	2	11	114	29	84	1	0
Dickinson	17,854	45	0	5	15	25	534	129	373	32	1
Dilley	3,589	8	0	0	2	6	55	23	28	4	0
Dimmitt	3,622	8	0	0	0	8	219	64	151	4	0
Donna	17,737	113	1	7	12	93	1,159	273	819	67	12
Double Oak	3,444	2	0	0	1	1	11	2	9	0	0
Driscoll	800	6	0	0	0	6	16	1	14	1	0
Dublin	3,769	11	0	0	0	11	58	21	36	1	0
Dumas	14,158	39	0	8	2	29	319	58	247	14	2
Duncanville	36,397	135	1	8	65	61	1,662	527	1,009	126	2
Eagle Lake	3,638	3	0	0	1	2	40	12	28	0	0
Eagle Pass	27,581	58	0	0	8	50	1,086	296	762	28	6
Early	2,707	10	0	2	2	6	69	19	47	3	0
Eastland	3,831	6	0	0	0	6	111	19	84	8	1
East Mountain	635	0	0	0	0	0	10	1	9	0	1
Edcouch	4,754	17	1	0	4	12	87	42	43	2	0
Edgewood	1,429	10	0	0	1	9	39	12	24	3	1
Edinburg	75,091	232	2	23	44	163	4,599	1,011	3,294	294	19
Edna	5,816	14	1	2	3	8	126	34	89	3	1
El Campo	10,729	39	0	2	7	30	331	79	232	20	4
Electra	2,864	6	0	0	0	6	72	21	50	1	0
Elgin	10,437	25	0	0	5	20	246	45	187	14	0
El Paso	624,322	2,861	5	179	479	2,198	17,404	1,953	13,899	1,552	101
Elsa	6,751	23	0	0	4	19	314	73	228	13	1
Ennis	20,103	65	0	2	19	44	893	173	682	38	3
Euless	53,950	141	1	22	50	68	2,008	486	1,385	137	2
Everman	5,828	27	0	4	8	15	214	66	140	8	1
Fairfield	3,755	8	0	0	1	7	40	18	22	0	1

[1] The FBI does not publish arson data unless it receives data from either the agency or the state for all 12 months of the calendar year.

Table 8.   Offenses Known to Law Enforcement, by State and City, 2010—*Continued*

(Number)

State/city	Population	Violent crime	Murder and non-negligent man-slaughter	Forcible rape	Robbery	Aggravated assault	Property crime	Burglary	Larceny-theft	Motor vehicle theft	Arson[1]
TEXAS—*Continued*											
Fair Oaks Ranch	6,595	2	0	1	0	1	41	25	15	1	0
Falfurrias	4,763	11	1	0	3	7	185	76	108	1	9
Farmers Branch	26,585	51	0	2	24	25	1,160	236	789	135	4
Farmersville	3,576	11	0	4	4	3	85	36	45	4	0
Farwell	1,238	3	0	0	0	3	18	0	18	0	0
Ferris	2,616	7	2	1	2	2	69	17	50	2	1
Flatonia	1,443	0	0	0	0	0	19	7	12	0	0
Florence	1,160	2	0	0	0	2	18	6	12	0	0
Floresville	7,818	14	0	3	1	10	246	49	194	3	0
Flower Mound	72,157	43	0	4	6	33	572	106	420	46	1
Floydada	3,003	19	1	1	2	15	81	32	46	3	1
Forest Hill	14,082	93	0	6	26	61	550	183	341	26	0
Forney	17,264	25	0	6	9	10	416	106	288	22	0
Fort Stockton	7,625	61	0	13	0	48	317	70	234	13	0
Fort Worth	746,433	4,293	63	318	1,330	2,582	35,090	9,352	23,274	2,464	138
Frankston	1,251	0	0	0	0	0	53	16	37	0	0
Fredericksburg	11,512	1	0	0	0	1	241	33	202	6	0
Freeport	12,570	35	0	5	4	26	388	102	266	20	2
Freer	2,902	7	0	0	0	7	109	27	77	5	0
Friendswood	34,530	25	0	4	10	11	390	87	286	17	2
Friona	3,499	19	0	0	1	18	40	16	20	4	1
Frisco	113,686	129	0	13	23	93	2,647	429	2,095	123	12
Gainesville	16,558	54	0	2	12	40	738	192	511	35	1
Galena Park	10,086	19	0	3	8	8	281	58	195	28	0
Galveston	55,835	373	1	77	128	167	3,181	787	2,144	250	291
Ganado	1,834	2	0	0	0	2	3	0	3	0	0
Garland	221,921	492	7	39	209	237	8,626	2,159	5,764	703	48
Gatesville	15,028	22	2	5	3	12	221	52	154	15	4
Georgetown	53,756	55	0	14	4	37	860	142	680	38	6
Giddings	5,373	40	0	4	5	31	171	40	127	4	1
Gilmer	5,148	18	2	1	0	15	197	29	156	12	0
Gladewater	6,316	22	0	2	3	17	291	62	210	19	2
Glenn Heights	11,808	49	0	3	6	40	256	115	122	19	3
Godley	1,040	3	0	1	0	2	16	2	14	0	0
Gonzales	7,471	83	0	6	7	70	276	66	207	3	0
Gorman	1,228	4	0	0	0	4	3	2	0	1	0
Graham	8,531	22	0	11	1	10	277	50	216	11	0
Granbury	9,153	12	0	1	0	11	464	58	399	7	1
Grand Prairie	166,866	599	4	66	193	336	7,483	1,967	4,596	920	30
Grand Saline	3,177	8	0	0	0	8	74	22	48	4	0
Granger	1,382	3	0	0	0	3	31	17	14	0	0
Granite Shoals	2,904	19	0	1	2	16	50	23	24	3	1
Grapeland	1,368	8	0	0	1	7	28	17	10	1	0
Grapevine	51,869	75	2	10	16	47	1,642	217	1,276	149	0
Greenville	25,629	210	0	19	41	150	1,283	277	939	67	1
Gregory	2,157	13	0	0	2	11	19	6	13	0	1
Groesbeck	4,295	15	0	3	2	10	75	32	40	3	0
Groves	14,122	52	0	2	12	38	503	148	333	22	0
Gruver	1,148	0	0	0	0	0	12	3	7	2	1
Gun Barrel City	6,073	30	0	1	1	28	298	67	227	4	0
Hale Center	2,140	0	0	0	0	0	32	13	16	3	0
Hallettsville	2,441	7	0	2	0	5	75	10	64	1	0
Hallsville	3,202	0	0	0	0	0	27	4	19	4	0
Haltom City	40,855	170	5	8	49	108	1,841	481	1,205	155	10
Hamlin	1,822	27	0	1	2	24	55	19	34	2	2
Harker Heights	26,971	45	1	9	8	27	880	248	607	25	3
Harlingen	65,765	399	3	34	87	275	4,405	850	3,375	180	32
Haskell	2,438	4	0	0	0	4	39	23	16	0	0
Hawk Cove	621	1	0	0	0	1	8	2	5	1	2
Hawkins	1,533	4	0	0	0	4	49	9	35	5	2
Hawley	559	0	0	0	0	0	5	4	1	0	1
Hearne	4,522	29	0	0	3	26	139	54	81	4	2
Heath	8,527	9	0	3	0	6	81	17	61	3	0
Hedwig Village	2,348	6	0	0	5	1	214	19	186	9	0
Helotes	8,263	4	0	1	1	2	91	10	79	2	0
Hemphill	1,027	4	0	1	0	3	34	7	26	1	2
Hempstead	7,974	18	0	0	7	11	249	92	149	8	3
Henderson	11,652	85	0	4	15	66	500	77	394	29	8
Hereford	14,304	62	0	2	3	57	400	101	273	26	2
Hewitt	13,810	34	0	2	2	30	123	33	78	12	1
Hickory Creek	4,110	6	0	2	1	3	104	9	89	6	0
Hidalgo	12,786	16	0	3	6	7	142	48	66	28	2
Highland Park	9,357	5	0	1	0	4	217	33	174	10	0

[1] The FBI does not publish arson data unless it receives data from either the agency or the state for all 12 months of the calendar year.

Table 8.   Offenses Known to Law Enforcement, by State and City, 2010—*Continued*

(Number)

State/city	Population	Violent crime	Murder and non-negligent man-slaughter	Forcible rape	Robbery	Aggravated assault	Property crime	Burglary	Larceny-theft	Motor vehicle theft	Arson[1]
TEXAS—*Continued*											
Highland Village	17,496	3	0	0	0	3	94	16	75	3	0
Hill Country Village	1,140	0	0	0	0	0	32	4	27	1	0
Hillsboro	8,968	23	0	2	7	14	262	52	203	7	0
Hitchcock	7,204	26	1	4	10	11	229	66	137	26	2
Holliday	1,768	0	0	0	0	0	15	7	8	0	0
Hollywood Park	3,335	3	0	1	2	0	114	9	102	3	0
Hondo	9,113	37	0	7	3	27	285	58	220	7	2
Hooks	3,012	3	0	0	2	1	23	9	14	0	0
Horizon City	15,025	18	0	0	1	17	200	91	86	23	0
Horseshoe Bay	2,492	12	0	2	0	10	67	16	48	3	0
Houston	2,280,859	22,491	269	712	9,449	12,061	115,323	27,924	74,582	12,817	865
Howe	2,731	4	0	0	1	3	29	6	19	4	0
Hubbard	1,759	3	0	0	1	2	10	1	8	1	0
Hudson	4,422	11	1	2	0	8	108	49	54	5	0
Hudson Oaks	2,230	2	0	0	2	0	88	15	70	3	0
Humble	14,843	153	0	26	74	53	2,027	184	1,691	152	2
Huntington	2,128	3	0	0	0	3	50	17	33	0	1
Huntsville	38,275	159	2	13	47	97	1,174	283	845	46	0
Hurst	39,147	167	0	10	44	113	2,125	276	1,770	79	0
Hutchins	3,192	14	0	0	2	12	206	28	150	28	0
Hutto	17,962	28	0	2	0	26	132	36	92	4	1
Idalou	2,128	3	0	0	0	3	24	5	17	2	0
Ingleside	8,927	18	0	5	6	7	230	81	136	13	1
Ingram	1,921	11	1	3	3	4	76	19	54	3	0
Iowa Park	6,295	3	0	0	0	3	61	16	41	4	0
Irving	206,308	529	6	36	170	317	7,744	1,632	5,488	624	28
Italy	2,177	8	0	0	0	8	45	10	33	2	0
Itasca	1,715	1	0	0	0	1	33	10	23	0	1
Jacinto City	9,797	25	0	0	10	15	389	70	285	34	4
Jacksboro	4,309	11	0	0	2	9	66	36	28	2	0
Jacksonville	14,447	95	0	11	25	59	858	302	520	36	5
Jamaica Beach	1,086	0	0	0	0	0	9	3	6	0	0
Jarrell	1,486	4	0	0	1	3	11	1	10	0	0
Jasper	7,269	26	0	1	1	24	339	55	276	8	0
Jefferson	1,849	6	0	0	0	6	55	11	42	2	0
Jersey Village	7,268	33	0	1	7	25	288	59	202	27	0
Johnson City	1,712	1	0	1	0	0	16	2	13	1	0
Jones Creek	2,128	2	0	0	0	2	5	1	3	1	0
Jonestown	2,654	10	0	1	2	7	50	17	30	3	0
Joshua	6,118	2	0	0	1	1	47	17	26	4	0
Jourdanton	4,445	8	0	0	1	7	38	13	23	2	1
Junction	2,606	16	0	2	0	14	98	13	84	1	0
Karnes City	3,294	9	0	0	1	8	68	14	54	0	3
Katy	14,070	36	0	1	23	12	605	72	512	21	1
Kaufman	9,186	19	0	0	4	15	163	45	112	6	0
Keene	6,516	2	0	0	1	1	94	26	64	4	0
Keller	41,396	18	0	5	0	13	506	94	406	6	1
Kemah	2,527	11	0	3	5	3	140	7	127	6	0
Kemp	1,380	5	0	1	0	4	28	4	21	3	0
Kenedy	3,262	11	0	0	0	11	192	78	114	0	0
Kennedale	7,403	25	0	0	7	18	230	76	146	8	0
Kerens	1,827	10	0	1	2	7	24	11	11	2	0
Kermit	5,251	7	0	1	0	6	46	13	33	0	0
Kerrville	22,998	44	0	0	8	36	629	67	541	21	7
Kilgore	12,229	51	0	9	7	35	688	78	574	36	1
Killeen	122,557	993	11	91	259	632	5,837	2,062	3,536	239	36
Kingsville	24,421	266	1	19	15	231	1,232	403	791	38	4
Kirby	8,669	18	0	1	3	14	169	52	100	17	0
Kirbyville	1,922	4	0	0	0	4	24	7	15	2	1
Kountze	2,227	5	0	1	2	2	42	15	21	6	0
Kress	735	0	0	0	0	0	4	3	1	0	0
Kyle	33,362	51	1	6	2	42	426	94	315	17	4
Lacy-Lakeview	5,947	42	1	8	6	27	244	73	145	26	0
La Feria	7,139	2	0	1	1	0	324	75	247	2	1
Lago Vista	6,637	9	0	1	2	6	101	20	80	1	0
La Grange	4,751	6	0	0	5	1	57	11	44	2	0
La Grulla	1,868	2	0	0	0	2	14	5	8	1	0
Laguna Vista	4,275	6	0	1	0	5	69	15	51	3	1
La Joya	4,977	1	0	0	1	0	38	14	22	2	0
Lake Dallas	8,333	13	0	4	1	8	190	35	136	19	1
Lake Jackson	29,037	49	2	7	13	27	685	120	547	18	3
Lakeside	1,377	1	0	1	0	0	25	8	16	1	0
Lakeview, Harris County	6,433	8	0	0	2	6	87	20	65	2	2

[1] The FBI does not publish arson data unless it receives data from either the agency or the state for all 12 months of the calendar year.

Table 8. Offenses Known to Law Enforcement, by State and City, 2010—*Continued*

(Number)

State/city	Population	Violent crime	Murder and non-negligent man-slaughter	Forcible rape	Robbery	Aggravated assault	Property crime	Burglary	Larceny-theft	Motor vehicle theft	Arson[1]
TEXAS—*Continued*											
Lakeway	11,829	20	0	3	2	15	196	38	150	8	0
Lake Worth	4,901	18	0	0	7	11	619	148	459	12	0
La Marque	14,199	138	2	15	35	86	704	202	475	27	3
Lamesa	8,684	27	1	1	2	23	214	59	146	9	3
Lampasas	7,897	20	0	9	0	11	190	33	152	5	0
La Porte	34,304	47	0	6	14	27	706	165	487	54	7
Laredo	230,674	1,142	9	78	209	846	11,464	1,821	8,740	903	72
La Vernia	1,259	3	0	0	0	3	42	7	34	1	0
La Villa	1,450	12	0	0	0	12	63	12	48	3	0
Lavon	437	5	0	0	0	5	35	9	26	0	0
League City	74,776	69	1	18	21	29	2,021	340	1,604	77	0
Leander	29,325	29	0	4	2	23	291	35	249	7	0
Leon Valley	11,181	38	0	3	19	16	857	129	667	61	0
Levelland	12,389	92	0	13	3	76	486	148	324	14	3
Lewisville	107,968	238	3	24	80	131	3,513	659	2,472	382	2
Lexington	1,225	3	0	0	0	3	4	0	4	0	0
Liberty	8,307	19	0	0	6	13	516	78	408	30	0
Lindale	5,028	12	0	1	4	7	182	28	146	8	0
Linden	2,076	7	0	0	1	6	39	16	21	2	0
Little Elm	30,854	11	0	0	2	9	309	46	254	9	0
Littlefield	5,654	35	0	1	1	33	258	95	151	12	2
Live Oak	15,079	21	0	6	7	8	590	67	501	22	0
Livingston	6,199	29	0	5	8	16	292	40	245	7	3
Llano	3,151	3	0	1	0	2	79	32	46	1	1
Lockhart	14,468	77	0	4	5	68	377	68	291	18	4
Lockney	1,634	1	0	0	0	1	51	23	24	4	1
Lone Star	1,537	6	0	0	1	5	79	42	37	0	0
Longview	78,319	581	10	41	134	396	4,290	857	3,073	360	30
Lorena	1,704	3	0	1	0	2	42	6	34	2	1
Lorenzo	1,149	1	0	0	0	1	9	8	1	0	2
Los Fresnos	5,704	17	0	0	0	17	119	49	66	4	3
Lott	660	2	0	0	1	1	13	8	5	0	0
Lubbock	227,867	2,001	10	91	328	1,572	12,391	3,083	8,802	506	54
Lufkin	34,611	183	3	12	52	116	2,272	577	1,622	73	5
Luling	5,526	34	0	3	7	24	225	64	149	12	3
Lumberton	10,832	11	0	1	2	8	225	47	173	5	0
Lyford	2,509	2	0	0	1	1	49	27	21	1	1
Lytle	2,941	8	0	0	4	4	89	14	73	2	0
Madisonville	4,343	21	0	3	7	11	193	33	150	10	1
Magnolia	1,298	4	0	0	0	4	54	9	42	3	0
Malakoff	2,328	10	0	0	1	9	79	14	52	13	0
Manor	4,107	21	0	0	3	18	170	46	116	8	0
Mansfield	49,677	79	0	13	19	47	991	214	711	66	5
Manvel	6,874	7	0	0	1	6	93	27	57	9	3
Marble Falls	7,765	7	0	3	0	4	314	37	262	15	1
Marlin	5,650	17	0	2	2	13	127	66	58	3	3
Marshall	24,038	150	2	10	28	110	1,102	308	729	65	8
Mart	2,507	8	0	1	0	7	35	10	25	0	1
Martindale	1,201	3	0	0	0	3	12	4	8	0	0
Mathis	5,216	22	0	1	7	14	186	59	121	6	3
McAllen	134,623	299	5	14	115	165	7,398	711	6,283	404	9
McGregor	4,912	19	0	2	1	16	93	39	54	0	0
McKinney	138,306	222	1	31	40	150	3,103	643	2,322	138	22
Meadows Place	6,529	7	0	0	4	3	144	31	107	6	1
Melissa	5,122	4	0	0	0	4	70	25	41	4	0
Memorial Villages	12,016	3	0	0	2	1	112	25	82	5	0
Memphis	2,115	12	0	1	0	11	53	27	22	4	0
Mercedes	15,488	88	0	5	7	76	808	191	567	50	6
Meridian	1,429	1	0	0	0	1	13	6	6	1	0
Merkel	2,619	4	0	0	0	4	48	10	36	2	0
Mesquite	133,964	482	7	8	165	302	6,516	1,457	4,345	714	20
Mexia	6,509	37	2	1	4	30	378	86	281	11	0
Midland[5]	109,791	407	2	44	65	296	3,599	893	2,558	148	13
Midlothian	19,220	35	0	3	3	29	363	53	296	14	0
Miles	746	4	0	0	0	4	31	8	22	1	0
Milford	767	6	0	1	0	5	7	2	5	0	0
Mineola	5,274	6	0	0	1	5	140	27	110	3	1
Mineral Wells	16,799	94	2	23	11	58	762	160	558	44	4
Mission	71,556	92	2	7	37	46	3,243	482	2,454	307	6
Missouri City	77,181	186	5	13	41	127	1,186	297	820	69	3
Monahans	6,442	52	0	1	2	49	171	64	99	8	0
Mont Belvieu	2,968	14	0	4	6	4	143	30	94	19	2
Montgomery	613	4	0	0	0	4	21	12	8	1	0

[1] The FBI does not publish arson data unless it receives data from either the agency or the state for all 12 months of the calendar year.

[5] Because of changes in the state/local agency's reporting practices, figures are not comparable to previous years' data.

Table 8.   Offenses Known to Law Enforcement, by State and City, 2010—*Continued*

(Number)

State/city	Population	Violent crime	Murder and non-negligent man-slaughter	Forcible rape	Robbery	Aggravated assault	Property crime	Burglary	Larceny-theft	Motor vehicle theft	Arson[1]
TEXAS—*Continued*											
Morgans Point Resort	4,536	1	0	0	0	1	44	10	31	3	0
Mount Pleasant	15,309	50	0	0	8	42	674	204	452	18	2
Muleshoe	4,208	17	2	4	0	11	127	58	63	6	2
Munday	1,154	1	0	1	0	0	17	4	13	0	1
Murphy	17,848	8	0	2	0	6	138	23	110	5	0
Mustang Ridge	973	1	0	0	0	1	2	2	0	0	0
Nacogdoches	33,402	329	2	9	44	274	1,406	330	1,035	41	2
Naples	1,365	12	0	1	1	10	59	39	19	1	1
Nash	2,474	3	0	0	2	1	66	27	38	1	0
Nassau Bay	3,988	7	1	2	2	2	108	21	81	6	0
Navasota	7,662	69	0	2	3	64	221	44	170	7	2
Nederland	15,875	63	0	15	14	34	513	124	361	28	0
Needville	3,554	4	0	1	0	3	37	8	25	4	1
New Boston	4,765	15	0	0	2	13	208	54	143	11	1
New Braunfels	57,796	121	0	10	25	86	1,966	373	1,530	63	6
New Deal	794	2	0	1	0	1	4	1	3	0	0
Nixon	2,277	2	0	0	0	2	5	1	3	1	0
Nocona	3,197	3	0	0	0	3	26	10	14	2	0
Nolanville	3,062	7	0	0	3	4	65	24	41	0	0
Northlake	2,328	6	0	0	0	6	48	1	40	7	0
North Richland Hills	66,897	226	0	31	40	155	2,111	411	1,611	89	0
Oak Ridge	268	0	0	0	0	0	2	0	1	1	0
Oak Ridge North	3,517	3	0	1	2	0	89	11	73	5	0
Odessa	101,580	726	3	36	96	591	3,523	824	2,508	191	16
O'Donnell	882	0	0	0	0	0	0	0	0	0	1
Olmos Park	2,338	1	0	0	1	0	72	9	62	1	0
Olney	3,234	3	0	0	0	3	84	33	47	4	1
Olton	2,066	5	0	0	0	5	21	7	12	2	1
Onalaska	1,462	0	0	0	0	0	0	0	0	0	0
Orange	19,452	146	1	3	49	93	1,017	417	551	49	15
Orange Grove	1,402	1	0	0	0	1	19	12	7	0	1
Overton	2,379	9	0	2	0	7	48	20	26	2	0
Ovilla	4,047	4	0	1	0	3	30	10	20	0	0
Oyster Creek	1,273	14	0	0	1	13	57	24	30	3	0
Paducah	1,188	0	0	0	0	0	21	19	2	0	0
Palacios	5,005	7	0	0	0	7	147	42	99	6	2
Palestine	18,485	72	1	19	14	38	729	190	517	22	5
Palmer	2,135	1	0	0	1	0	33	13	19	1	0
Palmhurst	2,732	8	0	0	4	4	315	37	267	11	1
Palm Valley	1,252	3	0	0	0	3	38	12	23	3	0
Palmview	5,658	3	0	0	3	0	328	24	284	20	0
Pampa	17,108	111	0	0	10	101	805	161	597	47	0
Panhandle	2,402	5	0	0	0	5	28	5	20	3	0
Pantego	2,416	15	0	1	3	11	129	25	97	7	0
Paris	25,671	146	1	6	27	112	1,607	390	1,171	46	0
Parker	3,197	0	0	0	0	0	17	7	8	2	0
Pasadena	145,713	611	7	68	149	387	5,551	1,113	4,066	372	15
Pearland	91,679	128	3	16	29	80	1,734	327	1,324	83	2
Pearsall	7,588	23	1	0	0	22	188	65	119	4	0
Pecos	7,611	24	0	3	1	20	222	54	164	4	0
Pelican Bay	1,695	2	0	0	1	1	23	6	15	2	0
Penitas	1,192	4	0	1	0	3	61	16	38	7	0
Perryton	8,494	18	0	2	0	16	122	38	78	6	3
Pflugerville	45,108	68	1	7	12	48	898	143	706	49	4
Pharr	68,274	251	6	13	55	177	3,692	698	2,697	297	14
Pilot Point	4,550	4	0	1	0	3	21	9	9	3	0
Pinehurst	2,082	4	0	0	2	2	107	39	63	5	0
Pittsburg	4,716	16	0	3	0	13	154	36	114	4	0
Plainview	21,231	72	1	9	12	50	926	193	705	28	4
Plano	278,244	503	4	53	152	294	6,716	1,237	5,093	386	10
Pleasanton	9,904	37	0	9	2	26	414	84	305	25	1
Point Comfort	702	0	0	0	0	0	6	3	3	0	0
Ponder	1,440	3	0	0	0	3	10	4	6	0	0
Port Aransas	3,947	23	1	0	3	19	366	66	286	14	0
Port Arthur	56,424	419	6	26	169	218	2,752	1,020	1,567	165	56
Port Isabel	5,333	24	0	2	4	18	387	100	276	11	1
Portland	16,559	18	0	2	4	12	480	62	407	11	1
Port Lavaca	11,405	119	0	13	4	102	351	72	266	13	3
Port Neches	12,385	34	1	3	3	27	345	102	227	16	1
Poteet	3,714	10	0	0	0	10	126	38	86	2	4
Poth	2,420	7	0	1	0	6	21	13	8	0	2
Pottsboro	2,181	7	0	0	2	5	39	10	24	5	0
Premont	2,768	6	1	2	0	3	50	29	19	2	0

[1] The FBI does not publish arson data unless it receives data from either the agency or the state for all 12 months of the calendar year.

Table 8. Offenses Known to Law Enforcement, by State and City, 2010—*Continued*

(Number)

State/city	Population	Violent crime	Murder and non-negligent man-slaughter	Forcible rape	Robbery	Aggravated assault	Property crime	Burglary	Larceny-theft	Motor vehicle theft	Arson[1]
TEXAS—*Continued*											
Presidio	4,736	0	0	0	0	0	16	11	4	1	0
Primera	4,339	6	0	1	0	5	27	15	12	0	0
Princeton	6,916	12	0	4	0	8	158	48	104	6	1
Progreso	5,702	25	0	4	2	19	134	31	89	14	1
Prosper	11,081	5	0	0	1	4	126	22	102	2	0
Queen City	1,529	18	0	7	1	10	51	15	32	4	0
Quinlan	1,429	8	0	0	5	3	111	19	81	11	0
Quitman	2,228	4	0	0	0	4	66	25	34	7	0
Ralls	1,906	2	0	0	0	2	23	12	9	2	0
Rancho Viejo	1,848	2	0	1	0	1	20	18	1	1	0
Ranger	2,556	9	0	0	2	7	64	31	32	1	0
Ransom Canyon	1,148	1	0	1	0	0	4	0	4	0	0
Raymondville	9,331	191	0	8	9	174	541	173	365	3	5
Red Oak	10,785	14	0	1	5	8	221	64	154	3	1
Refugio	2,627	5	0	0	0	5	36	18	17	1	0
Reno	3,108	5	0	1	1	3	75	19	54	2	1
Richardson	104,051	193	0	13	90	90	2,999	608	2,192	199	4
Richland Hills	8,196	8	0	1	2	5	336	78	220	38	0
Richmond	13,688	54	0	8	11	35	226	60	158	8	1
Richwood	3,644	0	0	0	0	0	46	11	34	1	0
Riesel	1,024	3	0	0	0	3	15	5	10	0	0
Rio Grande City	14,215	39	0	1	7	31	473	118	322	33	6
Rio Hondo	2,141	7	0	0	2	5	55	11	41	3	1
Rising Star	819	0	0	0	0	0	3	1	2	0	0
River Oaks	7,033	9	0	4	3	2	216	65	140	11	0
Roanoke	5,269	10	0	1	2	7	129	27	100	2	0
Robinson	10,796	8	0	0	2	6	200	28	162	10	1
Robstown	12,063	66	0	2	14	50	481	171	295	15	3
Rockdale	5,913	10	0	1	2	7	176	41	127	8	0
Rockport	10,012	14	0	2	1	11	373	93	269	11	0
Rockwall	39,232	25	0	7	3	15	971	139	758	74	0
Roma	11,470	25	1	4	3	17	199	39	140	20	2
Roman Forest	4,323	4	0	0	0	4	47	18	27	2	1
Ropesville	506	1	0	0	0	1	5	1	4	0	0
Roscoe	1,230	0	0	0	0	0	9	0	9	0	0
Rosebud	1,299	7	0	1	1	5	36	12	24	0	0
Rose City	487	1	0	0	1	0	8	3	5	0	0
Rosenberg	35,025	91	5	16	33	37	655	176	448	31	2
Round Rock	111,099	116	0	26	35	55	3,016	464	2,452	100	4
Rowlett	57,852	76	2	9	16	49	923	210	677	36	1
Royse City	10,734	30	0	9	2	19	146	20	119	7	1
Runaway Bay	1,485	2	0	1	0	1	3	1	2	0	0
Rusk	5,293	19	0	1	1	17	123	25	89	9	0
Sabinal	1,645	5	0	0	1	4	34	13	20	1	1
Sachse	20,548	12	0	5	1	6	233	62	166	5	0
Saginaw	21,770	45	0	5	5	35	575	86	450	39	1
Salado	2,042	0	0	0	0	0	30	7	21	2	0
San Angelo	92,234	276	1	48	50	177	4,169	1,035	2,976	158	16
San Antonio	1,392,198	8,434	79	467	2,360	5,528	88,353	17,301	65,395	5,657	327
San Augustine	2,306	6	0	0	0	6	18	3	14	1	0
San Benito	25,400	78	0	11	18	49	1,153	249	836	68	8
San Diego	4,357	38	1	0	0	37	108	41	65	2	2
San Felipe	995	1	0	1	0	0	9	6	2	1	0
Sanger	8,350	13	0	8	0	5	129	30	93	6	0
San Juan	35,326	223	3	31	31	158	1,680	309	1,257	114	1
San Marcos	55,100	152	1	13	34	104	1,726	263	1,390	73	1
San Saba	2,458	13	0	0	0	13	46	13	32	1	1
Sansom Park Village	4,242	11	1	0	3	7	112	43	63	6	1
Santa Anna	993	0	0	0	0	0	7	4	1	2	1
Santa Fe	11,915	21	0	4	3	14	255	97	144	14	1
Santa Rosa	3,155	11	0	1	2	8	82	15	66	1	0
Schertz	33,451	71	0	17	9	45	608	120	462	26	6
Schulenburg	2,743	16	0	4	0	12	141	32	106	3	1
Seabrook	11,663	20	0	4	5	11	230	37	181	12	0
Seagoville	12,436	13	0	0	5	8	539	158	327	54	0
Seagraves	2,375	3	0	1	0	2	11	3	6	2	0
Sealy	6,461	28	0	0	3	25	150	37	104	9	0
Seguin	27,087	110	2	17	37	54	1,219	235	956	28	4
Selma	6,049	10	0	3	1	6	257	24	227	6	0
Seminole	6,269	5	0	1	0	4	79	9	65	5	0
Seven Points	1,336	8	0	0	1	7	43	15	23	5	0
Seymour	2,533	21	0	0	0	21	31	8	23	0	0
Shallowater	2,384	1	0	0	0	1	20	4	16	0	0

[1] The FBI does not publish arson data unless it receives data from either the agency or the state for all 12 months of the calendar year.

Table 8.   Offenses Known to Law Enforcement, by State and City, 2010—*Continued*

(Number)

State/city	Population	Violent crime	Murder and non-negligent man-slaughter	Forcible rape	Robbery	Aggravated assault	Property crime	Burglary	Larceny-theft	Motor vehicle theft	Arson[1]
TEXAS—*Continued*											
Shamrock	1,805	2	0	0	2	0	22	7	12	3	0
Shavano Park	3,372	0	0	0	0	0	44	11	32	1	0
Shenandoah	2,160	7	0	2	2	3	260	4	250	6	0
Sherman	38,623	180	5	4	34	137	1,456	311	1,109	36	13
Silsbee	7,128	20	0	0	5	15	183	50	127	6	1
Sinton	5,250	26	0	0	0	26	184	53	128	3	0
Slaton	5,881	51	0	12	1	38	160	53	103	4	0
Smithville	4,603	8	0	0	1	7	129	23	99	7	0
Snyder	10,519	132	0	11	4	117	362	107	232	23	0
Socorro	32,790	91	0	6	16	69	604	143	400	61	8
Somerset	1,896	10	0	1	3	6	51	17	30	4	0
Somerville	1,671	4	0	0	2	2	26	8	17	1	0
Sonora	3,046	7	0	2	0	5	27	3	23	1	1
Sour Lake	1,777	3	0	0	0	3	55	6	45	4	0
South Houston	16,345	113	0	5	46	62	808	223	482	103	0
Southlake	27,811	16	0	1	3	12	541	139	390	12	2
South Padre Island	2,911	54	0	11	6	37	585	97	473	15	0
Southside Place	1,664	1	0	0	1	0	3	3	0	0	0
Spearman	3,002	3	0	0	0	3	22	4	18	0	0
Springtown	3,350	11	0	0	2	9	58	21	33	4	1
Spring Valley	3,982	5	0	0	3	2	122	15	103	4	0
Spur	910	2	0	0	0	2	3	1	1	1	1
Stafford	19,829	82	2	6	33	41	868	163	643	62	0
Stagecoach	520	0	0	0	0	0	7	3	2	2	0
Stamford	2,991	17	0	2	1	14	102	29	69	4	0
Stanton	2,192	5	0	1	1	3	42	17	21	4	0
Stephenville	17,646	44	0	8	4	32	512	89	419	4	3
Stratford	1,887	0	0	0	0	0	18	4	13	1	0
Sugar Land	83,368	142	0	7	60	75	1,879	235	1,556	88	1
Sullivan City	4,530	4	0	0	0	4	39	13	17	9	0
Sulphur Springs	15,798	43	0	1	7	35	289	70	203	16	2
Sunray	1,946	6	0	0	0	6	15	7	8	0	0
Sunrise Beach Village	740	0	0	0	0	0	13	6	6	1	0
Sunset Valley	938	1	0	0	1	0	141	4	135	2	0
Surfside Beach	912	2	0	0	0	2	29	9	14	6	1
Sweeny	3,651	4	0	1	1	2	106	29	75	2	0
Sweetwater	10,607	141	0	18	3	120	435	84	339	12	3
Taft	3,282	23	0	3	1	19	74	23	49	2	2
Tahoka	2,419	3	0	1	0	2	36	10	26	0	0
Tatum	1,220	3	0	0	0	3	17	11	6	0	0
Taylor	16,383	17	0	2	7	8	425	107	307	11	2
Teague	4,853	20	0	1	3	16	101	41	50	10	0
Temple	60,444	209	1	23	71	114	2,079	537	1,462	80	3
Terrell	20,241	121	0	16	25	80	783	266	466	51	4
Terrell Hills	5,298	3	0	1	1	1	96	24	72	0	0
Texarkana	37,220	527	3	26	98	400	2,350	647	1,592	111	21
Texas City	44,053	195	8	0	83	104	1,752	367	1,291	94	2
The Colony	46,873	53	2	11	9	31	617	165	418	34	7
Thorndale	1,308	3	0	0	0	3	9	4	5	0	0
Thrall	943	0	0	0	0	0	18	4	14	0	0
Three Rivers	1,568	5	0	0	0	5	24	9	15	0	0
Tioga	956	2	0	0	1	1	16	7	8	1	2
Tolar	706	0	0	0	0	0	2	0	2	0	0
Tomball	10,272	32	0	8	8	16	435	92	322	21	1
Tom Bean	1,038	7	0	1	0	6	10	4	6	0	0
Tool	2,434	3	0	1	0	2	67	20	46	1	0
Trenton	716	1	0	1	0	0	29	2	25	2	0
Trinity	2,641	15	0	1	0	14	117	22	88	7	0
Trophy Club	8,574	5	0	0	0	5	122	19	101	2	0
Troy	1,429	8	0	0	1	7	28	9	19	0	0
Tulia	4,362	22	0	6	1	15	116	34	80	2	0
Tye	1,165	2	0	2	0	0	26	6	18	2	0
Tyler	100,125	644	6	44	99	495	5,091	1,040	3,828	223	12
Universal City	18,511	70	0	3	18	49	475	121	320	34	3
University Park	25,389	12	0	0	8	4	430	68	344	18	0
Uvalde	16,318	39	1	0	7	31	575	215	360	0	0
Valley Mills	1,102	3	0	1	0	2	25	3	20	2	0
Valley View	831	0	0	0	0	0	3	2	0	1	0
Van	2,518	4	0	1	0	3	45	17	26	2	0
Van Alstyne	3,018	6	0	1	1	4	52	20	32	0	0
Vernon	10,686	61	0	6	5	50	361	78	270	13	2
Victoria	63,215	388	7	37	75	269	3,320	788	2,426	106	21
Vidor	10,611	42	0	0	6	36	570	112	431	27	0

[1] The FBI does not publish arson data unless it receives data from either the agency or the state for all 12 months of the calendar year.

Table 8. Offenses Known to Law Enforcement, by State and City, 2010—*Continued*

(Number)

State/city	Population	Violent crime	Murder and non-negligent man-slaughter	Forcible rape	Robbery	Aggravated assault	Property crime	Burglary	Larceny-theft	Motor vehicle theft	Arson[1]
TEXAS—*Continued*											
Waco	127,039	838	5	51	195	587	6,439	1,856	4,373	210	26
Waelder	1,025	10	0	1	1	8	14	8	6	0	0
Wake Village	5,672	1	0	0	1	0	81	39	34	8	1
Waller	2,205	8	0	1	1	6	90	24	60	6	1
Wallis	1,363	1	0	0	0	1	14	9	5	0	0
Watauga	24,494	60	0	1	7	52	550	132	388	30	0
Waxahachie	30,368	82	0	2	13	67	962	171	744	47	3
Weatherford	28,325	63	0	7	14	42	686	123	533	30	1
Webster	10,754	41	1	11	16	13	725	136	536	53	1
Weimar	2,001	4	0	1	1	2	23	10	11	2	0
Weslaco	35,244	196	1	20	40	135	2,725	505	1,998	222	6
West	2,710	1	0	1	0	0	42	13	28	1	0
West Columbia	4,185	20	0	1	2	17	77	15	55	7	2
West Lake Hills	3,224	3	0	0	2	1	89	18	70	1	0
West Orange	3,667	13	0	1	5	7	306	43	254	9	0
Westover Hills	739	0	0	0	0	0	13	5	8	0	0
West Tawakoni	1,621	5	0	0	0	5	61	30	26	5	0
West University Place	15,703	4	0	0	4	0	187	58	120	9	0
Westworth	3,167	4	0	0	3	1	118	38	77	3	0
Wharton	9,127	78	0	2	27	49	386	63	312	11	3
Whitehouse	8,183	9	0	1	2	6	103	32	70	1	1
White Oak	6,553	3	0	0	1	2	125	30	76	19	0
Whitesboro	4,061	4	0	3	0	1	63	14	48	1	0
White Settlement	16,670	41	0	0	10	31	694	153	508	33	1
Whitewright	1,705	5	0	0	0	5	55	10	40	5	0
Whitney	2,098	5	0	2	0	3	71	23	47	1	0
Wichita Falls	100,716	463	7	44	133	279	5,314	1,317	3,710	287	29
Willis	4,557	22	1	2	3	16	123	36	78	9	3
Willow Park	4,913	2	0	0	1	1	58	14	41	3	0
Wills Point	3,910	2	0	0	0	2	30	13	13	4	0
Wilmer	3,656	2	0	1	1	0	100	35	59	6	1
Windcrest	5,463	15	0	0	11	4	355	43	300	12	0
Winnsboro	3,907	16	0	1	0	15	42	17	25	0	0
Winters	2,498	3	0	1	0	2	32	15	16	1	0
Wolfe City	1,634	0	0	0	0	0	34	22	9	3	0
Wolfforth	3,701	1	0	1	0	0	49	18	27	4	0
Woodville	2,262	2	0	1	0	1	24	2	22	0	0
Woodway	8,824	16	0	4	1	11	167	18	144	5	0
Wortham	1,106	10	0	2	1	7	22	10	12	0	0
Wylie	43,508	35	1	11	5	18	703	141	527	35	1
Yoakum	5,398	4	0	0	1	3	149	69	78	2	0
Yorktown	2,145	2	0	0	0	2	40	15	23	2	0
UTAH											
American Fork/Cedar Hills	38,741	41	1	7	15	18	1,008	186	795	27	2
Big Water	400	0	0	0	0	0	1	0	1	0	0
Blanding	3,201	4	0	1	0	3	75	19	53	3	0
Bountiful	43,485	61	2	28	12	19	898	94	741	63	1
Brian Head	124	0	0	0	0	0	26	3	23	0	0
Brigham City	18,491	37	0	10	3	24	427	54	349	24	0
Cedar City	29,290	45	2	14	5	24	816	161	622	33	3
Centerville	15,862	8	0	2	1	5	374	54	311	9	0
Clearfield	27,788	41	0	12	14	15	846	125	685	36	1
Clinton	20,471	20	0	7	3	10	378	50	317	11	1
Cottonwood Heights	34,381	53	0	17	15	21	999	239	718	42	1
Draper	44,259	62	0	6	12	44	787	166	566	55	6
Enoch	5,275	1	0	0	0	1	44	15	29	0	0
Fairview	1,198	1	0	0	0	1	19	5	12	2	0
Farmington	17,977	5	0	1	1	3	171	27	137	7	0
Grantsville	9,358	8	0	2	1	5	160	32	114	14	1
Harrisville	6,356	9	0	0	5	4	361	29	316	16	0
Heber	10,101	2	0	0	0	2	115	26	82	7	0
Helper	1,840	1	0	0	0	1	64	20	41	3	1
Hildale	1,904	5	0	0	0	5	5	4	1	0	0
Hurricane[5]	13,587	17	0	3	0	14	295	78	205	12	3
Ivins	8,061	3	0	1	0	2	88	26	61	1	0
Kamas	1,535	1	0	0	1	0	34	6	27	1	0
Kaysville	26,200	14	0	10	0	4	567	193	357	17	0
La Verkin	4,342	18	0	1	0	17	62	15	43	4	0
Layton	65,610	103	3	24	12	64	2,317	398	1,859	60	2
Lehi	52,162	17	0	9	1	7	735	161	545	29	0
Lindon	11,047	5	0	3	0	2	265	45	210	10	1
Logan	48,819	22	0	5	2	15	616	111	486	19	0
Lone Peak	27,692	5	0	3	1	1	259	72	181	6	0

[1] The FBI does not publish arson data unless it receives data from either the agency or the state for all 12 months of the calendar year.

[5] Because of changes in the state/local agency's reporting practices, figures are not comparable to previous years' data.

Table 8. Offenses Known to Law Enforcement, by State and City, 2010—*Continued*

(Number)

State/city	Population	Violent crime	Murder and non-negligent man-slaughter	Forcible rape	Robbery	Aggravated assault	Property crime	Burglary	Larceny-theft	Motor vehicle theft	Arson[1]
UTAH—*Continued*											
Mapleton	8,495	2	0	2	0	0	96	6	90	0	0
Midvale	28,739	133	3	27	27	76	1,644	360	1,150	134	2
Moab	5,032	20	1	4	2	13	281	31	235	15	0
Monticello	1,975	0	0	0	0	0	24	5	19	0	0
Moroni	1,312	2	0	2	0	0	6	4	1	1	0
Murray	45,305	216	0	37	47	132	3,112	514	2,361	237	8
Naples	1,750	0	0	0	0	0	63	3	58	2	0
Nephi	5,438	2	0	1	0	1	165	60	98	7	0
North Ogden	17,721	14	0	5	1	8	273	51	215	7	2
North Park	12,554	19	0	9	0	10	230	21	200	9	1
North Salt Lake	14,475	22	0	1	4	17	460	63	350	47	1
Ogden	81,431	327	1	24	110	192	4,655	867	3,479	309	16
Orem	93,580	68	1	19	17	31	2,553	240	2,204	109	3
Park City	7,957	14	0	1	3	10	351	34	299	18	0
Payson	18,200	9	0	0	3	6	632	94	523	15	0
Perry	4,029	5	0	1	1	3	62	16	44	2	0
Pleasant Grove	35,589	24	0	9	6	9	521	75	419	27	2
Pleasant View	7,182	4	0	0	0	4	103	16	84	3	0
Price	7,979	23	0	5	1	17	376	80	292	4	2
Provo	117,734	194	2	46	27	119	2,739	370	2,266	103	17
Richfield	7,109	10	1	2	0	7	272	30	236	6	0
Riverdale	8,108	9	0	0	4	5	645	43	588	14	3
Roy	35,502	39	1	17	9	12	1,008	150	819	39	4
Salem	6,906	0	0	0	0	0	86	14	71	1	0
Salina	2,324	10	0	7	0	3	91	24	63	4	0
Salt Lake City	177,873	1,289	8	146	359	776	13,839	2,177	10,173	1,489	52
Sandy	95,173	160	1	20	34	105	2,839	551	2,146	142	7
Santaquin/Genola	9,895	4	0	0	0	4	149	31	111	7	0
Saratoga Springs	20,490	10	1	4	0	5	221	32	183	6	0
Smithfield	9,750	5	0	2	0	3	59	15	43	1	0
South Jordan	56,502	27	0	6	7	14	1,050	212	802	36	1
South Ogden	15,831	28	0	8	5	15	450	105	326	19	3
South Salt Lake	21,107	211	5	32	62	112	1,662	239	1,176	247	4
Spanish Fork	33,162	11	0	7	2	2	626	119	492	15	5
Springdale	621	2	0	0	0	2	26	3	21	2	0
Springville	29,784	39	0	10	6	23	888	131	736	21	1
St. George	73,086	68	0	12	10	46	1,616	315	1,224	77	5
Stockton	583	0	0	0	0	0	9	2	6	1	0
Sunset	4,844	3	0	1	1	1	135	11	118	6	0
Syracuse	23,780	15	0	4	0	11	347	62	278	7	0
Taylorsville City	57,376	222	2	24	66	130	2,518	355	1,938	225	10
Tooele	30,663	77	0	8	13	56	1,267	182	1,016	69	13
Tremonton	6,943	9	0	2	0	7	172	38	129	5	0
Vernal	9,121	27	1	4	2	20	403	66	326	11	2
Washington	18,755	23	0	3	4	16	384	72	301	11	0
Wellington	1,548	4	0	0	1	3	31	7	24	0	0
West Bountiful	5,354	7	0	3	1	3	198	11	173	14	0
West Jordan	104,783	257	1	37	54	165	3,103	469	2,410	224	14
West Valley	123,089	599	6	70	131	392	5,769	1,029	4,127	613	13
Woods Cross	8,899	8	0	4	1	3	238	38	181	19	1
VERMONT											
Barre	8,781	32	0	10	1	21	326	40	282	4	1
Barre Town	8,039	2	0	0	0	2	152	29	118	5	0
Bellows Falls	2,905	1	0	0	1	0	18	7	11	0	0
Bennington	15,086	47	0	5	2	40	400	67	309	24	5
Berlin	2,833	4	0	1	0	3	65	2	63	0	0
Bradford	832	0	0	0	0	0	29	4	24	1	0
Brandon	3,873	1	0	0	0	1	83	19	61	3	1
Brattleboro	11,573	48	0	1	16	31	477	83	374	20	0
Bristol	3,783	4	0	0	0	4	47	5	42	0	0
Castleton	4,649	4	0	0	0	4	39	29	9	1	0
Chester	3,005	3	0	0	1	2	37	16	21	0	0
Colchester	17,434	29	0	5	3	21	580	93	476	11	4
Dover	1,444	0	0	0	0	0	152	19	127	6	0
Essex	19,810	12	0	5	1	6	414	47	353	14	0
Fair Haven	2,921	1	0	0	0	1	100	33	65	2	0
Hardwick	3,195	11	0	0	0	11	87	31	53	3	0
Hartford	10,753	11	0	4	0	7	144	28	112	4	0
Hinesburg	4,660	0	0	0	0	0	49	12	37	0	0
Manchester	4,293	3	0	0	1	2	126	23	100	3	1
Middlebury	8,340	14	0	4	0	10	300	31	267	2	1
Milton	10,984	5	0	0	2	3	221	59	153	9	0
Montpelier	7,708	14	0	2	1	11	339	54	279	6	2

[1] The FBI does not publish arson data unless it receives data from either the agency or the state for all 12 months of the calendar year.

Table 8.   Offenses Known to Law Enforcement, by State and City, 2010—*Continued*

(Number)

State/city	Population	Violent crime	Murder and non-negligent man-slaughter	Forcible rape	Robbery	Aggravated assault	Property crime	Burglary	Larceny-theft	Motor vehicle theft	Arson[1]
VERMONT—*Continued*											
Morristown	5,892	4	0	0	0	4	72	12	59	1	0
Newport	5,159	10	0	4	1	5	102	34	68	0	0
Northfield	5,751	8	0	2	1	5	108	25	81	2	0
Randolph	5,080	1	0	0	0	1	33	9	22	2	0
Richmond	4,169	4	0	1	0	3	9	5	2	2	0
Shelburne	7,149	5	0	0	1	4	99	22	77	0	0
South Burlington	17,915	13	0	4	3	6	827	67	746	14	0
Springfield	8,577	34	0	4	2	28	189	40	142	7	2
St. Albans	7,235	22	0	4	4	14	280	46	230	4	2
St. Johnsbury	7,367	11	0	2	0	9	106	27	75	4	0
Stowe	5,238	4	0	1	1	2	143	34	109	0	0
Swanton	6,493	6	0	0	1	5	63	8	53	2	0
Thetford	2,812	0	0	0	0	0	14	1	13	0	0
Vergennes	2,675	3	0	1	1	1	45	5	39	1	2
Waterbury	5,416	3	0	0	0	3	31	3	28	0	0
Weathersfield	2,875	0	0	0	0	0	30	8	22	0	0
Williston	8,521	3	0	0	0	3	221	24	190	7	1
Wilmington	2,368	1	0	0	0	1	33	18	15	0	0
Windsor	3,596	3	0	0	0	3	45	8	36	1	0
Winooski	6,259	19	0	4	3	12	350	49	297	4	2
Woodstock	3,134	1	0	0	0	1	27	6	21	0	0
VIRGINIA											
Abingdon	8,059	15	1	1	5	8	286	28	250	8	0
Alexandria	152,801	276	2	21	125	128	3,242	317	2,639	286	7
Altavista	3,340	11	0	0	4	7	154	13	138	3	0
Amherst	2,207	1	0	0	0	1	14	0	14	0	0
Appalachia	1,719	3	0	2	0	1	69	6	62	1	1
Ashland	7,188	26	0	3	4	19	198	22	165	11	4
Bedford	6,377	15	0	0	4	11	219	22	194	3	1
Berryville	3,215	5	0	1	0	4	43	6	36	1	0
Big Stone Gap	5,653	12	0	3	1	8	159	19	137	3	0
Blacksburg	43,355	38	0	14	9	15	687	117	547	23	5
Blackstone	3,564	10	1	1	2	6	106	15	80	11	2
Bluefield	5,164	12	2	2	1	7	203	24	174	5	0
Bowling Green	1,036	0	0	0	0	0	0	0	0	0	0
Boykins	590	0	0	0	0	0	8	0	8	0	0
Bridgewater	5,464	0	0	0	0	0	36	6	29	1	0
Bristol	17,794	60	1	11	10	38	601	90	490	21	5
Broadway	3,343	1	0	0	0	1	6	1	2	3	0
Brookneal	1,242	2	0	0	1	1	21	3	18	0	0
Burkeville	472	0	0	0	0	0	11	0	11	0	0
Cape Charles	1,517	2	0	0	0	2	14	7	6	1	1
Cedar Bluff	1,046	0	0	0	0	0	19	3	15	1	0
Charlottesville	42,590	195	3	29	51	112	1,693	163	1,443	87	5
Chase City	2,287	7	0	2	0	5	84	14	69	1	0
Chatham	2,381	0	0	0	0	0	12	0	12	0	0
Chesapeake	225,627	866	9	26	276	555	7,494	1,180	5,922	392	23
Chilhowie	1,732	1	0	0	1	0	32	2	29	1	0
Chincoteague	4,331	6	0	1	0	5	77	10	62	5	1
Christiansburg	19,997	38	1	9	9	19	677	76	581	20	9
Clarksville	1,238	3	0	0	1	2	29	2	26	1	0
Clifton Forge	3,907	7	0	2	1	4	94	18	71	5	0
Clintwood	1,493	1	0	0	1	0	34	6	28	0	0
Colonial Beach	3,880	8	0	0	1	7	54	8	43	3	0
Colonial Heights	17,983	44	0	1	20	23	793	71	695	27	7
Covington	6,157	11	1	0	2	8	201	28	163	10	1
Crewe	2,268	6	0	0	2	4	58	9	48	1	0
Culpeper	14,633	68	0	4	21	43	386	22	347	17	3
Damascus	1,079	4	0	2	0	2	16	1	15	0	0
Danville	44,192	168	8	20	60	80	2,182	540	1,577	65	13
Dayton	1,366	2	0	0	0	2	6	1	4	1	0
Dublin	2,141	2	0	0	0	2	58	6	52	0	0
Dumfries	4,974	10	0	0	2	4	4	80	9	68	3	1
Edinburg	910	0	0	0	0	0	23	2	20	1	0
Elkton	2,650	0	0	0	0	0	41	11	26	4	0
Emporia	5,653	31	1	2	8	20	332	65	254	13	2
Exmore	1,350	2	0	0	1	1	34	8	25	1	0
Fairfax City	25,082	35	0	6	12	17	559	27	497	35	2
Falls Church	12,171	13	0	1	6	6	305	19	263	23	0
Farmville	7,778	22	0	2	9	11	208	45	159	4	1
Franklin	8,902	37	1	7	11	18	527	131	383	13	6
Fredericksburg	23,704	102	0	11	20	71	1,080	116	933	31	1
Fries	537	0	0	0	0	0	0	0	0	0	0

[1] The FBI does not publish arson data unless it receives data from either the agency or the state for all 12 months of the calendar year.

Table 8.   Offenses Known to Law Enforcement, by State and City, 2010—*Continued*

(Number)

State/city	Population	Violent crime	Murder and non-negligent man-slaughter	Forcible rape	Robbery	Aggravated assault	Property crime	Burglary	Larceny-theft	Motor vehicle theft	Arson[1]
VIRGINIA—*Continued*											
Front Royal	14,725	31	0	6	9	16	509	39	450	20	5
Galax	6,908	25	0	3	2	20	296	41	244	11	0
Gate City	2,009	7	0	2	1	4	37	10	25	2	0
Glasgow	991	0	0	0	0	0	7	1	6	0	0
Glen Lyn	165	0	0	0	0	0	2	1	1	0	0
Gordonsville	1,745	0	0	0	0	0	20	1	19	0	0
Gretna	1,203	1	0	1	0	0	17	5	11	1	1
Grottoes	2,212	3	0	0	1	2	66	47	18	1	0
Halifax	1,238	0	0	0	0	0	21	4	16	1	1
Hampton	144,545	395	14	29	175	177	5,334	759	4,230	345	24
Harrisonburg	45,804	91	1	11	13	66	1,072	135	901	36	11
Haymarket	1,298	1	0	0	1	0	12	0	12	0	0
Haysi	301	0	0	0	0	0	4	2	2	0	0
Herndon	22,751	49	0	3	10	36	413	39	361	13	0
Hillsville	2,610	5	0	0	1	4	68	7	57	4	0
Honaker	1,470	1	0	0	0	1	19	6	13	0	1
Hopewell	23,292	206	2	9	55	140	1,037	272	661	104	7
Hurt	1,206	1	0	1	0	0	21	4	12	5	0
Independence	876	1	0	0	0	1	6	0	6	0	0
Jonesville	961	2	0	0	0	2	7	1	6	0	0
Kenbridge	1,253	7	0	1	2	4	11	3	7	1	0
Kilmarnock	1,266	0	0	0	0	0	25	4	20	1	0
La Crosse	583	1	0	0	0	1	14	2	10	2	1
Lawrenceville	1,343	5	0	2	2	1	59	27	30	2	2
Lebanon	3,219	2	0	0	0	2	147	17	130	0	0
Leesburg	42,561	57	0	13	10	34	753	42	679	32	3
Lexington	6,934	3	0	0	1	2	44	7	35	2	0
Louisa	1,591	4	0	0	2	2	53	4	49	0	0
Luray	4,812	7	0	2	0	5	153	33	119	1	1
Lynchburg	75,137	323	4	26	75	218	2,594	433	2,067	94	16
Manassas	36,822	134	1	14	53	66	1,005	123	806	76	6
Manassas Park	12,275	18	0	7	6	5	202	14	175	13	0
Marion	5,907	35	0	6	5	24	241	33	202	6	0
Martinsville	14,618	39	3	6	13	17	448	71	364	13	4
Middleburg	1,017	0	0	0	0	0	13	2	10	1	0
Middletown	1,169	3	0	1	1	1	19	3	15	1	0
Mount Jackson	2,036	2	0	1	0	1	42	3	38	1	0
Narrows	2,160	0	0	0	0	0	28	12	16	0	0
New Market	1,878	2	0	0	0	2	22	4	17	1	0
Newport News	195,225	953	20	83	366	484	6,558	1,247	4,877	434	93
Norfolk	234,100	1,445	34	90	596	725	13,159	2,158	10,079	922	50
Norton	3,710	5	0	0	0	5	240	9	226	5	3
Occoquan	846	0	0	0	0	0	0	0	0	0	0
Onancock	1,378	0	0	0	0	0	23	8	14	1	1
Onley	472	1	0	0	1	0	10	1	9	0	0
Orange	4,749	8	0	2	1	5	141	11	126	4	1
Parksley	788	1	0	0	1	0	13	6	7	0	0
Pearisburg	2,773	2	0	0	0	2	58	4	54	0	0
Pembroke	1,176	0	0	0	0	0	17	4	13	0	0
Petersburg	33,048	189	12	6	63	108	1,500	434	930	136	6
Pocahontas	418	1	0	0	0	1	1	1	0	0	0
Poquoson	11,859	7	0	0	0	7	135	20	106	9	1
Portsmouth	99,576	609	14	17	265	313	5,474	1,318	3,885	271	24
Pound	1,076	1	0	0	0	1	35	10	25	0	0
Pulaski	8,918	21	0	3	7	11	320	59	253	8	7
Purcellville	5,533	2	0	0	0	2	62	5	55	2	1
Radford	16,277	64	1	6	6	51	458	103	340	15	5
Remington	694	0	0	0	0	0	2	0	2	0	0
Rich Creek	684	0	0	0	0	0	9	1	7	1	0
Richlands	5,647	10	0	1	2	7	251	32	213	6	2
Richmond	205,883	1,506	41	40	735	690	8,567	1,783	5,918	866	43
Roanoke	94,795	677	9	27	176	465	4,735	883	3,608	244	33
Rocky Mount	4,541	16	0	2	2	12	132	20	106	6	2
Rural Retreat	1,346	0	0	0	0	0	5	4	1	0	0
Salem	25,623	34	1	6	6	21	677	89	559	29	3
Saltville	2,192	3	0	1	1	1	36	2	34	0	0
Shenandoah	2,274	4	0	2	0	2	39	6	30	3	1
Smithfield	7,173	9	0	2	4	3	185	26	145	14	1
South Boston	7,770	35	1	6	12	16	352	66	280	6	0
South Hill	4,528	19	0	2	5	12	151	10	134	7	0
Stanley	1,560	1	0	0	1	0	42	3	39	0	0
Staunton	23,979	32	0	4	4	24	532	57	465	10	12
Stephens City	1,526	0	0	0	0	0	30	6	22	2	0

[1] The FBI does not publish arson data unless it receives data from either the agency or the state for all 12 months of the calendar year.

Table 8.   Offenses Known to Law Enforcement, by State and City, 2010—*Continued*

(Number)

State/city	Population	Violent crime	Murder and non-negligent man-slaughter	Forcible rape	Robbery	Aggravated assault	Property crime	Burglary	Larceny-theft	Motor vehicle theft	Arson[1]
VIRGINIA—*Continued*											
St. Paul	974	1	0	1	0	0	22	2	20	0	0
Strasburg	4,426	1	0	1	0	0	115	4	111	0	1
Suffolk	86,226	265	3	18	80	164	2,058	389	1,567	102	21
Tappahannock	2,219	6	1	2	2	1	108	12	89	7	0
Tazewell	4,282	9	1	1	1	6	127	23	103	1	0
Timberville	2,022	1	0	0	0	1	10	4	5	1	0
Victoria	1,693	5	0	0	0	5	16	1	15	0	0
Vienna	15,343	25	0	1	9	15	273	35	224	14	1
Vinton	7,851	31	1	2	2	26	288	35	250	3	6
Virginia Beach	435,873	820	14	55	422	329	13,232	2,151	10,431	650	133
Warrenton	9,367	27	0	4	4	19	270	46	216	8	1
Warsaw	1,321	0	0	0	0	0	8	0	8	0	0
Waverly	2,128	9	0	0	1	8	31	9	21	1	0
Waynesboro	22,606	71	2	8	19	42	651	104	523	24	8
Weber City	1,305	2	0	0	0	2	23	7	15	1	0
West Point	3,198	2	0	0	1	1	50	10	39	1	0
White Stone	327	0	0	0	0	0	5	1	4	0	0
Williamsburg	12,854	18	1	1	6	10	267	35	222	10	0
Winchester	26,698	56	0	8	20	28	1,125	146	956	23	1
Wise	3,235	2	0	0	0	2	90	11	77	2	2
Woodstock	4,340	3	0	0	3	0	123	11	107	5	2
Wytheville	8,298	12	0	1	3	8	254	19	227	8	1
WASHINGTON											
Aberdeen	15,917	52	0	6	15	31	1,143	185	898	60	7
Airway Heights	5,618	6	0	2	1	3	147	36	98	13	0
Algona	2,838	4	0	0	0	4	52	11	33	8	1
Anacortes	17,132	14	0	3	1	10	561	81	461	19	5
Arlington	17,749	26	0	4	6	16	731	94	542	95	0
Asotin	1,129	5	0	0	0	5	18	4	12	2	0
Auburn	64,139	235	3	15	79	138	3,828	725	2,533	570	23
Bainbridge Island	22,075	27	0	1	0	26	292	64	222	6	3
Battle Ground	18,076	34	0	10	7	17	485	86	367	32	3
Bellevue	127,735	138	0	10	59	69	3,769	657	2,905	207	31
Bellingham	81,139	282	2	37	73	170	3,653	589	2,931	133	6
Bingen	677	0	0	0	0	0	28	6	19	3	0
Black Diamond	4,090	1	1	0	0	0	52	18	32	2	0
Bonney Lake	17,760	30	0	3	9	18	468	85	349	34	5
Bothell	33,094	32	0	10	10	12	888	172	642	74	10
Bremerton	34,897	263	0	52	50	161	1,786	414	1,263	109	15
Brewster	2,123	6	0	0	4	2	99	29	63	7	0
Brier	6,393	6	0	1	0	5	141	36	100	5	2
Buckley	5,562	8	0	2	0	6	120	23	91	6	1
Burien	31,831	229	0	52	95	82	2,107	561	1,171	375	14
Burlington	8,883	13	0	3	7	3	1,135	105	992	38	2
Camas	18,850	18	0	9	1	8	337	48	274	15	4
Carnation	1,833	1	0	0	1	0	22	2	20	0	0
Castle Rock	2,114	2	0	0	0	2	62	14	44	4	0
Centralia	15,736	93	0	11	13	69	1,119	212	842	65	8
Chehalis	7,409	25	0	6	3	16	715	97	579	39	2
Cheney	11,030	35	0	7	6	22	349	73	256	20	1
Chewelah	2,314	3	0	0	1	2	101	31	65	5	0
Clarkston	7,135	18	0	8	2	8	383	50	326	7	4
Cle Elum	3,516	8	0	3	0	5	209	58	143	8	0
Clyde Hill	2,767	2	0	0	1	1	33	7	25	1	0
Colfax	2,804	2	0	1	0	1	15	3	10	2	0
College Place	9,186	4	0	2	1	1	195	29	160	6	0
Colton	403	0	0	0	0	0	0	0	0	0	0
Colville	4,889	5	0	0	3	2	163	13	142	8	0
Connell	3,484	10	0	2	1	7	33	6	22	5	1
Cosmopolis	1,660	1	0	0	1	0	19	7	11	1	0
Coulee Dam	1,048	3	0	1	1	1	20	6	13	1	0
Coupeville	1,878	6	0	0	2	4	53	15	36	2	1
Covington	18,933	47	0	11	21	15	653	139	460	54	0
Des Moines	29,134	83	1	9	47	26	979	192	615	172	2
Dupont	8,142	7	0	0	0	7	51	13	35	3	0
Duvall	6,349	3	0	2	1	0	38	8	30	0	0
East Wenatchee	12,620	29	0	5	8	16	536	63	446	27	2
Eatonville	2,608	1	0	0	1	0	40	12	27	1	0
Edgewood	9,885	12	1	1	4	6	223	79	122	22	0
Edmonds	40,769	68	0	9	23	36	847	183	616	48	14
Ellensburg	17,553	31	0	14	7	10	894	153	703	38	3
Elma	3,103	14	0	1	4	9	153	44	104	5	0
Enumclaw	10,787	6	0	2	2	2	297	49	224	24	1

[1] The FBI does not publish arson data unless it receives data from either the agency or the state for all 12 months of the calendar year.

Table 8.   Offenses Known to Law Enforcement, by State and City, 2010—*Continued*

(Number)

State/city	Population	Violent crime	Murder and non-negligent man-slaughter	Forcible rape	Robbery	Aggravated assault	Property crime	Burglary	Larceny-theft	Motor vehicle theft	Arson[1]
WASHINGTON—*Continued*											
Ephrata	7,620	19	0	1	5	13	539	120	399	20	0
Everett	99,387	535	5	76	181	273	7,672	994	5,536	1,142	29
Everson	2,254	3	0	2	0	1	72	16	50	6	0
Federal Way	85,623	325	5	50	152	118	4,710	828	3,141	741	11
Ferndale	11,962	16	0	3	5	8	393	72	312	9	0
Fife	8,607	45	0	3	8	34	593	112	398	83	2
Fircrest	6,299	10	0	1	2	7	130	29	90	11	2
Forks	3,345	15	1	3	0	11	92	15	75	2	2
Garfield	628	0	0	0	0	0	2	0	2	0	0
Gig Harbor	7,289	26	0	2	10	14	440	76	338	26	2
Goldendale	3,723	13	0	1	0	12	165	27	127	11	0
Grand Coulee	1,969	10	0	1	1	8	61	26	34	1	0
Grandview	9,614	20	0	4	2	14	366	104	220	42	2
Granger	3,148	16	1	1	4	10	145	35	89	21	2
Granite Falls	3,277	8	0	0	1	7	83	21	55	7	1
Hoquiam	8,749	18	0	2	5	11	439	90	324	25	5
Ilwaco	994	0	0	0	0	0	26	8	17	1	0
Issaquah	25,784	30	0	6	6	18	735	101	583	51	6
Kalama	2,292	2	0	0	0	2	52	14	35	3	0
Kelso	12,141	65	0	24	18	23	778	139	600	39	1
Kenmore	20,935	28	0	8	2	18	367	112	213	42	7
Kennewick	68,501	239	0	25	39	175	2,517	388	2,003	126	27
Kent	85,768	501	2	67	157	275	4,464	1,018	2,665	781	23
Kettle Falls	1,421	1	0	0	0	1	61	12	46	3	0
Kirkland	48,708	62	0	11	23	28	1,361	207	1,053	101	5
Kittitas	1,129	1	0	1	0	0	24	6	16	2	0
La Center	2,676	1	0	1	0	0	52	3	47	2	0
Lacey	43,130	81	0	5	18	58	1,560	278	1,195	87	3
Lake Forest Park	12,551	5	0	0	2	3	231	44	169	18	1
Lake Stevens	14,666	47	0	3	8	36	637	148	404	85	8
Lakewood	57,459	493	0	40	137	316	2,737	584	1,880	273	10
Langley	1,094	3	0	1	1	1	49	23	24	2	0
Liberty Lake	8,300	2	0	0	0	2	110	20	82	8	0
Long Beach	1,361	4	0	1	0	3	85	26	58	1	0
Longview	36,550	132	2	22	22	86	1,944	414	1,372	158	17
Lynden	12,377	10	0	2	0	8	219	33	185	1	0
Lynnwood	33,929	83	1	7	36	39	2,118	219	1,740	159	1
Maple Valley	21,797	38	0	19	7	12	292	96	181	15	8
Marysville	35,810	130	0	27	41	62	1,797	283	1,264	250	9
McCleary	1,628	0	0	0	0	0	28	5	18	5	0
Medina	3,704	0	0	0	0	0	42	7	34	1	0
Mercer Island	24,715	14	0	1	4	9	324	50	264	10	3
Mill Creek	17,697	39	0	6	16	17	505	91	369	45	0
Milton	6,086	24	1	1	12	10	307	64	219	24	2
Monroe	17,612	50	1	9	5	35	544	79	391	74	0
Montesano	3,643	2	0	1	1	0	95	21	68	6	6
Morton	1,084	2	0	1	0	1	43	10	31	2	0
Moses Lake	20,559	83	0	13	18	52	1,512	297	1,130	85	4
Mossyrock	712	3	0	1	0	2	15	4	10	1	0
Mountlake Terrace	19,978	49	0	5	17	27	543	114	378	51	8
Mount Vernon	32,630	89	0	15	23	51	2,109	290	1,756	63	8
Moxee	2,698	6	0	2	0	4	33	8	21	4	0
Mukilteo	21,177	18	0	3	2	13	571	137	382	52	2
Napavine	1,957	0	0	0	0	0	49	16	26	7	0
Newcastle	10,240	12	0	1	4	7	221	44	158	19	1
Normandy Park	6,342	3	0	0	1	2	182	43	130	9	1
North Bend	4,683	13	0	3	2	8	226	44	167	15	3
Oak Harbor	22,873	51	0	11	2	38	509	107	389	13	4
Oakville	733	2	0	0	0	2	28	10	14	4	0
Ocean Shores	5,257	10	0	3	2	5	189	94	92	3	3
Odessa	895	1	0	0	1	0	15	5	10	0	0
Olympia	46,264	150	0	37	29	84	2,562	425	1,987	150	5
Omak	4,734	19	0	4	4	11	134	22	104	8	1
Oroville	1,662	0	0	0	0	0	80	19	56	5	0
Orting	6,610	6	0	0	2	4	172	36	127	9	6
Othello	6,807	29	1	3	5	20	477	87	354	36	0
Pacific	6,072	14	0	3	2	9	159	49	79	31	0
Palouse	944	0	0	0	0	0	6	3	2	1	0
Pasco	61,747	183	3	22	38	120	1,448	324	1,006	118	27
Port Angeles	18,901	93	0	16	20	57	1,000	230	725	45	3
Port Orchard	8,013	50	0	14	3	33	590	102	450	38	2
Port Townsend	9,188	17	0	0	1	16	332	76	239	17	2
Poulsbo	8,386	31	0	2	3	26	285	41	241	3	1

[1] The FBI does not publish arson data unless it receives data from either the agency or the state for all 12 months of the calendar year.

Table 8.   Offenses Known to Law Enforcement, by State and City, 2010—*Continued*

(Number)

State/city	Population	Violent crime	Murder and non-negligent man-slaughter	Forcible rape	Robbery	Aggravated assault	Property crime	Burglary	Larceny-theft	Motor vehicle theft	Arson[1]
WASHINGTON—*Continued*											
Prosser	5,303	5	1	2	0	2	161	36	112	13	0
Pullman	27,806	42	0	10	9	23	608	198	393	17	1
Puyallup	37,964	117	1	17	53	46	2,517	398	1,836	283	11
Quincy	6,255	29	1	5	3	20	421	129	245	47	0
Rainier	1,713	2	0	0	0	2	26	5	20	1	1
Raymond	2,831	6	0	1	0	5	75	26	45	4	0
Reardan	586	0	0	0	0	0	9	3	6	0	0
Redmond	52,972	63	0	20	18	25	1,561	198	1,296	67	0
Renton	62,968	280	0	38	112	130	4,114	847	2,673	594	7
Republic	955	0	0	0	0	0	10	3	7	0	0
Richland	48,335	66	0	12	8	46	956	146	751	59	5
Ridgefield	4,739	3	0	0	2	1	61	17	39	5	0
Ritzville	1,759	4	0	0	1	3	67	12	51	4	0
Rosalia	593	1	0	0	0	1	5	1	4	0	0
Roy	802	3	0	0	0	3	16	5	10	1	0
Royal City	2,038	10	0	0	1	9	44	19	19	6	0
Ruston	747	2	0	0	1	1	33	11	20	2	0
Sammamish	43,048	17	0	6	4	7	381	95	275	11	0
SeaTac	26,667	118	2	18	49	49	1,317	294	724	299	8
Seattle	620,195	3,515	19	96	1,429	1,971	33,186	6,449	23,284	3,453	126
Sedro Woolley	11,221	15	0	3	8	4	568	152	399	17	3
Selah	7,361	6	0	3	0	3	263	74	165	24	0
Sequim	5,978	21	0	1	4	16	340	41	293	6	3
Shelton	9,309	79	0	15	19	45	849	148	603	98	5
Shoreline	52,567	108	1	21	43	43	1,405	311	994	100	8
Snohomish	9,223	19	0	4	10	5	396	50	306	40	5
Snoqualmie	10,246	7	0	0	2	5	188	10	171	7	2
Soap Lake	1,880	0	0	0	0	0	22	9	13	0	0
South Bend	1,799	2	0	0	0	2	22	2	19	1	0
Spokane	203,272	1,270	6	80	432	752	15,042	2,859	10,174	2,009	45
Spokane Valley	87,780	165	3	44	57	61	4,226	837	2,976	413	7
Stanwood	5,519	8	0	2	1	5	245	33	206	6	0
Steilacoom	6,115	13	0	3	1	9	88	19	65	4	0
Sultan	4,378	13	0	1	2	10	116	34	73	9	1
Sumas	1,295	2	1	0	0	1	39	7	31	1	0
Sumner	9,940	29	0	2	7	20	553	124	389	40	6
Sunnyside	15,297	52	6	7	12	27	724	188	450	86	2
Tacoma	199,595	1,700	14	141	535	1,010	12,670	2,893	7,741	2,036	64
Tenino	2,309	1	0	0	0	1	59	10	48	1	1
Tieton	1,175	4	1	1	0	2	17	8	8	1	0
Toledo	688	2	0	0	1	1	18	6	11	1	0
Tonasket	941	4	0	0	0	4	53	3	50	0	0
Toppenish	9,253	60	0	10	27	23	500	125	322	53	8
Tukwila	17,337	154	0	13	90	51	2,927	377	2,096	454	9
Tumwater	16,375	50	0	14	8	28	617	147	440	30	4
Twisp	900	0	0	0	0	0	45	12	32	1	0
Union Gap	5,782	7	0	2	2	3	735	92	611	32	1
University Place	30,655	111	0	14	31	66	914	226	617	71	8
Vancouver	167,264	671	0	112	173	386	6,544	939	4,682	923	48
Walla Walla	31,265	117	0	19	23	75	1,291	229	1,005	57	6
Wapato	4,570	23	0	2	11	10	271	96	140	35	1
Warden	2,651	3	0	0	0	3	65	9	49	7	0
Washougal	14,405	23	0	3	3	17	331	56	262	13	5
Wenatchee	30,287	80	1	16	10	53	1,181	150	971	60	2
Westport	2,668	1	0	0	0	1	98	43	50	5	1
West Richland	11,840	14	0	4	2	8	162	22	134	6	1
White Salmon	2,420	0	0	0	0	0	55	11	38	6	0
Wilbur	859	0	0	0	0	0	13	4	9	0	0
Winlock	1,235	2	0	0	0	2	34	13	21	0	0
Winthrop	397	0	0	0	0	0	12	5	5	2	0
Woodinville	11,558	18	0	1	9	8	369	66	283	20	2
Woodland	5,476	18	0	7	1	10	162	24	124	14	1
Woodway	1,163	2	0	2	0	0	14	5	9	0	0
Yakima	85,802	490	12	46	144	288	5,555	1,464	3,501	590	37
Yarrow Point	953	0	0	0	0	0	4	3	1	0	0
Yelm	6,642	10	0	5	4	1	234	45	172	17	0
Zillah	2,852	7	0	1	1	5	103	23	69	11	1
WEST VIRGINIA											
Barboursville	3,652	4	0	0	0	4	390	24	365	1	1
Beckley	16,990	188	1	12	38	137	1,472	335	1,093	44	10
Belington	1,843	16	0	0	1	15	17	6	11	0	0
Benwood	1,424	1	0	0	1	0	7	0	7	0	0
Bluefield	11,222	46	3	1	8	34	286	82	192	12	4

[1] The FBI does not publish arson data unless it receives data from either the agency or the state for all 12 months of the calendar year.

Table 8.   Offenses Known to Law Enforcement, by State and City, 2010—*Continued*

(Number)

State/city	Population	Violent crime	Murder and non-negligent man-slaughter	Forcible rape	Robbery	Aggravated assault	Property crime	Burglary	Larceny-theft	Motor vehicle theft	Arson[1]
WEST VIRGINIA—*Continued*											
Bridgeport	8,121	26	1	3	3	19	320	21	297	2	1
Buckhannon	5,601	3	0	1	0	2	80	25	50	5	3
Ceredo	1,608	0	0	0	0	0	24	2	21	1	0
Clarksburg	16,652	88	1	7	15	65	753	115	619	19	8
Dunbar	7,718	38	0	3	5	30	199	49	139	11	2
Eleanor	1,581	0	0	0	0	0	2	0	2	0	0
Elkins	7,114	66	1	1	7	57	224	58	159	7	1
Fairmont[2]	19,332	48	0	7	10	31		111		17	6
Follansbee	2,861	3	0	1	0	2	33	12	15	6	0
Glen Dale	1,389	2	0	0	0	2	35	9	25	1	0
Hurricane[2]	6,463	11	0	3	1	7		20		4	0
Kenova	3,297	12	0	0	6	6	149	30	111	8	2
Logan	1,500	16	0	0	2	14	251	34	209	8	1
Martinsburg	17,654	65	0	2	17	46	969	115	815	39	7
Matoaka	308	0	0	0	0	0	0	0	0	0	0
Moorefield	2,508	10	0	0	0	10	61	14	45	2	0
Morgantown[2]	31,247	100	1	9	22	68		187		22	3
Nitro	6,836	13	0	2	4	7	229	39	174	16	2
Nutter Fort	1,648	3	0	0	0	3	45	13	29	3	0
Oceana	1,401	30	0	1	2	27	118	9	107	2	0
Point Pleasant	4,445	24	0	0	9	15	180	39	131	10	0
Princeton	6,354	33	1	1	10	21	335	61	263	11	0
Ravenswood	3,958	8	0	0	1	7	31	7	24	0	0
Ripley	3,264	2	1	1	0	0	59	7	48	4	0
Shinnston	2,273	11	0	0	0	11	55	9	43	3	3
South Charleston	12,691	76	1	3	7	65	548	120	397	31	1
Summersville[3]	3,351		0	0	0		127	19	106	2	0
Vienna[2]	10,715	12	0	1	1	10		10		3	0
Weirton	18,717	18	1	1	5	11	196	46	143	7	4
Wellsburg	2,585	3	2	0	0	1	35	13	22	0	0
Weston	4,362	2	0	0	0	2	12	2	8	2	0
Williamson	3,039	7	0	0	3	4	33	11	18	4	0
WISCONSIN											
Albany	1,105	3	0	1	0	2	21	1	20	0	1
Algoma	3,130	3	0	2	0	1	100	2	95	3	0
Altoona	6,658	16	1	4	2	9	150	23	122	5	0
Amery	2,744	9	0	0	1	8	85	13	71	1	0
Antigo	7,846	31	0	0	1	30	501	64	430	7	0
Appleton	70,975	202	0	17	13	172	1,716	305	1,379	32	15
Arcadia	2,325	3	0	0	0	3	28	4	21	3	
Ashwaubenon	17,601	17	0	11	0	6	618	53	550	15	
Athens	1,047	1	0	1	0	0	8	0	8	0	0
Bangor	1,392	1	0	0	0	1	31	9	20	2	2
Baraboo	11,205	59	0	9	3	47	508	48	454	6	0
Bayside	4,455	3	0	0	2	1	25	5	20	0	0
Beaver Dam	15,258	7	0	0	5	2	487	84	398	5	0
Belleville	2,378	3	0	0	1	2	21	3	15	3	0
Beloit	36,651	151	3	14	60	74	1,398	296	1,028	74	11
Beloit Town	7,509	16	0	4	3	9	134	52	79	3	0
Berlin	4,932	5	0	0	1	4	174	18	153	3	0
Big Bend	1,326	1	0	0	0	1	33	8	25	0	0
Black River Falls	3,382	2	0	0	0	2	143	14	128	1	1
Blair	1,226	1	0	1	0	0	32	9	21	2	0
Bloomfield	6,382	12	0	4	4	4	121	8	112	1	1
Boscobel	3,148	36	0	0	0	36	111	58	53	0	0
Brillion	2,804	2	0	0	0	2	29	3	24	2	0
Brodhead	3,092	1	0	0	0	1	61	2	58	1	
Brookfield	39,262	30	0	2	11	17	1,174	103	1,055	16	
Brookfield Township	6,202	12	0	0	2	10	147	9	133	5	
Brown Deer	12,111	18	0	1	5	12	361	23	328	10	1
Burlington	10,628	0	0	0	0	0	250	24	219	7	0
Burlington Town	6,616	4	0	1	1	2	49	6	41	2	0
Butler	1,777	6	0	0	2	4	61	9	44	8	
Caledonia	26,154	59	0	5	8	46	359	73	273	13	2
Campbellsport	1,947	0	0	0	0	0	22	5	16	1	0
Campbell Township	4,575	9	0	0	1	8	67	12	52	3	0
Cedarburg	11,079	1	0	0	0	1	159	7	150	2	0
Chenequa	595	1	0	0	0	1	2	0	2	0	
Chetek	2,144	2	0	0	0	2	32	5	26	1	
Chilton	3,678	4	0	3	0	1	75	4	63	8	0
Chippewa Falls	12,862	18	1	1	0	16	225	47	158	20	
Cleveland	1,374	1	0	0	0	1	13	1	12	0	0
Clinton	2,238	0	0	0	0	0	54	4	50	0	0

[1] The FBI does not publish arson data unless it receives data from either the agency or the state for all 12 months of the calendar year.

[2] The FBI determined that the agency's data were underreported. Consequently, those data are not included in this table.

[3] The FBI determined that the agency's data were overreported. Consequently, those data are not included in this table.

Table 8.   Offenses Known to Law Enforcement, by State and City, 2010—*Continued*

(Number)

State/city	Population	Violent crime	Murder and non-negligent man-slaughter	Forcible rape	Robbery	Aggravated assault	Property crime	Burglary	Larceny-theft	Motor vehicle theft	Arson[1]
WISCONSIN—*Continued*											
Clintonville	4,289	4	0	3	0	1	232	28	198	6	0
Colby-Abbotsford	3,606	3	0	0	1	2	72	16	55	1	
Columbus	4,967	3	0	0	0	3	131	21	110	0	
Combined Locks	3,327	3	0	1	0	2	6	1	4	1	0
Cornell	1,398	0	0	0	0	0	26	2	24	0	
Cottage Grove	6,223	0	0	0	0	0	122	21	99	2	0
Crandon	1,806	4	0	0	0	4	68	15	49	4	0
Cross Plains	3,664	0	0	0	0	0	30	1	29	0	
Cuba City	1,967	0	0	0	0	0	25	6	19	0	3
Cudahy	19,048	47	1	2	10	34	517	96	396	25	5
Dane	1,026	0	0	0	0	0	0	0	0	0	
Darien	1,615	0	0	0	0	0	31	3	28	0	0
Darlington	2,229	1	0	1	0	0	34	3	30	1	
Deforest	9,260	6	0	2	0	4	122	20	101	1	
Delafield	6,970	5	0	0	4	1	170	11	157	2	
Delavan	8,309	11	0	0	2	9	330	36	287	7	0
Delavan Town	4,754	6	0	3	0	3	96	16	77	3	
Denmark	2,237	0	0	0	0	0	7	1	5	1	
Dodgeville	4,511	0	0	0	0	0	57	4	49	4	0
Durand	1,829	0	0	0	0	0	1	0	1	0	0
Eagle River	1,644	1	0	0	0	1	140	12	127	1	
Eagle Village	1,875	5	0	0	0	5	6	0	4	2	0
East Troy	4,506	6	0	3	1	2	128	10	115	3	5
Eau Claire	66,737	139	2	21	23	93	1,906	406	1,446	54	8
Edgerton	5,384	2	0	0	2	0	64	29	31	4	
Elkhart Lake	1,248	1	0	0	1	0	18	2	16	0	0
Elk Mound	806	0	0	0	0	0	17	3	14	0	
Ellsworth	3,116	0	0	0	0	0	86	24	61	1	0
Elm Grove	6,016	0	0	0	0	0	86	16	70	0	
Everest	16,425	26	0	1	3	22	340	83	247	10	2
Fall Creek	1,317	1	0	0	0	1	20	3	17	0	0
Fennimore	2,181	0	0	0	0	0	61	13	48	0	0
Fitchburg	24,537	85	1	3	31	50	851	66	735	50	
Fond du Lac	42,369	131	0	21	13	97	1,130	194	908	28	1
Fontana	1,837	5	0	0	0	5	36	1	35	0	0
Fort Atkinson	11,961	27	0	1	1	25	231	26	200	5	3
Fox Lake	1,453	0	0	0	0	0	19	5	14	0	0
Fox Point	6,861	4	0	1	3	0	78	9	68	1	1
Fox Valley Metro	17,757	9	0	1	1	7	347	49	292	6	1
Franklin	37,832	12	0	0	4	8	554	84	454	16	
Frederic	1,181	2	0	0	0	2	18	2	16	0	
Freedom	5,896	2	0	1	0	1	31	6	23	2	0
Geneva Town	4,692	4	0	0	2	2	116	22	92	2	0
Germantown	19,787	3	0	0	1	2	393	37	348	8	
Gillett	1,176	1	0	0	0	1	52	11	36	5	0
Glendale	13,029	27	0	1	21	5	812	42	745	25	0
Grafton	11,666	3	0	3	0	0	207	16	189	2	1
Grand Chute	21,194	42	0	6	10	26	1,192	119	1,052	21	1
Grantsburg	1,384	0	0	0	0	0	49	5	44	0	0
Green Bay[5]	101,320	370	2	54	67	247	2,595	568	1,917	110	6
Greendale	14,102	8	0	0	2	6	657	16	632	9	0
Greenfield	36,580	52	0	3	28	21	1,334	197	1,099	38	0
Hales Corners	7,775	5	0	1	2	2	163	13	144	6	1
Hartford	14,507	11	0	0	1	10	300	39	246	15	1
Hartland	8,772	11	0	1	0	10	80	13	66	1	
Hayward	2,260	7	0	0	0	7	160	12	138	10	0
Hazel Green	1,097	0	0	0	0	0	9	6	3	0	0
Highland	817	0	0	0	0	0	5	0	5	0	0
Hobart-Lawrence	10,975	0	0	0	0	0	60	13	46	1	
Holmen	8,644	9	0	0	0	9	177	50	123	4	1
Hortonville	2,833	2	0	1	0	1	148	18	129	1	
Hudson	12,832	11	0	0	0	11	621	73	534	14	1
Hurley	1,507	4	0	0	1	3	74	7	58	9	0
Independence	1,222	1	0	0	0	1	24	2	17	5	0
Iron Ridge	992	1	0	0	0	1	14	0	14	0	
Jackson	6,686	7	0	1	0	6	45	11	32	2	0
Janesville	63,651	170	1	30	39	100	2,411	383	1,980	48	12
Jefferson	7,950	12	0	4	4	4	230	11	214	5	2
Juneau	2,646	0	0	0	0	0	65	6	59	0	0
Kaukauna	15,948	17	0	1	2	14	193	18	168	7	0
Kenosha	98,961	270	2	41	89	138	2,968	602	2,239	127	9
Kewaskum	4,268	0	0	0	0	0	57	12	45	0	0
Kewaunee	2,740	1	0	0	0	1	30	0	28	2	0

[1] The FBI does not publish arson data unless it receives data from either the agency or the state for all 12 months of the calendar year.

[5] Because of changes in the state/local agency's reporting practices, figures are not comparable to previous years' data.

Table 8.   Offenses Known to Law Enforcement, by State and City, 2010—*Continued*

(Number)

State/city	Population	Violent crime	Murder and non-negligent man-slaughter	Forcible rape	Robbery	Aggravated assault	Property crime	Burglary	Larceny-theft	Motor vehicle theft	Arson[1]
WISCONSIN—*Continued*											
Kiel	3,516	3	0	0	0	3	61	5	54	2	0
Kohler	1,949	0	0	0	0	0	49	0	48	1	0
La Crosse	51,184	155	1	23	34	97	1,723	336	1,309	78	5
Ladysmith	3,209	1	0	1	0	0	127	16	111	0	0
Lake Delton	2,923	22	0	6	5	11	557	29	524	4	
Lake Hallie	6,190	7	0	0	0	7	186	27	150	9	
Lake Mills	5,589	18	0	0	1	17	64	13	51	0	1
Lancaster	3,770	0	0	0	0	0	41	4	37	0	
Lodi	2,909	2	0	0	0	2	67	6	60	1	
Lomira	2,422	3	0	1	2	0	42	5	34	3	0
Luxemburg	2,269	3	0	0	0	3	21	2	18	1	0
Madison[5]	238,224	933	2	87	326	518	8,037	1,647	6,025	365	30
Manitowoc	32,640	44	0	0	6	38	662	76	570	16	2
Marathon City	1,539	6	0	0	0	6	25	6	19	0	0
Marinette	10,395	7	0	2	2	3	436	66	361	9	0
Marion	1,165	2	0	1	0	1	31	11	19	1	0
Markesan	1,261	0	0	0	0	0	31	3	28	0	0
Marshall Village	3,800	8	0	0	2	6	73	15	55	3	
Marshfield	18,819	7	0	1	1	5	497	78	412	7	11
Mauston	4,233	24	0	1	1	22	128	35	87	6	0
Mayville	5,302	3	0	1	0	2	148	15	133	0	0
McFarland	8,040	2	0	0	0	2	190	21	167	2	
Medford	3,995	7	0	0	0	7	197	18	175	4	0
Menasha	17,052	41	0	8	2	31	389	72	308	9	4
Menomonee Falls	34,836	13	0	1	4	8	419	35	361	23	1
Menomonie	15,846	10	0	1	0	9	333	52	274	7	1
Mequon	23,569	7	0	1	2	4	140	25	111	4	1
Merrill	9,433	37	0	4	0	33	367	50	313	4	4
Middleton	17,444	18	0	3	10	5	415	58	346	11	1
Milton	5,809	11	0	0	4	7	78	10	63	5	
Milwaukee	605,921	6,329	94	197	2,932	3,106	31,720	6,181	21,212	4,327	248
Mineral Point	2,512	1	0	1	0	0	36	2	34	0	0
Minocqua	4,914	2	0	0	0	2	261	22	236	3	1
Mishicot	1,367	0	0	0	0	0	0	0	0	0	0
Mondovi	2,518	7	0	0	0	7	47	9	38	0	
Monona	8,588	11	0	0	7	4	509	24	481	4	
Monroe	10,482	31	0	3	1	27	313	35	271	7	0
Montello	1,411	4	0	1	1	2	46	8	38	0	0
Mount Horeb	7,120	5	0	0	0	5	137	29	108	0	
Mount Pleasant	26,991	37	0	3	10	24	658	79	558	21	2
Mukwonago	7,209	1	0	0	1	0	184	14	164	6	
Muskego	23,324	9	0	3	1	5	254	38	208	8	0
Neillsville	2,517	1	0	0	0	1	82	11	70	1	1
Neshkoro	427	0	0	0	0	0	10	1	9	0	0
New Glarus	2,057	1	0	0	0	1	58	7	48	3	0
New Holstein	3,082	2	0	0	0	2	106	14	90	2	0
New Lisbon	2,462	4	0	0	0	4	16	0	16	0	0
New London	6,837	13	0	1	0	12	186	16	167	3	0
New Richmond	8,541	0	0	0	0	0	246	15	226	5	0
Niagara	1,683	1	0	0	0	1	29	11	18	0	0
North Fond du Lac	5,108	3	0	0	0	3	85	11	72	2	0
North Hudson	3,840	1	0	1	0	0	33	3	30	0	0
North Prairie	2,098	0	0	0	0	0	3	1	2	0	
Oak Creek	34,572	40	0	7	10	23	1,124	110	966	48	3
Oconomowoc	14,984	3	0	0	0	3	132	19	109	4	
Oconto	4,512	13	0	2	3	8	136	22	108	6	
Oconto Falls	2,755	1	0	1	0	0	62	7	52	3	
Omro	3,441	7	0	0	0	7	7	6	0	1	0
Onalaska	17,367	14	0	2	2	10	438	37	395	6	0
Oregon	9,715	6	0	0	1	5	184	36	146	2	0
Osceola	2,712	13	0	0	1	12	38	5	33	0	0
Oshkosh	64,428	206	1	10	24	171	1,715	313	1,360	42	6
Osseo	1,579	5	0	0	0	5	67	8	59	0	
Oxford	538	1	0	1	0	0	6	1	5	0	
Park Falls	2,238	0	0	0	0	0	37	1	35	1	0
Pepin	903	1	0	1	0	0	23	2	20	1	0
Peshtigo	3,248	2	0	0	1	1	46	13	33	0	0
Pewaukee Village	8,998	8	0	0	2	6	146	10	135	1	
Phillips	1,465	6	0	0	0	6	65	0	63	2	0
Plainfield	836	0	0	0	0	0	19	6	13	0	
Pleasant Prairie	20,314	5	0	0	2	3	309	33	271	5	0
Plover	12,429	7	0	0	1	6	216	23	192	1	0

[1] The FBI does not publish arson data unless it receives data from either the agency or the state for all 12 months of the calendar year.

[5] Because of changes in the state/local agency's reporting practices, figures are not comparable to previous years' data.

Table 8. Offenses Known to Law Enforcement, by State and City, 2010—*Continued*

(Number)

State/city	Population	Violent crime	Murder and non-negligent man-slaughter	Forcible rape	Robbery	Aggravated assault	Property crime	Burglary	Larceny-theft	Motor vehicle theft	Arson[1]
WISCONSIN—*Continued*											
Plymouth	8,344	8	0	1	2	5	202	23	178	1	0
Portage[2]	9,815	27	0	2	2	23		23		6	
Port Washington	11,242	5	0	1	3	1	110	13	93	4	0
Poynette	2,504	1	0	0	0	1	28	1	27	0	
Prescott	3,933	3	0	0	0	3	122	17	104	1	
Pulaski	3,554	5	1	1	0	3	48	6	41	1	
Racine	82,059	387	8	19	201	159	3,406	971	2,279	156	
Reedsburg	8,761	12	0	5	1	6	169	2	165	2	0
Rhinelander	7,471	17	0	1	0	16	373	40	329	4	0
Rice Lake	8,356	34	0	16	0	18	332	31	293	8	1
Richland Center	4,969	2	0	1	0	1	102	11	91	0	0
Ripon	7,481	9	0	1	0	8	124	25	96	3	0
River Falls	14,745	36	0	5	0	31	407	37	361	9	5
River Hills	1,684	1	0	0	0	1	6	1	5	0	0
Rome Town	2,972	3	0	0	0	3	40	16	23	1	
Rothschild	5,330	6	0	0	1	5	141	5	132	4	0
Sauk Prairie	4,190	7	1	0	2	4	264	33	231	0	0
Saukville	4,386	5	0	0	0	5	88	1	83	4	
Seymour	3,396	8	0	3	0	5	33	6	27	0	0
Shawano	8,875	22	0	6	1	15	237	23	200	14	0
Sheboygan Falls	7,911	0	0	0	0	0	70	3	67	0	0
Shorewood	13,285	15	0	1	9	5	399	33	358	8	
Shorewood Hills	1,675	1	0	0	0	1	54	6	47	1	
Silver Lake	2,526	2	0	0	0	2	21	3	17	1	2
Slinger	4,913	0	0	0	0	0	77	6	68	3	0
Sparta	9,107	24	0	3	2	19	345	71	264	10	5
Spencer	1,812	0	0	0	0	0	26	2	24	0	
Spooner	726	1	0	0	0	1	82	8	71	3	0
Stanley	3,575	4	0	0	0	4	94	8	86	0	
St. Croix Falls	2,111	0	0	0	0	0	52	6	45	1	0
Stevens Point	25,235	37	0	2	5	30	694	99	584	11	5
St. Francis	9,985	9	0	1	4	4	284	32	240	12	0
Strum	1,001	0	0	0	0	0	17	5	12	0	0
Sturgeon Bay	8,916	4	0	0	0	4	120	18	99	3	0
Sturtevant	7,132	9	0	0	0	9	73	14	48	11	
Sun Prairie	30,122	36	0	2	9	25	725	93	616	16	2
Superior	26,726	74	2	14	18	40	1,668	297	1,301	70	8
Theresa	1,284	0	0	0	0	0	61	11	50	0	0
Thiensville	3,187	3	0	0	0	3	12	2	9	1	0
Three Lakes	2,229	3	0	0	0	3	26	3	23	0	0
Tomah	8,908	36	1	4	2	29	451	41	397	13	0
Tomahawk	3,580	5	0	0	0	5	110	14	86	10	0
Town of East Troy	3,872	1	0	0	0	1	45	14	31	0	0
Town of Madison	6,048	43	0	10	21	12	286	65	204	17	
Town of Menasha	17,512	21	0	3	0	18	250	57	182	11	0
Twin Lakes	5,726	6	0	1	0	5	132	21	111	0	0
Two Rivers	11,597	17	0	0	1	16	149	22	124	3	0
Valders	966	0	0	0	0	0	3	0	3	0	0
Verona	11,715	7	0	1	1	5	227	29	197	1	1
Viroqua	4,288	1	0	0	1	0	66	8	55	3	1
Washburn	2,051	3	0	0	0	3	27	3	24	0	
Waterloo	3,226	3	0	0	0	3	43	4	38	1	0
Watertown	23,069	112	0	16	9	87	539	127	400	12	6
Waukesha	68,680	93	1	16	18	58	1,075	176	854	45	1
Waunakee	11,920	9	0	0	2	7	116	18	95	3	0
Waupaca	5,868	18	0	0	1	17	229	15	207	7	1
Waupun	10,564	17	0	8	0	9	225	69	150	6	0
Wausau	38,429	102	0	19	14	69	1,187	267	894	26	6
Wautoma	2,047	5	0	0	0	5	68	9	59	0	0
Wauwatosa	45,229	76	1	6	42	27	1,840	263	1,526	51	
West Allis	60,502	190	1	13	90	86	2,975	481	2,319	175	22
West Bend	30,362	37	0	0	7	30	816	40	769	7	1
Westfield	1,158	0	0	0	0	0	21	1	18	2	0
West Milwaukee	4,038	18	0	0	6	12	304	34	250	20	1
West Salem	4,889	0	0	0	0	0	85	20	62	3	1
Whitefish Bay	13,695	4	0	0	4	0	237	28	202	7	
Whitehall	1,575	1	0	0	0	1	48	5	43	0	0
Whitewater	14,211	19	0	2	3	14	339	42	293	4	1
Williams Bay	2,630	1	0	1	0	0	29	3	26	0	0
Winneconne	2,520	3	0	0	0	3	17	5	12	0	0
Wisconsin Dells	2,432	31	0	4	2	25	287	24	260	3	0
Wisconsin Rapids	17,396	10	0	3	3	4	828	143	665	20	2
Woodruff	2,000	1	0	0	0	1	38	7	31	0	0

[1] The FBI does not publish arson data unless it receives data from either the agency or the state for all 12 months of the calendar year.

[2] The FBI determined that the agency's data were underreported. Consequently, those data are not included in this table.

Table 8.   Offenses Known to Law Enforcement, by State and City, 2010—*Continued*

(Number)

State/city	Population	Violent crime	Murder and non-negligent man-slaughter	Forcible rape	Robbery	Aggravated assault	Property crime	Burglary	Larceny-theft	Motor vehicle theft	Arson[1]
WYOMING											
Afton	1,960	3	0	0	0	3	25	6	19	0	0
Alpine	882	3	0	0	0	3	18	4	14	0	0
Basin	1,328	1	0	0	0	1	28	0	26	2	0
Buffalo	5,123	15	0	0	0	15	92	24	62	6	1
Casper	56,813	108	2	6	20	80	2,405	382	1,934	89	22
Cheyenne	59,361	131	0	27	21	83	2,269	236	1,948	85	15
Cody	9,730	14	0	1	1	12	271	30	239	2	2
Diamondville	693	3	1	0	0	2	4	2	2	0	0
Douglas	6,468	17	0	3	0	14	183	15	158	10	0
Evanston	12,311	7	0	3	1	3	387	30	334	23	1
Evansville	2,594	5	0	0	2	3	65	3	58	4	0
Gillette	30,473	29	0	6	2	21	893	127	747	19	6
Glenrock	2,552	3	0	0	0	3	41	8	33	0	0
Green River	12,793	89	0	6	1	82	246	36	202	8	1
Greybull	1,816	8	0	0	0	8	34	7	26	1	0
Guernsey	1,084	1	0	0	0	1	17	2	13	2	0
Hanna	893	1	0	1	0	0	4	4	0	0	0
Hulett	538	3	0	0	0	3	1	0	1	0	0
Jackson	10,301	41	0	13	1	27	235	23	204	8	0
Kemmerer	2,563	1	0	0	0	1	29	1	28	0	0
Lander	7,622	13	0	3	2	8	254	23	221	10	1
Laramie	29,742	42	0	10	1	31	667	113	521	33	4
Lovell	2,381	3	0	0	1	2	42	7	35	0	1
Lusk	1,465	7	0	2	0	5	12	2	9	1	0
Mills	3,707	17	0	0	0	17	99	32	61	6	0
Moorcroft	961	0	0	0	0	0	22	5	17	0	1
Newcastle	3,505	3	0	2	0	1	115	23	92	0	0
Pine Bluffs	1,198	5	0	0	0	5	27	8	19	0	1
Powell	5,953	10	0	0	0	10	204	22	179	3	0
Rawlins	8,993	25	0	3	0	22	267	31	229	7	0
Riverton	10,613	43	2	5	7	29	535	58	462	15	0
Rock Springs	21,689	100	0	20	3	77	590	91	473	26	1
Saratoga	1,829	0	0	0	0	0	23	5	17	1	0
Sheridan	18,070	24	1	4	0	19	459	84	360	15	1
Sundance	1,387	0	0	0	0	0	14	3	9	2	0
Thermopolis	3,002	1	0	0	0	1	53	5	48	0	0
Torrington	5,816	18	0	1	0	17	161	28	127	6	0
Wheatland	3,290	4	0	2	0	2	161	51	106	4	0
Worland	5,157	9	0	0	0	9	30	6	23	1	0

[1] The FBI does not publish arson data unless it receives data from either the agency or the state for all 12 months of the calendar year.

Table 9. Offenses Known to Law Enforcement, by State and University and College, 2010

(Number)

State and University/College	Student enroll-ment[1]	Violent crime	Murder and non-negligent man-slaughter	Forcible rape	Robbery	Aggra-vated assault	Property crime	Burglary	Larceny-theft	Motor vehicle theft	Arson[2]
ALABAMA											
Calhoun Community College[3]		2	0	0	1	1	23	0	23	0	
Jacksonville State University	9,351	3	0	1	1	1	93	14	79	0	
Troy University	29,328	3	0	1	1	1	98	8	88	2	
University of Alabama											
Birmingham	16,874	8	0	0	1	7	429	30	392	7	
Huntsville	7,681	0	0	0	0	0	104	13	89	2	
Tuscaloosa	28,699	15	0	5	7	3	456	113	340	3	
University of North Alabama	7,194	3	0	1	1	1	71	6	64	1	
University of South Alabama	14,522	10	0	1	3	6	236	40	191	5	
University of West Alabama	5,157	0	0	0	0	0	26	3	22	1	0
ALASKA											
University of Alaska											
Anchorage	17,276	1	0	0	0	1	115	2	111	2	0
Fairbanks	9,137	5	0	2	0	3	81	7	74	0	0
ARIZONA											
Arizona State University, Main Campus	68,064	26	0	4	5	17	1,210	119	1,073	18	7
Central Arizona College	6,795	1	0	0	0	1	67	21	42	4	0
Northern Arizona University	23,597	21	0	5	2	14	297	21	272	4	4
Pima Community College	35,880	1	0	0	1	0	216	13	175	28	0
University of Arizona	38,767	10	0	3	1	6	991	42	918	31	5
Yavapai College	8,276	3	0	3	0	0	34	7	27	0	0
ARKANSAS											
Arkansas State University, Jonesboro	12,156	11	1	4	0	6	177	68	107	2	0
Arkansas Tech University	8,814	2	0	0	0	2	95	16	74	5	0
Henderson State University	3,567	0	0	0	0	0	52	22	27	3	2
University of Arkansas											
Fayetteville	19,849	3	0	0	1	2	281	62	201	18	0
Little Rock	13,132	4	0	1	1	2	135	42	86	7	0
Medical Sciences	2,774	8	0	1	0	7	198	7	186	5	0
Monticello	3,479	0	0	0	0	0	24	14	10	0	0
Pine Bluff	3,792	2	0	0	2	0	53	14	39	0	1
University of Central Arkansas	11,781	8	0	2	1	5	162	53	106	3	0
CALIFORNIA											
Allan Hancock College	11,070	0	0	0	0	0	76	19	56	1	0
California State Polytechnic University											
Pomona	22,273	5	0	2	3	0	184	13	151	20	0
San Luis Obispo	19,325	0	0	0	0	0	189	31	155	3	1
California State University											
Bakersfield	8,003	2	0	0	0	2	66	13	51	2	0
Channel Islands	3,862	1	0	0	0	1	66	1	65	0	0
Chico	16,934	9	0	3	4	2	217	23	191	3	3
Dominguez Hills	14,477	7	0	1	1	5	106	32	68	6	0
East Bay	14,749	8	0	3	2	3	112	22	89	1	0
Fresno	21,500	10	0	0	8	2	372	49	310	13	1
Fullerton	36,262	8	0	2	1	5	282	65	201	16	0
Long Beach	35,557	3	0	0	1	2	263	16	237	10	1
Los Angeles	20,619	3	0	0	3	0	150	9	134	7	0
Monterey Bay	4,688	5	0	2	0	3	86	16	66	4	0
Northridge	35,198	11	0	4	4	3	370	37	322	11	1
Sacramento	29,241	8	0	1	2	5	241	15	222	4	0
San Bernardino	17,852	1	0	0	1	0	96	19	73	4	0
San Jose[3]		23	0	3	9	11	439	41	378	20	2
San Marcos	9,767	1	0	1	0	0	39	5	33	1	0
Stanislaus	8,586	1	0	1	0	0	103	10	79	14	2
College of the Sequoias	13,322	5	0	0	0	5	150	40	102	8	0
Contra Costa Community College	8,316	12	0	0	4	8	232	11	206	15	0
Cuesta College	12,025	0	0	0	0	0	38	1	37	0	0
El Camino College	27,237	6	0	0	4	2	148	15	120	13	0
Foothill-De Anza College	43,484	1	0	0	1	0	85	30	55	0	0
Humboldt State University	7,954	9	0	1	1	7	110	14	94	2	2
Marin Community College	7,066	1	0	0	0	1	28	2	26	0	0
Pasadena Community College	26,453	2	0	0	2	0	121	10	106	5	0
Riverside Community College	36,586	2	0	0	1	1	102	7	82	13	0
San Bernardino Community College	14,916	3	0	0	2	1	148	44	97	7	0
San Diego State University	32,817	32	0	9	7	16	540	84	424	32	7
San Francisco State University	30,469	8	0	3	5	0	269	42	210	17	0
San Jose/Evergreen Community College	23,550	3	0	1	1	1	53	2	50	1	0
Santa Rosa Junior College	25,877	2	0	0	1	1	82	6	75	1	2
Solano Community College	12,222	4	0	0	3	1	68	0	61	7	0

Note: Caution should be exercised in making any intercampus comparisons or ranking schools because university/college crime statistics are affected by a variety of factors. These include demographic characteristics of the surrounding community, ratio of male to female students, number of on-campus residents, accessibility of the campus to outside visitors, size of enrollment, and so on.

[1] The student enrollment figures provided by the United States Department of Education are for the 2009 school year, the most recent available. The enrollment figures include full-time and part-time students.

[2] The FBI does not publish arson data unless it receives data from either the agency or the state for all 12 months of the calendar year.

[3] Student enrollment figures were not available.

Table 9.   Offenses Known to Law Enforcement, by State and University and College, 2010—*Continued*

(Number)

State and University/College	Student enroll-ment[1]	Violent crime	Murder and non-negligent man-slaughter	Forcible rape	Robbery	Aggra-vated assault	Property crime	Burglary	Larceny-theft	Motor vehicle theft	Arson[2]
CALIFORNIA—*Continued*											
Sonoma State University	8,546	1	0	0	1	0	96	6	90	0	0
State Center Community College District	40,895	10	0	0	2	8	322	39	249	34	1
University of California											
Berkeley	35,830	33	0	0	15	18	892	80	794	18	9
Davis	31,247	9	0	6	1	2	751	55	686	10	2
Hastings College of Law	1,347	10	0	0	5	5	18	1	17	0	0
Irvine	27,142	16	0	1	0	15	476	32	438	6	4
Los Angeles	38,550	38	0	12	13	13	870	198	653	19	2
Medical Center, Sacramento[3]		5	0	1	1	3	136	15	119	2	0
Merced	3,414	1	0	0	0	1	18	0	18	0	0
Riverside	19,384	13	0	1	5	7	315	21	282	12	3
San Diego	28,418	6	1	3	0	2	504	48	434	22	2
San Francisco	3,119	9	0	1	3	5	277	15	255	7	1
Santa Barbara	22,850	5	0	4	0	1	454	51	401	2	1
Santa Cruz	16,775	5	0	0	2	3	215	35	176	4	1
Ventura County Community College District	14,395	0	0	0	0	0	113	0	113	0	2
West Valley-Mission College	23,847	2	0	0	2	0	70	4	62	4	0
COLORADO											
Adams State College	3,121	2	0	1	1	0	60	27	33	0	0
Auraria Higher Education Center[3]		3	0	0	1	2	293	4	279	10	0
Colorado School of Mines	5,124	4	0	1	0	3	42	7	35	0	0
Colorado State University											
Fort Collins	28,902	5	0	1	2	2	394	47	338	9	8
Pueblo	6,443	0	0	0	0	0	81	7	71	3	1
Fort Lewis College	3,770	0	0	0	0	0	50	6	43	1	2
Red Rocks Community College	9,143	0	0	0	0	0	21	0	20	1	0
University of Colorado											
Boulder	33,010	7	0	3	1	3	673	26	641	6	3
Colorado Springs	9,733	2	0	0	0	2	74	4	70	0	0
Denver Health Sciences Center[3]	23,715	0	0	0	0	0	46	3	43	0	1
University of Northern Colorado	12,711	3	0	1	0	2	194	13	179	2	0
CONNECTICUT											
Central Connecticut State University	12,461	6	0	3	1	2	109	18	90	1	0
Eastern Connecticut State University	5,610	7	0	0	1	6	92	8	84	0	0
Southern Connecticut State University	11,815	0	0	0	0	0	23	1	20	2	0
University of Connecticut											
Health Center[3]		0	0	0	0	0	10	1	9	0	0
Storrs, Avery Point, and Hartford[3]		7	0	2	3	2	325	28	296	1	6
Western Connecticut State University	6,617	1	0	1	0	0	72	16	55	1	0
Yale University	11,593	3	0	1	2	0	274	31	241	2	0
DELAWARE											
Delaware State University	3,609	9	0	1	4	4	54	15	38	1	0
University of Delaware	21,138	8	0	1	4	3	278	21	254	3	3
FLORIDA											
Edison State College	16,034	0	0	0	0	0	24	0	24	0	0
Florida A&M University	12,274	7	0	0	2	5	392	43	347	2	0
Florida Atlantic University	27,637	4	0	2	2	0	291	42	231	18	2
Florida Gulf Coast University	11,092	1	0	0	0	1	73	2	71	0	1
Florida International University	39,610	13	1	2	7	3	576	79	462	35	1
Florida State University											
Panama City[3]		0	0	0	0	0	17	0	17	0	0
Tallahassee	39,785	14	0	0	7	7	535	118	405	12	1
New College of Florida	825	1	0	1	0	0	54	7	47	0	1
Pensacola Junior College	11,598	1	0	0	0	1	38	1	37	0	0
Santa Fe College	15,043	2	0	0	2	0	55	3	49	3	0
Tallahassee Community College	14,526	0	0	0	0	0	117	9	108	0	0
University of Central Florida	53,401	16	0	2	1	13	411	43	336	32	3
University of Florida	50,691	16	0	2	7	7	516	30	474	12	0
University of North Florida	16,477	0	0	0	0	0	192	14	176	2	1
University of South Florida											
St. Petersburg	3,895	1	0	0	0	1	32	0	29	3	0
Tampa	40,022	11	0	7	1	3	400	68	321	11	0
University of West Florida	11,143	6	0	1	0	5	70	4	65	1	2
GEORGIA											
Abraham Baldwin Agricultural College	3,327	0	0	0	0	0	51	14	37	0	0
Albany State University	4,473	7	0	2	2	3	63	5	57	1	0
Armstrong Atlantic State University	7,538	1	0	0	1	0	89	13	75	1	0
Augusta State University	7,061	0	0	0	0	0	63	4	59	0	0
Berry College	1,922	0	0	0	0	0	33	5	28	0	0
Clark Atlanta University	3,873	8	0	1	7	0	174	73	95	6	1

Note: Caution should be exercised in making any intercampus comparisons or ranking schools because university/college crime statistics are affected by a variety of factors. These include demographic characteristics of the surrounding community, ratio of male to female students, number of on-campus residents, accessibility of the campus to outside visitors, size of enrollment, and so on.

[1] The student enrollment figures provided by the United States Department of Education are for the 2009 school year, the most recent available. The enrollment figures include full-time and part-time students.

[2] The FBI does not publish arson data unless it receives data from either the agency or the state for all 12 months of the calendar year.

[3] Student enrollment figures were not available.

Table 9. Offenses Known to Law Enforcement, by State and University and College, 2010—*Continued*

(Number)

State and University/College	Student enroll-ment[1]	Violent crime	Murder and non-negligent man-slaughter	Forcible rape	Robbery	Aggra-vated assault	Property crime	Burglary	Larceny-theft	Motor vehicle theft	Arson[2]
GEORGIA—*Continued*											
Coastal Georgia Community College[3]		0	0	0	0	0	32	3	29	0	0
Columbus State University	8,178	2	0	0	1	1	96	12	82	2	0
Dalton State College	5,722	0	0	0	0	0	42	0	42	0	0
Darton College	5,854	0	0	0	0	0	31	1	29	1	0
Emory University	12,930	7	0	2	2	3	495	26	454	15	0
Fort Valley State University	3,553	1	0	0	0	1	280	7	272	1	0
Gainesville State College	8,801	1	0	0	1	0	25	0	24	1	0
Georgia College and State University	6,633	0	0	0	0	0	12	1	11	0	0
Georgia Gwinette college	2,947	2	0	0	0	2	58	8	50	0	0
Georgia Institute of Technology	20,291	9	0	1	3	5	482	59	408	15	0
Georgia Military College[3]		0	0	0	0	0	5	0	3	2	0
Georgia Perimeter College	24,549	4	0	0	0	4	131	2	122	7	0
Georgia Southern University	19,086	3	0	0	3	0	283	10	272	1	0
Georgia Southwestern State University	2,903	1	0	0	0	1	41	14	27	0	0
Georgia State University	30,427	16	0	1	14	1	334	11	319	4	0
Gordon College	4,545	2	0	0	0	2	71	15	55	1	0
Kennesaw State University	22,389	3	0	2	1	0	162	21	138	3	0
Medical College of Georgia	2,515	1	0	0	1	0	108	2	102	4	0
Mercer University	8,072	2	0	1	1	0	84	15	63	6	0
Middle Georgia College	3,614	6	0	0	0	6	57	3	53	1	0
Morehouse College	2,689	10	0	0	10	0	126	24	102	0	0
Morehouse School of Medicine	326	0	0	0	0	0	0	0	0	0	0
Moorehouse Brown College[3]		0	0	0	0	0	4	0	4	0	0
North Georgia College and State University	5,652	0	0	0	0	0	34	1	33	0	0
Paine College	907	0	0	0	0	0	18	8	10	0	0
Piedmont College	2,811	0	0	0	0	0	0	0	0	0	0
Savannah State University	3,820	7	0	1	3	3	280	23	257	0	0
Southern Crescent Technology College[3]		1	0	1	0	0	18	0	17	1	0
Southern Polytechnic State University	5,183	2	0	1	1	0	56	13	41	2	0
South Georgia College	2,000	1	0	0	0	1	14	6	8	0	0
Spelman College	2,229	2	0	0	2	0	8	1	7	0	0
University of Georgia	34,885	10	0	1	3	6	372	74	282	16	9
University of West Georgia	11,500	8	0	2	2	4	148	14	133	1	1
Valdosta State University	12,391	4	0	1	1	2	301	52	248	1	0
Wesleyan College	685	0	0	0	0	0	6	1	5	0	0
Young Harris College	695	2	0	1	0	1	16	0	16	0	0
ILLINOIS[4]											
Benedictine University	5,836	1	0	0	1	0	12	1	11	0	0
Black Hawk College	6,267	0	0	0	0	0	14	0	14	0	0
Chicago State University	7,235	1	0	0	1	0	49	5	44	0	0
College of DuPage	27,083	5	0	2	0	3	80	3	77	0	0
College of Lake County	18,092	2	0	0	0	2	62	1	61	0	0
Elgin Community College	11,704	0	0	0	0	0	52	0	52	0	0
Illinois State University	21,184	27	0	4	4	19	138	23	114	1	1
Joliet Junior College	15,288	4	0	0	0	4	91	6	83	2	0
Lake Land College	7,945	0	0	0	0	0	5	2	3	0	0
Moraine Valley Community College	17,774	0	0	0	0	0	44	0	44	0	0
Northern Illinois University	24,424	5	0	1	2	2	206	41	164	1	0
Oakton Community College	12,087	4	0	0	0	4	15	0	15	0	0
Southern Illinois University											
Carbondale	20,350	17	0	3	6	8	262	44	217	1	0
Edwardsville	13,940	5	0	0	1	4	162	21	139	2	0
Southwestern Illinois College	14,440	0	0	0	0	0	37	0	36	1	0
Triton College	15,706	3	0	1	2	0	41	1	40	0	0
University of Illinois											
Chicago	26,840	10	0	0	8	2	505	5	494	6	0
Urbana	43,881	14	0	2	8	4	440	64	331	45	0
Western Illinois University	12,679	7	0	5	1	1	161	45	116	0	1
William Rainey Harper College[3]		1	0	0	0	1	76	14	62	0	0
INDIANA											
Ball State University	21,401	24	0	4	7	13	418	47	363	8	3
Indiana State University	10,534	4	0	0	0	4	226	4	216	6	0
Indiana University											
Bloomington	42,347	2	0	0	2	0	517	39	469	9	0
Gary	5,560	1	0	0	0	1	34	1	31	2	0
Indianapolis[3]		2	0	0	2	0	250	44	195	11	0
New Albany	6,840	0	0	0	0	0	29	3	26	0	0

Note: Caution should be exercised in making any intercampus comparisons or ranking schools because university/college crime statistics are affected by a variety of factors. These include demographic characteristics of the surrounding community, ratio of male to female students, number of on-campus residents, accessibility of the campus to outside visitors, size of enrollment, and so on.

[1] The student enrollment figures provided by the United States Department of Education are for the 2009 school year, the most recent available. The enrollment figures include full-time and part-time students.

[2] The FBI does not publish arson data unless it receives data from either the agency or the state for all 12 months of the calendar year.

[3] Student enrollment figures were not available.

[4] Because of changes in the state/local agency's reporting practices, figures are not comparable to previous years' data.

Table 9. Offenses Known to Law Enforcement, by State and University and College, 2010—*Continued*

(Number)

State and University/College	Student enroll-ment[1]	Violent crime	Murder and non-negligent man-slaughter	Forcible rape	Robbery	Aggra-vated assault	Property crime	Burglary	Larceny-theft	Motor vehicle theft	Arson[2]
INDIANA—*Continued*											
Marian University	2,277	2	0	0	1	1	28	3	25	0	0
Purdue University	41,052	8	0	3	1	4	494	46	446	2	0
IOWA											
Iowa State University	27,945	16	0	2	1	13	293	22	266	5	3
University of Iowa	28,987	8	0	1	1	6	168	26	142	0	4
University of Northern Iowa	13,303	4	0	2	0	2	74	9	64	1	0
KANSAS											
Emporia State University	6,314	0	0	0	0	0	21	1	20	0	0
Fort Hays State University	11,308	0	0	0	0	0	31	2	29	0	1
Kansas State University	23,581	12	0	3	1	8	179	26	150	3	0
Univeristy of Kansas, Main campus	29,242	3	0	1	0	2	260	43	213	4	0
Washburn University	6,652	2	0	2	0	0	58	4	53	1	0
Wichita State University	14,601	3	0	1	1	1	121	4	114	3	2
KENTUCKY											
Eastern Kentucky University	16,268	6	0	2	2	2	264	62	202	0	0
Kentucky State University	2,834	0	0	0	0	0	118	13	104	1	0
Morehead State University	8,822	1	0	0	1	0	56	16	40	0	0
Murray State University	10,071	1	0	1	0	0	142	7	134	1	0
Northern Kentucky University	15,378	1	0	1	0	0	146	22	123	1	2
University of Kentucky	26,295	15	0	2	11	2	638	26	607	5	2
University of Louisville	21,016	7	0	1	5	1	290	27	255	8	1
Western Kentucky University	20,712	4	0	1	1	2	248	78	169	1	1
LOUISIANA											
Delgado Community College	16,758	0	0	0	0	0	19	0	19	0	0
Grambling State University	4,992	2	0	0	1	1	102	19	80	3	0
Louisiana State University											
Baton Rouge[3]		19	0	2	4	13	489	61	416	12	3
Eunice	3,332	0	0	0	0	0	1	0	1	0	0
Health Sciences Center, Shreveport	823	4	0	1	0	3	34	4	27	3	0
Shreveport	4,667	4	0	0	1	3	30	6	24	0	0
Louisiana Tech University	11,264	4	0	0	1	3	127	21	100	6	2
McNeese State University	8,638	0	0	0	0	0	55	2	51	2	0
Nicholls State University	7,169	5	0	1	0	4	44	4	40	0	0
Northwestern State University	9,247	0	0	0	0	0	73	43	30	0	
Southeastern Louisiana University	15,151	0	0	0	0	0	136	7	128	1	0
Southern University and A&M College											
Baton Rouge	7,619	13	0	0	7	6	192	16	174	2	0
New Orleans	3,141	0	0	0	0	0	4	1	3	0	0
Shreveport	3,014	1	0	0	0	1	42	26	16	0	0
Tulane University	11,464	7	0	4	1	2	195	21	171	3	0
University of Louisiana											
Lafayette	16,361	11	0	1	3	7	183	17	166	0	2
Monroe	9,004	9	0	1	0	8	84	10	71	3	0
University of New Orleans	11,724	1	0	0	0	1	53	9	40	4	
MAINE											
University of Maine											
Farmington	2,361	0	0	0	0	0	34	5	29	0	0
Orono	11,894	2	0	0	0	2	204	5	199	0	11
University of Southern Maine	9,655	2	0	2	0	0	62	3	57	2	17
MARYLAND											
Bowie State University	5,617	13	0	1	2	10	92	39	50	3	3
Coppin State University	3,801	7	0	0	3	4	95	10	83	2	0
Frostburg State University	5,385	2	0	0	0	2	61	17	44	0	0
Morgan State University	7,226	24	0	1	21	2	159	61	91	7	0
Salisbury University	8,204	5	0	1	2	2	94	16	77	1	0
St. Mary's College	2,060	0	0	0	0	0	61	4	57	0	0
Towson University	21,177	7	0	0	2	5	156	14	142	0	1
University of Baltimore	6,265	1	0	0	1	0	48	2	46	0	0
University of Maryland											
Baltimore City	6,382	5	0	0	2	3	92	1	89	2	0
Baltimore County	12,870	1	0	0	1	0	161	10	151	0	0
College Park	37,195	15	0	1	8	6	457	79	358	20	3
Eastern Shore	4,433	17	0	2	5	10	84	23	59	2	0
MASSACHUSETTS											
Amherst College	1,744	1	0	0	1	0	51	2	49	0	0
Assumption College	2,794	2	0	1	0	1	48	7	41	0	1
Bentley College	5,628	8	0	3	0	5	60	17	43	0	3
Boston College	15,036	11	0	4	1	6	185	27	157	1	0

Note: Caution should be exercised in making any intercampus comparisons or ranking schools because university/college crime statistics are affected by a variety of factors. These include demographic characteristics of the surrounding community, ratio of male to female students, number of on-campus residents, accessibility of the campus to outside visitors, size of enrollment, and so on.

[1] The student enrollment figures provided by the United States Department of Education are for the 2009 school year, the most recent available. The enrollment figures include full-time and part-time students.

[2] The FBI does not publish arson data unless it receives data from either the agency or the state for all 12 months of the calendar year.

[3] Student enrollment figures were not available.

Table 9. Offenses Known to Law Enforcement, by State and University and College, 2010—*Continued*

(Number)

State and University/College	Student enroll-ment[1]	Violent crime	Murder and non-negligent man-slaughter	Forcible rape	Robbery	Aggra-vated assault	Property crime	Burglary	Larceny-theft	Motor vehicle theft	Arson[2]
MASSACHUSETTS—*Continued*											
Boston University	31,960	16	0	3	10	3	455	72	382	1	0
Brandeis University	5,598	2	0	0	0	2	78	20	58	0	0
Bridgewater State College	10,774	3	0	1	0	2	65	11	53	1	0
Bristol Community College	8,767	3	0	1	0	2	21	3	18	0	0
Bunker Hill Community College	11,009	0	0	0	0	0	47	2	43	2	
Clark University	3,416	4	0	3	1	0	48	12	36	0	0
Dean College	1,113	7	0	2	1	4	55	36	19	0	
Emerson College	4,556	3	0	0	0	3	42	16	25	1	1
Fitchburg State College	7,043	9	0	0	0	9	71	8	62	1	0
Framingham State College	5,989	2	0	0	0	2	12	5	7	0	0
Harvard University	27,651	21	0	9	8	4	577	39	534	4	0
Holyoke Community College	7,473	1	0	0	0	1	57	0	56	1	
Lasell College	1,672	5	0	1	1	3	70	12	58	0	0
Massachusetts College of Art	2,422	1	0	1	0	0	54	3	51	0	0
Massachusetts College of Liberal Arts	1,962	5	0	1	2	2	28	5	23	0	0
Massachusetts Institute of Technology	10,384	6	0	1	1	4	345	40	304	1	1
Merrimack College	2,090	3	0	1	0	2	42	10	32	0	1
Northeastern University	27,537	16	0	1	9	6	373	18	350	5	
North Shore Community College	7,968	0	0	0	0	0	17	0	17	0	0
Salem State College	10,125	0	0	0	0	0	106	21	82	3	0
Smith College	3,121	2	0	1	1	0	74	10	63	1	0
University of Massachusetts											
Dartmouth	9,302	18	0	2	1	15	203	40	157	6	
Harbor Campus, Boston	14,912	6	0	1	2	3	140	9	131	0	0
Wellesley College	2,324	0	0	0	0	0	53	12	40	1	0
Western New England College	3,710	2	0	2	0	0	36	2	34	0	0
MICHIGAN[6]											
Central Michigan University	27,247	10	0	1	2	7	193	8	174	11	0
Delta College	11,354	0	0	0	0	0	35	1	34	0	0
Eastern Michigan University	22,893	5	0	1	3	1	238	45	188	5	4
Ferris State University	13,865	3	0	0	3	0	111	16	93	2	0
Grand Valley State University	24,408	1	0	1	0	0	118	2	116	0	0
Lansing Community College	21,123	1	0	0	0	1	113	1	112	0	0
Michigan State University	47,071	23	0	7	8	8	858	84	753	21	2
Michigan Technological University	7,136	0	0	0	0	0	87	4	82	1	1
Mott Community College	12,151	9	0	0	5	4	127	7	119	1	0
Northern Michigan University	9,428	1	0	0	0	1	115	14	101	0	0
Oakland Community College	28,042	2	0	0	1	1	57	0	56	1	0
Oakland University	18,918	4	0	2	0	2	74	13	59	2	1
Saginaw Valley State University	10,498	3	0	0	0	3	113	14	98	1	0
University of Michigan											
Ann Arbor	41,674	18	0	2	7	9	910	29	868	13	1
Dearborn	8,379	0	0	0	0	0	36	1	32	3	0
Flint	7,773	2	0	0	2	0	79	2	74	3	0
MINNESOTA[5]											
University of Minnesota											
Duluth	11,664		0		0	0	52	2	50	0	0
Morris	1,705		0		0	0	31	2	28	1	0
Twin Cities	51,659		0		3	6	629	43	568	18	2
MISSISSIPPI											
Coahoma Community College	2,565	0	0	0	0	0	11	9	2	0	0
Jackson State University	8,783	9	0	0	5	4	286	19	259	8	0
Mississippi State University	18,601	3	0	0	3	0	204	18	185	1	0
Northeast Mississippi Community College	3,633	0	0	0	0	0	88	26	62	0	0
University of Mississippi											
Medical Center	2,412	0	0	0	0	0	171	1	164	6	0
Oxford	15,932	4	0	3	1	0	240	49	189	2	0
MISSOURI											
Lincoln University	3,314	21	0	0	7	14	59	33	26	0	0
Mineral Area College	3,671	0	0	0	0	0	14	10	4	0	0
Missouri Southern State University	5,701	0	0	0	0	0	48	10	37	1	0
Missouri University of Science and Technology	6,814	1	0	0	0	1	59	7	52	0	2
Missouri Western State University	5,703	5	0	1	1	3	83	19	63	1	0
Northwest Missouri State University	7,076	0	0	0	0	0	47	11	36	0	0
Southeast Missouri State University	10,801	1	0	1	0	0	41	9	30	2	0

Note: Caution should be exercised in making any intercampus comparisons or ranking schools because university/college crime statistics are affected by a variety of factors. These include demographic characteristics of the surrounding community, ratio of male to female students, number of on-campus residents, accessibility of the campus to outside visitors, size of enrollment, and so on.

[1] The student enrollment figures provided by the United States Department of Education are for the 2009 school year, the most recent available. The enrollment figures include full-time and part-time students.

[2] The FBI does not publish arson data unless it receives data from either the agency or the state for all 12 months of the calendar year.

[5] The data collection methodology for the offense of forcible rape used by the Minnesota state Uniform Crime Reporting (UCR) Program does not comply with national UCR Program guidelines. Consequently, its figures for forcible rape and violent crime (of which forcible rape is a part) are not published in this table.

Table 9. Offenses Known to Law Enforcement, by State and University and College, 2010—*Continued*

(Number)

State and University/College	Student enroll-ment[1]	Violent crime	Murder and non-negligent man-slaughter	Forcible rape	Robbery	Aggra-vated assault	Property crime	Burglary	Larceny-theft	Motor vehicle theft	Arson[2]
MISSOURI—*Continued*											
St. Louis Community College											
Florissant Valley	7,210	1	0	0	1	0	116	2	113	1	0
Meramec	11,186	0	0	0	0	0	42	0	42	0	
Three Rivers Community College	3,527	2	0	0	0	2	7	3	4	0	0
Truman State University	5,781	2	0	1	0	1	69	3	66	0	2
University of Central Missouri	11,191	6	0	1	1	4	145	40	103	2	0
University of Missouri											
Columbia	31,237	12	0	1	1	10	322	11	308	3	0
Kansas City	14,799	0	0	0	0	0	107	34	72	1	1
St. Louis	16,534	4	0	1	0	3	90	12	74	4	0
Washington University	13,575	1	0	1	0	0	126	14	110	2	0
MONTANA											
Montana State University	12,348	3	0	1	2	0	135	13	121	1	0
University of Montana	14,921	1	0	0	0	1	149	0	148	1	1
NEBRASKA											
University of Nebraska											
Kearney	6,650	1	0	1	0	0	44	9	35	0	0
Lincoln	24,100	7	0	2	1	4	299	17	279	3	0
NEVADA											
Truckee Meadows Community College	12,942	0	0	0	0	0	30	3	27	0	0
University of Nevada											
Las Vegas	29,080	10	0	0	6	4	249	50	181	18	1
Reno	16,875	10	0	0	0	10	208	31	169	8	0
NEW HAMPSHIRE											
University of New Hampshire	15,253	5	0	1	1	3	185	7	175	3	1
NEW JERSEY											
Brookdale Community College	15,639	1	0	0	0	1	52	3	49	0	0
Essex County College	13,314	4	0	0	3	1	82	0	80	2	0
Kean University	15,051	3	0	0	1	2	110	26	77	7	0
Middlesex County College	13,356	0	0	0	0	0	53	1	52	0	0
Monmouth University	6,499	0	0	0	0	0	57	3	53	1	1
Montclair State University	18,171	7	0	2	1	4	231	13	217	1	0
New Jersey Institute of Technology	8,840	14	0	0	10	4	172	16	148	8	0
Richard Stockton College of New Jersey	7,559	2	0	0	0	2	99	20	78	1	0
Rowan University	11,006	4	0	0	0	4	115	13	100	2	0
Rutgers University											
Camden	5,781	2	0	0	0	2	109	11	96	2	1
Newark	11,501	7	0	0	6	1	179	3	171	5	0
New Brunswick	37,366	17	0	2	7	8	572	82	483	7	1
Stevens Institute of Technology	5,757	0	0	0	0	0	39	3	36	0	0
The College of New Jersey	6,980	2	0	1	0	1	86	3	83	0	0
University of Medicine and Dentistry											
Camden[3]		0	0	0	0	0	6	0	6	0	0
Newark	6,055	32	0	0	14	18	164	2	144	18	0
New Brunswick[3]		1	0	0	0	1	39	0	39	0	0
Piscataway[3]		0	0	0	0	0	0	0	0	0	0
William Paterson University	10,820	3	0	2	0	1	64	6	58	0	0
NEW MEXICO											
Eastern New Mexico University	4,679	0	0	0	0	0	43	5	37	1	0
New Mexico State University	18,526	18	0	3	2	13	416	70	333	13	0
University of New Mexico	27,241	23	0	2	3	18	717	39	640	38	0
NEW YORK											
Cornell University	20,633	4	0	1	0	3	226	10	215	1	0
Ithaca College	6,894	0	0	0	0	0	123	10	113	0	1
Rensselaer Polytechnic Institute	6,901	2	0	0	2	0	105	0	105	0	0
State University of New York											
Albany	18,020	3	0	1	0	2	223	56	163	4	0
Buffalo[3]		11	0	1	5	5	450	94	351	5	1
Maritime College	1,756	0	0	0	0	0	20	9	11	0	0
Stony Brook[3]		11	0	1	1	9	560	99	453	8	
Upstate Medical Center[3]		2	0	0	0	2	97	1	95	1	0
State University of New York Agricultural and Technical College											
Alfred	3,530	8	0	1	1	6	62	10	51	1	0
Canton	3,320	1	0	0	0	1	61	3	58	0	0
Cobleskill	2,692	1	0	1	0	0	62	17	45	0	1
Farmingdale[3]		0	0	0	0	0	0	0	0	0	0
Morrisville[3]		3	0	1	0	2	85	17	68	0	0

Note: Caution should be exercised in making any intercampus comparisons or ranking schools because university/college crime statistics are affected by a variety of factors. These include demographic characteristics of the surrounding community, ratio of male to female students, number of on-campus residents, accessibility of the campus to outside visitors, size of enrollment, and so on.

[1] The student enrollment figures provided by the United States Department of Education are for the 2009 school year, the most recent available. The enrollment figures include full-time and part-time students.

[2] The FBI does not publish arson data unless it receives data from either the agency or the state for all 12 months of the calendar year.

[3] Student enrollment figures were not available.

Table 9.　Offenses Known to Law Enforcement, by State and University and College, 2010—*Continued*

(Number)

State and University/College	Student enroll-ment[1]	Violent crime	Murder and non-negligent man-slaughter	Forcible rape	Robbery	Aggra-vated assault	Property crime	Burglary	Larceny-theft	Motor vehicle theft	Arson[2]
NEW YORK—*Continued*											
State University of New York College											
Buffalo	11,714	9	0	1	1	7	175	48	126	1	0
Cortland	7,322	4	0	0	0	4	77	20	56	1	0
Fredonia		0	0	0	0	0	59	7	52	0	0
Geneseo[3]		1	0	1	0	0	116	15	101	0	0
New Paltz	7,907	3	0	0	1	2	78	6	70	2	2
Old Westbury	3,897	0	0	0	0	0	89	24	63	2	1
Oneonta	5,893	2	0	2	0	0	69	11	58	0	0
Optometry	301	0	0	0	0	0	12	1	11	0	0
Oswego	8,119	3	0	0	1	2	126	21	104	1	0
Plattsburgh	6,453	2	0	0	2	0	134	23	109	2	0
Potsdam	4,299	0	0	0	0	0	59	9	50	0	0
Purchase	4,192	8	0	5	1	2	127	23	104	0	0
Utica-Rome[3]		0	0	0	0	0	15	1	14	0	0
United States Merchant Marine Academy	982	0	0	0	0	0	44	38	5	1	0
NORTH CAROLINA											
Appalachian State University	16,968	0	0	0	0	0	152	12	139	1	0
East Carolina University	27,654	6	0	1	3	2	259	11	247	1	2
Elizabeth City State University	3,264	7	0	1	5	1	29	1	28	0	0
Elon University	5,666	1	0	0	0	1	40	9	31	0	0
North Carolina Agricultural and Technical											
State University	10,614	6	0	2	2	2	132	30	98	4	0
North Carolina Central University	8,587	3	0	1	0	2	202	26	174	2	1
North Carolina State University, Raleigh	33,819	18	0	0	1	17	432	34	383	15	1
University of North Carolina											
Chapel Hill	28,916	4	0	3	1	0	290	24	262	4	0
Greensboro	21,306	3	0	0	2	1	174	2	168	4	1
Pembroke	6,661	1	0	0	1	0	110	23	84	3	0
Wake Forest University	7,079	6	0	2	0	4	192	42	146	4	0
Western Carolina University	9,429	5	0	1	0	4	117	9	107	1	0
NORTH DAKOTA											
North Dakota State College of Science	2,650	1	0	1	0	0	21	1	20	0	0
North Dakota State University	14,189	2	0	1	0	1	123	10	111	2	0
University of North Dakota	13,172	0	0	0	0	0	158	11	145	2	0
OHIO											
Bowling Green State University	17,309	3	0	0	1	2	235	40	193	2	1
Capital University	3,540	0	0	0	0	0	39	11	21	7	0
Columbus State Community College	28,539	2	0	1	1	0	159	0	158	1	0
Cuyahoga Community College	29,807	1	0	0	1	0	150	4	141	5	0
Kent State University	25,127	2	0	1	1	0	269	30	235	4	0
Lakeland Community College	9,406	0	0	0	0	0	46	0	44	2	0
Miami University	16,884	9	0	3	0	6	194	15	176	3	2
Ohio State University, Columbus	55,014	14	1	2	7	4	1,107	142	957	8	7
Ohio University	22,647	10	0	5	1	4	237	36	200	1	3
Sinclair Community College	21,561	0	0	0	0	0	43	0	43	0	0
University of Akron	25,959	5	0	4	1	0	381	9	358	14	0
University of Cincinnati	31,134	49	0	5	6	38	631	91	538	2	1
University of Toledo	23,064	16	0	1	0	15	680	73	605	2	0
Wright State University	17,558	7	0	4	3	0	152	41	111	0	0
Youngstown State University	14,644	3	0	0	0	3	165	9	153	3	0
OKLAHOMA											
Cameron University	6,126	3	0	1	0	2	24	11	11	2	0
East Central University	4,612	1	0	0	0	1	11	5	6	0	
Northeastern Oklahoma A&M College	2,191	2	0	0	0	2	58	34	24	0	0
Northeastern State University, Tahlequah	9,239	0	0	0	0	0	47	4	43	0	0
Oklahoma City University	3,829	2	0	1	0	1	45	4	40	1	0
Oklahoma State University											
Main Campus	23,033	6	0	3	0	3	245	36	206	3	0
Okmulgee	4,129	1	0	0	0	1	11	0	8	3	0
Tulsa[3]		1	0	0	0	1	13	1	11	1	0
Rogers State University	4,235	0	0	0	0	0	16	1	15	0	0
Seminole State College	2,444	0	0	0	0	0	17	6	11	0	
Southeastern Oklahoma State University	4,229	0	0	0	0	0	33	13	20	0	0
Southwestern Oklahoma State University	5,010	0	0	0	0	0	32	6	26	0	0
Tulsa Community College	19,730	3	0	0	1	2	68	10	56	2	0
University of Central Oklahoma	16,092	3	0	1	0	2	164	31	132	1	0
University of Oklahoma											
Health Sciences Center	3,934	4	0	0	2	2	154	3	145	6	0
Norman	25,881	4	0	2	0	2	293	25	261	7	0

Note: Caution should be exercised in making any intercampus comparisons or ranking schools because university/college crime statistics are affected by a variety of factors. These include demographic characteristics of the surrounding community, ratio of male to female students, number of on-campus residents, accessibility of the campus to outside visitors, size of enrollment, and so on.

[1] The student enrollment figures provided by the United States Department of Education are for the 2009 school year, the most recent available. The enrollment figures include full-time and part-time students.

[2] The FBI does not publish arson data unless it receives data from either the agency or the state for all 12 months of the calendar year.

[3] Student enrollment figures were not available.

Table 9. Offenses Known to Law Enforcement, by State and University and College, 2010—*Continued*

(Number)

State and University/College	Student enroll-ment[1]	Violent crime	Murder and non-negligent man-slaughter	Forcible rape	Robbery	Aggra-vated assault	Property crime	Burglary	Larceny-theft	Motor vehicle theft	Arson[2]
PENNSYLVANIA											
Bloomsburg University	9,512	4	0	2	2	0	148	1	146	1	0
Cheyney University	1,488	10	0	3	0	7	68	29	38	1	1
Clarion University	7,346	4	0	0	0	4	36	6	30	0	0
Dickinson College	2,376	4	0	3	0	1	77	17	60	0	0
East Stroudsburg University	7,576	8	0	0	0	8	115	50	64	1	1
Edinboro University	8,286	6	0	3	0	3	65	4	61	0	0
Elizabethtown College	2,361	0	0	0	0	0	33	0	33	0	0
Indiana University	14,638	9	0	1	1	7	62	7	53	2	0
Kutztown University	10,634	2	0	1	0	1	104	4	100	0	0
Lehigh University	6,996	1	0	0	1	0	80	18	62	0	0
Lock Haven University	5,329	0	0	0	0	0	56	11	45	0	0
Mansfield University	3,569	1	0	0	0	1	17	4	13	0	0
Millersville University	8,427	3	0	1	0	2	41	6	35	0	0
Moravian College	2,057	1	0	0	0	1	46	5	41	0	0
Pennsylvania State University											
Altoona	4,182	2	0	2	0	0	38	5	33	0	0
Beaver	855	0	0	0	0	0	10	1	9	0	0
Behrend	4,400	1	0	1	0	0	30	8	22	0	0
Berks	2,759	1	0	0	0	1	27	4	23	0	0
Harrisburg	4,012	0	0	0	0	0	17	0	17	0	0
Hazelton	1,245	0	0	0	0	0	22	2	20	0	0
Mont Alto	1,182	0	0	0	0	0	11	0	11	0	0
University Park	45,185	15	0	0	2	13	544	53	490	1	14
Shippensburg University	8,253	5	0	4	0	1	35	12	23	0	0
Slippery Rock University	8,648	4	0	1	0	3	36	1	35	0	0
University of Pittsburgh											
Bradford	1,657	2	0	0	0	2	22	1	20	1	1
Pittsburgh	28,328	18	0	1	13	4	325	43	281	1	0
West Chester University	14,211	3	0	1	1	1	105	29	75	1	1
RHODE ISLAND											
Brown University	8,574	0	0	0	0	0	159	39	120	0	0
University of Rhode Island	16,389	4	0	1	3	0	157	7	147	3	2
SOUTH CAROLINA											
Benedict College	2,983	4	0	0	2	2	235	123	111	1	1
Bob Jones University	3,956	0	0	0	0	0	68	33	35	0	0
Clemson University	19,111	3	0	0	0	3	237	38	177	22	0
Coastal Carolina University	8,360	6	0	2	1	3	334	68	260	6	1
College of Charleston	11,772	5	0	2	0	3	108	4	103	1	0
Erskine College	874	0	0	0	0	0	1	0	1	0	0
Francis Marion University	3,957	4	0	0	0	4	43	1	42	0	0
Greenville Technical College	15,089	2	0	0	0	2	104	18	85	1	0
Lander University	2,838	5	0	1	0	4	35	2	33	0	0
Medical University of South Carolina	2,513	2	0	0	0	2	158	0	157	1	0
Midlands Technical College	11,890	1	0	0	1	0	16	2	13	1	0
South Carolina State University	4,538	18	0	1	11	6	229	101	122	6	0
Spartanburg Methodist College	808	0	0	0	0	0	2	0	2	0	0
The Citadel	3,339	0	0	0	0	0	27	3	24	0	0
University of South Carolina											
Aiken	3,269	1	0	0	0	1	20	0	18	2	0
Columbia	28,482	13	0	0	2	11	422	64	332	26	0
Upstate	5,403	2	0	0	0	2	37	1	36	0	0
Winthrop University	6,241	0	0	0	0	0	61	3	56	2	0
SOUTH DAKOTA											
South Dakota State University	12,376	2	0	2	0	0	58	4	54	0	0
TENNESSEE											
Austin Peay State University	10,188	1	0	1	0	0	98	7	91	0	0
Christian Brothers University	1,926	0	0	0	0	0	19	3	16	0	1
East Tennessee State University	14,421	8	0	0	3	5	143	22	118	3	1
Middle Tennessee State University	25,188	12	0	2	1	9	325	71	245	9	0
Northeast State Community College	6,270	0	0	0	0	0	18	1	17	0	0
Southwest Tennessee Community College	13,016	2	0	0	1	1	39	0	39	0	0
Tennessee State University	8,824	17	0	2	8	7	151	4	142	5	2
Tennessee Technological University	10,847	5	0	1	1	3	89	25	64	0	0
University of Memphis	21,424	6	0	0	4	2	181	44	134	3	0

Note: Caution should be exercised in making any intercampus comparisons or ranking schools because university/college crime statistics are affected by a variety of factors. These include demographic characteristics of the surrounding community, ratio of male to female students, number of on-campus residents, accessibility of the campus to outside visitors, size of enrollment, and so on.

[1] The student enrollment figures provided by the United States Department of Education are for the 2009 school year, the most recent available. The enrollment figures include full-time and part-time students.

[2] The FBI does not publish arson data unless it receives data from either the agency or the state for all 12 months of the calendar year.

Table 9.   Offenses Known to Law Enforcement, by State and University and College, 2010—*Continued*

(Number)

State and University/College	Student enroll-ment[1]	Violent crime	Murder and non-negligent man-slaughter	Forcible rape	Robbery	Aggra-vated assault	Property crime	Burglary	Larceny-theft	Motor vehicle theft	Arson[2]
TENNESSEE—*Continued*											
University of Tennessee											
Chattanooga	10,526	3	0	1	1	1	160	19	137	4	0
Health Science Center[3]		1	0	0	1	0	78	9	65	4	0
Knoxville	29,934	4	0	1	1	2	512	17	490	5	2
Martin	8,163	0	0	0	0	0	53	9	43	1	0
Vanderbilt University	12,506	10	0	1	1	8	558	33	523	2	1
Volunteer State Community College	8,430	0	0	0	0	0	40	1	39	0	0
Walters State Community College	6,853	0	0	0	0	0	11	0	11	0	0
TEXAS											
Abilene Christian University	4,813	1	0	0	0	1	125	5	116	4	0
Alamo Community College District[3]		30	0	0	10	20	387	6	367	14	0
Alvin Community College	5,240	1	0	1	0	0	14	0	14	0	0
Amarillo College	11,289	2	0	0	2	0	45	3	42	0	0
Angelo State University	6,387	2	0	1	0	1	75	4	71	0	0
Austin College	1,364	0	0	0	0	0	27	3	24	0	0
Baylor Health Care System[3]		2	0	0	0	2	437	5	429	3	0
Baylor University, Waco	14,614	11	0	0	2	9	159	12	144	3	0
Blinn College	17,173	4	0	1	1	2	111	24	86	1	0
Brookhaven College	11,814	0	0	0	0	0	41	2	38	1	0
Central Texas College	24,133	1	0	0	0	1	23	0	23	0	0
College of the Mainland	3,916	4	0	0	0	4	30	0	28	2	0
Eastfield College	11,944	1	0	0	1	0	45	8	31	6	0
El Paso Community College	28,168	3	0	0	0	3	151	3	133	15	0
Grayson County College	4,856	1	0	0	0	1	19	4	15	0	0
Hardin-Simmons University	2,305	0	0	0	0	0	22	5	17	0	0
Houston Baptist University	2,710	0	0	0	0	0	31	16	15	0	0
Houston Community College	54,942	7	0	0	5	2	378	52	315	11	3
Lamar University, Beaumont	13,992	3	0	1	1	1	125	9	115	1	0
Laredo Community College	9,361	0	0	0	0	0	18	1	15	2	0
McLennan Community College	9,128	0	0	0	0	0	19	0	19	0	0
Midwestern State University	6,341	1	0	0	1	0	87	11	76	0	0
Mountain View College	8,203	0	0	0	0	0	61	7	45	9	0
North Lake College	11,644	1	0	0	1	0	22	0	21	1	0
Paris Junior College	5,580	3	0	3	0	0	19	4	13	2	0
Prairie View A&M University	8,608	12	0	5	1	6	157	57	93	7	1
Rice University	5,576	2	0	0	0	2	252	30	218	4	0
Richland College	18,201	2	0	0	0	2	93	1	89	3	1
Southern Methodist University	10,891	0	0	0	0	0	226	40	184	2	0
South Plains College	10,011	1	0	0	0	1	16	7	9	0	0
Southwestern University	1,301	0	0	0	0	0	24	8	15	1	0
Stephen F. Austin State University	12,845	1	0	1	0	0	270	54	213	3	1
St. Mary's University	3,893	2	0	0	1	1	75	8	66	1	0
Sul Ross State University	3,047	1	0	1	0	0	25	7	18	0	2
Tarleton State University	10,424	2	0	1	0	1	53	9	44	0	0
Texas A&M International University	6,419	4	0	1	0	3	52	7	42	3	1
Texas A&M University											
College Station	48,702	3	0	0	0	3	556	16	532	8	1
Commerce	9,021	4	0	1	0	3	85	21	64	0	0
Corpus Christi	9,468	0	0	0	0	0	67	4	63	0	0
Galveston	1,774	1	0	1	0	0	20	3	17	0	0
Kingsville	8,194	4	0	1	0	3	154	43	111	0	6
Texas Christian University	8,853	2	0	1	0	1	215	3	211	1	0
Texas Southern University	9,394	18	0	0	12	6	294	83	207	4	1
Texas State Technical College											
Harlingen	5,988	1	0	0	0	1	27	1	25	1	0
Marshall	963	0	0	0	0	0	14	9	5	0	0
Waco	6,816	7	0	3	0	4	101	31	69	1	0
Texas State University, San Marcos	30,803	7	0	0	2	5	336	41	292	3	1
Texas Tech University, Lubbock	30,049	8	0	2	1	5	360	24	333	3	1
Texas Woman's University	13,338	1	0	1	0	0	40	4	35	1	0
Trinity University	2,693	2	0	1	1	0	78	13	57	8	1
Tyler Junior College	11,045	2	0	1	0	1	114	6	106	2	0
University of Houston											
Central Campus	37,000	19	0	2	10	7	455	23	417	15	0
Clearlake	7,643	0	0	0	0	0	14	0	14	0	0
Downtown Campus	12,742	2	0	0	2	0	62	0	57	5	0
University of Mary Hardin-Baylor	2,689	2	0	2	0	0	40	12	27	1	0

Note: Caution should be exercised in making any intercampus comparisons or ranking schools because university/college crime statistics are affected by a variety of factors. These include demographic characteristics of the surrounding community, ratio of male to female students, number of on-campus residents, accessibility of the campus to outside visitors, size of enrollment, and so on.

[1] The student enrollment figures provided by the United States Department of Education are for the 2009 school year, the most recent available. The enrollment figures include full-time and part-time students.

[2] The FBI does not publish arson data unless it receives data from either the agency or the state for all 12 months of the calendar year.

[3] Student enrollment figures were not available.

Table 9. Offenses Known to Law Enforcement, by State and University and College, 2010—*Continued*

(Number)

State and University/College	Student enroll-ment[1]	Violent crime	Murder and non-negligent man-slaughter	Forcible rape	Robbery	Aggra-vated assault	Property crime	Burglary	Larceny-theft	Motor vehicle theft	Arson[2]
TEXAS —*Continued*											
University of North Texas											
Denton	35,003	3	0	0	0	3	217	35	176	6	0
Health Science Center	1,395	0	0	0	0	0	19	2	17	0	0
University of Texas											
Arlington	28,085	10	0	2	6	2	264	27	229	8	0
Austin	50,995	4	0	1	1	2	591	38	543	10	1
Brownsville	17,151	1	0	0	0	1	65	0	62	3	0
Dallas	15,783	5	0	0	1	4	119	11	105	3	0
El Paso	21,011	20	0	0	3	17	240	72	162	6	0
Health Science Center, San Antonio	3,223	0	0	0	0	0	87	0	87	0	0
Health Science Center, Tyler[3]		1	0	0	0	1	18	0	18	0	0
Houston[3]		5	0	0	0	5	302	12	289	1	0
Medical Branch	2,430	2	0	0	0	2	118	3	112	3	0
Pan American	18,337	1	0	0	0	1	130	13	117	0	0
Permian Basin	3,546	0	0	0	0	0	43	11	29	3	0
San Antonio	28,955	1	0	1	0	0	187	3	182	2	0
Southwestern Medical School	2,459	4	0	0	2	2	196	5	178	13	0
Tyler	6,201	2	0	1	0	1	35	2	33	0	0
West Texas A&M University	7,634	2	0	2	0	0	42	7	35	0	0
UTAH											
Brigham Young University	34,130	2	0	0	0	2	270	19	250	1	1
College of Eastern Utah	2,419	0	0	0	0	0	9	0	9	0	0
Southern Utah University	8,066	1	0	0	0	1	37	7	30	0	0
University of Utah	29,284	8	0	0	1	7	613	37	556	20	0
Utah State University	15,612	2	0	1	0	1	85	3	82	0	0
Utah Valley University	28,765	1	0	0	0	1	101	5	95	1	0
Weber State University	23,001	1	0	0	0	1	57	7	50	0	0
VERMONT											
University of Vermont	13,391	6	0	3	1	2	199	28	171	0	0
VIRGINIA											
Christopher Newport University	4,952	1	0	0	0	1	125	5	119	1	0
College of William and Mary	7,874	3	0	2	0	1	224	23	199	2	1
Emory and Henry College	1,002	0	0	0	0	0	6	2	4	0	0
Ferrum College	1,425	2	0	2	0	0	41	9	31	1	0
George Mason University	32,067	4	0	2	1	1	217	14	197	6	1
Hampton University	5,402	5	0	0	2	3	71	31	40	0	0
James Madison University	18,971	3	0	2	0	1	179	19	159	1	1
J. Sargeant Reynolds Community College	12,729	0	0	0	0	0	35	0	35	0	0
Longwood University	4,832	2	0	0	0	2	51	4	47	0	0
Norfolk State University	6,993	6	0	0	6	0	241	58	173	10	1
Northern Virginia Community College	46,619	1	0	0	0	1	228	0	227	1	0
Radford University	8,878	5	0	4	0	1	84	10	74	0	1
Richard Bland College	1,579	0	0	0	0	0	14	1	13	0	0
University of Mary Washington	5,381	0	0	0	0	0	84	0	84	0	1
University of Richmond	4,344	5	0	3	1	1	149	28	117	4	3
University of Virginia	24,355	6	0	0	5	1	317	62	250	5	0
University of Virginia's College at Wise	2,015	0	0	0	0	0	1	0	1	0	0
Virginia Commonwealth University	32,172	14	0	0	6	8	644	5	634	5	1
Virginia Polytechnic Institute and State University	30,870	4	0	0	0	4	284	43	235	6	2
Virginia State University	5,366	9	0	1	4	4	125	0	121	4	0
Virginia Western Community College	8,927	0	0	0	0	0	13	0	13	0	0
WASHINGTON											
Central Washington University	11,357	3	0	3	0	0	179	15	161	3	1
Eastern Washington University	11,300	2	0	0	1	1	102	18	84	0	0
Evergreen State College	4,891	0	0	0	0	0	92	16	76	0	0
University of Washington	45,943	5	0	0	2	3	587	98	480	9	4
Washington State University											
Pullman	26,101	12	0	5	3	4	162	24	133	5	1
Vancouver[3]		0	0	0	0	0	16	0	14	2	0
Western Washington University	14,575	2	0	0	0	2	138	14	124	0	0
WEST VIRGINIA											
Concord University	2,882	2	0	1	0	1	12	7	5	0	0
Fairmont State University	4,574	0	0	0	0	0	20	1	19	0	0
Marshall University	13,776	3	0	1	2	0	129	2	126	1	0
Potomac State College	1,810	5	0	0	0	5	9	2	7	0	0
West Virginia University	28,898	40	0	3	3	34	161	4	154	3	3

Note: Caution should be exercised in making any intercampus comparisons or ranking schools because university/college crime statistics are affected by a variety of factors. These include demographic characteristics of the surrounding community, ratio of male to female students, number of on-campus residents, accessibility of the campus to outside visitors, size of enrollment, and so on.

[1] The student enrollment figures provided by the United States Department of Education are for the 2009 school year, the most recent available. The enrollment figures include full-time and part-time students.

[2] The FBI does not publish arson data unless it receives data from either the agency or the state for all 12 months of the calendar year.

[3] Student enrollment figures were not available.

Table 9.   Offenses Known to Law Enforcement, by State and University and College, 2010—*Continued*

(Number)

State and University/College	Student enroll-ment[1]	Violent crime	Murder and non-negligent man-slaughter	Forcible rape	Robbery	Aggra-vated assault	Property crime	Burglary	Larceny-theft	Motor vehicle theft	Arson[2]
WISCONSIN											
University of Wisconsin											
Eau Claire	11,216	0	0	0	0	0	77	2	75	0	0
Green Bay	6,638	2	0	1	0	1	25	1	24	0	
La Crosse	10,009	3	0	2	0	1	48	1	47	0	
Madison	41,654	8	0	5	3	0	438	56	374	8	
Milwaukee	30,418	2	0	1	0	1	269	13	255	1	0
Oshkosh	13,192	4	0	1	2	1	72	0	70	2	0
Parkside	5,303	0	0	0	0	0	65	2	63	0	0
Platteville	7,803	8	0	3	0	5	80	5	75	0	1
Stevens Point	9,209	0	0	0	0	0	80	10	70	0	0
Stout	9,017	3	0	0	0	3	98	20	78	0	0
Superior	2,794	0	0	0	0	0	34	1	33	0	0
Whitewater	11,139	3	0	1	1	1	127	12	114	1	0
WYOMING											
Sheridan College	3,899	0	0	0	0	0	7	0	7	0	0
University of Wyoming	12,427	0	0	0	0	0	219	9	210	0	0

Note: Caution should be exercised in making any intercampus comparisons or ranking schools because university/college crime statistics are affected by a variety of factors. These include demographic characteristics of the surrounding community, ratio of male to female students, number of on-campus residents, accessibility of the campus to outside visitors, size of enrollment, and so on.

[1] The student enrollment figures provided by the United States Department of Education are for the 2009 school year, the most recent available. The enrollment figures include full-time and part-time students.

[2] The FBI does not publish arson data unless it receives data from either the agency or the state for all 12 months of the calendar year.

Table 10. Offenses Known to Law Enforcement, by State Metropolitan and Nonmetropolitan Counties, 2010

(Number)

State/County	Violent crime	Murder and non-negligent man-slaughter	Forcible rape	Robbery	Aggravated assault	Property crime	Burglary	Larceny-theft	Motor vehicle theft	Arson[1]
ALABAMA—Metropolitan Counties										
Autauga	57	0	5	2	50	282	18	231	33	
Bibb	19	0	2	4	13	154	67	79	8	
Calhoun	38	0	8	7	23	813	286	525	2	
Etowah	62	1	4	0	57	485	73	383	29	
Geneva	51	1	8	2	40	265	13	229	23	
Hale	21	0	3	1	17	160	68	83	9	
Henry	31	2	3	2	24	111	40	54	17	
Houston	66	0	16	10	40	642	251	374	17	
Jefferson	349	5	51	109	184	5,857	2,345	3,073	439	36
Limestone	37	2	6	5	24	569	181	342	46	
Madison	308	7	17	55	229	2,420	839	1,421	160	9
Mobile	250	5	28	30	187	2,190	770	1,223	197	
Morgan	40	0	6	7	27	406	257	145	4	
Russell	110	0	5	3	102	429	167	221	41	
Shelby	222	1	19	14	188	1,291	323	862	106	
St. Clair	13	1	2	0	10	309	186	113	10	
Tuscaloosa	190	2	13	21	154	1,753	611	1,000	142	
Walker[2]	3	0	0	0	3		78		54	
ALABAMA—Nonmetropolitan Counties										
Barbour[3]	1	0	0	0	1				1	
Butler[2]	28	1	3	0	24			107	14	
Choctaw	4	0	0	0	4	13	8	5	0	
Clarke	63	7	5	2	49	43	26	9	8	
Clay	4	0	0	0	4	5	1	4	0	
Cleburne	24	0	9	1	14	189	78	94	17	
Coffee	21	0	2	0	19	148	57	76	15	
Conecuh	32	0	5	2	25	120	25	87	8	
Covington	36	0	4	0	32	215	87	122	6	
Crenshaw[2]	34	0	2	0	32			120	14	
Cullman	95	3	14	6	72	1,216	350	824	42	
Dale	29	0	9	0	20	148	10	127	11	
Dallas	72	0	5	6	61	454	143	276	35	
Escambia	27	1	4	1	21	183	51	128	4	
Fayette[3]	7	0	0	0	7			57	17	
Franklin	34	0	1	2	31	170	54	105	11	
Jackson[2]	38	0	4	1	33				20	
Lamar	1	0	0	0	1	2	2	0	0	
Macon	19	0	1	3	15	6	2	2	2	
Marengo	17	0	2	2	13	163	62	88	13	
Monroe	29	1	0	0	28	90	41	46	3	
Pickens	15	0	5	0	10	47	26	20	1	
Pike	14	1	2	0	11	99	35	53	11	
Randolph[2]	41	0	1	0	40			222	17	
Talladega	43	0	1	9	33	838	267	513	58	
Tallapoosa[2]	6	1	0	0	5			202	10	
Wilcox	3	0	0	0	3	44	9	31	4	
Winston	26	0	4	1	21	200	54	138	8	
ARIZONA—Metropolitan Counties										
Coconino	83	1	14	4	64	530	189	323	18	6
Maricopa	989	26	47	68	848	5,117	1,463	3,148	506	112
Mohave	135	4	7	14	110	2,140	772	1,212	156	8
Pima	644	27	56	168	393	11,752	2,363	8,469	920	120
Pinal	200	13	47	27	113	3,777	787	2,570	420	21
Yavapai	277	6	17	2	252	1,382	471	807	104	9
Yuma	80	5	5	6	64	879	401	403	75	5
ARIZONA—Nonmetropolitan Counties										
Cochise	404	7	8	17	372	903	382	427	94	17
Gila	45	0	5	0	40	321	43	245	33	0
La Paz	65	0	0	3	62	356	100	226	30	1
Navajo	60	1	3	4	52	749	473	206	70	5
ARKANSAS—Metropolitan Counties										
Benton	160	0	29	3	128	531	278	236	17	11
Cleveland	6	0	1	1	4	108	61	41	6	1
Craighead	35	2	5	0	28	287	101	170	16	8
Crawford	143	0	7	5	131	534	167	340	27	0
Crittenden	179	1	5	7	166	470	141	309	20	13
Faulkner	58	2	10	2	44	757	219	470	68	13
Franklin	17	0	1	0	16	190	66	112	12	2
Grant	15	2	2	0	11	229	76	136	17	4
Jefferson	75	2	12	3	58	422	190	182	50	10
Lincoln	5	0	0	0	5	79	56	22	1	2
Lonoke	138	0	11	3	124	664	306	299	59	8

[1] The FBI does not publish arson data unless it receives data from either the agency or the state for all 12 months of the calendar year.

[2] The FBI determined that the agency's data were overreported. Consequently, affected data are not included in this table.

[3] The FBI determined that the agency's data were underreported. Consequently, affected data are not included in this table.

Table 10.   Offenses Known to Law Enforcement, by State Metropolitan and Nonmetropolitan Counties, 2010—*Continued*

(Number)

State/County	Violent crime	Murder and non-negligent man-slaughter	Forcible rape	Robbery	Aggravated assault	Property crime	Burglary	Larceny-theft	Motor vehicle theft	Arson[1]
Madison	47	0	7	1	39	89	51	33	5	0
Perry	22	0	4	0	18	57	57	0	0	3
Poinsett	72	0	3	0	69	73	57	11	5	3
Pulaski	348	0	21	35	292	1,849	780	908	161	13
Sebastian	65	1	6	3	55	362	159	188	15	5
Washington	168	0	16	2	150	515	181	292	42	2
ARKANSAS—Nonmetropolitan Counties										
Arkansas	11	1	1	3	6	102	35	43	24	2
Ashley	32	2	1	2	27	226	92	122	12	0
Baxter	31	4	6	0	21	529	94	408	27	2
Carroll	39	0	0	0	39	225	66	132	27	2
Chicot	2	0	0	0	2	97	37	58	2	1
Clark	29	0	8	2	19	187	86	90	11	0
Cleburne	39	0	8	1	30	413	201	185	27	2
Columbia	58	1	0	2	55	173	54	113	6	3
Conway	36	0	8	2	26	342	107	204	31	13
Cross	38	0	3	0	35	56	20	36	0	0
Dallas	2	0	0	0	2	31	12	19	0	1
Drew	32	0	5	0	27	106	47	49	10	2
Fulton	27	0	2	0	25	79	35	42	2	2
Greene	7	0	1	2	4	185	48	126	11	3
Howard	13	0	1	0	12	46	28	18	0	0
Independence	210	1	22	9	178	1,414	546	774	94	21
Izard	7	1	1	0	5	124	60	64	0	4
Jackson	30	0	0	1	29	176	42	108	26	2
Johnson	36	1	3	0	32	173	130	43	0	16
Lawrence	19	0	2	0	17	184	78	106	0	1
Little River	12	0	0	0	12	72	20	46	6	4
Logan	23	0	1	2	20	248	84	151	13	2
Marion	26	0	1	1	24	147	64	77	6	4
Mississippi	29	1	9	1	18	389	106	246	37	0
Monroe	5	0	1	1	3	78	38	40	0	1
Montgomery	3	0	2	0	1	19	9	6	4	0
Nevada	5	0	1	0	4	42	21	18	3	0
Newton	7	1	2	0	4	104	41	62	1	2
Pike	4	0	1	0	3	44	19	17	8	0
Polk	50	0	4	0	46	232	114	112	6	5
Pope	38	0	4	1	33	340	145	166	29	3
Randolph	2	0	2	0	0	45	43	0	2	1
Scott	6	0	3	0	3	85	35	41	9	2
Searcy	8	0	1	1	6	30	14	14	2	1
Sevier	14	0	2	1	11	178	55	113	10	2
St. Francis	31	1	5	7	18	408	169	239	0	8
Stone	21	0	2	0	19	109	55	52	2	1
Union	46	1	3	6	36	370	91	252	27	0
Van Buren	53	0	1	0	52	226	49	150	27	6
White	70	4	11	0	55	775	312	369	94	7
Yell	6	0	1	0	5	16	13	3	0	2
CALIFORNIA—Metropolitan Counties										
Alameda	698	8	18	235	437	2,212	622	1,041	549	34
Butte	133	4	18	24	87	1,296	564	721	11	43
Contra Costa	449	12	28	119	290	2,754	1,011	1,729	14	23
El Dorado	256	3	15	34	204	1,990	864	1,114	12	7
Fresno	727	10	33	116	568	4,442	1,466	2,230	746	229
Imperial	265	2	9	13	241	600	283	295	22	10
Kern	1,977	34	95	463	1,385	10,246	3,368	5,152	1,726	297
Kings	140	1	9	12	118	594	243	306	45	10
Los Angeles	6,497	86	208	1,770	4,433	17,310	5,046	8,174	4,090	243
Madera	233	2	22	24	185	1,357	585	755	17	2
Marin	115	1	6	28	80	813	239	573	1	1
Merced	484	12	22	49	401	2,026	778	1,227	21	7
Monterey	228	11	19	51	147	1,316	567	735	14	15
Napa	56	0	3	2	51	379	157	219	3	0
Orange	187	0	8	32	147	1,275	255	910	110	7
Placer	298	0	24	30	244	1,950	645	1,275	30	8
Riverside	1,018	21	50	247	700	10,310	2,892	5,776	1,642	24
Sacramento	2,902	39	155	1,131	1,577	14,506	5,038	9,309	159	124
San Benito	53	0	4	5	44	336	134	197	5	0
San Bernardino	1,093	16	61	145	871	5,580	1,942	2,574	1,064	62
San Diego	1,432	13	87	278	1,054	5,985	1,755	3,106	1,124	38
San Joaquin	738	8	17	168	545	4,418	1,656	2,664	98	24

[1] The FBI does not publish arson data unless it receives data from either the agency or the state for all 12 months of the calendar year.

Table 10.   Offenses Known to Law Enforcement, by State Metropolitan and Nonmetropolitan Counties, 2010—*Continued*

(Number)

State/County	Violent crime	Murder and non-negligent man-slaughter	Forcible rape	Robbery	Aggravated assault	Property crime	Burglary	Larceny-theft	Motor vehicle theft	Arson[1]
San Luis Obispo	241	6	18	18	199	1,295	437	853	5	5
San Mateo	224	2	18	53	151	1,770	229	1,332	209	6
Santa Barbara	285	3	34	27	221	1,481	564	912	5	5
Santa Clara	254	1	28	24	201	1,762	438	1,113	211	2
Santa Cruz	301	7	18	36	240	2,232	812	1,419	1	20
Shasta	582	1	54	23	504	1,058	568	466	24	10
Sonoma	587	0	37	49	501	1,388	547	821	20	9
Stanislaus	414	11	33	106	264	3,002	1,320	1,421	261	152
Sutter	143	3	8	12	120	661	203	413	45	1
Tulare[4]	521	15	32	91	383		1,128	2,124		30
Ventura	192	1	18	31	142	1,323	349	894	80	20
Yolo	62	1	7	6	48	364	105	244	15	3
Yuba	159	1	14	28	116	1,031	390	634	7	14
CALIFORNIA—Nonmetropolitan Counties										
Alpine	10	0	3	0	7	73	15	58	0	0
Amador	60	1	9	6	44	485	180	301	4	0
Calaveras	82	1	10	12	59	654	282	361	11	2
Colusa	22	0	3	5	14	257	81	167	9	5
Del Norte	82	3	19	12	48	377	218	157	2	5
Glenn	16	1	0	0	15	180	85	85	10	1
Humboldt	242	5	33	33	171	1,208	450	732	26	15
Inyo	47	0	2	1	44	139	62	74	3	7
Lake	199	4	18	17	160	895	396	492	7	8
Lassen	36	0	2	1	33	129	47	78	4	4
Mariposa	37	0	5	2	30	294	124	170	0	1
Mendocino	310	3	24	19	264	551	260	286	5	12
Modoc	12	0	4	0	8	60	37	23	0	2
Mono	13	0	3	0	10	71	21	50	0	0
Nevada	137	1	17	4	115	578	250	324	4	3
Plumas	109	0	13	5	91	326	167	155	4	1
Sierra	19	0	0	0	19	44	10	34	0	0
Siskiyou	37	1	2	2	32	232	99	129	4	4
Tehama	181	1	3	11	166	278	165	112	1	2
Trinity	34	0	4	3	27	98	33	65	0	0
Tuolumne	97	1	21	15	60	757	325	422	10	5
COLORADO—Metropolitan Counties										
Adams	477	0	80	59	338	2,450	598	1,456	396	31
Arapahoe	204	2	19	31	152	1,403	420	861	122	16
Boulder	56	1	9	1	45	549	197	322	30	11
Clear Creek	21	0	1	0	20	80	15	58	7	2
Douglas	269	0	181	20	68	1,882	336	1,445	101	8
Gilpin	12	0	0	0	12	23	6	15	2	0
Jefferson[5]	183	1	31	21	130	2,572	501	1,929	142	17
Larimer	134	0	26	15	93	927	204	672	51	10
Mesa	163	0	25	15	123	1,243	264	905	74	14
Park	20	0	2	0	18	129	48	67	14	3
Pueblo	31	3	0	7	21	1,604	338	1,199	67	2
Teller	9	0	1	1	7	81	40	37	4	8
Weld	120	0	13	6	101	834	237	516	81	9
COLORADO—Nonmetropolitan Counties										
Alamosa	1	0	0	0	1	18	4	14	0	0
Baca	0	0	0	0	0	3	1	2	0	0
Bent	2	0	1	0	1	36	13	22	1	0
Chaffee	11	1	4	0	6	67	11	54	2	0
Cheyenne	0	0	0	0	0	3	0	3	0	0
Crowley	4	0	0	0	4	0	0	0	0	0
Delta	19	0	8	0	11	164	33	112	19	0
Dolores	0	0	0	0	0	28	15	10	3	0
Eagle	44	0	2	1	41	433	90	340	3	3
Fremont[6]		0	0	0		71	41	25	5	0
Grand	12	0	0	0	12	130	32	95	3	0
Gunnison	10	0	0	0	10	18	5	12	1	0
Kit Carson	2	0	1	0	1	29	8	17	4	1
Lake	2	1	0	0	1	20	7	12	1	1
Las Animas	0	0	0	0	0	0	0	0	0	0
Lincoln	2	0	0	0	2	2	0	1	1	0
Logan	10	1	1	0	8	65	16	42	7	1
Moffat	4	0	0	0	4	44	29	14	1	3
Montezuma	42	2	0	1	39	120	47	62	11	0
Montrose	21	2	3	1	15	157	43	104	10	1
Morgan	2	1	0	0	1	52	10	38	4	1
Otero	6	0	1	0	5	40	10	29	1	0

[1] The FBI does not publish arson data unless it receives data from either the agency or the state for all 12 months of the calendar year.

[4] The Tulare County Highway Patrol collects the motor vehicle thefts for this county. These data can be found in Table 11.

[5] Because of changes in the state/local agency's reporting practices, figures are not comparable to previous years' data.

[6] The FBI determined that the agency did not follow national Uniform Crime Reporting (UCR) Program guidelines for reporting an offense. Consequently, this figure is not included in this table.

Table 10. Offenses Known to Law Enforcement, by State Metropolitan and Nonmetropolitan Counties, 2010—*Continued*

(Number)

State/County	Violent crime	Murder and non-negligent man-slaughter	Forcible rape	Robbery	Aggravated assault	Property crime	Burglary	Larceny-theft	Motor vehicle theft	Arson[1]
Pitkin	7	0	0	0	7	56	12	40	4	0
Prowers	5	0	3	0	2	29	8	20	1	0
Rio Blanco	0	0	0	0	0	7	2	5	0	0
Routt	11	0	0	0	11	49	14	29	6	0
Saguache	12	0	0	0	12	26	11	14	1	0
San Miguel	3	0	0	0	3	19	2	15	2	0
Summit	12	0	4	1	7	289	23	245	21	1
Washington	5	0	2	0	3	79	15	59	5	1
DELAWARE—Metropolitan Counties										
New Castle County Police Department	1,251	7	63	352	829	6,625	2,052	4,044	529	7
FLORIDA—Metropolitan Counties										
Alachua	596	8	37	76	475	2,788	937	1,719	132	20
Baker	58	0	1	7	50	336	51	272	13	1
Bay	358	5	32	39	282	2,816	688	1,968	160	3
Brevard	926	4	72	125	725	5,348	1,311	3,816	221	20
Broward	292	1	13	92	186	956	234	665	57	7
Charlotte	353	1	22	45	285	3,822	977	2,735	110	9
Clay	710	9	52	99	550	3,918	793	2,991	134	39
Collier	977	10	50	195	722	4,947	1,090	3,675	182	17
Escambia	1,928	26	178	461	1,263	10,455	2,665	7,271	519	30
Flagler	173	0	15	29	129	1,952	489	1,399	64	2
Gadsden	294	3	7	15	269	742	336	370	36	0
Gilchrist	40	1	1	0	38	134	59	64	11	0
Hernando	592	9	55	82	446	4,479	1,247	3,077	155	15
Hillsborough	3,136	36	142	700	2,258	22,442	5,863	15,099	1,480	24
Indian River	313	0	17	55	241	2,953	818	2,030	105	7
Jefferson	126	0	5	4	117	171	94	62	15	3
Lake	595	7	35	24	529	2,813	794	1,837	182	8
Lee	1,347	17	84	387	859	9,358	3,218	5,540	600	59
Leon	273	2	23	38	210	1,363	427	835	101	7
Manatee	1,533	11	80	353	1,089	9,838	2,745	6,728	365	29
Marion	1,305	6	103	78	1,118	4,860	1,554	3,084	222	6
Martin	362	2	11	103	246	2,787	679	2,009	99	5
Miami-Dade	6,927	87	252	1,782	4,806	45,341	8,554	32,357	4,430	28
Nassau	163	0	4	9	150	1,137	382	705	50	4
Okaloosa	454	1	30	77	346	3,365	756	2,472	137	0
Orange	5,396	53	311	1,401	3,631	27,117	8,313	16,587	2,217	0
Osceola	885	6	15	101	763	5,814	2,123	3,427	264	1
Palm Beach	2,232	24	135	623	1,450	16,314	4,524	10,678	1,112	69
Pasco	1,292	8	76	321	887	12,773	3,673	8,504	596	71
Pinellas	1,119	11	124	227	757	7,609	1,847	5,416	346	26
Polk	1,308	12	82	202	1,012	10,070	3,377	6,159	534	0
Santa Rosa	222	6	33	17	166	1,598	508	1,024	66	7
Sarasota	697	3	39	140	515	7,714	2,182	5,249	283	10
Seminole	585	4	31	77	473	3,361	868	2,330	163	7
St. Johns	494	7	9	57	421	3,603	847	2,608	148	13
St. Lucie	257	6	28	42	181	1,743	570	1,087	86	2
Volusia	931	11	72	99	749	5,335	1,765	3,184	386	36
Wakulla	86	0	10	5	71	679	138	516	25	11
FLORIDA—Nonmetropolitan Counties										
Bradford	62	1	6	6	49	344	160	176	8	1
Calhoun	12	0	1	1	10	68	20	48	0	0
Citrus	452	7	26	49	370	3,203	884	2,191	128	25
Columbia	186	0	24	13	149	1,275	386	827	62	0
DeSoto	172	0	5	14	153	811	317	467	27	2
Dixie	69	1	10	4	54	524	226	270	28	3
Franklin	96	1	13	1	81	145	31	103	11	1
Glades	39	1	4	1	33	245	107	120	18	1
Gulf	34	1	0	0	33	125	44	77	4	0
Hamilton	52	1	4	9	38	211	73	129	9	2
Hardee	57	0	12	14	31	527	192	307	28	0
Hendry	212	3	8	35	166	1,130	656	435	39	14
Highlands	149	5	9	20	115	1,736	562	1,115	59	3
Holmes	56	1	6	1	48	203	66	120	17	0
Jackson	204	1	19	18	166	771	206	537	28	4
Lafayette	20	0	0	2	18	39	11	28	0	0
Levy	123	0	10	11	102	922	343	527	52	3
Liberty	16	0	0	0	16	56	18	32	6	0
Madison	123	1	5	9	108	306	125	163	18	1
Monroe	152	5	8	19	120	2,037	524	1,448	65	4
Okeechobee	193	2	14	26	151	976	490	460	26	1
Putnam	537	1	35	68	433	2,653	1,316	1,254	83	7
Sumter	144	3	23	9	109	654	221	398	35	1

[1] The FBI does not publish arson data unless it receives data from either the agency or the state for all 12 months of the calendar year.

Table 10. Offenses Known to Law Enforcement, by State Metropolitan and Nonmetropolitan Counties, 2010—*Continued*

(Number)

State/County	Violent crime	Murder and non-negligent man-slaughter	Forcible rape	Robbery	Aggravated assault	Property crime	Burglary	Larceny-theft	Motor vehicle theft	Arson[1]
Suwannee	118	4	4	6	104	553	201	306	46	5
Taylor	50	2	3	0	45	167	89	72	6	1
Union	55	0	2	1	52	142	73	66	3	0
Walton	158	2	9	8	139	1,145	374	702	69	4
Washington	9	3	0	0	6	241	97	132	12	0
GEORGIA—Metropolitan Counties										
Augusta-Richmond	1,084	36	127	648	273	14,303	4,222	8,530	1,551	63
Barrow	214	4	7	5	198	1,170	264	820	86	8
Bartow	224	1	23	34	166	2,470	740	1,515	215	0
Bibb	231	3	13	45	170	2,520	674	1,598	248	0
Brantley	32	0	4	4	24	284	194	90	0	
Brooks	43	0	0	0	43	302	113	153	36	6
Bryan	17	0	0	5	12	353	112	229	12	0
Burke	156	0	0	0	156	682	235	423	24	
Butts	36	1	8	5	22	550	126	376	48	3
Carroll	362	0	9	10	343	1,457	480	847	130	11
Catoosa	71	0	9	3	59	1,047	218	706	123	2
Chatham	0	0	0	0	0	0	0	0	0	0
Cherokee	133	1	12	26	94	2,010	525	1,367	118	5
Clarke	0	0	0	0	0	1	0	1	0	0
Clayton	0	0	0	0	0	0	0	0	0	0
Clayton County Police Department	1,031	12	74	434	511	9,418	4,266	3,849	1,303	33
Cobb	1	0	0	0	1	0	0	0	0	
Columbia	72	1	10	15	46	2,323	376	1,860	87	9
Coweta	91	1	19	14	57	1,436	497	845	94	6
Crawford	33	1	4	1	27	459	141	277	41	
Dade	37	1	4	0	32	200	49	124	27	0
Dawson	18	0	0	0	18	478	98	344	36	2
DeKalb	0	0	0	0	0	0	0	0	0	0
DeKalb County Police Department	3,469	80	155	1,927	1,307	29,924	9,612	15,739	4,573	114
Douglas	153	4	10	30	109	2,108	585	1,352	171	5
Echols	8	1	1	1	5	45	26	18	1	0
Effingham	57	1	29	9	18	297	201	66	30	2
Fayette	31	0	6	7	18	555	182	333	40	0
Floyd	34	0	0	1	33	24	14	10	0	
Floyd County Police Department	180	2	5	9	164	1,315	368	861	86	8
Forsyth	202	0	13	14	175	1,801	469	1,252	80	
Fulton	9	0	0	1	8	13	1	11	1	0
Fulton County Police Department	668	9	43	307	309	5,544	1,815	2,919	810	11
Glynn	0	0	0	0	0	0	0	0	0	0
Glynn County Police Department	253	2	12	61	178	3,033	750	2,199	84	2
Gwinnett County Police Department	1,675	20	176	726	753	16,909	5,370	10,082	1,457	85
Hall	187	3	19	45	120	2,603	774	1,602	227	15
Haralson	111	0	3	6	102	397	96	278	23	
Harris	8	0	2	2	4	407	16	380	11	
Heard	18	0	1	1	16	172	57	94	21	
Henry	18	0	0	0	18	123	1	119	3	
Henry County Police Department	286	6	27	96	157	4,051	1,255	2,416	380	17
Jasper	15	0	2	3	10	229	87	138	4	0
Jones	35	0	0	3	32	533	143	327	63	1
Lanier	8	0	4	0	4	99	23	72	4	0
Lee	14	1	0	2	11	528	168	322	38	0
Liberty	74	1	2	11	60	431	171	230	30	
Lowndes	37	0	4	9	24	941	279	591	71	
Madison	159	1	1	9	148	723	207	450	66	7
McDuffie	23	4	1	4	14	248	76	156	16	0
McIntosh	48	2	2	11	33	461	167	256	38	7
Meriwether	24	0	2	2	20	430	123	257	50	0
Murray	38	0	5	2	31	759	153	543	63	0
Muscogee	0	0	0	0	0	0	0	0	0	0
Newton	335	2	13	33	287	1,775	649	931	195	
Oconee	99	0	1	6	92	531	122	375	34	0
Oglethorpe	50	2	5	2	41	520	147	345	28	1
Paulding	152	0	16	12	124	2,418	617	1,616	185	18
Pickens	27	1	5	1	20	409	103	289	17	
Pike	8	2	2	1	3	109	35	69	5	0
Rockdale	325	5	13	34	273	2,223	591	1,458	174	6
Spalding	127	2	11	20	94	1,595	430	959	206	0
Terrell	21	0	2	0	19	105	31	61	13	0
Twiggs	12	0	0	1	11	166	54	95	17	
Walker	208	3	2	6	197	1,014	312	637	65	
Walton	112	1	7	7	97	1,007	258	664	85	0
Whitfield	180	5	23	9	143	1,729	479	1,133	117	10
Worth	2	1	0	1	0	191	56	108	27	1

[1] The FBI does not publish arson data unless it receives data from either the agency or the state for all 12 months of the calendar year.

Table 10. Offenses Known to Law Enforcement, by State Metropolitan and Nonmetropolitan Counties, 2010—*Continued*

(Number)

State/County	Violent crime	Murder and non-negligent man-slaughter	Forcible rape	Robbery	Aggravated assault	Property crime	Burglary	Larceny-theft	Motor vehicle theft	Arson[1]
GEORGIA—Nonmetropolitan Counties										
Baldwin	291	0	7	16	268	994	428	552	14	0
Banks	50	0	0	1	49	536	111	395	30	1
Ben Hill	15	0	5	0	10	223	58	147	18	0
Berrien	23	0	3	1	19	214	65	149	0	0
Bleckley	12	0	0	1	11	171	69	88	14	0
Bulloch	25	1	0	11	13	721	251	418	52	
Calhoun	4	0	0	0	4	46	21	16	9	
Camden	47	0	1	4	42	405	133	259	13	0
Candler	0	0	0	0	0	54	21	33	0	0
Charlton	9	0	1	0	8	105	40	53	12	0
Chattooga	24	0	3	0	21	213	60	143	10	0
Clinch	5	0	0	2	3	63	23	38	2	0
Coffee	46	0	6	9	31	703	207	451	45	3
Cook	21	0	0	0	21	180	51	118	11	0
Crisp	18	0	0	0	18	380	89	276	15	0
Decatur	28	0	2	2	24	263	72	181	10	6
Dodge	24	1	1	2	20	395	137	247	11	1
Dooly	16	0	0	1	15	72	22	50	0	0
Early	24	2	1	3	18	139	40	95	4	0
Elbert	43	0	4	4	35	690	218	449	23	0
Emanuel	7	1	0	0	6	397	235	130	32	0
Fannin	107	0	3	2	102	345	151	174	20	1
Franklin	8	0	3	1	4	381	141	211	29	
Gilmer	36	2	10	1	23	344	112	205	27	0
Gordon	159	2	3	11	143	737	229	505	3	0
Grady	14	1	1	2	10	196	87	97	12	0
Greene	23	1	1	4	17	212	57	150	5	0
Habersham	49	0	10	2	37	499	186	293	20	0
Hancock	1	0	0	1	0	56	22	32	2	
Hart	66	0	2	2	62	474	170	282	22	
Irwin	6	0	0	0	6	167	55	98	14	0
Jackson	31	3	5	5	18	915	258	605	52	
Jeff Davis	25	0	1	6	18	323	75	217	31	0
Jefferson	13	0	2	2	9	175	91	75	9	4
Johnson	37	0	0	0	37	82	41	34	7	
Laurens	39	0	2	14	23	775	186	502	87	3
Lumpkin	80	0	3	1	76	454	117	307	30	4
Macon	0	0	0	0	0	64	26	31	7	0
Miller	1	0	0	0	1	44	17	23	4	0
Mitchell	46	0	0	2	44	208	67	121	20	0
Morgan	13	0	0	0	13	160	47	84	29	1
Peach	20	1	2	2	15	309	109	158	42	0
Pierce[3]	0	0	0	0	0			96	3	0
Polk County Police Department	82	1	7	2	72	808	267	451	90	
Putnam	52	1	2	1	48	423	148	260	15	
Quitman	22	0	1	3	18	49	18	28	3	
Rabun	11	1	2	0	8	148	43	90	15	0
Schley	2	0	0	0	2	13	5	7	1	0
Seminole	13	0	1	0	12	76	30	41	5	2
Stephens	20	0	0	0	20	597	133	448	16	0
Sumter	29	0	4	2	23	297	94	178	25	0
Talbot	11	0	0	1	10	57	41	13	3	
Taliaferro	6	0	0	0	6	72	37	32	3	0
Tattnall	18	0	0	3	15	270	94	152	24	0
Taylor	2	0	0	1	1	71	20	40	11	
Telfair	10	0	0	1	9	80	33	41	6	
Thomas	39	2	7	10	20	570	233	295	42	10
Tift	137	1	5	28	103	817	262	504	51	
Toombs	20	0	3	0	17	275	95	144	36	3
Towns	7	0	0	0	7	122	55	62	5	1
Treutlen	4	1	0	0	3	76	33	38	5	
Troup	25	1	1	6	17	734	189	485	60	
Turner	7	0	0	1	6	86	16	65	5	0
Union	11	0	2	0	9	127	48	67	12	
Upson	18	0	0	2	16	433	151	271	11	0
Ware	36	0	11	4	21	672	167	465	40	
Washington	28	1	1	2	24	227	112	108	7	0
Wheeler	1	0	0	0	1	83	35	36	12	0
White	18	0	3	2	13	325	145	158	22	
Wilcox	4	0	2	0	2	66	25	37	4	0
Wilkes	4	0	0	0	4	17	5	10	2	0
Wilkinson	14	0	1	1	12	102	41	55	6	0

[1] The FBI does not publish arson data unless it receives data from either the agency or the state for all 12 months of the calendar year.

[3] The FBI determined that the agency's data were underreported. Consequently, affected data are not included in this table.

Table 10.   Offenses Known to Law Enforcement, by State Metropolitan and Nonmetropolitan Counties, 2010—*Continued*

(Number)

State/County	Violent crime	Murder and non-negligent man-slaughter	Forcible rape	Robbery	Aggravated assault	Property crime	Burglary	Larceny-theft	Motor vehicle theft	Arson[1]
HAWAII—Nonmetropolitan Counties										
Hawaii Police Department[5]	514	3	85	79	347	5,255	1,141	3,627	487	21
Kauai Police Department	246	2	40	18	186	2,476	714	1,652	110	10
IDAHO—Metropolitan Counties										
Ada	119	1	16	4	98	968	246	691	31	10
Bonneville	88	0	9	1	78	801	213	551	37	5
Canyon	61	1	9	1	50	598	226	335	37	2
Franklin	9	0	1	0	8	29	6	21	2	0
Gem	13	0	0	0	13	40	20	19	1	0
Jefferson	13	0	1	0	12	84	27	50	7	1
Kootenai	97	2	13	4	78	1,122	331	744	47	9
Nez Perce	10	0	2	0	8	119	25	89	5	0
Owyhee	13	0	4	0	9	132	26	96	10	1
Power	2	0	2	0	0	45	5	38	2	1
IDAHO—Nonmetropolitan Counties										
Adams	8	0	0	0	8	52	5	44	3	0
Bear Lake	1	0	0	0	1	39	6	31	2	0
Benewah	4	0	0	0	4	32	10	18	4	0
Bingham	32	0	12	2	18	271	80	174	17	1
Blaine	4	0	0	0	4	23	10	13	0	2
Bonner	37	1	5	1	30	434	150	238	46	4
Boundary	7	0	0	1	6	85	29	50	6	0
Butte	7	0	1	1	5	2	1	1	0	0
Camas	0	0	0	0	0	10	6	4	0	0
Caribou	2	0	1	0	1	13	8	5	0	0
Clearwater	16	0	0	0	16	97	17	76	4	0
Elmore	18	0	3	0	15	48	12	31	5	0
Fremont	4	0	0	0	4	66	3	58	5	0
Gooding	11	0	2	0	9	46	10	31	5	0
Idaho	8	0	2	0	6	91	19	65	7	1
Jerome	3	0	0	0	3	70	18	45	7	0
Latah	23	0	6	0	17	157	72	76	9	2
Lemhi	5	0	1	0	4	37	8	25	4	1
Lewis	5	0	0	0	5	36	13	22	1	1
Lincoln	5	0	1	0	4	13	3	8	2	0
Madison	9	0	6	0	3	74	24	49	1	0
Minidoka	3	0	1	0	2	145	45	91	9	0
Oneida	4	0	0	0	4	25	9	15	1	0
Payette	23	0	4	1	18	102	36	60	6	0
Shoshone	34	0	9	0	25	160	50	102	8	0
Teton	1	0	1	0	0	78	14	62	2	2
Twin Falls	35	0	3	1	31	205	78	104	23	6
Valley	16	0	6	0	10	73	22	47	4	2
Washington	2	0	0	0	2	16	9	7	0	0
ILLINOIS—Metropolitan Counties[5]										
Bond	6	0	0	0	6	142	46	91	5	0
Boone	21	0	5	0	16	295	72	211	12	137
Champaign	148	4	24	5	115	531	157	350	24	13
Clinton	9	0	5	0	4	162	19	141	2	0
De Kalb	33	0	8	1	24	268	58	199	11	2
Du Page	79	0	11	13	55	1,334	296	1,006	32	0
Grundy	2	0	0	0	2	210	58	148	4	3
Henry	0	0	0	0	0	79	19	56	4	0
Jersey	28	0	9	1	18	137	31	105	1	0
Kendall	63	1	9	3	50	399	109	283	7	7
Lake	83	2	13	10	58	1,714	459	1,178	77	15
Macon	66	0	9	0	57	432	147	273	12	1
Macoupin	10	0	3	0	7	245	75	167	3	2
Madison	90	1	8	5	76	1,108	316	766	26	4
Marshall	0	0	0	0	0	45	17	26	2	0
McLean	42	0	15	4	23	206	67	122	17	3
Mercer	26	0	8	0	18	152	57	88	7	0
Peoria	180	2	40	19	119	743	180	522	41	12
Piatt	22	0	6	0	16	121	33	85	3	1
Rock Island	51	0	11	4	36	313	95	209	9	1
Sangamon	170	1	29	19	121	944	406	499	39	14
Stark	11	0	2	0	9	72	18	50	4	3
St. Clair	85	1	23	15	46	1,050	281	679	90	17
Tazewell	1	0	0	0	1	243	85	142	16	1
Vermilion	69	0	13	4	52	487	168	304	15	0
Winnebago	120	1	22	16	81	1,200	399	735	66	3
Woodford	4	0	0	1	3	141	33	101	7	0

[1] The FBI does not publish arson data unless it receives data from either the agency or the state for all 12 months of the calendar year.

[5] Because of changes in the state/local agency's reporting practices, figures are not comparable to previous years' data.

Table 10. Offenses Known to Law Enforcement, by State Metropolitan and Nonmetropolitan Counties, 2010—*Continued*

(Number)

State/County	Violent crime	Murder and non-negligent man-slaughter	Forcible rape	Robbery	Aggravated assault	Property crime	Burglary	Larceny-theft	Motor vehicle theft	Arson[1]
ILLINOIS—Nonmetropolitan Counties[5]										
Adams	22	0	3	0	19	223	63	151	9	0
Bureau	15	0	0	0	15	221	61	157	3	1
Cass	2	0	0	0	2	64	27	36	1	0
Christian	72	0	0	0	72	148	28	113	7	3
Clark	3	0	0	0	3	72	33	37	2	2
Clay	4	0	0	0	4	64	20	43	1	8
Coles	5	0	0	0	5	105	24	77	4	1
Crawford	1	0	0	0	1	59	23	33	3	0
Douglas	13	0	0	0	13	28	3	24	1	0
Edgar	26	0	5	0	21	65	29	32	4	0
Effingham	9	0	0	0	9	166	54	99	13	2
Franklin	12	0	0	1	11	283	102	172	9	4
Fulton	8	0	0	0	8	133	34	89	10	0
Gallatin	3	0	0	0	3	66	19	46	1	0
Iroquois	5	0	0	0	5	150	75	73	2	0
Jackson	47	0	11	5	31	336	162	161	13	3
Jefferson	52	0	4	2	46	339	130	177	32	7
Johnson	23	0	1	0	22	105	28	67	10	1
La Salle	32	0	15	1	16	400	130	258	12	10
Lawrence	15	0	0	0	15	24	14	9	1	0
Livingston	15	0	6	2	7	278	54	215	9	47
Marion	18	0	8	1	9	277	93	165	19	0
Mason	20	0	5	0	15	132	31	99	2	2
Massac	9	0	0	0	9	146	49	92	5	1
McDonough	6	0	0	0	6	91	31	58	2	1
Montgomery	108	0	0	0	108	153	74	79	0	0
Morgan	10	1	2	0	7	112	42	66	4	3
Moultrie	8	0	2	1	5	54	13	41	0	0
Ogle	13	0	6	0	7	308	74	221	13	1
Perry	22	3	1	2	16	88	50	38	0	0
Pike	1	0	1	0	0	7	3	4	0	0
Pope	13	0	0	0	13	45	25	19	1	0
Pulaski	79	0	5	2	72	104	38	55	11	0
Putnam	4	0	3	0	1	48	13	35	0	0
Richland	6	0	1	1	4	91	32	52	7	0
Schuyler	5	0	0	0	5	10	2	8	0	0
Shelby	12	0	0	0	12	66	28	38	0	0
Stephenson	6	1	1	1	3	208	56	144	8	1
Union	15	0	2	0	13	107	18	82	7	0
Warren	11	0	0	0	11	89	31	56	2	0
Washington	37	0	0	0	37	66	27	38	1	0
White	6	0	0	0	6	168	53	113	2	3
Whiteside	22	0	11	0	11	233	81	144	8	0
Williamson	9	0	1	1	7	359	139	207	13	8
INDIANA—Metropolitan Counties										
Allen	65	2	14	10	39	872	187	635	50	0
Bartholomew	30	0	10	1	19	497	138	322	37	1
Boone	1	0	0	1	0	170	42	118	10	0
Brown	2	0	1	0	1	97	42	54	1	1
Carroll	12	0	3	0	9	174	63	98	13	
Clark	70	0	10	8	52	745	268	435	42	3
Delaware	19	0	6	1	12	490	113	316	61	0
Elkhart	42	1	9	23	9	1,646	533	987	126	13
Floyd	0	0	0	0	0	651	150	469	32	1
Franklin	1	0	0	0	1	126	80	41	5	3
Gibson	5	0	0	1	4	139	31	105	3	6
Greene	6	0	3	1	2	159	47	99	13	1
Hancock	11	0	3	3	5	286	78	192	16	0
Harrison	11	1	0	3	7	422	106	298	18	
Howard	37	0	4	3	30	453	208	230	15	0
Lake	32	1	3	15	13	1,023	176	773	74	0
La Porte	28	0	6	9	13	816	312	458	46	1
Madison	30	0	4	3	23	478	200	246	32	0
Monroe	60	3	12	6	39	1,025	349	613	63	3
Newton	14	0	2	0	12	206	77	117	12	4
Porter	42	0	0	4	38	771	124	604	43	1
Putnam	9	2	1	1	5	245	106	114	25	2
Shelby	28	0	4	2	22	279	103	157	19	2
St. Joseph	116	1	13	21	81	2,107	603	1,440	64	0
Sullivan	13	0	0	0	13	187	43	121	23	0
Tippecanoe	31	0	9	6	16	909	253	608	48	6

[1] The FBI does not publish arson data unless it receives data from either the agency or the state for all 12 months of the calendar year.

[5] Because of changes in the state/local agency's reporting practices, figures are not comparable to previous years' data.

Table 10.   Offenses Known to Law Enforcement, by State Metropolitan and Nonmetropolitan Counties, 2010—*Continued*

(Number)

State/County	Violent crime	Murder and non-negligent man-slaughter	Forcible rape	Robbery	Aggravated assault	Property crime	Burglary	Larceny-theft	Motor vehicle theft	Arson[1]
Tipton	9	0	2	1	6	71	24	42	5	0
Vanderburgh[6]		2	7	9		790	124	631	35	4
Warrick	92	0	4	0	88	600	85	490	25	3
Wells	2	0	1	0	1	150	40	102	8	0
INDIANA—Nonmetropolitan Counties										
Blackford	4	0	0	0	4	57	14	39	4	0
Cass	10	0	2	0	8	216	34	177	5	0
Clinton	11	0	1	3	7	360	76	264	20	0
Daviess	7	0	0	1	6	103	35	55	13	3
Fulton	16	0	4	1	11	94	38	50	6	3
Grant	9	0	4	4	1	384	131	224	29	
Henry	6	0	4	1	1	566	193	345	28	0
Huntington	9	1	1	4	3	131	37	87	7	0
Jackson	18	0	2	0	16	412	105	294	13	3
Jay	4	0	0	0	4	104	24	72	8	0
Jennings	21	0	4	1	16	310	137	154	19	0
Knox	0	0	0	0	0	0	0	0	0	0
Kosciusko	34	0	4	2	28	710	133	539	38	2
LaGrange	6	0	0	4	2	202	47	134	21	0
Lawrence	13	0	9	0	4	305	130	160	15	5
Marshall[6]		0	5	0		110			16	0
Martin	0	0	0	0	0	70	15	48	7	0
Montgomery	24	0	1	1	22	447	178	259	10	0
Noble	16	0	3	0	13	168	78	82	8	1
Parke	0	0	0	0	0	140	37	100	3	2
Pulaski	46	0	3	0	43	179	43	123	13	4
Randolph	1	1	0	0	0	272	92	167	13	2
Ripley	9	0	1	0	8	229	64	157	8	1
Rush	2	0	0	0	2	268	67	193	8	1
Scott	12	0	0	0	12	137	54	76	7	1
Starke	30	0	5	0	25	442	81	324	37	7
Steuben	19	0	6	5	8	467	123	329	15	2
Wayne	0	0	0	0	0	166	64	98	4	2
IOWA—Metropolitan Counties										
Black Hawk	34	0	12	1	21	157	60	84	13	0
Bremer	12	0	1	0	11	43	14	25	4	1
Dallas	18	0	2	0	16	136	29	93	14	2
Dubuque	63	0	3	0	60	209	86	103	20	4
Grundy	3	0	0	0	3	83	25	57	1	1
Harrison	6	0	0	1	5	98	35	56	7	0
Johnson	52	1	7	0	44	218	75	125	18	2
Jones	0	0	0	0	0	88	19	61	8	0
Linn	23	0	7	0	16	364	167	167	30	4
Mills	30	0	9	1	20	206	77	110	19	2
Polk	104	0	9	9	86	668	215	380	73	3
Pottawattamie	39	0	3	2	34	437	155	235	47	2
Scott	24	0	0	0	24	128	33	86	9	1
Story	17	0	5	0	12	177	67	98	12	1
Warren	46	0	6	2	38	246	83	144	19	4
Washington	34	0	13	0	21	85	21	59	5	0
Woodbury	19	0	0	0	19	130	52	71	7	0
IOWA—Nonmetropolitan Counties										
Adair	5	0	0	0	5	54	19	33	2	0
Adams	26	2	1	0	23	57	25	30	2	0
Appanoose	13	0	0	0	13	82	34	43	5	0
Boone	8	0	1	0	7	12	7	5	0	0
Buchanan	5	0	0	0	5	122	33	84	5	0
Buena Vista	7	0	0	0	7	63	21	39	3	4
Butler	6	0	1	0	5	5	3	2	0	0
Calhoun	6	0	1	0	5	74	14	53	7	0
Cass	15	0	1	0	14	69	24	41	4	1
Cedar	8	0	1	0	7	95	12	77	6	3
Cerro Gordo	6	0	0	0	6	152	53	93	6	1
Clarke	7	0	0	0	7	40	12	28	0	0
Clay	10	0	3	0	7	38	19	16	3	1
Clayton	7	0	1	0	6	54	13	37	4	0
Clinton	24	0	1	0	23	184	100	75	9	1
Davis	9	1	0	0	8	9	3	6	0	0
Delaware	15	0	2	0	13	24	14	9	1	0
Des Moines	14	0	1	0	13	101	32	63	6	1
Fayette	10	0	2	0	8	39	9	25	5	0
Floyd	1	0	0	0	1	23	7	13	3	0
Hamilton	14	0	0	0	14	72	37	33	2	0

[1] The FBI does not publish arson data unless it receives data from either the agency or the state for all 12 months of the calendar year.

[6] The FBI determined that the agency did not follow national Uniform Crime Reporting (UCR) Program guidelines for reporting an offense. Consequently, this figure is not included in this table.

Table 10. Offenses Known to Law Enforcement, by State Metropolitan and Nonmetropolitan Counties, 2010—*Continued*

(Number)

State/County	Violent crime	Murder and non-negligent man-slaughter	Forcible rape	Robbery	Aggravated assault	Property crime	Burglary	Larceny-theft	Motor vehicle theft	Arson[1]
Hancock	4	0	1	0	3	75	48	26	1	0
Hardin	10	0	0	0	10	97	39	48	10	2
Henry	17	0	0	1	16	85	31	47	7	4
Howard	6	0	2	0	4	66	24	41	1	1
Humboldt	0	0	0	0	0	35	21	11	3	0
Ida	2	0	0	0	2	55	13	42	0	0
Iowa	15	1	3	0	11	93	20	59	14	0
Jasper	37	0	2	0	35	151	72	62	17	0
Jefferson	4	0	0	1	3	66	19	40	7	2
Kossuth	8	0	1	0	7	69	41	27	1	0
Lee	27	1	0	0	26	106	43	40	23	1
Louisa	10	0	0	0	10	74	25	44	5	1
Lucas	6	1	2	1	2	59	19	35	5	4
Lyon	20	2	2	1	15	56	13	36	7	0
Mahaska	21	0	0	0	21	83	40	39	4	0
Marion	28	0	9	0	19	125	58	56	11	1
Marshall	15	0	1	0	14	117	59	55	3	2
Mitchell	3	0	0	0	3	12	7	4	1	0
Monroe	4	0	0	0	4	22	8	14	0	0
Muscatine	17	0	3	0	14	110	45	53	12	0
O'Brien	5	0	0	0	5	45	19	24	2	0
Osceola	1	0	0	0	1	15	4	6	5	0
Page	3	0	0	0	3	56	9	45	2	1
Palo Alto	11	0	0	0	11	48	19	27	2	1
Plymouth	10	0	0	0	10	47	15	27	5	0
Pocahontas	6	0	0	0	6	39	15	21	3	2
Poweshiek	4	0	1	0	3	110	40	61	9	2
Sioux	18	0	1	0	17	77	37	35	5	1
Tama	36	0	1	0	35	140	74	57	9	1
Taylor	1	0	0	0	1	35	14	18	3	0
Union	3	0	0	0	3	32	11	14	7	1
Wapello	15	0	0	0	15	105	43	53	9	0
Wayne	4	0	0	0	4	31	13	17	1	1
Webster	35	0	1	1	33	221	93	110	18	1
Winneshiek	0	0	0	0	0	25	6	19	0	0
Worth	2	0	0	0	2	108	32	71	5	0
Wright	4	1	0	0	3	32	13	19	0	0
KANSAS—Metropolitan Counties										
Butler	35	1	4	0	30	451	151	271	29	9
Doniphan	5	0	1	0	4	54	19	34	1	0
Douglas	25	0	3	1	21	233	67	159	7	4
Franklin	35	0	6	0	29	212	103	97	12	9
Geary	6	0	1	0	5	32	8	23	1	1
Harvey	9	0	0	2	7	102	31	63	8	0
Jackson	22	0	2	1	19	128	46	71	11	2
Jefferson	27	0	1	0	26	424	101	290	33	8
Johnson	40	0	6	2	32	294	68	204	22	5
Leavenworth	62	0	3	2	57	353	149	171	33	11
Miami	18	0	0	1	17	237	103	119	15	11
Osage	12	0	1	0	11	85	29	46	10	2
Pottawatomie	35	0	0	2	33	251	93	144	14	4
Riley County Police Department	187	2	29	16	140	1,400	244	1,139	17	18
Sedgwick	150	0	10	5	135	792	246	486	60	9
Shawnee	71	0	5	6	60	1,163	302	802	59	17
Sumner	9	0	1	1	7	127	42	78	7	0
Wabaunsee	16	0	0	1	15	77	26	44	7	2
Wyandotte	4	0	0	1	3	11	4	7	0	2
KANSAS—Nonmetropolitan Counties										
Allen	18	1	3	0	14	79	31	43	5	6
Anderson	8	0	2	1	5	68	32	29	7	0
Atchison	4	0	1	0	3	14	11	1	2	0
Barber	3	0	0	0	3	16	3	13	0	0
Barton	31	0	5	0	26	134	47	77	10	0
Bourbon	11	0	2	0	9	100	56	39	5	8
Brown	10	0	3	0	7	49	15	31	3	0
Chautauqua	2	0	0	0	2	11	6	5	0	1
Cherokee	33	0	0	0	33	206	91	101	14	17
Cheyenne	2	0	0	0	2	19	5	9	5	0
Clark	2	0	0	0	2	25	4	20	1	0
Clay	4	0	1	0	3	27	11	12	4	2
Cloud	9	1	2	0	6	56	17	35	4	0
Coffey	8	0	4	0	4	44	13	25	6	0
Cowley	34	0	2	1	31	169	67	95	7	0
Crawford	18	1	1	2	14	253	79	158	16	21

[1] The FBI does not publish arson data unless it receives data from either the agency or the state for all 12 months of the calendar year.

Table 10.   Offenses Known to Law Enforcement, by State Metropolitan and Nonmetropolitan Counties, 2010—*Continued*

(Number)

State/County	Violent crime	Murder and non-negligent man-slaughter	Forcible rape	Robbery	Aggravated assault	Property crime	Burglary	Larceny-theft	Motor vehicle theft	Arson[1]
Dickinson	13	1	2	0	10	125	56	59	10	4
Edwards	1	0	0	0	1	29	8	18	3	1
Ellis	14	0	2	1	11	78	22	53	3	2
Ellsworth	4	0	0	0	4	45	13	27	5	1
Finney	23	0	5	0	18	255	74	170	11	2
Ford	27	1	6	3	17	123	25	87	11	1
Graham	0	0	0	0	0	30	9	20	1	0
Grant	2	0	0	0	2	23	8	13	2	0
Gray	2	0	0	0	2	34	8	26	0	0
Greenwood	9	0	4	1	4	78	24	46	8	1
Harper	7	0	1	0	6	20	7	11	2	0
Hodgeman	2	0	1	0	1	33	10	21	2	0
Kingman	3	0	0	0	3	51	17	29	5	1
Kiowa	2	0	1	0	1	57	19	36	2	0
Labette	14	0	1	0	13	103	40	52	11	2
Lincoln	6	0	0	0	6	40	14	25	1	0
Logan	1	0	0	0	1	13	4	9	0	0
Lyon	8	0	2	0	6	108	10	95	3	3
Marion	6	0	0	0	6	6	1	4	1	0
Marshall	1	0	0	0	1	41	24	15	2	0
McPherson	14	0	4	0	10	93	42	45	6	3
Montgomery	42	0	2	0	40	162	58	88	16	8
Morris	8	0	0	0	8	42	14	26	2	2
Morton	8	0	0	0	8	30	11	18	1	1
Nemaha	16	0	0	0	16	49	16	30	3	1
Neosho	9	1	5	0	3	105	46	55	4	3
Ness	4	0	1	0	3	16	3	10	3	0
Norton	1	0	0	0	1	20	16	4	0	0
Osborne	2	0	0	0	2	18	9	8	1	0
Ottawa	6	0	0	0	6	71	21	50	0	0
Pawnee	1	0	0	0	1	20	3	15	2	0
Phillips	1	0	0	0	1	24	10	13	1	3
Pratt	13	0	1	1	11	79	18	58	3	0
Reno	40	0	1	0	39	337	151	169	17	3
Republic	5	0	0	0	5	28	3	25	0	2
Rice	7	0	2	0	5	52	24	25	3	0
Rush	7	0	4	0	3	21	6	14	1	0
Russell	10	0	1	0	9	69	29	31	9	0
Saline	36	6	5	0	25	175	86	77	12	9
Seward	14	0	2	0	12	42	15	25	2	0
Sherman	1	0	1	0	0	11	1	8	2	0
Smith	1	0	0	0	1	15	4	10	1	0
Stafford	7	0	0	0	7	24	5	18	1	0
Thomas	9	0	1	0	8	27	14	11	2	1
Washington	1	0	0	0	1	15	6	6	3	0
Wichita	6	1	0	0	5	32	11	19	2	0
Wilson	4	0	0	2	2	50	21	22	7	1
Woodson	3	0	1	0	2	66	23	40	3	3
KENTUCKY—Metropolitan Counties										
Boone	63	2	12	14	35	1,496	350	1,086	60	3
Bourbon	0	0	0	0	0	48	19	29	0	0
Boyd	23	0	2	8	13	210	62	139	9	0
Bracken	1	0	0	0	1	103	53	47	3	0
Bullitt	28	1	7	4	16	703	303	356	44	2
Christian	14	1	2	3	8	393	173	193	27	4
Clark	5	0	0	2	3	194	83	102	9	0
Edmonson	3	0	1	0	2	52	23	27	2	0
Gallatin	1	0	0	0	1	22	9	10	3	0
Grant	2	0	1	0	1	161	68	85	8	2
Greenup	3	1	2	0	0	48	37	9	2	0
Hancock	0	0	0	0	0	24	8	15	1	0
Hardin	2	0	0	1	1	83	34	44	5	0
Henderson	9	0	2	1	6	165	68	84	13	1
Henry	0	0	0	0	0	4	4	0	0	1
Jessamine	12	0	2	1	9	294	121	157	16	0
Kenton	1	0	0	0	1	2	0	2	0	0
Kenton County Police Department	23	0	1	3	19	186	60	120	6	2
Larue	1	0	1	0	0	40	27	11	2	0
McLean	2	0	0	1	1	35	16	12	7	0
Meade	4	0	0	2	2	108	68	36	4	0
Nelson	16	1	1	1	13	265	134	116	15	0
Oldham	0	0	0	0	0	4	1	3	0	0
Oldham County Police Department	33	0	11	10	12	400	157	226	17	1
Pendleton	2	0	2	0	0	149	47	85	17	2

[1] The FBI does not publish arson data unless it receives data from either the agency or the state for all 12 months of the calendar year.

Table 10. Offenses Known to Law Enforcement, by State Metropolitan and Nonmetropolitan Counties, 2010—*Continued*

(Number)

State/County	Violent crime	Murder and non-negligent man-slaughter	Forcible rape	Robbery	Aggravated assault	Property crime	Burglary	Larceny-theft	Motor vehicle theft	Arson[1]
Scott	11	0	1	3	7	205	89	106	10	1
Shelby	16	0	3	5	8	373	96	254	23	6
Spencer	0	0	0	0	0	23	15	8	0	0
Trigg	5	0	0	2	3	68	30	35	3	0
Trimble	0	0	0	0	0	21	13	8	0	0
Warren	24	0	7	3	14	434	171	232	31	2
Webster	2	0	1	0	1	14	6	4	4	0
Woodford	0	0	0	0	0	22	1	21	0	0
KENTUCKY—Nonmetropolitan Counties										
Adair	1	0	1	0	0	32	18	12	2	0
Allen	14	0	10	0	4	129	61	62	6	2
Anderson	5	0	2	1	2	89	38	49	2	0
Ballard	5	0	0	1	4	200	54	137	9	3
Barren	8	0	0	2	6	148	85	44	19	1
Bell	3	0	0	0	3	74	21	38	15	0
Boyle	7	0	0	0	7	60	23	33	4	0
Breckinridge	2	1	0	1	0	38	21	12	5	0
Butler	1	0	0	0	1	17	6	5	6	0
Caldwell	4	0	0	0	4	82	39	37	6	1
Calloway	13	1	4	1	7	416	173	225	18	1
Carlisle	0	0	0	0	0	12	5	6	1	0
Carter	3	0	0	0	3	36	14	16	6	1
Casey	3	0	0	1	2	121	76	41	4	0
Clay	12	0	0	1	11	96	23	57	16	0
Crittenden	0	0	0	0	0	15	7	7	1	1
Cumberland	0	0	0	0	0	7	1	5	1	0
Estill	9	0	0	4	5	108	53	51	4	0
Fleming	0	0	0	0	0	32	14	15	3	0
Floyd	0	0	0	0	0	103	41	51	11	1
Franklin	13	0	4	4	5	177	67	103	7	0
Fulton	3	0	0	0	3	33	8	21	4	2
Garrard	0	0	0	0	0	63	17	39	7	0
Graves	15	0	3	3	9	188	92	87	9	0
Grayson	1	0	0	1	0	119	44	62	13	0
Green	1	0	1	0	0	4	3	1	0	0
Harlan	10	0	2	1	7	78	29	49	0	3
Harrison	11	0	0	6	5	244	106	133	5	0
Hart	2	0	0	0	2	15	8	5	2	0
Hopkins	21	0	14	2	5	274	114	133	27	1
Jackson	1	0	0	1	0	99	43	50	6	0
Johnson	2	1	1	0	0	34	12	11	11	0
Knott	0	0	0	0	0	22	6	14	2	0
Knox	7	0	1	0	6	229	121	94	14	1
Laurel	11	0	1	1	9	287	125	132	30	4
Lawrence	3	0	0	2	1	58	27	22	9	0
Letcher	6	0	1	1	4	31	19	11	1	0
Lewis	5	0	0	2	3	59	42	13	4	2
Lincoln	6	0	0	3	3	90	65	19	6	0
Livingston	3	0	2	0	1	100	47	44	9	0
Logan	10	0	4	1	5	180	78	88	14	3
Lyon	0	0	0	0	0	62	36	23	3	0
Madison	17	0	1	6	10	514	159	340	15	0
Magoffin	5	0	1	2	2	44	11	29	4	0
Marion	2	0	0	0	2	79	40	34	5	1
Marshall	26	0	7	2	17	334	143	172	19	1
Martin	3	0	0	1	2	68	24	31	13	0
Mason	5	0	0	0	5	145	87	53	5	0
McCracken	38	2	12	7	17	589	227	325	37	1
McCreary	9	1	1	5	2	172	90	70	12	0
Menifee	0	0	0	0	0	30	10	19	1	0
Mercer	4	2	1	0	1	78	45	28	5	1
Metcalfe	1	0	0	1	0	54	11	35	8	1
Montgomery	24	0	1	10	13	509	228	258	23	1
Muhlenberg	1	0	0	0	1	37	12	18	7	0
Ohio	6	1	1	0	4	112	48	56	8	1
Owen	0	0	0	0	0	64	34	27	3	0
Perry	13	0	0	1	12	26	4	10	12	0
Pike	1	0	0	1	0	27	11	15	1	0
Powell	1	0	0	0	1	83	39	40	4	0
Pulaski	16	2	5	4	5	642	325	291	26	2
Rockcastle	4	0	0	3	1	71	37	25	9	0
Rowan	5	0	1	1	3	55	13	38	4	0
Russell	4	0	0	0	4	31	13	15	3	0
Simpson	9	0	4	1	4	104	45	54	5	0

[1] The FBI does not publish arson data unless it receives data from either the agency or the state for all 12 months of the calendar year.

Table 10.   Offenses Known to Law Enforcement, by State Metropolitan and Nonmetropolitan Counties, 2010—*Continued*

(Number)

State/County	Violent crime	Murder and non-negligent man-slaughter	Forcible rape	Robbery	Aggravated assault	Property crime	Burglary	Larceny-theft	Motor vehicle theft	Arson[1]
Taylor	8	0	2	1	5	182	80	100	2	2
Todd	0	0	0	0	0	3	0	3	0	0
Union	11	1	2	3	5	38	11	23	4	1
Washington	0	0	0	0	0	25	13	9	3	1
Wayne	7	0	0	0	7	52	28	17	7	0
LOUISIANA—Metropolitan Counties										
Ascension	371	5	23	42	301	2,657	738	1,727	192	1
Bossier	92	0	5	2	85	535	87	417	31	0
Caddo	111	4	10	7	90	843	230	567	46	2
Calcasieu	442	9	77	40	316	3,847	968	2,614	265	13
Cameron	13	0	1	1	11	139	35	96	8	3
De Soto	139	2	2	4	131	269	79	149	41	1
East Baton Rouge	539	10	19	208	302	7,767	2,060	5,448	259	20
East Feliciana	1	0	0	0	1	64	17	44	3	0
Grant	18	0	0	0	18	267	74	182	11	0
Jefferson	1,870	52	67	431	1,320	12,782	2,809	8,896	1,077	130
Lafayette	339	3	15	40	281	1,593	431	1,055	107	
Lafourche	78	2	2	23	51	1,620	404	1,154	62	1
Livingston	202	6	7	29	160	2,478	688	1,642	148	12
Ouachita	159	8	9	18	124	2,651	913	1,654	84	1
Plaquemines	38	0	0	1	37	284	44	225	15	2
Pointe Coupee	106	1	8	5	92	320	107	206	7	4
Rapides	281	4	23	9	245	2,006	653	1,198	155	2
St. Bernard[3]	100	0	12	12	76		330	986		7
St. Charles	121	3	7	24	87	1,413	366	959	88	16
St. Helena	88	2	0	2	84	265	103	134	28	0
St. John the Baptist	87	3	5	44	35	1,235	327	813	95	0
St. Martin	126	1	1	9	115	519	48	464	7	
St. Tammany	275	7	19	25	224	2,374	568	1,658	148	15
Terrebonne	369	6	27	35	301	2,998	490	2,315	193	12
West Baton Rouge	81	0	6	11	64	433	46	371	16	0
West Feliciana	37	2	2	3	30	167	54	105	8	1
LOUISIANA—Nonmetropolitan Counties										
Allen	26	1	8	1	16	392	87	302	3	0
Assumption	108	0	0	2	106	431	123	272	36	0
Avoyelles	69	2	21	1	45	390	124	243	23	1
Beauregard	27	0	0	1	26	308	118	159	31	0
Bienville	20	0	0	4	16	183	47	125	11	
Caldwell	26	0	0	5	21	312	106	177	29	1
Catahoula	224	0	16	1	207	236	56	171	9	0
Claiborne	66	1	13	2	50	225	84	124	17	34
Concordia	60	0	6	3	51	251	60	182	9	0
East Carroll	15	0	0	3	12	60	20	33	7	1
Evangeline	27	0	4	1	22	448	79	362	7	0
Franklin	11	0	1	0	10	202	85	107	10	0
Iberia	405	3	18	118	266	2,177	838	1,245	94	
Jackson	2	0	0	0	2	134	54	77	3	0
Jefferson Davis	51	0	9	1	41	347	37	275	35	0
La Salle	23	0	0	1	22	91	11	79	1	1
Lincoln	65	0	5	2	58	273	139	129	5	0
Madison	33	1	0	0	32	100	36	56	8	0
Morehouse[3]	25	0	0	2	23		56		22	1
Natchitoches	86	2	1	5	78	453	116	309	28	0
Red River	50	0	0	2	48	81	29	46	6	0
Richland	18	0	1	1	16	212	70	123	19	0
Sabine	37	0	1	0	36	426	75	324	27	0
St. James	112	0	1	3	108	378	77	274	27	5
St. Landry	125	1	12	12	100	864	381	409	74	
St. Mary	127	0	12	28	87	964	220	700	44	
Tangipahoa	874	5	8	69	792	4,211	1,699	2,400	112	
Tensas	7	1	0	0	6	45	20	25	0	0
Vermilion	28	1	2	0	25	179	30	149	0	0
Vernon	116	1	9	3	103	620	32	562	26	
Washington	92	2	14	11	65	786	316	423	47	0
Webster	46	0	7	1	38	252	120	108	24	2
West Carroll	99	0	1	1	97	428	108	296	24	2
Winn	19	0	2	0	17	153	28	117	8	
MAINE—Metropolitan Counties										
Androscoggin	10	0	6	1	3	210	52	153	5	2
Cumberland	40	0	8	6	26	716	314	373	29	5
Penobscot	2	0	0	2	0	738	227	464	47	0
Sagadahoc	2	0	0	0	2	154	52	97	5	0
York	20	0	4	2	14	545	169	342	34	3

[1] The FBI does not publish arson data unless it receives data from either the agency or the state for all 12 months of the calendar year.

[3] The FBI determined that the agency's data were underreported. Consequently, affected data are not included in this table.

Table 10. Offenses Known to Law Enforcement, by State Metropolitan and Nonmetropolitan Counties, 2010—*Continued*

(Number)

State/County	Violent crime	Murder and non-negligent man-slaughter	Forcible rape	Robbery	Aggravated assault	Property crime	Burglary	Larceny-theft	Motor vehicle theft	Arson[1]
MAINE—Nonmetropolitan Counties										
Aroostook	3	0	0	0	3	75	27	47	1	0
Franklin	7	0	2	0	5	108	39	63	6	0
Hancock	6	0	1	2	3	261	84	167	10	0
Kennebec	13	0	7	2	4	357	134	206	17	0
Knox	7	0	2	0	5	213	69	125	19	0
Lincoln	18	0	7	4	7	286	105	177	4	1
Oxford	21	0	14	0	7	332	143	172	17	1
Piscataquis	0	0	0	0	0	97	41	52	4	0
Somerset	13	0	6	3	4	325	153	155	17	1
Waldo	7	0	4	1	2	337	136	182	19	2
Washington	34	0	1	5	28	165	47	108	10	0
MARYLAND—Metropolitan Counties										
Allegany	0	0	0	0	0	0	0	0	0	0
Allegany County Bureau of Police	50	1	4	2	43	331	68	258	5	0
Anne Arundel	2	0	0	0	2	0	0	0	0	0
Anne Arundel County Police Department	2,693	14	106	570	2,003	14,682	2,662	10,901	1,119	70
Baltimore County	0	0	0	0	0	0	0	0	0	0
Baltimore County Police Department	4,305	20	126	1,335	2,824	23,765	4,089	17,817	1,859	220
Calvert	173	0	18	30	125	1,762	460	1,210	92	6
Carroll	61	0	34	3	24	303	75	218	10	0
Cecil	146	2	21	16	107	946	369	515	62	0
Charles	658	2	34	156	466	3,334	663	2,392	279	0
Frederick	204	1	12	28	163	1,559	272	1,220	67	4
Harford	579	5	51	112	411	2,688	677	1,859	152	7
Howard	0	0	0	0	0	0	0	0	0	0
Howard County Police Department	558	4	25	222	307	6,771	1,393	4,998	380	58
Prince George's	74	0	1	1	72	0	0	0	0	0
Prince George's County Police Department	4,941	81	169	2,472	2,219	28,275	6,427	16,251	5,597	281
Queen Anne's	69	0	7	6	56	741	153	570	18	6
Somerset	1	0	0	0	1	58	8	49	1	0
Washington	227	0	13	15	199	1,270	316	906	48	0
Wicomico	137	1	3	25	108	862	328	486	48	
MARYLAND—Nonmetropolitan Counties										
Caroline	22	0	1	8	13	333	143	174	16	0
Dorchester	18	0	1	1	16	278	70	199	9	0
Garrett	25	1	1	1	22	239	84	144	11	0
Kent	14	0	0	5	9	115	51	55	9	0
St. Mary's	280	4	11	38	227	1,956	432	1,429	95	3
Talbot	13	2	2	3	6	214	53	157	4	0
Worcester	74	2	2	4	66	193	56	129	8	1
MICHIGAN—Metropolitan Counties										
Barry	37	0	12	1	24	384	126	235	23	4
Bay	40	0	10	2	28	701	129	547	25	6
Berrien	108	0	21	8	79	729	182	515	32	5
Calhoun	65	0	8	2	55	488	163	300	25	8
Cass	39	0	19	6	14	699	214	456	29	7
Clinton	7	0	3	0	4	202	75	120	7	2
Eaton	91	0	25	17	49	1,536	307	1,187	42	1
Genesee	35	0	11	2	22	520	138	351	31	1
Ingham	97	0	15	11	71	801	245	513	43	4
Ionia	43	1	19	1	22	352	158	178	16	4
Jackson	122	3	13	5	101	519	129	363	27	2
Kalamazoo	176	2	29	34	111	2,103	547	1,466	90	17
Kent	401	2	65	48	286	3,304	935	2,229	140	31
Lapeer	41	1	2	0	38	450	121	295	34	0
Livingston	67	1	15	9	42	733	185	515	33	7
Macomb	399	0	52	37	310	2,306	438	1,740	128	12
Monroe	229	2	53	41	133	2,381	640	1,587	154	25
Muskegon	36	1	11	3	21	780	180	570	30	2
Newaygo	33	0	11	0	22	402	179	203	20	4
Oakland	293	2	43	45	203	3,809	853	2,802	154	85
Ottawa	304	0	110	15	179	3,096	739	2,296	61	21
Saginaw	92	0	18	11	63	483	136	327	20	1
St. Clair	146	1	19	17	109	1,507	414	1,018	75	21
Van Buren	106	0	24	1	81	580	155	386	39	2
Washtenaw	460	4	57	77	322	2,439	953	1,260	226	17
Wayne	6	0	1	1	4	5	0	3	2	0
MICHIGAN—Nonmetropolitan Counties										
Alcona	18	1	6	0	11	102	42	60	0	0
Allegan	96	0	30	4	62	810	280	489	41	8
Alpena	5	0	2	0	3	77	21	55	1	0
Antrim	37	0	11	1	25	378	158	210	10	0

[1] The FBI does not publish arson data unless it receives data from either the agency or the state for all 12 months of the calendar year.

Table 10.   Offenses Known to Law Enforcement, by State Metropolitan and Nonmetropolitan Counties, 2010—*Continued*

(Number)

State/County	Violent crime	Murder and non-negligent man-slaughter	Forcible rape	Robbery	Aggravated assault	Property crime	Burglary	Larceny-theft	Motor vehicle theft	Arson[1]
Arenac	25	0	0	1	24	100	44	53	3	1
Baraga	1	0	0	0	1	28	11	17	0	2
Benzie	21	0	3	1	17	232	58	170	4	2
Branch	19	0	5	2	12	193	35	149	9	0
Charlevoix	24	0	7	2	15	154	46	100	8	4
Cheboygan	8	0	1	1	6	183	96	74	13	2
Chippewa	6	0	3	0	3	116	40	64	12	0
Crawford	38	0	5	0	33	213	97	103	13	0
Delta	2	0	0	0	2	67	15	45	7	1
Emmet	20	0	3	0	17	189	30	155	4	2
Gladwin	13	0	3	1	9	208	62	138	8	1
Grand Traverse	70	1	17	8	44	764	120	621	23	4
Gratiot	10	0	5	0	5	135	28	95	12	1
Hillsdale	34	0	12	4	18	184	69	101	14	2
Houghton	4	0	4	0	0	113	23	83	7	0
Huron	12	0	1	0	11	102	28	70	4	2
Iosco	1	0	0	0	1	7	4	3	0	0
Iron	7	0	2	1	4	44	13	30	1	1
Isabella	46	0	12	3	31	391	129	249	13	2
Kalkaska	60	0	12	0	48	332	108	207	17	0
Lenawee	50	0	17	3	30	362	121	232	9	6
Luce	10	0	3	0	7	66	17	48	1	0
Mackinac	4	0	0	0	4	109	42	64	3	1
Manistee	8	0	4	0	4	105	28	74	3	1
Marquette	5	0	1	0	4	196	38	151	7	0
Mecosta	144	0	8	0	136	684	272	389	23	6
Midland	64	0	26	0	38	473	124	343	6	2
Missaukee	1	0	1	0	0	151	43	108	0	0
Montcalm	66	2	16	1	47	463	184	261	18	4
Montmorency	4	1	1	0	2	24	10	11	3	1
Oceana	31	0	12	0	19	324	96	220	8	0
Ogemaw	17	0	3	0	14	236	115	113	8	0
Ontonagon	6	0	1	0	5	18	7	9	2	0
Osceola	23	0	6	0	17	201	87	105	9	1
Oscoda	30	0	1	0	29	177	70	101	6	0
Otsego	6	1	2	0	3	77	17	57	3	0
Presque Isle	4	0	1	0	3	55	28	24	3	0
Roscommon	18	0	8	0	10	176	53	118	5	1
Sanilac	25	0	11	0	14	195	71	115	9	2
Shiawassee	51	1	8	1	41	441	134	281	26	1
St. Joseph	45	2	12	1	30	281	83	176	22	5
Tuscola	34	0	3	1	30	277	111	149	17	1
Wexford	45	0	11	3	31	430	94	315	21	4
MINNESOTA—Metropolitan Counties[7]										
Anoka		0		5	44	1,472	278	1,124	70	3
Benton		0		1	8	223	47	158	18	2
Blue Earth		1		0	14	160	55	93	12	1
Carlton		0		2	5	307	69	227	11	1
Chisago		0		0	11	482	82	372	28	0
Clay		0		0	4	69	27	39	3	0
Dakota		0		2	14	199	59	128	12	1
Dodge		0		0	32	261	34	220	7	0
Hennepin		0		0	26	164	27	129	8	0
Houston		0		0	8	79	24	45	10	0
Isanti		0		0	7	291	84	165	42	0
Nicollet		0		0	3	77	21	54	2	0
Olmsted		0		5	24	304	82	194	28	6
Polk		0		1	14	204	80	115	9	6
Ramsey		3		0	9	201	18	170	13	1
Scott		0		0	11	160	43	108	9	0
Sherburne		1		1	26	415	64	319	32	2
Stearns		0		1	19	397	66	314	17	1
St. Louis		0		2	37	801	300	463	38	3
Washington		3		1	30	1,131	194	887	50	4
Wright		1		3	61	1,736	151	1,526	59	6
MINNESOTA—Nonmetropolitan Counties[7]										
Aitkin		0		0	13	366	124	224	18	2
Becker		0		0	10	144	54	64	26	0
Beltrami		0		4	52	467	117	308	42	6
Big Stone		0		0	1	46	16	28	2	0
Brown		0		0	0	2	1	0	1	0
Cass		0		2	18	1,041	244	727	70	1
Chippewa		0		0	6	55	35	18	2	0

[1] The FBI does not publish arson data unless it receives data from either the agency or the state for all 12 months of the calendar year.

[7] The data collection methodology for the offense of forcible rape used by the Minnesota state UCR Program does not comply with national UCR Program guidelines. Consequently, its figures for forcible rape and violent crime (of which forcible rape is a part) are not published in this table.

Table 10. Offenses Known to Law Enforcement, by State Metropolitan and Nonmetropolitan Counties, 2010—*Continued*

(Number)

State/County	Violent crime	Murder and non-negligent man-slaughter	Forcible rape	Robbery	Aggravated assault	Property crime	Burglary	Larceny-theft	Motor vehicle theft	Arson[1]
Clearwater		0		0	27	192	41	139	12	0
Cook		0		1	8	165	30	128	7	1
Cottonwood		0		0	3	38	10	26	2	0
Crow Wing		0		2	19	389	112	251	26	0
Douglas		0		0	15	309	83	212	14	5
Faribault		0		0	8	60	21	35	4	1
Fillmore		0		0	5	66	20	38	8	0
Freeborn		0		0	8	116	42	69	5	0
Goodhue		0		1	7	217	76	121	20	0
Grant		0		0	5	91	30	58	3	0
Hubbard		0		1	4	314	131	167	16	0
Itasca		0		2	20	385	113	251	21	2
Jackson		0		0	1	22	2	19	1	0
Kanabec		0		0	27	486	151	302	33	2
Kandiyohi		0		0	20	317	57	245	15	7
Kittson		0		0	0	34	6	26	2	0
Koochiching		0		0	3	89	25	59	5	0
Lac Qui Parle		0		0	1	35	6	28	1	0
Lake		0		0	2	33	12	18	3	0
Lake of the Woods		0		0	2	13	2	10	1	0
Le Sueur		1		1	4	119	35	77	7	1
Lincoln		0		0	1	5	0	5	0	0
Lyon		0		0	5	38	9	27	2	1
Martin		0		0	1	32	6	23	3	0
McLeod		0		0	15	82	24	52	6	0
Meeker		0		0	15	317	105	205	7	0
Mille Lacs		0		2	14	401	94	277	30	1
Morrison		0		0	16	210	36	166	8	2
Mower		0		0	5	184	67	101	16	2
Murray		0		0	2	39	12	24	3	0
Nobles		0		1	3	54	27	25	2	0
Norman		0		0	4	42	14	22	6	0
Otter Tail		0		0	6	363	123	224	16	2
Pennington		0		0	0	37	14	18	5	0
Pine		0		2	25	773	256	427	90	13
Pipestone		0		0	1	117	9	106	2	0
Pope		0		0	3	65	23	41	1	1
Red Lake		0		0	2	17	3	14	0	0
Redwood		0		0	3	68	22	43	3	0
Renville		0		1	5	141	44	94	3	2
Roseau		0		0	3	37	8	29	0	0
Steele		0		0	2	117	34	68	15	2
Stevens		0		0	0	51	23	26	2	0
Swift		0		0	0	31	16	11	4	0
Todd		0		0	1	7	254	98	147	9	1
Traverse		0		0	3	30	10	18	2	0
Wadena		0		0	12	94	28	63	3	0
Waseca		0		0	4	66	28	34	4	1
Watonwan		2		0	3	60	14	41	5	1
Wilkin		0		0	0	46	11	34	1	0
Winona		1		1	6	118	45	63	10	0
Yellow Medicine		0		0	9	52	13	38	1	0
MISSISSIPPI—Metropolitan Counties										
DeSoto	18	2	4	0	12	540	273	222	45	8
Forrest	32	0	3	3	26	485	166	309	10	3
Harrison	20	2	1	6	11	1,199	346	740	113	9
Hinds	69	6	9	18	36	992	311	528	153	0
Jackson	137	1	38	16	82	1,633	650	867	116	8
Lamar	38	1	23	6	8	571	244	299	28	1
Madison	40	2	5	8	25	470	173	255	42	0
Rankin	32	4	3	5	20	587	148	387	52	0
Simpson	51	0	7	2	42	295	125	148	22	0
Tate	6	1	0	1	4	236	95	116	25	1
Tunica	69	1	12	25	31	526	83	403	40	1
MISSISSIPPI—Nonmetropolitan Counties										
Adams	59	0	2	16	41	692	332	336	24	3
Bolivar	18	2	5	4	7	97	54	41	2	0
Carroll	7	0	0	2	5	76	55	18	3	1
Chickasaw	31	2	3	7	19	58	33	25	0	0
Choctaw	17	0	3	0	14	79	34	39	6	0
Claiborne	79	0	1	10	68	59	29	28	2	0
Franklin	16	0	1	3	12	39	18	14	7	0
Greene	7	0	0	1	6	47	10	31	6	0

[1] The FBI does not publish arson data unless it receives data from either the agency or the state for all 12 months of the calendar year.

Table 10. Offenses Known to Law Enforcement, by State Metropolitan and Nonmetropolitan Counties, 2010—*Continued*

(Number)

State/County	Violent crime	Murder and non-negligent man-slaughter	Forcible rape	Robbery	Aggravated assault	Property crime	Burglary	Larceny-theft	Motor vehicle theft	Arson[1]
Grenada	17	0	0	3	14	122	58	48	16	0
Jefferson	27	0	1	1	25	22	6	15	1	0
Jones	101	2	40	6	53	772	272	481	19	0
Kemper	8	2	0	1	5	31	12	18	1	5
Lauderdale	46	7	13	7	19	571	310	231	30	2
Lee	35	0	2	2	31	778	278	465	35	9
Leflore	83	0	3	17	63	404	167	209	28	2
Lincoln	20	2	4	5	9	324	106	194	24	7
Lowndes	45	1	12	10	22	574	221	331	22	1
Marion	29	1	3	4	21	419	189	205	25	2
Oktibbeha	27	0	4	4	19	225	75	143	7	2
Panola	95	2	0	4	89	674	394	262	18	0
Pearl River	41	1	17	4	19	827	411	373	43	1
Pike	48	2	0	7	39	477	248	227	2	
Pontotoc	4	1	0	2	1	20	8	11	1	5
Scott	41	3	0	1	37	256	97	141	18	2
Sharkey	2	0	0	1	1	11	5	4	2	0
Tippah	8	1	0	1	6	2	1	1	0	0
Union	5	1	1	0	3	199	74	110	15	3
Walthall	7	2	0	0	5	201	105	83	13	0
Warren	23	0	7	5	11	495	261	190	44	1
Washington	15	1	1	5	8	550	184	315	51	4
Winston	5	1	1	0	3	20	5	15	0	1
MISSOURI—Metropolitan Counties										
Andrew	3	0	0	0	3	94	28	58	8	0
Bates	18	0	6	1	11	186	82	104	0	7
Bollinger	3	0	0	0	3	66	28	32	6	8
Boone	116	1	8	6	101	642	156	451	35	
Buchanan	24	1	1	1	21	203	89	103	11	4
Caldwell	30	1	3	0	26	95	50	43	2	0
Callaway	71	3	8	6	54	720	193	473	54	7
Cape Girardeau	135	0	3	3	129	231	92	124	15	8
Cass	41	3	3	1	34	333	117	191	25	0
Christian	145	0	0	0	145	323	132	164	27	0
Clay	31	1	3	2	25	253	106	136	11	4
Clinton	22	0	0	0	22	137	48	78	11	0
Cole	45	0	1	2	42	304	96	199	9	1
Dallas	23	0	3	0	20	158	60	88	10	
De Kalb	6	0	2	0	4	91	40	42	9	1
Franklin	70	0	1	2	67	562	157	357	48	1
Greene	129	0	13	19	97	1,745	559	1,095	91	17
Jackson	77	3	4	11	59	538	168	329	41	6
Jasper	184	0	11	6	167	545	161	310	74	2
Jefferson	406	2	29	13	362	2,379	462	1,750	167	22
Lafayette	18	0	1	0	17	131	61	64	6	0
Lincoln	90	1	1	0	88	233	89	120	24	0
McDonald	51	0	0	1	50	234	39	164	31	2
Moniteau	14	0	0	0	14	49	20	26	3	1
Newton	101	1	13	5	82	661	172	422	67	4
Osage	19	0	1	0	18	100	30	60	10	0
Platte	29	0	2	2	25	386	87	289	10	3
Polk	83	0	1	2	80	377	136	209	32	1
Ray	18	0	2	0	16	140	61	66	13	5
St. Charles	157	0	7	10	140	1,063	277	748	38	9
St. Louis County Police Department	1,090	17	70	286	717	9,538	2,162	6,589	787	60
Warren	42	0	8	0	34	190	70	110	10	0
Washington	40	1	3	0	36	186	49	99	38	1
Webster	19	0	0	0	19	273	137	109	27	4
MISSOURI—Nonmetropolitan Counties										
Adair	22	1	1	0	20	130	27	95	8	2
Atchison	1	0	0	0	1	23	10	8	5	0
Audrain	20	0	0	1	19	117	50	61	6	0
Barry	69	0	2	2	65	434	187	230	17	8
Barton	7	0	1	0	6	89	32	54	3	0
Benton	32	0	0	0	32	245	95	130	20	2
Butler	99	1	7	3	88	410	138	267	5	1
Camden	46	5	1	2	38	415	123	275	17	1
Carroll	4	1	0	0	3	33	12	18	3	0
Carter	7	0	0	0	7	32	7	22	3	2
Cedar	5	1	0	0	4	140	39	95	6	0
Chariton	21	0	0	0	21	88	22	65	1	0
Clark	6	0	0	0	6	49	24	22	3	0
Cooper	10	0	0	2	8	161	47	104	10	0

[1] The FBI does not publish arson data unless it receives data from either the agency or the state for all 12 months of the calendar year.

Table 10. Offenses Known to Law Enforcement, by State Metropolitan and Nonmetropolitan Counties, 2010—*Continued*

(Number)

State/County	Violent crime	Murder and non-negligent man-slaughter	Forcible rape	Robbery	Aggravated assault	Property crime	Burglary	Larceny-theft	Motor vehicle theft	Arson[1]
Crawford	15	1	1	0	13	208	88	109	11	4
Dade	7	0	0	0	7	37	15	19	3	1
Daviess	8	0	0	1	7	62	25	34	3	0
Dent	23	0	6	1	16	120	62	56	2	0
Douglas	20	0	0	0	20	70	27	38	5	0
Dunklin	38	0	2	1	35	177	50	115	12	1
Gasconade	22	0	2	0	20	108	49	47	12	0
Grundy	1	0	0	0	1	38	10	25	3	0
Harrison	1	0	0	0	1	42	17	25	0	1
Henry	39	0	0	2	37	321	104	192	25	1
Hickory	4	1	0	0	3	130	71	53	6	1
Holt	0	0	0	0	0	78	35	39	4	0
Howell	39	2	0	1	36	366	126	217	23	0
Iron	20	0	3	0	17	72	28	32	12	0
Johnson	36	0	5	3	28	334	125	194	15	0
Knox	3	0	0	0	3	97	37	54	6	0
Laclede[6]		5	5	0		279	101	156	22	1
Lawrence	47	0	0	1	46	375	131	226	18	2
Lewis	1	0	0	0	1	53	15	33	5	1
Linn	7	0	0	1	6	71	43	25	3	1
Livingston	1	0	0	0	1	53	15	33	5	0
Macon	12	0	2	0	10	116	62	42	12	0
Madison	2	0	0	0	2	57	21	29	7	0
Maries	7	0	0	0	7	52	22	28	2	0
Marion	15	0	1	0	14	87	22	65	0	0
Mercer	11	0	1	0	10	18	10	8	0	3
Miller	34	2	3	0	29	182	74	98	10	0
Mississippi	13	1	0	0	12	69	24	38	7	2
Monroe	6	0	2	0	4	102	58	34	10	
Montgomery	4	0	0	1	3	61	30	29	2	0
Morgan	34	1	1	0	32	270	129	127	14	0
New Madrid	17	2	0	1	14	41	18	17	6	2
Nodaway	5	0	2	0	3	95	42	49	4	1
Oregon	17	1	0	3	13	63	25	28	10	0
Ozark	21	1	4	1	15	102	41	53	8	1
Pemiscot	19	0	3	3	13	167	56	104	7	2
Perry	11	0	0	1	10	74	29	35	10	0
Pettis	21	0	2	0	19	267	69	184	14	1
Phelps	50	2	3	3	42	379	137	217	25	1
Pike	25	0	3	0	22	94	43	40	11	4
Pulaski	66	0	1	2	63	269	132	120	17	1
Ralls	8	0	5	0	3	152	34	112	6	0
Randolph	7	0	0	0	7	95	31	60	4	0
Reynolds	11	0	3	0	8	61	19	33	9	0
Ripley	19	4	0	0	15	166	45	116	5	2
Scotland	1	0	0	0	1	29	11	17	1	1
Scott	23	0	1	0	22	103	39	59	5	0
Shannon	14	0	2	0	12	83	20	51	12	3
Shelby	0	0	0	0	0	61	22	36	3	0
St. Clair	11	2	0	0	9	125	45	79	1	0
Ste. Genevieve	33	0	2	1	30	119	34	74	11	1
St. Francois	75	0	4	0	71	392	104	233	55	5
Stoddard	29	0	2	0	27	181	86	84	11	0
Stone	79	0	1	3	75	531	222	266	43	1
Sullivan	14	0	0	0	14	52	23	28	1	0
Taney	96	0	5	1	90	555	191	328	36	0
Texas	7	1	0	0	6	143	50	75	18	6
Vernon	27	1	1	0	25	227	55	155	17	2
Wayne	6	0	0	0	6	108	55	49	4	0
Worth	8	0	0	0	8	29	19	8	2	1
Wright	15	0	1	0	14	105	60	30	15	1
MONTANA—Metropolitan Counties										
Carbon	6	0	2	0	4	42	5	35	2	2
Missoula	79	1	6	4	68	613	99	470	44	5
Yellowstone	35	0	4	3	28	666	126	479	61	5
MONTANA—Nonmetropolitan Counties										
Beaverhead	11	0	0	0	11	52	25	26	1	2
Big Horn	26	0	0	0	26	96	7	80	9	0
Blaine	6	0	1	0	5	28	2	23	3	1
Broadwater	13	0	2	0	11	46	1	36	9	1
Carter	1	0	1	0	0	4	1	3	0	0
Chouteau	5	0	1	0	4	13	2	10	1	0
Custer	5	0	2	0	3	36	2	32	2	0

[1] The FBI does not publish arson data unless it receives data from either the agency or the state for all 12 months of the calendar year.

Table 10.   Offenses Known to Law Enforcement, by State Metropolitan and Nonmetropolitan Counties, 2010—*Continued*

(Number)

State/County	Violent crime	Murder and non-negligent man-slaughter	Forcible rape	Robbery	Aggravated assault	Property crime	Burglary	Larceny-theft	Motor vehicle theft	Arson[1]
Daniels	4	0	0	0	4	3	0	2	1	0
Dawson	7	0	0	0	7	48	6	41	1	0
Deer Lodge	43	1	5	0	37	204	23	168	13	0
Fallon	1	0	1	0	0	8	1	7	0	0
Fergus	10	0	4	0	6	31	7	22	2	0
Flathead	200	5	18	3	174	940	177	698	65	4
Gallatin	50	1	10	1	38	393	50	310	33	3
Garfield	0	0	0	0	0	2	0	1	1	0
Glacier	6	0	0	0	6	18	3	15	0	0
Granite	4	0	0	0	4	72	4	67	1	5
Hill	15	0	1	1	13	138	15	113	10	0
Jefferson	18	0	1	0	17	59	13	43	3	0
Judith Basin	0	0	0	0	0	7	2	4	1	0
Lake	84	0	3	1	80	223	55	148	20	3
Lewis and Clark	55	0	11	0	44	354	69	268	17	5
Lincoln	29	1	4	1	23	157	30	121	6	4
Madison	4	0	0	0	4	53	15	31	7	2
McCone	2	0	1	0	1	10	4	6	0	0
Meagher	1	1	0	0	0	15	4	11	0	0
Mineral	2	0	0	0	2	5	1	4	0	0
Musselshell	8	0	0	0	8	80	13	62	5	0
Park	17	0	5	0	12	69	8	54	7	2
Phillips	12	0	0	0	12	49	8	34	7	0
Pondera	0	0	0	0	0	7	0	7	0	0
Prairie	1	0	0	0	1	4	3	1	0	0
Richland	0	0	0	0	0	24	5	18	1	0
Roosevelt	6	0	0	0	6	39	10	25	4	0
Rosebud	13	0	0	0	13	48	4	42	2	2
Sanders	23	0	4	0	19	77	13	58	6	2
Sheridan	7	1	1	0	5	49	6	38	5	0
Silver Bow	92	0	5	10	77	1,463	252	1,092	119	16
Stillwater	8	0	1	0	7	52	16	33	3	0
Sweet Grass	10	0	0	0	10	34	5	27	2	0
Teton	5	0	0	0	5	55	3	51	1	0
Toole	28	0	1	0	27	80	13	62	5	0
Valley	3	0	3	0	0	21	5	13	3	0
Wibaux	0	0	0	0	0	2	1	1	0	0
NEBRASKA—Metropolitan Counties										
Cass	7	0	3	1	3	232	50	159	23	4
Dakota	1	0	0	0	1	44	11	29	4	0
Dixon	6	0	2	0	4	54	17	34	3	4
Douglas	153	2	4	4	143	1,156	313	756	87	0
Lancaster	24	0	2	0	22	272	69	194	9	2
Sarpy	17	0	7	5	5	743	131	553	59	2
Saunders	7	0	1	0	6	68	24	43	1	1
NEBRASKA—Nonmetropolitan Counties										
Adams	4	0	2	0	2	117	35	66	16	1
Antelope	1	0	0	0	1	19	2	15	2	1
Arthur	0	0	0	0	0	0	0	0	0	0
Box Butte	1	0	0	0	1	13	3	9	1	0
Boyd	2	0	1	0	1	16	11	5	0	0
Brown	1	0	0	0	1	35	8	27	0	0
Buffalo	12	0	2	0	10	179	30	144	5	0
Burt	4	1	0	0	3	27	9	15	3	0
Butler	9	0	0	2	7	61	15	46	0	0
Cedar	5	0	0	1	4	16	3	12	1	1
Chase	1	0	0	0	1	23	8	13	2	0
Cherry	4	0	0	0	4	5	2	3	0	0
Colfax	7	0	0	0	7	39	16	19	4	0
Cuming	2	0	0	0	2	20	2	18	0	0
Custer	2	0	2	0	0	66	17	44	5	1
Dawes	6	0	1	0	5	14	4	7	3	1
Dawson	6	0	2	0	4	93	30	54	9	0
Deuel	0	0	0	0	0	21	5	15	1	0
Dodge	4	0	0	0	4	174	40	127	7	0
Franklin	0	0	0	0	0	10	6	4	0	0
Gage	17	0	1	0	16	112	34	76	2	0
Hall	7	0	2	0	5	220	64	148	8	1
Hamilton	4	0	1	1	2	32	12	19	1	0
Hitchcock	3	0	0	0	3	22	8	12	2	0
Hooker	0	0	0	0	0	0	0	0	0	0
Johnson	1	0	1	0	0	15	7	8	0	0
Kearney	3	0	0	0	3	46	4	39	3	0

[1] The FBI does not publish arson data unless it receives data from either the agency or the state for all 12 months of the calendar year.

Table 10.   Offenses Known to Law Enforcement, by State Metropolitan and Nonmetropolitan Counties, 2010—*Continued*

(Number)

State/County	Violent crime	Murder and non-negligent man-slaughter	Forcible rape	Robbery	Aggravated assault	Property crime	Burglary	Larceny-theft	Motor vehicle theft	Arson[1]
Keith	0	0	0	0	0	47	5	39	3	0
Keya Paha	0	0	0	0	0	0	0	0	0	0
Kimball	0	0	0	0	0	7	0	7	0	0
Knox	0	0	0	0	0	25	7	15	3	0
Lincoln	14	0	5	1	8	154	31	118	5	1
Madison	4	0	3	0	1	63	15	44	4	0
Merrick	14	0	0	0	14	66	11	55	0	0
Morrill	0	0	0	0	0	31	7	19	5	0
Nemaha	3	0	2	0	1	30	6	22	2	0
Pawnee	3	0	0	0	3	24	5	17	2	0
Perkins	0	0	0	0	0	25	7	17	1	0
Pierce	1	0	0	0	1	9	0	8	1	0
Platte	16	0	7	0	9	115	33	78	4	0
Red Willow	3	0	1	0	2	9	3	4	2	0
Rock	0	0	0	0	0	3	2	1	0	0
Saline	4	0	0	0	4	36	18	16	2	0
Scotts Bluff	10	0	3	0	7	91	14	64	13	0
Sheridan	4	0	1	0	3	42	8	31	3	0
Stanton	2	0	0	0	2	46	13	32	1	0
Thayer	1	0	0	0	1	81	36	43	2	0
Webster	7	0	0	0	7	38	17	21	0	0
Wheeler	0	0	0	0	0	4	1	3	0	0
York	0	0	0	0	0	30	3	18	9	0
NEVADA—Metropolitan Counties										
Carson City	162	0	1	20	141	1,133	281	768	84	3
Storey	5	0	0	0	5	50	17	30	3	2
Washoe	232	1	23	11	197	1,097	386	596	115	7
NEVADA—Nonmetropolitan Counties										
Churchill	39	1	6	1	31	213	88	92	33	2
Douglas	61	0	3	4	54	818	176	605	37	8
Elko	12	0	1	0	11	49	27	18	4	1
Esmeralda	2	0	0	0	2	1	1	0	0	1
Eureka	8	0	0	0	8	18	6	11	1	0
Humboldt	50	1	0	0	49	53	20	27	6	0
Lander	43	0	11	0	32	95	47	40	8	0
Lincoln	7	0	0	0	7	39	4	34	1	0
Lyon	95	2	3	11	79	707	210	439	58	5
Mineral	22	0	0	0	22	31	18	11	2	0
Nye	334	4	15	39	276	1,255	468	653	134	11
Pershing	25	0	7	0	18	49	18	28	3	0
White Pine	33	1	7	1	24	136	50	77	9	4
NEW HAMPSHIRE—Metropolitan Counties										
Rockingham	10	0	0	0	10	1	0	1	0	0
NEW HAMPSHIRE—Nonmetropolitan Counties										
Carroll	1	0	0	0	1	44	6	36	2	1
Cheshire	8	0	0	0	8	8	1	7	0	0
Merrimack	5	0	3	0	2	7	1	6	0	0
NEW JERSEY—Metropolitan Counties										
Atlantic	0	0	0	0	0	0	0	0	0	0
Bergen	0	0	0	0	0	0	0	0	0	0
Bergen County Police Department	0	0	0	0	0	0	0	0	0	0
Burlington	0	0	0	0	0	0	0	0	0	0
Camden	0	0	0	0	0	0	0	0	0	0
Cape May	0	0	0	0	0	0	0	0	0	0
Cumberland	0	0	0	0	0	0	0	0	0	0
Essex	0	0	0	0	0	0	0	0	0	0
Gloucester	0	0	0	0	0	0	0	0	0	0
Hudson	0	0	0	0	0	0	0	0	0	0
Hunterdon	0	0	0	0	0	0	0	0	0	0
Mercer	0	0	0	0	0	0	0	0	0	0
Middlesex	0	0	0	0	0	0	0	0	0	0
Monmouth	0	0	0	0	0	0	0	0	0	0
Morris	0	0	0	0	0	0	0	0	0	0
Ocean	0	0	0	0	0	0	0	0	0	0
Passaic	0	0	0	0	0	0	0	0	0	0
Salem	0	0	0	0	0	0	0	0	0	0
Somerset	0	0	0	0	0	0	0	0	0	0
Sussex	0	0	0	0	0	0	0	0	0	0
Union	0	0	0	0	0	0	0	0	0	0
Warren	0	0	0	0	0	0	0	0	0	0
NEW MEXICO—Metropolitan Counties										
Bernalillo	795	7	29	109	650	2,471	902	1,338	231	54
Dona Ana	277	6	44	9	218	1,333	518	697	118	8
Sandoval	10	0	0	1	9	151	79	68	4	0

[1] The FBI does not publish arson data unless it receives data from either the agency or the state for all 12 months of the calendar year.

Table 10.   Offenses Known to Law Enforcement, by State Metropolitan and Nonmetropolitan Counties, 2010—*Continued*

(Number)

State/County	Violent crime	Murder and non-negligent man-slaughter	Forcible rape	Robbery	Aggravated assault	Property crime	Burglary	Larceny-theft	Motor vehicle theft	Arson[1]
San Juan	214	1	23	6	184	766	257	444	65	12
Santa Fe	95	1	3	4	87	1,208	776	385	47	9
Torrance	13	1	0	0	12	91	55	14	22	0
Valencia	115	0	6	6	103	1,176	612	456	108	10
NEW MEXICO—Nonmetropolitan Counties										
Catron	1	0	0	0	1	12	5	6	1	0
Chaves	38	0	13	3	22	399	224	138	37	4
Cibola[6]		0	3	0		91	45	29	17	1
Colfax	3	0	0	0	3	3	2	1	0	0
Curry	16	0	1	2	13	106	66	28	12	1
Eddy	48	2	8	2	36	421	142	263	16	5
Grant	13	1	1	0	11	149	95	54	0	2
Lea	32	1	8	2	21	374	136	213	25	3
Lincoln	40	0	2	2	36	97	31	62	4	0
Luna[6]		1	0	0		174	77	79	18	0
McKinley	91	1	10	5	75	258	88	149	21	7
Mora	3	0	0	0	3	4	1	3	0	0
Otero	105	0	19	0	86	255	118	120	17	0
Quay	1	0	0	0	1	29	10	18	1	0
Rio Arriba	18	0	1	0	17	81	64	11	6	1
Roosevelt	11	0	4	0	7	58	32	24	2	0
Sierra	7	0	1	0	6	47	15	30	2	0
Socorro	30	0	0	0	30	68	34	32	2	0
Taos[6]		2	2	0		170	117	48	5	0
Union	2	0	0	0	2	22	12	9	1	0
NEW YORK—Metropolitan Counties										
Albany	12	0	2	0	10	157	21	121	15	0
Broome	58	0	9	8	41	790	144	627	19	0
Chemung	26	0	1	5	20	345	71	266	8	3
Dutchess	71	3	3	9	56	714	202	492	20	6
Erie	126	1	8	12	105	1,033	211	793	29	3
Herkimer	0	0	0	0	0	1	0	1	0	0
Livingston	16	2	2	1	11	494	89	402	3	2
Madison	12	0	1	1	10	244	59	178	7	1
Monroe	205	1	18	41	145	3,947	671	3,187	89	10
Nassau	1,496	15	70	672	739	13,879	1,925	11,117	837	
Niagara	73	0	12	20	41	1,184	310	835	39	4
Oneida	28	1	4	4	19	458	137	309	12	2
Onondaga	157	1	29	36	91	2,111	357	1,685	69	4
Ontario	62	0	13	12	37	931	168	749	14	4
Orange	15	0	0	0	15	35	0	35	0	0
Orleans	24	0	2	2	20	384	103	256	25	0
Oswego	45	3	6	4	32	602	189	383	30	3
Putnam	21	2	0	3	16	349	94	250	5	6
Rensselaer	34	0	1	2	31	248	64	168	16	5
Rockland	7	0	0	1	6	46	1	45	0	0
Saratoga	39	0	6	8	25	1,300	254	1,009	37	6
Schenectady	0	0	0	0	0	17	1	16	0	0
Schoharie	2	0	0	0	2	66	24	41	1	1
Suffolk	119	0	0	2	117	13	1	3	9	0
Suffolk County Police Department	2,031	50	55	814	1,112	25,515	4,031	20,038	1,446	201
Tioga	13	0	1	2	10	236	63	170	3	0
Tompkins	26	1	6	2	17	337	60	273	4	0
Ulster	48	1	4	5	38	359	75	272	12	2
Warren	40	0	9	5	26	789	126	655	8	2
Washington	27	0	6	2	19	350	110	225	15	2
Wayne	50	0	5	3	42	640	183	433	24	1
Westchester Public Safety	67	0	0	2	65	211	15	190	6	0
NEW YORK—Nonmetropolitan Counties										
Allegany	1	0	0	0	1	4	1	3	0	0
Cattaraugus	47	0	8	4	35	522	182	325	15	5
Cayuga	33	0	4	1	28	327	65	260	2	2
Chautauqua	28	0	8	6	14	810	262	535	13	3
Chenango	18	0	4	2	12	380	71	306	3	1
Clinton	7	0	1	0	6	20	6	13	1	0
Columbia	17	1	2	1	13	296	73	218	5	1
Cortland	12	0	3	1	8	323	69	243	11	1
Franklin	0	0	0	0	0	0	0	0	0	0
Fulton	17	0	5	1	11	452	176	255	21	1
Genesee	38	0	8	7	23	646	109	513	24	4
Greene	15	0	0	1	14	84	29	50	5	1
Hamilton	1	0	0	0	1	3	3	0	0	0
Jefferson	39	0	1	1	37	202	39	154	9	1
Lewis	9	0	0	1	8	264	125	130	9	0

[1] The FBI does not publish arson data unless it receives data from either the agency or the state for all 12 months of the calendar year.

[6] The FBI determined that the agency did not follow national Uniform Crime Reporting (UCR) Program guidelines for reporting an offense. Consequently, this figure is not included in this table.

Table 10. Offenses Known to Law Enforcement, by State Metropolitan and Nonmetropolitan Counties, 2010—*Continued*

(Number)

State/County	Violent crime	Murder and non-negligent man-slaughter	Forcible rape	Robbery	Aggravated assault	Property crime	Burglary	Larceny-theft	Motor vehicle theft	Arson[1]
Montgomery	15	0	0	0	15	346	32	299	15	3
Otsego	17	0	3	0	14	155	81	68	6	1
Schuyler	6	0	1	1	4	49	12	33	4	1
Seneca	11	0	2	1	8	221	49	168	4	1
Steuben[5]	20	0	1	0	19	175	61	100	14	0
St. Lawrence	26	1	2	0	23	97	29	62	6	1
Sullivan	41	0	3	10	28	542	143	386	13	3
Wyoming	7	0	2	0	5	184	51	128	5	0
Yates	10	0	3	2	5	242	83	156	3	0
NORTH CAROLINA—Metropolitan Counties										
Alamance	115	5	6	12	92	1,095	446	583	66	2
Alexander	54	0	6	11	37	749	265	460	24	17
Anson	64	0	6	21	37	597	290	269	38	4
Brunswick	151	0	16	26	109	2,000	990	909	101	4
Buncombe	149	3	12	33	101	1,940	831	949	160	8
Burke	85	4	7	10	64	1,326	556	698	72	3
Cabarrus	35	2	2	6	25	916	436	436	44	10
Caldwell	62	4	7	7	44	1,513	575	864	74	13
Catawba	176	3	7	18	148	1,910	797	1,007	106	10
Chatham	81	1	6	7	67	820	389	392	39	6
Cumberland	499	5	18	106	370	3,929	1,512	2,213	204	90
Currituck	49	1	3	0	45	638	160	463	15	3
Davie	74	1	10	5	58	691	230	408	53	2
Edgecombe	68	2	7	8	51	557	252	280	25	2
Forsyth	275	2	20	22	231	2,754	763	1,891	100	17
Franklin	58	3	8	10	37	970	404	457	109	2
Gaston	7	0	0	0	7	3	0	3	0	0
Greene	59	4	10	10	35	652	304	320	28	1
Guilford	167	5	11	30	121	1,853	728	1,008	117	20
Haywood	97	2	6	7	82	820	366	405	49	4
Henderson	99	0	18	12	69	1,214	552	579	83	4
Johnston	141	8	21	17	95	2,358	878	1,320	160	16
Madison	9	0	4	1	4	204	92	95	17	2
Onslow	259	7	38	41	173	2,901	910	1,861	130	24
Orange	42	2	4	13	23	693	377	266	50	3
Person	59	5	9	4	41	718	326	360	32	6
Randolph	94	1	3	22	68	2,289	708	1,490	91	6
Rockingham	84	1	2	19	62	1,368	500	772	96	1
Stokes	150	2	2	1	145	886	340	489	57	1
Union	186	8	20	25	133	2,283	735	1,449	99	15
Wake	229	6	25	33	165	2,673	986	1,476	211	11
Wayne	156	1	2	35	118	2,090	1,041	938	111	3
Yadkin	67	1	5	5	56	733	331	359	43	1
NORTH CAROLINA—Nonmetropolitan Counties										
Avery	13	0	2	1	10	205	67	131	7	1
Beaufort	84	3	4	11	66	702	292	385	25	9
Bertie	18	0	1	1	16	257	95	140	22	2
Camden	6	0	0	2	4	84	28	55	1	5
Carteret	90	1	18	2	69	958	319	602	37	2
Caswell	50	1	3	5	41	510	199	293	18	7
Clay	16	0	0	1	15	178	70	94	14	2
Cleveland	34	0	11	18	5	1,528	699	735	94	4
Columbus	148	3	6	31	108	1,585	760	692	133	7
Craven	155	2	14	12	127	1,464	749	637	78	4
Dare	37	0	3	2	32	730	263	447	20	1
Davidson	134	6	8	33	87	2,026	776	1,143	107	14
Duplin	167	0	5	7	155	870	401	397	72	6
Granville	73	1	1	12	59	889	366	472	51	8
Halifax	144	2	6	26	110	961	435	483	43	15
Harnett	214	11	14	21	168	2,237	818	1,270	149	14
Hertford	19	0	2	7	10	300	145	128	27	0
Iredell	176	3	12	11	150	1,867	750	959	158	19
Lee	28	1	5	4	18	610	190	376	44	2
Lincoln	75	4	12	18	41	1,530	610	870	50	4
Macon	22	0	1	1	20	491	212	256	23	2
Martin	62	0	6	5	51	352	148	181	23	4
McDowell	25	2	3	5	15	557	231	293	33	3
Montgomery	38	0	6	3	29	452	192	249	11	1
Moore	66	3	5	9	49	921	431	440	50	3
Northampton	46	0	3	8	35	424	211	184	29	2
Pamlico	20	0	3	3	14	258	84	165	9	0
Perquimans	10	0	2	2	6	107	57	41	9	2
Robeson	589	6	17	115	451	4,380	2,287	1,842	251	47

[1] The FBI does not publish arson data unless it receives data from either the agency or the state for all 12 months of the calendar year.

[5] Because of changes in the state/local agency's reporting practices, figures are not comparable to previous years' data.

Table 10. Offenses Known to Law Enforcement, by State Metropolitan and Nonmetropolitan Counties, 2010—*Continued*

(Number)

State/County	Violent crime	Murder and non-negligent man-slaughter	Forcible rape	Robbery	Aggravated assault	Property crime	Burglary	Larceny-theft	Motor vehicle theft	Arson[1]
Rowan	147	4	12	20	111	1,410	508	842	60	12
Rutherford	105	1	9	14	81	1,216	559	590	67	19
Sampson	104	4	15	19	66	1,321	617	614	90	22
Stanly	33	0	5	3	25	537	213	306	18	1
Surry	75	1	8	7	59	1,284	618	571	95	13
Swain	32	0	5	0	27	365	142	202	21	0
Transylvania	42	1	9	5	27	399	200	180	19	5
Tyrrell	3	0	0	1	2	65	10	53	2	0
Vance	68	1	3	17	47	1,425	694	633	98	4
Watauga	24	2	1	1	20	486	110	344	32	0
Wilkes	113	2	3	12	96	1,181	521	602	58	6
Wilson	89	0	8	9	72	769	254	462	53	12
Yancey	4	3	0	0	1	116	63	51	2	1
NORTH DAKOTA—Metropolitan Counties										
Burleigh	16	0	4	0	12	135	29	95	11	0
Cass	15	0	4	0	11	190	75	100	15	2
Grand Forks	3	1	1	0	1	65	17	37	11	0
Morton	1	0	1	0	0	48	9	31	8	0
NORTH DAKOTA—Nonmetropolitan Counties										
Adams	1	0	0	0	1	11	5	5	1	0
Barnes	0	0	0	0	0	17	2	13	2	1
Benson	4	0	1	0	3	15	6	7	2	0
Billings	0	0	0	0	0	3	1	2	0	0
Bottineau	0	0	0	0	0	21	6	12	3	0
Burke	3	0	1	0	2	23	4	16	3	0
Cavalier	0	0	0	0	0	38	5	29	4	0
Dickey	1	0	0	0	1	8	1	6	1	1
Eddy	0	0	0	0	0	12	2	10	0	0
Emmons	0	0	0	0	0	28	5	23	0	2
Golden Valley	0	0	0	0	0	11	2	9	0	0
Grant	1	0	1	0	0	10	3	5	2	0
Griggs	1	0	0	0	1	5	1	4	0	0
Hettinger	0	0	0	0	0	8	2	5	1	0
Kidder	0	0	0	0	0	2	0	2	0	0
Lamoure	2	0	2	0	0	1	1	0	0	0
Logan	0	0	0	0	0	7	1	6	0	0
McHenry	0	0	0	0	0	10	1	8	1	0
McIntosh	1	1	0	0	0	5	1	2	2	0
McLean	6	0	3	0	3	93	35	57	1	0
Mercer	3	0	3	0	0	33	12	14	7	1
Mountrail	0	0	0	0	0	76	10	61	5	0
Nelson	4	0	1	1	2	47	6	37	4	1
Oliver	0	0	0	0	0	1	1	0	0	0
Ramsey	4	0	3	0	1	17	1	11	5	0
Ransom	1	0	1	0	0	9	3	4	2	0
Richland	5	1	0	0	4	55	16	37	2	1
Rolette	6	0	1	1	4	21	12	5	4	1
Sargent	0	0	0	0	0	32	7	22	3	0
Sheridan	1	0	1	0	0	17	4	13	0	1
Sioux	0	0	0	0	0	0	0	0	0	0
Slope	0	0	0	0	0	2	0	1	1	0
Stark	4	0	0	0	4	30	4	21	5	0
Stutsman	1	0	0	0	1	15	3	11	1	0
Towner	0	0	0	0	0	14	4	8	2	0
Traill	0	0	0	0	0	46	13	26	7	1
Walsh	4	0	0	0	4	60	15	37	8	1
Ward	16	1	1	0	14	163	29	118	16	0
Wells	2	0	0	0	2	9	3	5	1	0
Williams	6	0	1	0	5	87	21	51	15	0
OHIO—Metropolitan Counties										
Allen	60	1	12	19	28	943	233	673	37	4
Belmont	34	0	10	5	19	546	172	341	33	2
Butler	88	0	10	5	73	813	218	595	0	1
Carroll	2	0	2	0	0	118	34	80	4	0
Clark	17	0	3	4	10	972	242	704	26	10
Clermont	74	0	12	9	53	1,817	604	1,162	51	13
Delaware	21	1	5	5	10	1,083	433	642	8	6
Erie	41	0	6	1	34	406	117	288	1	1
Fairfield	39	0	7	12	20	1,507	454	1,009	44	9
Fulton	18	0	4	1	13	379	147	218	14	6
Geauga	10	0	2	1	7	247	61	172	14	0
Hamilton	278	7	38	185	48	6,923	1,207	5,491	225	35
Jefferson	18	1	2	1	14	240	70	151	19	3

[1] The FBI does not publish arson data unless it receives data from either the agency or the state for all 12 months of the calendar year.

Table 10.   Offenses Known to Law Enforcement, by State Metropolitan and Nonmetropolitan Counties, 2010—*Continued*

(Number)

State/County	Violent crime	Murder and non-negligent man-slaughter	Forcible rape	Robbery	Aggravated assault	Property crime	Burglary	Larceny-theft	Motor vehicle theft	Arson[1]
Lake	280	1	16	3	260	500	112	386	2	2
Lawrence	70	0	5	5	60	853	276	516	61	11
Licking[5]	117	2	17	6	92	923	318	569	36	4
Lorain	38	1	9	13	15	809	404	379	26	8
Lucas	64	1	11	13	39	1,345	364	893	88	10
Madison	9	1	2	1	5	409	163	228	18	6
Mahoning	4	0	1	0	3	217	67	147	3	1
Medina	12	1	1	1	9	141	122	19	0	1
Miami	11	0	5	2	4	504	168	316	20	10
Montgomery	340	4	22	120	194	1,918	756	999	163	20
Morrow	8	0	2	3	3	329	99	211	19	1
Ottawa	8	3	1	2	2	342	52	279	11	0
Pickaway	49	1	4	10	34	1,080	499	564	17	10
Portage	25	0	12	5	8	1,528	522	932	74	5
Preble	13	0	5	2	6	328	122	180	26	2
Richland	36	1	5	16	14	1,091	438	607	46	4
Stark	98	2	21	36	39	1,468	503	861	104	10
Summit	58	2	21	16	19	1,119	275	788	56	4
Trumbull	12	0	3	1	8	479	198	253	28	1
Warren	62	0	17	16	29	1,067	283	777	7	4
Washington	26	2	21	1	2	342	138	189	15	3
Wood	12	0	5	1	6	517	176	327	14	4
OHIO—Nonmetropolitan Counties										
Ashland	12	0	4	2	6	337	130	189	18	1
Champaign	24	0	5	3	16	459	150	274	35	6
Columbiana	8	1	1	1	5	81	65	13	3	0
Coshocton	16	0	2	6	8	624	145	470	9	5
Crawford	6	0	1	0	5	264	108	153	3	0
Defiance	2	0	0	1	1	165	44	117	4	1
Fayette	19	0	3	6	10	556	183	356	17	3
Gallia	18	1	6	3	8	748	323	403	22	9
Guernsey	6	0	1	3	2	431	210	210	11	3
Hancock	10	0	2	0	8	194	59	129	6	2
Harrison	8	0	1	0	7	130	72	51	7	0
Henry	7	0	2	1	4	291	92	193	6	1
Highland	73	0	1	3	69	562	209	323	30	5
Hocking	3	0	0	0	3	304	137	163	4	1
Holmes	5	0	2	0	3	234	61	159	14	1
Logan	14	0	5	0	9	493	169	312	12	0
Meigs	9	0	3	2	4	344	145	177	22	1
Mercer	12	0	3	2	7	220	58	156	6	1
Monroe	10	0	2	2	6	88	34	54	0	1
Morgan	6	0	0	1	5	188	70	102	16	1
Muskingum	40	2	19	9	10	1,298	406	816	76	14
Paulding	6	0	1	0	5	174	65	109	0	1
Pike	5	0	1	0	4	431	141	268	22	7
Putnam	1	0	1	0	0	85	33	51	1	0
Ross	45	0	13	22	10	1,915	517	1,305	93	4
Sandusky	68	0	6	3	59	122	80	39	3	0
Scioto	24	2	4	10	8	1,053	386	622	45	8
Seneca	3	0	2	0	1	222	75	145	2	0
Shelby[5]	15	0	1	1	13	169	60	94	15	0
Tuscarawas	16	0	5	3	8	283	125	139	19	1
Van Wert	4	0	1	2	1	221	102	113	6	1
Vinton	15	0	1	5	9	263	122	123	18	1
Wayne	26	1	12	1	12	630	250	338	42	6
Williams	12	0	8	1	3	261	98	153	10	1
Wyandot	6	0	1	0	5	6	3	3	0	0
OKLAHOMA—Metropolitan Counties										
Canadian[2]		0	3	3		140	57	58	25	1
Cleveland	40	0	6	0	34	309	118	154	37	9
Comanche	47	2	4	1	40	378	114	229	35	1
Creek	59	0	9	3	47	578	211	302	65	9
Grady	27	0	0	3	24	364	145	192	27	1
Le Flore	57	0	2	1	54	410	174	207	29	13
Lincoln	30	0	6	0	24	315	88	204	23	2
Logan	47	1	9	0	37	298	114	170	14	2
McClain	23	3	5	2	13	303	102	170	31	3
Oklahoma	36	1	3	0	32	226	83	121	22	0
Okmulgee	19	1	5	1	12	244	85	147	12	19
Osage	37	0	6	0	31	441	168	252	21	15
Pawnee	15	0	0	0	15	129	56	65	8	0
Rogers	41	0	4	1	36	489	160	253	76	1

[1] The FBI does not publish arson data unless it receives data from either the agency or the state for all 12 months of the calendar year.

[2] The FBI determined that the agency's data were overreported. Consequently, affected data are not included in this table.

[5] Because of changes in the state/local agency's reporting practices, figures are not comparable to previous years' data.

Table 10.   Offenses Known to Law Enforcement, by State Metropolitan and Nonmetropolitan Counties, 2010—*Continued*

(Number)

State/County	Violent crime	Murder and non-negligent man-slaughter	Forcible rape	Robbery	Aggravated assault	Property crime	Burglary	Larceny-theft	Motor vehicle theft	Arson[1]
Sequoyah	62	5	10	2	45	432	147	276	9	6
Tulsa	188	1	8	6	173	519	255	211	53	6
Wagoner	43	0	4	2	37	547	153	340	54	9
OKLAHOMA—Nonmetropolitan Counties										
Adair	66	1	2	0	63	215	121	83	11	5
Alfalfa	1	0	0	0	1	29	11	16	2	1
Atoka	8	0	3	0	5	132	64	51	17	2
Beaver	6	0	2	1	3	47	5	38	4	1
Beckham	6	0	0	0	6	38	12	17	9	1
Blaine	4	0	2	1	1	48	9	37	2	1
Bryan	60	0	4	1	55	349	133	168	48	7
Caddo[2]		0	8	2		205	76	118	11	1
Carter[2]		0	3	1		189	81	93	15	1
Cherokee[5]	38	1	3	1	33	212	104	84	24	2
Choctaw	19	0	1	1	17	137	53	68	16	4
Cimarron	0	0	0	0	0	0	0	0	0	0
Coal	8	0	1	0	7	77	12	60	5	1
Cotton	7	1	1	0	5	30	8	21	1	0
Craig	5	0	0	0	5	103	40	55	8	7
Custer	9	0	2	0	7	115	60	48	7	0
Delaware	62	2	18	2	40	395	183	180	32	5
Dewey	2	0	0	0	2	14	2	10	2	0
Ellis	8	0	0	1	7	43	26	11	6	0
Garfield	6	0	1	1	4	66	16	50	0	21
Garvin	25	0	7	1	17	184	39	134	11	4
Grant	1	0	0	0	1	48	11	35	2	3
Greer	1	0	0	0	1	14	10	4	0	0
Harmon	1	0	0	0	1	17	5	11	1	0
Harper	2	0	0	0	2	11	2	8	1	0
Haskell[2]		0	0	0		68	19	34	15	4
Hughes	13	0	1	0	12	151	58	71	22	1
Jackson	7	0	0	0	7	76	30	39	7	2
Jefferson	3	0	1	0	2	23	5	17	1	0
Johnston	22	2	1	0	19	4	4	0	0	2
Kay	27	0	3	1	23	73	35	34	4	5
Kingfisher	3	0	1	0	2	96	19	68	9	2
Kiowa	9	0	0	0	9	68	30	37	1	0
Latimer	6	0	1	0	5	90	37	45	8	3
Love	2	0	0	0	2	82	25	41	16	4
Major	0	0	0	0	0	35	2	32	1	1
Marshall[2]		0	3	1		68	29	33	6	1
Mayes	33	0	3	0	30	287	106	163	18	0
McCurtain	50	0	5	2	43	526	194	293	39	27
McIntosh	29	1	5	0	23	266	102	150	14	5
Murray	6	0	1	0	5	38	25	12	1	1
Muskogee	72	2	7	2	61	376	144	186	46	10
Noble	1	0	0	0	1	51	15	35	1	2
Nowata	16	0	3	0	13	120	67	47	6	2
Okfuskee	11	1	0	1	9	59	27	26	6	5
Ottawa	3	0	0	1	2	114	58	42	14	4
Payne	27	0	9	3	15	290	122	151	17	13
Pittsburg	34	3	7	0	24	369	164	189	16	12
Pontotoc	22	1	2	0	19	284	110	158	16	7
Pottawatomie	39	1	3	3	32	601	227	308	66	2
Pushmataha	20	1	0	0	19	130	58	57	15	3
Roger Mills	2	0	0	0	2	36	8	26	2	0
Seminole	19	0	2	0	17	308	109	180	19	5
Stephens	38	1	7	1	29	259	70	157	32	2
Texas	2	0	1	0	1	29	10	18	1	0
Tillman	8	0	0	0	8	64	15	45	4	0
Washington	11	0	4	1	6	165	69	88	8	9
Washita	13	0	4	0	9	64	17	36	11	3
Woods	2	0	0	0	2	4	0	3	1	0
Woodward	14	0	0	0	14	66	19	42	5	3
OREGON—Metropolitan Counties[5]										
Benton	26	0	5	1	20	184	51	121	12	3
Clackamas	225	4	35	107	79	6,102	1,097	4,582	423	18
Deschutes	156	2	15	7	132	983	215	705	63	12
Jackson	177	0	12	6	159	989	228	686	75	7
Lane	242	3	25	15	199	1,039	474	461	104	13
Multnomah	81	0	3	21	57	1,015	120	835	60	2
Polk	47	2	7	1	37	261	71	173	17	3
Washington	267	2	73	33	159	2,509	515	1,824	170	29
Yamhill	25	0	3	1	21	569	137	398	34	10

[1] The FBI does not publish arson data unless it receives data from either the agency or the state for all 12 months of the calendar year.

[2] The FBI determined that the agency's data were overreported. Consequently, affected data are not included in this table.

[5] Because of changes in the state/local agency's reporting practices, figures are not comparable to previous years' data.

Table 10.   Offenses Known to Law Enforcement, by State Metropolitan and Nonmetropolitan Counties, 2010—*Continued*

(Number)

State/County	Violent crime	Murder and non-negligent man-slaughter	Forcible rape	Robbery	Aggravated assault	Property crime	Burglary	Larceny-theft	Motor vehicle theft	Arson[1]
OREGON—Nonmetropolitan Counties[5]										
Baker	1	0	1	0	0	19	6	11	2	0
Clatsop	6	0	2	0	4	182	60	110	12	3
Coos	77	3	7	3	64	488	160	290	38	6
Crook	22	0	3	2	17	120	55	63	2	2
Curry	22	0	0	0	22	251	72	161	18	1
Douglas	42	2	13	8	19	823	242	507	74	19
Gilliam	0	0	0	0	0	16	2	13	1	0
Grant	0	0	0	0	0	32	4	24	4	1
Harney	3	0	0	0	3	22	12	9	1	1
Jefferson	4	0	2	1	1	242	68	145	29	1
Lake	1	0	0	0	1	31	10	21	0	0
Lincoln	42	1	8	1	32	357	129	211	17	3
Linn	40	2	11	7	20	1,017	276	668	73	8
Morrow	11	1	3	1	6	122	17	100	5	1
Sherman	0	0	0	0	0	45	3	39	3	0
Tillamook	8	2	1	2	3	293	90	179	24	0
Umatilla	62	1	6	4	51	411	119	249	43	2
Union	10	0	0	0	10	175	44	124	7	3
Wasco	3	1	0	1	1	171	51	107	13	1
PENNSYLVANIA—Metropolitan Counties										
Allegheny	5	0	0	0	5	0	0	0	0	0
Allegheny County Police Department	25	0	0	0	25	115	0	105	10	126
Beaver	0	0	0	0	0	0	0	0	0	0
Blair	1	0	0	0	1	0	0	0	0	0
Butler	0	0	0	0	0	0	0	0	0	0
Cumberland	1	0	0	0	1	0	0	0	0	0
Erie	2	0	0	0	2	1	0	1	0	0
Luzerne	1	0	0	0	1	4	0	4	0	0
Mercer	2	0	0	0	2	0	0	0	0	0
Montgomery	0	0	0	0	0	0	0	0	0	0
Washington	0	0	0	0	0	0	0	0	0	0
York	0	0	0	0	0	0	0	0	0	0
PENNSYLVANIA—Nonmetropolitan Counties										
Clarion	0	0	0	0	0	3	2	1	0	0
Elk	0	0	0	0	0	0	0	0	0	0
Franklin	0	0	0	0	0	0	0	0	0	0
Greene	0	0	0	0	0	0	0	0	0	0
Jefferson	0	0	0	0	0	0	0	0	0	0
Snyder	0	0	0	0	0	1	0	1	0	0
Tioga	0	0	0	0	0	0	0	0	0	0
SOUTH CAROLINA—Metropolitan Counties										
Aiken	380	4	42	64	270	3,543	1,426	1,813	304	3
Anderson	795	4	47	101	643	6,278	1,829	3,928	521	27
Berkeley	534	3	36	88	407	3,424	976	2,081	367	19
Calhoun	50	1	1	5	43	338	109	183	46	10
Charleston	577	9	18	98	452	2,374	776	1,364	234	8
Darlington	371	8	19	54	290	1,866	658	1,078	130	11
Dorchester	370	1	9	74	286	2,536	833	1,481	222	8
Edgefield	30	2	3	4	21	435	144	251	40	2
Fairfield	155	0	2	10	143	661	173	419	69	2
Florence	342	9	24	70	239	2,784	800	1,806	178	7
Greenville	1,748	17	111	323	1,297	10,103	2,797	6,521	785	43
Horry	2	0	1	0	1	54	1	53	0	0
Horry County Police Department	943	14	52	149	728	7,375	1,876	4,688	811	30
Laurens	238	1	16	20	201	1,336	499	683	154	12
Lexington	505	6	52	96	351	3,902	981	2,574	347	10
Pickens	267	4	26	12	225	1,968	600	1,201	167	6
Richland	2,390	12	94	311	1,973	9,681	2,784	5,913	984	42
Saluda	47	0	9	0	38	252	89	141	22	1
Spartanburg	631	8	52	103	468	5,955	1,646	3,859	450	36
York	420	1	43	43	333	2,772	723	1,877	172	17
SOUTH CAROLINA—Nonmetropolitan Counties										
Abbeville	44	0	2	1	41	346	87	235	24	9
Allendale	16	0	0	0	16	106	38	61	7	0
Bamberg	51	0	5	3	43	294	104	168	22	6
Barnwell	103	0	4	6	93	382	115	246	21	3
Beaufort	713	4	17	96	596	3,914	1,120	2,576	218	21
Chester	154	3	5	13	133	903	258	581	64	6
Chesterfield	140	3	9	6	122	842	222	564	56	6
Clarendon	125	1	10	9	105	912	268	575	69	2
Colleton	208	7	17	28	156	1,332	421	728	183	16
Dillon	263	2	1	41	219	1,154	488	602	64	10

[1] The FBI does not publish arson data unless it receives data from either the agency or the state for all 12 months of the calendar year.

[5] Because of changes in the state/local agency's reporting practices, figures are not comparable to previous years' data.

Table 10. Offenses Known to Law Enforcement, by State Metropolitan and Nonmetropolitan Counties, 2010—*Continued*

(Number)

State/County	Violent crime	Murder and non-negligent man-slaughter	Forcible rape	Robbery	Aggravated assault	Property crime	Burglary	Larceny-theft	Motor vehicle theft	Arson[1]
Georgetown	208	2	9	19	178	1,592	491	971	130	7
Greenwood	287	0	12	14	261	1,642	394	1,174	74	1
Hampton	92	0	1	7	84	345	133	195	17	3
Jasper	65	2	4	19	40	715	226	438	51	2
Lancaster	273	3	17	51	202	2,064	639	1,301	124	3
Lee	77	1	4	4	68	545	233	268	44	7
Marion	124	0	4	13	107	724	241	432	51	2
Marlboro	186	2	14	17	153	732	257	415	60	4
McCormick	19	0	1	3	15	119	37	65	17	1
Newberry	63	3	3	11	46	437	98	312	27	1
Oconee	269	0	25	10	234	1,386	475	787	124	6
Orangeburg	392	15	15	101	261	3,674	1,122	2,067	485	12
Union	104	1	0	7	96	532	170	348	14	3
Williamsburg	128	5	8	22	93	879	291	483	105	7
SOUTH DAKOTA—Metropolitan Counties										
Lincoln	12	0	1	0	11	127	40	80	7	1
Meade	4	0	0	1	3	41	11	27	3	0
Minnehaha	38	0	2	2	34	373	180	175	18	2
Pennington	85	2	25	0	58	396	105	278	13	3
Turner	5	0	1	0	4	44	11	25	8	2
Union	3	0	2	0	1	33	0	31	2	0
SOUTH DAKOTA—Nonmetropolitan Counties										
Beadle	1	0	0	0	1	33	11	21	1	0
Bennett	2	0	0	0	2	15	4	11	0	0
Bon Homme	0	0	0	0	0	1	1	0	0	0
Brookings	3	0	0	0	3	84	20	63	1	0
Brown	4	0	0	0	4	30	4	23	3	0
Butte	0	0	0	0	0	23	10	12	1	1
Campbell	0	0	0	0	0	3	2	1	0	0
Charles Mix	16	0	1	0	15	43	21	17	5	2
Clark	0	0	0	0	0	13	8	4	1	0
Clay	1	0	0	0	1	18	1	15	2	0
Codington	10	0	4	0	6	33	5	24	4	0
Custer	5	0	0	0	5	63	21	38	4	0
Davison	1	0	0	0	1	6	1	4	1	0
Deuel	0	0	0	0	0	21	7	11	3	0
Dewey	1	0	1	0	0	9	2	5	2	0
Edmunds	0	0	0	0	0	2	1	0	1	0
Faulk	0	0	0	0	0	12	4	8	0	0
Hamlin	9	1	1	1	6	43	24	17	2	1
Hanson	0	0	0	0	0	15	3	10	2	0
Harding	0	0	0	0	0	1	1	0	0	0
Hughes	2	1	1	0	0	12	9	3	0	0
Jerauld	0	0	0	0	0	1	0	1	0	0
Lawrence	2	0	0	0	2	29	14	15	0	1
Marshall	5	0	2	0	3	55	23	29	3	0
Mellette	8	0	0	1	7	11	6	5	0	0
Miner	1	0	0	0	1	10	5	5	0	0
Moody	2	0	0	1	1	15	2	11	2	0
Roberts	10	0	1	0	9	15	7	5	3	2
Spink	9	0	0	0	9	38	12	26	0	0
Stanley	1	0	0	0	1	49	7	41	1	0
Sully	1	0	0	0	1	1	0	0	1	0
Tripp	1	0	0	0	1	12	4	7	1	2
Yankton	7	0	3	0	4	111	32	73	6	0
Ziebach	0	0	0	0	0	0	0	0	0	0
TENNESSEE—Metropolitan Counties										
Anderson	111	1	7	13	90	1,021	453	503	65	7
Bradley	243	0	6	10	227	884	268	552	64	3
Cannon	19	0	1	0	18	133	63	54	16	2
Carter	63	0	0	1	62	710	275	390	45	10
Cheatham	84	6	9	1	68	669	205	390	74	1
Chester	26	1	3	1	21	145	40	79	26	0
Dickson	75	2	16	1	56	558	183	325	50	5
Fayette	119	0	0	3	116	610	209	355	46	0
Hamblen	121	0	3	21	97	950	365	551	34	9
Hamilton	259	1	15	20	223	1,712	579	1,041	92	5
Hartsville/Trousdale	45	0	2	0	43	271	73	195	3	3
Hawkins	75	3	5	9	58	1,302	558	644	100	5
Hickman	41	2	4	1	34	243	79	132	32	0
Jefferson	93	3	7	9	74	952	375	510	67	3
Knox	650	8	27	129	486	5,996	1,847	3,750	399	23
Loudon	84	2	2	16	64	677	229	398	50	5
Macon	36	0	2	0	34	189	34	141	14	1

[1] The FBI does not publish arson data unless it receives data from either the agency or the state for all 12 months of the calendar year.

Table 10. Offenses Known to Law Enforcement, by State Metropolitan and Nonmetropolitan Counties, 2010—*Continued*

(Number)

State/County	Violent crime	Murder and non-negligent man-slaughter	Forcible rape	Robbery	Aggravated assault	Property crime	Burglary	Larceny-theft	Motor vehicle theft	Arson[1]
Madison	155	2	13	10	130	893	281	530	82	7
Marion	79	1	2	5	71	400	124	219	57	1
Montgomery	92	1	9	0	82	741	154	548	39	3
Polk	32	0	0	0	32	234	56	156	22	4
Robertson	84	0	9	1	74	449	155	256	38	5
Rutherford	241	0	13	11	217	1,504	451	933	120	4
Sequatchie	26	0	4	0	22	132	36	71	25	4
Shelby	474	6	39	69	360	3,538	1,291	1,987	260	16
Smith	17	0	2	0	15	59	31	25	3	0
Stewart	24	0	2	1	21	194	78	99	17	0
Sullivan	280	1	34	12	233	1,633	607	929	97	18
Tipton	347	2	15	7	323	765	222	453	90	6
Unicoi	12	1	1	1	9	145	39	100	6	3
Union	33	1	1	3	28	330	141	161	28	1
Washington	243	3	18	11	211	1,120	460	608	52	4
Williamson	47	2	2	2	41	539	174	345	20	2
Wilson	257	3	65	11	178	1,071	449	570	52	0
TENNESSEE—Nonmetropolitan Counties										
Bedford	41	0	0	4	37	259	113	133	13	2
Benton	36	1	2	0	33	247	63	175	9	1
Bledsoe	4	0	0	0	4	111	64	37	10	0
Campbell	65	1	7	5	52	1,035	424	553	58	16
Carroll	38	0	1	1	36	193	97	83	13	0
Claiborne	105	1	1	17	86	827	347	433	47	3
Clay	15	1	1	0	13	97	58	34	5	1
Cocke	145	2	0	20	123	1,084	469	520	95	9
Coffee	106	0	6	4	96	507	94	367	46	7
Crockett	28	1	0	1	26	107	37	62	8	2
Cumberland	77	2	5	8	62	1,036	432	523	81	4
Decatur	17	0	1	4	12	178	68	97	13	3
DeKalb	29	0	3	3	23	351	143	189	19	1
Dyer	42	0	0	1	41	349	100	226	23	1
Fentress	22	0	0	1	21	338	147	176	15	0
Franklin	37	2	9	2	24	356	63	255	38	10
Gibson	66	0	3	4	59	358	181	152	25	5
Giles	39	1	4	2	32	243	102	125	16	3
Greene	168	1	11	15	141	1,406	602	724	80	6
Hancock	13	0	1	0	12	142	55	83	4	0
Hardeman	82	1	4	3	74	412	205	161	46	4
Hardin	76	1	3	1	71	397	146	211	40	8
Haywood	44	1	2	2	39	198	69	104	25	2
Henderson	103	0	8	5	90	421	126	254	41	5
Henry	46	3	2	2	39	455	140	298	17	2
Houston	19	0	0	0	19	149	57	82	10	1
Humphreys	20	1	1	0	18	153	44	100	9	0
Jackson	24	0	1	5	18	222	63	141	18	4
Johnson	70	1	2	3	64	217	103	90	24	4
Lake	3	0	0	0	3	21	3	16	2	0
Lauderdale	60	1	2	4	53	406	179	183	44	1
Lawrence	101	1	7	2	91	570	257	267	46	13
Lewis	21	0	4	0	17	161	53	95	13	3
Lincoln	102	0	0	2	100	475	197	254	24	4
Marshall	23	0	1	0	22	138	35	98	5	1
Maury	140	4	11	8	117	743	185	489	69	6
McMinn	77	1	3	3	70	756	230	441	85	4
McNairy	39	1	5	1	32	299	94	166	39	1
Meigs	41	1	5	0	35	285	89	165	31	2
Monroe	99	1	2	1	95	721	184	478	59	8
Moore	5	0	2	0	3	110	21	88	1	0
Obion	16	0	2	1	13	225	50	151	24	2
Overton	27	1	1	0	25	214	99	107	8	0
Perry	25	0	1	0	24	141	54	82	5	3
Putnam	86	2	4	0	80	784	173	559	52	6
Rhea	87	0	9	4	74	363	116	209	38	3
Roane	56	0	0	2	54	705	227	423	55	0
Scott	80	0	4	2	74	560	287	254	19	1
Sevier	152	4	25	15	108	2,038	917	1,036	85	1
Van Buren	15	0	0	0	15	80	29	45	6	2
Warren	42	0	1	2	39	390	166	186	38	3
Wayne	20	2	0	1	17	75	14	52	9	1
Weakley	45	0	0	1	44	222	83	125	14	0
White	53	1	3	1	48	458	126	288	44	2

[1] The FBI does not publish arson data unless it receives data from either the agency or the state for all 12 months of the calendar year.

Table 10.   Offenses Known to Law Enforcement, by State Metropolitan and Nonmetropolitan Counties, 2010—*Continued*

(Number)

State/County	Violent crime	Murder and non-negligent man-slaughter	Forcible rape	Robbery	Aggravated assault	Property crime	Burglary	Larceny-theft	Motor vehicle theft	Arson[1]
TEXAS—Metropolitan Counties										
Aransas	21	0	6	3	12	319	116	181	22	0
Archer	8	0	1	0	7	70	23	45	2	1
Armstrong	0	0	0	0	0	22	11	10	1	0
Atascosa	29	0	0	0	29	378	119	239	20	1
Austin	18	5	4	0	9	194	98	83	13	0
Bandera	13	0	0	0	13	208	103	105	0	0
Bastrop	329	3	21	10	295	1,076	497	520	59	6
Bell	40	0	18	6	16	837	294	516	27	17
Bexar	546	11	73	110	352	6,999	2,151	4,417	431	90
Bowie	113	1	9	2	101	728	243	415	70	11
Brazoria	133	0	26	31	76	1,514	573	836	105	0
Brazos	49	0	2	1	46	405	131	255	19	2
Burleson	27	0	17	0	10	130	76	39	15	0
Caldwell	16	0	2	0	14	210	71	132	7	0
Calhoun	20	0	2	0	18	127	37	86	4	0
Callahan	12	0	0	0	12	83	31	41	11	0
Cameron	157	1	6	31	119	1,734	754	873	107	14
Carson	4	0	0	1	3	41	4	35	2	0
Chambers	49	2	3	5	39	523	159	305	59	4
Clay	10	0	0	2	8	130	43	83	4	1
Collin	86	0	9	4	73	809	417	315	77	1
Comal	230	2	32	12	184	930	350	552	28	1
Coryell	9	0	0	0	9	137	59	65	13	0
Crosby	1	0	0	0	1	16	5	9	2	0
Dallas	23	0	3	3	17	286	89	176	21	15
Delta	5	0	0	3	2	116	39	72	5	0
Denton	85	1	9	5	70	878	292	514	72	5
Ector	154	4	0	12	138	1,172	362	750	60	3
Ellis	68	1	6	4	57	733	258	417	58	7
El Paso	310	2	34	23	251	1,374	369	872	133	18
Fort Bend	896	8	50	132	706	4,440	1,579	2,625	236	22
Galveston	112	0	13	13	86	873	288	516	69	19
Goliad	18	0	4	0	14	52	21	29	2	0
Grayson	42	5	10	6	21	704	244	409	51	10
Gregg	109	3	26	3	77	623	200	322	101	5
Guadalupe	59	1	5	3	50	750	318	386	46	6
Hardin	38	1	6	2	29	376	114	210	52	4
Harris	8,089	77	212	3,059	4,741	55,841	15,240	35,318	5,283	401
Hays	116	3	7	4	102	1,119	332	750	37	4
Hidalgo	640	14	77	156	393	7,208	2,835	3,876	497	191
Hunt	93	3	0	17	73	1,194	659	465	70	2
Irion	1	0	0	0	1	18	2	15	1	0
Jefferson	25	2	2	3	18	474	126	287	61	0
Johnson	100	3	0	4	93	1,107	370	705	32	6
Jones	4	0	1	0	3	73	23	47	3	0
Kaufman	189	2	25	8	154	1,337	587	618	132	1
Kendall	17	0	7	4	6	202	67	127	8	2
Lampasas	1	0	1	0	0	101	29	69	3	2
Liberty	189	3	4	5	177	1,270	438	644	188	11
Lubbock	174	0	25	9	140	662	199	394	69	4
McLennan	109	0	38	7	64	765	304	405	56	14
Medina	41	0	2	0	39	255	117	120	18	0
Midland	29	1	0	4	24	527	194	301	32	1
Montgomery	862	7	50	146	659	7,561	2,184	4,824	553	27
Nueces	62	1	2	5	54	250	95	147	8	0
Orange	81	0	6	6	69	852	328	446	78	1
Parker	104	3	6	4	91	1,128	437	626	65	0
Potter	30	3	4	1	22	211	67	128	16	1
Randall	31	0	3	1	27	348	114	199	35	3
Robertson	2	0	0	0	2	195	50	129	16	2
Rockwall	33	1	5	1	26	199	77	99	23	0
Rusk	68	5	2	3	58	567	248	262	57	5
San Jacinto	82	2	4	10	66	761	362	340	59	3
San Patricio	31	1	1	8	21	298	111	171	16	3
Smith	184	7	64	23	90	2,021	629	1,229	163	27
Tarrant	105	1	27	14	63	1,245	445	722	78	0
Taylor	17	0	4	1	12	190	95	79	16	0
Tom Green	24	1	9	4	10	296	84	205	7	3
Travis	495	9	15	57	414	3,692	1,168	2,367	157	28
Upshur	41	0	9	3	29	554	184	332	38	2
Victoria	109	1	7	7	94	555	175	351	29	0
Waller	38	2	2	2	32	323	118	178	27	0

[1] The FBI does not publish arson data unless it receives data from either the agency or the state for all 12 months of the calendar year.

Table 10. Offenses Known to Law Enforcement, by State Metropolitan and Nonmetropolitan Counties, 2010—*Continued*

(Number)

State/County	Violent crime	Murder and non-negligent man-slaughter	Forcible rape	Robbery	Aggravated assault	Property crime	Burglary	Larceny-theft	Motor vehicle theft	Arson[1]
Webb	90	2	3	2	83	311	120	155	36	3
Wichita	29	0	2	3	24	154	48	102	4	8
Williamson	129	2	26	6	95	1,572	392	1,129	51	10
Wilson	15	1	1	2	11	238	86	135	17	0
Wise	117	0	9	2	106	449	175	262	12	0
TEXAS—Nonmetropolitan Counties										
Anderson	78	4	6	3	65	396	165	213	18	13
Andrews	5	0	0	0	5	90	36	52	2	0
Angelina	54	0	7	7	40	371	176	180	15	1
Bailey	3	0	1	0	2	41	20	18	3	0
Baylor	3	0	0	0	3	21	10	10	1	1
Bee	43	0	9	2	32	148	47	85	16	2
Blanco	13	0	0	0	13	94	45	35	14	0
Borden	0	0	0	0	0	2	2	0	0	0
Bosque	5	0	0	0	5	133	45	83	5	0
Brewster	8	1	1	0	6	32	14	17	1	0
Briscoe	2	0	0	0	2	8	5	2	1	0
Brooks	9	0	2	0	7	5	1	2	2	1
Brown	37	0	0	0	37	193	75	115	3	2
Burnet	14	0	5	0	9	307	119	155	33	1
Camp	7	0	5	0	2	139	73	61	5	1
Cass	39	0	8	1	30	394	160	197	37	0
Castro	3	1	0	0	2	70	24	44	2	1
Cherokee	66	2	3	7	54	539	192	292	55	4
Childress	5	0	1	0	4	13	6	5	2	4
Cochran	0	0	0	0	0	73	22	46	5	1
Coke	1	0	0	0	1	16	15	0	1	0
Coleman	1	0	0	0	1	47	17	26	4	1
Collingsworth	0	0	0	0	0	0	0	0	0	0
Colorado	11	0	1	1	9	160	55	91	14	0
Comanche	15	0	0	0	15	127	40	84	3	1
Concho	3	0	2	0	1	14	7	5	2	0
Cooke	29	2	6	3	18	280	102	159	19	2
Cottle	0	0	0	0	0	4	3	1	0	0
Crane	1	0	0	0	1	25	11	13	1	1
Culberson	5	0	1	0	4	10	0	8	2	0
Dallam	1	0	0	0	1	26	8	17	1	0
Dawson	0	0	0	0	0	44	14	26	4	1
Deaf Smith	7	0	1	1	5	82	33	46	3	3
DeWitt	18	0	0	0	18	98	36	60	2	1
Dickens	0	0	0	0	0	1	1	0	0	0
Dimmit	47	0	0	5	42	157	55	91	11	1
Donley	9	0	0	0	9	40	14	25	1	0
Duval	39	1	1	3	34	99	37	47	15	0
Eastland	4	0	0	0	4	19	6	12	1	1
Edwards	3	0	0	0	3	31	14	17	0	0
Erath	20	0	8	0	12	134	35	83	16	0
Falls	7	0	0	0	7	92	40	39	13	1
Fannin	23	1	3	0	19	218	91	116	11	0
Fayette	6	2	0	0	4	180	67	101	12	2
Fisher	10	0	0	0	10	54	22	32	0	0
Floyd	4	0	1	0	3	9	3	6	0	0
Foard	1	0	0	0	1	6	2	4	0	0
Franklin	19	0	4	2	13	108	57	42	9	0
Freestone	8	1	0	0	7	135	36	88	11	0
Frio	4	0	0	0	4	83	38	41	4	0
Gaines	6	1	0	0	5	70	24	41	5	4
Garza	2	0	0	0	2	36	15	18	3	0
Gillespie	8	1	3	0	4	89	30	58	1	0
Glasscock	1	0	0	0	1	13	3	10	0	0
Gonzales	13	1	2	2	8	133	54	62	17	2
Gray	11	0	2	1	8	100	33	64	3	0
Grimes	16	1	2	2	11	309	117	170	22	2
Hale	3	0	1	0	2	98	45	47	6	0
Hall	3	0	0	1	2	6	2	3	1	0
Hamilton	24	0	1	2	21	184	98	79	7	3
Hansford	1	0	0	0	1	20	4	15	1	3
Hardeman	7	0	1	0	6	98	45	51	2	16
Harrison	112	1	3	4	104	590	235	332	23	1
Hartley	9	0	1	0	8	34	13	19	2	0
Haskell	2	0	1	0	1	15	4	11	0	0
Hemphill	14	0	1	1	12	42	7	32	3	0
Henderson	168	3	34	11	120	1,324	527	672	125	2

[1] The FBI does not publish arson data unless it receives data from either the agency or the state for all 12 months of the calendar year.

Table 10.   Offenses Known to Law Enforcement, by State Metropolitan and Nonmetropolitan Counties, 2010—*Continued*

(Number)

State/County	Violent crime	Murder and non-negligent man-slaughter	Forcible rape	Robbery	Aggravated assault	Property crime	Burglary	Larceny-theft	Motor vehicle theft	Arson[1]
Hill	5	1	4	0	0	377	160	200	17	4
Hockley	5	0	1	0	4	88	37	46	5	0
Hood	86	1	8	5	72	710	202	445	63	8
Hopkins	12	0	6	0	6	131	65	55	11	0
Houston	14	1	0	0	13	209	73	112	24	0
Howard	22	0	0	0	22	167	65	88	14	0
Hudspeth	10	0	0	1	9	44	20	10	14	1
Hutchinson	16	0	1	0	15	135	34	88	13	0
Jack	7	0	0	0	7	42	20	16	6	1
Jackson	18	0	0	1	17	69	18	49	2	0
Jasper	80	0	9	0	71	306	121	173	12	0
Jeff Davis	5	0	2	0	3	9	5	4	0	0
Jim Hogg	10	0	0	0	10	25	10	15	0	0
Jim Wells	79	1	9	2	67	326	147	152	27	2
Karnes	17	0	0	0	17	140	65	62	13	3
Kenedy	0	0	0	0	0	4	1	2	1	0
Kent	2	0	0	0	2	21	4	17	0	0
Kerr	33	0	5	0	28	364	110	235	19	2
Kimble	3	1	2	0	0	14	6	5	3	0
King	1	0	0	0	1	4	4	0	0	0
Kinney	7	1	0	0	6	11	6	3	2	2
Kleberg	6	0	1	0	5	185	31	151	3	0
Knox	0	0	0	0	0	17	5	10	2	0
Lamar	30	1	6	0	23	377	155	203	19	0
Lamb	14	0	2	0	12	114	29	76	9	0
La Salle	13	0	0	1	12	60	16	43	1	0
Lavaca	7	1	1	0	5	65	28	33	4	0
Lee	22	1	6	1	14	117	62	47	8	1
Leon	19	0	2	1	16	177	76	92	9	0
Limestone	81	0	24	1	56	374	165	198	11	5
Lipscomb	0	0	0	0	0	16	1	13	2	0
Live Oak	3	0	1	0	2	71	34	36	1	0
Llano	11	1	4	1	5	312	102	203	7	1
Loving	0	0	0	0	0	0	0	0	0	0
Lynn	2	0	1	0	1	27	12	13	2	1
Madison	23	2	1	0	20	139	55	70	14	0
Marion	48	0	8	3	37	239	104	122	13	2
Martin	1	0	0	0	1	36	15	17	4	0
Mason	2	0	1	0	1	35	5	30	0	0
Matagorda	44	0	2	1	41	332	139	184	9	1
Maverick	73	0	5	1	67	464	203	234	27	1
McCulloch	2	0	0	1	1	39	16	22	1	0
McMullen	2	0	1	0	1	6	0	5	1	0
Menard	1	1	0	0	0	8	2	5	1	0
Milam	11	0	2	0	9	186	52	124	10	2
Mills	2	0	0	0	2	53	20	31	2	1
Mitchell	1	0	0	0	1	26	7	19	0	0
Montague	14	0	0	0	14	210	88	103	19	1
Moore	2	0	1	0	1	77	25	46	6	0
Morris	41	0	6	4	31	125	66	52	7	2
Motley	2	0	0	0	2	19	6	12	1	1
Nacogdoches	73	2	5	4	62	504	203	269	32	2
Navarro	47	0	18	3	26	603	245	337	21	1
Newton	10	0	0	1	9	139	50	80	9	2
Nolan	8	1	0	0	7	62	26	31	5	1
Ochiltree	6	1	0	0	5	33	9	21	3	0
Oldham	2	0	0	0	2	17	3	12	2	0
Palo Pinto	30	0	1	1	28	191	106	71	14	1
Panola	30	2	7	2	19	247	79	141	27	2
Parmer	1	0	0	1	0	42	11	30	1	0
Pecos	9	1	1	1	6	35	10	23	2	1
Polk	70	3	27	8	32	741	311	386	44	3
Presidio	4	0	0	1	3	9	7	1	1	0
Rains	17	0	1	2	14	119	47	67	5	0
Reagan	2	0	0	0	2	7	2	5	0	0
Real	5	0	0	0	5	12	8	4	0	0
Red River	19	0	1	0	18	132	70	54	8	1
Reeves	13	0	2	0	11	81	29	48	4	1
Refugio	8	0	2	0	6	33	12	20	1	0
Roberts	3	0	1	0	2	25	5	17	3	0
Runnels	0	0	0	0	0	26	0	23	3	0
Sabine	26	1	2	1	22	68	30	37	1	2
San Augustine	17	0	1	0	16	107	38	64	5	1

[1] The FBI does not publish arson data unless it receives data from either the agency or the state for all 12 months of the calendar year.

Table 10.   Offenses Known to Law Enforcement, by State Metropolitan and Nonmetropolitan Counties, 2010—*Continued*

(Number)

State/County	Violent crime	Murder and non-negligent man-slaughter	Forcible rape	Robbery	Aggravated assault	Property crime	Burglary	Larceny-theft	Motor vehicle theft	Arson[1]
San Saba	9	0	1	1	7	15	10	5	0	1
Schleicher	1	0	0	0	1	11	3	8	0	0
Scurry	4	1	0	0	3	90	26	55	9	0
Shackelford	4	0	2	0	2	36	14	19	3	0
Shelby	36	2	2	7	25	270	69	182	19	5
Sherman	0	0	0	0	0	0	0	0	0	0
Somervell	7	0	2	2	3	95	25	67	3	2
Starr	113	3	11	8	91	418	178	203	37	4
Stephens	8	1	0	0	7	55	26	23	6	0
Sterling	3	0	0	0	3	15	5	9	1	2
Stonewall	5	0	0	0	5	10	8	2	0	0
Sutton	0	0	0	0	0	7	0	7	0	0
Swisher	7	0	4	0	3	30	14	14	2	1
Terrell	4	0	0	0	4	30	21	7	2	0
Terry	1	0	0	0	1	44	13	28	3	0
Throckmorton	0	0	0	0	0	5	5	0	0	0
Titus	51	2	6	4	39	281	119	144	18	5
Trinity	15	1	6	1	7	257	97	140	20	0
Tyler	93	2	12	4	75	401	221	153	27	8
Upton	2	0	1	0	1	20	3	17	0	0
Uvalde	28	0	3	1	24	161	71	85	5	0
Val Verde	14	1	1	3	9	167	64	91	12	1
Van Zandt	88	1	0	4	83	699	289	338	72	5
Walker	87	0	11	9	67	467	191	244	32	0
Ward	10	0	0	0	10	71	26	41	4	0
Washington	27	0	6	2	19	196	85	103	8	1
Wharton	54	0	0	11	43	358	171	161	26	8
Wheeler	12	1	0	1	10	49	13	32	4	1
Wilbarger	1	0	0	0	1	21	7	11	3	2
Willacy	66	0	9	1	56	291	113	166	12	5
Winkler	5	0	1	0	4	31	4	22	5	0
Wood	22	1	3	0	18	469	176	266	27	5
Yoakum	7	0	1	1	5	39	8	30	1	0
Young	8	0	0	0	8	96	42	49	5	0
Zapata	37	2	5	3	27	279	156	112	11	1
Zavala	22	0	0	1	21	73	23	43	7	1
UTAH—Metropolitan Counties										
Cache	21	0	10	3	8	388	61	314	13	2
Davis	21	0	7	1	13	287	63	207	17	0
Juab	5	0	1	0	4	78	13	56	9	1
Morgan	7	0	3	0	4	68	29	36	3	0
Salt Lake	561	6	71	115	369	7,577	1,590	5,320	667	27
Summit	16	0	5	2	9	530	99	390	41	0
Tooele	24	0	5	2	17	145	58	64	23	5
Utah	13	1	3	0	9	312	67	236	9	3
Washington	15	0	3	0	12	154	38	90	26	0
Weber	36	1	7	6	22	1,277	267	953	57	6
UTAH—Nonmetropolitan Counties										
Beaver	4	0	2	0	2	32	7	24	1	0
Box Elder	10	0	3	0	7	184	36	142	6	0
Carbon	6	0	2	0	4	140	55	84	1	1
Daggett	0	0	0	0	0	19	9	9	1	0
Duchesne	15	0	1	1	13	170	42	114	14	1
Emery	1	0	1	0	0	87	26	60	1	0
Grand	2	0	0	0	2	72	18	52	2	0
Iron	24	0	4	1	19	188	52	116	20	6
Millard	16	1	1	0	14	232	43	181	8	1
Rich	2	0	0	0	2	46	17	29	0	0
San Juan	7	0	3	0	4	40	15	22	3	0
Sevier	14	0	4	1	9	151	47	100	4	1
Uintah	29	0	3	0	26	311	120	169	22	1
Wasatch	7	0	0	0	7	118	22	87	9	0
Wayne	5	0	2	0	3	17	1	16	0	0
VERMONT—Metropolitan Counties										
Franklin	4	0	0	0	4	199	45	150	4	0
Grand Isle	0	0	0	0	0	71	39	30	2	0
VERMONT—Nonmetropolitan Counties										
Addison	0	0	0	0	0	0	0	0	0	0
Bennington	2	0	0	0	2	3	0	2	1	0
Lamoille	5	0	2	0	3	136	22	111	3	0
Orange	5	0	5	0	0	67	14	51	2	0
Orleans	0	0	0	0	0	43	13	29	1	0
Rutland	1	0	0	0	1	74	4	68	2	0

[1] The FBI does not publish arson data unless it receives data from either the agency or the state for all 12 months of the calendar year.

Table 10. Offenses Known to Law Enforcement, by State Metropolitan and Nonmetropolitan Counties, 2010—*Continued*

(Number)

State/County	Violent crime	Murder and non-negligent man-slaughter	Forcible rape	Robbery	Aggravated assault	Property crime	Burglary	Larceny-theft	Motor vehicle theft	Arson[1]
Washington	0	0	0	0	0	0	0	0	0	0
Windham	0	0	0	0	0	10	1	8	1	0
VIRGINIA—Metropolitan Counties										
Albemarle County Police Department	126	2	27	21	76	1,803	294	1,432	77	11
Amelia	21	1	3	5	12	156	47	95	14	4
Amherst	29	0	7	3	19	461	53	388	20	3
Appomattox	21	8	4	1	8	96	20	71	5	0
Arlington County Police Department	329	1	25	142	161	4,419	303	3,904	212	3
Bedford	244	2	6	2	234	735	187	496	52	3
Botetourt	26	0	2	3	21	348	86	246	16	4
Campbell	69	2	12	9	46	713	157	513	43	4
Caroline	44	0	9	10	25	428	65	338	25	10
Charles City	7	0	3	0	4	34	10	19	5	0
Chesterfield County Police Department	479	10	60	217	192	6,980	1,533	5,133	314	59
Clarke	18	0	1	1	16	142	22	117	3	1
Craig	0	0	0	0	0	18	10	8	0	0
Cumberland	12	0	0	2	10	40	16	18	6	2
Dinwiddie	49	1	9	8	31	471	137	279	55	4
Fairfax County Police Department	953	22	120	379	432	15,523	1,191	13,365	967	44
Fauquier	42	0	12	5	25	597	111	448	38	3
Fluvanna	17	0	1	1	15	269	57	196	16	3
Franklin	33	2	9	3	19	604	114	444	46	1
Frederick	93	1	42	22	28	1,512	375	1,044	93	3
Giles	12	0	1	1	10	144	27	111	6	0
Gloucester	18	0	5	2	11	583	80	487	16	3
Goochland	20	2	2	2	14	183	31	145	7	1
Greene	50	0	4	2	44	241	33	197	11	2
Hanover	53	1	9	7	36	930	122	742	66	1
Henrico County Police Department	498	12	26	248	212	7,593	1,206	6,031	356	91
Isle of Wight	32	0	1	10	21	440	131	283	26	2
James City County Police Department	63	0	7	11	45	964	195	727	42	14
King and Queen	14	0	1	1	12	65	18	38	9	4
King William	8	0	0	0	8	90	26	60	4	0
Loudoun	187	0	28	36	123	2,786	308	2,342	136	37
Mathews	7	0	1	0	6	90	29	56	5	4
Montgomery	39	0	3	2	34	580	183	364	33	8
Nelson	10	1	1	0	8	218	55	141	22	0
New Kent	18	0	0	0	18	278	80	187	11	3
Pittsylvania	46	4	5	8	29	696	251	403	42	4
Powhatan	12	2	3	0	7	246	68	169	9	2
Prince George County Police Department	27	2	5	8	12	488	87	377	24	1
Prince William County Police Department	623	9	42	229	343	7,419	1,018	5,953	448	29
Pulaski	52	2	6	7	37	664	156	489	19	1
Roanoke County Police Department	98	6	19	14	59	1,186	250	902	34	11
Rockingham	40	0	14	1	25	279	79	192	8	4
Scott	17	5	3	1	8	427	135	276	16	3
Spotsylvania	262	7	29	49	177	2,370	217	2,030	123	15
Stafford	208	2	36	54	116	2,085	204	1,751	130	13
Surry	21	1	2	5	13	59	25	33	1	0
Sussex	19	0	1	2	16	170	57	106	7	1
Warren	11	0	5	1	5	341	53	262	26	1
Washington	40	1	9	2	28	972	167	789	16	5
York	84	0	3	21	60	1,201	203	963	35	13
VIRGINIA—Nonmetropolitan Counties										
Accomack	53	2	7	28	16	467	123	313	31	2
Alleghany	8	0	2	0	6	168	44	112	12	8
Augusta	75	2	8	3	62	745	160	540	45	3
Bath	1	0	1	0	0	38	13	23	2	0
Bland	3	0	0	1	2	30	12	17	1	0
Brunswick	18	0	3	0	15	127	45	63	19	0
Buchanan	31	3	4	2	22	422	119	278	25	1
Buckingham	28	0	5	3	20	203	75	115	13	2
Carroll	28	1	7	3	17	435	128	274	33	5
Charlotte	13	0	1	2	10	117	22	81	14	0
Culpeper	21	0	4	1	16	312	77	211	24	2
Dickenson	15	1	0	0	14	175	39	128	8	2
Essex	5	0	1	0	4	46	4	38	4	3
Floyd	10	0	4	1	5	161	47	105	9	4
Grayson	20	0	3	0	17	120	29	83	8	4
Greensville	18	0	0	5	13	148	50	88	10	0
Halifax	35	1	10	8	16	458	133	278	47	5
Henry	155	6	6	26	117	1,044	287	690	67	3
Highland	1	0	0	0	1	12	2	10	0	1

[1] The FBI does not publish arson data unless it receives data from either the agency or the state for all 12 months of the calendar year.

Table 10. Offenses Known to Law Enforcement, by State Metropolitan and Nonmetropolitan Counties, 2010—*Continued*

(Number)

State/County	Violent crime	Murder and non-negligent man-slaughter	Forcible rape	Robbery	Aggravated assault	Property crime	Burglary	Larceny-theft	Motor vehicle theft	Arson[1]
King George	26	0	5	2	19	397	59	320	18	3
Lancaster	8	2	3	0	3	122	29	87	6	1
Lee	30	4	4	2	20	255	81	168	6	0
Lunenburg	15	0	2	0	13	110	45	55	10	2
Madison	7	1	1	0	5	105	11	86	8	0
Mecklenburg	39	1	6	7	25	366	105	218	43	4
Middlesex	12	1	7	0	4	149	35	100	14	0
Northampton	12	2	1	3	6	187	88	92	7	1
Northumberland	14	0	2	0	12	117	35	77	5	3
Nottoway	3	0	1	0	2	69	13	48	8	2
Orange	17	0	5	3	9	177	34	130	13	1
Page	17	1	5	0	11	227	70	146	11	4
Patrick	22	0	2	1	19	297	75	193	29	3
Prince Edward	13	0	1	3	9	109	57	49	3	3
Rappahannock	4	2	0	0	2	60	19	38	3	2
Richmond	9	0	0	1	8	52	14	31	7	1
Rockbridge	8	1	1	2	4	280	64	204	12	1
Russell	21	0	10	0	11	275	93	166	16	4
Shenandoah	18	0	3	2	13	369	111	244	14	7
Smyth	22	0	6	0	16	327	59	246	22	7
Southampton	27	2	2	4	19	296	86	183	27	3
Tazewell	19	3	3	0	13	569	150	384	35	1
Westmoreland	6	0	0	1	5	100	27	67	6	0
Wise	36	1	9	2	24	393	115	256	22	6
Wythe	16	0	2	1	13	220	37	172	11	0
WASHINGTON—Metropolitan Counties										
Asotin	16	1	0	0	15	170	35	131	4	0
Benton	58	1	5	5	47	561	198	316	47	0
Chelan	37	0	18	4	15	867	174	650	43	1
Clark	239	0	60	54	125	4,288	926	2,894	468	40
Cowlitz	102	0	45	7	50	583	189	339	55	5
Franklin	18	0	4	2	12	186	43	131	12	2
King	471	7	92	124	248	6,242	2,095	3,420	727	94
Kitsap	628	1	95	60	472	3,503	1,035	2,262	206	37
Pierce	1,134	10	101	263	760	9,533	3,180	5,174	1,179	52
Skagit	116	0	25	13	78	1,443	490	878	75	12
Skamania	10	0	2	0	8	222	45	157	20	0
Snohomish	487	4	77	98	308	5,445	1,772	2,979	694	39
Spokane	155	3	14	29	109	3,834	1,181	2,298	355	6
Thurston	335	4	25	27	279	2,935	1,115	1,682	138	27
Whatcom	126	2	28	16	80	1,355	501	765	89	6
Yakima	128	4	24	29	71	2,357	1,115	933	309	28
WASHINGTON—Nonmetropolitan Counties										
Adams	23	0	5	4	14	321	129	160	32	6
Clallam	63	0	8	4	51	653	196	429	28	2
Columbia	4	0	0	1	3	193	50	136	7	2
Ferry	8	0	0	0	8	32	12	16	4	0
Garfield	3	0	3	0	0	54	11	43	0	1
Grant	93	2	14	16	61	1,661	618	876	167	25
Grays Harbor	32	1	1	6	24	482	213	237	32	2
Island	40	0	6	3	31	547	190	324	33	1
Jefferson	44	1	6	4	33	380	116	252	12	1
Kittitas	14	0	2	5	7	484	157	286	41	5
Klickitat	3	0	0	0	3	167	125	14	28	0
Lewis	48	6	3	5	34	729	256	429	44	2
Lincoln	6	0	2	0	4	127	31	90	6	3
Mason	108	1	24	20	63	1,705	542	939	224	5
Okanogan	33	1	4	5	23	351	114	192	45	2
Pacific	22	0	4	3	15	439	189	225	25	5
Pend Oreille	16	0	0	0	16	422	140	243	39	2
San Juan	14	0	4	0	10	187	68	107	12	5
Stevens	46	0	20	4	22	818	349	380	89	1
Wahkiakum	2	0	1	0	1	31	10	18	3	0
Walla Walla	31	1	10	2	18	342	117	209	16	0
Whitman	5	1	1	1	2	127	44	73	10	1
WEST VIRGINIA—Metropolitan Counties										
Berkeley	68	2	11	12	43	757	220	477	60	13
Boone	14	0	1	1	12	68	28	33	7	0
Brooke	3	0	0	2	1	124	63	51	10	1
Cabell	44	0	6	15	23	864	274	524	66	3
Hampshire	35	0	0	0	35	113	56	52	5	1
Jefferson	34	0	1	2	31	350	60	279	11	3
Kanawha	240	6	8	23	203	1,390	509	756	125	21

[1] The FBI does not publish arson data unless it receives data from either the agency or the state for all 12 months of the calendar year.

Table 10.   Offenses Known to Law Enforcement, by State Metropolitan and Nonmetropolitan Counties, 2010—*Continued*

(Number)

State/County	Violent crime	Murder and non-negligent man-slaughter	Forcible rape	Robbery	Aggravated assault	Property crime	Burglary	Larceny-theft	Motor vehicle theft	Arson[1]
Marshall	8	0	2	1	5	234	70	146	18	4
Mineral	44	0	3	3	38	39	8	31	0	0
Monongalia[2]			1	2	8	476	133	328	15	1
Morgan	15	0	2	3	10	169	73	81	15	0
Ohio[2]		0	2	0		113	34	75	4	1
Preston[2]		0	3	1		231	98	118	15	2
Putnam	41	0	2	1	38	180	40	127	13	1
Wirt	15	0	0	0	15	36	22	14	0	1
Wood	204	0	8	4	192	333	91	226	16	15
WEST VIRGINIA—Nonmetropolitan Counties										
Barbour	6	0	0	0	6	12	3	9	0	0
Braxton	18	0	0	0	18	25	3	18	4	0
Fayette	61	1	7	6	47	337	145	165	27	6
Grant	10	0	0	0	10	27	8	19	0	0
Hardy	3	0	1	1	1	32	15	16	1	0
Harrison	55	0	0	8	47	339	127	191	21	1
Jackson	8	1	0	1	6	40	12	23	5	0
Lewis	11	2	0	0	9	12	3	8	1	0
Logan[2]		1	0	1		76	34	34	8	6
Mason	6	0	0	0	6	148	0	132	16	0
McDowell	28	0	0	5	23	114	35	70	9	8
Mercer	69	2	1	11	55	605	229	322	54	4
Monroe	2	0	1	0	1	15	3	12	0	1
Nicholas[2]		0	0	1		248	67	172	9	2
Raleigh	105	3	7	15	80	664	307	323	34	4
Randolph	40	0	0	2	38	59	31	28	0	0
Ritchie	6	0	1	1	4	44	18	23	3	0
Roane	0	0	0	0	0	0	0	0	0	0
Tyler	0	0	0	0	0	1	1	0	0	0
Upshur	3	0	3	0	0	37	8	29	0	0
Wyoming	31	0	1	4	26	299	95	182	22	3
WISCONSIN—Metropolitan Counties										
Brown	44	0	16	0	28	1,028	220	793	15	
Calumet	12	0	1	4	7	335	138	189	8	1
Chippewa	42	2	13	1	26	318	108	198	12	3
Columbia	30	0	5	0	25	365	86	254	25	3
Dane	66	0	2	2	62	980	215	714	51	3
Douglas	8	0	4	2	2	317	133	168	16	1
Eau Claire	17	1	5	2	9	208	67	129	12	5
Fond du Lac	26	1	6	0	19	287	79	185	23	0
Iowa	20	1	12	0	7	197	52	138	7	1
Kenosha	37	0	10	4	23	810	209	558	43	6
Kewaunee	5	0	2	0	3	87	20	65	2	2
La Crosse	14	2	1	0	11	218	68	145	5	1
Marathon	19	0	2	2	15	442	112	320	10	2
Milwaukee	10	0	0	9	1	28	2	25	1	0
Oconto	5	0	0	5	0	476	153	298	25	
Outagamie	37	0	12	1	24	505	160	324	21	1
Pierce	17	0	1	0	16	190	56	124	10	
Racine	15	0	4	1	10	616	86	491	39	
Rock	35	0	5	0	30	549	193	341	15	5
Sheboygan	55	1	3	0	51	556	107	438	11	
St. Croix	26	0	3	1	22	417	88	301	28	0
Waukesha	49	0	1	6	42	854	128	698	28	1
Winnebago	28	1	1	0	26	362	102	248	12	
WISCONSIN—Nonmetropolitan Counties										
Adams	25	1	8	1	15	357	161	179	17	
Ashland	13	0	0	0	13	36	12	23	1	
Barron	4	2	1	1	0	224	98	119	7	4
Bayfield	21	0	0	0	21	219	93	117	9	
Buffalo	1	0	1	0	0	51	19	28	4	
Burnett	18	0	3	0	15	204	70	123	11	2
Clark	92	0	1	1	90	229	73	141	15	
Dodge	24	0	6	1	17	232	72	148	12	1
Door	4	0	1	0	3	147	27	114	6	0
Dunn	13	0	2	0	11	163	55	102	6	0
Florence	9	0	1	0	8	127	43	78	6	0
Forest	4	0	0	1	3	181	67	107	7	
Grant	28	0	4	0	24	299	113	173	13	5
Green	11	0	2	0	9	223	65	144	14	0
Green Lake	4	0	2	0	2	92	32	59	1	0
Iron	14	0	0	0	14	69	25	44	0	0
Jackson	10	0	5	1	4	233	85	132	16	1

[1] The FBI does not publish arson data unless it receives data from either the agency or the state for all 12 months of the calendar year.

[2] The FBI determined that the agency's data were overreported. Consequently, affected data are not included in this table.

Table 10. Offenses Known to Law Enforcement, by State Metropolitan and Nonmetropolitan Counties, 2010—*Continued*

(Number)

State/County	Violent crime	Murder and non-negligent man-slaughter	Forcible rape	Robbery	Aggravated assault	Property crime	Burglary	Larceny-theft	Motor vehicle theft	Arson[1]
Jefferson	35	0	5	0	30	422	84	323	15	7
Juneau	37	0	8	1	28	310	114	170	26	3
Lafayette	2	0	0	0	2	167	39	124	4	0
Langlade	8	0	0	0	8	264	96	155	13	0
Lincoln	8	1	0	0	7	131	57	68	6	1
Manitowoc	27	1	7	0	19	172	39	124	9	5
Marinette	17	0	10	1	6	512	309	181	22	1
Marquette	4	0	4	0	0	184	55	119	10	0
Menominee	3	0	0	0	3	59	24	28	7	1
Monroe	15	1	3	2	9	225	56	152	17	0
Oneida	10	0	1	0	9	264	109	143	12	2
Pepin	1	0	0	0	1	21	14	6	1	0
Polk	102	0	7	2	93	376	99	259	18	2
Portage	23	0	3	1	19	278	85	185	8	1
Price	6	0	3	0	3	132	48	78	6	2
Rusk	13	0	1	0	12	140	39	90	11	3
Sauk	20	1	6	0	13	568	71	467	30	1
Sawyer	21	0	2	1	18	377	129	214	34	0
Shawano	14	0	5	4	5	418	152	236	30	1
Taylor	5	0	3	0	2	152	40	109	3	
Trempealeau	4	0	3	0	1	153	61	88	4	0
Vilas	11	1	3	1	6	197	49	134	14	0
Walworth	14	0	6	1	7	301	52	238	11	0
Washburn	16	1	5	0	10	211	53	146	12	1
Waupaca	18	0	3	0	15	497	174	300	23	0
Waushara	16	0	3	1	12	351	114	229	8	
Wood	2	0	0	1	1	161	62	87	12	2
WYOMING—Metropolitan Counties										
Laramie	47	0	14	2	31	493	93	366	34	5
Natrona	15	1	4	2	8	279	95	148	36	2
WYOMING—Nonmetropolitan Counties										
Albany	8	0	3	0	5	74	10	60	4	0
Big Horn	11	0	2	0	9	22	12	8	2	0
Campbell	18	0	0	2	16	284	84	185	15	0
Carbon	4	0	0	1	3	48	11	32	5	2
Converse	17	0	7	0	10	47	6	39	2	0
Crook	2	0	1	0	1	51	16	35	0	0
Fremont	11	0	1	0	10	195	54	127	14	0
Goshen	13	0	1	0	12	63	14	48	1	0
Hot Springs	1	0	0	0	1	26	5	21	0	0
Johnson	3	0	0	0	3	42	12	26	4	0
Lincoln	11	0	2	1	8	109	15	92	2	1
Niobrara	1	0	0	0	1	3	2	0	1	0
Park	42	0	5	1	36	88	21	66	1	0
Platte	1	0	0	0	1	32	7	23	2	0
Sheridan	1	0	0	1	0	63	17	42	4	0
Sublette	8	0	0	0	8	149	22	120	7	0
Sweetwater	18	1	2	2	13	161	49	95	17	0
Teton	13	0	0	1	12	100	15	81	4	1
Uinta	0	0	0	0	0	87	11	70	6	0
Washakie	1	0	0	0	1	4	2	2	0	0
Weston	3	0	0	0	3	8	3	3	2	0

[1] The FBI does not publish arson data unless it receives data from either the agency or the state for all 12 months of the calendar year.

Table 11.   Offenses Known to Law Enforcement, by State, Tribal, and Other Agencies, 2010

(Number)

State/Other Agency	Unit/Office	Violent crime	Murder and non-negligent man-slaughter	Forcible rape	Robbery	Aggra-vated assault	Property crime	Burglary	Larceny-theft	Motor vehicle theft	Arson[1]
ALABAMA—Tribal Agencies											
Poarch Creek Tribal		13	0	1	3	9	262	38	212	12	0
ALABAMA—Other Agencies											
22nd Judicial Circuit Drug Task Force		0	0	0	0	0	1	0	1	0	
ALASKA—State Agencies											
Alaska State Troopers...............		994	15	61	40	878	3,361	1,056	1,975	330	49
Alcohol Beverage Control Board		0	0	0	0	0	0	0	0	0	0
ALASKA—Tribal Agencies											
Metlakatla Tribal		0	0	0	0	0	4	2	1	1	0
ALASKA—Other Agencies											
Anchorage International Airport...............		1	0	0	0	1	66	3	62	1	0
Fairbanks International Airport		1	0	0	0	1	8	1	7	0	0
ARIZONA—State Agencies											
Arizona Department of Public Safety		23	0	0	0	23	9	0	9	0	0
ARIZONA—Tribal Agencies											
Cocopah Tribal...............		12	0	1	0	11	51	14	34	3	0
Colorado River Agency...............		12	0	4	0	8	1	1	0	0	7
Colorado River Tribal...............		34	2	5	0	27	40	12	3	25	14
Fort Apache Agency...............		129	13	57	0	59	1	1	0	0	10
Fort McDowell Tribal...............		20	0	0	2	18	49	12	32	5	2
Fort Mojave Tribal...............		37	0	1	0	36	120	25	85	10	5
Hopi Tribal		214	0	0	0	214	80	0	72	8	0
Kaibab Paiute Tribal		0	0	0	0	0	0	0	0	0	0
Navajo Nation...............		830	17	336	25	452	2,397	958	896	543	294
Quechan Tribal...............		3	0	0	0	3	35	10	23	2	4
Salt River Tribal...............		78	5	4	20	49	533	89	377	67	2
San Carlos Apache...............		75	2	6	1	66	443	125	299	19	125
Truxton Canon Agency...............		6	0	0	0	6	15	10	5	0	0
White Mountain Apache Tribal		102	0	28	0	74	352	303	29	20	8
Yavapai-Prescott Tribal...............		2	0	0	0	2	44	1	41	2	0
ARIZONA—Other Agencies											
Tucson Airport Authority...............		1	1	0	0	0	82	10	48	24	0
CALIFORNIA—State Agencies											
Atascadero State Hospital		60	0	0	1	59	23	0	23	0	1
California State Fair...............		1	0	0	0	1	38	0	38	0	0
Coalinga State Hospital...............		51	0	0	0	51	24	7	17	0	1
Department of Parks and Recreation:	Angeles	0	0	0	0	0	0	0	0	0	0
	Bay Area[2]	7	0	0	2	5		18		3	0
	Calaveras County	0	0	0	0	0	1	1	0	0	0
	Capital	1	0	0	0	1	7	1	6	0	0
	Channel Coast	3	0	0	1	2	60	1	59	0	0
	Colorado	0	0	0	0	0	0	0	0	0	0
	Four Rivers District	1	0	0	1	0	7	0	7	0	0
	Gold Fields District	4	0	0	0	4	66	1	63	2	3
	Hollister Hills	1	0	0	0	1	5	0	4	1	0
	Hungry Valley	0	0	0	0	0	1	0	1	0	0
	Inland Empire	1	0	0	0	1	5	0	5	0	1
	Marin County	0	0	0	0	0	0	0	0	0	0
	Mendocino Headquarters	0	0	0	0	0	29	4	23	2	1
	Monterey County	0	0	0	0	0	27	1	26	0	0
	North Coast Redwoods	0	0	0	0	0	31	23	8	0	0
	Northern Buttes	0	0	0	0	0	30	0	26	4	0
	Oceano Dunes	3	0	1	0	2	47	2	39	6	0
	Ocotillo Wells	0	0	0	0	0	0	0	0	0	0
	Orange Coast	0	0	0	0	0	82	12	69	1	0
	Russian River	0	0	0	0	0	10	0	10	0	0
	San Diego Coast	0	0	0	0	0	60	3	57	0	0
	San Joaquin	0	0	0	0	0	19	3	16	0	0
	San Luis Obispo Coast	2	0	0	0	2	4	0	4	0	0
	Santa Cruz Mountains	1	0	0	0	1	51	0	50	1	0
	Sierra	0	0	0	0	0	9	0	9	0	0
	Silverado	0	0	0	0	0	0	0	0	0	0
	Tehachapi District	1	0	0	0	1	10	3	6	1	0
	Twin Cities	0	0	0	0	0	1	0	1	0	0
Fairview Developmental Center		0	0	0	0	0	18	4	13	1	0
Highway Patrol:	Alameda County	5	0	0	0	5	252	1	22	229	0
	Alpine County	0	0	0	0	0	4	0	0	4	0
	Amador County	0	0	0	0	0	29	0	0	29	0
	Butte County	0	0	0	0	0	224	0	28	196	0
	Calaveras County	0	0	0	0	0	103	0	18	85	0
	Colusa County	0	0	0	0	0	25	0	5	20	0
	Contra Costa County	0	0	0	0	0	848	0	14	834	0

[1] The FBI does not publish arson data unless it receives data from either the agency or the state for all 12 months of the calendar year.
[2] The FBI determined that the agency's data were overreported. Consequently, affected data are not included in this table.

Table 11. Offenses Known to Law Enforcement, by State, Tribal, and Other Agencies, 2010—*Continued*

(Number)

State/Other Agency	Unit/Office	Violent crime	Murder and non-negligent man-slaughter	Forcible rape	Robbery	Aggra-vated assault	Property crime	Burglary	Larceny-theft	Motor vehicle theft	Arson[1]
	Del Norte County	1	0	0	0	1	83	0	0	83	0
	El Dorado County	0	0	0	0	0	166	0	34	132	0
	Fresno County	1	0	0	0	1	217	1	23	193	0
	Glenn County	0	0	0	0	0	31	0	3	28	0
	Humboldt County	1	0	0	0	1	207	1	26	180	0
	Imperial County	0	0	0	0	0	91	0	11	80	0
	Inyo County	0	0	0	0	0	22	0	8	14	0
	Kern County	1	0	0	0	1	249	0	30	219	0
	Kings County	0	0	0	0	0	73	0	0	73	0
	Lake County	0	0	0	0	0	99	0	17	82	0
	Lassen County	0	0	0	0	0	17	0	3	14	0
	Los Angeles County	11	0	0	0	11	476	14	21	441	0
	Madera County	0	0	0	0	0	295	0	52	243	0
	Marin County	1	0	0	0	1	74	0	14	60	0
	Mariposa County	0	0	0	0	0	19	0	2	17	0
	Mendocino County	1	0	0	0	1	128	0	11	117	0
	Merced County	1	0	0	0	1	507	1	72	434	0
	Modoc County	0	0	0	0	0	4	0	0	4	0
	Mono County	0	0	0	0	0	2	0	0	2	0
	Monterey County	2	0	0	0	2	283	0	29	254	0
	Napa County	0	0	0	0	0	50	0	15	35	0
	Nevada County	1	0	0	0	1	68	0	17	51	0
	Orange County	7	0	0	0	7	28	0	0	28	0
	Placer County	3	0	0	0	3	207	0	43	164	0
	Plumas County	0	0	0	0	0	36	0	13	23	0
	Riverside County	10	0	0	1	9	74	25	0	49	0
	Sacramento County	5	0	0	0	5	3,918	19	888	3,011	0
	San Benito County	0	0	0	0	0	32	0	0	32	0
	San Bernardino County	4	0	0	0	4	58	4	8	46	0
	San Diego County	9	0	0	0	9	73	0	18	55	0
	San Francisco County	0	0	0	0	0	8	0	0	8	0
	San Joaquin County	3	0	0	0	3	722	0	253	469	0
	San Luis Obispo County	1	0	0	0	1	117	0	8	109	0
	San Mateo County	1	0	0	0	1	10	0	0	10	0
	Santa Barbara County	1	0	0	0	1	115	0	23	92	0
	Santa Clara County	0	0	0	0	0	55	0	10	45	0
	Santa Cruz County	0	0	0	0	0	337	0	71	266	0
	Shasta County	4	0	0	0	4	173	0	40	133	0
	Sierra County	0	0	0	0	0	1	0	1	0	0
	Siskiyou County	0	0	0	0	0	36	0	2	34	0
	Solano County	2	0	0	0	2	90	0	0	90	0
	Sonoma County	0	0	0	0	0	224	1	51	172	0
	Stanislaus County	1	0	0	0	1	595	1	14	580	0
	Sutter County	0	0	0	0	0	31	0	1	30	0
	Tehama County	0	0	0	0	0	98	2	10	86	0
	Trinity County	0	0	0	0	0	36	0	3	33	0
	Tulare County	5	0	0	0	5	745	0	117	628	0
	Tuolumne County	0	0	0	0	0	78	0	15	63	0
	Ventura County	5	0	0	1	4	54	0	10	44	0
	Yolo County	2	0	0	0	2	47	2	1	44	0
	Yuba County	1	0	0	0	1	210	0	21	189	0
Lanterman State Hospital		0	0	0	0	0	1	0	1	0	0
Napa State Hospital		287	1	0	0	286	13	4	9	0	0
Patton State Hospital		514	0	5	6	503	12	4	8	0	1
Porterville Developmental Center		3	0	0	0	3	9	0	9	0	0
Sonoma Developmental Center		0	0	0	0	0	9	4	5	0	0
CALIFORNIA—Tribal Agencies											
Hoopa Valley Tribal		107	0	1	0	106	162	87	69	6	0
CALIFORNIA—Other Agencies											
East Bay Municipal Utility		0	0	0	0	0	22	0	19	3	0
East Bay Regional Parks:	Alameda County	6	0	1	2	3	151	0	147	4	6
	Contra Costa County	12	0	1	10	1	236	2	227	7	3
Fontana Unified School District		23	0	2	7	14	108	35	68	5	7
Los Angeles County Metropolitan Transportation Authority		13	0	0	3	10	22	0	22	0	0
Los Angeles Transportation Services Bureau		532	2	1	292	237	738	12	582	144	2
Monterey Peninsula Airport		0	0	0	0	0	16	5	10	1	0
Port of San Diego Harbor		20	0	0	7	13	384	22	362	0	0
San Bernardino Unified School District		99	0	0	88	11	423	230	177	16	16
San Francisco Bay Area Rapid Transit:	Alameda County	103	0	1	84	18	1,223	4	1,043	176	2
	Contra Costa County	40	0	1	27	12	858	4	701	153	3
	San Francisco County	34	0	0	28	6	262	3	257	2	0
	San Mateo County	4	0	0	1	3	86	1	65	20	0

[1] The FBI does not publish arson data unless it receives data from either the agency or the state for all 12 months of the calendar year.

[2] The FBI determined that the agency's data were overreported. Consequently, affected data are not included in this table.

Table 11.   Offenses Known to Law Enforcement, by State, Tribal, and Other Agencies, 2010—*Continued*

(Number)

State/Other Agency	Unit/Office	Violent crime	Murder and non-negligent man-slaughter	Forcible rape	Robbery	Aggra-vated assault	Property crime	Burglary	Larceny-theft	Motor vehicle theft	Arson[1]
Santa Clara Transit District		43	0	1	15	27	84	2	74	8	0
Stockton Unified School District		84	0	2	23	59	423	114	304	5	12
Twin Rivers Unified School District		45	0	1	13	31	149	59	80	10	3
Union Pacific Railroad:	Alameda County	5	0	0	0	5	124	109	15	0	0
	Amador County	0	0	0	0	0	0	0	0	0	0
	Butte County	2	0	0	0	2	5	0	5	0	0
	Calaveras County	0	0	0	0	0	0	0	0	0	0
	Colusa County	0	0	0	0	0	0	0	0	0	0
	Contra Costa County	5	0	0	0	5	15	5	10	0	0
	El Dorado County	0	0	0	0	0	0	0	0	0	0
	Fresno County	0	0	0	0	0	2	1	1	0	0
	Glenn County	0	0	0	0	0	0	0	0	0	0
	Humboldt County	0	0	0	0	0	0	0	0	0	0
	Imperial County	0	0	0	0	0	22	20	2	0	0
	Inyo County	0	0	0	0	0	0	0	0	0	0
	Kern County	0	0	0	0	0	7	3	4	0	0
	Kings County	0	0	0	0	0	0	0	0	0	0
	Lassen County	0	0	0	0	0	2	0	2	0	0
	Los Angeles County	5	0	0	0	5	203	186	17	0	0
	Madera County	0	0	0	0	0	2	0	2	0	0
	Marin County	0	0	0	0	0	0	0	0	0	0
	Mendocino County	0	0	0	0	0	0	0	0	0	0
	Merced County	0	0	0	0	0	8	0	8	0	0
	Modoc County	0	0	0	0	0	0	0	0	0	0
	Monterey County	0	0	0	0	0	1	0	1	0	0
	Napa County	0	0	0	0	0	0	0	0	0	0
	Nevada County	1	0	0	0	1	0	0	0	0	0
	Orange County	0	0	0	0	0	0	0	0	0	0
	Placer County	4	0	0	0	4	24	8	16	0	0
	Plumas County	0	0	0	0	0	2	0	2	0	0
	Riverside County	4	0	0	0	4	20	14	6	0	0
	Sacramento County	7	0	0	0	7	15	2	13	0	0
	San Benito County	0	0	0	0	0	0	0	0	0	0
	San Bernardino County	4	0	0	0	4	48	26	22	0	0
	San Francisco County	0	0	0	0	0	1	0	1	0	0
	San Joaquin County	10	0	0	0	10	136	118	18	0	0
	San Luis Obispo County	0	0	0	0	0	3	0	3	0	0
	San Mateo County	0	0	0	0	0	0	0	0	0	0
	Santa Barbara County	0	0	0	0	0	7	0	7	0	0
	Santa Clara County	0	0	0	0	0	6	0	6	0	0
	Santa Cruz County	0	0	0	0	0	2	0	2	0	0
	Shasta County	1	0	0	0	1	2	0	2	0	0
	Sierra County	0	0	0	0	0	1	0	1	0	0
	Siskiyou County	0	0	0	0	0	0	0	0	0	0
	Solano County	2	0	0	0	2	3	0	3	0	0
	Sonoma County	0	0	0	0	0	0	0	0	0	0
	Stanislaus County	1	0	0	0	1	5	3	2	0	0
	Sutter County	0	0	0	0	0	1	0	1	0	0
	Tehama County	0	0	0	0	0	0	0	0	0	0
	Trinity County	0	0	0	0	0	0	0	0	0	0
	Tulare County	0	0	0	0	0	4	2	2	0	0
	Ventura County	0	0	0	0	0	0	0	0	0	0
	Yolo County	1	0	0	0	1	4	0	4	0	0
	Yuba County	2	0	0	0	2	4	0	4	0	0
COLORADO—State Agencies											
Colorado Mental Health Institute		0	0	0	0	0	1	0	1	0	0
State Patrol		14	0	0	0	14	28	0	9	19	0
COLORADO—Tribal Agencies											
Southern Ute Tribal		2	0	0	0	2	21	10	0	11	2
Ute Mountain Tribal		0	0	0	0	0	1	0	0	1	6
COLORADO—Other Agencies											
Southwest Drug Task Force		0	0	0	0	0	1	0	1	0	0
CONNECTICUT—State Agencies											
Connecticut State Police		303	5	40	55	203	4,924	1,583	3,023	318	71
State Capitol Police		0	0	0	0	0	6	0	6	0	0
CONNECTICUT—Tribal Agencies											
Mashantucket Pequot Tribal		6	0	0	1	5	20	1	17	2	0
Mohegan Tribal		12	0	1	2	9	71	2	67	2	0
CONNECTICUT—Other Agencies											
Metropolitan Transportation Authority		4	0	0	4	0	62	0	61	1	0

[1] The FBI does not publish arson data unless it receives data from either the agency or the state for all 12 months of the calendar year.

Table 11.   Offenses Known to Law Enforcement, by State, Tribal, and Other Agencies, 2010—*Continued*

(Number)

State/Other Agency	Unit/Office	Violent crime	Murder and non-negligent man-slaughter	Forcible rape	Robbery	Aggra-vated assault	Property crime	Burglary	Larceny-theft	Motor vehicle theft	Arson[1]
DELAWARE—State Agencies											
Attorney General:	Kent County	0	0	0	0	0	0	0	0	0	0
	New Castle County	0	0	0	0	0	1	0	1	0	0
Division of Alcohol and Tobacco Enforcement............		0	0	0	0	0	0	0	0	0	0
Environmental Control		0	0	0	0	0	3	0	3	0	0
Fish and Wildlife..		0	0	0	0	0	23	2	21	0	0
Park Rangers		3	0	0	0	3	56	21	34	1	1
River and Bay Authority		1	0	0	0	1	17	1	16	0	0
State Capitol Police		1	0	0	0	1	24	7	16	1	1
State Fire Marshal...		33	0	0	0	33	23	21	1	1	224
State Police:	Kent County	458	5	42	82	329	2,192	732	1,324	136	1
	New Castle County	709	2	27	386	294	5,604	621	4,725	258	1
	Sussex County	629	3	76	99	451	4,354	1,585	2,578	191	5
DELAWARE—Other Agencies											
Amtrak Police..		0	0	0	0	0	0	0	0	0	0
Drug Enforcement Administration	Wilmington Resident Office	0	0	0	0	0	0	0	0	0	0
FLORIDA—State Agencies											
Capitol Police..		0	0	0	0	0	14	0	14	0	0
Department of Environmental Protection, Division of Law Enforcement:	Alachua County	1	0	0	0	1	2	1	1	0	0
	Bay County	1	0	0	0	1	10	0	10	0	0
	Brevard County	0	0	0	0	0	4	0	4	0	0
	Broward County	0	0	0	0	0	46	0	46	0	0
	Charlotte County	0	0	0	0	0	0	0	0	0	0
	Citrus County	0	0	0	0	0	0	0	0	0	0
	Clay County	0	0	0	0	0	2	0	2	0	0
	Collier County	0	0	0	0	0	1	0	1	0	0
	Columbia County	0	0	0	0	0	0	0	0	0	0
	DeSoto County	0	0	0	0	0	0	0	0	0	0
	Dixie County	0	0	0	0	0	0	0	0	0	0
	Duval County	0	0	0	0	0	2	0	2	0	0
	Escambia County	0	0	0	0	0	2	0	1	1	0
	Flagler County	0	0	0	0	0	0	0	0	0	0
	Franklin County	0	0	0	0	0	0	0	0	0	0
	Gadsden County	0	0	0	0	0	0	0	0	0	0
	Gilchrist County	0	0	0	0	0	0	0	0	0	0
	Gulf County	0	0	0	0	0	0	0	0	0	0
	Hendry County	0	0	0	0	0	0	0	0	0	0
	Hernando County	0	0	0	0	0	3	1	2	0	0
	Highlands County	0	0	0	0	0	1	0	1	0	0
	Hillsborough County	0	0	0	0	0	4	0	4	0	0
	Holmes County	0	0	0	0	0	0	0	0	0	0
	Indian River County	0	0	0	0	0	0	0	0	0	0
	Lafayette County	0	0	0	0	0	0	0	0	0	0
	Lake County	0	0	0	0	0	6	4	2	0	0
	Lee County	0	0	0	0	0	0	0	0	0	0
	Leon County	0	0	0	0	0	0	0	0	0	0
	Levy County	0	0	0	0	0	6	0	6	0	0
	Liberty County	0	0	0	0	0	0	0	0	0	0
	Manatee County	0	0	0	0	0	0	0	0	0	0
	Marion County	1	0	0	0	1	0	0	0	0	0
	Martin County	0	0	0	0	0	3	1	2	0	0
	Miami-Dade County	1	0	0	0	1	40	2	38	0	0
	Monroe County	0	0	0	0	0	6	0	6	0	0
	Nassau County	0	0	0	0	0	0	0	0	0	0
	Okaloosa County	0	0	0	0	0	1	0	1	0	0
	Okeechobee County	0	0	0	0	0	0	0	0	0	0
	Orange County	0	0	0	0	0	6	1	4	1	0
	Osceola County	0	0	0	0	0	0	0	0	0	0
	Palm Beach County	0	0	0	0	0	3	1	2	0	0
	Pasco County	0	0	0	0	0	0	0	0	0	0
	Pinellas County	0	0	0	0	0	7	1	6	0	0
	Polk County	0	0	0	0	0	0	0	0	0	0
	Santa Rosa County	0	0	0	0	0	3	0	3	0	0
	Sarasota County	0	0	0	0	0	1	0	0	1	0
	Seminole County	0	0	0	0	0	1	0	1	0	0
	St. Johns County	0	0	0	0	0	0	0	0	0	0
	St. Lucie County	0	0	0	0	0	3	0	3	0	0
	Sumter County	0	0	0	0	0	0	0	0	0	0
	Volusia County	0	0	0	0	0	19	2	17	0	0
	Walton County	0	0	0	0	0	2	0	2	0	0

[1] The FBI does not publish arson data unless it receives data from either the agency or the state for all 12 months of the calendar year.

Table 11.   Offenses Known to Law Enforcement, by State, Tribal, and Other Agencies, 2010—*Continued*

(Number)

State/Other Agency	Unit/Office	Violent crime	Murder and non-negligent man-slaughter	Forcible rape	Robbery	Aggra-vated assault	Property crime	Burglary	Larceny-theft	Motor vehicle theft	Arson[1]
Department of Insurance:	Broward County	0	0	0	0	0	0	0	0	0	0
	Duval County	0	0	0	0	0	0	0	0	0	0
	Escambia County	0	0	0	0	0	0	0	0	0	0
	Hillsborough County	0	0	0	0	0	0	0	0	0	0
	Lee County	0	0	0	0	0	0	0	0	0	0
	Miami-Dade County	0	0	0	0	0	0	0	0	0	0
	Orange County	0	0	0	0	0	0	0	0	0	0
	Palm Beach County	0	0	0	0	0	0	0	0	0	0
	Pinellas County	0	0	0	0	0	0	0	0	0	0
Department of Law Enforcement:	Duval County, Jacksonville	0	0	0	0	0	0	0	0	0	0
	Escambia County, Pensacola	0	0	0	0	0	0	0	0	0	0
	Hillsborough County, Tampa	0	0	0	0	0	0	0	0	0	0
	Lee County, Fort Myers	0	0	0	0	0	0	0	0	0	0
	Leon County, Tallahassee	0	0	0	0	0	0	0	0	0	0
	Miami-Dade County, Miami	0	0	0	0	0	1	0	1	0	0
	Orange County, Orlando	0	0	0	0	0	0	0	0	0	0
Division of Alcoholic Beverages and Tobacco:	Alachua County	0	0	0	0	0	0	0	0	0	0
	Baker County	0	0	0	0	0	0	0	0	0	0
	Bay County	0	0	0	0	0	0	0	0	0	0
	Bradford County	0	0	0	0	0	0	0	0	0	0
	Brevard County	0	0	0	0	0	0	0	0	0	0
	Broward County	0	0	0	0	0	0	0	0	0	0
	Calhoun County	0	0	0	0	0	0	0	0	0	0
	Charlotte County	0	0	0	0	0	0	0	0	0	0
	Citrus County	0	0	0	0	0	0	0	0	0	0
	Clay County	0	0	0	0	0	0	0	0	0	0
	Collier County	0	0	0	0	0	0	0	0	0	0
	Columbia County	0	0	0	0	0	0	0	0	0	0
	DeSoto County	0	0	0	0	0	0	0	0	0	0
	Dixie County	0	0	0	0	0	0	0	0	0	0
	Duval County	0	0	0	0	0	0	0	0	0	0
	Escambia County	0	0	0	0	0	0	0	0	0	0
	Franklin County	0	0	0	0	0	0	0	0	0	0
	Gadsden County	0	0	0	0	0	0	0	0	0	0
	Gilchrist County	0	0	0	0	0	0	0	0	0	0
	Glades County	0	0	0	0	0	0	0	0	0	0
	Gulf County	0	0	0	0	0	0	0	0	0	0
	Hamilton County	0	0	0	0	0	0	0	0	0	0
	Hendry County	0	0	0	0	0	0	0	0	0	0
	Hernando County	0	0	0	0	0	0	0	0	0	0
	Highlands County	0	0	0	0	0	0	0	0	0	0
	Hillsborough County	0	0	0	0	0	0	0	0	0	0
	Holmes County	0	0	0	0	0	0	0	0	0	0
	Indian River County	0	0	0	0	0	0	0	0	0	0
	Jackson County	0	0	0	0	0	0	0	0	0	0
	Jefferson County	0	0	0	0	0	0	0	0	0	0
	Lake County	0	0	0	0	0	0	0	0	0	0
	Lee County	0	0	0	0	0	0	0	0	0	0
	Leon County	0	0	0	0	0	0	0	0	0	0
	Levy County	0	0	0	0	0	0	0	0	0	0
	Liberty County	0	0	0	0	0	0	0	0	0	0
	Madison County	0	0	0	0	0	0	0	0	0	0
	Manatee County	0	0	0	0	0	0	0	0	0	0
	Marion County	0	0	0	0	0	0	0	0	0	0
	Martin County	0	0	0	0	0	0	0	0	0	0
	Miami-Dade County	0	0	0	0	0	0	0	0	0	0
	Nassau County	0	0	0	0	0	0	0	0	0	0
	Okaloosa County	0	0	0	0	0	0	0	0	0	0
	Okeechobee County	0	0	0	0	0	0	0	0	0	0
	Orange County	0	0	0	0	0	0	0	0	0	0
	Osceola County	0	0	0	0	0	0	0	0	0	0
	Palm Beach County	0	0	0	0	0	0	0	0	0	0
	Pasco County	0	0	0	0	0	0	0	0	0	0
	Pinellas County	0	0	0	0	0	0	0	0	0	0
	Polk County	0	0	0	0	0	0	0	0	0	0
	Putnam County	0	0	0	0	0	0	0	0	0	0
	Santa Rosa County	0	0	0	0	0	0	0	0	0	0
	Sarasota County	0	0	0	0	0	0	0	0	0	0
	Seminole County	0	0	0	0	0	0	0	0	0	0

[1] The FBI does not publish arson data unless it receives data from either the agency or the state for all 12 months of the calendar year.

Table 11.   Offenses Known to Law Enforcement, by State, Tribal, and Other Agencies, 2010—*Continued*

(Number)

State/Other Agency	Unit/Office	Violent crime	Murder and non-negligent man-slaughter	Forcible rape	Robbery	Aggra-vated assault	Property crime	Burglary	Larceny-theft	Motor vehicle theft	Arson[1]
	St. Johns County	0	0	0	0	0	0	0	0	0	0
	St. Lucie County	0	0	0	0	0	0	0	0	0	0
	Sumter County	0	0	0	0	0	0	0	0	0	0
	Suwannee County	0	0	0	0	0	0	0	0	0	0
	Taylor County	0	0	0	0	0	0	0	0	0	0
	Union County	0	0	0	0	0	0	0	0	0	0
	Volusia County	0	0	0	0	0	0	0	0	0	0
	Wakulla County	0	0	0	0	0	0	0	0	0	0
	Walton County	0	0	0	0	0	0	0	0	0	0
	Washington County	0	0	0	0	0	0	0	0	0	0
Florida Game Commission:	Alachua County	0	0	0	0	0	0	0	0	0	0
	Baker County	0	0	0	0	0	0	0	0	0	0
	Bay County	0	0	0	0	0	0	0	0	0	0
	Bradford County	0	0	0	0	0	0	0	0	0	0
	Brevard County	0	0	0	0	0	0	0	0	0	0
	Broward County	0	0	0	0	0	0	0	0	0	0
	Calhoun County	0	0	0	0	0	0	0	0	0	0
	Charlotte County	0	0	0	0	0	0	0	0	0	0
	Citrus County	0	0	0	0	0	0	0	0	0	0
	Clay County	0	0	0	0	0	0	0	0	0	0
	Collier County	0	0	0	0	0	0	0	0	0	0
	Columbia County	0	0	0	0	0	0	0	0	0	0
	DeSoto County	0	0	0	0	0	0	0	0	0	0
	Dixie County	0	0	0	0	0	0	0	0	0	0
	Duval County	0	0	0	0	0	0	0	0	0	0
	Escambia County	0	0	0	0	0	0	0	0	0	0
	Flagler County	0	0	0	0	0	0	0	0	0	0
	Franklin County	0	0	0	0	0	0	0	0	0	0
	Gadsden County	0	0	0	0	0	0	0	0	0	0
	Gilchrist County	0	0	0	0	0	0	0	0	0	0
	Glades County	0	0	0	0	0	0	0	0	0	0
	Gulf County	0	0	0	0	0	0	0	0	0	0
	Hamilton County	0	0	0	0	0	0	0	0	0	0
	Hardee County	0	0	0	0	0	0	0	0	0	0
	Hendry County	0	0	0	0	0	0	0	0	0	0
	Hernando County	0	0	0	0	0	0	0	0	0	0
	Highlands County	0	0	0	0	0	0	0	0	0	0
	Hillsborough County	0	0	0	0	0	0	0	0	0	0
	Holmes County	0	0	0	0	0	0	0	0	0	0
	Indian River County	0	0	0	0	0	0	0	0	0	0
	Jackson County	0	0	0	0	0	0	0	0	0	0
	Jefferson County	0	0	0	0	0	0	0	0	0	0
	Lafayette County	0	0	0	0	0	0	0	0	0	0
	Lake County	0	0	0	0	0	0	0	0	0	0
	Lee County	0	0	0	0	0	0	0	0	0	0
	Leon County	0	0	0	0	0	0	0	0	0	0
	Levy County	0	0	0	0	0	0	0	0	0	0
	Liberty County	0	0	0	0	0	0	0	0	0	0
	Madison County	0	0	0	0	0	0	0	0	0	0
	Manatee County	0	0	0	0	0	0	0	0	0	0
	Marion County	0	0	0	0	0	0	0	0	0	0
	Martin County	0	0	0	0	0	0	0	0	0	0
	Miami-Dade County	0	0	0	0	0	0	0	0	0	0
	Monroe County	0	0	0	0	0	0	0	0	0	0
	Nassau County	0	0	0	0	0	0	0	0	0	0
	Okaloosa County	0	0	0	0	0	0	0	0	0	0
	Okeechobee County	0	0	0	0	0	0	0	0	0	0
	Orange County	0	0	0	0	0	0	0	0	0	0
	Osceola County	0	0	0	0	0	0	0	0	0	0
	Palm Beach County	0	0	0	0	0	0	0	0	0	0
	Pasco County	0	0	0	0	0	0	0	0	0	0
	Pinellas County	0	0	0	0	0	0	0	0	0	0
	Polk County	0	0	0	0	0	0	0	0	0	0
	Putnam County	0	0	0	0	0	0	0	0	0	0
	Santa Rosa County	0	0	0	0	0	0	0	0	0	0
	Sarasota County	0	0	0	0	0	0	0	0	0	0
	Seminole County	0	0	0	0	0	0	0	0	0	0
	St. Johns County	0	0	0	0	0	0	0	0	0	0
	St. Lucie County	0	0	0	0	0	0	0	0	0	0
	Sumter County	0	0	0	0	0	0	0	0	0	0
	Suwannee County	0	0	0	0	0	0	0	0	0	0
	Taylor County	0	0	0	0	0	0	0	0	0	0
	Union County	0	0	0	0	0	0	0	0	0	0
	Volusia County	0	0	0	0	0	0	0	0	0	0

[1] The FBI does not publish arson data unless it receives data from either the agency or the state for all 12 months of the calendar year.

Table 11.   Offenses Known to Law Enforcement, by State, Tribal, and Other Agencies, 2010—*Continued*

(Number)

State/Other Agency	Unit/Office	Violent crime	Murder and non-negligent man-slaughter	Forcible rape	Robbery	Aggra-vated assault	Property crime	Burglary	Larceny-theft	Motor vehicle theft	Arson[1]
	Wakulla County	0	0	0	0	0	0	0	0	0	0
	Walton County	0	0	0	0	0	0	0	0	0	0
	Washington County	0	0	0	0	0	0	0	0	0	0
Highway Patrol:	Alachua County	3	0	0	0	3	1	0	1	0	0
	Baker County	0	0	0	0	0	0	0	0	0	0
	Bay County	0	0	0	0	0	0	0	0	0	0
	Braford County	0	0	0	0	0	0	0	0	0	0
	Brevard County	0	0	0	0	0	0	0	0	0	0
	Broward County	31	0	0	0	31	70	0	45	25	0
	Calhoun County	0	0	0	0	0	0	0	0	0	0
	Charlotte County	1	0	0	0	1	1	0	1	0	0
	Citrus County	1	0	0	0	1	0	0	0	0	0
	Clay County	0	0	0	0	0	0	0	0	0	0
	Collier County	1	0	0	0	1	0	0	0	0	0
	Columbia County	1	0	0	0	1	1	0	0	1	0
	DeSoto County	0	0	0	0	0	0	0	0	0	0
	Dixie County	0	0	0	0	0	0	0	0	0	0
	Duval County	2	0	0	0	2	0	0	0	0	0
	Escambia County	2	0	0	0	2	1	0	0	1	0
	Flagler County	0	0	0	0	0	1	0	1	0	0
	Franklin County	0	0	0	0	0	0	0	0	0	0
	Gadsden County	3	0	0	0	3	0	0	0	0	0
	Gilchrist County	0	0	0	0	0	0	0	0	0	0
	Glades County	0	0	0	0	0	0	0	0	0	0
	Gulf County	0	0	0	0	0	0	0	0	0	0
	Hamilton County	0	0	0	0	0	0	0	0	0	0
	Hardee County	0	0	0	0	0	0	0	0	0	0
	Hendry County	1	0	0	0	1	0	0	0	0	0
	Hernando County	0	0	0	0	0	0	0	0	0	0
	Highlands County	0	0	0	0	0	0	0	0	0	0
	Hillsborough County	16	0	0	0	16	9	0	4	5	0
	Holmes County	0	0	0	0	0	0	0	0	0	0
	Indian River County	0	0	0	0	0	1	0	1	0	0
	Jackson County	0	0	0	0	0	0	0	0	0	0
	Jefferson County	0	0	0	0	0	0	0	0	0	0
	Lafayette County	0	0	0	0	0	0	0	0	0	0
	Lake County	3	0	0	0	3	3	0	3	0	0
	Lee County	2	0	0	0	2	2	0	1	1	0
	Leon County	0	0	0	0	0	0	0	0	0	0
	Levy County	0	0	0	0	0	0	0	0	0	0
	Liberty County	0	0	0	0	0	0	0	0	0	0
	Madison County	0	0	0	0	0	0	0	0	0	0
	Manatee County	5	0	0	0	5	0	0	0	0	0
	Marion County	0	0	0	0	0	0	0	0	0	0
	Martin County	0	0	0	0	0	0	0	0	0	0
	Miami-Dade County	26	0	0	0	26	61	0	40	21	0
	Monroe County	1	0	0	0	1	0	0	0	0	0
	Nassau County	0	0	0	0	0	0	0	0	0	0
	Okaloosa County	0	0	0	0	0	0	0	0	0	0
	Okeechobee County	0	0	0	0	0	0	0	0	0	0
	Orange County	5	0	0	0	5	6	0	3	3	1
	Osceola County	2	0	0	0	2	4	0	4	0	0
	Palm Beach County	18	0	0	0	18	38	0	19	19	0
	Pasco County	7	0	0	0	7	2	0	0	2	0
	Pinellas County	0	0	0	0	0	0	0	0	0	0
	Polk County	1	0	0	0	1	0	0	0	0	0
	Putnam County	0	0	0	0	0	0	0	0	0	0
	Santa Rosa County	2	0	0	0	2	2	0	1	1	0
	Sarasota County	2	0	0	0	2	2	0	1	1	0
	Seminole County	0	0	0	0	0	0	0	0	0	0
	St. Johns County	1	0	0	0	1	3	0	3	0	0
	St. Lucie County	2	0	0	0	2	2	0	1	1	0
	Sumter County	1	0	0	0	1	2	0	2	0	0
	Suwannee County	1	0	0	0	1	0	0	0	0	0
	Taylor County	0	0	0	0	0	0	0	0	0	0
	Union County	0	0	0	0	0	0	0	0	0	0
	Volusia County	2	0	0	0	2	0	0	0	0	0
	Wakulla County	0	0	0	0	0	0	0	0	0	0
	Walton County	0	0	0	0	0	0	0	0	0	0
	Washington County	0	0	0	0	0	0	0	0	0	0
State Treasurer's Office	Division of Insurance Fraud	0	0	0	0	0	0	0	0	0	0

[1] The FBI does not publish arson data unless it receives data from either the agency or the state for all 12 months of the calendar year.

Table 11. Offenses Known to Law Enforcement, by State, Tribal, and Other Agencies, 2010—*Continued*

(Number)

State/Other Agency	Unit/Office	Violent crime	Murder and non-negligent man-slaughter	Forcible rape	Robbery	Aggra-vated assault	Property crime	Burglary	Larceny-theft	Motor vehicle theft	Arson[1]
FLORIDA—Tribal Agencies											
Miccosukee Tribal		5	0	0	1	4	146	6	138	2	2
Seminole Tribal		116	1	7	38	70	821	54	695	72	2
FLORIDA—Other Agencies											
Duval County Schools		76	0	0	20	56	649	122	515	12	6
Florida School for the Deaf and Blind		2	0	0	0	2	0	0	0	0	0
Fort Lauderdale Airport		9	0	0	2	7	298	1	265	32	0
Jacksonville Airport Authority		0	0	0	0	0	54	4	35	15	0
Lee County Port Authority		0	0	0	0	0	157	0	151	6	0
Melbourne International Airport		0	0	0	0	0	0	0	0	0	0
Miami-Dade County Public Schools		282	0	7	112	163	1,808	621	1,170	17	21
Palm Beach County School District		82	0	0	17	65	861	114	743	4	3
Port Everglades		1	0	0	0	1	31	0	31	0	0
Sarasota-Bradenton International Airport		0	0	0	0	0	8	0	6	2	0
St. Petersburg-Clearwater International Airport		0	0	0	0	0	0	0	0	0	0
Tampa International Airport		2	0	0	1	1	154	12	127	15	0
Volusia County Beach Management		12	0	0	3	9	204	0	196	8	0
GEORGIA—State Agencies											
Atlanta State Farmers Market		0	0	0	0	0	43	5	27	11	0
Georgia Department of Public Safety		1	0	1	0	0	94	0	92	2	0
Georgia Department of Transportation	Office of Investigations	0	0	0	0	0	7	0	7	0	0
Georgia Public Safety Training Center		0	0	0	0	0	0	0	0	0	0
Georgia World Congress		9	0	0	2	7	214	2	207	5	0
Ports Authority	Savannah	0	0	0	0	0	8	0	7	1	0
State Board of Workers Compensation	Fraud Investigation Division	0	0	0	0	0	0	0	0	0	0
GEORGIA—Other Agencies											
Atlanta Public Schools		0	0	0	0	0	0	0	0	0	0
Augusta Board of Education		34	0	0	0	34	30	4	26	0	1
Bibb County Board of Education		7	0	0	1	6	167	23	139	5	1
Chatham County Board of Education		15	0	2	6	7	130	22	108	0	4
Cherokee County Board of Education		4	0	1	0	3	135	8	127	0	
Cherokee County Marshal		0	0	0	0	0	0	0	0	0	0
Cobb County Board of Education		10	0	0	6	4	435	22	410	3	
Fayette County Marshal		0	0	0	0	0	0	0	0	0	0
Fulton County Marshal		1	0	0	1	0	6	1	5	0	
Fulton County School System		16	0	4	11	1	263	22	235	6	3
Glynn County School System		0	0	0	0	0	94	13	81	0	0
Gwinnett County Public Schools		11	0	1	2	8	252	24	223	5	6
Hartsfield-Jackson Atlanta International Airport		6	0	0	1	5	302	4	263	35	0
Metropolitan Atlanta Rapid Transit Authority		157	1	1	47	108	281	5	231	45	4
Muscogee City Marshal		0	0	0	0	0	0	0	0	0	0
Richmond County Marshal		0	0	0	0	0	0	0	0	0	0
Washington County Board of Education		0	0	0	0	0	0	0	0	0	0
IDAHO—State Agencies											
Idaho State Police		12	0	2	0	10	13	1	5	7	0
IDAHO—Tribal Agencies											
Coeur d'Alene Tribal		142	0	7	0	135	82	28	47	7	4
Fort Hall Tribal		29	0	1	0	28	84	35	21	28	5
Nez Perce Tribal		21	0	2	3	16	132	33	87	12	0
ILLINOIS—State Agencies[3]											
Illinois Department of Natural Resources		9	0	0	2	7	34	2	32	0	1
Secretary of State Police		0	0	0	0	0	23	1	22	0	0
State Fire Marshal		0	0	0	0	0	0	0	0	0	416
ILLINOIS—Other Agencies[3]											
Canadian National Railway		0	0	0	0	0	30	5	24	1	0
Capitol Airport Authority		0	0	0	0	0	0	0	0	0	0
Indiana Harbor Belt Railroad		0	0	0	0	0	17	3	14	0	0
Pekin Park District		5	0	0	0	5	5	4	1	0	0
Springfield Park District		40	0	2	8	30	37	3	31	3	0
INDIANA—State Agencies											
Indiana State Excise Police		3	0	0	0	3	6	1	5	0	0
Northern Indiana Commuter Transportation District		2	0	0	1	1	79	0	76	3	0
State Police:	Adams County	2	0	0	0	2	2	1	1	0	0
	Allen County	10	0	0	3	7	67	4	59	4	1
	Bartholomew County	0	0	0	0	0	16	1	15	0	0
	Benton County	0	0	0	0	0	0	0	0	0	0
	Blackford County	0	0	0	0	0	0	0	0	0	0
	Boone County	0	0	0	0	0	0	0	0	0	0

[1] The FBI does not publish arson data unless it receives data from either the agency or the state for all 12 months of the calendar year.

[3] Because of changes in the state/local agency's reporting practices, figures are not comparable to previous years' data.

Table 11. Offenses Known to Law Enforcement, by State, Tribal, and Other Agencies, 2010—*Continued*

(Number)

State/Other Agency	Unit/Office	Violent crime	Murder and non-negligent man-slaughter	Forcible rape	Robbery	Aggra-vated assault	Property crime	Burglary	Larceny-theft	Motor vehicle theft	Arson[1]
	Brown County	2	0	1	0	1	0	0	0	0	0
	Carroll County	0	0	0	0	0	0	0	0	0	0
	Cass County	5	0	1	1	3	17	3	12	2	0
	Clark County	34	0	0	0	34	123	8	97	18	0
	Clay County	3	0	1	0	2	12	2	8	2	0
	Clinton County	2	0	0	0	2	12	0	11	1	0
	Crawford County	8	0	1	0	7	11	1	10	0	3
	Daviess County	6	0	2	0	4	9	2	4	3	0
	Dearborn County	4	0	2	1	1	18	5	11	2	0
	Decatur County	3	0	1	0	2	18	1	16	1	0
	De Kalb County	4	1	0	0	3	16	3	11	2	0
	Delaware County	3	0	0	0	3	27	3	24	0	0
	Dubois County	18	0	2	0	16	49	8	38	3	0
	Elkhart County	2	0	0	2	0	36	0	31	5	0
	Fayette County	2	0	0	0	2	10	0	10	0	0
	Floyd County	14	0	0	0	14	29	3	23	3	0
	Fountain County	5	0	0	1	4	11	3	6	2	0
	Franklin County	6	0	2	2	2	29	5	23	1	2
	Fulton County	0	0	0	0	0	9	0	9	0	0
	Gibson County	9	1	0	0	8	36	2	32	2	0
	Grant County	3	1	0	0	2	12	0	12	0	0
	Greene County	9	0	1	0	8	21	7	12	2	0
	Hamilton County	0	0	0	0	0	5	0	3	2	0
	Hancock County	2	0	0	2	0	11	0	10	1	0
	Harrison County	25	1	3	0	21	87	16	65	6	0
	Hendricks County	4	0	1	0	3	14	0	10	4	0
	Henry County	3	0	0	0	3	100	0	100	0	0
	Howard County	3	0	0	0	3	17	3	13	1	0
	Huntington County	2	0	0	1	1	22	3	19	0	0
	Jackson County	10	0	2	2	6	62	15	44	3	0
	Jasper County	11	0	1	0	10	25	3	16	6	0
	Jay County	1	0	1	0	0	5	1	4	0	0
	Jefferson County	5	0	1	0	4	28	8	17	3	0
	Jennings County	7	0	3	0	4	13	3	9	1	0
	Johnson County	0	0	0	0	0	3	0	3	0	0
	Knox County	7	0	1	0	6	28	6	20	2	1
	Kosciusko County	0	0	0	0	0	21	2	18	1	1
	LaGrange County	4	0	0	3	1	32	4	22	6	0
	Lake County	26	1	1	3	21	108	5	52	51	0
	La Porte County	13	3	1	2	7	31	2	21	8	2
	Lawrence County	15	0	9	0	6	35	8	24	3	0
	Madison County	14	0	1	0	13	9	2	5	2	0
	Marion County	14	0	1	0	13	79	1	63	15	0
	Marshall County	1	0	1	0	0	28	1	25	2	0
	Martin County	6	0	2	0	4	14	2	12	0	5
	Miami County	7	0	1	0	6	44	13	27	4	0
	Monroe County	16	0	2	4	10	61	5	43	13	0
	Montgomery County	6	0	3	0	3	10	1	7	2	0
	Morgan County	5	0	0	0	5	14	4	7	3	0
	Newton County	2	0	1	0	1	5	0	5	0	0
	Noble County	5	0	1	1	3	23	5	18	0	1
	Ohio County	1	0	0	0	1	1	0	1	0	0
	Orange County	13	0	2	3	8	35	13	22	0	0
	Owen County	7	0	1	0	6	11	6	5	0	0
	Parke County	4	0	1	0	3	5	1	3	1	0
	Perry County	2	0	2	0	0	8	0	8	0	0
	Pike County	3	0	1	0	2	12	1	11	0	0
	Porter County	7	0	0	1	6	35	0	27	8	0
	Posey County	7	0	1	1	5	30	11	14	5	1
	Pulaski County	0	0	0	0	0	6	0	6	0	0
	Putnam County	5	0	1	0	4	25	5	15	5	0
	Randolph County	1	0	0	1	0	4	1	3	0	0
	Ripley County	15	0	6	0	9	83	29	52	2	3
	Rush County	0	0	0	0	0	8	1	6	1	0
	Scott County	12	2	1	2	7	46	10	33	3	0
	Shelby County	1	0	0	0	1	4	0	4	0	0
	Spencer County	3	0	2	0	1	19	2	15	2	0
	Starke County	0	0	0	0	0	8	3	5	0	0
	Steuben County	10	0	1	3	6	19	1	17	1	0
	St. Joseph County	5	0	1	0	4	56	5	49	2	0
	Sullivan County	4	0	0	0	4	17	2	14	1	0
	Switzerland County	0	0	0	0	0	12	2	8	2	0
	Tippecanoe County	15	0	1	1	13	38	2	33	3	0
	Tipton County	1	0	1	0	0	5	2	3	0	0

[1] The FBI does not publish arson data unless it receives data from either the agency or the state for all 12 months of the calendar year.

Table 11. Offenses Known to Law Enforcement, by State, Tribal, and Other Agencies, 2010—*Continued*

(Number)

State/Other Agency	Unit/Office	Violent crime	Murder and non-negligent man-slaughter	Forcible rape	Robbery	Aggra-vated assault	Property crime	Burglary	Larceny-theft	Motor vehicle theft	Arson[1]
	Union County	0	0	0	0	0	5	1	4	0	0
	Vanderburgh County	4	0	1	1	2	19	1	17	1	0
	Vermillion County	0	0	0	0	0	8	1	6	1	0
	Vigo County	10	0	3	1	6	57	6	40	11	0
	Wabash County	1	0	0	0	1	8	0	7	1	0
	Warren County	1	0	1	0	0	6	1	5	0	0
	Warrick County	2	0	0	0	2	14	1	11	2	0
	Washington County	33	0	12	1	20	39	10	26	3	0
	Wayne County	5	0	0	1	4	9	4	5	0	0
	Wells County	1	0	0	0	1	1	0	1	0	0
	White County	13	0	1	1	11	26	1	23	2	0
	Whitley County	3	0	0	0	3	13	2	9	2	0
INDIANA—Other Agencies											
Indianapolis International Airport		0	0	0	0	0	72	1	68	3	1
St. Joseph County Airport Authority		0	0	0	0	0	12	0	10	2	0
KANSAS—State Agencies											
Kansas Alcoholic Beverage Control		0	0	0	0	0	0	0	0	0	0
Kansas Bureau of Investigation		2	0	0	0	2	0	0	0	0	0
Kansas Department of Wildlife and Parks		2	0	0	0	2	24	2	22	0	0
Kansas Highway Patrol		39	0	0	3	36	66	4	53	9	0
Kansas Racing Commission	Security Division	0	0	0	0	0	0	0	0	0	0
State Fire Marshal		0	0	0	0	0	0	0	0	0	0
KANSAS—Tribal Agencies											
Kickapoo Tribal		0	0	0	0	0	1	1	0	0	0
Potawatomi Tribal		6	0	0	0	6	40	4	34	2	3
Sac and Fox Tribal		1	0	0	0	1	26	3	23	0	0
KANSAS—Other Agencies											
Blue Valley School District		1	0	0	0	1	55	0	55	0	0
Shawnee Mission Public Schools		0	0	0	0	0	7	0	7	0	0
Unified School District	Goddard	0	0	0	0	0	28	2	26	0	0
KENTUCKY—State Agencies[5]											
Kentucky Fairgrounds Security		0	0	0	0	0	12	0	11	1	0
Kentucky Horse Park		0	0	0	0	0	35	0	35	0	0
Motor Vehicle Enforcement		1	0	0	0	1	12	2	7	3	0
Park Security		0	0	0	0	0	22	5	17	0	0
State Police:	Ashland	33	1	13	1	18	412	198	183	31	5
	Bowling Green	56	2	23	2	29	272	131	95	46	6
	Campbellsburg	67	2	25	6	34	246	132	102	12	7
	Cannabis Suppression Section	0	0	0	0	0	0	0	0	0	0
	Columbia	86	6	47	3	30	216	127	77	12	21
	Drug Enforcement Area 2	2	0	0	0	2	11	2	9	0	0
	Dry Ridge	41	0	20	6	15	346	169	156	21	8
	Elizabethtown	56	4	29	2	21	299	130	117	52	10
	Frankfort	35	2	14	7	12	208	70	113	25	14
	Harlan	38	1	11	5	21	431	216	185	30	4
	Hazard	82	11	27	7	37	447	226	171	50	6
	Henderson	38	4	9	5	20	183	71	105	7	7
	London	70	4	26	6	34	455	209	186	60	39
	Madisonville	32	1	10	5	16	243	107	108	28	10
	Mayfield	56	0	25	4	27	284	121	143	20	4
	Morehead	73	5	28	11	29	595	333	204	58	8
	Pikeville	109	6	23	30	50	824	357	374	93	12
	Richmond	66	9	22	7	28	564	296	231	37	29
	Special Investigations	0	0	0	0	0	1	0	0	1	0
	West Drug Enforcement Branch	1	0	0	0	1	3	0	3	0	0
Unlawful Narcotics Investigation	Treatment and Education	0	0	0	0	0	0	0	0	0	0
KENTUCKY—Other Agencies											
Barren County Drug Task Force		0	0	0	0	0	2	1	1	0	0
Buffalo Trace-Gateway Narcotics Task Force		1	0	0	0	1	0	0	0	0	0
Central Kentucky Area Drug Task Force		0	0	0	0	0	2	0	2	0	0
Cincinnati-Northern Kentucky International Airport		0	0	0	0	0	91	0	86	5	0
Clark County School System		1	0	0	0	1	5	0	5	0	0
Fayette County Schools		5	0	0	3	2	249	7	242	0	0
FIVCO Area Drug Task Force		0	0	0	0	0	4	0	4	0	0
Greater Hardin County Narcotics Task Force		0	0	0	0	0	1	0	1	0	0
Jefferson County Board of Education		16	0	0	0	16	112	64	48	0	3
Lake Cumberland Area Drug Enforcement Task Force		0	0	0	0	0	0	0	0	0	0

[1] The FBI does not publish arson data unless it receives data from either the agency or the state for all 12 months of the calendar year.

[5] Tribal figures represented throughout Table 11 are included in the aggregated totals listed under the Bureau of Indian Affairs data.

Table 11. Offenses Known to Law Enforcement, by State, Tribal, and Other Agencies, 2010—*Continued*

(Number)

State/Other Agency	Unit/Office	Violent crime	Murder and non-negligent man-slaughter	Forcible rape	Robbery	Aggra-vated assault	Property crime	Burglary	Larceny-theft	Motor vehicle theft	Arson[1]
Louisville Regional Airport Authority		0	0	0	0	0	31	0	14	17	0
Montgomery County School District		0	0	0	0	0	10	0	10	0	0
Northern Kentucky Narcotics Enforcement Unit		1	0	0	1	0	2	0	2	0	0
Ohio County School System		0	0	0	0	0	1	0	1	0	1
Pennyrile Narcotics Task Force		1	0	0	1	0	5	0	5	0	0
South Central Kentucky Drug Task Force		0	0	0	0	0	20	1	19	0	0
LOUISIANA—State Agencies											
Department of Public Safety	State Capitol Detail	4	0	1	1	2	27	0	27	0	0
Tensas Basin Levee District		0	0	0	0	0	1	1	0	0	0
LOUISIANA—Tribal Agencies											
Chitimacha Tribal		0	0	0	0	0	52	7	43	2	0
Coushatta Tribal		2	0	2	0	0	192	4	184	4	0
Tunica Biloxi Tribal		25	0	0	0	25	127	0	126	1	0
MAINE—State Agencies											
Drug Enforcement Agency:	Androscoggin County	0	0	0	0	0	0	0	0	0	0
	Aroostook County	0	0	0	0	0	0	0	0	0	0
	Cumberland County	0	0	0	0	0	0	0	0	0	0
	Franklin County	0	0	0	0	0	0	0	0	0	0
	Hancock County	0	0	0	0	0	0	0	0	0	0
	Kennebec County	0	0	0	0	0	0	0	0	0	0
	Knox County	0	0	0	0	0	0	0	0	0	0
	Lincoln County	0	0	0	0	0	0	0	0	0	0
	Oxford County	0	0	0	0	0	0	0	0	0	0
	Penobscot County	0	0	0	0	0	0	0	0	0	0
	Piscataquis County	0	0	0	0	0	0	0	0	0	0
	Sagadahoc County	0	0	0	0	0	0	0	0	0	0
	Somerset County	0	0	0	0	0	0	0	0	0	0
	Waldo County	0	0	0	0	0	0	0	0	0	0
	Washington County	0	0	0	0	0	0	0	0	0	0
	York County	0	0	0	0	0	0	0	0	0	0
State Police:	Androscoggin County	12	1	0	1	10	114	42	62	10	2
	Aroostook County	7	3	2	1	1	297	64	216	17	3
	Cumberland County	12	1	2	1	8	119	51	61	7	2
	Franklin County	8	0	3	0	5	86	34	50	2	1
	Hancock County	14	0	2	2	10	258	117	131	10	2
	Kennebec County	12	0	3	1	8	430	156	259	15	4
	Knox County	4	0	0	0	4	77	19	55	3	2
	Lincoln County	0	0	0	0	0	24	12	12	0	0
	Oxford County	8	0	2	1	5	211	95	101	15	2
	Penobscot County	16	0	7	3	6	389	146	227	16	5
	Piscataquis County	0	0	0	0	0	32	14	18	0	0
	Sagadahoc County	2	0	0	0	2	8	4	3	1	1
	Somerset County	12	1	2	2	7	242	103	129	10	7
	Waldo County	12	2	3	0	7	144	43	91	10	3
	Washington County	23	0	1	1	21	163	78	77	8	4
	York County	8	2	1	0	5	287	126	153	8	4
MAINE—Tribal Agencies											
Passamaquoddy Indian Township		0	0	0	0	0	57	12	43	2	6
Passamaquoddy Pleasant Point Tribal		29	0	1	0	28	12	8	2	2	0
Penobscot Nation		3	0	0	0	3	33	10	23	0	1
MARYLAND—State Agencies											
Comptroller of the Treasury	Field Enforcement Division	0	0	0	0	0	0	0	0	0	0
Department of Public Safety and Correctional Services	Internal Investigations Unit	104	0	0	1	103	1	0	1	0	0
General Services:	Annapolis, Anne Arundel County	0	0	0	0	0	12	0	12	0	0
	Baltimore City	0	0	0	0	0	17	1	15	1	0
Maryland State Police Statewide		1	0	0	0	1	3	0	3	0	0
Natural Resources Police		7	0	0	1	6	247	22	223	2	41
Springfield Hospital		2	0	0	0	2	17	0	17	0	0
State Fire Marshal		0	0	0	0	0	0	0	0	0	1
State Police:	Allegany County	45	1	3	3	38	494	104	373	17	5
	Anne Arundel County	8	1	0	0	7	33	1	19	13	1
	Baltimore City	1	0	0	0	1	1	0	1	0	0
	Baltimore County	36	0	0	3	33	46	6	19	21	0
	Calvert County	23	1	1	4	17	276	61	194	21	15
	Caroline County	26	1	0	8	17	161	63	83	15	9
	Carroll County	162	2	0	19	141	1,402	336	995	71	6
	Cecil County	161	3	2	27	129	933	301	586	46	34
	Charles County	4	0	1	0	3	37	0	36	1	40
	Dorchester County	14	0	0	2	12	51	23	23	5	8

[1] The FBI does not publish arson data unless it receives data from either the agency or the state for all 12 months of the calendar year.

Table 11.   Offenses Known to Law Enforcement, by State, Tribal, and Other Agencies, 2010—*Continued*

(Number)

State/Other Agency	Unit/Office	Violent crime	Murder and non-negligent man-slaughter	Forcible rape	Robbery	Aggra-vated assault	Property crime	Burglary	Larceny-theft	Motor vehicle theft	Arson[1]
	Frederick County	63	0	4	15	44	505	106	377	22	8
	Garrett County	24	0	1	1	22	196	64	115	17	5
	Harford County	65	0	3	24	38	253	47	186	20	25
	Howard County	8	1	1	0	6	34	0	25	9	0
	Kent County	10	0	1	0	9	53	20	30	3	6
	Montgomery County	2	0	0	0	2	14	0	7	7	0
	Prince George's County	6	1	1	0	4	90	0	34	56	0
	Queen Anne's County	44	2	4	1	37	182	51	122	9	9
	Somerset County	24	0	0	3	21	222	80	129	13	5
	St. Mary's County	43	0	1	2	40	227	50	169	8	22
	Talbot County	5	0	0	0	5	96	34	59	3	5
	Washington County	33	0	1	2	30	209	55	133	21	24
	Wicomico County	77	3	2	9	63	332	135	181	16	14
	Worcester County	19	0	3	3	13	202	44	143	15	3
Transportation Administration...........................		0	0	0	0	0	0	0	0	0	0
Transportation Authority.................................		11	0	0	0	11	180	2	158	20	0
MARYLAND—Other Agencies											
Maryland-National Capital Park Police:	Montgomery County	19	0	2	15	2	173	6	164	3	1
	Prince George's County	79	1	4	49	25	283	11	257	15	0
MASSACHUSETTS—State Agencies................	Environmental Police										
Massachusetts Bay Transportation Authority:	Bristol County	0	0	0	0	0	1	0	0	1	0
	Essex County	10	0	1	4	5	42	0	38	4	0
	Middlesex County	32	0	1	16	15	125	2	116	7	0
	Norfolk County	20	0	0	7	13	76	0	71	5	0
	Plymouth County	0	0	0	0	0	50	0	46	4	0
	Suffolk County	288	1	1	197	89	266	10	246	10	0
	Worcester County	0	0	0	0	0	16	0	15	1	0
State Police:	Barnstable County	7	0	0	1	6	0	0	0	0	0
	Berkshire County	14	0	0	0	14	67	32	34	1	0
	Bristol County	18	0	0	2	16	14	3	3	8	0
	Dukes County	1	0	0	0	1	2	1	1	0	0
	Essex County	3	0	0	0	3	7	0	2	5	0
	Franklin County	31	0	1	1	29	1	1	0	0	0
	Hampden County	24	0	1	2	21	51	3	32	16	0
	Hampshire County	2	0	0	0	2	2	2	0	0	0
	Middlesex County	9	0	0	0	9	7	1	4	2	0
	Norfolk County	6	0	0	0	6	5	0	1	4	0
	Plymouth County	10	0	0	0	10	4	0	0	4	0
	Worcester County	29	0	0	0	29	0	0	0	0	0
MASSACHUSETTS—Other Agencies											
Beth Israel Deaconess Medical Center		6	0	0	0	6	158	1	156	1	0
MICHIGAN—State Agencies											
State Police:	Alcona County	1	0	0	0	1	19	4	15	0	0
	Alger County	13	0	5	0	8	69	32	30	7	1
	Allegan County	58	0	21	1	36	370	123	227	20	3
	Alpena County	23	1	6	1	15	234	70	152	12	2
	Antrim County	6	0	3	0	3	26	13	13	0	0
	Arenac County	4	0	2	0	2	23	7	12	4	0
	Baraga County	13	0	1	1	11	44	14	29	1	0
	Barry County	37	0	14	1	22	242	91	133	18	1
	Bay County	35	0	17	4	14	394	123	251	20	2
	Benzie County	4	0	1	0	3	45	11	33	1	0
	Berrien County	31	1	12	0	18	327	68	242	17	0
	Branch County	42	1	6	0	35	140	53	78	9	4
	Calhoun County	35	0	18	2	15	207	84	112	11	2
	Cass County	12	1	3	0	8	118	42	67	9	1
	Charlevoix County	6	0	3	0	3	21	3	18	0	0
	Cheboygan County	9	0	4	0	5	70	22	42	6	0
	Chippewa County	17	0	3	1	13	139	55	79	5	1
	Clare County	14	0	7	0	7	83	32	47	4	0
	Clinton County	8	0	4	0	4	46	10	36	0	0
	Crawford County	4	0	2	0	2	28	12	15	1	0
	Delta County	10	0	7	0	3	90	35	50	5	1
	Dickinson County	10	0	4	0	6	59	21	34	4	0
	Eaton County	14	0	7	0	7	80	35	42	3	1
	Emmet County	15	1	8	0	6	125	28	96	1	1
	Genesee County	58	0	26	2	30	230	98	112	20	1
	Gladwin County	11	1	7	0	3	44	11	30	3	0
	Gogebic County	13	2	3	0	8	21	7	11	3	1
	Grand Traverse County	21	0	10	2	9	152	29	121	2	1
	Gratiot County	22	0	4	0	18	135	55	75	5	1

[1] The FBI does not publish arson data unless it receives data from either the agency or the state for all 12 months of the calendar year.

Table 11.   Offenses Known to Law Enforcement, by State, Tribal, and Other Agencies, 2010—*Continued*

(Number)

State/Other Agency	Unit/Office	Violent crime	Murder and non-negligent man-slaughter	Forcible rape	Robbery	Aggra-vated assault	Property crime	Burglary	Larceny-theft	Motor vehicle theft	Arson[1]
	Hillsdale County	41	0	24	1	16	204	69	120	15	1
	Houghton County	11	0	5	0	6	145	44	95	6	1
	Huron County	8	0	4	0	4	79	28	48	3	0
	Ingham County	20	0	14	1	5	61	24	30	7	1
	Ionia County	27	0	11	3	13	303	108	176	19	2
	Iosco County	34	0	14	1	19	211	109	98	4	1
	Iron County	10	1	1	1	7	69	34	33	2	0
	Isabella County	22	0	9	1	12	188	59	127	2	2
	Jackson County	88	1	19	2	66	364	104	241	19	6
	Kalamazoo County	10	0	8	0	2	10	2	8	0	0
	Kalkaska County	19	0	6	0	13	81	40	37	4	1
	Kent County	25	0	16	0	9	42	1	37	4	0
	Keweenaw County	0	0	0	0	0	2	0	2	0	0
	Lake County	17	0	8	1	8	35	12	23	0	1
	Lapeer County	23	0	4	0	19	75	28	42	5	0
	Leelanau County	1	0	1	0	0	9	1	8	0	0
	Lenawee County	42	0	15	0	27	211	91	105	15	2
	Livingston County	50	1	13	6	30	492	97	365	30	2
	Luce County	22	0	6	0	16	55	17	35	3	1
	Mackinac County	12	0	4	2	6	96	36	52	8	0
	Macomb County	16	0	10	0	6	56	19	30	7	0
	Manistee County	16	0	3	0	13	173	63	107	3	1
	Marquette County	28	1	8	0	19	385	131	234	20	8
	Mason County	12	0	3	1	8	84	26	56	2	0
	Mecosta County	17	0	7	0	10	131	48	76	7	0
	Menominee County	17	0	1	0	16	97	38	53	6	0
	Midland County	4	0	1	0	3	45	18	26	1	1
	Missaukee County	3	0	1	0	2	26	12	14	0	0
	Monroe County	31	0	11	5	15	200	66	119	15	1
	Montcalm County	39	1	15	0	23	295	96	177	22	7
	Montmorency County	5	0	2	0	3	33	15	18	0	0
	Muskegon County	52	0	21	1	30	299	85	201	13	1
	Newaygo County	53	2	20	2	29	315	138	154	23	0
	Oakland County	41	1	10	9	21	258	82	156	20	2
	Oceana County	10	0	4	0	6	130	52	75	3	0
	Ogemaw County	15	0	7	0	8	169	62	100	7	2
	Ontonagon County	0	0	0	0	0	39	13	24	2	0
	Osceola County	23	0	10	0	13	116	57	52	7	0
	Oscoda County	5	0	1	0	4	24	12	11	1	1
	Otsego County	31	0	18	1	12	222	75	139	8	0
	Ottawa County	7	0	4	0	3	63	10	53	0	0
	Presque Isle County	9	1	6	0	2	18	5	13	0	0
	Roscommon County	17	0	11	0	6	127	49	73	5	1
	Saginaw County	76	2	28	4	42	249	95	136	18	3
	Sanilac County	26	0	10	1	15	160	61	88	11	2
	Schoolcraft County	12	0	5	0	7	104	50	52	2	2
	Shiawassee County	22	0	8	2	12	198	63	118	17	2
	St. Clair County	24	0	3	1	20	343	132	186	25	2
	St. Joseph County	31	1	9	1	20	184	63	102	19	1
	Tuscola County	30	0	17	0	13	172	70	89	13	0
	Van Buren County	65	0	16	4	45	407	156	221	30	7
	Washtenaw County	50	1	7	2	40	276	138	116	22	3
	Wayne County	67	1	10	4	52	114	4	82	28	1
	Wexford County	18	0	11	0	7	149	46	99	4	1
MICHIGAN—Tribal Agencies											
Bay Mills Tribal		1	0	0	0	1	48	4	41	3	0
Hannahville Tribal		18	0	10	0	8	121	17	100	4	0
Lac Vieux Desert Tribal		4	0	1	0	3	51	13	32	6	0
Little River Band of Ottawa Indians		1	0	0	0	1	90	1	84	5	0
Little Traverse Bay Bands of Odawa Indians		2	0	0	0	2	48	1	47	0	
Nottawaseppi Huron Band of Potawatomi		1	0	0	0	1	22	1	21	0	0
Pokagon Tribal		6	0	1	0	5	179	3	176	0	1
Saginaw Chippewa Tribal		29	3	5	1	20	282	44	218	20	
Saulte Ste. Marie Tribal		23	0	13	3	7	96	15	78	3	1
MICHIGAN—Other Agencies											
Capitol Region Airport Authority		0	0	0	0	0	5	0	3	2	0
Gerald R. Ford International Airport		0	0	0	0	0	15	0	12	3	0
Gerald R. Ford International Airport		2	0	2	0	0	2	0	0	2	0
Huron-Clinton Metropolitan Authority:	Lower Huron Metropark	2	0	0	0	2	15	0	15	0	0
	Stony Creek Metropark	5	0	0	0	5	40	2	37	1	0
Wayne County Airport		5	0	3	0	2	257	0	183	74	0

[1] The FBI does not publish arson data unless it receives data from either the agency or the state for all 12 months of the calendar year.

Table 11.   Offenses Known to Law Enforcement, by State, Tribal, and Other Agencies, 2010—*Continued*

(Number)

State/Other Agency	Unit/Office	Violent crime	Murder and non-negligent man-slaughter	Forcible rape	Robbery	Aggra-vated assault	Property crime	Burglary	Larceny-theft	Motor vehicle theft	Arson[1]
MINNESOTA—State Agencies[4]											
Capitol Security	St. Paul		0		0	0	41	0	41	0	0
Minnesota State Patrol			0		0	0	0	0	0	0	0
State Patrol:	Brainerd		0		0	0	0	0	0	0	0
	Detroit Lakes		0		0	0	0	0	0	0	0
	Duluth		0		0	0	0	0	0	0	0
	Golden Valley		0		0	0	0	0	0	0	0
	Mankato		0		0	0	0	0	0	0	0
	Marshall		0		0	0	0	0	0	0	0
	Oakdale		0		0	0	0	0	0	0	0
	Rochester		0		0	0	0	0	0	0	0
	St. Cloud		0		0	0	0	0	0	0	0
	Thief River Falls		0		0	0	0	0	0	0	0
	Virginia		0		0	0	0	0	0	0	0
MINNESOTA—Tribal Agencies											
Nett Lake Tribal		4	0	0	0	4	2	0	0	2	1
Red Lake Agency		175	0	12	1	162	451	87	284	80	45
White Earth Tribal		30	2	2	3	23	223	74	120	29	2
MINNESOTA—Other Agencies[4]											
Minneapolis-St. Paul International Airport			0		0	0	0	0	0	0	0
Three Rivers Park District			0		0	0	130	1	127	2	1
MISSISSIPPI—State Agencies											
State Capitol Police		0	0	0	0	0	23	1	20	2	0
MISSISSIPPI—Tribal Agencies											
Choctaw Tribal		40	0	6	1	33	133	96	36	1	0
MISSOURI—State Agencies											
Capitol Police		0	0	0	0	0	25	0	25	0	0
Department of Conservation		0	0	0	0	0	2	0	2	0	0
Department of Social Services	State Technical Assistance Team	12	0	10	0	2	0	0	0	0	0
Division of Alcohol and Tobacco Control		0	0	0	0	0	0	0	0	0	0
Gaming Commission	Enforcement Division	16	0	0	0	16	217	0	216	1	0
State Fire Marshal		0	0	0	0	0	0	0	0	0	221
State Highway Patrol:	Jefferson City	11	0	0	0	11	13	1	7	5	0
	Kirkwood	12	0	1	1	10	9	0	6	3	0
	Lee's Summit	9	0	0	0	9	18	1	11	6	0
	Macon	13	2	4	0	7	8	0	6	2	0
	Poplar Bluff	16	1	1	0	14	9	0	3	6	0
	Rolla	5	4	0	0	1	4	0	1	3	0
	Springfield	11	0	0	1	10	9	0	5	4	0
	St. Joseph	17	2	3	2	10	25	3	15	7	1
	Willow Springs	4	0	0	0	4	13	9	0	4	0
State Park Rangers		5	0	0	0	5	90	5	82	3	4
State Water Patrol		8	0	0	0	8	194	0	194	0	0
MISSOURI—Other Agencies											
Bootheel Drug Task Force		1	0	0	0	1	0	0	0	0	0
Clay County Drug Task Force		0	0	0	0	0	0	0	0	0	0
Clay County Park Authority		1	0	0	0	1	16	1	15	0	0
Jackson County Drug Task Force		0	0	0	0	0	0	0	0	0	0
Jackson County Park Rangers		0	0	0	0	0	0	0	0	0	0
Lambert-St. Louis International Airport		10	0	0	0	10	144	0	141	3	0
Platte County Multi-Jurisdictional Enforcement Group		0	0	0	0	0	0	0	0	0	0
Springfield-Branson Airport		0	0	0	0	0	5	0	4	1	0
St. Charles County Park Rangers		0	0	0	0	0	1	0	1	0	0
St. Peters Ranger Division		3	0	0	0	3	63	1	62	0	0
Western Missouri Cyber Crimes Task Force		0	0	0	0	0	0	0	0	0	0
MONTANA—Tribal Agencies											
Crow Agency		31	0	7	0	24	221	50	143	28	1
Fort Peck Assiniboine and Sioux Tribes		49	2	12	1	34	148	50	91	7	9
Northern Cheyenne Agency		46	2	5	0	39	90	29	50	11	8
Rocky Boys Tribal		28	1	13	3	11	77	36	35	6	1
NEBRASKA—State Agencies											
Nebraska State Patrol		1	0	0	0	1	6	2	4	0	0
State Patrol:	Adams County	0	0	0	0	0	1	1	0	0	0
	Antelope County	0	0	0	0	0	0	0	0	0	0
	Arthur County	0	0	0	0	0	0	0	0	0	0
	Banner County	0	0	0	0	0	0	0	0	0	0
	Blaine County	0	0	0	0	0	0	0	0	0	0
	Boone County	0	0	0	0	0	0	0	0	0	0
	Box Butte County	0	0	0	0	0	0	0	0	0	0
	Boyd County	0	0	0	0	0	0	0	0	0	0
	Brown County	0	0	0	0	0	0	0	0	0	0
	Buffalo County	0	0	0	0	0	2	0	2	0	0

[1] The FBI does not publish arson data unless it receives data from either the agency or the state for all 12 months of the calendar year.

[4] The data collection methodology for the offense of forcible rape used by the Minnesota state Uniform Crime Reporting (UCR) Program does not comply with national UCR Program guidelines. Consequently, its figures for forcible rape and violent crime (of which forcible rape is a part) are not published in this table.

Table 11.   Offenses Known to Law Enforcement, by State, Tribal, and Other Agencies, 2010—*Continued*

(Number)

State/Other Agency	Unit/Office	Violent crime	Murder and non-negligent man-slaughter	Forcible rape	Robbery	Aggra-vated assault	Property crime	Burglary	Larceny-theft	Motor vehicle theft	Arson[1]
	Burt County	0	0	0	0	0	0	0	0	0	0
	Butler County	0	0	0	0	0	0	0	0	0	0
	Cass County	0	0	0	0	0	4	1	3	0	0
	Cedar County	0	0	0	0	0	0	0	0	0	0
	Chase County	0	0	0	0	0	0	0	0	0	0
	Cherry County	0	0	0	0	0	0	0	0	0	0
	Cheyenne County	0	0	0	0	0	0	0	0	0	0
	Clay County	0	0	0	0	0	0	0	0	0	0
	Colfax County	0	0	0	0	0	0	0	0	0	0
	Cuming County	0	0	0	0	0	0	0	0	0	0
	Custer County	1	1	0	0	0	1	0	1	0	0
	Dakota County	1	0	0	1	0	0	0	0	0	0
	Dawes County	0	0	0	0	0	1	0	1	0	0
	Dawson County	1	0	0	0	1	2	0	1	1	0
	Deuel County	0	0	0	0	0	0	0	0	0	0
	Dixon County	0	0	0	0	0	0	0	0	0	0
	Dodge County	0	0	0	0	0	0	0	0	0	0
	Douglas County	0	0	0	0	0	4	0	3	1	0
	Dundy County	0	0	0	0	0	0	0	0	0	0
	Fillmore County	0	0	0	0	0	0	0	0	0	0
	Franklin County	0	0	0	0	0	0	0	0	0	0
	Frontier County	0	0	0	0	0	0	0	0	0	0
	Furnas County	0	0	0	0	0	0	0	0	0	0
	Gage County	0	0	0	0	0	0	0	0	0	0
	Garden County	0	0	0	0	0	0	0	0	0	0
	Garfield County	0	0	0	0	0	0	0	0	0	0
	Gosper County	0	0	0	0	0	0	0	0	0	0
	Grant County	0	0	0	0	0	0	0	0	0	0
	Greeley County	0	0	0	0	0	2	2	0	0	0
	Hall County	1	0	0	0	1	21	4	17	0	0
	Hamilton County	0	0	0	0	0	0	0	0	0	0
	Harlan County	1	0	0	0	1	0	0	0	0	0
	Hayes County	0	0	0	0	0	0	0	0	0	0
	Hitchcock County	0	0	0	0	0	2	1	0	1	0
	Holt County	0	0	0	0	0	1	0	1	0	0
	Hooker County	0	0	0	0	0	1	1	0	0	0
	Howard County	0	0	0	0	0	0	0	0	0	0
	Jefferson County	0	0	0	0	0	1	0	1	0	0
	Johnson County	0	0	0	0	0	0	0	0	0	0
	Kearney County	1	1	0	0	0	0	0	0	0	0
	Keith County	1	0	0	0	1	1	1	0	0	0
	Keya Paha County	0	0	0	0	0	0	0	0	0	0
	Kimball County	0	0	0	0	0	1	0	1	0	0
	Knox County	0	0	0	0	0	0	0	0	0	0
	Lancaster County	0	0	0	0	0	4	0	4	0	0
	Lincoln County	0	0	0	0	0	2	0	2	0	0
	Logan County	0	0	0	0	0	4	3	1	0	0
	Loup County	0	0	0	0	0	0	0	0	0	0
	Madison County	1	0	0	0	1	7	3	4	0	
	McPherson County	0	0	0	0	0	0	0	0	0	0
	Merrick County	0	0	0	0	0	1	1	0	0	1
	Morrill County	0	0	0	0	0	1	0	0	1	0
	Nance County	0	0	0	0	0	0	0	0	0	0
	Nemaha County	0	0	0	0	0	1	0	1	0	0
	Nuckolls County	0	0	0	0	0	0	0	0	0	0
	Otoe County	0	0	0	0	0	0	0	0	0	0
	Pawnee County	0	0	0	0	0	0	0	0	0	0
	Perkins County	0	0	0	0	0	0	0	0	0	0
	Phelps County	0	0	0	0	0	0	0	0	0	0
	Pierce County	0	0	0	0	0	0	0	0	0	0
	Platte County	0	0	0	0	0	0	0	0	0	0
	Polk County	0	0	0	0	0	0	0	0	0	0
	Red Willow County	0	0	0	0	0	1	0	1	0	0
	Richardson County	1	0	0	0	1	0	0	0	0	0
	Rock County	0	0	0	0	0	1	1	0	0	0
	Saline County	0	0	0	0	0	0	0	0	0	0
	Sarpy County	1	0	0	0	1	0	0	0	0	0
	Saunders County	0	0	0	0	0	0	0	0	0	0
	Scotts Bluff County	0	0	0	0	0	1	0	1	0	0
	Seward County	0	0	0	0	0	1	0	1	0	0
	Sheridan County	1	0	0	0	1	1	0	0	1	0
	Sherman County	1	0	0	0	1	0	0	0	0	0
	Sioux County	0	0	0	0	0	0	0	0	0	0

[1] The FBI does not publish arson data unless it receives data from either the agency or the state for all 12 months of the calendar year.

Table 11. Offenses Known to Law Enforcement, by State, Tribal, and Other Agencies, 2010—*Continued*

(Number)

State/Other Agency	Unit/Office	Violent crime	Murder and non-negligent man-slaughter	Forcible rape	Robbery	Aggra-vated assault	Property crime	Burglary	Larceny-theft	Motor vehicle theft	Arson[1]
	Stanton County	0	0	0	0	0	0	0	0	0	0
	Thayer County	0	0	0	0	0	0	0	0	0	0
	Thomas County	0	0	0	0	0	0	0	0	0	0
	Thurston County	0	0	0	0	0	0	0	0	0	0
	Valley County	0	0	0	0	0	0	0	0	0	0
	Washington County	0	0	0	0	0	0	0	0	0	0
	Wayne County	0	0	0	0	0	1	1	0	0	0
	Webster County	0	0	0	0	0	0	0	0	0	0
	Wheeler County	0	0	0	0	0	1	0	1	0	0
	York County	1	0	0	1	0	0	0	0	0	0
NEBRASKA—Tribal Agencies											
Omaha Tribal		55	0	8	0	47	82	50	15	17	12
Santee Tribal		30	1	1	1	27	10	7	0	3	4
Winnebago Tribal		46	0	0	0	46	6	4	1	1	0
NEVADA—State Agencies											
Taxicab Authority		2	0	0	0	2	465	3	462	0	0
NEVADA—Tribal Agencies											
Eastern Nevada Agency		6	0	0	0	6	3	2	0	1	0
Ely Shoshone Tribal		1	0	0	0	1	7	4	3	0	0
Las Vegas Paiute Tribal		7	0	0	1	6	121	0	120	1	0
Lovelock Paiute Tribal		5	0	0	0	5	2	2	0	0	0
Pyramid Lake Tribal		23	0	3	0	20	30	14	9	7	4
Yomba Shoshone Tribal		0	0	0	0	0	2	0	2	0	0
NEVADA—Other Agencies											
Clark County School District		78	0	2	37	39	934	166	749	19	34
Washoe County School District		4	0	0	0	4	155	5	148	2	12
NEW HAMPSHIRE—State Agencies											
Liquor Commission		1	0	0	1	0	32	1	31	0	0
NEW JERSEY—State Agencies											
Division of Fish and Wildlife		0	0	0	0	0	0	0	0	0	0
New Jersey Transit Police		36	1	0	24	11	372	7	363	2	0
Palisades Interstate Parkway		2	0	0	0	2	2	0	2	0	0
State Park Police		0	0	0	0	0	0	0	0	0	0
State Police:	Atlantic County	38	0	1	18	19	971	109	841	21	1
	Bergen County	10	0	0	1	9	94	5	84	5	1
	Burlington County	26	1	1	5	19	572	130	415	27	4
	Camden County	9	0	0	1	8	34	2	32	0	0
	Cape May County	35	0	0	5	30	413	145	254	14	2
	Cumberland County	79	2	1	13	63	883	290	560	33	4
	Essex County	9	0	1	4	4	30	1	27	2	1
	Gloucester County	1	0	0	0	1	6	1	5	0	0
	Hudson County	2	0	0	1	1	14	0	13	1	0
	Hunterdon County	8	0	0	1	7	185	47	133	5	0
	Mercer County	3	0	0	1	2	116	9	104	3	0
	Middlesex County	8	1	0	2	5	65	1	59	5	0
	Monmouth County	24	0	0	3	21	254	73	171	10	4
	Morris County	12	0	2	1	9	23	6	13	4	0
	Ocean County	7	0	0	0	7	110	11	91	8	2
	Salem County	30	0	1	2	27	454	167	266	21	4
	Somerset County	2	0	0	1	1	9	1	7	1	0
	Sussex County	25	0	0	3	22	538	161	368	9	4
	Union County	4	0	0	2	2	15	0	15	0	0
	Warren County	14	0	0	0	14	233	65	155	13	2
NEW JERSEY—Other Agencies											
Park Police:	Camden County	8	0	1	4	3	32	8	23	1	0
	Morris County	0	0	0	0	0	0	0	0	0	0
	Union County	0	0	0	0	0	0	0	0	0	0
Prosecutor:	Atlantic County	0	0	0	0	0	0	0	0	0	0
	Bergen County	0	0	0	0	0	0	0	0	0	0
	Burlington County	0	0	0	0	0	0	0	0	0	0
	Camden County	0	0	0	0	0	0	0	0	0	0
	Cape May County	0	0	0	0	0	0	0	0	0	0
	Cumberland County	0	0	0	0	0	0	0	0	0	0
	Essex County	0	0	0	0	0	0	0	0	0	0
	Gloucester County	0	0	0	0	0	0	0	0	0	0
	Hudson County	0	0	0	0	0	0	0	0	0	0
	Hunterdon County	0	0	0	0	0	0	0	0	0	0
	Mercer County	0	0	0	0	0	0	0	0	0	0
	Middlesex County	0	0	0	0	0	0	0	0	0	0
	Monmouth County	0	0	0	0	0	0	0	0	0	0
	Morris County	0	0	0	0	0	0	0	0	0	0
	Ocean County	0	0	0	0	0	0	0	0	0	0
	Passaic County	0	0	0	0	0	0	0	0	0	0

[1] The FBI does not publish arson data unless it receives data from either the agency or the state for all 12 months of the calendar year.

Table 11. Offenses Known to Law Enforcement, by State, Tribal, and Other Agencies, 2010—*Continued*

(Number)

State/Other Agency	Unit/Office	Violent crime	Murder and non-negligent manslaughter	Forcible rape	Robbery	Aggravated assault	Property crime	Burglary	Larceny-theft	Motor vehicle theft	Arson[1]
	Salem County	0	0	0	0	0	0	0	0	0	0
	Somerset County	0	0	0	0	0	0	0	0	0	0
	Sussex County	0	0	0	0	0	0	0	0	0	0
	Union County	0	0	0	0	0	0	0	0	0	0
	Warren County	0	0	0	0	0	0	0	0	0	0
NEW MEXICO—State Agencies											
New Mexico State Police		114	9	20	24	61	1,056	654	294	108	6
NEW MEXICO—Tribal Agencies											
Acoma Tribal		26	0	2	0	24	18	9	6	3	0
Isleta Tribal		68	0	1	1	66	136	32	87	17	1
Jemez Pueblo		21	0	0	0	21	10	7	2	1	0
Jicarilla Tribal		55	1	1	0	53	0	0	0	0	0
Laguna Tribal		98	0	8	0	90	86	16	60	10	0
Mescalero Tribal		89	0	4	3	82	32	14	9	9	3
Northern Pueblos Agency		53	5	0	1	47	69	35	32	2	1
Ohkay Owingeh Tribal		7	1	0	1	5	47	16	30	1	0
Pojoaque Tribal		10	0	2	3	5	117	30	73	14	0
Ramah Navajo Tribal		26	1	0	0	25	24	19	1	4	0
Santa Ana Tribal		4	0	0	2	2	11	7	0	4	0
Santa Clara Pueblo		3	0	0	0	3	37	9	24	4	0
Southern Pueblos Agency		20	11	6	0	3	22	14	8	0	1
Taos Pueblo		5	0	0	0	5	10	4	6	0	0
Zuni Tribal		47	2	2	5	38	20	13	6	1	0
NEW YORK—State Agencies											
State Park:	Allegany Region	4	0	0	0	4	20	3	16	1	1
	Central Region	1	0	0	0	1	33	3	30	0	0
	Finger Lakes Region	0	0	0	0	0	43	1	42	0	0
	Genesee Region	0	0	0	0	0	28	1	27	0	0
	Long Island Region	2	0	0	0	2	160	7	145	8	0
	New York City Region	6	0	0	5	1	43	0	43	0	0
	Niagara Region	0	0	0	0	0	34	1	32	1	0
	Palisades Region	9	0	0	0	9	44	6	37	1	1
	Saratoga/Capital Region	4	0	0	2	2	47	2	44	1	0
	Taconic Region	0	0	0	0	0	3	0	3	0	0
	Thousand Island Region	0	0	0	0	0	27	0	27	0	0
State Police:	Albany County	14	0	3	2	9	228	21	199	8	0
	Allegany County[3]	35	0	6	1	28	338	96	233	9	3
	Broome County	48	1	9	7	31	578	117	434	27	3
	Cattaraugus County	19	0	3	1	15	302	77	210	15	0
	Cayuga County	28	0	1	1	26	252	63	181	8	0
	Chautauqua County	10	1	0	0	9	153	35	113	5	0
	Chemung County	49	0	4	1	44	238	33	199	6	1
	Chenango County	23	0	8	0	15	166	60	101	5	1
	Clinton County[3]	48	3	12	2	31	974	182	769	23	5
	Columbia County	23	0	4	2	17	313	100	207	6	4
	Cortland County	3	0	1	0	2	185	28	149	8	0
	Delaware County	21	0	1	2	18	296	109	175	12	1
	Dutchess County	97	1	14	13	69	736	177	531	28	5
	Erie County[3]	26	1	4	2	19	457	37	407	13	0
	Essex County	22	0	5	0	17	339	122	209	8	2
	Franklin County	37	0	9	0	28	358	135	207	16	11
	Fulton County	10	0	2	0	8	166	22	139	5	1
	Genesee County	13	0	1	1	11	80	11	68	1	0
	Greene County	57	0	7	4	46	405	150	229	26	3
	Hamilton County	3	0	1	1	1	35	10	23	2	0
	Herkimer County[3]	40	0	8	0	32	338	146	178	14	5
	Jefferson County	50	2	5	5	38	620	143	456	21	3
	Lewis County	10	0	3	0	7	82	45	33	4	0
	Livingston County[3]	8	0	2	1	5	77	16	60	1	1
	Madison County	17	0	7	2	8	228	58	164	6	2
	Monroe County	19	0	10	0	9	70	0	66	4	0
	Montgomery County	6	0	1	2	3	97	14	81	2	0
	Nassau County	5	0	1	1	3	21	3	18	0	1
	New York County	1	0	0	0	1	137	0	137	0	0
	Niagara County	15	0	7	2	6	242	37	201	4	0
	Oneida County[3]	67	3	9	6	49	615	192	396	27	3
	Onondaga County	26	0	4	6	16	686	124	532	30	2
	Ontario County	13	1	8	1	3	230	46	178	6	0
	Orange County	70	1	16	15	38	946	85	830	31	4
	Orleans County	10	0	1	0	9	54	11	39	4	1
	Oswego County	41	0	11	2	28	990	281	658	51	3
	Otsego County	32	0	6	5	21	411	87	313	11	1
	Putnam County	29	0	6	4	19	132	26	102	4	0
	Rensselaer County	27	0	9	4	14	552	96	429	27	2

[1] The FBI does not publish arson data unless it receives data from either the agency or the state for all 12 months of the calendar year.

[3] Because of changes in the state/local agency's reporting practices, figures are not comparable to previous years' data.

Table 11. Offenses Known to Law Enforcement, by State, Tribal, and Other Agencies, 2010—*Continued*

(Number)

State/Other Agency	Unit/Office	Violent crime	Murder and non-negligent man-slaughter	Forcible rape	Robbery	Aggra-vated assault	Property crime	Burglary	Larceny-theft	Motor vehicle theft	Arson[1]
	Rockland County	11	0	3	1	7	19	1	17	1	0
	Saratoga County	52	0	11	2	39	699	97	584	18	1
	Schenectady County	6	0	0	1	5	101	18	80	3	0
	Schoharie County	8	0	0	1	7	151	37	109	5	1
	Schuyler County	4	0	0	1	3	38	8	29	1	0
	Seneca County[3]	17	0	6	1	10	150	36	110	4	0
	Steuben County	43	0	8	2	33	500	137	346	17	16
	St. Lawrence County[3]	46	0	12	6	28	575	173	377	25	5
	Suffolk County	11	2	4	0	5	79	6	69	4	0
	Sullivan County	63	0	12	5	46	375	123	232	20	2
	Tioga County	15	0	3	1	11	104	30	68	6	0
	Tompkins County	18	0	4	1	13	263	40	214	9	1
	Ulster County	108	0	14	6	88	497	131	332	34	3
	Warren County	11	0	6	1	4	169	26	139	4	1
	Washington County	29	0	8	0	21	145	45	95	5	1
	Wayne County	39	0	10	5	24	496	160	321	15	2
	Westchester County	61	1	10	9	41	470	100	351	19	4
	Wyoming County	14	0	1	0	13	39	10	27	2	1
	Yates County	4	0	1	0	3	35	9	23	3	0
NEW YORK—Tribal Agencies											
Oneida Indian Nation		9	1	0	4	4	291	7	284	0	0
St. Regis Tribal		10	1	3	5	1	124	50	64	10	2
NEW YORK—Other Agencies											
Board of Water:	Delaware County	0	0	0	0	0	0	0	0	0	0
	Sullivan County	0	0	0	0	0	1	0	1	0	0
	Ulster County	0	0	0	0	0	5	0	5	0	0
	Westchester County	0	0	0	0	0	15	0	15	0	0
Broome County Special Investigations Task Force		0	0	0	0	0	0	0	0	0	0
New York City Metropolitan Transportation Authority		87	0	0	49	38	555	11	533	11	0
Onondaga County Parks		1	0	0	0	1	46	3	43	0	0
Suffolk County Parks		1	0	0	1	0	44	5	36	3	0
NORTH CAROLINA—State Agencies											
Department of Human Resources		0	0	0	0	0	17	0	17	0	0
North Carolina Highway Patrol		0	0	0	0	0	0	0	0	0	0
State Park Rangers:	Cliffs of the Neuse	0	0	0	0	0	1	0	1	0	0
	Crowders Mountain	0	0	0	0	0	0	0	0	0	0
	Eno River	0	0	0	0	0	5	0	5	0	0
	Goose Creek	0	0	0	0	0	0	0	0	0	0
	Hanging Rock	0	0	0	0	0	3	0	3	0	0
	Lake James	0	0	0	0	0	2	0	2	0	0
	Morrow Mountain	1	0	0	0	1	4	0	4	0	0
	New River-Mount Jefferson	0	0	0	0	0	0	0	0	0	0
	Stone Mountain	0	0	0	0	0	0	0	0	0	0
State Capitol Police		2	0	0	0	2	68	11	54	3	0
NORTH CAROLINA—Tribal Agencies											
Cherokee Tribal		104	4	10	16	74	480	139	303	38	4
NORTH CAROLINA—Other Agencies											
Beaufort County Alcohol Beverage Control Enforcement		0	0	0	0	0	7	2	5	0	0
Pitt County Memorial Hospital		4	0	0	0	4	38	6	32	0	0
Raleigh-Durham International Airport		2	0	0	0	2	47	1	44	2	0
Triad Alcohol Beverage Control Law Enforcement		0	0	0	0	0	15	2	13	0	0
NORTH DAKOTA—Tribal Agencies											
Fort Totten Tribal		95	0	8	0	87	142	34	88	20	3
Standing Rock Agency		99	0	11	5	83	107	19	73	15	8
Three Affiliated Tribes		70	0	0	0	70	30	4	0	26	2
Turtle Mountain Agency		85	1	7	1	76	373	126	196	51	7
OHIO—State Agencies											
Ohio Department of Natural Resources		5	0	0	2	3	38	2	35	1	14
Ohio State Highway Patrol		304	3	6	7	288	466	18	376	72	6
OHIO—Other Agencies											
Cleveland Metropolitan Park District		3	0	0	3	0	81	2	77	2	3
Lake Metroparks		0	0	0	0	0	12	2	10	0	0
Lorain County Metropolitan Park District		0	0	0	0	0	2	0	2	0	0
Robinson Memorial Hospital		0	0	0	0	0	6	0	5	1	0
OKLAHOMA—State Agencies											
Capitol Park Police		1	0	0	0	1	7	1	6	0	0
OKLAHOMA—Tribal Agencies											
Absentee Shawnee Tribal		18	1	1	4	12	58	36	11	11	1
Anadarko Agency		5	0	0	1	4	39	7	32	0	1
Cherokee Nation		13	0	0	3	10	18	13	4	1	2

[1] The FBI does not publish arson data unless it receives data from either the agency or the state for all 12 months of the calendar year.

[3] Because of changes in the state/local agency's reporting practices, figures are not comparable to previous years' data.

Table 11. Offenses Known to Law Enforcement, by State, Tribal, and Other Agencies, 2010—*Continued*

(Number)

State/Other Agency	Unit/Office	Violent crime	Murder and non-negligent man-slaughter	Forcible rape	Robbery	Aggra-vated assault	Property crime	Burglary	Larceny-theft	Motor vehicle theft	Arson[1]
Choctaw Nation		2	0	1	0	1	285	37	235	13	0
Citizen Potawatomi Nation		9	0	0	1	8	63	9	41	13	0
Comanche Nation		11	0	0	1	10	103	11	79	13	1
Concho Agency		3	0	0	2	1	6	3	2	1	0
Eastern Shawnee Tribal		5	0	1	2	2	37	6	26	5	0
Iowa Tribal		1	1	0	0	0	8	0	8	0	0
Kaw Tribal		0	0	0	0	0	15	2	13	0	0
Kickapoo Tribal		8	0	0	0	8	17	6	9	2	1
Miami Agency		4	0	0	0	4	86	3	77	6	9
Miami Tribal		0	0	0	0	0	0	0	0	0	0
Muscogee Nation Tribal		10	1	0	0	9	60	7	44	9	5
Osage Nation		4	0	0	2	2	44	16	20	8	0
Otoe-Missouria Tribal		4	0	0	1	3	24	7	12	5	0
Pawnee Agency		1	1	0	0	0	5	2	3	0	1
Pawnee Tribal		3	0	1	0	2	9	0	9	0	0
Ponca Tribal		7	0	0	0	7	22	5	15	2	1
Sac and Fox Tribal		4	2	0	0	2	19	3	12	4	2
Seminole Nation Lighthorse		0	0	0	0	0	17	3	11	3	0
Tonkawa Tribal		0	0	0	0	0	5	2	3	0	0
Wyandotte Nation		7	0	0	3	4	57	2	54	1	0
OKLAHOMA—Other Agencies											
Jenks Public Schools		0	0	0	0	0	18	0	18	0	0
Madill Public Schools		1	0	0	0	1	1	1	0	0	0
Norman Public Schools		1	0	0	0	1	30	5	25	0	0
Putnam City Campus		4	0	0	2	2	48	4	44	0	
OREGON—Tribal Agencies											
Burns Paiute Tribal		0	0	0	0	0	1	0	0	1	0
Coquille Tribal		0	0	0	0	0	8	3	5	0	4
Umatilla Tribal		35	2	2	1	30	91	23	62	6	2
Warm Springs Tribal		22	2	5	4	11	122	63	45	14	7
OREGON—Other Agencies[3]											
Blue Mountain Enforcement Narcotics Team:	Morrow County	0	0	0	0	0	0	0	0	0	0
	Umatilla County	0	0	0	0	0	0	0	0	0	0
Port of Portland		4	0	1	0	3	316	1	301	14	0
PENNSYLVANIA—State Agencies											
Bureau of Forestry:	Adams County	0	0	0	0	0	0	0	0	0	4
	Armstrong County	0	0	0	0	0	0	0	0	0	4
	Beaver County	0	0	0	0	0	0	0	0	0	0
	Bedford County	0	0	0	0	0	0	0	0	0	4
	Berks County	0	0	0	0	0	0	0	0	0	2
	Blair County	0	0	0	0	0	0	0	0	0	6
	Bradford County	0	0	0	0	0	0	0	0	0	3
	Bucks County	0	0	0	0	0	0	0	0	0	0
	Butler County	0	0	0	0	0	0	0	0	0	0
	Cambria County	0	0	0	0	0	0	0	0	0	0
	Cameron County	0	0	0	0	0	0	0	0	0	5
	Carbon County	0	0	0	0	0	0	0	0	0	6
	Centre County	0	0	0	0	0	0	0	0	0	0
	Chester County	0	0	0	0	0	0	0	0	0	0
	Clarion County	0	0	0	0	0	0	0	0	0	0
	Clearfield County	0	0	0	0	0	0	0	0	0	12
	Clinton County	0	0	0	0	0	0	0	0	0	3
	Columbia County	0	0	0	0	0	0	0	0	0	0
	Cumberland County	0	0	0	0	0	0	0	0	0	0
	Dauphin County	0	0	0	0	0	0	0	0	0	0
	Delaware County	0	0	0	0	0	0	0	0	0	0
	Elk County	0	0	0	0	0	0	0	0	0	0
	Fayette County	0	0	0	0	0	0	0	0	0	3
	Forest County	0	0	0	0	0	0	0	0	0	0
	Franklin County	0	0	0	0	0	0	0	0	0	0
	Fulton County	0	0	0	0	0	0	0	0	0	0
	Greene County	0	0	0	0	0	0	0	0	0	0
	Huntingdon County	0	0	0	0	0	0	0	0	0	10
	Indiana County	0	0	0	0	0	0	0	0	0	0
	Jefferson County	0	0	0	0	0	0	0	0	0	0
	Juniata County	0	0	0	0	0	0	0	0	0	0
	Lackawanna County	0	0	0	0	0	0	0	0	0	4
	Lancaster County	0	0	0	0	0	0	0	0	0	0
	Lawrence County	0	0	0	0	0	0	0	0	0	0
	Lebanon County	0	0	0	0	0	0	0	0	0	0
	Lehigh County	0	0	0	0	0	0	0	0	0	0
	Luzerne County	0	0	0	0	0	0	0	0	0	31

[1] The FBI does not publish arson data unless it receives data from either the agency or the state for all 12 months of the calendar year.

[3] Because of changes in the state/local agency's reporting practices, figures are not comparable to previous years' data.

Table 11.   Offenses Known to Law Enforcement, by State, Tribal, and Other Agencies, 2010—*Continued*

(Number)

State/Other Agency	Unit/Office	Violent crime	Murder and non-negligent man-slaughter	Forcible rape	Robbery	Aggra-vated assault	Property crime	Burglary	Larceny-theft	Motor vehicle theft	Arson[1]
	Lycoming County	0	0	0	0	0	0	0	0	0	0
	McKean County	0	0	0	0	0	0	0	0	0	0
	Mifflin County	0	0	0	0	0	0	0	0	0	2
	Monroe County	0	0	0	0	0	0	0	0	0	7
	Montgomery County	0	0	0	0	0	0	0	0	0	3
	Montour County	0	0	0	0	0	0	0	0	0	0
	Northampton County	0	0	0	0	0	0	0	0	0	0
	Northumberland County	0	0	0	0	0	0	0	0	0	15
	Perry County	0	0	0	0	0	0	0	0	0	0
	Pike County	0	0	0	0	0	0	0	0	0	5
	Potter County	0	0	0	0	0	0	0	0	0	0
	Snyder County	0	0	0	0	0	0	0	0	0	0
	Somerset County	0	0	0	0	0	0	0	0	0	5
	Sullivan County	0	0	0	0	0	0	0	0	0	0
	Susquehanna County	0	0	0	0	0	0	0	0	0	0
	Tioga County	0	0	0	0	0	0	0	0	0	0
	Union County	0	0	0	0	0	0	0	0	0	0
	Venango County	0	0	0	0	0	0	0	0	0	0
	Warren County	0	0	0	0	0	0	0	0	0	0
	Wayne County	0	0	0	0	0	0	0	0	0	0
	Westmoreland County	0	0	0	0	0	0	0	0	0	7
	Wyoming County	0	0	0	0	0	0	0	0	0	0
	York County	0	0	0	0	0	0	0	0	0	0
Bureau of Narcotics:	Adams County	0	0	0	0	0	0	0	0	0	0
	Allegheny County	0	0	0	0	0	0	0	0	0	0
	Armstrong County	0	0	0	0	0	0	0	0	0	0
	Beaver County	0	0	0	0	0	0	0	0	0	0
	Bedford County	0	0	0	0	0	0	0	0	0	0
	Berks County	0	0	0	0	0	0	0	0	0	0
	Blair County	0	0	0	0	0	0	0	0	0	0
	Bradford County	0	0	0	0	0	0	0	0	0	0
	Bucks County	0	0	0	0	0	0	0	0	0	0
	Butler County	0	0	0	0	0	0	0	0	0	0
	Cambria County	0	0	0	0	0	0	0	0	0	0
	Cameron County	0	0	0	0	0	0	0	0	0	0
	Carbon County	0	0	0	0	0	0	0	0	0	0
	Centre County	0	0	0	0	0	0	0	0	0	0
	Chester County	0	0	0	0	0	0	0	0	0	0
	Clarion County	0	0	0	0	0	0	0	0	0	0
	Clearfield County	0	0	0	0	0	0	0	0	0	0
	Clinton County	0	0	0	0	0	0	0	0	0	0
	Columbia County	0	0	0	0	0	0	0	0	0	0
	Crawford County	0	0	0	0	0	0	0	0	0	0
	Cumberland County	0	0	0	0	0	0	0	0	0	0
	Dauphin County	0	0	0	0	0	0	0	0	0	0
	Delaware County	0	0	0	0	0	0	0	0	0	0
	Elk County	0	0	0	0	0	0	0	0	0	0
	Erie County	0	0	0	0	0	0	0	0	0	0
	Fayette County	0	0	0	0	0	0	0	0	0	0
	Forest County	0	0	0	0	0	0	0	0	0	0
	Franklin County	0	0	0	0	0	0	0	0	0	0
	Fulton County	0	0	0	0	0	0	0	0	0	0
	Greene County	0	0	0	0	0	0	0	0	0	0
	Huntingdon County	0	0	0	0	0	0	0	0	0	0
	Indiana County	0	0	0	0	0	0	0	0	0	0
	Jefferson County	0	0	0	0	0	0	0	0	0	0
	Juniata County	0	0	0	0	0	0	0	0	0	0
	Lackawanna County	0	0	0	0	0	0	0	0	0	0
	Lancaster County	0	0	0	0	0	0	0	0	0	0
	Lawrence County	0	0	0	0	0	0	0	0	0	0
	Lebanon County	0	0	0	0	0	0	0	0	0	0
	Lehigh County	0	0	0	0	0	0	0	0	0	0
	Luzerne County	0	0	0	0	0	0	0	0	0	0
	Lycoming County	0	0	0	0	0	0	0	0	0	0
	McKean County	0	0	0	0	0	0	0	0	0	0
	Mercer County	0	0	0	0	0	0	0	0	0	0
	Mifflin County	0	0	0	0	0	0	0	0	0	0
	Monroe County	0	0	0	0	0	0	0	0	0	0
	Montgomery County	0	0	0	0	0	0	0	0	0	0
	Montour County	0	0	0	0	0	0	0	0	0	0
	Northampton County	0	0	0	0	0	0	0	0	0	0
	Northumberland County	0	0	0	0	0	0	0	0	0	0
	Perry County	0	0	0	0	0	0	0	0	0	0

[1] The FBI does not publish arson data unless it receives data from either the agency or the state for all 12 months of the calendar year.

Table 11. Offenses Known to Law Enforcement, by State, Tribal, and Other Agencies, 2010—*Continued*
(Number)

State/Other Agency	Unit/Office	Violent crime	Murder and non-negligent man-slaughter	Forcible rape	Robbery	Aggra-vated assault	Property crime	Burglary	Larceny-theft	Motor vehicle theft	Arson[1]
	Philadelphia County	0	0	0	0	0	0	0	0	0	0
	Pike County	0	0	0	0	0	0	0	0	0	0
	Potter County	0	0	0	0	0	0	0	0	0	0
	Schuylkill County	0	0	0	0	0	0	0	0	0	0
	Snyder County	0	0	0	0	0	0	0	0	0	0
	Somerset County	0	0	0	0	0	0	0	0	0	0
	Sullivan County	0	0	0	0	0	0	0	0	0	0
	Susquehanna County	0	0	0	0	0	0	0	0	0	0
	Tioga County	0	0	0	0	0	0	0	0	0	0
	Union County	0	0	0	0	0	0	0	0	0	0
	Venango County	0	0	0	0	0	0	0	0	0	0
	Warren County	0	0	0	0	0	0	0	0	0	0
	Washington County	0	0	0	0	0	0	0	0	0	0
	Wayne County	0	0	0	0	0	0	0	0	0	0
	Westmoreland County	0	0	0	0	0	0	0	0	0	0
	Wyoming County	0	0	0	0	0	0	0	0	0	0
	York County	0	0	0	0	0	0	0	0	0	0
Department of Environmental Resources		0	0	0	0	0	6	0	6	0	0
State Capitol Police		3	0	0	0	3	55	2	52	1	0
State Park Police:	Pine Grove Furnace	0	0	0	0	0	2	1	1	0	1
	Pymatuning	0	0	0	0	0	47	0	47	0	0
State Police, Bureau of Criminal Investigation:	Adams County	0	0	0	0	0	0	0	0	0	0
	Allegheny County	1	0	1	0	0	6	1	3	2	0
	Armstrong County	0	0	0	0	0	1	0	1	0	0
	Beaver County	0	0	0	0	0	0	0	0	0	0
	Bedford County	0	0	0	0	0	0	0	0	0	0
	Berks County	0	0	0	0	0	0	0	0	0	0
	Blair County	0	0	0	0	0	0	0	0	0	0
	Bradford County	0	0	0	0	0	0	0	0	0	0
	Bucks County	1	0	0	1	0	0	0	0	0	0
	Butler County	0	0	0	0	0	1	0	1	0	0
	Cambria County	0	0	0	0	0	1	0	1	0	0
	Cameron County	0	0	0	0	0	0	0	0	0	0
	Carbon County	0	0	0	0	0	0	0	0	0	0
	Centre County	0	0	0	0	0	0	0	0	0	0
	Chester County	0	0	0	0	0	0	0	0	0	0
	Clarion County	0	0	0	0	0	0	0	0	0	0
	Clearfield County	0	0	0	0	0	0	0	0	0	0
	Clinton County	0	0	0	0	0	0	0	0	0	0
	Columbia County	0	0	0	0	0	1	0	0	1	0
	Crawford County	0	0	0	0	0	0	0	0	0	0
	Cumberland County	0	0	0	0	0	3	0	3	0	0
	Dauphin County	0	0	0	0	0	3	0	1	2	0
	Delaware County	0	0	0	0	0	0	0	0	0	0
	Elk County	0	0	0	0	0	0	0	0	0	0
	Erie County	0	0	0	0	0	3	0	3	0	0
	Fayette County	0	0	0	0	0	1	0	1	0	0
	Forest County	0	0	0	0	0	0	0	0	0	0
	Franklin County	0	0	0	0	0	0	0	0	0	0
	Fulton County	0	0	0	0	0	0	0	0	0	0
	Greene County	0	0	0	0	0	1	0	1	0	0
	Huntingdon County	0	0	0	0	0	0	0	0	0	0
	Indiana County	0	0	0	0	0	0	0	0	0	0
	Jefferson County	0	0	0	0	0	0	0	0	0	0
	Juniata County	0	0	0	0	0	0	0	0	0	0
	Lackawanna County	0	0	0	0	0	0	0	0	0	0
	Lancaster County	0	0	0	0	0	1	0	1	0	0
	Lawrence County	0	0	0	0	0	1	0	1	0	0
	Lebanon County	0	0	0	0	0	0	0	0	0	0
	Lehigh County	0	0	0	0	0	0	0	0	0	0
	Luzerne County	0	0	0	0	0	0	0	0	0	0
	Lycoming County	0	0	0	0	0	0	0	0	0	0
	McKean County	0	0	0	0	0	0	0	0	0	0
	Mercer County	0	0	0	0	0	0	0	0	0	0
	Mifflin County	0	0	0	0	0	0	0	0	0	0
	Monroe County	0	0	0	0	0	0	0	0	0	0
	Montgomery County	0	0	0	0	0	0	0	0	0	0
	Montour County	0	0	0	0	0	0	0	0	0	0
	Northampton County	0	0	0	0	0	0	0	0	0	0
	Northumberland County	0	0	0	0	0	1	0	0	1	0
	Perry County	0	0	0	0	0	0	0	0	0	0
	Philadelphia County	1	0	0	0	1	0	0	0	0	0
	Pike County	0	0	0	0	0	0	0	0	0	0

[1] The FBI does not publish arson data unless it receives data from either the agency or the state for all 12 months of the calendar year.

Table 11.   Offenses Known to Law Enforcement, by State, Tribal, and Other Agencies, 2010—*Continued*

(Number)

State/Other Agency	Unit/Office	Violent crime	Murder and non-negligent man-slaughter	Forcible rape	Robbery	Aggra-vated assault	Property crime	Burglary	Larceny-theft	Motor vehicle theft	Arson[1]
	Potter County	0	0	0	0	0	0	0	0	0	0
	Schuylkill County	0	0	0	0	0	0	0	0	0	0
	Snyder County	0	0	0	0	0	0	0	0	0	0
	Somerset County	0	0	0	0	0	0	0	0	0	0
	Sullivan County	0	0	0	0	0	0	0	0	0	0
	Susquehanna County	0	0	0	0	0	0	0	0	0	0
	Tioga County	0	0	0	0	0	0	0	0	0	0
	Union County	0	0	0	0	0	0	0	0	0	0
	Venango County	0	0	0	0	0	0	0	0	0	0
	Warren County	0	0	0	0	0	0	0	0	0	0
	Washington County	0	0	0	0	0	4	0	4	0	0
	Wayne County	0	0	0	0	0	0	0	0	0	0
	Westmoreland County	0	0	0	0	0	0	0	0	0	0
	Wyoming County	0	0	0	0	0	0	0	0	0	0
	York County	0	0	0	0	0	0	0	0	0	0
State Police:	Adams County	123	4	62	7	50	497	127	346	24	10
	Allegheny County	27	0	1	3	23	678	3	668	7	1
	Armstrong County	55	0	13	12	30	417	143	259	15	7
	Beaver County	41	0	3	0	38	263	137	105	21	10
	Bedford County	36	0	9	5	22	388	124	240	24	3
	Berks County	206	0	18	8	180	715	210	468	37	9
	Blair County	32	0	8	5	19	258	83	142	33	9
	Bradford County	70	0	22	2	46	443	156	271	16	5
	Bucks County	30	1	7	3	19	384	56	309	19	0
	Butler County	88	2	10	3	73	609	205	367	37	14
	Cambria County	59	1	8	6	44	275	112	138	25	5
	Cameron County	3	0	1	0	2	92	44	48	0	1
	Carbon County	47	2	2	3	40	382	117	249	16	6
	Centre County	42	0	11	8	23	487	134	330	23	4
	Chester County	130	1	17	30	82	1,263	454	754	55	7
	Clarion County	30	0	17	3	10	446	121	304	21	4
	Clearfield County	57	0	19	8	30	541	174	338	29	10
	Clinton County	27	0	14	1	12	349	110	226	13	2
	Columbia County	8	0	2	1	5	127	48	78	1	0
	Crawford County	35	4	14	3	14	698	300	372	26	3
	Cumberland County	47	0	10	8	29	676	142	513	21	6
	Delaware County	77	0	1	22	54	1,246	172	1,038	36	1
	Elizabethville	69	0	14	12	43	1,099	181	891	27	20
	Elk County	6	0	2	1	3	233	79	141	13	2
	Erie County	95	0	27	20	48	1,529	338	1,130	61	9
	Fayette County	166	1	28	45	92	1,593	380	1,079	134	47
	Franklin County	76	6	17	13	40	890	213	639	38	3
	Fulton County	30	0	6	6	18	197	79	116	2	5
	Greene County	23	0	4	7	12	496	152	317	27	12
	Huntingdon County	82	1	12	3	66	453	142	300	11	7
	Indiana County	87	3	20	27	37	951	278	630	43	12
	Jefferson County	24	2	10	1	11	270	108	140	22	5
	Juniata County	36	1	15	1	19	231	88	138	5	0
	Lackawanna County	33	0	9	1	23	197	99	87	11	19
	Lancaster County	60	0	23	7	30	896	329	530	37	9
	Lawrence County	48	0	16	6	26	419	150	246	23	10
	Lebanon County	91	0	9	4	78	349	106	233	10	3
	Lehigh County	43	0	10	3	30	777	168	588	21	7
	Luzerne County	106	4	9	14	79	1,008	232	731	45	27
	Lycoming County	49	0	16	6	27	731	203	509	19	5
	McKean County	13	0	6	0	7	159	58	93	8	1
	Mercer County	31	1	7	5	18	416	180	220	16	7
	Mifflin County	9	1	2	0	6	95	30	58	7	0
	Monroe County	398	2	21	20	355	1,508	481	949	78	3
	Montour County	13	0	2	3	8	91	41	42	8	2
	Northampton County	29	6	3	1	19	594	77	503	14	3
	Northumberland County	70	1	12	3	54	209	64	137	8	1
	Perry County	61	1	18	12	30	585	152	413	20	6
	Philadelphia County	9	1	0	0	8	6	0	4	2	0
	Pike County	67	0	12	10	45	750	390	336	24	9
	Potter County	41	0	18	0	23	155	55	93	7	0
	Schuylkill County	116	3	17	11	85	628	155	435	38	28
	Skippack	67	1	2	2	62	423	91	317	15	8
	Snyder County	21	1	7	0	13	359	74	271	14	1
	Somerset County	40	0	14	3	23	494	119	352	23	10
	Sullivan County	16	0	5	1	10	144	71	71	2	0
	Susquehanna County	43	0	23	2	18	440	129	279	32	11
	Tioga County	25	1	7	1	16	269	86	166	17	7

[1] The FBI does not publish arson data unless it receives data from either the agency or the state for all 12 months of the calendar year.

Table 11.   Offenses Known to Law Enforcement, by State, Tribal, and Other Agencies, 2010—*Continued*

(Number)

State/Other Agency	Unit/Office	Violent crime	Murder and non-negligent man-slaughter	Forcible rape	Robbery	Aggra-vated assault	Property crime	Burglary	Larceny-theft	Motor vehicle theft	Arson[1]
	Tionesta	18	0	1	0	17	86	40	44	2	1
	Union County	19	1	11	3	4	180	48	129	3	4
	Venango County	32	2	6	2	22	409	111	273	25	3
	Warren County	20	0	10	2	8	272	105	154	13	6
	Washington County	115	7	17	28	63	1,101	268	770	63	30
	Wayne County	50	2	9	2	37	461	166	274	21	8
	Westmoreland County	158	2	34	43	79	1,442	340	1,023	79	33
	Wyoming County	17	1	6	1	9	142	39	91	12	0
	York County	64	1	15	18	30	692	182	465	45	13
PENNSYLVANIA—Other Agencies											
Allegheny County District Attorney	Criminal Investigation Division	0	0	0	0	0	73	0	73	0	0
Allegheny County Port Authority		121	0	1	28	92	98	0	92	6	0
Altoona Hospital		1	0	0	0	1	4	1	2	1	0
County Detective:	Bucks County	2	0	1	0	1	7	0	7	0	0
	Butler County	0	0	0	0	0	0	0	0	0	0
	Chester County	25	0	16	0	9	5	0	5	0	0
	Clarion County	0	0	0	0	0	1	0	1	0	0
	Dauphin County	33	0	3	0	30	15	1	14	0	0
	Lackawanna County	11	0	0	0	11	6	0	6	0	0
	Lebanon County	2	0	2	0	0	2	0	2	0	0
	Lehigh County	5	0	3	2	0	52	2	0	50	0
	Pike County	0	0	0	0	0	4	1	3	0	0
	Schuylkill County	0	0	0	0	0	0	0	0	0	0
	Westmoreland County	2	0	0	0	2	72	0	72	0	0
	York County	0	0	0	0	0	3	0	2	1	0
Delaware County District Attorney	Criminal Investigation Division	22	0	3	0	19	8	0	7	1	0
Delaware County Park		4	0	0	0	4	90	1	88	1	0
Easton Area School District		5	0	0	0	5	183	0	183	0	0
Erie City School District		27	0	0	2	25	14	1	13	0	0
Fort Cherry School District		0	0	0	0	0	0	0	0	0	0
Fort Indiantown Gap		0	0	0	0	0	15	2	13	0	0
Harrisburg International Airport		0	0	0	0	0	5	0	1	4	0
Uniontown Hospital		0	0	0	0	0	10	0	10	0	0
Westmoreland County Park		0	0	0	0	0	26	0	26	0	0
Wilkes-Barre Area School District		2	0	0	0	2	3	0	3	0	0
RHODE ISLAND—State Agencies											
Department of Environmental Management		1	0	0	0	1	56	5	46	5	5
Rhode Island State Airport...		1	0	0	0	1	24	0	15	9	0
Rhode Island State Police Headquarters		5	1	0	0	4	79	0	23	56	0
State Police:	Chepachet	6	0	4	0	2	28	4	20	4	0
	Hope Valley	8	0	4	0	4	54	9	39	6	1
	Lincoln	13	0	3	0	10	78	1	54	23	0
	Portsmouth	0	0	0	0	0	11	1	10	0	0
	Wickford	7	0	3	0	4	43	9	30	4	0
RHODE ISLAND—Tribal Agencies											
Narragansett Tribal		1	0	0	0	1	7	7	0	0	0
SOUTH CAROLINA—State Agencies											
Bureau of Protective Services..		1	0	0	0	1	31	3	24	4	0
Department of Natural Resources:	Abbeville County	0	0	0	0	0	0	0	0	0	0
	Aiken County	0	0	0	0	0	0	0	0	0	0
	Allendale County	0	0	0	0	0	0	0	0	0	0
	Anderson County	0	0	0	0	0	0	0	0	0	0
	Bamberg County	0	0	0	0	0	0	0	0	0	0
	Barnwell County	0	0	0	0	0	0	0	0	0	0
	Beaufort County	0	0	0	0	0	0	0	0	0	0
	Berkeley County	0	0	0	0	0	0	0	0	0	0
	Calhoun County	0	0	0	0	0	0	0	0	0	0
	Charleston County	0	0	0	0	0	0	0	0	0	0
	Cherokee County	0	0	0	0	0	0	0	0	0	0
	Chester County	0	0	0	0	0	0	0	0	0	0
	Chesterfield County	0	0	0	0	0	0	0	0	0	0
	Clarendon County	0	0	0	0	0	0	0	0	0	0
	Colleton County	0	0	0	0	0	0	0	0	0	0
	Darlington County	0	0	0	0	0	0	0	0	0	0
	Dillon County	0	0	0	0	0	0	0	0	0	0
	Dorchester County	0	0	0	0	0	0	0	0	0	0
	Edgefield County	0	0	0	0	0	0	0	0	0	0
	Fairfield County	0	0	0	0	0	0	0	0	0	0
	Florence County	0	0	0	0	0	0	0	0	0	0
	Georgetown County	0	0	0	0	0	0	0	0	0	0
	Greenville County	0	0	0	0	0	0	0	0	0	0

[1] The FBI does not publish arson data unless it receives data from either the agency or the state for all 12 months of the calendar year.

Table 11.   Offenses Known to Law Enforcement, by State, Tribal, and Other Agencies, 2010—*Continued*

(Number)

State/Other Agency	Unit/Office	Violent crime	Murder and non-negligent man-slaughter	Forcible rape	Robbery	Aggra-vated assault	Property crime	Burglary	Larceny-theft	Motor vehicle theft	Arson[1]
	Greenwood County	0	0	0	0	0	0	0	0	0	0
	Hampton County	0	0	0	0	0	0	0	0	0	0
	Horry County	0	0	0	0	0	0	0	0	0	0
	Jasper County	0	0	0	0	0	0	0	0	0	0
	Kershaw County	0	0	0	0	0	0	0	0	0	0
	Lancaster County	0	0	0	0	0	0	0	0	0	0
	Laurens County	0	0	0	0	0	0	0	0	0	0
	Lee County	0	0	0	0	0	0	0	0	0	0
	Lexington County	0	0	0	0	0	0	0	0	0	0
	Marion County	0	0	0	0	0	0	0	0	0	0
	Marlboro County	0	0	0	0	0	0	0	0	0	0
	McCormick County	0	0	0	0	0	0	0	0	0	0
	Newberry County	0	0	0	0	0	0	0	0	0	0
	Oconee County	0	0	0	0	0	0	0	0	0	0
	Orangeburg County	0	0	0	0	0	0	0	0	0	0
	Pickens County	0	0	0	0	0	0	0	0	0	0
	Richland County	0	0	0	0	0	0	0	0	0	0
	Saluda County	0	0	0	0	0	0	0	0	0	0
	Spartanburg County	0	0	0	0	0	0	0	0	0	0
	Sumter County	0	0	0	0	0	0	0	0	0	0
	Union County	0	0	0	0	0	0	0	0	0	0
	Williamsburg County	0	0	0	0	0	0	0	0	0	0
	York County	0	0	0	0	0	0	0	0	0	0
Forestry Commission:	Abbeville County	0	0	0	0	0	0	0	0	0	1
	Aiken County	0	0	0	0	0	0	0	0	0	1
	Allendale County	0	0	0	0	0	0	0	0	0	3
	Anderson County	0	0	0	0	0	2	0	2	0	0
	Bamberg County	0	0	0	0	0	0	0	0	0	1
	Barnwell County	0	0	0	0	0	0	0	0	0	0
	Beaufort County	0	0	0	0	0	0	0	0	0	3
	Berkeley County	0	0	0	0	0	0	0	0	0	32
	Calhoun County	0	0	0	0	0	0	0	0	0	0
	Charleston County	0	0	0	0	0	0	0	0	0	4
	Cherokee County	0	0	0	0	0	0	0	0	0	0
	Chester County	0	0	0	0	0	0	0	0	0	0
	Chesterfield County	0	0	0	0	0	6	1	5	0	3
	Clarendon County	0	0	0	0	0	3	0	3	0	5
	Colleton County	0	0	0	0	0	1	0	1	0	6
	Darlington County	0	0	0	0	0	2	0	2	0	0
	Dillon County	0	0	0	0	0	0	0	0	0	0
	Dorchester County	0	0	0	0	0	0	0	0	0	3
	Edgefield County	0	0	0	0	0	0	0	0	0	0
	Fairfield County	0	0	0	0	0	5	0	5	0	0
	Florence County	0	0	0	0	0	1	0	1	0	1
	Georgetown County	0	0	0	0	0	2	0	2	0	0
	Greenville County	0	0	0	0	0	3	0	3	0	0
	Greenwood County	0	0	0	0	0	0	0	0	0	0
	Hampton County	0	0	0	0	0	0	0	0	0	4
	Horry County	0	0	0	0	0	0	0	0	0	2
	Jasper County	0	0	0	0	0	0	0	0	0	0
	Kershaw County	0	0	0	0	0	3	0	3	0	0
	Lancaster County	0	0	0	0	0	1	0	1	0	0
	Laurens County	0	0	0	0	0	0	0	0	0	0
	Lee County	0	0	0	0	0	0	0	0	0	0
	Lexington County	0	0	0	0	0	0	0	0	0	3
	Marion County	0	0	0	0	0	0	0	0	0	0
	Marlboro County	0	0	0	0	0	0	0	0	0	0
	McCormick County	0	0	0	0	0	0	0	0	0	0
	Newberry County	0	0	0	0	0	1	0	1	0	0
	Oconee County	0	0	0	0	0	0	0	0	0	1
	Orangeburg County	0	0	0	0	0	2	0	2	0	2
	Pickens County	0	0	0	0	0	1	0	1	0	0
	Richland County	0	0	0	0	0	4	1	3	0	0
	Saluda County	0	0	0	0	0	0	0	0	0	0
	Spartanburg County	0	0	0	0	0	2	0	2	0	1
	Sumter County	0	0	0	0	0	2	0	2	0	3
	Union County	0	0	0	0	0	0	0	0	0	0
	Williamsburg County	0	0	0	0	0	1	0	1	0	2
	York County	0	0	0	0	0	0	0	0	0	0
Highway Patrol:	Abbeville County	0	0	0	0	0	0	0	0	0	0
	Aiken County	0	0	0	0	0	1	0	0	1	0
	Allendale County	0	0	0	0	0	0	0	0	0	0
	Anderson County	1	0	0	0	1	2	0	1	1	0

[1] The FBI does not publish arson data unless it receives data from either the agency or the state for all 12 months of the calendar year.

Table 11.   Offenses Known to Law Enforcement, by State, Tribal, and Other Agencies, 2010—*Continued*

(Number)

State/Other Agency	Unit/Office	Violent crime	Murder and non-negligent man-slaughter	Forcible rape	Robbery	Aggra-vated assault	Property crime	Burglary	Larceny-theft	Motor vehicle theft	Arson[1]
	Bamberg County	0	0	0	0	0	0	0	0	0	0
	Barnwell County	0	0	0	0	0	0	0	0	0	0
	Beaufort County	0	0	0	0	0	0	0	0	0	0
	Berkeley County	0	0	0	0	0	1	0	1	0	0
	Calhoun County	0	0	0	0	0	0	0	0	0	0
	Charleston County	0	0	0	0	0	0	0	0	0	0
	Cherokee County	0	0	0	0	0	0	0	0	0	0
	Chester County	0	0	0	0	0	0	0	0	0	0
	Chesterfield County	0	0	0	0	0	0	0	0	0	0
	Clarendon County	0	0	0	0	0	0	0	0	0	0
	Colleton County	0	0	0	0	0	0	0	0	0	0
	Darlington County	0	0	0	0	0	0	0	0	0	0
	Dillon County	0	0	0	0	0	0	0	0	0	0
	Dorchester County	0	0	0	0	0	0	0	0	0	0
	Edgefield County	0	0	0	0	0	0	0	0	0	0
	Fairfield County	0	0	0	0	0	1	0	0	1	0
	Florence County	0	0	0	0	0	0	0	0	0	0
	Georgetown County	0	0	0	0	0	0	0	0	0	0
	Greenville County	0	0	0	0	0	0	0	0	0	0
	Greenwood County	0	0	0	0	0	0	0	0	0	0
	Hampton County	0	0	0	0	0	0	0	0	0	0
	Horry County	1	0	0	0	1	0	0	0	0	0
	Jasper County	0	0	0	0	0	0	0	0	0	0
	Kershaw County	0	0	0	0	0	1	0	1	0	0
	Lancaster County	0	0	0	0	0	0	0	0	0	0
	Laurens County	0	0	0	0	0	0	0	0	0	0
	Lee County	0	0	0	0	0	0	0	0	0	0
	Lexington County	0	0	0	0	0	0	0	0	0	0
	Marion County	0	0	0	0	0	0	0	0	0	0
	Marlboro County	0	0	0	0	0	0	0	0	0	0
	McCormick County	0	0	0	0	0	0	0	0	0	0
	Newberry County	0	0	0	0	0	0	0	0	0	0
	Oconee County	0	0	0	0	0	0	0	0	0	0
	Orangeburg County	2	2	0	0	0	1	0	0	1	0
	Pickens County	0	0	0	0	0	0	0	0	0	0
	Richland County	0	0	0	0	0	0	0	0	0	0
	Saluda County	0	0	0	0	0	0	0	0	0	0
	Spartanburg County	0	0	0	0	0	0	0	0	0	0
	Sumter County	1	0	0	0	1	0	0	0	0	0
	Union County	0	0	0	0	0	0	0	0	0	0
	Williamsburg County	0	0	0	0	0	0	0	0	0	0
	York County	0	0	0	0	0	1	0	0	1	0
South Carolina School for the Deaf and Blind............		0	0	0	0	0	0	0	0	0	0
State Ports Authority..		0	0	0	0	0	6	1	5	0	0
State Transport Police:	Abbeville County	0	0	0	0	0	0	0	0	0	0
	Aiken County	0	0	0	0	0	0	0	0	0	0
	Allendale County	0	0	0	0	0	0	0	0	0	0
	Anderson County	0	0	0	0	0	0	0	0	0	0
	Bamberg County	0	0	0	0	0	0	0	0	0	0
	Barnwell County	0	0	0	0	0	0	0	0	0	0
	Beaufort County	0	0	0	0	0	0	0	0	0	0
	Berkeley County	0	0	0	0	0	0	0	0	0	0
	Calhoun County	0	0	0	0	0	0	0	0	0	0
	Charleston County	0	0	0	0	0	0	0	0	0	0
	Cherokee County	0	0	0	0	0	0	0	0	0	0
	Chester County	0	0	0	0	0	0	0	0	0	0
	Chesterfield County	0	0	0	0	0	0	0	0	0	0
	Clarendon County	0	0	0	0	0	0	0	0	0	0
	Colleton County	0	0	0	0	0	0	0	0	0	0
	Darlington County	0	0	0	0	0	0	0	0	0	0
	Dillon County	0	0	0	0	0	0	0	0	0	0
	Dorchester County	0	0	0	0	0	0	0	0	0	0
	Edgefield County	0	0	0	0	0	0	0	0	0	0
	Fairfield County	0	0	0	0	0	0	0	0	0	0
	Florence County	0	0	0	0	0	0	0	0	0	0
	Georgetown County	0	0	0	0	0	0	0	0	0	0
	Greenville County	0	0	0	0	0	0	0	0	0	0
	Greenwood County	0	0	0	0	0	0	0	0	0	0
	Hampton County	0	0	0	0	0	0	0	0	0	0
	Horry County	0	0	0	0	0	0	0	0	0	0
	Jasper County	0	0	0	0	0	0	0	0	0	0
	Kershaw County	0	0	0	0	0	0	0	0	0	0
	Lancaster County	0	0	0	0	0	0	0	0	0	0

[1] The FBI does not publish arson data unless it receives data from either the agency or the state for all 12 months of the calendar year.

Table 11.   Offenses Known to Law Enforcement, by State, Tribal, and Other Agencies, 2010—*Continued*

(Number)

State/Other Agency	Unit/Office	Violent crime	Murder and non-negligent man-slaughter	Forcible rape	Robbery	Aggra-vated assault	Property crime	Burglary	Larceny-theft	Motor vehicle theft	Arson[1]
	Laurens County	0	0	0	0	0	0	0	0	0	0
	Lee County	0	0	0	0	0	0	0	0	0	0
	Lexington County	0	0	0	0	0	0	0	0	0	0
	Marion County	0	0	0	0	0	0	0	0	0	0
	Marlboro County	0	0	0	0	0	0	0	0	0	0
	McCormick County	0	0	0	0	0	0	0	0	0	0
	Newberry County	0	0	0	0	0	0	0	0	0	0
	Oconee County	0	0	0	0	0	0	0	0	0	0
	Orangeburg County	0	0	0	0	0	0	0	0	0	0
	Pickens County	0	0	0	0	0	0	0	0	0	0
	Richland County	0	0	0	0	0	0	0	0	0	0
	Saluda County	0	0	0	0	0	0	0	0	0	0
	Spartanburg County	0	0	0	0	0	0	0	0	0	0
	Sumter County	0	0	0	0	0	0	0	0	0	0
	Union County	0	0	0	0	0	0	0	0	0	0
	Williamsburg County	0	0	0	0	0	0	0	0	0	0
	York County	0	0	0	0	0	0	0	0	0	0
United States Department of Energy	Savannah River Plant	0	0	0	0	0	27	1	26	0	0
SOUTH CAROLINA—Other Agencies		0	0	0	0	0	0	0	0	0	0
Charleston County Aviation Authority		0	0	0	0	0	33	0	33	0	0
Columbia Metropolitan Airport		0	0	0	0	0	4	0	3	1	0
Lexington County Medical Center		4	0	0	0	4	51	0	50	1	0
SOUTH DAKOTA—State Agencies											
Division of Criminal Investigation		25	4	9	2	10	7	7	0	0	5
SOUTH DAKOTA—Tribal Agencies											
Crow Creek Tribal		9	0	3	0	6	25	7	0	18	4
Flandreau Tribal		5	0	0	0	5	11	1	4	6	0
Lower Brule Tribal		9	0	5	0	4	11	8	0	3	2
Oglala Sioux Tribal		40	5	10	3	22	186	75	88	23	6
Pine Ridge Sioux Tribal		83	1	7	13	62	19	8	11	0	2
Sisseton-Wahpeton Tribal		10	0	2	0	8	157	30	90	37	3
Yankton Tribal		3	0	0	0	3	8	8	0	0	1
TENNESSEE—State Agencies											
Alcoholic Beverage Commission		0	0	0	0	0	0	0	0	0	0
Department of Correction	Internal Affairs	7	1	0	0	6	1	0	1	0	2
Department of Safety		56	0	0	1	55	36	0	8	28	0
State Fire Marshal		0	0	0	0	0	0	0	0	0	18
State Park Rangers:	Bicentennial Capitol Mall	0	0	0	0	0	0	0	0	0	0
	Big Hill Pond	0	0	0	0	0	0	0	0	0	0
	Big Ridge	0	0	0	0	0	3	0	3	0	0
	Bledsoe Creek	0	0	0	0	0	0	0	0	0	0
	Booker T. Washington	0	0	0	0	0	0	0	0	0	0
	Burgess Falls Natural Area	1	0	0	1	0	0	0	0	0	0
	Cedars of Lebanon	0	0	0	0	0	0	0	0	0	0
	Chickasaw	0	0	0	0	0	1	0	1	0	0
	Chief Rangers Office	0	0	0	0	0	0	0	0	0	0
	Cove Lake	0	0	0	0	0	0	0	0	0	0
	Cumberland Mountain	0	0	0	0	0	0	0	0	0	0
	Cumberland Trail	0	0	0	0	0	0	0	0	0	0
	David Crockett	0	0	0	0	0	0	0	0	0	0
	Davy Crockett Birthplace	0	0	0	0	0	0	0	0	0	0
	Dunbar Cave Natural Area	0	0	0	0	0	1	0	1	0	0
	Edgar Evins	0	0	0	0	0	2	0	2	0	0
	Fall Creek Falls	0	0	0	0	0	2	0	2	0	0
	Fort Loudon State Historic Park	0	0	0	0	0	0	0	0	0	0
	Fort Pillow State Historic Park	0	0	0	0	0	0	0	0	0	0
	Frozen Head Natural Area	0	0	0	0	0	0	0	0	0	0
	Harpeth Scenic Rivers	0	0	0	0	0	0	0	0	0	0
	Harrison Bay	0	0	0	0	0	2	1	0	1	0
	Henry Horton	0	0	0	0	0	1	0	1	0	0
	Hiwassee/Ocoee State Scenic Rivers	0	0	0	0	0	0	0	0	0	0
	Indian Mountain	0	0	0	0	0	0	0	0	0	0
	Johnsonville State Historic Park	0	0	0	0	0	0	0	0	0	0
	Long Hunter	0	0	0	0	0	0	0	0	0	0

[1] The FBI does not publish arson data unless it receives data from either the agency or the state for all 12 months of the calendar year.

Table 11. Offenses Known to Law Enforcement, by State, Tribal, and Other Agencies, 2010—*Continued*

(Number)

State/Other Agency	Unit/Office	Violent crime	Murder and non-negligent man-slaughter	Forcible rape	Robbery	Aggra-vated assault	Property crime	Burglary	Larceny-theft	Motor vehicle theft	Arson[1]
	Meeman-Shelby Forest	0	0	0	0	0	1	0	1	0	0
	Montgomery Bell	0	0	0	0	0	2	1	1	0	0
	Mousetail Landing	0	0	0	0	0	0	0	0	0	0
	Natchez Trace	0	0	0	0	0	1	0	1	0	0
	Nathan Bedford Forrest	0	0	0	0	0	0	0	0	0	0
	Norris Dam	0	0	0	0	0	0	0	0	0	0
	Old Stone Fort State Archaeological Park	0	0	0	0	0	0	0	0	0	0
	Panther Creek	0	0	0	0	0	2	0	2	0	0
	Paris Landing	0	0	0	0	0	0	0	0	0	0
	Pickett	0	0	0	0	0	0	0	0	0	0
	Pickwick Landing	0	0	0	0	0	0	0	0	0	0
	Pinson Mounds State Archaeological Park	0	0	0	0	0	0	0	0	0	0
	Radnor Lake Natural Area	0	0	0	0	0	0	0	0	0	0
	Red Clay State Historic Park	0	0	0	0	0	0	0	0	0	0
	Reelfoot Lake	0	0	0	0	0	0	0	0	0	0
	Roan Mountain	0	0	0	0	0	0	0	0	0	0
	Rock Island	0	0	0	0	0	1	0	1	0	0
	Sgt. Alvin C. York	0	0	0	0	0	0	0	0	0	0
	South Cumberland Recreation Area	0	0	0	0	0	1	0	1	0	0
	Standing Stone	0	0	0	0	0	0	0	0	0	1
	Sycamore Shoals State Historic Park	0	0	0	0	0	0	0	0	0	0
	Tim's Ford	0	0	0	0	0	2	0	2	0	0
	T.O. Fuller	0	0	0	0	0	0	0	0	0	0
	Warrior's Path	0	0	0	0	0	3	0	3	0	0
TennCare Office of Inspector General		0	0	0	0	0	0	0	0	0	0
Tennessee Bureau of Investigation		33	10	4	1	18	10	2	8	0	1
Tennessee Department of Revenue	Special Investigations Unit	0	0	0	0	0	0	0	0	0	0
Wildlife Resources Agency:	Region 1	0	0	0	0	0	0	0	0	0	0
	Region 2	0	0	0	0	0	0	0	0	0	0
	Region 3	0	0	0	0	0	0	0	0	0	0
	Region 4	0	0	0	0	0	0	0	0	0	0
TENNESSEE—Other Agencies											
Chattanooga Housing Authority		1	0	1	0	0	4	1	3	0	0
Chattanooga Metropolitan Airport		0	0	0	0	0	2	0	2	0	0
Dickson Parks and Recreation		0	0	0	0	0	0	0	0	0	0
Drug Task Force:	1st Judicial District	0	0	0	0	0	0	0	0	0	0
	2nd Judicial District	0	0	0	0	0	0	0	0	0	0
	3rd Judicial District	0	0	0	0	0	0	0	0	0	0
	4th Judicial District	0	0	0	0	0	2	0	2	0	0
	5th Judicial District	0	0	0	0	0	1	0	1	0	0
	8th Judicial District	0	0	0	0	0	0	0	0	0	0
	9th Judicial District	0	0	0	0	0	0	0	0	0	0
	10th Judicial District	0	0	0	0	0	4	0	1	3	0
	12th Judicial District	0	0	0	0	0	0	0	0	0	0
	13th Judicial District	0	0	0	0	0	0	0	0	0	0
	14th Judicial District	0	0	0	0	0	0	0	0	0	0
	15th Judicial District	0	0	0	0	0	0	0	0	0	0
	17th Judicial District	0	0	0	0	0	0	0	0	0	0
	18th Judicial District	1	0	0	0	1	0	0	0	0	0
	19th Judicial District	0	0	0	0	0	0	0	0	0	0
	21st Judicial District	0	0	0	0	0	2	0	1	1	0
	22nd Judicial District	0	0	0	0	0	0	0	0	0	0
	23rd Judicial District	0	0	0	0	0	0	0	0	0	0
	24th Judicial District	0	0	0	0	0	0	0	0	0	0
	25th Judicial District	0	0	0	0	0	0	0	0	0	0
	27th Judicial District	0	0	0	0	0	0	0	0	0	0
	31st Judicial District	0	0	0	0	0	0	0	0	0	0
Knoxville Metropolitan Airport		0	0	0	0	0	21	0	20	1	0
Memphis International Airport		3	0	0	1	2	142	0	135	7	0
Metropolitan Nashville Park Police		13	0	0	3	10	138	5	131	2	4
Nashville International Airport		0	0	0	0	0	28	0	12	16	0
Smyrna/Rutherford County Airport Authority		0	0	0	0	0	0	0	0	0	0
Tri-Cities Regional Airport		0	0	0	0	0	2	0	2	0	0
West Tennessee Violent Crime Task Force		0	0	0	0	0	0	0	0	0	0
TEXAS—Tribal Agencies											
Ysleta Del Sur Pueblo Tribal		51	0	0	0	51	48	3	42	3	11

[1] The FBI does not publish arson data unless it receives data from either the agency or the state for all 12 months of the calendar year.

Table 11.   Offenses Known to Law Enforcement, by State, Tribal, and Other Agencies, 2010—*Continued*

(Number)

State/Other Agency	Unit/Office	Violent crime	Murder and non-negligent man-slaughter	Forcible rape	Robbery	Aggra-vated assault	Property crime	Burglary	Larceny-theft	Motor vehicle theft	Arson[1]
TEXAS—Other Agencies											
Amarillo International Airport		0	0	0	0	0	2	1	1	0	0
Dallas-Fort Worth International Airport..........		4	0	0	0	4	403	5	372	26	0
Hospital District:	Dallas County	6	0	0	3	3	370	6	361	3	0
	Tarrant County	5	0	0	1	4	160	0	156	4	0
Houston Metropolitan Transit Authority		2	0	0	2	0	37	0	32	5	0
Independent School District:..........	Aldine	5	0	0	3	2	110	13	87	10	0
	Alvin	11	0	0	1	10	120	7	112	1	0
	Angleton	2	0	0	0	2	23	1	21	1	0
	Austin	26	0	0	12	14	841	50	785	6	16
	Barbers Hill	1	0	0	0	1	31	2	29	0	0
	Cedar Hill	5	0	0	0	5	28	3	25	0	1
	Conroe	12	0	1	0	11	288	2	282	4	2
	Corpus Christi	60	0	0	2	58	247	22	224	1	2
	Ector County	24	0	0	3	21	137	3	134	0	1
	Edinburg	5	0	1	0	4	280	6	274	0	3
	El Paso	30	0	2	3	25	401	37	361	3	4
	Floresville	0	0	0	0	0	24	1	23	0	0
	Fort Bend	9	0	0	3	6	400	10	390	0	0
	Humble	22	0	2	1	19	150	11	139	0	0
	Judson	0	0	0	0	0	27	3	24	0	0
	Katy	6	0	4	1	1	299	4	292	3	3
	Killeen	9	0	2	1	6	102	14	88	0	3
	Klein	0	0	0	0	0	36	2	34	0	0
	Laredo	33	0	0	0	33	28	6	20	2	0
	Lyford	0	0	0	0	0	10	4	6	0	0
	Mexia	0	0	0	0	0	4	1	3	0	0
	Midland	2	0	0	0	2	62	3	59	0	0
	North East	23	0	1	0	22	406	2	404	0	0
	Pasadena	2	0	0	1	1	213	10	189	14	0
	Pflugerville	12	0	0	1	11	81	1	80	0	1
	Rio Grande City	0	0	0	0	0	37	6	30	1	3
	Socorro	11	0	0	0	11	129	10	117	2	4
	Spring	44	0	1	8	35	119	9	105	5	1
	Spring Branch	1	0	0	0	1	121	13	103	5	0
	Taft	0	0	0	0	0	1	0	1	0	0
	United	4	0	0	0	4	71	2	69	0	1
Port of Houston Authority		0	0	0	0	0	24	0	21	3	0
UTAH—State Agencies											
Parks and Recreation.............		0	0	0	0	0	16	4	12	0	0
UTAH—Other Agencies.............		0	0	0	0	0	0	0	0	0	0
Cache-Rich Drug Task Force		1	0	0	0	1	5	3	2	0	0
Davis Metropolitan Narcotics Strike Force		0	0	0	0	0	0	0	0	0	0
Granite School District.............		10	0	1	0	9	152	23	127	2	9
Utah County Attorney	Investigations Division	0	0	0	0	0	0	0	0	0	0
Utah County Major Crime Task Force		0	0	0	0	0	2	0	2	0	0
Utah Transit Authority.............		13	0	0	4	9	1,459	1	1,447	11	0
VERMONT—State Agencies		6	0	0	3	3	513	8	478	27	0
State Police:	Bradford	10	1	0	0	9	208	96	98	14	0
	Brattleboro	5	0	2	0	3	133	64	60	9	0
	Derby	24	0	2	0	22	335	142	176	17	3
	Middlesex	7	0	0	0	7	315	154	155	6	5
	Rockingham	17	0	4	1	12	232	102	116	14	2
	Royalton	22	1	7	0	14	244	106	124	14	0
	Rutland	17	1	6	0	10	488	219	246	23	3
	Shaftsbury	12	1	2	0	9	188	64	114	10	2
	St. Albans	36	0	4	3	29	490	190	257	43	0
	St. Johnsbury	17	1	4	1	11	357	157	193	7	2
	Williston	20	1	7	1	11	227	63	153	11	2
Vermont State Police		0	0	0	0	0	0	0	0	0	0
Vermont State Police Headquarters	Bureau of Criminal Investigations	0	0	0	0	0	1	0	1	0	0
VIRGINIA—State Agencies											
Alcoholic Beverage Control Commission..........		0	0	0	0	0	45	1	44	0	0
Department of Conservation and Recreation		0	0	0	0	0	38	4	34	0	0
Department of Game and Inland Fisheries	Enforcement Division	4	0	0	0	4	9	0	7	2	0
Department of Motor Vehicles..........		0	0	0	0	0	46	0	8	38	0
Southside Virginia Training Center..........		1	1	0	0	0	22	0	22	0	1
State Police:	Accomack County	0	0	0	0	0	9	0	6	3	2
	Alexandria	0	0	0	0	0	2	0	1	1	0
	Alleghany County	0	0	0	0	0	3	0	2	1	0
	Amherst County	0	0	0	0	0	0	0	0	0	0
	Augusta County	1	0	1	0	0	1	0	0	1	0

[1] The FBI does not publish arson data unless it receives data from either the agency or the state for all 12 months of the calendar year.

Table 11.   Offenses Known to Law Enforcement, by State, Tribal, and Other Agencies, 2010—*Continued*

(Number)

State/Other Agency	Unit/Office	Violent crime	Murder and non-negligent man-slaughter	Forcible rape	Robbery	Aggra-vated assault	Property crime	Burglary	Larceny-theft	Motor vehicle theft	Arson[1]
	Bath County	0	0	0	0	0	9	2	7	0	1
	Bedford County	2	0	0	0	2	8	0	7	1	0
	Bland County	2	0	0	0	2	7	1	6	0	0
	Botetourt County	0	0	0	0	0	2	0	2	0	0
	Brunswick County	0	0	0	0	0	3	0	1	2	0
	Buchanan County	1	0	0	0	1	23	4	18	1	3
	Buckingham County	0	0	0	0	0	0	0	0	0	0
	Campbell County	2	0	0	0	2	3	0	3	0	0
	Caroline County	0	0	0	0	0	8	0	3	5	2
	Carroll County	0	0	0	0	0	2	0	1	1	0
	Charlotte County	1	0	0	0	1	0	0	0	0	0
	Chesapeake	5	1	0	0	4	4	0	2	2	0
	Chesterfield County	15	0	0	0	15	25	1	14	10	0
	Craig County	0	0	0	0	0	4	0	4	0	0
	Culpeper County	5	0	0	0	5	3	1	2	0	0
	Essex County	1	0	0	0	1	0	0	0	0	0
	Fairfax County	20	1	0	1	18	41	0	22	19	0
	Fauquier County	1	0	0	0	1	5	0	5	0	0
	Fluvanna County	2	0	0	0	2	2	0	2	0	0
	Franklin County	0	0	0	0	0	9	0	7	2	0
	Frederick County	1	1	0	0	0	3	0	1	2	0
	Fredericksburg	1	0	1	0	0	1	0	1	0	0
	Gloucester County	0	0	0	0	0	5	0	4	1	0
	Goochland County	1	0	0	0	1	1	0	1	0	0
	Greene County	0	0	0	0	0	0	0	0	0	0
	Greensville County	0	0	0	0	0	0	0	0	0	0
	Halifax County	0	0	0	0	0	8	0	7	1	0
	Hampton	2	0	0	0	2	2	0	1	1	0
	Hanover County	0	0	0	0	0	4	1	1	2	2
	Harrisonburg	1	0	1	0	0	4	0	4	0	0
	Henrico County	2	0	0	0	2	11	1	9	1	1
	Henry County	1	1	0	0	0	4	0	2	2	0
	Isle of Wight County	0	0	0	0	0	2	0	2	0	1
	James City County	0	0	0	0	0	0	0	0	0	0
	King George County	0	0	0	0	0	2	0	1	1	0
	Lancaster County	0	0	0	0	0	1	0	1	0	0
	Lee County	0	0	0	0	0	2	0	0	2	1
	Loudoun County	0	0	0	0	0	3	1	1	1	0
	Louisa County	2	2	0	0	0	5	0	3	2	0
	Lunenburg County	0	0	0	0	0	0	0	0	0	0
	Lynchburg	0	0	0	0	0	2	0	0	2	0
	Madison County	3	0	0	0	3	0	0	0	0	0
	Mecklenburg County	1	0	0	0	1	6	1	5	0	0
	Montgomery County	1	1	0	0	0	1	0	1	0	0
	Newport News	2	0	0	0	2	8	0	2	6	0
	Norfolk	5	0	0	0	5	8	0	3	5	0
	Northampton County	0	0	0	0	0	7	0	6	1	0
	Northumberland County	0	0	0	0	0	0	0	0	0	0
	Nottoway County	0	0	0	0	0	4	1	2	1	0
	Orange County	2	1	0	1	0	1	0	1	0	0
	Page County	0	0	0	0	0	4	1	2	1	0
	Patrick County	0	0	0	0	0	0	0	0	0	0
	Petersburg	1	0	0	0	1	0	0	0	0	0
	Pittsylvania County	2	0	0	0	2	36	0	13	23	1
	Powhatan County	12	0	0	0	12	0	0	0	0	0
	Prince George County	0	0	0	0	0	1	0	1	0	0
	Prince William County	3	0	0	0	3	10	0	8	2	0
	Pulaski County	0	0	0	0	0	11	2	6	3	0
	Rappahannock County	0	0	0	0	0	0	0	0	0	0
	Richmond	4	0	0	0	4	9	0	5	4	0
	Roanoke	0	0	0	0	0	1	0	1	0	0
	Roanoke County	0	0	0	0	0	1	0	1	0	0
	Rockbridge County	1	0	1	0	0	7	0	7	0	0
	Rockingham County	0	0	0	0	0	22	0	10	12	0
	Russell County	0	0	0	0	0	7	1	5	1	0
	Shenandoah County	1	0	0	0	1	2	0	2	0	0
	Smyth County	3	0	0	0	3	12	0	9	3	0
	Southampton County	0	0	0	0	0	3	0	2	1	0
	Spotsylvania County	0	0	0	0	0	3	1	2	0	0
	Stafford County	0	0	0	0	0	0	0	0	0	0
	Tazewell County	1	0	0	0	1	14	4	8	2	0
	Virginia Beach	2	0	0	0	2	8	1	2	5	0
	Warren County	1	0	0	0	1	1	0	0	1	0

[1] The FBI does not publish arson data unless it receives data from either the agency or the state for all 12 months of the calendar year.

Table 11. Offenses Known to Law Enforcement, by State, Tribal, and Other Agencies, 2010—*Continued*

(Number)

State/Other Agency	Unit/Office	Violent crime	Murder and non-negligent man-slaughter	Forcible rape	Robbery	Aggra-vated assault	Property crime	Burglary	Larceny-theft	Motor vehicle theft	Arson[1]
	Washington County	0	0	0	0	0	4	0	4	0	0
	Winchester	1	0	0	1	0	2	0	2	0	0
	Wise County	2	1	1	0	0	6	0	6	0	0
	Wythe County	1	0	0	0	1	15	1	13	1	0
	York County	0	0	0	0	0	2	0	0	2	0
Virginia State Capitol		0	0	0	0	0	31	2	29	0	0
VIRGINIA—Other Agencies											
Norfolk Airport Authority		0	0	0	0	0	50	0	41	9	0
Port Authority	Norfolk	0	0	0	0	0	3	1	2	0	0
Reagan National Airport..........................		1	0	0	0	1	332	0	261	71	1
Richmond International Airport...................		1	0	0	0	1	15	0	13	2	0
WASHINGTON—State Agencies											
State Insurance Commissioner	Special Investigations Unit	0	0	0	0	0	0	0	0	0	0
WASHINGTON—Tribal Agencies											
Chehalis Tribal...............................		1	0	0	0	1	99	20	75	4	0
Colville Tribal................................		75	0	7	4	64	208	73	102	33	18
Kalispel Tribal................................		6	0	0	0	6	47	10	28	9	0
Lummi Tribal.................................		95	0	15	8	72	442	146	273	23	0
Makah Tribal.................................		20	0	0	0	20	10	6	4	0	1
Nisqually Tribal..............................		2	0	0	0	2	47	10	33	4	0
Nooksack Tribal..............................		4	0	1	1	2	52	16	32	4	0
Port Gamble S'Klallam Tribal...................		4	0	0	0	4	60	25	35	0	0
Puyallup Tribal...............................		42	0	4	19	19	396	35	223	138	1
Quinault Indian Nation		3	0	3	0	0	28	20	0	8	1
Shoalwater Bay Tribal..........................		1	0	0	0	1	10	2	8	0	0
Spokane Agency...............................		43	0	0	1	42	27	19	1	7	7
Stillaguamish Tribal...........................		1	0	0	0	1	13	5	8	0	0
Suquamish Tribal.............................		17	0	1	1	15	102	26	59	17	2
Swinomish Tribal.............................		5	0	1	2	2	148	26	119	3	0
Upper Skagit Tribal...........................		1	0	0	0	1	17	13	3	1	0
Yakima Tribal................................		50	0	35	4	11	410	193	167	50	11
WASHINGTON—Other Agencies	Port of Seattle	26	0	0	3	23	781	17	729	35	1
WEST VIRGINIA—State Agencies											
Division of Natural Resources:	Harrison County	0	0	0	0	0	0	0	0	0	0
	Kanawha County	0	0	0	0	0	0	0	0	0	0
	Ritchie County	0	0	0	0	0	0	0	0	0	0
	Roane County	0	0	0	0	0	0	0	0	0	0
	Taylor County	0	0	0	0	0	0	0	0	0	0
	Wood County	0	0	0	0	0	0	0	0	0	0
State Police:	Berkeley Springs	7	0	0	0	7	96	26	64	6	0
	Bridgeport	21	2	1	2	16	256	69	160	27	1
	Buckhannon	9	0	1	0	8	55	15	35	5	0
	Clay	10	0	1	0	9	48	20	21	7	2
	Danville	29	0	3	0	26	224	43	158	23	3
	Elizabeth	8	0	0	0	8	35	11	21	3	0
	Elkins	25	0	3	2	20	232	58	159	15	0
	Fairmont	10	0	1	2	7	145	46	89	10	1
	Franklin	9	0	2	0	7	18	8	10	0	1
	Gauley Bridge	3	0	0	0	3	32	9	21	2	1
	Gilbert	14	0	1	2	11	102	36	54	12	3
	Glenville	13	0	2	0	11	38	11	26	1	0
	Grantsville	6	0	1	1	4	29	9	13	7	4
	Hamlin	40	1	7	2	30	395	165	194	36	5
	Harrisville	9	0	2	0	7	57	17	37	3	1
	Hinton	10	0	1	0	9	87	43	37	7	0
	Hundred	6	0	0	0	6	49	14	34	1	0
	Huntington	17	0	5	5	7	449	63	365	21	4
	Jesse	1	0	0	0	1	26	4	19	3	0
	Kearneysville	25	0	1	1	23	209	50	130	29	1
	Keyser	16	1	2	1	12	258	125	123	10	4
	Kingwood	16	0	1	0	15	128	61	55	12	1
	Lewisburg	6	0	0	0	6	78	22	52	4	0
	Logan	74	1	2	5	66	617	176	367	74	6
	Marlinton	14	1	0	0	13	42	9	29	4	2
	Martinsburg	68	0	8	14	46	575	165	361	49	1
	Moorefield	14	0	5	0	9	43	18	19	6	1
	Morgantown	69	1	3	8	57	637	198	398	41	2
	Moundsville	3	0	1	0	2	27	6	18	3	0
	New Cumberland	1	0	1	0	0	17	1	14	2	0
	Oak Hill	11	0	2	0	9	106	23	74	9	2
	Paden City	2	0	0	0	2	20	5	11	4	1
	Parkersburg	6	0	2	1	3	100	18	76	6	0
	Parsons	6	0	1	0	5	38	8	26	4	0

[1] The FBI does not publish arson data unless it receives data from either the agency or the state for all 12 months of the calendar year.

Table 11.   Offenses Known to Law Enforcement, by State, Tribal, and Other Agencies, 2010—*Continued*

(Number)

State/Other Agency	Unit/Office	Violent crime	Murder and non-negligent man-slaughter	Forcible rape	Robbery	Aggra-vated assault	Property crime	Burglary	Larceny-theft	Motor vehicle theft	Arson[1]
	Petersburg	10	0	5	0	5	41	22	18	1	2
	Philippi	10	0	0	0	10	60	21	33	6	1
	Point Pleasant	3	0	1	0	2	84	30	46	8	0
	Princeton	41	0	3	3	35	419	110	289	20	0
	Quincy	7	0	0	1	6	132	23	100	9	2
	Rainelle	1	0	0	0	1	61	15	44	2	0
	Richwood	3	0	0	0	3	31	4	26	1	0
	Ripley	6	0	0	0	6	60	22	37	1	0
	Romney	8	0	6	0	2	105	34	65	6	1
	South Charleston	43	0	6	4	33	576	84	455	37	1
	Spencer	9	0	0	0	9	43	12	23	8	0
	Summersville	0	0	0	0	0	56	10	44	2	0
	Sutton	15	0	1	0	14	103	18	79	6	2
	Union	3	0	0	0	3	66	25	37	4	0
	Upperglade	14	1	0	0	13	46	9	34	3	0
	Wayne	29	0	4	4	21	444	177	230	37	4
	Welch	25	0	1	0	24	63	25	29	9	2
	Wellsburg	5	0	2	0	3	14	3	11	0	0
	Weston	11	0	3	0	8	88	16	65	7	0
	West Union	3	0	0	0	3	39	14	23	2	1
	Wheeling	10	0	2	0	8	66	5	59	2	0
	Whitesville	15	0	0	2	13	44	17	26	1	1
	Williamson	31	0	3	3	25	132	37	72	23	3
	Winfield	17	1	0	0	16	254	39	196	19	0
WEST VIRGINIA—Other Agencies											
Eastern Panhandle Drug and Violent Crime Task Force		0	0	0	0	0	0	0	0	0	0
Metropolitan Drug Enforcement Network Team		0	0	0	0	0	1	1	0	0	0
Ohio Valley Drug and Violent Crime Task Force		0	0	0	0	0	1	0	1	0	0
Potomac Highlands Drug and Violent Crime Task Force		0	0	0	0	0	0	0	0	0	0
WISCONSIN—State Agencies											
Department of Natural Resources		0	0	0	0	0	0	0	0	0	0
WISCONSIN—Tribal Agencies											
Lac du Flambeau Tribal		15	1	0	2	12	377	59	296	22	0
Oneida Tribal		27	4	1	0	22	135	23	97	15	0
Red Cliff Tribal		4	0	0	0	4	118	23	89	6	1
St. Croix Tribal		4	0	1	1	2	38	5	29	4	0
Stockbridge Munsee Tribal		4	0	1	0	3	49	14	35	0	0
WYOMING—Tribal Agencies											
Wind River Tribal		37	0	2	0	35	113	10	69	34	2
OTHER OUTLYING AREAS											
Virgin Islands:	St. Croix	573	29	21	118	405	1,385	585	659	141	31
	St. Thomas	1,176	31	45	252	848	1,609	788	699	122	36
FEDERAL AGENCIES											
National Institutes of Health		0	0	0	0	0	96	1	95	0	0
United States Department of the Interior:	Bureau of Indian Affairs[5]	5,532	133	852	280	4,267	17,713	4,990	10,495	2,228	818
	Bureau of Land Management	16	3	0	1	12	353	17	317	19	35
	Bureau of Reclamation	0	0	0	0	0	1	0	1	0	0
	Fish and Wildlife Service	16	3	1	1	11	389	81	265	43	52
	National Park Service	369	15	45	58	251	2,777	346	2,323	108	82

[1] The FBI does not publish arson data unless it receives data from either the agency or the state for all 12 months of the calendar year.

[5] Tribal figures represented throughout Table 11 are included in the aggregated totals listed under the Bureau of Indian Affairs data.

Table 12.   Crime Trends, by Population Group, 2009–2010

(Number, percent change)

Population group	Violent crime	Murder and non-negligent man-slaughter	Forcible rape	Robbery	Aggra-vated assault	Property crime	Burglary	Larceny-theft	Motor vehicle theft	Arson	Number of agencies	2010 estimated population
TOTAL ALL AGENCIES												
2009	1,253,786	14,668	79,306	394,107	765,705	8,783,560	2,068,376	5,950,908	764,276	56,477		
2010	1,181,579	14,077	76,322	355,795	735,385	8,543,699	2,034,268	5,801,900	707,531	52,191	14,706	291,385,855
Percent change	-5.8	-4.0	-3.8	-9.7	-4.0	-2.7	-1.6	-2.5	-7.4	-7.6		
Total Cities												
2009	998,731	11,318	58,265	343,360	585,788	6,875,514	1,515,174	4,754,923	605,417	41,914		
2010	943,322	10,861	56,651	310,450	565,360	6,666,087	1,489,019	4,615,865	561,203	39,169	10,611	197,239,780
Percent change	-5.5	-4.0	-2.8	-9.6	-3.5	-3.0	-1.7	-2.9	-7.3	-6.5		
GROUP I (250,000 and over)												
2009	453,671	5,808	18,889	184,802	244,172	2,240,358	521,170	1,440,506	278,682	15,164		
2010	428,565	5,731	18,673	167,555	236,606	2,164,781	509,242	1,392,700	262,839	14,006	75	57,354,512
Percent change	-5.5	-1.3	-1.1	-9.3	-3.1	-3.4	-2.3	-3.3	-5.7	-7.6		
1,000,000 and over (Group I subset)												
2009	193,010	2,369	6,105	85,436	99,100	842,014	178,035	555,477	108,502	4,587		
2010	183,262	2,316	6,062	78,293	96,591	810,287	172,991	535,650	101,646	3,890	10	25,823,829
Percent change	-5.1	-2.2	-0.7	-8.4	-2.5	-3.8	-2.8	-3.6	-6.3	-15.2		
500,000 to 999,999 (Group I subset)												
2009	146,001	1,903	6,501	55,448	82,149	798,436	192,180	509,521	96,735	5,405		
2010	138,348	1,813	6,658	49,429	80,448	767,672	185,280	491,214	91,178	5,291	25	17,415,371
Percent change	-5.2	-4.7	2.4	-10.9	-2.1	-3.9	-3.6	-3.6	-5.7	-2.1		
250,000 to 499,999 (Group I subset)												
2009	114,660	1,536	6,283	43,918	62,923	599,908	150,955	375,508	73,445	5,172		
2010	106,955	1,602	5,953	39,833	59,567	586,822	150,971	365,836	70,015	4,825	40	14,115,312
Percent change	-6.7	4.3	-5.3	-9.3	-5.3	-2.2	*	-2.6	-4.7	-6.7		
GROUP II (100,000 to 249,999)												
2009	165,046	1,875	10,022	56,341	96,808	1,198,242	275,636	808,869	113,737	6,686		
2010	156,707	1,744	9,481	51,275	94,207	1,155,269	273,363	778,735	103,171	6,426	203	30,280,703
Percent change	-5.1	-7.0	-5.4	-9.0	-2.7	-3.6	-0.8	-3.7	-9.3	-3.9		
GROUP III (50,000 to 99,999)												
2009	131,509	1,272	8,769	42,113	79,355	1,040,159	228,051	728,515	83,593	6,346		
2010	123,175	1,248	8,492	37,895	75,540	1,006,803	223,639	706,049	77,115	5,886	458	31,381,299
Percent change	-6.3	-1.9	-3.2	-10.0	-4.8	-3.2	-1.9	-3.1	-7.7	-7.2		
GROUP IV (25,000 to 49,999)												
2009	95,293	934	7,198	28,129	59,032	861,663	177,532	630,329	53,802	4,881		
2010	89,599	914	7,107	25,031	56,547	839,961	178,140	612,266	49,555	4,427	808	27,927,972
Percent change	-6.0	-2.1	-1.3	-11.0	-4.2	-2.5	0.3	-2.9	-7.9	-9.3		
GROUP V (10,000 to 24,999)												
2009	82,409	748	6,906	20,435	54,320	819,189	170,827	604,783	43,579	3,985		
2010	77,803	700	6,481	18,285	52,337	796,254	166,235	590,495	39,524	3,754	1,743	27,712,113
Percent change	-5.6	-6.4	-6.2	-10.5	-3.7	-2.8	-2.7	-2.4	-9.3	-5.8		
GROUP VI (under 10,000)												
2009	70,803	681	6,481	11,540	52,101	715,903	141,958	541,921	32,024	4,852		
2010	67,473	524	6,417	10,409	50,123	703,019	138,400	535,620	28,999	4,670	7,324	22,583,181
Percent change	-4.7	-23.1	-1.0	-9.8	-3.8	-1.8	-2.5	-1.2	-9.4	-3.8		
Metropolitan Counties												
2009	200,546	2,407	14,784	46,206	137,149	1,489,728	405,436	953,993	130,299	10,893		
2010	186,939	2,369	13,844	41,111	129,615	1,450,064	396,185	934,912	118,967	9,608	1,710	67,489,063
Percent change	-6.8	-1.6	-6.4	-11.0	-5.5	-2.7	-2.3	-2.0	-8.7	-11.8		
Nonmetropolitan Counties[1]												
2009	54,509	943	6,257	4,541	42,768	418,318	147,766	241,992	28,560	3,670		
2010	51,318	847	5,827	4,234	40,410	427,548	149,064	251,123	27,361	3,414	2,385	26,657,012
Percent change	-5.9	-10.2	-6.9	-6.8	-5.5	2.2	0.9	3.8	-4.2	-7.0		
SUBURBAN AREAS[2]												
2009	348,688	3,684	25,803	86,425	232,776	3,018,216	702,080	2,093,365	222,771	18,895		
2010	326,791	3,606	24,748	77,080	221,357	2,940,843	688,618	2,049,413	202,812	16,860	7,765	123,142,328
Percent change	-6.3	-2.1	-4.1	-10.8	-4.9	-2.6	-1.9	-2.1	-9.0	-10.8		

[1] Includes state police agencies that report aggregately for the entire state.

[2] Suburban areas include law enforcement agencies in cities with less than 50,000 inhabitants and county law enforcement agencies that are within a Metropolitan Statistical Area. Suburban areas exclude all metropolitan agencies associated with a principal city. The agencies associated with suburban areas also appear in other groups within this table.

* Less than one-tenth of 1 percent.

Table 13.   Crime Trends, by Suburban and Nonsuburban Cities, by Population Group, 2009–2010[1]

(Number, percent change)

Population group	Violent crime	Murder and non-negligent man-slaughter	Forcible rape	Robbery	Aggra-vated assault	Property crime	Burglary	Larceny-theft	Motor vehicle theft	Arson	Number of agencies	2010 estimated population
TOTAL SUBURBAN CITIES												
2009	148,119	1,277	10,996	40,219	95,627	1,528,488	296,644	1,139,372	92,472	8,002		
2010	139,702	1,237	10,754	35,969	91,742	1,490,779	292,433	1,114,501	83,845	7,252	6,055	55,653,265
Percent change	-5.7	-3.1	-2.2	-10.6	-4.1	-2.5	-1.4	-2.2	-9.3	-9.4		
GROUP IV (25,000 to 49,999)												
2009	58,671	536	3,987	18,127	36,021	560,288	110,453	410,349	39,486	3,045		
2010	54,326	562	3,864	16,020	33,880	545,861	111,058	398,311	36,492	2,714	612	20,999,217
Percent change	-7.4	4.9	-3.1	-11.6	-5.9	-2.6	0.5	-2.9	-7.6	-10.9		
GROUP V (10,000 to 24,999)												
2009	51,629	437	3,970	14,352	32,870	533,259	106,851	393,735	32,673	2,661		
2010	49,513	435	3,809	13,036	32,233	518,139	104,311	384,508	29,320	2,453	1,297	20,845,416
Percent change	-4.1	-0.5	-4.1	-9.2	-1.9	-2.8	-2.4	-2.3	-10.3	-7.8		
GROUP VI (under 10,000)												
2009	37,819	304	3,039	7,740	26,736	434,941	79,340	335,288	20,313	2,296		
2010	35,863	240	3,081	6,913	25,629	426,779	77,064	331,682	18,033	2,085	4,146	13,808,632
Percent change	-5.2	-21.1	1.4	-10.7	-4.1	-1.9	-2.9	-1.1	-11.2	-9.2		
TOTAL NONSUBURBAN CITIES												
2009	100,386	1,086	9,589	19,885	69,826	868,267	193,673	637,661	36,933	5,716		
2010	95,175	901	9,253	17,756	67,265	848,455	190,342	623,880	34,233	5,599	3,820	22,570,001
Percent change	-5.2	-17.0	-3.5	-10.7	-3.7	-2.3	-1.7	-2.2	-7.3	-2.0		
GROUP IV (25,000 to 49,999)												
2009	36,622	398	3,211	10,002	23,011	301,375	67,079	219,980	14,316	1,836		
2010	35,273	352	3,243	9,011	22,667	294,100	67,082	213,955	13,063	1,713	196	6,928,755
Percent change	-3.7	-11.6	1.0	-9.9	-1.5	-2.4	*	-2.7	-8.8	-6.7		
GROUP V (10,000 to 24,999)												
2009	30,780	311	2,936	6,083	21,450	285,930	63,976	211,048	10,906	1,324		
2010	28,290	265	2,672	5,249	20,104	278,115	61,924	205,987	10,204	1,301	446	6,866,697
Percent change	-8.1	-14.8	-9.0	-13.7	-6.3	-2.7	-3.2	-2.4	-6.4	-1.7		
GROUP VI (under 10,000)												
2009	32,984	377	3,442	3,800	25,365	280,962	62,618	206,633	11,711	2,556		
2010	31,612	284	3,338	3,496	24,494	276,240	61,336	203,938	10,966	2,585	3,178	8,774,549
Percent change	-4.2	-24.7	-3.0	-8.0	-3.4	-1.7	-2.0	-1.3	-6.4	1.1		

[1] Suburban cities include law enforcement agencies in cities with less than 50,000 inhabitants that are within a Metropolitan Statistical Area. Suburban cities exclude all metropolitan agencies associated with a principal city. Nonsuburban cities include law enforcement agencies in cities with less than 50,000 inhabitants that are not associated with a Metropolitan Statistical Area.
* Less than one-tenth of 1 percent.

Table 14. Crime Trends, by Metropolitan and Nonmetropolitan Counties, by Population Group, 2009–2010[1]

(Number, Percent change)

Population group and range	Violent crime	Murder and non-negligent man-slaughter	Forcible rape	Robbery	Aggra-vated assault	Property crime	Burglary	Larceny-theft	Motor vehicle theft	Arson	Number of agencies	2010 estimated population
METROPOLITAN COUNTIES												
100,000 and over												
2009	140,563	1,650	8,679	38,936	91,298	998,597	258,474	651,369	88,754	6,798		
2010	130,199	1,635	8,166	34,690	85,708	957,763	250,812	627,292	79,659	6,051	152	40,546,466
Percent change	-7.4	-0.9	-5.9	-10.9	-6.1	-4.1	-3.0	-3.7	-10.2	-11.0		
25,000 to 99,999												
2009	43,548	566	4,488	5,088	33,406	368,887	114,941	229,738	24,208	2,614		
2010	40,484	534	4,129	4,321	31,500	370,265	115,042	232,619	22,604	2,237	426	22,168,732
Percent change	-7.0	-5.7	-8.0	-15.1	-5.7	0.4	0.1	1.3	-6.6	-14.4		
Under 25,000												
2009	16,177	190	1,608	2,161	12,218	119,687	31,239	71,204	17,244	1,471		
2010	15,958	200	1,491	2,086	12,181	119,366	29,437	73,301	16,628	1,312	1,121	4,574,163
Percent change	-1.4	5.3	-7.3	-3.5	-0.3	-0.3	-5.8	2.9	-3.6	-10.8		
NONMETROPOLITAN COUNTIES												
25,000 and over												
2009	23,635	360	2,434	2,352	18,489	186,361	68,141	106,225	11,995	1,311		
2010	22,125	352	2,284	2,227	17,262	190,651	68,558	110,657	11,436	1,250	292	11,495,405
Percent change	-6.4	-2.2	-6.2	-5.3	-6.6	2.3	0.6	4.2	-4.7	-4.7		
10,000 to 24,999												
2009	15,862	310	1,583	1,041	12,928	124,095	43,639	72,449	8,007	951		
2010	14,849	226	1,560	962	12,101	127,417	44,876	74,864	7,677	928	571	9,159,539
Percent change	-6.4	-27.1	-1.5	-7.6	-6.4	2.7	2.8	3.3	-4.1	-2.4		
Under 10,000												
2009	8,677	162	1,233	419	6,863	61,483	20,884	35,712	4,887	843		
2010	8,375	141	1,192	358	6,684	62,858	20,271	37,835	4,752	748	1,345	3,972,118
Percent change	-3.5	-13.0	-3.3	-14.6	-2.6	2.2	-2.9	5.9	-2.8	-11.3		

[1] Metropolitan counties include sheriffs and county law enforcement agencies associated with a Metropolitan Statistical Area. Nonmetropolitan counties include sheriffs and county law enforcement agencies that are not associated with a Metropolitan Statistical Area. The offenses from state police agencies are not included in this table.

Table 15. Crime Trends, by Population Group, 2009–2010

(Number, percent change)

Population group	Forcible rape		Robbery				Aggravated assault			
	Rape by force	Assault to rape-attempts	Firearm	Knife or cutting instrument	Other weapon	Strong-arm	Firearm	Knife or cutting instrument	Other weapon	Hands, fists, feet, etc.
TOTAL ALL AGENCIES										
2009	72,041	5,423	147,510	26,707	30,317	142,628	146,461	131,251	235,043	189,907
2010	68,934	5,293	128,793	24,388	27,170	130,839	138,403	127,857	222,892	185,029
Percent change	-4.3	-2.4	-12.7	-8.7	-10.4	-8.3	-5.5	-2.6	-5.2	-2.6
Total Cities										
2009	52,545	4,268	125,099	22,966	25,718	124,606	114,283	102,879	175,421	132,504
2010	50,714	4,219	109,059	21,130	23,105	114,092	108,048	100,557	167,723	130,313
Percent change	-3.5	-1.1	-12.8	-8.0	-10.2	-8.4	-5.5	-2.3	-4.4	-1.7
GROUP I (250,000 and over)										
2009	16,176	1,686	67,462	10,551	11,111	56,640	57,058	38,543	69,050	30,700
2010	15,611	1,702	58,034	9,530	9,704	52,477	53,771	37,530	66,687	31,095
Percent change	-3.5	0.9	-14.0	-9.7	-12.7	-7.3	-5.8	-2.6	-3.4	1.3
1,000,000 and over (Group I subset)										
2009	4,610	663	23,022	4,216	3,867	19,857	15,865	12,223	20,897	7,931
2010	4,345	681	19,193	3,746	3,469	18,064	14,729	11,927	20,680	8,189
Percent change	-5.7	2.7	-16.6	-11.1	-10.3	-9.0	-7.2	-2.4	-1.0	3.3
500,000 to 999,999 (Group I subset)										
2009	5,817	526	25,387	3,510	4,027	18,817	22,823	15,067	27,957	10,741
2010	5,870	523	21,296	3,286	3,581	17,930	21,258	15,133	27,325	11,240
Percent change	0.9	-0.6	-16.1	-6.4	-11.1	-4.7	-6.9	0.4	-2.3	4.6
250,000 to 499,999 (Group I subset)										
2009	5,749	497	19,053	2,825	3,217	17,966	18,370	11,253	20,196	12,028
2010	5,396	498	17,545	2,498	2,654	16,483	17,784	10,470	18,682	11,666
Percent change	-6.1	0.2	-7.9	-11.6	-17.5	-8.3	-3.2	-7.0	-7.5	-3.0
GROUP II (100,000 to 249,999)										
2009	9,145	607	21,761	4,349	5,137	22,641	20,484	20,442	32,900	18,671
2010	8,672	597	19,954	4,096	4,732	20,224	19,671	19,394	31,783	19,003
Percent change	-5.2	-1.6	-8.3	-5.8	-7.9	-10.7	-4.0	-5.1	-3.4	1.8
GROUP III (50,000 to 99,999)										
2009	8,111	598	14,554	3,408	3,894	19,253	13,910	15,669	25,935	22,108
2010	7,895	530	12,661	3,307	3,531	17,463	12,748	15,390	24,766	21,021
Percent change	-2.7	-11.4	-13.0	-3.0	-9.3	-9.3	-8.4	-1.8	-4.5	-4.9
GROUP IV (25,000 to 49,999)										
2009	6,764	415	9,864	2,162	2,628	11,927	9,018	10,579	18,167	17,564
2010	6,675	407	8,509	1,869	2,412	10,969	8,689	10,832	17,037	16,737
Percent change	-1.3	-1.9	-13.7	-13.6	-8.2	-8.0	-3.6	2.4	-6.2	-4.7
GROUP V (10,000 to 24,999)										
2009	6,425	440	7,361	1,572	1,897	8,810	7,772	9,685	16,132	19,318
2010	6,044	406	6,355	1,465	1,750	8,061	7,288	9,410	15,403	18,958
Percent change	-5.9	-7.7	-13.7	-6.8	-7.7	-8.5	-6.2	-2.8	-4.5	-1.9
GROUP VI (under 10,000)										
2009	5,924	522	4,097	924	1,051	5,335	6,041	7,961	13,237	24,143
2010	5,817	577	3,546	863	976	4,898	5,881	8,001	12,047	23,499
Percent change	-1.8	10.5	-13.4	-6.6	-7.1	-8.2	-2.6	0.5	-9.0	-2.7
Metropolitan Counties										
2009	13,610	819	20,510	3,351	4,013	16,373	24,544	22,360	47,607	40,751
2010	12,757	737	17,997	2,886	3,544	15,165	23,226	21,354	43,855	39,097
Percent change	-6.3	-10.0	-12.3	-13.9	-11.7	-7.4	-5.4	-4.5	-7.9	-4.1
Nonmetropolitan Counties										
2009	5,886	336	1,901	390	586	1,649	7,634	6,012	12,015	16,652
2010	5,463	337	1,737	372	521	1,582	7,129	5,946	11,314	15,619
Percent change	-7.2	0.3	-8.6	-4.6	-11.1	-4.1	-6.6	-1.1	-5.8	-6.2
SUBURBAN AREAS[1]										
2009	23,921	1,503	34,771	6,309	7,674	33,933	37,040	37,981	76,097	75,764
2010	22,938	1,440	30,311	5,607	6,849	31,288	35,043	36,991	70,222	73,603
Percent change	-4.1	-4.2	-12.8	-11.1	-10.8	-7.8	-5.4	-2.6	-7.7	-2.9

[1] Suburban areas include law enforcement agencies in cities with less than 50,000 inhabitants and county law enforcement agencies that are within a Metropolitan Statistical Area. Suburban areas exclude all metropolitan agencies associated with a principal city. The agencies associated with suburban areas also appear in other groups within this table.

Table 15.   Crime Trends, by Population Group, 2009–2010—*Continued*

(Number, percent change)

Population group	Burglary			Motor vehicle theft			Arson			Number of agencies	2010 estimated population
	Forcible entry	Unlawful entry	Attempted forcible entry	Autos	Trucks and buses	Other vehicles	Structure	Mobile	Other		
TOTAL ALL AGENCIES											
2009	1,194,238	640,096	126,393	518,407	123,101	77,793	23,713	15,009	14,647		
2010	1,166,754	636,558	122,434	481,236	109,266	70,074	22,470	12,680	13,931	14,439	272,150,917
Percent change	-2.3	-0.6	-3.1	-7.2	-11.2	-9.9	-5.2	-15.5	-4.9		
Total Cities											
2009	864,431	460,892	96,826	420,677	94,940	49,219	17,796	10,507	10,934		
2010	843,526	459,032	93,263	388,351	84,541	45,184	16,911	8,994	10,601	10,386	180,156,135
Percent change	-2.4	-0.4	-3.7	-7.7	-11.0	-8.2	-5.0	-14.4	-3.0		
GROUP I (250,000 and over)											
2009	319,484	115,224	29,674	178,417	51,657	16,871	6,359	4,976	3,113		
2010	310,714	115,308	27,645	165,380	46,788	15,838	6,029	4,103	3,207	71	45,289,754
Percent change	-2.7	0.1	-6.8	-7.3	-9.4	-6.1	-5.2	-17.5	3.0		
1,000,000 and over (Group I subset)											
2009	94,331	31,731	6,699	51,675	23,518	7,146	1,737	1,848	1,002		
2010	90,745	31,873	6,244	45,235	20,837	6,177	1,512	1,394	984	8	14,654,178
Percent change	-3.8	0.4	-6.8	-12.5	-11.4	-13.6	-13.0	-24.6	-1.8		
500,000 to 999,999 (Group I subset)											
2009	129,354	41,897	13,131	68,942	17,348	5,821	2,176	1,517	1,121		
2010	123,501	42,035	12,171	64,963	16,040	5,766	2,353	1,368	1,019	24	16,775,442
Percent change	-4.5	0.3	-7.3	-5.8	-7.5	-0.9	8.1	-9.8	-9.1		
250,000 to 499,999 (Group I subset)											
2009	95,799	41,596	9,844	57,800	10,791	3,904	2,446	1,611	990		
2010	96,468	41,400	9,230	55,182	9,911	3,895	2,164	1,341	1,204	39	13,860,134
Percent change	0.7	-0.5	-6.2	-4.5	-8.2	-0.2	-11.5	-16.8	21.6		
GROUP II (100,000 to 249,999)											
2009	157,457	86,173	18,769	82,606	18,314	9,234	2,838	1,680	1,759		
2010	154,456	86,225	18,134	75,680	15,885	8,265	2,838	1,475	1,658	194	28,854,065
Percent change	-1.9	0.1	-3.4	-8.4	-13.3	-10.5	0.0	-12.2	-5.7		
GROUP III (50,000 to 99,999)											
2009	126,335	79,137	15,763	63,946	10,548	7,538	2,537	1,566	1,854		
2010	123,843	77,490	15,391	59,436	9,293	7,028	2,495	1,248	1,818	444	30,436,777
Percent change	-2.0	-2.1	-2.4	-7.1	-11.9	-6.8	-1.7	-20.3	-1.9		
GROUP IV (25,000 to 49,999)											
2009	94,994	62,658	11,811	40,192	5,663	5,824	1,908	943	1,609		
2010	94,879	63,251	11,769	37,244	5,018	5,157	1,660	840	1,504	770	26,639,832
Percent change	-0.1	+0.9	-0.4	-7.3	-11.4	-11.5	-13.0	-10.9	-6.5		
GROUP V (10,000 to 24,999)											
2009	91,642	61,899	11,417	32,122	5,228	5,098	1,884	718	1,148		
2010	87,879	61,582	11,012	29,392	4,374	4,688	1,732	705	1,098	1,684	26,749,154
Percent change	-4.1	-0.5	-3.5	-8.5	-16.3	-8.0	-8.1	-1.8	-4.4		
GROUP VI (under 10,000)											
2009	74,519	55,801	9,392	23,394	3,530	4,654	2,270	624	1,451		
2010	71,755	55,176	9,312	21,219	3,183	4,208	2,157	623	1,316	7,223	22,186,553
Percent change	-3.7	-1.1	-0.9	-9.3	-9.8	-9.6	-5.0	-0.2	-9.3		
Metropolitan Counties											
2009	239,492	129,516	23,274	81,003	23,771	21,334	4,063	3,651	2,866		
2010	234,110	125,713	22,691	76,357	20,491	18,494	3,771	2,946	2,557	1,687	65,686,356
Percent change	-2.2	-2.9	-2.5	-5.7	-13.8	-13.3	-7.2	-19.3	-10.8		
Nonmetropolitan Counties											
2009	90,315	49,688	6,293	16,727	4,390	7,240	1,854	851	847		
2010	89,118	51,813	6,480	16,528	4,234	6,396	1,788	740	773	2,366	26,308,426
Percent change	-1.3	4.3	3.0	-1.2	-3.6	-11.7	-3.6	-13.0	-8.7		
SUBURBAN AREAS[1]											
2009	395,668	238,887	44,589	149,486	34,555	31,670	7,525	5,056	5,510		
2010	386,691	235,012	43,636	138,980	29,724	27,625	6,801	4,210	5,001	7,591	119,228,798
Percent change	-2.3	-1.6	-2.1	-7.0	-14.0	-12.8	-9.6	-16.7	-9.2		

[1] Suburban areas include law enforcement agencies in cities with less than 50,000 inhabitants and county law enforcement agencies that are within a Metropolitan Statistical Area. Suburban areas exclude all metropolitan agencies associated with a principal city. The agencies associated with suburban areas also appear in other groups within this table.

Table 16.   Crime per 100,000 Population, by Population Group, 2010

(Number, rate)

Population group	Violent crime		Murder and nonnegligent manslaughter		Forcible rape		Robbery		Aggravated assault	
	Number of offenses known	Rate	Number of offenses known	Rate	Number of offenses known	Rate	Number of offenses known	Rate	Number of offenses known	Rate
TOTAL ALL AGENCIES	1,180,839	410.9	13,941	4.9	80,031	27.8	352,613	122.7	734,254	255.5
Total Cities	941,873	481.7	10,735	5.5	59,648	30.5	308,033	157.5	563,457	288.2
GROUP I (250,000 and over)	424,782	751.4	5,677	10.0	19,192	34.0	166,024	293.7	233,889	413.7
1,000,000 and over (Group I subset)	184,009	712.6	2,316	9.0	6,809	26.4	78,293	303.2	96,591	374.0
500,000 to 999,999 (Group I subset)	133,818	806.6	1,759	10.6	6,430	38.8	47,898	288.7	77,731	468.5
250,000 to 499,999 (Group I subset)	106,955	757.7	1,602	11.3	5,953	42.2	39,833	282.2	59,567	422.0
GROUP II (100,000 to 249,999)	153,984	519.6	1,691	5.7	9,799	33.1	50,371	170.0	92,123	310.8
GROUP III (50,000 to 99,999)	122,835	394.6	1,211	3.9	8,839	28.4	37,534	120.6	75,251	241.8
GROUP IV (25,000 to 49,999)	91,298	326.3	913	3.3	7,923	28.3	25,104	89.7	57,358	205.0
GROUP V (10,000 to 24,999)	80,752	285.4	711	2.5	7,223	25.5	18,593	65.7	54,225	191.7
GROUP VI (under 10,000)	68,222	310.6	532	2.4	6,672	30.4	10,407	47.4	50,611	230.5
Metropolitan Counties	187,381	284.1	2,357	3.6	14,322	21.7	40,447	61.3	130,255	197.5
Nonmetropolitan Counties[1]	51,585	199.3	849	3.3	6,061	23.4	4,133	16.0	40,542	156.6
SUBURBAN AREAS[2]	330,785	271.0	3,612	3.0	26,437	21.7	76,755	62.9	223,981	183.5

Population group	Property crime		Burglary		Larceny-theft		Motor vehicle theft		Number of agencies	2010 estimated population
	Number of offenses known	Rate	Number of offenses known	Rate	Number of offenses known	Rate	Number of offenses known	Rate		
TOTAL ALL AGENCIES:	8,544,651	2,973.3	2,025,747	704.9	5,814,440	2,023.3	704,464	245.1	14,442	287,379,482
Total Cities	6,673,837	3,413.3	1,479,919	756.9	4,634,938	2,370.5	558,980	285.9	10,348	195,526,478
GROUP I (250,000 and over)	2,166,752	3,833.0	502,925	889.7	1,403,073	2,482.0	260,754	461.3	74	56,529,440
1,000,000 and over (Group I subset)	810,287	3,137.7	172,991	669.9	535,650	2,074.2	101,646	393.6	10	25,823,829
500,000 to 999,999 (Group I subset)	761,275	4,588.7	178,963	1,078.7	493,219	2,972.9	89,093	537.0	24	16,590,299
250,000 to 499,999 (Group I subset)	595,190	4,216.6	150,971	1,069.6	374,204	2,651.1	70,015	496.0	40	14,115,312
GROUP II (100,000 to 249,999)	1,140,095	3,846.8	267,891	903.9	770,502	2,599.8	101,702	343.2	200	29,637,257
GROUP III (50,000 to 99,999)	1,001,762	3,218.5	221,656	712.1	702,145	2,255.9	77,961	250.5	456	31,125,270
GROUP IV (25,000 to 49,999)	848,255	3,031.6	179,255	640.6	619,623	2,214.5	49,377	176.5	810	27,980,645
GROUP V (10,000 to 24,999)	814,729	2,879.7	169,757	600.0	604,823	2,137.7	40,149	141.9	1,778	28,292,601
GROUP VI (under 10,000)	702,244	3,197.6	138,435	630.4	534,772	2,435.1	29,037	132.2	7,030	21,961,265
Metropolitan Counties	1,444,787	2,190.2	397,131	602.0	929,084	1,408.4	118,572	179.7	1,745	65,965,840
Nonmetropolitan Counties[1]	426,027	1,645.7	148,697	574.4	250,418	967.3	26,912	104.0	2,349	25,887,164
SUBURBAN AREAS[2]	2,958,589	2,423.8	692,827	567.6	2,062,795	1,689.9	202,967	166.3	7,732	122,065,067

[1] Includes state police agencies that report aggregately for the entire state.

[2] Suburban areas include law enforcement agencies in cities with less than 50,000 inhabitants and county law enforcement agencies that are within a Metropolitan Statistical Area. Suburban areas exclude all metropolitan agencies associated with a principal city. The agencies associated with suburban areas also appear in other groups within this table.

Table 17. Crime per 100,000 Population, by Suburban and Nonsuburban Cities, by Population Group, 2010[1]

(Number, rate)

Population group	Violent crime		Murder and nonnegligent manslaughter		Forcible rape		Robbery		Aggravated assault	
	Number of offenses known	Rate	Number of offenses known	Rate	Number of offenses known	Rate	Number of offenses known	Rate	Number of offenses known	Rate
TOTAL SUBURBAN CITIES:............................	143,420	255.7	1,255	2.2	12,131	21.6	36,308	64.7	93,726	167.1
GROUP IV (25,000 to 49,999)...............................	55,544	263.5	567	2.7	4,554	21.6	16,053	76.2	34,370	163.1
GROUP V (10,000 to 24,999)	51,200	239.3	440	2.1	4,307	20.1	13,256	62.0	33,197	155.2
GROUP VI (under 10,000)	36,676	269.2	248	1.8	3,270	24.0	6,999	51.4	26,159	192.0
TOTAL NONSUBURBAN CITIES:...................	96,852	437.5	901	4.1	9,687	43.8	17,796	80.4	68,468	309.3
GROUP IV (25,000 to 49,999)...............................	35,754	518.0	346	5.0	3,369	48.8	9,051	131.1	22,988	333.1
GROUP V (10,000 to 24,999)	29,552	428.5	271	3.9	2,916	42.3	5,337	77.4	21,028	304.9
GROUP VI (under 10,000)	31,546	378.4	284	3.4	3,402	40.8	3,408	40.9	24,452	293.3

Population group	Property crime		Burglary		Larceny-theft		Motor vehicle theft		Number of agencies	2010 estimated population
	Number of offenses known	Rate	Number of offenses known	Rate	Number of offenses known	Rate	Number of offenses known	Rate		
TOTAL SUBURBAN CITIES:............................	1,513,802	2,698.4	295,696	527.1	1,133,711	2,020.9	84,395	150.4	5,987	56,099,227
GROUP IV (25,000 to 49,999)...............................	551,851	2,618.1	111,615	529.5	403,868	1,916.0	36,368	172.5	615	21,078,672
GROUP V (10,000 to 24,999)	528,681	2,471.0	106,039	495.6	393,010	1,836.9	29,632	138.5	1,332	21,395,517
GROUP VI (under 10,000)	433,270	3,180.0	78,042	572.8	336,833	2,472.2	18,395	135.0	4,040	13,625,038
TOTAL NONSUBURBAN CITIES:...................	851,426	3,846.5	191,751	866.3	625,507	2,825.8	34,168	154.4	3,631	22,135,284
GROUP IV (25,000 to 49,999)...............................	296,404	4,294.5	67,640	980.0	215,755	3,126.0	13,009	188.5	195	6,901,973
GROUP V (10,000 to 24,999)	286,048	4,147.4	63,718	923.8	211,813	3,071.1	10,517	152.5	446	6,897,084
GROUP VI (under 10,000)	268,974	3,226.6	60,393	724.5	197,939	2,374.4	10,642	127.7	2,990	8,336,227

[1] Suburban cities include law enforcement agencies in cities with less than 50,000 inhabitants that are within a Metropolitan Statistical Area. Suburban cities exclude all metropolitan agencies associated with a principal city. Nonsuburban cities include law enforcement agencies in cities with less than 50,000 inhabitants that are not associated with a Metropolitan Statistical Area.

Table 18. Crime per 100,000 Population, by Metropolitan and Nonmetropolitan Counties, by Population Group, 2010[1]

(Number, rate)

Population group	Violent crime		Murder and nonnegligent manslaughter		Forcible rape		Robbery		Aggravated assault	
	Number of offenses known	Rate	Number of offenses known	Rate	Number of offenses known	Rate	Number of offenses known	Rate	Number of offenses known	Rate
METROPOLITAN COUNTIES										
100,000 and over	129,069	329.1	1,619	4.1	8,137	20.7	33,996	86.7	85,317	217.5
25,000 to 99,999	41,896	190.5	541	2.5	4,470	20.3	4,361	19.8	32,524	147.9
Under 25,000	16,416	344.9	197	4.1	1,715	36.0	2,090	43.9	12,414	260.8
NONMETROPOLITAN COUNTIES										
25,000 and over	21,753	197.3	354	3.2	2,332	21.2	2,176	19.7	16,891	153.2
10,000 to 24,999	15,339	168.8	226	2.5	1,691	18.6	968	10.7	12,454	137.0
Under 10,000	8,645	221.9	139	3.6	1,261	32.4	337	8.6	6,908	177.3

Population group	Property crime		Burglary		Larceny-theft		Motor vehicle theft		Number of agencies	2010 estimated population
	Number of offenses known	Rate	Number of offenses known	Rate	Number of offenses known	Rate	Number of offenses known	Rate		
METROPOLITAN COUNTIES										
100,000 and over	945,209	2,410.1	249,534	636.3	616,885	1,573.0	78,790	200.9	151	39,218,196
25,000 to 99,999	375,738	1,708.9	116,578	530.2	236,067	1,073.6	23,093	105.0	422	21,987,528
Under 25,000	123,840	2,601.6	31,019	651.6	76,132	1,599.4	16,689	350.6	1,172	4,760,116
NONMETROPOLITAN COUNTIES										
25,000 and over	188,856	1,712.9	67,432	611.6	110,120	998.8	11,304	102.5	280	11,025,413
10,000 to 24,999	129,670	1,426.7	45,702	502.8	76,310	839.6	7,658	84.3	568	9,088,802
Under 10,000	63,535	1,630.7	20,629	529.5	38,167	979.6	4,739	121.6	1,336	3,896,245

[1] Metropolitan counties include sheriffs and county law enforcement agencies associated with a Metropolitan Statistical Area. Nonmetropolitan counties include sheriffs and county law enforcement agencies that are not associated with a Metropolitan Statistical Area. The offenses from state police agencies are not included in this table.

Table 19.   Crime per 100,000 Population, Selected Known Offenses, by Population Group, 2010

(Number, rate)

Population group	Forcible rape		Robbery				Aggravated assault			
	Rape by force	Assault to rape-attempts	Firearm	Knife or cutting instrument	Other weapon	Strong-arm	Firearm	Knife or cutting instrument	Other weapon	Hands, fists, feet, etc.
TOTAL ALL AGENCIES										
Number of offenses known	69,896	5,298	127,521	24,204	26,978	129,606	137,857	127,509	221,620	183,457
Rate	26.3	2.0	47.9	9.1	10.1	48.7	51.8	47.9	83.3	69.0
Total Cities										
Number of offenses known	51,223	4,229	107,747	20,983	22,964	113,085	107,397	100,257	166,228	128,948
Rate	29.0	2.4	60.9	11.9	13.0	63.9	60.7	56.7	94.0	72.9
GROUP I (250,000 and over)										
Number of offenses known	15,410	1,675	57,349	9,430	9,628	51,807	53,307	37,102	65,515	30,442
Rate	34.7	3.8	129.0	21.2	21.7	116.5	119.9	83.4	147.3	68.5
1,000,000 and over (Group I subset)										
Number of offenses known	4,345	681	19,193	3,746	3,469	18,064	14,729	11,927	20,680	8,189
Rate	29.7	4.6	131.0	25.6	23.7	123.3	100.5	81.4	141.1	55.9
500,000 to 999,999 (Group I subset)										
Number of offenses known	5,669	496	20,611	3,186	3,505	17,260	20,794	14,705	26,153	10,587
Rate	35.5	3.1	129.2	20.0	22.0	108.2	130.4	92.2	164.0	66.4
250,000 to 499,999 (Group I subset)										
Number of offenses known	5,396	498	17,545	2,498	2,654	16,483	17,784	10,470	18,682	11,666
Rate	38.9	3.6	126.6	18.0	19.1	118.9	128.3	75.5	134.8	84.2
GROUP II (100,000 to 249,999)										
Number of offenses known	8,749	603	19,708	4,088	4,671	20,058	19,528	19,377	31,197	18,558
Rate	30.6	2.1	68.9	14.3	16.3	70.2	68.3	67.8	109.1	64.9
GROUP III (50,000 to 99,999)										
Number of offenses known	8,101	533	12,485	3,281	3,487	17,324	12,630	15,366	24,668	21,023
Rate	27.0	1.8	41.6	10.9	11.6	57.7	42.0	51.1	82.1	70.0
GROUP IV (25,000 to 49,999)										
Number of offenses known	6,820	422	8,388	1,863	2,393	10,934	8,662	10,857	16,986	16,722
Rate	26.1	1.6	32.0	7.1	9.1	41.8	33.1	41.5	64.9	63.9
GROUP V (10,000 to 24,999)										
Number of offenses known	6,306	411	6,341	1,474	1,825	8,123	7,424	9,621	15,926	18,990
Rate	23.8	1.5	23.9	5.6	6.9	30.6	28.0	36.2	60.0	71.5
GROUP VI (under 10,000)										
Number of offenses known	5,837	585	3,476	847	960	4,839	5,846	7,934	11,936	23,213
Rate	27.8	2.8	16.5	4.0	4.6	23.0	27.8	37.7	56.8	110.4
Metropolitan Counties										
Number of offenses known	13,059	733	18,068	2,858	3,514	14,983	23,368	21,331	44,111	39,091
Rate	20.4	1.1	28.3	4.5	5.5	23.4	36.5	33.4	69.0	61.1
Nonmetropolitan Counties										
Number of offenses known	5,614	336	1,706	363	500	1,538	7,092	5,921	11,281	15,418
Rate	22.2	1.3	6.8	1.4	2.0	6.1	28.1	23.5	44.7	61.1
SUBURBAN AREAS[1]										
Number of offenses known	23,518	1,457	30,254	5,573	6,816	31,093	35,231	37,050	70,686	73,526
Rate	20.2	1.3	26.0	4.8	5.9	26.7	30.3	31.8	60.7	63.2

[1] Suburban areas include law enforcement agencies in cities with less than 50,000 inhabitants and county law enforcement agencies that are within a Metropolitan Statistical Area. Suburban areas exclude all metropolitan agencies associated with a principal city. The agencies associated with suburban areas also appear in other groups within this table.

Table 19.   Crime per 100,000 Population, Selected Known Offenses, by Population Group, 2010—*Continued*

(Number, rate)

Population group	Burglary			Motor vehicle theft			Number of agencies	2010 estimated population
	Forcible entry	Unlawful entry	Attempted forcible entry	Autos	Trucks and buses	Other vehicles		
TOTAL ALL AGENCIES								
Number of offenses known	1,157,212	634,943	121,163	479,677	108,709	69,432	13,893	266,040,636
Rate	435.0	238.7	45.5	180.3	40.9	26.1		
Total Cities								
Number of offenses known	833,823	456,908	92,134	386,578	83,968	44,791	9,877	176,845,269
Rate	471.5	258.4	52.1	218.6	47.5	25.3		
GROUP I (250,000 and over)								
Number of offenses known	306,179	114,112	27,059	163,818	46,441	15,662	70	44,464,682
Rate	688.6	256.6	60.9	368.4	104.4	35.2		
1,000,000 and over (Group I subset)								
Number of offenses known	90,745	31,873	6,244	45,235	20,837	6,177	8	14,654,178
Rate	619.2	217.5	42.6	308.7	142.2	42.2		
500,000 to 999,999 (Group I subset)								
Number of offenses known	118,966	40,839	11,585	63,401	15,693	5,590	23	15,950,370
Rate	745.9	256.0	72.6	397.5	98.4	35.0		
250,000 to 499,999 (Group I subset)								
Number of offenses known	96,468	41,400	9,230	55,182	9,911	3,895	39	13,860,134
Rate	696.0	298.7	66.6	398.1	71.5	28.1		
GROUP II (100,000 to 249,999)								
Number of offenses known	152,344	85,738	18,024	75,282	15,678	8,172	193	28,585,285
Rate	532.9	299.9	63.1	263.4	54.8	28.6		
GROUP III (50,000 to 99,999)								
Number of offenses known	122,060	77,413	15,341	60,294	9,340	6,969	439	30,046,974
Rate	406.2	257.6	51.1	200.7	31.1	23.2		
GROUP IV (25,000 to 49,999)								
Number of offenses known	94,299	62,835	11,658	36,785	5,014	5,101	757	26,176,528
Rate	360.2	240.0	44.5	140.5	19.2	19.5		
GROUP V (10,000 to 24,999)								
Number of offenses known	88,104	62,519	10,906	29,426	4,360	4,756	1,670	26,541,488
Rate	331.9	235.6	41.1	110.9	16.4	17.9		
GROUP VI (under 10,000)								
Number of offenses known	70,837	54,291	9,146	20,973	3,135	4,131	6,748	21,030,312
Rate	336.8	258.2	43.5	99.7	14.9	19.6		
Metropolitan Counties								
Number of offenses known	235,173	126,586	22,647	76,922	20,556	18,422	1,713	63,953,300
Rate	367.7	197.9	35.4	120.3	32.1	28.8		
Nonmetropolitan Counties								
Number of offenses known	88,216	51,449	6,382	16,177	4,185	6,219	2,303	25,242,067
Rate	349.5	203.8	25.3	64.1	16.6	24.6		
SUBURBAN AREAS[1]								
Number of offenses known	386,615	235,492	43,320	139,080	29,736	27,480	7,379	116,412,187
Rate	332.1	202.3	37.2	119.5	25.5	23.6		

[1] Suburban areas include law enforcement agencies in cities with less than 50,000 inhabitants and county law enforcement agencies that are within a Metropolitan Statistical Area. Suburban areas exclude all metropolitan agencies associated with a principal city. The agencies associated with suburban areas also appear in other groups within this table.

Table 20.   Murder, by State and Type of Weapon, 2010

(Number)

State	Total murders[1]	Total firearms	Handguns	Rifles	Shotguns	Firearms (type unknown)	Knives or cutting instruments	Other weapons	Hands, fists, feet, etc.[2]
Alabama	199	135	112	0	23	0	23	24	17
Alaska	31	19	3	5	1	10	4	4	4
Arizona	352	232	152	14	10	56	51	62	7
Arkansas	130	93	49	7	4	33	12	21	4
California	1,811	1,257	953	59	44	201	250	201	103
Colorado	117	65	34	0	4	27	20	21	11
Connecticut	131	97	72	0	1	24	20	8	6
Delaware	48	38	25	0	2	11	8	0	2
District of Columbia	131	99	32	0	0	67	20	7	5
Georgia	527	376	315	19	21	21	64	85	2
Hawaii	24	7	6	0	0	1	6	5	6
Idaho	21	12	12	0	0	0	4	2	3
Illinois[3]	453	364	355	3	1	5	30	43	16
Indiana	198	142	83	11	7	41	19	25	12
Iowa	38	21	9	1	4	7	4	9	4
Kansas	100	63	30	4	1	28	13	18	6
Kentucky	180	116	76	6	16	18	19	25	20
Louisiana	437	351	263	19	11	58	42	31	13
Maine	24	11	4	2	1	4	6	1	6
Maryland	424	293	272	3	12	6	59	53	19
Massachusetts	209	118	52	0	1	65	50	31	10
Michigan	558	413	239	25	14	135	43	71	31
Minnesota	91	53	43	2	8	0	14	16	8
Mississippi	165	120	98	3	12	7	21	19	5
Missouri	419	321	189	26	4	102	35	49	14
Montana	21	12	6	2	4	0	3	5	1
Nebraska	51	32	29	1	2	0	8	5	6
Nevada	158	84	57	5	6	16	22	34	18
New Hampshire	13	5	2	0	2	1	5	3	0
New Jersey	363	246	216	7	2	21	50	39	28
New Mexico	118	67	36	6	2	23	29	15	7
New York	860	517	135	6	12	364	173	148	22
North Carolina	445	286	188	21	25	52	56	72	31
North Dakota	9	4	3	0	1	0	0	4	1
Ohio	460	310	176	7	2	125	40	93	17
Oklahoma	188	111	86	8	7	10	24	32	21
Oregon	78	36	20	1	2	13	16	17	9
Pennsylvania	646	457	367	8	11	71	67	94	28
Rhode Island	29	16	2	1	1	12	5	6	2
South Carolina	280	207	136	8	7	56	22	34	17
South Dakota	14	8	3	0	1	4	2	4	0
Tennessee	356	219	146	12	11	50	35	83	19
Texas	1,246	805	581	34	48	142	202	130	109
Utah	52	22	16	0	1	5	7	12	11
Vermont	7	2	1	1	0	0	1	2	2
Virginia	369	250	137	9	12	92	47	50	22
Washington	151	93	73	4	2	14	24	22	12
West Virginia	55	27	16	0	4	7	11	9	8
Wisconsin	151	97	63	5	6	23	13	22	19
Wyoming	8	5	0	2	0	3	1	1	1

[1] Total number of murders for which supplemental homicide data were received.
[2] Pushed is included in hands, fists, feet, etc.
[3] Limited supplemental homicide data were received.

Table 21. Robbery, by State and Type of Weapon, 2010

(Number)

State	Total robberies[1]	Firearms	Knives or cutting instruments	Other weapons	Strong-arm	Agency count	Population
Alabama	1,511	817	91	113	490	303	2,573,716
Alaska	584	153	53	55	323	35	694,439
Arizona	6,864	3,036	645	599	2,584	96	6,084,911
Arkansas	2,283	1,067	137	227	852	199	2,498,547
California	58,035	18,053	5,044	5,357	29,581	729	37,180,162
Colorado	3,068	1,119	308	383	1,258	171	4,579,863
Connecticut	3,483	1,164	377	297	1,645	99	3,431,851
Delaware	1,829	839	146	136	708	53	897,934
District of Columbia	3,914	1,563	246	209	1,896	1	601,723
Florida	26,071	11,105	1,730	2,206	11,030	663	18,791,299
Georgia	10,551	6,192	474	876	3,009	458	7,659,917
Hawaii	988	97	80	92	719	3	1,207,055
Idaho	213	61	26	25	101	102	1,466,441
Illinois[2]	495	240	20	60	175	1	156,180
Indiana	2,665	1,122	199	311	1,033	286	4,464,937
Iowa	995	274	95	104	522	188	2,719,028
Kansas	1,511	695	120	161	535	236	2,641,509
Kentucky	3,673	1,716	301	323	1,333	330	4,066,139
Louisiana	4,067	2,121	248	300	1,398	172	3,916,237
Maine	414	75	70	52	217	167	1,328,361
Maryland	6,809	3,266	552	342	2,649	153	4,166,837
Massachusetts	6,712	1,626	1,298	880	2,908	320	6,135,892
Michigan	11,238	5,523	524	909	4,282	515	9,294,572
Minnesota	3,088	1,011	234	399	1,444	305	4,764,748
Mississippi	2,278	1,422	97	190	569	121	2,040,999
Missouri	6,029	3,180	322	382	2,145	578	5,819,912
Montana	122	20	16	41	45	96	839,025
Nebraska	1,018	439	70	76	433	211	1,669,683
Nevada	4,844	1,722	450	427	2,245	40	2,460,734
New Hampshire	427	94	50	71	212	150	1,153,610
New Jersey	11,720	3,944	964	777	6,035	578	8,713,262
New Mexico	1,581	626	229	140	586	88	1,873,990
New York	8,770	2,540	1,004	970	4,256	533	10,706,971
North Carolina	8,540	4,419	551	769	2,801	308	8,077,998
North Dakota	89	12	5	10	62	87	633,347
Ohio	15,644	6,479	738	1,491	6,936	444	9,605,351
Oklahoma	3,293	1,503	268	262	1,260	302	3,610,830
Oregon	2,237	580	236	213	1,208	140	3,347,382
Pennsylvania	16,194	6,574	1,111	1,022	7,487	1,264	12,290,455
Rhode Island	780	198	78	106	398	49	1,052,567
South Carolina	4,780	2,656	313	388	1,423	407	4,393,517
South Dakota	147	18	24	27	78	107	696,093
Tennessee	8,309	4,682	598	711	2,318	457	6,136,858
Texas	32,809	16,280	2,716	2,745	11,068	1,020	25,077,044
Utah	1,262	349	173	132	608	119	2,705,776
Vermont	54	13	14	7	20	67	524,847
Virginia	5,651	2,955	365	552	1,779	354	7,951,616
Washington	5,906	1,446	537	583	3,340	254	6,684,514
West Virginia	235	66	32	34	103	127	830,296
Wisconsin	4,453	2,344	215	428	1,466	342	5,262,535
Wyoming	76	25	10	8	33	65	559,126

[1] The number of robberies from agencies that submitted 12 months of data in 2010 for which breakdowns by type of weapon were included.

[2] Limited data were received.

Table 22. Aggravated Assault, by State and Type of Weapon, 2010

(Number)

State	Total aggravated assaults[1]	Firearms	Knives or cutting instruments	Other weapons	Personal weapons	Agency count	Population
Alabama	5,700	1,529	912	1,273	1,986	303	2,573,716
Alaska	3,309	543	780	795	1,191	35	694,439
Arizona	15,337	3,618	2,604	4,577	4,538	96	6,084,911
Arkansas	10,044	2,548	1,522	2,163	3,811	199	2,498,547
California	95,678	16,937	15,178	33,074	30,489	729	37,180,162
Colorado	9,535	1,936	2,323	2,659	2,617	171	4,579,863
Connecticut	5,703	792	1,250	2,026	1,635	99	3,431,851
Delaware	3,376	824	763	1,400	389	53	897,934
District of Columbia	3,238	606	944	1,233	455	1	601,723
Florida	69,482	13,295	12,385	25,994	17,808	663	18,791,299
Georgia	20,287	5,160	3,580	5,553	5,994	458	7,659,917
Hawaii	1,953	170	421	642	720	3	1,207,055
Idaho	2,556	361	472	847	876	102	1,466,441
Illinois[2]	1,646	805	219	311	311	1	156,180
Indiana	5,496	514	662	1,171	3,149	286	4,464,937
Iowa	6,010	566	1,143	1,369	2,932	188	2,719,028
Kansas	7,354	2,016	1,545	2,274	1,519	236	2,641,509
Kentucky	5,056	1,060	869	1,976	1,151	330	4,066,139
Louisiana	14,895	3,501	2,409	3,742	5,243	172	3,916,237
Maine	794	48	157	235	354	167	1,328,361
Maryland	12,754	1,761	2,872	4,610	3,511	153	4,166,837
Massachusetts	20,904	2,043	4,770	10,749	3,342	320	6,135,892
Michigan	30,673	8,231	6,005	10,926	5,511	515	9,294,572
Minnesota	6,606	1,058	1,307	1,876	2,365	305	4,764,748
Mississippi	2,910	888	521	781	720	121	2,040,999
Missouri	18,676	5,368	2,407	4,750	6,151	578	5,819,912
Montana	1,781	278	256	532	715	96	839,025
Nebraska	3,230	531	505	1,378	816	211	1,669,683
Nevada	10,336	1,554	1,893	5,192	1,697	40	2,460,734
New Hampshire	1,220	202	401	328	289	150	1,153,610
New Jersey	13,764	2,101	3,113	4,320	4,230	578	8,713,262
New Mexico	8,578	1,669	1,474	2,779	2,656	88	1,873,990
New York	16,331	2,311	5,182	4,675	4,163	533	10,706,971
North Carolina	19,087	5,677	3,911	5,270	4,229	308	8,077,998
North Dakota	1,134	21	105	228	780	87	633,347
Ohio	14,061	3,511	2,687	4,463	3,400	444	9,605,351
Oklahoma	12,194	2,347	2,016	4,416	3,415	302	3,610,830
Oregon	5,499	614	1,033	1,894	1,958	140	3,347,382
Pennsylvania	25,145	4,984	3,841	6,324	9,996	1,264	12,290,455
Rhode Island	1,596	302	426	676	192	49	1,052,567
South Carolina	20,187	5,274	3,663	5,614	5,636	407	4,393,517
South Dakota	1,098	144	378	353	223	107	696,093
Tennessee	27,640	8,231	6,137	10,644	2,628	457	6,136,858
Texas	71,380	15,544	15,836	25,244	14,756	1,020	25,077,044
Utah	3,530	603	954	1,148	825	119	2,705,776
Vermont	439	49	84	72	234	67	524,847
Virginia	9,472	1,872	2,189	3,011	2,400	354	7,951,616
Washington	12,248	1,678	2,180	3,824	4,566	254	6,684,514
West Virginia	1,712	339	269	402	702	127	830,296
Wisconsin	7,962	1,764	800	1,564	3,834	342	5,262,535
Wyoming	847	79	156	263	349	65	559,126

[1] The number of aggravated assaults from agencies that submitted 12 months of data in 2010 for which breakdowns by type of weapon were included.

[2] Limited data were received.

Table 23.   Offense Analysis, Number and Percent Change, 2009–2010

(Number, percent, dollars; 14,153 agencies; 2010 estimated population 270,682,616)

Classification	Number of offenses 2010	Percent change from 2009	Percent distribution[1]	Average value (dollars)
Murder..	12,990	-4.2	...	
Forcible rape...	72,117	-4.5	...	
Robbery..	300,274	-10.6	100.0	1,239
By location				
Street/highway..	129,605	-9.6	43.2	908
Commercial house...	39,705	-13.4	13.2	1,858
Gas or service station...	6,955	-14.6	2.3	939
Convenience store...	15,687	-14.3	5.2	782
Residence...	51,888	-8.8	17.3	1,491
Bank..	6,536	-8.8	2.2	4,410
Miscellaneous..	49,898	-11.0	16.6	1,115
Burglary..	1,897,963	-2.0	100.0	2,119
By location				
Residence (dwelling):	1,402,214	-0.2	73.9	2,137
Residence Night...	389,910	-0.8	20.5	1,868
Residence Day...	722,231	+0.2	38.1	2,158
Residence Unknown..	290,073	-0.5	15.3	2,445
Nonresidence (store, office, etc.):	495,749	-6.6	26.1	2,070
Nonresidence Night..	204,605	-8.8	10.8	1,765
Nonresidence Day...	168,912	-4.7	8.9	2,010
Nonresidence Unknown..	122,232	-5.5	6.4	2,662
Larceny-theft (except motor vehicle theft)	5,391,580	-2.6	100.0	988
By type				
Pocket-picking	21,056	-8.3	0.4	526
Purse-snatching..	24,450	-7.1	0.5	400
Shoplifting...	925,107	-7.1	17.2	174
From motor vehicles (except accessories)...............................	1,423,947	-5.6	26.4	704
Motor vehicle accessories..	477,848	-5.5	8.9	681
Bicycles..	179,595	-1.7	3.3	351
From buildings..	607,927	-0.4	11.3	1,406
From coin-operated machines	17,648	-20.8	0.3	365
All others...	1,714,002	+3.2	31.8	1,654
By value				
Over $200	2,443,142	-0.9	45.3	2,089
$50 to $200..	1,235,096	-1.8	22.9	111
Under $50..	1,713,342	-5.5	31.8	17
Motor vehicle theft..	641,874	-8.4	...	6,152

[1] Because of rounding, the percentages may not add to 100.0.

Table 24.   Property Stolen and Recovered, by Type and Value, 2010

(Dollars, percent; 13,573 agencies; 2010 estimated population 261,890,722)

Type of property	Value of property		Percent recovered
	Stolen	Recovered	
Total	13,270,998,162	2,788,437,110	21.0
Currency, notes, etc.	1,154,196,924	37,392,343	3.2
Jewelry and precious metals.................................	1,556,364,665	65,166,103	4.2
Clothing and furs...	278,993,083	32,002,758	11.5
Locally stolen motor vehicles	3,970,565,871	2,225,549,279	56.1
Office equipment...	726,685,261	37,042,533	5.1
Televisions, radios, stereos, etc.	955,054,564	39,812,451	4.2
Firearms...	143,477,530	12,027,921	8.4
Household goods..	330,123,170	11,031,184	3.3
Consumable goods...	225,549,642	15,845,262	7.0
Livestock	19,093,096	2,448,651	12.8
Miscellaneous	3,910,894,356	310,118,625	7.9

SECTION III:
OFFENSES CLEARED

OFFENSES CLEARED

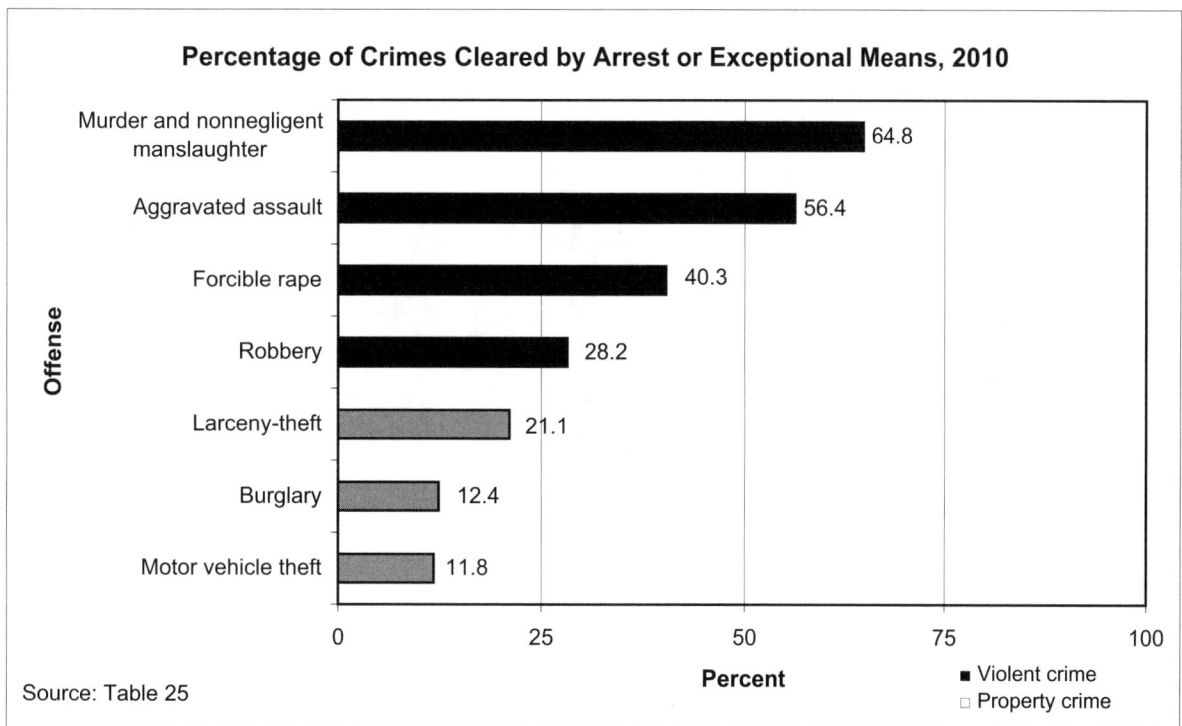

Percentage of Crimes Cleared by Arrest or Exceptional Means, 2010

Offense	Percent
Murder and nonnegligent manslaughter	64.8
Aggravated assault	56.4
Forcible rape	40.3
Robbery	28.2
Larceny-theft	21.1
Burglary	12.4
Motor vehicle theft	11.8

Source: Table 25

■ Violent crime
□ Property crime

Law enforcement agencies that report crime to the Federal Bureau of Investigation (FBI) can clear, or "close," offenses in one of two ways: by arrest or by exceptional means. However, the administrative closing of a case by a local law enforcement agency does not necessarily mean that the agency can clear an offense for UCR purposes. To clear an offense within the program's guidelines, the reporting agency must adhere to certain criteria, which are outlined in this section. (*Note:* The UCR Program does not distinguish between offenses cleared by arrest and those cleared by exceptional means in its data presentations. The distinction is made solely for the purpose of a definition and not for data collection and publication.) See Appendix I for information on the UCR Program's statistical methodology.

Cleared by Arrest

In the UCR Program, a law enforcement agency reports that an offense is cleared by arrest, or solved for crime reporting purposes, when at least one person is arrested, charged with the commission of the offense, and turned over to the court for prosecution (whether following arrest, court summons, or police notice). To qualify as a clearance, *all* of these conditions must be met.

In its calculations, the UCR Program counts the number of offenses that are cleared, not the number of arrestees. Therefore, the arrest of one person may clear several crimes, and the arrest of many persons may clear only one offense. In addition, some clearances recorded by an agency during a particular calendar year, such as 2010, may pertain to offenses that occurred in previous years.

Cleared by Exceptional Means

In certain situations, elements beyond law enforcement's control prevent the agency from arresting and formally charging the offender. When this occurs, the agency can clear the offense *exceptionally*. There are four UCR Program requirements that law enforcement must meet in order to clear an offense by exceptional means. The agency must have:

• Identified the offender

• Gathered enough evidence to support an arrest, make a charge, and turn over the offender to the court for prosecution

• Identified the offender's exact location so that the suspect could be taken into custody immediately

• Encountered a circumstance outside the control of law enforcement that prohibits the agency from arresting, charging, and prosecuting the offender

Examples of exceptional clearances include, but are not limited to, the death of the offender (e.g., suicide or justifiably killed by a law enforcement officer or a citizen), the victim's refusal to cooperate with the prosecution after the offender has been identified, or the denial of extradition because the offender committed a crime in another jurisdiction and is being prosecuted for that offense. In the UCR Program, the recovery of property does not clear an offense.

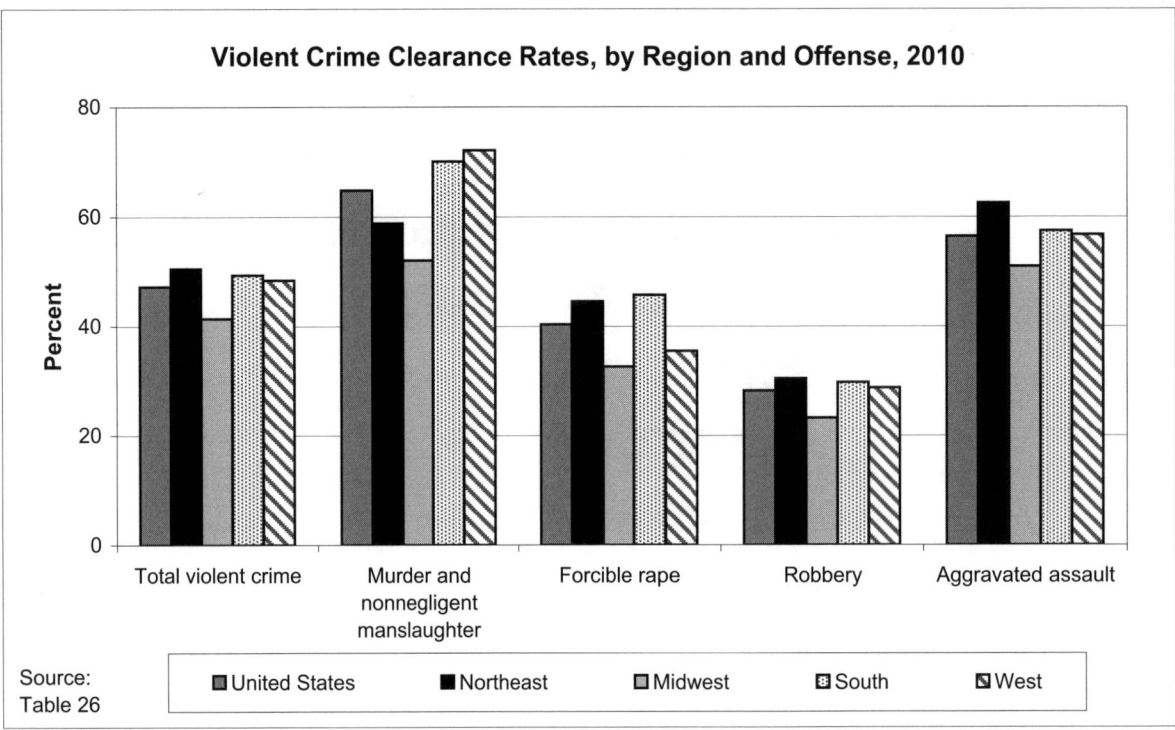

Violent Crime Clearance Rates, by Region and Offense, 2010

Source: Table 26

Legend: ■ United States   ■ Northeast   ▦ Midwest   ▧ South   ▨ West

National Clearances

A review of the data for 2010 revealed law enforcement agencies in the United States cleared 47.2 percent of violent crimes (murder, forcible rape, robbery, and aggravated assault) and 18.3 percent of property crimes (burglary, larceny-theft, and motor vehicle theft) brought to their attention. In addition, law enforcement cleared 19.0 percent of arson offenses, which are reported in a slightly different manner than the other property crimes. (Table 26) (More details concerning this offense are furnished in the arson text in this section.)

As in most years, law enforcement agencies cleared a higher percentage of violent crimes than property crimes in 2010. As a rule, this long-term trend is attributed to the more vigorous investigative efforts put forth for violent crimes. In addition, violent crimes more often involve victims and/or witnesses who are able to identify the perpetrators.

A breakdown of the clearances for violent crimes for 2010 revealed that the nation's law enforcement agencies cleared 64.8 percent of murder offenses, 56.4 percent of aggravated assault offenses, 40.3 percent of forcible rape offenses, and 28.2 percent of robbery offenses. (Table 25)

For property crime offenses, law enforcement agencies throughout the nation collectively cleared 18.3 percent of all offenses in 2010, including 12.4 percent of burglary offenses, 21.1 percent of larceny-theft offenses, 11.8 percent of motor vehicle theft offenses, and 19.0 percent of arson offenses. (Table 25)

Regional Clearances

The UCR Program divides the nation into four regions: the Northeast, the Midwest, the South, and the West. (See

Appendix III for further details.) A review of clearance data for 2010 by region showed that agencies in the Northeast cleared the greatest proportion of their violent crime offenses (50.5 percent). Law enforcement agencies in the South cleared 49.3 percent of their violent crimes, while agencies in the West and Midwest cleared 45.4 percent and 41.4 percent, respectively. (Table 26)

For murder and nonnegligent manslaughter, the South cleared 70.1 percent of offenses, followed by the West (66.3 percent), the Northeast (58.8 percent), and the Midwest (52.0 percent each). Forcible rape offenses were cleared 45.7 percent of the time in the South, 44.5 percent of the time in the Northeast, 36.1 percent in the West, and 32.6 percent in the Midwest. For robbery, the Northeast had the highest clearance rate, at 30.4 percent. The Northeast also had the highest proportion of clearances for aggravated assault (62.5 percent). (Table 26)

Clearance data for 2010 showed that, among the regions, law enforcement agencies in the Northeast cleared the highest percentage of their property crimes (21.1 percent). Agencies in the South and Midwest cleared 18.7 percent and 17.9 percent, respectively. Agencies in the West cleared 16.3 percent of their property crimes. (Table 26) Agencies in the Northeast cleared the highest percentage of burglary offenses at 15.0 percent, followed by the South at 13.0 percent, the West at 11.7 percent, and the Midwest at 10.2 percent. For larceny-theft, the Northeast (23.4 percent) was followed by the Midwest and the South, both at 21.3 percent, and then the West (19.4 percent). The Northeast also cleared the highest proportion of motor vehicle thefts at 14.8 percent, followed closely by the South, which cleared 14.5 percent. The South cleared the greatest percentage of arson offenses (24.4 percent), followed closely by the Northeast (23.8 percent). (Table 26)

Clearances by Population Groups

The UCR Program uses the following population group designations in its data presentations: cities (grouped according to population size) and counties (classified as either metropolitan or nonmetropolitan counties). (A breakdown of these classifications is furnished in Appendix III.)

Cities

In 2010, the clearance data collected showed that law enforcement agencies in the nation's cities cleared 45.3 percent of their violent crime offenses. Among the city population groups, agencies in the smallest cities, those with fewer than 10,000 inhabitants, cleared the greatest proportion of their violent crime offenses (53.9 percent), and law enforcement in cities with 1,000,000 and more inhabitants cleared the smallest proportion of their violent crime offenses (39.2 percent). (Table 25)

The clearance data for murder showed that among the city population groups, cities with populations of 10,000 to 24,999 inhabitants cleared the greatest percentage of their murders (72.3 percent). Law enforcement agencies in cities with 500,000 to 999,999 inhabitants cleared the lowest percentage of their murders (56.7 percent). For forcible rape, cities with 1,000,000 or more inhabitants cleared the largest percentage of offenses at 44.1 percent, while cities with 25,000 to 49,999 inhabitants cleared the lowest percentage of offenses at 34.9 percent. Cities with 10,000 to 24,999 inhabitants cleared the greatest percentage of their robbery offenses at 36.9 percent, and cities with 500,000 to 999,999 inhabitants cleared the lowest proportion of their robbery offenses at 23.6 percent. For aggravated assault, cities with fewer than 10,000 inhabitants cleared the highest proportion of offenses (63.0 percent); cities with 500,000 to 999,999 inhabitants cleared the lowest percentage of offenses (48.8 percent). (Table 25)

In 2010, agencies in the nation's cities collectively cleared 18.3 percent of their property crime offenses. Law enforcement in cities with 10,000 to 24,999 inhabitants cleared the highest proportion of the property crimes brought to their attention (23.0 percent); cities with 500,000 to 999,999 or more inhabitants cleared the smallest proportion of their property crimes (12.8 percent). (Table 25)

Law enforcement agencies in cities cleared 12.4 percent of burglaries, 21.1 percent of larceny-thefts, 11.8 percent of motor vehicle thefts, and 19.0 percent of arsons in 2010. (Table 25) For burglaries, cities with fewer than 10,000 inhabitants cleared the largest percentage of their offenses, at 16.5 percent, while cities with 1,000,000 or more inhabitants cleared the smallest percentage of their offenses, at 7.6 percent. Cities with 10,000 to 24,999 inhabitants cleared the greatest percentage of their larceny-theft offenses (25.6 percent), and cities with 500,000 to 999,999 inhabitants cleared the lowest proportion of larceny-theft offenses (15.3 percent). For motor vehicle theft, cities with fewer than 10,000 inhabitants cleared the highest percentages of their offenses, at 22.8 percent. (Table 25) Cities with 10,000 to 24,999 inhabitants cleared the great-

est percentage of their arson offenses, at 25.1 percent. (Table 25)

Metropolitan and Nonmetropolitan Counties

In 2010, law enforcement agencies in metropolitan counties cleared 52.1 percent of their violent crime offenses. Of the violent crimes made known to law enforcement agencies in metropolitan counties, murder offenses had the highest proportion of clearance (64.7 percent), followed by aggravated assaults (59.3 percent), forcible rapes (44.7 percent), and robberies (30.8 percent). Law enforcement agencies in metropolitan counties cleared 17.7 percent of their total property crimes, 13.2 percent of burglaries, 19.9 percent of larceny-thefts, 14.5 percent of motor vehicle thefts, and 18.7 percent of their arsons. (Table 25)

Like their counterparts in metropolitan counties, nonmetropolitan counties collectively cleared a greater proportion of their violent crimes than did the nation as a whole in 2010. Nonmetropolitan counties cleared 61.1 percent of their violent crime offenses and 18.2 percent of property crimes. Of the violent crimes known to them, law enforcement in nonmetropolitan counties had the highest number of clearances for murder (75.0 percent), with 46.3 percent of forcible rapes, 43.6 percent of robberies, and 64.8 percent of aggravated assaults being cleared. Agencies in nonmetropolitan counties reported clearing 15.4 percent of their burglaries, 19.3 percent of their larceny-thefts, 23.2 percent of their motor vehicle thefts, and 24.3 percent of their arsons. (Table 25)

Clearances by Classification Group and Type

For forcible rape, by classification group and type, law enforcement agencies cleared 41.6 percent of assault to rape attempts and 39.2 percent of rapes by force in 2010. Cleared robbery offenses included 31.8 percent of offenses involving strong-arm tactics, 29.9 percent of offenses involving knives or other cutting instruments, 28.8 percent of offenses involving other weapons, and 22.3 percent of offenses involving firearms. For aggravated assaults, agencies cleared 63.4 percent of offenses involving knives or other cutting instruments; 61.2 percent of offenses involving hands, feet, fists, and so on; 56.9 percent of offenses involving other weapons; and 41.1 percent of offenses involving firearms. (Table 27)

For property crime clearances grouped by classification and type, data showed that the highest percentage of burglary clearances in the nation in 2010 (13.6 percent) were of offenses that involved unlawful entry of structures. Law enforcement agencies cleared 11.4 percent of burglaries involving forcible entry and 10.8 percent of attempted forcible entry offenses. For motor vehicle theft, agencies cleared 12.1 percent of motor vehicle theft offenses involving automobiles and 9.1 percent of motor vehicle theft offenses involving trucks and buses. (Table 27)

In 2010, 21.8 percent of structural arson offenses were cleared by arrest or exceptional means, while 9.4 percent of mobile arson offenses and 21.8 percent of other arson crimes were cleared. (Table 27)

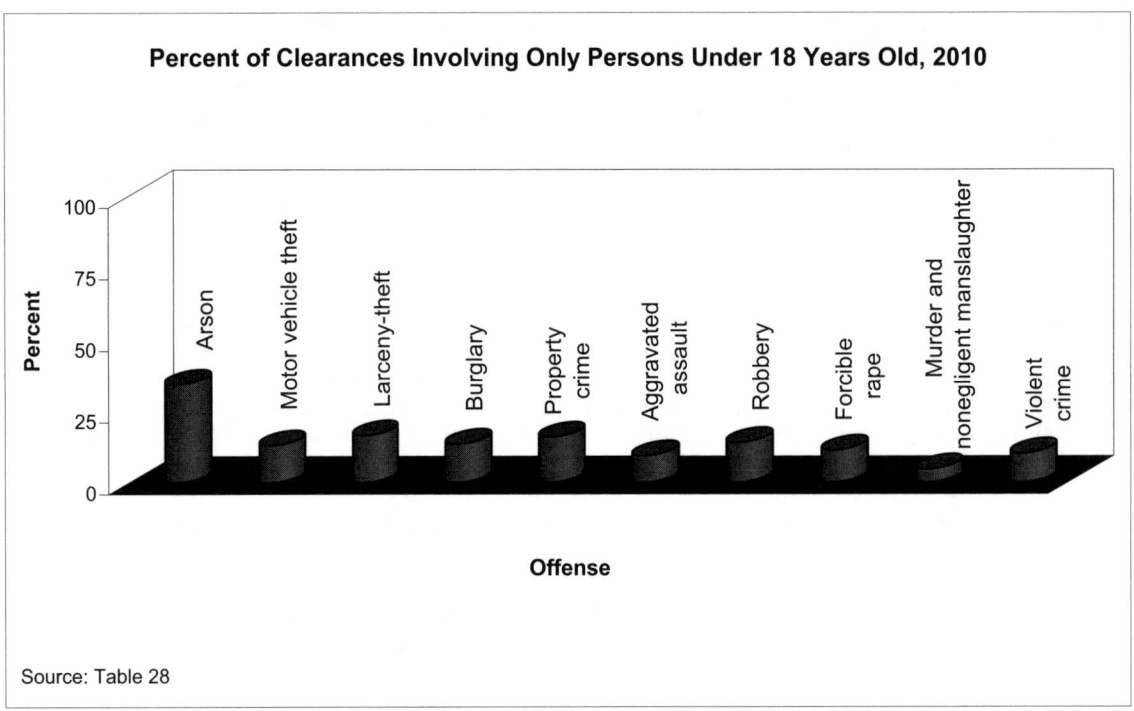

Percent of Clearances Involving Only Persons Under 18 Years Old, 2010

Source: Table 28

Clearances and Juveniles

When an offender under 18 years of age is cited to appear in juvenile court or before other juvenile authorities, the UCR Program considers the incident for which the juvenile is being held responsible to be cleared by arrest, although a physical arrest may not have occurred. In addition, according to program definitions, clearances that include both adult and juvenile offenders are classified as clearances for crimes committed by adults. Therefore, the juvenile clearance data are limited to those clearances involving juveniles only, and the figures in this publication should not be used to present a definitive picture of juvenile involvement in crime.

Of the clearances for violent crimes that were reported in the nation in 2010, 10.2 percent involved only juveniles, down from 11.0 percent in 2009. In the nation's cities, collectively, 10.4 percent of violent crime clearances involved only juveniles, with juveniles in cities exclusively involved in 4.6 percent of murder clearances, 10.6 percent of forcible rape clearances, 14.3 percent of robbery clearances, and 9.5 percent of aggravated assault clearances. Of the nation's city population groups, cities with fewer than 10,000 inhabitants had the highest percentage of overall clearances for violent crime only involving juveniles (11.8 percent); cities with 1,000,000 or more inhabitants had the lowest percentage (7.9 percent). (Table 28)

Law enforcement agencies in metropolitan counties reported that 10.4 percent of their violent crime clearances—including 5.1 percent of their murder clearances, 13.3 percent of their forcible rape clearances, 13.6 percent of their robbery clearances, and 9.8 percent of their aggravated assault clearances—involved only juveniles. Agencies in nonmetropolitan counties reported that 7.3 percent of their clearances for violent crime involved only juveniles,

including 4.1 percent of their murder clearances, 14.0 percent of their forcible rape clearances, 6.2 percent of their robbery clearances, and 10.7 percent of their aggravated assault clearances. (Table 28)

In 2010, 15.9 percent of clearances for property crime involved only juveniles. In cities collectively, 16.5 percent of the clearances for property crime, 14.3 percent of clearances for burglary, 17.1 percent of clearances for larceny-theft, 13.3 percent of clearances for motor vehicle theft, and 37.3 percent of clearances for arson involved juveniles only. Among the population groups labeled *city*, the percentages of clearances involving only juveniles for overall property crime ranged from a low of 13.8 percent in cities with fewer than 10,000 inhabitants to a high of 19.2 percent in cities with populations of 100,000 to 249,999.

Metropolitan counties reported 14.3 percent of property crime clearances, 12.6 percent of burglary clearances, 14.9 percent of larceny-theft clearances, 12.6 percent of motor vehicle theft clearances, and 28.4 percent of arson clearances involved persons under 18 years of age. In nonmetropolitan counties, 10.6 percent of property crime clearances, 9.5 percent of burglary clearances, 11.1 percent of larceny-theft clearances, 11.5 percent of motor vehicle theft clearances, and 20.6 percent of arson clearances involved juveniles exclusively. In suburban areas, 35.9 percent of arson clearances involved only juveniles. (Table 28)

Arson offenses had the highest percentage of clearances involving only juveniles—34.3 percent—nationally in 2010. (Table 28) Of clearances for structural arsons, 32.5 percent involved only juveniles. Approximately 10.8 percent of clearances for mobile arsons and 45.1 percent of other property type arsons involved only juveniles. (Expanded Arson Table 2; see Section I for more information)

Table 25. Number and Percent of Offenses Cleared by Arrest or Exceptional Means, by Population Group, 2010

(Number, percent)

Population group	Violent crime	Murder and non-negligent man-slaughter	Forcible rape	Robbery	Aggra-vated assault	Property crime	Burglary	Larceny-theft	Motor vehicle theft	Arson[1]	Number of agencies	2010 estimated population
TOTAL ALL AGENCIES												
Offenses known	1,080,242	12,760	73,934	315,115	678,433	8,064,964	1,936,341	5,466,667	661,956	50,567	14,565	271,571,110
Percent cleared by arrest	47.2	64.8	40.3	28.2	56.4	18.3	12.4	21.1	11.8	19.0		
Total Cities												
Offenses known	845,386	9,579	54,586	270,811	510,410	6,229,128	1,401,687	4,309,372	518,069	37,375	10,457	180,504,683
Percent cleared by arrest	45.3	63.9	38.6	27.6	55.1	18.4	11.9	21.5	10.6	18.6		
GROUP I (250,000 and over)												
Offenses known	347,014	4,728	17,236	132,178	192,872	1,861,697	456,470	1,177,739	227,488	13,529	71	44,953,427
Percent cleared by arrest	39.9	61.1	41.3	24.5	49.8	13.8	9.3	16.8	7.5	14.4		
1,000,000 and over (Group I subset)												
Offenses known	106,371	1,348	5,026	44,472	55,525	550,627	128,862	349,516	72,249	3,890	8	14,654,178
Percent cleared by arrest	39.2	69.3	44.1	24.6	49.7	13.1	7.6	16.6	5.7	13.0		
500,000 to 999,999 (Group I subset)												
Offenses known	135,800	1,794	6,440	48,538	79,028	736,004	179,520	469,207	87,277	4,942	24	16,465,103
Percent cleared by arrest	39.5	56.7	40.6	23.6	48.8	12.8	8.9	15.3	7.7	14.4		
250,000 to 499,999 (Group I subset)												
Offenses known	104,843	1,586	5,770	39,168	58,319	575,066	148,088	359,016	67,962	4,697	39	13,834,146
Percent cleared by arrest	41.0	59.0	39.8	25.3	51.1	15.7	11.2	18.9	9.0	15.6		
GROUP II (100,000 to 249,999)												
Offenses known	151,801	1,683	9,505	49,851	90,762	1,115,390	263,754	751,059	100,577	6,254	196	29,191,226
Percent cleared by arrest	44.3	62.5	36.6	27.6	54.0	17.6	11.0	20.9	10.0	16.6		
GROUP III (50,000 to 99,999)												
Offenses known	122,519	1,219	8,595	37,337	75,368	997,549	219,527	700,032	77,990	5,908	451	30,903,160
Percent cleared by arrest	47.6	67.8	37.1	30.1	57.2	20.0	12.6	23.4	11.2	19.2		
GROUP IV (25,000 to 49,999)												
Offenses known	84,032	836	6,996	23,350	52,850	797,465	167,143	584,108	46,214	4,114	766	26,508,712
Percent cleared by arrest	49.9	66.4	34.9	32.0	59.5	21.3	12.8	24.3	13.7	22.4		
GROUP V (10,000 to 24,999)												
Offenses known	77,050	685	6,592	17,796	51,977	777,824	162,578	576,615	38,631	3,784	1,685	26,752,794
Percent cleared by arrest	53.9	72.3	38.3	36.0	61.8	23.0	15.0	25.6	17.6	25.1		
GROUP VI (under 10,000)												
Offenses known	62,970	428	5,662	10,299	46,581	679,203	132,215	519,819	27,169	3,786	7,288	22,195,364
Percent cleared by arrest	56.5	70.8	40.9	35.1	63.0	21.7	16.5	22.9	22.8	24.7		
Metropolitan Counties												
Offenses known	185,397	2,337	13,815	40,210	129,035	1,426,858	390,869	918,318	117,671	9,817	1,761	65,773,804
Percent cleared by arrest	52.1	64.7	44.7	30.7	59.3	17.7	13.2	19.9	14.5	18.7		
Nonmetropolitan Counties												
Offenses known	49,459	844	5,533	4,094	38,988	408,978	143,785	238,977	26,216	3,375	2,347	25,292,623
Percent cleared by arrest	61.1	75.0	46.3	43.6	64.8	18.2	15.4	19.3	23.2	24.3		
SUBURBAN AREAS[2]												
Offenses known	320,825	3,509	24,740	74,711	217,865	2,864,008	673,000	1,993,229	197,779	16,926	7,746	119,065,296
Percent cleared by arrest	52.6	65.5	41.7	32.0	60.6	19.6	13.7	22.0	14.8	20.9		

[1] Not all agencies submit reports for arson to the FBI. As a result, the number of reports the FBI uses to compute the percent of offenses cleared for arson is less than the number it uses to compute the percent of offenses cleared for all other offenses.

[2] Suburban areas include law enforcement agencies in cities with less than 50,000 inhabitants and county law enforcement agencies that are within a Metropolitan Statistical Area. Suburban areas exclude all metropolitan agencies associated with a principal city. The agencies associated with suburban areas also appear in other groups within this table.

Table 26. Number and Percent of Offenses Cleared by Arrest or Exceptional Means, by Region and Geographic Division, 2010

(Number, percent)

Geographic region/division	Violent crime	Murder and non-negligent man-slaughter	Forcible rape	Robbery	Aggra-vated assault	Property crime	Burglary	Larceny-theft	Motor vehicle theft	Arson[1]	Number of agencies	2010 estimated population
TOTAL ALL AGENCIES												
Offenses known	1,080,242	12,760	73,934	315,115	678,433	8,064,964	1,936,341	5,466,667	661,956	50,567	14,565	271,571,110
Percent cleared by arrest	47.2	64.8	40.3	28.2	56.4	18.3	12.4	21.1	11.8	19.0		
Northeast												
Offenses known	144,316	1,738	9,307	48,353	84,918	986,715	208,150	714,652	63,913	5,945	3,241	44,904,941
Percent cleared by arrest	50.5	58.8	44.5	30.4	62.5	21.1	15.0	23.4	14.8	23.8		
New England												
Offenses known	46,824	410	3,452	11,974	30,988	324,804	72,690	229,547	22,567	1,893	886	13,984,258
Percent cleared by arrest	50.0	49.8	33.9	27.5	60.4	16.4	12.5	18.2	10.8	21.9		
Middle Atlantic												
Offenses known	97,492	1,328	5,855	36,379	53,930	661,911	135,460	485,105	41,346	4,052	2,355	30,920,683
Percent cleared by arrest	50.8	61.6	50.7	31.3	63.7	23.4	16.4	25.9	17.0	24.7		
Midwest												
Offenses known	171,142	2,059	15,098	48,606	105,379	1,404,806	338,207	966,971	99,628	11,425	3,598	49,299,959
Percent cleared by arrest	41.4	52.0	32.6	23.2	50.9	17.9	10.2	21.3	11.8	15.7		
East North Central												
Offenses known	109,773	1,350	10,228	36,059	62,136	862,236	226,863	572,242	63,131	7,731	1,714	29,721,234
Percent cleared by arrest	35.5	46.0	30.1	21.5	44.3	16.2	9.5	19.5	10.2	14.0		
West North Central												
Offenses known	61,369	709	4,870	12,547	43,243	542,570	111,344	394,729	36,497	3,694	1,884	19,578,725
Percent cleared by arrest	52.0	63.5	38.0	28.3	60.3	20.7	11.8	23.8	14.6	19.4		
South												
Offenses known	488,421	6,062	29,871	133,437	319,051	3,708,735	947,810	2,503,874	257,051	19,093	5,774	108,009,812
Percent cleared by arrest	49.3	70.1	45.7	29.7	57.4	18.7	13.0	21.3	14.5	21.1		
South Atlantic												
Offenses known	258,388	3,202	13,692	73,379	168,115	1,878,157	474,079	1,270,844	133,234	8,881	2,826	56,470,869
Percent cleared by arrest	51.8	69.6	50.8	31.7	60.3	20.5	15.2	22.9	15.7	24.4		
East South Central												
Offenses known	68,235	867	5,082	17,585	44,701	535,921	146,705	356,234	32,982	2,737	1,267	16,808,518
Percent cleared by arrest	45.2	66.7	40.3	26.5	52.7	18.5	12.1	21.4	15.9	20.4		
West South Central												
Offenses known	161,798	1,993	11,097	42,473	106,235	1,294,657	327,026	876,796	90,835	7,475	1,681	34,730,425
Percent cleared by arrest	46.9	72.3	41.8	27.6	54.7	16.3	10.1	19.0	12.3	17.4		
West												
Offenses known	276,363	2,901	19,658	84,719	169,085	1,964,708	442,174	1,281,170	241,364	14,104	1,952	69,356,398
Percent cleared by arrest	45.4	66.3	36.1	27.5	55.0	16.3	11.7	19.4	8.2	16.7		
Mountain												
Offenses known	78,522	831	7,275	18,028	52,388	611,125	138,485	418,592	54,048	3,792	802	21,211,428
Percent cleared by arrest	48.4	72.1	35.5	28.7	56.7	19.0	10.5	22.9	10.3	21.1		
Pacific												
Offenses known	197,841	2,070	12,383	66,691	116,697	1,353,583	303,689	862,578	187,316	10,312	1,150	48,144,970
Percent cleared by arrest	44.1	64.0	36.5	27.2	54.3	15.1	12.3	17.7	7.6	15.0		

[1] Not all agencies submit reports for arson to the FBI. As a result, the number of reports the FBI uses to compute the percent of offenses cleared for arson is less than the number it uses to compute the percent of offenses cleared for all other offenses.

Table 27.   Number and Percent of Offenses Cleared by Arrest or Exceptional Means, by Population Group, 2010

(Number, percent)

Population group	Forcible rape		Robbery				Aggravated assault			
	Rape by force	Assault to rape-attempts	Firearm	Knife or cutting instrument	Other weapon	Strong-arm	Firearm	Knife or cutting instrument	Other weapon	Hands, fists, feet, etc.
TOTAL ALL AGENCIES										
Offenses known	63,267	4,791	117,447	22,567	24,848	118,886	124,968	115,129	196,668	164,724
Percent cleared by arrest	39.2	41.6	22.3	29.9	29.8	31.8	41.1	63.6	56.7	61.2
Total Cities										
Offenses known	47,387	3,871	101,234	19,895	21,589	105,514	99,956	92,856	153,464	118,483
Percent cleared by arrest	37.7	41.6	22.2	29.1	29.3	31.1	38.5	62.8	55.5	60.8
GROUP I (250,000 and over)										
Offenses known	14,859	1,644	55,521	9,130	9,330	49,975	51,155	35,482	63,816	28,261
Percent cleared by arrest	40.5	42.4	19.8	25.4	25.5	27.8	34.4	61.1	52.0	53.7
1,000,000 and over (Group I subset)										
Offenses known	4,345	681	19,193	3,746	3,469	18,064	14,729	11,927	20,680	8,189
Percent cleared by arrest	43.7	46.7	19.6	24.7	26.7	29.5	35.5	61.8	52.2	51.3
500,000 to 999,999 (Group I subset)										
Offenses known	5,360	499	20,174	3,117	3,372	16,846	19,701	14,157	25,900	10,398
Percent cleared by arrest	39.5	35.3	18.6	25.3	24.5	25.1	34.8	58.5	49.4	50.8
250,000 to 499,999 (Group I subset)										
Offenses known	5,154	464	16,154	2,267	2,489	15,065	16,725	9,398	17,236	9,674
Percent cleared by arrest	38.8	43.8	21.5	26.8	25.2	28.6	32.9	64.2	55.5	58.7
GROUP II (100,000 to 249,999)										
Offenses known	7,944	543	17,865	3,777	4,360	18,013	17,542	17,246	27,366	16,851
Percent cleared by arrest	34.8	42.5	22.4	29.8	31.6	31.2	37.4	62.0	55.0	59.9
GROUP III (50,000 to 99,999)										
Offenses known	7,460	491	11,265	3,074	3,193	15,595	11,396	14,129	21,890	19,598
Percent cleared by arrest	36.7	34.8	24.7	30.4	31.4	33.0	41.3	61.5	57.0	63.4
GROUP IV (25,000 to 49,999)										
Offenses known	6,263	382	7,565	1,728	2,197	9,819	7,816	9,807	15,196	15,423
Percent cleared by arrest	34.2	41.1	27.8	32.3	30.5	34.9	45.5	65.5	59.8	61.9
GROUP V (10,000 to 24,999)										
Offenses known	5,849	370	5,655	1,367	1,640	7,418	6,728	8,902	14,397	17,299
Percent cleared by arrest	37.4	41.4	30.0	39.7	34.5	40.4	50.0	67.2	61.1	64.7
GROUP VI (under 10,000)										
Offenses known	5,012	441	3,363	819	869	4,694	5,319	7,290	10,799	21,051
Percent cleared by arrest	40.0	46.0	28.5	36.6	38.3	38.2	51.9	67.0	60.6	64.9
Metropolitan Counties										
Offenses known	10,903	641	14,606	2,349	2,782	12,034	18,496	16,889	32,975	32,306
Percent cleared by arrest	43.0	42.6	21.4	34.1	31.9	35.6	47.7	66.2	60.2	61.7
Nonmetropolitan Counties										
Offenses known	4,977	279	1,607	323	477	1,338	6,516	5,384	10,229	13,935
Percent cleared by arrest	45.6	38.4	37.1	53.3	39.2	46.8	61.9	68.9	63.8	62.8
SUBURBAN AREAS[2]										
Offenses known	20,459	1,297	25,501	4,839	5,783	26,528	29,142	31,130	56,587	63,756
Percent cleared by arrest	40.2	42.9	23.8	34.7	32.7	36.9	48.1	67.0	61.0	63.3

[2] Suburban areas include law enforcement agencies in cities with less than 50,000 inhabitants and county law enforcement agencies that are within a Metropolitan Statistical Area. Suburban areas exclude all metropolitan agencies associated with a principal city. The agencies associated with suburban areas also appear in other groups within this table.

Table 27.   Number and Percent of Offenses Cleared by Arrest or Exceptional Means, by Population Group, 2010—
Continued

(Number, percent)

Population group	Burglary			Motor vehicle theft			Arson[1]			Number of agencies	2010 estimated population
	Forcible entry	Unlawful entry	Attempted forcible entry	Autos	Trucks and buses	Other vehicles	Structure	Mobile	Other		
TOTAL ALL AGENCIES											
Offenses known	1,056,872	579,671	107,692	451,940	98,358	61,865	21,286	12,184	13,580	13,888	251,147,923
Percent cleared by arrest	11.4	13.6	10.8	12.1	9.1	10.4	21.8	9.4	21.8		
Total Cities											
Offenses known	778,448	425,951	83,871	366,951	78,109	40,540	16,069	8,590	10,151	10,120	169,966,285
Percent cleared by arrest	10.9	13.3	10.8	11.0	8.1	9.3	21.4	8.7	22.1		
GROUP I (250,000 and over)											
Offenses known	292,520	109,326	25,855	157,742	44,871	14,179	5,687	3,888	2,977	66	42,447,594
Percent cleared by arrest	8.4	10.4	9.1	7.8	5.6	7.3	17.7	5.8	19.4		
1,000,000 and over (Group I subset)											
Offenses known	90,745	31,873	6,244	45,235	20,837	6,177	1,512	1,394	984	8	14,654,178
Percent cleared by arrest	7.2	8.2	9.6	6.7	3.8	5.2	20.0	5.5	13.0		
500,000 to 999,999 (Group I subset)											
Offenses known	112,111	39,069	11,179	61,634	14,729	4,532	2,217	1,253	822	22	15,002,760
Percent cleared by arrest	8.0	10.1	8.3	7.6	6.1	10.1	16.0	5.3	23.5		
250,000 to 499,999 (Group I subset)											
Offenses known	89,664	38,384	8,432	50,873	9,305	3,470	1,958	1,241	1,171	36	12,790,656
Percent cleared by arrest	10.1	12.7	9.9	9.1	9.0	7.2	17.9	6.7	21.9		
GROUP II (100,000 to 249,999)											
Offenses known	137,965	77,229	15,062	70,251	13,489	7,158	2,664	1,411	1,639	177	26,247,156
Percent cleared by arrest	10.1	12.3	10.0	9.8	9.1	8.4	17.9	7.7	21.8		
GROUP III (50,000 to 99,999)											
Offenses known	112,193	71,640	13,721	57,486	8,564	6,189	2,430	1,223	1,844	419	28,758,695
Percent cleared by arrest	11.3	14.2	11.8	11.2	9.8	9.2	21.8	10.5	21.4		
GROUP IV (25,000 to 49,999)											
Offenses known	86,609	58,187	10,441	34,274	4,339	4,766	1,562	792	1,512	731	25,287,278
Percent cleared by arrest	12.1	13.6	11.4	14.4	11.2	8.8	25.7	13.1	22.4		
GROUP V (10,000 to 24,999)											
Offenses known	82,573	57,899	10,221	28,122	3,894	4,309	1,728	713	1,130	1,612	25,583,045
Percent cleared by arrest	14.4	15.7	12.6	18.6	16.7	12.1	29.3	11.6	26.5		
GROUP VI (under 10,000)											
Offenses known	66,588	51,670	8,571	19,076	2,952	3,939	1,998	563	1,049	7,115	21,642,517
Percent cleared by arrest	16.5	16.7	12.9	24.6	19.8	16.0	25.6	16.7	26.5		
Metropolitan Counties											
Offenses known	195,520	107,051	17,832	69,327	16,461	15,490	3,522	2,896	2,602	1,547	56,839,183
Percent cleared by arrest	12.2	14.2	10.1	15.1	11.1	11.2	22.6	9.6	19.3		
Nonmetropolitan Counties											
Offenses known	82,904	46,669	5,989	15,662	3,788	5,835	1,695	698	827	2,221	24,342,455
Percent cleared by arrest	15.1	15.0	13.1	25.3	22.2	15.9	24.1	17.9	26.1		
SUBURBAN AREAS[2]											
Offenses known	334,787	208,018	36,448	127,670	24,530	23,831	6,453	4,145	5,067	7,313	107,741,763
Percent cleared by arrest	12.8	14.9	11.0	15.4	11.8	11.2	25.2	10.4	21.4		

[1] Not all agencies submit reports for arson to the FBI. As a result, the number of reports the FBI uses to compute the percent of offenses cleared for arson is less than the number it uses to compute the percent of offenses cleared for all other offenses. Agencies must report arson clearances by detailed property classification as specified on the Monthly Return of Arson Offenses Known to Law Enforcement to be included in this table; therefore, clearances in this table may differ from other clearance tables.

[2] Suburban areas include law enforcement agencies in cities with less than 50,000 inhabitants and county law enforcement agencies that are within a Metropolitan Statistical Area. Suburban areas exclude all metropolitan agencies associated with a principal city. The agencies associated with suburban areas also appear in other groups within this table.

Table 28.   Number of Offenses Cleared by Arrest or Exceptional Means and Percent Involving Persons Under 18 Years of Age, by Population Group, 2010

(Number, percent)

Population group	Violent crime	Murder and non-negligent man-slaughter	Forcible rape	Robbery	Aggra-vated assault	Property crime	Burglary	Larceny-theft	Motor vehicle theft	Arson[1]	Number of agencies	2010 estimated population
TOTAL ALL AGENCIES												
Offenses known	440,345	7,234	26,387	76,532	330,192	1,301,561	206,676	1,025,905	68,980	8,871	13,617	247,007,886
Percent under 18 years old	10.2	4.7	11.3	14.0	9.4	15.9	13.5	16.5	13.0	34.3		
Total Cities												
Offenses known	339,442	5,406	19,137	65,975	248,924	1,038,276	146,993	841,690	49,593	6,502	9,981	167,156,718
Percent under 18 years old	10.4	4.6	10.4	14.3	9.5	16.5	14.3	17.1	13.3	37.3		
GROUP I (250,000 and over)												
Offenses known	123,629	2,530	6,601	28,764	85,734	237,466	37,938	183,799	15,729	1,848	65	41,845,871
Percent under 18 years old	9.1	4.7	8.0	13.3	7.9	15.2	14.3	15.6	13.1	34.6		
1,000,000 and over (Group I subset)												
Offenses known	41,682	934	2,216	10,939	27,593	72,113	9,780	58,183	4,150	507	8	14,654,178
Percent under 18 years old	7.9	3.9	7.2	10.7	6.9	12.5	11.2	13.0	9.6	28.2		
500,000 to 999,999 (Group I subset)												
Offenses known	43,092	731	2,184	8,808	31,369	83,381	13,422	64,071	5,888	639	21	14,401,037
Percent under 18 years old	9.2	5.5	8.4	14.3	8.0	15.4	16.4	15.3	14.0	39.7		
250,000 to 499,999 (Group I subset)												
Offenses known	38,855	865	2,201	9,017	26,772	81,972	14,736	61,545	5,691	702	36	12,790,656
Percent under 18 years old	10.3	5.1	8.3	15.4	8.8	17.4	14.4	18.4	14.8	34.6		
GROUP II (100,000 to 249,999)												
Offenses known	57,600	912	2,950	11,988	41,750	169,579	24,525	136,491	8,563	945	175	26,015,237
Percent under 18 years old	11.0	4.2	10.5	16.5	9.6	19.2	16.3	20.1	13.5	39.9		
GROUP III (50,000 to 99,999)												
Offenses known	51,427	745	2,895	9,728	38,059	177,612	24,086	145,805	7,721	1,071	412	28,310,820
Percent under 18 years old	11.2	4.7	11.3	15.8	10.1	18.4	14.0	19.4	13.8	33.7		
GROUP IV (25,000 to 49,999)												
Offenses known	37,500	492	2,262	6,586	28,160	154,135	19,108	129,353	5,674	847	717	24,817,340
Percent under 18 years old	11.1	4.5	12.4	14.6	10.3	16.8	13.8	17.3	14.6	41.9		
GROUP V (10,000 to 24,999)												
Offenses known	36,557	443	2,252	5,622	28,240	162,127	21,433	134,518	6,176	892	1,567	24,841,849
Percent under 18 years old	11.0	5.2	12.6	12.4	10.7	15.4	13.3	15.9	12.5	40.6		
GROUP VI (under 10,000)												
Offenses known	32,729	284	2,177	3,287	26,981	137,357	19,903	111,724	5,730	899	7,045	21,325,601
Percent under 18 years old	11.8	4.2	12.2	13.0	11.7	13.8	14.0	13.8	12.2	36.8		
Metropolitan Counties												
Offenses known	74,258	1,236	4,912	9,046	59,064	196,676	40,081	142,771	13,824	1,594	1,483	56,028,893
Percent under 18 years old	10.4	5.1	13.3	13.6	9.8	14.3	12.6	14.9	12.6	28.4		
Nonmetropolitan Counties												
Offenses known	26,645	592	2,338	1,511	22,204	66,609	19,602	41,444	5,563	775	2,153	23,822,275
Percent under 18 years old	7.3	4.1	14.0	6.2	6.8	10.6	9.5	11.1	11.5	20.6		
SUBURBAN AREAS[2]												
Offenses known	137,484	1,924	8,645	19,108	107,807	475,532	75,979	374,837	24,716	3,175	7,166	105,897,801
Percent under 18 years old	11.3	4.7	13.2	14.1	10.7	15.1	13.2	15.7	12.5	35.9		

[1] Not all agencies submit reports for arson to the FBI. As a result, the number of reports the FBI uses to compute the percent of offenses cleared for arson is less than the number it uses to compute the percent of offenses cleared for all other offenses.

[2] Suburban areas include law enforcement agencies in cities with less than 50,000 inhabitants and county law enforcement agencies that are within a Metropolitan Statistical Area. Suburban areas exclude all metropolitan agencies associated with a principal city. The agencies associated with suburban areas also appear in other groups within this table.

SECTION IV:
PERSONS ARRESTED

PERSONS ARRESTED

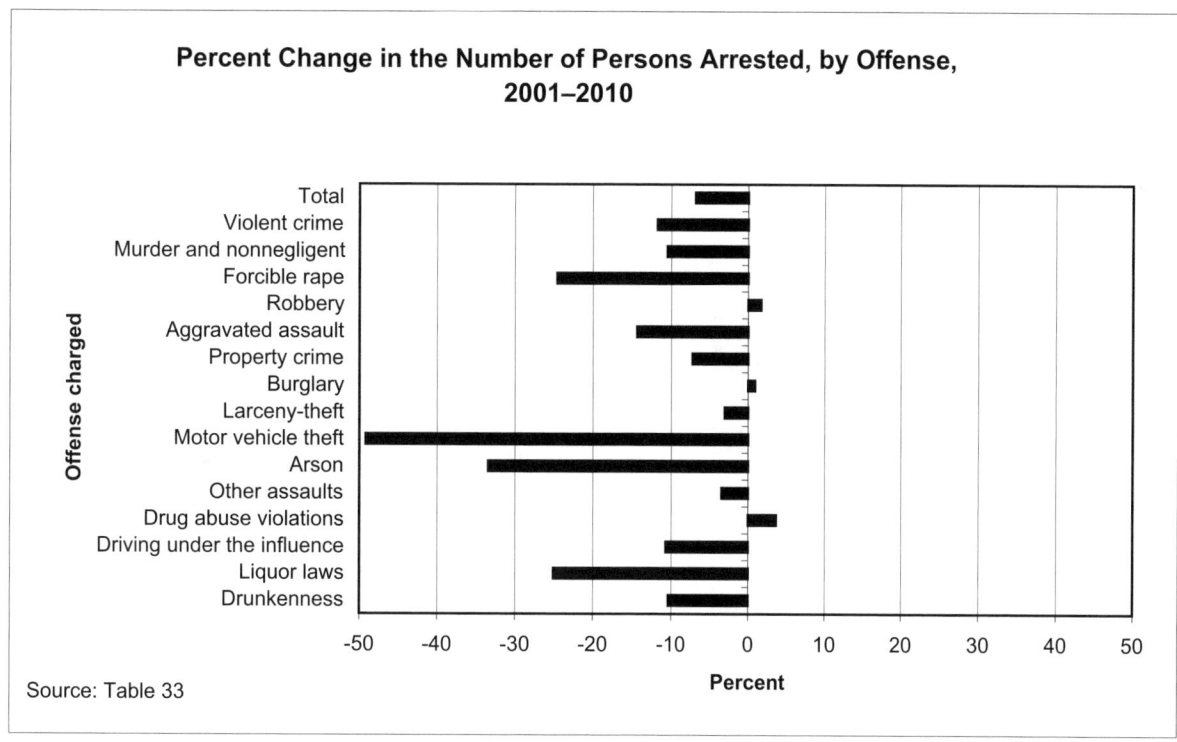

Percent Change in the Number of Persons Arrested, by Offense, 2001–2010

Source: Table 33

In the Uniform Crime Reporting (UCR) Program, one arrest is counted for each separate instance in which an individual is arrested, cited, or summoned for criminal acts in Part I and Part II crimes. (See Appendix II for additional information concerning Part I and Part II crimes.) One person may be arrested multiple times during the year; as a result, the arrest figures in this section should not be taken as the total number of individuals arrested. Instead, it provides the number of arrest occurrences reported by law enforcement. Information regarding the UCR Program's statistical methodology and table construction can be found in Appendix I.

National Volume, Trends, and Rates

Volume

The FBI estimated that 13,120,947 arrests occurred in 2010 for all offenses (except traffic violations). Of these arrests, 522,077 were for violent crimes and 1,643,962 were for property crimes. Of the total violent crimes in 2010, aggravated assaults accounted for 74.0 percent, or 408,488 incidents. Robbery had the next highest proportion with 20.3 percent, or 112,300 incidents; followed by forcible rape, 3.6 percent (or 20,088 incidents); and murder and non-negligent manslaughter, 2.1 percent (or 11,201 incidents). Of the estimated 1,643,962 arrests for property crimes in 2010, 1,271,410 (77.3 percent) were for larceny-theft, 289,769 (17.6 percent) were for burglary, 71,487 (4.3 percent) were for motor vehicle theft, and 11,296 (0.7 percent) were for arson. (Table 29) The most frequent identifiable arrests

made in 2010 were for drug abuse violations (estimated at 1,638,846 arrests). These arrests compose 12.5 percent of the total number of all arrests.

A comparison of arrest figures from 2009 to 2010 revealed a 4.5 percent decrease. Arrests for violent crimes decreased 5.3 percent, and arrests for property crimes decreased 4.7 percent during the 2-year period. (Table 36) An examination of the 5-year and 10-year arrest trends showed that the total number of arrests in 2010 fell 9.0 percent from the 2006 total. Arrests for violent crimes showed a 9.9 percent decrease from 2006 to 2010 while property crimes showed a 6.7 percent increase. (Table 34) In the 10-year trend data (2001 to 2010), the number of arrests decreased 2.9 percent. For violent crimes, the number of arrests fell 9.6 percent, while arrests for property crimes increased 3.3 percent. (Tables 32)

The number of adults arrested for violent crime (arrestees age 18 years and over) decreased 4.3 percent from 2009 to 2010, decreased 6.8 percent from 2006 to 2010, and decreased 7.5 percent from 2001 to 2010. The number of juveniles arrested for violent crime (arrestees under 18 years of age) decreased 11.6 percent from 2009 to 2010, decreased 25.3 percent from 2006 to 2010, and decreased 21.6 percent from 2001 to 2010. (Tables 32, 34, and 36)

Trends

The trend data for murder showed that the number of arrests for this offense decreased 8.3 percent from 2009 to

2010, decreased 15.0 percent from 2006 to 2010, and decreased 12.9 percent from 2001 to 2010. The number of adults arrested for murder declined 8.4 percent from 2009 to 2010, decreased 14.2 percent from 2006 to 2010, and fell 11.7 percent from 2001 to 2010. The number of juveniles arrested for murder fell 7.1 percent from 2009 to 2010, decreased 22.3 percent from 2006 to 2010, and fell 23.7 percent from 2001 to 2010. (Tables 32, 34, and 36)

For forcible rape, the 2-year trend data showed that arrests decreased 4.6 percent from 2009 to 2010, with adult arrests decreasing 4.1 percent and juvenile arrests dropping 7.2 percent. The 5-year trend data showed that arrests decreased 13.0 percent from 2006 to 2010; adult arrests decreased 12.3 percent and juvenile arrests declined 17.1 percent during this period. The 10-year trend data showed that forcible rape arrests dropped 24.8 percent from 2001 to 2010, with adult arrests falling 22.9 percent and juvenile arrests falling 34.7 percent. (Tables 32, 34, and 36)

For robbery, the 2-year trend data showed that arrests decreased 10.8 percent from 2009 to 2010, with adult arrests decreasing 9.8 percent and juvenile arrests falling 14.1 percent. The 5-year trend data showed that total robbery arrests fell 10.7 percent from 2006 to 2010; adult arrests decreased 6.1 percent and juvenile arrests dropped 22.3 percent during this period. The 10-year trend data showed that arrests rose 4.5 percent from 2001 to 2010, with adult arrests increasing 4.2 percent and juvenile arrests increasing 5.6 percent. (Tables 32, 34, and 36)

The aggravated assault trend data showed that the number of arrests for this offense fell 3.6 percent from 2009 to 2010, dropped 9.3 percent from 2006 to 2010, and fell 11.9 percent from 2001 to 2010. The number of adults arrested for aggravated assault decreased 2.2 percent from 2009 to 2010, declined 6.5 percent from 2006 to 2010, and declined 8.9 percent from 2001 to 2010. The number of juveniles arrested for aggravated assault dropped 10.4 percent from 2009 to 2010, fell 27.6 percent from 2006 to 2010, and dropped 31.3 percent from 2001 to 2010. (Tables 32, 34, and 36)

The 2-year, 5-year, and 10-year trend data showed that the number of arrests for property crime decreased 4.76 percent from 2009 to 2010, increased 6.7 percent from 2006 to 2010, and increased 3.3 percent from 2001 to 2010. The number of adults arrested for property crime offenses (arrestees age 18 years and over) decreased 2.3 percent from 2009 to 2010, increased 12.4 percent from 2006 to 2010, and increased 16.0 percent from 2001 to 2010. The number of juveniles arrested for property crime (arrestees under 18 years of age) decreased 12.0 percent from 2009 to 2010, decreased 9.0 percent from 2006 to 2010, and decreased 24.8 percent from 2001 to 2010. (Tables 32, 34, and 36)

The trend data for burglary showed that the number of arrests for this offense decreased 2.7 percent from 2009 to 2010, decreased 3.3 percent from 2006 to 2010, and increased 3.5 percent from 2001 to 2010. The number of

adults arrested for burglary rose 0.4 percent from 2009 to 2010, rose 3.3 percent from 2006 to 2010, and rose 16.7 percent from 2001 to 2010. The number of juveniles arrested for burglary decreased 12.0 percent from 2009 to 2010, decreased 20.7 percent from 2006 to 2010, and fell 25.9 percent from 2001 to 2010. (Tables 32, 34, and 36)

For larceny-theft, the 2-year trend data showed that arrests decreased 4.7 percent from 2009 to 2010, with adult arrests decreasing 2.6 percent and juvenile arrests decreasing 11.5 percent. The 5-year trend data showed that total larceny-theft arrests increased 16.4 percent from 2006 to 2010; adult arrests increased 21.9 percent and juvenile arrests rose 0.6 percent during this period. The 10-year trend data showed that larceny-theft arrests rose 9.8 percent from 2001 to 2010, with adult arrests increasing 22.4 percent and juvenile arrests falling 18.9 percent. (Tables 32, 34, and 36)

For motor vehicle theft, the 2-year trend data showed that arrests declined 10.7 percent from 2009 to 2010, with adult arrests decreasing 7.6 percent and juvenile arrests decreasing 20.2 percent. The 5-year trend data showed that total motor vehicle theft arrests dropped 45.5 percent from 2006 to 2010; adult arrests fell 43.0 percent and juvenile arrests dropped 52.8 percent during this period. The 10-year trend data showed that arrests dropped 48.3 percent from 2001 to 2010, with adult arrests falling 39.7 percent and juvenile arrests dropping 66.1 percent. (Tables 32, 34, and 36)

The arson trend data showed that the number of arrests for this offense decreased 7.1 percent from 2009 to 2010, fell 29.6 percent from 2006 to 2010, and fell 32.1 percent from 2001 to 2010. The number of adults arrested for arson decreased 1.4 percent from 2009 to 2010, fell 17.9 percent from 2006 to 2010, and fell 15.0 percent from 2001 to 2010. The number of juveniles arrested for arson dropped 14.1 percent from 2009 to 2010, dropped 41.6 percent from 2006 to 2010, and dropped 46.9 percent from 2001 to 2010. (Tables 32, 34, and 36)

Rates

The rate of arrests was estimated at 4,257.6 arrests per 100,000 inhabitants in 2010. The arrest rate for violent crime was 179.2 per 100,000 inhabitants, and the arrest rate for property crime was 538.5 per 100,000 inhabitants. Law enforcement agencies throughout the nation reported 3.6 murder arrests, 6.5 forcible rape arrests, 36.6 robbery arrests, and 132.6 aggravated assault arrests per 100,000 inhabitants in 2010. Rates for all violent crimes were down from the 2009 rates. Law enforcement agencies throughout the nation reported 538.5 property crime arrests, 94.3 burglary arrests, 417.5 larceny-theft arrests, 23.1 motor vehicle theft arrests, and 3.7 arson arrests per 100,000 inhabitants in 2010. Rates for all property crimes were also down from the 2009 rates. (Table 30)

By Age, Sex, and Race

Law enforcement agencies that contributed arrest data to the UCR Program reported information on the age, sex,

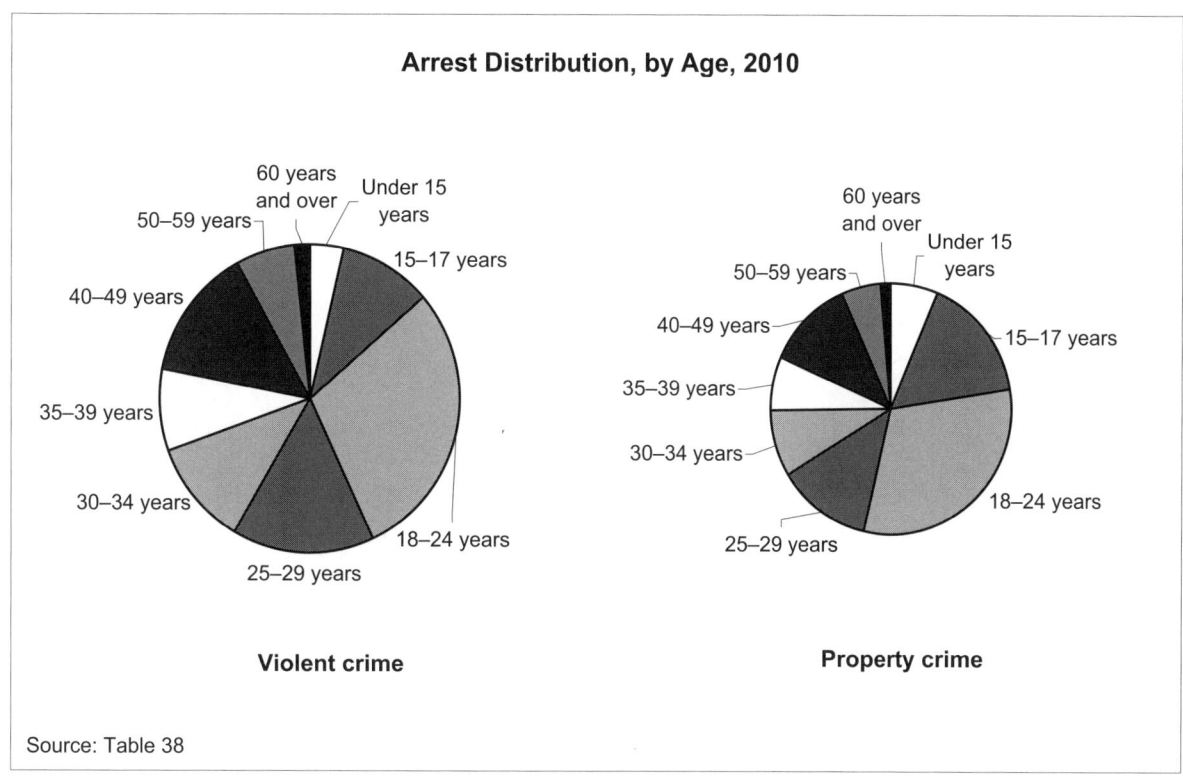

Arrest Distribution, by Age, 2010

Violent crime

Property crime

Source: Table 38

and race of the persons they arrested. According to the 2010 data, adults accounted for 87.4 percent of arrestees nationally. (Table 38)

A review of arrest data by age from 2009 to 2010 showed that arrests of adults decreased 3.7 percent during this period. Arrests of adults for property crimes decreased 2.3 percent, and arrests of adults for violent crimes decreased 4.3 percent over the same time span. The arrest total for juveniles (those under 18 years of age) decreased 9.7 percent from 2009 to 2010. Over the 2-year period, arrests of juveniles for violent crimes fell 11.6 percent; juvenile arrests for property crimes decreased 12.0 percent. (Table 36)

By sex, males accounted for 74.5 percent of all persons arrested. Males represented 80.5 percent of arrestees for violent crime, 89.1 percent of arrestees for murder, 98.9 percent of arrestees for forcible rape, 87.8 percent for robbery, and 77.4 percent for aggravated assault. Females accounted for 19.5 percent of violent crime arrestees, 10.9 percent of murder arrestees, 1.1 percent of forcible rape arrestees, 12.2 percent of robbery arrestees, and 22.6 percent of aggravated assault arrestees. (Table 42)

In 2010, most arrestees for property crime (77.5 percent) were over 18 years of age. By sex, males accounted for 62.4 percent of arrestees for property crime, 84.7 percent of arrestees for burglary, 56.1 percent of arrestees for larceny-theft, 82.5 percent of arrestees for motor vehicle theft, and 82.6 percent of arrestees for arson. Females accounted for 37.6 percent of property crime arrestees. Of the four property crimes, larceny-theft had the highest proportion of female arrestees at 43.9 percent. (Tables 38 and 42)

In 2010, 69.4 percent of all persons arrested were White; 28.0 percent were Black; and the remaining 2.6 percent were of other races (American Indian or Alaskan Native and Asian or Pacific Islander). Of all arrestees for violent crimes, 59.3 percent were White, 38.1 percent were Black, and 2.5 percent were of other races. For murder, 49.3 percent of arrestees were White, 48.7 percent were Black, and 2.0 percent were of other races. For forcible rape, 65.7 percent of arrestees were White, 31.8 percent were Black, and 2.6 percent were of other races. For robbery, 43.3 percent of arrestees were White, 55.0 percent of arrestees were Black, and 1.7 percent were of other races. For aggravated assault, 63.7 percent of arrestees were White, 33.5 percent of arrestees were Black, and 2.7 percent were of other races. (Table 43)

Of all arrestees for property crimes, 68.4 percent were White, 28.9 percent were Black, and 2.6 percent were of other races. For burglary, 67.4 percent of arrestees were White, 30.8 percent were Black, and 1.8 percent were of other races. For larceny-theft, 68.9 percent of arrestees were White, 28.3 percent were Black, and 2.8 percent were of other races. For motor vehicle theft, 63.3 percent of arrestees were White, 34.0 percent of arrestees were Black, and 2.7 percent were of other races. For arson, 75.2 percent of arrestees were White, 22.6 percent of arrestees were Black, and 2.2 percent were of other races. (Table 43)

White adults were most commonly arrested for driving under the influence (927,516 arrests) and drug abuse violations (846,736 arrests). Black adults were most frequently arrested for drug abuse violations (404,609 arrests) and other assaults (simple) (318,117 arrests). (Table 43)

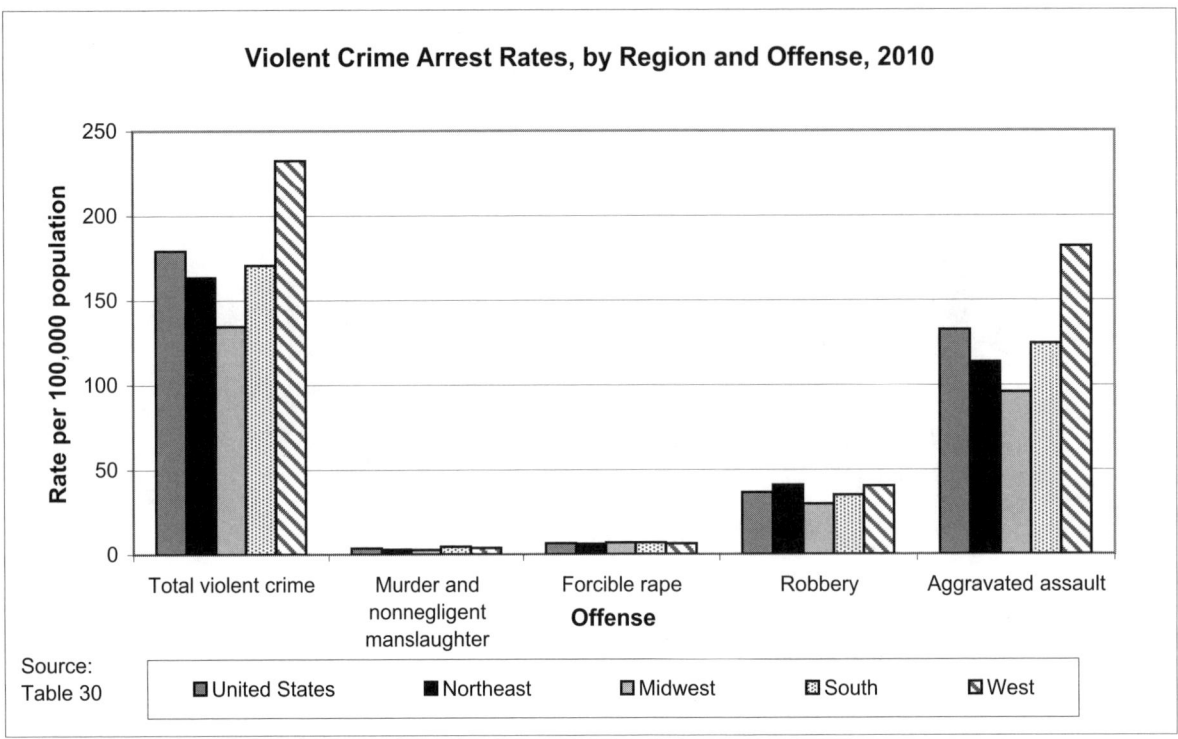

Violent Crime Arrest Rates, by Region and Offense, 2010

Source: Table 30

Regional Arrest Rates

The UCR Program divides the United States into four regions: the Northeast, the Midwest, the South, and the West. (Appendix III provides more information about the regions.) Law enforcement agencies in the Northeast had an overall arrest rate of 3,557.0 arrests per 100,000 inhabitants, well below the national rate (4,257.6 arrests per 100,000 inhabitants). In this region, the arrest rate for violent crimes was 163.4 arrests per 100,000 inhabitants, and for property crime, the arrest rate was 460.8 arrests per 100,000 inhabitants. In the Midwest, law enforcement agencies reported an arrest rate of 4,024.4 arrests per 100,000 inhabitants. The arrest rate for violent crimes was 134.7 and the arrest rate for property crime was 530.1. Law enforcement agencies in the South, the nation's most populous region, reported an arrest rate of 4,813.8 per 100,000 inhabitants. Arrests for violent crime occurred at a rate of 170.7 arrests per 100,000 residents, and for property crime, the arrest rate was 605.9 arrests per 100,000 inhabitants. In the Western states, law enforcement agencies reported an overall arrest rate of 4,209.2 arrests per 100,000 inhabitants. The region's violent crime arrest rate was 232.4, while its property crime arrest rate was 513.6. (Table 30)

The regional murder arrest rates were 2.9 in the Northeast, 2.6 in the Midwest, 4.5 in the South, and 3.7 in the West. For forcible rape, the regional arrest rates were 6.1 in the Northeast, 6.8 in the Midwest, 6.7 in the South, and 6.3 in the West. Regional arrest rates for robbery were 40.9 in the Northeast, 29.8 in the Midwest, 35.1 in the South, and 40.3 in the West. For aggravated assault, the regional arrest rates were 113.5 in the Northeast, 95.5 in the Midwest, 124.5 in the South, and 182.0 in the West. (Table 30)

The regional burglary arrest rates were 76.1 in the Northeast, 74.4 in the Midwest, 102.2 in the South, and 111.0 in the West. For larceny-theft, the regional arrest rates were 364.4 in the Northeast, 428.7 in the Midwest, 479.7 in the South, and 368.5 in the West. Regional arrest rates for motor vehicle theft were 16.4 in the Northeast, 23.9 in the Midwest, 20.3 in the South, and 30.3 in the West. For arson, the regional arrest rates were 4.0 in the Northeast, 3.3 in the Midwest, 3.6 in the South, and 3.8 in the West. (Table 30)

By population group, law enforcement agencies in the nation's cities collectively reported 201.0 violent crime arrests per 100,000 inhabitants in 2010. In the city population groups, cities with 250,000 or more inhabitants reported the highest violent crime arrest rate (275.2) and cities with 10,000 to 24,999 inhabitants reported the lowest violent crime arrest rate (142.9). Cities reported an overall murder arrest rate of 3.9 per 100,000 inhabitants; cities with 250,000 or more inhabitants had the highest murder arrest rate (6.5) and cities with under 10,000 inhabitants had the lowest murder arrest rate (1.7). The collective city forcible rape arrest rate was 6.9 per 100,000 inhabitants, with the highest rate in cities with 250,000 or more inhabitants (9.1), and the lowest rate in cities with 10,000 to 24,999 inhabitants (5.5). The overall robbery arrest rate for cities was 45.1 per 100,000 inhabitants; cities with 250,000 or more inhabitants had the highest robbery arrest rate (74.2) and cities with fewer than 10,000 inhabitants had the lowest robbery arrest rate (19.3). For aggravated assault, the collective city arrest rate was 145.2 per 100,000 inhabitants, with the greatest arrest rate in cities with 250,000 or more inhabitants (185.4) and the lowest arrest rate in cities with 10,000 to 24,999 inhabitants (108.0). (Table 31)

Agencies in metropolitan counties reported a violent crime arrest rate of 140.9 per 100,000 inhabitants, with arrest rates of 3.2 for murder, 5.1 for forcible rape, 21.2 for robbery, and 111.5 for aggravated assault. Agencies in nonmetropolitan counties reported arrest rates of 107.7 for violent crime, 2.9 for murder, 6.7 for forcible rape, 9.4 for robbery, and 88.8 for aggravated assault. (Table 31)

By population group, law enforcement agencies in the nation's cities collectively reported 634.9 property crime arrests per 100,000 inhabitants in 2010. In the city population groups, cities with 100,000 to 249,999 inhabitants reported the highest property crime arrest rate (665.0) and cities with 250,000 or more inhabitants reported the lowest property crime arrest rate (594.6). Cities reported an overall burglary arrest rate of 100.6 per 100,000 inhabitants; cities with 100,000 to 249,999 inhabitants had the highest burglary arrest rate (118.7) and cities with 25,000 to 49,999 inhabitants had the lowest burglary arrest rate (87.2). The collective city larceny-theft arrest rate was 505.5 per 100,000 inhabitants, with the highest rate in cities with 25,000 to 49,999 inhabitants (549.2) and the lowest rate in cities with 250,000 or more inhabitants (452.2). The overall motor vehicle theft arrest rate for cities was 24.9 per 100,000 inhabitants; cities with 250,000 or more inhabitants had the highest motor vehicle theft arrest rate (37.6), and cities with 25,000 to 49,999 inhabitants had the lowest motor vehicle theft arrest rate (16.0). For arson, the collective city arrest rate was 3.9 per 100,000 inhabitants, with the greatest arrest rate in cities with fewer than 10,000 inhabitants (5.4) and the lowest arrest rate in cities with 250,000 or more inhabitants (3.4). (Table 31)

Agencies in metropolitan counties reported a property crime arrest rate of 346.3 per 100,000 inhabitants, with arrest rates of 77.1 for burglary, 246.4 for larceny-theft, 19.9 for motor vehicle theft, and 2.9 for arson. Agencies in nonmetropolitan counties reported arrest rates of 275.2 for property crime, 87.3 for burglary, 167.0 for larceny-theft, 17.3 for motor vehicle theft, and 3.6 for arson. (Table 31)

Community Types

In 2010, law enforcement agencies in the nation's cities reported that 86.1 percent of arrests in their jurisdictions were of adults and 13.9 percent of arrests were of juveniles. Adults accounted for 85.4 percent of arrestees for violent crimes, while juveniles accounted for 14.6 percent. Adults made up 76.5 percent of the arrestees for property crimes, and juveniles accounted for 23.5 percent. (Table 46) Of all arrests in the nation's cities in 2010, 44.0 percent were of individuals under 25 years of age. (Table 47) In metropolitan counties, 37.9 percent of arrests were of individuals under 25 years of age. (Table 53) In nonmetropolitan counties, 33.9 percent of persons arrested were individuals under 25 years of age. (Table 59)

Males accounted for 74.2 percent and females accounted for 25.8 percent of arrestees in the nation's cities in 2010. (Table 48) In metropolitan counties, males composed 75.3 percent of arrestees, and in nonmetropolitan counties, males represented 75.9 percent of all arrestees. (Tables 54 and 60)

By race, 67.1 percent of arrestees in the nation's cities in 2010 were White, 30.2 percent were Black, and 2.7 percent were of other races (American Indian or Alaska Native and Asian or Pacific Islander). (Table 49) Whites accounted for 73.9 percent of arrestees in metropolitan counties in 2010, Blacks made up 24.7 percent of arrestees, and persons of other races made up 1.4 percent of the total. (Table 55) In nonmetropolitan counties, Whites made up 81.7 percent of arrestees, Blacks accounted for 14.1 percent of arrestees, and other races made up 4.2 percent of the total. (Table 61)

Population Groups: Trends and Rates

The national UCR Program aggregates data by various population groups, which include cities, metropolitan counties, and nonmetropolitan counties. Definitions of these groups can be found in Appendix III. The total number of arrests in U.S. cities fell 4.9 percent from 2009 to 2010. The number of arrests for violent crimes declined 5.5 percent and arrests for property crimes decreased 5.3 percent during the 2-year time frame. (Table 44)

In 2010, law enforcement agencies in cities collectively recorded an arrest rate of 4,593.3 arrests per 100,000 inhabitants. The nation's smallest cities, those with fewer than 10,000 inhabitants, had the highest arrest rate among the city population groups with 5,630.8 arrests per 100,000 inhabitants. Law enforcement agencies in cities with 25,000 to 49,999 inhabitants recorded the lowest rate, 4,115.0. In the nation's metropolitan counties, law enforcement agencies reported an arrest rate of 3,462.7 per 100,000 inhabitants. Agencies in nonmetropolitan counties reported an arrest rate of 3,636.2. (Table 31)

Table 29.   Estimated Number of Arrests, 2010

(Number)

Offense	Arrests
TOTAL[1]	13,120,947
Violent Crime	552,077
Murder and nonnegligent manslaughter	11,201
Forcible rape	20,088
Robbery	112,300
Aggravated assault	408,488
Property Crime	1,643,962
Burglary	289,769
Larceny-theft	1,271,410
Motor vehicle theft	71,487
Arson	11,296
Other	
Other assaults	1,292,449
Forgery and counterfeiting	78,101
Fraud	187,887
Embezzlement	16,616
Stolen property; buying, receiving, possessing	94,802
Vandalism	252,753
Weapons; carrying, possessing, etc.	159,020
Prostitution and commercialized vice	62,668
Sex offenses (except forcible rape and prostitution)	72,628
Drug abuse violations	1,638,846
Gambling	9,941
Offenses against the family and children	111,062
Driving under the influence	1,412,223
Liquor laws	512,790
Drunkenness	560,718
Disorderly conduct	615,172
Vagrancy	32,033
All other offenses	3,720,402
Suspicion	1,166
Curfew and loitering law violations	94,797

[1] Does not include suspicion.

Table 30.   Number and Rate of Arrests, by Geographic Region, 2010

(Number, rate per 100,000)

Offense charged	United States total (12,222 agencies; population 240,103,394)		Northeast (3,079 agencies; population 44,091,861)		Midwest (2,881 agencies; population 48,046,513)		South (4,464 agencies; population 81,479,421)		West (1,798 agencies; population 66,485,599)	
	Total	Rate	Total	Rate	Total	Rate	Total	Rate	Total	Rate
TOTAL[1]	10,222,654	4,257.6	1,568,336	3,557.0	1,933,601	4,024.4	3,922,224	4,813.8	2,798,493	4,209.2
Violent Crime	430,364	179.2	72,030	163.4	64,727	134.7	139,110	170.7	154,497	232.4
Murder and nonnegligent manslaughter	8,667	3.6	1,274	2.9	1,264	2.6	3,639	4.5	2,490	3.7
Forcible rape	15,586	6.5	2,677	6.1	3,252	6.8	5,440	6.7	4,217	6.3
Robbery	87,771	36.6	18,051	40.9	14,337	29.8	28,565	35.1	26,818	40.3
Aggravated assault	318,340	132.6	50,028	113.5	45,874	95.5	101,466	124.5	120,972	182.0
Property Crime	1,293,023	538.5	203,180	460.8	254,709	530.1	493,681	605.9	341,453	513.6
Burglary	226,325	94.3	33,537	76.1	35,729	74.4	83,258	102.2	73,801	111.0
Larceny-theft	1,002,466	417.5	160,657	364.4	205,952	428.7	390,887	479.7	244,970	368.5
Motor vehicle theft	55,426	23.1	7,236	16.4	11,465	23.9	16,566	20.3	20,159	30.3
Arson	8,806	3.7	1,750	4.0	1,563	3.3	2,970	3.6	2,523	3.8
Other										
Other assaults	1,008,509	420.0	177,993	403.7	199,405	415.0	407,970	500.7	223,141	335.6
Forgery and counterfeiting	60,841	25.3	9,272	21.0	9,386	19.5	27,909	34.3	14,274	21.5
Fraud	144,956	60.4	22,782	51.7	23,912	49.8	78,704	96.6	19,558	29.4
Embezzlement	13,020	5.4	1,222	2.8	1,791	3.7	7,424	9.1	2,583	3.9
Stolen property; buying, receiving, possessing	74,313	31.0	14,295	32.4	13,742	28.6	21,961	27.0	24,315	36.6
Vandalism	197,850	82.4	42,973	97.5	39,577	82.4	51,126	62.7	64,174	96.5
Weapons; carrying, possessing, etc.	123,719	51.5	16,220	36.8	23,038	47.9	42,770	52.5	41,691	62.7
Prostitution and commercialized vice	48,281	20.1	5,722	13.0	7,043	14.7	16,690	20.5	18,826	28.3
Sex offenses (except forcible rape and prostitution)	56,332	23.5	9,629	21.8	10,450	21.7	16,345	20.1	19,908	29.9
Drug abuse violations	1,273,963	530.6	211,413	479.5	231,927	482.7	455,864	559.5	374,759	563.7
Gambling	7,533	3.1	445	1.0	3,542	7.4	2,664	3.3	882	1.3
Offenses against the family and children	85,213	35.5	19,445	44.1	18,700	38.9	34,521	42.4	12,547	18.9
Driving under the influence	1,087,987	453.1	150,844	342.1	222,527	463.1	344,874	423.3	369,742	556.1
Liquor laws	400,608	166.8	50,305	114.1	135,973	283.0	98,632	121.1	115,698	174.0
Drunkenness	442,392	184.3	36,050	81.8	27,348	56.9	263,285	323.1	115,709	174.0
Disorderly conduct	482,991	201.2	121,727	276.1	140,170	291.7	147,598	181.1	73,496	110.5
Vagrancy	24,839	10.3	3,147	7.1	4,584	9.5	8,665	10.6	8,443	12.7
All other offenses (except traffic)	2,892,023	1,204.5	376,941	854.9	488,258	1,016.2	1,244,984	1,528.0	781,840	1,176.0
Suspicion	904	0.4	54	0.1	235	0.5	481	0.6	134	0.2
Curfew and loitering law violations	73,897	30.8	22,701	51.5	12,792	26.6	17,447	21.4	20,957	31.5

[1] Does not include suspicion.

Table 31.   Number and Rate of Arrests, by Population Group, 2010

(Number, rate per 100,000 population)

Offense charged	Cities									
	Total (12,222 agencies; population 240,103,394)		Total cities (8,912 cities; population 165,417,960)		Group I (62 cities, 250,000 and over; population 43,269,361)		Group II (169 cities, 100,000 to 249,999; population 24,902,643)		Group III (406 cities, 50,000 to 99,999; population 27,899,693)	
	Total	Rate	Total	Rate	Total	Rate	Total	Rate	Total	Rate
TOTAL[2]	10,222,654	4,257.6	7,598,178	4,593.3	2,053,643	4,746.2	1,096,552	4,403.4	1,211,726	4,343.2
Violent Crime	430,364	179.2	332,509	201.0	119,068	275.2	56,725	227.8	54,680	196.0
Murder and nonnegligent manslaughter	8,667	3.6	6,373	3.9	2,820	6.5	1,035	4.2	961	3.4
Forcible rape	15,586	6.5	11,424	6.9	3,940	9.1	1,634	6.6	1,727	6.2
Robbery	87,771	36.6	74,578	45.1	32,103	74.2	12,789	51.4	11,343	40.7
Aggravated assault	318,340	132.6	240,134	145.2	80,205	185.4	41,267	165.7	40,649	145.7
Property Crime	1,293,023	538.5	1,050,227	634.9	257,269	594.6	165,606	665.0	183,200	656.6
Burglary	226,325	94.3	166,483	100.6	43,850	101.3	29,569	118.7	29,782	106.7
Larceny-theft	1,002,466	417.5	836,119	505.5	195,675	452.2	128,138	514.6	146,545	525.3
Motor vehicle theft	55,426	23.1	41,138	24.9	16,274	37.6	6,962	28.0	5,736	20.6
Arson	8,806	3.7	6,487	3.9	1,470	3.4	937	3.8	1,137	4.1
Other										
Other assaults	1,008,509	420.0	758,138	458.3	204,418	472.4	121,628	488.4	120,166	430.7
Forgery and counterfeiting	60,841	25.3	44,909	27.1	11,186	25.9	6,038	24.2	7,084	25.4
Fraud	144,956	60.4	90,104	54.5	18,080	41.8	11,649	46.8	13,190	47.3
Embezzlement	13,020	5.4	9,640	5.8	1,956	4.5	1,789	7.2	1,702	6.1
Stolen property; buying, receiving, possessing	74,313	31.0	55,086	33.3	12,739	29.4	8,357	33.6	10,699	38.3
Vandalism	197,850	82.4	155,565	94.0	39,868	92.1	22,659	91.0	26,441	94.8
Weapons; carrying, possessing, etc.	123,719	51.5	97,015	58.6	37,563	86.8	15,167	60.9	14,787	53.0
Prostitution and commercialized vice	48,281	20.1	45,248	27.4	32,306	74.7	6,278	25.2	3,200	11.5
Sex offenses (except forcible rape and prostitution)	56,332	23.5	39,756	24.0	13,290	30.7	5,401	21.7	6,241	22.4
Drug abuse violations	1,273,963	530.6	943,847	570.6	307,848	711.5	141,187	567.0	150,731	540.3
Gambling	7,533	3.1	6,152	3.7	4,637	10.7	427	1.7	183	0.7
Offenses against the family and children	85,213	35.5	41,654	25.2	6,288	14.5	6,890	27.7	6,734	24.1
Driving under the influence	1,087,987	453.1	646,531	390.8	144,490	333.9	80,007	321.3	99,563	356.9
Liquor laws	400,608	166.8	321,909	194.6	59,585	137.7	34,536	138.7	47,229	169.3
Drunkenness	442,392	184.3	380,484	230.0	85,373	197.3	61,928	248.7	68,164	244.3
Disorderly conduct	482,991	201.2	411,718	248.9	91,921	212.4	48,901	196.4	64,311	230.5
Vagrancy	24,839	10.3	22,053	13.3	12,457	28.8	2,149	8.6	3,709	13.3
All other offenses (except traffic)	2,892,023	1,204.5	2,076,357	1,255.2	558,167	1,290.0	293,036	1,176.7	320,214	1,147.7
Suspicion	904	0.4	672	0.4	5	0.0	1	0.0	179	0.6
Curfew and loitering law violations	73,897	30.8	69,276	41.9	35,134	81.2	6,194	24.9	9,498	34.0

[1] Suburban areas include law enforcement agencies in cities with less than 50,000 inhabitants and county law enforcement agencies that are within a Metropolitan Statistical Area. Suburban areas exclude all metropolitan agencies associated with a principal city. The agencies associated with suburban areas also appear in other groups within this table.

[2] Does not include suspicion.

Table 31.   Number and Rate of Arrests, by Population Group, 2010—*Continued*

(Number, rate per 100,000 population)

Offense charged	Cities						Counties				Suburban areas[1] (6,634 agencies; population 104,853,682)	
	Group IV (707 cities, 25,000 to 49,999; population 24,374,008)		Group V (1,575 cities, 10,000 to 24,999; population 25,033,333)		Group VI (5,993 cities, under 10,000; population 19,938,922)		Metropolitan counties (1,352 agencies; population 52,433,613)		Nonmetropolitan counties (1,958 agencies; population 22,251,821)			
	Total	Rate	Total	Rate	Total	Rate	Total	Rate	Total	Rate	Total	Rate
TOTAL[2]	1,002,986	4,115.0	1,110,545	4,436.3	1,122,726	5,630.8	1,815,350	3,462.2	809,126	3,636.2	4,096,307	3,864.4
Violent Crime	37,035	151.9	35,767	142.9	29,234	146.6	73,884	140.9	23,971	107.7	146,917	138.6
Murder and nonnegligent manslaughter	610	2.5	610	2.4	337	1.7	1,657	3.2	637	2.9	2,679	2.5
Forcible rape	1,370	5.6	1,375	5.5	1,378	6.9	2,679	5.1	1,483	6.7	5,449	5.1
Robbery	7,742	31.8	6,751	27.0	3,850	19.3	11,108	21.2	2,085	9.4	25,602	24.2
Aggravated assault	27,313	112.1	27,031	108.0	23,669	118.7	58,440	111.5	19,766	88.8	113,187	106.8
Property Crime	159,877	655.9	161,152	643.7	123,123	617.5	181,557	346.3	61,239	275.2	500,311	472.0
Burglary	21,260	87.2	22,849	91.3	19,173	96.2	40,413	77.1	19,429	87.3	85,116	80.3
Larceny-theft	133,850	549.2	132,989	531.2	98,922	496.1	129,188	246.4	37,159	167.0	392,605	370.4
Motor vehicle theft	3,909	16.0	4,303	17.2	3,954	19.8	10,432	19.9	3,856	17.3	18,921	17.8
Arson	858	3.5	1,011	4.0	1,074	5.4	1,524	2.9	795	3.6	3,669	3.5
Other												
Other assaults	102,006	418.5	108,509	433.5	101,411	508.6	175,126	334.0	75,245	338.2	388,235	366.3
Forgery and counterfeiting	6,277	25.8	7,633	30.5	6,691	33.6	11,735	22.4	4,197	18.9	26,004	24.5
Fraud	13,288	54.5	14,352	57.3	19,545	98.0	35,737	68.2	19,115	85.9	67,273	63.5
Embezzlement	1,549	6.4	1,463	5.8	1,181	5.9	2,393	4.6	987	4.4	5,155	4.9
Stolen property; buying, receiving, possessing	8,166	33.5	8,724	34.8	6,401	32.1	14,235	27.1	4,992	22.4	32,399	30.6
Vandalism	21,600	88.6	22,584	90.2	22,413	112.4	30,077	57.4	12,208	54.9	76,171	71.9
Weapons; carrying, possessing, etc.	10,015	41.1	9,657	38.6	9,826	49.3	19,868	37.9	6,836	30.7	42,133	39.7
Prostitution and commercialized vice	2,059	8.4	932	3.7	473	2.4	2,822	5.4	211	0.9	5,918	5.6
Sex offenses (except forcible rape and prostitution)	4,930	20.2	4,963	19.8	4,931	24.7	11,502	21.9	5,074	22.8	22,011	20.8
Drug abuse violations	110,419	453.0	112,774	450.5	120,888	606.3	231,600	441.7	98,516	442.7	486,332	458.8
Gambling	118	0.5	445	1.8	342	1.7	1,190	2.3	191	0.9	1,558	1.5
Offenses against the family and children	6,811	27.9	7,728	30.9	7,203	36.1	31,142	59.4	12,417	55.8	45,174	42.6
Driving under the influence	89,479	367.1	110,915	443.1	122,077	612.3	263,087	501.8	178,369	801.6	494,513	466.5
Liquor laws	43,787	179.6	55,454	221.5	81,318	407.8	49,220	93.9	29,479	132.5	168,371	158.8
Drunkenness	51,524	211.4	56,067	224.0	57,428	288.0	43,619	83.2	18,289	82.2	153,565	144.9
Disorderly conduct	54,538	223.8	69,399	277.2	82,648	414.5	49,473	94.4	21,800	98.0	191,791	180.9
Vagrancy	1,062	4.4	961	3.8	1,715	8.6	2,457	4.7	329	1.5	5,206	4.9
All other offenses (except traffic)	272,749	1,119.0	314,558	1,256.6	317,633	1,593.0	580,443	1,107.0	235,223	1,057.1	1,219,293	1,150.3
Suspicion	119	0.5	101	0.4	267	1.3	81	0.2	151	0.7	371	0.3
Curfew and loitering law violations	5,697	23.4	6,508	26.0	6,245	31.3	4,183	8.0	438	2.0	17,977	17.0

[1] Suburban areas include law enforcement agencies in cities with less than 50,000 inhabitants and county law enforcement agencies that are within a Metropolitan Statistical Area. Suburban areas exclude all metropolitan agencies associated with a principal city. The agencies associated with suburban areas also appear in other groups within this table.

[2] Does not include suspicion.

Table 32.   Ten-Year Arrest Trends, 2001 and 2010

(Number, percent change; 8,726 agencies; 2010 estimated population 194,771,628; 2001 estimated population 180,336,272)

Offense charged	Number of persons arrested								
	Total all ages			Under 18 years of age			18 years of age and over		
	2001	2010	Percent change	2001	2010	Percent change	2001	2010	Percent change
TOTAL[1]	8,468,019	8,221,468	-2.9	1,360,895	1,040,453	-23.5	7,107,124	7,181,015	1.0
Violent Crime	397,801	359,520	-9.6	60,558	47,450	-21.6	337,243	312,070	-7.5
Murder and nonnegligent manslaughter	8,071	7,027	-12.9	822	627	-23.7	7,249	6,400	-11.7
Forcible rape	16,745	12,588	-24.8	2,788	1,821	-34.7	13,957	10,767	-22.9
Robbery	68,293	71,393	4.5	15,946	16,841	5.6	52,347	54,552	4.2
Aggravated assault	304,692	268,512	-11.9	41,002	28,161	-31.3	263,690	240,351	-8.9
Property Crime	1,021,601	1,055,572	3.3	317,955	239,170	-24.8	703,646	816,402	16.0
Burglary	184,076	190,440	3.5	57,329	42,478	-25.9	126,747	147,962	16.7
Larceny-theft	741,163	813,493	9.8	227,017	184,154	-18.9	514,146	629,339	22.4
Motor vehicle theft	85,303	44,125	-48.3	27,707	9,406	-66.1	57,596	34,719	-39.7
Arson	11,059	7,514	-32.1	5,902	3,132	-46.9	5,157	4,382	-15.0
Other									
Other assaults	819,796	829,525	1.2	150,182	134,420	-10.5	669,614	695,105	3.8
Forgery and counterfeiting	73,248	47,845	-34.7	3,849	1,046	-72.8	69,399	46,799	-32.6
Fraud	216,503	120,764	-44.2	5,578	3,634	-34.9	210,925	117,130	-44.5
Embezzlement	13,690	11,301	-17.5	1,308	310	-76.3	12,382	10,991	-11.2
Stolen property; buying, receiving, possessing	75,552	62,274	-17.6	16,494	9,850	-40.3	59,058	52,424	-11.2
Vandalism	172,579	161,668	-6.3	68,771	50,326	-26.8	103,808	111,342	7.3
Weapons; carrying, possessing, etc.	99,723	98,067	-1.7	23,108	19,715	-14.7	76,615	78,352	2.3
Prostitution and commercialized vice	47,256	36,805	-22.1	882	654	-25.9	46,374	36,151	-22.0
Sex offenses (except forcible rape and prostitution)	57,263	46,089	-19.5	11,885	8,056	-32.2	45,378	38,033	-16.2
Drug abuse violations	961,056	1,014,383	5.5	123,686	107,164	-13.4	837,370	907,219	8.3
Gambling	4,913	3,046	-38.0	402	244	-39.3	4,511	2,802	-37.9
Offenses against the family and children	88,528	69,571	-21.4	6,097	2,275	-62.7	82,431	67,296	-18.4
Driving under the influence	860,398	836,018	-2.8	12,509	7,238	-42.1	847,889	828,780	-2.3
Liquor laws	403,068	321,255	-20.3	90,293	61,561	-31.8	312,775	259,694	-17.0
Drunkenness	399,835	373,886	-6.5	13,160	8,859	-32.7	386,675	365,027	-5.6
Disorderly conduct	380,646	350,773	-7.8	105,894	89,340	-15.6	274,752	261,433	-4.8
Vagrancy	16,788	21,252	26.6	1,674	1,490	-11.0	15,114	19,762	30.8
All other offenses (except traffic)	2,261,825	2,339,901	3.5	250,660	185,698	-25.9	2,011,165	2,154,203	7.1
Suspicion	2,300	537	-76.7	620	86	-86.1	1,680	451	-73.2
Curfew and loitering law violations	95,950	61,953	-35.4	95,950	61,953	-35.4	...	...	...

[1] Does not include suspicion.

Table 33.   Ten-Year Arrest Trends, by Sex, 2001 and 2010

(Number, percent change; 8,726 agencies; 2010 estimated population 194,771,628; 2001 estimated population 180,336,272)

Offense charged	Male						Female					
	Total			Under 18			Total			Under 18		
	2001	2010	Percent change	2001	2010	Percent change	2001	2010	Percent change	2001	2010	Percent change
TOTAL[1]	6,568,579	6,122,413	-6.8	998,238	733,955	-26.5	1,899,440	2,099,055	10.5	362,657	306,498	-15.5
Violent Crime	328,259	289,501	-11.8	49,544	38,721	-21.8	69,542	70,019	0.7	11,014	8,729	-20.7
Murder and nonnegligent manslaughter	7,011	6,276	-10.5	738	561	-24.0	1,060	751	-29.2	84	66	-21.4
Forcible rape	16,552	12,475	-24.6	2,748	1,793	-34.8	193	113	-41.5	40	28	-30.0
Robbery	61,315	62,383	1.7	14,556	15,091	3.7	6,978	9,010	29.1	1,390	1,750	25.9
Aggravated assault	243,381	208,367	-14.4	31,502	21,276	-32.5	61,311	60,145	-1.9	9,500	6,885	-27.5
Property Crime	707,452	656,367	-7.2	216,535	147,222	-32.0	314,149	399,205	27.1	101,420	91,948	-9.3
Burglary	158,422	159,813	0.9	50,286	37,216	-26.0	25,654	30,627	19.4	7,043	5,262	-25.3
Larceny-theft	468,276	454,079	-3.0	138,056	99,440	-28.0	272,887	359,414	31.7	88,961	84,714	-4.8
Motor vehicle theft	71,385	36,238	-49.2	22,939	7,846	-65.8	13,918	7,887	-43.3	4,768	1,560	-67.3
Arson	9,369	6,237	-33.4	5,254	2,720	-48.2	1,690	1,277	-24.4	648	412	-36.4
Other												
Other assaults	624,982	603,501	-3.4	102,570	86,903	-15.3	194,814	226,024	16.0	47,612	47,517	-0.2
Forgery and counterfeiting	43,623	29,878	-31.5	2,457	761	-69.0	29,625	17,967	-39.4	1,392	285	-79.5
Fraud	116,414	69,079	-40.7	3,666	2,360	-35.6	100,089	51,685	-48.4	1,912	1,274	-33.4
Embezzlement	6,940	5,538	-20.2	763	180	-76.4	6,750	5,763	-14.6	545	130	-76.1
Stolen property; buying, receiving, possessing	62,888	50,045	-20.4	14,109	8,240	-41.6	12,664	12,229	-3.4	2,385	1,610	-32.5
Vandalism	144,703	131,349	-9.2	59,745	43,037	-28.0	27,876	30,319	8.8	9,026	7,289	-19.2
Weapons; carrying, possessing, etc.	91,440	89,693	-1.9	20,676	17,607	-14.8	8,283	8,374	1.1	2,432	2,108	-13.3
Prostitution and commercialized vice	16,245	10,844	-33.2	255	112	-56.1	31,011	25,961	-16.3	627	542	-13.6
Sex offenses (except forcible rape and prostitution)	52,815	42,833	-18.9	10,982	7,346	-33.1	4,448	3,256	-26.8	903	710	-21.4
Drug abuse violations	786,831	816,307	3.7	103,696	89,066	-14.1	174,225	198,076	13.7	19,990	18,098	-9.5
Gambling	4,365	2,614	-40.1	376	234	-37.8	548	432	-21.2	26	10	-61.5
Offenses against the family and children	68,431	52,116	-23.8	3,881	1,468	-62.2	20,097	17,455	-13.1	2,216	807	-63.6
Driving under the influence	715,610	639,291	-10.7	10,287	5,424	-47.3	144,788	196,727	35.9	2,222	1,814	-18.4
Liquor laws	307,444	230,230	-25.1	61,056	38,030	-37.7	95,624	91,025	-4.8	29,237	23,531	-19.5
Drunkenness	344,649	308,784	-10.4	10,348	6,503	-37.2	55,186	65,102	18.0	2,812	2,356	-16.2
Disorderly conduct	287,509	251,193	-12.6	74,442	58,055	-22.0	93,137	99,580	6.9	31,452	31,285	-0.5
Vagrancy	13,512	16,981	25.7	1,305	1,142	-12.5	3,276	4,271	30.4	369	348	-5.7
All other offenses (except traffic)	1,777,951	1,782,491	0.3	185,029	137,766	-25.5	483,874	557,410	15.2	65,631	47,932	-27.0
Suspicion	1,772	427	-75.9	407	68	-83.3	528	110	-79.2	213	18	-91.5
Curfew and loitering law violations	66,516	43,778	-34.2	66,516	43,778	-34.2	29,434	18,175	-38.3	29,434	18,175	-38.3

[1] Does not include suspicion.

Table 34.   Five-Year Arrest Trends, by Age, 2006 and 2010

(Number, percent change; 10,062 agencies; 2010 estimated population 212,437,594; 2006 estimated population 206,552,492)

Offense charged	Number of persons arrested								
	Total all ages			Under 18 years of age			18 years of age and over		
	2006	2010	Percent change	2006	2010	Percent change	2006	2010	Percent change
TOTAL[1]	9,829,216	8,949,384	-9.0	1,479,342	1,154,096	-22.0	8,349,874	7,795,288	-6.6
Violent Crime	422,596	380,841	-9.9	70,142	52,378	-25.3	352,454	328,463	-6.8
Murder and nonnegligent manslaughter	8,853	7,528	-15.0	846	657	-22.3	8,007	6,871	-14.2
Forcible rape	16,165	14,063	-13.0	2,451	2,033	-17.1	13,714	12,030	-12.3
Robbery	86,809	77,530	-10.7	24,538	19,054	-22.3	62,271	58,476	-6.1
Aggravated assault	310,769	281,720	-9.3	42,307	30,634	-27.6	268,462	251,086	-6.5
Property Crime	1,073,158	1,144,997	6.7	285,486	259,847	-9.0	787,672	885,150	12.4
Burglary	210,075	203,142	-3.3	57,601	45,673	-20.7	152,474	157,469	3.3
Larceny-theft	759,274	883,467	16.4	198,497	199,654	0.6	560,777	683,813	21.9
Motor vehicle theft	92,201	50,220	-45.5	23,643	11,165	-52.8	68,558	39,055	-43.0
Arson	11,608	8,168	-29.6	5,745	3,355	-41.6	5,863	4,813	-17.9
Other									
Other assaults	899,187	890,356	-1.0	172,603	143,813	-16.7	726,584	746,543	2.7
Forgery and counterfeiting	73,738	50,939	-30.9	2,437	1,169	-52.0	71,301	49,770	-30.2
Fraud	202,396	131,678	-34.9	5,609	4,250	-24.2	196,787	127,428	-35.2
Embezzlement	13,947	11,273	-19.2	976	317	-67.5	12,971	10,956	-15.5
Stolen property; buying, receiving, possessing	85,516	66,205	-22.6	15,229	10,570	-30.6	70,287	55,635	-20.8
Vandalism	212,137	178,946	-15.6	83,825	55,042	-34.3	128,312	123,904	-3.4
Weapons; carrying, possessing, etc.	136,015	109,314	-19.6	32,829	22,053	-32.8	103,186	87,261	-15.4
Prostitution and commercialized vice	50,144	38,032	-24.2	1,060	671	-36.7	49,084	37,361	-23.9
Sex offenses (except forcible rape and prostitution)	59,187	50,375	-14.9	11,133	9,139	-17.9	48,054	41,236	-14.2
Drug abuse violations	1,294,016	1,127,915	-12.8	137,200	119,927	-12.6	1,156,816	1,007,988	-12.9
Gambling	8,028	6,448	-19.7	1,527	902	-40.9	6,501	5,546	-14.7
Offenses against the family and children	89,387	75,756	-15.2	3,693	2,567	-30.5	85,694	73,189	-14.6
Driving under the influence	986,752	938,176	-4.9	13,600	8,333	-38.7	973,152	929,843	-4.5
Liquor laws	443,660	360,622	-18.7	100,370	69,536	-30.7	343,290	291,086	-15.2
Drunkenness	399,218	390,220	-2.3	11,746	8,890	-24.3	387,472	381,330	-1.6
Disorderly conduct	489,436	426,974	-12.8	142,810	107,040	-25.0	346,626	319,934	-7.7
Vagrancy	24,431	22,129	-9.4	3,638	1,602	-56.0	20,793	20,527	-1.3
All other offenses (except traffic)	2,756,544	2,480,652	-10.0	273,706	208,514	-23.8	2,482,838	2,272,138	-8.5
Suspicion	1,639	638	-61.1	297	90	-69.7	1,342	548	-59.2
Curfew and loitering law violations	109,723	67,536	-38.4	109,723	67,536	-38.4	...	...	...

[1] Does not include suspicion.

Table 35. Five-Year Arrest Trends, by Age and Sex, 2006 and 2010

(Number, percent change; 10,062 agencies; 2010 estimated population 212,437,594; 2006 estimated population 206,552,492)

Offense charged	Male						Female					
	Total			Under 18			Total			Under 18		
	2006	2010	Percent change	2006	2010	Percent change	2006	2010	Percent change	2006	2010	Percent change
TOTAL[1]	7,511,192	6,677,859	-11.1	1,074,248	816,646	-24.0	2,318,024	2,271,525	-2.0	405,094	337,450	-16.7
Violent Crime	347,413	308,047	-11.3	57,878	43,049	-25.6	75,183	72,794	-3.2	12,264	9,329	-23.9
Murder and nonnegligent manslaughter	7,894	6,729	-14.8	807	591	-26.8	959	799	-16.7	39	66	69.2
Forcible rape	15,962	13,920	-12.8	2,407	1,989	-17.4	203	143	-29.6	44	44	0.0
Robbery	76,953	67,952	-11.7	22,218	17,196	-22.6	9,856	9,578	-2.8	2,320	1,858	-19.9
Aggravated assault	246,604	219,446	-11.0	32,446	23,273	-28.3	64,165	62,274	-2.9	9,861	7,361	-25.4
Property Crime	736,210	715,032	-2.9	192,836	161,068	-16.5	336,948	429,965	27.6	92,650	98,779	6.6
Burglary	179,301	171,367	-4.4	51,090	40,173	-21.4	30,774	31,775	3.3	6,511	5,500	-15.5
Larceny-theft	471,341	495,513	5.1	117,126	108,601	-7.3	287,933	387,954	34.7	81,371	91,053	11.9
Motor vehicle theft	75,908	41,395	-45.5	19,655	9,380	-52.3	16,293	8,825	-45.8	3,988	1,785	-55.2
Arson	9,660	6,757	-30.1	4,965	2,914	-41.3	1,948	1,411	-27.6	780	441	-43.5
Other												
Other assaults	673,130	651,068	-3.3	114,674	93,252	-18.7	226,057	239,288	5.9	57,929	50,561	-12.7
Forgery and counterfeiting	44,254	31,639	-28.5	1,607	853	-46.9	29,484	19,300	-34.5	830	316	-61.9
Fraud	110,841	76,246	-31.2	3,685	2,789	-24.3	91,555	55,432	-39.5	1,924	1,461	-24.1
Embezzlement	6,556	5,504	-16.0	537	186	-65.4	7,391	5,769	-21.9	439	131	-70.2
Stolen property; buying, receiving, possessing	69,387	53,154	-23.4	13,056	8,838	-32.3	16,129	13,051	-19.1	2,173	1,732	-20.3
Vandalism	176,980	145,401	-17.8	72,893	47,033	-35.5	35,157	33,545	-4.6	10,932	8,009	-26.7
Weapons; carrying, possessing, etc.	124,972	100,169	-19.8	29,501	19,734	-33.1	11,043	9,145	-17.2	3,328	2,319	-30.3
Prostitution and commercialized vice	18,776	12,085	-35.6	270	130	-51.9	31,368	25,947	-17.3	790	541	-31.5
Sex offenses (except forcible rape and prostitution)	54,029	46,610	-13.7	10,040	8,201	-18.3	5,158	3,765	-27.0	1,093	938	-14.2
Drug abuse violations	1,047,464	912,088	-12.9	115,277	100,056	-13.2	246,552	215,827	-12.5	21,923	19,871	-9.4
Gambling	7,443	5,903	-20.7	1,485	889	-40.1	585	545	-6.8	42	13	-69.0
Offenses against the family and children	67,676	56,616	-16.3	2,254	1,682	-25.4	21,711	19,140	-11.8	1,439	885	-38.5
Driving under the influence	787,736	716,398	-9.1	10,426	6,226	-40.3	199,016	221,778	11.4	3,174	2,107	-33.6
Liquor laws	321,904	256,309	-20.4	63,867	42,649	-33.2	121,756	104,313	-14.3	36,503	26,887	-26.3
Drunkenness	336,923	322,054	-4.4	8,748	6,466	-26.1	62,295	68,166	9.4	2,998	2,424	-19.1
Disorderly conduct	361,726	308,868	-14.6	96,260	70,499	-26.8	127,710	118,106	-7.5	46,550	36,541	-21.5
Vagrancy	18,793	17,801	-5.3	2,527	1,246	-50.7	5,638	4,328	-23.2	1,111	356	-68.0
All other offenses (except traffic)	2,123,239	1,889,330	-11.0	200,687	154,263	-23.1	633,305	591,322	-6.6	73,019	54,251	-25.7
Suspicion	1,276	498	-61.0	231	68	-70.6	363	140	-61.4	66	22	-66.7
Curfew and loitering law violations	75,740	47,537	-37.2	75,740	47,537	-37.2	33,983	19,999	-41.1	33,983	19,999	-41.1

[1] Does not include suspicion.

Table 36. Current Year Over Previous Year Arrest Trends, 2009–2010

(Number, percent change; 11,631 agencies; 2010 estimated population 228,914,576; 2009 estimated population 227,500,540)

Offense charged	Number of persons arrested											
	Total all ages			Under 15 years of age			Under 18 years of age			18 years of age and over		
	2009	2010	Percent change	2009	2010	Percent change	2009	2010	Percent change	2009	2010	Percent change
TOTAL[1]	10,098,934	9,641,603	-4.5	356,463	331,690	-6.9	1,348,012	1,217,454	-9.7	8,750,922	8,424,149	-3.7
Violent Crime	428,113	405,412	-5.3	15,650	14,194	-9.3	60,949	53,884	-11.6	367,164	351,528	-4.3
Murder and nonnegligent manslaughter	8,728	8,007	-8.3	75	70	-6.7	773	718	-7.1	7,955	7,289	-8.4
Forcible rape	15,163	14,470	-4.6	724	683	-5.7	2,233	2,072	-7.2	12,930	12,398	-4.1
Robbery	91,409	81,521	-10.8	4,085	3,547	-13.2	22,259	19,118	-14.1	69,150	62,403	-9.8
Aggravated assault	312,813	301,414	-3.6	10,766	9,894	-8.1	35,684	31,976	-10.4	277,129	269,438	-2.8
Property Crime	1,287,265	1,227,192	-4.7	86,764	78,530	-9.5	314,047	276,461	-12.0	973,218	950,731	-2.3
Burglary	222,317	216,340	-2.7	15,030	13,386	-10.9	55,158	48,557	-12.0	167,159	167,783	0.4
Larceny-theft	998,821	951,441	-4.7	66,593	60,844	-8.6	241,158	213,508	-11.5	757,663	737,933	-2.6
Motor vehicle theft	56,936	50,869	-10.7	2,731	2,230	-18.3	13,649	10,890	-20.2	43,287	39,979	-7.6
Arson	9,191	8,542	-7.1	2,410	2,070	-14.1	4,082	3,506	-14.1	5,109	5,036	-1.4
Other												
Other assaults	968,889	951,142	-1.8	58,882	57,841	-1.8	159,905	153,159	-4.2	808,984	797,983	-1.4
Forgery and counterfeiting	63,479	57,520	-9.4	209	154	-26.3	1,592	1,236	-22.4	61,887	56,284	-9.1
Fraud	164,758	139,005	-15.6	811	741	-8.6	4,920	4,419	-10.2	159,838	134,586	-15.8
Embezzlement	13,723	12,301	-10.4	32	18	-43.8	478	340	-28.9	13,245	11,961	-9.7
Stolen property; buying, receiving, possessing	74,770	71,886	-3.9	2,789	2,493	-10.6	13,195	11,285	-14.5	61,575	60,601	-1.6
Vandalism	201,174	187,883	-6.6	26,271	22,483	-14.4	68,046	57,724	-15.2	133,128	130,159	-2.2
Weapons; carrying, possessing, etc.	119,204	113,838	-4.5	7,732	7,567	-2.1	24,582	22,562	-8.2	94,622	91,276	-3.5
Prostitution and commercialized vice	47,103	41,996	-10.8	122	85	-30.3	978	723	-26.1	46,125	41,273	-10.5
Sex offenses (except forcible rape and prostitution)	56,735	53,385	-5.9	4,812	4,666	-3.0	9,990	9,632	-3.6	46,745	43,753	-6.4
Drug abuse violations	1,197,396	1,177,176	-1.7	19,762	21,690	9.8	123,555	122,713	-0.7	1,073,841	1,054,463	-1.8
Gambling	4,585	3,986	-13.1	69	43	-37.7	493	352	-28.6	4,092	3,634	-11.2
Offenses against the family and children	86,883	82,878	-4.6	936	941	0.5	3,308	2,906	-12.2	83,575	79,972	-4.3
Driving under the influence	1,088,388	1,035,708	-4.8	219	162	-26.0	10,430	8,931	-14.4	1,077,958	1,026,777	-4.7
Liquor laws	432,693	386,234	-10.7	7,785	7,273	-6.6	85,755	74,013	-13.7	346,938	312,221	-10.0
Drunkenness	451,019	418,929	-7.1	1,232	1,207	-2.0	10,709	9,679	-9.6	440,310	409,250	-7.1
Disorderly conduct	475,630	448,496	-5.7	43,433	41,168	-5.2	121,059	111,555	-7.9	354,571	336,941	-5.0
Vagrancy	24,929	24,558	-1.5	511	470	-8.0	2,020	1,675	-17.1	22,909	22,883	-0.1
All other offenses (except traffic)	2,825,544	2,730,492	-3.4	57,154	52,254	-8.6	245,347	222,619	-9.3	2,580,197	2,507,873	-2.8
Suspicion	813	810	-0.4	26	23	-11.5	98	98	0.0	715	712	-0.4
Curfew and loitering law violations	86,654	71,586	-17.4	21,288	17,710	-16.8	86,654	71,586	-17.4	...	...	...

[1] Does not include suspicion.

Table 37. Current Year Over Previous Year Arrest Trends, by Age and Sex, 2009–2010

(Number, percent change; 11,631 agencies; 2010 estimated population 228,914,576; 2009 estimated population 227,500,540)

Offense charged	Male						Female					
	Total			Under 18			Total			Under 18		
	2009	2010	Percent change	2009	2010	Percent change	2009	2010	Percent change	2009	2010	Percent change
TOTAL[1]	7,546,481	7,167,015	-5.0	952,228	856,807	-10.0	2,552,453	2,474,588	-3.1	395,784	360,647	-8.9
Violent Crime	346,970	326,440	-5.9	49,774	43,968	-11.7	81,143	78,972	-2.7	11,175	9,916	-11.3
Murder and nonnegligent manslaughter	7,771	7,118	-8.4	708	643	-9.2	957	889	-7.1	65	75	15.4
Forcible rape	14,970	14,323	-4.3	2,191	2,026	-7.5	193	147	-23.8	42	46	9.5
Robbery	80,327	71,295	-11.2	19,967	17,186	-13.9	11,082	10,226	-7.7	2,292	1,932	-15.7
Aggravated assault	243,902	233,704	-4.2	26,908	24,113	-10.4	68,911	67,710	-1.7	8,776	7,863	-10.4
Property Crime	803,772	763,821	-5.0	194,454	170,606	-12.3	483,493	463,371	-4.2	119,593	105,855	-11.5
Burglary	188,504	182,762	-3.0	48,624	42,782	-12.0	33,813	33,578	-0.7	6,534	5,775	-11.6
Larceny-theft	560,876	532,115	-5.1	131,009	115,702	-11.7	437,945	419,326	-4.3	110,149	97,806	-11.2
Motor vehicle theft	46,752	41,877	-10.4	11,275	9,078	-19.5	10,184	8,992	-11.7	2,374	1,812	-23.7
Arson	7,640	7,067	-7.5	3,546	3,044	-14.2	1,551	1,475	-4.9	536	462	-13.8
Other												
Other assaults	715,014	693,925	-2.9	105,126	98,980	-5.8	253,875	257,217	1.3	54,779	54,179	-1.1
Forgery and counterfeiting	39,698	35,832	-9.7	1,117	891	-20.2	23,781	21,688	-8.8	475	345	-27.4
Fraud	92,730	80,328	-13.4	3,176	2,898	-8.8	72,028	58,677	-18.5	1,744	1,521	-12.8
Embezzlement	6,717	6,068	-9.7	275	198	-28.0	7,006	6,233	-11.0	203	142	-30.0
Stolen property; buying, receiving, .possessing	60,378	57,653	-4.5	11,043	9,402	-14.9	14,392	14,233	-1.1	2,152	1,883	-12.5
Vandalism	165,008	152,379	-7.7	58,713	49,191	-16.2	36,166	35,504	-1.8	9,333	8,533	-8.6
Weapons; carrying, possessing, etc.	109,312	104,123	-4.7	21,991	20,134	-8.4	9,892	9,715	-1.8	2,591	2,428	-6.3
Prostitution and commercialized vice	14,041	12,868	-8.4	211	132	-37.4	33,062	29,128	-11.9	767	591	-22.9
Sex offenses (except forcible rape and prostitution)	51,654	49,264	-4.6	8,935	8,657	-3.1	5,081	4,121	-18.9	1,055	975	-7.6
Drug abuse violations	969,123	946,430	-2.3	103,502	101,788	-1.7	228,273	230,746	1.1	20,053	20,925	4.3
Gambling	3,765	3,346	-11.1	466	323	-30.7	820	640	-22.0	27	29	7.4
Offenses against the family and children	65,349	62,097	-5.0	2,123	1,895	-10.7	21,534	20,781	-3.5	1,185	1,011	-14.7
Driving under the influence	840,440	789,552	-6.1	7,827	6,664	-14.9	247,948	246,156	-0.7	2,603	2,267	-12.9
Liquor laws	307,599	275,093	-10.6	52,696	45,403	-13.8	125,094	111,141	-11.2	33,059	28,610	-13.5
Drunkenness	374,877	345,107	-7.9	7,961	7,081	-11.1	76,142	73,822	-3.0	2,748	2,598	-5.5
Disorderly conduct	345,477	321,617	-6.9	80,569	72,983	-9.4	130,153	126,879	-2.5	40,490	38,572	-4.7
Vagrancy	19,569	19,628	0.3	1,459	1,299	-11.0	5,360	4,930	-8.0	561	376	-33.0
All other offenses (except traffic)	2,154,855	2,071,085	-3.9	180,677	163,955	-9.3	670,689	659,407	-1.7	64,670	58,664	-9.3
Suspicion	589	616	4.6	79	73	-7.6	224	194	-13.4	19	25	31.6
Curfew and loitering law violations	60,133	50,359	-16.3	60,133	50,359	-16.3	26,521	21,227	-20.0	26,521	21,227	-20.0

[1] Does not include suspicion.

Table 38.   Arrests, Distribution by Age, 2010

(Number, percent; 12,222 agencies; 2010 estimated population 240,103,394)

Offense charged	Total all ages	Ages under 15	Ages under 18	Ages 18 and over	Under 10	10–12	13–14	15	16	17	18	19	20
TOTAL	10,223,558	349,695	1,288,615	8,934,943	8,205	75,408	266,082	244,042	317,280	377,598	468,670	499,103	478,530
Total percent distribution[1]	100.0	3.4	12.6	87.4	0.1	0.7	2.6	2.4	3.1	3.7	4.6	4.9	4.7
Violent Crime	430,364	15,643	59,093	371,271	345	3,609	11,689	11,046	15,041	17,363	20,375	20,371	19,175
Violent crime percent distribution[1]	100.0	3.6	13.7	86.3	0.1	0.8	2.7	2.6	3.5	4.0	4.7	4.7	4.5
Murder and nonnegligent manslaughter	8,667	73	784	7,883	0	7	66	119	239	353	543	581	515
Forcible rape	15,586	717	2,198	13,388	7	195	515	393	505	583	730	787	692
Robbery	87,771	3,936	21,110	66,661	36	558	3,342	4,179	6,052	6,943	7,724	6,938	5,769
Aggravated assault	318,340	10,917	35,001	283,339	302	2,849	7,766	6,355	8,245	9,484	11,378	12,065	12,199
Property Crime	1,293,023	81,843	290,351	1,002,672	1,759	18,024	62,060	56,316	70,944	81,248	87,461	75,770	63,016
Property crime percent distribution[1]	100.0	6.3	22.5	77.5	0.1	1.4	4.8	4.4	5.5	6.3	6.8	5.9	4.9
Burglary	226,325	14,019	51,298	175,027	438	3,024	10,557	9,832	12,539	14,908	17,244	15,315	12,597
Larceny-theft	1,002,466	63,254	223,207	779,259	1,097	14,001	48,156	43,189	54,510	62,254	66,064	56,984	47,531
Motor vehicle theft	55,426	2,465	12,268	43,158	20	273	2,172	2,707	3,443	3,653	3,798	3,176	2,605
Arson	8,806	2,105	3,578	5,228	204	726	1,175	588	452	433	355	295	283
Other													
Other assaults	1,008,509	61,754	163,370	845,139	1,750	16,329	43,675	31,534	35,546	34,536	32,388	33,398	34,214
Forgery and counterfeiting	60,841	163	1,314	59,527	5	31	127	173	304	674	1,663	2,358	2,807
Fraud	144,956	756	4,585	140,371	20	117	619	690	1,203	1,936	3,403	4,725	5,173
Embezzlement	13,020	19	349	12,671	0	1	18	20	80	230	584	804	828
Stolen property; buying, receiving, possessing	74,313	2,561	11,608	62,705	46	414	2,101	2,335	3,069	3,643	4,973	4,621	3,935
Vandalism	197,850	23,470	60,591	137,259	1,091	6,369	16,010	11,416	12,822	12,883	12,098	10,397	9,180
Weapons; carrying, possessing, etc.	123,719	8,170	24,518	99,201	418	2,202	5,550	4,331	5,434	6,583	7,550	7,411	6,345
Prostitution and commercialized vice	48,281	91	804	47,477	1	5	85	112	208	393	1,392	1,885	2,159
Sex offenses (except forcible rape and prostitution)	56,332	4,896	10,147	46,185	181	1,392	3,323	1,738	1,767	1,746	2,303	2,110	1,843
Drug abuse violations	1,273,963	23,016	132,921	1,141,042	152	2,799	20,065	23,223	35,320	51,362	78,870	81,842	75,454
Gambling	7,533	118	1,040	6,493	1	5	112	161	305	456	501	507	463
Offenses against the family and children	85,213	964	2,982	82,231	50	222	692	556	717	745	1,483	1,698	1,887
Driving under the influence	1,087,987	171	9,352	1,078,635	25	20	126	335	2,141	6,705	19,764	29,313	34,499
Liquor laws	400,608	7,451	75,889	324,719	54	653	6,744	11,353	21,337	35,748	65,538	73,739	62,188
Drunkenness	442,392	1,231	10,030	432,362	19	88	1,124	1,659	2,357	4,783	11,511	13,333	13,572
Disorderly conduct	482,991	44,481	121,276	361,715	616	10,720	33,145	24,762	26,675	25,358	21,257	19,305	18,748
Vagrancy	24,839	474	1,690	23,149	6	66	402	404	474	338	1,162	1,134	948
All other offenses (except traffic)	2,892,023	54,165	232,702	2,659,321	1,422	9,477	43,266	45,685	60,060	72,792	94,346	114,338	122,037
Suspicion	904	25	106	798	1	1	23	15	33	33	48	44	59
Curfew and loitering law violations	73,897	18,233	73,897	...	243	2,864	15,126	16,178	21,443	18,043	...	...	...

[1] Because of rounding, the percentages may not add to 100.0.

Table 38. Arrests, Distribution by Age, 2010—*Continued*

(Number, percent; 12,222 agencies; 2010 estimated population 240,103,394)

Offense charged	21	22	23	24	25–29	30–34	35–39	40–44	45–49	50–54	55–59	60–64	65 and over
TOTAL	437,741	400,218	373,511	356,577	1,517,930	1,118,681	868,570	791,328	715,851	481,553	242,547	108,665	75,468
Total percent distribution[1]	4.3	3.9	3.7	3.5	14.8	10.9	8.5	7.7	7.0	4.7	2.4	1.1	0.7
Violent Crime	18,670	16,949	15,854	14,876	65,279	48,229	36,735	32,416	27,905	17,882	8,793	4,314	3,448
Violent crime percent distribution[1]	4.3	3.9	3.7	3.5	15.2	11.2	8.5	7.5	6.5	4.2	2.0	1.0	0.8
Murder and nonnegligent manslaughter	523	426	393	347	1,430	938	643	469	418	292	180	95	90
Forcible rape	686	552	534	466	2,123	1,682	1,514	1,240	1,012	652	340	200	178
Robbery	4,751	3,894	3,318	2,836	10,827	6,689	4,553	3,875	2,970	1,546	647	225	99
Aggravated assault	12,710	12,077	11,609	11,227	50,899	38,920	30,025	26,832	23,505	15,392	7,626	3,794	3,081
Property Crime	53,095	45,731	40,840	38,332	158,400	114,124	88,722	81,902	70,750	45,424	21,948	9,823	7,334
Property crime percent distribution[1]	4.1	3.5	3.2	3.0	12.3	8.8	6.9	6.3	5.5	3.5	1.7	0.8	0.6
Burglary	10,622	8,861	7,896	7,345	28,587	19,461	14,373	12,881	10,375	5,940	2,252	851	427
Larceny-theft	39,961	34,635	30,887	29,023	121,393	88,339	69,742	65,086	57,350	37,858	18,986	8,692	6,728
Motor vehicle theft	2,269	2,021	1,872	1,791	7,663	5,650	4,150	3,476	2,533	1,322	537	181	114
Arson	243	214	185	173	757	674	457	459	492	304	173	99	65
Other													
Other assaults	37,215	36,052	34,773	33,563	150,766	117,254	94,565	84,132	72,242	45,331	21,460	9,742	8,044
Forgery and counterfeiting	2,540	2,581	2,642	2,603	11,730	9,371	6,988	5,580	4,339	2,504	1,107	453	261
Fraud	4,764	4,828	4,728	4,781	23,806	21,537	18,715	15,726	12,578	7,996	4,169	2,016	1,426
Embezzlement	730	630	572	557	1,962	1,486	1,344	1,156	850	614	320	166	68
Stolen property; buying, receiving, possessing	3,602	2,983	2,665	2,601	10,968	8,045	5,786	4,922	3,853	2,213	935	356	247
Vandalism	8,684	7,505	6,565	6,059	23,568	15,710	11,040	9,522	7,900	4,823	2,254	1,040	914
Weapons; carrying, possessing, etc.	5,934	5,478	4,911	4,607	18,450	11,749	7,684	6,067	5,281	3,714	2,034	1,094	892
Prostitution and commercialized vice	2,068	2,097	1,830	1,778	7,691	6,262	5,858	5,486	4,600	2,435	1,040	472	424
Sex offenses (except forcible rape and prostitution)	1,854	1,625	1,445	1,269	5,969	5,338	4,798	4,770	4,415	3,336	2,133	1,389	1,588
Drug abuse violations	66,334	58,533	53,265	50,088	205,638	140,490	97,100	83,584	72,150	46,057	20,732	7,651	3,254
Gambling	371	298	288	242	883	598	461	505	375	437	229	159	176
Offenses against the family and children	2,290	2,372	2,580	2,755	14,803	14,692	12,477	10,373	7,615	4,262	1,795	678	471
Driving under the influence	50,104	49,872	48,905	47,523	198,928	140,950	111,499	102,248	98,081	70,997	40,360	21,013	14,579
Liquor laws	10,469	7,346	5,570	4,758	17,850	13,222	11,794	13,734	15,094	12,138	6,685	2,931	1,663
Drunkenness	20,295	18,149	16,586	15,602	66,140	49,173	41,725	45,697	50,741	38,159	19,690	7,913	4,076
Disorderly conduct	22,141	19,131	16,686	15,566	58,233	40,419	31,512	29,816	29,909	20,695	10,195	4,617	3,485
Vagrancy	765	671	604	557	2,461	1,989	2,005	2,542	3,192	2,713	1,506	567	333
All other offenses (except traffic)	125,767	117,348	112,156	108,422	474,259	357,948	277,672	251,097	223,940	149,797	75,149	32,263	22,782
Suspicion	49	39	46	38	146	95	90	53	41	26	13	8	3
Curfew and loitering law violations	…	…	…	…	…	…	…	…	…	…	…	…	…

[1] Because of rounding, the percentages may not add to 100.0.

Table 39. Male Arrests, Distribution by Age, 2010

(Number, percent; 12,222 agencies; 2010 estimated population 240,103,394)

Offense charged	Total all ages	Ages under 15	Ages under 18	Ages 18 and over	Under 10	10–12	13–14	15	16	17	18	19	20
TOTAL	7,621,103	240,167	910,798	6,710,305	6,732	53,702	179,733	168,328	225,500	276,803	350,731	372,174	355,982
Total percent distribution[1]	100.0	3.2	12.0	88.0	0.1	0.7	2.4	2.2	3.0	3.6	4.6	4.9	4.7
Violent Crime	346,519	12,353	48,273	298,246	305	2,893	9,155	8,889	12,427	14,604	17,235	16,874	15,607
Violent crime percent distribution[1]	100.0	3.6	13.9	86.1	0.1	0.8	2.6	2.6	3.6	4.2	5.0	4.9	4.5
Murder and nonnegligent manslaughter	7,726	59	707	7,019	0	5	54	103	222	323	508	532	470
Forcible rape	15,419	692	2,150	13,269	7	185	500	381	496	581	728	781	688
Robbery	77,077	3,520	19,080	57,997	31	500	2,989	3,739	5,521	6,300	6,976	6,173	5,118
Aggravated assault	246,297	8,082	26,336	219,961	267	2,203	5,612	4,666	6,188	7,400	9,023	9,388	9,331
Property Crime	807,467	51,189	179,957	627,510	1,373	11,481	38,335	34,615	43,680	50,473	55,537	47,994	39,275
Property crime percent distribution[1]	100.0	6.3	22.3	77.7	0.2	1.4	4.7	4.3	5.4	6.3	6.9	5.9	4.9
Burglary	191,663	12,234	45,285	146,378	367	2,635	9,232	8,606	11,112	13,333	15,335	13,386	10,780
Larceny-theft	562,812	35,118	121,278	441,534	796	7,976	26,346	23,281	29,302	33,577	36,599	31,634	26,080
Motor vehicle theft	45,721	2,018	10,290	35,431	18	232	1,768	2,224	2,876	3,172	3,293	2,711	2,163
Arson	7,271	1,819	3,104	4,167	192	638	989	504	390	391	310	263	252
Other													
Other assaults	737,206	40,071	105,890	631,316	1,443	11,375	27,253	19,756	22,815	23,248	22,440	23,101	23,829
Forgery and counterfeiting	37,984	122	954	37,030	4	25	93	135	231	466	1,051	1,506	1,706
Fraud	84,840	454	3,021	81,819	16	70	368	459	823	1,285	2,269	2,929	3,196
Embezzlement	6,446	14	205	6,241	0	1	13	11	52	128	323	418	446
Stolen property; buying, receiving, possessing	59,637	2,073	9,640	49,997	41	345	1,687	1,887	2,568	3,112	4,242	3,822	3,177
Vandalism	160,376	19,837	51,693	108,683	980	5,328	13,529	9,827	10,987	11,042	10,210	8,461	7,391
Weapons; carrying, possessing, etc.	113,315	7,138	21,880	91,435	378	1,920	4,840	3,832	4,874	6,036	7,089	6,958	5,934
Prostitution and commercialized vice	15,095	22	148	14,947	1	5	16	20	36	70	192	275	390
Sex offenses (except forcible rape and prostitution)	51,996	4,385	9,104	42,892	156	1,264	2,965	1,545	1,570	1,604	2,102	1,949	1,693
Drug abuse violations	1,030,078	18,145	111,127	918,951	132	2,262	15,751	19,170	29,953	43,859	67,152	68,717	62,278
Gambling	6,831	117	1,007	5,824	1	5	111	155	293	442	487	495	439
Offenses against the family and children	63,710	623	1,955	61,755	39	147	437	360	452	520	1,050	1,132	1,226
Driving under the influence	830,026	113	6,988	823,038	16	14	83	259	1,555	5,061	14,895	22,130	26,157
Liquor laws	286,311	3,760	46,644	239,667	39	319	3,402	6,274	13,089	23,521	44,221	51,094	44,422
Drunkenness	365,981	775	7,357	358,624	18	64	693	1,113	1,743	3,726	9,131	10,691	11,059
Disorderly conduct	348,958	28,144	79,677	269,281	508	7,250	20,386	15,752	17,969	17,812	15,593	14,113	13,656
Vagrancy	19,902	351	1,313	18,589	6	44	301	304	377	281	872	858	682
All other offenses (except traffic)	2,195,691	38,125	171,843	2,023,848	1,081	6,895	30,149	32,786	44,739	56,193	74,609	88,620	93,374
Suspicion	693	13	81	612	1	1	11	15	28	25	31	37	45
Curfew and loitering law violations	52,041	12,343	52,041	...	194	1,994	10,155	11,164	15,239	13,295	...	...	...

[1] Because of rounding, the percentages may not add to 100.0.

Table 39.　Male Arrests, Distribution by Age, 2010—*Continued*

(Number, percent; 12,222 agencies; 2010 estimated population 240,103,394)

Offense charged	21	22	23	24	25–29	30–34	35–39	40–44	45–49	50–54	55–59	60–64	65 and over
TOTAL	328,000	299,145	278,913	265,981	1,132,499	833,541	638,963	586,323	542,098	378,374	197,119	88,986	61,476
Total percent distribution[1]	4.3	3.9	3.7	3.5	14.9	10.9	8.4	7.7	7.1	5.0	2.6	1.2	0.8
Violent Crime	15,001	13,529	12,646	11,878	52,176	38,258	28,832	25,421	22,084	14,637	7,375	3,725	2,968
Violent crime percent distribution[1]	4.3	3.9	3.6	3.4	15.1	11.0	8.3	7.3	6.4	4.2	2.1	1.1	0.9
Murder and nonnegligent manslaughter	489	388	348	308	1,271	815	562	402	350	251	163	83	79
Forcible rape	682	546	527	463	2,103	1,662	1,491	1,231	1,006	647	338	200	176
Robbery	4,162	3,402	2,894	2,464	9,248	5,666	3,829	3,295	2,566	1,359	564	193	88
Aggravated assault	9,668	9,193	8,877	8,643	39,554	30,115	22,950	20,493	18,162	12,380	6,310	3,249	2,625
Property Crime	33,051	28,144	25,244	23,606	96,594	69,709	54,710	52,798	46,685	29,849	14,140	5,870	4,304
Property crime percent distribution[1]	4.1	3.5	3.1	2.9	12.0	8.6	6.8	6.5	5.8	3.7	1.8	0.7	0.5
Burglary	8,918	7,432	6,611	6,154	23,476	15,743	11,497	10,561	8,556	4,982	1,898	715	334
Larceny-theft	22,052	18,876	16,989	15,882	66,396	48,899	39,534	39,087	35,657	23,497	11,627	4,917	3,808
Motor vehicle theft	1,871	1,656	1,485	1,432	6,132	4,529	3,352	2,815	2,106	1,143	480	159	104
Arson	210	180	159	138	590	538	327	335	366	227	135	79	58
Other													
Other assaults	26,436	25,915	25,176	24,751	112,973	89,083	71,133	63,572	55,487	35,533	17,270	7,959	6,658
Forgery and counterfeiting	1,571	1,579	1,655	1,619	7,061	5,648	4,253	3,456	2,864	1,722	786	344	209
Fraud	2,921	2,885	2,821	2,808	13,487	11,850	10,119	9,065	7,592	5,033	2,670	1,269	905
Embezzlement	376	343	264	289	957	718	616	513	395	270	180	91	42
Stolen property; buying, receiving, possessing	2,881	2,336	2,076	2,036	8,447	6,237	4,508	3,978	3,105	1,844	812	291	205
Vandalism	6,929	6,032	5,105	4,730	18,494	12,275	8,462	7,265	6,056	3,887	1,803	827	756
Weapons; carrying, possessing, etc.	5,525	5,063	4,559	4,243	16,988	10,739	6,969	5,448	4,748	3,427	1,882	1,019	844
Prostitution and commercialized vice	391	444	454	445	2,394	2,219	1,934	1,746	1,546	1,073	659	394	391
Sex offenses (except forcible rape and prostitution)	1,681	1,474	1,323	1,149	5,444	4,896	4,425	4,424	4,130	3,189	2,078	1,368	1,567
Drug abuse violations	54,572	47,872	43,385	40,463	165,344	112,045	75,102	63,389	55,085	36,705	17,399	6,641	2,802
Gambling	348	290	277	231	810	537	383	416	305	353	182	133	138
Offenses against the family and children	1,498	1,586	1,681	1,880	10,328	11,073	9,689	8,307	6,276	3,594	1,503	549	383
Driving under the influence	36,853	37,038	36,567	35,843	152,305	109,399	85,279	76,412	73,151	54,799	32,445	17,393	12,372
Liquor laws	8,187	5,852	4,472	3,729	14,273	10,553	9,269	10,921	12,325	10,415	5,908	2,600	1,426
Drunkenness	16,585	15,021	13,731	13,027	54,792	40,672	33,990	36,942	41,797	32,625	17,604	7,201	3,756
Disorderly conduct	16,553	14,348	12,428	11,683	42,950	29,730	22,641	21,626	22,421	16,487	8,391	3,847	2,814
Vagrancy	617	516	473	434	1,938	1,565	1,537	1,973	2,628	2,350	1,341	522	283
All other offenses (except traffic)	95,986	88,848	84,537	81,109	354,636	266,258	205,044	188,610	173,388	120,564	62,679	26,936	18,650
Suspicion	38	30	39	28	108	77	68	41	30	18	12	7	3
Curfew and loitering law violations	...	...	...	...	...	...	...	...	...	...	...	...	...

[1] Because of rounding, the percentages may not add to 100.0.

Table 40. Female Arrests, Distribution by Age, 2010

(Number, percent; 12,222 agencies; 2010 estimated population 240,103,394)

Offense charged	Total all ages	Ages under 15	Ages under 18	Ages 18 and over	Under 10	10–12	13–14	15	16	17	18	19	20
TOTAL	2,602,455	109,528	377,817	2,224,638	1,473	21,706	86,349	75,714	91,780	100,795	117,939	126,929	122,548
Total percent distribution[1]	100.0	4.2	14.5	85.5	0.1	0.8	3.3	2.9	3.5	3.9	4.5	4.9	4.7
Violent Crime	83,845	3,290	10,820	73,025	40	716	2,534	2,157	2,614	2,759	3,140	3,497	3,568
Violent crime percent distribution[1]	100.0	3.9	12.9	87.1	*	0.9	3.0	2.6	3.1	3.3	3.7	4.2	4.3
Murder and nonnegligent manslaughter	941	14	77	864	0	2	12	16	17	30	35	49	45
Forcible rape	167	25	48	119	0	10	15	12	9	2	2	6	4
Robbery	10,694	416	2,030	8,664	5	58	353	440	531	643	748	765	651
Aggravated assault	72,043	2,835	8,665	63,378	35	646	2,154	1,689	2,057	2,084	2,355	2,677	2,868
Property Crime	485,556	30,654	110,394	375,162	386	6,543	23,725	21,701	27,264	30,775	31,924	27,776	23,741
Property crime percent distribution[1]	100.0	6.3	22.7	77.3	0.1	1.3	4.9	4.5	5.6	6.3	6.6	5.7	4.9
Burglary	34,662	1,785	6,013	28,649	71	389	1,325	1,226	1,427	1,575	1,909	1,929	1,817
Larceny-theft	439,654	28,136	101,929	337,725	301	6,025	21,810	19,908	25,208	28,677	29,465	25,350	21,451
Motor vehicle theft	9,705	447	1,978	7,727	2	41	404	483	567	481	505	465	442
Arson	1,535	286	474	1,061	12	88	186	84	62	42	45	32	31
Other													
Other assaults	271,303	21,683	57,480	213,823	307	4,954	16,422	11,778	12,731	11,288	9,948	10,297	10,385
Forgery and counterfeiting	22,857	41	360	22,497	1	6	34	38	73	208	612	852	1,101
Fraud	60,116	302	1,564	58,552	4	47	251	231	380	651	1,134	1,796	1,977
Embezzlement	6,574	5	144	6,430	0	0	5	9	28	102	261	386	382
Stolen property; buying, receiving, possessing	14,676	488	1,968	12,708	5	69	414	448	501	531	731	799	758
Vandalism	37,474	3,633	8,898	28,576	111	1,041	2,481	1,589	1,835	1,841	1,888	1,936	1,789
Weapons; carrying, possessing, etc.	10,404	1,032	2,638	7,766	40	282	710	499	560	547	461	453	411
Prostitution and commercialized vice	33,186	69	656	32,530	0	0	69	92	172	323	1,200	1,610	1,769
Sex offenses (except forcible rape and prostitution)	4,336	511	1,043	3,293	25	128	358	193	197	142	201	161	150
Drug abuse violations	243,885	4,871	21,794	222,091	20	537	4,314	4,053	5,367	7,503	11,718	13,125	13,176
Gambling	702	1	33	669	0	0	1	6	12	14	14	12	24
Offenses against the family and children	21,503	341	1,027	20,476	11	75	255	196	265	225	433	566	661
Driving under the influence	257,961	58	2,364	255,597	9	6	43	76	586	1,644	4,869	7,183	8,342
Liquor laws	114,297	3,691	29,245	85,052	15	334	3,342	5,079	8,248	12,227	21,317	22,645	17,766
Drunkenness	76,411	456	2,673	73,738	1	24	431	546	614	1,057	2,380	2,642	2,513
Disorderly conduct	134,033	16,337	41,599	92,434	108	3,470	12,759	9,010	8,706	7,546	5,664	5,192	5,092
Vagrancy	4,937	123	377	4,560	0	22	101	100	97	57	290	276	266
All other offenses (except traffic)	696,332	16,040	60,859	635,473	341	2,582	13,117	12,899	15,321	16,599	19,737	25,718	28,663
Suspicion	211	12	25	186	0	0	12	0	5	8	17	7	14
Curfew and loitering law violations	21,856	5,890	21,856	…	49	870	4,971	5,014	6,204	4,748	…	…	…

[1] Because of rounding, the percentages may not add to 100.0.

* Less than one-tenth of 1 percent.

Table 40. Female Arrests, Distribution by Age, 2010—*Continued*

(Number, percent; 12,222 agencies; 2010 estimated population 240,103,394)

Offense charged	21	22	23	24	25–29	30–34	35–39	40–44	45–49	50–54	55–59	60–64	65 and over
TOTAL	109,741	101,073	94,598	90,596	385,431	285,140	229,607	205,005	173,753	103,179	45,428	19,679	13,992
Total percent distribution[1]	4.2	3.9	3.6	3.5	14.8	11.0	8.8	7.9	6.7	4.0	1.7	0.8	0.5
Violent Crime	3,669	3,420	3,208	2,998	13,103	9,971	7,903	6,995	5,821	3,245	1,418	589	480
Violent crime percent distribution[1]	4.4	4.1	3.8	3.6	15.6	11.9	9.4	8.3	6.9	3.9	1.7	0.7	0.6
Murder and nonnegligent manslaughter	34	38	45	39	159	123	81	67	68	41	17	12	11
Forcible rape	4	6	7	3	20	20	23	9	6	5	2	0	2
Robbery	589	492	424	372	1,579	1,023	724	580	404	187	83	32	11
Aggravated assault	3,042	2,884	2,732	2,584	11,345	8,805	7,075	6,339	5,343	3,012	1,316	545	456
Property Crime	20,044	17,587	15,596	14,726	61,806	44,415	34,012	29,104	24,065	15,575	7,808	3,953	3,030
Property crime percent distribution[1]	4.1	3.6	3.2	3.0	12.7	9.1	7.0	6.0	5.0	3.2	1.6	0.8	0.6
Burglary	1,704	1,429	1,285	1,191	5,111	3,718	2,876	2,320	1,819	958	354	136	93
Larceny-theft	17,909	15,759	13,898	13,141	54,997	39,440	30,208	25,999	21,693	14,361	7,359	3,775	2,920
Motor vehicle theft	398	365	387	359	1,531	1,121	798	661	427	179	57	22	10
Arson	33	34	26	35	167	136	130	124	126	77	38	20	7
Other													
Other assaults	10,779	10,137	9,597	8,812	37,793	28,171	23,432	20,560	16,755	9,798	4,190	1,783	1,386
Forgery and counterfeiting	969	1,002	987	984	4,669	3,723	2,735	2,124	1,475	782	321	109	52
Fraud	1,843	1,943	1,907	1,973	10,319	9,687	8,596	6,661	4,986	2,963	1,499	747	521
Embezzlement	354	287	308	268	1,005	768	728	643	455	344	140	75	26
Stolen property; buying, receiving, possessing	721	647	589	565	2,521	1,808	1,278	944	748	369	123	65	42
Vandalism	1,755	1,473	1,460	1,329	5,074	3,435	2,578	2,257	1,844	936	451	213	158
Weapons; carrying, possessing, etc.	409	415	352	364	1,462	1,010	715	619	533	287	152	75	48
Prostitution and commercialized vice	1,677	1,653	1,376	1,333	5,297	4,043	3,924	3,740	3,054	1,362	381	78	33
Sex offenses (except forcible rape and prostitution)	173	151	122	120	525	442	373	346	285	147	55	21	21
Drug abuse violations	11,762	10,661	9,880	9,625	40,294	28,445	21,998	20,195	17,065	9,352	3,333	1,010	452
Gambling	23	8	11	11	73	61	78	89	70	84	47	26	38
Offenses against the family and children	792	786	899	875	4,475	3,619	2,788	2,066	1,339	668	292	129	88
Driving under the influence	13,251	12,834	12,338	11,680	46,623	31,551	26,220	25,836	24,930	16,198	7,915	3,620	2,207
Liquor laws	2,282	1,494	1,098	1,029	3,577	2,669	2,525	2,813	2,769	1,723	777	331	237
Drunkenness	3,710	3,128	2,855	2,575	11,348	8,501	7,735	8,755	8,944	5,534	2,086	712	320
Disorderly conduct	5,588	4,783	4,258	3,883	15,283	10,689	8,871	8,190	7,488	4,208	1,804	770	671
Vagrancy	148	155	131	123	523	424	468	569	564	363	165	45	50
All other offenses (except traffic)	29,781	28,500	27,619	27,313	119,623	91,690	72,628	62,487	50,552	29,233	12,470	5,327	4,132
Suspicion	11	9	7	10	38	18	22	12	11	8	1	1	0
Curfew and loitering law violations	...	...	...	...	...	...	...	...	...	...	...	...	...

[1] Because of rounding, the percentages may not add to 100.0.

Table 41. Arrests of Persons Under 15, 18, 21, and 25 Years of Age, 2010

(Number, percent; 12,222 agencies; 2010 estimated population 240,103,394)

Offense charged	Total all ages	Number of persons arrested				Percent of total all ages			
		Under 15	Under 18	Under 21	Under 25	Under 15	Under 18	Under 21	Under 25
TOTAL	10,223,558	349,695	1,288,615	2,734,918	4,302,965	3.4	12.6	26.8	42.1
Violent Crime	430,364	15,643	59,093	119,014	185,363	3.6	13.7	27.7	43.1
Murder and nonnegligent manslaughter	8,667	73	784	2,423	4,112	0.8	9.0	28.0	47.4
Forcible rape	15,586	717	2,198	4,407	6,645	4.6	14.1	28.3	42.6
Robbery	87,771	3,936	21,110	41,541	56,340	4.5	24.1	47.3	64.2
Aggravated assault	318,340	10,917	35,001	70,643	118,266	3.4	11.0	22.2	37.2
Property Crime	1,293,023	81,843	290,351	516,598	694,596	6.3	22.5	40.0	53.7
Burglary	226,325	14,019	51,298	96,454	131,178	6.2	22.7	42.6	58.0
Larceny-theft	1,002,466	63,254	223,207	393,786	528,292	6.3	22.3	39.3	52.7
Motor vehicle theft	55,426	2,465	12,268	21,847	29,800	4.4	22.1	39.4	53.8
Arson	8,806	2,105	3,578	4,511	5,326	23.9	40.6	51.2	60.5
Other									
Other assaults	1,008,509	61,754	163,370	263,370	404,973	6.1	16.2	26.1	40.2
Forgery and counterfeiting	60,841	163	1,314	8,142	18,508	0.3	2.2	13.4	30.4
Fraud	144,956	756	4,585	17,886	36,987	0.5	3.2	12.3	25.5
Embezzlement	13,020	19	349	2,565	5,054	0.1	2.7	19.7	38.8
Stolen property; buying, receiving, possessing	74,313	2,561	11,608	25,137	36,988	3.4	15.6	33.8	49.8
Vandalism	197,850	23,470	60,591	92,266	121,079	11.9	30.6	46.6	61.2
Weapons; carrying, possessing, etc.	123,719	8,170	24,518	45,824	66,754	6.6	19.8	37.0	54.0
Prostitution and commercialized vice	48,281	91	804	6,240	14,013	0.2	1.7	12.9	29.0
Sex offenses (except forcible rape and prostitution)	56,332	4,896	10,147	16,403	22,596	8.7	18.0	29.1	40.1
Drug abuse violations	1,273,963	23,016	132,921	369,087	597,307	1.8	10.4	29.0	46.9
Gambling	7,533	118	1,040	2,511	3,710	1.6	13.8	33.3	49.2
Offenses against the family and children	85,213	964	2,982	8,050	18,047	1.1	3.5	9.4	21.2
Driving under the influence	1,087,987	171	9,352	92,928	289,332	*	0.9	8.5	26.6
Liquor laws	400,608	7,451	75,889	277,354	305,497	1.9	18.9	69.2	76.3
Drunkenness	442,392	1,231	10,030	48,446	119,078	0.3	2.3	11.0	26.9
Disorderly conduct	482,991	44,481	121,276	180,586	254,110	9.2	25.1	37.4	52.6
Vagrancy	24,839	474	1,690	4,934	7,531	1.9	6.8	19.9	30.3
All other offenses (except traffic)	2,892,023	54,165	232,702	563,423	1,027,116	1.9	8.0	19.5	35.5
Suspicion	904	25	106	257	429	2.8	11.7	28.4	47.5
Curfew and loitering law violations	73,897	18,233	73,897	73,897	73,897	24.7	100.0	100.0	100.0

* Less than one-tenth of 1 percent.

Table 42. Arrests, Distribution by Sex, 2010

(Number, percent; 12,222 agencies; 2010 estimated population 240,103,394)

Offense charged	Number of persons arrested			Percent male	Percent female	Percent distribution[1]		
	Total	Male	Female			Total	Male	Female
TOTAL	10,223,558	7,621,103	2,602,455	74.5	25.5	100.0	100.0	100.0
Violent Crime	430,364	346,519	83,845	80.5	19.5	4.2	4.5	3.2
Murder and nonnegligent manslaughter	8,667	7,726	941	89.1	10.9	0.1	0.1	*
Forcible rape	15,586	15,419	167	98.9	1.1	0.2	0.2	*
Robbery	87,771	77,077	10,694	87.8	12.2	0.9	1.0	0.4
Aggravated assault	318,340	246,297	72,043	77.4	22.6	3.1	3.2	2.8
Property Crime	1,293,023	807,467	485,556	62.4	37.6	12.6	10.6	18.7
Burglary	226,325	191,663	34,662	84.7	15.3	2.2	2.5	1.3
Larceny-theft	1,002,466	562,812	439,654	56.1	43.9	9.8	7.4	16.9
Motor vehicle theft	55,426	45,721	9,705	82.5	17.5	0.5	0.6	0.4
Arson	8,806	7,271	1,535	82.6	17.4	0.1	0.1	0.1
Other								
Other assaults	1,008,509	737,206	271,303	73.1	26.9	9.9	9.7	10.4
Forgery and counterfeiting	60,841	37,984	22,857	62.4	37.6	0.6	0.5	0.9
Fraud	144,956	84,840	60,116	58.5	41.5	1.4	1.1	2.3
Embezzlement	13,020	6,446	6,574	49.5	50.5	0.1	0.1	0.3
Stolen property; buying, receiving, possessing	74,313	59,637	14,676	80.3	19.7	0.7	0.8	0.6
Vandalism	197,850	160,376	37,474	81.1	18.9	1.9	2.1	1.4
Weapons; carrying, possessing, etc.	123,719	113,315	10,404	91.6	8.4	1.2	1.5	0.4
Prostitution and commercialized vice	48,281	15,095	33,186	31.3	68.7	0.5	0.2	1.3
Sex offenses (except forcible rape and prostitution)	56,332	51,996	4,336	92.3	7.7	0.6	0.7	0.2
Drug abuse violations	1,273,963	1,030,078	243,885	80.9	19.1	12.5	13.5	9.4
Gambling	7,533	6,831	702	90.7	9.3	0.1	0.1	*
Offenses against the family and children	85,213	63,710	21,503	74.8	25.2	0.8	0.8	0.8
Driving under the influence	1,087,987	830,026	257,961	76.3	23.7	10.6	10.9	9.9
Liquor laws	400,608	286,311	114,297	71.5	28.5	3.9	3.8	4.4
Drunkenness	442,392	365,981	76,411	82.7	17.3	4.3	4.8	2.9
Disorderly conduct	482,991	348,958	134,033	72.2	27.8	4.7	4.6	5.2
Vagrancy	24,839	19,902	4,937	80.1	19.9	0.2	0.3	0.2
All other offenses (except traffic)	2,892,023	2,195,691	696,332	75.9	24.1	28.3	28.8	26.8
Suspicion	904	693	211	76.7	23.3	*	*	*
Curfew and loitering law violations	73,897	52,041	21,856	70.4	29.6	0.7	0.7	0.8

[1] Because of rounding, the percentages may not add to 100.0.

* Less than one-tenth of 1 percent.

Table 43.   Arrests, Distribution by Race, 2010

(Number, percent; 12,221 agencies; 2010 estimated population 240,100,189)

Offense charged	Total arrests					Percent distribution[1]				
	Total	White	Black	American Indian or Alaskan Native	Asian or Pacific Islander	Total	White	Black	American Indian or Alaskan Native	Asian or Pacific Islander
TOTAL	10,177,907	7,066,154	2,846,862	145,612	119,279	100.0	69.4	28.0	1.4	1.2
Violent Crime	429,166	254,620	163,670	5,776	5,100	100.0	59.3	38.1	1.3	1.2
Murder and nonnegligent manslaughter	8,641	4,261	4,209	91	80	100.0	49.3	48.7	1.1	0.9
Forcible rape	15,503	10,178	4,925	214	186	100.0	65.7	31.8	1.4	1.2
Robbery	87,587	37,906	48,154	617	910	100.0	43.3	55.0	0.7	1.0
Aggravated assault	317,435	202,275	106,382	4,854	3,924	100.0	63.7	33.5	1.5	1.2
Property Crime	1,288,295	881,420	372,562	17,080	17,233	100.0	68.4	28.9	1.3	1.3
Burglary	225,775	152,210	69,541	1,961	2,063	100.0	67.4	30.8	0.9	0.9
Larceny-theft	998,476	687,609	282,246	14,323	14,298	100.0	68.9	28.3	1.4	1.4
Motor vehicle theft	55,278	35,009	18,797	696	776	100.0	63.3	34.0	1.3	1.4
Arson	8,766	6,592	1,978	100	96	100.0	75.2	22.6	1.1	1.1
Other										
Other assaults	1,004,273	659,171	318,117	14,848	12,137	100.0	65.6	31.7	1.5	1.2
Forgery and counterfeiting	60,538	40,167	19,350	342	679	100.0	66.4	32.0	0.6	1.1
Fraud	144,214	95,126	46,493	1,253	1,342	100.0	66.0	32.2	0.9	0.9
Embezzlement	12,930	8,568	4,037	88	237	100.0	66.3	31.2	0.7	1.8
Stolen property; buying, receiving, possessing	74,122	48,303	24,494	598	727	100.0	65.2	33.0	0.8	1.0
Vandalism	197,015	145,284	46,306	3,279	2,146	100.0	73.7	23.5	1.7	1.1
Weapons; carrying, possessing, etc.	123,278	71,772	49,443	874	1,189	100.0	58.2	40.1	0.7	1.0
Prostitution and commercialized vice	48,154	26,156	20,405	342	1,251	100.0	54.3	42.4	0.7	2.6
Sex offenses (except forcible rape and prostitution)	56,125	41,406	13,182	744	793	100.0	73.8	23.5	1.3	1.4
Drug abuse violations	1,270,443	846,736	404,609	8,766	10,332	100.0	66.6	31.8	0.7	0.8
Gambling	7,512	2,160	5,071	32	249	100.0	28.8	67.5	0.4	3.3
Offenses against the family and children	84,812	56,233	26,470	1,533	576	100.0	66.3	31.2	1.8	0.7
Driving under the influence	1,082,301	927,516	124,467	13,980	16,338	100.0	85.7	11.5	1.3	1.5
Liquor laws	396,942	329,895	47,529	14,129	5,389	100.0	83.1	12.0	3.6	1.4
Drunkenness	440,688	362,396	66,837	8,583	2,872	100.0	82.2	15.2	1.9	0.7
Disorderly conduct	480,080	305,154	162,521	8,415	3,990	100.0	63.6	33.9	1.8	0.8
Vagrancy	24,759	14,092	9,935	567	165	100.0	56.9	40.1	2.3	0.7
All other offenses (except traffic)	2,877,687	1,905,436	893,018	43,634	35,599	100.0	66.2	31.0	1.5	1.2
Suspicion	903	582	310	5	6	100.0	64.5	34.3	0.6	0.7
Curfew and loitering law violations	73,670	43,961	28,036	744	929	100.0	59.7	38.1	1.0	1.3

[1] Because of rounding, the percentages may not add to 100.0.

Table 43. Arrests, Distribution by Race, 2010—*Continued*

(Number, percent; 12,221 agencies; 2010 estimated population 240,100,189)

Offense charged	Arrests under 18					Percent distribution[1]				
	Total	White	Black	American Indian or Alaskan Native	Asian or Pacific Islander	Total	White	Black	American Indian or Alaskan Native	Asian or Pacific Islander
TOTAL	1,281,738	849,251	399,249	15,760	17,478	100.0	66.3	31.1	1.2	1.4
Violent Crime	58,903	27,983	29,754	538	628	100.0	47.5	50.5	0.9	1.1
Murder and nonnegligent manslaughter	781	332	439	4	6	100.0	42.5	56.2	0.5	0.8
Forcible rape	2,181	1,369	787	15	10	100.0	62.8	36.1	0.7	0.5
Robbery	21,062	6,670	14,046	101	245	100.0	31.7	66.7	0.5	1.2
Aggravated assault	34,879	19,612	14,482	418	367	100.0	56.2	41.5	1.2	1.1
Property Crime	288,811	184,728	95,440	3,523	5,120	100.0	64.0	33.0	1.2	1.8
Burglary	51,135	31,539	18,657	400	539	100.0	61.7	36.5	0.8	1.1
Larceny-theft	221,901	143,791	70,833	2,912	4,365	100.0	64.8	31.9	1.3	2.0
Motor vehicle theft	12,223	6,721	5,166	172	164	100.0	55.0	42.3	1.4	1.3
Arson	3,552	2,677	784	39	52	100.0	75.4	22.1	1.1	1.5
Other										
Other assaults	162,389	96,994	61,847	1,694	1,854	100.0	59.7	38.1	1.0	1.1
Forgery and counterfeiting	1,306	873	404	8	21	100.0	66.8	30.9	0.6	1.6
Fraud	4,557	2,700	1,753	52	52	100.0	59.2	38.5	1.1	1.1
Embezzlement	341	212	119	3	7	100.0	62.2	34.9	0.9	2.1
Stolen property; buying, receiving, possessing	11,564	6,486	4,865	80	133	100.0	56.1	42.1	0.7	1.2
Vandalism	60,265	46,992	11,858	747	668	100.0	78.0	19.7	1.2	1.1
Weapons; carrying, possessing, etc.	24,355	15,112	8,771	178	294	100.0	62.0	36.0	0.7	1.2
Prostitution and commercialized vice	804	306	476	9	13	100.0	38.1	59.2	1.1	1.6
Sex offenses (except forcible rape and prostitution)	10,082	7,228	2,640	71	143	100.0	71.7	26.2	0.7	1.4
Drug abuse violations	132,481	98,039	31,575	1,425	1,442	100.0	74.0	23.8	1.1	1.1
Gambling	1,039	86	942	3	8	100.0	8.3	90.7	0.3	0.8
Offenses against the family and children	2,948	2,114	746	72	16	100.0	71.7	25.3	2.4	0.5
Driving under the influence	9,290	8,468	532	156	134	100.0	91.2	5.7	1.7	1.4
Liquor laws	75,397	66,720	5,288	2,360	1,029	100.0	88.5	7.0	3.1	1.4
Drunkenness	10,003	8,862	850	221	70	100.0	88.6	8.5	2.2	0.7
Disorderly conduct	120,514	69,470	48,808	1,283	953	100.0	57.6	40.5	1.1	0.8
Vagrancy	1,690	1,282	391	5	12	100.0	75.9	23.1	0.3	0.7
All other offenses (except traffic)	231,223	160,564	64,120	2,588	3,951	100.0	69.4	27.7	1.1	1.7
Suspicion	106	71	34	0	1	100.0	67.0	32.1	0.0	0.9
Curfew and loitering law violations	73,670	43,961	28,036	744	929	100.0	59.7	38.1	1.0	1.3

[1] Because of rounding, the percentages may not add to 100.0.

Table 43. Arrests, Distribution by Race, 2010—*Continued*

(Number, percent; 12,221 agencies; 2010 estimated population 240,100,189)

Offense charged	Arrests 18 and over					Percent distribution[1]				
	Total	White	Black	American Indian or Alaskan Native	Asian or Pacific Islander	Total	White	Black	American Indian or Alaskan Native	Asian or Pacific Islander
TOTAL	8,896,169	6,216,903	2,447,613	129,852	101,801	100.0	69.9	27.5	1.5	1.1
Violent Crime	370,263	226,637	133,916	5,238	4,472	100.0	61.2	36.2	1.4	1.2
Murder and nonnegligent manslaughter	7,860	3,929	3,770	87	74	100.0	50.0	48.0	1.1	0.9
Forcible rape	13,322	8,809	4,138	199	176	100.0	66.1	31.1	1.5	1.3
Robbery	66,525	31,236	34,108	516	665	100.0	47.0	51.3	0.8	1.0
Aggravated assault	282,556	182,663	91,900	4,436	3,557	100.0	64.6	32.5	1.6	1.3
Property Crime	999,484	696,692	277,122	13,557	12,113	100.0	69.7	27.7	1.4	1.2
Burglary	174,640	120,671	50,884	1,561	1,524	100.0	69.1	29.1	0.9	0.9
Larceny-theft	776,575	543,818	211,413	11,411	9,933	100.0	70.0	27.2	1.5	1.3
Motor vehicle theft	43,055	28,288	13,631	524	612	100.0	65.7	31.7	1.2	1.4
Arson	5,214	3,915	1,194	61	44	100.0	75.1	22.9	1.2	0.8
Other										
Other assaults	841,884	562,177	256,270	13,154	10,283	100.0	66.8	30.4	1.6	1.2
Forgery and counterfeiting	59,232	39,294	18,946	334	658	100.0	66.3	32.0	0.6	1.1
Fraud	139,657	92,426	44,740	1,201	1,290	100.0	66.2	32.0	0.9	0.9
Embezzlement	12,589	8,356	3,918	85	230	100.0	66.4	31.1	0.7	1.8
Stolen property; buying, receiving, possessing	62,558	41,817	19,629	518	594	100.0	66.8	31.4	0.8	0.9
Vandalism	136,750	98,292	34,448	2,532	1,478	100.0	71.9	25.2	1.9	1.1
Weapons; carrying, possessing, etc.	98,923	56,660	40,672	696	895	100.0	57.3	41.1	0.7	0.9
Prostitution and commercialized vice	47,350	25,850	19,929	333	1,238	100.0	54.6	42.1	0.7	2.6
Sex offenses (except forcible rape and prostitution)	46,043	34,178	10,542	673	650	100.0	74.2	22.9	1.5	1.4
Drug abuse violations	1,137,962	748,697	373,034	7,341	8,890	100.0	65.8	32.8	0.6	0.8
Gambling	6,473	2,074	4,129	29	241	100.0	32.0	63.8	0.4	3.7
Offenses against the family and children	81,864	54,119	25,724	1,461	560	100.0	66.1	31.4	1.8	0.7
Driving under the influence	1,073,011	919,048	123,935	13,824	16,204	100.0	85.7	11.6	1.3	1.5
Liquor laws	321,545	263,175	42,241	11,769	4,360	100.0	81.8	13.1	3.7	1.4
Drunkenness	430,685	353,534	65,987	8,362	2,802	100.0	82.1	15.3	1.9	0.7
Disorderly conduct	359,566	235,684	113,713	7,132	3,037	100.0	65.5	31.6	2.0	0.8
Vagrancy	23,069	12,810	9,544	562	153	100.0	55.5	41.4	2.4	0.7
All other offenses (except traffic)	2,646,464	1,744,872	828,898	41,046	31,648	100.0	65.9	31.3	1.6	1.2
Suspicion	797	511	276	5	5	100.0	64.1	34.6	0.6	0.6
Curfew and loitering law violations	…	…	…	…	…	…	…	…	…	…

[1] Because of rounding, the percentages may not add to 100.0.

Table 44.   City Arrest Trends, 2009–2010

(Number, percent change; 8,436 agencies; 2010 estimated population 157,943,246; 2009 estimated population 156,998,017)

Offense charged	Number of persons arrested								
	Total all ages			Under 18 years of age			18 years of age and over		
	2009	2010	Percent change	2009	2010	Percent change	2009	2010	Percent change
TOTAL[1]	7,514,218	7,144,759	-4.9	1,111,456	1,001,610	-9.9	6,402,762	6,143,149	-4.1
Violent Crime	333,295	315,088	-5.5	49,829	44,217	-11.3	283,466	270,871	-4.4
Murder and nonnegligent manslaughter	6,347	5,909	-6.9	635	578	-9.0	5,712	5,331	-6.7
Forcible rape	10,815	10,598	-2.0	1,594	1,521	-4.6	9,221	9,077	-1.6
Robbery	78,378	69,778	-11.0	19,568	16,928	-13.5	58,810	52,850	-10.1
Aggravated assault	237,755	228,803	-3.8	28,032	25,190	-10.1	209,723	203,613	-2.9
Property Crime	1,054,900	999,433	-5.3	265,686	234,734	-11.6	789,214	764,699	-3.1
Burglary	163,691	160,160	-2.2	42,866	38,490	-10.2	120,825	121,670	0.7
Larceny-theft	842,080	795,457	-5.5	209,059	184,891	-11.6	633,021	610,566	-3.5
Motor vehicle theft	42,497	37,510	-11.7	10,555	8,476	-19.7	31,942	29,034	-9.1
Arson	6,632	6,306	-4.9	3,206	2,877	-10.3	3,426	3,429	0.1
Other									
Other assaults	726,896	714,495	-1.7	122,460	116,756	-4.7	604,436	597,739	-1.1
Forgery and counterfeiting	47,629	42,891	-9.9	1,253	990	-21.0	46,376	41,901	-9.6
Fraud	99,561	85,535	-14.1	3,877	3,457	-10.8	95,684	82,078	-14.2
Embezzlement	10,470	9,321	-11.0	374	265	-29.1	10,096	9,056	-10.3
Stolen property; buying, receiving, possessing	56,707	54,700	-3.5	11,037	9,506	-13.9	45,670	45,194	-1.0
Vandalism	157,732	147,252	-6.6	55,299	46,930	-15.1	102,433	100,322	-2.1
Weapons; carrying, possessing, etc.	93,725	89,821	-4.2	20,353	18,605	-8.6	73,372	71,216	-2.9
Prostitution and commercialized vice	44,197	39,247	-11.2	894	649	-27.4	43,303	38,598	-10.9
Sex offenses (except forcible rape and prostitution)	40,620	37,951	-6.6	7,119	6,838	-3.9	33,501	31,113	-7.1
Drug abuse violations	894,406	871,870	-2.5	98,459	97,945	-0.5	795,947	773,925	-2.8
Gambling	3,128	2,838	-9.3	432	312	-27.8	2,696	2,526	-6.3
Offenses against the family and children	41,635	40,347	-3.1	2,521	2,205	-12.5	39,114	38,142	-2.5
Driving under the influence	661,039	621,518	-6.0	7,099	5,954	-16.1	653,940	615,564	-5.9
Liquor laws	346,402	309,545	-10.6	65,721	56,961	-13.3	280,681	252,584	-10.0
Drunkenness	384,113	358,926	-6.6	9,253	8,479	-8.4	374,860	350,447	-6.5
Disorderly conduct	407,181	380,930	-6.4	104,866	95,834	-8.6	302,315	285,096	-5.7
Vagrancy	22,310	21,823	-2.2	1,847	1,498	-18.9	20,463	20,325	-0.7
All other offenses (except traffic)	2,006,289	1,934,398	-3.6	201,094	182,645	-9.2	1,805,195	1,751,753	-3.0
Suspicion	637	648	1.7	83	84	1.2	554	564	1.8
Curfew and loitering law violations	81,983	66,830	-18.5	81,983	66,830	-18.5	…	…	…

[1] Does not include suspicion.

Table 45.   City Arrest Trends, by Age and Sex, 2009–2010

(Number, percent change; 8,436 agencies; 2010 estimated population 157,943,246; 2009 estimated population 156,998,017)

Offense charged	Male						Female					
	Total			Under 18			Total			Under 18		
	2009	2010	Percent change	2009	2010	Percent change	2009	2010	Percent change	2009	2010	Percent change
TOTAL[1]	5,589,498	5,286,295	-5.4	780,257	701,263	-10.1	1,924,720	1,858,464	-3.4	331,199	300,347	-9.3
Violent Crime	269,303	252,847	-6.1	40,725	36,104	-11.3	63,992	62,241	-2.7	9,104	8,113	-10.9
Murder and nonnegligent manslaughter	5,694	5,284	7.2	578	521	9.9	653	625	4.3	57	57	0.0
Forcible rape	10,692	10,502	-1.8	1,568	1,486	-5.2	123	96	-22.0	26	35	34.6
Robbery	68,739	61,007	-11.2	17,486	15,177	-13.2	9,639	8,771	-9.0	2,082	1,751	-15.9
Aggravated assault	184,178	176,054	-4.4	21,093	18,920	-10.3	53,577	52,749	-1.5	6,939	6,270	-9.6
Property Crime	642,857	606,974	-5.6	160,541	141,672	-11.8	412,043	392,459	-4.8	105,145	93,062	-11.5
Burglary	138,182	134,735	-2.5	37,709	33,695	-10.6	25,509	25,425	-0.3	5,157	4,795	-7.0
Larceny-theft	464,331	436,103	-6.1	111,292	98,332	-11.6	377,749	359,354	-4.9	97,767	86,559	-11.5
Motor vehicle theft	34,822	30,918	-11.2	8,750	7,139	-18.4	7,675	6,592	-14.1	1,805	1,337	-25.9
Arson	5,522	5,218	-5.5	2,790	2,506	-10.2	1,110	1,088	-2.0	416	371	-10.8
Other												
Other assaults	535,753	520,329	-2.9	79,935	74,965	-6.2	191,143	194,166	1.6	42,525	41,791	-1.7
Forgery and counterfeiting	29,835	26,625	-10.8	873	698	-20.0	17,794	16,266	-8.6	380	292	-23.2
Fraud	58,416	51,254	-12.3	2,501	2,270	-9.2	41,145	34,281	-16.7	1,376	1,187	-13.7
Embezzlement	5,060	4,585	-9.4	216	144	-33.3	5,410	4,736	-12.5	158	121	-23.4
Stolen property; buying, receiving, possessing	45,608	43,749	-4.1	9,218	7,917	-14.1	11,099	10,951	-1.3	1,819	1,589	-12.6
Vandalism	129,546	119,402	-7.8	47,862	40,146	-16.1	28,186	27,850	-1.2	7,437	6,784	-8.8
Weapons; carrying, possessing, etc.	86,037	82,273	-4.4	18,307	16,673	-8.9	7,688	7,548	-1.8	2,046	1,932	-5.6
Prostitution and commercialized vice	12,996	11,742	-9.6	181	109	-39.8	31,201	27,505	-11.8	713	540	-24.3
Sex offenses (except forcible rape and prostitution)	36,675	34,896	-4.9	6,338	6,138	-3.2	3,945	3,055	-22.6	781	700	-10.4
Drug abuse violations	729,670	706,886	-3.1	82,907	81,592	-1.6	164,736	164,984	0.2	15,552	16,353	5.2
Gambling	2,787	2,432	-12.7	426	297	-30.3	341	406	19.1	6	15	150.0
Offenses against the family and children	27,915	26,941	-3.5	1,589	1,420	-10.6	13,720	13,406	-2.3	932	785	-15.8
Driving under the influence	506,530	470,604	-7.1	5,292	4,405	-16.8	154,509	150,914	-2.3	1,807	1,549	-14.3
Liquor laws	247,174	221,483	-10.4	40,413	35,125	-13.1	99,228	88,062	-11.3	25,308	21,836	-13.7
Drunkenness	320,459	297,002	-7.3	6,878	6,202	-9.8	63,654	61,924	-2.7	2,375	2,277	-4.1
Disorderly conduct	295,988	272,976	-7.8	69,539	62,503	-10.1	111,193	107,954	-2.9	35,327	33,331	-5.7
Vagrancy	17,815	17,567	-1.4	1,345	1,168	-13.2	4,495	4,256	-5.3	502	330	-34.3
All other offenses (except traffic)	1,531,965	1,468,481	-4.1	148,062	134,468	-9.2	474,324	465,917	-1.8	53,032	48,177	-9.2
Suspicion	472	485	2.8	66	61	-7.6	165	163	-1.2	17	23	35.3
Curfew and loitering law violations	57,109	47,247	-17.3	57,109	47,247	-17.3	24,874	19,583	-21.3	24,874	19,583	-21.3

[1] Does not include suspicion.

Table 46.   City Arrests, Distribution by Age, 2010

(Number, percent; 8,912 agencies; 2010 estimated population 165,417,960)

Offense charged	Total all ages	Ages under 15	Ages under 18	Ages 18 and over	Under 10	10–12	13–14	15	16	17	18	19	20
TOTAL	7,598,850	291,325	1,060,014	6,538,836	6,280	62,315	222,730	204,389	261,093	303,207	366,166	384,955	363,348
Total percent distribution[1]	100.0	3.8	13.9	86.1	0.1	0.8	2.9	2.7	3.4	4.0	4.8	5.1	4.8
Violent Crime	332,509	12,726	48,634	283,875	268	2,802	9,656	9,225	12,503	14,180	16,129	16,165	15,046
Violent crime percent distribution[1]	100.0	3.8	14.6	85.4	0.1	0.8	2.9	2.8	3.8	4.3	4.9	4.9	4.5
Murder and nonnegligent manslaughter	6,373	54	618	5,755	0	4	50	82	190	292	420	458	401
Forcible rape	11,424	513	1,607	9,817	7	135	371	285	386	423	537	561	509
Robbery	74,578	3,537	18,669	55,909	32	498	3,007	3,733	5,327	6,072	6,505	5,808	4,759
Aggravated assault	240,134	8,622	27,740	212,394	229	2,165	6,228	5,125	6,600	7,393	8,667	9,338	9,377
Property Crime	1,050,227	70,448	246,384	803,843	1,461	15,635	53,352	48,373	60,238	67,325	71,430	61,272	50,550
Property crime percent distribution[1]	100.0	6.7	23.5	76.5	0.1	1.5	5.1	4.6	5.7	6.4	6.8	5.8	4.8
Burglary	166,483	11,373	40,607	125,876	335	2,454	8,584	7,972	9,925	11,337	12,518	10,935	8,914
Larceny-theft	836,119	55,345	193,120	642,999	946	12,338	42,061	37,712	47,251	52,812	55,814	47,710	39,457
Motor vehicle theft	41,138	1,953	9,715	31,423	12	222	1,719	2,187	2,716	2,859	2,862	2,429	1,989
Arson	6,487	1,777	2,942	3,545	168	621	988	502	346	317	236	198	190
Other													
Other assaults	758,138	47,423	124,260	633,878	1,187	12,440	33,796	24,192	26,713	25,932	24,836	25,936	26,695
Forgery and counterfeiting	44,909	134	1,052	43,857	4	24	106	140	237	541	1,309	1,820	2,139
Fraud	90,104	555	3,584	86,520	10	86	459	549	952	1,528	2,611	3,564	3,859
Embezzlement	9,640	9	274	9,366	0	1	8	16	66	183	461	640	673
Stolen property; buying, receiving, possessing	55,086	2,191	9,618	45,468	38	367	1,786	1,958	2,552	2,917	3,898	3,539	3,007
Vandalism	155,565	19,458	49,267	106,298	877	5,274	13,307	9,356	10,288	10,165	9,470	8,104	7,210
Weapons; carrying, possessing, etc.	97,015	6,379	20,007	77,008	274	1,648	4,457	3,612	4,519	5,497	6,254	6,119	5,179
Prostitution and commercialized vice	45,248	72	722	44,526	0	4	68	100	186	364	1,322	1,769	2,009
Sex offenses (except forcible rape and prostitution)	39,756	3,426	7,113	32,643	113	962	2,351	1,244	1,264	1,179	1,592	1,422	1,292
Drug abuse violations	943,847	18,868	106,801	837,046	111	2,270	16,487	19,073	28,570	40,290	60,446	61,671	55,927
Gambling	6,152	115	999	5,153	1	5	109	155	293	436	478	479	428
Offenses against the family and children	41,654	742	2,270	39,384	23	169	550	427	552	549	1,068	1,191	1,230
Driving under the influence	646,531	120	6,131	640,400	16	12	92	240	1,427	4,344	12,420	17,891	20,950
Liquor laws	321,909	6,038	58,407	263,502	39	532	5,467	9,022	16,412	26,935	52,290	59,569	49,792
Drunkenness	380,484	1,104	8,818	371,666	17	81	1,006	1,466	2,065	4,183	9,656	11,310	11,450
Disorderly conduct	411,718	38,761	104,156	307,562	507	9,373	28,881	21,318	22,726	21,351	18,263	16,813	16,361
Vagrancy	22,053	436	1,507	20,546	4	64	368	369	427	275	1,068	1,025	859
All other offenses (except traffic)	2,076,357	45,077	190,642	1,885,715	1,096	7,817	36,164	38,387	49,198	57,980	71,125	84,616	88,644
Suspicion	672	23	92	580	1	0	22	15	28	26	40	40	48
Curfew and loitering law violations	69,276	17,220	69,276	…	233	2,749	14,238	15,152	19,877	17,027	…	…	…

[1] Because of rounding, the percentages may not add to 100.0.

Table 46.   City Arrests, Distribution by Age, 2010—*Continued*

(Number, percent; 8,912 agencies; 2010 estimated population 165,417,960)

Offense charged	21	22	23	24	25–29	30–34	35–39	40–44	45–49	50–54	55–59	60–64	65 and over
TOTAL	329,611	298,542	276,197	261,287	1,099,456	798,884	614,352	565,858	518,930	352,709	178,030	77,932	52,579
Total percent distribution[1]	4.3	3.9	3.6	3.4	14.5	10.5	8.1	7.4	6.8	4.6	2.3	1.0	0.7
Violent Crime	14,773	13,295	12,435	11,587	50,256	36,662	27,570	24,305	20,819	13,154	6,405	2,809	2,311
Violent crime percent distribution[1]	4.4	4.0	3.7	3.5	15.1	11.0	8.3	7.3	6.3	4.0	1.9	0.8	0.6
Murder and nonnegligent manslaughter	393	333	297	264	1,081	674	440	325	268	171	117	62	51
Forcible rape	492	393	399	364	1,607	1,253	1,093	912	742	466	259	127	103
Robbery	3,981	3,247	2,772	2,383	8,985	5,531	3,850	3,322	2,576	1,356	551	204	79
Aggravated assault	9,907	9,322	8,967	8,576	38,583	29,204	22,187	19,746	17,233	11,161	5,478	2,619	2,029
Property Crime	42,408	36,441	32,615	30,113	124,978	90,535	70,624	65,841	57,565	37,360	18,129	8,046	5,936
Property crime percent distribution[1]	4.0	3.5	3.1	2.9	11.9	8.6	6.7	6.3	5.5	3.6	1.7	0.8	0.6
Burglary	7,457	6,228	5,590	5,201	19,926	13,865	10,545	9,595	7,890	4,533	1,726	651	302
Larceny-theft	33,107	28,551	25,515	23,474	98,947	72,173	56,884	53,437	47,577	31,695	15,922	7,219	5,517
Motor vehicle theft	1,674	1,517	1,381	1,306	5,575	4,056	2,882	2,502	1,765	931	362	112	80
Arson	170	145	129	132	530	441	313	307	333	201	119	64	37
Other													
Other assaults	29,326	28,213	27,168	26,059	115,787	87,854	69,014	60,778	52,006	32,792	15,395	6,784	5,235
Forgery and counterfeiting	1,932	1,949	1,934	1,916	8,575	6,925	4,954	4,120	3,142	1,829	812	315	186
Fraud	3,336	3,317	3,127	3,160	14,851	12,601	10,561	9,054	7,491	4,679	2,445	1,100	764
Embezzlement	593	510	425	426	1,501	1,097	898	781	582	412	220	106	41
Stolen property; buying, receiving, possessing	2,655	2,177	1,971	1,849	7,916	5,680	4,037	3,496	2,664	1,541	650	230	158
Vandalism	6,871	5,964	5,195	4,711	18,543	12,080	8,355	7,170	5,951	3,632	1,698	741	603
Weapons; carrying, possessing, etc.	4,870	4,368	3,888	3,681	14,427	9,049	5,658	4,406	3,730	2,626	1,446	751	556
Prostitution and commercialized vice	1,945	1,943	1,697	1,650	7,181	5,892	5,529	5,213	4,334	2,297	948	419	378
Sex offenses (except forcible rape and prostitution)	1,273	1,143	1,024	924	4,259	3,826	3,355	3,404	3,172	2,431	1,548	942	1,036
Drug abuse violations	49,065	43,113	38,887	36,389	149,803	101,429	69,920	61,362	52,797	33,541	14,953	5,497	2,246
Gambling	357	287	260	217	756	484	317	289	251	216	142	93	99
Offenses against the family and children	1,443	1,462	1,541	1,569	7,787	6,675	5,025	4,089	3,091	1,776	845	325	267
Driving under the influence	30,946	30,625	29,662	28,825	119,078	83,868	65,939	59,150	56,610	40,907	23,110	11,983	8,436
Liquor laws	8,551	5,934	4,417	3,821	14,228	10,627	9,559	11,503	12,923	10,596	5,795	2,520	1,377
Drunkenness	17,611	15,824	14,389	13,409	56,475	41,778	35,544	39,189	43,925	33,426	17,324	6,875	3,481
Disorderly conduct	19,536	16,757	14,505	13,408	49,757	34,015	26,318	24,661	24,800	17,253	8,525	3,819	2,771
Vagrancy	670	587	531	489	2,076	1,711	1,752	2,268	2,863	2,479	1,382	508	278
All other offenses (except traffic)	91,407	84,608	80,492	77,062	331,111	246,029	189,365	174,744	160,190	109,745	56,250	23,861	16,466
Suspicion	43	25	34	22	111	67	58	35	24	17	8	5	3
Curfew and loitering law violations	...	...	...	...	...	...	...	...	...	...	...	...	...

[1] Because of rounding, the percentages may not add to 100.0.

Table 47. City Arrests of Persons Under 15, 18, 21, and 25 Years of Age, 2010

(Number, percent; 8,912 agencies; 2010 estimated population 165,417,960)

Offense charged	Total all ages	Number of persons arrested				Percent of total all ages			
		Under 15	Under 18	Under 21	Under 25	Under 15	Under 18	Under 21	Under 25
TOTAL	7,598,850	291,325	1,060,014	2,174,483	3,340,120	3.8	13.9	28.6	44.0
Violent Crime	332,509	12,726	48,634	95,974	148,064	3.8	14.6	28.9	44.5
Murder and nonnegligent manslaughter	6,373	54	618	1,897	3,184	0.8	9.7	29.8	50.0
Forcible rape	11,424	513	1,607	3,214	4,862	4.5	14.1	28.1	42.6
Robbery	74,578	3,537	18,669	35,741	48,124	4.7	25.0	47.9	64.5
Aggravated assault	240,134	8,622	27,740	55,122	91,894	3.6	11.6	23.0	38.3
Property Crime	1,050,227	70,448	246,384	429,636	571,213	6.7	23.5	40.9	54.4
Burglary	166,483	11,373	40,607	72,974	97,450	6.8	24.4	43.8	58.5
Larceny-theft	836,119	55,345	193,120	336,101	446,748	6.6	23.1	40.2	53.4
Motor vehicle theft	41,138	1,953	9,715	16,995	22,873	4.7	23.6	41.3	55.6
Arson	6,487	1,777	2,942	3,566	4,142	27.4	45.4	55.0	63.9
Other									
Other assaults	758,138	47,423	124,260	201,727	312,493	6.3	16.4	26.6	41.2
Forgery and counterfeiting	44,909	134	1,052	6,320	14,051	0.3	2.3	14.1	31.3
Fraud	90,104	555	3,584	13,618	26,558	0.6	4.0	15.1	29.5
Embezzlement	9,640	9	274	2,048	4,002	0.1	2.8	21.2	41.5
Stolen property; buying, receiving, possessing	55,086	2,191	9,618	20,062	28,714	4.0	17.5	36.4	52.1
Vandalism	155,565	19,458	49,267	74,051	96,792	12.5	31.7	47.6	62.2
Weapons; carrying, possessing, etc.	97,015	6,379	20,007	37,559	54,366	6.6	20.6	38.7	56.0
Prostitution and commercialized vice	45,248	72	722	5,822	13,057	0.2	1.6	12.9	28.9
Sex offenses (except forcible rape and prostitution)	39,756	3,426	7,113	11,419	15,783	8.6	17.9	28.7	39.7
Drug abuse violations	943,847	18,868	106,801	284,845	452,299	2.0	11.3	30.2	47.9
Gambling	6,152	115	999	2,384	3,505	1.9	16.2	38.8	57.0
Offenses against the family and children	41,654	742	2,270	5,759	11,774	1.8	5.4	13.8	28.3
Driving under the influence	646,531	120	6,131	57,392	177,450	*	0.9	8.9	27.4
Liquor laws	321,909	6,038	58,407	220,058	242,781	1.9	18.1	68.4	75.4
Drunkenness	380,484	1,104	8,818	41,234	102,467	0.3	2.3	10.8	26.9
Disorderly conduct	411,718	38,761	104,156	155,593	219,799	9.4	25.3	37.8	53.4
Vagrancy	22,053	436	1,507	4,459	6,736	2.0	6.8	20.2	30.5
All other offenses (except traffic)	2,076,357	45,077	190,642	435,027	768,596	2.2	9.2	21.0	37.0
Suspicion	672	23	92	220	344	3.4	13.7	32.7	51.2
Curfew and loitering law violations	69,276	17,220	69,276	69,276	69,276	24.9	100.0	100.0	100.0

* Less than one-tenth of 1 percent.

Table 48.   City Arrests, Distribution by Sex, 2010

(Number, percent; 8,912 agencies; 2010 estimated population 165,417,960)

Offense charged	Number of persons arrested			Percent male	Percent female	Percent distribution[1]		
	Total	Male	Female			Total	Male	Female
TOTAL	7,598,850	5,639,500	1,959,350	74.2	25.8	100.0	100.0	100.0
Violent Crime	332,509	266,892	65,617	80.3	19.7	4.4	4.7	3.3
Murder and nonnegligent manslaughter	6,373	5,712	661	89.6	10.4	0.1	0.1	*
Forcible rape	11,424	11,317	107	99.1	0.9	0.2	0.2	*
Robbery	74,578	65,503	9,075	87.8	12.2	1.0	1.2	0.5
Aggravated assault	240,134	184,360	55,774	76.8	23.2	3.2	3.3	2.8
Property Crime	1,050,227	640,286	409,941	61.0	39.0	13.8	11.4	20.9
Burglary	166,483	140,507	25,976	84.4	15.6	2.2	2.5	1.3
Larceny-theft	836,119	460,412	375,707	55.1	44.9	11.0	8.2	19.2
Motor vehicle theft	41,138	34,012	7,126	82.7	17.3	0.5	0.6	0.4
Arson	6,487	5,355	1,132	82.5	17.5	0.1	0.1	0.1
Other								
Other assaults	758,138	553,711	204,427	73.0	27.0	10.0	9.8	10.4
Forgery and counterfeiting	44,909	27,916	16,993	62.2	37.8	0.6	0.5	0.9
Fraud	90,104	54,732	35,372	60.7	39.3	1.2	1.0	1.8
Embezzlement	9,640	4,784	4,856	49.6	50.4	0.1	0.1	0.2
Stolen property; buying, receiving, possessing	55,086	44,041	11,045	79.9	20.1	0.7	0.8	0.6
Vandalism	155,565	126,003	29,562	81.0	19.0	2.0	2.2	1.5
Weapons; carrying, possessing, etc.	97,015	89,012	8,003	91.8	8.2	1.3	1.6	0.4
Prostitution and commercialized vice	45,248	13,807	31,441	30.5	69.5	0.6	0.2	1.6
Sex offenses (except forcible rape and prostitution)	39,756	36,572	3,184	92.0	8.0	0.5	0.6	0.2
Drug abuse violations	943,847	770,070	173,777	81.6	18.4	12.4	13.7	8.9
Gambling	6,152	5,692	460	92.5	7.5	0.1	0.1	*
Offenses against the family and children	41,654	27,679	13,975	66.4	33.6	0.5	0.5	0.7
Driving under the influence	646,531	490,509	156,022	75.9	24.1	8.5	8.7	8.0
Liquor laws	321,909	231,063	90,846	71.8	28.2	4.2	4.1	4.6
Drunkenness	380,484	315,802	64,682	83.0	17.0	5.0	5.6	3.3
Disorderly conduct	411,718	297,637	114,081	72.3	27.7	5.4	5.3	5.8
Vagrancy	22,053	17,798	4,255	80.7	19.3	0.3	0.3	0.2
All other offenses (except traffic)	2,076,357	1,575,978	500,379	75.9	24.1	27.3	27.9	25.5
Suspicion	672	506	166	75.3	24.7	*	*	*
Curfew and loitering law violations	69,276	49,010	20,266	70.7	29.3	0.9	0.9	1.0

[1] Because of rounding, the percentages may not add to 100.0.
* Less than one-tenth of 1 percent.

Table 49.　City Arrests, Distribution by Race, 2010

(Number, percent; 8,911 agencies; 2010 estimated population 165,414,755)

Offense charged	Total arrests					Percent distribution[1]				
	Total	White	Black	American Indian or Alaskan Native	Asian or Pacific Islander	Total	White	Black	American Indian or Alaskan Native	Asian or Pacific Islander
TOTAL	7,564,496	5,073,139	2,285,782	109,286	96,289	100.0	67.1	30.2	1.4	1.3
Violent Crime	331,518	186,838	136,163	4,132	4,385	100.0	56.4	41.1	1.2	1.3
Murder and nonnegligent manslaughter	6,350	2,832	3,406	46	66	100.0	44.6	53.6	0.7	1.0
Forcible rape	11,358	6,901	4,148	152	157	100.0	60.8	36.5	1.3	1.4
Robbery	74,413	31,475	41,643	493	802	100.0	42.3	56.0	0.7	1.1
Aggravated assault	239,397	145,630	86,966	3,441	3,360	100.0	60.8	36.3	1.4	1.4
Property Crime	1,046,162	704,549	312,186	14,605	14,822	100.0	67.3	29.8	1.4	1.4
Burglary	166,057	106,171	56,924	1,235	1,727	100.0	63.9	34.3	0.7	1.0
Larceny-theft	832,619	569,397	238,037	12,820	12,365	100.0	68.4	28.6	1.5	1.5
Motor vehicle theft	41,032	24,297	15,610	484	641	100.0	59.2	38.0	1.2	1.6
Arson	6,454	4,684	1,615	66	89	100.0	72.6	25.0	1.0	1.4
Other										
Other assaults	754,701	472,572	261,011	11,144	9,974	100.0	62.6	34.6	1.5	1.3
Forgery and counterfeiting	44,688	28,894	15,008	242	544	100.0	64.7	33.6	0.5	1.2
Fraud	89,599	55,475	32,276	793	1,055	100.0	61.9	36.0	0.9	1.2
Embezzlement	9,567	6,189	3,119	61	198	100.0	64.7	32.6	0.6	2.1
Stolen property; buying, receiving, possessing	54,941	34,184	19,731	426	600	100.0	62.2	35.9	0.8	1.1
Vandalism	154,889	111,594	38,888	2,596	1,811	100.0	72.0	25.1	1.7	1.2
Weapons; carrying, possessing, etc.	96,634	53,658	41,392	583	1,001	100.0	55.5	42.8	0.6	1.0
Prostitution and commercialized vice	45,125	24,289	19,383	330	1,123	100.0	53.8	43.0	0.7	2.5
Sex offenses (except forcible rape and prostitution)	39,608	27,837	10,541	571	659	100.0	70.3	26.6	1.4	1.7
Drug abuse violations	941,447	596,719	330,565	6,081	8,082	100.0	63.4	35.1	0.6	0.9
Gambling	6,137	1,262	4,739	21	115	100.0	20.6	77.2	0.3	1.9
Offenses against the family and children	41,384	28,487	11,639	863	395	100.0	68.8	28.1	2.1	1.0
Driving under the influence	643,860	546,731	78,160	8,137	10,832	100.0	84.9	12.1	1.3	1.7
Liquor laws	319,018	260,920	41,021	12,461	4,616	100.0	81.8	12.9	3.9	1.4
Drunkenness	378,889	308,175	60,794	7,369	2,551	100.0	81.3	16.0	1.9	0.7
Disorderly conduct	409,109	254,922	143,563	7,087	3,537	100.0	62.3	35.1	1.7	0.9
Vagrancy	21,973	12,026	9,243	547	157	100.0	54.7	42.1	2.5	0.7
All other offenses (except traffic)	2,065,504	1,316,953	689,081	30,512	28,958	100.0	63.8	33.4	1.5	1.4
Suspicion	672	436	225	5	6	100.0	64.9	33.5	0.7	0.9
Curfew and loitering law violations	69,071	40,429	27,054	720	868	100.0	58.5	39.2	1.0	1.3

[1] Because of rounding, the percentages may not add to 100.0.

Table 49.   City Arrests, Distribution by Race, 2010—*Continued*

(Number, percent; 8,911 agencies; 2010 estimated population 165,414,755)

Offense charged	Arrests under 18					Percent distribution[1]				
	Total	White	Black	American Indian or Alaskan Native	Asian or Pacific Islander	Total	White	Black	American Indian or Alaskan Native	Asian or Pacific Islander
TOTAL	1,054,150	691,188	335,039	12,928	14,995	100.0	65.6	31.8	1.2	1.4
Violent Crime	48,474	22,239	25,284	411	540	100.0	45.9	52.2	0.8	1.1
Murder and nonnegligent manslaughter	616	243	365	2	6	100.0	39.4	59.3	0.3	1.0
Forcible rape	1,596	926	654	8	8	100.0	58.0	41.0	0.5	0.5
Robbery	18,626	5,929	12,389	89	219	100.0	31.8	66.5	0.5	1.2
Aggravated assault	27,636	15,141	11,876	312	307	100.0	54.8	43.0	1.1	1.1
Property Crime	245,017	156,544	80,817	3,164	4,492	100.0	63.9	33.0	1.3	1.8
Burglary	40,484	24,037	15,693	297	457	100.0	59.4	38.8	0.7	1.1
Larceny-theft	191,934	125,357	60,020	2,703	3,854	100.0	65.3	31.3	1.4	2.0
Motor vehicle theft	9,679	4,984	4,433	130	132	100.0	51.5	45.8	1.3	1.4
Arson	2,920	2,166	671	34	49	100.0	74.2	23.0	1.2	1.7
Other										
Other assaults	123,430	73,449	47,166	1,284	1,531	100.0	59.5	38.2	1.0	1.2
Forgery and counterfeiting	1,046	687	334	7	18	100.0	65.7	31.9	0.7	1.7
Fraud	3,564	1,962	1,516	42	44	100.0	55.1	42.5	1.2	1.2
Embezzlement	268	163	95	3	7	100.0	60.8	35.4	1.1	2.6
Stolen property; buying, receiving, possessing	9,584	5,252	4,148	69	115	100.0	54.8	43.3	0.7	1.2
Vandalism	49,012	38,043	9,785	596	588	100.0	77.6	20.0	1.2	1.2
Weapons; carrying, possessing, etc.	19,852	12,267	7,202	128	255	100.0	61.8	36.3	0.6	1.3
Prostitution and commercialized vice	722	265	437	8	12	100.0	36.7	60.5	1.1	1.7
Sex offenses (except forcible rape and prostitution)	7,061	4,835	2,061	44	121	100.0	68.5	29.2	0.6	1.7
Drug abuse violations	106,451	77,570	26,610	1,116	1,155	100.0	72.9	25.0	1.0	1.1
Gambling	998	65	928	3	2	100.0	6.5	93.0	0.3	0.2
Offenses against the family and children	2,236	1,540	622	63	11	100.0	68.9	27.8	2.8	0.5
Driving under the influence	6,089	5,538	361	103	87	100.0	91.0	5.9	1.7	1.4
Liquor laws	58,057	50,631	4,552	2,037	837	100.0	87.2	7.8	3.5	1.4
Drunkenness	8,792	7,783	771	176	62	100.0	88.5	8.8	2.0	0.7
Disorderly conduct	103,455	59,770	41,826	1,013	846	100.0	57.8	40.4	1.0	0.8
Vagrancy	1,507	1,133	361	4	9	100.0	75.2	24.0	0.3	0.6
All other offenses (except traffic)	189,372	130,959	53,082	1,937	3,394	100.0	69.2	28.0	1.0	1.8
Suspicion	92	64	27	0	1	100.0	69.6	29.3	0.0	1.1
Curfew and loitering law violations	69,071	40,429	27,054	720	868	100.0	58.5	39.2	1.0	1.3

[1] Because of rounding, the percentages may not add to 100.0.

Table 49. City Arrests, Distribution by Race, 2010—*Continued*

(Number, percent; 8,911 agencies; 2010 estimated population 165,414,755)

Offense charged	Arrests 18 and over					Percent distribution[1]				
	Total	White	Black	American Indian or Alaskan Native	Asian or Pacific Islander	Total	White	Black	American Indian or Alaskan Native	Asian or Pacific Islander
TOTAL	6,510,346	4,381,951	1,950,743	96,358	81,294	100.0	67.3	30.0	1.5	1.2
Violent Crime	283,044	164,599	110,879	3,721	3,845	100.0	58.2	39.2	1.3	1.4
Murder and nonnegligent manslaughter	5,734	2,589	3,041	44	60	100.0	45.2	53.0	0.8	1.0
Forcible rape	9,762	5,975	3,494	144	149	100.0	61.2	35.8	1.5	1.5
Robbery	55,787	25,546	29,254	404	583	100.0	45.8	52.4	0.7	1.0
Aggravated assault	211,761	130,489	75,090	3,129	3,053	100.0	61.6	35.5	1.5	1.4
Property Crime	801,145	548,005	231,369	11,441	10,330	100.0	68.4	28.9	1.4	1.3
Burglary	125,573	82,134	41,231	938	1,270	100.0	65.4	32.8	0.7	1.0
Larceny-theft	640,685	444,040	178,017	10,117	8,511	100.0	69.3	27.8	1.6	1.3
Motor vehicle theft	31,353	19,313	11,177	354	509	100.0	61.6	35.6	1.1	1.6
Arson	3,534	2,518	944	32	40	100.0	71.3	26.7	0.9	1.1
Other										
Other assaults	631,271	399,123	213,845	9,860	8,443	100.0	63.2	33.9	1.6	1.3
Forgery and counterfeiting	43,642	28,207	14,674	235	526	100.0	64.6	33.6	0.5	1.2
Fraud	86,035	53,513	30,760	751	1,011	100.0	62.2	35.8	0.9	1.2
Embezzlement	9,299	6,026	3,024	58	191	100.0	64.8	32.5	0.6	2.1
Stolen property; buying, receiving, possessing	45,357	28,932	15,583	357	485	100.0	63.8	34.4	0.8	1.1
Vandalism	105,877	73,551	29,103	2,000	1,223	100.0	69.5	27.5	1.9	1.2
Weapons; carrying, possessing, etc.	76,782	41,391	34,190	455	746	100.0	53.9	44.5	0.6	1.0
Prostitution and commercialized vice	44,403	24,024	18,946	322	1,111	100.0	54.1	42.7	0.7	2.5
Sex offenses (except forcible rape and prostitution)	32,547	23,002	8,480	527	538	100.0	70.7	26.1	1.6	1.7
Drug abuse violations	834,996	519,149	303,955	4,965	6,927	100.0	62.2	36.4	0.6	0.8
Gambling	5,139	1,197	3,811	18	113	100.0	23.3	74.2	0.4	2.2
Offenses against the family and children	39,148	26,947	11,017	800	384	100.0	68.8	28.1	2.0	1.0
Driving under the influence	637,771	541,193	77,799	8,034	10,745	100.0	84.9	12.2	1.3	1.7
Liquor laws	260,961	210,289	36,469	10,424	3,779	100.0	80.6	14.0	4.0	1.4
Drunkenness	370,097	300,392	60,023	7,193	2,489	100.0	81.2	16.2	1.9	0.7
Disorderly conduct	305,654	195,152	101,737	6,074	2,691	100.0	63.8	33.3	2.0	0.9
Vagrancy	20,466	10,893	8,882	543	148	100.0	53.2	43.4	2.7	0.7
All other offenses (except traffic)	1,876,132	1,185,994	635,999	28,575	25,564	100.0	63.2	33.9	1.5	1.4
Suspicion	580	372	198	5	5	100.0	64.1	34.1	0.9	0.9
Curfew and loitering law violations	...	...	...	...	...	...	...	...	...	...

[1] Because of rounding, the percentages may not add to 100.0.

Table 50.   Metropolitan County Arrest Trends, 2009–2010

(Number, percent change; 1,283 agencies; 2010 estimated population 48,782,563; 2009 estimated population 48,289,105)

Offense charged	Number of persons arrested								
	Total all ages			Under 18 years of age			18 years of age and over		
	2009	2010	Percent change	2009	2010	Percent change	2009	2010	Percent change
TOTAL[1]	1,757,319	1,702,415	-3.1	180,350	165,564	-8.2	1,576,969	1,536,851	-2.5
Violent Crime	69,787	66,789	-4.3	9,097	7,986	-12.2	60,690	58,803	-3.1
Murder and nonnegligent manslaughter	1,587	1,489	-6.2	92	117	27.2	1,495	1,372	-8.2
Forcible rape	2,745	2,428	-11.5	414	366	-11.6	2,331	2,062	-11.5
Robbery	10,958	9,759	-10.9	2,468	2,014	-18.4	8,490	7,745	-8.8
Aggravated assault	54,497	53,113	-2.5	6,123	5,489	-10.4	48,374	47,624	-1.6
Property Crime	173,812	168,640	-3.0	38,615	33,273	-13.8	135,197	135,367	0.1
Burglary	39,523	37,739	-4.5	8,876	7,303	-17.7	30,647	30,436	-0.7
Larceny-theft	122,102	119,930	-1.8	26,768	23,772	-11.2	95,334	96,158	0.9
Motor vehicle theft	10,456	9,512	-9.0	2,311	1,739	-24.8	8,145	7,773	-4.6
Arson	1,731	1,459	-15.7	660	459	-30.5	1,071	1,000	-6.6
Other									
Other assaults	165,991	162,745	-2.0	29,040	28,336	-2.4	136,951	134,409	-1.9
Forgery and counterfeiting	11,551	10,494	-9.2	264	192	-27.3	11,287	10,302	-8.7
Fraud	40,806	33,913	-16.9	775	698	-9.9	40,031	33,215	-17.0
Embezzlement	2,465	2,125	-13.8	87	68	-21.8	2,378	2,057	-13.5
Stolen property; buying, receiving, possessing	13,459	12,629	-6.2	1,682	1,410	-16.2	11,777	11,219	-4.7
Vandalism	30,049	28,537	-5.0	9,263	8,149	-12.0	20,786	20,388	-1.9
Weapons; carrying, possessing, etc.	18,535	17,603	-5.0	3,572	3,359	-6.0	14,963	14,244	-4.8
Prostitution and commercialized vice	2,738	2,543	-7.1	76	70	-7.9	2,662	2,473	-7.1
Sex offenses (except forcible rape and prostitution)	11,107	10,565	-4.9	1,970	1,891	-4.0	9,137	8,674	-5.1
Drug abuse violations	211,446	211,021	-0.2	19,719	19,392	-1.7	191,727	191,629	-0.1
Gambling	1,148	963	-16.1	52	33	-36.5	1,096	930	-15.1
Offenses against the family and children	32,156	30,478	-5.2	538	500	-7.1	31,618	29,978	-5.2
Driving under the influence	257,247	254,068	-1.2	1,810	1,689	-6.7	255,437	252,379	-1.2
Liquor laws	54,344	47,598	-12.4	13,072	10,898	-16.6	41,272	36,700	-11.1
Drunkenness	43,931	40,193	-8.5	1,013	861	-15.0	42,918	39,332	-8.4
Disorderly conduct	46,015	46,162	0.3	12,055	11,991	-0.5	33,960	34,171	0.6
Vagrancy	2,241	2,403	7.2	147	164	11.6	2,094	2,239	6.9
All other offenses (except traffic)	564,309	548,652	-2.8	33,321	30,310	-9.0	530,988	518,342	-2.4
Suspicion	87	80	-8.0	4	12	200.0	83	68	-18.1
Curfew and loitering law violations	4,182	4,294	2.7	4,182	4,294	2.7	...	...	...

[1] Does not include suspicion.

Table 51. Metropolitan County Arrest Trends, by Age and Sex, 2009–2010

(Number, percent change; 1,283 agencies; 2010 estimated population 48,782,563; 2009 estimated population 48,289,105)

Offense charged	Male						Female					
	Total			Under 18			Total			Under 18		
	2009	2010	Percent change	2009	2010	Percent change	2009	2010	Percent change	2009	2010	Percent change
TOTAL[1]	1,326,295	1,278,398	-3.6	130,579	119,093	-8.8	431,024	424,017	-1.6	49,771	46,471	-6.6
Violent Crime	56,968	54,153	-4.9	7,388	6,465	-12.5	12,819	12,636	-1.4	1,709	1,521	-11.0
Murder and nonnegligent manslaughter	1,401	1,307	-6.7	87	102	17.2	186	182	-2.2	5	15	200.0
Forcible rape	2,704	2,402	-11.2	403	360	-10.7	41	26	-36.6	11	6	-45.5
Robbery	9,757	8,566	-12.2	2,270	1,848	-18.6	1,201	1,193	-0.7	198	166	-16.2
Aggravated assault	43,106	41,878	-2.8	4,628	4,155	-10.2	11,391	11,235	-1.4	1,495	1,334	-10.8
Property Crime	117,195	112,741	-3.8	26,344	22,457	-14.8	56,617	55,899	-1.3	12,271	10,816	-11.9
Burglary	33,749	32,095	-4.9	7,818	6,581	-15.8	5,774	5,644	-2.3	1,058	722	-31.8
Larceny-theft	73,375	71,629	-2.4	16,040	14,077	-12.2	48,727	48,301	-0.9	10,728	9,695	-9.6
Motor vehicle theft	8,644	7,803	-9.7	1,917	1,410	-26.4	1,812	1,709	-5.7	394	329	-16.5
Arson	1,427	1,214	-14.9	569	389	-31.6	304	245	-19.4	91	70	-23.1
Other												
Other assaults	122,424	118,891	-2.9	19,390	18,679	-3.7	43,567	43,854	0.7	9,650	9,657	0.1
Forgery and counterfeiting	7,312	6,701	-8.4	198	152	-23.2	4,239	3,793	-10.5	66	40	-39.4
Fraud	21,963	18,794	-14.4	524	458	-12.6	18,843	15,119	-19.8	251	240	-4.4
Embezzlement	1,265	1,102	-12.9	45	47	4.4	1,200	1,023	-14.8	42	21	-50.0
Stolen property; buying, receiving, possessing	10,929	10,118	-7.4	1,432	1,170	-18.3	2,530	2,511	-0.8	250	240	-4.0
Vandalism	24,417	23,076	-5.5	7,829	6,824	-12.8	5,632	5,461	-3.0	1,434	1,325	-7.6
Weapons; carrying, possessing, etc.	16,838	15,905	-5.5	3,095	2,913	-5.9	1,697	1,698	0.1	477	446	-6.5
Prostitution and commercialized vice	945	1,007	6.6	24	19	-20.8	1,793	1,536	-14.3	52	51	-1.9
Sex offenses (except forcible rape and prostitution)	10,294	9,805	-4.8	1,784	1,698	-4.8	813	760	-6.5	186	193	3.8
Drug abuse violations	167,608	166,552	-0.6	16,311	15,874	-2.7	43,838	44,469	1.4	3,408	3,518	3.2
Gambling	725	759	4.7	32	20	-37.5	423	204	-51.8	20	13	-35.0
Offenses against the family and children	26,883	25,586	-4.8	369	342	-7.3	5,273	4,892	-7.2	169	158	-6.5
Driving under the influence	199,823	194,023	-2.9	1,359	1,248	-8.2	57,424	60,045	4.6	451	441	-2.2
Liquor laws	37,909	33,235	-12.3	7,894	6,596	-16.4	16,435	14,363	-12.6	5,178	4,302	-16.9
Drunkenness	36,119	32,604	-9.7	749	644	-14.0	7,812	7,589	-2.9	264	217	-17.8
Disorderly conduct	33,269	33,176	-0.3	8,190	8,008	-2.2	12,746	12,986	1.9	3,865	3,983	3.1
Vagrancy	1,454	1,795	23.5	99	122	23.2	787	608	-22.7	48	42	-12.5
All other offenses (except traffic)	429,216	415,549	-3.2	24,784	22,531	-9.1	135,093	133,103	-1.5	8,537	7,779	-8.9
Suspicion	60	61	1.7	4	11	175.0	27	19	-29.6	0	1	
Curfew and loitering law violations	2,739	2,826	3.2	2,739	2,826	3.2	1,443	1,468	1.7	1,443	1,468	1.7

[1] Does not include suspicion.

Table 52. Metropolitan County Arrests, Distribution by Age, 2010

(Number, percent; 1,352 agencies; 2010 estimated population 52,433,613)

Offense charged	Total all ages	Ages under 15	Ages under 18	Ages 18 and over	Under 10	10–12	13–14	15	16	17	18	19	20
TOTAL	1,815,431	46,664	176,428	1,639,003	1,426	10,440	34,798	31,428	43,147	55,189	72,413	79,287	80,004
Total percent distribution[1]	100.0	2.6	9.7	90.3	0.1	0.6	1.9	1.7	2.4	3.0	4.0	4.4	4.4
Violent Crime	73,884	2,425	8,681	65,203	63	653	1,709	1,567	2,105	2,584	3,299	3,262	3,197
Violent crime percent distribution[1]	100.0	3.3	11.7	88.3	0.1	0.9	2.3	2.1	2.8	3.5	4.5	4.4	4.3
Murder and nonnegligent manslaughter	1,657	12	140	1,517	0	1	11	33	43	52	96	97	88
Forcible rape	2,679	143	402	2,277	0	45	98	69	80	110	115	150	113
Robbery	11,108	377	2,247	8,861	3	57	317	422	676	772	1,029	955	852
Aggravated assault	58,440	1,893	5,892	52,548	60	550	1,283	1,043	1,306	1,650	2,059	2,060	2,144
Property Crime	181,557	9,174	35,124	146,433	222	1,868	7,084	6,489	8,600	10,861	12,037	10,715	9,367
Property crime percent distribution[1]	100.0	5.1	19.3	80.7	0.1	1.0	3.9	3.6	4.7	6.0	6.6	5.9	5.2
Burglary	40,413	1,908	7,747	32,666	76	394	1,438	1,402	1,905	2,532	3,163	2,913	2,532
Larceny-theft	129,188	6,648	25,060	104,128	111	1,359	5,178	4,633	6,094	7,685	8,122	7,188	6,320
Motor vehicle theft	10,432	370	1,858	8,574	8	36	326	385	524	579	675	556	457
Arson	1,524	248	459	1,065	27	79	142	69	77	65	77	58	58
Other													
Other assaults	175,126	11,740	30,724	144,402	460	3,247	8,033	5,774	6,780	6,430	5,338	5,216	5,246
Forgery and counterfeiting	11,735	26	209	11,526	1	7	18	27	49	107	268	395	498
Fraud	35,737	141	707	35,030	4	20	117	108	181	277	551	773	888
Embezzlement	2,393	7	68	2,325	0	0	7	4	13	44	106	138	132
Stolen property; buying, receiving, possessing	14,235	302	1,583	12,652	4	36	262	308	403	570	835	812	713
Vandalism	30,077	3,092	8,617	21,460	150	840	2,102	1,588	1,916	2,021	1,873	1,582	1,347
Weapons; carrying, possessing, etc.	19,868	1,562	3,838	16,030	117	484	961	622	756	898	1,052	1,034	905
Prostitution and commercialized vice	2,822	17	78	2,744	1	1	15	12	22	27	67	112	146
Sex offenses (except forcible rape and prostitution)	11,502	1,049	2,100	9,402	40	304	705	352	322	377	455	453	368
Drug abuse violations	231,600	3,362	20,527	211,073	28	428	2,906	3,378	5,354	8,433	13,422	14,445	13,813
Gambling	1,190	3	33	1,157	0	0	3	5	8	17	16	17	22
Offenses against the family and children	31,142	141	482	30,660	19	34	88	99	109	133	256	316	413
Driving under the influence	263,087	26	1,734	261,353	5	3	18	55	374	1,279	4,230	6,594	7,977
Liquor laws	49,220	932	11,286	37,934	10	79	843	1,502	3,115	5,737	8,276	8,843	7,687
Drunkenness	43,619	100	890	42,729	0	5	95	145	211	434	1,303	1,428	1,466
Disorderly conduct	49,473	4,536	13,225	36,248	71	1,074	3,391	2,752	2,984	2,953	2,105	1,696	1,677
Vagrancy	2,457	36	170	2,287	2	1	33	35	43	56	83	95	78
All other offenses (except traffic)	580,443	7,082	32,157	548,286	223	1,252	5,607	5,685	8,345	11,045	16,836	21,360	24,059
Suspicion	81	1	12	69	0	1	0	0	5	6	5	1	5
Curfew and loitering law violations	4,183	910	4,183	...	6	103	801	921	1,452	900	...	...	...

[1] Because of rounding, the percentages may not add to 100.0.

Table 52.   Metropolitan County Arrests, Distribution by Age, 2010—*Continued*

(Number, percent; 1,352 agencies; 2010 estimated population 52,433,613)

Offense charged	21	22	23	24	25–29	30–34	35–39	40–44	45–49	50–54	55–59	60–64	65 and over
TOTAL	75,866	70,904	67,675	66,115	287,435	218,484	172,527	153,667	133,298	85,891	42,100	19,353	13,984
Total percent distribution[1]	4.2	3.9	3.7	3.6	15.8	12.0	9.5	8.5	7.3	4.7	2.3	1.1	0.8
Violent Crime	2,982	2,760	2,574	2,457	11,183	8,593	6,803	5,961	5,297	3,398	1,726	917	794
Violent crime percent distribution[1]	4.0	3.7	3.5	3.3	15.1	11.6	9.2	8.1	7.2	4.6	2.3	1.2	1.1
Murder and nonnegligent manslaughter	99	71	69	63	254	181	137	91	101	78	44	22	26
Forcible rape	113	107	82	63	328	287	281	215	179	117	42	42	43
Robbery	642	518	455	359	1,483	969	552	449	325	160	83	13	17
Aggravated assault	2,128	2,064	1,968	1,972	9,118	7,156	5,833	5,206	4,692	3,043	1,557	840	708
Property Crime	7,931	6,867	5,974	6,011	24,049	17,167	13,179	11,933	9,939	6,074	2,876	1,304	1,010
Property crime percent distribution[1]	4.4	3.8	3.3	3.3	13.2	9.5	7.3	6.6	5.5	3.3	1.6	0.7	0.6
Burglary	2,102	1,787	1,524	1,432	5,641	3,687	2,513	2,177	1,723	922	359	123	68
Larceny-theft	5,341	4,679	4,052	4,196	16,748	12,138	9,668	8,969	7,542	4,789	2,367	1,110	899
Motor vehicle theft	451	356	354	359	1,507	1,192	910	698	581	291	113	49	25
Arson	37	45	44	24	153	150	88	89	93	72	37	22	18
Other													
Other assaults	5,456	5,453	5,269	5,164	24,104	20,073	17,434	16,024	13,622	8,446	3,992	1,852	1,713
Forgery and counterfeiting	443	482	532	502	2,239	1,786	1,498	1,117	881	499	220	105	61
Fraud	950	1,006	991	1,033	5,745	5,766	5,300	4,458	3,385	2,128	1,097	548	411
Embezzlement	121	92	96	104	331	262	245	268	193	113	62	41	21
Stolen property; buying, receiving, possessing	710	570	488	551	2,255	1,716	1,293	1,026	881	480	201	68	53
Vandalism	1,286	1,057	942	919	3,464	2,522	1,880	1,646	1,339	810	409	187	197
Weapons; carrying, possessing, etc.	814	863	779	688	2,978	1,941	1,412	1,135	1,003	671	352	203	200
Prostitution and commercialized vice	118	147	127	123	474	342	304	254	246	123	82	42	37
Sex offenses (except forcible rape and prostitution)	397	334	310	241	1,204	1,045	985	966	909	642	395	313	385
Drug abuse violations	12,347	10,867	10,058	9,644	38,445	27,032	18,504	15,342	13,202	8,313	3,711	1,340	588
Gambling	10	10	23	19	106	95	125	199	110	200	76	56	73
Offenses against the family and children	533	606	712	788	4,788	5,731	5,449	4,697	3,417	1,880	711	255	108
Driving under the influence	11,924	12,055	12,178	11,933	50,208	34,829	26,837	24,717	23,503	16,823	9,569	4,785	3,191
Liquor laws	1,131	850	736	554	2,228	1,584	1,393	1,397	1,339	958	552	248	158
Drunkenness	1,976	1,672	1,560	1,537	6,872	5,201	4,289	4,482	4,785	3,335	1,691	722	410
Disorderly conduct	1,772	1,625	1,504	1,446	5,664	4,260	3,392	3,392	3,379	2,303	1,098	510	425
Vagrancy	82	78	63	61	335	229	212	245	296	209	113	54	54
All other offenses (except traffic)	24,880	23,504	22,757	22,337	100,752	78,303	61,983	54,402	45,565	28,485	13,166	5,802	4,095
Suspicion	3	6	2	3	11	7	10	6	7	1	1	1	0
Curfew and loitering law violations	…	…	…	…	…	…	…	…	…	…	…	…	…

[1] Because of rounding, the percentages may not add to 100.0.

Table 53.   Metropolitan County Arrests of Persons Under 15, 18, 21, and 25 Years of Age, 2010

(Number, percent; 1,352 agencies; 2010 estimated population 52,433,613)

Offense charged	Total all ages	Number of persons arrested				Percent of total all ages			
		Under 15	Under 18	Under 21	Under 25	Under 15	Under 18	Under 21	Under 25
TOTAL	1,815,431	46,664	176,428	408,132	688,692	2.6	9.7	22.5	37.9
Violent Crime	73,884	2,425	8,681	18,439	29,212	3.3	11.7	25.0	39.5
Murder and nonnegligent manslaughter	1,657	12	140	421	723	0.7	8.4	25.4	43.6
Forcible rape	2,679	143	402	780	1,145	5.3	15.0	29.1	42.7
Robbery	11,108	377	2,247	5,083	7,057	3.4	20.2	45.8	63.5
Aggravated assault	58,440	1,893	5,892	12,155	20,287	3.2	10.1	20.8	34.7
Property Crime	181,557	9,174	35,124	67,243	94,026	5.1	19.3	37.0	51.8
Burglary	40,413	1,908	7,747	16,355	23,200	4.7	19.2	40.5	57.4
Larceny-theft	129,188	6,648	25,060	46,690	64,958	5.1	19.4	36.1	50.3
Motor vehicle theft	10,432	370	1,858	3,546	5,066	3.5	17.8	34.0	48.6
Arson	1,524	248	459	652	802	16.3	30.1	42.8	52.6
Other									
Other assaults	175,126	11,740	30,724	46,524	67,866	6.7	17.5	26.6	38.8
Forgery and counterfeiting	11,735	26	209	1,370	3,329	0.2	1.8	11.7	28.4
Fraud	35,737	141	707	2,919	6,899	0.4	2.0	8.2	19.3
Embezzlement	2,393	7	68	444	857	0.3	2.8	18.6	35.8
Stolen property; buying, receiving, possessing	14,235	302	1,583	3,943	6,262	2.1	11.1	27.7	44.0
Vandalism	30,077	3,092	8,617	13,419	17,623	10.3	28.6	44.6	58.6
Weapons; carrying, possessing, etc.	19,868	1,562	3,838	6,829	9,973	7.9	19.3	34.4	50.2
Prostitution and commercialized vice	2,822	17	78	403	918	0.6	2.8	14.3	32.5
Sex offenses (except forcible rape and prostitution)	11,502	1,049	2,100	3,376	4,658	9.1	18.3	29.4	40.5
Drug abuse violations	231,600	3,362	20,527	62,207	105,123	1.5	8.9	26.9	45.4
Gambling	1,190	3	33	88	150	0.3	2.8	7.4	12.6
Offenses against the family and children	31,142	141	482	1,467	4,106	0.5	1.5	4.7	13.2
Driving under the influence	263,087	26	1,734	20,535	68,625	*	0.7	7.8	26.1
Liquor laws	49,220	932	11,286	36,092	39,363	1.9	22.9	73.3	80.0
Drunkenness	43,619	100	890	5,087	11,832	0.2	2.0	11.7	27.1
Disorderly conduct	49,473	4,536	13,225	18,703	25,050	9.2	26.7	37.8	50.6
Vagrancy	2,457	36	170	426	710	1.5	6.9	17.3	28.9
All other offenses (except traffic)	580,443	7,082	32,157	94,412	187,890	1.2	5.5	16.3	32.4
Suspicion	81	1	12	23	37	1.2	14.8	28.4	45.7
Curfew and loitering law violations	4,183	910	4,183	4,183	4,183	21.8	100.0	100.0	100.0

* Less than one-tenth of 1 percent.

Table 54.   Metropolitan County Arrests, Distribution by Sex, 2010

(Number, percent; 1,352 agencies; 2010 estimated population 52,433,613)

Offense charged	Number of persons arrested			Percent male	Percent female	Percent distribution[1]		
	Total	Male	Female			Total	Male	Female
TOTAL	1,815,431	1,367,190	448,241	75.3	24.7	100.0	100.0	100.0
Violent Crime	73,884	59,860	14,024	81.0	19.0	4.1	4.4	3.1
Murder and nonnegligent manslaughter	1,657	1,456	201	87.9	12.1	0.1	0.1	*
Forcible rape	2,679	2,645	34	98.7	1.3	0.1	0.2	*
Robbery	11,108	9,754	1,354	87.8	12.2	0.6	0.7	0.3
Aggravated assault	58,440	46,005	12,435	78.7	21.3	3.2	3.4	2.8
Property Crime	181,557	121,368	60,189	66.8	33.2	10.0	8.9	13.4
Burglary	40,413	34,352	6,061	85.0	15.0	2.2	2.5	1.4
Larceny-theft	129,188	77,198	51,990	59.8	40.2	7.1	5.6	11.6
Motor vehicle theft	10,432	8,551	1,881	82.0	18.0	0.6	0.6	0.4
Arson	1,524	1,267	257	83.1	16.9	0.1	0.1	0.1
Other								
Other assaults	175,126	127,897	47,229	73.0	27.0	9.6	9.4	10.5
Forgery and counterfeiting	11,735	7,534	4,201	64.2	35.8	0.6	0.6	0.9
Fraud	35,737	19,901	15,836	55.7	44.3	2.0	1.5	3.5
Embezzlement	2,393	1,258	1,135	52.6	47.4	0.1	0.1	0.3
Stolen property; buying, receiving, possessing	14,235	11,446	2,789	80.4	19.6	0.8	0.8	0.6
Vandalism	30,077	24,383	5,694	81.1	18.9	1.7	1.8	1.3
Weapons; carrying, possessing, etc.	19,868	17,986	1,882	90.5	9.5	1.1	1.3	0.4
Prostitution and commercialized vice	2,822	1,166	1,656	41.3	58.7	0.2	0.1	0.4
Sex offenses (except forcible rape and prostitution)	11,502	10,665	837	92.7	7.3	0.6	0.8	0.2
Drug abuse violations	231,600	183,566	48,034	79.3	20.7	12.8	13.4	10.7
Gambling	1,190	981	209	82.4	17.6	0.1	0.1	*
Offenses against the family and children	31,142	26,208	4,934	84.2	15.8	1.7	1.9	1.1
Driving under the influence	263,087	201,200	61,887	76.5	23.5	14.5	14.7	13.8
Liquor laws	49,220	34,591	14,629	70.3	29.7	2.7	2.5	3.3
Drunkenness	43,619	35,783	7,836	82.0	18.0	2.4	2.6	1.7
Disorderly conduct	49,473	35,521	13,952	71.8	28.2	2.7	2.6	3.1
Vagrancy	2,457	1,839	618	74.8	25.2	0.1	0.1	0.1
All other offenses (except traffic)	580,443	441,218	139,225	76.0	24.0	32.0	32.3	31.1
Suspicion	81	61	20	75.3	24.7	*	*	*
Curfew and loitering law violations	4,183	2,758	1,425	65.9	34.1	0.2	0.2	0.3

[1] Because of rounding, the percentages may not add to 100.0.

* Less than one-tenth of 1 percent.

Table 55.   Metropolitan County Arrests, Distribution by Race, 2010

(Number, percent; 1,352 agencies; 2010 estimated population 52,443,613)

Offense charged	Total arrests					Percent distribution[1]				
	Total	White	Black	American Indian or Alaskan Native	Asian or Pacific Islander	Total	White	Black	American Indian or Alaskan Native	Asian or Pacific Islander
TOTAL	1,810,107	1,336,891	447,793	12,385	13,038	100.0	73.9	24.7	0.7	0.7
Violent Crime	73,784	50,224	22,555	538	467	100.0	68.1	30.6	0.7	0.6
Murder and nonnegligent manslaughter	1,655	997	636	11	11	100.0	60.2	38.4	0.7	0.7
Forcible rape	2,670	2,054	574	26	16	100.0	76.9	21.5	1.0	0.6
Robbery	11,097	5,289	5,689	56	63	100.0	47.7	51.3	0.5	0.6
Aggravated assault	58,362	41,884	15,656	445	377	100.0	71.8	26.8	0.8	0.6
Property Crime	181,182	127,083	51,655	907	1,537	100.0	70.1	28.5	0.5	0.8
Burglary	40,355	30,302	9,698	152	203	100.0	75.1	24.0	0.4	0.5
Larceny-theft	128,899	87,956	38,996	675	1,272	100.0	68.2	30.3	0.5	1.0
Motor vehicle theft	10,407	7,592	2,687	71	57	100.0	73.0	25.8	0.7	0.5
Arson	1,521	1,233	274	9	5	100.0	81.1	18.0	0.6	0.3
Other										
Other assaults	174,748	126,766	45,630	1,128	1,224	100.0	72.5	26.1	0.6	0.7
Forgery and counterfeiting	11,708	7,950	3,613	38	107	100.0	67.9	30.9	0.3	0.9
Fraud	35,602	24,576	10,644	173	209	100.0	69.0	29.9	0.5	0.6
Embezzlement	2,380	1,516	828	8	28	100.0	63.7	34.8	0.3	1.2
Stolen property; buying, receiving, possessing	14,217	10,207	3,870	59	81	100.0	71.8	27.2	0.4	0.6
Vandalism	30,011	23,600	5,991	229	191	100.0	78.6	20.0	0.8	0.6
Weapons; carrying, possessing, etc.	19,830	12,956	6,644	100	130	100.0	65.3	33.5	0.5	0.7
Prostitution and commercialized vice	2,818	1,708	990	6	114	100.0	60.6	35.1	0.2	4.0
Sex offenses (except forcible rape and prostitution)	11,471	9,147	2,168	59	97	100.0	79.7	18.9	0.5	0.8
Drug abuse violations	231,081	169,812	58,762	1,087	1,420	100.0	73.5	25.4	0.5	0.6
Gambling	1,186	765	293	10	118	100.0	64.5	24.7	0.8	9.9
Offenses against the family and children	31,058	18,774	11,999	128	157	100.0	60.4	38.6	0.4	0.5
Driving under the influence	262,167	228,164	29,809	1,620	2,574	100.0	87.0	11.4	0.6	1.0
Liquor laws	48,825	42,501	5,248	593	483	100.0	87.0	10.7	1.2	1.0
Drunkenness	43,567	38,305	4,583	396	283	100.0	87.9	10.5	0.9	0.6
Disorderly conduct	49,329	33,342	15,348	360	279	100.0	67.6	31.1	0.7	0.6
Vagrancy	2,457	1,849	600	2	6	100.0	75.3	24.4	0.1	0.2
All other offenses (except traffic)	578,436	404,424	165,584	4,936	3,492	100.0	69.9	28.6	0.9	0.6
Suspicion	81	60	21	0	0	100.0	74.1	25.9	0.0	0.0
Curfew and loitering law violations	4,169	3,162	958	8	41	100.0	75.8	23.0	0.2	1.0

[1] Because of rounding, the percentages may not add to 100.0.

Table 55. Metropolitan County Arrests, Distribution by Race, 2010—*Continued*

(Number, percent; 1,352 agencies; 2010 estimated population 52,443,613)

Offense charged	Arrests under 18					Percent distribution[1]				
	Total	White	Black	American Indian or Alaskan Native	Asian or Pacific Islander	Total	White	Black	American Indian or Alaskan Native	Asian or Pacific Islander
TOTAL	175,872	116,527	57,060	956	1,329	100.0	66.3	32.4	0.5	0.8
Violent Crime	8,668	4,543	4,014	59	52	100.0	52.4	46.3	0.7	0.6
Murder and nonnegligent manslaughter	139	71	67	1	0	100.0	51.1	48.2	0.7	0.0
Forcible rape	400	294	102	4	0	100.0	73.5	25.5	1.0	0.0
Robbery	2,245	665	1,558	9	13	100.0	29.6	69.4	0.4	0.6
Aggravated assault	5,884	3,513	2,287	45	39	100.0	59.7	38.9	0.8	0.7
Property Crime	35,024	21,067	13,443	145	369	100.0	60.2	38.4	0.4	1.1
Burglary	7,727	5,128	2,526	23	50	100.0	66.4	32.7	0.3	0.6
Larceny-theft	24,988	14,428	10,147	106	307	100.0	57.7	40.6	0.4	1.2
Motor vehicle theft	1,852	1,158	670	15	9	100.0	62.5	36.2	0.8	0.5
Arson	457	353	100	1	3	100.0	77.2	21.9	0.2	0.7
Other										
Other assaults	30,656	17,426	12,921	149	160	100.0	56.8	42.1	0.5	0.5
Forgery and counterfeiting	207	142	62	0	3	100.0	68.6	30.0	0.0	1.4
Fraud	703	490	202	4	7	100.0	69.7	28.7	0.6	1.0
Embezzlement	66	44	22	0	0	100.0	66.7	33.3	0.0	0.0
Stolen property; buying, receiving, possessing	1,577	925	637	4	11	100.0	58.7	40.4	0.3	0.7
Vandalism	8,587	6,670	1,819	51	47	100.0	77.7	21.2	0.6	0.5
Weapons; carrying, possessing, etc.	3,830	2,349	1,414	33	34	100.0	61.3	36.9	0.9	0.9
Prostitution and commercialized vice	78	37	39	1	1	100.0	47.4	50.0	1.3	1.3
Sex offenses (except forcible rape and prostitution)	2,092	1,566	502	9	15	100.0	74.9	24.0	0.4	0.7
Drug abuse violations	20,470	15,755	4,403	151	161	100.0	77.0	21.5	0.7	0.8
Gambling	33	18	14	0	1	100.0	54.5	42.4	0.0	3.0
Offenses against the family and children	482	368	108	2	4	100.0	76.3	22.4	0.4	0.8
Driving under the influence	1,727	1,598	105	8	16	100.0	92.5	6.1	0.5	0.9
Liquor laws	11,212	10,374	616	98	124	100.0	92.5	5.5	0.9	1.1
Drunkenness	889	806	66	11	6	100.0	90.7	7.4	1.2	0.7
Disorderly conduct	13,198	7,037	6,030	66	65	100.0	53.3	45.7	0.5	0.5
Vagrancy	170	137	30	0	3	100.0	80.6	17.6	0.0	1.8
All other offenses (except traffic)	32,022	22,006	9,650	157	209	100.0	68.7	30.1	0.5	0.7
Suspicion	12	7	5	0	0	100.0	58.3	41.7	0.0	0.0
Curfew and loitering law violations	4,169	3,162	958	8	41	100.0	75.8	23.0	0.2	1.0

[1] Because of rounding, the percentages may not add to 100.0.

Table 55.   Metropolitan County Arrests, Distribution by Race, 2010—*Continued*

(Number, percent; 1,352 agencies; 2010 estimated population 52,443,613)

Offense charged	Arrests 18 and over					Percent distribution[1]				
	Total	White	Black	American Indian or Alaskan Native	Asian or Pacific Islander	Total	White	Black	American Indian or Alaskan Native	Asian or Pacific Islander
TOTAL	1,634,235	1,220,364	390,733	11,429	11,709	100.0	74.7	23.9	0.7	0.7
Violent Crime...	65,116	45,681	18,541	479	415	100.0	70.2	28.5	0.7	0.6
Murder and nonnegligent manslaughter	1,516	926	569	10	11	100.0	61.1	37.5	0.7	0.7
Forcible rape	2,270	1,760	472	22	16	100.0	77.5	20.8	1.0	0.7
Robbery...	8,852	4,624	4,131	47	50	100.0	52.2	46.7	0.5	0.6
Aggravated assault	52,478	38,371	13,369	400	338	100.0	73.1	25.5	0.8	0.6
Property Crime...	146,158	106,016	38,212	762	1,168	100.0	72.5	26.1	0.5	0.8
Burglary	32,628	25,174	7,172	129	153	100.0	77.2	22.0	0.4	0.5
Larceny-theft...	103,911	73,528	28,849	569	965	100.0	70.8	27.8	0.5	0.9
Motor vehicle theft...	8,555	6,434	2,017	56	48	100.0	75.2	23.6	0.7	0.6
Arson...	1,064	880	174	8	2	100.0	82.7	16.4	0.8	0.2
Other										
Other assaults...	144,092	109,340	32,709	979	1,064	100.0	75.9	22.7	0.7	0.7
Forgery and counterfeiting	11,501	7,808	3,551	38	104	100.0	67.9	30.9	0.3	0.9
Fraud...	34,899	24,086	10,442	169	202	100.0	69.0	29.9	0.5	0.6
Embezzlement...	2,314	1,472	806	8	28	100.0	63.6	34.8	0.3	1.2
Stolen property; buying, receiving, possessing.......................	12,640	9,282	3,233	55	70	100.0	73.4	25.6	0.4	0.6
Vandalism...	21,424	16,930	4,172	178	144	100.0	79.0	19.5	0.8	0.7
Weapons; carrying, possessing, etc.	16,000	10,607	5,230	67	96	100.0	66.3	32.7	0.4	0.6
Prostitution and commercialized vice	2,740	1,671	951	5	113	100.0	61.0	34.7	0.2	4.1
Sex offenses (except forcible rape and prostitution)............	9,379	7,581	1,666	50	82	100.0	80.8	17.8	0.5	0.9
Drug abuse violations	210,611	154,057	54,359	936	1,259	100.0	73.1	25.8	0.4	0.6
Gambling	1,153	747	279	10	117	100.0	64.8	24.2	0.9	10.1
Offenses against the family and children............................	30,576	18,406	11,891	126	153	100.0	60.2	38.9	0.4	0.5
Driving under the influence	260,440	226,566	29,704	1,612	2,558	100.0	87.0	11.4	0.6	1.0
Liquor laws...	37,613	32,127	4,632	495	359	100.0	85.4	12.3	1.3	1.0
Drunkenness...	42,678	37,499	4,517	385	277	100.0	87.9	10.6	0.9	0.6
Disorderly conduct...	36,131	26,305	9,318	294	214	100.0	72.8	25.8	0.8	0.6
Vagrancy...	2,287	1,712	570	2	3	100.0	74.9	24.9	0.1	0.1
All other offenses (except traffic)	546,414	382,418	155,934	4,779	3,283	100.0	70.0	28.5	0.9	0.6
Suspicion...	69	53	16	0	0	100.0	76.8	23.2	0.0	0.0
Curfew and loitering law violations.................................	...	...	...	...	...	...	...	...	...	...

[1] Because of rounding, the percentages may not add to 100.0.

Table 56.   Nonmetropolitan County Arrest Trends, 2009–2010

(Number, percent change; 1,912 agencies; 2010 estimated population 22,188,767; 2009 estimated population 22,213,418)

Offense charged	Number of persons arrested								
	Total all ages			Under 18 years of age			18 years of age and over		
	2009	2010	Percent change	2009	2010	Percent change	2009	2010	Percent change
TOTAL[1]	827,397	794,429	-4.0	56,206	50,280	-10.5	771,191	744,149	-3.5
Violent Crime	25,031	23,535	-6.0	2,023	1,681	-16.9	23,008	21,854	-5.0
Murder and nonnegligent manslaughter	794	609	-23.3	46	23	-50.0	748	586	-21.7
Forcible rape	1,603	1,444	-9.9	225	185	-17.8	1,378	1,259	-8.6
Robbery	2,073	1,984	-4.3	223	176	-21.1	1,850	1,808	-2.3
Aggravated assault	20,561	19,498	-5.2	1,529	1,297	-15.2	19,032	18,201	-4.4
Property Crime	58,553	59,119	1.0	9,746	8,454	-13.3	48,807	50,665	3.8
Burglary	19,103	18,441	-3.5	3,416	2,764	-19.1	15,687	15,677	-0.1
Larceny-theft	34,639	36,054	4.1	5,331	4,845	-9.1	29,308	31,209	6.5
Motor vehicle theft	3,983	3,847	-3.4	783	675	-13.8	3,200	3,172	-0.9
Arson	828	777	-6.2	216	170	-21.3	612	607	-0.8
Other									
Other assaults	76,002	73,902	-2.8	8,405	8,067	-4.0	67,597	65,835	-2.6
Forgery and counterfeiting	4,299	4,135	-3.8	75	54	-28.0	4,224	4,081	-3.4
Fraud	24,391	19,557	-19.8	268	264	-1.5	24,123	19,293	-20.0
Embezzlement	788	855	8.5	17	7	-58.8	771	848	10.0
Stolen property; buying, receiving, possessing	4,604	4,557	-1.0	476	369	-22.5	4,128	4,188	1.5
Vandalism	13,393	12,094	-9.7	3,484	2,645	-24.1	9,909	9,449	-4.6
Weapons; carrying, possessing, etc.	6,944	6,414	-7.6	657	598	-9.0	6,287	5,816	-7.5
Prostitution and commercialized vice	168	206	22.6	8	4	-50.0	160	202	26.3
Sex offenses (except forcible rape and prostitution)	5,008	4,869	-2.8	901	903	0.2	4,107	3,966	-3.4
Drug abuse violations	91,544	94,285	3.0	5,377	5,376	*	86,167	88,909	3.2
Gambling	309	185	-40.1	9	7	-22.2	300	178	-40.7
Offenses against the family and children	13,092	12,053	-7.9	249	201	-19.3	12,843	11,852	-7.7
Driving under the influence	170,102	160,122	-5.9	1,521	1,288	-15.3	168,581	158,834	-5.8
Liquor laws	31,947	29,091	-8.9	6,962	6,154	-11.6	24,985	22,937	-8.2
Drunkenness	22,975	19,810	-13.8	443	339	-23.5	22,532	19,471	-13.6
Disorderly conduct	22,434	21,404	-4.6	4,138	3,730	-9.9	18,296	17,674	-3.4
Vagrancy	378	332	-12.2	26	13	-50.0	352	319	-9.4
All other offenses (except traffic)	254,946	247,442	-2.9	10,932	9,664	-11.6	244,014	237,778	-2.6
Suspicion	89	82	-7.9	11	2	-81.8	78	80	2.6
Curfew and loitering law violations	489	462	-5.5	489	462	-5.5	...	...	...

[1] Does not include suspicion.
* Less than one-tenth of 1 percent.

Table 57.   Nonmetropolitan County Arrest Trends, by Age and Sex, 2009–2010

(Number, percent; 1,912 agencies; 2010 estimated population 22,188,767; 2009 estimated population 22,213,418)

Offense charged	Male						Female					
	Total			Under 18			Total			Under 18		
	2009	2010	Percent change	2009	2010	Percent change	2009	2010	Percent change	2009	2010	Percent change
Violent Crime	20,699	19,440	-6.1	1,661	1,399	-15.8	4,332	4,095	-5.5	362	282	-22.1
Murder and nonnegligent manslaughter	676	527	-22.0	43	20	-53.5	118	82	-30.5	3	3	0.0
Forcible rape	1,574	1,419	-9.8	220	180	-18.2	29	25	-13.8	5	5	0.0
Robbery	1,831	1,722	-6.0	211	161	-23.7	242	262	8.3	12	15	25.0
Aggravated assault	16,618	15,772	-5.1	1,187	1,038	-12.6	3,943	3,726	-5.5	342	259	-24.3
Property Crime	43,720	44,106	0.9	7,569	6,477	-14.4	14,833	15,013	1.2	2,177	1,977	-9.2
Burglary	16,573	15,932	-3.9	3,097	2,506	-19.1	2,530	2,509	-0.8	319	258	-19.1
Larceny-theft	23,170	24,383	5.2	3,677	3,293	-10.4	11,469	11,671	1.8	1,654	1,552	-6.2
Motor vehicle theft	3,286	3,156	-4.0	608	529	-13.0	697	691	-0.9	175	146	-16.6
Arson	691	635	-8.1	187	149	-20.3	137	142	3.6	29	21	-27.6
Other												
Other assaults	56,837	54,705	-3.8	5,801	5,336	-8.0	19,165	19,197	0.2	2,604	2,731	4.9
Forgery and counterfeiting	2,551	2,506	-1.8	46	41	-10.9	1,748	1,629	-6.8	29	13	-55.2
Fraud	12,351	10,280	-16.8	151	170	12.6	12,040	9,277	-22.9	117	94	-19.7
Embezzlement	392	381	-2.8	14	7	-50.0	396	474	19.7	3	0	-100.0
Stolen property; buying, receiving, possessing	3,841	3,786	-1.4	393	315	-19.8	763	771	1.0	83	54	-34.9
Vandalism	11,045	9,901	-10.4	3,022	2,221	-26.5	2,348	2,193	-6.6	462	424	-8.2
Weapons; carrying, possessing, etc.	6,437	5,945	-7.6	589	548	-7.0	507	469	-7.5	68	50	-26.5
Prostitution and commercialized vice	100	119	19.0	6	4	-33.3	68	87	27.9	2	0	-100.0
Sex offenses (except forcible rape and prostitution)	4,685	4,563	-2.6	813	821	1.0	323	306	-5.3	88	82	-6.8
Drug abuse violations	71,845	72,992	1.6	4,284	4,322	0.9	19,699	21,293	8.1	1,093	1,054	-3.6
Gambling	253	155	-38.7	8	6	-25.0	56	30	-46.4	1	1	0.0
Offenses against the family and children	10,551	9,570	-9.3	165	133	-19.4	2,541	2,483	-2.3	84	68	-19.0
Driving under the influence	134,087	124,925	-6.8	1,176	1,011	-14.0	36,015	35,197	-2.3	345	277	-19.7
Liquor laws	22,516	20,375	-9.5	4,389	3,682	-16.1	9,431	8,716	-7.6	2,573	2,472	-3.9
Drunkenness	18,299	15,501	-15.3	334	235	-29.6	4,676	4,309	-7.8	109	104	-4.6
Disorderly conduct	16,220	15,465	-4.7	2,840	2,472	-13.0	6,214	5,939	-4.4	1,298	1,258	-3.1
Vagrancy	300	266	-11.3	15	9	-40.0	78	66	-15.4	11	4	-63.6
All other offenses (except traffic)	193,674	187,055	-3.4	7,831	6,956	-11.2	61,272	60,387	-1.4	3,101	2,708	-12.7
Suspicion	57	70	22.8	9	1	-88.9	32	12	-62.5	2	1	-50.0
Curfew and loitering law violations	285	286	0.4	285	286	0.4	204	176	-13.7	204	176	-13.7

[1] Does not include suspicion.

Table 58.   Nonmetropolitan County Arrests, Distribution by Age, 2010

(Number, percent; 1,958 agencies; 2010 estimated population 22,251,821)

Offense charged	Total all ages	Ages under 15	Ages under 18	Ages 18 and over	Under 10	10–12	13–14	15	16	17	18	19	20
TOTAL	809,277	11,706	52,173	757,104	499	2,653	8,554	8,225	13,040	19,202	30,091	34,861	35,178
Total percent distribution[1]	100.0	1.4	6.4	93.6	0.1	0.3	1.1	1.0	1.6	2.4	3.7	4.3	4.3
Violent Crime	23,971	492	1,778	22,193	14	154	324	254	433	599	947	944	932
Violent crime percent distribution[1]	100.0	2.1	7.4	92.6	0.1	0.6	1.4	1.1	1.8	2.5	4.0	3.9	3.9
Murder and nonnegligent manslaughter	637	7	26	611	0	2	5	4	6	9	27	26	26
Forcible rape	1,483	61	189	1,294	0	15	46	39	39	50	78	76	70
Robbery	2,085	22	194	1,891	1	3	18	24	49	99	190	175	158
Aggravated assault	19,766	402	1,369	18,397	13	134	255	187	339	441	652	667	678
Property Crime	61,239	2,221	8,843	52,396	76	521	1,624	1,454	2,106	3,062	3,994	3,783	3,099
Property crime percent distribution[1]	100.0	3.6	14.4	85.6	0.1	0.9	2.7	2.4	3.4	5.0	6.5	6.2	5.1
Burglary	19,429	738	2,944	16,485	27	176	535	458	709	1,039	1,563	1,467	1,151
Larceny-theft	37,159	1,261	5,027	32,132	40	304	917	844	1,165	1,757	2,128	2,086	1,754
Motor vehicle theft	3,856	142	695	3,161	0	15	127	135	203	215	261	191	159
Arson	795	80	177	618	9	26	45	17	29	51	42	39	35
Other													
Other assaults	75,245	2,591	8,386	66,859	103	642	1,846	1,568	2,053	2,174	2,214	2,246	2,273
Forgery and counterfeiting	4,197	3	53	4,144	0	0	3	6	18	26	86	143	170
Fraud	19,115	60	294	18,821	6	11	43	33	70	131	241	388	426
Embezzlement	987	3	7	980	0	0	3	0	1	3	17	26	23
Stolen property; buying, receiving, possession	4,992	68	407	4,585	4	11	53	69	114	156	240	270	215
Vandalism	12,208	920	2,707	9,501	64	255	601	472	618	697	755	711	623
Weapons; carrying, possessing, etc.	6,836	229	673	6,163	27	70	132	97	159	188	244	258	261
Prostitution and commercialized vice	211	2	4	207	0	0	2	0	0	2	3	4	4
Sex offenses (except forcible rape and prostitution)	5,074	421	934	4,140	28	126	267	142	181	190	256	235	183
Drug abuse violations	98,516	786	5,593	92,923	13	101	672	772	1,396	2,639	5,002	5,726	5,714
Gambling	191	0	8	183	0	0	0	1	4	3	7	11	13
Offenses against the family and children	12,417	81	230	12,187	8	19	54	30	56	63	159	191	244
Driving under the influence	178,369	25	1,487	176,882	4	5	16	40	340	1,082	3,114	4,828	5,572
Liquor laws	29,479	481	6,196	23,283	5	42	434	829	1,810	3,076	4,972	5,327	4,709
Drunkenness	18,289	27	322	17,967	2	2	23	48	81	166	552	595	656
Disorderly conduct	21,800	1,184	3,895	17,905	38	273	873	692	965	1,054	889	796	710
Vagrancy	329	2	13	316	0	1	1	0	4	7	11	14	11
All other offenses (except traffic)	235,223	2,006	9,903	225,320	103	408	1,495	1,613	2,517	3,767	6,385	8,362	9,334
Suspicion	151	1	2	149	0	0	1	0	0	1	3	3	6
Curfew and loitering law violations	438	103	438	...	4	12	87	105	114	116	...	...	...

[1] Because of rounding, the percentages may not add to 100.0.

Table 58.   Nonmetropolitan County Arrests, Distribution by Age, 2010—*Continued*

(Number, percent; 1,958 agencies; 2010 estimated population 22,251,821)

Offense charged	21	22	23	24	25–29	30–34	35–39	40–44	45–49	50–54	55–59	60–64	65 and over
TOTAL	32,264	30,772	29,639	29,175	131,039	101,313	81,691	71,803	63,623	42,953	22,417	11,380	8,905
Total percent distribution[1]	4.0	3.8	3.7	3.6	16.2	12.5	10.1	8.9	7.9	5.3	2.8	1.4	1.1
Violent Crime	915	894	845	832	3,840	2,974	2,362	2,150	1,789	1,330	662	385	392
Violent crime percent distribution[1]	3.8	3.7	3.5	3.5	16.0	12.4	9.9	9.0	7.5	5.5	2.8	1.6	1.6
Murder and nonnegligent manslaughter	31	22	27	20	95	83	66	53	49	43	19	11	13
Forcible rape	81	52	53	39	188	142	140	113	91	69	39	31	32
Robbery	128	129	91	94	359	189	151	104	69	30	13	8	3
Aggravated assault	675	691	674	679	3,198	2,560	2,005	1,880	1,580	1,188	591	335	344
Property Crime	2,756	2,423	2,251	2,208	9,373	6,422	4,919	4,128	3,246	1,990	943	473	388
Property crime percent distribution[1]	4.5	4.0	3.7	3.6	15.3	10.5	8.0	6.7	5.3	3.2	1.5	0.8	0.6
Burglary	1,063	846	782	712	3,020	1,909	1,315	1,109	762	485	167	77	57
Larceny-theft	1,513	1,405	1,320	1,353	5,698	4,028	3,190	2,680	2,231	1,374	697	363	312
Motor vehicle theft	144	148	137	126	581	402	358	276	187	100	62	20	9
Arson	36	24	12	17	74	83	56	63	66	31	17	13	10
Other													
Other assaults	2,433	2,386	2,336	2,340	10,875	9,327	8,117	7,330	6,614	4,093	2,073	1,106	1,096
Forgery and counterfeiting	165	150	176	185	916	660	536	343	316	176	75	33	14
Fraud	478	505	610	588	3,210	3,170	2,854	2,214	1,702	1,189	627	368	251
Embezzlement	16	28	51	27	130	127	201	107	75	89	38	19	6
Stolen property; buying, receiving, possessing	237	236	206	201	797	649	456	400	308	192	84	58	36
Vandalism	527	484	428	429	1,561	1,108	805	706	610	381	147	112	114
Weapons; carrying, possessing, etc.	250	247	244	238	1,045	759	614	526	548	417	236	140	136
Prostitution and commercialized vice	5	7	6	5	36	28	25	19	20	15	10	11	9
Sex offenses (except forcible rape and prostitution)	184	148	111	104	506	467	458	400	334	263	190	134	167
Drug abuse violations	4,922	4,553	4,320	4,055	17,390	12,029	8,676	6,880	6,151	4,203	2,068	814	420
Gambling	4	1	5	6	21	19	19	17	14	21	11	10	4
Offenses against the family and children	314	304	327	398	2,228	2,286	2,003	1,587	1,107	606	239	98	96
Driving under the influence	7,234	7,192	7,065	6,765	29,642	22,253	18,723	18,381	17,968	13,267	7,681	4,245	2,952
Liquor laws	787	562	417	383	1,394	1,011	842	834	832	584	338	163	128
Drunkenness	708	653	637	656	2,793	2,194	1,892	2,026	2,031	1,398	675	316	185
Disorderly conduct	833	749	677	712	2,812	2,144	1,802	1,763	1,730	1,139	572	288	289
Vagrancy	13	6	10	7	50	49	41	29	33	25	11	5	1
All other offenses (except traffic)	9,480	9,236	8,907	9,023	42,396	33,616	26,324	21,951	18,185	11,567	5,733	2,600	2,221
Suspicion	3	8	10	13	24	21	22	12	10	8	4	2	0
Curfew and loitering law violations	…	…	…	…	…	…	…	…	…	…	…	…	…

[1] Because of rounding, the percentages may not add to 100.0.

Table 59.　Nonmetropolitan County Arrests of Persons Under 15, 18, 21, and 25 Years of Age, 2010

(Number, percent; 1,958 agencies; 2010 estimated population 22,251,821)

Offense charged	Total all ages	Number of persons arrested				Percent of total all ages			
		Under 15	Under 18	Under 21	Under 25	Under 15	Under 18	Under 21	Under 25
TOTAL	809,277	11,706	52,173	152,303	274,153	1.4	6.4	18.8	33.9
Violent Crime..	23,971	492	1,778	4,601	8,087	2.1	7.4	19.2	33.7
Murder and nonnegligent manslaughter	637	7	26	105	205	1.1	4.1	16.5	32.2
Forcible rape	1,483	61	189	413	638	4.1	12.7	27.8	43.0
Robbery	2,085	22	194	717	1,159	1.1	9.3	34.4	55.6
Aggravated assault	19,766	402	1,369	3,366	6,085	2.0	6.9	17.0	30.8
Property Crime	61,239	2,221	8,843	19,719	29,357	3.6	14.4	32.2	47.9
Burglary	19,429	738	2,944	7,125	10,528	3.8	15.2	36.7	54.2
Larceny-theft	37,159	1,261	5,027	10,995	16,586	3.4	13.5	29.6	44.6
Motor vehicle theft	3,856	142	695	1,306	1,861	3.7	18.0	33.9	48.3
Arson	795	80	177	293	382	10.1	22.3	36.9	48.1
Other									
Other assaults..	75,245	2,591	8,386	15,119	24,614	3.4	11.1	20.1	32.7
Forgery and counterfeiting	4,197	3	53	452	1,128	0.1	1.3	10.8	26.9
Fraud	19,115	60	294	1,349	3,530	0.3	1.5	7.1	18.5
Embezzlement	987	3	7	73	195	0.3	0.7	7.4	19.8
Stolen property; buying, receiving, possessing........	4,992	68	407	1,132	2,012	1.4	8.2	22.7	40.3
Vandalism...	12,208	920	2,707	4,796	6,664	7.5	22.2	39.3	54.6
Weapons; carrying, possessing, etc.	6,836	229	673	1,436	2,415	3.3	9.8	21.0	35.3
Prostitution and commercialized vice	211	2	4	15	38	0.9	1.9	7.1	18.0
Sex offenses (except forcible rape and prostitution).............	5,074	421	934	1,608	2,155	8.3	18.4	31.7	42.5
Drug abuse violations	98,516	786	5,593	22,035	39,885	0.8	5.7	22.4	40.5
Gambling	191	0	8	39	55	0.0	4.2	20.4	28.8
Offenses against the family and children..................	12,417	81	230	824	2,167	0.7	1.9	6.6	17.5
Driving under the influence	178,369	25	1,487	15,001	43,257	*	0.8	8.4	24.3
Liquor laws...	29,479	481	6,196	21,204	23,353	1.6	21.0	71.9	79.2
Drunkenness	18,289	27	322	2,125	4,779	0.1	1.8	11.6	26.1
Disorderly conduct	21,800	1,184	3,895	6,290	9,261	5.4	17.9	28.9	42.5
Vagrancy...	329	2	13	49	85	0.6	4.0	14.9	25.8
All other offenses (except traffic)	235,223	2,006	9,903	33,984	70,630	0.9	4.2	14.4	30.0
Suspicion..	151	1	2	14	48	0.7	1.3	9.3	31.8
Curfew and loitering law violations........................	438	103	438	438	438	23.5	100.0	100.0	100.0

* Less than one-tenth of 1 percent.

Table 60.   Nonmetropolitan County Arrests, Distribution by Sex, 2010

(Number, percent; 1,958 agencies; 2010 estimated population 22,251,821)

Offense charged	Number of persons arrested			Percent male	Percent female	Percent distribution[1]		
	Total	Male	Female			Total	Male	Female
TOTAL	809,277	614,413	194,864	75.9	24.1	100.0	100.0	100.0
Violent Crime	23,971	19,767	4,204	82.5	17.5	3.0	3.2	2.2
Murder and nonnegligent manslaughter	637	558	79	87.6	12.4	0.1	0.1	*
Forcible rape	1,483	1,457	26	98.2	1.8	0.2	0.2	*
Robbery	2,085	1,820	265	87.3	12.7	0.3	0.3	0.1
Aggravated assault	19,766	15,932	3,834	80.6	19.4	2.4	2.6	2.0
Property Crime	61,239	45,813	15,426	74.8	25.2	7.6	7.5	7.9
Burglary	19,429	16,804	2,625	86.5	13.5	2.4	2.7	1.3
Larceny-theft	37,159	25,202	11,957	67.8	32.2	4.6	4.1	6.1
Motor vehicle theft	3,856	3,158	698	81.9	18.1	0.5	0.5	0.4
Arson	795	649	146	81.6	18.4	0.1	0.1	0.1
Other								
Other assaults	75,245	55,598	19,647	73.9	26.1	9.3	9.0	10.1
Forgery and counterfeiting	4,197	2,534	1,663	60.4	39.6	0.5	0.4	0.9
Fraud	19,115	10,207	8,908	53.4	46.6	2.4	1.7	4.6
Embezzlement	987	404	583	40.9	59.1	0.1	0.1	0.3
Stolen property; buying, receiving, possessing	4,992	4,150	842	83.1	16.9	0.6	0.7	0.4
Vandalism	12,208	9,990	2,218	81.8	18.2	1.5	1.6	1.1
Weapons; carrying, possessing, etc.	6,836	6,317	519	92.4	7.6	0.8	1.0	0.3
Prostitution and commercialized vice	211	122	89	57.8	42.2	*	*	*
Sex offenses (except forcible rape and prostitution)	5,074	4,759	315	93.8	6.2	0.6	0.8	0.2
Drug abuse violations	98,516	76,442	22,074	77.6	22.4	12.2	12.4	11.3
Gambling	191	158	33	82.7	17.3	*	*	*
Offenses against the family and children	12,417	9,823	2,594	79.1	20.9	1.5	1.6	1.3
Driving under the influence	178,369	138,317	40,052	77.5	22.5	22.0	22.5	20.6
Liquor laws	29,479	20,657	8,822	70.1	29.9	3.6	3.4	4.5
Drunkenness	18,289	14,396	3,893	78.7	21.3	2.3	2.3	2.0
Disorderly conduct	21,800	15,800	6,000	72.5	27.5	2.7	2.6	3.1
Vagrancy	329	265	64	80.5	19.5	*	*	*
All other offenses (except traffic)	235,223	178,495	56,728	75.9	24.1	29.1	29.1	29.1
Suspicion	151	126	25	83.4	16.6	*	*	*
Curfew and loitering law violations	438	273	165	62.3	37.7	0.1	*	0.1

[1] Because of rounding, the percentages may not add to 100.0.

* Less than one-tenth of 1 percent.

Table 61. Nonmetropolitan County Arrests, Distribution by Race, 2010

(Number, percent; 1,958 agencies; 2010 estimated population 22,251,821)

Offense charged	Total arrests					Percent distribution[1]				
	Total	White	Black	American Indian or Alaskan Native	Asian or Pacific Islander	Total	White	Black	American Indian or Alaskan Native	Asian or Pacific Islander
TOTAL	803,304	656,124	113,287	23,941	9,952	100.0	81.7	14.1	3.0	1.2
Violent Crime	23,864	17,558	4,952	1,106	248	100.0	73.6	20.8	4.6	1.0
Murder and nonnegligent manslaughter	636	432	167	34	3	100.0	67.9	26.3	5.3	0.5
Forcible rape	1,475	1,223	203	36	13	100.0	82.9	13.8	2.4	0.9
Robbery	2,077	1,142	822	68	45	100.0	55.0	39.6	3.3	2.2
Aggravated assault	19,676	14,761	3,760	968	187	100.0	75.0	19.1	4.9	1.0
Property Crime	60,951	49,788	8,721	1,568	874	100.0	81.7	14.3	2.6	1.4
Burglary	19,363	15,737	2,919	574	133	100.0	81.3	15.1	3.0	0.7
Larceny-theft	36,958	30,256	5,213	828	661	100.0	81.9	14.1	2.2	1.8
Motor vehicle theft	3,839	3,120	500	141	78	100.0	81.3	13.0	3.7	2.0
Arson	791	675	89	25	2	100.0	85.3	11.3	3.2	0.3
Other										
Other assaults	74,824	59,833	11,476	2,576	939	100.0	80.0	15.3	3.4	1.3
Forgery and counterfeiting	4,142	3,323	729	62	28	100.0	80.2	17.6	1.5	0.7
Fraud	19,013	15,075	3,573	287	78	100.0	79.3	18.8	1.5	0.4
Embezzlement	983	863	90	19	11	100.0	87.8	9.2	1.9	1.1
Stolen property; buying, receiving, possessing	4,964	3,912	893	113	46	100.0	78.8	18.0	2.3	0.9
Vandalism	12,115	10,090	1,427	454	144	100.0	83.3	11.8	3.7	1.2
Weapons; carrying, possessing, etc.	6,814	5,158	1,407	191	58	100.0	75.7	20.6	2.8	0.9
Prostitution and commercialized vice	211	159	32	6	14	100.0	75.4	15.2	2.8	6.6
Sex offenses (except forcible rape and prostitution)	5,046	4,422	473	114	37	100.0	87.6	9.4	2.3	0.7
Drug abuse violations	97,915	80,205	15,282	1,598	830	100.0	81.9	15.6	1.6	0.8
Gambling	189	133	39	1	16	100.0	70.4	20.6	0.5	8.5
Offenses against the family and children	12,370	8,972	2,832	542	24	100.0	72.5	22.9	4.4	0.2
Driving under the influence	176,274	152,621	16,498	4,223	2,932	100.0	86.6	9.4	2.4	1.7
Liquor laws	29,099	26,474	1,260	1,075	290	100.0	91.0	4.3	3.7	1.0
Drunkenness	18,232	15,916	1,460	818	38	100.0	87.3	8.0	4.5	0.2
Disorderly conduct	21,642	16,890	3,610	968	174	100.0	78.0	16.7	4.5	0.8
Vagrancy	329	217	92	18	2	100.0	66.0	28.0	5.5	0.6
All other offenses (except traffic)	233,747	184,059	38,353	8,186	3,149	100.0	78.7	16.4	3.5	1.3
Suspicion	150	86	64	0	0	100.0	57.3	42.7	0.0	0.0
Curfew and loitering law violations	430	370	24	16	20	100.0	86.0	5.6	3.7	4.7

[1] Because of rounding, the percentages may not add to 100.0.

Table 61. Nonmetropolitan County Arrests, Distribution by Race, 2010—*Continued*

(Number, percent; 1,958 agencies; 2010 estimated population 22,251,821)

Offense charged	Arrests under 18					Percent distribution[1]				
	Total	White	Black	American Indian or Alaskan Native	Asian or Pacific Islander	Total	White	Black	American Indian or Alaskan Native	Asian or Pacific Islander
TOTAL	51,716	41,536	7,150	1,876	1,154	100.0	80.3	13.8	3.6	2.2
Violent Crime	1,761	1,201	456	68	36	100.0	68.2	25.9	3.9	2.0
Murder and nonnegligent manslaughter	26	18	7	1	0	100.0	69.2	26.9	3.8	0.0
Forcible rape	185	149	31	3	2	100.0	80.5	16.8	1.6	1.1
Robbery	191	76	99	3	13	100.0	39.8	51.8	1.6	6.8
Aggravated assault	1,359	958	319	61	21	100.0	70.5	23.5	4.5	1.5
Property Crime	8,770	7,117	1,180	214	259	100.0	81.2	13.5	2.4	3.0
Burglary	2,924	2,374	438	80	32	100.0	81.2	15.0	2.7	1.1
Larceny-theft	4,979	4,006	666	103	204	100.0	80.5	13.4	2.1	4.1
Motor vehicle theft	692	579	63	27	23	100.0	83.7	9.1	3.9	3.3
Arson	175	158	13	4	0	100.0	90.3	7.4	2.3	0.0
Other										
Other assaults	8,303	6,119	1,760	261	163	100.0	73.7	21.2	3.1	2.0
Forgery and counterfeiting	53	44	8	1	0	100.0	83.0	15.1	1.9	0.0
Fraud	290	248	35	6	1	100.0	85.5	12.1	2.1	0.3
Embezzlement	7	5	2	0	0	100.0	71.4	28.6	0.0	0.0
Stolen property; buying, receiving, possessing	403	309	80	7	7	100.0	76.7	19.9	1.7	1.7
Vandalism	2,666	2,279	254	100	33	100.0	85.5	9.5	3.8	1.2
Weapons; carrying, possessing, etc.	673	496	155	17	5	100.0	73.7	23.0	2.5	0.7
Prostitution and commercialized vice	4	4	0	0	0	100.0	100.0	0.0	0.0	0.0
Sex offenses (except forcible rape and prostitution)	929	827	77	18	7	100.0	89.0	8.3	1.9	0.8
Drug abuse violations	5,560	4,714	562	158	126	100.0	84.8	10.1	2.8	2.3
Gambling	8	3	0	0	5	100.0	37.5	0.0	0.0	62.5
Offenses against the family and children	230	206	16	7	1	100.0	89.6	7.0	3.0	0.4
Driving under the influence	1,474	1,332	66	45	31	100.0	90.4	4.5	3.1	2.1
Liquor laws	6,128	5,715	120	225	68	100.0	93.3	2.0	3.7	1.1
Drunkenness	322	273	13	34	2	100.0	84.8	4.0	10.6	0.6
Disorderly conduct	3,861	2,663	952	204	42	100.0	69.0	24.7	5.3	1.1
Vagrancy	13	12	0	1	0	100.0	92.3	0.0	7.7	0.0
All other offenses (except traffic)	9,829	7,599	1,388	494	348	100.0	77.3	14.1	5.0	3.5
Suspicion	2	0	2	0	0	100.0	0.0	100.0	0.0	0.0
Curfew and loitering law violations	430	370	24	16	20	100.0	86.0	5.6	3.7	4.7

[1] Because of rounding, the percentages may not add to 100.0.

Table 61.   Nonmetropolitan County Arrests, Distribution by Race, 2010—*Continued*

(Number, percent; 1,958 agencies; 2010 estimated population 22,251,821)

Offense charged	Arrests 18 and over					Percent distribution[1]				
	Total	White	Black	American Indian or Alaskan Native	Asian or Pacific Islander	Total	White	Black	American Indian or Alaskan Native	Asian or Pacific Islander
TOTAL	751,588	614,588	106,137	22,065	8,798	100.0	81.8	14.1	2.9	1.2
Violent Crime..................	22,103	16,357	4,496	1,038	212	100.0	74.0	20.3	4.7	1.0
Murder and nonnegligent manslaughter	610	414	160	33	3	100.0	67.9	26.2	5.4	0.5
Forcible rape	1,290	1,074	172	33	11	100.0	83.3	13.3	2.6	0.9
Robbery	1,886	1,066	723	65	32	100.0	56.5	38.3	3.4	1.7
Aggravated assault	18,317	13,803	3,441	907	166	100.0	75.4	18.8	5.0	0.9
Property Crime..................	52,181	42,671	7,541	1,354	615	100.0	81.8	14.5	2.6	1.2
Burglary............................	16,439	13,363	2,481	494	101	100.0	81.3	15.1	3.0	0.6
Larceny-theft.....................	31,979	26,250	4,547	725	457	100.0	82.1	14.2	2.3	1.4
Motor vehicle theft............	3,147	2,541	437	114	55	100.0	80.7	13.9	3.6	1.7
Arson................................	616	517	76	21	2	100.0	83.9	12.3	3.4	0.3
Other										
Other assaults....................	66,521	53,714	9,716	2,315	776	100.0	80.7	14.6	3.5	1.2
Forgery and counterfeiting........	4,089	3,279	721	61	28	100.0	80.2	17.6	1.5	0.7
Fraud................................	18,723	14,827	3,538	281	77	100.0	79.2	18.9	1.5	0.4
Embezzlement....................	976	858	88	19	11	100.0	87.9	9.0	1.9	1.1
Stolen property; buying, receiving, possessing........	4,561	3,603	813	106	39	100.0	79.0	17.8	2.3	0.9
Vandalism.........................	9,449	7,811	1,173	354	111	100.0	82.7	12.4	3.7	1.2
Weapons; carrying, possessing, etc.	6,141	4,662	1,252	174	53	100.0	75.9	20.4	2.8	0.9
Prostitution and commercialized vice	207	155	32	6	14	100.0	74.9	15.5	2.9	6.8
Sex offenses (except forcible rape and prostitution)...........	4,117	3,595	396	96	30	100.0	87.3	9.6	2.3	0.7
Drug abuse violations	92,355	75,491	14,720	1,440	704	100.0	81.7	15.9	1.6	0.8
Gambling	181	130	39	1	11	100.0	71.8	21.5	0.6	6.1
Offenses against the family and children............	12,140	8,766	2,816	535	23	100.0	72.2	23.2	4.4	0.2
Driving under the influence	174,800	151,289	16,432	4,178	2,901	100.0	86.5	9.4	2.4	1.7
Liquor laws.......................	22,971	20,759	1,140	850	222	100.0	90.4	5.0	3.7	1.0
Drunkenness......................	17,910	15,643	1,447	784	36	100.0	87.3	8.1	4.4	0.2
Disorderly conduct.............	17,781	14,227	2,658	764	132	100.0	80.0	14.9	4.3	0.7
Vagrancy...........................	316	205	92	17	2	100.0	64.9	29.1	5.4	0.6
All other offenses (except traffic)	223,918	176,460	36,965	7,692	2,801	100.0	78.8	16.5	3.4	1.3
Suspicion	148	86	62	0	0	100.0	58.1	41.9	0.0	0.0
Curfew and loitering law violations...........................	...	...	...	...	...	...	...	...	...	...

[1] Because of rounding, the percentages may not add to 100.0.

Table 62. Suburban Area Arrest Trends, 2009–2010[1]

(Number, percent change; 6,161 agencies; 2010 estimated population 96,704,770; 2009 estimated population 95,920,094)

Offense charged	Number of persons arrested								
	Total all ages			Under 18 years of age			18 years of age and over		
	2009	2010	Percent change	2009	2010	Percent change	2009	2010	Percent change
TOTAL[2]	3,748,069	3,617,502	-3.5	496,287	453,257	-8.7	3,251,782	3,164,245	-2.7
Violent Crime	133,927	127,637	-4.7	19,640	17,324	-11.8	114,287	110,313	-3.5
Murder and nonnegligent manslaughter	2,400	2,275	-5.2	181	194	7.2	2,219	2,081	-6.2
Forcible rape	5,055	4,649	-8.0	815	737	-9.6	4,240	3,912	-7.7
Robbery	24,220	21,471	-11.4	5,591	4,675	-16.4	18,629	16,796	-9.8
Aggravated assault	102,252	99,242	-2.9	13,053	11,718	-10.2	89,199	87,524	-1.9
Property Crime	448,932	434,966	-3.1	107,493	93,848	-12.7	341,439	341,118	-0.1
Burglary	78,070	75,988	-2.7	19,166	16,406	-14.4	58,904	59,582	1.2
Larceny-theft	348,102	338,736	-2.7	82,071	72,540	-11.6	266,031	266,196	0.1
Motor vehicle theft	19,004	16,904	-11.1	4,454	3,408	-23.5	14,550	13,496	-7.2
Arson	3,756	3,338	-11.1	1,802	1,494	-17.1	1,954	1,844	-5.6
Other									
Other assaults	343,733	337,865	-1.7	64,901	62,274	-4.0	278,832	275,591	-1.2
Forgery and counterfeiting	24,572	22,482	-8.5	633	548	-13.4	23,939	21,934	-8.4
Fraud	73,790	62,174	-15.7	1,895	1,784	-5.9	71,895	60,390	-16.0
Embezzlement	4,783	4,298	-10.1	162	125	-22.8	4,621	4,173	-9.7
Stolen property; buying, receiving, possessing	29,657	28,215	-4.9	5,163	4,323	-16.3	24,494	23,892	-2.5
Vandalism	72,608	67,459	-7.1	26,004	22,148	-14.8	46,604	45,311	-2.8
Weapons; carrying, possessing, etc.	37,886	36,017	-4.9	8,473	7,781	-8.2	29,413	28,236	-4.0
Prostitution and commercialized vice	4,877	4,573	-6.2	152	117	-23.0	4,725	4,456	-5.7
Sex offenses (except forcible rape and prostitution)	20,031	19,425	-3.0	3,888	3,787	-2.6	16,143	15,638	-3.1
Drug abuse violations	429,685	431,362	0.4	50,275	50,276	*	379,410	381,086	0.4
Gambling	1,548	1,312	-15.2	125	69	-44.8	1,423	1,243	-12.6
Offenses against the family and children	44,301	42,229	-4.7	1,414	1,256	-11.2	42,887	40,973	-4.5
Driving under the influence	477,474	458,882	-3.9	4,400	3,938	-10.5	473,074	454,944	-3.8
Liquor laws	164,990	147,230	-10.8	37,670	32,320	-14.2	127,320	114,910	-9.7
Drunkenness	140,773	130,638	-7.2	4,260	3,804	-10.7	136,513	126,834	-7.1
Disorderly conduct	173,654	167,137	-3.8	49,252	46,733	-5.1	124,402	120,404	-3.2
Vagrancy	4,605	4,764	3.5	408	448	9.8	4,197	4,316	2.8
All other offenses (except traffic)	1,097,959	1,072,242	-2.3	91,795	83,759	-8.8	1,006,164	988,483	-1.8
Suspicion	298	357	19.8	42	53	26.2	256	304	18.8
Curfew and loitering law violations	18,284	16,595	-9.2	18,284	16,595	-9.2	...	...	...

[1] Suburban areas include law enforcement agencies in cities with less than 50,000 inhabitants and county law enforcement agencies that are within a metropolitan statistical area. Suburban areas exclude all metropolitan agencies associated with a principal city.

[2] Does not include suspicion.

* Less than one-tenth of 1 percent.

Table 63.   Suburban Area Arrest Trends, by Age and Sex, 2009–2010[1]

(Number, percent change; 6,161 agencies; 2010 estimated population 96,704,770; 2009 estimated population 95,920,094)

Offense charged	Male Total			Male Under 18			Female Total			Female Under 18		
	2009	2010	Percent change	2009	2010	Percent change	2009	2010	Percent change	2009	2010	Percent change
TOTAL[2]	2,791,832	2,679,079	-4.0	353,920	321,507	-9.2	956,237	938,423	-1.9	142,367	131,750	-7.5
Violent Crime	108,940	103,150	-5.3	15,916	13,980	-12.2	24,987	24,487	-2.0	3,724	3,344	-10.2
Murder and nonnegligent manslaughter	2,109	1,987	-5.8	164	171	4.3	291	288	-1.0	17	23	35.3
Forcible rape	4,989	4,599	-7.8	799	723	-9.5	66	50	-24.2	16	14	-12.5
Robbery	21,409	18,861	-11.9	5,091	4,281	-15.9	2,811	2,610	-7.2	500	394	-21.2
Aggravated assault	80,433	77,703	-3.4	9,862	8,805	-10.7	21,819	21,539	-1.3	3,191	2,913	-8.7
Property Crime	284,565	274,149	-3.7	69,224	60,148	-13.1	164,367	160,817	-2.2	38,269	33,700	-11.9
Burglary	66,673	64,529	-3.2	17,000	14,635	-13.9	11,397	11,459	0.5	2,166	1,771	-18.2
Larceny-theft	199,165	192,988	-3.1	46,983	41,405	-11.9	148,937	145,748	-2.1	35,088	31,135	-11.3
Motor vehicle theft	15,549	13,801	-11.2	3,658	2,797	-23.5	3,455	3,103	-10.2	796	611	-23.2
Arson	3,178	2,831	-10.9	1,583	1,311	-17.2	578	507	-12.3	219	183	-16.4
Other												
Other assaults	252,453	245,270	-2.8	43,302	40,748	-5.9	91,280	92,595	1.4	21,599	21,526	-0.3
Forgery and counterfeiting	15,286	14,139	-7.5	469	403	-14.1	9,286	8,343	-10.2	164	145	-11.6
Fraud	40,998	35,715	-12.9	1,240	1,194	-3.7	32,792	26,459	-19.3	655	590	-9.9
Embezzlement	2,323	2,179	-6.2	80	80	0.0	2,460	2,119	-13.9	82	45	-45.1
Stolen property; buying, receiving, possessing	23,648	22,266	-5.8	4,218	3,500	-17.0	6,009	5,949	-1.0	945	823	-12.9
Vandalism	60,109	55,151	-8.2	22,339	18,744	-16.1	12,499	12,308	-1.5	3,665	3,404	-7.1
Weapons; carrying, possessing, etc.	34,407	32,698	-5.0	7,441	6,857	-7.8	3,479	3,319	-4.6	1,032	924	-10.5
Prostitution and commercialized vice	1,742	1,874	7.6	61	43	-29.5	3,135	2,699	-13.9	91	74	-18.7
Sex offenses (except forcible rape and prostitution)	18,560	17,979	-3.1	3,493	3,400	-2.7	1,471	1,446	-1.7	395	387	-2.0
Drug abuse violations	343,243	342,381	-0.3	41,618	41,239	-0.9	86,442	88,981	2.9	8,657	9,037	4.4
Gambling	1,054	1,026	-2.7	105	48	-54.3	494	286	-42.1	20	21	5.0
Offenses against the family and children	35,257	33,751	-4.3	915	842	-8.0	9,044	8,478	-6.3	499	414	-17.0
Driving under the influence	366,377	347,045	-5.3	3,313	2,924	-11.7	111,097	111,837	0.7	1,087	1,014	-6.7
Liquor laws	114,809	102,605	-10.6	23,124	19,673	-14.9	50,181	44,625	-11.1	14,546	12,647	-13.1
Drunkenness	115,097	105,784	-8.1	3,104	2,730	-12.0	25,676	24,854	-3.2	1,156	1,074	-7.1
Disorderly conduct	126,089	119,688	-5.1	33,534	31,353	-6.5	47,565	47,449	-0.2	15,718	15,380	-2.2
Vagrancy	3,382	3,715	9.8	305	361	18.4	1,223	1,049	-14.2	103	87	-15.5
All other offenses (except traffic)	831,285	807,249	-2.9	67,911	61,975	-8.7	266,674	264,993	-0.6	23,884	21,784	-8.8
Suspicion	198	278	40.4	36	43	19.4	100	79	-21.0	6	10	66.7
Curfew and loitering law violations	12,208	11,265	-7.7	12,208	11,265	-7.7	6,076	5,330	-12.3	6,076	5,330	-12.3

[1] Suburban areas include law enforcement agencies in cities with less than 50,000 inhabitants and county law enforcement agencies that are within a metropolitan statistical area. Suburban areas exclude all metropolitan agencies associated with a principal city.
[2] Does not include suspicion.

Table 64. Suburban Area Arrests, Distribution by Age, 2010[1]

(Number, percent; 6,634 agencies; 2010 estimated population 106,002,095)

Offense charged	Total all ages	Ages under 15	Ages under 18	Ages 18 and over	Under 10	10–12	13–14	15	16	17	18	19	20
TOTAL	4,096,678	139,476	508,739	3,587,939	3,555	30,825	105,096	94,256	123,078	151,929	198,651	209,325	197,013
Total percent distribution[2]	100.0	3.4	12.4	87.6	0.1	0.8	2.6	2.3	3.0	3.7	4.8	5.1	4.8
Violent Crime	146,917	5,563	19,819	127,098	137	1,410	4,016	3,658	4,781	5,817	6,939	6,877	6,462
Violent crime percent distribution[2]	100.0	3.8	13.5	86.5	0.1	1.0	2.7	2.5	3.3	4.0	4.7	4.7	4.4
Murder and nonnegligent manslaughter	2,679	18	229	2,450	0	1	17	53	66	92	148	162	154
Forcible rape	5,449	277	857	4,592	4	74	199	166	175	239	278	316	240
Robbery	25,602	997	5,576	20,026	11	152	834	1,072	1,622	1,885	2,307	2,112	1,773
Aggravated assault	113,187	4,271	13,157	100,030	122	1,183	2,966	2,367	2,918	3,601	4,206	4,287	4,295
Property Crime	500,311	29,073	106,946	393,365	674	6,331	22,068	20,245	26,224	31,404	34,400	30,124	25,212
Property crime percent distribution[2]	100.0	5.8	21.4	78.6	0.1	1.3	4.4	4.0	5.2	6.3	6.9	6.0	5.0
Burglary	85,116	4,989	18,391	66,725	168	1,078	3,743	3,421	4,485	5,496	6,566	5,939	5,026
Larceny-theft	392,605	22,399	83,139	309,466	407	4,872	17,120	15,698	20,467	24,575	26,453	22,970	19,203
Motor vehicle theft	18,921	767	3,827	15,094	14	80	673	864	1,055	1,141	1,210	1,087	859
Arson	3,669	918	1,589	2,080	85	301	532	262	217	192	171	128	124
Other													
Other assaults	388,235	27,573	70,811	317,424	850	7,478	19,245	13,628	15,164	14,446	12,684	12,590	12,514
Forgery and counterfeiting	26,004	87	603	25,401	1	17	69	76	130	310	693	984	1,168
Fraud	67,273	312	1,944	65,329	5	53	254	266	480	886	1,569	2,115	2,309
Embezzlement	5,155	10	141	5,014	0	0	10	7	27	97	227	299	299
Stolen property; buying, receiving, possessing	32,399	1,084	4,953	27,446	16	167	901	980	1,288	1,601	2,159	2,063	1,765
Vandalism	76,171	9,520	24,512	51,659	409	2,627	6,484	4,560	5,086	5,346	5,002	4,226	3,460
Weapons; carrying, possessing, etc.	42,133	3,513	9,011	33,122	220	1,014	2,279	1,528	1,800	2,170	2,539	2,384	2,049
Prostitution and commercialized vice	5,918	22	130	5,788	1	2	19	16	41	51	129	200	265
Sex offenses (except forcible rape and prostitution)	22,011	2,162	4,375	17,636	84	614	1,464	717	727	769	1,032	910	743
Drug abuse violations	486,332	9,495	55,209	431,123	61	1,160	8,274	9,509	14,541	21,664	34,561	35,078	30,850
Gambling	1,558	9	70	1,488	0	0	9	10	25	26	27	30	33
Offenses against the family and children	45,174	426	1,407	43,767	28	91	307	274	318	389	586	717	778
Driving under the influence	494,513	73	4,209	490,304	14	7	52	135	908	3,093	8,974	13,219	15,597
Liquor laws	168,371	3,185	35,651	132,720	23	255	2,907	5,142	9,931	17,393	32,362	34,661	27,676
Drunkenness	153,565	509	4,081	149,484	6	42	461	674	961	1,937	4,927	5,357	5,167
Disorderly conduct	191,791	18,868	52,370	139,421	279	4,506	14,083	10,755	11,558	11,189	9,082	7,845	7,495
Vagrancy	5,206	114	481	4,725	2	17	95	113	119	135	245	270	210
All other offenses (except traffic)	1,219,293	23,168	93,986	1,125,307	701	4,348	18,119	17,792	23,603	29,423	40,498	49,360	52,936
Suspicion	371	12	53	318	1	1	10	9	17	15	16	16	25
Curfew and loitering law violations	17,977	4,698	17,977	...	43	685	3,970	4,162	5,349	3,768	...	...	...

[1] Suburban areas include law enforcement agencies in cities with less than 50,000 inhabitants and county law enforcement agencies that are within a metropolitan statistical area. Suburban areas exclude all metropolitan agencies associated with a principal city.

[2] Because of rounding, the percentages may not add to 100.0.

Table 64.   Suburban Area Arrests, Distribution by Age, 2010[1]—*Continued*

(Number, percent; 6,634 agencies; 2010 estimated population 106,002,095)

Offense charged	21	22	23	24	25–29	30–34	35–39	40–44	45–49	50–54	55–59	60–64	65 and over
TOTAL	176,866	161,166	149,895	143,572	608,396	450,054	349,740	316,700	279,585	183,128	90,837	41,851	31,160
Total percent distribution[2]	4.3	3.9	3.7	3.5	14.9	11.0	8.5	7.7	6.8	4.5	2.2	1.0	0.8
Violent Crime	6,229	5,641	5,181	4,913	22,148	16,441	12,689	11,354	9,837	6,306	3,136	1,573	1,372
Violent crime percent distribution[2]	4.2	3.8	3.5	3.3	15.1	11.2	8.6	7.7	6.7	4.3	2.1	1.1	0.9
Murder and nonnegligent manslaughter	161	112	117	105	446	290	196	145	165	109	64	37	39
Forcible rape	250	203	177	137	691	568	522	423	334	215	105	66	67
Robbery	1,437	1,178	1,003	839	3,352	2,084	1,281	1,150	809	423	194	52	32
Aggravated assault	4,381	4,148	3,884	3,832	17,659	13,499	10,690	9,636	8,529	5,559	2,773	1,418	1,234
Property Crime	21,195	18,360	16,109	15,598	63,187	45,491	34,252	31,338	26,509	16,787	8,015	3,766	3,022
Property crime percent distribution[2]	4.2	3.7	3.2	3.1	12.6	9.1	6.8	6.3	5.3	3.4	1.6	0.8	0.6
Burglary	4,256	3,539	3,065	2,925	11,188	7,579	5,261	4,601	3,624	1,948	760	277	171
Larceny-theft	16,089	14,081	12,327	11,981	49,036	35,594	27,292	25,342	21,728	14,213	7,007	3,377	2,773
Motor vehicle theft	773	647	638	627	2,670	2,061	1,528	1,220	966	498	185	75	50
Arson	77	93	79	65	293	257	171	175	191	128	63	37	28
Other													
Other assaults	13,180	12,779	12,281	11,911	53,736	43,453	36,685	33,457	28,823	17,640	8,428	3,868	3,395
Forgery and counterfeiting	1,080	1,147	1,153	1,085	4,954	3,937	3,071	2,367	1,885	1,072	454	220	131
Fraud	2,189	2,168	2,055	2,153	10,747	10,089	9,060	7,588	6,055	3,701	1,909	935	687
Embezzlement	276	226	213	224	745	583	518	525	378	245	145	76	35
Stolen property; buying, receiving, possessing	1,632	1,346	1,133	1,137	4,711	3,446	2,545	2,099	1,749	993	399	149	120
Vandalism	3,307	2,737	2,383	2,215	8,397	5,776	4,116	3,602	2,960	1,802	857	400	419
Weapons; carrying, possessing, etc.	1,858	1,784	1,633	1,465	5,944	3,836	2,655	2,185	1,885	1,368	736	426	375
Prostitution and commercialized vice	250	276	234	232	995	781	621	630	527	307	167	83	91
Sex offenses (except forcible rape and prostitution)	748	660	594	479	2,312	1,932	1,781	1,744	1,601	1,172	720	522	686
Drug abuse violations	26,407	22,815	20,567	19,423	76,310	51,214	34,582	29,056	24,760	15,312	6,704	2,420	1,064
Gambling	20	16	35	28	141	137	158	233	150	230	96	66	88
Offenses against the family and children	1,009	1,063	1,161	1,289	7,293	7,839	7,159	6,208	4,497	2,533	1,042	370	223
Driving under the influence	22,763	22,786	22,379	21,688	90,573	63,156	49,726	46,888	45,296	32,739	18,640	9,417	6,463
Liquor laws	4,116	2,842	2,097	1,754	6,227	4,381	3,722	3,695	3,765	2,809	1,497	677	439
Drunkenness	7,692	6,589	5,753	5,351	22,625	16,873	14,142	15,440	16,935	12,340	6,251	2,601	1,441
Disorderly conduct	8,258	7,175	6,322	5,854	21,888	15,498	12,208	11,661	11,524	7,637	3,658	1,791	1,525
Vagrancy	194	172	151	129	617	438	409	461	555	441	233	124	76
All other offenses (except traffic)	54,441	50,564	48,444	46,635	204,783	154,718	119,611	106,146	89,873	57,684	27,743	12,364	9,507
Suspicion	22	20	17	9	63	35	30	23	21	10	7	3	1
Curfew and loitering law violations	...	...	...	...	...	...	...	...	...	...	...	...	...

[1] Suburban areas include law enforcement agencies in cities with less than 50,000 inhabitants and county law enforcement agencies that are within a metropolitan statistical area. Suburban areas exclude all metropolitan agencies associated with a principal city.
[2] Because of rounding, the percentages may not add to 100.0.

Table 65. Suburban Area Arrests of Persons Under 15, 18, 21, and 25 Years of Age, 2010[1]

(Number, percent; 6,634 agencies; 2010 estimated population 106,002,095)

Offense charged	Total all ages	Number of persons arrested				Percent of total all ages			
		Under 15	Under 18	Under 21	Under 25	Under 15	Under 18	Under 21	Under 25
TOTAL	4,096,678	139,476	508,739	1,113,728	1,745,227	3.4	12.4	27.2	42.6
Violent Crime	146,917	5,563	19,819	40,097	62,061	3.8	13.5	27.3	42.2
Murder and nonnegligent manslaughter	2,679	18	229	693	1,188	0.7	8.5	25.9	44.3
Forcible rape	5,449	277	857	1,691	2,458	5.1	15.7	31.0	45.1
Robbery	25,602	997	5,576	11,768	16,225	3.9	21.8	46.0	63.4
Aggravated assault	113,187	4,271	13,157	25,945	42,190	3.8	11.6	22.9	37.3
Property Crime	500,311	29,073	106,946	196,682	267,944	5.8	21.4	39.3	53.6
Burglary	85,116	4,989	18,391	35,922	49,707	5.9	21.6	42.2	58.4
Larceny-theft	392,605	22,399	83,139	151,765	206,243	5.7	21.2	38.7	52.5
Motor vehicle theft	18,921	767	3,827	6,983	9,668	4.1	20.2	36.9	51.1
Arson	3,669	918	1,589	2,012	2,326	25.0	43.3	54.8	63.4
Other									
Other assaults	388,235	27,573	70,811	108,599	158,750	7.1	18.2	28.0	40.9
Forgery and counterfeiting	26,004	87	603	3,448	7,913	0.3	2.3	13.3	30.4
Fraud	67,273	312	1,944	7,937	16,502	0.5	2.9	11.8	24.5
Embezzlement	5,155	10	141	966	1,905	0.2	2.7	18.7	37.0
Stolen property; buying, receiving, possessing	32,399	1,084	4,953	10,940	16,188	3.3	15.3	33.8	50.0
Vandalism	76,171	9,520	24,512	37,200	47,842	12.5	32.2	48.8	62.8
Weapons; carrying, possessing, etc.	42,133	3,513	9,011	15,983	22,723	8.3	21.4	37.9	53.9
Prostitution and commercialized vice	5,918	22	130	724	1,716	0.4	2.2	12.2	29.0
Sex offenses (except forcible rape and prostitution)	22,011	2,162	4,375	7,060	9,541	9.8	19.9	32.1	43.3
Drug abuse violations	486,332	9,495	55,209	155,698	244,910	2.0	11.4	32.0	50.4
Gambling	1,558	9	70	160	259	0.6	4.5	10.3	16.6
Offenses against the family and children	45,174	426	1,407	3,488	8,010	0.9	3.1	7.7	17.7
Driving under the influence	494,513	73	4,209	41,999	131,615	*	0.9	8.5	26.6
Liquor laws	168,371	3,185	35,651	130,350	141,159	1.9	21.2	77.4	83.8
Drunkenness	153,565	509	4,081	19,532	44,917	0.3	2.7	12.7	29.2
Disorderly conduct	191,791	18,868	52,370	76,792	104,401	9.8	27.3	40.0	54.4
Vagrancy	5,206	114	481	1,206	1,852	2.2	9.2	23.2	35.6
All other offenses (except traffic)	1,219,293	23,168	93,986	236,780	436,864	1.9	7.7	19.4	35.8
Suspicion	371	12	53	110	178	3.2	14.3	29.6	48.0
Curfew and loitering law violations	17,977	4,698	17,977	17,977	17,977	26.1	100.0	100.0	100.0

[1] Suburban areas include law enforcement agencies in cities with less than 50,000 inhabitants and county law enforcement agencies that are within a metropolitan statistical area. Suburban areas exclude all metropolitan agencies associated with a principal city.
* Less than one-tenth of 1 percent.

Table 66. Suburban Area Arrests, Distribution by Sex, 2010[1]

(Number, percent; 6,634 agencies; 2010 estimated population 106,002,095)

Offense charged	Number of persons arrested			Percent male	Percent female	Percent distribution[2]		
	Total	Male	Female			Total	Male	Female
TOTAL	4,096,678	3,034,589	1,062,089	74.1	25.9	100.0	100.0	100.0
Violent Crime	146,917	118,676	28,241	80.8	19.2	3.6	3.9	2.7
Murder and nonnegligent manslaughter	2,679	2,346	333	87.6	12.4	0.1	0.1	*
Forcible rape	5,449	5,387	62	98.9	1.1	0.1	0.2	*
Robbery	25,602	22,494	3,108	87.9	12.1	0.6	0.7	0.3
Aggravated assault	113,187	88,449	24,738	78.1	21.9	2.8	2.9	2.3
Property Crime	500,311	313,341	186,970	62.6	37.4	12.2	10.3	17.6
Burglary	85,116	72,433	12,683	85.1	14.9	2.1	2.4	1.2
Larceny-theft	392,605	222,340	170,265	56.6	43.4	9.6	7.3	16.0
Motor vehicle theft	18,921	15,457	3,464	81.7	18.3	0.5	0.5	0.3
Arson	3,669	3,111	558	84.8	15.2	0.1	0.1	0.1
Other								
Other assaults	388,235	281,650	106,585	72.5	27.5	9.5	9.3	10.0
Forgery and counterfeiting	26,004	16,378	9,626	63.0	37.0	0.6	0.5	0.9
Fraud	67,273	38,802	28,471	57.7	42.3	1.6	1.3	2.7
Embezzlement	5,155	2,607	2,548	50.6	49.4	0.1	0.1	0.2
Stolen property; buying, receiving, possessing	32,399	25,608	6,791	79.0	21.0	0.8	0.8	0.6
Vandalism	76,171	62,099	14,072	81.5	18.5	1.9	2.0	1.3
Weapons; carrying, possessing, etc.	42,133	38,283	3,850	90.9	9.1	1.0	1.3	0.4
Prostitution and commercialized vice	5,918	2,262	3,656	38.2	61.8	0.1	0.1	0.3
Sex offenses (except forcible rape and prostitution)	22,011	20,368	1,643	92.5	7.5	0.5	0.7	0.2
Drug abuse violations	486,332	387,203	99,129	79.6	20.4	11.9	12.8	9.3
Gambling	1,558	1,266	292	81.3	18.7	*	*	*
Offenses against the family and children	45,174	35,816	9,358	79.3	20.7	1.1	1.2	0.9
Driving under the influence	494,513	374,079	120,434	75.6	24.4	12.1	12.3	11.3
Liquor laws	168,371	117,722	50,649	69.9	30.1	4.1	3.9	4.8
Drunkenness	153,565	125,036	28,529	81.4	18.6	3.7	4.1	2.7
Disorderly conduct	191,791	137,243	54,548	71.6	28.4	4.7	4.5	5.1
Vagrancy	5,206	4,067	1,139	78.1	21.9	0.1	0.1	0.1
All other offenses (except traffic)	1,219,293	919,514	299,779	75.4	24.6	29.8	30.3	28.2
Suspicion	371	288	83	77.6	22.4	*	*	*
Curfew and loitering law violations	17,977	12,281	5,696	68.3	31.7	0.4	0.4	0.5

[1] Suburban areas include law enforcement agencies in cities with less than 50,000 inhabitants and county law enforcement agencies that are within a metropolitan statistical area. Suburban areas exclude all metropolitan agencies associated with a principal city.

[2] Because of rounding, the percentages may not add to 100.0.

* Less than one-tenth of 1 percent.

Table 67. Suburban Area Arrests, Distribution by Race, 2010[1]

(Number, percent; 6,633 agencies; 2010 estimated population 105,998,890)

Offense charged	Total arrests					Percent distribution[2]				
	Total	White	Black	American Indian or Alaskan Native	Asian or Pacific Islander	Total	White	Black	American Indian or Alaskan Native	Asian or Pacific Islander
TOTAL	4,081,054	3,034,236	979,073	34,096	33,649	100.0	74.3	24.0	0.8	0.8
Violent Crime	146,549	97,706	46,504	1,204	1,135	100.0	66.7	31.7	0.8	0.8
Murder and nonnegligent manslaughter	2,675	1,560	1,075	18	22	100.0	58.3	40.2	0.7	0.8
Forcible rape	5,424	4,029	1,296	55	44	100.0	74.3	23.9	1.0	0.8
Robbery	25,561	12,390	12,878	127	166	100.0	48.5	50.4	0.5	0.6
Aggravated assault	112,889	79,727	31,255	1,004	903	100.0	70.6	27.7	0.9	0.8
Property Crime	498,602	355,105	134,816	3,888	4,793	100.0	71.2	27.0	0.8	1.0
Burglary	84,936	62,979	21,058	367	532	100.0	74.1	24.8	0.4	0.6
Larceny-theft	391,134	275,543	108,107	3,371	4,113	100.0	70.4	27.6	0.9	1.1
Motor vehicle theft	18,870	13,649	4,971	131	119	100.0	72.3	26.3	0.7	0.6
Arson	3,662	2,934	680	19	29	100.0	80.1	18.6	0.5	0.8
Other										
Other assaults	387,050	280,335	100,821	2,819	3,075	100.0	72.4	26.0	0.7	0.8
Forgery and counterfeiting	25,889	17,450	8,138	86	215	100.0	67.4	31.4	0.3	0.8
Fraud	66,931	44,858	21,284	280	509	100.0	67.0	31.8	0.4	0.8
Embezzlement	5,114	3,396	1,642	15	61	100.0	66.4	32.1	0.3	1.2
Stolen property; buying, receiving, possessing	32,321	22,336	9,593	162	230	100.0	69.1	29.7	0.5	0.7
Vandalism	75,879	60,010	14,695	618	556	100.0	79.1	19.4	0.8	0.7
Weapons; carrying, possessing, etc.	42,021	27,846	13,650	202	323	100.0	66.3	32.5	0.5	0.8
Prostitution and commercialized vice	5,907	3,794	1,842	26	245	100.0	64.2	31.2	0.4	4.1
Sex offenses (except forcible rape and prostitution)	21,932	17,113	4,466	132	221	100.0	78.0	20.4	0.6	1.0
Drug abuse violations	485,043	361,520	117,693	2,404	3,426	100.0	74.5	24.3	0.5	0.7
Gambling	1,554	956	442	21	135	100.0	61.5	28.4	1.4	8.7
Offenses against the family and children	44,996	29,586	14,778	331	301	100.0	65.8	32.8	0.7	0.7
Driving under the influence	492,560	429,984	53,666	3,406	5,504	100.0	87.3	10.9	0.7	1.1
Liquor laws	166,500	145,687	15,965	2,734	2,114	100.0	87.5	9.6	1.6	1.3
Drunkenness	153,088	132,595	17,939	1,632	922	100.0	86.6	11.7	1.1	0.6
Disorderly conduct	190,954	132,839	55,160	1,608	1,347	100.0	69.6	28.9	0.8	0.7
Vagrancy	5,204	3,682	1,477	16	29	100.0	70.8	28.4	0.3	0.6
All other offenses (except traffic)	1,214,667	853,600	340,220	12,461	8,386	100.0	70.3	28.0	1.0	0.7
Suspicion	371	244	124	0	3	100.0	65.8	33.4	0.0	0.8
Curfew and loitering law violations	17,922	13,594	4,158	51	119	100.0	75.9	23.2	0.3	0.7

[1] Suburban areas include law enforcement agencies in cities with less than 50,000 inhabitants and county law enforcement agencies that are within a metropolitan statistical area. Suburban areas exclude all metropolitan agencies associated with a principal city.

[2] Because of rounding, the percentages may not add to 100.0.

Table 67.   Suburban Area Arrests, Distribution by Race, 2010[1]—*Continued*

(Number, percent; 6,633 agencies; 2010 estimated population 105,998,890)

Offense charged	Arrests under 18					Percent distribution[2]				
	Total	White	Black	American Indian or Alaskan Native	Asian or Pacific Islander	Total	White	Black	American Indian or Alaskan Native	Asian or Pacific Islander
TOTAL	506,719	358,584	140,303	3,276	4,556	100.0	70.8	27.7	0.6	0.9
Violent Crime	19,765	10,634	8,858	151	122	100.0	53.8	44.8	0.8	0.6
Murder and nonnegligent manslaughter	228	117	108	2	1	100.0	51.3	47.4	0.9	0.4
Forcible rape	849	613	227	7	2	100.0	72.2	26.7	0.8	0.2
Robbery	5,568	1,865	3,645	22	36	100.0	33.5	65.5	0.4	0.6
Aggravated assault	13,120	8,039	4,878	120	83	100.0	61.3	37.2	0.9	0.6
Property Crime	106,410	69,170	35,211	698	1,331	100.0	65.0	33.1	0.7	1.3
Burglary	18,344	12,564	5,573	66	141	100.0	68.5	30.4	0.4	0.8
Larceny-theft	82,672	52,866	28,060	599	1,147	100.0	63.9	33.9	0.7	1.4
Motor vehicle theft	3,809	2,483	1,271	27	28	100.0	65.2	33.4	0.7	0.7
Arson	1,585	1,257	307	6	15	100.0	79.3	19.4	0.4	0.9
Other										
Other assaults	70,581	44,778	25,059	342	402	100.0	63.4	35.5	0.5	0.6
Forgery and counterfeiting	598	428	157	2	11	100.0	71.6	26.3	0.3	1.8
Fraud	1,934	1,180	728	8	18	100.0	61.0	37.6	0.4	0.9
Embezzlement	137	95	41	1	0	100.0	69.3	29.9	0.7	0.0
Stolen property; buying, receiving, possessing	4,935	2,945	1,930	21	39	100.0	59.7	39.1	0.4	0.8
Vandalism	24,407	19,637	4,458	139	173	100.0	80.5	18.3	0.6	0.7
Weapons; carrying, possessing, etc.	8,976	6,051	2,777	52	96	100.0	67.4	30.9	0.6	1.1
Prostitution and commercialized vice	130	70	56	2	2	100.0	53.8	43.1	1.5	1.5
Sex offenses (except forcible rape and prostitution)	4,354	3,261	1,035	18	40	100.0	74.9	23.8	0.4	0.9
Drug abuse violations	55,046	44,564	9,602	379	501	100.0	81.0	17.4	0.7	0.9
Gambling	70	36	31	2	1	100.0	51.4	44.3	2.9	1.4
Offenses against the family and children	1,400	1,063	318	10	9	100.0	75.9	22.7	0.7	0.6
Driving under the influence	4,185	3,896	225	25	39	100.0	93.1	5.4	0.6	0.9
Liquor laws	35,429	32,244	2,278	435	472	100.0	91.0	6.4	1.2	1.3
Drunkenness	4,074	3,709	295	45	25	100.0	91.0	7.2	1.1	0.6
Disorderly conduct	52,243	31,921	19,691	244	387	100.0	61.1	37.7	0.5	0.7
Vagrancy	481	354	118	1	8	100.0	73.6	24.5	0.2	1.7
All other offenses (except traffic)	93,589	68,917	23,261	650	761	100.0	73.6	24.9	0.7	0.8
Suspicion	53	37	16	0	0	100.0	69.8	30.2	0.0	0.0
Curfew and loitering law violations	17,922	13,594	4,158	51	119	100.0	75.9	23.2	0.3	0.7

[1] Suburban areas include law enforcement agencies in cities with less than 50,000 inhabitants and county law enforcement agencies that are within a metropolitan statistical area. Suburban areas exclude all metropolitan agencies associated with a principal city.

[2] Because of rounding, the percentages may not add to 100.0.

Table 67. Suburban Area Arrests, Distribution by Race, 2010[1]—*Continued*

(Number, percent; 6,633 agencies; 2010 estimated population 105,998,890)

Offense charged	Arrests 18 and over					Percent distribution[2]				
	Total	White	Black	American Indian or Alaskan Native	Asian or Pacific Islander	Total	White	Black	American Indian or Alaskan Native	Asian or Pacific Islander
TOTAL	3,574,335	2,675,652	838,770	30,820	29,093	100.0	74.9	23.5	0.9	0.8
Violent Crime	126,784	87,072	37,646	1,053	1,013	100.0	68.7	29.7	0.8	0.8
Murder and nonnegligent manslaughter	2,447	1,443	967	16	21	100.0	59.0	39.5	0.7	0.9
Forcible rape	4,575	3,416	1,069	48	42	100.0	74.7	23.4	1.0	0.9
Robbery	19,993	10,525	9,233	105	130	100.0	52.6	46.2	0.5	0.7
Aggravated assault	99,769	71,688	26,377	884	820	100.0	71.9	26.4	0.9	0.8
Property Crime	392,192	285,935	99,605	3,190	3,462	100.0	72.9	25.4	0.8	0.9
Burglary	66,592	50,415	15,485	301	391	100.0	75.7	23.3	0.5	0.6
Larceny-theft	308,462	222,677	80,047	2,772	2,966	100.0	72.2	26.0	0.9	1.0
Motor vehicle theft	15,061	11,166	3,700	104	91	100.0	74.1	24.6	0.7	0.6
Arson	2,077	1,677	373	13	14	100.0	80.7	18.0	0.6	0.7
Other										
Other assaults	316,469	235,557	75,762	2,477	2,673	100.0	74.4	23.9	0.8	0.8
Forgery and counterfeiting	25,291	17,022	7,981	84	204	100.0	67.3	31.6	0.3	0.8
Fraud	64,997	43,678	20,556	272	491	100.0	67.2	31.6	0.4	0.8
Embezzlement	4,977	3,301	1,601	14	61	100.0	66.3	32.2	0.3	1.2
Stolen property; buying, receiving, possessing	27,386	19,391	7,663	141	191	100.0	70.8	28.0	0.5	0.7
Vandalism	51,472	40,373	10,237	479	383	100.0	78.4	19.9	0.9	0.7
Weapons; carrying, possessing, etc.	33,045	21,795	10,873	150	227	100.0	66.0	32.9	0.5	0.7
Prostitution and commercialized vice	5,777	3,724	1,786	24	243	100.0	64.5	30.9	0.4	4.2
Sex offenses (except forcible rape and prostitution)	17,578	13,852	3,431	114	181	100.0	78.8	19.5	0.6	1.0
Drug abuse violations	429,997	316,956	108,091	2,025	2,925	100.0	73.7	25.1	0.5	0.7
Gambling	1,484	920	411	19	134	100.0	62.0	27.7	1.3	9.0
Offenses against the family and children	43,596	28,523	14,460	321	292	100.0	65.4	33.2	0.7	0.7
Driving under the influence	488,375	426,088	53,441	3,381	5,465	100.0	87.2	10.9	0.7	1.1
Liquor laws	131,071	113,443	13,687	2,299	1,642	100.0	86.6	10.4	1.8	1.3
Drunkenness	149,014	128,886	17,644	1,587	897	100.0	86.5	11.8	1.1	0.6
Disorderly conduct	138,711	100,918	35,469	1,364	960	100.0	72.8	25.6	1.0	0.7
Vagrancy	4,723	3,328	1,359	15	21	100.0	70.5	28.8	0.3	0.4
All other offenses (except traffic)	1,121,078	784,683	316,959	11,811	7,625	100.0	70.0	28.3	1.1	0.7
Suspicion	318	207	108	0	3	100.0	65.1	34.0	0.0	0.9
Curfew and loitering law violations	...	...	...	...	...	...	...	...	...	...

[1] Suburban areas include law enforcement agencies in cities with less than 50,000 inhabitants and county law enforcement agencies that are within a metropolitan statistical area. Suburban areas exclude all metropolitan agencies associated with a principal city.

[2] Because of rounding, the percentages may not add to 100.0.

Table 68.　Police Disposition of Juvenile Offenders Taken into Custody, 2010

(Number, percent)

Population group	Total[1]	Handled within department and released	Referred to juvenile court jurisdiction	Referred to welfare agency	Referred to other police agency	Referred to criminal or adult court	Number of agencies	2010 estimated population
TOTAL AGENCIES:								
Number	495,453	111,876	335,279	2,365	6,856	39,077	5,209	121,215,136
Percent[2]	100.0	22.6	67.7	0.5	1.4	7.9		
Total Cities								
Number	423,659	100,313	284,961	2,019	5,688	30,678	3,960	88,280,366
Percent[2]	100.0	23.7	67.3	0.5	1.3	7.2		
GROUP I (250,000 and over)								
Number	112,738	36,606	72,666	146	1,161	2,159	36	26,155,247
Percent[2]	100.0	32.5	64.5	0.1	1.0	1.9		
GROUP II (100,000 to 249,999)								
Number	58,916	12,823	43,703	453	783	1,154	83	12,315,412
Percent[2]	100.0	21.8	74.2	0.8	1.3	2.0		
GROUP III (50,000 to 99,999)								
Number	82,159	16,782	58,634	476	1,317	4,950	238	16,101,572
Percent[2]	100.0	20.4	71.4	0.6	1.6	6.0		
GROUP IV (25,000 to 49,999)								
Number	55,665	10,247	38,421	166	1,135	5,696	348	12,006,184
Percent[2]	100.0	18.4	69.0	0.3	2.0	10.2		
GROUP V (10,000 to 24,999)								
Number	63,086	13,113	40,264	404	741	8,564	808	12,877,732
Percent[2]	100.0	20.8	63.8	0.6	1.2	13.6		
GROUP VI (under 10,000)								
Number	51,095	10,742	31,273	374	551	8,155	2,447	8,824,219
Percent[2]	100.0	21.0	61.2	0.7	1.1	16.0		
Metropolitan Counties								
Number	56,598	9,259	40,317	232	999	5,791	655	24,543,709
Percent[2]	100.0	16.4	71.2	0.4	1.8	10.2		
Nonmetropolitan Counties								
Number	15,196	2,304	10,001	114	169	2,608	594	8,391,061
Percent[2]	100.0	15.2	65.8	0.8	1.1	17.2		
SUBURBAN AREAS[3]								
Number	209,287	43,383	137,399	1,193	2,714	24,598	3,337	59,279,363
Percent[2]	100.0	20.7	65.7	0.6	1.3	11.8		

[1] Includes all offenses except traffic and neglect cases.

[2] Because of rounding, the percentages may not add to 100.0.

[3] Suburban areas include law enforcement agencies in cities with less than 50,000 inhabitants and county law enforcement agencies that are within a Metropolitan Statistical Area. Suburban areas exclude all metropolitan agencies associated with a principal city. The agencies associated with suburban areas also appear in other groups within this table.

Table 69. State Arrests, 2010

(Number)

State	Total all classes[1]	Violent crime[2]	Property crime[2]	Murder and non-negligent man-slaughter	Forcible rape	Robbery	Aggra-vated assault	Burglary	Larceny-theft	Motor vehicle theft	Arson	Other assaults
ALABAMA												
Under 18	6,100	298	1,833	7	15	100	176	256	1,526	43	8	849
Total all ages	155,266	3,772	15,640	176	230	688	2,678	2,183	12,691	658	108	17,457
ALASKA												
Under 18	3,665	203	1,088	0	5	41	157	139	870	59	20	441
Total all ages	42,084	2,462	3,940	25	88	264	2,085	486	3,141	280	33	5,220
ARIZONA												
Under 18	38,852	1,185	9,265	37	19	264	865	1,232	7,639	285	109	4,123
Total all ages	286,906	8,099	38,616	315	193	1,708	5,883	4,185	32,822	1,411	198	24,471
ARKANSAS												
Under 18	9,091	306	2,311	7	19	55	225	409	1,856	33	13	1,438
Total all ages	114,029	3,272	11,546	67	164	398	2,643	2,027	9,179	286	54	9,193
CALIFORNIA												
Under 18	177,206	12,446	37,775	175	183	5,053	7,035	12,007	22,938	2,279	551	17,102
Total all ages	1,357,573	109,722	152,408	1,548	1,909	18,163	88,102	51,601	86,717	12,957	1,133	84,758
COLORADO[4]												
Under 18	32,054	741	6,765	8	56	148	529	573	5,832	248	112	1,943
Total all ages	210,253	5,939	23,172	120	441	907	4,471	2,483	19,510	971	208	13,880
CONNECTICUT												
Under 18	15,060	789	3,163	5	35	281	468	487	2,471	150	55	3,753
Total all ages	128,670	5,413	17,101	104	234	1,431	3,644	2,787	13,514	646	154	23,722
DELAWARE												
Under 18	5,197	343	1,352	4	16	109	214	278	1,022	41	11	1,198
Total all ages	37,917	2,467	7,079	31	86	600	1,750	1,145	5,773	117	44	7,672
FLORIDA[4,5]												
Under 18	95,756	6,310	28,164	74	207	2,017	4,012	7,838	18,830	1,357	139	13,963
Total all ages	1,038,651	45,087	131,328	852	1,546	9,419	33,270	28,392	96,923	5,607	406	90,096
GEORGIA												
Under 18	39,326	1,718	10,720	46	43	583	1,046	2,183	7,959	501	77	5,524
Total all ages	340,098	13,514	50,215	410	341	2,892	9,871	8,602	39,197	2,176	240	32,790
HAWAII												
Under 18	6,420	256	1,516	2	13	128	113	103	1,333	65	15	919
Total all ages	46,875	1,378	5,197	22	111	375	870	512	4,229	426	30	4,862
IDAHO												
Under 18	10,654	161	2,528	0	18	18	125	344	2,078	66	40	1,090
Total all ages	65,624	1,345	6,693	13	104	105	1,123	986	5,473	183	51	5,667
ILLINOIS[6]												
Under 18	26,605	2,717	4,830	29	55	1,262	1,371	1,022	2,691	1,100	17	4,156
Total all ages	145,657	7,565	19,083	264	434	2,594	4,273	2,721	13,185	3,118	59	21,421
INDIANA												
Under 18	19,715	611	5,131	4	20	137	450	590	4,339	173	29	2,600
Total all ages	139,062	4,333	21,074	115	109	762	3,347	2,902	17,392	688	92	12,163
IOWA												
Under 18	16,561	579	4,602	5	23	65	486	686	3,715	135	66	2,235
Total all ages	106,800	4,058	13,988	20	105	273	3,660	1,871	11,615	387	115	10,061
KANSAS												
Under 18	8,127	328	2,152	4	26	45	253	243	1,779	96	34	1,194
Total all ages	79,565	2,562	7,230	43	179	284	2,056	1,003	5,815	339	73	11,615
KENTUCKY												
Under 18	7,334	401	2,416	6	26	200	169	520	1,811	63	22	1,046
Total all ages	148,208	3,428	16,773	113	222	1,075	2,018	3,216	13,066	407	84	9,553
LOUISIANA												
Under 18	16,582	1,438	4,336	32	34	205	1,167	855	3,305	145	31	3,159
Total all ages	142,872	9,304	22,610	163	192	906	8,043	3,812	18,008	688	102	15,633
MAINE												
Under 18	6,557	72	1,757	0	8	19	45	348	1,294	70	45	898
Total all ages	54,566	691	8,039	19	68	201	403	1,493	6,209	234	103	6,637
MARYLAND												
Under 18	35,339	2,692	8,751	21	40	1,347	1,284	1,479	6,449	656	167	6,716
Total all ages	251,633	11,078	29,541	271	305	3,385	7,117	5,813	21,528	1,791	409	27,873
MASSACHUSETTS												
Under 18	14,623	1,613	2,792	7	36	324	1,246	611	1,982	128	71	2,390
Total all ages	148,282	12,987	20,037	87	383	1,850	10,667	3,934	15,199	768	136	22,612
MICHIGAN												
Under 18	30,678	1,850	9,107	14	107	655	1,074	1,563	6,851	562	131	4,004
Total all ages	275,769	13,152	35,262	187	665	2,567	9,733	6,211	26,782	1,988	281	30,457

[1] Does not include traffic arrests.

[2] Violent crimes are offenses of murder and nonnegligent manslaughter, forcible rape, robbery, and aggravated assault. Property crimes are offenses of burglary, larceny-theft, motor vehicle theft, and arson.

[4] See Appendix I for details.

[5] The arrest category *All other offenses* also includes the arrest counts for offenses against the family and children, drunkenness, disorderly conduct, vagrancy, suspicion, curfew and loitering law violations, and runaways.

[6] Forcible rape figures for Illinois include only those data provided by Rockford. The forcible rape figures for Minnesota include only those provided by the cities of St. Paul and Minneapolis. See Appendix I for details.

NOTE: Because the number of agencies submitting arrest data varies from year to year, users are cautioned about making direct comparisons between 2010 arrest totals and those published in previous years' editions of *Crime in the United States*. Further, arrest figures may vary widely from state to state because some Part II crimes are not considered crimes in some states.

Table 69.   State Arrests, 2010—*Continued*

(Number)

State	Forgery and counter-feiting	Fraud	Embezzle-ment	Stolen property; buying, receiving, possessing	Vandal-ism	Weapons; carrying, possessing, etc.	Prostitu-tion and commer-cialized vice	Sex offenses (except forcible rape and prosti-tution)	Drug abuse violations	Gamb-ling	Offenses against the family and children	Driving under the influence
ALABAMA												
Under 18	5	29	2	79	156	72	1	14	314	1	5	82
Total all ages	1,178	6,370	163	1,496	1,878	1,084	74	412	8,213	47	1,022	13,191
ALASKA												
Under 18	6	10	4	2	132	29	3	43	320	0	5	64
Total all ages	118	283	96	35	903	420	161	324	2,491	10	315	4,997
ARIZONA												
Under 18	29	102	8	138	2,735	320	11	263	5,183	11	184	437
Total all ages	1,901	2,062	213	1,145	11,026	2,701	956	1,626	30,349	268	2,336	36,200
ARKANSAS												
Under 18	13	27	10	97	318	115	1	37	765	1	1	88
Total all ages	670	2,001	44	777	1,249	796	269	163	9,753	10	85	8,616
CALIFORNIA												
Under 18	166	429	26	2,367	10,878	6,626	363	1,823	22,921	27	6	1,080
Total all ages	6,932	8,367	1,264	16,356	24,795	28,374	11,344	11,949	241,547	497	246	195,276
COLORADO[4]												
Under 18	28	74	5	102	1,487	426	9	195	3,249	0	61	383
Total all ages	752	1,861	112	647	5,201	1,690	417	841	15,294	4	3,057	27,833
CONNECTICUT												
Under 18	14	44	8	67	661	247	1	127	1,536	2	73	57
Total all ages	747	1,357	174	463	2,548	1,385	445	574	17,092	31	1,519	9,621
DELAWARE												
Under 18	4	63	3	85	239	118	0	48	593	0	1	0
Total all ages	480	1,678	183	448	941	391	27	156	5,395	12	187	211
FLORIDA[4,5]												
Under 18	80	493	14	209	1,918	1,232	46	299	10,847	63		245
Total all ages	3,562	14,989	815	3,160	7,717	6,018	5,048	2,990	141,831	384		52,346
GEORGIA												
Under 18	82	326	13	516	804	925	28	541	3,289	14	197	229
Total all ages	5,083	7,735	419	3,592	3,765	4,208	1,414	3,910	41,312	585	4,421	28,712
HAWAII												
Under 18	0	15	4	32	224	21	3	63	431	7	0	56
Total all ages	129	403	51	141	694	225	296	263	2,078	38	26	5,922
IDAHO												
Under 18	8	20	2	43	463	133	0	96	876	0	13	127
Total all ages	218	440	65	227	1,094	502	13	300	6,349	0	756	10,458
ILLINOIS[6]												
Under 18	3	22	0	13	1,280	916	33	54	5,303	657	8	23
Total all ages	246	282	1	47	4,041	3,932	2,525	700	42,934	3,059	377	3,966
INDIANA												
Under 18	36	52	1	183	773	216	1	134	1,863	0	224	121
Total all ages	1,069	1,441	6	889	1,763	1,176	203	903	16,728	18	1,428	17,405
IOWA												
Under 18	27	35	8	56	1,138	115	2	46	1,213	1	3	152
Total all ages	465	851	101	179	2,751	484	123	210	9,031	8	947	11,548
KANSAS												
Under 18	14	26	12	41	389	82	0	74	1,103	0	11	166
Total all ages	465	1,216	167	299	1,818	646	185	296	8,122	1	232	12,969
KENTUCKY												
Under 18	10	16	2	166	220	107	1	65	749	2	12	125
Total all ages	1,452	811	295	1,660	991	1,012	275	360	18,277	15	3,630	21,148
LOUISIANA												
Under 18	16	32	3	206	544	233	9	86	1,480	8	69	44
Total all ages	629	1,884	159	1,279	2,301	1,750	257	593	19,324	61	1,092	8,143
MAINE												
Under 18	5	25	3	19	463	58	1	56	574	0	6	41
Total all ages	319	742	43	211	1,522	413	10	285	5,933	2	107	6,203
MARYLAND												
Under 18	18	46	14	12	1,490	955	15	237	5,424	29	8	122
Total all ages	1,082	1,794	275	181	3,654	3,655	1,465	1,252	44,888	240	2,064	18,526
MASSACHUSETTS												
Under 18	15	31	5	230	757	218	4	93	663	2	164	78
Total all ages	676	1,422	148	1,478	3,541	1,597	905	657	12,086	15	2,134	11,634
MICHIGAN												
Under 18	17	342	9	354	911	647	8	252	3,237	11	7	452
Total all ages	764	5,152	925	1,799	3,406	4,120	446	1,010	34,513	118	2,774	34,882

[4] See Appendix I for details.

[5] The arrest category *All other offenses* also includes the arrest counts for offenses against the family and children, drunkenness, disorderly conduct, vagrancy, suspicion, curfew and loitering law violations, and runaways.

[6] Forcible rape figures for Illinois include only those data provided by Rockford. The forcible rape figures for Minnesota include only those provided by the cities of St. Paul and Minneapolis. See Appendix I for details.

NOTE: Because the number of agencies submitting arrest data varies from year to year, users are cautioned about making direct comparisons between 2010 arrest totals and those published in previous years' editions of *Crime in the United States*. Further, arrest figures may vary widely from state to state because some Part II crimes are not considered crimes in some states.

Table 69. State Arrests, 2010—*Continued*

(Number)

State	Liquor laws	Drunken-ness[3]	Disorderly conduct	Vagrancy	All other offenses (except traffic)	Suspi-cion	Curfew and loitering law violations	Number of agencies	2010 estimated population
ALABAMA									
Under 18	462	49	532	1	1,220	0	96	344	3,421,075
Total all ages	3,697	6,140	3,192	97	70,047	0	96		
ALASKA									
Under 18	539	16	59	2	678	1	20	35	705,910
Total all ages	2,492	496	1,083	16	16,191	11	20		
ARIZONA									
Under 18	4,754	0	2,658	17	4,343	0	3,086	80	5,783,974
Total all ages	24,236	3	16,653	1,368	79,591	0	3,086		
ARKANSAS									
Under 18	194	189	814	0	1,904	0	462	173	2,166,546
Total all ages	1,950	7,168	2,755	333	52,917	0	462		
CALIFORNIA									
Under 18	4,275	3,583	8,288	358	36,601	0	10,066	691	35,923,361
Total all ages	17,007	105,388	12,433	4,640	314,204	0	10,066		
COLORADO[4]									
Under 18	3,195	14	2,876	19	8,992	6	1,484	162	4,498,950
Total all ages	12,479	1,723	10,213	370	83,255	29	1,484		
CONNECTICUT									
Under 18	218	0	2,170	0	2,098	0	32	95	3,402,212
Total all ages	1,077	1	14,206	30	31,132	0	32		
DELAWARE									
Under 18	232	15	415	0	383	0	105	53	897,934
Total all ages	1,821	607	2,316	876	4,865	0	105		
FLORIDA[4,5]									
Under 18	1,313				30,560			663	18,791,299
Total all ages	32,637				500,643				
GEORGIA									
Under 18	1,205	69	4,075	77	8,437	11	526	408	7,826,626
Total all ages	10,077	3,432	26,197	1,544	96,605	42	526		
HAWAII									
Under 18	158	0	121	0	2,430	0	164	3	1,207,055
Total all ages	1,157	0	791	0	23,060	0	164		
IDAHO									
Under 18	1,230	16	542	0	2,844	0	462	99	1,466,441
Total all ages	4,934	305	2,544	11	23,241	0	462		
ILLINOIS[6]									
Under 18	144	0	3,109	0	3,052	0	285	2	2,989,829
Total all ages	1,256	0	13,990	141	19,806	0	285		
INDIANA									
Under 18	2,089	173	1,493	2	3,294	9	709	158	3,819,446
Total all ages	10,131	10,686	4,353	100	32,330	154	709		
IOWA									
Under 18	1,312	252	2,035	0	2,143	0	607	186	2,674,284
Total all ages	7,509	11,549	6,400	13	25,917	0	607		
KANSAS									
Under 18	982	3	506	0	1,044	0	0	217	1,978,746
Total all ages	6,354	340	3,175	0	21,873	0	0		
KENTUCKY									
Under 18	92	172	481	21	1,179	0	51	282	3,042,574
Total all ages	469	19,213	5,357	496	42,942	0	51		
LOUISIANA									
Under 18	154	21	1,765	31	2,804	11	133	106	2,616,792
Total all ages	2,176	2,406	7,229	212	45,602	95	133		
MAINE									
Under 18	1,107	10	266	0	1,137	0	59	164	1,328,361
Total all ages	4,961	35	1,924	10	16,420	0	59		
MARYLAND									
Under 18	708	0	1,823	11	5,915	32	321	153	4,804,436
Total all ages	6,748	1	6,544	161	90,034	256	321		
MASSACHUSETTS									
Under 18	975	231	1,104	0	3,246	8	4	319	6,131,066
Total all ages	4,601	7,443	7,942	10	36,299	54	4		
MICHIGAN									
Under 18	2,759	6	1,166	0	4,653	0	886	505	9,249,545
Total all ages	16,732	348	9,709	332	78,982	0	886		

[3] Drunkenness is not considered a crime in some states; therefore, the figures vary widely from state to state.

[4] See Appendix I for details.

[5] The arrest category *All other offenses* also includes the arrest counts for offenses against the family and children, drunkenness, disorderly conduct, vagrancy, suspicion, curfew and loitering law violations, and runaways.

[6] Forcible rape figures for Illinois include only those data provided by Rockford. The forcible rape figures for Minnesota include only those provided by the cities of St. Paul and Minneapolis. See Appendix I for details.

NOTE: Because the number of agencies submitting arrest data varies from year to year, users are cautioned about making direct comparisons between 2010 arrest totals and those published in previous years' editions of *Crime in the United States*. Further, arrest figures may vary widely from state to state because some Part II crimes are not considered crimes in some states.

Table 69.   State Arrests, 2010—*Continued*

(Number)

State	Total all classes[1]	Violent crime[2]	Property crime[2]	Murder and non-negligent man-slaughter	Forcible rape	Robbery	Aggra-vated assault	Burglary	Larceny-theft	Motor vehicle theft	Arson	Other assaults
MINNESOTA[6]												
Under 18	34,201		8,613	9		310	594	783	7,501	229	100	3,279
Total all ages	180,703		28,542	90		1,037	4,019	2,833	24,552	980	177	16,873
MISSISSIPPI												
Under 18	9,038	213	2,412	7	20	126	60	656	1,680	64	12	1,336
Total all ages	109,802	1,973	11,921	116	142	612	1,103	2,525	8,970	352	74	11,391
MISSOURI												
Under 18	34,168	1,326	9,199	25	45	405	851	1,309	7,504	317	69	5,393
Total all ages	289,495	10,219	40,653	145	374	1,851	7,849	6,066	32,812	1,473	302	29,970
MONTANA												
Under 18	5,552	104	1,363	0	6	14	84	78	1,193	73	19	562
Total all ages	25,058	760	3,719	9	25	54	672	233	3,259	198	29	3,270
NEBRASKA												
Under 18	13,662	193	3,414	3	26	75	89	260	3,022	102	30	1,921
Total all ages	83,132	2,039	10,081	60	163	332	1,484	863	8,782	358	78	8,870
NEVADA												
Under 18	20,239	781	3,891	4	17	291	469	560	3,220	74	37	2,462
Total all ages	152,050	6,277	15,672	113	143	1,576	4,445	2,521	12,513	538	100	16,820
NEW HAMPSHIRE												
Under 18	6,675	113	998	0	10	28	75	117	836	25	20	1,138
Total all ages	46,438	765	4,200	5	63	187	510	587	3,507	69	37	6,438
NEW JERSEY												
Under 18	35,989	2,274	6,885	25	65	1,067	1,117	1,118	5,472	146	149	3,049
Total all ages	351,747	12,663	33,508	254	313	3,825	8,271	5,951	26,635	642	280	26,206
NEW MEXICO												
Under 18	11,787	484	3,000	8	28	44	404	340	2,502	112	46	1,722
Total all ages	110,709	4,316	12,362	86	122	330	3,778	1,636	10,178	384	164	10,545
NEW YORK[4]												
Under 18	38,765	2,189	10,733	21	80	888	1,200	1,917	8,249	465	102	4,898
Total all ages	338,474	13,833	56,095	234	503	3,372	9,724	8,256	45,462	2,051	326	37,980
NORTH CAROLINA												
Under 18	36,762	1,763	9,830	51	82	608	1,022	2,677	6,830	208	115	7,100
Total all ages	425,700	18,611	60,533	553	598	3,671	13,789	15,196	43,788	1,180	369	54,262
NORTH DAKOTA												
Under 18	5,075	54	991	0	15	5	34	68	872	47	4	372
Total all ages	24,900	428	2,820	7	39	31	351	232	2,449	129	10	1,846
OHIO												
Under 18	33,821	1,037	7,187	15	83	558	381	1,282	5,547	271	87	6,234
Total all ages	272,655	7,424	38,592	183	511	2,790	3,940	6,725	30,710	935	222	36,172
OKLAHOMA												
Under 18	16,365	596	4,671	21	23	135	417	759	3,700	94	118	1,174
Total all ages	153,958	5,660	18,604	161	243	761	4,495	3,017	14,892	442	253	9,387
OREGON												
Under 18	20,820	499	5,559	4	19	160	316	535	4,718	162	144	1,596
Total all ages	123,440	4,013	23,706	82	222	971	2,738	2,343	19,943	1,165	255	12,414
PENNSYLVANIA												
Under 18	81,412	4,486	11,054	44	173	1,709	2,560	1,708	8,491	621	234	7,825
Total all ages	452,862	24,263	58,803	556	975	6,896	15,836	9,389	46,175	2,595	644	48,237
RHODE ISLAND												
Under 18	5,033	207	943	0	20	72	115	227	646	39	31	716
Total all ages	35,893	946	3,785	9	61	270	606	834	2,748	151	52	4,815
SOUTH CAROLINA												
Under 18	19,258	850	5,068	18	47	219	566	968	3,949	131	20	3,159
Total all ages	195,496	8,819	26,256	239	305	1,486	6,789	4,484	20,805	838	129	21,652
SOUTH DAKOTA												
Under 18	4,833	74	1,235	0	6	7	61	75	1,118	36	6	461
Total all ages	26,717	548	3,419	11	47	39	451	353	2,942	112	12	3,469
TENNESSEE												
Under 18	33,399	2,008	7,084	16	59	526	1,407	1,444	5,216	329	95	5,511
Total all ages	327,693	14,979	40,437	253	335	2,296	12,095	6,384	32,097	1,737	219	29,574
TEXAS												
Under 18	145,129	4,325	31,130	58	237	1,372	2,658	4,779	25,342	823	186	21,861
Total all ages	1,120,190	33,072	139,877	767	1,851	7,612	22,842	19,493	115,161	4,656	567	112,198
UTAH												
Under 18	23,810	311	6,019	2	52	63	194	332	5,541	108	38	2,095
Total all ages	125,124	2,070	20,683	43	238	444	1,345	1,406	18,872	325	80	11,330
VERMONT												
Under 18	1,030	36	255	0	14	0	22	58	170	18	9	185
Total all ages	11,458	469	1,612	6	77	19	367	306	1,208	80	18	1,346

[1] Does not include traffic arrests.

[2] Violent crimes are offenses of murder and nonnegligent manslaughter, forcible rape, robbery, and aggravated assault. Property crimes are offenses of burglary, larceny-theft, motor vehicle theft, and arson.

[4] See Appendix I for details.

[6] Forcible rape figures for Illinois include only those data provided by Rockford. The forcible rape figures for Minnesota include only those provided by the cities of St. Paul and Minneapolis. See Appendix I for details.

NOTE: Because the number of agencies submitting arrest data varies from year to year, users are cautioned about making direct comparisons between 2010 arrest totals and those published in previous years' editions of *Crime in the United States*. Further, arrest figures may vary widely from state to state because some Part II crimes are not considered crimes in some states.

Table 69. State Arrests, 2010—*Continued*

(Number)

State	Forgery and counter-feiting	Fraud	Embezzle-ment	Stolen property; buying, receiving, possessing	Vandal-ism	Weapons; carrying, possessing, etc.	Prostitu-tion and commer-cialized vice	Sex offenses (except forcible rape and prosti-tution)	Drug abuse violations	Gamb-ling	Offenses against the family and children	Driving under the influence
MINNESOTA[6]												
Under 18	43	197	2	436	1,401	526	13	273	2,847	0	14	310
Total all ages	1,179	2,721	39	1,736	3,908	1,690	966	1,463	17,501	19	664	24,978
MISSISSIPPI												
Under 18	5	55	7	87	152	223	0	33	578	13	159	72
Total all ages	662	1,662	497	662	1,071	959	149	393	11,004	126	3,480	11,005
MISSOURI												
Under 18	35	65	9	516	1,492	416	3	426	3,081	4	80	312
Total all ages	1,986	2,894	230	2,847	5,387	3,294	338	2,010	33,964	99	4,138	29,655
MONTANA												
Under 18	2	9	1	5	292	20	0	14	351	0	48	49
Total all ages	38	153	21	15	801	83	1	66	1,494	0	347	3,659
NEBRASKA												
Under 18	13	84	4	154	1,062	153	1	100	1,368	1	21	205
Total all ages	497	1,425	54	790	2,807	870	148	609	10,177	10	1,386	12,488
NEVADA												
Under 18	6	38	3	231	1,214	273	52	135	2,030	2	9	84
Total all ages	880	1,545	408	1,494	2,514	1,597	3,738	1,355	16,268	19	1,327	13,412
NEW HAMPSHIRE												
Under 18	4	28	0	131	371	20	0	41	771	0	12	72
Total all ages	211	762	38	663	1,284	116	24	162	3,915	5	178	4,355
NEW JERSEY												
Under 18	43	77	3	652	1,734	1,109	15	267	4,837	18	80	298
Total all ages	1,681	3,798	169	3,182	5,488	4,300	1,489	1,441	49,072	106	13,284	26,016
NEW MEXICO												
Under 18	9	49	9	82	398	242	5	34	1,628	8	34	131
Total all ages	296	613	207	585	1,368	708	347	210	8,814	37	1,351	11,307
NEW YORK[4]												
Under 18	82	307	4	928	3,381	571	5	717	5,009	8	66	208
Total all ages	2,742	6,487	103	5,008	16,304	3,699	783	3,708	62,519	147	623	36,578
NORTH CAROLINA												
Under 18	36	386	26	526	1,440	1,433	12	193	2,830	4	73	460
Total all ages	2,064	17,435	1,473	4,543	7,407	6,727	1,145	1,504	33,170	81	6,577	50,907
NORTH DAKOTA												
Under 18	5	14	2	59	222	13	0	32	336	0	49	30
Total all ages	77	613	35	143	475	118	5	82	1,938	0	113	3,945
OHIO												
Under 18	32	153	3	492	1,468	499	8	224	2,538	6	499	136
Total all ages	1,509	2,902	37	3,436	4,516	3,228	1,724	799	31,465	45	4,172	36,259
OKLAHOMA												
Under 18	24	42	20	320	467	262	4	76	1,706	6	76	163
Total all ages	795	2,278	487	2,233	1,431	1,922	247	660	19,714	46	895	17,446
OREGON												
Under 18	16	96	0	63	1,517	187	5	122	2,409	0	8	117
Total all ages	745	1,586	37	339	4,438	1,491	296	1,102	15,600	1	468	13,600
PENNSYLVANIA												
Under 18	75	214	39	498	3,289	1,251	8	578	5,223	4	33	459
Total all ages	2,703	7,404	400	2,792	10,642	4,293	1,958	2,681	55,858	139	1,206	51,402
RHODE ISLAND												
Under 18	3	19	7	67	411	152	1	33	483	0	79	22
Total all ages	143	585	110	393	1,305	408	103	107	3,782	0	101	2,574
SOUTH CAROLINA												
Under 18	24	84	7	227	712	519	2	119	2,679	0	18	122
Total all ages	1,676	7,358	403	2,063	3,386	2,406	624	562	30,435	321	1,136	19,245
SOUTH DAKOTA												
Under 18	11	32	2	27	203	66	2	20	513	0	104	72
Total all ages	102	598	32	94	537	162	22	57	2,903	0	254	4,883
TENNESSEE												
Under 18	49	169	6	71	1,379	628	17	190	3,098	96	51	114
Total all ages	2,478	6,438	719	775	4,306	3,109	2,387	737	37,512	408	2,359	20,589
TEXAS												
Under 18	158	317	22	157	4,598	1,200	92	599	15,883	21	47	866
Total all ages	6,958	13,033	522	908	13,205	10,664	7,554	4,301	136,966	624	5,414	93,533
UTAH												
Under 18	21	49	1	134	1,762	342	16	284	1,894	0	31	96
Total all ages	953	1,091	20	774	4,300	1,260	414	848	10,728	1	1,562	7,170
VERMONT												
Under 18	2	2	2	12	83	5	0	4	102	0	4	22
Total all ages	50	225	37	105	339	9	5	14	1,156	0	293	2,461

[4] See Appendix I for details.

[6] Forcible rape figures for Illinois include only those data provided by Rockford. The forcible rape figures for Minnesota include only those provided by the cities of St. Paul and Minneapolis. See Appendix I for details.

NOTE: Because the number of agencies submitting arrest data varies from year to year, users are cautioned about making direct comparisons between 2010 arrest totals and those published in previous years' editions of *Crime in the United States*. Further, arrest figures may vary widely from state to state because some Part II crimes are not considered crimes in some states.

Table 69. State Arrests, 2010—*Continued*

(Number)

State	Liquor laws	Drunken-ness[3]	Disorderly conduct	Vagrancy	All other offenses (except traffic)	Suspi-cion	Curfew and loitering law violations	Number of agencies	2010 estimated population
MINNESOTA[6]									
Under 18	4,287	0	3,906	23	5,027	0	2,091	327	5,303,925
Total all ages	22,990	1	13,095	554	34,547	0	2,091		
MISSISSIPPI									
Under 18	104	39	1,475	0	1,604	5	466	93	1,569,211
Total all ages	1,858	5,200	7,081	136	38,018	88	466		
MISSOURI									
Under 18	1,899	16	2,188	13	5,748	0	1,947	379	5,574,070
Total all ages	10,241	553	12,951	219	95,900	0	1,947		
MONTANA									
Under 18	1,033	0	566	0	774	0	359	92	858,976
Total all ages	3,040	0	2,830	4	4,398	0	359		
NEBRASKA									
Under 18	1,748	0	736	1	2,191	0	292	199	1,641,088
Total all ages	10,526	0	3,730	37	16,296	0	292		
NEVADA									
Under 18	1,867	58	1,014	34	3,890	1	2,164	32	2,397,300
Total all ages	8,557	228	2,634	1,686	53,453	2	2,164		
NEW HAMPSHIRE									
Under 18	799	208	254	0	1,698	0	17	149	1,144,113
Total all ages	4,411	3,602	1,450	52	13,790	0	17		
NEW JERSEY									
Under 18	2,032	0	3,319	20	5,858	0	3,419	513	8,598,088
Total all ages	6,640	0	19,974	839	138,472	0	3,419		
NEW MEXICO									
Under 18	857	13	621	0	2,439	12	10	80	1,807,829
Total all ages	5,189	845	3,522	50	47,950	77	10		
NEW YORK[4]									
Under 18	788	0	2,081	41	6,749	0	0	528	9,600,548
Total all ages	4,620	0	14,017	868	72,360	0	0		
NORTH CAROLINA									
Under 18	1,216	0	3,592	0	5,842	0	0	292	7,886,978
Total all ages	9,634	0	13,958	279	135,390	0	0		
NORTH DAKOTA									
Under 18	808	1	858	0	980	0	249	81	605,751
Total all ages	5,072	196	2,167	1	4,577	0	249		
OHIO									
Under 18	1,848	61	2,789	1	7,334	5	1,267	412	8,539,835
Total all ages	11,723	3,602	19,318	39	64,347	79	1,267		
OKLAHOMA									
Under 18	362	665	1,062	0	2,695	0	1,974	269	3,706,617
Total all ages	2,551	21,859	2,846	1,111	41,812	0	1,974		
OREGON									
Under 18	2,878	0	1,314	0	2,930	0	1,504	128	3,337,173
Total all ages	14,350	0	9,421	5	18,324	0	1,504		
PENNSYLVANIA									
Under 18	5,758	305	14,824	130	6,193	0	19,166	1,197	12,300,834
Total all ages	22,405	24,949	58,285	1,338	53,938	0	19,166		
RHODE ISLAND									
Under 18	98	0	939	0	849	0	4	47	1,040,938
Total all ages	1,162	17	3,376	0	12,177	0	4		
SOUTH CAROLINA									
Under 18	726	115	2,563	0	2,149	0	115	404	4,393,409
Total all ages	9,613	11,706	15,479	961	31,280	0	115		
SOUTH DAKOTA									
Under 18	1,058	10	328	0	419	0	196	95	632,552
Total all ages	5,066	68	1,765	171	2,371	0	196		
TENNESSEE									
Under 18	857	253	3,617	0	6,263	0	1,938	397	4,932,498
Total all ages	6,102	17,104	9,884	35	125,823	0	1,938		
TEXAS									
Under 18	4,646	3,048	19,936	773	26,991	0	8,459	1,007	24,862,112
Total all ages	26,607	130,295	37,961	2,184	335,855	0	8,459		
UTAH									
Under 18	2,108	170	1,805	54	5,443	0	1,175	116	2,669,959
Total all ages	10,063	4,337	5,224	212	40,909	0	1,175		
VERMONT									
Under 18	126	1	59	0	130	0	0	67	545,701
Total all ages	428	3	553	0	2,353	0	0		

[3] Drunkenness is not considered a crime in some states; therefore, the figures vary widely from state to state.

[4] See Appendix I for details.

[6] Forcible rape figures for Illinois include only those data provided by Rockford. The forcible rape figures for Minnesota include only those provided by the cities of St. Paul and Minneapolis. See Appendix I for details.

NOTE: Because the number of agencies submitting arrest data varies from year to year, users are cautioned about making direct comparisons between 2010 arrest totals and those published in previous years' editions of *Crime in the United States*. Further, arrest figures may vary widely from state to state because some Part II crimes are not considered crimes in some states.

Table 69.   State Arrests, 2010—*Continued*

(Number)

State	Total all classes[1]	Violent crime[2]	Property crime[2]	Murder and non-negligent man-slaughter	Forcible rape	Robbery	Aggra-vated assault	Burglary	Larceny-theft	Motor vehicle theft	Arson	Other assaults
VIRGINIA												
Under 18	31,261	915	6,221	17	44	382	472	825	5,065	215	116	5,069
Total all ages	353,473	7,272	36,689	293	366	2,005	4,608	4,486	30,893	1,045	265	42,988
WASHINGTON												
Under 18	23,325	1,172	6,678	6	86	426	654	1,126	5,192	272	88	3,786
Total all ages	217,761	7,627	32,414	108	583	1,898	5,038	5,059	25,895	1,237	223	26,736
WEST VIRGINIA												
Under 18	1,954	84	491	2	5	15	62	55	409	22	5	352
Total all ages	46,370	1,889	5,960	26	60	178	1,625	875	4,839	193	53	6,347
WISCONSIN												
Under 18	63,925	1,284	10,299	15	137	557	575	1,201	8,692	340	66	2,717
Total all ages	309,381	7,253	33,965	139	626	1,777	4,711	3,949	28,916	958	142	16,488
WYOMING												
Under 18	5,581	55	938	0	2	9	44	113	790	27	8	619
Total all ages	35,170	489	2,871	6	38	23	422	350	2,418	84	19	3,168

[1] Does not include traffic arrests.

[2] Violent crimes are offenses of murder and nonnegligent manslaughter, forcible rape, robbery, and aggravated assault. Property crimes are offenses of burglary, larceny-theft, motor vehicle theft, and arson.

Table 69. State Arrests, 2010—*Continued*

(Number)

State	Forgery and counter-feiting	Fraud	Embezzle-ment	Stolen property; buying, receiving, possessing	Vandal-ism	Weapons; carrying, possessing, etc.	Prostitu-tion and commer-cialized vice	Sex offenses (except forcible rape and prosti-tution)	Drug abuse violations	Gamb-ling	Offenses against the family and children	Driving under the influence
VIRGINIA												
Under 18	40	154	22	162	1,019	434	2	240	2,539	1	57	159
Total all ages	2,268	7,425	1,646	999	4,719	3,777	689	1,217	33,666	78	2,072	28,680
WASHINGTON												
Under 18	25	40	1	278	1,656	509	33	154	2,615	3	11	384
Total all ages	1,238	954	85	2,489	6,292	2,541	836	876	20,644	7	562	34,098
WEST VIRGINIA												
Under 18	7	3	1	13	81	11	0	8	222	0	0	17
Total all ages	434	802	139	345	822	310	114	125	6,235	10	87	4,922
WISCONSIN												
Under 18	26	130	3	468	2,459	828	14	868	3,659	72	252	381
Total all ages	1,027	3,817	164	1,483	8,168	3,318	358	2,311	22,651	165	2,215	29,549
WYOMING												
Under 18	2	6	1	4	266	47	0	16	606	0	9	64
Total all ages	74	200	4	68	748	99	7	148	3,103	0	194	5,810

Table 69.   State Arrests, 2010—*Continued*

(Number)

State	Liquor laws	Drunken-ness[3]	Disorderly conduct	Vagrancy	All other offenses (except traffic)	Suspi-cion	Curfew and loitering law violations	Number of agencies	2010 estimated population
VIRGINIA									
Under 18	2,119	218	1,172	0	7,981	0	2,737	329	7,864,147
Total all ages	13,618	34,766	5,701	233	122,233	0	2,737		
WASHINGTON									
Under 18	2,354	2	570	19	3,001	0	34	216	5,269,545
Total all ages	8,434	10	4,835	54	66,995	0	34		
WEST VIRGINIA									
Under 18	119	12	59	0	410	0	64	154	1,488,466
Total all ages	1,711	3,388	1,098	7	11,561	0	64		
WISCONSIN									
Under 18	5,613	1	13,110	37	17,439	2	4,263	320	5,037,442
Total all ages	28,373	5	49,517	2,977	91,312	2	4,263		
WYOMING									
Under 18	997	15	221	5	1,278	3	429	64	559,126
Total all ages	3,760	2,374	1,313	27	10,269	15	429		

[3] Drunkenness is not considered a crime in some states; therefore, the figures vary widely from state to state.

SECTION V:
LAW ENFORCEMENT PERSONNEL

LAW ENFORCEMENT PERSONNEL

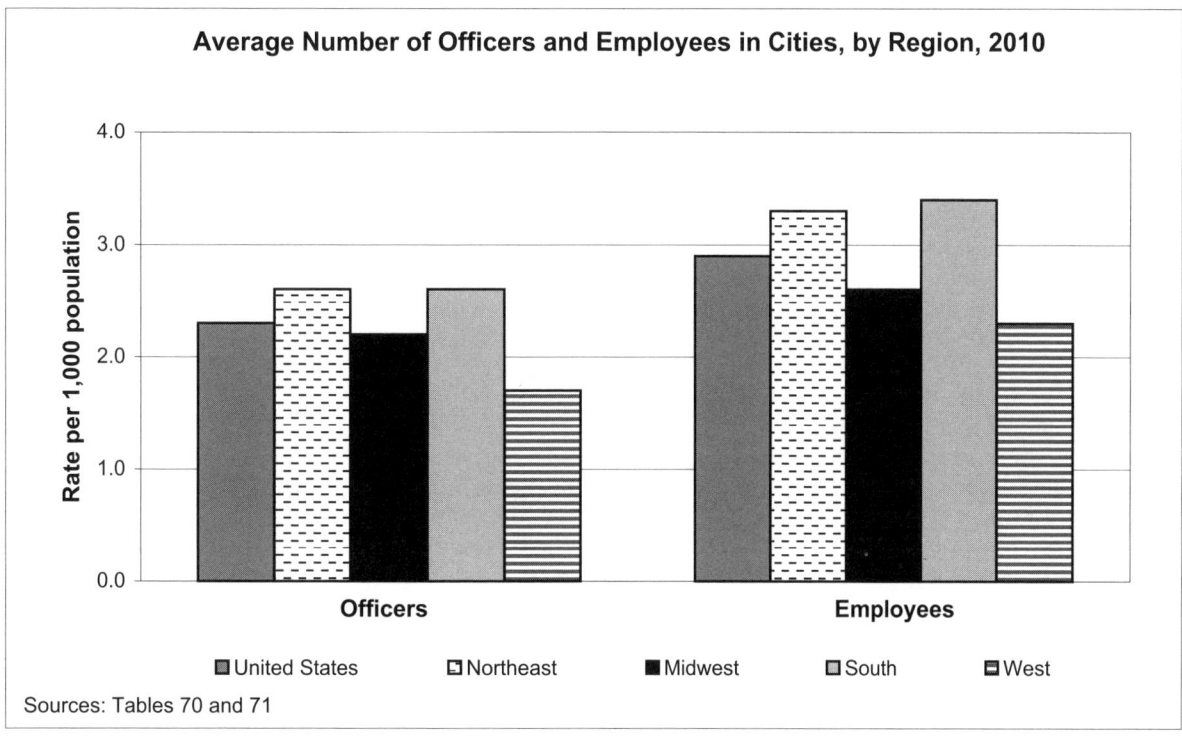

Average Number of Officers and Employees in Cities, by Region, 2010

Sources: Tables 70 and 71

The Uniform Crime Reporting (UCR) Program defines law enforcement officers as individuals who ordinarily carry a firearm and a badge, have full arrest powers, and are paid from governmental funds set aside specifically for sworn law enforcement representatives. Because of law enforcement's varied service requirements and functions, as well as the distinct demographic traits and characteristics of jurisdictions, readers should use caution when comparing staffing levels between agencies based on police employment data from the UCR Program. In addition, the data presented here reflect existing staff levels and should not be interpreted as preferred officer strengths recommended by the FBI. Also note that the totals given for sworn officers for any particular agency reflect not only the patrol officers on the street but also officers assigned to various other duties such as those in administrative and investigative positions and those assigned to special teams.

Each year, law enforcement agencies across the United States report the total number of sworn law enforcement officers and civilians in their agencies as of October 31 to the UCR Program. Civilian employees include personnel such as clerks, radio dispatchers, meter attendants, stenographers, jailers, correctional officers, and mechanics provided that they are full-time employees of the agency.

This section of *Crime in the United States* presents those data as the number and rate of law enforcement officers and civilian employees throughout the United States. In 2010, 705,009 sworn officers and 308,599 civilians, provided law enforcement services to more than 291 million people nationwide.

These law enforcement personnel were employed by 14,744 state, city, university and college, metropolitan and nonmetropolitan county, and other law enforcement agencies. Of the slightly more than 1 million law enforcement employees, 73.3 percent were male. (Table 74)

The data in this section are broken down by geographic region and division, population group, state, city, university and college, metropolitan and nonmetropolitan county, and other law enforcement agencies. (Information about geographic regions and divisions and population groups can be found in Appendix III.) UCR Program staff compute the rate of sworn officers and law enforcement employees by taking the number of employees (sworn officers only or in combination with civilians), dividing by the population for which the agency provides law enforcement service, and multiplying by 1,000.

• Tables 70 and 71 present the number and rate of law enforcement personnel per 1,000 inhabitants collectively employed by agencies, broken down by geographic region and division by population group.

• Tables 72 and 73 provide a count of law enforcement agencies by population group, based on the employment rate ranges for sworn officer and civilian employees per 1,000 inhabitants.

• Table 74 provides the number and percentage of male and female sworn officers and civilian employees by population group.

- Table 75 lists the percentage of full-time civilian law enforcement employees by population group.

- Table 76 breaks down by state the number of sworn law enforcement officers and civilians employed by state law enforcement agencies.

- Tables 78 to 80 list the number of law enforcement employees for cities, universities and colleges, and metropolitan and nonmetropolitan counties.

- Table 81 supplies employee data for those law enforcement agencies that serve the nation's transit systems, parks and forests, schools and school districts, hospitals, and so on.

The demographic traits and characteristics of a jurisdiction affect its requirements for law enforcement service. For instance, a village between two large cities may require more law enforcement than a community of the same size with no urban center nearby. A town with legal gambling may have different law enforcement needs than a town near a military base. A city largely made up of college students may have different law enforcement needs than a city whose residents are mainly retirees.

Similarly, the functions of law enforcement agencies are diverse. Employees of these agencies patrol local streets and major highways, protect citizens in the nation's smallest towns and largest cities, and conduct investigations on offenses at the local and state level. State police in one area may enforce traffic laws on state highways and interstates; in another area, they may be responsible for investigating violent crimes. Sheriff's departments may collect tax monies, serve as the enforcement authority for local and state courts, administer jail facilities, or carry out some combination of these duties. This has an impact on an agency's staffing levels.

Because of the differing service requirements and functions, care should be taken when drawing comparisons between and among the staffing levels of law enforcement agencies. The data in this section are not intended as recommended or preferred officer strength; they should be used merely as guides. Adequate staffing levels can be determined only after careful study of the conditions that affect the service requirements in a particular jurisdiction.

Rate

The UCR Program computes these rates by taking the number of employees, dividing by the population of the agency's jurisdiction, and multiplying by 1,000. The rate of full-time law enforcement employees (civilian and sworn) per 1,000 inhabitants in the nation for 2010 was 3.5.

Among the nation's four regions, law enforcement agencies in the south had the highest rate of law enforcement employees in 2010, with 3.4 per 1,000 inhabitants. The Northeast followed closely with 3.3 per 1,000 inhabitants.

Agencies in the Midwest had 2.6 law enforcement employees per 1,000 inhabitants, followed by the West at 2.3. (Table 70)

An examination of the 2010 law enforcement employee data by population group showed that the nation's cities had a collective rate of 2.9 law enforcement employees per 1,000 inhabitants. Cities with fewer than 10,000 inhabitants had the highest rate of law enforcement employees, with a rate of 4.5 per 1,000 inhabitants. Cities with 50,000 to 99,999 inhabitants had the lowest rate of law enforcement employees (2.2 per 1,000 in population). The nation's largest cities, those with 250,000 or more inhabitants, averaged 3.6 law enforcement employees for every 1,000 inhabitants. (Table 70)

Sworn Personnel

An analysis of the 2010 data showed that law enforcement agencies in the cities in the Northeast and the South had the highest rate of sworn officers—each at a rate of 2.7 per 1,000 inhabitants, followed by the Midwest (2.2), and the West (1.7). (Table 71)

By population group in 2010, there were 2.3 sworn officers for each 1,000 resident population in the nation's cities collectively. This rate has remained constant since 2007. Cities with fewer than 10,000 inhabitants had the highest rate at 3.5 sworn officers per 1,000 inhabitants. The nation's largest cities, those with 250,000 or more inhabitants, averaged 2.7 officers per 1,000 inhabitants, slightly lower than in 2009. (Table 71)

Males accounted for 88.2 percent of all full-time sworn law enforcement officers in 2010. Cities with populations of 1 million and over employed the highest percentage (18.1) of full-time female officers. Of the city population groups, cities with populations of 10,000 to 24,999 inhabitants employed the highest percentage (92.2) of male officers. In metropolitan counties, 86.6 percent of officers were male, and in nonmetropolitan counties, 92.3 percent of officers were male. (Table 74)

Civilian Employees

Civilian employees provide a myriad of services to the nation's law enforcement and criminal justice agencies. Among other duties, they dispatch officers, provide administrative and record-keeping support, and query local, state, and national databases.

In 2010, 30.4 percent of all law enforcement employees in the nation were civilians. Female employees accounted for 60.8 percent of all full-time civilian law enforcement employees in 2010. In cities, civilians made up 22.3 percent of law enforcement agencies employees. Civilians made up 41.6 percent of law enforcement employees in metropolitan counties, 40.1 percent of law enforcement employees in nonmetropolitan counties, and 34.5 percent of law enforcement employees in suburban areas. (Table 74)

Table 70.   Full-Time Law Enforcement Employees, by Geographic Region and Division and Population Group, 2010[1]

(Number, rate per 1,000 population)

Geographic region/division	Total (11,356 cities; population 197,172,429)	Group I (74 cities, 250,000 and over; population 56,581,538)	Group II (193 cities, 100,000 to 249,999; population 28,908,827)	Group III (437 cities, 50,000 to 99,999; population 29,978,412)	Group IV (812 cities, 25,000 to 49,999; population 27,951,300)	Group V (1,853 cities, 10,000 to 24,999; population 29,350,253)
TOTAL						
Number of employees	577,677	201,067	68,705	65,955	62,927	69,615
Average number of employees per 1,000 inhabitants	2.9	3.6	2.4	2.2	2.3	2.4
Northeast						
Number of employees	149,760	63,818	9,577	15,425	18,498	19,902
Average number of employees per 1,000 inhabitants	3.3	5.6	3.3	2.5	2.3	2.1
New England						
Number of employees	34,296	2,680	4,596	5,797	6,966	7,445
Average number of employees per 1,000 inhabitants	2.6	4.2	3.2	2.3	2.2	2.2
Middle Atlantic						
Number of employees	115,464	61,138	4,981	9,628	11,532	12,457
Average number of employees per 1,000 inhabitants	3.6	5.7	3.4	2.6	2.3	2.1
Midwest						
Number of employees	116,895	33,118	9,134	13,651	16,125	19,021
Average number of employees per 1,000 inhabitants	2.6	3.6	2.2	1.9	2.0	2.2
East North Central						
Number of employees	83,756	25,293	5,872	9,547	12,593	13,780
Average number of employees per 1,000 inhabitants	2.7	3.9	2.2	2.0	2.1	2.2
West North Central						
Number of employees	33,139	7,825	3,262	4,104	3,532	5,241
Average number of employees per 1,000 inhabitants	2.5	3.0	2.2	1.7	1.9	2.2
South						
Number of employees	195,386	54,420	30,309	20,475	18,723	23,586
Average number of employees per 1,000 inhabitants	3.4	3.2	2.7	2.7	2.8	3.0
South Atlantic						
Number of employees	90,964	21,951	15,450	11,567	8,577	10,772
Average number of employees per 1,000 inhabitants	3.9	4.1	2.9	3.0	3.1	3.2
East South Central						
Number of employees	34,395	7,127	4,584	2,350	4,478	5,582
Average number of employees per 1,000 inhabitants	3.4	2.9	3.3	3.0	2.8	3.1
West South Central						
Number of employees	70,027	25,342	10,275	6,558	5,668	7,232
Average number of employees per 1,000 inhabitants	2.9	2.7	2.3	2.2	2.4	2.7
West						
Number of employees	115,636	49,711	19,685	16,404	9,581	7,106
Average number of employees per 1,000 inhabitants	2.3	2.6	1.8	1.8	1.9	2.1
Mountain						
Number of employees	41,906	17,164	6,867	5,034	3,673	2,663
Average number of employees per 1,000 inhabitants	2.6	2.8	2.1	2.0	2.0	2.4
Pacific						
Number of employees	73,730	32,547	12,818	11,370	5,908	4,443
Average number of employees per 1,000 inhabitants	2.2	2.5	1.7	1.7	1.8	2.0

[1] Full-time law enforcement employees include civilians.

Table 70.   Full-Time Law Enforcement Employees, by Geographic Region and Division and Population Group, 2010[1]—*Continued*

(Number, rate per 1,000 population)

Geographic region/division	Group VI (7,987 cities, under 10,000; population 24,402,099)	Total city agencies	2010 estimated city population	County[2] (3,388 agencies; population 94,242,165)	Total city and county agencies	2010 estimated total agency population	Suburban Area[3] (7,675 agencies; population 124,334,967)
TOTAL							
Number of employees	109,408	11,356	197,172,429	435,931	14,744	291,414,594	469,656
Average number of employees per 1,000 inhabitants	4.5			4.6			3.8
Northeast							
Number of employees	22,540	2,648	44,886,743				
Average number of employees per 1,000 inhabitants	3.3						
New England							
Number of employees	6,812	808	12,956,907				
Average number of employees per 1,000 inhabitants	3.7						
Middle Atlantic							
Number of employees	15,728	1,840	31,929,836				
Average number of employees per 1,000 inhabitants	3.2						
Midwest							
Number of employees	25,846	3,374	44,558,939				
Average number of employees per 1,000 inhabitants	3.4						
East North Central							
Number of employees	16,671	2,141	31,209,169				
Average number of employees per 1,000 inhabitants	3.4						
West North Central							
Number of employees	9,175	1,233	13,349,770				
Average number of employees per 1,000 inhabitants	3.5						
South							
Number of employees	47,873	3,922	58,174,704				
Average number of employees per 1,000 inhabitants	6.3						
South Atlantic							
Number of employees	22,647	1,634	23,617,349				
Average number of employees per 1,000 inhabitants	7.7						
East South Central							
Number of employees	10,274	972	9,987,963				
Average number of employees per 1,000 inhabitants	5.3						
West South Central							
Number of employees	14,952	1,316	24,569,392				
Average number of employees per 1,000 inhabitants	5.5						
West							
Number of employees	13,149	1,412	49,552,043				
Average number of employees per 1,000 inhabitants	5.2						
Mountain							
Number of employees	6,505	634	16,079,899				
Average number of employees per 1,000 inhabitants	5.0						
Pacific							
Number of employees	6,644	778	33,472,144				
Average number of employees per 1,000 inhabitants	5.5						

[2] The designation county is a combination of both metropolitan and nonmetropolitan counties.

[3] Suburban areas include law enforcement agencies in cities with less than 50,000 inhabitants and county law enforcement agencies that are within a Metropolitan Statistical Area. Suburban areas exclude all metropolitan agencies associated with a principal city. The agencies associated with suburban areas also appear in other groups within this table.

Table 71.   Full-Time Law Enforcement Officers, by Geographic Region and Division and Population Group, 2010

(Number, rate per 1,000 population)

Geographic region/division	Total (11,356 cities; population 197,172,429)	Group I (74 cities, 250,000 and over; population 56,581,538)	Group II (193 cities, 100,000 to 249,999; population 28,908,827)	Group III (437 cities, 50,000 to 99,999; population 29,978,412)	Group IV (812 cities, 25,000 to 49,999; population 27,951,300)	Group V (1,853 cities, 10,000 to 24,999; population 29,350,253)
TOTAL						
Number of officers..	448,905	154,306	52,541	51,072	49,883	55,959
Average number of officers per 1,000 inhabitants................................	2.3	2.7	1.8	1.7	1.8	1.9
Northeast						
Number of officers..	118,708	46,608	8,134	12,850	15,536	16,808
Average number of officers per 1,000 inhabitants................................	2.6	4.1	2.8	2.1	1.9	1.8
New England						
Number of officers..	28,236	2,094	3,910	4,941	5,784	6,051
Average number of officers per 1,000 inhabitants................................	2.2	3.3	2.7	2.0	1.9	1.8
Middle Atlantic						
Number of officers..	90,472	44,514	4,224	7,909	9,752	10,757
Average number of officers per 1,000 inhabitants................................	2.8	4.1	2.9	2.1	1.9	1.8
Midwest						
Number of officers..	96,472	28,645	7,375	10,990	12,841	15,398
Average number of officers per 1,000 inhabitants................................	2.2	3.1	1.8	1.6	1.6	1.8
East North Central						
Number of officers..	69,972	22,662	4,816	7,692	10,037	11,181
Average number of officers per 1,000 inhabitants................................	2.2	3.5	1.8	1.6	1.6	1.8
West North Central						
Number of officers..	26,500	5,983	2,559	3,298	2,804	4,217
Average number of officers per 1,000 inhabitants................................	2.0	2.3	1.7	1.4	1.5	
South						
Number of officers..	150,276	42,513	23,265	15,688	14,579	18,410
Average number of officers per 1,000 inhabitants................................	2.6	2.5	2.1	2.1	2.2	2.4
South Atlantic						
Number of officers..	69,799	16,494	11,883	8,857	6,779	8,591
Average number of officers per 1,000 inhabitants................................	3.0	3.1	2.2	2.3	2.4	2.6
East South Central						
Number of officers..	27,158	5,902	3,464	1,808	3,577	4,357
Average number of officers per 1,000 inhabitants................................	2.7	2.4	2.5	2.3	2.3	2.4
West South Central						
Number of officers..	53,319	20,117	7,918	5,023	4,223	5,462
Average number of officers per 1,000 inhabitants................................	2.2	2.1	1.8	1.7	1.8	2.0
West						
Number of officers..	83,449	36,540	13,767	11,544	6,927	5,343
Average number of officers per 1,000 inhabitants................................	1.7	1.9	1.3	1.3	1.4	1.6
Mountain						
Number of officers..	29,586	11,724	4,886	3,558	2,702	2,026
Average number of officers per 1,000 inhabitants................................	1.8	1.9	1.5	1.4	1.5	1.8
Pacific						
Number of officers..	53,863	24,816	8,881	7,986	4,225	3,317
Average number of officers per 1,000 inhabitants................................	1.6	1.9	1.2	1.2	1.3	1.5

Table 71. Full-Time Law Enforcement Officers, by Geographic Region and Division and Population Group, 2010—*Continued*

(Number, rate per 1,000 population)

Geographic region/division	Group VI (7,987 cities, under 10,000; population 24,402,099)	Total city agencies	2010 estimated city population	County[1] (3,388 agencies; population 94,242,165)	Total city and county agencies	2010 estimated total agency population	Suburban Area[2] (7,675 agencies; population 124,334,967)
TOTAL							
Number of officers	85,144	11,356	197,172,429	256,104	14,744	291,414,594	307,593
Average number of officers per 1,000 inhabitants	3.5			2.7			2.5
Northeast							
Number of officers	18,772	2,648	44,886,743				
Average number of officers per 1,000 inhabitants	2.8						
New England							
Number of officers	5,456	808	12,956,907				
Average number of officers per 1,000 inhabitants	2.9						
Middle Atlantic							
Number of officers	13,316	1,840	31,929,836				
Average number of officers per 1,000 inhabitants	2.7						
Midwest							
Number of officers	21,223	3,374	44,558,939				
Average number of officers per 1,000 inhabitants	2.8						
East North Central							
Number of officers	13,584	2,141	31,209,169				
Average number of officers per 1,000 inhabitants	2.8						
West North Central							
Number of officers	7,639	1,233	13,349,770				
Average number of officers per 1,000 inhabitants	2.9						
South							
Number of officers	35,821	3,922	58,174,704				
Average number of officers per 1,000 inhabitants	4.7						
South Atlantic							
Number of officers	17,195	1,634	23,617,349				
Average number of officers per 1,000 inhabitants	5.9						
East South Central							
Number of officers	8,050	972	9,987,963				
Average number of officers per 1,000 inhabitants	4.1						
West South Central							
Number of officers	10,576	1,316	24,569,392				
Average number of officers per 1,000 inhabitants	3.9						
West							
Number of officers	9,328	1,412	49,552,043				
Average number of officers per 1,000 inhabitants	3.7						
Mountain							
Number of officers	4,690	634	16,079,899				
Average number of officers per 1,000 inhabitants	3.6						
Pacific							
Number of officers	4,638	778	33,472,144				
Average number of officers per 1,000 inhabitants	3.8						

[1] The designation county is a combination of both metropolitan and nonmetropolitan counties.

[2] Suburban areas include law enforcement agencies in cities with less than 50,000 inhabitants and county law enforcement agencies that are within a Metropolitan Statistical Area. Suburban areas exclude all metropolitan agencies associated with a principal city. The agencies associated with suburban areas also appear in other groups within this table.

Table 72.   Full-Time Law Enforcement Employees, by Rate Range, 2010[1]

(Number, rate per 1,000 population.)

Rate range	Total cities[2] (10,204 cities; population 197,172,429)	Group I (74 cities, 250,000 and over; population 56,581,538)	Group II (193 cities, 100,000 to 249,999; population 28,908,827)	Group III (437 cities; 50,000 to 99,999; population 29,978,412)	Group IV (812 cities, 25,000 to 49,999; population 27,951,300)	Group V (1,853 cities, 10,000 to 24,999; population 29,350,253)	Group VI (6,835 cities, under 10,000; population 24,402,099)
Total Cities							
Number	10,204	74	193	437	812	1,853	6,835
Percent[3]	100.0	100.0	100.0	100.0	100.0	100.0	100.0
0.1–0.5							
Number	123	0	0	0	2	5	116
Percent	1.2	0.0	0.0	0.0	0.2	0.3	1.7
0.6–1.0							
Number	523	0	1	7	21	51	443
Percent	5.1	0.0	0.5	1.6	2.6	2.8	6.5
1.1–1.5							
Number	1,206	1	29	68	111	214	783
Percent	11.8	1.4	15.0	15.6	13.7	11.5	11.5
1.6–2.0							
Number	1,992	12	57	134	227	436	1,126
Percent	19.5	16.2	29.5	30.7	28.0	23.5	16.5
2.1–2.5							
Number	1,992	20	44	121	220	486	1,101
Percent	19.5	27.0	22.8	27.7	27.1	26.2	16.1
2.6–3.0							
Number	1,368	14	28	53	116	306	851
Percent	13.4	18.9	14.5	12.1	14.3	16.5	12.5
3.1–3.5							
Number	908	7	17	33	74	165	612
Percent	8.9	9.5	8.8	7.6	9.1	8.9	9.0
3.6–4.0							
Number	620	6	9	10	25	95	475
Percent	6.1	8.1	4.7	2.3	3.1	5.1	6.9
4.1–4.5							
Number	426	6	6	5	6	49	354
Percent	4.2	8.1	3.1	1.1	0.7	2.6	5.2
4.6–5.0							
Number	260	3	2	2	5	22	226
Percent	2.5	4.1	1.0	0.5	0.6	1.2	3.3
5.1 and over							
Number	786	5	0	4	5	24	748
Percent	7.7	6.8	0.0	0.9	0.6	1.3	10.9

[1] Full-time law enforcement employees include civilians.

[2] The number of agencies used to compile these figures differs from other tables that include data about law enforcement employees because agencies with no resident population are excluded from this table. These agencies include those associated with universities and colleges (see Table 79) and other agencies (see Table 81), as well as some state agencies that have concurrent jurisdiction with other local law enforcement.

[3] Because of rounding, the percentages may not add to 100.0.

Table 73. Full-Time Law Enforcement Officers, by Rate Range, 2010

(Number, rate per 1,000 population)

Rate range	Total cities[1] (10,204 cities; population 197,172,429)	Group I (74 cities, 250,000 and over; population 56,581,538)	Group II (193 cities, 100,000 to 249,999; population 28,908,827)	Group III (437 cities, 50,000 to 99,999; population 29,978,412)	Group IV (812 cities, 25,000 to 49,999; population 27,951,300)	Group V (1,853 cities, 10,000 to 24,999; population 29,350,253)	Group VI (6,835 cities, under 10,000; population 24,402,099)
Total Cities							
Number	10,204	74	193	437	812	1,853	6,835
Percent[2]	100.0	100.0	100.0	100.0	100.0	100.0	100.0
0.1–0.5							
Number	142	0	0	0	3	7	132
Percent	1.4	0.0	0.0	0.0	0.4	0.4	1.9
0.6–1.0							
Number	721	2	17	49	61	91	501
Percent	7.1	2.7	8.8	11.2	7.5	4.9	7.3
1.1–1.5							
Number	1,973	11	65	152	249	460	1,036
Percent	19.3	14.9	33.7	34.8	30.7	24.8	15.2
1.6–2.0							
Number	2,621	28	59	130	284	658	1,462
Percent	25.7	37.8	30.6	29.7	35.0	35.5	21.4
2.1–2.5							
Number	1,764	11	25	72	122	356	1,178
Percent	17.3	14.9	13.0	16.5	15.0	19.2	17.2
2.6–3.0							
Number	1,062	8	15	16	69	153	801
Percent	10.4	10.8	7.8	3.7	8.5	8.3	11.7
3.1–3.5							
Number	690	5	7	12	16	77	573
Percent	6.8	6.8	3.6	2.7	2.0	4.2	8.4
3.6–4.0							
Number	359	2	5	1	5	35	311
Percent	3.5	2.7	2.6	0.2	0.6	1.9	4.6
4.1–4.5							
Number	269	4	0	3	0	10	252
Percent	2.6	5.4	0.0	0.7	0.0	0.5	3.7
4.6–5.0							
Number	140	2	0	2	0	2	134
Percent	1.4	2.7	0.0	0.5	0.0	0.1	2.0
5.1 and over							
Number	463	1	0	0	3	4	455
Percent	4.5	1.4	0.0	0.0	0.4	0.2	6.7

[1] The number of agencies used to compile these figures differs from other tables that include data about law enforcement officers because agencies with no resident population are excluded from this table. These agencies include those associated with universities and colleges (see Table 79) and other agencies (see Table 81), as well as some state agencies that have concurrent jurisdiction with other local law enforcement.
[2] Because of rounding, the percentages may not add to 100.0.

Table 74. Full-Time Law Enforcement Employees, by Population Group, Percent Male and Female, 2010

(Number, percent)

Population group	Total law enforcement employees	Percent law enforcement employees		Total officers	Percent officers		Total civilians	Percent civilians		Number of agencies	2010 estimated population
		Male	Female		Male	Female		Male	Female		
TOTAL AGENCIES...................................	1,013,608	73.3	26.7	705,009	88.2	11.8	308,599	39.2	60.8	14,744	291,414,594
Total Cities..	577,677	75.5	24.5	448,905	88.2	11.8	128,772	31.4	68.6	11,356	197,172,429
GROUP I (250,000 and over)	201,067	71.6	28.4	154,306	83.2	16.8	46,761	33.6	66.4	74	56,581,538
1,000,000 and over (Group I subset)	109,760	70.3	29.7	82,949	81.9	18.1	26,811	34.5	65.5	10	25,823,829
500,000 to 999,999 (Group I subset)	53,777	74.1	25.9	42,239	84.3	15.7	11,538	36.8	63.2	24	16,642,397
250,000 to 499,999 (Group I subset)	37,530	72.0	28.0	29,118	85.1	14.9	8,412	26.6	73.4	40	14,115,312
GROUP II (100,000 to 249,999)...................	68,705	73.3	26.7	52,541	87.9	12.1	16,164	25.9	74.1	193	28,908,827
GROUP III (50,000 to 99,999)	65,955	76.2	23.8	51,072	90.3	9.7	14,883	27.9	72.1	437	29,978,412
GROUP IV (25,000 to 49,999)	62,927	78.2	21.8	49,883	91.4	8.6	13,044	27.6	72.4	812	27,951,300
GROUP V (10,000 to 24,999)	69,615	79.4	20.6	55,959	92.2	7.8	13,656	26.8	73.2	1,853	29,350,253
GROUP VI (under 10,000)..........................	109,408	79.5	20.5	85,144	91.5	8.5	24,264	37.5	62.5	7,987	24,402,099
Metropolitan Counties.................................	302,405	69.6	30.4	176,658	86.6	13.4	125,747	45.7	54.3	1,254	66,864,768
Nonmetropolitan Counties.........................	133,526	72.1	27.9	79,446	92.3	7.7	54,080	42.5	57.5	2,134	27,377,397
SUBURBAN AREAS[1]..............................	469,656	73.0	27.0	307,593	88.6	11.4	162,063	43.2	56.8	7,675	124,334,967

[1] Suburban areas include law enforcement agencies in cities with less than 50,000 inhabitants and county law enforcement agencies that are within a Metropolitan Statistical Area. Suburban areas exclude all metropolitan agencies associated with a principal city. The agencies associated with suburban areas also appear in other groups within this table.

Table 75. Full-Time Civilian Law Enforcement Employees, by Population Group, 2010

(Number, percent)

Population group	Percent civilian employees	Number of Agencies	2010 estimated population
TOTAL AGENCIES...	30.4	14,744	291,414,594
Total Cities...	22.3	11,356	197,172,429
GROUP I (250,000 and over)	23.3	74	56,581,538
1,000,000 and over (Group I subset)	24.4	10	25,823,829
500,000 to 999,999 (Group I subset).......................	21.5	24	16,642,397
250,000 to 499,999 (Group I subset).......................	22.4	40	14,115,312
GROUP II (100,000 to 249,999)	23.5	193	28,908,827
GROUP III (50,000 to 99,999).............................	22.6	437	29,978,412
GROUP IV (25,000 to 49,999)..............................	20.7	812	27,951,300
GROUP V (10,000 to 24,999)	19.6	1,853	29,350,253
GROUP VI (under 10,000)	22.2	7,987	24,402,099
Metropolitan Counties..	41.6	1,254	66,864,768
Nonmetropolitan Counties.....................................	40.5	2,134	27,377,397
SUBURBAN AREAS[1]	34.5	7,675	124,334,967

[1] Suburban areas include law enforcement agencies in cities with less than 50,000 inhabitants and county law enforcement agencies that are within a Metropolitan Statistical Area. Suburban areas exclude all metropolitan agencies associated with a principal city. The agencies associated with suburban areas also appear in other groups within this table.

Table 76.   Full-Time State Law Enforcement Employees, by State, 2010

(Number)

State/agency	Total law enforcement employees	Total officers		Total civilians	
		Male	Female	Male	Female
Alabama					
Highway Patrol....................	643	510	9	36	88
Other state agencies..................	306	248	11	7	40
Alaska					
State Troopers.....................	589	324	11	123	131
Arizona					
Department of Public Safety	1,907	1,074	59	299	475
Other state agencies..................	55	28	1	14	12
Arkansas					
State Police	943	506	25	118	294
Other state agencies..................	32	28	1	0	3
California					
Highway Patrol....................	11,101	7,050	610	1,477	1,964
Other state agencies..................	1,235	914	225	18	78
Colorado					
State Patrol	998	680	48	87	183
Other state agencies..................	285	74	33	71	107
Connecticut					
State Police	1,690	1,084	86	243	277
Other state agencies..................	36	26	1	7	2
Delaware					
State Police	891	588	74	101	128
Other state agencies..................	656	275	101	58	222
Florida					
Highway Patrol....................	2,077	1,392	180	165	340
Other state agencies..................	2,933	1,251	171	520	991
Georgia					
Department of Public Safety	1,457	1,002	48	168	239
Other state agencies..................	1,209	233	296	136	544
Idaho					
State Police	459	246	10	58	145
Illinois					
State Police	3,275	1,777	211	486	801
Other state agencies..................	434	276	23	75	60
Indiana					
State Police	1,861	1,226	64	226	345
Other state agencies..................	102	78	16	0	8
Iowa					
Department of Public Safety	941	594	41	146	160
Kansas					
Highway Patrol....................	820	517	17	108	178
Other state agencies..................	553	298	19	86	150
Kentucky					
State Police	1,897	1,088	30	390	389
Other state agencies..................	430	346	29	20	35
Louisiana					
State Police	1,710	1,129	52	166	363
Other state agencies..................	44	34	3	0	7
Maine					
State Police	428	280	21	58	69
Other state agencies[1]	53	23	1	19	10
Maryland					
State Police	2,151	1,294	102	410	345
Other state agencies..................	1,695	882	143	325	345
Massachusetts					
State Police	2,388	1,754	163	185	286
Other state agencies[1]	277	226	41	3	7
Michigan					
State Police	2,475	1,449	205	336	485
Minnesota					
State Patrol	769	486	56	118	109
Other state agencies..................	58	17	1	33	7
Mississippi					
Highway Safety Patrol..................	1,094	518	9	176	391
Other State Agencies..................	74	56	5	1	12
Missouri					
State Highway Patrol..................	2,209	1,058	51	489	611
Other state agencies..................	516	453	30	1	32
Montana					
Highway Patrol....................	279	217	9	15	38
Other state agencies..................	24	21	0	0	3
Nebraska					
State Patrol	715	450	25	85	155
Nevada					
Highway Patrol....................	943	470	65	122	286
Other state agencies..................	55	24	3	13	15

Note: Caution should be used when comparing data from one state to that of another. The responsibilities of the various state police, highway patrol, and department of public safety agencies range from full law enforcement duties to only traffic patrol, which can impact both the level of employment for agencies as well as the ratio of sworn officers to civilians employed. Any valid comparison must take these factors and the other identified variables affecting crime into consideration.

[1] The total employee count includes employees from agencies that are not represented in other law enforcement employee tables.

Table 76. Full-Time State Law Enforcement Employees, by State, 2009 *(Contd.)*

(Number)

State/agency	Total law enforcement employees	Total officers		Total civilians	
		Male	Female	Male	Female
New Hampshire					
State Police	501	304	33	54	110
Other state agencies	33	18	3	4	8
New Jersey					
State Police	4,233	2,826	110	605	692
Other state agencies	566	452	43	41	30
Port Authority of New York and New Jersey[2]	965	830	65	12	58
New Mexico					
State Police	643	479	21	43	100
New York					
State Police	5,736	4,317	391	440	588
Other state agencies	276	226	23	11	16
North Carolina					
Highway Patrol	2,218	1,657	46	276	239
Other state agencies	744	546	59	63	76
North Dakota					
Highway Patrol	187	133	6	19	29
Ohio					
Highway Patrol	2,486	1,361	132	496	497
Other state agencies	495	365	28	29	73
Oklahoma					
Department of Public Safety	1,437	812	15	246	364
Other state agencies	67	31	4	22	10
Oregon					
State Police	815	582	47	70	116
Other state agencies	48	31	10	0	7
Pennsylvania					
State Police	4,277	3,549	173	240	315
Other state agencies	174	142	7	16	9
Rhode Island					
State Police	285	216	19	32	18
Other state agencies	89	68	4	12	5
South Carolina					
Highway Patrol	1,001	792	23	67	119
Other state agencies[1]	1,198	751	144	179	124
South Dakota					
Highway Patrol	265	161	5	65	34
Other state agencies	154	40	4	41	69
Tennessee					
Department of Safety	1,621	800	33	224	564
Other state agencies	1,023	562	75	121	265
Texas					
Department of Public Safety	8,208	3,291	195	1,626	3,096
Utah					
Highway Patrol	544	405	18	30	91
Other state agencies	158	136	12	6	4
Vermont					
State Police	430	301	26	35	68
Other state agencies	107	83	4	4	16
Virginia					
State Police	2,521	1,754	104	200	463
Other state agencies	754	478	57	82	137
Washington					
State Patrol	2,233	995	76	574	588
Other State Agencies	6	4	0	0	2
West Virginia					
State Police	1,005	627	19	124	235
Other state agencies	184	153	1	13	17
Wisconsin					
State Patrol	646	442	54	61	89
Other state agencies	510	404	59	19	28
Wyoming					
Highway Patrol	360	192	9	59	100

Note: Caution should be used when comparing data from one state to that of another. The responsibilities of the various state police, highway patrol, and department of public safety agencies range from full law enforcement duties to only traffic patrol, which can impact both the level of employment for agencies as well as the ratio of sworn officers to civilians employed. Any valid comparison must take these factors and the other identified variables affecting crime into consideration.

[1] The total employee count includes employees from agencies that are not represented in other law enforcement employee tables.

[2] Data reported are the number of law enforcement employees for the state of New Jersey.

Table 77.   Full-Time Law Enforcement Employees, by State, 2010

(Number)

State	Total law enforcement employees	Total officers		Total civilians		Number of agencies	2010 estimated population
		Male	Female	Male	Female		
Alabama	16,205	10,134	796	2,016	3,259	346	4,637,287
Alaska	1,944	1,116	103	256	469	40	709,604
Arizona	22,130	11,261	1,345	4,336	5,188	106	6,304,972
Arkansas	9,964	5,671	504	1,471	2,318	280	2,913,580
California	118,884	68,635	10,361	14,336	25,552	460	32,115,492
Colorado	17,071	10,074	1,462	1,892	3,643	234	5,026,084
Connecticut	10,476	7,812	807	788	1,069	103	3,574,097
Delaware	3,170	2,006	317	311	536	54	897,563
District of Columbia	4,477	3,046	899	210	322	1	601,723
Florida	72,390	37,849	6,389	10,229	17,923	361	17,887,439
Georgia	32,780	20,552	4,029	2,668	5,531	426	8,639,939
Hawaii	3,725	2,654	293	235	543	4	1,360,301
Idaho	4,341	2,603	190	314	1,234	110	1,565,006
Illinois	49,849	29,991	5,452	6,968	7,438	778	12,749,781
Indiana	15,577	9,808	761	2,315	2,693	237	5,852,251
Iowa	8,085	4,875	428	1,079	1,703	238	3,038,644
Kansas	10,565	6,388	609	1,390	2,178	337	2,600,455
Kentucky	10,104	7,526	525	773	1,280	344	4,098,561
Louisiana	18,493	11,270	2,554	1,712	2,957	147	3,407,020
Maine	2,839	2,109	141	242	347	134	1,327,392
Maryland	20,467	13,410	2,085	1,891	3,081	132	5,593,253
Massachusetts	19,574	14,786	1,366	1,356	2,066	347	6,493,971
Michigan	24,426	15,772	2,457	2,737	3,460	629	9,709,589
Minnesota	13,509	7,761	1,064	1,936	2,748	322	5,220,467
Mississippi	10,325	5,636	518	1,715	2,456	190	2,795,693
Missouri	20,375	13,156	1,444	2,185	3,590	564	5,882,476
Montana	2,941	1,754	105	477	605	115	988,583
Nebraska	4,835	3,134	393	346	962	158	1,778,848
Nevada	9,873	5,301	580	1,430	2,562	44	2,700,551
New Hampshire	3,441	2,401	205	255	580	153	1,192,506
New Jersey	39,996	28,461	2,604	3,297	5,634	545	8,491,420
New Mexico	6,030	3,957	436	549	1,088	109	2,008,152
New York	83,394	53,432	8,481	7,664	13,817	466	19,194,379
North Carolina	32,755	20,401	2,519	4,426	5,409	510	9,530,637
North Dakota	1,840	1,205	134	193	308	107	668,266
Ohio	27,987	17,782	1,901	3,465	4,839	607	9,362,390
Oklahoma	11,667	7,073	569	1,692	2,333	330	3,749,477
Oregon	10,195	5,524	606	1,746	2,319	209	3,794,249
Pennsylvania	29,488	22,509	2,646	1,536	2,797	987	9,609,935
Rhode Island	3,164	2,356	182	286	340	48	1,052,567
South Carolina	14,030	9,134	1,220	1,349	2,327	274	4,220,787
South Dakota	2,411	1,413	98	384	516	142	812,168
Tennessee	25,671	14,474	1,543	4,405	5,249	453	6,341,016
Texas	89,897	48,620	6,272	15,209	19,796	1,011	25,006,973
Utah	6,987	4,499	371	871	1,246	135	2,763,885
Vermont	1,516	1,059	99	119	239	69	365,443
Virginia	23,390	16,199	2,181	1,368	3,642	279	7,998,552
Washington	14,555	9,451	954	1,460	2,690	259	6,708,828
West Virginia	4,415	3,361	112	360	582	351	1,841,354
Wisconsin	19,423	11,328	1,767	2,544	3,784	393	5,671,361
Wyoming	1,962	1,295	108	125	434	66	559,627

NOTE: Caution should be used when comparing data from one state to that of another. The responsibilities of the various state police, highway patrol, and department of public safety agencies range from full law enforcement duties to only traffic patrol which can impact both the level of employment for agencies as well as the ratio of sworn officers to civilians employed. Any valid comparison must take these factors and the other identified variables affecting crime into consideration.

Table 78. Full-Time Law Enforcement Employees by State and City, 2010

(Number)

State/city	Population	Total law enforcement employees	Total officers	Total civilians	State/city	Population	Total law enforcement employees	Total officers	Total civilians
ALABAMA					Enterprise	26,649	71	54	17
Abbeville	2,950	14	7	7	Eufaula	14,709	48	33	15
Adamsville	4,796	27	17	10	Eutaw	2,833	10	9	1
Addison	714	3	3	0	Evergreen	3,468	18	16	2
Alabaster	30,781	77	63	14	Excel	609	1	1	0
Albertville	20,588	58	38	20	Fairfield	11,344	47	33	14
Alexander City	15,229	67	49	18	Falkville	1,229	4	4	0
Aliceville	2,423	8	7	1	Fayette	4,676	11	11	0
Andalusia	8,946	39	29	10	Flomaton	1,547	8	4	4
Anniston	23,703	138	98	40	Florala	1,878	6	6	0
Arab	8,438	38	25	13	Florence	38,643	131	106	25
Ardmore	1,328	11	7	4	Foley	15,044	84	58	26
Argo	2,005	5	5	0	Fort Deposit	1,154	4	4	0
Ariton	750	1	1	0	Fort Payne	14,418	36	32	4
Arley	320	3	1	2	Fultondale	7,095	28	24	4
Ashford	2,146	9	5	4	Gadsden	36,835	129	98	31
Ashland	1,900	11	6	5	Gardendale	14,048	35	27	8
Ashville	2,708	5	5	0	Geneva	4,488	16	11	5
Athens	24,989	56	45	11	Geraldine	857	3	3	0
Atmore	10,182	34	27	7	Glencoe	5,393	9	7	2
Attalla	6,621	25	20	5	Goodwater	1,476	7	4	3
Auburn	59,651	113	107	6	Gordo	1,520	4	4	0
Autaugaville	891	1	1	0	Grant	732	2	2	0
Bay Minette	8,468	34	25	9	Greensboro	2,529	10	9	1
Bayou La Batre	3,253	19	14	5	Greenville	6,961	33	26	7
Beatrice	384	1	1	0	Guin	2,146	5	5	0
Berry	1,176	3	3	0	Gulf Shores	10,999	48	36	12
Bessemer	28,881	137	104	33	Guntersville	8,775	43	30	13
Birmingham	231,009	1,163	858	305	Gurley	885	5	4	1
Blountsville	2,042	5	5	0	Hackleburg	1,432	4	4	0
Boaz	8,656	33	23	10	Haleyville	4,080	16	11	5
Brantley	912	4	4	0	Hamilton	6,324	13	12	1
Brent	4,361	5	5	0	Hammondville	556	2	2	0
Brewton	5,262	34	26	8	Hanceville	3,531	19	13	6
Brighton	3,381	13	7	6	Harpersville	1,869	9	9	0
Brundidge	2,271	14	9	5	Hartford	2,447	13	8	5
Butler	1,681	5	5	0	Hartselle	14,258	37	29	8
Calera	12,424	32	26	6	Hayneville	1,090	4	4	0
Camden	2,153	8	7	1	Headland	4,061	17	12	5
Carbon Hill	2,040	9	5	4	Heflin	3,592	11	11	0
Carrollton	911	4	4	0	Helena	15,845	25	21	4
Cedar Bluff	1,666	4	4	0	Henagar	2,654	9	5	4
Centre	3,515	8	7	1	Hokes Bluff	4,531	7	7	0
Centreville	2,646	6	6	0	Hollywood	923	2	2	0
Chatom	1,153	6	6	0	Homewood	24,101	113	74	39
Cherokee	1,164	4	4	0	Hoover	74,687	210	152	58
Chickasaw	5,948	27	21	6	Hueytown	15,942	43	35	8
Childersburg	4,967	17	15	2	Huntsville	183,357	482	377	105
Clanton	9,109	28	25	3	Hurtsboro	546	4	4	0
Clayhatchee	496	1	1	0	Ider	733	5	4	1
Cleveland	1,460	1	1	0	Irondale	9,865	33	27	6
Collinsville	2,026	9	4	5	Jackson	5,112	23	17	6
Columbia	866	2	2	0	Jacksonville	10,467	31	26	5
Columbiana	4,210	12	8	4	Jasper	14,138	75	57	18
Coosada	1,731	3	3	0	Jemison	3,077	12	12	0
Cordova	2,265	7	5	2	Killen	1,154	6	5	1
Cottonwood	1,231	3	3	0	Kimberly	3,027	6	5	1
Creola	2,100	11	6	5	Kinsey	2,058	3	2	1
Crossville	1,535	4	4	0	Kinston	630	1	1	0
Cullman	15,540	66	48	18	Lafayette	2,875	17	16	1
Dadeville	3,265	15	14	1	Lake View	2,630	5	4	1
Daleville	4,561	24	18	6	Lanett	7,026	30	27	3
Daphne	20,018	76	46	30	Leeds	11,679	30	24	6
Dauphin Island	1,640	14	9	5	Leesburg	827	3	3	0
Decatur	57,153	153	132	21	Level Plains	1,537	4	4	0
Dora	2,431	6	3	3	Lincoln	6,279	16	15	1
Dothan	69,134	214	150	64	Linden	2,225	6	6	0
Double Springs	975	6	6	0	Lineville	2,333	12	8	4
Douglas	643	5	5	0	Lipscomb	2,036	9	6	3
Dozier	398	1	1	0	Littleville	1,056	8	4	4
East Brewton	2,491	6	4	2	Livingston	2,869	10	6	4
Eclectic	1,183	9	5	4	Louisville	573	4	4	0
Elba	4,254	22	13	9	Loxley	2,063	18	11	7
Elberta	1,527	6	5	1	Luverne	2,777	14	10	4

Table 78. Full-Time Law Enforcement Employees by State and City, 2010—*Continued*

(Number)

State/city	Population	Total law enforcement employees	Total officers	Total civilians	State/city	Population	Total law enforcement employees	Total officers	Total civilians
Madison	41,426	100	73	27	Southside	8,731	15	10	5
Maplesville	706	6	5	1	Spanish Fort	7,873	24	20	4
Margaret	1,313	5	5	0	Springville	3,906	9	9	0
Marion	3,291	9	9	0	St. Florian	538	2	2	0
Mentone	492	1	1	0	Sulligent	1,949	6	6	0
Midfield	5,215	15	11	4	Sumiton	2,566	14	8	6
Midland City	1,927	7	4	3	Summerdale	787	6	5	1
Millbrook	17,750	39	29	10	Sylacauga	13,159	37	36	1
Millry	588	3	3	0	Sylvania	1,425	3	3	0
Mobile	255,178	766	523	243	Talladega	16,826	41	37	4
Monroeville	6,285	27	21	6	Tallassee	5,315	25	19	6
Montevallo	6,657	16	12	4	Tarrant	6,529	27	22	5
Montgomery	203,966	648	506	142	Taylor	2,059	2	2	0
Moody	14,726	18	17	1	Thomasville	4,433	21	15	6
Morris	1,927	8	6	2	Thorsby	2,148	5	5	0
Moulton	3,259	11	11	0	Town Creek	1,213	3	3	0
Mountain Brook	21,312	63	50	13	Triana	510	2	2	0
Mount Vernon	819	12	6	6	Trinity	2,079	7	7	0
Muscle Shoals	13,277	43	34	9	Troy	15,395	68	48	20
Napier Field	398	2	2	0	Trussville	19,962	53	42	11
New Brockton	1,258	4	2	2	Tuscaloosa	95,570	355	282	73
New Hope	2,901	4	4	0	Tuscumbia	8,490	28	21	7
New Site	843	1	1	0	Tuskegee	11,065	28	17	11
Newton	1,662	4	4	0	Union Springs	4,801	20	12	8
North Courtland	805	6	5	1	Valley	9,966	38	28	10
Northport	24,019	80	61	19	Valley Head	667	3	2	1
Oakman	921	1	1	0	Vance	1,307	3	3	0
Odenville	2,968	9	9	0	Vernon	1,863	7	7	0
Ohatchee	1,285	5	5	0	Vestavia Hills	31,420	70	68	2
Oneonta	7,317	21	20	1	Warrior	3,171	17	12	5
Opelika	28,815	103	82	21	Weaver	2,972	12	9	3
Opp	6,552	27	20	7	Webb	1,417	2	2	0
Orange Beach	6,575	48	31	17	Wedowee	823	7	7	0
Oxford	21,171	59	50	9	West Blocton	1,422	5	5	0
Ozark	14,669	36	31	5	Wetumpka	8,101	39	30	9
Parrish	1,252	10	6	4	Winfield	4,573	10	9	1
Pelham	22,777	81	66	15	Woodstock	1,099	3	3	0
Pell City	13,637	35	32	3	Woodville	748	2	2	0
Phenix City	31,662	107	83	24	**ALASKA**				
Phil Campbell	1,061	2	2	0	Anchorage	290,334	526	373	153
Pickensville	626	2	1	1	Bethel	6,667	22	12	10
Piedmont	4,994	14	10	4	Bristol Bay Borough	856	8	3	5
Pinckard	623	2	2	0	Cordova	2,231	10	4	6
Pine Hill	878	4	4	0	Craig	1,184	11	5	6
Pleasant Grove	10,407	25	19	6	Dillingham	2,496	17	6	11
Powell	1,002	1	1	0	Fairbanks	35,989	51	48	3
Prattville	33,738	91	81	10	Haines	2,412	10	5	5
Priceville	3,072	5	5	0	Homer	6,158	20	11	9
Prichard	27,725	48	34	14	Hoonah	686	5	2	3
Ragland	2,232	4	4	0	Houston	2,412	3	2	1
Rainbow City	9,569	33	22	11	Juneau	30,966	85	49	36
Rainsville	5,141	15	11	4	Kenai	8,094	28	19	9
Ranburne	488	2	2	0	Ketchikan	7,479	33	21	12
Red Bay	3,338	11	7	4	Klawock	739	4	4	0
Reform	1,751	5	5	0	Kodiak	6,387	36	17	19
Riverside	2,146	3	3	0	Kotzebue	3,173	19	9	10
Roanoke	6,716	26	21	5	Nome	3,688	16	9	7
Robertsdale	5,320	26	13	13	North Pole	2,318	15	14	1
Rockford	386	2	1	1	North Slope Borough	6,728	61	36	25
Rogersville	1,219	5	5	0	Palmer	8,964	30	15	15
Russellville	9,041	26	22	4	Petersburg	2,797	13	7	6
Samson	2,039	7	6	1	Sand Point	969	8	4	4
Saraland	13,238	43	32	11	Seldovia	325	1	1	0
Sardis City	2,227	4	4	0	Seward	3,224	24	10	14
Satsuma	6,120	17	13	4	Sitka	8,783	29	15	14
Scottsboro	15,018	70	46	24	Skagway	930	7	3	4
Section	757	2	2	0	Soldotna	4,621	15	13	2
Selma	18,238	75	53	22	St. Paul	431	6	3	3
Sheffield	9,053	34	29	5	Togiak	819	2	2	0
Shorter	372	7	4	3	Unalaska	3,539	24	12	12
Silas	472	2	1	1	Valdez	3,786	20	11	9
Sipsey	550	2	2	0	Wasilla	11,471	46	22	24
Skyline	883	3	1	2	Whittier	156	4	4	0
Slocomb	2,065	8	6	2	Wrangell	2,130	14	7	7
Snead	879	4	4	0					
Somerville	662	3	3	0					

Table 78. Full-Time Law Enforcement Employees by State and City, 2010—*Continued*

(Number)

State/city	Population	Total law enforcement employees	Total officers	Total civilians	State/city	Population	Total law enforcement employees	Total officers	Total civilians
ARIZONA					**ARKANSAS**				
Apache Junction	33,225	88	51	37	Alma	5,318	19	11	8
Avondale	82,580	163	113	50	Altheimer	1,102	1	1	0
Benson	4,985	25	15	10	Arkadelphia	11,213	27	22	5
Bisbee	5,778	22	15	7	Arkansas City	506	2	1	1
Buckeye	50,008	83	63	20	Ashdown	4,448	12	11	1
Bullhead City	39,488	130	77	53	Ash Flat	1,099	3	3	0
Camp Verde	10,535	30	19	11	Atkins	2,992	7	6	1
Casa Grande	42,522	103	74	29	Augusta	2,176	4	4	0
Chandler	241,826	478	320	158	Austin	2,260	3	3	0
Chino Valley	10,837	38	27	11	Bald Knob	3,456	10	6	4
Clarkdale	4,121	9	7	2	Barling	4,587	10	10	0
Clifton	2,490	9	5	4	Bay	2,085	4	3	1
Colorado City	4,524	4	4	0	Bearden	999	1	1	0
Coolidge	10,737	41	31	10	Beebe	7,173	17	10	7
Cottonwood	11,010	47	30	17	Bella Vista	26,745	29	20	9
Douglas	16,912	47	34	13	Benton	30,692	64	54	10
Eagar	4,376	11	8	3	Bentonville	39,161	83	57	26
El Mirage	24,047	51	44	7	Berryville	5,391	13	11	2
Eloy	12,897	39	29	10	Blytheville	15,787	61	42	19
Flagstaff	58,739	161	112	49	Bono	1,634	4	4	0
Florence	21,096	37	26	11	Booneville	4,024	12	8	4
Fredonia	1,110	3	3	0	Bradford	973	3	3	0
Gilbert	215,215	320	214	106	Brinkley	3,004	16	12	4
Glendale	245,387	553	408	145	Bryant	16,740	42	31	11
Globe	6,936	31	24	7	Bull Shoals	2,138	3	3	0
Goodyear	61,721	127	94	33	Cabot	24,900	46	36	10
Hayden	1,194	9	8	1	Caddo Valley	654	4	4	0
Holbrook	4,926	21	15	6	Camden	11,163	39	24	15
Huachuca City	1,896	9	4	5	Cammack Village	782	3	2	1
Jerome	366	5	5	0	Caraway	1,417	3	3	0
Kearny	3,340	8	5	3	Carlisle	2,470	9	5	4
Kingman	26,671	80	55	25	Cave City	2,028	3	3	0
Lake Havasu City	53,938	116	86	30	Cave Springs	1,892	5	4	1
Mammoth	2,618	11	5	6	Centerton	9,788	11	10	1
Marana	34,039	99	74	25	Charleston	2,999	4	4	0
Maricopa	43,310	59	53	6	Cherokee Village	4,710	10	9	1
Mesa	452,725	1,186	776	410	Clarendon	1,564	4	4	0
Miami	1,710	9	6	3	Clarksville	8,843	22	18	4
Nogales	19,399	84	65	19	Clinton	2,609	8	7	1
Oro Valley	42,644	125	97	28	Conway	61,425	154	111	43
Page	6,854	31	19	12	Corning	3,217	14	9	5
Paradise Valley	14,715	35	27	8	Cotter	1,096	2	2	0
Parker	3,024	13	11	2	Crossett	5,349	26	15	11
Payson	15,067	43	28	15	Danville	2,529	6	5	1
Peoria	158,184	279	184	95	Dardanelle	4,548	14	10	4
Phoenix	1,544,427	4,198	3,146	1,052	Decatur	2,143	6	6	0
Pima	2,130	6	6	0	De Queen	6,251	16	13	3
Pinetop-Lakeside	4,382	23	14	9	Dermott	3,158	14	8	6
Prescott	41,428	85	64	21	Des Arc	1,687	4	4	0
Prescott Valley	37,275	73	58	15	De Witt	3,175	14	9	5
Quartzsite	3,359	14	13	1	Diaz	1,108	2	2	0
Safford	9,528	23	19	4	Dierks	1,235	3	3	0
Sahuarita	24,067	51	43	8	Dover	1,412	4	4	0
Scottsdale	230,496	676	423	253	Dumas	4,496	24	12	12
Sedona	11,240	34	26	8	Earle	2,732	8	6	2
Show Low	11,965	44	30	14	El Dorado	19,441	71	54	17
Sierra Vista	41,892	89	62	27	Elkins	2,703	6	6	0
Snowflake-Taylor	9,563	21	13	8	England	3,086	11	6	5
Somerton	12,360	29	20	9	Etowah	342	1	1	0
South Tucson	5,855	18	15	3	Eudora	2,248	9	5	4
Springerville	1,943	9	7	2	Eureka Springs	2,402	15	10	5
St. Johns	3,561	13	10	3	Fairfield Bay	2,460	16	7	9
Surprise	92,294	175	124	51	Farmington	4,795	11	10	1
Tempe	173,004	487	338	149	Fayetteville	79,237	160	113	47
Thatcher	4,913	12	11	1	Flippin	1,357	5	5	0
Tolleson	7,103	40	30	10	Fordyce	4,087	10	6	4
Tombstone	1,514	9	5	4	Forrest City	13,052	42	31	11
Tucson	527,107	1,295	974	321	Fort Smith	86,096	209	164	45
Wellton	1,891	8	8	0	Gassville	2,210	4	4	0
Wickenburg	6,448	20	14	6	Gentry	3,200	10	8	2
Willcox	3,704	20	11	9	Glenwood	1,986	3	3	0
Williams	3,233	17	9	8	Gosnell	3,541	9	9	0
Winslow	9,529	36	27	9	Gould	1,114	1	1	0
Youngtown	4,759	9	8	1	Gravette	2,756	8	7	1
Yuma	88,291	235	155	80	Greenbrier	4,746	13	9	4

Table 78. Full-Time Law Enforcement Employees by State and City, 2010—*Continued*

(Number)

State/city	Population	Total law enforcement employees	Total officers	Total civilians	State/city	Population	Total law enforcement employees	Total officers	Total civilians
Green Forest	3,106	8	6	2	Plummerville	867	4	4	0
Greenland	1,278	4	4	0	Pocahontas	6,631	14	13	1
Greenwood	8,937	22	20	2	Pottsville	2,941	5	5	0
Greers Ferry	973	4	3	1	Prairie Grove	3,986	8	8	0
Gurdon	2,251	4	3	1	Prescott	4,406	10	9	1
Guy	569	2	1	1	Quitman	742	4	4	0
Hamburg	2,644	5	4	1	Ravenden	493	1	1	0
Hampton	1,392	2	2	0	Redfield	1,191	5	4	1
Hardy	799	3	3	0	Rison	1,241	3	3	0
Harrisburg	2,100	4	4	0	Rockport	809	6	5	1
Harrison	13,285	40	28	12	Rogers	61,417	135	100	35
Hazen	1,441	5	4	1	Rose Bud	460	3	2	1
Heber Springs	7,392	24	14	10	Russellville	27,992	62	54	8
Helena-West Helena	11,502	44	29	15	Salem	1,591	3	3	0
Hermitage	741	3	3	0	Searcy	23,791	63	45	18
Highfill	862	2	2	0	Sheridan	4,670	27	14	13
Highland	1,099	3	3	0	Sherwood	29,370	92	69	23
Hope	10,368	35	23	12	Siloam Springs	15,337	48	32	16
Horseshoe Bend	2,226	5	5	0	Smackover	1,843	5	4	1
Hot Springs	40,081	129	99	30	Springdale	71,047	166	117	49
Hoxie	2,619	5	4	1	Stamps	1,835	3	3	0
Huntsville	2,450	8	7	1	Star City	2,187	5	4	1
Jacksonville	31,833	83	69	14	Stuttgart	8,750	24	17	7
Jonesboro	67,382	159	148	11	Sulphur Springs	724	2	2	0
Judsonia	2,207	2	2	0	Swifton	757	1	1	0
Keiser	790	1	1	0	Texarkana	30,488	121	80	41
Kensett	1,874	3	3	0	Trumann	6,766	23	16	7
Lake City	2,197	4	4	0	Tuckerman	1,580	4	3	1
Lakeview	849	2	2	0	Van Buren	23,072	57	43	14
Lake Village	2,301	16	9	7	Vilonia	3,753	8	8	0
Leachville	1,824	3	3	0	Waldron	3,523	10	9	1
Lepanto	2,001	8	4	4	Walnut Ridge	4,700	9	8	1
Lewisville	1,105	2	2	0	Ward	4,311	6	5	1
Lincoln	2,114	6	6	0	Warren	6,015	21	15	6
Little Flock	3,328	7	7	0	Weiner	715	1	1	0
Little Rock	192,922	635	525	110	West Fork	2,365	6	5	1
Lonoke	4,721	16	11	5	West Memphis	27,196	95	75	20
Lowell	7,660	22	15	7	White Hall	5,216	16	14	2
Luxora	1,210	2	2	0	Wynne	8,317	18	17	1
Magnolia	10,882	29	21	8	**CALIFORNIA**				
Malvern	8,842	24	21	3	Alameda	71,016	130	85	45
Mammoth Spring	1,090	2	2	0	Albany	16,096	34	25	9
Mansfield	1,126	4	4	0	Alhambra	84,987	128	84	44
Marianna	4,079	30	15	15	Alturas	2,733	8	7	1
Marion	12,769	27	24	3	Anaheim	338,492	548	389	159
Marked Tree	2,601	12	8	4	Anderson	10,851	26	16	10
Marmaduke	1,177	4	4	0	Antioch	102,125	133	104	29
Marvell	1,065	9	5	4	Arcadia	56,465	95	65	30
Maumelle	17,331	37	27	10	Arcata	17,172	36	26	10
Mayflower	2,332	8	6	2	Arroyo Grande	17,358	31	25	6
McCrory	1,509	5	5	0	Arvin	15,410	27	18	9
McGehee	3,821	25	9	16	Atascadero	28,468	35	26	9
McRae	749	2	2	0	Atherton	7,527	22	17	5
Mena	5,605	14	13	1	Atwater	26,495	46	36	10
Mineral Springs	1,287	3	3	0	Auburn	13,432	29	22	7
Monette	1,255	3	3	0	Azusa	46,824	87	59	28
Monticello	9,207	26	21	5	Bakersfield	333,458	469	349	120
Morrilton	6,571	32	22	10	Baldwin Park	77,127	100	72	28
Mountain Home	12,642	34	27	7	Banning	29,563	44	33	11
Mountain View	3,121	9	8	1	Barstow	24,704	52	39	13
Mulberry	1,739	3	3	0	Bear Valley	4,655	17	8	9
Murfreesboro	1,625	2	2	0	Beaumont	37,399	73	56	17
Nashville	4,855	17	16	1	Bell	36,506	45	32	13
Newport	7,303	22	15	7	Bell Gardens	44,591	72	53	19
North Little Rock	60,129	219	188	31	Belmont	24,881	43	31	12
Ola	1,272	3	3	0	Belvedere	2,050	10	9	1
Osceola	7,807	37	24	13	Benicia	26,082	51	36	15
Ozark	3,532	10	8	2	Berkeley	102,700	267	171	96
Pangburn	708	1	1	0	Beverly Hills	34,329	181	127	54
Paragould	25,350	51	41	10	Bishop	3,412	18	12	6
Paris	3,553	14	9	5	Blythe	21,365	31	22	9
Pea Ridge	5,098	11	11	0	Brawley	23,464	52	38	14
Perryville	1,438	4	4	0	Brea	38,725	134	97	37
Piggott	3,372	10	8	2	Brentwood	53,312	77	61	16
Pine Bluff	49,971	161	136	25	Brisbane	3,712	16	13	3
Plainview	799	1	1	0	Broadmoor	4,428	9	9	0

Table 78.   Full-Time Law Enforcement Employees by State and City, 2010—*Continued*

(Number)

State/city	Population	Total law enforcement employees	Total officers	Total civilians	State/city	Population	Total law enforcement employees	Total officers	Total civilians
Buena Park	79,929	135	90	45	Galt	24,517	46	35	11
Burbank	103,304	236	149	87	Gardena	58,358	120	89	31
Burlingame	27,838	52	36	16	Garden Grove	166,287	229	161	68
Calexico	40,186	59	40	19	Gilroy	51,108	86	58	28
California City	15,573	22	15	7	Glendale	196,877	367	254	113
Calipatria	7,715	4	4	0	Glendora	49,720	92	49	43
Calistoga	5,252	15	11	4	Gonzales	8,830	12	9	3
Campbell	38,854	62	40	22	Grass Valley	12,330	31	23	8
Capitola	9,747	29	21	8	Greenfield	15,626	19	15	4
Carlsbad	100,461	157	110	47	Gridley	6,528	20	15	5
Carmel	3,882	20	13	7	Grover Beach	13,199	28	18	10
Cathedral City	53,449	91	53	38	Guadalupe	6,692	13	11	2
Ceres	43,505	66	49	17	Gustine	5,130	8	6	2
Chico	85,630	146	97	49	Half Moon Bay	12,648	15	12	3
Chino	84,170	150	102	48	Hanford	50,903	74	51	23
Chowchilla	19,795	23	17	6	Hawthorne	83,849	133	96	37
Chula Vista	229,060	312	230	82	Hayward	144,509	312	199	113
Citrus Heights	84,476	133	87	46	Healdsburg	11,146	24	16	8
City of Angels	3,774	7	6	1	Hemet	73,111	90	66	24
Claremont	35,527	58	35	23	Hercules	25,192	33	29	4
Clayton	11,487	13	11	2	Hermosa Beach	19,408	57	34	23
Clearlake	15,352	27	18	9	Hillsborough	10,951	34	25	9
Cloverdale	8,357	23	15	8	Hollister	35,056	33	25	8
Clovis	95,901	142	94	48	Huntington Beach	193,545	339	215	124
Coalinga	18,833	30	21	9	Huntington Park	60,514	119	69	50
Colma	1,456	24	17	7	Huron	8,220	15	11	4
Colton	50,706	81	58	23	Imperial	14,727	19	16	3
Colusa	5,952	9	8	1	Indio	89,621	106	70	36
Concord	122,119	196	147	49	Inglewood	112,100	270	188	82
Corcoran	25,112	31	19	12	Ione	7,744	7	6	1
Corning	7,323	25	15	10	Irvine	217,193	289	200	89
Corona	153,311	244	172	72	Irwindale	1,431	35	26	9
Coronado	22,033	61	43	18	Isleton	843	1	1	0
Costa Mesa	110,424	201	147	54	Jackson	4,258	10	9	1
Cotati	7,306	15	9	6	Kensington	5,430	10	10	0
Covina	46,728	85	55	30	Kerman	13,293	21	18	3
Crescent City	7,809	15	14	1	King City	11,704	22	19	3
Culver City	38,342	146	99	47	Kingsburg	11,461	21	14	7
Cypress	47,320	75	56	19	Laguna Beach	24,147	84	47	37
Daly City	101,939	152	108	44	La Habra	59,355	95	62	33
Davis	63,292	90	58	32	Lakeport	5,256	13	11	2
Delano	54,298	74	46	28	Lake Shastina	2,409	5	4	1
Del Rey Oaks	1,529	6	6	0	La Mesa	55,580	97	67	30
Desert Hot Springs	25,309	31	25	6	La Palma	15,733	32	24	8
Dinuba	21,094	45	35	10	La Verne	34,066	59	40	19
Dixon	17,518	28	24	4	Lemoore	24,766	34	27	7
Dos Palos	4,951	8	7	1	Lincoln	50,936	41	31	10
Downey	106,992	165	118	47	Lindsay	10,725	26	18	8
East Palo Alto	34,294	47	37	10	Livermore	81,769	128	83	45
El Cajon	94,311	184	120	64	Livingston	13,679	29	19	10
El Centro	41,535	75	52	23	Lodi	61,812	111	72	39
El Cerrito	22,263	51	43	8	Lompoc	41,049	70	50	20
Elk Grove	142,330	197	123	74	Long Beach	462,267	1,252	889	363
El Monte	121,884	172	127	45	Los Alamitos	11,698	26	22	4
El Segundo	16,181	88	63	25	Los Altos	28,652	47	30	17
Emeryville	10,207	55	38	17	Los Angeles	3,841,707	12,754	9,858	2,896
Escalon	7,463	13	10	3	Los Banos	36,124	58	38	20
Escondido	140,662	214	160	54	Los Gatos	29,558	61	42	19
Etna	764	2	1	1	Madera	58,147	77	59	18
Eureka	25,143	75	48	27	Mammoth Lakes	7,413	21	18	3
Exeter	10,048	18	17	1	Manhattan Beach	36,803	99	65	34
Fairfax	7,071	16	11	5	Manteca	67,344	86	59	27
Fairfield	104,202	182	114	68	Marina	17,921	39	30	9
Farmersville	10,211	16	14	2	Martinez	35,344	55	39	16
Ferndale	1,383	4	4	0	Marysville	11,548	30	20	10
Firebaugh	7,079	16	12	4	McFarland	12,452	10	7	3
Folsom	69,497	99	74	25	Mendota	10,690	14	12	2
Fontana	192,595	275	184	91	Menlo Park	30,202	73	48	25
Fort Bragg	6,550	21	16	5	Merced	77,484	132	96	36
Fortuna	11,434	27	18	9	Millbrae	21,295	22	18	4
Foster City	29,283	50	35	15	Mill Valley	13,372	26	21	5
Fountain Valley	55,879	76	56	20	Milpitas	68,371	106	84	22
Fowler	5,769	11	10	1	Modesto	203,890	319	236	83
Fremont	205,477	277	178	99	Monrovia	37,544	75	48	27
Fresno	484,734	1,007	793	214	Montclair	36,508	72	50	22
Fullerton	133,139	216	147	69	Montebello	61,570	109	71	38

Table 78.   Full-Time Law Enforcement Employees by State and City, 2010—*Continued*

(Number)

State/city	Population	Total law enforcement employees	Total officers	Total civilians	State/city	Population	Total law enforcement employees	Total officers	Total civilians
Monterey	27,619	66	50	16	San Marino	12,725	35	28	7
Monterey Park	61,662	102	72	30	San Mateo	92,724	142	106	36
Moraga	17,334	12	11	1	San Pablo	31,122	74	52	22
Morgan Hill	38,986	53	36	17	San Rafael	55,832	86	65	21
Morro Bay	10,382	22	16	6	San Ramon	50,006	78	58	20
Mountain View	72,321	137	94	43	Santa Ana	340,240	623	353	270
Mount Shasta	3,509	11	8	3	Santa Barbara	85,967	189	131	58
Murrieta	104,343	129	86	43	Santa Clara	112,917	219	137	82
Napa	75,482	107	66	41	Santa Cruz	56,860	109	88	21
National City	56,270	120	85	35	Santa Maria	87,803	149	105	44
Nevada City	2,936	13	12	1	Santa Monica	87,817	387	204	183
Newark	42,099	72	51	21	Santa Paula	28,810	40	30	10
Newman	10,544	15	12	3	Santa Rosa	158,182	244	168	76
Newport Beach	81,882	216	137	79	Sausalito	7,180	23	18	5
Novato	54,009	71	55	16	Scotts Valley	11,243	25	18	7
Oakdale	21,023	30	21	9	Seal Beach	24,225	49	30	19
Oakland	409,723	935	674	261	Seaside	34,057	50	41	9
Oceanside	173,901	292	208	84	Sebastopol	7,574	20	14	6
Ontario	172,814	329	224	105	Selma	23,169	39	31	8
Orange	137,606	232	158	74	Shafter	16,247	31	23	8
Orland	7,326	12	10	2	Sierra Madre	10,796	23	18	5
Oroville	14,718	36	23	13	Signal Hill	10,981	48	35	13
Oxnard	189,051	377	236	141	Simi Valley	121,755	173	115	58
Pacifica	37,917	48	36	12	Soledad	28,655	26	21	5
Pacific Grove	14,537	30	22	8	Sonora	4,627	17	12	5
Palm Springs	48,696	125	88	37	South Gate	96,182	125	84	41
Palo Alto	60,288	143	86	57	South Lake Tahoe	23,540	60	39	21
Palos Verdes Estates	13,553	31	21	10	South Pasadena	24,320	49	35	14
Paradise	26,424	37	24	13	South San Francisco	63,006	100	72	28
Parlier	13,532	19	16	3	Stallion Springs	1,674	3	3	0
Pasadena	144,496	359	240	119	St. Helena	5,908	15	11	4
Paso Robles	29,089	44	32	12	Stockton	292,047	532	342	190
Petaluma	55,168	93	67	26	Suisun City	27,053	37	25	12
Piedmont	10,519	27	19	8	Sunnyvale	134,073	286	213	73
Pinole	18,899	47	31	16	Susanville	17,067	18	16	2
Pismo Beach	8,639	34	23	11	Sutter Creek	2,690	5	5	0
Pittsburg	65,930	94	72	22	Taft	9,046	26	16	10
Placentia	50,237	64	46	18	Tehachapi	12,137	16	14	2
Placerville	10,124	25	18	7	Tiburon	8,728	17	13	4
Pleasant Hill	33,048	58	43	15	Torrance	140,411	335	217	118
Pleasanton	67,823	113	81	32	Tracy	81,712	127	85	42
Pomona	152,673	262	154	108	Truckee	16,491	30	26	4
Porterville	52,777	83	58	25	Tulare	58,790	101	73	28
Port Hueneme	21,510	32	24	8	Tulelake	949	4	4	0
Red Bluff	13,836	32	22	10	Turlock	69,961	122	81	41
Redding	91,414	138	105	33	Tustin	72,982	130	90	40
Redlands	70,552	117	77	40	Twin Cities	21,067	38	30	8
Redondo Beach	66,985	150	94	56	Ukiah	14,781	41	27	14
Redwood City	74,355	116	90	26	Union City	73,356	99	74	25
Reedley	23,893	47	33	14	Upland	73,341	121	80	41
Rialto	99,232	153	110	43	Vacaville	92,177	159	101	58
Richmond	103,442	289	188	101	Vallejo	114,258	116	89	27
Ridgecrest	25,973	48	32	16	Ventura	104,661	161	122	39
Rio Dell	3,181	9	8	1	Vernon	89	65	50	15
Rio Vista	8,340	11	10	1	Visalia	125,036	193	135	58
Ripon	15,271	33	23	10	Walnut Creek	63,897	108	76	32
Riverside	301,859	512	361	151	Watsonville	51,488	85	66	19
Rocklin	55,524	76	51	25	Weed	3,023	15	10	5
Rohnert Park	40,843	79	60	19	West Covina	105,395	170	107	63
Roseville	119,755	176	119	57	Westminster	89,604	137	93	44
Ross	2,281	9	9	0	Westmorland	2,231	5	5	0
Sacramento	472,469	1,019	696	323	West Sacramento	49,816	96	67	29
Salinas	144,242	210	157	53	Wheatland	3,715	7	7	0
San Anselmo	12,016	26	19	7	Whittier	81,611	173	123	50
San Bernardino	199,214	484	319	165	Williams	4,896	14	11	3
San Bruno	41,517	58	44	14	Willits	4,931	18	12	6
San Carlos	27,371	37	30	7	Willows	6,234	11	10	1
Sand City	372	11	10	1	Winters	7,096	11	9	2
San Diego	1,313,433	2,516	1,863	653	Woodlake	7,791	15	13	2
San Fernando	23,719	54	35	19	Woodland	55,814	82	64	18
San Francisco	818,594	2,629	2,250	379	Yreka	7,345	20	14	6
San Gabriel	40,281	68	53	15	Yuba City	62,694	89	64	25
Sanger	26,246	42	35	7	**COLORADO**				
San Jose	970,252	1,624	1,259	365	Alamosa	8,660	28	24	4
San Leandro	78,447	127	87	40	Arvada	107,227	211	151	60
San Luis Obispo	44,008	83	57	26	Aspen	6,012	34	26	8

Table 78.   Full-Time Law Enforcement Employees by State and City, 2010—*Continued*

(Number)

State/city	Population	Total law enforcement employees	Total officers	Total civilians	State/city	Population	Total law enforcement employees	Total officers	Total civilians
Ault	1,449	6	6	0	Idaho Springs	1,648	9	7	2
Aurora	323,483	765	644	121	Ignacio	781	6	6	0
Avon	6,737	20	17	3	Johnstown	10,277	15	13	2
Basalt	3,347	11	8	3	Kersey	1,472	3	3	0
Bayfield	2,114	5	5	0	Kiowa	607	2	2	0
Berthoud	5,440	10	9	1	Kremmling	1,451	4	4	0
Black Hawk	112	31	22	9	Lafayette	26,055	47	39	8
Boulder	99,255	253	167	86	La Junta	6,845	21	14	7
Breckenridge	3,557	25	18	7	Lakeside	19	4	4	0
Brighton	33,166	73	53	20	Lakewood	139,615	424	279	145
Broomfield	57,126	189	107	82	Lamar	7,670	28	22	6
Brush	5,338	14	11	3	La Salle	2,000	6	6	0
Buena Vista	2,107	9	7	2	Las Animas	2,262	7	6	1
Burlington	4,414	10	9	1	La Veta	814	3	3	0
Calhan	868	3	3	0	Leadville	2,693	10	8	2
Campo	119	3	2	1	Limon	1,644	6	5	1
Canon City	15,706	46	34	12	Littleton	40,544	89	67	22
Carbondale	6,333	17	14	3	Lochbuie	5,455	6	5	1
Castle Rock	48,715	70	50	20	Lone Tree	9,718	47	42	5
Cedaredge	2,284	8	6	2	Longmont	88,913	195	137	58
Centennial	98,902	156	118	38	Louisville	19,429	36	31	5
Center	2,347	10	5	5	Loveland	66,857	131	91	40
Central City	650	4	4	0	Mancos	1,256	3	3	0
Cherry Hills Village	6,389	27	22	5	Manitou Springs	5,169	20	14	6
Collbran	437	1	1	0	Manzanola	459	3	2	1
Colorado Springs	397,886	894	617	277	Meeker	2,457	8	6	2
Columbine Valley	1,331	6	6	0	Milliken	6,593	10	9	1
Commerce City	46,771	117	93	24	Minturn	1,208	4	3	1
Cortez	8,570	51	27	24	Monte Vista	3,879	17	12	5
Craig	9,178	31	24	7	Montrose	18,758	56	41	15
Crested Butte	1,663	9	7	2	Monument	5,257	16	13	3
Cripple Creek	1,002	17	14	3	Morrison	409	3	2	1
Dacono	4,237	11	9	2	Mountain View	511	2	2	0
De Beque	542	2	2	0	Mount Crested Butte	866	7	6	1
Del Norte	1,543	6	5	1	Nederland	1,381	4	3	1
Delta	9,270	20	17	3	New Castle	4,383	9	8	1
Denver	607,051	1,705	1,470	235	Northglenn	34,467	79	64	15
Dillon	799	11	9	2	Oak Creek	828	1	1	0
Durango	16,608	63	53	10	Olathe	1,755	3	3	0
Eagle	6,367	12	10	2	Ouray	936	4	4	0
Eaton	4,387	9	8	1	Pagosa Springs	1,814	8	7	1
Edgewater	5,055	18	15	3	Palisade	2,924	8	7	1
Elizabeth	1,443	6	5	1	Palmer Lake	2,344	6	5	1
Empire	311	1	1	0	Paonia	1,637	5	5	0
Englewood	32,494	98	71	27	Parachute	1,301	6	5	1
Erie	18,772	23	21	2	Parker	46,794	80	58	22
Estes Park	6,553	28	18	10	Platteville	2,685	8	8	0
Evans	20,440	32	30	2	Pueblo	103,612	250	201	49
Fairplay	640	3	3	0	Rangely	2,166	10	5	5
Federal Heights	12,114	36	24	12	Ridgway	800	3	3	0
Firestone	9,436	23	19	4	Rifle	9,391	21	18	3
Florence	3,533	18	9	9	Rocky Ford	3,830	9	8	1
Fort Collins	138,689	245	166	79	Salida	5,337	17	14	3
Fort Lupton	7,677	20	17	3	Sheridan	6,150	32	27	5
Fort Morgan	10,262	30	25	5	Silt	2,767	7	6	1
Fountain	25,197	40	37	3	Silverthorne	4,094	18	15	3
Fowler	1,060	3	2	1	Simla	688	2	2	0
Fraser/Winter Park	1,825	9	8	1	Snowmass Village	2,009	12	9	3
Frederick	9,196	17	16	1	South Fork	511	5	3	2
Frisco	2,736	15	13	2	Springfield	1,221	4	4	0
Fruita	12,848	18	16	2	Steamboat Springs	12,426	36	23	13
Georgetown	979	3	3	0	Sterling	12,517	24	21	3
Glendale	4,790	36	24	12	Stratton	599	1	1	0
Glenwood Springs	9,105	31	24	7	Telluride	2,380	13	9	4
Golden	17,226	60	43	17	Thornton	119,989	218	159	59
Granby	1,636	7	6	1	Trinidad	8,933	31	19	12
Grand Junction	59,029	186	101	85	Vail	4,794	55	27	28
Greeley	92,804	244	142	102	Victor	396	3	3	0
Green Mountain Falls	755	2	2	0	Walsenburg	3,545	11	10	1
Greenwood Village	14,430	92	67	25	Westminster	108,383	255	175	80
Gunnison	5,451	24	13	11	Wheat Ridge	30,400	99	72	27
Haxtun	949	3	3	0	Wiggins	939	2	2	0
Hayden	1,623	5	4	1	Windsor	18,088	23	20	3
Holyoke	2,190	4	4	0	Woodland Park	6,540	29	20	9
Hotchkiss	1,088	3	3	0	Wray	2,093	8	7	1
Hugo	699	3	3	0	Yuma	3,240	8	7	1

Table 78. Full-Time Law Enforcement Employees by State and City, 2010—*Continued*

(Number)

State/city	Population	Total law enforcement employees	Total officers	Total civilians	State/city	Population	Total law enforcement employees	Total officers	Total civilians
CONNECTICUT					Vernon	30,785	63	50	13
Ansonia	18,743	51	44	7	Wallingford	45,636	93	66	27
Avon	17,734	37	28	9	Waterbury	108,489	352	285	67
Berlin	20,963	52	40	12	Waterford	19,161	53	46	7
Bethel	18,814	46	36	10	Watertown	22,552	50	40	10
Bloomfield	21,086	57	46	11	West Hartford	61,603	147	126	21
Branford	29,415	62	50	12	West Haven	53,746	127	114	13
Bridgeport	138,810	457	406	51	Weston	10,344	15	14	1
Bristol	61,879	141	118	23	Westport	27,242	87	68	19
Brookfield	16,994	40	30	10	Wethersfield	26,042	58	47	11
Canton	10,392	18	13	5	Willimantic	16,605	45	41	4
Cheshire	29,569	58	46	12	Wilton	18,007	47	43	4
Clinton	13,832	33	24	9	Winchester	10,927	23	19	4
Coventry	12,546	19	14	5	Windsor	29,447	61	49	12
Cromwell	13,919	34	25	9	Windsor Locks	12,722	30	24	6
Danbury	81,242	159	152	7	Wolcott	16,799	28	19	9
Darien	20,617	57	51	6	Woodbridge	9,324	34	25	9
Derby	12,542	32	30	2	**DELAWARE**				
East Hampton	13,122	16	14	2	Bethany Beach	988	10	9	1
East Hartford	49,156	160	124	36	Blades	1,206	3	3	0
East Haven	28,973	52	49	3	Bridgeville	1,724	8	8	0
Easton	7,483	19	16	3	Camden	2,642	13	12	1
East Windsor	11,310	30	23	7	Cheswold	526	3	3	0
Enfield	45,837	120	96	24	Clayton	1,520	8	7	1
Fairfield	58,331	109	103	6	Dagsboro	596	2	2	0
Farmington	25,615	61	45	16	Delaware City	1,542	3	3	0
Glastonbury	33,921	71	55	16	Delmar	1,597	13	12	1
Granby	11,451	20	15	5	Dewey Beach	325	9	8	1
Greenwich	63,281	177	150	27	Dover	37,113	118	90	28
Groton	9,492	40	31	9	Elsmere	5,726	12	11	1
Groton Long Point	703	7	7	0	Felton	922	4	4	0
Groton Town	29,842	70	66	4	Fenwick Island	375	6	5	1
Guilford	22,861	45	37	8	Frankford	800	1	1	0
Hamden	58,988	131	106	25	Georgetown	5,313	18	16	2
Hartford	125,626	498	452	46	Greenwood	931	2	1	1
Madison	19,155	33	26	7	Harrington	3,580	11	10	1
Manchester	57,271	148	117	31	Laurel	4,087	14	13	1
Meriden	60,032	131	117	14	Lewes	3,222	13	12	1
Middlebury	7,588	17	11	6	Middletown	13,710	31	27	4
Middletown	49,281	113	98	15	Milford	8,792	40	30	10
Milford	57,565	127	110	17	Millsboro	2,831	13	12	1
Monroe	19,696	50	39	11	Milton	1,882	10	9	1
Naugatuck	32,529	69	57	12	Newark	30,543	80	64	16
New Britain	71,344	164	151	13	New Castle	5,049	19	17	2
New Canaan	20,312	50	45	5	Newport	1,138	7	7	0
New Haven	124,856	511	452	59	Ocean View	1,178	8	7	1
Newington	30,246	64	50	14	Rehoboth Beach	1,624	26	15	11
New London	26,517	105	89	16	Seaford	7,403	38	27	11
New Milford	29,006	60	47	13	Selbyville	1,935	9	8	1
Newtown	27,366	50	45	5	Smyrna	9,322	29	22	7
North Branford	14,619	29	23	6	South Bethany	538	6	6	0
North Haven	24,306	55	46	9	Wilmington	73,270	396	334	62
Norwalk	84,944	210	175	35	Wyoming	1,468	3	3	0
Norwich	37,157	89	75	14	**DISTRICT OF COLUMBIA**				
Old Saybrook	10,696	30	23	7	Washington	601,723	4,477	3,945	532
Orange	14,003	53	42	11	**FLORIDA**				
Plainfield	15,720	19	16	3	Alachua	9,757	29	21	8
Plainville	17,511	42	34	8	Altamonte Springs	39,774	115	97	18
Plymouth	12,202	22	22	0	Altha	514	1	1	0
Portland	9,785	12	11	1	Apalachicola	2,192	8	7	1
Putnam	9,458	18	15	3	Apopka	40,095	124	89	35
Redding	9,003	21	15	6	Arcadia	6,926	24	18	6
Ridgefield	24,591	45	40	5	Astatula	1,908	5	5	0
Rocky Hill	19,152	40	33	7	Atlantic Beach	13,139	38	26	12
Seymour	16,616	42	40	2	Atlantis	2,088	18	13	5
Shelton	41,037	62	55	7	Auburndale	14,204	44	35	9
Simsbury	23,988	42	34	8	Aventura	30,874	118	82	36
Southington	43,354	87	66	21	Avon Park	8,850	25	22	3
South Windsor	26,781	53	39	14	Bal Harbour Village	3,230	36	27	9
Stamford	122,933	328	277	51	Bartow	17,072	64	41	23
Stonington	18,807	47	36	11	Bay Harbor Islands	5,126	26	21	5
Stratford	49,469	109	102	7	Belleair	4,052	14	13	1
Suffield	15,524	24	19	5	Belle Isle	6,603	12	11	1
Thomaston	7,928	14	11	3	Belleview	4,538	16	14	2
Torrington	35,876	99	85	14	Biscayne Park	3,054	9	8	1
Trumbull	35,425	82	71	11	Blountstown	2,475	12	9	3

Table 78. Full-Time Law Enforcement Employees by State and City, 2010—*Continued*

(Number)

State/city	Population	Total law enforcement employees	Total officers	Total civilians	State/city	Population	Total law enforcement employees	Total officers	Total civilians
Boca Raton	86,707	281	191	90	Holmes Beach	5,130	21	14	7
Bonifay	2,696	6	5	1	Homestead	63,761	144	102	42
Bowling Green	2,986	7	7	0	Howey-in-the-Hills	1,270	6	6	0
Boynton Beach	70,574	233	161	72	Indialantic	2,905	16	11	5
Bradenton	54,337	148	119	29	Indian Creek Village	40	16	10	6
Bradenton Beach	1,585	10	10	0	Indian Harbour Beach	8,253	26	19	7
Brooksville	8,333	26	23	3	Indian River Shores	3,449	22	19	3
Bunnell	3,096	14	12	2	Indian Shores	4,213	12	10	2
Bushnell	2,279	10	9	1	Inglis	1,630	6	5	1
Cape Coral	160,432	320	228	92	Interlachen	1,497	4	4	0
Carrabelle	1,222	5	5	0	Jacksonville	822,414	3,310	1,751	1,559
Casselberry	24,802	59	48	11	Jacksonville Beach	22,140	79	59	20
Cedar Key	970	4	4	0	Jasper	2,063	8	7	1
Center Hill	1,117	3	3	0	Jennings	861	2	2	0
Chattahoochee	3,661	10	9	1	Juno Beach	3,369	19	14	5
Chiefland	2,193	13	11	2	Jupiter	51,785	139	109	30
Chipley	3,780	11	10	1	Jupiter Inlet Colony	392	5	5	0
Clearwater	105,647	333	232	101	Jupiter Island	684	19	15	4
Clermont	13,802	69	55	14	Kenneth City	4,257	15	14	1
Clewiston	7,168	25	18	7	Key Biscayne	10,097	42	30	12
Cocoa	16,469	91	68	23	Key Colony Beach	760	5	5	0
Cocoa Beach	11,790	56	34	22	Key West	22,167	113	88	25
Coconut Creek	51,184	132	92	40	Kissimmee	64,122	194	124	70
Coleman	815	1	1	0	Lady Lake	15,487	43	30	13
Coral Gables	44,559	239	170	69	Lake Alfred	4,652	15	10	5
Coral Springs	127,113	301	201	100	Lake City	12,850	47	35	12
Cottondale	878	3	3	0	Lake Clarke Shores	3,341	10	10	0
Crescent City	1,779	7	6	1	Lake Hamilton	1,494	7	6	1
Crestview	20,424	62	47	15	Lake Helen	2,767	7	6	1
Cross City	1,776	5	5	0	Lakeland	94,569	314	210	104
Dade City	7,268	34	24	10	Lake Mary	15,641	54	38	16
Davenport	3,002	9	8	1	Lake Placid	1,996	9	7	2
Davie	92,661	226	161	65	Lake Wales	14,593	48	43	5
Daytona Beach	63,736	278	232	46	Lantana	10,229	33	28	5
Daytona Beach Shores	5,137	36	29	7	Largo	73,019	183	137	46
De Funiak Springs	5,122	27	20	7	Lauderhill	67,442	129	113	16
Deland	27,926	76	58	18	Lawtey	698	1	1	0
Delray Beach	65,087	217	149	68	Leesburg	22,949	97	72	25
Doral	32,645	127	88	39	Lighthouse Point	11,232	41	32	9
Dunnellon	1,941	11	8	3	Live Oak	7,232	21	17	4
Eatonville	2,359	17	15	2	Longboat Key	7,223	24	17	7
Edgewater	21,456	30	28	2	Longwood	13,443	47	40	7
Edgewood	2,116	13	12	1	Lynn Haven	15,678	39	29	10
El Portal	2,393	7	7	0	Madison	2,992	16	15	1
Eustis	19,455	55	43	12	Maitland	15,489	50	44	6
Fellsmere	5,194	10	9	1	Manalapan	345	15	10	5
Fernandina Beach	11,721	45	34	11	Marco Island	15,820	34	32	2
Flagler Beach	5,467	16	14	2	Margate	54,478	166	107	59
Florida City	10,883	44	33	11	Marianna	6,170	24	17	7
Fort Lauderdale	186,170	686	504	182	Mascotte	6,042	12	11	1
Fort Myers	66,053	234	168	66	Medley	1,077	47	37	10
Fort Pierce	42,797	147	108	39	Melbourne	77,861	235	168	67
Fort Walton Beach	18,432	55	42	13	Melbourne Beach	3,107	10	9	1
Fruitland Park	4,914	14	13	1	Melbourne Village	666	5	5	0
Gainesville	116,880	342	283	59	Mexico Beach	1,304	7	6	1
Golden Beach	909	19	18	1	Miami	440,482	1,453	1,098	355
Graceville	2,411	9	6	3	Miami Beach	87,990	506	358	148
Greenacres City	33,244	67	49	18	Miami Gardens	110,130	256	199	57
Green Cove Springs	6,731	23	18	5	Miami Shores	10,132	44	34	10
Greensboro	593	1	1	0	Miami Springs	12,924	54	43	11
Gretna	1,749	5	5	0	Milton	8,805	26	19	7
Groveland	8,353	29	22	7	Miramar	113,385	271	193	78
Gulf Breeze	6,704	25	17	8	Monticello	2,426	13	9	4
Gulfport	12,212	38	29	9	Mount Dora	14,053	47	32	15
Gulf Stream	744	11	11	0	Naples	22,239	97	68	29
Haines City	19,411	68	45	23	Neptune Beach	6,707	26	18	8
Hallandale	39,359	123	91	32	New Port Richey	17,634	47	35	12
Hampton	460	2	2	0	New Smyrna Beach	23,656	59	49	10
Havana	1,668	13	10	3	Niceville	12,145	24	19	5
Hialeah	217,995	401	342	59	North Bay Village	8,316	32	26	6
Hialeah Gardens	20,554	56	38	18	North Miami	57,796	164	133	31
Highland Beach	4,016	15	14	1	North Miami Beach	41,170	164	115	49
High Springs	4,775	13	8	5	North Palm Beach	12,255	43	31	12
Hillsboro Beach	2,279	18	15	3	North Port	59,076	122	97	25
Holly Hill	13,204	32	29	3	Oak Hill	1,654	7	7	0
Hollywood	142,793	472	315	157	Ocala	56,396	236	157	79

Table 78. Full-Time Law Enforcement Employees by State and City, 2010—*Continued*

(Number)

State/city	Population	Total law enforcement employees	Total officers	Total civilians	State/city	Population	Total law enforcement employees	Total officers	Total civilians
Ocean Ridge	1,654	19	14	5	West Melbourne	15,969	43	33	10
Ocoee	33,650	88	77	11	West Miami	5,739	22	18	4
Okeechobee	5,924	26	20	6	West Palm Beach	101,267	372	280	92
Opa Locka	16,762	57	47	10	White Springs	843	3	3	0
Orange City	10,149	24	21	3	Wildwood	12,797	25	18	7
Orange Park	9,066	28	21	7	Williston	2,919	19	11	8
Orlando	240,222	939	719	220	Wilton Manors	12,873	44	30	14
Ormond Beach	37,923	85	65	20	Windermere	2,689	13	12	1
Oviedo	33,670	78	60	18	Winter Garden	32,096	83	67	16
Palatka	10,726	42	36	6	Winter Haven	33,981	101	79	22
Palm Bay	103,350	241	159	82	Winter Park	28,069	109	83	26
Palm Beach	9,607	107	71	36	Winter Springs	32,862	85	69	16
Palm Beach Gardens	51,458	139	109	30	Zephyrhills	13,360	47	32	15
Palm Beach Shores	1,576	15	11	4	**GEORGIA**				
Palmetto	14,554	46	35	11	Acworth	19,939	56	52	4
Palm Springs	17,223	50	38	12	Adairsville	3,358	15	13	2
Panama City	36,593	126	89	37	Adel	5,236	22	20	2
Panama City Beach	15,482	65	51	14	Alamo	2,671	4	3	1
Parker	4,557	10	9	1	Albany	73,034	207	177	30
Pembroke Pines	147,343	284	231	53	Alma	3,435	13	11	2
Pensacola	53,476	214	166	48	Alpharetta	50,392	114	104	10
Perry	6,647	24	22	2	Americus	15,694	46	38	8
Pinellas Park	47,180	121	100	21	Aragon	1,051	5	4	1
Plantation	85,000	266	173	93	Arcade	1,908	4	4	0
Plant City	33,421	86	68	18	Ashburn	4,075	16	16	0
Ponce Inlet	3,165	17	11	6	Athens-Clarke County	112,851	293	228	65
Port Orange	55,381	93	78	15	Atlanta	536,472	1,973	1,612	361
Port Richey	3,426	18	12	6	Attapulgus	433	1	1	0
Port St. Joe	3,479	7	7	0	Auburn	7,600	22	15	7
Port St. Lucie	163,089	261	206	55	Austell	7,024	39	30	9
Punta Gorda	17,389	49	34	15	Avondale Estates	2,788	11	11	0
Riviera Beach	37,637	147	111	36	Bainbridge	11,641	50	46	4
Rockledge	25,230	68	49	19	Ball Ground	1,003	3	3	0
Sanford	52,325	143	126	17	Barnesville	6,159	19	17	2
Sanibel	5,526	35	24	11	Baxley	4,377	13	11	2
Sarasota	51,928	227	174	53	Berlin	602	4	3	1
Satellite Beach	11,792	31	23	8	Blackshear	3,461	15	12	3
Sea Ranch Lakes	741	7	3	4	Blairsville	697	8	7	1
Sebastian	21,063	51	35	16	Bloomingdale	2,591	13	11	2
Sebring	10,518	39	33	6	Blythe	814	1	1	0
Sewall's Point	2,019	8	8	0	Boston	1,407	4	4	0
Shalimar	687	4	4	0	Bowdon	2,008	10	7	3
Sneads	1,944	9	5	4	Braselton	6,538	13	12	1
South Daytona	13,513	35	27	8	Bremen	5,586	21	19	2
South Miami	11,154	56	48	8	Brooklet	1,329	4	4	0
South Palm Beach	1,474	8	8	0	Brunswick	15,871	70	62	8
Springfield	8,858	21	15	6	Buchanan	982	8	7	1
Starke	5,928	20	18	2	Buena Vista	1,584	6	6	0
St. Augustine	12,794	60	48	12	Butler	1,705	7	6	1
St. Augustine Beach	6,522	17	15	2	Byron	4,405	24	21	3
St. Cloud	30,245	106	70	36	Cairo	9,607	26	23	3
St. Pete Beach	9,855	33	26	7	Calhoun	14,710	49	42	7
St. Petersburg	243,666	774	538	236	Camilla	5,149	22	19	3
Stuart	15,986	63	44	19	Canton	24,697	48	43	5
Sunny Isles Beach	17,052	55	43	12	Carrollton	23,014	77	64	13
Sunrise	90,016	253	171	82	Cartersville	18,646	67	56	11
Surfside	4,684	36	27	9	Cave Spring	1,020	14	13	1
Sweetwater	13,563	25	19	6	Centerville	7,332	17	14	3
Tallahassee	174,516	473	350	123	Chamblee	10,990	44	32	12
Tampa	347,830	1,245	952	293	Chatsworth	4,086	16	14	2
Tarpon Springs	23,695	58	47	11	Chattahoochee Hills	2,315	8	8	0
Tavares	14,353	37	26	11	Clarkesville	1,708	7	6	1
Temple Terrace	22,760	69	49	20	Clarkston	7,677	21	15	6
Tequesta	5,799	24	17	7	Claxton	2,289	9	8	1
Titusville	44,839	134	87	47	Cleveland	2,856	14	13	1
Treasure Island	7,399	27	19	8	Climax	269	1	1	0
Umatilla	3,564	9	8	1	College Park	19,917	129	88	41
Valparaiso	5,783	14	10	4	Colquitt	1,871	10	9	1
Venice	20,997	66	50	16	Columbus	184,576	582	480	102
Vero Beach	17,254	77	54	23	Commerce	6,477	27	21	6
Village of Pinecrest	19,367	66	48	18	Conyers	13,738	77	57	20
Virginia Gardens	2,241	7	6	1	Coolidge	545	4	4	0
Waldo	819	8	7	1	Cordele	11,110	35	29	6
Wauchula	4,640	19	16	3	Cornelia	3,725	20	18	2
Webster	922	3	3	0	Covington	15,181	60	52	8
Welaka	800	1	1	0	Crawfordville	477	1	1	0

Table 78. Full-Time Law Enforcement Employees by State and City, 2010—*Continued*

(Number)

State/city	Popula-tion	Total law enforce-ment employees	Total officers	Total civilians	State/city	Popula-tion	Total law enforce-ment employees	Total officers	Total civilians
Cumming	5,891	20	14	6	Leslie	410	6	6	0
Cuthbert	3,286	10	10	0	Lilburn	11,645	39	29	10
Dallas	11,260	25	19	6	Lincolnton	1,443	4	4	0
Dalton	33,064	98	83	15	Lithonia	2,335	6	5	1
Danielsville	423	2	2	0	Locust Grove	5,136	21	19	2
Davisboro	1,975	2	1	1	Loganville	11,256	27	25	2
Decatur	18,391	55	42	13	Lookout Mountain	1,459	7	7	0
Dillard	228	3	3	0	Louisville	2,621	7	7	0
Doerun	813	6	5	1	Ludowici	1,578	11	7	4
Donalsonville	2,589	10	9	1	Lumber City	1,114	1	1	0
Douglas	11,120	50	40	10	Lumpkin	1,136	5	4	1
Douglasville	32,033	107	88	19	Macon	89,125	363	285	78
Duluth	26,199	74	53	21	Manchester	3,609	16	11	5
East Dublin	2,748	8	8	0	Marietta	65,318	169	134	35
East Point	42,311	163	117	46	Maysville	1,681	10	2	8
Eatonton	6,118	23	16	7	McCaysville	957	4	4	0
Elberton	4,471	24	21	3	McDonough	21,010	44	40	4
Emerson	1,513	6	6	0	McIntyre	693	5	5	0
Enigma	855	4	4	0	McRae	4,385	8	7	1
Ephesus	374	1	1	0	Meigs	1,053	8	5	3
Eton	470	6	6	0	Metter	4,309	14	13	1
Fairburn	11,644	39	33	6	Midville	434	1	1	0
Fairmount	790	4	4	0	Midway	1,514	6	5	1
Fayetteville	15,019	44	40	4	Milan	717	5	4	1
Fitzgerald	8,812	38	31	7	Milledgeville	20,543	59	37	22
Flowery Branch	4,287	15	13	2	Millen	3,260	9	9	0
Folkston	3,076	7	6	1	Milton	15,747	28	26	2
Forsyth	5,111	23	18	5	Molena	460	5	5	0
Fort Gaines	922	7	7	0	Monroe	13,305	43	39	4
Fort Oglethorpe	9,863	29	28	1	Montezuma	3,547	12	10	2
Franklin Springs	708	5	5	0	Monticello	2,532	15	14	1
Gainesville	35,657	106	94	12	Morrow	5,423	36	32	4
Garden City	9,134	48	40	8	Morven	565	6	6	0
Glennville	5,515	17	12	5	Mountain City	718	3	3	0
Glenwood	883	4	3	1	Mount Airy	1,285	2	1	1
Gordon	2,028	10	10	0	Mount Vernon	2,071	7	5	2
Grantville	2,840	9	8	1	Mount Zion	1,574	2	2	0
Greensboro	3,136	21	18	3	Nashville	4,671	19	16	3
Greenville	884	7	6	1	Newnan	32,623	82	70	12
Griffin	23,186	107	94	13	Newton	729	3	3	0
Grovetown	9,970	31	22	9	Nicholls	2,787	6	5	1
Guyton	1,969	4	3	1	Norcross	10,870	46	36	10
Hagan	1,027	7	5	2	Oakwood	5,414	15	13	2
Hampton	5,342	20	18	2	Ocilla	3,009	14	13	1
Hapeville	6,624	37	23	14	Oxford	2,548	4	4	0
Harlem	2,119	12	7	5	Patterson	675	1	1	0
Hartwell	4,152	23	18	5	Peachtree City	33,956	68	64	4
Hazlehurst	3,780	13	11	2	Pearson	1,906	4	4	0
Helen	879	11	9	2	Pembroke	2,575	8	6	2
Helena	2,268	3	3	0	Perry	13,406	41	36	5
Hephzibah	4,531	54	54	0	Pine Lake	636	18	18	0
Hiawassee	828	4	4	0	Pine Mountain	1,301	8	7	1
Hilltonia	350	3	2	1	Pooler	17,306	35	29	6
Hinesville	29,764	93	80	13	Porterdale	1,835	8	7	1
Hiram	2,102	25	17	8	Port Wentworth	4,928	25	21	4
Hoboken	511	3	2	1	Powder Springs	15,768	34	30	4
Hogansville	2,841	20	15	5	Quitman	4,173	16	14	2
Holly Springs	9,708	16	16	0	Reidsville	2,412	9	7	2
Homeland	759	2	2	0	Richmond Hill	11,455	36	29	7
Homerville	2,583	12	11	1	Rincon	8,354	16	15	1
Irwinton	566	2	2	0	Ringgold	2,777	9	9	0
Ivey	1,048	2	2	0	Riverdale	15,112	59	44	15
Jackson	4,481	17	12	5	Roberta	696	4	4	0
Jefferson	8,232	24	20	4	Rockmart	4,489	17	15	2
Jesup	10,175	28	26	2	Roswell	85,461	205	139	66
Johns Creek	59,893	68	60	8	Royston	2,640	16	13	3
Jonesboro	4,082	26	21	5	Sandersville	5,890	22	19	3
Keysville	225	1	1	0	Sandy Springs	82,898	144	128	16
Kingsland	14,033	47	44	3	Savannah-Chatham Metropolitan	210,744	808	579	229
Kingston	660	2	2	0	Senoia	3,866	12	11	1
LaGrange	27,712	93	78	15	Shiloh	432	2	1	1
Lake Park	550	2	2	0	Smyrna	49,693	98	88	10
Lavonia	2,009	13	12	1	Snellville	20,323	51	41	10
Lawrenceville	29,625	91	71	20	Social Circle	4,858	20	17	3
Leary	582	1	1	0	Sparta	1,193	14	8	6
Leesburg	2,932	12	11	1	Springfield	2,353	8	7	1

Table 78. Full-Time Law Enforcement Employees by State and City, 2010—*Continued*

(Number)

State/city	Population	Total law enforcement employees	Total officers	Total civilians	State/city	Population	Total law enforcement employees	Total officers	Total civilians
Statham	3,041	8	8	0	Kimberly	3,302	6	6	0
St. Marys	16,424	36	34	2	Lewiston	31,860	67	46	21
Stone Mountain	7,525	19	18	1	McCall	2,595	19	14	5
Suwanee	17,028	43	36	7	Meridian	72,688	102	79	23
Sylvania	2,610	16	11	5	Montpelier	2,302	9	7	2
Sylvester	5,540	23	20	3	Moscow	24,550	41	33	8
Tallapoosa	3,006	14	13	1	Mountain Home	12,301	36	28	8
Tennille	1,386	8	8	0	Nampa	84,179	173	120	53
Thomaston	8,804	23	20	3	Orofino	2,951	7	6	1
Thomasville	18,922	73	65	8	Osburn	1,341	2	2	0
Thomson	6,630	14	13	1	Parma	1,884	4	4	0
Thunderbolt	2,575	11	8	3	Payette	7,688	13	11	2
Tifton	17,012	55	46	9	Pinehurst	1,541	1	1	0
Tignall	591	2	1	1	Pocatello	55,215	126	89	37
Toccoa	8,747	30	29	1	Ponderay	733	7	6	1
Toomsboro	598	1	1	0	Post Falls	27,882	66	40	26
Trenton	2,325	8	8	0	Preston	5,133	6	5	1
Trion	1,968	9	8	1	Priest River	1,978	5	3	2
Tunnel Hill	1,199	3	3	0	Rathdrum	7,174	15	12	3
Tybee Island	3,817	24	16	8	Rexburg	30,200	36	29	7
Tyrone	6,653	14	13	1	Rigby	3,568	9	8	1
Union City	17,584	74	55	19	Rupert	5,166	14	12	2
Union Point	1,467	7	7	0	Salmon	3,120	9	8	1
Uvalda	532	2	1	1	Sandpoint	8,503	26	21	5
Valdosta	51,089	165	144	21	Shelley	4,403	8	8	0
Varnell	1,558	12	12	0	Soda Springs	3,062	8	7	1
Vidalia	10,973	41	32	9	Spirit Lake	1,788	6	5	1
Vienna	2,712	9	8	1	St. Anthony	3,443	4	4	0
Villa Rica	13,906	41	34	7	St. Maries	2,593	4	4	0
Wadley	1,857	17	13	4	Sun Valley	1,483	11	10	1
Warm Springs	461	7	7	0	Twin Falls	43,434	99	69	30
Warner Robins	61,332	142	109	33	Weiser	5,181	16	13	3
Warrenton	1,800	8	8	0	Wendell	2,426	6	5	1
Warwick	381	8	8	0	Wilder	1,482	3	3	0
Washington	3,851	15	15	0	**ILLINOIS**				
Watkinsville	2,941	7	7	0	Abingdon	3,189	5	5	0
Waverly Hall	773	3	3	0	Addison	36,581	94	68	26
Waycross	14,182	68	58	10	Albany	917	1	1	0
Waynesboro	5,602	24	18	6	Albion	1,765	3	3	0
Whigham	561	4	3	1	Aledo	3,466	7	7	0
Whitesburg	577	4	4	0	Algonquin	30,848	59	49	10
Willacoochee	1,492	6	5	1	Alorton	2,500	3	3	0
Winder	14,658	48	42	6	Alsip	18,278	53	38	15
Woodstock	24,370	65	53	12	Altamont	2,224	6	6	0
Wrens	2,111	9	9	0	Alton	28,841	86	61	25
HAWAII					Amboy	2,523	3	3	0
Honolulu	950,268	2,554	2,066	488	Anna	4,870	8	8	0
IDAHO					Annawan	891	1	1	0
Aberdeen	1,762	6	3	3	Antioch	14,266	42	28	14
American Falls	4,075	8	7	1	Arcola	2,685	6	5	1
Bellevue	2,259	5	4	1	Arlington Heights	72,061	140	109	31
Blackfoot	11,176	29	26	3	Arthur	2,084	4	4	0
Boise	205,902	364	296	68	Ashland	1,299	1	1	0
Bonners Ferry	2,550	6	6	0	Ashton	1,143	1	1	0
Buhl	4,105	10	8	2	Assumption	1,167	1	1	0
Caldwell	45,089	76	61	15	Athens	1,763	3	3	0
Cascade	964	5	4	1	Atkinson	934	1	1	0
Chubbuck	12,745	33	20	13	Atlanta	1,617	1	1	0
Coeur d'Alene	44,626	85	68	17	Atwood	1,194	2	2	0
Cottonwood	1,039	1	1	0	Auburn	4,398	9	5	4
Emmett	6,329	14	13	1	Aurora	174,255	356	290	66
Filer	2,268	5	5	0	Aviston	1,754	1	1	0
Fruitland	4,853	10	8	2	Bannockburn	1,919	7	7	0
Garden City	11,969	32	25	7	Barrington	10,240	27	23	4
Gooding	3,179	8	7	1	Barrington Hills	4,373	29	19	10
Grangeville	3,099	6	6	0	Bartlett	42,962	71	54	17
Hagerman	825	1	1	0	Bartonville	6,142	15	12	3
Hailey	8,242	17	16	1	Batavia	27,759	48	42	6
Heyburn	2,747	6	5	1	Beardstown	5,794	9	9	0
Homedale	2,525	5	5	0	Beckemeyer	1,049	1	1	0
Idaho City	474	1	1	0	Bedford Park	520	44	36	8
Idaho Falls	55,524	132	90	42	Beecher	3,159	8	7	1
Jerome	9,714	21	18	3	Belleville	40,747	96	78	18
Kamiah	1,123	3	3	0	Bellwood	18,500	42	39	3
Kellogg	2,146	8	7	1	Belvidere	26,712	45	42	3
Ketchum	3,401	14	10	4	Benld	1,424	4	4	0

Table 78.   Full-Time Law Enforcement Employees by State and City, 2010—*Continued*

(Number)

State/city	Popula-tion	Total law enforce-ment employees	Total officers	Total civilians	State/city	Popula-tion	Total law enforce-ment employees	Total officers	Total civilians
Bensenville	19,890	41	31	10	Cortland	4,501	3	3	0
Benton	6,836	11	10	1	Coulterville	1,130	2	2	0
Berkeley	4,800	20	16	4	Country Club Hills	16,472	62	44	18
Berwyn	48,737	136	108	28	Countryside	5,698	30	23	7
Bethalto	9,896	17	13	4	Crest Hill	21,199	27	25	2
Bloomingdale	21,638	59	43	16	Crestwood	10,845	4	3	1
Bloomington	74,304	148	117	31	Crete	9,154	18	17	1
Blue Island	21,898	60	39	21	Creve Coeur	5,145	7	5	2
Blue Mound	996	1	1	0	Crystal Lake	42,137	78	65	13
Bolingbrook	71,696	146	113	33	Dallas City	938	1	1	0
Bourbonnais	19,340	31	24	7	Danvers	1,149	2	2	0
Bradley	15,131	43	31	12	Danville	31,942	74	62	12
Braidwood	6,886	9	8	1	Darien	22,097	52	35	17
Breese	4,263	7	6	1	Decatur	74,857	188	157	31
Bridgeport	2,018	1	1	0	Deer Creek-Goodfield	1,616	1	1	0
Bridgeview	14,816	43	41	2	Deerfield	19,543	51	37	14
Brighton	2,348	4	4	0	Deer Park	3,339	9	9	0
Broadview	7,432	31	25	6	De Kalb	45,959	73	60	13
Brookfield	17,675	35	30	5	Delavan	1,738	3	3	0
Brooklyn	611	8	7	1	De Pue	1,707	3	3	0
Buffalo Grove	42,361	81	70	11	De Soto	1,517	4	3	1
Bull Valley	1,129	2	2	0	Des Plaines	56,188	110	90	20
Bunker Hill	1,706	4	3	1	Divernon	1,112	3	3	0
Burbank	27,135	69	52	17	Dixmoor	3,783	9	8	1
Burnham	3,892	13	8	5	Dixon	14,696	32	28	4
Burr Ridge	11,359	31	28	3	Dolton	23,335	53	43	10
Byron	3,903	8	7	1	Downers Grove	48,574	100	73	27
Cahokia	14,826	36	29	7	Dupo	4,056	6	6	0
Cairo	2,909	15	10	5	Du Quoin	6,222	14	10	4
Calumet City	36,004	105	81	24	Durand	1,070	1	1	0
Calumet Park	7,817	26	23	3	Dwight	4,223	10	9	1
Cambridge	2,054	1	1	0	Earlville	1,836	2	2	0
Camp Point	1,187	2	2	0	East Alton	6,450	17	11	6
Campton Hills	9,739	7	6	1	East Carondelet	610	1	1	0
Canton	14,269	33	23	10	East Dubuque	1,870	6	6	0
Carbondale	25,959	83	64	19	East Dundee	3,133	12	11	1
Carlinville	5,837	17	12	5	East Hazel Crest	1,503	11	10	1
Carlyle	3,292	8	7	1	East Moline	20,589	50	40	10
Carmi	5,116	11	9	2	Easton	338	1	1	0
Carol Stream	39,577	82	60	22	East Peoria	22,638	52	40	12
Carpentersville	38,387	75	64	11	East St. Louis	28,188	83	62	21
Carrier Mills	1,796	2	2	0	Edinburg	1,085	1	1	0
Carrollton	2,395	6	6	0	Edwardsville	24,437	56	41	15
Carterville	5,549	7	7	0	Effingham	12,442	35	22	13
Carthage	2,404	4	4	0	Elburn	5,564	9	8	1
Cary	19,906	30	26	4	Eldorado	4,304	11	7	4
Casey	2,829	8	7	1	Elgin	107,731	219	179	40
Caseyville	4,159	13	11	2	Elizabeth	633	1	1	0
Central City	1,285	4	4	0	Elk Grove Village	32,620	102	89	13
Centralia	13,237	35	26	9	Elmhurst	46,160	87	67	20
Centreville	5,555	14	11	3	Elmwood	1,862	1	1	0
Cerro Gordo	1,321	1	1	0	Elmwood Park	23,536	41	35	6
Chadwick	459	1	1	0	El Paso	2,853	5	5	0
Champaign	80,489	153	122	31	Elwood	2,417	10	9	1
Channahon	14,727	29	25	4	Energy	1,197	4	4	0
Charleston	21,538	32	30	2	Erie	1,523	2	2	0
Chatham	10,950	21	15	6	Essex	705	1	1	0
Chenoa	3,265	4	4	0	Eureka	5,421	6	6	0
Cherry Valley	2,272	16	15	1	Evanston	77,418	216	163	53
Chester	7,677	11	8	3	Evergreen Park	18,888	76	62	14
Chicago	2,833,649	13,318	12,515	803	Fairbury	3,734	7	7	0
Chicago Heights	29,870	106	77	29	Fairfield	4,996	17	13	4
Chicago Ridge	13,094	33	29	4	Fairmont City	2,216	11	8	3
Chillicothe	5,944	14	9	5	Fairview	472	1	1	0
Christopher	2,765	5	5	0	Fairview Heights	16,712	45	35	10
Cicero	78,746	177	150	27	Farmer City	1,884	4	4	0
Clarendon Hills	8,581	15	14	1	Farmington	2,385	4	4	0
Clayton	814	1	1	0	Fisher	1,757	2	2	0
Clinton	6,867	15	13	2	Flora	4,595	16	11	5
Coal City	5,817	12	11	1	Flossmoor	9,152	25	19	6
Coal Valley	4,026	8	7	1	Forest Park	14,926	53	37	16
Cobden	1,071	3	3	0	Forest View	700	12	9	3
Colfax	1,003	1	1	0	Fox Lake	11,125	27	23	4
Collinsville	25,851	63	44	19	Fox River Grove	5,168	14	12	2
Colona	5,150	11	10	1	Frankfort	19,115	34	30	4
Columbia	9,520	20	13	7	Franklin Park	17,562	43	42	1

Table 78. Full-Time Law Enforcement Employees by State and City, 2010—*Continued*

(Number)

State/city	Population	Total law enforcement employees	Total officers	Total civilians	State/city	Population	Total law enforcement employees	Total officers	Total civilians
Freeburg	4,545	10	9	1	Jerome	1,267	8	8	0
Freeport	24,277	66	51	15	Jerseyville	8,285	20	14	6
Fulton	3,775	9	8	1	Johnsburg	6,887	10	9	1
Galena	3,251	12	9	3	Johnston City	3,449	5	5	0
Galesburg	30,424	77	51	26	Joliet	150,723	341	263	78
Galva	2,588	3	3	0	Jonesboro	1,759	2	2	0
Geneseo	6,322	17	12	5	Justice	12,280	30	24	6
Geneva	24,648	46	36	10	Kankakee	26,481	84	70	14
Genoa	5,190	7	6	1	Kenilworth	2,354	13	10	3
Georgetown	3,356	4	4	0	Kewanee	12,042	32	24	8
Germantown	1,126	1	1	0	Kildeer	4,131	10	9	1
Gibson City	3,221	9	7	2	Kincaid	1,430	2	2	0
Gifford	998	1	1	0	Kingston	1,067	2	2	0
Gilberts	7,297	9	8	1	Kirkland	1,758	3	3	0
Gillespie	3,088	10	7	3	Knoxville	2,860	5	5	0
Gilman	1,649	3	3	0	Lacon	1,797	3	3	0
Girard	2,120	5	5	0	La Grange	14,987	43	28	15
Glasford	1,029	1	1	0	La Grange Park	12,119	26	20	6
Glen Carbon	12,760	26	19	7	Lake Bluff	6,173	20	15	5
Glencoe	8,920	44	33	11	Lake Forest	20,854	56	39	17
Glendale Heights	31,532	77	54	23	Lake in the Hills	30,023	57	40	17
Glen Ellyn	26,950	46	38	8	Lakemoor	6,129	7	6	1
Glenview	46,036	78	73	5	Lake Villa	8,922	18	17	1
Glenwood	8,310	22	21	1	Lakewood	3,835	9	8	1
Golf	436	4	4	0	Lake Zurich	20,408	50	34	16
Grafton	678	3	3	0	La Moille	725	1	1	0
Grand Tower	564	1	1	0	Lanark	1,420	2	2	0
Grandview	1,381	2	2	0	Lansing	26,075	74	55	19
Granite City	30,254	70	60	10	La Salle	9,359	30	24	6
Grant Park	1,717	3	3	0	Lawrenceville	4,201	7	7	0
Granville	1,320	2	2	0	Lebanon	4,606	10	10	0
Grayslake	21,790	37	33	4	Leland	949	1	1	0
Grayville	1,554	2	2	0	Leland Grove	1,408	5	5	0
Greenfield	1,046	2	2	0	Lemont	16,379	33	27	6
Greenup	1,444	4	4	0	Lenzburg	525	1	1	0
Greenville	7,233	13	9	4	Le Roy	3,551	6	6	0
Gurnee	30,415	86	59	27	Lewistown	2,324	3	3	0
Hamilton	2,672	4	4	0	Lexington	1,954	1	1	0
Hampshire	6,006	11	11	0	Libertyville	21,709	51	38	13
Hampton	1,776	4	4	0	Lincoln	14,291	25	24	1
Hanover	768	1	1	0	Lincolnshire	8,080	33	24	9
Hanover Park	36,166	92	57	35	Lincolnwood	11,560	43	32	11
Harrisburg	9,395	15	14	1	Lindenhurst	14,743	18	16	2
Hartford	1,451	5	4	1	Lisle	22,976	54	43	11
Harvard	10,063	24	18	6	Litchfield	6,482	20	15	5
Harvey	27,461	92	66	26	Livingston	778	1	1	0
Harwood Heights	7,896	33	24	9	Lockport	25,986	41	35	6
Havana	3,196	13	8	5	Lombard	42,394	85	69	16
Hawthorn Woods	8,205	10	9	1	Loves Park	24,660	36	33	3
Hazel Crest	13,771	35	30	5	Ludlow	360	1	1	0
Hebron	1,444	3	3	0	Lynwood	8,627	24	19	5
Henry	2,385	4	4	0	Lyons	10,075	36	28	8
Herrin	12,421	23	16	7	Machesney Park	22,686	27	26	1
Herscher	1,611	3	3	0	Mackinaw	1,749	1	1	0
Hickory Hills	13,050	36	28	8	Macomb	19,674	30	27	3
Highland	9,841	27	20	7	Madison	4,498	14	10	4
Highland Park	31,306	74	53	21	Mahomet	6,784	9	8	1
Highwood	5,317	10	9	1	Manhattan	7,858	10	9	1
Hillsboro	6,017	8	8	0	Manito	1,565	3	3	0
Hillside	8,194	32	25	7	Manteno	8,718	18	17	1
Hinckley	2,079	3	3	0	Maple Park	1,352	1	1	0
Hinsdale	18,362	28	26	2	Marengo	7,665	20	15	5
Hodgkins	2,010	22	20	2	Marion	17,405	40	30	10
Hoffman Estates	53,500	113	95	18	Marissa	1,965	4	4	0
Homer	1,111	1	1	0	Markham	11,987	46	39	7
Hometown	4,004	5	1	4	Maroa	1,538	4	4	0
Homewood	18,062	41	36	5	Marquette Heights	2,810	5	5	0
Hoopeston	5,507	16	11	5	Marseilles	4,947	14	9	5
Hopedale	923	2	2	0	Marshall	3,840	10	9	1
Huntley	26,256	36	31	5	Martinsville	1,178	2	2	0
Indian Head Park	3,547	9	8	1	Maryville	7,795	16	12	4
Inverness	7,636	13	12	1	Mascoutah	6,838	14	13	1
Irving	468	1	1	0	Mason City	2,278	5	5	0
Island Lake	8,570	21	15	6	Matteson	17,627	42	34	8
Itasca	8,573	32	24	8	Mattoon	16,834	40	36	4
Jacksonville	18,937	47	37	10	Maywood	24,448	66	55	11

Table 78. Full-Time Law Enforcement Employees by State and City, 2010—Continued

(Number)

State/city	Population	Total law enforcement employees	Total officers	Total civilians	State/city	Population	Total law enforcement employees	Total officers	Total civilians
McCook	232	21	17	4	Orland Hills	7,108	14	13	1
McHenry	27,477	58	44	14	Orland Park	55,051	123	96	27
McLean	790	1	1	0	Oswego	31,336	57	48	9
McLeansboro	2,670	5	5	0	Ottawa	19,198	47	36	11
Medora	471	1	1	0	Palatine	66,024	138	111	27
Melrose Park	21,405	80	71	9	Palestine	1,296	2	2	0
Mendota	6,908	20	15	5	Palmyra	691	2	2	0
Meredosia	942	1	1	0	Palos Heights	12,369	29	26	3
Metamora	3,480	5	5	0	Palos Hills	16,571	34	31	3
Metropolis	6,414	22	17	5	Palos Park	5,007	10	9	1
Midlothian	13,361	28	25	3	Pana	5,601	13	9	4
Milan	5,124	19	14	5	Paris	8,446	23	17	6
Milledgeville	903	2	2	0	Park City	6,644	12	10	2
Millstadt	3,413	8	8	0	Park Forest	22,125	51	42	9
Minier	1,243	2	2	0	Park Ridge	36,324	66	55	11
Minonk	2,153	3	3	0	Pawnee	2,514	10	6	4
Minooka	11,652	24	20	4	Paxton	4,406	6	6	0
Mokena	19,567	33	30	3	Pecatonica	2,201	2	2	0
Moline	42,510	105	83	22	Pekin	33,196	64	55	9
Momence	3,022	7	7	0	Peoria	114,557	254	218	36
Monee	5,195	14	13	1	Peoria Heights	6,181	16	12	4
Monmouth	9,092	26	16	10	Peotone	4,374	10	9	1
Montgomery	16,835	31	23	8	Peru	9,683	32	25	7
Monticello	5,341	7	6	1	Petersburg	2,151	4	4	0
Morris	14,035	34	25	9	Phoenix	2,001	2	1	1
Morrison	4,245	6	6	0	Pinckneyville	5,303	8	7	1
Morton	16,115	28	21	7	Piper City	714	1	1	0
Morton Grove	22,177	58	45	13	Pittsfield	4,328	6	6	0
Mound City	558	2	1	1	Plainfield	40,084	70	51	19
Mount Carmel	7,227	17	12	5	Plano	13,645	22	20	2
Mount Carroll	1,615	3	3	0	Polo	2,454	4	4	0
Mount Morris	3,065	5	4	1	Pontiac	11,076	24	22	2
Mount Olive	2,020	5	3	2	Pontoon Beach	6,094	22	16	6
Mount Prospect	52,190	108	84	24	Posen	4,838	18	16	2
Mount Pulaski	1,549	2	2	0	Potomac	644	1	1	0
Mount Sterling	1,876	6	4	2	Princeton	7,378	17	16	1
Mount Vernon	15,998	54	42	12	Prophetstown	1,886	3	3	0
Mount Zion	5,214	12	10	2	Prospect Heights	15,688	17	15	2
Moweaqua	1,798	2	2	0	Quincy	39,579	88	75	13
Mundelein	33,921	68	50	18	Rantoul	12,053	39	30	9
Murphysboro	7,964	22	16	6	Red Bud	3,600	6	6	0
Naperville	143,657	270	173	97	Richmond	2,467	4	4	0
Nashville	2,947	8	7	1	Richton Park	12,694	35	30	5
Nauvoo	1,136	3	3	0	Ridge Farm	836	1	1	0
Neoga	1,702	3	3	0	Ridgway	801	2	2	0
New Athens	1,979	4	4	0	Riverdale	13,841	43	38	5
New Baden	3,243	5	5	0	River Forest	10,964	30	27	3
New Lenox	24,716	41	37	4	River Grove	9,758	30	23	7
Newman	874	1	1	0	Riverside	8,086	23	18	5
Newton	2,843	7	6	1	Riverton	3,013	7	7	0
Niles	28,068	68	53	15	Riverwoods	4,051	7	7	0
Nokomis	2,192	4	3	1	Robbins	6,235	9	3	6
Normal	53,014	91	78	13	Robinson	6,191	14	13	1
Norridge	13,664	51	35	16	Rochelle	9,772	26	19	7
North Aurora	16,276	31	29	2	Rochester	3,250	8	8	0
Northbrook	33,432	93	66	27	Rockdale	1,995	3	3	0
North Chicago	32,018	77	57	20	Rock Falls	9,139	26	19	7
Northfield	5,396	27	19	8	Rockford	156,180	307	277	30
Northlake	11,213	58	40	18	Rock Island	37,534	105	79	26
North Pekin	1,717	4	4	0	Rockton	5,474	16	15	1
North Riverside	6,092	34	26	8	Rolling Meadows	22,952	60	51	9
Oak Brook	8,753	52	42	10	Romeoville	39,759	81	61	20
Oakbrook Terrace	2,371	23	20	3	Roodhouse	1,881	8	4	4
Oak Forest	27,339	53	42	11	Roscoe	9,016	13	12	1
Oak Lawn	52,172	152	104	48	Roselle	22,945	43	33	10
Oak Park	52,629	138	111	27	Rosemont	3,836	99	76	23
Oakwood	1,405	1	1	0	Rossville	1,125	2	2	0
Oblong	1,491	1	1	0	Round Lake	18,435	28	22	6
O'Fallon	28,102	61	45	16	Round Lake Beach	27,668	50	42	8
Oglesby	3,644	12	9	3	Round Lake Heights	2,988	6	6	0
Okawville	1,312	3	3	0	Round Lake Park	6,124	13	11	2
Old Shawneetown	245	4	4	0	Roxana	1,530	7	6	1
Olney	8,267	20	13	7	Royalton	1,145	1	1	0
Olympia Fields	4,665	22	19	3	Rushville	2,959	4	4	0
Oregon	4,092	9	8	1	Salem	7,180	22	14	8
Orion	1,654	3	3	0	Sandwich	7,389	21	14	7

Table 78.   Full-Time Law Enforcement Employees by State and City, 2010—*Continued*

(Number)

State/city	Population	Total law enforcement employees	Total officers	Total civilians	State/city	Population	Total law enforcement employees	Total officers	Total civilians
Sauget	236	14	13	1	Warrenville	12,882	38	30	8
Sauk Village	10,095	31	24	7	Warsaw	1,536	3	3	0
Savanna	3,122	8	8	0	Washburn	1,095	1	1	0
Schaumburg	70,170	157	116	41	Washington	14,425	28	21	7
Schiller Park	11,279	39	31	8	Washington Park	5,460	7	5	2
Seneca	2,110	8	4	4	Waterloo	10,073	17	15	2
Sesser	2,093	6	5	1	Waterman	1,546	2	2	0
Shannon	775	1	1	0	Watseka	5,290	9	9	0
Shawneetown	1,219	4	4	0	Wauconda	12,456	36	25	11
Shelbyville	4,569	8	7	1	Waukegan	89,900	192	148	44
Sheridan	2,007	2	2	0	Wayne	2,407	5	5	0
Sherman	3,945	6	6	0	Wayne City	1,034	1	1	0
Shiloh	11,750	17	16	1	Westchester	15,331	42	31	11
Shorewood	16,666	30	26	4	West Chicago	26,470	55	47	8
Silvis	7,728	21	14	7	West City	761	9	5	4
Skokie	66,088	142	109	33	West Dundee	8,220	21	19	2
Sleepy Hollow	3,688	8	7	1	Western Springs	12,520	28	21	7
Smithton	3,550	7	6	1	West Frankfort	8,029	17	12	5
Somonauk	1,847	5	5	0	Westmont	24,745	48	36	12
South Barrington	4,525	22	19	3	West Salem	912	1	1	0
South Beloit	5,425	16	15	1	Westville	2,922	3	3	0
South Chicago Heights	3,701	11	7	4	Wheaton	53,898	78	63	15
South Elgin	21,632	38	29	9	Wheeling	35,500	86	62	24
Southern View	1,609	4	4	0	White Hall	2,397	7	5	2
South Holland	20,710	48	46	2	Williamsfield	559	1	1	0
South Jacksonville	3,145	6	5	1	Williamsville	1,367	3	3	0
South Pekin	1,191	2	2	0	Willowbrook	8,674	27	24	3
South Roxana	1,778	5	5	0	Willow Springs	5,872	24	18	6
Sparta	4,247	15	10	5	Wilmette	25,898	57	43	14
Springfield	117,383	293	251	42	Wilmington	6,253	16	15	1
Spring Grove	5,966	11	9	2	Winchester	1,520	2	2	0
Spring Valley	5,356	13	10	3	Winfield	10,005	20	18	2
St. Anne	1,238	2	2	0	Winnebago	3,228	5	5	0
Staunton	5,025	10	7	3	Winnetka	12,242	36	27	9
St. Charles	32,992	64	51	13	Winthrop Harbor	7,171	15	10	5
Steger	10,387	22	15	7	Wood Dale	13,765	52	35	17
Sterling	14,823	39	27	12	Woodhull	775	1	1	0
St. Francisville	705	1	1	0	Woodridge	34,137	75	52	23
Stickney	5,643	21	15	6	Wood River	10,787	25	19	6
Stockton	1,747	7	4	3	Woodstock	24,517	50	37	13
Stone Park	4,774	17	14	3	Worden	1,043	2	2	0
Stonington	877	2	2	0	Worth	10,210	23	21	2
Streamwood	36,621	65	56	9	Yates City	651	1	1	0
Streator	13,579	31	25	6	Yorkville	18,182	30	26	4
Sugar Grove	10,523	15	14	1	Zeigler	1,639	4	4	0
Sullivan	4,353	10	8	2	Zion	25,171	58	45	13
Summit	10,018	33	27	6	**INDIANA**				
Sumner	3,321	2	2	0	Albion	2,366	7	6	1
Swansea	13,142	27	21	6	Alexandria	5,609	17	13	4
Sycamore	18,283	32	29	3	Anderson	57,156	130	117	13
Taylorville	11,966	23	18	5	Angola	8,347	20	16	4
Thomson	513	1	1	0	Attica	3,239	6	6	0
Thornton	2,331	12	11	1	Auburn	13,229	28	22	6
Tilden	864	4	1	3	Aurora	4,120	13	10	3
Tilton	3,008	4	4	0	Austin	4,590	7	7	0
Tinley Park	59,607	101	74	27	Avon	13,259	24	22	2
Tolono	2,869	3	3	0	Bargersville	3,644	8	7	1
Toluca	1,228	1	1	0	Batesville	6,474	17	12	5
Tremont	2,066	3	3	0	Bedford	13,438	33	25	8
Trenton	2,600	5	5	0	Beech Grove	14,487	34	31	3
Troy	9,891	24	18	6	Berne	4,451	7	6	1
Tuscola	4,531	8	7	1	Bloomington	72,286	127	92	35
University Park	8,301	21	17	4	Bluffton	9,160	33	20	13
Urbana	39,784	64	50	14	Boonville	6,863	15	14	1
Valmeyer	1,234	2	2	0	Brazil	8,266	17	13	4
Vandalia	6,170	18	13	5	Bremen	4,682	16	12	4
Venice	2,383	13	9	4	Brownsburg	21,380	47	40	7
Vernon Hills	24,585	64	44	20	Burns Harbor	1,231	6	5	1
Vienna	1,295	4	4	0	Cannelton	1,127	2	2	0
Villa Grove	2,349	5	4	1	Carmel	71,647	128	107	21
Villa Park	21,984	49	36	13	Cedar Lake	11,411	21	16	5
Virden	3,289	9	6	3	Charlestown	7,548	20	15	5
Virginia	1,637	1	1	0	Chesterfield	2,786	6	6	0
Wamac	1,237	2	2	0	Chesterton	13,140	26	22	4
Warren	1,329	4	3	1	Clarksville	22,347	47	39	8
Warrensburg	1,136	2	2	0	Columbia City	8,501	20	18	2

Table 78.   Full-Time Law Enforcement Employees by State and City, 2010—*Continued*

(Number)

State/city	Popula-tion	Total law enforce-ment employees	Total officers	Total civilians	State/city	Popula-tion	Total law enforce-ment employees	Total officers	Total civilians
Columbus	40,554	81	73	8	North Vernon	6,274	20	18	2
Corydon	2,819	7	7	0	Oakland City	2,516	4	4	0
Covington	2,389	6	6	0	Peru	12,184	30	28	2
Crawfordsville	15,139	42	30	12	Plainfield	29,592	47	42	5
Crown Point	25,011	53	40	13	Plymouth	11,294	28	23	5
Culver	1,515	4	4	0	Portage	37,852	69	61	8
Danville	8,652	17	15	2	Porter	5,475	12	9	3
Decatur	9,682	21	17	4	Portland	6,050	17	13	4
Delphi	2,828	7	7	0	Princeton	8,477	18	17	1
Dyer	16,198	32	25	7	Rensselaer	6,372	15	10	5
East Chicago	29,773	118	105	13	Richmond	36,455	83	72	11
Elkhart	53,296	148	123	25	Rochester	6,454	17	12	5
Elwood	9,042	21	16	5	Rushville	5,979	18	13	5
Evansville	116,541	311	280	31	Schererville	29,332	60	48	12
Fairmount	2,712	9	5	4	Scottsburg	5,935	13	13	0
Fishers	75,734	101	94	7	Sellersburg	6,507	20	15	5
Fort Wayne	257,009	493	458	35	Seymour	19,507	54	38	16
Fowler	2,141	4	4	0	Shelbyville	18,797	60	48	12
Frankfort	16,533	36	28	8	South Bend	104,182	328	259	69
Franklin	24,118	55	39	16	South Whitley	1,856	4	4	0
Garrett	5,714	17	13	4	Speedway	12,770	45	31	14
Gas City	5,661	14	10	4	St. John	13,874	25	19	6
Georgetown	3,378	4	4	0	Tell City	7,465	20	12	8
Goshen	32,812	64	58	6	Terre Haute	60,156	144	134	10
Greencastle	10,098	17	15	2	Tipton	4,982	14	12	2
Greendale	4,427	13	10	3	Union City	3,296	9	8	1
Greenfield	19,972	41	38	3	Valparaiso	30,981	57	51	6
Greenwood	49,847	73	53	20	Vincennes	17,883	40	36	4
Griffith	16,252	39	31	8	Wabash	10,677	28	27	1
Hagerstown	1,618	5	5	0	Walkerton	2,175	10	6	4
Hammond	76,216	247	202	45	Warsaw	13,844	42	35	7
Hartford City	6,273	12	11	1	Washington	11,706	24	17	7
Highland	22,583	46	39	7	Waterloo	2,177	4	4	0
Hobart	28,136	69	55	14	Westfield	23,334	44	39	5
Huntingburg	6,113	11	10	1	West Lafayette	31,945	65	47	18
Huntington	16,803	40	32	8	West Terre Haute	2,242	9	8	1
Indianapolis	825,072	1,913	1,648	265	Westville	5,034	3	3	0
Jasonville	2,432	5	5	0	Whitestown	1,462	13	13	0
Jasper	14,292	27	21	6	Whiting	4,740	23	18	5
Jeffersonville	33,421	76	62	14	Winchester	4,554	11	11	0
Kendallville	10,628	26	18	8	Winona Lake	4,334	5	5	0
Kingsford Heights	1,411	4	4	0	Zionsville	14,472	25	24	1
Knox	3,818	7	7	0	**IOWA**				
Kokomo	45,412	131	102	29	Adel	4,462	10	9	1
Lafayette	66,388	163	130	33	Albia	3,541	7	6	1
Lake Station	13,253	29	24	5	Algona	5,229	14	10	4
La Porte	21,282	46	40	6	Altoona	15,012	25	23	2
Lawrenceburg	4,856	24	20	4	Ames	57,817	75	52	23
Lebanon	15,904	30	29	1	Anamosa	5,825	7	6	1
Ligonier	4,600	10	9	1	Ankeny	44,995	56	47	9
Linton	5,679	20	11	9	Atlantic	6,742	14	12	2
Logansport	18,544	39	38	1	Audubon	2,115	3	3	0
Long Beach	1,561	6	5	1	Belle Plaine	2,856	4	4	0
Loogootee	2,575	4	4	0	Belmond	2,263	5	5	0
Lowell	8,599	19	14	5	Bettendorf	33,690	49	45	4
Madison	13,018	34	27	7	Bloomfield	2,586	4	4	0
Marion	30,342	88	72	16	Boone	12,565	16	15	1
Martinsville	12,054	30	21	9	Burlington	25,650	59	43	16
Merrillville	33,839	63	49	14	Camanche	4,315	8	8	0
Michigan City	32,482	97	89	8	Carlisle	3,776	6	5	1
Mishawaka	50,632	123	101	22	Carroll	9,953	16	15	1
Mitchell	4,575	11	7	4	Carter Lake	3,235	10	9	1
Monticello	5,162	19	13	6	Cedar Falls	39,350	43	41	2
Mooresville	11,970	28	22	6	Cedar Rapids	129,605	264	203	61
Mount Vernon	6,917	15	14	1	Centerville	5,367	18	13	5
Muncie	67,736	104	99	5	Chariton	4,366	8	7	1
Munster	22,188	46	38	8	Charles City	7,373	21	14	7
Nappanee	7,249	22	15	7	Cherokee	4,654	9	8	1
New Albany	37,619	68	64	4	Clarinda	5,316	14	9	5
New Castle	18,093	34	32	2	Clarion	2,669	8	7	1
New Chicago	1,994	5	2	3	Clear Lake	7,822	22	16	6
New Haven	13,914	28	20	8	Clinton	26,591	52	44	8
New Whiteland	6,031	13	8	5	Clive	15,894	26	24	2
Noblesville	44,661	81	72	9	Coralville	19,419	37	33	4
North Liberty	1,404	3	3	0	Council Bluffs	61,181	131	111	20
North Manchester	5,775	16	11	5	Cresco	3,714	7	7	0

Table 78.   Full-Time Law Enforcement Employees by State and City, 2010—*Continued*

(Number)

State/city	Population	Total law enforcement employees	Total officers	Total civilians	State/city	Population	Total law enforcement employees	Total officers	Total civilians
Creston	7,627	15	11	4	Sioux Center	6,836	7	7	0
Davenport	102,628	195	167	28	Sioux City	83,494	155	127	28
Decorah	7,800	18	11	7	Spencer	11,045	28	19	9
Denison	7,241	18	13	5	Spirit Lake	4,672	10	9	1
Des Moines	202,564	480	374	106	St. Ansgar	1,036	1	1	0
De Witt	5,313	10	10	0	State Center	1,348	1	1	0
Dubuque	57,744	106	100	6	Storm Lake	9,582	23	19	4
Dyersville	4,236	10	6	4	Story City	3,438	5	5	0
Eagle Grove	3,246	7	7	0	Tama	2,492	4	4	0
Eldora	2,706	4	4	0	Tipton	3,028	6	6	0
Eldridge	5,078	8	8	0	Urbandale	40,124	52	47	5
Emmetsburg	3,581	7	6	1	Vinton	5,144	8	8	0
Estherville	6,211	12	12	0	Washington	7,280	12	11	1
Evansdale	5,177	8	7	1	Waterloo	67,203	138	126	12
Fairfield	9,251	20	13	7	Waukee	14,091	17	15	2
Forest City	3,961	7	7	0	Waukon	3,883	7	7	0
Fort Dodge	25,204	43	38	5	Waverly	9,261	16	15	1
Fort Madison	10,901	20	18	2	Webster City	7,664	17	13	4
Garner	2,900	5	5	0	West Branch	2,339	4	3	1
Glenwood	5,737	10	9	1	West Burlington	3,383	11	10	1
Grinnell	9,147	17	15	2	West Des Moines	58,600	80	64	16
Grundy Center	2,540	4	4	0	West Liberty	3,725	8	7	1
Hampton	4,187	12	7	5	West Union	2,405	3	3	0
Harlan	4,905	8	7	1	Williamsburg	2,865	6	6	0
Hawarden	2,380	4	4	0	Wilton	2,867	4	4	0
Hiawatha	6,779	13	12	1	Windsor Heights	4,657	13	12	1
Humboldt	4,205	6	6	0	Winterset	4,883	8	8	0
Independence	6,133	12	11	1	**KANSAS**				
Indianola	14,785	21	19	2	Abilene	6,284	16	13	3
Iowa City	70,411	103	80	23	Altamont	1,054	3	3	0
Iowa Falls	4,911	13	9	4	Andale	929	2	2	0
Jefferson	4,109	7	7	0	Andover	11,091	29	21	8
Johnston	17,024	24	23	1	Anthony	2,130	6	5	1
Keokuk	10,413	28	24	4	Argonia	465	1	1	0
Knoxville	7,286	13	12	1	Arkansas City	10,960	33	23	10
Le Claire	3,666	8	7	1	Arma	1,519	5	5	0
Le Mars	9,199	15	14	1	Atchison	10,483	22	21	1
Leon	1,838	3	3	0	Attica	568	1	1	0
Lisbon	2,048	2	2	0	Atwood	1,021	2	2	0
Manchester	4,880	13	9	4	Augusta	8,830	36	23	13
Maquoketa	5,823	16	10	6	Baldwin City	4,533	10	8	2
Marion	34,562	50	41	9	Basehor	4,713	14	12	2
Marshalltown	26,041	56	41	15	Baxter Springs	4,132	14	9	5
Mason City	27,344	53	48	5	Bel Aire	7,009	13	12	1
Missouri Valley	2,749	6	6	0	Belle Plaine	1,512	5	5	0
Monticello	3,742	6	5	1	Belleville	1,806	5	5	0
Mount Pleasant	8,751	16	14	2	Beloit	3,659	10	10	0
Mount Vernon	4,263	6	6	0	Benton	812	2	2	0
Muscatine	22,866	40	37	3	Blue Rapids	1,013	1	1	0
Nevada	6,806	9	8	1	Bonner Springs	7,349	27	24	3
New Hampton	3,401	7	7	0	Buhler	1,337	3	3	0
New London	1,797	3	3	0	Burden	526	1	1	0
Newton	14,909	28	23	5	Burlingame	942	2	2	0
North Liberty	13,609	14	13	1	Burlington	2,685	9	7	2
Norwalk	9,331	15	13	2	Burrton	913	3	2	1
Oelwein	5,985	15	10	5	Caldwell	1,128	3	3	0
Ogden	1,945	3	3	0	Caney	1,969	10	6	4
Onawa	2,695	6	6	0	Canton	788	1	1	0
Orange City	5,889	7	7	0	Carbondale	1,350	2	2	0
Osage	3,461	6	5	1	Cedar Vale	606	1	1	0
Osceola	4,814	11	10	1	Chapman	1,383	4	4	0
Oskaloosa	10,990	18	17	1	Chase	447	1	1	0
Ottumwa	24,501	47	40	7	Cheney	2,128	5	5	0
Pella	10,332	21	15	6	Cherokee	722	1	1	0
Perry	9,568	20	13	7	Chetopa	1,234	4	4	0
Pleasant Hill	8,922	18	16	2	Claflin	631	1	1	0
Pleasantville	1,600	1	1	0	Clay Center	4,378	9	7	2
Polk City	3,398	6	6	0	Clearwater	2,477	6	5	1
Prairie City	1,446	3	3	0	Coffeyville	10,241	32	25	7
Red Oak	5,623	12	10	2	Colby	4,811	18	12	6
Rock Rapids	2,445	1	1	0	Columbus	3,179	11	9	2
Rock Valley	3,220	5	5	0	Colwich	1,459	3	3	0
Sac City	2,073	4	4	0	Concordia	5,091	17	11	6
Sergeant Bluff	4,142	9	8	1	Conway Springs	1,181	2	2	0
Sheldon	4,866	7	7	0	Council Grove	2,274	7	7	0
Shenandoah	4,814	11	8	3	Derby	23,607	53	39	14

Table 78. Full-Time Law Enforcement Employees by State and City, 2010—*Continued*

(Number)

State/city	Population	Total law enforcement employees	Total officers	Total civilians	State/city	Population	Total law enforcement employees	Total officers	Total civilians
Dodge City	26,213	66	50	16	Marquette	584	1	1	0
Eastborough	815	6	6	0	Marysville	3,103	9	8	1
Edwardsville	4,595	17	15	2	McLouth	822	2	2	0
El Dorado	12,712	26	23	3	McPherson	13,371	34	28	6
Elkhart	1,938	4	4	0	Meade	1,569	3	3	0
Ellinwood	1,974	5	5	0	Medicine Lodge	1,869	7	6	1
Ellis	1,952	5	5	0	Merriam	11,224	33	28	5
Ellsworth	2,823	7	6	1	Minneapolis	1,956	5	5	0
Elwood	1,119	5	5	0	Mission	9,920	31	29	2
Emporia	24,856	69	46	23	Mission Hills	3,651	11	8	3
Erie	1,150	3	2	1	Moran	521	1	1	0
Eskridge	563	1	1	0	Mound City	762	2	2	0
Eudora	6,540	11	10	1	Moundridge	1,635	3	3	0
Fairway	3,912	11	9	2	Mount Hope	880	2	2	0
Florence	587	1	1	0	Mulberry	571	2	2	0
Fort Scott	7,959	27	18	9	Mulvane	6,033	17	11	6
Frontenac	3,244	9	6	3	Neodesha	2,559	8	7	1
Galena	3,126	11	7	4	Newton	18,637	38	33	5
Galva	813	1	1	0	Nickerson	1,151	3	3	0
Garden City	28,736	91	58	33	North Newton	1,632	2	2	0
Garden Plain	881	2	2	0	Norton	2,643	6	6	0
Gardner	19,112	35	31	4	Norwich	487	1	1	0
Garnett	3,166	9	9	0	Oakley	1,794	11	6	5
Girard	2,719	7	6	1	Oberlin	1,600	3	3	0
Goddard	4,352	11	10	1	Olathe	126,090	188	162	26
Goodland	4,245	9	8	1	Onaga	686	1	1	0
Grandview Plaza	1,432	6	6	0	Osage City	2,766	6	6	0
Great Bend	15,794	35	30	5	Osawatomie	4,554	18	13	5
Halstead	1,935	6	6	0	Osborne	1,363	4	4	0
Haven	1,163	3	3	0	Oswego	1,752	5	5	0
Havensville	146	1	1	0	Ottawa	13,073	32	28	4
Hays	20,537	54	33	21	Oxford	1,064	2	2	0
Haysville	10,765	31	26	5	Paola	5,415	20	15	5
Herington	2,396	8	7	1	Park City	8,295	19	17	2
Hesston	3,881	7	6	1	Parsons	11,026	30	23	7
Hiawatha	3,178	7	6	1	Peabody	1,182	3	3	0
Highland	936	1	1	0	Pittsburg	19,817	54	38	16
Hill City	1,292	4	4	0	Plainville	1,741	5	5	0
Hillsboro	2,607	5	5	0	Pleasanton	1,275	2	2	0
Hoisington	2,802	9	7	2	Prairie Village	21,821	58	45	13
Holcomb	2,176	4	3	1	Pratt	6,336	21	14	7
Holton	3,306	6	6	0	Protection	527	1	1	0
Holyrood	444	1	1	0	Roeland Park	7,059	17	15	2
Horton	1,777	10	6	4	Rolla	417	1	1	0
Howard	746	1	1	0	Rose Hill	4,187	11	9	2
Hoxie	1,076	2	2	0	Rossville	1,143	2	2	0
Hugoton	3,456	7	5	2	Russell	4,167	10	8	2
Humboldt	1,812	7	6	1	Sabetha	2,454	9	5	4
Hutchinson	40,981	88	67	21	Salina	46,547	105	75	30
Independence	9,203	29	21	8	Scott City	3,475	12	7	5
Inman	1,184	2	2	0	Scranton	672	1	1	0
Iola	5,704	17	16	1	Sedgwick	1,721	2	2	0
Junction City	21,298	65	45	20	Seneca	1,988	5	5	0
Kansas City	143,867	494	370	124	Shawnee	63,652	105	84	21
Kechi	1,849	4	3	1	Silver Lake	1,404	1	1	0
Kingman	2,907	7	7	0	Smith Center	1,566	3	3	0
La Crosse	1,202	3	3	0	South Hutchinson	2,559	10	8	2
La Cygne	1,078	2	2	0	Spring Hill	5,644	15	13	2
Lake Quivira	962	1	1	0	Stafford	1,028	3	3	0
Lansing	11,003	19	18	1	Sterling	2,541	4	4	0
Larned	3,504	13	9	4	St. Francis	1,250	4	3	1
Lawrence	93,945	168	138	30	St. George	607	1	1	0
Leavenworth	35,290	92	66	26	St. John	1,170	4	4	0
Leawood	32,422	83	61	22	St. Marys	2,326	5	5	0
Lebo	912	1	1	0	Stockton	1,352	5	5	0
Lenexa	49,282	125	86	39	Tonganoxie	4,657	11	10	1
Liberal	20,226	52	37	15	Topeka	125,306	345	281	64
Lindsborg	3,237	7	6	1	Troy	994	1	1	0
Linn Valley	572	2	2	0	Udall	739	1	1	0
Little River	524	1	1	0	Ulysses	5,512	12	12	0
Louisburg	4,093	8	8	0	Valley Center	6,799	18	13	5
Lyndon	1,000	2	2	0	Valley Falls	1,140	2	2	0
Lyons	3,394	7	6	1	Victoria	1,202	2	2	0
Macksville	477	1	1	0	Wa Keeney	1,730	5	5	0
Maize	3,477	9	8	1	Wakefield	907	1	1	0
Marion	1,849	4	4	0	Walton	295	1	1	0

Table 78.   Full-Time Law Enforcement Employees by State and City, 2010—*Continued*

(Number)

State/city	Population	Total law enforcement employees	Total officers	Total civilians	State/city	Population	Total law enforcement employees	Total officers	Total civilians
Wamego	4,414	13	8	5	Franklin	7,944	25	24	1
Waterville	610	1	1	0	Fulton	2,388	13	10	3
Wathena	1,280	2	2	0	Georgetown	22,441	50	47	3
Wellington	7,639	20	17	3	Glasgow	14,381	42	30	12
Westwood	1,879	8	7	1	Glencoe	384	1	1	0
Wichita	376,880	802	630	172	Graymoor-Devondale	3,156	2	2	0
Winfield	11,126	32	23	9	Greensburg	2,389	11	7	4
Yates Center	1,341	3	3	0	Greenup	1,200	3	3	0
KENTUCKY					Greenville	4,286	9	9	0
Adairville	918	1	1	0	Guthrie	1,455	4	4	0
Albany	2,266	8	8	0	Hardinsburg	2,420	5	5	0
Alexandria	8,509	15	13	2	Harlan	1,838	14	12	2
Allen	147	1	1	0	Harrodsburg	8,154	21	10	11
Anchorage	3,414	14	10	4	Hartford	2,632	5	5	0
Ashland	21,209	55	49	6	Hawesville	972	1	1	0
Auburn	1,508	1	1	0	Hazard	4,736	23	18	5
Audubon Park	1,680	7	6	1	Henderson	27,978	73	61	12
Augusta	1,261	3	3	0	Highland Heights Southgate	10,660	16	16	0
Barbourville	3,625	17	14	3	Hillview	7,601	13	13	0
Bardstown	11,339	24	23	1	Hindman	744	2	2	0
Beattyville	1,096	6	5	1	Hodgenville	2,732	5	5	0
Beaver Dam	3,120	5	5	0	Hopkinsville	32,265	86	78	8
Bellefonte	855	4	4	0	Horse Cave	2,292	4	4	0
Bellevue	5,822	12	11	1	Hurstbourne Acres	1,650	2	2	0
Benham	524	2	2	0	Hustonville	350	1	1	0
Benton	4,346	8	7	1	Independence	22,935	28	26	2
Berea	15,130	32	30	2	Indian Hills	3,555	8	8	0
Bloomfield	900	1	1	0	Inez	419	2	2	0
Booneville	147	3	3	0	Irvine	2,616	7	5	2
Bowling Green	57,308	140	103	37	Irvington	1,398	4	4	0
Brandenburg	2,155	5	5	0	Jackson	2,361	12	9	3
Brooksville	609	1	1	0	Jamestown	1,755	5	5	0
Burkesville	1,632	9	5	4	Jeffersontown	26,411	61	51	10
Burnside	995	4	4	0	Jenkins	2,190	5	4	1
Butler	615	1	1	0	Junction City	2,211	3	3	0
Cadiz	2,602	10	9	1	La Center	1,015	1	1	0
Calhoun	774	1	1	0	La Grange	6,638	13	13	0
Calvert City	2,753	7	6	1	Lakeside Park-Crestview Hills	6,458	11	10	1
Campbellsville	11,340	24	22	2	Lancaster	4,459	9	9	0
Caneyville	663	1	1	0	Lawrenceburg	10,225	24	16	8
Carlisle	2,071	9	5	4	Lebanon	6,371	21	14	7
Carrollton	3,933	11	10	1	Lebanon Junction	2,045	5	5	0
Catlettsburg	1,824	8	8	0	Leitchfield	6,562	17	16	1
Cave City	2,009	6	6	0	Lewisburg	912	1	1	0
Central City	5,655	12	12	0	Lexington	300,069	623	544	79
Clarkson	841	1	1	0	London	7,958	34	31	3
Clay City	1,328	2	2	0	Louisa	2,091	6	6	0
Clinton	1,296	4	4	0	Louisville Metro	637,428	1,379	1,211	168
Cloverport	1,222	2	2	0	Loyall	697	2	2	0
Coal Run Village	626	3	2	1	Ludlow	4,845	10	9	1
Cold Spring	6,172	12	11	1	Lynch	812	2	2	0
Corbin	8,335	28	21	7	Lynnview	1,046	3	3	0
Covington	43,054	141	116	25	Madisonville	18,920	53	43	10
Cumberland	2,329	6	6	0	Manchester	1,962	12	12	0
Cynthiana	6,281	15	14	1	Marion	3,031	9	6	3
Danville	15,646	28	26	2	Martin	621	4	4	0
Dawson Springs	2,872	7	5	2	Maysville	9,207	30	23	7
Dayton	5,418	9	8	1	McKee	821	1	1	0
Earlington	1,550	1	1	0	Meadow Vale	861	1	1	0
Eddyville	2,409	6	6	0	Middlesboro	9,775	24	21	3
Edgewood	8,885	14	14	0	Millersburg	860	1	1	0
Edmonton	1,606	6	6	0	Monticello	6,152	11	10	1
Elizabethtown	24,712	57	43	14	Morehead	7,714	27	20	7
Elkhorn City	995	4	4	0	Morganfield	3,240	14	8	6
Elkton	1,988	7	7	0	Morgantown	2,558	6	6	0
Elsmere	7,999	14	13	1	Mortons Gap	931	1	1	0
Eminence	2,245	6	6	0	Mount Sterling	7,145	23	21	2
Erlanger	21,384	54	41	13	Mount Vernon	2,555	8	8	0
Ferguson	940	1	1	0	Mount Washington	12,414	15	14	1
Flatwoods	7,678	11	10	1	Muldraugh	1,211	4	4	0
Flemingsburg	2,654	8	8	0	Munfordville	1,588	5	5	0
Florence	28,869	62	58	4	Murray	16,677	37	31	6
Fort Mitchell	7,539	12	12	0	Newport	15,738	41	37	4
Fort Thomas	15,141	24	23	1	Nicholasville	27,686	71	64	7
Fort Wright	5,436	12	12	0	Nortonville	1,223	1	1	0
Frankfort	27,319	65	60	5	Oak Grove	9,673	23	17	6

Table 78.   Full-Time Law Enforcement Employees by State and City, 2010—*Continued*

(Number)

State/city	Popula-tion	Total law enforce-ment employees	Total officers	Total civilians	State/city	Popula-tion	Total law enforce-ment employees	Total officers	Total civilians
Olive Hill	1,758	5	5	0	Clarence	501	3	3	0
Owensboro	55,848	139	101	38	Clinton	1,867	9	8	1
Owingsville	1,645	5	5	0	Covington	9,325	51	39	12
Paducah	25,643	88	77	11	Crowley	13,878	43	37	6
Paintsville	4,152	12	12	0	Denham Springs	10,504	43	35	8
Paris	9,189	23	21	2	Dixie Inn	341	2	2	0
Park Hills	2,770	6	6	0	Epps	1,090	5	3	2
Perryville	758	1	1	0	Erath	2,160	10	7	3
Pewee Valley	1,632	1	1	0	Farmerville	3,574	14	14	0
Pikeville	6,407	30	22	8	Franklin	7,538	22	20	2
Pineville	2,041	9	9	0	Franklinton	3,771	23	17	6
Pioneer Village	2,733	5	5	0	Georgetown	320	3	2	1
Powderly	880	2	2	0	Glenmora	1,567	3	3	0
Prestonsburg	3,825	16	16	0	Golden Meadow	2,095	6	5	1
Princeton	6,366	16	15	1	Gonzales	9,738	44	40	4
Prospect	5,972	10	9	1	Grambling	4,931	15	10	5
Providence	3,399	7	7	0	Gretna	17,901	129	99	30
Radcliff	22,251	54	41	13	Hammond	20,386	104	80	24
Ravenna	658	1	1	0	Haughton	3,032	7	7	0
Richmond	34,068	71	60	11	Iowa	2,634	12	9	3
Russell	3,632	12	12	0	Jeanerette	5,848	14	14	0
Russell Springs	2,335	9	8	1	Jena	2,845	7	6	1
Russellville	7,254	19	19	0	Jennings	10,418	35	23	12
Salyersville	1,557	3	3	0	Kaplan	4,996	23	17	6
Scottsville	4,558	20	13	7	Kenner	67,889	235	169	66
Sebree	1,504	1	1	0	Kentwood	2,315	8	7	1
Shelbyville	11,637	24	23	1	Kinder	2,403	17	12	5
Shepherdsville	9,424	28	26	2	Krotz Springs	1,300	6	5	1
Shively	16,609	32	26	6	Lafayette	115,378	321	259	62
Silver Grove	1,150	1	1	0	Lake Charles	71,795	183	180	3
Simpsonville	1,500	4	4	0	Lecompte	1,321	5	5	0
Smiths Grove	805	1	1	0	Mandeville	12,825	52	38	14
Somerset	12,266	46	42	4	Many	2,698	11	9	2
South Shore	1,277	1	1	0	Marion	753	2	2	0
Stamping Ground	709	1	1	0	Marksville	5,690	25	21	4
Stanford	3,379	10	10	0	McNary	200	2	1	1
Stanton	3,070	7	7	0	Minden	12,799	34	34	0
St. Matthews	18,885	37	31	6	Moreauville	931	3	3	0
Strathmoor Village	738	2	2	0	Morgan City	11,367	55	53	2
Sturgis	1,889	3	3	0	Natchitoches	17,667	64	49	15
Taylor Mill	7,123	11	10	1	New Orleans	356,317	1,715	1,452	263
Taylorsville	1,300	5	5	0	Oak Grove	1,918	6	6	0
Tompkinsville	2,603	12	9	3	Oil City	1,212	4	4	0
Uniontown	1,017	2	2	0	Olla	1,328	4	4	0
Vanceburg	1,681	6	6	0	Pineville	15,064	67	58	9
Versailles	7,924	48	39	9	Plaquemine	6,646	29	26	3
Villa Hills	7,704	8	7	1	Ponchatoula	6,524	28	23	5
Vine Grove	4,558	8	8	0	Port Allen	4,892	20	19	1
Warsaw	1,798	5	5	0	Port Barre	2,442	18	12	6
Wayland	286	1	1	0	Port Vincent	541	4	3	1
West Liberty	3,356	15	8	7	Ruston	21,391	51	42	9
West Point	968	4	4	0	Scott	9,335	24	23	1
Wheelwright	1,206	1	1	0	Shreveport	199,900	736	637	99
Wilder	2,956	6	6	0	Sicily Island	442	2	2	0
Williamsburg	5,176	13	12	1	Simmesport	2,207	5	5	0
Williamstown	3,533	7	6	1	Springhill	5,064	17	17	0
Wilmore	6,028	10	9	1	Sterlington	1,447	6	6	0
Winchester	16,754	45	33	12	St. Francisville	1,466	8	8	0
Wingo	596	1	1	0	St. Gabriel	5,562	20	12	8
Worthington	1,700	4	4	0	Sulphur	19,632	67	42	25
LOUISIANA					Tallulah	7,218	16	11	5
Abbeville	12,310	43	41	2	Thibodaux	14,487	67	56	11
Addis	4,043	12	11	1	Tickfaw	703	6	6	0
Alexandria	49,283	188	155	33	Vidalia	4,070	29	21	8
Baker	13,460	39	37	2	Ville Platte	8,066	31	26	5
Baldwin	2,639	9	8	1	Vinton	3,385	11	8	3
Baton Rouge	226,001	832	728	104	Walker	6,567	21	17	4
Bernice	1,618	7	7	0	West Monroe	12,930	80	77	3
Berwick	4,266	13	12	1	Westwego	10,226	40	39	1
Blanchard	2,734	6	5	1	Youngsville	7,719	15	15	0
Bogalusa	12,581	57	36	21	Zachary	15,696	45	44	1
Bossier City	64,232	214	173	41	**MAINE**				
Breaux Bridge	8,109	23	18	5	Ashland	1,457	2	2	0
Brusly	2,129	9	8	1	Auburn	22,953	57	50	7
Bunkie	4,444	12	9	3	Augusta	18,514	55	40	15
Carencro	6,897	26	24	2	Baileyville	1,524	4	4	0

Table 78.   Full-Time Law Enforcement Employees by State and City, 2010—*Continued*

(Number)

State/city	Population	Total law enforcement employees	Total officers	Total civilians
Bangor	31,587	98	81	17
Bar Harbor	5,243	17	13	4
Bath	8,879	21	18	3
Belfast	6,748	14	13	1
Berwick	7,707	12	11	1
Biddeford	21,511	70	47	23
Boothbay Harbor	2,252	8	7	1
Brewer	9,097	22	21	1
Bridgton	5,608	11	8	3
Brownville	1,288	2	2	0
Brunswick	22,171	51	36	15
Bucksport	4,951	11	7	4
Buxton	8,179	13	8	5
Calais	3,145	9	8	1
Camden	5,279	15	13	2
Cape Elizabeth	8,825	14	13	1
Caribou	8,063	17	16	1
Carrabassett Valley	474	1	1	0
Clinton	3,328	3	3	0
Cumberland	7,744	12	11	1
Damariscotta	1,905	7	6	1
Dexter	3,687	5	5	0
Dixfield	2,532	4	4	0
Dover-Foxcroft	4,165	6	6	0
East Millinocket	3,177	4	4	0
Eastport	1,509	4	4	0
Eliot	6,358	11	10	1
Ellsworth	7,243	20	16	4
Fairfield	6,695	12	11	1
Falmouth	10,921	24	17	7
Farmington	7,602	14	13	1
Fort Fairfield	3,443	4	4	0
Fort Kent	4,212	8	4	4
Freeport	8,392	14	12	2
Fryeburg	3,313	6	6	0
Gardiner	6,103	14	12	2
Gorham	15,940	25	23	2
Gouldsboro	2,011	2	2	0
Greenville	1,721	2	2	0
Hallowell	2,434	5	5	0
Hampden	7,052	12	11	1
Holden	3,048	3	3	0
Houlton	6,105	20	14	6
Jay	4,739	8	7	1
Kennebunk	11,577	27	20	7
Kennebunkport	4,031	16	11	5
Kittery	10,632	28	20	8
Lewiston	35,153	94	81	13
Limestone	2,252	3	3	0
Lincoln	5,318	7	6	1
Lincolnville	2,205	1	1	0
Lisbon	9,355	18	14	4
Livermore Falls	3,134	7	6	1
Machias	2,124	3	3	0
Madawaska	4,319	6	5	1
Madison	4,578	7	6	1
Mechanic Falls	3,254	5	5	0
Mexico	2,828	5	5	0
Milbridge	1,289	2	2	0
Millinocket	4,891	9	9	0
Milo	2,313	3	3	0
Monmouth	3,959	4	4	0
Mount Desert	2,188	11	7	4
Newport	3,151	7	7	0
North Berwick	4,921	9	8	1
Norway	4,755	8	7	1
Oakland	6,236	11	10	1
Ogunquit	1,264	10	9	1
Old Orchard Beach	9,494	24	18	6
Old Town	7,731	18	16	2
Orono	10,290	15	14	1
Oxford	3,935	6	5	1
Paris	4,942	7	6	1
Phippsburg	2,185	1	1	0
Pittsfield	4,186	6	6	0
Portland	63,166	215	159	56
Presque Isle	9,050	21	19	2
Rangeley	1,183	3	3	0
Richmond	3,457	4	4	0
Rockland	7,458	21	18	3
Rockport	3,563	6	5	1
Rumford	6,236	13	12	1
Sabattus	4,744	8	7	1
Saco	18,417	46	33	13
Sanford	21,216	45	40	5
Scarborough	19,549	51	35	16
Searsport	2,588	4	4	0
Skowhegan	8,611	15	15	0
South Berwick	7,221	12	8	4
South Portland	24,144	67	50	17
Southwest Harbor	1,962	9	5	4
Swan's Island	302	1	1	0
Thomaston	3,652	5	5	0
Topsham	9,953	14	13	1
Van Buren	2,464	3	3	0
Veazie	1,910	4	4	0
Waldoboro	5,007	9	8	1
Washburn	1,572	2	2	0
Waterville	16,076	41	31	10
Wells	10,005	29	21	8
Westbrook	16,762	41	37	4
Wilton	4,167	8	7	1
Windham	17,187	27	23	4
Winslow	7,825	10	9	1
Winthrop	6,419	13	9	4
Wiscasset	3,798	4	3	1
Yarmouth	8,157	13	12	1
York	14,201	38	27	11
MARYLAND				
Aberdeen	14,198	55	45	10
Annapolis	37,180	156	111	45
Baltimore	639,929	3,503	2,960	543
Baltimore City Sheriff		173	128	45
Bel Air	9,894	43	31	12
Berlin	4,125	18	13	5
Berwyn Heights	2,997	8	7	1
Bladensburg	7,732	23	17	6
Boonsboro	3,417	4	4	0
Bowie	53,840	54	48	6
Brentwood	2,853	1	1	0
Brunswick	5,338	11	9	2
Cambridge	12,167	57	45	12
Capitol Heights	4,188	4	4	0
Centreville	3,766	10	9	1
Chestertown	5,101	11	10	1
Cheverly	6,510	19	16	3
Chevy Chase Village	2,180	17	10	7
Colmar Manor	1,286	5	4	1
Cottage City	1,147	7	5	2
Crisfield	2,734	14	11	3
Cumberland	20,449	50	47	3
Delmar	3,524	13	12	1
Denton	4,189	13	12	1
District Heights	6,164	15	11	4
Easton	15,252	61	46	15
Edmonston	1,359	7	5	2
Elkton	15,144	46	39	7
Fairmount Heights	1,529	1	1	0
Federalsburg	2,660	9	9	0
Forest Heights	2,608	7	5	2
Frederick	60,686	172	130	42
Frostburg	7,831	18	14	4
Fruitland	4,606	20	18	2
Glenarden	6,451	11	10	1
Greenbelt	21,585	68	53	15
Greensboro	2,053	3	3	0
Hagerstown	40,564	110	98	12
Hampstead	5,510	10	9	1
Hancock	1,763	4	3	1
Havre de Grace	13,585	44	35	9
Hurlock	2,043	11	9	2
Hyattsville	15,688	51	38	13
Landover Hills	1,545	5	4	1
La Plata	9,266	17	15	2

Table 78. Full-Time Law Enforcement Employees by State and City, 2010—*Continued*

(Number)

State/city	Popula-tion	Total law enforce-ment employees	Total officers	Total civilians	State/city	Popula-tion	Total law enforce-ment employees	Total officers	Total civilians
Laurel	22,960	83	65	18	Brookfield	3,405	1	1	0
Luke	72	1	1	0	Brookline	55,751	154	127	27
Manchester	3,511	7	6	1	Buckland	1,963	2	2	0
Morningside	1,284	7	6	1	Burlington	25,782	70	64	6
Mount Rainier	8,497	21	17	4	Cambridge	108,356	307	267	40
New Carrollton	12,734	22	17	5	Canton	22,291	43	42	1
North East	2,898	10	9	1	Carlisle	4,839	10	10	0
Oakland	2,002	5	4	1	Carver	11,999	19	15	4
Ocean City	7,020	139	108	31	Charlton	12,626	23	19	4
Ocean Pines	11,442	17	13	4	Chatham	6,689	27	21	6
Oxford	696	3	3	0	Chelmsford	33,785	60	48	12
Perryville	3,852	12	10	2	Chelsea	37,335	101	96	5
Pocomoke City	3,880	19	12	7	Chicopee	55,444	130	126	4
Port Deposit	713	2	2	0	Chilmark	892	4	4	0
Preston	685	3	2	1	Clinton	14,101	32	27	5
Princess Anne	3,079	15	13	2	Cohasset	7,347	22	16	6
Ridgely	1,550	4	4	0	Concord	17,457	39	31	8
Rising Sun	1,835	7	6	1	Dalton	6,449	11	10	1
Riverdale Park	6,484	28	18	10	Danvers	27,165	59	46	13
Rock Hall	1,493	5	5	0	Dartmouth	34,450	77	62	15
Salisbury	29,046	115	82	33	Dedham	24,687	56	56	0
Seat Pleasant	4,932	16	14	2	Deerfield	4,627	8	7	1
Smithsburg	3,011	5	4	1	Dennis	15,212	47	38	9
Snow Hill	2,280	9	8	1	Dighton	6,760	9	9	0
St. Michaels	1,047	8	7	1	Douglas	8,109	20	15	5
Sykesville	4,489	8	7	1	Dover	5,685	16	15	1
Takoma Park	18,200	66	43	23	Dracut	29,179	42	37	5
Taneytown	5,496	12	11	1	Dudley	11,227	15	11	4
Thurmont	6,179	12	10	2	Dunstable	3,410	7	7	0
Trappe	1,142	1	1	0	Duxbury	14,222	33	26	7
University Park	2,330	7	7	0	East Bridgewater	14,060	22	20	2
Upper Marlboro	673	4	4	0	East Brookfield	2,062	4	4	0
Westminster	18,196	57	45	12	Eastham	5,402	20	14	6
MASSACHUSETTS					Easthampton	16,116	34	27	7
Abington	16,836	28	23	5	East Longmeadow	15,916	24	23	1
Acton	21,090	43	33	10	Easton	22,807	40	33	7
Acushnet	10,275	18	16	2	Edgartown	4,049	16	15	1
Adams	8,120	19	15	4	Egremont	1,329	3	3	0
Agawam	28,215	56	48	8	Erving	1,538	4	4	0
Amesbury	16,549	33	26	7	Essex	3,310	12	8	4
Amherst	36,004	44	42	2	Everett	37,897	99	91	8
Andover	33,505	68	50	18	Fairhaven	15,916	35	28	7
Aquinnah	370	4	4	0	Fall River	89,741	256	204	52
Arlington	41,212	79	63	16	Falmouth	32,471	67	60	7
Ashburnham	6,050	13	9	4	Fitchburg	42,046	80	73	7
Ashby	3,115	5	5	0	Foxborough	17,023	37	28	9
Ashland	15,279	32	26	6	Framingham	66,493	120	114	6
Athol	11,773	29	24	5	Franklin	31,979	53	45	8
Attleboro	43,385	89	76	13	Freetown	9,027	16	16	0
Auburn	16,335	44	33	11	Gardner	20,743	39	31	8
Avon	4,323	15	15	0	Georgetown	8,772	15	11	4
Ayer	7,828	22	17	5	Gill	1,381	2	2	0
Barnstable	45,599	126	110	16	Gloucester	30,226	61	57	4
Barre	5,599	11	7	4	Goshen	971	1	1	0
Becket	1,788	2	2	0	Grafton	17,897	23	18	5
Bedford	13,794	37	28	9	Granby	6,228	11	9	2
Belchertown	14,252	22	17	5	Granville	1,639	1	1	0
Bellingham	15,728	33	26	7	Great Barrington	7,263	17	17	0
Belmont	23,430	60	46	14	Greenfield	17,625	36	33	3
Berkley	6,526	6	6	0	Groton	10,793	22	17	5
Berlin	2,978	11	7	4	Groveland	7,533	11	8	3
Bernardston	2,214	3	3	0	Hadley	4,674	15	11	4
Beverly	39,064	71	67	4	Halifax	7,745	12	11	1
Billerica	39,519	72	61	11	Hamilton	8,155	13	13	0
Blackstone	9,725	19	16	3	Hampden	5,346	15	10	5
Blandford	1,292	1	1	0	Hanover	14,051	30	27	3
Bolton	4,595	14	9	5	Hanson	10,091	24	20	4
Boston	644,064	2,680	2,094	586	Hardwick	2,648	3	3	0
Bourne	19,239	43	37	6	Harvard	6,100	13	9	4
Boxborough	5,154	11	10	1	Harwich	12,104	35	33	2
Boxford	8,194	13	13	0	Hatfield	3,212	2	2	0
Boylston	4,384	13	10	3	Haverhill	61,179	97	87	10
Braintree	35,298	79	72	7	Hingham	23,433	43	41	2
Brewster	9,854	42	19	23	Hinsdale	1,890	1	1	0
Bridgewater	27,185	44	26	18	Holbrook	10,615	21	20	1
Brockton	92,383	195	176	19	Holden	17,657	26	24	2

Table 78.   Full-Time Law Enforcement Employees by State and City, 2010—*Continued*

(Number)

State/city	Population	Total law enforcement employees	Total officers	Total civilians	State/city	Population	Total law enforcement employees	Total officers	Total civilians
Holliston	14,076	24	23	1	Oak Bluffs	3,948	17	15	2
Holyoke	40,026	131	118	13	Oakham	1,951	3	3	0
Hopedale	6,215	13	12	1	Orange	7,614	13	12	1
Hopkinton	14,627	25	20	5	Orleans	6,177	27	21	6
Hubbardston	4,483	56	20	36	Oxford	13,690	24	19	5
Hudson	19,985	37	31	6	Palmer	13,021	24	18	6
Hull	11,008	38	24	14	Paxton	4,820	12	8	4
Ipswich	13,307	32	25	7	Peabody	51,517	106	92	14
Kingston	12,419	28	22	6	Pelham	1,377	1	1	0
Lakeville	10,587	17	13	4	Pembroke	18,843	29	27	2
Lancaster	7,013	11	10	1	Pepperell	11,418	17	16	1
Lanesboro	2,807	7	7	0	Petersham	1,330	2	2	0
Lawrence	69,679	130	108	22	Phillipston	1,784	2	2	0
Lee	5,654	12	11	1	Pittsfield	41,666	108	89	19
Leicester	11,072	23	18	5	Plainville	8,271	19	14	5
Lenox	5,027	10	10	0	Plymouth	56,751	113	96	17
Leominster	41,884	86	69	17	Plympton	2,787	7	7	0
Leverett	1,778	2	2	0	Princeton	3,504	9	6	3
Lexington	30,649	61	47	14	Provincetown	3,378	23	14	9
Lincoln	8,622	19	13	6	Quincy	90,304	218	187	31
Littleton	8,959	22	16	6	Randolph	30,701	58	55	3
Longmeadow	15,324	28	23	5	Raynham	13,601	34	25	9
Lowell	103,065	287	222	65	Reading	23,233	49	40	9
Ludlow	22,028	37	32	5	Rehoboth	11,516	30	23	7
Lunenburg	10,111	13	13	0	Revere	51,597	100	89	11
Lynn	86,340	193	173	20	Rochester	5,304	10	10	0
Lynnfield	11,954	25	18	7	Rockland	17,932	39	31	8
Malden	55,540	107	99	8	Rockport	7,580	16	15	1
Manchester-by-the-Sea	5,144	18	15	3	Rowley	5,795	12	11	1
Mansfield	23,749	46	34	12	Rutland	8,189	9	8	1
Marblehead	19,705	39	31	8	Salem	41,017	90	81	9
Marion	5,131	14	14	0	Salisbury	8,612	22	17	5
Marlborough	38,250	76	65	11	Sandwich	19,721	34	32	2
Marshfield	24,675	45	42	3	Saugus	27,830	70	54	16
Mashpee	14,347	45	34	11	Scituate	18,143	35	28	7
Mattapoisett	6,474	18	17	1	Seekonk	13,635	36	34	2
Maynard	10,534	23	21	2	Sharon	17,903	40	30	10
Medfield	12,134	21	17	4	Sheffield	3,257	5	5	0
Medford	54,984	101	99	2	Shelburne	2,003	2	2	0
Medway	12,820	21	19	2	Sherborn	4,251	16	15	1
Melrose	26,796	53	44	9	Shirley	8,073	13	9	4
Mendon	5,676	18	12	6	Shrewsbury	33,796	54	42	12
Merrimac	6,583	11	7	4	Somerset	18,364	38	32	6
Methuen	43,938	101	89	12	Somerville	75,585	147	122	25
Middleboro	21,286	41	37	4	Southampton	5,957	8	8	0
Middleton	9,284	15	13	2	Southborough	9,704	19	14	5
Milford	27,375	54	44	10	Southbridge	17,305	37	34	3
Millbury	13,483	24	19	5	South Hadley	17,138	31	26	5
Millis	7,955	19	15	4	Southwick	9,673	22	16	6
Millville	2,949	6	5	1	Spencer	11,909	21	17	4
Milton	25,922	65	51	14	Springfield	154,314	536	436	100
Monson	9,031	16	11	5	Sterling	7,745	18	13	5
Montague	8,045	20	15	5	Stockbridge	2,164	6	6	0
Monterey	952	2	2	0	Stoneham	21,285	36	34	2
Nahant	3,590	13	12	1	Stoughton	26,866	54	47	7
Nantucket	11,393	37	33	4	Stow	6,678	16	11	5
Natick	32,017	63	51	12	Sturbridge	8,865	23	18	5
Needham	28,765	53	44	9	Sudbury	17,552	32	27	5
New Bedford	89,613	299	253	46	Sunderland	3,902	4	4	0
New Braintree	1,144	1	1	0	Sutton	9,161	20	15	5
Newbury	6,865	13	12	1	Swampscott	13,883	33	32	1
Newburyport	17,447	37	31	6	Swansea	16,012	35	29	6
Newton	83,781	181	139	42	Taunton	55,156	109	104	5
Norfolk	11,136	22	16	6	Templeton	7,993	11	10	1
North Adams	13,590	33	26	7	Tewksbury	30,447	69	55	14
Northampton	28,184	63	57	6	Tisbury	3,901	13	12	1
North Andover	27,581	51	38	13	Topsfield	6,077	14	10	4
North Attleboro	27,559	56	43	13	Townsend	9,630	16	14	2
Northborough	14,774	27	20	7	Truro	2,104	14	9	5
Northbridge	14,705	22	17	5	Tyngsboro	11,952	29	20	9
North Brookfield	5,034	5	5	0	Upton	6,745	17	12	5
Northfield	3,003	2	2	0	Uxbridge	12,909	23	18	5
North Reading	14,417	29	28	1	Wakefield	24,973	42	42	0
Norton	19,217	29	28	1	Walpole	23,257	41	35	6
Norwell	10,279	30	23	7	Waltham	60,106	171	144	27
Norwood	28,130	70	59	11	Ware	9,748	17	17	0

Table 78. Full-Time Law Enforcement Employees by State and City, 2010—*Continued*

(Number)

State/city	Population	Total law enforcement employees	Total officers	Total civilians	State/city	Population	Total law enforcement employees	Total officers	Total civilians
Wareham	21,218	51	41	10	Bloomfield Hills	3,731	28	24	4
Warren	5,279	6	6	0	Bloomfield Township	40,490	93	72	21
Watertown	32,780	76	63	13	Boyne City	3,049	8	7	1
Wayland	13,396	29	20	9	Breckenridge	1,257	2	2	0
Webster	16,721	34	30	4	Bridgeport Township	10,570	9	8	1
Wellesley	27,143	59	43	16	Bridgman	2,384	4	4	0
Wellfleet	2,820	17	12	5	Brighton	7,238	19	17	2
Wenham	4,705	10	9	1	Bronson	2,216	4	4	0
Westborough	18,214	36	29	7	Brown City	1,203	2	2	0
West Boylston	8,085	14	13	1	Brownstown Township	28,102	44	34	10
West Bridgewater	6,619	20	19	1	Buchanan	4,288	10	9	1
West Brookfield	3,821	7	6	1	Buena Vista Township	9,156	18	16	2
Westfield	41,899	90	78	12	Burr Oak	730	1	1	0
Westford	22,582	49	39	10	Burton	29,143	38	35	3
Westminster	7,447	18	13	5	Byron	545	1	1	0
West Newbury	4,393	7	7	0	Cadillac	10,101	16	15	1
Weston	11,815	29	25	4	Calumet	787	1	1	0
Westport	15,496	36	29	7	Cambridge Township	5,737	3	3	0
West Springfield	27,861	90	80	10	Canton Township	80,039	118	86	32
West Tisbury	2,652	9	8	1	Capac	2,052	1	1	0
Westwood	14,190	36	27	9	Carleton	2,537	4	3	1
Weymouth	53,400	105	88	17	Caro	3,889	7	7	0
Whately	1,554	2	2	0	Carrollton Township	5,810	8	7	1
Whitman	14,062	27	26	1	Carson City	1,159	1	1	0
Wilbraham	14,070	26	25	1	Caseville	805	2	2	0
Williamsburg	2,491	2	2	0	Caspian-Gaastra	2,211	1	1	0
Williamstown	7,902	16	12	4	Cass City	2,408	4	4	0
Wilmington	22,230	48	46	2	Cassopolis	1,872	5	5	0
Winchendon	10,261	18	14	4	Cedar Springs	3,254	7	7	0
Winchester	21,331	45	38	7	Center Line	8,017	22	20	2
Winthrop	19,127	35	32	3	Central Lake	941	1	1	0
Woburn	38,731	79	74	5	Charlevoix	2,570	8	7	1
Worcester	181,908	467	421	46	Charlotte	8,839	18	17	1
Wrentham	11,166	20	18	2	Cheboygan	4,806	8	7	1
Yarmouth	23,498	68	57	11	Chelsea	5,051	12	8	4
MICHIGAN					Chesterfield Township	45,027	59	47	12
Adrian	20,997	35	32	3	Chikaming Township	3,641	6	5	1
Adrian Township	7,329	2	2	0	Chocolay Township	5,993	5	4	1
Albion	9,021	21	21	0	Clare	3,021	9	8	1
Algonac	4,445	8	7	1	Clawson	12,025	18	17	1
Allegan	4,770	10	9	1	Clayton Township	7,590	7	7	0
Allen Park	24,833	53	45	8	Clay Township	9,280	16	12	4
Alma	9,107	14	14	0	Clinton	2,358	4	4	0
Almont	2,691	7	7	0	Clinton Township	95,167	126	97	29
Alpena	10,184	19	17	2	Clio	2,434	3	3	0
Ann Arbor	111,745	171	124	47	Coldwater	10,335	19	18	1
Argentine Township	6,937	5	4	1	Coleman	1,211	2	2	0
Armada	1,644	2	2	0	Coloma Township	6,483	11	8	3
Auburn	2,008	2	2	0	Colon	1,137	3	3	0
Auburn Hills	20,870	66	53	13	Columbia Township	7,431	6	6	0
Au Gres-Sims	1,914	2	2	0	Concord	1,055	2	2	0
Augusta	849	5	4	1	Constantine	2,066	6	5	1
Bad Axe	2,942	8	8	0	Corunna	3,218	3	2	1
Bancroft	571	1	1	0	Covert Township	3,047	6	6	0
Bangor	1,814	5	5	0	Croswell	2,365	5	5	0
Baraga	1,174	2	2	0	Crystal Falls	1,513	3	3	0
Baroda Lake Township	870	5	4	1	Davison	4,985	9	7	2
Barry Township	3,457	2	2	0	Davison Township	18,214	20	18	2
Bath Township	11,955	12	11	1	Dearborn	82,612	223	193	30
Battle Creek	60,386	134	116	18	Dearborn Heights	49,674	109	83	26
Bay City	33,200	57	54	3	Decatur	1,806	5	5	0
Beaverton	1,036	1	1	0	Deckerville	856	1	1	0
Belding	5,599	8	8	0	Denton Township	5,247	5	5	0
Bellaire	1,093	2	2	0	Detroit	899,447	3,210	2,890	320
Belleville	3,392	9	7	2	Dewitt	4,355	7	6	1
Bellevue	1,329	2	2	0	Dewitt Township	13,074	16	15	1
Benton Harbor	10,683	24	20	4	Dowagiac	5,550	15	14	1
Benton Township	14,959	28	23	5	Dryden Township	4,490	4	4	0
Berkley	14,609	33	27	6	Dundee	4,283	1	1	0
Berrien Springs-Oronoko Township	9,759	10	9	1	Durand	3,618	4	4	0
Beverly Hills	9,739	27	23	4	East Grand Rapids	10,423	32	29	3
Big Rapids	10,170	20	19	1	East Jordan	2,168	4	4	0
Birch Run	1,624	6	5	1	East Lansing	45,058	89	58	31
Birmingham	18,823	39	30	9	Eastpointe	32,016	53	48	5
Blackman Township	37,751	29	28	1	East Tawas	2,657	5	4	1
Blissfield	3,103	6	6	0	Eaton Rapids	5,146	11	10	1

Table 78.   Full-time Law Enforcement Employees, by State, by City, 2010—*Continued*

(Number)

State/city	Population	Total law enforcement employees	Total officers	Total civilians	State/city	Population	Total law enforcement employees	Total officers	Total civilians
Ecorse	9,399	23	22	1	Imlay City	3,600	10	9	1
Elk Rapids	1,630	4	4	0	Inkster	25,428	70	61	9
Elkton	724	2	2	0	Ionia	11,342	16	14	2
Elsie	962	2	2	0	Iron Mountain	7,612	14	14	0
Emmett Township	11,684	22	18	4	Iron River	2,845	7	6	1
Erie Township	4,586	1	1	0	Ironwood	5,192	12	12	0
Escanaba	11,918	42	31	11	Ishpeming	6,402	11	10	1
Essexville	3,421	7	7	0	Ishpeming Township	3,594	1	1	0
Evart	1,622	4	4	0	Ithaca	2,960	4	4	0
Fair Haven Township	1,081	1	1	0	Jackson	32,741	73	59	14
Farmington	9,713	29	22	7	Jonesville	2,164	5	5	0
Farmington Hills	77,646	137	105	32	Kalamazoo	71,775	287	243	44
Fenton	11,542	17	14	3	Kalamazoo Township	21,977	36	29	7
Ferndale	20,847	46	38	8	Kalkaska	2,115	3	2	1
Flat Rock	8,563	21	21	0	Keego Harbor	2,828	4	4	0
Flint	109,245	155	132	23	Kentwood	47,441	76	63	13
Flint Township	30,778	47	39	8	Kingsford	5,181	18	18	0
Flushing	7,584	10	10	0	Kingston	408	1	1	0
Flushing Township	9,880	7	6	1	Kinross Township	8,656	3	3	0
Forsyth Township	4,870	7	6	1	Laingsburg	1,220	2	2	0
Fowlerville	3,083	8	7	1	Lake Angelus	309	1	1	0
Frankenmuth	4,556	7	7	0	Lake Linden	1,035	1	1	0
Frankfort	1,414	3	3	0	Lake Odessa	2,180	4	4	0
Franklin	2,898	10	10	0	Lake Orion	2,696	8	4	4
Fraser	14,770	45	39	6	Lakeview	1,070	2	2	0
Fremont	4,077	9	8	1	L'Anse	1,861	4	4	0
Frost Township	1,093	1	1	0	Lansing	112,254	301	226	75
Fruitport	1,058	10	8	2	Lansing Township	7,769	16	15	1
Galesburg	1,935	3	2	1	Lapeer	8,947	24	21	3
Garden City	25,549	36	29	7	Lapeer Township	4,864	1	1	0
Gaylord	3,484	13	11	2	Lathrup Village	4,012	8	8	0
Genesee Township	22,571	14	12	2	Laurium	1,973	4	4	0
Gerrish Township	2,996	7	7	0	Lawton	1,780	6	6	0
Gibraltar	4,731	9	8	1	Leslie	2,280	3	3	0
Gladstone	4,976	10	9	1	Lexington	1,009	3	3	0
Gladwin	2,813	5	5	0	Lincoln Park	33,702	57	50	7
Grand Beach	243	4	4	0	Lincoln Township	14,281	12	11	1
Grand Blanc	7,312	19	17	2	Linden	3,341	8	5	3
Grand Blanc Township	34,634	45	42	3	Litchfield	1,351	2	2	0
Grand Haven	10,574	37	32	5	Livonia	87,434	165	137	28
Grand Ledge	7,530	15	14	1	Lowell	4,156	8	6	2
Grand Rapids	191,566	392	315	77	Ludington	8,153	15	14	1
Grandville	16,653	26	24	2	Luna Pier	1,507	4	4	0
Grant	839	1	1	0	Mackinac Island	449	6	5	1
Green Oak Township	17,817	16	14	2	Mackinaw City	830	6	6	0
Greenville	7,957	21	17	4	Madison Heights	29,174	64	52	12
Grosse Ile Township	9,470	24	17	7	Madison Township	7,824	2	2	0
Grosse Pointe	4,765	26	24	2	Mancelona	1,318	2	2	0
Grosse Pointe Farms	8,218	44	32	12	Manistee	5,985	13	13	0
Grosse Pointe Park	10,498	46	40	6	Manistique	2,969	8	8	0
Grosse Pointe Shores	2,400	20	17	3	Manton	1,145	1	1	0
Grosse Pointe Woods	14,470	39	34	5	Marenisco Township	1,757	1	1	0
Hamburg Township	21,608	14	13	1	Marine City	4,264	4	4	0
Hampton Township	9,583	11	10	1	Marion	782	1	1	0
Hamtramck	19,615	43	43	0	Marlette	1,910	3	3	0
Hancock	4,100	7	7	0	Marquette	20,849	37	31	6
Harbor Beach	1,550	4	4	0	Marshall	7,005	14	14	0
Harbor Springs	1,535	6	5	1	Marysville	9,784	16	13	3
Harper Woods	12,012	36	34	2	Mason	8,169	14	13	1
Hart	1,885	4	4	0	Mattawan	2,846	5	5	0
Hartford	2,437	5	5	0	Mayville	952	2	2	0
Hastings	6,685	14	12	2	Melvindale	9,443	22	20	2
Hazel Park	17,715	39	34	5	Memphis	1,095	1	1	0
Hesperia	933	1	1	0	Mendon	887	2	2	0
Hillsdale	7,574	15	13	2	Menominee	8,037	14	13	1
Holland	33,652	68	58	10	Meridian Township	38,105	44	39	5
Holly	6,226	16	12	4	Metamora Township	4,540	5	5	0
Homer	1,725	3	3	0	Michiana	191	3	3	0
Home Township	1,504	1	1	0	Midland	40,346	49	47	2
Hopkins	543	2	2	0	Milan	5,752	12	8	4
Houghton	6,922	8	7	1	Milford	16,562	24	18	6
Howard City	1,554	3	3	0	Millington	1,032	1	1	0
Howell	9,636	20	18	2	Monroe	21,062	42	37	5
Hudson	2,244	3	3	0	Montague	2,251	5	5	0
Huntington Woods	5,732	18	17	1	Montrose Township	7,508	9	8	1
Huron Township	15,652	23	18	5	Morenci	2,195	3	3	0

Table 78.   Full-Time Law Enforcement Employees by State and City, 2010—*Continued*

(Number)

State/city	Popula-tion	Total law enforce-ment employees	Total officers	Total civilians	State/city	Popula-tion	Total law enforce-ment employees	Total officers	Total civilians
Morrice	859	2	2	0	Saginaw	54,155	113	104	9
Mount Morris	3,091	7	6	1	Saginaw Township	37,872	50	45	5
Mount Morris Township	21,614	28	25	3	Saline	8,942	18	14	4
Mount Pleasant	26,580	39	33	6	Sandusky	2,504	4	3	1
Mundy Township	13,810	18	15	3	Saugatuck-Douglas	2,161	8	7	1
Munising	2,280	5	5	0	Sault Ste. Marie	13,849	25	23	2
Muskegon	38,829	88	79	9	Schoolcraft	1,502	3	3	0
Muskegon Heights	11,420	19	17	2	Scottville	1,224	3	3	0
Muskegon Township	18,159	15	14	1	Sebewaing	1,674	3	3	0
Napoleon Township	6,871	2	2	0	Shelby	1,860	3	3	0
Nashville	1,620	2	2	0	Shelby Township	71,589	91	70	21
Negaunee	4,405	9	8	1	Shepherd	1,333	2	2	0
Newaygo	1,668	5	4	1	Somerset Township	4,584	5	4	1
New Baltimore	11,701	20	16	4	Southfield	74,587	187	150	37
New Buffalo	2,441	8	7	1	Southgate	26,575	48	41	7
New Haven	5,368	10	9	1	South Haven	5,112	24	18	6
Niles	11,084	26	18	8	South Lyon	10,983	18	17	1
North Branch	951	2	2	0	South Rockwood	1,678	2	2	0
Northfield Township	8,484	11	10	1	Sparta	4,021	5	5	0
North Muskegon	3,842	7	7	0	Spaulding Township	2,132	1	1	0
Northville	5,839	14	14	0	Spring Arbor Township	8,397	2	2	0
Northville Township	23,641	46	34	12	Springfield	4,968	14	13	1
Norton Shores	23,127	27	25	2	Spring Lake-Ferrysburg	5,419	10	9	1
Norway	2,764	4	4	0	Springport Township	2,183	2	2	0
Novi	54,857	85	64	21	Standish	1,774	1	1	0
Oak Park	30,131	70	61	9	Stanton	1,459	1	1	0
Olivet	1,819	2	2	0	St. Charles	1,967	3	3	0
Onaway	871	1	1	0	St. Clair	5,646	9	9	0
Ontwa Township-Edwardsburg	5,889	9	8	1	St. Clair Shores	59,522	99	83	16
Orchard Lake	2,205	9	8	1	Sterling Heights	126,291	208	162	46
Oscoda Township	6,668	12	11	1	St. Ignace	2,270	7	6	1
Otsego	3,762	7	6	1	St. Johns	7,191	11	10	1
Ovid	1,376	3	3	0	St. Joseph	8,386	23	17	6
Owosso	14,526	22	19	3	St. Joseph Township	9,519	12	11	1
Oxford	3,498	19	11	8	St. Louis	6,895	7	6	1
Parchment	1,791	6	3	3	Stockbridge	1,265	2	2	0
Paw Paw	3,179	7	6	1	Sturgis	10,544	23	18	5
Pentwater	928	3	3	0	Sumpter Township	10,737	19	14	5
Perry	1,966	6	6	0	Suttons Bay	573	1	1	0
Petoskey	5,971	21	18	3	Swartz Creek	5,118	7	6	1
Pigeon	1,021	1	1	0	Sylvan Lake	1,616	4	4	0
Pinckney	2,429	4	4	0	Taylor	58,158	96	81	15
Pinconning	1,295	2	2	0	Tecumseh	8,385	14	12	2
Pittsfield Township	34,681	50	38	12	Thetford Township	7,657	2	2	0
Plainwell	3,801	8	7	1	Thomas Township	12,096	8	7	1
Pleasant Ridge	2,436	6	6	0	Three Oaks	1,676	1	1	0
Plymouth	8,297	16	15	1	Three Rivers	6,974	21	17	4
Plymouth Township	24,291	39	25	14	Tittabawassee Township	8,754	6	5	1
Pontiac	65,517	97	76	21	Traverse City	14,012	32	30	2
Portage	46,192	69	53	16	Trenton	17,217	30	29	1
Port Austin	624	1	1	0	Troy	79,794	172	121	51
Port Huron	30,132	60	51	9	Tuscarora Township	2,946	8	7	1
Portland	3,612	5	5	0	Ubly	740	2	2	0
Potterville	2,121	3	3	0	Unadilla Township	3,420	2	2	0
Prairieville Township	3,438	3	3	0	Union City	1,679	4	4	0
Raisin Township	7,294	6	5	1	Utica	4,911	19	15	4
Redford Township	43,827	64	54	10	Van Buren Township	25,627	60	45	15
Reed City	2,266	4	4	0	Vassar	2,578	4	4	0
Reese	1,304	2	2	0	Vernon	764	1	1	0
Richfield Township, Genesee County	8,408	9	7	2	Vicksburg	2,178	8	8	0
Richfield Township, Roscommon County	3,971	7	7	0	Walker	23,773	34	33	1
Richland	770	2	2	0	Walled Lake	6,833	13	12	1
Richland Township, Saginaw County	4,190	4	4	0	Warren	132,266	250	214	36
Richmond	5,615	12	9	3	Waterford Township	70,013	88	67	21
River Rouge	8,036	21	20	1	Waterloo Township	2,933	3	3	0
Riverview	11,306	29	26	3	Watervliet	1,719	2	2	0
Rochester	10,982	27	21	6	Wayland	3,772	6	5	1
Rockford	5,525	11	10	1	Wayne	16,454	35	29	6
Rockwood	3,026	7	7	0	West Bloomfield Township	63,345	103	75	28
Rogers City	2,921	7	7	0	West Branch	1,799	5	4	1
Romeo	3,702	11	8	3	Westland	75,726	99	78	21
Romulus	22,214	58	45	13	White Cloud	1,365	2	2	0
Roosevelt Park	3,706	5	5	0	Whitehall	2,756	8	8	0
Rose City	680	1	1	0	White Lake Township	29,890	35	25	10
Roseville	46,221	90	82	8	White Pigeon	1,522	4	4	0
Royal Oak	56,408	75	63	12	Williamston	3,781	6	5	1

Table 78.   Full-Time Law Enforcement Employees by State and City, 2010—*Continued*

(Number)

State/city	Population	Total law enforcement employees	Total officers	Total civilians	State/city	Population	Total law enforcement employees	Total officers	Total civilians
Wixom	13,344	23	20	3	Fergus Falls	13,531	26	21	5
Wolverine Lake	4,263	5	5	0	Floodwood	499	2	2	0
Woodhaven	12,239	28	27	1	Forest Lake	18,030	28	25	3
Wyandotte	23,607	46	37	9	Fridley	25,857	43	37	6
Wyoming	70,160	96	83	13	Gilbert	1,748	7	7	0
Yale	1,912	4	4	0	Glencoe	5,517	10	9	1
Ypsilanti	21,245	36	31	5	Glenwood	2,467	3	3	0
Zeeland	5,383	10	9	1	Golden Valley	20,527	40	30	10
Zilwaukee	1,610	2	2	0	Goodview	3,737	4	4	0
MINNESOTA					Grand Rapids	9,457	20	17	3
Albany	2,239	3	2	1	Granite Falls	2,857	4	4	0
Albert Lea	17,304	39	28	11	Hallock	981	1	1	0
Alexandria	12,003	25	20	5	Hastings	22,688	34	29	5
Annandale	3,212	4	4	0	Hermantown	9,755	14	12	2
Anoka	17,323	33	27	6	Hibbing	16,157	32	29	3
Appleton	2,971	3	3	0	Hokah	553	1	1	0
Apple Valley	50,579	56	48	8	Hopkins	17,020	39	26	13
Aurora	1,745	4	4	0	Houston	943	1	1	0
Austin	22,929	34	31	3	Hoyt Lakes	1,953	5	5	0
Avon	1,342	3	3	0	Hutchinson	13,901	31	22	9
Babbitt	1,579	4	4	0	International Falls	5,763	12	11	1
Baxter	8,748	16	15	1	Inver Grove Heights	34,457	40	34	6
Bayport	3,335	5	5	0	Jackson	3,302	7	7	0
Becker	4,387	6	5	1	Janesville	2,259	2	2	0
Belgrade	720	1	1	0	Jordan	5,731	9	7	2
Belle Plaine	7,244	10	8	2	Kasson	5,703	8	8	0
Bemidji	13,911	33	31	2	Kimball	718	4	4	0
Benson	2,930	7	6	1	La Crescent	4,897	8	7	1
Big Lake	10,240	13	11	2	Lake City	5,313	12	10	2
Blackduck	790	2	2	0	Lake Crystal	2,635	4	4	0
Blaine	57,561	70	58	12	Lakefield	1,614	2	2	0
Blooming Prairie	1,983	3	3	0	Lakes Area	8,654	13	11	2
Bloomington	82,715	140	111	29	Lakeville	57,470	59	51	8
Blue Earth	3,183	5	5	0	Lester Prairie	1,769	3	3	0
Brainerd	13,779	29	23	6	Le Sueur	4,271	8	7	1
Breckenridge	3,151	7	7	0	Lewiston	1,461	1	1	0
Brooklyn Center	27,378	58	46	12	Lino Lakes	20,953	27	24	3
Brooklyn Park	72,682	131	104	27	Litchfield	6,554	10	9	1
Brownton	777	2	2	0	Little Falls	8,049	15	13	2
Buffalo	14,881	20	17	3	Long Prairie	2,757	5	5	0
Burnsville	59,028	83	75	8	Madison	1,527	3	3	0
Caledonia	2,795	4	4	0	Mankato	36,921	59	49	10
Cambridge	7,986	14	13	1	Maple Grove	64,861	77	64	13
Cannon Falls	4,050	9	8	1	Mapleton	1,672	3	3	0
Centennial Lakes	11,423	18	16	2	Maplewood	36,907	57	52	5
Champlin	24,139	29	24	5	Marshall	12,754	23	20	3
Chaska	25,424	27	24	3	Medina	5,297	11	10	1
Chisholm	4,559	11	10	1	Melrose	3,261	6	5	1
Cloquet	11,486	21	19	2	Mendota Heights	11,697	20	17	3
Cold Spring	5,108	9	8	1	Milaca	3,015	6	5	1
Columbia Heights	18,427	34	28	6	Minneapolis	385,704	1,009	880	129
Coon Rapids	62,419	71	63	8	Minnetonka	50,753	73	55	18
Corcoran	5,749	8	7	1	Minnetrista	8,796	15	12	3
Cottage Grove	34,276	46	39	7	Montevideo	5,148	11	10	1
Crookston	7,829	16	14	2	Montgomery	3,305	5	4	1
Crosby	2,245	9	8	1	Moorhead	37,274	66	52	14
Crystal	21,753	35	29	6	Moose Lake	2,576	4	4	0
Dawson	1,323	2	2	0	Morris	5,074	10	8	2
Dayton	4,650	6	5	1	Mound	9,654	14	12	2
Deephaven-Woodland	4,339	8	7	1	Mounds View	12,000	19	17	2
Detroit Lakes	8,329	17	15	2	Mountain Iron	2,925	5	5	0
Dilworth	3,787	7	6	1	Mountain Lake	1,878	4	4	0
Duluth	84,249	179	144	35	New Brighton	21,689	35	27	8
Eagan	64,239	80	69	11	New Hope	20,644	37	30	7
Eagle Lake	2,416	2	2	0	Newport	3,495	7	7	0
East Grand Forks	7,878	24	21	3	New Prague	7,065	11	9	2
Eden Prairie	63,159	88	63	25	New Richland	1,148	2	2	0
Edina	46,503	68	51	17	New Ulm	12,843	25	22	3
Elk River	24,025	39	31	8	North Branch	10,732	12	10	2
Elmore	642	1	1	0	Northfield	19,918	26	21	5
Ely	3,459	8	7	1	North Mankato	12,748	13	12	1
Eveleth	3,559	10	9	1	North St. Paul	11,433	19	17	2
Fairmont	10,029	20	17	3	Oakdale	27,358	42	31	11
Faribault	22,272	37	30	7	Oak Park Heights	4,839	10	9	1
Farmington	20,229	28	25	3	Olivia	2,320	5	5	0

Table 78.   Full-Time Law Enforcement Employees by State and City, 2010—*Continued*

(Number)

State/city	Population	Total law enforcement employees	Total officers	Total civilians	State/city	Population	Total law enforcement employees	Total officers	Total civilians
Orono	12,294	21	18	3	Baldwyn	3,335	17	9	8
Ortonville	1,911	3	3	0	Batesville	7,776	47	38	9
Osakis	1,566	3	3	0	Bay St. Louis	8,190	35	28	7
Osseo	2,597	6	5	1	Belzoni	2,315	16	10	6
Owatonna	25,210	37	34	3	Biloxi	45,350	178	126	52
Park Rapids	3,654	11	10	1	Booneville	8,786	39	29	10
Paynesville	2,290	5	4	1	Brandon	22,877	55	41	14
Plainview	3,245	5	5	0	Brookhaven	13,240	39	34	5
Plymouth	73,579	78	67	11	Bruce	1,973	5	5	0
Princeton	4,839	13	11	2	Byhalia	1,302	14	9	5
Prior Lake	26,241	25	22	3	Carthage	4,904	19	15	4
Proctor	2,840	7	6	1	Charleston	1,793	11	10	1
Ramsey	24,681	27	23	4	Clarksdale	17,484	45	36	9
Red Wing	15,641	31	26	5	Cleveland	11,874	53	46	7
Redwood Falls	5,050	11	9	2	Clinton	26,390	61	45	16
Richfield	33,188	56	44	12	Collins	2,881	13	9	4
Robbinsdale	13,822	25	21	4	Columbia	6,516	30	21	9
Rochester	105,027	187	132	55	Columbus	23,638	79	69	10
Rogers	8,288	16	14	2	Como	1,290	4	4	0
Roseau	2,752	6	5	1	Corinth	14,322	52	38	14
Rosemount	22,870	24	21	3	Crystal Springs	5,899	21	14	7
Roseville	33,176	55	48	7	De Kalb	851	6	5	1
Sartell	15,018	18	17	1	D'Iberville	9,082	28	26	2
Sauk Centre	4,073	7	6	1	Edwards	1,290	1	1	0
Sauk Rapids	12,130	14	13	1	Eupora	2,175	6	5	1
Savage	29,151	41	32	9	Fayette	1,953	5	2	3
Shakopee	36,290	51	44	7	Florence	3,869	15	10	5
Silver Bay	1,804	5	5	0	Flowood	7,238	63	48	15
Silver Lake	794	2	2	0	Forest	6,043	24	16	8
Slayton	1,809	4	4	0	Fulton	4,049	9	9	0
Sleepy Eye	3,363	6	6	0	Gautier	16,435	53	43	10
South Lake Minnetonka	12,329	16	14	2	Gloster	996	6	4	2
South St. Paul	19,434	28	26	2	Greenville	34,826	141	100	41
Springfield	2,103	5	5	0	Greenwood	15,578	73	57	16
Spring Grove	1,233	2	2	0	Grenada	14,650	46	43	3
Spring Lake Park	6,577	12	10	2	Gulfport	70,806	249	185	64
St. Anthony	8,484	25	22	3	Hattiesburg	53,678	208	115	93
Staples	2,984	6	5	1	Heidelberg	795	6	5	1
St. Charles	3,566	4	4	0	Hernando	13,380	41	31	10
St. Cloud	67,942	122	97	25	Holly Springs	7,868	25	18	7
St. Francis	7,644	12	10	2	Horn Lake	25,693	70	53	17
Stillwater	18,208	23	21	2	Houston	3,808	12	10	2
St. James	4,271	8	7	1	Indianola	10,370	30	22	8
St. Joseph	6,298	8	7	1	Itta Bena	1,807	8	8	0
St. Louis Park	45,690	67	51	16	Iuka	2,926	12	9	3
St. Paul	281,166	773	592	181	Jackson	174,153	706	449	257
St. Paul Park	5,262	9	9	0	Kosciusko	7,351	19	19	0
St. Peter	11,063	18	13	5	Laurel	18,928	82	57	25
Thief River Falls	8,575	15	13	2	Leakesville	1,025	3	2	1
Tracy	2,063	3	3	0	Leland	4,678	22	16	6
Two Harbors	3,245	9	8	1	Long Beach	11,937	50	35	15
Virginia	8,419	20	19	1	Louisville	6,557	27	21	6
Wabasha	2,513	6	5	1	Lucedale	3,154	19	14	5
Wadena	3,920	9	8	1	Macon	2,651	9	8	1
Waite Park	6,873	16	13	3	Madison	22,275	88	70	18
Warroad	1,649	7	6	1	Magee	4,347	17	13	4
Waseca	8,668	16	14	2	Magnolia	2,062	8	8	0
Wayzata	3,953	11	10	1	McComb	13,689	63	31	32
Wells	2,299	4	4	0	Mendenhall	2,537	12	7	5
West Hennepin	5,680	10	8	2	Meridian	39,566	114	99	15
West St. Paul	18,737	34	29	5	Morton	3,482	14	14	0
Wheaton	1,362	3	3	0	Moss Point	13,788	46	29	17
White Bear Lake	24,365	34	27	7	Natchez	15,841	70	45	25
Willmar	17,854	37	33	4	New Albany	8,206	25	24	1
Windom	4,101	9	8	1	Ocean Springs	17,388	52	39	13
Winnebago	1,308	3	3	0	Okolona	2,813	7	7	0
Winona	26,447	41	37	4	Olive Branch	33,964	86	67	19
Winsted	2,425	3	3	0	Oxford	18,105	66	59	7
Woodbury	58,503	74	65	9	Pascagoula	23,479	97	62	35
Worthington	11,114	32	23	9	Pass Christian	3,967	23	21	2
Wyoming	8,148	9	8	1	Pearl	25,078	72	55	17
Zumbrota	3,109	4	4	0	Petal	10,906	30	24	6
					Philadelphia	7,964	36	28	8
MISSISSIPPI					Picayune	12,194	51	35	16
Aberdeen	5,966	22	17	5	Poplarville	3,045	13	12	1
Ackerman	1,485	5	5	0	Port Gibson	1,596	10	6	4
Amory	7,123	26	19	7					

Table 78. Full-Time Law Enforcement Employees by State and City, 2010—*Continued*

(Number)

State/city	Population	Total law enforcement employees	Total officers	Total civilians	State/city	Population	Total law enforcement employees	Total officers	Total civilians
Purvis	2,757	11	8	3	Calverton Park	1,255	6	6	0
Quitman	2,270	6	6	0	Camdenton	3,659	17	13	4
Ridgeland	21,847	94	65	29	Cameron	8,946	26	18	8
Ripley	5,773	12	11	1	Canton	2,403	4	3	1
Rosedale	2,275	7	6	1	Cape Girardeau	37,627	92	74	18
Saltillo	4,438	12	11	1	Cardwell	701	2	2	0
Senatobia	7,468	21	16	5	Carl Junction	7,649	17	12	5
Shaw	2,092	9	5	4	Carrollton	3,665	9	8	1
Southaven	47,435	125	103	22	Carterville	1,994	7	7	0
Starkville	24,588	63	53	10	Carthage	14,099	36	29	7
Stonewall	1,048	1	1	0	Caruthersville	5,912	22	21	1
Summit	1,606	6	5	1	Cassville	3,253	11	11	0
Tchula	2,158	6	4	2	Center	623	1	1	0
Tupelo	36,574	129	115	14	Centralia	3,672	11	6	5
Tylertown	1,887	7	6	1	Chaffee	2,928	11	6	5
Vaiden	847	4	2	2	Charlack	1,329	11	10	1
Vicksburg	24,773	105	78	27	Charleston	5,008	19	13	6
Water Valley	4,007	11	11	0	Chesterfield	45,709	92	82	10
Waveland	5,592	26	25	1	Chillicothe	8,622	23	17	6
Waynesboro	5,608	20	17	3	Clarkton	1,206	4	4	0
West Point	11,082	28	24	4	Claycomo	1,376	15	11	4
Wiggins	5,162	20	16	4	Clayton	15,979	61	53	8
Winona	4,350	11	9	2	Cleveland	686	1	1	0
Yazoo City	11,055	32	23	9	Clever	1,894	6	6	0
MISSOURI					Clinton	9,316	23	22	1
Adrian	1,863	3	3	0	Cole Camp	1,140	3	3	0
Advance	1,180	3	3	0	Columbia	103,417	189	158	31
Anderson	2,084	2	2	0	Concordia	2,333	6	6	0
Appleton City	1,246	2	2	0	Conway	773	2	2	0
Arbyrd	473	1	1	0	Cool Valley	990	10	10	0
Archie	1,036	3	3	0	Cooter	402	1	1	0
Arnold	20,535	61	49	12	Cottleville	3,359	13	13	0
Ash Grove	1,532	3	3	0	Country Club Hills	1,258	12	12	0
Ashland	2,230	6	6	0	Country Club Village	2,437	2	2	0
Aurora	7,430	23	16	7	Crane	1,353	2	2	0
Ava	3,180	14	7	7	Crestwood	11,289	35	28	7
Ballwin	29,774	59	49	10	Creve Coeur	16,786	60	49	11
Bates City	261	1	1	0	Crystal City	4,517	22	16	6
Battlefield	4,534	6	5	1	Cuba	3,563	12	11	1
Bella Villa	626	4	4	0	Dellwood	4,837	18	17	1
Bellefontaine Neighbors	10,103	33	32	1	Delta	547	1	1	0
Bellerive	250	22	21	1	Desloge	5,213	10	10	0
Bellflower	380	1	1	0	De Soto	6,439	19	15	4
Bel-Nor	1,457	7	6	1	Des Peres	8,541	46	38	8
Bel-Ridge	2,852	20	16	4	Dexter	7,493	23	17	6
Belton	24,941	66	46	20	Diamond	896	4	4	0
Berkeley	9,245	54	44	10	Dixon	1,624	8	5	3
Bernie	1,740	9	5	4	Doniphan	1,845	12	8	4
Bethany	3,020	5	5	0	Doolittle	664	1	1	0
Beverly Hills	549	5	3	2	Drexel	1,099	2	2	0
Billings	1,139	4	4	0	Duenweg	1,261	3	3	0
Birmingham	233	1	1	0	Duquesne	1,762	6	6	0
Bismarck	1,541	3	3	0	East Prairie	3,002	10	7	3
Bloomfield	1,812	3	3	0	Edina	1,092	3	2	1
Blue Springs	56,226	119	87	32	Edmundson	772	10	9	1
Bolivar	11,308	24	20	4	Eldon	4,905	11	10	1
Bonne Terre	7,456	13	10	3	El Dorado Springs	3,598	11	7	4
Boonville	8,622	28	21	7	Ellisville	9,162	21	20	1
Bourbon	1,523	7	6	1	Elsberry	2,694	4	4	0
Bowling Green	5,268	15	11	4	Eureka	9,472	27	23	4
Branson	8,621	60	44	16	Everton	297	1	1	0
Branson West	514	7	6	1	Excelsior Springs	12,674	34	23	11
Braymer	931	1	1	0	Fair Grove	1,433	4	4	0
Breckenridge Hills	4,413	15	14	1	Fair Play	458	1	1	0
Brentwood	7,086	34	26	8	Farmington	16,461	34	26	8
Bridgeton	14,900	62	51	11	Fayette	2,647	7	7	0
Brookfield	4,254	18	11	7	Ferguson	20,657	61	52	9
Brunswick	822	1	1	0	Ferrelview	601	1	1	0
Bucklin	470	1	1	0	Festus	11,457	39	28	11
Buckner	2,900	6	6	0	Flordell Hills	848	12	12	0
Buffalo	3,250	8	7	1	Florissant	49,886	112	88	24
Butler	4,178	15	10	5	Foley	215	1	1	0
Butterfield Village	414	2	1	1	Fordland	765	2	2	0
Byrnes Mill	2,977	5	5	0	Foristell	374	8	7	1
Cabool	2,118	10	6	4	Forsyth	1,703	8	7	1
California	4,123	7	6	1	Frankford	350	1	1	0

Table 78.   Full-Time Law Enforcement Employees by State and City, 2010—*Continued*

(Number)

State/city	Population	Total law enforcement employees	Total officers	Total civilians	State/city	Population	Total law enforcement employees	Total officers	Total civilians
Fredericktown	4,152	7	7	0	Laurie	707	5	5	0
Freeman	609	1	1	0	Lawson	2,316	6	5	1
Frontenac	3,838	27	21	6	Leadington	422	6	5	1
Fulton	12,796	36	29	7	Leadwood	1,159	6	5	1
Gallatin	1,745	2	2	0	Leasburg	336	1	1	0
Garden City	1,677	4	4	0	Lebanon	14,403	39	28	11
Gerald	1,255	5	5	0	Lee's Summit	87,707	188	132	56
Gideon	932	3	3	0	Lexington	4,424	10	9	1
Gladstone	29,745	56	40	16	Liberal	759	1	1	0
Glasgow	1,175	3	3	0	Liberty	32,496	53	38	15
Glendale	5,421	16	12	4	Licking	2,957	4	4	0
Glen Echo Park	156	5	3	2	Lincoln	1,082	3	3	0
Gower	1,414	3	3	0	Linn	1,433	4	4	0
Grain Valley	11,384	25	20	5	Linn Creek	310	2	2	0
Granby	2,224	3	3	0	Lone Jack	1,002	5	5	0
Grandview	24,552	66	51	15	Macon	5,349	17	15	2
Greendale	681	7	6	1	Malden	4,347	15	15	0
Greenfield	1,199	3	3	0	Manchester	18,396	42	37	5
Greenwood	4,836	5	5	0	Mansfield	1,303	4	4	0
Hallsville	962	2	2	0	Maplewood	8,510	34	32	2
Hamilton	1,748	4	4	0	Marble Hill	1,441	5	5	0
Hannibal	17,379	49	40	9	Marceline	2,270	8	5	3
Hardin	543	1	1	0	Marionville	2,157	3	3	0
Harrisonville	9,880	30	22	8	Marshall	12,127	37	25	12
Hartville	580	2	2	0	Marshfield	7,368	10	10	0
Hayti	2,870	9	8	1	Marston	518	1	1	0
Hazelwood	25,070	85	70	15	Marthasville	857	1	1	0
Herculaneum	3,728	12	11	1	Maryland Heights	25,591	98	79	19
Hermann	2,671	12	7	5	Maryville	10,782	26	20	6
Higginsville	4,448	15	9	6	Matthews	520	2	2	0
Highlandville	973	1	1	0	Maysville	1,120	1	1	0
Hillsboro	2,579	6	6	0	Memphis	1,934	3	3	0
Hillsdale	1,392	13	12	1	Merriam Woods	1,477	2	2	0
Holcomb	657	2	2	0	Mexico	10,736	37	35	2
Holden	2,556	6	5	1	Milan	1,799	4	4	0
Hollister	4,041	16	11	5	Mill Spring	200	1	1	0
Holt	482	1	1	0	Miner	1,335	13	9	4
Holts Summit	3,882	10	9	1	Moberly	14,011	43	31	12
Hornersville	639	3	2	1	Moline Acres	2,487	16	15	1
Houston	2,015	6	6	0	Monett	8,884	29	20	9
Howardville	307	1	1	0	Monroe City	2,413	7	7	0
Humansville	1,021	1	1	0	Montgomery City	2,427	6	6	0
Huntsville	1,620	3	3	0	Morehouse	900	2	2	0
Iberia	657	2	2	0	Morley	801	1	1	0
Independence	121,141	302	204	98	Mosby	255	1	1	0
Indian Point	728	2	2	0	Moscow Mills	2,749	7	7	0
Ironton	1,297	5	4	1	Mound City	1,045	2	2	0
Jackson	14,043	30	22	8	Mountain View	2,584	8	7	1
Jasper	1,077	2	2	0	Mount Vernon	4,605	11	11	0
Jefferson City	41,092	118	87	31	Napoleon	192	1	1	0
Jennings	14,423	40	37	3	Naylor	586	1	1	0
Jonesburg	714	1	1	0	Neosho	11,245	15	14	1
Joplin	50,346	156	111	45	Nevada	8,287	20	17	3
Kahoka	2,143	3	3	0	Newburg	461	1	1	0
Kansas City	483,191	1,993	1,404	589	New Florence	737	2	2	0
Kearney	9,442	15	14	1	New Franklin	1,093	1	1	0
Kennett	10,409	29	24	5	New Haven	2,053	6	6	0
Kimberling City	2,408	8	7	1	New London	986	1	1	0
King City	860	1	1	0	New Madrid	2,945	6	5	1
Kinloch	420	4	4	0	New Melle	302	3	3	0
Kirksville	17,406	29	26	3	Niangua	496	1	1	0
Kirkwood	26,573	71	59	12	Noel	1,619	4	4	0
Knob Noster	3,359	12	7	5	Norborne	722	1	1	0
Ladue	8,111	31	25	6	Normandy	4,834	22	21	1
La Grange	899	7	7	0	North Kansas City	6,116	51	38	13
Lake Lotawana	2,191	7	6	1	Northwoods	4,244	19	17	2
Lake Ozark	2,048	17	11	6	Norwood	558	1	1	0
Lakeshire	1,266	4	4	0	Oak Grove	7,154	16	15	1
Lake St. Louis	14,734	39	30	9	Oakland	1,544	71	59	12
Lake Tapawingo	802	3	3	0	Oakview Village	414	4	3	1
Lake Winnebago	1,167	5	5	0	Odessa	4,632	11	10	1
Lamar	4,385	12	10	2	O'Fallon	81,851	136	107	29
La Monte	1,102	2	2	0	Old Monroe	326	1	1	0
Lanagan	434	1	1	0	Olivette	7,414	25	23	2
La Plata	1,434	3	3	0	Oran	1,247	1	1	0
Lathrop	2,319	4	4	0	Oronogo	2,963	5	5	0

Table 78.   Full-Time Law Enforcement Employees by State and City, 2010—*Continued*

(Number)

State/city	Popula-tion	Total law enforce-ment employees	Total officers	Total civilians	State/city	Popula-tion	Total law enforce-ment employees	Total officers	Total civilians
Orrick	805	2	2	0	St. Marys	374	1	1	0
Osage Beach	4,787	39	25	14	Stover	1,023	3	3	0
Osceola	771	2	2	0	St. Peters	56,518	110	86	24
Overland	15,400	59	45	14	Strafford	2,232	8	7	1
Owensville	2,527	6	6	0	St. Robert	3,702	27	20	7
Ozark	19,449	34	29	5	Sturgeon	923	2	2	0
Pacific	7,332	24	17	7	Sugar Creek	3,606	22	16	6
Pagedale	3,360	15	14	1	Sullivan	6,757	25	17	8
Palmyra	3,428	7	7	0	Summersville	548	2	2	0
Parkville	5,584	16	15	1	Sunset Hills	8,131	32	26	6
Parma	744	4	3	1	Sweet Springs	1,518	3	3	0
Pasadena Park	452	22	21	1	Tarkio	1,787	3	3	0
Peculiar	4,977	9	8	1	Thayer	2,143	11	7	4
Perry	647	1	1	0	Tipton	3,278	3	3	0
Perryville	8,185	29	26	3	Town and Country	10,626	35	30	5
Pevely	6,112	20	14	6	Tracy	218	1	1	0
Piedmont	1,840	7	7	0	Trenton	5,945	19	12	7
Pierce City	1,459	2	2	0	Troy	13,056	24	22	2
Pilot Grove	740	1	1	0	Union	9,904	23	21	2
Pilot Knob	676	1	1	0	Unionville	1,788	6	6	0
Pine Lawn	3,938	30	25	5	University City	35,875	89	73	16
Pineville	915	5	5	0	Uplands Park	432	11	9	2
Platte City	5,034	9	8	1	Urbana	427	1	1	0
Platte Woods	467	2	2	0	Vandalia	4,344	8	6	2
Plattsburg	2,390	6	6	0	Velda City	1,474	12	11	1
Pleasant Hill	7,409	18	12	6	Velda Village Hills	1,022	5	3	2
Pleasant Hope	605	1	1	0	Verona	718	2	2	0
Pleasant Valley	3,721	14	9	5	Versailles	2,654	10	10	0
Polo	591	1	1	0	Viburnum	777	2	2	0
Poplar Bluff	16,938	55	43	12	Vienna	625	2	2	0
Portageville	2,831	16	12	4	Vinita Park	1,760	13	12	1
Purdy	1,135	2	2	0	Walnut Grove	666	2	2	0
Puxico	1,121	2	2	0	Wardell	385	1	1	0
Qulin	482	1	1	0	Warrensburg	19,376	38	34	4
Randolph	54	2	2	0	Warrenton	7,714	25	22	3
Raymore	19,420	37	26	11	Warsaw	2,226	7	7	0
Raytown	28,616	73	51	22	Warson Woods	1,817	7	7	0
Reeds Spring	810	1	1	0	Washington	14,366	31	28	3
Republic	14,880	34	23	11	Waverly	771	1	1	0
Rich Hill	1,460	2	2	0	Waynesville	4,337	11	10	1
Richland	1,844	6	5	1	Weatherby Lake	1,915	5	5	0
Richmond	5,787	10	8	2	Webb City	11,795	26	21	5
Richmond Heights	8,985	42	41	1	Webster Groves	22,106	40	38	2
Risco	342	1	1	0	Wellston	2,284	10	8	2
Riverside	3,075	32	24	8	Wellsville	1,288	3	3	0
Riverview	2,874	12	11	1	Wentzville	27,351	75	56	19
Rockaway Beach	586	2	2	0	Weston	1,720	5	5	0
Rock Hill	4,530	10	9	1	West Plains	12,034	29	25	4
Rock Port	1,275	3	3	0	Wheaton	744	1	1	0
Rogersville	3,261	7	7	0	Willard	3,368	11	10	1
Salem	4,898	19	14	5	Willow Springs	2,147	7	6	1
Salisbury	1,513	4	3	1	Winfield	1,180	4	4	0
Sarcoxie	1,382	3	3	0	Winona	1,309	4	4	0
Savannah	5,104	6	6	0	Woodson Terrace	3,963	20	17	3
Scott City	4,525	22	16	6	Wright City	3,256	9	8	1
Sedalia	21,091	58	45	13	**MONTANA**				
Senath	1,547	3	3	0	Baker	1,647	3	3	0
Seneca	2,248	6	6	0	Belgrade	8,518	18	15	3
Seymour	2,092	5	5	0	Billings	108,039	157	136	21
Shelbina	1,743	6	6	0	Boulder	1,503	2	2	0
Shrewsbury	6,150	20	18	2	Bozeman	40,892	61	57	4
Sikeston	16,953	77	67	10	Bridger	740	2	2	0
Slater	1,898	5	4	1	Brockton	244	1	1	0
Smithville	8,800	14	14	0	Chinook	1,270	3	3	0
Southwest City	939	3	3	0	Colstrip	2,395	11	6	5
Sparta	1,246	3	3	0	Columbia Falls	5,569	10	9	1
Springfield	157,110	357	285	72	Columbus	2,078	5	4	1
St. Ann	12,475	48	36	12	Conrad	2,481	5	5	0
St. Charles	65,729	155	111	44	Cut Bank	3,179	7	7	0
St. Clair	4,445	16	14	2	Dillon	4,250	9	8	1
Steele	2,017	5	5	0	East Helena	2,204	5	5	0
Steelville	1,486	6	6	0	Ennis	1,077	1	1	0
Ste. Genevieve	4,316	10	9	1	Eureka	1,002	3	3	0
St. John	6,283	25	23	2	Fort Benton	1,438	4	4	0
St. Joseph	75,922	158	115	43	Glasgow	2,854	13	10	3
St. Louis	355,151	1,920	1,363	557	Glendive	4,635	14	9	5

Table 78. Full-Time Law Enforcement Employees by State and City, 2010—*Continued*

(Number)

State/city	Population	Total law enforcement employees	Total officers	Total civilians	State/city	Population	Total law enforcement employees	Total officers	Total civilians
Great Falls	59,984	122	85	37	Papillion	25,213	43	39	4
Hamilton	5,129	16	15	1	Pierce	1,666	3	3	0
Havre	9,726	25	19	6	Plainview	1,185	2	2	0
Helena	30,520	73	50	23	Plattsmouth	6,941	17	14	3
Hot Springs	590	2	2	0	Ralston	6,178	15	13	2
Joliet	650	1	1	0	Schuyler	5,392	10	8	2
Kalispell	22,568	40	34	6	Scottsbluff	15,053	36	31	5
Laurel	6,841	17	13	4	Scribner	956	1	1	0
Lewistown	5,936	23	14	9	Seward	6,842	11	9	2
Libby	2,898	6	6	0	Sidney	6,399	14	12	2
Livingston	7,461	15	14	1	South Sioux City	12,374	28	27	1
Manhattan	1,712	2	1	1	St. Paul	2,148	4	4	0
Miles City	8,141	19	17	2	Superior	1,729	4	4	0
Missoula	70,559	121	100	21	Tekamah	1,693	3	3	0
Plains	1,268	3	3	0	Valentine	2,530	6	5	1
Polson	5,383	13	12	1	Valley	1,994	4	4	0
Poplar	886	3	3	0	Wahoo	4,212	6	6	0
Red Lodge	2,531	7	7	0	Wayne	5,386	14	9	5
Ronan City	2,030	5	5	0	West Point	3,291	7	6	1
Sidney	4,855	11	10	1	Wilber	1,765	4	4	0
Stevensville	2,087	2	2	0	Wymore	1,566	3	3	0
St. Ignatius	814	2	2	0	York	7,681	19	13	6
Thompson Falls	1,450	3	3	0	York	7,847	20	14	6
Three Forks	2,004	2	2	0	**NEVADA**				
Troy	969	3	3	0	Boulder City	14,794	45	32	13
West Yellowstone	1,549	10	5	5	Carlin	2,103	7	6	1
Whitefish	8,776	18	17	1	Elko	17,374	43	39	4
Wolf Point	2,562	9	8	1	Fallon	8,552	36	22	14
NEBRASKA					Henderson	264,280	550	346	204
Albion	1,601	3	3	0	Las Vegas Metropolitan Police Department	1,416,401	5,130	2,696	2,434
Alliance	8,005	24	17	7	Lovelock	1,813	7	6	1
Auburn	3,237	6	6	0	Mesquite	18,130	55	32	23
Aurora	4,240	9	8	1	North Las Vegas	238,004	468	308	160
Bayard	1,095	4	4	0	Reno	222,242	392	323	69
Beatrice	12,706	31	21	10	Sparks	91,433	150	108	42
Bellevue	52,330	119	101	18	West Wendover	5,091	21	13	8
Bennington	1,029	2	2	0	Winnemucca	8,361	18	15	3
Blair	7,805	19	17	2	Yerington	3,912	7	6	1
Bridgeport	1,431	3	3	0	**NEW HAMPSHIRE**				
Broken Bow	3,140	7	6	1	Alexandria	1,541	2	2	0
Central City	2,827	6	5	1	Alstead	2,090	2	2	0
Chadron	5,480	20	14	6	Alton	5,114	14	12	2
Columbus	22,246	48	33	15	Amherst	11,903	19	18	1
Cozad	4,355	7	7	0	Antrim	2,630	6	5	1
Crete	6,380	16	10	6	Ashland	2,065	5	5	0
David City	2,522	4	4	0	Auburn	5,177	9	7	2
Emerson	837	2	2	0	Barnstead	4,619	6	6	0
Fairbury	3,644	5	4	1	Barrington	8,576	10	9	1
Falls City	3,910	12	8	4	Bartlett	2,930	4	3	1
Fremont	25,262	49	39	10	Bedford	21,304	47	33	14
Gering	7,825	18	15	3	Belmont	7,051	18	15	3
Gordon	1,468	5	4	1	Bennington	1,469	2	2	0
Gothenburg	3,753	7	6	1	Berlin	9,155	29	21	8
Grand Island	47,736	82	72	10	Bethlehem	2,450	6	6	0
Hastings	25,705	48	36	12	Boscawen	3,958	7	6	1
Holdrege	5,128	16	10	6	Bow	8,107	20	14	6
Imperial	1,759	4	4	0	Bradford	1,524	2	2	0
Kearney	31,436	66	52	14	Brentwood	3,998	5	5	0
Kimball	2,217	6	5	1	Bristol	3,110	10	9	1
La Vista	17,702	36	33	3	Campton	3,006	6	5	1
Lexington	10,415	18	16	2	Candia	4,177	8	7	1
Lincoln	259,672	410	325	85	Canterbury	2,316	3	3	0
Lyons	841	2	2	0	Carroll	726	4	4	0
Madison	2,218	4	4	0	Center Harbor	1,102	3	3	0
McCook	7,437	20	16	4	Charlestown	4,804	8	5	3
Milford	2,069	4	4	0	Chester	4,769	7	6	1
Minden	2,800	5	5	0	Claremont	12,788	29	24	5
Mitchell	1,816	4	4	0	Colebrook	2,282	5	5	0
Nebraska City	6,912	16	15	1	Concord	42,190	89	78	11
Neligh	1,448	3	3	0	Conway	9,195	30	21	9
Norfolk	23,523	54	39	15	Danville	4,326	6	5	1
North Platte	24,429	66	41	25	Deerfield	4,243	8	7	1
Ogallala	4,373	11	10	1	Deering	2,059	2	2	0
Omaha	464,628	918	789	129	Derry	34,075	70	56	14
O'Neill	3,242	8	7	1	Dover	28,627	62	45	17
Ord	1,986	4	4	0	Dublin	1,574	4	3	1

Table 78. Full-Time Law Enforcement Employees by State and City, 2010—*Continued*

(Number)

State/city	Popula-tion	Total law enforce-ment employees	Total officers	Total civilians	State/city	Popula-tion	Total law enforce-ment employees	Total officers	Total civilians
Dunbarton	2,676	3	3	0	Plymouth	6,647	16	10	6
Durham	14,465	21	19	2	Portsmouth	20,281	84	65	19
Enfield	4,811	8	7	1	Raymond	10,260	25	17	8
Epping	6,435	14	13	1	Rindge	6,451	9	8	1
Epsom	4,619	6	5	1	Rochester	30,827	72	54	18
Exeter	14,924	33	23	10	Rollinsford	2,611	4	4	0
Farmington	6,764	16	14	2	Rye	5,097	10	9	1
Fitzwilliam	2,296	3	3	0	Salem	29,146	74	58	16
Franconia	1,047	3	3	0	Sandown	5,907	7	7	0
Franklin	8,662	24	16	8	Sandwich	1,318	2	2	0
Freedom	1,443	3	3	0	Seabrook	8,471	34	27	7
Fremont	4,188	5	4	1	Somersworth	11,940	33	26	7
Gilford	7,427	23	17	6	South Hampton	871	2	2	0
Gilmanton	3,506	6	5	1	Strafford	4,076	4	4	0
Goffstown	17,774	42	28	14	Stratham	7,328	11	10	1
Gorham	2,718	10	7	3	Sugar Hill	610	2	2	0
Grantham	2,544	4	3	1	Sunapee	3,365	5	5	0
Greenland	3,435	7	7	0	Thornton	2,144	4	3	1
Hampstead	8,981	8	8	0	Tilton	3,542	16	14	2
Hampton	15,270	43	34	9	Troy	2,045	4	4	0
Hancock	1,807	3	3	0	Tuftonboro	2,442	4	4	0
Hanover	10,922	34	21	13	Wakefield	5,455	11	10	1
Haverhill	4,672	7	6	1	Walpole	3,637	4	3	1
Henniker	5,021	10	8	2	Warner	2,932	5	4	1
Hillsborough	5,592	19	13	6	Washington	1,087	1	1	0
Hinsdale	4,124	8	7	1	Waterville Valley	267	5	5	0
Hooksett	14,075	32	22	10	Weare	9,240	12	11	1
Hopkinton	5,561	7	7	0	Webster	1,891	3	3	0
Hudson	24,901	60	45	15	Wilton	3,938	7	6	1
Jaffrey	5,603	12	11	1	Winchester	4,252	8	7	1
Keene	22,093	58	43	15	Windham	13,484	26	19	7
Kingston	6,199	10	9	1	Wolfeboro	6,569	17	12	5
Laconia	16,973	47	38	9	Woodstock	1,155	4	4	0
Lancaster	3,151	8	7	1	**NEW JERSEY**				
Lebanon	12,765	48	35	13	Aberdeen Township	18,575	41	34	7
Lee	4,461	8	7	1	Absecon	8,728	30	23	7
Lincoln	1,337	13	8	5	Allendale	6,641	18	13	5
Lisbon	1,648	4	4	0	Allenhurst	699	13	9	4
Litchfield	8,852	12	10	2	Allentown	1,847	5	4	1
Littleton	6,111	14	13	1	Alpha	2,382	15	14	1
Londonderry	25,014	77	62	15	Alpine	2,552	13	13	0
Loudon	5,213	7	6	1	Andover Township	6,623	18	12	6
Madison	2,350	4	3	1	Asbury Park	16,625	103	93	10
Manchester	108,101	271	209	62	Atlantic City	39,787	346	283	63
Marlborough	2,052	3	3	0	Atlantic Highlands	4,609	19	14	5
Meredith	6,617	18	14	4	Audubon	8,908	19	17	2
Merrimack	26,501	54	40	14	Avalon	2,094	26	21	5
Middleton	1,861	3	3	0	Avon-by-the-Sea	2,252	11	11	0
Milford	15,089	29	24	5	Barnegat Township	23,692	56	45	11
Milton	4,633	8	7	1	Barrington	6,972	15	14	1
Mont Vernon	2,378	2	2	0	Bay Head	1,284	9	8	1
Moultonborough	5,028	14	11	3	Bayonne	58,393	228	195	33
Nashua	86,523	228	169	59	Beach Haven	1,425	13	11	2
New Boston	5,209	7	6	1	Beachwood	11,001	21	19	2
Newbury	2,120	4	4	0	Bedminster Township	8,456	17	15	2
New Durham	2,569	6	5	1	Belleville	33,849	109	99	10
Newfields	1,625	4	4	0	Bellmawr	11,275	25	23	2
New Hampton	2,256	6	6	0	Belmar	5,917	24	21	3
Newington	797	11	10	1	Belvidere	2,638	7	6	1
New Ipswich	5,438	6	6	0	Bergenfield	25,680	52	44	8
New London	4,402	13	8	5	Berkeley Heights Township	13,523	30	24	6
Newmarket	9,497	20	13	7	Berkeley Township	43,531	89	70	19
Newport	6,474	16	11	5	Berlin	8,194	17	16	1
Newton	4,587	8	5	3	Berlin Township	5,509	21	20	1
Northfield	5,120	11	10	1	Bernards Township	26,990	54	39	15
North Hampton	4,509	13	12	1	Bernardsville	7,872	24	18	6
Northumberland	2,242	4	4	0	Beverly	2,580	8	6	2
Northwood	4,164	9	8	1	Blairstown Township	5,985	7	5	2
Nottingham	4,601	7	6	1	Bloomfield	43,669	133	122	11
Orford	1,039	2	2	0	Bloomingdale	7,485	18	17	1
Ossipee	4,706	10	9	1	Bogota	7,933	20	15	5
Pelham	12,770	26	19	7	Boonton	8,552	25	21	4
Pembroke	7,317	13	11	2	Boonton Township	4,539	13	13	0
Peterborough	6,176	13	11	2	Bordentown	3,830	14	12	2
Pittsfield	4,348	9	8	1	Bordentown Township	10,300	30	24	6
Plaistow	7,522	25	17	8	Bound Brook	10,523	26	21	5

Table 78.   Full-Time Law Enforcement Employees by State and City, 2010—*Continued*

(Number)

State/city	Population	Total law enforcement employees	Total officers	Total civilians	State/city	Population	Total law enforcement employees	Total officers	Total civilians
Bradley Beach	5,046	19	15	4	Ewing Township	36,612	89	74	15
Branchburg Township	15,263	26	26	0	Fairfield Township, Essex County	7,531	40	39	1
Brick Township	79,569	175	125	50	Fair Haven	5,984	13	13	0
Bridgeton	25,243	74	63	11	Fair Lawn	30,607	67	54	13
Bridgewater Township	45,176	91	75	16	Fairview	13,709	34	31	3
Brielle	4,925	14	14	0	Fanwood	7,164	18	17	1
Brigantine	12,729	46	35	11	Far Hills	910	9	8	1
Brooklawn	2,262	8	8	0	Flemington	4,452	15	15	0
Buena	3,733	15	10	5	Florence Township	11,663	27	24	3
Burlington	9,423	35	32	3	Florham Park	12,669	40	33	7
Burlington Township	21,558	52	42	10	Fort Lee	36,580	110	91	19
Butler	8,248	18	17	1	Franklin	5,115	13	13	0
Byram Township	8,544	17	16	1	Franklin Lakes	11,816	26	21	5
Caldwell	7,115	20	20	0	Franklin Township, Gloucester County	17,679	31	28	3
Califon	1,043	32	28	4	Franklin Township, Hunterdon County	3,289	6	5	1
Camden	79,081	452	366	86	Franklin Township, Somerset County	61,185	119	103	16
Cape May	3,691	28	23	5	Freehold	11,548	37	31	6
Carlstadt	6,111	24	22	2	Freehold Township	35,117	71	67	4
Carney's Point Township	8,076	25	20	5	Frenchtown	1,474	3	3	0
Carteret	24,246	68	57	11	Galloway Township	37,367	75	61	14
Cedar Grove Township	12,774	32	30	2	Garfield	29,068	69	61	8
Chatham	8,263	25	19	6	Garwood	4,599	20	16	4
Chatham Township	10,302	25	20	5	Gibbsboro	2,447	6	6	0
Cherry Hill Township	71,338	154	129	25	Glassboro	20,047	44	40	4
Chesilhurst	1,997	8	7	1	Glen Ridge	6,642	28	22	6
Chester	1,700	10	9	1	Glen Rock	11,158	22	21	1
Chesterfield Township	7,860	11	10	1	Gloucester City	11,614	29	27	2
Chester Township	7,866	16	15	1	Gloucester Township	65,239	128	106	22
Cinnaminson Township	15,718	24	24	0	Green Brook Township	7,098	26	22	4
Clark Township	14,505	51	41	10	Greenwich Township, Gloucester County	5,040	19	18	1
Clayton	7,682	18	17	1	Greenwich Township, Warren County	5,193	11	11	0
Clementon	4,914	12	11	1	Guttenberg	10,643	23	19	4
Cliffside Park	23,139	46	46	0	Hackensack	43,111	128	102	26
Clifton	78,632	177	148	29	Hackettstown	9,653	18	17	1
Clinton	2,576	10	10	0	Haddonfield	11,499	23	21	2
Clinton Township	14,075	28	26	2	Haddon Heights	7,736	16	15	1
Closter	8,759	25	20	5	Haddon Township	14,432	30	28	2
Collingswood	13,880	30	26	4	Haledon	8,806	19	16	3
Colts Neck Township	10,180	21	20	1	Hamburg	3,514	9	9	0
Cranbury Township	4,023	18	17	1	Hamilton Township, Atlantic County	24,892	83	63	20
Cranford Township	22,147	63	48	15	Hamilton Township, Mercer County	91,439	208	176	32
Cresskill	8,760	26	21	5	Hammonton	13,603	38	31	7
Deal	1,051	21	17	4	Hanover Township	13,905	37	30	7
Delanco Township	5,000	10	9	1	Harding Township	3,375	13	12	1
Delaware Township	4,760	8	7	1	Hardyston Township	8,621	25	19	6
Delran Township	16,957	35	31	4	Harrington Park	4,914	10	10	0
Demarest	5,216	15	15	0	Harrison	15,393	61	47	14
Denville Township	16,708	42	33	9	Harrison Township	13,122	18	17	1
Deptford Township	31,340	72	67	5	Harvey Cedars	404	8	8	0
Dover	17,948	36	33	3	Hasbrouck Heights	11,497	32	29	3
Dumont	17,022	43	34	9	Haworth	3,447	12	11	1
Dunellen	7,150	16	16	0	Hawthorne	18,083	36	31	5
Eastampton Township	6,597	15	14	1	Hazlet Township	21,013	48	42	6
East Brunswick Township	47,620	107	84	23	Helmetta	2,039	5	5	0
East Greenwich Township	8,733	22	20	2	High Bridge	3,712	7	7	0
East Hanover Township	11,500	41	33	8	Highland Park	14,455	33	26	7
East Newark	2,116	10	7	3	Highlands	5,299	18	14	4
East Orange	65,118	325	265	60	Hightstown	5,370	16	11	5
East Rutherford	8,846	40	40	0	Hillsborough Township	40,011	70	55	15
East Windsor Township	27,424	56	44	12	Hillsdale	9,884	22	20	2
Eatontown	14,428	47	37	10	Hillside Township	21,346	82	69	13
Edgewater	9,875	31	30	1	Hi-Nella	1,003	5	5	0
Edgewater Park Township	7,757	11	10	1	Hoboken	41,515	161	149	12
Edison Township	100,395	239	183	56	Ho-Ho-Kus	4,024	18	15	3
Egg Harbor City	4,391	15	14	1	Holland Township	5,314	7	6	1
Egg Harbor Township	41,573	111	85	26	Holmdel Township	17,066	50	41	9
Elizabeth	126,494	425	341	84	Hopatcong	15,579	34	26	8
Elk Township	4,084	13	12	1	Hopewell Township	18,060	39	31	8
Elmer	1,346	2	2	0	Howell Township	52,130	109	92	17
Elmwood Park	18,736	42	40	2	Independence Township	5,724	9	8	1
Emerson	7,504	20	17	3	Irvington	56,019	196	167	29
Englewood	30,023	100	79	21	Island Heights	1,917	5	5	0
Englewood Cliffs	5,946	24	23	1	Jackson Township	54,638	89	80	9
Englishtown	1,944	6	6	0	Jamesburg	6,437	18	13	5
Essex Fells	2,149	13	13	0	Jefferson Township	21,997	44	37	7
Evesham Township	45,959	80	72	8	Jersey City	244,201	984	831	153

Table 78. Full-Time Law Enforcement Employees by State and City, 2010—*Continued*

(Number)

State/city	Population	Total law enforcement employees	Total officers	Total civilians	State/city	Population	Total law enforcement employees	Total officers	Total civilians
Keansburg	10,579	39	33	6	Morris Plains	5,954	18	16	2
Kearny	36,400	125	118	7	Morristown	19,085	57	51	6
Kenilworth	7,711	30	28	2	Morris Township	21,418	48	40	8
Keyport	7,516	24	18	6	Mountain Lakes	4,306	13	13	0
Kinnelon	9,703	16	15	1	Mountainside	6,638	25	21	4
Lacey Township	26,852	57	43	14	Mount Arlington	5,862	14	13	1
Lake Como	1,784	10	10	0	Mount Ephraim	4,443	14	13	1
Lakehurst	2,743	11	10	1	Mount Holly Township	10,246	25	23	2
Lakewood Township	72,960	153	128	25	Mount Laurel Township	39,696	67	61	6
Lambertville	3,802	13	11	2	Mount Olive Township	26,431	60	52	8
Laurel Springs	1,912	7	7	0	Mullica Township	6,104	13	12	1
Lavallette	2,802	17	12	5	Neptune City	5,116	23	17	6
Lawnside	2,870	9	8	1	Neptune Township	28,586	84	65	19
Lawrence Township, Mercer County	32,104	80	67	13	Netcong	3,244	10	9	1
Lebanon Township	6,291	10	9	1	Newark	280,379	1,666	1,308	358
Leonia	8,636	23	17	6	New Brunswick	52,245	161	132	29
Lincoln Park	10,663	29	23	6	Newfield	1,689	6	6	0
Linden	39,680	154	125	29	New Hanover Township	9,455	3	3	0
Lindenwold	17,875	45	42	3	New Milford	16,005	35	32	3
Linwood	7,275	21	20	1	New Providence	12,126	29	23	6
Little Egg Harbor Township	21,508	43	36	7	Newton	8,161	47	24	23
Little Falls Township	11,703	28	23	5	North Arlington	14,721	39	31	8
Little Ferry	10,510	28	25	3	North Bergen Township	54,933	130	118	12
Little Silver	6,175	21	16	5	North Brunswick Township	40,123	96	78	18
Livingston Township	27,775	85	72	13	North Caldwell	7,086	19	14	5
Loch Arbour	274	75	61	14	Northfield	7,965	24	23	1
Lodi	23,895	50	40	10	North Haledon	9,058	22	18	4
Logan Township	6,352	20	19	1	North Hanover Township	7,421	10	9	1
Long Beach Township	3,628	52	40	12	North Plainfield	21,373	52	46	6
Long Branch	33,368	115	95	20	Northvale	4,874	13	13	0
Long Hill Township	8,676	26	23	3	North Wildwood	4,840	38	28	10
Longport	1,104	18	14	4	Norwood	6,290	13	12	1
Lopatcong Township	8,744	15	14	1	Nutley Township	26,145	80	67	13
Lower Alloways Creek Township	1,908	16	12	4	Oakland	13,454	32	26	6
Lower Township	20,114	55	41	14	Oaklyn	4,047	13	12	1
Lumberton Township	12,184	23	20	3	Ocean City	14,725	72	59	13
Lyndhurst Township	19,403	56	50	6	Ocean Gate	2,171	8	7	1
Madison	15,849	37	31	6	Oceanport	5,755	17	14	3
Magnolia	4,353	11	11	0	Ocean Township, Monmouth County	28,503	75	61	14
Mahwah Township	24,346	60	51	9	Ocean Township, Ocean County	9,501	23	18	5
Manalapan Township	40,301	74	61	13	Ogdensburg	2,565	6	6	0
Manasquan	6,309	23	17	6	Old Bridge Township	66,913	131	100	31
Manchester Township	42,400	81	64	17	Old Tappan	6,151	13	12	1
Mansfield Township, Burlington County	8,405	14	12	2	Oradell	7,811	21	20	1
Mansfield Township, Warren County	8,139	15	14	1	Orange	31,057	135	106	29
Mantoloking	461	8	7	1	Palisades Park	19,789	38	28	10
Mantua Township	15,414	28	26	2	Palmyra	7,400	17	15	2
Manville	10,996	28	22	6	Paramus	26,340	113	85	28
Maple Shade Township	19,297	39	35	4	Park Ridge	9,013	18	17	1
Maplewood Township	21,944	73	61	12	Parsippany-Troy Hills Township	50,760	120	101	19
Margate City	8,612	43	33	10	Passaic	67,356	193	163	30
Marlboro Township	41,231	90	71	19	Paterson	146,356	593	497	96
Matawan	9,175	25	23	2	Paulsboro	6,121	20	19	1
Maywood	9,166	26	22	4	Peapack and Gladstone	2,600	8	7	1
Medford Lakes	4,129	9	8	1	Pemberton	1,634	7	7	0
Medford Township	22,914	57	46	11	Pemberton Township	28,107	62	54	8
Mendham	5,110	13	12	1	Pennington	2,674	6	6	0
Mendham Township	5,564	18	15	3	Pennsauken Township	35,105	111	93	18
Merchantville	3,784	15	13	2	Penns Grove	4,686	16	12	4
Metuchen	13,200	32	27	5	Pennsville Township	13,402	23	22	1
Middlesex	13,732	27	27	0	Pequannock Township	17,494	35	30	5
Middle Township	16,580	61	47	14	Perth Amboy	49,156	123	100	23
Middletown Township	66,915	131	105	26	Phillipsburg	14,500	36	35	1
Midland Park	6,783	14	13	1	Pine Beach	2,110	6	5	1
Millburn Township	18,548	61	51	10	Pine Hill	11,449	20	18	2
Milltown	7,007	18	15	3	Pine Valley	24	4	4	0
Millville	29,497	89	77	12	Piscataway Township	52,897	102	86	16
Monmouth Beach	3,590	9	9	0	Pitman	9,271	16	15	1
Monroe Township, Gloucester County	33,950	73	66	7	Plainfield	46,459	178	148	30
Monroe Township, Middlesex County	38,777	69	49	20	Plainsboro Township	21,407	42	32	10
Montclair	37,425	127	106	21	Pleasantville	18,996	66	52	14
Montgomery Township	23,760	35	30	5	Plumsted Township	8,446	12	11	1
Montvale	7,746	23	21	2	Pohatcong Township	3,331	15	14	1
Montville Township	21,253	44	38	6	Point Pleasant	20,569	40	32	8
Moonachie	2,770	20	18	2	Point Pleasant Beach	5,492	27	22	5
Moorestown Township	19,653	40	35	5	Pompton Lakes	11,150	27	23	4

Table 78. Full-Time Law Enforcement Employees by State and City, 2010—*Continued*

(Number)

State/city	Population	Total law enforcement employees	Total officers	Total civilians	State/city	Population	Total law enforcement employees	Total officers	Total civilians
Princeton	13,448	38	29	9	Union City	61,855	190	158	32
Princeton Township	17,581	39	30	9	Union Township	53,945	172	131	41
Prospect Park	5,623	15	15	0	Upper Saddle River	8,612	21	17	4
Rahway	29,443	82	73	9	Ventnor City	12,177	49	37	12
Ramsey	14,846	34	29	5	Vernon Township	24,993	39	29	10
Randolph Township	25,391	44	37	7	Verona	12,636	32	28	4
Raritan	7,487	22	18	4	Vineland	59,924	181	153	28
Raritan Township	22,934	34	31	3	Voorhees Township	32,441	63	50	13
Readington Township	16,302	25	23	2	Waldwick	9,643	23	18	5
Red Bank	11,992	46	40	6	Wallington	11,355	21	20	1
Ridgefield	10,953	29	27	2	Wall Township	26,387	79	64	15
Ridgefield Park	12,426	37	29	8	Wanaque	12,430	26	22	4
Ridgewood	24,260	45	40	5	Warren Township	16,356	32	25	7
Ringwood	12,822	25	21	4	Washington Township, Bergen County	9,664	21	21	0
Riverdale	3,590	22	18	4	Washington Township, Gloucester County	52,251	87	80	7
River Edge	10,733	26	21	5	Washington Township, Morris County	18,615	32	28	4
Riverside Township	7,703	16	16	0	Washington Township, Warren County	6,949	30	28	2
Riverton	2,633	5	5	0	Watchung	6,752	36	29	7
River Vale Township	9,730	23	21	2	Waterford Township	10,774	24	21	3
Robbinsville Township	12,573	33	25	8	Wayne Township	54,234	140	114	26
Rochelle Park Township	6,159	23	20	3	Weehawken Township	12,351	55	51	4
Rockaway	6,276	15	14	1	Wenonah	2,376	8	8	0
Rockaway Township	25,860	67	56	11	Westampton Township	8,877	24	22	2
Roseland	5,390	28	27	1	West Amwell Township	3,002	5	5	0
Roselle	20,721	70	58	12	West Caldwell Township	10,392	33	27	6
Roselle Park	12,899	41	34	7	West Deptford Township	22,482	44	41	3
Roxbury Township	23,485	49	46	3	Westfield	29,867	68	55	13
Rumson	7,371	21	16	5	West Long Branch	8,482	25	20	5
Runnemede	8,449	18	17	1	West Milford Township	28,049	47	40	7
Rutherford	17,491	40	37	3	West New York	46,907	119	107	12
Saddle Brook Township	14,371	31	28	3	West Orange	42,590	137	121	16
Saddle River	3,883	22	17	5	Westville	4,490	16	15	1
Salem	5,855	25	22	3	West Wildwood	404	8	8	0
Sayreville	42,680	104	86	18	West Windsor Township	27,202	58	47	11
Scotch Plains Township	23,231	51	45	6	Westwood	10,739	28	27	1
Sea Bright	1,818	12	11	1	Wharton	6,108	21	20	1
Sea Girt	2,107	14	12	2	Wildwood	5,222	49	40	9
Sea Isle City	2,938	34	21	13	Wildwood Crest	4,058	27	21	6
Seaside Heights	3,397	32	23	9	Willingboro Township	36,888	81	72	9
Seaside Park	2,351	16	15	1	Winfield Township	1,445	8	8	0
Secaucus	15,852	67	59	8	Winslow Township	40,393	85	69	16
Ship Bottom	1,479	12	11	1	Woodbridge Township	98,576	244	195	49
Shrewsbury	3,815	21	16	5	Woodbury	10,527	31	28	3
Somerdale	5,116	13	13	0	Woodbury Heights	3,079	8	7	1
Somers Point	11,401	32	27	5	Woodcliff Lake	6,020	17	16	1
Somerville	12,847	36	31	5	Woodland Park	12,383	30	25	5
South Amboy	7,802	30	25	5	Woodlynne	2,693	10	9	1
South Bound Brook	5,242	13	12	1	Wood-Ridge	7,491	33	19	14
South Brunswick Township	41,861	103	74	29	Woodstown	3,392	10	9	1
South Hackensack Township	2,271	15	14	1	Woolwich Township	10,659	21	20	1
South Harrison Township	3,298	5	5	0	Wyckoff Township	17,056	29	23	6
South Orange	16,024	56	52	4	**NEW MEXICO**				
South Plainfield	22,848	65	51	14	Alamogordo	36,555	112	70	42
South River	15,809	38	32	6	Albuquerque	545,389	1,441	1,055	386
South Toms River	3,759	12	11	1	Angel Fire	976	3	3	0
Sparta Township	19,466	46	35	11	Artesia	11,414	54	33	21
Spotswood	8,261	23	19	4	Aztec	7,135	16	14	2
Springfield	15,353	42	36	6	Bayard	2,423	5	5	0
Springfield Township	3,498	9	8	1	Belen	7,522	22	19	3
Spring Lake	3,561	16	13	3	Bernalillo	9,878	22	19	3
Spring Lake Heights	5,164	12	12	0	Bloomfield	7,462	25	21	4
Stafford Township	27,444	68	48	20	Bosque Farms	4,154	14	13	1
Stanhope	3,586	10	9	1	Capitan	1,552	3	3	0
Stone Harbor	1,011	27	16	11	Carlsbad	26,801	84	54	30
Stratford	7,067	16	15	1	Carrizozo	1,065	4	3	1
Summit	20,783	55	46	9	Cimarron	799	2	2	0
Surf City	1,590	10	10	0	Clayton	2,321	15	8	7
Teaneck Township	38,666	100	87	13	Cloudcroft	944	3	3	0
Tenafly	14,864	41	34	7	Clovis	33,359	83	59	24
Tewksbury Township	6,168	11	10	1	Corrales	8,107	18	15	3
Tinton Falls	20,257	35	34	1	Cuba	1,550	5	4	1
Toms River Township	98,282	197	150	47	Deming	15,655	37	32	5
Totowa	10,809	31	27	4	Dexter	1,257	4	4	0
Trenton	83,552	445	356	89	Edgewood	4,823	9	8	1
Tuckerton	3,984	9	9	0	Espanola	9,846	36	25	11
Union Beach	6,647	18	14	4	Estancia	1,606	6	5	1

Table 78.   Full-Time Law Enforcement Employees by State and City, 2010—*Continued*

(Number)

State/city	Popula-tion	Total law enforce-ment employees	Total officers	Total civilians	State/city	Popula-tion	Total law enforce-ment employees	Total officers	Total civilians
Eunice	2,905	15	8	7	Cambridge Village	1,786	6	6	0
Gallup	19,825	75	59	16	Camden Village	2,219	3	3	0
Grants	8,845	20	17	3	Camillus Town and Village	23,245	24	22	2
Hobbs	32,642	102	62	40	Canajoharie Village	2,124	3	3	0
Hurley	1,427	6	5	1	Canandaigua	11,054	25	23	2
Jal	2,133	10	5	5	Canastota Village	4,225	7	6	1
Las Cruces	97,065	251	168	83	Canisteo Village	2,175	1	1	0
Las Vegas	13,797	53	35	18	Canton Village	6,065	10	8	2
Logan	1,002	4	4	0	Carmel Town	34,119	42	35	7
Lordsburg	2,886	12	10	2	Carthage Village	3,734	3	3	0
Los Alamos	18,311	71	31	40	Catskill Village	4,128	16	15	1
Los Lunas	15,054	39	34	5	Cayuga Heights Village	3,626	7	6	1
Lovington	10,422	29	20	9	Cazenovia Village	2,956	5	4	1
Magdalena	984	4	4	0	Centre Island Village	441	6	6	0
Mesilla	2,547	6	6	0	Chatham Village	1,639	5	4	1
Milan	2,566	11	6	5	Cheektowaga Town	76,671	170	126	44
Moriarty	2,014	11	10	1	Chester Town	9,972	14	14	0
Portales	12,468	36	25	11	Chester Village	3,548	16	15	1
Raton	6,330	22	13	9	Chittenango Village	4,811	5	4	1
Red River	523	4	4	0	Cicero Town	28,288	14	13	1
Rio Rancho	87,608	181	108	73	Clarkstown Town	78,365	188	163	25
Roswell	47,238	119	89	30	Clayton Village	1,877	3	3	0
Ruidoso	9,504	38	25	13	Clifton Springs Village	2,117	2	2	0
Ruidoso Downs	2,740	16	8	8	Cobleskill Village	4,486	11	11	0
Santa Clara	1,875	4	3	1	Coeymans Town	7,939	9	6	3
Santa Fe	76,442	205	163	42	Cohoes	14,884	45	34	11
Santa Rosa	2,593	13	6	7	Colchester Town	1,988	2	2	0
Silver City	10,459	38	33	5	Colonie Town	77,078	150	106	44
Socorro	9,056	30	21	9	Cooperstown Village	1,849	7	6	1
Springer	1,123	2	2	0	Corning	10,046	24	20	4
Sunland Park	15,224	24	21	3	Cornwall-on-Hudson Village	3,039	2	2	0
Taos	5,689	41	22	19	Cornwall Town	9,724	15	12	3
Taos Ski Valley	59	3	3	0	Cortland	17,930	45	42	3
Tatum	793	8	2	6	Crawford Town	9,492	14	12	2
Texico	997	3	3	0	Croton-on-Hudson Village	7,909	23	21	2
Truth or Consequences	7,194	18	14	4	Cuba Town	3,217	4	4	0
Tucumcari	5,255	25	16	9	Dansville Village	4,363	6	6	0
Tularosa	3,078	12	7	5	Deerpark Town	8,495	6	6	0
NEW YORK					Delhi Village	2,749	4	4	0
Addison Town and Village	2,466	2	2	0	Depew Village	14,966	32	26	6
Akron Village	2,923	1	1	0	Deposit Village	1,547	2	2	0
Albany	92,713	465	327	138	Dewitt Town	21,202	38	34	4
Albion Village	5,437	12	12	0	Dobbs Ferry Village	11,151	28	26	2
Alexandria Bay Village	1,114	2	2	0	Dolgeville Village	1,973	2	2	0
Alfred Village	4,933	6	6	0	Dryden Village	1,807	6	5	1
Allegany Village	1,715	3	2	1	Dunkirk	11,801	38	37	1
Altamont Village	1,676	1	1	0	East Aurora-Aurora Town	13,307	22	17	5
Amherst Town	109,138	193	157	36	Eastchester Town	18,612	54	49	5
Amity Town and Belmont Village	2,187	1	1	0	East Fishkill Town	28,798	41	32	9
Amityville Village	9,962	29	27	2	East Greenbush Town	16,873	32	24	8
Amsterdam	17,187	43	41	2	East Hampton Town	19,860	88	62	26
Andover Village	970	1	1	0	East Hampton Village	1,395	29	24	5
Arcade Village	1,836	6	6	0	East Rochester Village	6,153	9	8	1
Ardsley Village	4,855	20	20	0	East Syracuse Village	2,924	9	8	1
Asharoken Village	658	3	3	0	Eden Town	7,604	5	4	1
Attica Village	2,348	5	5	0	Ellenville Village	3,851	11	11	0
Auburn	26,448	76	68	8	Ellicott Town	5,162	13	12	1
Avon Village	2,850	5	5	0	Ellicottville	518	2	2	0
Baldwinsville Village	7,201	14	12	2	Elmira	28,823	89	77	12
Ballston Spa Village	5,444	6	6	0	Elmira Heights Village	3,849	9	9	0
Batavia	14,871	33	31	2	Elmira Town	5,808	3	3	0
Bath Village	5,330	14	12	2	Elmsford Village	4,722	18	18	0
Beacon	14,342	37	35	2	Endicott Village	12,103	38	35	3
Bethlehem Town	32,862	59	42	17	Evans Town	16,561	30	24	6
Binghamton	43,628	135	123	12	Fairport Village	5,382	10	9	1
Blooming Grove Town	12,219	17	15	2	Fallsburg Town	12,285	23	19	4
Bolivar Village	1,069	1	1	0	Floral Park Village	15,699	43	35	8
Boonville Village	1,996	3	3	0	Florida Village	2,811	1	1	0
Briarcliff Manor Village	7,864	19	19	0	Fort Edward Village	2,965	5	5	0
Brighton Town	33,701	45	39	6	Fort Plain Village	2,144	4	4	0
Brockport Village	8,269	12	11	1	Frankfort Town	4,704	3	3	0
Bronxville Village	6,452	24	22	2	Frankfort Village	2,308	4	4	0
Buchanan Village	2,223	6	6	0	Franklinville Village	1,659	2	2	0
Buffalo	265,128	918	768	150	Fredonia Village	10,982	18	14	4
Cairo Town	6,411	2	2	0	Freeport Village	43,458	103	87	16
Caledonia Village	2,080	2	2	0	Fulton City	10,956	37	35	2

Table 78. Full-Time Law Enforcement Employees by State and City, 2010—*Continued*

(Number)

State/city	Popula-tion	Total law enforce-ment employees	Total officers	Total civilians	State/city	Popula-tion	Total law enforce-ment employees	Total officers	Total civilians
Garden City Village	22,314	61	48	13	Malone Village	5,649	14	14	0
Gates Town	28,357	36	30	6	Malverne Village	8,785	25	24	1
Geddes Town	10,269	16	14	2	Mamaroneck Town	11,466	40	39	1
Geneseo Village	7,679	8	8	0	Mamaroneck Village	18,309	59	51	8
Geneva	13,090	41	36	5	Manlius Town	24,597	45	37	8
Glen Cove	26,661	56	52	4	Marlborough Town	8,178	8	6	2
Glens Falls	13,650	37	31	6	Massena Village	10,286	26	21	5
Glenville Town	21,844	36	22	14	Maybrook Village	4,049	3	3	0
Gloversville	14,713	32	30	2	Mechanicville	4,827	13	12	1
Goshen Town	8,257	12	11	1	Medina Village	5,933	12	11	1
Goshen Village	5,553	20	17	3	Menands Village	3,734	13	10	3
Gouverneur Village	3,925	8	5	3	Middleport Village	1,746	3	3	0
Granville Village	2,490	5	5	0	Middletown	25,701	80	68	12
Great Neck Estates Village	2,760	15	12	3	Mohawk Village	2,418	4	4	0
Greece Town	92,282	102	96	6	Monroe Village	8,172	23	18	5
Greenburgh Town	43,314	147	116	31	Montgomery Town	8,685	16	14	2
Greene Village	1,597	1	1	0	Monticello Village	6,240	28	25	3
Green Island Village	2,529	1	1	0	Moriah Town	3,400	2	2	0
Greenwich Village	1,791	6	6	0	Mount Hope Town	7,540	2	2	0
Greenwood Lake Village	3,382	7	5	2	Mount Kisco Village	10,314	38	34	4
Groton Village	2,380	1	1	0	Mount Morris Village	2,804	5	5	0
Guilderland Town	32,840	51	35	16	Mount Pleasant Town	26,257	53	44	9
Hamburg Town	43,642	79	63	16	Mount Vernon	68,081	224	194	30
Hamburg Village	9,231	14	13	1	Nassau Village	1,098	1	1	0
Hamilton Village	3,766	3	3	0	Newark Village	8,871	19	18	1
Harriman Village	2,312	7	7	0	Newburgh	27,836	91	79	12
Harrison Town	26,710	69	59	10	Newburgh Town	31,293	61	52	9
Hastings-on-Hudson Village	7,887	20	20	0	New Castle Town	17,598	41	37	4
Haverstraw Town	37,489	79	72	7	New Hartford Town and Village	18,875	30	19	11
Hempstead Village	53,443	154	126	28	New Paltz Town and Village	14,279	26	23	3
Herkimer Village	6,824	22	21	1	New Rochelle	73,648	238	178	60
Highland Falls Village	3,674	11	8	3	New Windsor Town	25,211	52	43	9
Holley Village	1,645	2	2	0	New York	8,336,002	50,068	34,817	15,251
Homer Village	3,135	4	4	0	New York Mills Village	3,245	5	5	0
Hoosick Falls Village	3,216	5	3	2	Niagara Falls	50,321	170	149	21
Hornell	8,441	20	20	0	Niagara Town	8,215	6	5	1
Horseheads Village	6,193	14	13	1	Niskayuna Town	21,735	39	28	11
Hudson	6,691	32	26	6	Nissequogue Village	1,608	3	3	0
Hudson Falls Village	6,491	16	13	3	North Castle Town	12,173	37	34	3
Hunter Town	2,650	1	1	0	North Greenbush Town	11,833	19	17	2
Huntington Bay Village	1,504	6	6	0	Northport Village	7,633	19	15	4
Hyde Park Town	19,992	15	12	3	North Syracuse Village	6,477	11	10	1
Ilion Village	7,844	20	18	2	North Tonawanda	30,564	55	45	10
Inlet Town	363	3	2	1	Norwich	6,778	21	20	1
Irondequoit Town	49,101	64	53	11	Ocean Beach Village	147	5	5	0
Irvington Village	6,615	23	22	1	Ogdensburg	10,814	28	24	4
Ithaca	29,791	79	67	12	Ogden Town	19,177	15	12	3
Jamestown	28,785	70	60	10	Old Brookville Village	2,310	51	40	11
Johnson City Village	14,384	36	33	3	Old Westbury Village	5,329	31	26	5
Johnstown	8,354	27	25	2	Olean	13,778	35	34	1
Kenmore Village	14,652	25	25	0	Olive Town	4,573	1	1	0
Kensington Village	1,193	6	6	0	Oneida	10,508	26	22	4
Kent Town	13,999	25	20	5	Oneonta City	12,785	33	28	5
Kings Point Village	5,351	25	23	2	Orangetown Town	36,021	98	88	10
Kingston	22,012	83	80	3	Orchard Park Town	28,384	34	30	4
Kirkland Town	8,238	6	6	0	Ossining Town	5,678	16	16	0
Lackawanna	17,202	52	46	6	Ossining Village	23,687	65	56	9
Lake Placid Village	2,700	17	14	3	Oswego City	16,897	53	45	8
Lake Success Village	2,869	26	23	3	Owego Village	3,622	9	8	1
Lakewood-Busti	7,273	10	9	1	Oxford Village	1,493	1	1	0
Lancaster Town	23,380	64	49	15	Oyster Bay Cove Village	2,290	11	11	0
Larchmont Village	6,517	28	25	3	Painted Post Village	1,738	3	3	0
Le Roy Village	4,057	8	8	0	Palmyra Village	3,389	6	5	1
Lewisboro Town	12,425	1	1	0	Peekskill	24,699	74	60	14
Lewiston Town and Village	16,604	10	9	1	Pelham Manor Village	5,397	29	28	1
Liberty Village	3,804	20	17	3	Pelham Village	6,418	28	25	3
Little Falls	4,751	11	10	1	Penn Yan Village	5,025	13	12	1
Liverpool Village	2,305	6	5	1	Perry Village	3,571	3	3	0
Lloyd Harbor Village	3,722	14	13	1	Piermont Village	2,541	8	8	0
Lloyd Town	10,623	13	10	3	Plattsburgh City	19,219	53	48	5
Lockport	20,175	52	49	3	Pleasantville Village	7,069	23	21	2
Long Beach	35,527	94	77	17	Port Chester Village	27,939	61	59	2
Lowville Village	3,077	6	6	0	Port Dickinson Village	1,557	5	4	1
Lynbrook Village	19,656	55	47	8	Port Jervis	9,061	33	32	1
Lyons Village	3,334	11	9	2	Port Washington	18,808	69	61	8
Macedon Town and Village	8,770	5	4	1	Potsdam Village	9,798	18	14	4

Table 78. Full-Time Law Enforcement Employees by State and City, 2010—*Continued*

(Number)

State/city	Population	Total law enforcement employees	Total officers	Total civilians	State/city	Population	Total law enforcement employees	Total officers	Total civilians
Poughkeepsie	29,175	135	100	35	Webb Town	1,915	5	5	0
Poughkeepsie Town	42,538	96	85	11	Webster Town and Village	41,839	37	31	6
Pound Ridge Town	4,915	3	2	1	Wellsville Village	4,728	12	10	2
Pulaski Village	2,244	1	1	0	Westfield Village	3,303	5	5	0
Quogue Village	1,174	14	13	1	Westhampton Beach Village	2,009	18	15	3
Ramapo Town	77,482	136	112	24	West Seneca Town	43,061	79	66	13
Red Hook Village	1,991	3	2	1	Whitehall Village	2,518	4	4	0
Rensselaer City	7,760	31	26	5	White Plains	57,254	207	195	12
Riverhead Town	36,120	100	85	15	Whitesboro Village	3,661	7	7	0
Rochester	203,802	917	772	145	Whitestown Town	9,088	7	7	0
Rockville Centre Village	24,188	62	52	10	Windham Town	1,880	2	2	0
Rome	32,930	80	76	4	Wolcott Village	1,561	1	1	0
Rosendale Town	6,138	3	2	1	Woodbury Town	10,242	26	21	5
Rotterdam Town	30,025	59	42	17	Woodridge Village	1,064	1	1	0
Rouses Point Village	2,265	1	1	0	Woodstock Town	6,009	10	10	0
Rye	14,987	39	34	5	Yonkers	199,296	659	589	70
Rye Brook Village	9,575	28	27	1	Yorktown Town	37,684	67	58	9
Sag Harbor Village	2,423	15	14	1	Yorkville Village	2,503	3	3	0
Salamanca	5,521	15	15	0	**NORTH CAROLINA**				
Sands Point Village	2,848	19	19	0	Aberdeen	6,116	28	26	2
Saranac Lake Village	4,689	12	12	0	Ahoskie	4,617	22	17	5
Saratoga Springs	29,080	78	65	13	Albemarle	15,446	53	47	6
Saugerties Town	19,375	19	14	5	Andrews	1,610	5	5	0
Scarsdale Village	17,530	51	45	6	Angier	4,555	12	12	0
Schenectady	60,751	201	153	48	Apex	35,709	68	54	14
Schodack Town	11,453	11	10	1	Archdale	9,344	31	25	6
Schoharie Village	957	1	1	0	Asheboro	25,017	85	78	7
Scotia Village	7,978	14	13	1	Asheville	77,067	268	193	75
Seneca Falls Village	6,539	15	13	2	Atlantic Beach	1,855	22	18	4
Shandaken Town	2,990	4	4	0	Aurora	575	2	2	0
Shawangunk Town	12,570	7	7	0	Ayden	5,078	22	18	4
Shelter Island Town	2,555	10	9	1	Badin	1,329	5	5	0
Sherrill	3,077	3	3	0	Bailey	691	3	3	0
Sidney Village	3,541	8	8	0	Bakersville	342	1	1	0
Silver Creek Village	2,757	5	5	0	Bald Head Island	309	19	13	6
Skaneateles Village	2,544	5	5	0	Banner Elk	944	10	9	1
Sleepy Hollow Village	10,212	27	27	0	Beaufort	4,368	18	17	1
Sodus Village	1,572	1	1	0	Beech Mountain	348	14	10	4
Solvay Village	6,318	16	14	2	Belhaven	2,050	11	7	4
Southampton Town	52,425	125	106	19	Belmont	9,601	42	32	10
Southampton Village	4,502	44	31	13	Benson	3,632	15	14	1
South Glens Falls Village	3,371	6	6	0	Bethel	1,759	5	5	0
South Nyack Village	3,306	7	6	1	Beulaville	1,133	5	5	0
Southold Town	20,444	66	52	14	Biltmore Forest	1,576	14	12	2
Spring Valley Village	24,965	64	56	8	Biscoe	1,685	9	8	1
St. Johnsville Village	1,574	2	2	0	Black Creek	709	2	2	0
Stony Point Town	15,050	30	29	1	Black Mountain	7,953	22	18	4
Suffern Village	10,917	30	25	5	Bladenboro	1,659	6	6	0
Syracuse	136,284	552	484	68	Blowing Rock	1,484	15	11	4
Tarrytown Village	11,047	39	33	6	Boiling Spring Lakes	5,012	9	8	1
Ticonderoga Town	4,853	7	7	0	Boiling Springs	3,959	8	8	0
Tonawanda	14,475	33	28	5	Boone	14,209	43	35	8
Tonawanda Town	55,706	157	106	51	Boonville	1,098	5	5	0
Troy	46,861	138	124	14	Brevard	6,722	29	23	6
Tuckahoe Village	6,196	28	25	3	Broadway	1,194	4	4	0
Tupper Lake Village	3,740	9	9	0	Brookford	431	1	1	0
Tuxedo Park Village	713	5	2	3	Bryson City	1,348	7	6	1
Tuxedo Town	2,960	15	12	3	Bunn	421	3	3	0
Ulster Town	12,469	29	25	4	Burgaw	4,478	13	12	1
Utica	57,153	202	182	20	Burlington	52,210	160	117	43
Vernon Village	1,125	1	1	0	Burnsville	1,674	8	8	0
Vestal Town	27,146	41	37	4	Butner	6,389	46	41	5
Walden Village	6,991	17	14	3	Cameron	310	1	1	0
Wallkill Town	27,941	42	37	5	Candor	843	5	5	0
Walton Village	2,739	7	6	1	Canton	3,841	18	12	6
Wappingers Falls Village	6,072	7	4	3	Cape Carteret	1,429	7	7	0
Warsaw Village	3,527	6	6	0	Carolina Beach	5,968	30	28	2
Warwick Town	19,824	38	31	7	Carrboro	18,448	42	39	3
Washingtonville Village	6,122	15	13	2	Carthage	2,080	10	9	1
Waterford Town and Village	8,520	13	10	3	Cary	141,461	201	165	36
Waterloo Village	4,905	9	8	1	Caswell Beach	483	4	4	0
Watertown	27,267	70	66	4	Catawba	836	2	2	0
Watervliet	9,320	30	26	4	Chadbourn	2,043	10	9	1
Watkins Glen Village	1,951	5	5	0	Chapel Hill	54,164	139	113	26
Waverly Village	4,216	11	10	1	Charlotte-Mecklenburg[1]	797,733	2,187	1,696	491
Wayland Village	1,746	2	2	0	Cherryville	5,862	21	16	5

[1] The employee data presented in this table for Charlotte-Mecklenburg represent only Charlotte-Mecklenburg Police Department and exclude Mecklenburg County Sheriff's Office.

Table 78.   Full-Time Law Enforcement Employees by State and City, 2010—*Continued*

(Number)

State/city	Population	Total law enforcement employees	Total officers	Total civilians	State/city	Population	Total law enforcement employees	Total officers	Total civilians
China Grove	3,772	13	13	0	Huntersville	47,537	89	80	9
Chocowinity	720	3	3	0	Indian Beach	95	4	4	0
Claremont	1,163	9	8	1	Jackson	626	2	1	1
Clayton	17,472	45	41	4	Jacksonville	82,254	142	114	28
Cleveland	846	5	5	0	Jefferson	1,341	3	3	0
Clinton	8,753	35	31	4	Jonesville	2,233	11	10	1
Clyde	1,282	4	4	0	Kannapolis	44,084	94	75	19
Coats	2,218	7	7	0	Kenansville	1,168	5	5	0
Columbus	1,056	6	6	0	Kenly	2,028	8	8	0
Concord	68,461	178	154	24	Kernersville	23,695	83	64	19
Conover	7,503	26	25	1	Kill Devil Hills	6,929	35	29	6
Conway	640	1	1	0	King	7,092	23	20	3
Cooleemee	990	4	4	0	Kings Mountain	11,243	36	30	6
Cornelius	26,180	67	52	15	Kinston	21,900	93	84	9
Cramerton	3,184	11	11	0	Kitty Hawk	3,351	17	15	2
Creedmoor	3,898	17	13	4	Knightdale	10,686	26	25	1
Dallas	3,899	16	12	4	Kure Beach	2,642	11	10	1
Davidson	10,958	18	17	1	Lake Lure	1,001	11	10	1
Denton	1,669	6	6	0	Lake Royale		5	5	0
Dobson	1,452	6	6	0	Lake Waccamaw	1,435	5	5	0
Drexel	1,865	5	5	0	Landis	3,130	11	10	1
Duck	504	9	8	1	Laurel Park	2,185	7	7	0
Dunn	10,272	50	35	15	Laurinburg	15,325	47	40	7
Durham	233,790	598	485	113	Leland	6,165	32	29	3
East Bend	657	2	2	0	Lenoir	17,840	67	52	15
East Spencer	1,801	5	5	0	Lexington	20,255	75	67	8
Eden	15,310	54	46	8	Liberty	2,738	10	9	1
Edenton	5,052	18	16	2	Lilesville	415	1	1	0
Elizabeth City	20,801	74	61	13	Lillington	3,489	13	12	1
Elizabethtown	3,677	17	16	1	Lincolnton	11,017	36	31	5
Elkin	4,117	21	17	4	Littleton	633	4	4	0
Elon	7,198	16	15	1	Locust	2,705	13	12	1
Emerald Isle	3,719	18	13	5	Long View	5,005	15	15	0
Enfield	2,319	18	17	1	Louisburg	3,755	14	13	1
Erwin	4,954	11	10	1	Lowell	2,817	9	9	0
Fair Bluff	1,140	3	3	0	Lumberton	22,019	86	76	10
Fairmont	2,625	15	12	3	Madison	2,245	15	14	1
Farmville	4,679	20	15	5	Maggie Valley	906	10	9	1
Fayetteville	208,263	518	366	152	Magnolia	988	2	2	0
Fletcher	4,819	15	14	1	Maiden	3,521	15	14	1
Forest City	6,913	34	32	2	Manteo	1,503	8	7	1
Four Oaks	2,146	4	4	0	Marion	7,015	28	23	5
Foxfire Village	496	2	2	0	Marshall	827	4	4	0
Franklin	3,980	19	18	1	Mars Hill	1,803	4	4	0
Franklinton	2,041	10	9	1	Marshville	3,389	7	7	0
Fremont	1,420	6	4	2	Matthews	27,989	69	57	12
Fuquay-Varina	19,387	33	28	5	Maxton	2,727	17	12	5
Garner	28,620	69	64	5	Mayodan	2,625	15	12	3
Garysburg	1,093	2	2	0	Maysville	947	3	3	0
Gaston	852	2	2	0	Mebane	11,196	26	20	6
Gastonia	73,533	201	173	28	Middlesex	872	4	4	0
Gibsonville	4,905	15	14	1	Mint Hill	21,032	31	29	2
Glen Alpine	1,079	3	3	0	Misenheimer	702	4	4	0
Goldsboro	38,179	122	111	11	Mocksville	4,683	23	21	2
Graham	14,826	38	35	3	Monroe	34,132	100	89	11
Granite Falls	4,571	17	14	3	Montreat	718	5	5	0
Granite Quarry	2,314	6	6	0	Mooresville	22,430	78	58	20
Greensboro	257,237	746	641	105	Morehead City	9,888	46	36	10
Greenville	84,044	238	187	51	Morganton	17,001	95	63	32
Grifton	2,265	7	7	0	Morrisville	15,446	34	33	1
Hamlet	5,725	23	19	4	Mount Airy	10,612	51	38	13
Havelock	21,934	35	28	7	Mount Gilead	1,403	6	6	0
Haw River	2,050	8	8	0	Mount Holly	10,228	35	27	8
Henderson	15,730	63	54	9	Mount Olive	4,344	16	15	1
Hendersonville	12,311	50	38	12	Murfreesboro	2,413	15	10	5
Hertford	2,170	9	8	1	Murphy	1,526	9	6	3
Hickory	41,892	140	110	30	Nags Head	3,097	22	20	2
Highlands	964	11	10	1	Nashville	4,582	14	13	1
High Point	105,278	250	215	35	Navassa	1,977	4	4	0
Hillsborough	5,831	29	27	2	New Bern	29,657	125	82	43
Holden Beach	859	8	8	0	Newland	648	5	5	0
Holly Ridge	1,000	9	8	1	Newport	4,492	9	9	0
Holly Springs	23,506	51	41	10	Newton	13,676	43	34	9
Hope Mills	14,008	34	31	3	Newton Grove	626	3	3	0
Hot Springs	634	1	1	0	Norlina	1,006	4	4	0
Hudson	3,013	12	11	1	North Topsail Beach	982	12	11	1

Table 78.   Full-Time Law Enforcement Employees by State and City, 2010—Continued

(Number)

State/city	Population	Total law enforcement employees	Total officers	Total civilians	State/city	Population	Total law enforcement employees	Total officers	Total civilians
Northwest	1,013	2	2	0	Tabor City	2,773	10	9	1
North Wilkesboro	4,133	25	23	2	Tarboro	9,930	33	27	6
Norwood	2,451	7	6	1	Taylorsville	1,815	11	11	0
Oakboro	1,166	6	6	0	Taylortown	901	1	1	0
Oak Island	8,487	31	24	7	Thomasville	26,850	71	65	6
Ocean Isle Beach	540	13	13	0	Topsail Beach	593	8	7	1
Old Fort	961	3	2	1	Trent Woods	4,007	5	5	0
Oxford	8,699	39	32	7	Troutman	2,024	14	14	0
Parkton	434	2	2	0	Troy	3,458	12	11	1
Pembroke	2,752	15	11	4	Tryon	1,705	10	8	2
Pikeville	715	3	3	0	Valdese	4,530	13	12	1
Pilot Mountain	1,260	9	8	1	Vanceboro	857	2	2	0
Pinebluff	1,447	4	4	0	Vass	815	3	3	0
Pinehurst	12,749	28	24	4	Wadesboro	5,145	31	26	5
Pine Knoll Shores	1,569	7	5	2	Wagram	761	2	2	0
Pine Level	1,854	5	5	0	Wake Forest	30,155	63	53	10
Pinetops	1,228	9	6	3	Wallace	3,589	17	14	3
Pineville	7,313	49	38	11	Walnut Cove	1,604	7	7	0
Pink Hill	524	2	2	0	Walnut Creek	847	2	2	0
Pittsboro	2,820	13	13	0	Warrenton	827	5	4	1
Plymouth	3,768	12	12	0	Warsaw	3,193	15	13	2
Princeton	1,347	3	3	0	Washington	10,228	47	36	11
Raeford	4,149	19	17	2	Waxhaw	4,355	21	19	2
Raleigh	419,700	883	770	113	Waynesville	10,261	42	34	8
Ramseur	1,772	6	6	0	Weaverville	3,118	15	14	1
Randleman	3,692	14	14	0	Weldon	1,641	9	9	0
Ranlo	2,335	7	7	0	Wendell	5,612	20	18	2
Red Springs	3,503	17	13	4	West Jefferson	1,132	7	7	0
Reidsville	14,739	58	50	8	Whispering Pines	2,180	8	7	1
Richlands	964	5	5	0	Whitakers	766	3	3	0
Rich Square	972	2	2	0	White Lake	606	6	6	0
River Bend	3,161	5	5	0	Whiteville	5,231	25	22	3
Roanoke Rapids	16,121	43	39	4	Wilkesboro	3,123	23	21	2
Robbins	1,248	5	5	0	Williamston	5,313	21	19	2
Robersonville	1,520	8	8	0	Wilmington	102,649	315	261	54
Rockingham	8,727	37	32	5	Wilson	49,134	134	117	17
Rockwell	2,024	5	5	0	Wilson's Mills	1,757	4	4	0
Rocky Mount	59,688	207	165	42	Windsor	3,131	9	9	0
Rolesville	3,512	11	10	1	Wingate	4,186	8	8	0
Rose Hill	1,399	4	4	0	Winston-Salem	232,928	688	528	160
Rowland	1,154	7	6	1	Winterville	4,886	21	19	2
Roxboro	8,683	36	32	4	Woodfin	5,861	15	15	0
Rutherfordton	4,050	15	15	0	Woodland	739	2	2	0
Salisbury	31,106	101	86	15	Wrightsville Beach	2,660	25	23	2
Saluda	590	4	4	0	Yadkinville	2,825	13	12	1
Sanford	30,679	105	84	21	Youngsville	798	9	8	1
Scotland Neck	2,122	8	7	1	Zebulon	4,964	23	22	1
Selma	7,172	25	23	2	**NORTH DAKOTA**				
Seven Devils	175	5	5	0	Belfield	844	2	2	0
Shallotte	2,260	14	13	1	Beulah	2,976	6	5	1
Sharpsburg	2,412	9	9	0	Bismarck	64,142	129	101	28
Shelby	21,430	85	71	14	Bowman	1,563	3	3	0
Siler City	8,938	28	23	5	Burlington	1,043	2	2	0
Smithfield	13,448	49	45	4	Cando	1,033	3	3	0
Southern Pines	13,060	40	31	9	Carrington	2,001	4	4	0
Southern Shores	2,668	11	10	1	Cavalier	1,351	4	4	0
Southport	3,339	11	10	1	Crosby	954	2	2	0
Sparta	1,760	6	6	0	Devils Lake	6,917	18	16	2
Spencer	3,408	12	11	1	Dickinson	16,917	40	27	13
Spindale	3,809	12	12	0	Ellendale	1,500	2	2	0
Spring Hope	1,310	5	5	0	Emerado	497	1	1	0
Spring Lake	12,303	25	23	2	Fargo	99,694	161	144	17
Spruce Pine	1,947	12	12	0	Fessenden	493	1	1	0
Stallings	9,612	21	19	2	Grafton	4,052	9	8	1
Stanfield	1,118	3	3	0	Grand Forks	53,382	97	82	15
Stanley	3,228	13	10	3	Harvey	1,604	3	3	0
Stantonsburg	726	3	3	0	Hazen	2,260	4	4	0
Star	796	4	4	0	Hillsboro	1,522	2	2	0
Statesville	26,994	93	72	21	Jamestown	15,164	34	29	5
Stoneville	969	4	4	0	Kenmare	1,125	3	3	0
St. Pauls	2,036	18	13	5	Killdeer	704	2	2	0
Sugar Mountain	208	5	5	0	Lamoure	807	5	4	1
Sunset Beach	2,721	14	14	0	Lincoln	3,140	3	3	0
Surf City	2,132	19	17	2	Linton	1,031	1	1	0
Swansboro	2,071	9	9	0	Lisbon	2,185	3	3	0
Sylva	2,460	13	13	0	Mandan	19,134	36	27	9

Table 78. Full-Time Law Enforcement Employees by State and City, 2010—*Continued*

(Number)

State/city	Population	Total law enforcement employees	Total officers	Total civilians	State/city	Population	Total law enforcement employees	Total officers	Total civilians
Medora	99	2	2	0	Brooklyn	10,175	39	33	6
Minot	37,605	84	60	24	Brooklyn Heights	1,428	15	15	0
Napoleon	702	1	1	0	Brook Park	18,806	53	43	10
Northwood	944	2	2	0	Brookville	5,455	12	11	1
Oakes	1,797	2	2	0	Brunswick	35,166	52	39	13
Rolla	1,483	4	4	0	Brunswick Hills Township	7,587	8	8	0
Rugby	2,566	4	4	0	Bryan	8,157	26	19	7
Sherwood	216	2	2	0	Buckeye Lake	3,078	2	2	0
South Heart	314	1	1	0	Bucyrus	12,009	26	20	6
Stanley	1,329	2	2	0	Burton	1,489	2	2	0
Steele	632	1	1	0	Butler Township	8,038	16	15	1
Surrey	924	1	1	0	Cadiz	3,239	5	5	0
Thompson	985	1	1	0	Caldwell	2,339	2	2	0
Valley City	6,477	20	14	6	Cambridge	11,085	29	23	6
Wahpeton	7,592	16	14	2	Camden	2,143	3	3	0
Watford City	1,450	5	5	0	Campbell	8,277	13	13	0
West Fargo	26,409	45	35	10	Canal Fulton	5,037	10	9	1
Williston	13,569	32	24	8	Canfield	6,754	20	15	5
Wishek	866	2	2	0	Canton	77,938	189	157	32
OHIO					Carey	3,770	10	7	3
Aberdeen	1,489	5	4	1	Carlisle	6,195	9	8	1
Ada	6,104	11	8	3	Carrollton	3,205	7	7	0
Addyston	1,001	1	1	0	Centerville	22,745	53	42	11
Akron	205,760	492	447	45	Chagrin Falls	3,574	18	11	7
Alliance	22,467	55	42	13	Champion Township	9,059	9	8	1
Amberley Village	3,563	22	18	4	Chardon	5,452	16	10	6
Amelia	3,644	6	5	1	Chester Township	11,417	13	13	0
American Township	12,206	1	1	0	Cheviot	8,350	9	9	0
Amherst	11,705	26	20	6	Chillicothe	22,143	51	46	5
Ansonia	1,065	2	2	0	Cincinnati	332,365	1,214	1,090	124
Arcanum	1,938	3	3	0	Circleville	13,686	29	22	7
Archbold	4,430	8	8	0	Clayton	12,769	14	14	0
Arlington Heights	836	4	3	1	Clearcreek Township	13,005	14	14	0
Ashland	21,737	35	26	9	Cleveland	426,042	1,805	1,559	246
Ashtabula	19,512	36	32	4	Cleveland Heights	44,799	118	102	16
Ashville	3,294	10	10	0	Cleves	2,724	4	4	0
Athens	22,161	33	26	7	Clinton Township	4,075	9	9	0
Aurora	14,712	34	26	8	Clyde	6,060	15	11	4
Austintown	34,548	45	37	8	Coitsville Township	1,614	2	2	0
Avon Lake	24,989	34	29	5	Coldwater	4,374	8	8	0
Bainbridge Township	11,705	27	19	8	Columbiana	6,037	12	9	3
Baltimore	2,939	5	5	0	Commercial Point	838	1	1	0
Barberton	26,332	51	38	13	Conneaut	12,337	23	18	5
Barnesville	3,987	7	6	1	Copley Township	14,009	23	23	0
Batavia	1,761	3	3	0	Covington	2,623	6	5	1
Bath Township, Summit County	10,214	28	20	8	Crestline	4,842	13	9	4
Bay Village	14,298	28	24	4	Cridersville	1,700	3	3	0
Bazetta Township	5,905	6	6	0	Cuyahoga Falls	51,140	72	66	6
Beach City	1,094	2	2	0	Dalton	1,709	2	2	0
Beachwood	10,904	56	43	13	Danville	1,074	2	2	0
Beavercreek	42,247	63	46	17	Dayton	152,319	456	383	73
Beaver Township	6,017	15	11	4	Deer Park	5,745	15	11	4
Bedford	12,694	43	32	11	Defiance	15,912	30	27	3
Bedford Heights	10,328	58	31	27	Delaware	35,468	54	48	6
Bellaire	4,502	10	10	0	Delhi Township	31,310	31	29	2
Bellbrook	6,792	17	12	5	Delphos	6,720	17	13	4
Bellefontaine	12,735	30	23	7	Delta	2,880	7	7	0
Bellville	1,680	3	3	0	Dover	12,408	20	19	1
Belpre	6,437	14	9	5	Doylestown	2,905	7	6	1
Berea	17,858	38	31	7	Dresden	1,415	3	3	0
Berlin Heights	627	1	1	0	Dublin	40,073	84	61	23
Bethel	2,648	3	3	0	Eastlake	19,635	46	33	13
Bethesda	1,337	1	1	0	East Liverpool	11,826	24	19	5
Beverly	1,320	1	1	0	East Palestine	4,654	8	6	2
Blanchester	4,284	7	7	0	Eaton	7,899	21	15	6
Blendon Township	7,880	12	11	1	Edgerton	1,916	3	3	0
Blue Ash	12,764	43	37	6	Elida	1,887	2	2	0
Bluffton	3,882	6	6	0	Elmwood Place	2,472	2	2	0
Boardman	38,524	60	47	13	Elyria	54,701	99	82	17
Bowling Green	28,617	58	43	15	Englewood	12,647	25	20	5
Bratenahl	1,242	13	10	3	Enon	2,518	4	4	0
Brecksville	12,675	34	29	5	Euclid	46,357	137	94	43
Brewster	2,308	5	5	0	Evendale	3,007	21	19	2
Bridgeport	2,031	4	4	0	Fairborn	31,731	55	40	15
Brimfield Township	7,959	15	13	2	Fairfax	1,854	10	9	1
Brookfield Township	9,310	9	9	0	Fairfield	42,494	81	61	20

Table 78. Full-Time Law Enforcement Employees by State and City, 2010—*Continued*

(Number)

State/city	Population	Total law enforcement employees	Total officers	Total civilians	State/city	Population	Total law enforcement employees	Total officers	Total civilians
Fairfield Township	17,538	18	17	1	Lakewood	49,526	113	94	19
Fairlawn	6,961	33	23	10	Lancaster	37,330	83	66	17
Fairport Harbor	3,246	8	7	1	Lawrence Township	8,437	6	6	0
Fairview Park	15,405	27	26	1	Lebanon	21,099	38	29	9
Fayette	1,272	3	3	0	Leipsic	2,149	4	4	0
Findlay	36,324	80	62	18	Lexington	4,057	13	9	4
Forest	1,441	2	2	0	Liberty Township	11,649	22	16	6
Forest Park	18,476	45	39	6	Lima	37,182	98	79	19
Fort Recovery	1,331	2	2	0	Linndale	86	4	3	1
Fort Shawnee	3,663	5	5	0	Lisbon	2,967	10	6	4
Fostoria	12,741	24	19	5	Lithopolis	1,175	3	3	0
Franklin	13,260	31	24	7	Liverpool Township	4,108	4	4	0
Frazeysburg	1,295	1	1	0	Lockland	3,463	15	14	1
Fredericktown	2,500	4	4	0	Logan	7,418	20	15	5
Fremont	16,305	36	31	5	London	9,692	21	17	4
Gahanna	34,335	72	58	14	Lorain	70,242	114	90	24
Galion	10,553	21	17	4	Lordstown	3,502	13	9	4
Garfield Heights	27,109	71	57	14	Loudonville	3,055	11	7	4
Gates Mills	2,231	14	10	4	Luckey	989	1	1	0
Geneva	6,245	15	11	4	Lynchburg	1,369	1	1	0
Geneva-on-the-Lake	1,479	5	5	0	Lyndhurst	13,551	35	27	8
Genoa Township	15,960	28	25	3	Madeira	9,078	13	12	1
Germantown	4,990	12	11	1	Madison	3,159	5	5	0
German Township, Clark County	7,208	3	3	0	Madison Township, Franklin County	18,751	16	14	2
Gibsonburg	2,395	5	5	0	Madison Township, Lake County	17,187	18	15	3
Girard	9,896	17	16	1	Magnolia	921	2	2	0
Glendale	2,224	7	7	0	Maineville	1,066	2	2	0
Glenwillow	633	4	4	0	Manchester	2,092	2	2	0
Gnadenhutten	1,271	2	2	0	Maple Heights	23,180	58	41	17
Golf Manor	3,756	10	9	1	Marblehead	831	4	4	0
Goshen Township, Clermont County	16,559	13	12	1	Mariemont	3,169	9	8	1
Goshen Township, Mahoning County	3,407	7	7	0	Marietta	14,007	36	29	7
Grandview Heights	6,342	22	18	4	Marion	35,540	76	61	15
Granville	5,229	13	10	3	Marlboro Township	4,747	4	3	1
Greenfield	4,997	12	9	3	Martins Ferry	6,560	15	12	3
Greenhills	3,819	7	7	0	Marysville	18,580	36	30	6
Green Springs	1,192	2	2	0	Mason	30,805	50	43	7
Greenville	12,713	30	24	6	Maumee	13,651	59	44	15
Greenwich	1,499	3	3	0	Mayfield Heights	17,396	46	37	9
Grove City	35,339	76	59	17	Mayfield Village	3,059	24	16	8
Hamilton	62,805	140	118	22	McArthur	2,011	4	4	0
Hanging Rock	291	6	4	2	McComb	1,580	3	3	0
Harrisburg	314	1	1	0	McConnelsville	1,556	4	4	0
Harrison	9,697	24	22	2	Mechanicsburg	1,693	4	4	0
Haskins	642	2	2	0	Mentor	51,924	111	80	31
Heath	8,950	25	18	7	Mentor-on-the-Lake	8,392	15	10	5
Hebron	2,161	8	7	1	Miamisburg	19,679	40	36	4
Hicksville	3,358	8	7	1	Miami Township, Clermont County	40,101	42	39	3
Highland Heights	8,665	29	22	7	Miami Township, Montgomery County	24,822	44	37	7
Highland Hills	1,374	7	5	2	Middleburg Heights	14,705	41	34	7
Hilliard	29,204	65	48	17	Middlefield	2,515	12	9	3
Hinckley Township	8,211	11	10	1	Middleport	2,448	8	5	3
Holland	1,323	9	9	0	Middletown	51,464	115	79	36
Howland Township	16,106	21	20	1	Midvale	606	1	1	0
Hubbard Township	5,612	8	7	1	Milford	6,324	16	14	2
Huber Heights	36,736	66	50	16	Millersport	934	1	1	0
Hudson	23,023	35	28	7	Milton Township	2,814	4	4	0
Huron	7,251	15	11	4	Minerva	3,900	13	8	5
Independence	6,662	44	32	12	Minerva Park	1,212	5	5	0
Indian Hill	6,095	25	20	5	Mingo Junction	3,233	1	1	0
Ironton	11,252	20	16	4	Minster	2,767	7	6	1
Jackson Center	1,439	2	2	0	Monroe	15,513	36	29	7
Jackson Township, Mahoning County	2,246	5	5	0	Montgomery	10,606	24	21	3
Jackson Township, Montgomery County	3,826	5	5	0	Montpelier	3,928	9	8	1
Jamestown	1,804	4	4	0	Montville Township	6,669	12	12	0
Jefferson	3,389	6	5	1	Moraine	6,376	38	31	7
Johnstown	4,100	14	10	4	Moreland Hills	3,010	15	14	1
Junction City	845	1	1	0	Mount Gilead	3,558	7	7	0
Kalida	1,249	1	1	0	Mount Healthy	6,062	11	10	1
Kent	27,823	56	42	14	Mount Sterling	1,823	9	5	4
Kenton	7,970	13	13	0	Munroe Falls	5,119	9	8	1
Kettering	52,931	117	85	32	Napoleon	8,664	22	16	6
Kirtland	7,524	14	9	5	Navarre	1,883	5	5	0
Kirtland Hills	824	10	9	1	Nelsonville	5,717	14	14	0
Lagrange	2,035	6	6	0	New Albany	7,766	22	16	6
Lake Township	7,478	16	15	1	Newark	47,409	95	78	17

Table 78.   Full-Time Law Enforcement Employees by State and City, 2010—*Continued*

(Number)

State/city	Population	Total law enforcement employees	Total officers	Total civilians	State/city	Population	Total law enforcement employees	Total officers	Total civilians
New Boston	2,131	12	8	4	Richmond Heights	10,048	23	17	6
New Bremen	3,085	6	6	0	Richwood	2,195	6	6	0
Newburgh Heights	2,080	4	2	2	Rio Grande	849	1	1	0
New Concord	2,548	4	4	0	Rittman	6,257	12	8	4
New Franklin	14,976	18	13	5	Riverside	24,938	29	28	1
New Lebanon	4,059	8	8	0	Roaming Shores Village	1,186	2	2	0
New Lexington	4,539	12	8	4	Rockford	1,075	2	2	0
New London	2,586	4	4	0	Rossford	6,399	12	11	1
New Middletown	1,494	4	4	0	Ross Township	8,072	2	2	0
New Philadelphia	17,238	26	22	4	Russells Point	1,518	3	3	0
New Richmond	2,545	5	5	0	Russell Township	5,840	9	8	1
Newton Falls	4,558	10	7	3	Russia	614	1	1	0
Newtown	4,153	8	7	1	Sabina	2,764	5	5	0
New Washington	901	2	2	0	Salem	11,676	18	18	0
North Baltimore	3,354	5	5	0	Saline Township	1,316	5	5	0
North Canton	16,737	32	24	8	Sandusky	25,380	53	47	6
North College Hill	9,515	14	13	1	Seaman	1,054	2	2	0
Northfield	3,616	10	10	0	Sebring	4,451	9	6	3
North Kingsville	2,550	4	4	0	Seven Hills	11,457	20	18	2
North Olmsted	30,689	59	46	13	Seville	2,438	5	5	0
North Randall	813	10	6	4	Shadyside	3,490	5	5	0
North Ridgeville	29,437	47	39	8	Shaker Heights	25,852	90	66	24
North Royalton	29,210	59	38	21	Sharon Township	2,395	10	10	0
Northwood	5,542	21	17	4	Sharonville	13,337	47	37	10
Norton	11,451	20	19	1	Shawnee Hills	598	2	2	0
Norwalk	16,838	29	22	7	Shawnee Township	8,742	18	11	7
Norwood	20,240	60	52	8	Sheffield Lake	8,848	13	10	3
Oak Harbor	2,793	8	5	3	Shelby	9,195	19	15	4
Oak Hill	1,603	3	3	0	Sidney	19,809	50	39	11
Oakwood, Montgomery County	8,295	37	32	5	Silverton	5,134	13	10	3
Oakwood Village	3,698	12	10	2	Smith Township	4,774	5	5	0
Olmsted Falls	8,092	16	10	6	Smithville	1,294	4	4	0
Olmsted Township	9,997	19	16	3	Solon	21,837	74	48	26
Ontario	5,157	24	20	4	Somerset	1,558	2	2	0
Orange Village	3,222	15	14	1	South Bloomfield	1,682	3	3	0
Oregon	18,912	59	45	14	South Charleston	1,762	1	1	0
Orrville	8,367	18	13	5	South Euclid	20,750	51	40	11
Orwell	1,469	5	5	0	South Point	4,058	6	6	0
Ottawa	4,371	8	8	0	South Russell	4,059	10	10	0
Owensville	850	4	4	0	South Zanesville	2,030	2	2	0
Oxford	23,202	40	25	15	Spencer	841	1	1	0
Oxford Township	2,715	3	3	0	Spencerville	2,130	4	4	0
Painesville	19,084	43	39	4	Springboro	18,460	28	25	3
Parma	76,303	151	95	56	Springdale	10,436	42	35	7
Parma Heights	19,343	36	30	6	Springfield	61,540	149	131	18
Pataskala	12,950	16	15	1	Springfield Township, Hamilton County	39,931	56	50	6
Paulding	3,299	5	4	1	Springfield Township, Mahoning County	5,985	8	8	0
Payne	1,152	1	1	0	Springfield Township, Summit County	18,150	26	23	3
Pemberville	1,358	1	1	0	St. Bernard	4,623	18	17	1
Peninsula	699	3	3	0	St. Clairsville	5,007	12	8	4
Pepper Pike	5,667	21	16	5	Steubenville	18,522	47	40	7
Perkins Township	12,747	24	19	5	St. Henry	2,414	2	2	0
Perrysburg	17,658	43	32	11	St. Marys	8,111	19	14	5
Perrysville	813	1	1	0	Stow	33,938	49	39	10
Perry Township, Columbiana County	4,561	5	5	0	St. Paris	1,957	3	3	0
Perry Township, Franklin County	3,719	11	10	1	Strasburg	2,744	4	4	0
Perry Township, Montgomery County	3,812	4	4	0	Streetsboro	14,937	36	28	8
Perry Township, Stark County	27,930	30	24	6	Strongsville	42,134	106	77	29
Pickerington	18,460	36	26	10	Struthers	10,548	19	15	4
Pierce Township	11,189	17	17	0	Sugarcreek	2,190	5	5	0
Pioneer	1,357	4	4	0	Sugarcreek Township	6,821	17	16	1
Piqua	20,478	35	31	4	Sunbury	3,555	12	11	1
Plain City	3,630	8	8	0	Swanton	3,639	6	5	1
Poland Township	10,929	12	11	1	Sycamore	862	1	1	0
Poland Village	2,620	5	5	0	Sylvania	19,195	43	36	7
Pomeroy	1,940	11	6	5	Sylvania Township	25,964	61	45	16
Port Clinton	6,087	19	14	5	Tallmadge	17,397	25	22	3
Portsmouth	20,254	46	42	4	Terrace Park	2,224	6	6	0
Powell	14,121	19	17	2	Thornville	1,184	1	1	0
Powhatan Point	1,642	3	3	0	Tipp City	9,238	22	19	3
Ravenna	11,378	29	22	7	Toledo	315,647	677	566	111
Reading	10,469	24	20	4	Toronto	5,080	10	10	0
Reminderville	2,864	6	6	0	Trenton	11,162	18	14	4
Republic	567	1	1	0	Trotwood	25,685	38	34	4
Reynoldsburg	34,208	67	53	14	Troy	21,950	45	40	5
Richfield	3,611	23	16	7	Twinsburg	17,325	43	31	12

Table 78.   Full-Time Law Enforcement Employees by State and City, 2010—*Continued*

(Number)

State/city	Population	Total law enforcement employees	Total officers	Total civilians	State/city	Population	Total law enforcement employees	Total officers	Total civilians
Uhrichsville	5,437	8	8	0	Bixby	22,683	32	25	7
Union City	1,622	4	4	0	Blackwell	7,238	22	16	6
Uniontown	2,847	9	7	2	Blanchard	7,061	19	13	6
Union Township, Clermont County	44,619	71	57	14	Boise City	1,207	3	3	0
Union Township, Licking County	3,903	2	2	0	Boley	1,097	1	1	0
University Heights	12,396	36	30	6	Bristow	4,425	12	8	4
Upper Arlington	32,111	63	50	13	Broken Arrow	97,581	163	120	43
Upper Sandusky	6,327	17	13	4	Broken Bow	4,135	18	13	5
Urbana	11,334	19	19	0	Caddo	1,009	3	3	0
Utica	2,103	9	4	5	Calera	1,940	11	8	3
Vandalia	14,015	39	31	8	Calumet	553	2	2	0
Van Wert	10,022	27	19	8	Caney	212	4	3	1
Vermilion	10,708	23	18	5	Carnegie	1,619	8	4	4
Vienna Township	3,808	1	1	0	Catoosa	8,193	13	12	1
Wadsworth	21,212	36	28	8	Chandler	2,874	12	8	4
Waite Hill	575	6	6	0	Checotah	3,496	15	10	5
Wakeman	929	1	1	0	Chelsea	2,261	5	1	4
Walbridge	3,110	6	5	1	Cherokee	1,376	7	3	4
Walton Hills	2,244	20	13	7	Chickasha	17,507	37	28	9
Wapakoneta	9,433	19	14	5	Choctaw	11,942	12	11	1
Warren	42,850	79	63	16	Chouteau	2,208	9	8	1
Warrensville Heights	13,341	44	33	11	Claremore	17,741	54	38	16
Warren Township	5,940	7	7	0	Clayton	744	6	2	4
Washington Court House	13,468	27	22	5	Cleveland	3,270	7	7	0
Waterville Township	5,812	2	2	0	Clinton	8,948	27	17	10
Wauseon	7,209	18	14	4	Coalgate	1,926	6	6	0
Waverly	4,459	13	9	4	Colbert	1,151	5	4	1
Waynesville	3,141	4	3	1	Colcord	887	2	2	0
Weathersfield	8,071	9	8	1	Collinsville	5,380	16	10	6
Wellington	4,740	8	6	2	Comanche	1,528	3	3	0
Wellston	5,923	11	8	3	Cordell	2,983	11	6	5
Wells Township	2,764	4	4	0	Coweta	9,248	22	15	7
Wellsville	3,845	9	9	0	Crescent	1,463	5	4	1
West Alexandria	1,275	3	3	0	Cushing	9,838	22	16	6
West Carrollton	12,556	30	24	6	Davenport	875	1	1	0
West Chester Township	56,305	115	88	27	Davis	2,699	10	9	1
Westerville	36,966	88	74	14	Del City	22,549	42	30	12
West Jefferson	4,255	14	11	3	Dewar	910	2	2	0
Westlake	30,122	71	53	18	Dewey	3,367	12	10	2
West Liberty	1,719	2	2	0	Dibble	674	4	3	1
West Unity	1,714	4	4	0	Drumright	2,908	6	6	0
Whitehall	18,332	59	46	13	Duncan	22,814	53	46	7
Wickliffe	13,050	40	30	10	Durant	17,357	38	35	3
Willard	6,553	18	14	4	Edmond	83,337	139	112	27
Williamsburg	2,390	5	5	0	Elk City	11,748	30	21	9
Willoughby	22,909	59	44	15	El Reno	17,262	36	25	11
Willowick	13,802	33	24	9	Enid	48,581	116	95	21
Wilmington	12,578	25	23	2	Eufaula	2,808	16	12	4
Winchester	1,069	3	3	0	Fairfax	1,429	6	4	2
Windham	2,718	7	4	3	Fairview	2,561	8	5	3
Wintersville	3,809	9	8	1	Fletcher	1,100	1	1	0
Woodlawn	2,636	15	15	0	Forest Park	1,193	4	4	0
Woodsfield	2,362	6	6	0	Fort Gibson	4,440	13	9	4
Woodville	1,965	5	5	0	Frederick	3,778	13	11	2
Wooster	26,244	39	36	3	Geary	1,243	10	5	5
Worthington	13,401	46	33	13	Glenpool	10,685	23	18	5
Wyoming	8,331	21	19	2	Goodwell	1,251	4	4	0
Xenia	27,702	62	40	22	Grove	6,575	28	20	8
Yellow Springs	3,223	10	7	3	Guthrie	11,797	28	20	8
Zanesville	24,776	88	52	36	Guymon	11,294	24	16	8
OKLAHOMA					Haileyville	911	4	3	1
Achille	549	6	3	3	Harrah	5,402	8	8	0
Ada	17,298	42	35	7	Hartshorne	2,088	5	5	0
Allen	1,015	4	3	1	Haskell	2,014	6	6	0
Altus	18,983	60	44	16	Healdton	2,816	5	3	2
Alva	4,822	11	9	2	Heavener	3,254	11	7	4
Anadarko	6,422	22	14	8	Henryetta	6,053	17	12	5
Antlers	2,547	10	5	5	Hinton	3,746	5	5	0
Apache	1,540	8	4	4	Hobart	3,512	14	8	6
Ardmore	25,238	74	51	23	Holdenville	5,638	14	9	5
Arkoma	2,194	6	3	3	Hollis	1,949	11	6	5
Atoka	3,092	16	15	1	Hominy	3,588	9	5	4
Bartlesville	36,586	72	52	20	Hooker	1,815	3	3	0
Beaver	1,366	4	3	1	Howe	728	4	2	2
Beggs	1,374	8	4	4	Hugo	5,434	24	17	7
Bethany	19,923	41	30	11	Hulbert	544	2	2	0

Table 78. Full-Time Law Enforcement Employees by State and City, 2010—*Continued*

(Number)

State/city	Population	Total law enforcement employees	Total officers	Total civilians	State/city	Population	Total law enforcement employees	Total officers	Total civilians
Hydro	1,014	2	2	0	Sparks	137	1	1	0
Idabel	6,829	26	20	6	Spencer	4,150	9	8	1
Jay	3,051	11	7	4	Spiro	2,362	4	4	0
Jenks	17,170	23	17	6	Stigler	2,979	16	9	7
Jones	2,805	5	5	0	Stillwater	47,414	109	74	35
Kaw City	375	1	1	0	Stilwell	3,530	18	13	5
Kiefer	1,713	4	4	0	Stonewall	506	2	2	0
Kingfisher	4,418	11	10	1	Stratford	1,497	3	3	0
Kingston	1,652	7	7	0	Stringtown	421	5	4	1
Krebs	2,164	8	6	2	Stroud	2,722	11	8	3
Lawton	92,025	193	164	29	Sulphur	4,964	13	11	2
Lexington	2,185	11	6	5	Tahlequah	17,067	37	30	7
Lindsay	2,916	11	7	4	Talihina	1,245	10	6	4
Locust Grove	1,615	10	5	5	Tecumseh	6,857	12	11	1
Lone Grove	5,496	10	7	3	The Village	9,923	27	21	6
Luther	1,201	7	6	1	Tishomingo	3,266	8	7	1
Madill	3,855	11	10	1	Tonkawa	3,194	12	6	6
Mangum	2,709	7	4	3	Tryon	452	1	1	0
Mannford	2,938	9	7	2	Tulsa	393,412	822	736	86
Marietta	2,540	6	5	1	Tushka	380	3	3	0
Marlow	4,639	14	10	4	Tuttle	6,450	16	10	6
Maysville	1,306	3	2	1	Valliant	743	6	3	3
McAlester	18,675	60	45	15	Verdigris	3,245	3	3	0
McCurtain	491	2	2	0	Vian	1,562	3	3	0
McLoud	4,784	13	8	5	Vinita	6,115	19	14	5
Medicine Park	396	2	2	0	Wagoner	8,270	19	13	6
Meeker	983	4	4	0	Walters	2,468	4	4	0
Miami	12,967	44	31	13	Warner	1,560	4	4	0
Midwest City	58,095	119	93	26	Warr Acres	9,579	28	22	6
Minco	1,850	4	4	0	Washington	570	3	3	0
Moore	55,788	85	80	5	Watonga	5,833	9	7	2
Mooreland	1,270	2	2	0	Waukomis	1,237	3	3	0
Morris	1,325	2	2	0	Waurika	1,950	2	2	0
Mountain View	758	2	2	0	Waynoka	906	4	4	0
Muldrow	3,201	11	7	4	Weatherford	10,551	30	19	11
Muskogee	40,499	112	86	26	Weleetka	903	8	4	4
Mustang	19,200	28	21	7	Westville	1,658	11	6	5
Newcastle	7,845	22	16	6	Wetumka	1,416	5	5	0
Newkirk	2,158	7	6	1	Wewoka	3,320	10	7	3
Nichols Hills	4,147	21	16	5	Wilburton	2,928	7	6	1
Nicoma Park	2,464	6	6	0	Wilson	1,669	4	4	0
Noble	6,046	16	11	5	Woodward	12,535	39	25	14
Norman	111,534	213	160	53	Wright City	788	3	3	0
Nowata	3,956	7	5	2	Wynnewood	2,286	4	3	1
Oilton	1,141	2	2	0	Yale	1,504	8	4	4
Okemah	2,833	11	7	4	Yukon	24,023	56	35	21
Oklahoma City	571,865	1,254	1,015	239	**OREGON**				
Okmulgee	12,648	33	26	7	Adair Village	800	8	6	2
Oologah	1,180	3	3	0	Albany	48,777	95	63	32
Owasso	30,431	62	46	16	Amity	1,431	2	2	0
Pauls Valley	6,112	20	13	7	Ashland	20,942	35	28	7
Pawhuska	3,350	11	7	4	Astoria	9,639	27	16	11
Pawnee	2,160	6	5	1	Athena	1,172	2	2	0
Perkins	2,680	7	7	0	Aumsville	3,727	7	6	1
Perry	4,972	22	13	9	Aurora	1,056	9	8	1
Piedmont	6,079	13	10	3	Baker City	9,309	16	15	1
Pocola	4,581	8	5	3	Bandon	3,222	7	6	1
Ponca City	24,928	83	54	29	Beaverton	93,993	167	134	33
Porum	748	2	2	0	Bend	79,556	112	88	24
Poteau	8,408	32	25	7	Black Butte		7	6	1
Prague	2,153	12	7	5	Brookings	6,003	20	13	7
Pryor	9,400	33	25	8	Burns	2,596	5	4	1
Purcell	6,359	21	18	3	Canby	15,935	30	25	5
Ringling	1,065	1	1	0	Cannon Beach	1,714	9	8	1
Roland	3,605	8	5	3	Carlton	1,720	3	3	0
Rush Springs	1,381	3	3	0	Central Point	16,819	28	22	6
Sallisaw	8,985	32	24	8	Clatskanie	1,615	6	5	1
Sand Springs	19,204	40	30	10	Columbia City	1,991	1	1	0
Sapulpa	21,567	58	47	11	Condon	610	2	1	1
Sawyer	269	2	2	0	Coos Bay	15,227	37	24	13
Sayre	4,137	13	8	5	Coquille	3,926	8	7	1
Seminole	6,895	16	12	4	Cornelius	11,703	15	14	1
Shawnee	31,002	74	53	21	Corvallis	51,276	80	53	27
Skiatook	7,118	26	19	7	Cottage Grove	9,173	23	16	7
Snyder	1,329	2	2	0	Dallas	16,416	31	20	11
South Coffeyville	777	4	4	0	Eagle Point	8,673	15	13	2

Table 78.   Full-Time Law Enforcement Employees by State and City, 2010—*Continued*

(Number)

State/city	Popula-tion	Total law enforce-ment employees	Total officers	Total civilians	State/city	Popula-tion	Total law enforce-ment employees	Total officers	Total civilians
Elgin	1,641	4	3	1	Talent	6,242	8	7	1
Enterprise	1,728	4	4	0	The Dalles	12,186	23	21	2
Eugene	153,269	308	185	123	Tigard	49,466	89	72	17
Fairview	10,070	15	14	1	Tillamook	4,333	11	8	3
Florence	8,824	23	14	9	Toledo	3,239	16	10	6
Forest Grove	21,600	32	28	4	Troutdale	15,692	29	25	4
Gearhart	1,196	3	3	0	Tualatin	26,897	47	39	8
Gervais	2,488	5	4	1	Turner	1,782	3	3	0
Gladstone	12,162	19	16	3	Umatilla	6,387	10	8	2
Gold Beach	1,878	7	6	1	Veneta	4,565	4	3	1
Grants Pass	32,871	74	46	28	Vernonia	2,294	3	3	0
Gresham	102,540	162	128	34	Warrenton	4,481	9	8	1
Hermiston	15,399	33	23	10	West Linn	25,614	36	31	5
Hillsboro	97,423	181	130	51	Weston	686	2	2	0
Hines	1,341	3	3	0	Winston	5,463	8	7	1
Hood River	6,971	14	12	2	Woodburn	23,032	40	32	8
Hubbard	2,861	5	4	1	Yamhill	923	3	3	0
Independence	9,835	16	14	2	**PENNSYLVANIA**				
Jacksonville	2,182	6	5	1	Abington Township	54,235	116	89	27
John Day	1,440	9	4	5	Adams Township, Butler County	10,107	6	6	0
Junction City	5,754	16	10	6	Adams Township, Cambria County	6,024	3	3	0
Keizer	36,191	48	40	8	Akron	4,053	6	5	1
King City	2,993	6	5	1	Albion	1,509	2	2	0
Klamath Falls	19,922	45	39	6	Alburtis	2,449	4	4	0
La Grande	12,600	33	18	15	Aldan	4,284	6	6	0
Lake Oswego	37,349	69	42	27	Aleppo Township	1,220	14	11	3
Lakeview	2,319	6	5	1	Aliquippa	10,497	17	17	0
Lebanon	16,084	38	26	12	Allegheny Township, Blair County	6,967	7	6	1
Lincoln City	8,144	35	24	11	Allegheny Township, Westmoreland County	8,288	9	8	1
Madras	5,815	11	10	1	Allentown	108,473	220	197	23
Malin	608	2	1	1	Altoona	46,213	82	74	8
Manzanita	851	3	3	0	Ambler	6,228	16	14	2
McMinnville	31,748	43	33	10	Ambridge	6,948	13	13	0
Medford	73,525	155	103	52	Amity Township	12,299	14	13	1
Merrill	857	2	1	1	Annville Township	4,808	8	5	3
Milton-Freewater	6,242	17	11	6	Apollo	1,598	1	1	0
Milwaukie	20,674	40	36	4	Archbald	6,584	5	5	0
Molalla	7,727	15	12	3	Arnold	5,178	11	10	1
Monmouth	9,851	14	12	2	Ashland	3,088	3	3	0
Mount Angel	3,374	8	5	3	Ashley	2,670	3	3	0
Myrtle Creek	3,401	9	7	2	Aspinwall	2,692	6	6	0
Myrtle Point	2,390	5	5	0	Aston Township	17,100	18	16	2
Newberg-Dundee	26,738	35	22	13	Athens	3,175	5	4	1
Newport	9,877	23	19	4	Athens Township	5,042	10	9	1
North Bend	9,441	23	16	7	Auburn	799	1	1	0
North Plains	1,933	2	2	0	Austin	559	1	1	0
Nyssa	2,920	8	8	0	Avalon	4,751	6	6	0
Oakridge	3,195	12	6	6	Avoca	2,659	2	2	0
Ontario	10,822	32	24	8	Avonmore Boro	761	2	2	0
Oregon City	32,045	47	40	7	Baden	3,965	5	5	0
Pendleton	16,263	24	21	3	Baldwin Borough	18,450	25	23	2
Philomath	4,542	10	9	1	Baldwin Township	1,992	5	5	0
Phoenix	4,387	11	9	2	Bally	1,108	2	2	0
Pilot Rock	1,487	3	3	0	Bangor	5,343	10	9	1
Portland	564,392	1,186	957	229	Barrett Township	4,327	6	6	0
Port Orford	1,073	2	2	0	Beaver	4,321	11	10	1
Prineville	9,951	25	15	10	Beaver Falls	8,926	19	18	1
Rainier	1,798	6	5	1	Beaver Meadows	951	1	1	0
Redmond	25,480	52	37	15	Bedford	2,967	5	5	0
Reedsport	4,093	15	10	5	Bedminster Township	6,480	7	6	1
Rockaway Beach	1,351	3	3	0	Bell Acres	1,357	3	3	0
Rogue River	1,918	5	4	1	Bellefonte	6,179	12	10	2
Roseburg	20,169	42	37	5	Bellevue	7,969	17	14	3
Salem	155,820	349	206	143	Bellwood	1,871	2	2	0
Sandy	9,426	16	12	4	Ben Avon	1,764	14	11	3
Scappoose	6,480	11	10	1	Ben Avon Heights	358	14	11	3
Seaside	6,157	28	19	9	Bensalem Township	59,028	132	101	31
Sherwood	18,483	27	24	3	Berks-Lehigh Regional	31,334	31	30	1
Silverton	9,900	19	18	1	Berlin	2,046	1	1	0
Springfield	57,081	120	68	52	Bern Township	7,311	14	13	1
Stanfield	1,924	4	4	0	Berwick	10,169	16	15	1
Stayton	7,369	19	16	3	Bethel Park	31,514	44	38	6
St. Helens	12,708	21	19	2	Bethel Township, Berks County	4,572	2	2	0
Sunriver		12	11	1	Bethlehem	73,634	186	159	27
Sutherlin	7,064	17	15	2	Bethlehem Township	24,220	35	33	2
Sweet Home	8,950	23	16	7	Biglerville	1,168	2	2	0

Table 78.   Full-Time Law Enforcement Employees by State and City, 2010—*Continued*

(Number)

State/city	Population	Total law enforcement employees	Total officers	Total civilians	State/city	Population	Total law enforcement employees	Total officers	Total civilians
Birdsboro	5,237	8	7	1	Coaldale	2,104	4	4	0
Birmingham Township	4,366	4	4	0	Coal Township	10,195	13	12	1
Blairsville	3,333	3	1	2	Cochranton	1,059	2	2	0
Blair Township	4,781	5	5	0	Colebrookdale District	6,483	10	9	1
Blakely	6,716	5	5	0	Collegeville	5,117	9	8	1
Blawnox	1,435	4	4	0	Collier Township	6,588	15	14	1
Bloomsburg Town	12,873	21	15	6	Collingdale	8,436	9	8	1
Boyertown	3,960	8	7	1	Colonial Regional	20,560	26	24	2
Brackenridge	3,234	4	4	0	Columbia	10,116	20	17	3
Braddock	2,662	1	1	0	Colwyn	2,416	1	1	0
Braddock Hills	1,816	2	2	0	Conemaugh Township, Cambria County	2,441	2	2	0
Bradford	8,271	22	22	0	Conemaugh Township, Somerset County	7,171	7	6	1
Bradford Township	4,927	5	5	0	Conewago Township, Adams County	6,215	9	8	1
Branch Township	1,812	1	1	0	Conewango Township	3,542	4	4	0
Brecknock Township, Berks County	5,008	5	5	0	Conneaut Lake Regional	3,501	4	3	1
Brentwood	9,470	16	14	2	Connellsville	8,313	17	16	1
Briar Creek Township	3,128	8	8	0	Conshohocken	8,593	21	19	2
Bridgeport	4,425	10	9	1	Conway	2,112	3	3	0
Bridgeville	4,869	9	8	1	Conyngham	1,840	1	1	0
Bridgewater	871	3	3	0	Coopersburg	2,586	7	7	0
Brighton Township	7,956	6	6	0	Coplay	3,401	4	4	0
Bristol	9,699	17	15	2	Coraopolis	5,575	13	10	3
Bristol Township	54,171	88	75	13	Cornwall	3,562	8	7	1
Brockway	2,022	2	2	0	Corry	6,315	13	11	2
Brookhaven	8,024	9	8	1	Coudersport	2,357	4	4	0
Brookville	3,932	7	6	1	Covington Township	2,215	3	3	0
Brownsville	2,586	2	2	0	Crafton	6,508	9	8	1
Bryn Athyn	1,346	5	5	0	Cranberry Township	28,107	33	28	5
Buckingham Township	20,119	24	22	2	Crescent Township	2,778	4	4	0
Buffalo Township	7,411	5	5	0	Cresson	1,463	10	10	0
Bushkill Township	8,546	11	10	1	Cresson Township	4,533	3	2	1
Butler	13,916	24	23	1	Croyle Township	2,220	1	1	0
Butler Township, Butler County	16,659	23	21	2	Cumberland Township, Adams County	6,469	6	6	0
Butler Township, Luzerne County	9,568	9	8	1	Cumberland Township, Greene County	6,351	4	4	0
Butler Township, Schuykill County	6,105	4	4	0	Cumru Township	15,163	27	25	2
Caernarvon Township, Berks County	3,650	9	8	1	Curwensville	2,431	1	1	0
California	6,411	8	7	1	Dale	1,342	2	2	0
Caln Township	12,496	21	19	2	Dallas	2,477	4	4	0
Cambria Township	6,168	3	3	0	Dallas Township	9,187	8	8	0
Cambridge Springs	2,651	3	3	0	Dalton	1,231	2	2	0
Camp Hill	7,454	11	10	1	Danville	4,410	10	9	1
Canonsburg	8,776	17	17	0	Darby	9,980	13	12	1
Canton	1,681	3	3	0	Darby Township	9,624	14	14	0
Carbondale	9,155	12	12	0	Decatur Township	5,884	1	1	0
Carlisle	18,708	37	32	5	Delmont	2,449	4	4	0
Carnegie	7,929	13	12	1	Derry	2,763	3	3	0
Carrolltown	955	2	2	0	Derry Township, Dauphin County	22,348	47	39	8
Carroll Township, Washington County	5,481	2	2	0	Dickson City	5,876	7	7	0
Carroll Township, York County	6,070	10	10	0	Donegal Township	2,923	1	1	0
Carroll Valley	3,604	4	3	1	Donora	5,242	6	6	0
Castle Shannon	8,069	13	12	1	Dormont	8,411	16	15	1
Catasauqua	6,628	9	8	1	Douglass Township, Berks County	3,603	3	3	0
Catawissa	1,532	2	2	0	Downingtown	8,093	19	16	3
Cecil Township	10,821	18	17	1	Doylestown	8,169	21	16	5
Center Township	11,649	26	26	0	Doylestown Township	18,844	23	21	2
Centerville	3,216	3	3	0	Dublin Borough	2,162	2	2	0
Central Berks Regional	9,487	15	14	1	Du Bois	7,558	14	14	0
Chalfont	4,221	7	6	1	Duboistown	1,187	1	1	0
Chambersburg	18,711	3	3	0	Duncannon	1,498	2	2	0
Charleroi	5,692	8	6	2	Duncansville	1,235	2	2	0
Chartiers Township	7,507	11	11	0	Dunmore	13,943	19	19	0
Cheltenham Township	36,084	95	83	12	Dupont	2,580	1	1	0
Chester	37,308	113	102	11	Duquesne	6,678	14	13	1
Chester Township	4,495	12	11	1	Duryea	4,332	2	2	0
Cheswick	1,691	2	2	0	East Bangor	1,222	1	1	0
Chippewa Township	9,777	9	8	1	East Berlin	1,452	1	1	0
Churchill	3,216	10	10	0	East Bethlehem Township	2,351	1	1	0
Clairton	7,768	7	7	0	East Brandywine Township	7,133	11	10	1
Clarion	5,177	9	8	1	East Buffalo Township	5,945	8	8	0
Clarks Summit	6,485	6	5	1	East Cocalico Township	10,642	25	23	2
Clay Township	6,114	5	4	1	East Coventry Township	7,177	8	7	1
Clearfield	6,088	8	7	1	East Deer Township	1,321	2	2	0
Cleona	2,150	4	4	0	East Earl Township	6,720	7	7	0
Clifford Township	2,449	1	1	0	Eastern Adams Regional	10,116	11	10	1
Clifton Heights	6,594	10	9	1	Eastern Pike Regional	5,602	10	9	1
Clymer	1,413	1	1	0	East Fallowfield Township	8,075	7	7	0

Table 78. Full-Time Law Enforcement Employees by State and City, 2010—*Continued*

(Number)

State/city	Population	Total law enforcement employees	Total officers	Total civilians	State/city	Population	Total law enforcement employees	Total officers	Total civilians
East Franklin Township	3,910	3	2	1	Gilpin Township	2,480	1	1	0
East Hempfield Township	24,035	37	33	4	Girard	2,932	4	4	0
East Lampeter Township	15,465	43	39	4	Glassport	4,511	6	6	0
East Lansdowne	2,498	5	3	2	Glenolden	7,264	11	10	1
East Marlborough Township	8,316	1	1	0	Granville Township	4,933	9	7	2
East McKeesport	2,918	3	3	0	Greencastle	4,135	6	5	1
East Norriton Township	13,787	29	26	3	Greenfield Township, Blair County	3,775	4	4	0
East Pennsboro Township	20,147	20	19	1	Greensburg	15,271	38	28	10
East Penn Township	2,786	2	2	0	Green Tree	4,407	12	11	1
East Pikeland Township	7,113	8	7	1	Greenville	6,057	10	9	1
East Pittsburgh	1,937	1	1	0	Greenwood Township	2,083	1	1	0
East Taylor Township	2,514	1	1	0	Grove City	7,670	11	10	1
Easttown Township	10,706	15	14	1	Hamburg	4,260	5	4	1
East Union Township	1,431	1	1	0	Hamiltonban Township	2,834	1	1	0
East Vincent Township	6,688	7	7	0	Hampden Township	27,801	24	23	1
East Washington	1,859	1	1	0	Hampton Township	17,361	19	18	1
East Whiteland Township	10,899	22	20	2	Hanover	15,234	27	25	2
Ebensburg	2,898	3	3	0	Hanover Township, Luzerne County	11,014	15	14	1
Economy	9,150	12	11	1	Hanover Township, Washington County	2,747	9	3	6
Eddystone	2,360	10	9	1	Harmar Township	3,088	7	7	0
Edgewood	3,116	12	10	2	Harmony Township	3,016	5	5	0
Edgeworth	1,586	6	4	2	Harrisburg	47,509	230	179	51
Edinboro	6,567	8	8	0	Harrison Township	9,962	21	18	3
Edwardsville	4,651	1	1	0	Harveys Lake	2,952	6	6	0
Elizabeth	1,435	2	2	0	Hastings	1,285	1	1	0
Elizabethtown	12,186	18	16	2	Hatboro	7,166	17	14	3
Elizabeth Township	12,902	11	10	1	Hatfield Township	20,276	32	27	5
Elkland	1,660	2	2	0	Haverford Township	48,500	81	69	12
Ellwood City	7,887	12	10	2	Hazleton	21,705	41	38	3
Emlenton Borough	726	1	1	0	Hegins Township	3,368	2	2	0
Emmaus	11,485	19	17	2	Heidelberg	1,141	3	3	0
Emporium	2,140	2	2	0	Heidelberg Township, Berks County	1,787	1	1	0
Emsworth	2,381	14	11	3	Heidelberg Township, Lebanon County	4,274	1	1	0
Ephrata	13,247	34	29	5	Hellam Township	9,222	10	8	2
Erie	104,077	199	173	26	Hellertown	5,781	11	10	1
Etna	3,612	8	7	1	Hemlock Township	2,285	6	6	0
Evans City	1,887	2	2	0	Hempfield Township, Mercer County	3,835	6	5	1
Everett	1,838	3	3	0	Highspire	2,630	6	6	0
Exeter	5,965	4	3	1	Hilltown Township	13,752	20	17	3
Exeter Township, Berks County	25,876	33	30	3	Hollidaysburg	5,519	11	8	3
Exeter Township, Luzerne County	2,546	7	7	0	Homer City	1,690	2	2	0
Fairchance	2,025	1	1	0	Homestead	3,638	13	12	1
Fairview Township, Luzerne County	4,328	5	5	0	Honesdale	4,740	9	9	0
Fairview Township, York County	17,419	18	16	2	Honey Brook	1,636	1	1	0
Fallowfield Township	4,200	2	2	0	Hooversville	695	1	1	0
Falls Township, Bucks County	33,850	60	53	7	Hopewell Township	12,292	16	15	1
Fawn Township	2,337	2	2	0	Horsham Township	24,983	49	40	9
Ferguson Township	16,966	23	20	3	Hughestown	1,442	1	1	0
Ferndale	1,630	1	1	0	Hughesville	2,034	1	1	0
Findlay Township	5,090	23	16	7	Hummelstown	4,476	7	7	0
Fleetwood	4,038	6	6	0	Huntingdon	6,790	12	12	0
Folcroft	6,901	10	10	0	Independence Township, Beaver County	2,690	3	3	0
Ford City	3,108	3	3	0	Indiana	15,062	24	22	2
Forest City	1,702	2	2	0	Indiana Township	7,036	10	10	0
Forest Hills	6,459	11	10	1	Industry	1,770	12	12	0
Forks Township	15,331	24	23	1	Ingram	3,375	4	4	0
Forty Fort	4,231	2	2	0	Irwin	4,031	3	3	0
Forward Township	3,495	4	4	0	Ivyland	852	2	2	0
Foster Township	4,187	4	4	0	Jackson Township, Butler County	3,782	10	8	2
Fountain Hill	4,622	11	10	1	Jackson Township, Cambria County	4,691	1	1	0
Fox Chapel	5,430	12	12	0	Jackson Township, Luzerne County	4,742	4	4	0
Frackville	4,106	4	4	0	Jeannette	9,824	17	14	3
Franconia Township	13,128	17	15	2	Jefferson Hills Borough	9,862	18	16	2
Franklin	6,590	23	17	6	Jefferson Township, Mercer County	2,315	1	1	0
Franklin Park	12,529	13	12	1	Jenkins Township	4,949	2	2	0
Franklin Township, Carbon County	4,914	4	4	0	Jenkintown	4,334	13	11	2
Frazer Township	1,195	3	3	0	Jermyn	2,227	1	1	0
Freedom Township	3,334	2	2	0	Jim Thorpe	4,915	7	6	1
Freeland	3,385	2	2	0	Johnsonburg	2,625	3	3	0
Freemansburg	2,091	4	3	1	Johnstown	22,900	42	38	4
Freeport	1,771	2	2	0	Kane	3,705	6	5	1
Galeton	1,200	2	2	0	Kennedy Township	9,723	15	11	4
Gallitzin	1,855	5	5	0	Kennett Square	5,339	12	9	3
Geistown	2,322	1	1	0	Kennett Township	8,124	1	1	0
Gettysburg	8,172	17	13	4	Kidder Township	1,490	10	10	0
Gilberton	822	1	1	0	Kilbuck Township	626	14	11	3

Table 78. Full-Time Law Enforcement Employees by State and City, 2010—*Continued*

(Number)

State/city	Population	Total law enforcement employees	Total officers	Total civilians	State/city	Population	Total law enforcement employees	Total officers	Total civilians
Kingston	12,912	24	19	5	Martinsburg	2,139	2	2	0
Kingston Township	7,086	11	11	0	Marysville	2,456	1	1	0
Kiskiminetas Township	4,731	1	1	0	Masontown	3,334	5	5	0
Kittanning	4,261	9	8	1	Mayfield	1,697	1	1	0
Knox	1,072	3	3	0	McAdoo	2,074	3	3	0
Koppel	764	1	1	0	McCandless	27,188	29	27	2
Kulpmont	2,752	1	1	0	McDonald Borough	2,115	3	3	0
Kutztown	5,159	12	10	2	McKeesport	22,009	55	52	3
Laflin Borough	1,493	3	3	0	McKees Rocks	6,038	12	11	1
Lake City	2,916	3	3	0	McSherrystown	2,839	4	4	0
Lancaster	55,582	168	145	23	Meadville	13,229	25	22	3
Lancaster Township, Butler County	2,632	1	1	0	Mechanicsburg	8,744	17	16	1
Lansdale	15,622	27	20	7	Media	5,448	24	16	8
Lansdowne	10,737	19	16	3	Mercer	2,184	4	4	0
Lansford	4,152	10	9	1	Mercersburg	1,593	2	2	0
Larksville	4,437	4	4	0	Meyersdale	2,242	2	2	0
Latimore Township	2,915	1	1	0	Middleburg	1,333	3	2	1
Latrobe	8,307	14	13	1	Middlesex Township, Butler County	5,518	3	3	0
Laureldale	3,772	5	5	0	Middletown	8,781	21	16	5
Lawrence Park Township	3,690	8	7	1	Middletown Township	47,432	57	52	5
Lawrence Township, Clearfield County	7,424	10	9	1	Midland	2,809	4	4	0
Lebanon	24,357	48	42	6	Mifflin	600	1	1	0
Leechburg	2,163	3	3	0	Mifflinburg	3,514	10	9	1
Leetsdale	1,111	5	5	0	Mifflin County Regional	30,294	23	22	1
Leet Township	1,479	5	5	0	Mifflin Township	2,272	4	4	0
Lehighton	5,450	10	9	1	Milford	2,930	2	2	0
Lehigh Township, Northampton County	11,215	13	12	1	Millbourne	914	1	1	0
Lehman Township	3,377	2	2	0	Millcreek Township, Erie County	52,537	70	58	12
Lewisburg	5,515	10	8	2	Millcreek Township, Lebanon County	3,274	3	3	0
Liberty	2,413	1	1	0	Millersburg	2,479	5	4	1
Liberty Township, Adams County	1,331	1	1	0	Millersville	7,350	14	12	2
Ligonier	1,598	3	3	0	Millvale	3,643	5	5	0
Ligonier Township	6,763	4	4	0	Millville	941	1	1	0
Limerick Township	17,476	17	16	1	Milton	6,360	9	8	1
Lincoln	1,075	1	1	0	Minersville	4,187	6	6	0
Lititz	9,107	17	13	4	Mohnton	3,110	4	4	0
Littlestown	4,190	8	7	1	Monaca	5,675	9	9	0
Locust Township	2,563	3	3	0	Monessen	7,977	12	12	0
Logan Township	12,341	18	16	2	Monongahela	4,409	9	7	2
Lower Allen Township	18,025	21	20	1	Monroeville	27,622	56	46	10
Lower Burrell	12,078	16	16	0	Montgomery	5,379	3	3	0
Lower Chichester Township	3,467	4	4	0	Montgomery Township	24,720	43	33	10
Lower Frederick Township	4,859	3	3	0	Montrose	1,509	1	1	0
Lower Gwynedd Township	11,627	19	18	1	Moon Township	23,197	36	30	6
Lower Heidelberg Township	5,620	10	9	1	Moore Township	9,775	8	7	1
Lower Makefield Township	32,410	42	38	4	Moosic	5,811	10	10	0
Lower Merion Township	57,561	155	136	19	Morris-Cooper Regional	5,623	1	1	0
Lower Milford Township	3,973	2	2	0	Morrisville	9,639	12	11	1
Lower Moreland Township	12,940	28	23	5	Morton	2,658	5	4	1
Lower Paxton Township	46,144	67	60	7	Moscow	1,941	3	3	0
Lower Pottsgrove Township	12,361	19	17	2	Mount Carmel	5,869	9	9	0
Lower Providence Township	26,475	35	31	4	Mount Carmel Township	2,582	6	6	0
Lower Salford Township	14,832	19	17	2	Mount Holly Springs	1,923	3	3	0
Lower Saucon Township	11,625	16	14	2	Mount Jewett	983	1	1	0
Lower Southampton Township	19,137	34	31	3	Mount Joy	7,426	15	13	2
Lower Swatara Township	8,829	11	10	1	Mount Lebanon	30,380	53	44	9
Lower Windsor Township	7,996	11	10	1	Mount Oliver	3,644	10	10	0
Luzerne Township	6,684	1	1	0	Mount Pleasant	4,357	3	3	0
Lykens	1,867	1	1	0	Mount Pleasant Township	3,667	3	3	0
Macungie	3,165	5	5	0	Mount Union	2,313	5	5	0
Mahanoy City	4,359	4	4	0	Muhlenberg Township	19,028	33	30	3
Mahoning Township, Carbon County	4,493	4	4	0	Muncy	2,444	3	3	0
Mahoning Township, Lawrence County	3,306	2	2	0	Munhall	11,048	25	21	4
Mahoning Township, Montour County	4,248	7	6	1	Murrysville	19,688	26	21	5
Malvern	3,174	6	5	1	Myerstown	3,163	3	3	0
Manheim	4,680	10	9	1	Nanticoke	10,183	14	13	1
Manheim Township	36,619	79	63	16	Nanty Glo	2,763	2	2	0
Manor	2,966	3	3	0	Narberth	4,063	6	6	0
Manor Township, Lancaster County	20,161	19	17	2	Neshannock Township	9,282	7	7	0
Mansfield	3,266	5	5	0	Nether Providence Township	13,298	17	16	1
Marcus Hook	2,249	7	6	1	Neville Township	1,120	14	11	3
Marion Township, Beaver County	883	2	2	0	Newberry Township	15,825	18	16	2
Marion Township, Berks County	1,827	3	3	0	New Bethlehem	960	3	3	0
Marlborough Township	3,337	3	3	0	New Brighton	9,246	9	7	2
Marple Township	23,682	35	30	5	New Britain	2,279	6	5	1
Mars	1,658	1	1	0	New Britain Township	11,109	14	12	2

Table 78.　Full-Time Law Enforcement Employees by State and City, 2010—*Continued*

(Number)

State/city	Popula-tion	Total law enforce-ment employees	Total officers	Total civilians	State/city	Popula-tion	Total law enforce-ment employees	Total officers	Total civilians
New Castle	23,968	41	37	4	Penn Township, Butler County	5,212	5	4	1
New Castle Township	396	1	1	0	Penn Township, Lancaster County	8,973	11	10	1
New Cumberland	7,061	9	8	1	Penn Township, Perry County	3,284	6	5	1
New Garden Township	12,307	11	10	1	Penn Township, Westmoreland County	20,387	21	19	2
New Hanover Township	10,029	10	9	1	Penn Township, York County	16,193	25	23	2
New Holland	5,223	13	12	1	Pequea Township	4,581	9	9	0
New Hope	2,298	11	9	2	Perkasie	8,695	20	18	2
New Kensington	13,583	23	23	0	Perryopolis	1,693	2	2	0
New Philadelphia	1,085	1	1	0	Peters Township	20,731	23	21	2
Newport	1,469	1	1	0	Philadelphia	1,558,378	7,532	6,734	798
Newport Township	4,872	2	2	0	Phoenixville	16,923	29	28	1
New Sewickley Township	7,651	7	7	0	Pine Grove	2,036	2	2	0
Newton Township	2,812	1	1	0	Pitcairn	3,308	4	4	0
Newtown	2,404	5	5	0	Pittsburgh	312,737	954	887	67
Newtown Township, Bucks County	19,713	32	28	4	Pittston	7,539	7	7	0
Newtown Township, Delaware County	11,937	19	17	2	Plainfield Township	6,370	13	12	1
Newville	1,309	2	2	0	Plains Township	10,460	17	16	1
New Wilmington	2,334	4	4	0	Pleasant Hills	7,959	20	18	2
Norristown	32,217	83	70	13	Plum	26,311	30	24	6
Northampton	10,064	14	12	2	Plumstead Township	11,937	17	15	2
Northampton Township	41,145	47	41	6	Plymouth Township, Montgomery County	16,534	53	46	7
North Belle Vernon	1,941	2	2	0	Pocono Mountain Regional	36,242	50	44	6
North Braddock	5,694	3	3	0	Pocono Township	11,430	19	18	1
North Catasauqua	2,919	5	5	0	Point Marion	1,225	1	1	0
North Charleroi	1,308	1	1	0	Point Township	3,940	5	5	0
North Cornwall Township	6,683	10	9	1	Polk	992	2	2	0
North Coventry Township	7,924	14	13	1	Portage	2,555	2	2	0
North East, Erie County	4,186	7	6	1	Port Allegany	2,160	3	3	0
Northeastern Regional	11,441	13	11	2	Port Carbon	1,766	2	2	0
Northern Berks Regional	12,828	15	14	1	Port Vue	3,838	4	4	0
Northern Cambria Borough	3,875	4	4	0	Pottstown	21,491	58	46	12
Northern Regional	29,057	30	28	2	Pottsville	14,300	29	28	1
Northern York Regional	68,116	50	46	4	Pringle	937	24	19	5
North Fayette Township	13,375	25	20	5	Prospect Park	6,545	9	9	0
North Franklin Township	4,642	6	6	0	Pulaski Township, Lawrence County	3,393	2	2	0
North Huntingdon Township	29,816	35	29	6	Punxsutawney	5,855	11	8	3
North Lebanon Township	11,141	12	10	2	Pymatuning Township	3,555	5	5	0
North Londonderry Township	7,114	9	8	1	Quakertown	8,690	23	15	8
North Middleton Township	11,191	10	9	1	Quarryville	2,184	4	4	0
North Sewickley Township	5,628	1	1	0	Raccoon Township	3,218	4	4	0
North Strabane Township	12,876	20	19	1	Radnor Township	31,260	57	47	10
Northumberland	3,505	5	5	0	Ralpho Township	3,938	6	6	0
North Versailles Township	12,051	22	18	4	Rankin	2,101	1	1	0
North Wales	3,245	5	4	1	Reading	81,370	193	172	21
Northwest Lancaster County Regional	18,254	16	15	1	Redstone Township	5,959	2	2	0
Norwood	5,825	8	7	1	Reilly Township	831	1	1	0
Oakmont	6,411	7	7	0	Reserve Township	3,621	6	6	0
O'Hara Township	9,361	15	15	0	Reynoldsville	2,512	2	2	0
Ohio Township	4,397	14	11	3	Rice Township	3,098	5	5	0
Ohioville	3,611	2	2	0	Richland Township, Bucks County	13,124	14	12	2
Oil City	10,461	23	18	5	Richland Township, Cambria County	12,562	21	20	1
Old Forge	8,525	5	5	0	Ridgway	4,013	6	5	1
Old Lycoming Township	5,276	9	8	1	Ridley Park	7,048	14	10	4
Oley Township	3,750	5	5	0	Ridley Township	30,135	37	32	5
Oliver Township	2,087	1	1	0	Riverside	1,871	3	3	0
Olyphant	4,973	5	5	0	Roaring Brook Township	1,815	2	2	0
Orangeville Area	1,697	1	1	0	Roaring Spring	2,259	3	3	0
Orwigsburg	2,970	4	4	0	Robeson Township	7,807	6	6	0
Overfield Township	1,556	4	4	0	Robinson Township, Allegheny County	13,742	26	21	5
Oxford	4,776	12	11	1	Robinson Township, Washington County	2,144	4	3	1
Paint Township	3,156	5	4	1	Rochester	3,622	10	8	2
Palmerton	5,235	9	8	1	Rochester Township	2,839	3	3	0
Palmer Township	21,029	34	31	3	Rockledge	2,491	5	5	0
Palmyra	7,099	10	9	1	Roseto	1,675	1	1	0
Palo Alto	1,073	1	1	0	Rosslyn Farms	421	2	2	0
Parkesburg	3,514	11	10	1	Ross Township	30,615	45	43	2
Parkside	2,199	3	3	0	Rostraver Township	11,729	15	14	1
Parks Township	2,546	2	2	0	Royersford	4,763	8	7	1
Patterson Township	2,930	4	4	0	Rush Township	3,756	3	3	0
Patton	1,829	2	2	0	Rye Township	2,567	1	1	0
Patton Township	13,570	20	18	2	Sadsbury Township, Chester County	3,443	2	2	0
Paxtang	1,493	3	3	0	Salem Township, Luzerne County	4,121	4	4	0
Pen Argyl	3,693	5	5	0	Salisbury Township	14,197	19	17	2
Penbrook	2,937	8	8	0	Sandy Lake	685	1	1	0
Penn Hills	44,001	57	53	4	Sandy Township	11,527	8	7	1
Pennridge Regional	10,783	14	12	2	Saxton	756	1	1	0

Table 78.   Full-Time Law Enforcement Employees by State and City, 2010—*Continued*

(Number)

State/city	Population	Total law enforcement employees	Total officers	Total civilians	State/city	Population	Total law enforcement employees	Total officers	Total civilians
Sayre	5,388	14	14	0	Stoneboro	1,007	1	1	0
Schuylkill Haven	5,128	8	8	0	Stonycreek Township	2,865	2	2	0
Schuylkill Township, Chester County	7,881	13	11	2	Stowe Township	6,029	8	7	1
Scottdale	4,391	7	7	0	Strasburg	2,802	4	4	0
Scott Township, Allegheny County	15,778	22	21	1	Stroud Area Regional	35,282	61	55	6
Scott Township, Columbia County	5,049	6	6	0	Sugarcreek	4,932	5	5	0
Scott Township, Lackawanna County	4,911	5	5	0	Sugarloaf Township, Luzerne County	4,112	3	3	0
Scranton	71,920	170	150	20	Sugar Notch	957	4	1	3
Selinsgrove	5,465	7	6	1	Summerhill Township	2,554	2	2	0
Seven Springs	99	7	6	1	Summit Hill	2,981	6	4	2
Sewickley	4,074	13	12	1	Summit Township	2,229	1	1	0
Sewickley Heights	975	4	3	1	Sunbury	9,784	14	11	3
Shaler Township	27,862	24	24	0	Susquehanna Regional	7,673	17	15	2
Shamokin	7,337	12	12	0	Susquehanna Township, Dauphin County	23,556	41	39	2
Shamokin Dam	1,451	3	3	0	Swarthmore	6,161	9	9	0
Sharon Hill	5,367	10	9	1	Swatara Township	22,781	52	49	3
Sharpsburg	3,281	6	6	0	Swissvale	8,721	14	14	0
Sharpsville	4,040	6	5	1	Swoyersville	4,830	6	6	0
Sheffield Township	2,196	1	1	0	Sykesville	1,152	2	2	0
Shenandoah	5,121	3	3	0	Tamaqua	6,525	10	9	1
Shenango Township, Lawrence County	7,652	6	6	0	Tarentum	4,501	8	7	1
Shillington	5,042	8	7	1	Tatamy	1,112	1	1	0
Shinglehouse	1,094	1	1	0	Taylor	6,134	7	7	0
Shippensburg	5,609	11	10	1	Telford	4,632	7	6	1
Shippingport	221	2	2	0	Throop	4,061	3	3	0
Shiremanstown	1,466	2	2	0	Tiadaghton Valley Regional	6,613	10	9	1
Shohola Township	2,541	1	1	0	Tidioute	713	1	1	0
Silver Lake Township	1,719	2	2	0	Tilden Township	3,895	2	2	0
Silver Spring Township	14,067	17	16	1	Tinicum Township, Bucks County	4,259	5	5	0
Sinking Spring	3,767	7	6	1	Tinicum Township, Delaware County	4,237	17	15	2
Slatington	4,452	7	7	0	Titusville	5,687	10	10	0
Slippery Rock	2,957	4	4	0	Towamencin Township	17,830	36	24	12
Smethport	1,547	2	2	0	Towanda	2,796	6	6	0
Smithton Borough	406	1	1	0	Trafford	3,080	3	3	0
Smith Township	4,508	1	1	0	Trainer	1,856	6	6	0
Solebury Township	8,957	15	13	2	Tredyffrin Township	29,336	53	47	6
Somerset	6,294	8	7	1	Troy	1,445	3	3	0
Souderton	6,601	7	6	1	Tullytown	1,967	7	6	1
South Abington Township	9,588	12	10	2	Tulpehocken Township	3,611	3	3	0
South Beaver Township	2,845	4	4	0	Tunkhannock	1,760	4	4	0
South Buffalo Township	2,771	2	2	0	Tunkhannock Township, Wyoming County	4,294	4	4	0
South Centre Township	1,924	10	10	0	Turtle Creek	5,489	7	6	1
South Coatesville	1,185	2	2	0	Tyrone	5,216	14	11	3
South Connellsville Borough	2,121	2	2	0	Union City	3,295	3	3	0
Southern Regional Lancaster County	3,914	9	9	0	Uniontown	11,514	21	20	1
Southern Regional York County	10,136	11	10	1	Union Township, Lawrence County	4,992	4	4	0
South Fayette Township	13,359	18	17	1	Upland	2,889	6	5	1
South Fork	1,018	2	2	0	Upper Allen Township	18,659	21	20	1
South Greensburg	2,216	2	2	0	Upper Burrell Township	2,128	2	2	0
South Heidelberg Township	7,542	7	7	0	Upper Chichester Township	17,847	24	22	2
South Lebanon Township	8,867	8	7	1	Upper Darby Township	79,046	145	126	19
South Londonderry Township	7,691	6	6	0	Upper Dublin Township	26,118	47	40	7
South Park Township	14,057	18	17	1	Upper Gwynedd Township	16,481	24	21	3
South Pymatuning Township	2,781	2	2	0	Upper Makefield Township	8,691	17	16	1
South Waverly	959	3	3	0	Upper Merion Township	26,693	83	64	19
Southwestern Regional	18,477	14	13	1	Upper Moreland Township	24,291	47	37	10
Southwest Greensburg	2,187	2	2	0	Upper Nazareth Township	6,181	4	3	1
Southwest Mercer County Regional	11,071	24	23	1	Upper Perkiomen	6,422	10	9	1
Southwest Regional	2,918	3	2	1	Upper Pottsgrove Township	5,455	9	8	1
South Whitehall Township	20,110	37	34	3	Upper Providence Township, Delaware County	11,280	13	12	1
South Williamsport	5,988	7	7	0	Upper Providence Township, Montgomery County	20,416	27	25	2
Spring City	3,438	4	3	1	Upper Saucon Township	15,514	20	19	1
Springdale	3,474	4	4	0	Upper Southampton Township	15,349	25	21	4
Springdale Township	1,650	4	4	0	Upper St. Clair Township	18,666	33	27	6
Springettsbury Township	25,205	35	32	3	Upper Uwchlan Township	12,202	10	10	0
Springfield Township, Bucks County	5,127	4	4	0	Upper Yoder Township	5,450	13	13	0
Springfield Township, Delaware County	22,990	40	34	6	Uwchlan Township	19,079	24	22	2
Springfield Township, Montgomery County	18,926	30	29	1	Valley Township	7,223	4	4	0
Spring Garden Township	12,218	23	20	3	Vandergrift	4,970	8	8	0
Spring Township, Berks County	27,157	31	30	1	Vernon Township	5,453	5	4	1
Spring Township, Centre County	7,243	8	7	1	Verona	2,634	4	3	1
State College	54,649	74	61	13	Walker Township	985	1	1	0
St. Clair Boro	2,962	6	6	0	Walnutport	2,240	4	4	0
Steelton	5,636	9	8	1	Warminster Township	35,027	56	51	5
Stewartstown	2,036	7	6	1	Warren	9,302	18	15	3
St. Marys City	13,273	15	14	1	Warrington Township	23,663	32	30	2

Table 78. Full-Time Law Enforcement Employees by State and City, 2010—*Continued*

(Number)

State/city	Population	Total law enforcement employees	Total officers	Total civilians	State/city	Population	Total law enforcement employees	Total officers	Total civilians
Warwick Township, Bucks County	15,090	21	19	2	York Area Regional	59,342	55	50	5
Warwick Township, Lancaster County	17,596	16	15	1	Youngsville	1,652	2	2	0
Washington, Washington County	14,745	31	29	2	Zelienople	3,958	10	9	1
Washington Township, Fayette County	4,095	3	3	0	**RHODE ISLAND**				
Washington Township, Franklin County	12,440	16	14	2	Barrington	16,276	31	24	7
Washington Township, Northampton County	5,022	5	5	0	Bristol	22,266	51	40	11
Washington Township, Westmoreland County	7,409	6	6	0	Burrillville	16,637	31	23	8
Watsontown	2,107	5	5	0	Central Falls	18,676	48	40	8
Waynesboro	10,259	20	18	2	Charlestown	8,093	25	20	5
Waynesburg	4,196	9	8	1	Coventry	35,021	73	57	16
Weatherly	2,604	4	4	0	Cranston	80,125	166	138	28
Weissport	427	1	1	0	Cumberland	34,589	57	46	11
Wellsboro	3,254	6	6	0	East Greenwich	13,361	38	31	7
Wesleyville	3,310	11	10	1	East Providence	48,507	115	97	18
West Brandywine Township	8,049	5	5	0	Foster	4,561	12	8	4
West Brownsville	1,022	1	1	0	Glocester	10,602	19	13	6
West Caln Township	8,657	2	2	0	Hopkinton	8,021	20	15	5
West Chester	18,578	60	47	13	Jamestown	5,451	17	13	4
West Conshohocken	1,513	8	8	0	Johnston	28,623	84	69	15
West Deer Township	12,079	12	11	1	Lincoln	22,133	44	37	7
West Earl Township	7,975	6	6	0	Little Compton	3,516	13	9	4
Western Berks Regional	4,569	4	4	0	Middletown	15,895	41	36	5
West Fallowfield Township	2,621	1	1	0	Narragansett	16,485	48	37	11
Westfield	1,123	2	2	0	Newport	23,173	97	79	18
West Goshen Township	22,211	33	29	4	New Shoreham	1,036	9	5	4
West Grove Borough	2,808	2	2	0	North Kingstown	26,656	57	45	12
West Hazleton	3,295	3	2	1	North Providence	32,740	83	62	21
West Hempfield Township	16,388	23	20	3	North Smithfield	11,629	25	22	3
West Hills Regional	10,549	12	11	1	Pawtucket	71,782	178	151	27
West Homestead	1,984	7	6	1	Portsmouth	16,845	33	31	2
West Lampeter Township	15,972	17	15	2	Providence	171,565	582	483	99
West Lebanon Township	857	12	10	2	Richmond	7,678	17	13	4
West Mahanoy Township	2,982	3	3	0	Scituate	10,894	23	17	6
West Manchester Township	18,665	29	26	3	Smithfield	21,242	55	41	14
West Manheim Township	7,965	9	8	1	South Kingstown	29,291	69	51	18
West Mead Township	5,051	2	2	0	Tiverton	14,836	37	27	10
West Mifflin	20,352	42	36	6	Warren	10,840	28	22	6
West Newton	2,840	2	2	0	Warwick	84,568	207	158	49
West Norriton Township	14,593	33	28	5	Westerly	23,524	61	46	15
West Penn Township	4,389	3	3	0	West Greenwich	6,531	15	11	4
West Pikeland Township	4,136	4	4	0	West Warwick	29,251	66	56	10
West Pittston	4,932	3	3	0	Woonsocket	43,320	109	94	15
West Pottsgrove Township	3,789	10	9	1	**SOUTH CAROLINA**				
West Reading	4,075	16	15	1	Abbeville	5,443	23	19	4
West Sadsbury Township	2,560	4	3	1	Aiken	29,875	115	90	25
West Shore Regional	6,620	12	10	2	Anderson	27,325	130	95	35
Westtown-East Goshen Regional	32,298	31	28	3	Bamberg	3,303	12	10	2
West View	6,628	12	8	4	Barnwell	4,714	17	15	2
West Vincent Township	5,164	6	5	1	Batesburg-Leesville	5,670	26	21	5
West Whiteland Township	18,636	29	27	2	Beaufort	12,076	47	43	4
West Wyoming	2,687	1	1	0	Belton	4,709	14	12	2
West York	4,219	9	9	0	Bennettsville	8,941	38	35	3
Whitehall	13,364	26	21	5	Bishopville	3,773	15	13	2
Whitehall Township	27,352	53	46	7	Bluffton	14,899	35	32	3
White Haven Borough	1,143	2	2	0	Bonneau	403	5	3	2
White Oak	8,116	12	11	1	Bowman	1,130	4	4	0
White Township	1,295	3	3	0	Burnettown	2,701	2	2	0
Whitpain Township	19,018	38	30	8	Camden	7,152	32	29	3
Wiconisco Township	1,114	1	1	0	Cayce	13,161	68	51	17
Wilkes-Barre	40,970	92	88	4	Central	4,127	10	9	1
Wilkes-Barre Township	3,081	17	15	2	Chapin	770	6	6	0
Wilkinsburg	17,047	27	24	3	Charleston	117,551	535	398	137
Wilkins Township	6,483	12	12	0	Cheraw	5,372	28	22	6
Williamsburg	1,250	1	1	0	Chesnee	1,115	5	5	0
Williamsport	29,320	55	51	4	Chester	5,915	28	25	3
Willistown Township	10,984	19	17	2	Chesterfield	1,321	6	5	1
Wilson	7,760	9	8	1	Clemson	13,134	36	26	10
Windber	3,953	3	2	1	Clinton	8,910	42	33	9
Womelsdorf	2,856	1	1	0	Columbia	130,498	402	340	62
Wrightsville	2,255	3	3	0	Conway	16,742	65	50	15
Wright Township	5,945	7	7	0	Darlington	6,482	30	27	3
Wyoming	2,988	4	4	0	Denmark	2,900	11	9	2
Wyomissing	10,533	28	23	5	Dillon	6,468	28	26	2
Yardley	2,524	2	2	0	Due West	1,266	7	6	1
Yeadon	11,462	17	15	2	Duncan	3,258	12	10	2
York	40,553	116	103	13	Easley	20,818	53	41	12

Table 78.   Full-Time Law Enforcement Employees by State and City, 2010—*Continued*

(Number)

State/city	Popula-tion	Total law enforce-ment employees	Total officers	Total civilians	State/city	Popula-tion	Total law enforce-ment employees	Total officers	Total civilians
Edgefield	4,357	9	9	0	Summerville	47,479	101	81	20
Edisto Beach	724	4	4	0	Sumter	38,228	129	115	14
Elgin	1,320	6	6	0	Surfside Beach	4,884	25	19	6
Elloree	674	3	3	0	Swansea	828	5	4	1
Eutawville	294	3	2	1	Tega Cay	5,293	26	19	7
Fairfax	3,081	7	6	1	Timmonsville	2,403	5	4	1
Florence	32,273	130	103	27	Travelers Rest	4,685	21	15	6
Folly Beach	2,511	15	13	2	Turbeville	700	4	3	1
Forest Acres	9,871	32	26	6	Union	7,832	30	25	5
Fort Lawn	801	3	3	0	Wagener	885	4	4	0
Fort Mill	11,024	40	34	6	Walhalla	3,477	16	14	2
Fountain Inn	8,063	30	24	6	Walterboro	5,841	43	28	15
Gaffney	13,155	45	41	4	Wellford	2,618	9	9	0
Georgetown	8,393	42	35	7	West Columbia	14,145	64	54	10
Goose Creek	39,955	85	62	23	Whitmire	1,583	4	4	0
Great Falls	2,001	5	5	0	Williamston	4,015	19	15	4
Greenville	62,368	220	177	43	Williston	3,121	9	8	1
Greenwood	22,762	57	50	7	Winnsboro	3,615	25	23	2
Greer	26,760	70	53	17	Woodruff	4,169	15	12	3
Hampton	2,730	11	11	0	Yemassee	874	8	8	0
Hanahan	16,639	40	33	7	York	8,327	32	25	7
Hardeeville	3,795	20	18	2	**SOUTH DAKOTA**				
Hartsville	7,326	40	37	3	Aberdeen	24,818	51	43	8
Hemingway	475	6	5	1	Alcester	913	2	2	0
Honea Path	3,734	15	15	0	Armour	637	1	1	0
Inman	2,154	9	9	0	Avon	499	1	1	0
Irmo	12,023	25	23	2	Belle Fourche	4,972	11	10	1
Isle of Palms	4,736	29	20	9	Beresford	2,295	8	4	4
Iva	1,216	6	5	1	Box Elder	4,340	9	8	1
Jackson	1,669	4	4	0	Brandon	8,330	12	11	1
Jamestown	108	4	4	0	Brookings	20,200	40	31	9
Johnsonville	1,505	6	5	1	Burke	544	1	1	0
Johnston	2,334	7	7	0	Canton	4,378	4	4	0
Jonesville	878	3	3	0	Centerville	818	1	1	0
Kingstree	3,139	21	19	2	Chamberlain	2,273	6	6	0
Lake City	6,719	23	19	4	Corsica	559	1	1	0
Lancaster	10,376	49	38	11	Deadwood	1,254	14	11	3
Landrum	2,693	10	9	1	Eagle Butte	928	2	2	0
Lane	498	2	2	0	Elk Point	2,014	4	4	0
Laurens	9,464	36	29	7	Estelline	663	1	1	0
Liberty	3,079	15	10	5	Eureka	904	1	1	0
Loris	2,412	14	12	2	Faith	431	1	1	0
Lyman	3,065	10	8	2	Flandreau	2,171	9	8	1
Mauldin	23,218	51	41	10	Freeman	1,157	2	2	0
McColl	2,284	7	6	1	Gettysburg	987	2	2	0
McCormick	2,689	7	7	0	Gregory	1,130	3	3	0
Moncks Corner	7,390	27	24	3	Groton	1,413	4	4	0
Mount Pleasant	68,555	183	141	42	Hot Springs	4,063	8	7	1
Mullins	4,595	26	24	2	Hoven	367	1	1	0
Myrtle Beach	32,907	272	202	70	Huron	11,155	32	25	7
Newberry	11,144	30	30	0	Jefferson	617	2	2	0
New Ellenton	2,252	6	6	0	Kadoka	611	1	1	0
North	788	3	3	0	Kimball	692	1	1	0
North Augusta	21,242	76	53	23	Lead	2,813	6	5	1
North Charleston	99,447	398	315	83	Lemmon	1,142	3	3	0
North Myrtle Beach	16,832	124	73	51	Lennox	2,920	4	4	0
Orangeburg	13,252	95	69	26	Leola	374	1	1	0
Pacolet	2,886	8	6	2	Madison	6,573	12	11	1
Pageland	2,508	16	11	5	Martin	966	2	2	0
Pelion	613	3	3	0	McIntosh	201	1	1	0
Pickens	3,039	14	13	1	McLaughlin	714	4	2	2
Pine Ridge	2,025	2	1	1	Menno	633	1	1	0
Port Royal	11,663	20	19	1	Milbank	3,105	6	6	0
Prosperity	1,063	3	3	0	Miller	1,296	4	4	0
Ridgeland	2,577	17	16	1	Mitchell	14,669	40	28	12
Ridgeville	2,060	1	1	0	Mobridge	3,085	14	7	7
Rock Hill	71,456	171	127	44	North Sioux City	2,619	9	7	2
Saluda	2,980	11	10	1	Parkston	1,430	3	3	0
Scranton	1,093	2	2	0	Philip	696	2	2	0
Seneca	7,852	44	32	12	Pierre	14,003	37	24	13
Simpsonville	18,119	46	36	10	Platte	1,282	2	2	0
South Congaree	2,458	7	6	1	Rapid City	67,436	134	105	29
Spartanburg	40,448	147	122	25	Rosholt	425	1	1	0
Springdale	2,819	8	8	0	Scotland	762	1	1	0
St. George	2,156	9	9	0	Selby	635	1	1	0
Sullivans Island	1,891	9	8	1	Sioux Falls	160,679	261	223	38

Table 78. Full-Time Law Enforcement Employees by State and City, 2010—*Continued*

(Number)

State/city	Popula-tion	Total law enforce-ment employees	Total officers	Total civilians	State/city	Popula-tion	Total law enforce-ment employees	Total officers	Total civilians
Sisseton	2,430	7	7	0	Dandridge	2,784	12	12	0
Spearfish	10,057	29	20	9	Dayton	6,945	19	17	2
Springfield	1,456	2	2	0	Decatur	1,512	5	5	0
Sturgis	5,897	19	16	3	Decaturville	832	1	1	0
Summerset	434	1	1	0	Decherd	2,113	10	9	1
Tea	5,058	5	5	0	Dickson	14,100	50	44	6
Tripp	606	1	1	0	Dover	1,642	6	6	0
Tyndall	1,061	2	2	0	Dresden	2,810	10	9	1
Vermillion	10,369	18	17	1	Dunlap	5,672	13	11	2
Viborg	747	1	1	0	Dyer	2,396	6	6	0
Wagner	1,487	5	5	0	Dyersburg	17,104	69	60	9
Watertown	20,232	53	35	18	Eagleville	533	1	1	0
Webster	1,625	5	5	0	East Ridge	19,882	41	37	4
Whitewood	852	2	2	0	Elizabethton	13,694	42	38	4
Winner	2,614	9	8	1	Elkton	591	2	2	0
Worthing	1,249	1	1	0	Englewood	1,815	5	5	0
Yankton	13,817	38	26	12	Erin	1,448	5	4	1
TENNESSEE					Erwin	5,759	13	13	0
Adamsville	2,134	9	6	3	Estill Springs	2,232	6	6	0
Alamo	2,402	3	3	0	Etowah	3,770	15	10	5
Alcoa	8,775	45	38	7	Fairview	8,324	18	18	0
Alexandria	957	3	3	0	Fayetteville	7,216	27	25	2
Algood	3,472	13	13	0	Franklin	62,127	151	128	23
Ardmore	1,177	11	7	4	Friendship	604	1	1	0
Ashland City	4,707	17	15	2	Gainesboro	835	8	4	4
Athens	14,352	31	29	2	Gallatin	31,229	88	63	25
Atoka	7,978	16	15	1	Gallaway	760	2	2	0
Baileyton	492	3	2	1	Gates	836	2	2	0
Bartlett	48,358	142	109	33	Gatlinburg	6,104	52	42	10
Baxter	1,435	4	4	0	Germantown	41,347	109	88	21
Bean Station	3,085	7	7	0	Gibson	415	4	3	1
Belle Meade	3,572	19	15	4	Gleason	1,397	5	5	0
Bells	2,283	5	5	0	Goodlettsville	17,658	50	35	15
Benton	1,182	8	7	1	Gordonsville	1,311	4	4	0
Berry Hill	830	17	13	4	Grand Junction	298	1	1	0
Bethel Springs	778	3	1	2	Graysville	1,468	6	5	1
Big Sandy	502	2	2	0	Greenbrier	6,899	12	11	1
Blaine	1,777	3	1	2	Greeneville	15,294	47	45	2
Bluff City	1,689	8	8	0	Greenfield	2,011	8	7	1
Bolivar	5,516	26	20	6	Halls	2,145	7	7	0
Bradford	1,061	3	3	0	Harriman	6,612	20	19	1
Brentwood	38,371	70	55	15	Henderson	6,445	16	15	1
Brighton	2,782	7	6	1	Hendersonville	49,010	115	88	27
Bristol	25,799	90	67	23	Henning	1,251	4	4	0
Brownsville	10,138	37	32	5	Henry	551	2	2	0
Bruceton	1,418	4	4	0	Hohenwald	3,808	12	11	1
Burns	1,461	3	3	0	Hollow Rock	924	2	2	0
Calhoun	525	3	3	0	Hornbeak	410	1	1	0
Camden	3,545	19	15	4	Humboldt	9,114	34	28	6
Carthage	2,222	11	7	4	Huntingdon	4,074	16	12	4
Caryville	2,373	5	5	0	Huntland	862	4	4	0
Celina	1,342	8	6	2	Jacksboro	2,086	7	7	0
Centerville	3,947	21	13	8	Jackson	63,969	252	212	40
Chapel Hill	1,368	5	5	0	Jamestown	1,916	10	10	0
Charleston	674	3	3	0	Jasper	3,060	8	8	0
Chattanooga	172,460	509	406	103	Jefferson City	8,232	21	19	2
Church Hill	6,876	11	10	1	Jellico	2,511	7	6	1
Clarksville	126,548	299	243	56	Johnson City	63,750	166	141	25
Cleveland	40,452	98	87	11	Jonesborough	5,583	21	17	4
Clifton	2,673	5	5	0	Kenton	1,286	5	5	0
Clinton	9,715	27	25	2	Kimball	1,390	9	9	0
Collegedale	8,343	21	20	1	Kingsport	44,587	170	112	58
Collierville	40,286	135	96	39	Kingston	5,609	12	11	1
Collinwood	995	3	3	0	Kingston Springs	2,996	6	5	1
Columbia	35,364	97	87	10	Knoxville	185,554	503	405	98
Cookeville	30,179	88	69	19	Lafayette	4,588	20	14	6
Coopertown	3,520	3	2	1	La Follette	8,082	28	20	8
Copperhill	428	1	1	0	Lake City	1,848	10	7	3
Cornersville	986	4	4	0	Lakewood	2,659	5	5	0
Covington	9,396	33	32	1	La Vergne	32,335	59	43	16
Cowan	1,705	5	5	0	Lawrenceburg	10,877	41	37	4
Cross Plains	1,728	3	3	0	Lebanon	25,446	83	69	14
Crossville	12,084	44	41	3	Lenoir City	8,202	24	23	1
Crump	1,464	4	3	1	Lewisburg	11,126	41	29	12
Cumberland City	329	3	3	0	Lexington	7,876	34	29	5
Cumberland Gap	208	1	1	0	Livingston	3,552	22	17	5

Table 78.   Full-Time Law Enforcement Employees by State and City, 2010—*Continued*

(Number)

State/city	Population	Total law enforcement employees	Total officers	Total civilians	State/city	Population	Total law enforcement employees	Total officers	Total civilians
Lookout Mountain	1,884	20	16	4	Smyrna	41,071	104	77	27
Loretto	1,800	4	4	0	Sneedville	1,282	1	1	0
Loudon	4,995	15	15	0	Soddy-Daisy	12,967	31	25	6
Madisonville	4,761	20	16	4	Somerville	2,970	11	10	1
Manchester	10,210	41	35	6	South Carthage	1,355	4	4	0
Martin	10,145	36	28	8	South Fulton	2,373	7	6	1
Maryville	27,638	56	49	7	South Pittsburg	3,079	9	9	0
Mason	1,356	6	6	0	Sparta	5,012	16	15	1
Maynardville	1,940	4	4	0	Spencer	1,687	3	3	0
McEwen	1,678	9	4	5	Spring City	2,140	7	7	0
McKenzie	5,283	19	15	4	Springfield	17,903	61	38	23
McMinnville	13,647	34	30	4	Spring Hill	30,829	45	36	9
Medina	2,465	11	10	1	St. Joseph	864	1	1	0
Memphis	673,650	2,775	2,335	440	Surgoinsville	1,834	2	2	0
Middleton	605	4	4	0	Sweetwater	6,740	22	20	2
Milan	7,913	28	22	6	Tazewell	2,185	6	6	0
Millersville	6,565	18	12	6	Tellico Plains	973	6	5	1
Millington	10,875	50	37	13	Tiptonville	3,959	5	5	0
Minor Hill	446	2	2	0	Townsend	549	4	4	0
Monteagle	1,204	6	6	0	Tracy City	1,605	5	5	0
Monterey	2,944	7	7	0	Trenton	4,480	26	20	6
Morristown	28,147	94	87	7	Trezevant	868	1	1	0
Moscow	559	4	4	0	Trimble	721	1	1	0
Mountain City	2,360	9	9	0	Troy	1,201	4	4	0
Mount Carmel	5,525	9	8	1	Tullahoma	18,535	41	36	5
Mount Juliet	24,544	57	45	12	Tusculum	2,317	2	2	0
Mount Pleasant	4,532	16	12	4	Union City	10,486	39	33	6
Munford	6,880	15	14	1	Vonore	1,516	11	10	1
Murfreesboro	109,199	274	220	54	Wartburg	912	4	4	0
Nashville	616,366	1,584	1,289	295	Wartrace	614	2	1	1
Newbern	3,173	20	13	7	Watertown	1,422	7	4	3
New Hope	1,049	1	1	0	Waverly	4,192	14	13	1
New Johnsonville	1,961	4	4	0	Waynesboro	2,090	8	8	0
New Market	1,397	4	3	1	Westmoreland	2,243	9	6	3
Newport	7,556	33	27	6	White Bluff	2,570	4	4	0
New Tazewell	2,845	10	10	0	White House	10,626	26	18	8
Niota	811	3	3	0	White Pine	2,202	9	8	1
Nolensville	3,178	7	7	0	Whiteville	4,480	7	7	0
Norris	1,490	7	7	0	Whitwell	1,572	5	5	0
Oakland	5,878	22	20	2	Winchester	7,911	25	23	2
Oak Ridge	27,728	77	61	16	Winfield	994	3	3	0
Obion	1,074	3	3	0	Woodbury	2,619	9	8	1
Oliver Springs	3,346	14	9	5	**TEXAS**				
Oneida	3,812	16	11	5	Abernathy	2,748	4	4	0
Paris	9,946	36	25	11	Abilene	116,938	250	183	67
Parsons	2,480	7	7	0	Addison	15,862	86	60	26
Petersburg	610	2	2	0	Alamo	17,687	39	28	11
Pigeon Forge	6,532	64	52	12	Alamo Heights	7,488	31	21	10
Pikeville	1,863	3	3	0	Alice	19,690	46	36	10
Piperton	1,508	9	9	0	Allen	89,459	154	107	47
Pittman Center	716	1	1	0	Alpine	6,490	17	9	8
Plainview	2,062	1	1	0	Alto	1,157	5	5	0
Pleasant View	4,304	5	5	0	Alton	12,349	17	13	4
Portland	11,682	33	26	7	Alvarado	4,379	22	16	6
Powells Crossroads	1,246	1	1	0	Alvin	23,399	76	49	27
Pulaski	7,790	29	26	3	Amarillo	190,393	357	309	48
Puryear	676	2	2	0	Andrews	10,508	25	16	9
Red Bank	11,680	23	21	2	Angleton	19,138	49	37	12
Red Boiling Springs	1,114	5	5	0	Anna	1,999	13	11	2
Ridgely	1,486	6	5	1	Anson	2,194	6	5	1
Ridgetop	1,796	6	6	0	Anthony	4,550	17	16	1
Ripley	7,473	31	24	7	Aransas Pass	8,787	34	26	8
Rockwood	5,536	17	16	1	Archer City	1,778	2	2	0
Rogersville	4,340	12	11	1	Arcola	1,252	7	6	1
Rossville	637	5	5	0	Argyle	3,753	10	9	1
Rutherford	1,248	3	3	0	Arlington	383,715	817	629	188
Rutledge	1,294	4	4	0	Arp	981	4	4	0
Saltillo	350	3	2	1	Athens	12,173	34	26	8
Savannah	7,330	20	18	2	Atlanta	5,380	18	14	4
Selmer	4,699	20	18	2	Austin	796,310	2,141	1,605	536
Sevierville	17,854	68	54	14	Azle	11,689	31	24	7
Sewanee	2,634	13	9	4	Baird	1,644	2	2	0
Sharon	901	1	1	0	Balch Springs	20,265	48	33	15
Shelbyville	20,527	51	40	11	Balcones Heights	2,997	27	22	5
Signal Mountain	7,217	16	15	1	Ballinger	3,607	6	6	0
Smithville	4,465	12	11	1	Bangs	1,532	3	3	0

Table 78.　Full-Time Law Enforcement Employees by State and City, 2010—*Continued*

(Number)

State/city	Popula-tion	Total law enforce-ment employees	Total officers	Total civilians	State/city	Popula-tion	Total law enforce-ment employees	Total officers	Total civilians
Bastrop	8,790	24	20	4	College Station	88,416	156	112	44
Bay City	17,523	55	35	20	Colleyville	25,480	43	38	5
Bayou Vista	1,663	5	5	0	Collinsville	1,539	2	2	0
Baytown	71,082	195	137	58	Colorado City	3,895	10	5	5
Beaumont	109,430	292	252	40	Columbus	3,854	11	10	1
Bedford	49,993	130	80	50	Comanche	4,173	10	8	2
Bee Cave	3,435	15	14	1	Combes	2,925	4	4	0
Beeville	12,439	27	22	5	Commerce	9,187	20	15	5
Bellaire	18,378	54	41	13	Conroe	60,677	148	96	52
Bellmead	9,659	23	16	7	Converse	18,890	48	34	14
Bellville	4,552	11	10	1	Coppell	39,870	78	61	17
Belton	17,955	37	29	8	Copperas Cove	30,791	70	49	21
Benbrook	23,589	50	39	11	Corinth	22,185	30	28	2
Bertram	1,455	5	4	1	Corpus Christi	287,559	657	445	212
Beverly Hills	2,031	13	8	5	Corrigan	1,881	9	6	3
Big Sandy	1,348	6	6	0	Corsicana	26,344	58	45	13
Big Spring	24,357	60	47	13	Cottonwood Shores	1,235	3	3	0
Bishop	3,100	11	6	5	Crandall	4,036	13	13	0
Blanco	1,673	4	4	0	Crane	3,318	12	7	5
Bloomburg	359	1	1	0	Crockett	6,623	18	17	1
Blue Mound	2,385	9	5	4	Crosbyton	1,561	3	3	0
Boerne	11,152	44	29	15	Crowell	912	1	1	0
Bogata	1,209	4	4	0	Crowley	13,600	36	27	9
Bonham	10,547	26	18	8	Crystal City	7,052	9	5	4
Borger	12,469	40	27	13	Cuero	6,445	14	13	1
Bovina	1,697	5	4	1	Cumby	730	7	5	2
Bowie	5,487	22	15	7	Daingerfield	2,354	8	7	1
Brackettville	1,769	1	1	0	Dalhart	7,101	18	15	3
Brady	5,286	15	9	6	Dallas	1,306,775	4,241	3,666	575
Brazoria	3,021	12	7	5	Dalworthington Gardens	2,473	19	14	5
Breckenridge	5,606	18	12	6	Danbury	1,707	3	3	0
Bremond	851	6	5	1	Dayton	7,828	24	17	7
Brenham	16,267	38	33	5	Decatur	6,641	25	20	5
Bridge City	8,421	19	14	5	Deer Park	31,087	80	55	25
Bridgeport	6,263	22	15	7	De Kalb	1,842	6	6	0
Brookshire	4,010	17	13	4	De Leon	2,329	4	4	0
Brookside Village	1,823	5	5	0	Del Rio	36,840	92	67	25
Brownfield	8,863	24	18	6	Denison	24,196	59	45	14
Brownsville	180,040	312	239	73	Denton	127,251	199	150	49
Brownwood	18,725	58	38	20	Denver City	4,146	13	8	5
Bruceville-Eddy	1,562	4	3	1	DeSoto	49,328	90	65	25
Bryan	75,350	168	132	36	Devine	4,610	11	9	2
Bullard	1,979	8	7	1	Diboll	5,519	21	15	6
Bulverde	4,894	14	14	0	Dickinson	17,854	44	31	13
Burkburnett	10,424	25	19	6	Dilley	3,589	7	6	1
Burleson	37,902	73	55	18	Dimmitt	3,622	8	7	1
Burnet	6,114	14	13	1	Donna	17,737	36	27	9
Cactus	2,699	7	5	2	Double Oak	3,444	6	6	0
Caddo Mills	1,216	3	3	0	Driscoll	800	5	4	1
Caldwell	3,693	13	12	1	Dublin	3,769	9	5	4
Calvert	1,340	3	3	0	Dumas	14,158	31	26	5
Cameron	5,608	14	8	6	Duncanville	36,397	71	55	16
Canton	3,639	20	20	0	Eagle Lake	3,638	9	8	1
Canyon	14,634	23	20	3	Eagle Pass	27,581	84	68	16
Carrollton	130,862	201	161	40	Early	2,707	8	7	1
Carthage	6,650	23	16	7	Eastland	3,831	11	9	2
Castle Hills	4,227	30	23	7	East Mountain	635	1	1	0
Castroville	3,083	10	8	2	Edcouch	4,754	18	13	5
Cedar Hill	46,674	83	64	19	Eden	2,338	2	2	0
Cedar Park	70,363	93	72	21	Edgewood	1,429	3	2	1
Celina	6,115	7	7	0	Edinburg	75,091	164	117	47
Center	5,769	27	19	8	Edna	5,816	11	9	2
Childress	6,463	10	9	1	El Campo	10,729	39	28	11
Chillicothe	655	2	2	0	Electra	2,864	14	7	7
Cibolo	18,403	21	19	2	Elgin	10,437	24	18	6
Cisco	3,684	9	7	2	El Paso	624,322	1,279	1,078	201
Clarksville	3,301	12	8	4	Elsa	6,751	19	15	4
Cleburne	30,209	74	55	19	Ennis	20,103	41	34	7
Cleveland	7,903	29	18	11	Euless	53,950	124	85	39
Clifton	3,488	8	7	1	Everman	5,828	15	11	4
Clint	972	1	1	0	Fairfield	3,755	16	12	4
Clute	10,930	38	27	11	Fair Oaks Ranch	6,595	17	16	1
Clyde	3,774	9	8	1	Falfurrias	4,763	15	14	1
Cockrell Hill	4,287	19	13	6	Farmers Branch	26,585	113	75	38
Coffee City	208	3	3	0	Farmersville	3,576	9	8	1
Coleman	4,573	14	10	4	Farwell	1,238	3	3	0

Table 78. Full-Time Law Enforcement Employees by State and City, 2010—*Continued*

(Number)

State/city	Population	Total law enforcement employees	Total officers	Total civilians	State/city	Population	Total law enforcement employees	Total officers	Total civilians
Ferris	2,616	10	6	4	Horizon City	15,025	22	19	3
Flatonia	1,443	4	4	0	Horseshoe Bay	2,492	18	16	2
Florence	1,160	2	2	0	Houston	2,280,859	7,054	5,351	1,703
Floresville	7,818	17	15	2	Howe	2,731	6	6	0
Flower Mound	72,157	120	84	36	Hubbard	1,759	4	4	0
Floydada	3,003	6	6	0	Hudson	4,422	5	5	0
Forest Hill	14,082	28	22	6	Hudson Oaks	2,230	12	11	1
Forney	17,264	33	22	11	Humble	14,843	78	57	21
Fort Stockton	7,625	30	18	12	Huntington	2,128	5	5	0
Fort Worth	746,433	1,918	1,505	413	Huntsville	38,275	57	50	7
Frankston	1,251	6	5	1	Hurst	39,147	118	74	44
Fredericksburg	11,512	34	30	4	Hutchins	3,192	21	17	4
Freeport	12,570	40	28	12	Hutto	17,962	30	25	5
Freer	2,902	12	9	3	Idalou	2,128	5	5	0
Friendswood	34,530	75	57	18	Ingleside	8,927	23	16	7
Friona	3,499	10	6	4	Ingram	1,921	7	6	1
Frisco	113,686	191	135	56	Iowa Park	6,295	18	12	6
Gainesville	16,558	52	38	14	Irving	206,308	503	339	164
Galena Park	10,086	23	17	6	Italy	2,177	5	4	1
Galveston	55,835	164	132	32	Itasca	1,715	3	3	0
Ganado	1,834	3	3	0	Jacinto City	9,797	27	20	7
Garland	221,921	448	323	125	Jacksboro	4,309	10	8	2
Gatesville	15,028	24	16	8	Jacksonville	14,447	36	27	9
Georgetown	53,756	98	68	30	Jamaica Beach	1,086	5	5	0
Giddings	5,373	19	14	5	Jarrell	1,486	3	3	0
Gilmer	5,148	19	15	4	Jasper	7,269	31	23	8
Gladewater	6,316	23	17	6	Jefferson	1,849	7	6	1
Glenn Heights	11,808	25	17	8	Jersey Village	7,268	38	28	10
Godley	1,040	6	6	0	Johnson City	1,712	4	4	0
Gonzales	7,471	21	15	6	Jonestown	2,654	9	8	1
Gorman	1,228	4	4	0	Joshua	6,118	16	11	5
Graham	8,531	23	22	1	Jourdanton	4,445	9	9	0
Granbury	9,153	38	32	6	Junction	2,606	5	5	0
Grand Prairie	166,866	320	211	109	Karnes City	3,294	7	6	1
Grand Saline	3,177	7	7	0	Katy	14,070	60	43	17
Granger	1,382	4	3	1	Kaufman	9,186	25	18	7
Grapeland	1,368	3	2	1	Keene	6,516	16	10	6
Grapevine	51,869	126	91	35	Keller	41,396	81	50	31
Greenville	25,629	73	52	21	Kemah	2,527	20	15	5
Gregory	2,157	3	3	0	Kemp	1,380	5	5	0
Groesbeck	4,295	8	7	1	Kenedy	3,262	8	7	1
Groves	14,122	23	21	2	Kennedale	7,403	27	19	8
Gruver	1,148	1	1	0	Kerens	1,827	5	5	0
Gun Barrel City	6,073	20	15	5	Kermit	5,251	17	10	7
Hale Center	2,140	3	3	0	Kerrville	22,998	66	51	15
Hallettsville	2,441	8	7	1	Kilgore	12,229	51	35	16
Hallsville	3,202	6	5	1	Killeen	122,557	281	207	74
Haltom City	40,855	92	71	21	Kingsville	24,421	61	47	14
Hamlin	1,822	8	4	4	Kirby	8,669	21	13	8
Harker Heights	26,971	59	47	12	Kirbyville	1,922	5	5	0
Harlingen	65,765	169	131	38	Kountze	2,227	6	6	0
Haskell	2,438	4	4	0	Kress	735	1	1	0
Hawk Cove	621	2	2	0	Kyle	33,362	37	25	12
Hawkins	1,533	4	4	0	Lacoste	1,441	1	1	0
Hawley	559	4	4	0	Lacy-Lakeview	5,947	24	16	8
Hearne	4,522	19	13	6	La Feria	7,139	17	13	4
Heath	8,527	17	16	1	Lago Vista	6,637	23	16	7
Hedwig Village	2,348	22	17	5	La Grange	4,751	10	10	0
Helotes	8,263	21	19	2	La Grulla	1,868	5	4	1
Hemphill	1,027	3	3	0	Laguna Vista	4,275	7	7	0
Hempstead	7,974	19	16	3	La Joya	4,977	18	12	6
Henderson	11,652	42	34	8	Lake Dallas	8,333	23	15	8
Hereford	14,304	30	24	6	Lake Jackson	29,037	61	45	16
Hewitt	13,810	30	22	8	Lakeside	1,377	4	4	0
Hickory Creek	4,110	12	12	0	Lakeview, Harris County	6,433	17	13	4
Hidalgo	12,786	44	32	12	Lakeway	11,829	39	28	11
Highland Park	9,357	68	51	17	Lake Worth	4,901	35	26	9
Highland Village	17,496	37	29	8	La Marque	14,199	41	29	12
Hill Country Village	1,140	11	11	0	Lamesa	8,684	25	19	6
Hillsboro	8,968	33	24	9	Lampasas	7,897	26	18	8
Hitchcock	7,204	21	15	6	Lancaster	37,349	66	51	15
Holland	1,136	1	1	0	La Porte	34,304	105	75	30
Holliday	1,768	3	3	0	Laredo	230,674	501	419	82
Hollywood Park	3,335	12	11	1	La Vernia	1,259	7	7	0
Hondo	9,113	21	19	2	La Villa	1,450	5	5	0
Hooks	3,012	7	7	0	Lavon	437	9	8	1

Table 78. Full-Time Law Enforcement Employees by State and City, 2010—*Continued*

(Number)

State/city	Population	Total law enforcement employees	Total officers	Total civilians	State/city	Population	Total law enforcement employees	Total officers	Total civilians
League City	74,776	136	101	35	New Deal	794	2	2	0
Leander	29,325	48	35	13	Nixon	2,277	3	3	0
Leon Valley	11,181	32	24	8	Nocona	3,197	9	5	4
Levelland	12,389	32	22	10	Nolanville	3,062	5	5	0
Lewisville	107,968	190	133	57	Northlake	2,328	9	9	0
Lexington	1,225	5	4	1	North Richland Hills	66,897	157	108	49
Liberty	8,307	25	17	8	Oak Ridge	268	2	2	0
Lindale	5,028	20	14	6	Oak Ridge North	3,517	15	15	0
Linden	2,076	6	5	1	Odessa	101,580	218	171	47
Little Elm	30,854	39	34	5	O'Donnell	882	1	1	0
Littlefield	5,654	20	12	8	Olmos Park	2,338	12	12	0
Live Oak	15,079	43	29	14	Olney	3,234	9	5	4
Livingston	6,199	24	17	7	Olton	2,066	3	3	0
Llano	3,151	10	9	1	Onalaska	1,462	6	6	0
Lockhart	14,468	30	21	9	Orange	19,452	55	41	14
Lockney	1,634	2	2	0	Orange Grove	1,402	4	4	0
Lone Star	1,537	5	4	1	Ore City	1,158	4	4	0
Longview	78,319	225	159	66	Overton	2,379	9	6	3
Lorena	1,704	4	3	1	Ovilla	4,047	10	9	1
Lorenzo	1,149	2	2	0	Oyster Creek	1,273	9	5	4
Los Fresnos	5,704	22	15	7	Paducah	1,188	6	1	5
Lott	660	3	3	0	Palacios	5,005	21	15	6
Lubbock	227,867	513	382	131	Palestine	18,485	46	37	9
Lufkin	34,611	95	73	22	Palmer	2,135	12	9	3
Luling	5,526	22	15	7	Palmhurst	2,732	13	10	3
Lumberton	10,832	18	15	3	Palm Valley	1,252	5	5	0
Lyford	2,509	2	2	0	Pampa	17,108	35	25	10
Lytle	2,941	6	6	0	Panhandle	2,402	4	4	0
Madisonville	4,343	12	11	1	Pantego	2,416	17	12	5
Magnolia	1,298	11	9	2	Paris	25,671	83	61	22
Malakoff	2,328	6	6	0	Parker	3,197	7	7	0
Manor	4,107	16	14	2	Pasadena	145,713	343	265	78
Mansfield	49,677	205	87	118	Pearland	91,679	176	131	45
Manvel	6,874	13	8	5	Pearsall	7,588	14	13	1
Marble Falls	7,765	36	23	13	Pecos	7,611	40	18	22
Marfa	1,884	5	4	1	Penitas	1,192	12	7	5
Marlin	5,650	22	16	6	Perryton	8,494	17	11	6
Marshall	24,038	72	54	18	Pflugerville	45,108	97	74	23
Mart	2,507	4	4	0	Pharr	68,274	163	118	45
Mathis	5,216	14	8	6	Pilot Point	4,550	5	5	0
McAllen	134,623	407	270	137	Pinehurst	2,082	8	6	2
McGregor	4,912	18	12	6	Pittsburg	4,716	12	10	2
McKinney	138,306	199	155	44	Plainview	21,231	40	33	7
Meadows Place	6,529	15	14	1	Plano	278,244	495	332	163
Melissa	5,122	8	7	1	Pleasanton	9,904	25	19	6
Memorial Villages	12,016	39	33	6	Point Comfort	702	1	1	0
Memphis	2,115	4	4	0	Ponder	1,440	1	1	0
Mercedes	15,488	40	33	7	Port Aransas	3,947	22	13	9
Meridian	1,429	3	2	1	Port Arthur	56,424	163	126	37
Merkel	2,619	5	5	0	Port Isabel	5,333	24	17	7
Mesquite	133,964	300	226	74	Portland	16,559	35	24	11
Mexia	6,509	29	19	10	Port Lavaca	11,405	26	20	6
Midland	109,791	240	170	70	Port Neches	12,385	21	18	3
Midlothian	19,220	51	31	20	Poteet	3,714	10	9	1
Miles	746	2	2	0	Poth	2,420	3	3	0
Milford	767	5	5	0	Pottsboro	2,181	7	7	0
Mineola	5,274	18	12	6	Premont	2,768	6	6	0
Mineral Wells	16,799	38	28	10	Presidio	4,736	8	4	4
Missouri City	77,181	107	83	24	Primera	4,339	7	6	1
Mont Belvieu	2,968	15	10	5	Princeton	6,916	12	11	1
Montgomery	613	8	8	0	Progreso	5,702	9	9	0
Morgans Point Resort	4,536	8	7	1	Prosper	11,081	15	10	5
Mount Pleasant	15,309	39	28	11	Queen City	1,529	6	6	0
Muleshoe	4,208	15	8	7	Quinlan	1,429	4	4	0
Munday	1,154	2	2	0	Quitman	2,228	6	6	0
Murphy	17,848	31	21	10	Ralls	1,906	3	3	0
Mustang Ridge	973	3	3	0	Rancho Viejo	1,848	7	7	0
Nacogdoches	33,402	72	57	15	Ranger	2,556	5	5	0
Naples	1,365	4	4	0	Ransom Canyon	1,148	3	3	0
Nash	2,474	9	8	1	Raymondville	9,331	19	12	7
Nassau Bay	3,988	13	12	1	Red Oak	10,785	23	21	2
Navasota	7,662	27	19	8	Refugio	2,627	7	6	1
Nederland	15,875	34	24	10	Reno	3,108	5	4	1
Needville	3,554	6	6	0	Richardson	104,051	230	144	86
New Boston	4,765	12	9	3	Richland Hills	8,196	27	19	8
New Braunfels	57,796	120	98	22	Richmond	13,688	38	28	10

Table 78. Full-Time Law Enforcement Employees by State and City, 2010—*Continued*

(Number)

State/city	Popula-tion	Total law enforce-ment employees	Total officers	Total civilians	State/city	Popula-tion	Total law enforce-ment employees	Total officers	Total civilians
Richwood	3,644	8	8	0	Stanton	2,192	5	5	0
Riesel	1,024	3	3	0	Stephenville	17,646	52	39	13
Rio Grande City	14,215	36	27	9	Stratford	1,887	3	3	0
Rio Hondo	2,141	6	6	0	Sugar Land	83,368	171	146	25
Rising Star	819	1	1	0	Sullivan City	4,530	15	10	5
River Oaks	7,033	24	18	6	Sulphur Springs	15,798	41	30	11
Roanoke	5,269	33	27	6	Sunray	1,946	4	3	1
Robinson	10,796	30	21	9	Sunrise Beach Village	740	4	4	0
Robstown	12,063	33	25	8	Sunset Valley	938	13	13	0
Rockdale	5,913	15	9	6	Surfside Beach	912	6	6	0
Rockport	10,012	26	24	2	Sweeny	3,651	7	7	0
Rockwall	39,232	88	68	20	Sweetwater	10,607	27	22	5
Roma	11,470	35	27	8	Taft	3,282	10	9	1
Roman Forest	4,323	8	8	0	Tahoka	2,419	4	4	0
Ropesville	506	2	2	0	Tatum	1,220	7	6	1
Roscoe	1,230	1	1	0	Taylor	16,383	37	27	10
Rosebud	1,299	3	3	0	Teague	4,853	8	7	1
Rose City	487	1	1	0	Temple	60,444	157	131	26
Rosenberg	35,025	76	59	17	Terrell	20,241	50	33	17
Round Rock	111,099	206	143	63	Terrell Hills	5,298	14	13	1
Rowlett	57,852	120	75	45	Texarkana	37,220	96	86	10
Royse City	10,734	15	14	1	Texas City	44,053	114	89	25
Runaway Bay	1,485	7	7	0	The Colony	46,873	75	52	23
Rusk	5,293	16	14	2	Thorndale	1,308	2	2	0
Sabinal	1,645	6	5	1	Thrall	943	2	2	0
Sachse	20,548	42	29	13	Three Rivers	1,568	7	6	1
Saginaw	21,770	44	37	7	Tioga	956	2	2	0
San Angelo	92,234	180	149	31	Tolar	706	2	1	1
San Antonio	1,392,198	2,949	2,303	646	Tomball	10,272	49	34	15
San Augustine	2,306	7	6	1	Tom Bean	1,038	5	4	1
San Benito	25,400	169	131	38	Tool	2,434	11	7	4
San Diego	4,357	8	7	1	Trenton	716	2	2	0
Sanger	8,350	14	13	1	Trinity	2,641	10	6	4
San Juan	35,326	56	45	11	Trophy Club	8,574	15	14	1
San Marcos	55,100	128	95	33	Troup	2,141	9	8	1
San Saba	2,458	4	4	0	Troy	1,429	4	4	0
Sansom Park Village	4,242	12	7	5	Tulia	4,362	12	7	5
Santa Anna	993	2	2	0	Tye	1,165	4	4	0
Santa Fe	11,915	27	22	5	Tyler	100,125	238	186	52
Santa Rosa	3,155	6	6	0	Universal City	18,511	38	28	10
Schertz	33,451	60	45	15	University Park	25,389	52	39	13
Schulenburg	2,743	8	7	1	Uvalde	16,318	50	38	12
Seabrook	11,663	39	32	7	Valley Mills	1,102	2	2	0
Seadrift	1,460	2	2	0	Valley View	831	1	1	0
Seagoville	12,436	28	21	7	Van	2,518	6	6	0
Seagraves	2,375	6	5	1	Van Alstyne	3,018	14	9	5
Sealy	6,461	20	18	2	Vernon	10,686	32	21	11
Seguin	27,087	65	50	15	Victoria	63,215	143	107	36
Selma	6,049	27	24	3	Vidor	10,611	29	21	8
Seminole	6,269	12	11	1	Waco	127,039	324	244	80
Seven Points	1,336	12	8	4	Wake Village	5,672	7	6	1
Seymour	2,533	8	6	2	Waller	2,205	9	8	1
Shallowater	2,384	5	5	0	Wallis	1,363	4	4	0
Shavano Park	3,372	16	15	1	Watauga	24,494	53	36	17
Shenandoah	2,160	21	20	1	Waxahachie	30,368	70	54	16
Sherman	38,623	83	59	24	Weatherford	28,325	71	56	15
Silsbee	7,128	21	16	5	Webster	10,754	62	47	15
Sinton	5,250	12	11	1	Weimar	2,001	9	8	1
Slaton	5,881	17	12	5	Weslaco	35,244	76	58	18
Smithville	4,603	14	10	4	West	2,710	7	7	0
Snyder	10,519	22	20	2	West Columbia	4,185	15	8	7
Socorro	32,790	29	18	11	West Lake Hills	3,224	20	14	6
Somerville	1,671	5	5	0	West Orange	3,667	11	9	2
Sonora	3,046	7	5	2	Westover Hills	739	19	11	8
Sour Lake	1,777	7	6	1	West Tawakoni	1,621	5	5	0
South Houston	16,345	41	32	9	West University Place	15,703	29	21	8
Southlake	27,811	57	51	6	Westworth	3,167	18	13	5
South Padre Island	2,911	35	26	9	Wharton	9,127	33	23	10
Southside Place	1,664	12	7	5	Whitehouse	8,183	22	15	7
Spearman	3,002	4	4	0	White Oak	6,553	19	15	4
Springtown	3,350	16	11	5	Whitesboro	4,061	13	8	5
Spring Valley	3,982	23	18	5	White Settlement	16,670	46	32	14
Spur	910	6	2	4	Whitewright	1,705	4	4	0
Stafford	19,829	62	45	17	Whitney	2,098	7	6	1
Stagecoach	520	3	3	0	Wichita Falls	100,716	275	192	83
Stamford	2,991	8	7	1	Willis	4,557	16	14	2

Table 78. Full-Time Law Enforcement Employees by State and City, 2010—*Continued*

(Number)

State/city	Population	Total law enforcement employees	Total officers	Total civilians	State/city	Population	Total law enforcement employees	Total officers	Total civilians
Willow Park	4,913	17	12	5	Provo	117,734	140	91	49
Wills Point	3,910	13	10	3	Richfield	7,109	13	11	2
Wilmer	3,656	16	11	5	Riverdale	8,108	22	18	4
Windcrest	5,463	24	17	7	Roosevelt	5,441	13	11	2
Wink	925	1	1	0	Roy	35,502	47	40	7
Winnsboro	3,907	14	9	5	Salem	6,906	10	9	1
Winters	2,498	4	4	0	Salina	2,324	5	4	1
Wolfe City	1,634	2	2	0	Salt Lake City	177,873	579	426	153
Wolfforth	3,701	10	9	1	Sandy	95,173	148	112	36
Woodville	2,262	10	9	1	Santaquin/Genola	9,895	10	10	0
Woodway	8,824	40	27	13	Saratoga Springs	20,490	22	18	4
Wortham	1,106	3	3	0	Smithfield	9,750	9	8	1
Wylie	43,508	52	47	5	South Jordan	56,502	57	49	8
Yoakum	5,398	17	10	7	South Ogden	15,831	27	23	4
Yorktown	2,145	4	4	0	South Salt Lake	21,107	72	62	10
UTAH					Spanish Fork	33,162	33	29	4
Alta	363	8	4	4	Springdale	621	4	3	1
American Fork/Cedar Hills	38,741	39	32	7	Springville	29,784	38	27	11
Big Water	400	1	1	0	St. George	73,086	141	102	39
Blanding	3,201	6	5	1	Stockton	583	1	1	0
Bluffdale	8,246	5	5	0	Sunset	4,844	8	8	0
Bountiful	43,485	51	36	15	Syracuse	23,780	21	19	2
Brian Head	124	5	5	0	Taylorsville City	57,376	64	59	5
Brigham City	18,491	28	24	4	Tooele	30,663	36	32	4
Cedar City	29,290	41	34	7	Tremonton	6,943	12	10	2
Centerville	15,862	20	17	3	Vernal	9,121	24	21	3
Clearfield	27,788	42	29	13	Washington	18,755	23	19	4
Clinton	20,471	17	16	1	Wellington	1,548	3	3	0
Cottonwood Heights	34,381	40	34	6	West Bountiful	5,354	10	9	1
Draper	44,259	41	34	7	West Jordan	104,783	139	98	41
East Carbon	1,223	4	4	0	West Valley	123,089	232	190	42
Enoch	5,275	4	3	1	Willard	1,738	2	2	0
Ephraim	5,349	5	5	0	Woods Cross	8,899	14	12	2
Fairview	1,198	1	1	0	**VERMONT**				
Farmington	17,977	16	13	3	Barre	8,781	25	18	7
Garland	2,037	4	4	0	Barre Town	8,039	7	6	1
Grantsville	9,358	13	10	3	Bellows Falls	2,905	12	8	4
Gunnison	3,020	3	3	0	Bennington	15,086	30	23	7
Harrisville	6,356	10	9	1	Berlin	2,833	7	6	1
Heber	10,101	13	11	2	Bradford	832	1	1	0
Helper	1,840	6	6	0	Brandon	3,873	7	7	0
Hildale	1,904	11	7	4	Brattleboro	11,573	38	26	12
Hurricane	13,587	20	18	2	Bristol	3,783	3	3	0
Ivins	8,061	12	10	2	Burlington	38,699	128	88	40
Kamas	1,535	2	2	0	Castleton	4,649	3	3	0
Kanab	3,714	8	6	2	Chester	3,005	5	4	1
Kaysville	26,200	22	20	2	Colchester	17,434	32	24	8
La Verkin	4,342	4	4	0	Dover	1,444	6	5	1
Layton	65,610	105	76	29	Essex	19,810	32	26	6
Lehi	52,162	41	37	4	Fair Haven	2,921	4	4	0
Lindon	11,047	15	14	1	Hardwick	3,195	8	7	1
Logan	48,819	94	61	33	Hartford	10,753	31	22	9
Lone Peak	27,692	20	18	2	Hinesburg	4,660	5	5	0
Mantua	749	1	1	0	Ludlow	2,661	9	5	4
Mapleton	8,495	9	8	1	Lyndonville	1,205	3	3	0
Midvale	28,739	57	47	10	Manchester	4,293	12	8	4
Minersville	807	1	1	0	Middlebury	8,340	16	14	2
Moab	5,032	18	13	5	Milton	10,984	13	12	1
Monticello	1,975	3	3	0	Montpelier	7,708	23	15	8
Moroni	1,312	2	2	0	Morristown	5,892	9	9	0
Mount Pleasant	2,784	4	4	0	Newport	5,159	13	11	2
Murray	45,305	94	79	15	Northfield	5,751	7	6	1
Naples	1,750	7	6	1	Norwich	3,527	4	3	1
Nephi	5,438	10	8	2	Randolph	5,080	7	7	0
North Ogden	17,721	20	17	3	Richmond	4,169	3	3	0
North Park	12,554	10	9	1	Rutland	16,643	46	36	10
North Salt Lake	14,475	18	16	2	Shelburne	7,149	19	10	9
Ogden	81,431	162	131	31	South Burlington	17,915	45	39	6
Orem	93,580	122	88	34	Springfield	8,577	22	17	5
Park City	7,957	41	30	11	St. Albans	7,235	31	21	10
Parowan	2,572	4	4	0	St. Johnsbury	7,367	16	11	5
Payson	18,200	19	17	2	Stowe	5,238	12	11	1
Perry	4,029	5	5	0	Swanton	6,493	6	5	1
Pleasant Grove	35,589	33	25	8	Thetford	2,812	3	3	0
Pleasant View	7,182	9	8	1	Vergennes	2,675	5	5	0
Price	7,979	20	17	3	Vernon	2,047	3	2	1

Table 78. Full-Time Law Enforcement Employees by State and City, 2010—*Continued*

(Number)

State/city	Popula-tion	Total law enforce-ment employees	Total officers	Total civilians	State/city	Popula-tion	Total law enforce-ment employees	Total officers	Total civilians
Waterbury	5,416	4	4	0	Hillsville	2,610	12	11	1
Weathersfield	2,875	1	1	0	Honaker	1,470	3	2	1
Williston	8,521	15	11	4	Hopewell	23,292	69	57	12
Wilmington	2,368	7	6	1	Hurt	1,206	2	2	0
Windsor	3,596	8	7	1	Independence	876	2	2	0
Winhall	801	7	6	1	Jonesville	961	3	3	0
Winooski	6,259	19	13	6	Kenbridge	1,253	5	5	0
Woodstock	3,134	7	6	1	Kilmarnock	1,266	4	4	0
VIRGINIA					La Crosse	583	1	1	0
Abingdon	8,059	27	25	2	Lawrenceville	1,343	6	6	0
Alexandria	152,801	433	308	125	Lebanon	3,219	12	11	1
Altavista	3,340	14	13	1	Leesburg	42,561	96	80	16
Amherst	2,207	4	4	0	Lexington	6,934	19	17	2
Appalachia	1,719	7	6	1	Louisa	1,591	5	5	0
Ashland	7,188	27	24	3	Luray	4,812	13	11	2
Bedford	6,377	23	20	3	Lynchburg	75,137	180	157	23
Berryville	3,215	10	9	1	Manassas	36,822	114	83	31
Big Stone Gap	5,653	15	13	2	Manassas Park	12,275	42	30	12
Blacksburg	43,355	77	62	15	Marion	5,907	21	19	2
Blackstone	3,564	16	12	4	Martinsville	14,618	60	54	6
Bluefield	5,164	20	15	5	Middleburg	1,017	5	5	0
Bridgewater	5,464	9	9	0	Middletown	1,169	2	2	0
Bristol	17,794	71	51	20	Mount Jackson	2,036	4	4	0
Broadway	3,343	4	4	0	Narrows	2,160	4	4	0
Brookneal	1,242	1	1	0	New Market	1,878	5	5	0
Buena Vista	6,232	16	14	2	Newport News	195,225	542	412	130
Burkeville	472	1	1	0	Norfolk	234,100	842	759	83
Cape Charles	1,517	5	5	0	Norton	3,710	23	17	6
Cedar Bluff	1,046	2	2	0	Onancock	1,378	4	4	0
Charlottesville	42,590	143	115	28	Onley	472	3	3	0
Chase City	2,287	10	8	2	Orange	4,749	17	15	2
Chatham	2,381	4	4	0	Parksley	788	3	3	0
Chesapeake	225,627	484	365	119	Pearisburg	2,773	8	7	1
Chilhowie	1,732	6	6	0	Pembroke	1,176	2	2	0
Chincoteague	4,331	14	10	4	Pennington Gap	1,761	6	6	0
Christiansburg	19,997	71	55	16	Petersburg	33,048	161	115	46
Clarksville	1,238	8	7	1	Pocahontas	418	1	1	0
Clifton Forge	3,907	12	10	2	Poquoson	11,859	23	22	1
Clintwood	1,493	4	4	0	Portsmouth	99,576	329	236	93
Coeburn	1,982	7	7	0	Pound	1,076	4	4	0
Colonial Beach	3,880	15	10	5	Pulaski	8,918	37	27	10
Colonial Heights	17,983	52	48	4	Purcellville	5,533	15	14	1
Covington	6,157	26	16	10	Quantico	4,531	2	2	0
Crewe	2,268	3	3	0	Radford	16,277	46	33	13
Culpeper	14,633	46	39	7	Remington	694	1	1	0
Damascus	1,079	5	5	0	Rich Creek	684	1	1	0
Danville	44,192	136	126	10	Richlands	5,647	22	16	6
Dayton	1,366	8	7	1	Richmond	205,883	893	729	164
Dublin	2,141	10	9	1	Roanoke	94,795	299	251	48
Dumfries	4,974	10	7	3	Rocky Mount	4,541	18	16	2
Edinburg	910	2	2	0	Rural Retreat	1,346	1	1	0
Elkton	2,650	7	6	1	Salem	25,623	93	65	28
Emporia	5,653	36	26	10	Saltville	2,192	5	5	0
Exmore	1,350	7	7	0	Shenandoah	2,274	5	5	0
Fairfax City	25,082	79	62	17	Smithfield	7,173	25	22	3
Falls Church	12,171	40	32	8	South Boston	7,770	31	29	2
Farmville	7,778	28	27	1	South Hill	4,528	22	20	2
Franklin	8,902	43	30	13	Stanley	1,560	4	4	0
Fredericksburg	23,704	95	70	25	Staunton	23,979	58	44	14
Fries	537	1	1	0	Stephens City	1,526	4	4	0
Front Royal	14,725	45	35	10	St. Paul	974	5	5	0
Galax	6,908	38	24	14	Strasburg	4,426	22	20	2
Gate City	2,009	4	4	0	Suffolk	86,226	238	185	53
Glade Spring	1,547	3	3	0	Tappahannock	2,219	10	9	1
Glasgow	991	1	1	0	Tazewell	4,282	17	15	2
Glen Lyn	165	1	1	0	Timberville	2,022	4	4	0
Gordonsville	1,745	6	6	0	Victoria	1,693	7	6	1
Gretna	1,203	4	4	0	Vienna	15,343	50	39	11
Grottoes	2,212	6	5	1	Vinton	7,851	24	22	2
Grundy	918	5	5	0	Virginia Beach	435,873	938	775	163
Halifax	1,238	5	5	0	Warrenton	9,367	19	17	2
Hampton	144,545	340	285	55	Warsaw	1,321	3	3	0
Harrisonburg	45,804	96	81	15	Waverly	2,128	12	6	6
Haymarket	1,298	6	5	1	Waynesboro	22,606	53	43	10
Haysi	301	2	2	0	Weber City	1,305	5	5	0
Herndon	22,751	71	55	16	West Point	3,198	8	7	1

Table 78.   Full-Time Law Enforcement Employees by State and City, 2010—*Continued*

(Number)

State/city	Population	Total law enforcement employees	Total officers	Total civilians	State/city	Population	Total law enforcement employees	Total officers	Total civilians
White Stone	327	1	1	0	Kennewick	68,501	105	87	18
Williamsburg	12,854	37	34	3	Kent	85,768	182	131	51
Winchester	26,698	100	76	24	Kettle Falls	1,421	5	4	1
Wise	3,235	14	13	1	Kirkland	48,708	107	80	27
Woodstock	4,340	15	14	1	Kittitas	1,129	2	2	0
Wytheville	8,298	42	28	14	La Center	2,676	11	9	2
WASHINGTON					Lacey	43,130	67	56	11
Aberdeen	15,917	47	34	13	Lake Forest Park	12,551	22	18	4
Airway Heights	5,618	13	13	0	Lake Stevens	14,666	33	28	5
Algona	2,838	9	8	1	Lakewood	57,459	118	102	16
Anacortes	17,132	30	23	7	Langley	1,094	4	4	0
Arlington	17,749	30	25	5	Liberty Lake	8,300	10	9	1
Asotin	1,129	1	1	0	Long Beach	1,361	7	6	1
Auburn	64,139	125	95	30	Longview	36,550	64	52	12
Bainbridge Island	22,075	27	21	6	Lynden	12,377	18	14	4
Battle Ground	18,076	31	25	6	Lynnwood	33,929	114	80	34
Bellevue	127,735	214	173	41	Mabton	2,220	2	2	0
Bellingham	81,139	154	110	44	Maple Valley	21,797	17	13	4
Black Diamond	4,090	11	10	1	Marysville	35,810	84	53	31
Blaine	5,195	15	11	4	Mattawa	3,272	4	4	0
Bonney Lake	17,760	37	29	8	McCleary	1,628	3	3	0
Bothell	33,094	84	58	26	Medina	3,704	9	8	1
Bremerton	34,897	72	60	12	Mercer Island	24,715	35	32	3
Brewster	2,123	8	6	2	Mill Creek	17,697	30	23	7
Brier	6,393	8	6	2	Milton	6,086	12	11	1
Buckley	5,562	19	9	10	Monroe	17,612	41	31	10
Burien	31,831	67	48	19	Montesano	3,643	9	7	2
Burlington	8,883	29	24	5	Morton	1,084	4	3	1
Camas	18,850	29	25	4	Moses Lake	20,559	42	34	8
Castle Rock	2,114	6	5	1	Mossyrock	712	2	2	0
Centralia	15,736	40	33	7	Mountlake Terrace	19,978	38	28	10
Chehalis	7,409	22	17	5	Mount Vernon	32,630	51	40	11
Cheney	11,030	20	14	6	Moxee	2,698	4	4	0
Chewelah	2,314	6	5	1	Mukilteo	21,177	32	28	4
Clarkston	7,135	15	14	1	Napavine	1,957	2	2	0
Cle Elum	3,516	10	8	2	Newcastle	10,240	10	8	2
Clyde Hill	2,767	9	8	1	Normandy Park	6,342	12	11	1
Colfax	2,804	7	6	1	North Bend	4,683	9	7	2
College Place	9,186	13	10	3	Oak Harbor	22,873	40	27	13
Colton	403	1	1	0	Ocean Shores	5,257	12	11	1
Colville	4,889	12	10	2	Odessa	895	2	2	0
Connell	3,484	6	6	0	Olympia	46,264	89	62	27
Cosmopolis	1,660	4	3	1	Omak	4,734	14	11	3
Coulee City	650	1	1	0	Oroville	1,662	6	5	1
Coulee Dam	1,048	7	7	0	Orting	6,610	10	9	1
Coupeville	1,878	5	5	0	Othello	6,807	21	15	6
Covington	18,933	20	15	5	Pacific	6,072	13	11	2
Des Moines	29,134	49	37	12	Palouse	944	3	3	0
Dupont	8,142	10	8	2	Pasco	61,747	77	65	12
Duvall	6,349	17	15	2	Port Angeles	18,901	57	31	26
East Wenatchee	12,620	25	22	3	Port Orchard	8,013	23	21	2
Eatonville	2,608	6	5	1	Port Townsend	9,188	19	15	4
Edgewood	9,885	6	6	0	Poulsbo	8,386	20	16	4
Edmonds	40,769	63	54	9	Prosser	5,303	17	11	6
Ellensburg	17,553	37	27	10	Pullman	27,806	39	28	11
Elma	3,103	8	7	1	Puyallup	37,964	77	57	20
Enumclaw	10,787	28	16	12	Quincy	6,255	16	14	2
Ephrata	7,620	20	16	4	Raymond	2,831	7	6	1
Everett	99,387	233	193	40	Reardan	586	1	1	0
Everson	2,254	6	6	0	Redmond	52,972	123	83	40
Federal Way	85,623	160	130	30	Renton	62,968	163	122	41
Ferndale	11,962	21	19	2	Republic	955	4	3	1
Fife	8,607	54	29	25	Richland	48,335	70	59	11
Fircrest	6,299	9	9	0	Ridgefield	4,739	8	7	1
Forks	3,345	14	7	7	Ritzville	1,759	4	4	0
Gig Harbor	7,289	18	16	2	Rosalia	593	1	1	0
Goldendale	3,723	10	9	1	Roy	802	2	2	0
Grand Coulee	1,969	8	8	0	Royal City	2,038	3	3	0
Grandview	9,614	24	18	6	Ruston	747	3	3	0
Granger	3,148	6	6	0	Sammamish	43,048	31	24	7
Granite Falls	3,277	8	7	1	SeaTac	26,667	60	43	17
Hoquiam	8,749	21	19	2	Seattle	620,195	1,861	1,344	517
Issaquah	25,784	59	31	28	Sedro Woolley	11,221	17	14	3
Kalama	2,292	5	5	0	Selah	7,361	15	14	1
Kelso	12,141	32	28	4	Sequim	5,978	21	18	3
Kenmore	20,935	19	14	5	Shelton	9,309	22	19	3

Table 78.   Full-Time Law Enforcement Employees by State and City, 2010—*Continued*

(Number)

State/city	Population	Total law enforcement employees	Total officers	Total civilians	State/city	Population	Total law enforcement employees	Total officers	Total civilians
Shoreline	52,567	69	50	19	East Bank	905	3	3	0
Snohomish	9,223	24	19	5	Eleanor	1,581	2	2	0
Snoqualmie	10,246	17	14	3	Elkins	7,114	11	8	3
Soap Lake	1,880	4	4	0	Fairmont	19,332	41	35	6
South Bend	1,799	5	4	1	Fairview	455	1	1	0
Spokane	203,272	400	290	110	Farmington	395	1	1	0
Spokane Valley	87,780	107	104	3	Fayetteville	2,710	12	11	1
Springdale	277	1	1	0	Follansbee	2,861	7	7	0
Stanwood	5,519	13	11	2	Fort Gay	813	3	3	0
Steilacoom	6,115	14	13	1	Gary	729	2	2	0
Sumas	1,295	6	6	0	Gassaway	864	2	2	0
Sumner	9,940	32	19	13	Gauley Bridge	690	4	3	1
Sunnyside	15,297	49	27	22	Gilbert	393	4	4	0
Tacoma	199,595	419	377	42	Glasgow	741	2	2	0
Tenino	2,309	7	6	1	Glen Dale	1,389	8	5	3
Tieton	1,175	2	2	0	Glenville	1,454	4	3	1
Toledo	688	2	2	0	Grafton	5,463	7	6	1
Tonasket	941	5	4	1	Grantsville	529	1	1	0
Toppenish	9,253	27	16	11	Grant Town	647	1	1	0
Tukwila	17,337	81	66	15	Granville	854	14	13	1
Tumwater	16,375	29	24	5	Hamlin	1,094	4	4	0
Twisp	900	2	2	0	Handley	346	1	1	0
Union Gap	5,782	20	17	3	Harpers Ferry/Bolivar	1,414	5	4	1
University Place	30,655	16	15	1	Harrisville	1,827	1	1	0
Vader	616	1	1	0	Hinton	2,545	8	8	0
Vancouver	167,264	209	188	21	Huntington	49,703	113	106	7
Walla Walla	31,265	75	45	30	Hurricane	6,463	17	15	2
Wapato	4,570	18	11	7	Iaeger	287	1	1	0
Warden	2,651	6	4	2	Kenova	3,297	10	7	3
Washougal	14,405	21	19	2	Kermit	239	1	1	0
Wenatchee	30,287	51	40	11	Keyser	5,349	17	12	5
Westport	2,668	9	7	2	Keystone	356	1	1	0
West Richland	11,840	15	12	3	Kimball	328	3	3	0
White Salmon	2,420	5	4	1	Kingwood	3,097	3	3	0
Wilbur	859	2	2	0	Lewisburg	3,545	13	11	2
Winlock	1,235	2	2	0	Logan	1,500	12	8	4
Winthrop	397	3	3	0	Lumberport	985	2	2	0
Woodinville	11,558	17	13	4	Mabscott	1,350	3	2	1
Woodland	5,476	12	10	2	Madison	2,615	6	5	1
Yakima	85,802	180	137	43	Man	691	3	3	0
Yelm	6,642	15	13	2	Mannington	2,118	4	4	0
Zillah	2,852	9	7	2	Marmet	1,628	5	5	0
WEST VIRGINIA					Martinsburg	17,654	57	44	13
Alderson	1,079	1	1	0	Mason	1,055	3	3	0
Anmoore	790	2	2	0	Matewan	481	1	1	0
Ansted	1,598	1	1	0	Matoaka	308	1	1	0
Athens	1,200	1	1	0	McMechen	1,715	3	3	0
Barboursville	3,652	20	18	2	Milton	2,489	3	3	0
Barrackville	1,315	1	1	0	Monongah	974	2	2	0
Bayard	284	1	1	0	Montgomery	1,943	7	5	2
Beckley	16,990	68	49	19	Moorefield	2,508	7	6	1
Belington	1,843	2	2	0	Morgantown	31,247	73	63	10
Belle	1,164	4	4	0	Moundsville	9,121	22	18	4
Benwood	1,424	12	6	6	Mount Hope	1,376	6	5	1
Berkeley Springs	699	4	3	1	Mullens	1,556	6	6	0
Bethlehem	2,504	4	4	0	New Cumberland	987	4	3	1
Bluefield	11,222	28	20	8	New Haven	1,531	2	2	0
Bradshaw	244	1	1	0	New Martinsville	5,592	14	11	3
Bramwell	420	1	1	0	Nitro	6,836	17	16	1
Bridgeport	8,121	30	27	3	Northfork	409	1	1	0
Buckhannon	5,601	10	10	0	Nutter Fort	1,648	6	6	0
Burnsville	462	2	2	0	Oak Hill	7,231	15	13	2
Cameron	1,073	5	3	2	Oceana	1,401	5	5	0
Capon Bridge	294	1	1	0	Paden City	2,575	4	3	1
Ceredo	1,608	9	6	3	Parkersburg	32,001	70	61	9
Chapmanville	1,120	5	5	0	Parsons	1,378	1	1	0
Charleston	50,822	201	175	26	Paw Paw	491	2	2	0
Charles Town	5,183	18	15	3	Pennsboro	1,155	1	1	0
Chesapeake	1,564	3	3	0	Petersburg	2,821	6	3	3
Chester	2,325	7	6	1	Philippi	2,833	7	7	0
Clarksburg	16,652	49	44	5	Piedmont	934	1	1	0
Clendenin	1,063	4	4	0	Pineville	648	3	3	0
Danville	557	2	2	0	Point Pleasant	4,445	10	9	1
Delbarton	466	2	2	0	Pratt	539	1	1	0
Dunbar	7,718	19	16	3	Princeton	6,354	24	20	4

Table 78. Full-Time Law Enforcement Employees by State and City, 2010—*Continued*

(Number)

State/city	Population	Total law enforcement employees	Total officers	Total civilians	State/city	Population	Total law enforcement employees	Total officers	Total civilians
Rainelle	1,478	3	2	1	Brookfield	39,262	82	65	17
Ranson	5,078	14	13	1	Brookfield Township	6,202	13	12	1
Ravenswood	3,958	6	5	1	Brown Deer	12,111	34	28	6
Rhodell	231	2	2	0	Burlington	10,628	28	22	6
Richwood	2,323	5	5	0	Burlington Town	6,616	10	9	1
Ridgeley	694	3	3	0	Butler	1,777	8	7	1
Ripley	3,264	10	9	1	Caledonia	26,154	58	43	15
Rivesville	921	1	1	0	Campbellsport	1,947	2	2	0
Romney	1,936	4	3	1	Campbell Township	4,575	5	5	0
Ronceverte	1,520	6	6	0	Cashton	1,052	2	2	0
Rowlesburg	621	2	2	0	Cedarburg	11,079	26	19	7
Salem	2,078	4	3	1	Chenequa	595	8	8	0
Shepherdstown	1,173	6	4	2	Chetek	2,144	6	5	1
Shinnston	2,273	8	8	0	Chilton	3,678	6	6	0
Sistersville	1,389	4	4	0	Chippewa Falls	12,862	31	24	7
Smithers	844	5	4	1	Cleveland	1,374	3	2	1
Sophia	1,238	4	4	0	Clinton	2,238	6	6	0
South Charleston	12,691	45	40	5	Clintonville	4,289	15	11	4
Spencer	2,114	5	5	0	Colby-Abbotsford	3,606	7	6	1
St. Albans	11,117	21	20	1	Columbus	4,967	12	11	1
Star City	1,764	5	5	0	Combined Locks	3,327	5	5	0
St. Marys	1,925	5	4	1	Coon Valley	694	1	1	0
Stonewood	1,892	2	2	0	Cornell	1,398	2	2	0
Summersville	3,351	15	14	1	Cottage Grove	6,223	12	11	1
Sutton	971	1	1	0	Crandon	1,806	4	3	1
Sylvester	516	1	1	0	Cross Plains	3,664	6	5	1
Terra Alta	1,537	1	1	0	Cuba City	1,967	4	3	1
Triadelphia	813	1	1	0	Cudahy	19,048	39	28	11
Vienna	10,715	22	17	5	Cumberland	2,242	4	4	0
War	655	2	2	0	Darien	1,615	5	5	0
Wardensville	261	2	2	0	Darlington	2,229	5	5	0
Webster Springs	753	2	2	0	DeForest	9,260	20	17	3
Weirton	18,717	39	36	3	Delafield	6,970	17	15	2
Welch	2,174	10	9	1	Delavan	8,309	25	19	6
Wellsburg	2,585	6	6	0	Delavan Town	4,754	12	11	1
West Logan	390	1	1	0	Denmark	2,237	2	2	0
Weston	4,362	8	6	2	De Pere	23,724	38	33	5
Westover	4,238	9	9	0	Dodgeville	4,511	10	9	1
West Union	785	1	1	0	Durand	1,829	3	3	0
Wheeling	29,054	83	80	3	Eagle River	1,644	6	6	0
White Sulphur Springs	2,296	7	6	1	Eagle Village	1,875	3	3	0
Williamson	3,039	9	7	2	East Troy	4,506	7	7	0
Williamstown	3,044	7	6	1	Eau Claire	66,737	132	96	36
Winfield	2,088	2	2	0	Edgar	1,461	1	1	0
WISCONSIN					Edgerton	5,384	11	10	1
Adams	1,707	4	4	0	Eleva	630	1	1	0
Albany	1,105	3	3	0	Elkhart Lake	1,248	3	3	0
Algoma	3,130	6	6	0	Elkhorn	9,314	19	16	3
Altoona	6,658	13	12	1	Elk Mound	806	1	1	0
Amery	2,744	8	7	1	Ellsworth	3,116	6	5	1
Antigo	7,846	19	16	3	Elm Grove	6,016	25	18	7
Appleton	70,975	135	109	26	Elroy	1,419	2	2	0
Arcadia	2,325	5	5	0	Evansville	5,081	10	9	1
Ashland	7,886	21	19	2	Everest	16,425	28	25	3
Ashwaubenon	17,601	54	47	7	Fall Creek	1,317	2	2	0
Athens	1,047	1	1	0	Fall River	1,591	2	2	0
Avoca	578	1	1	0	Fennimore	2,181	5	5	0
Bangor	1,392	2	2	0	Fitchburg	24,537	53	41	12
Baraboo	11,205	34	28	6	Fond du Lac	42,369	79	73	6
Barron	3,078	6	6	0	Fontana	1,837	7	6	1
Bayfield	545	3	3	0	Fort Atkinson	11,961	26	20	6
Bayside	4,455	19	12	7	Fountain City	945	1	1	0
Beaver Dam	15,258	35	30	5	Fox Lake	1,453	2	2	0
Belleville	2,378	5	5	0	Fox Point	6,861	18	17	1
Beloit	36,651	88	76	12	Fox Valley Metro	17,757	28	25	3
Beloit Town	7,509	10	9	1	Franklin	37,832	72	57	15
Berlin	4,932	13	12	1	Frederic	1,181	2	2	0
Big Bend	1,326	3	3	0	Geneva Town	4,692	7	6	1
Black River Falls	3,382	7	6	1	Genoa City	2,956	6	5	1
Blair	1,226	2	2	0	Germantown	19,787	42	31	11
Blanchardville	732	97	40	57	Gillett	1,176	4	4	0
Bloomer	3,317	8	7	1	Glendale	13,029	47	43	4
Bloomfield	6,382	7	7	0	Grafton	11,666	29	22	7
Boscobel	3,148	6	6	0	Grand Chute	21,194	33	29	4
Brillion	2,804	7	6	1	Grand Rapids	7,640	6	4	2
Brodhead	3,092	12	8	4	Grantsburg	1,384	3	3	0

Table 78. Full-Time Law Enforcement Employees by State and City, 2010—*Continued*

(Number)

State/city	Popula-tion	Total law enforce-ment employees	Total officers	Total civilians	State/city	Popula-tion	Total law enforce-ment employees	Total officers	Total civilians
Green Bay	101,320	220	180	40	New Berlin	39,385	85	67	18
Greendale	14,102	37	29	8	New Glarus	2,057	3	3	0
Greenfield	36,580	80	58	22	New Holstein	3,082	7	6	1
Green Lake	1,120	4	4	0	New Lisbon	2,462	4	4	0
Hales Corners	7,775	20	17	3	New London	6,837	18	16	2
Hartford	14,507	29	25	4	New Richmond	8,541	18	16	2
Hartland	8,772	18	16	2	Niagara	1,683	4	4	0
Hayward	2,260	9	8	1	North Fond du Lac	5,108	13	12	1
Hazel Green	1,097	2	2	0	North Hudson	3,840	6	5	1
Highland	817	1	1	0	Oak Creek	34,572	85	60	25
Hillsboro	1,315	2	2	0	Oconomowoc	14,984	28	22	6
Hobart-Lawrence	10,975	6	5	1	Oconomowoc Town	8,300	13	11	2
Holmen	8,644	10	9	1	Oconto	4,512	8	8	0
Horicon	3,499	11	9	2	Oconto Falls	2,755	5	5	0
Hortonville	2,833	6	5	1	Omro	3,441	7	6	1
Hudson	12,832	26	23	3	Onalaska	17,367	29	26	3
Hurley	1,507	7	6	1	Oregon	9,715	18	16	2
Independence	1,222	2	2	0	Osceola	2,712	6	5	1
Iron Ridge	992	1	1	0	Oshkosh	64,428	111	93	18
Jackson	6,686	12	11	1	Osseo	1,579	4	4	0
Janesville	63,651	110	97	13	Oxford	538	18	18	0
Jefferson	7,950	17	14	3	Palmyra	1,740	5	5	0
Juneau	2,646	5	4	1	Park Falls	2,238	8	7	1
Kaukauna	15,948	26	24	2	Pepin	903	1	1	0
Kendall	458	2	2	0	Peshtigo	3,248	7	6	1
Kenosha	98,961	208	199	9	Pewaukee Village	8,998	20	18	2
Kewaskum	4,268	7	7	0	Phillips	1,465	5	5	0
Kewaunee	2,740	6	6	0	Plainfield	836	2	2	0
Kiel	3,516	8	7	1	Platteville	10,322	24	18	6
Kohler	1,949	8	7	1	Pleasant Prairie	20,314	30	28	2
Kronenwetter	7,109	7	6	1	Plover	12,429	22	19	3
La Crosse	51,184	107	89	18	Plymouth	8,344	16	16	0
Ladysmith	3,209	11	10	1	Portage	9,815	29	22	7
Lake Delton	2,923	20	18	2	Port Washington	11,242	24	19	5
Lake Geneva	7,608	31	22	9	Poynette	2,504	5	4	1
Lake Hallie	6,190	7	6	1	Prairie du Chien	5,606	14	13	1
Lancaster	3,770	7	7	0	Prescott	3,933	8	7	1
Lodi	2,909	6	5	1	Princeton	1,378	5	5	0
Lomira	2,422	2	2	0	Pulaski	3,554	7	6	1
Luxemburg	2,269	2	2	0	Racine	82,059	260	199	61
Madison	238,224	548	443	105	Readstown	372	1	1	0
Manitowoc	32,640	75	65	10	Reedsburg	8,761	28	20	8
Maple Bluff	1,380	6	6	0	Rhinelander	7,471	20	17	3
Marathon City	1,539	2	2	0	Rice Lake	8,356	20	18	2
Marinette	10,395	28	23	5	Richland Center	4,969	13	11	2
Marion	1,165	3	3	0	Ripon	7,481	20	14	6
Markesan	1,261	3	3	0	River Falls	14,745	24	22	2
Marshall Village	3,800	8	8	0	River Hills	1,684	12	12	0
Marshfield	18,819	47	39	8	Rome Town	2,972	7	6	1
Mauston	4,233	9	8	1	Rosendale	1,022	1	1	0
Mayville	5,302	10	8	2	Rothschild	5,330	12	10	2
McFarland	8,040	15	13	2	Sauk Prairie	4,190	16	14	2
Medford	3,995	10	9	1	Saukville	4,386	13	11	2
Menasha	17,052	37	30	7	Seymour	3,396	6	6	0
Menomonee Falls	34,836	81	59	22	Shawano	8,875	21	19	2
Menomonie	15,846	37	28	9	Sheboygan	47,516	102	76	26
Mequon	23,569	43	35	8	Sheboygan Falls	7,911	16	14	2
Merrill	9,433	25	22	3	Shiocton	943	1	1	0
Middleton	17,444	44	35	9	Shorewood	13,285	30	25	5
Milton	5,809	11	9	2	Shorewood Hills	1,675	7	6	1
Milwaukee	605,921	2,663	1,936	727	Silver Lake	2,526	5	4	1
Mineral Point	2,512	6	6	0	Siren	742	3	3	0
Minocqua	4,914	16	11	5	Slinger	4,913	10	9	1
Mishicot	1,367	1	1	0	Somerset	2,433	6	5	1
Mondovi	2,518	4	4	0	South Milwaukee	21,366	39	33	6
Monona	8,588	25	20	5	Sparta	9,107	20	18	2
Monroe	10,482	35	26	9	Spencer	1,812	3	3	0
Montello	1,411	20	18	2	Spooner	726	7	6	1
Mosinee	4,037	8	7	1	Spring Green	1,457	4	3	1
Mount Horeb	7,120	11	10	1	Stanley	3,575	4	4	0
Mount Pleasant	26,991	53	40	13	St. Croix Falls	2,111	5	5	0
Mukwonago	7,209	21	14	7	Stevens Point	25,235	57	44	13
Muskego	23,324	46	36	10	St. Francis	9,985	26	21	5
Neenah	25,641	49	40	9	Stoughton	13,184	26	20	6
Neillsville	2,517	7	6	1	Strum	1,001	9	9	0
Neshkoro	427	2	2	0	Sturgeon Bay	8,916	23	21	2

Table 78.　Full-Time Law Enforcement Employees by State and City, 2010—*Continued*

(Number)

State/city	Popula-tion	Total law enforce-ment employees	Total officers	Total civilians	State/city	Popula-tion	Total law enforce-ment employees	Total officers	Total civilians
Sturtevant	7,132	10	9	1	**WYOMING**				
Summit	5,140	8	8	0	Afton	1,960	4	4	0
Sun Prairie	30,122	73	51	22	Alpine	882	1	1	0
Superior	26,726	64	58	6	Basin	1,328	4	4	0
Theresa	1,284	2	2	0	Buffalo	5,123	21	12	9
Thiensville	3,187	8	7	1	Casper	56,813	102	88	14
Three Lakes	2,229	97	40	57	Cheyenne	59,361	115	96	19
Tomah	8,908	22	20	2	Cody	9,730	24	21	3
Tomahawk	3,580	8	7	1	Diamondville	693	5	3	2
Town of East Troy	3,872	6	6	0	Douglas	6,468	24	16	8
Town of Madison	6,048	19	17	2	Evanston	12,311	34	28	6
Town of Menasha	17,512	30	24	6	Evansville	2,594	11	9	2
Trempealeau	1,500	2	2	0	Gillette	30,473	83	53	30
Twin Lakes	5,726	17	13	4	Glenrock	2,552	13	7	6
Two Rivers	11,597	28	25	3	Green River	12,793	40	30	10
Valders	966	1	1	0	Greybull	1,816	6	5	1
Verona	11,715	19	17	2	Guernsey	1,084	4	4	0
Viroqua	4,288	11	9	2	Hanna	893	3	3	0
Walworth	2,651	7	6	1	Hulett	538	2	2	0
Washburn	2,051	5	5	0	Jackson	10,301	26	21	5
Waterloo	3,226	9	8	1	Kemmerer	2,563	8	7	1
Watertown	23,069	52	38	14	La Barge	501	3	3	0
Waukesha	68,680	145	111	34	Lander	7,622	19	18	1
Waunakee	11,920	19	17	2	Laramie	29,742	76	49	27
Waupaca	5,868	15	14	1	Lovell	2,381	10	6	4
Waupun	10,564	20	18	2	Lusk	1,465	4	4	0
Wausau	38,429	74	68	6	Mills	3,707	14	12	2
Wautoma	2,047	7	6	1	Moorcroft	961	5	4	1
Wauwatosa	45,229	122	94	28	Newcastle	3,505	16	8	8
West Allis	60,502	150	127	23	Pine Bluffs	1,198	9	3	6
West Bend	30,362	75	56	19	Powell	5,953	22	15	7
Westby	2,137	3	3	0	Rawlins	8,993	29	19	10
Westfield	1,158	3	3	0	Riverton	10,613	35	24	11
West Milwaukee	4,038	23	18	5	Rock Springs	21,689	67	48	19
West Salem	4,889	7	6	1	Saratoga	1,829	10	5	5
Whitefish Bay	13,695	27	24	3	Sheridan	18,070	50	29	21
Whitehall	1,575	4	4	0	Sundance	1,387	4	4	0
Whitewater	14,211	35	24	11	Thermopolis	3,002	13	7	6
Williams Bay	2,630	8	7	1	Torrington	5,816	22	16	6
Winneconne	2,520	6	5	1	Wheatland	3,290	8	7	1
Wisconsin Dells	2,432	17	12	5	Worland	5,157	11	11	0
Wisconsin Rapids	17,396	42	37	5					
Woodruff	2,000	6	5	1					

Table 79.   Full-Time Law Enforcement Employees, by State and University or College, 2010

(Number)

State, University/College	Campus	Student enrollment[1]	Total law enforcement employees	Total officers	Total civilians
ALABAMA					
Alabama State University		5,564	30	20	10
Auburn University:	Montgomery	5,567	18	11	7
Calhoun Community College[2]			8	7	1
George C. Wallace State Community College		4,653	2	2	0
Jacksonville State University		9,351	19	14	5
Troy University		29,328	15	11	4
University of Alabama:	Birmingham	16,874	162	85	77
	Huntsville	7,681	20	13	7
	Tuscaloosa	28,699	75	63	12
University of Montevallo		3,044	18	10	8
University of North Alabama		7,194	15	13	2
University of South Alabama		14,522	44	30	14
University of West Alabama		5,157	9	6	3
ALASKA					
University of Alaska:	Anchorage	17,276	21	15	6
	Fairbanks	9,137	17	10	7
ARIZONA					
Arizona State University:	Main Campus	68,064	136	71	65
Arizona Western College		7,984	12	7	5
Central Arizona College		6,795	10	7	3
Northern Arizona University		23,597	27	17	10
Pima Community College		35,880	36	28	8
Yavapai College		8,276	9	8	1
ARKANSAS					
Arkansas State University:	Beebe	4,491	5	4	1
	Jonesboro	12,156	21	17	4
Arkansas Tech University		8,814	13	11	2
Henderson State University		3,567	9	8	1
Northwest Arkansas Community College		8,006	28	10	18
Southern Arkansas University		3,226	8	7	1
University of Arkansas:	Fayetteville	19,849	37	30	7
	Little Rock	13,132	39	25	14
	Medical Sciences	2,774	50	37	13
	Monticello	3,479	7	6	1
	Pine Bluff	3,792	20	15	5
University of Central Arkansas		11,781	33	26	7
CALIFORNIA					
Allan Hancock College		11,070	5	4	1
California State Polytechnic University:	Pomona	22,273	30	18	12
	San Luis Obispo	19,325	37	18	19
Allan Hancock College		11,552	5	4	1
California State Polytechnic University:	Pomona	21,190	31	20	11
	San Luis Obispo	19,471	39	19	20
California State University:	Bakersfield	7,684	15	11	4
	Channel Islands	3,783	24	12	12
	Chico	17,132	24	16	8
	Dominguez Hills	12,851	22	16	6
	East Bay	14,167	23	14	9
	Fresno	22,613	30	21	9
	Fullerton	36,996	27	22	5
	Long Beach	37,891	53	26	27
	Los Angeles	20,743	34	20	14
	Monterey Bay	4,340	17	15	2
	Northridge	36,208	38	23	15
	Sacramento	29,011	28	22	6
	San Bernardino	17,646	25	16	9
	San Jose[2]		51	28	23
	San Marcos	9,148	37	16	21
	Stanislaus	8,601	21	11	10
College of the Sequoias		13,322	6	5	1
Contra Costa Community College		8,316	33	23	10
Cuesta College		12,025	5	4	1
El Camino College		27,237	32	25	7
Foothill-De Anza College		43,484	17	9	8
Humboldt State University		7,954	20	12	8
Marin Community College		7,066	7	6	1
Pasadena Community College		26,453	17	9	8
Riverside Community College		36,586	29	19	10
San Bernardino Community College		14,916	16	9	7
San Diego State University		32,817	46	26	20
San Francisco State University		30,469	46	25	21
San Jose/Evergreen Community College		23,550	10	4	6
Santa Rosa Junior College		25,877	28	13	15
Solano Community College		12,222	6	4	2

[1] The student enrollment figures provided by the United States Department of Education are for the 2009 school year, the most recent available. The enrollment figures include full-time and part-time students.

[2] Student enrollment figures were not available.

Table 79. Full-Time Law Enforcement Employees, by State and University or College, 2010—*Continued*

(Number)

State, University/College	Campus	Student enrollment[1]	Total law enforcement employees	Total officers	Total civilians
Sonoma State University		8,546	20	11	9
State Center Community College District		40,895	18	15	3
University of California:	Berkeley	35,830	110	65	45
	Davis	31,247	78	46	32
	Hastings College of Law	1,347	14	14	0
	Irvine	27,142	45	31	14
	Los Angeles	38,550	94	57	37
	Merced	3,414	19	10	9
	Riverside	19,384	37	27	10
	San Diego	28,418	66	32	34
	San Francisco	3,119	118	43	75
	Santa Barbara	22,850	46	30	16
	Santa Cruz	16,775	44	19	25
Ventura County Community College District		14,395	17	16	1
West Valley-Mission College		23,847	12	8	4
COLORADO					
Adams State College		3,121	5	5	0
Arapahoe Community College		9,969	10	7	3
Auraria Higher Education Center[2]			38	25	13
Colorado School of Mines		5,124	9	8	1
Colorado State University:	Fort Collins	28,902	48	36	12
	Pueblo	6,443	3	2	1
Fort Lewis College		3,770	8	6	2
Pikes Peak Community College		13,572	19	17	2
Red Rocks Community College		9,143	2	2	0
University of Colorado:	Boulder	33,010	56	40	16
	Colorado Springs	9,733	24	14	10
	Denver	23,715	58	26	32
University of Northern Colorado		12,711	23	13	10
CONNECTICUT					
Central Connecticut State University		12,461	28	21	7
Eastern Connecticut State University		5,610	23	17	6
Southern Connecticut State University		11,815	33	26	7
University of Connecticut:	Health Center[2]		28	14	14
	Storrs, Avery Point, and Hartford[2]		88	70	18
Western Connecticut State University		6,617	24	17	7
Yale University		11,593	101	85	16
DELAWARE					
Delaware State University		3,609	38	19	19
University of Delaware		21,138	77	51	26
FLORIDA					
Edison State College		16,034	12	6	6
Florida A&M University		12,274	62	37	25
Florida Atlantic University		27,637	66	42	24
Florida Gulf Coast University		11,092	22	16	6
Florida International University		39,610	64	44	20
Florida State University		39,785	82	61	21
New College of Florida		825	18	12	6
Pensacola Junior College		11,598	11	7	4
Santa Fe College		15,043	21	16	5
Tallahassee Community College		14,526	23	9	14
University of Central Florida		53,401	106	54	52
University of Florida		50,691	142	81	61
University of North Florida		16,477	42	29	13
University of South Florida:	St. Petersburg	3,895	15	11	4
	Tampa	40,022	56	40	16
University of West Florida		11,143	30	20	10
GEORGIA					
Abraham Baldwin Agricultural College		3,327	10	10	0
Albany State University		4,473	29	18	11
Armstrong Atlantic State University		7,538	21	14	7
Clark Atlanta University		3,873	41	16	25
Columbus State University		8,178	38	24	14
Darton College		5,854	8	7	1
Emory University		12,930	70	52	18
Fort Valley State University		3,553	41	13	28
Gainesville State College		8,801	10	10	0
Georgia College and State University		6,633	24	18	6
Georgia Gwinnett College		2,947	24	17	7
Georgia Institute of Technology		20,291	96	73	23
Georgia Military College[2]			4	3	1
Georgia Perimeter College		24,549	124	44	80
Georgia Southern University		19,086	42	35	7

[1] The student enrollment figures provided by the United States Department of Education are for the 2009 school year, the most recent available. The enrollment figures include full-time and part-time students.

[2] Student enrollment figures were not available.

Table 79.   Full-Time Law Enforcement Employees, by State and University or College, 2010—*Continued*

(Number)

State, University/College	Campus	Student enrollment[1]	Total law enforcement employees	Total officers	Total civilians
Georgia State University		30,427	123	60	63
Kennesaw State University		22,389	62	35	27
Medical College of Georgia		2,515	43	32	11
Mercer University		8,072	34	25	9
Middle Georgia College		3,614	17	16	1
Morehouse College		2,689	44	17	27
Morehouse School of Medicine[2]		326	19	5	14
Morris-Brown College[2]			5	2	3
Savannah State University		3,820	37	20	17
Southern Crescent Technology College[2]			3	3	0
Spelman College		2,229	24	12	12
University of Georgia		34,885	96	74	22
University of West Georgia		11,500	28	19	9
Valdosta State University		12,391	30	22	8
Young Harris College		695	5	4	1
ILLINOIS					
Benedictine University		5,836	20	13	7
Black Hawk College		6,267	10	9	1
Chicago State University		7,235	37	26	11
College of DuPage		27,083	19	14	5
College of Lake County		18,092	21	14	7
Eastern Illinois University		11,966	22	19	3
Elgin Community College		11,704	16	12	4
Governors State University		5,674	13	9	4
Illinois State University		21,184	27	21	6
John A. Logan College		8,568	9	7	2
Joliet Junior College		15,288	21	12	9
Lake Land College		7,945	5	5	0
Loyola University		15,879	32	32	0
Moraine Valley Community College		17,774	18	12	6
Morton College		5,290	6	4	2
Northeastern Illinois University		11,631	27	22	5
Northern Illinois University		24,424	71	56	15
Northwestern University:	Chicago[2]		14	14	0
	Evanston[2]		72	31	41
Oakton Community College		12,087	12	11	1
Parkland College		9,633	20	14	6
Rock Valley College		8,659	16	13	3
Southern Illinois University:	Carbondale	20,350	54	36	18
	Edwardsville	13,940	44	35	9
	School of Medicine[2]		13	3	10
South Suburban College		7,279	13	9	4
Southwestern Illinois College		14,440	23	17	6
Triton College		15,706	14	9	5
University of Illinois:	Chicago	26,840	128	74	54
	Springfield	4,977	21	15	6
	Urbana	43,881	64	53	11
Waubonsee College		10,532	3	3	0
Western Illinois University		12,679	30	25	5
William Rainey Harper College[2]			16	11	5
INDIANA					
Ball State University		21,401	53	30	23
Indiana State University		10,534	29	20	9
Indiana University:	Bloomington	42,347	52	41	11
	Gary	5,560	17	13	4
	Indianapolis[2]		54	40	14
	New Albany	6,840	13	10	3
Marian University		2,277	9	6	3
Purdue University		41,052	54	42	12
IOWA					
Iowa State University		27,945	37	31	6
University of Iowa		28,987	69	39	30
University of Northern Iowa		13,303	27	18	9
KANSAS					
Emporia State University		6,314	9	9	0
Fort Hays State University		11,308	11	9	2
Kansas City Community College		7,137	15	14	1
Kansas State University		23,581	40	19	21
Pittsburg State University		7,277	16	13	3
University of Kansas:	Main Campus	29,242	47	25	22
	Medical Center[2]		63	29	34
Washburn University		6,652	20	15	5
Wichita State University		14,601	33	21	12
KENTUCKY					
Eastern Kentucky University		16,268	28	24	4
Kentucky State University		2,834	20	12	8

[1] The student enrollment figures provided by the United States Department of Education are for the 2009 school year, the most recent available. The enrollment figures include full-time and part-time students.

[2] Student enrollment figures were not available.

Table 79. Full-Time Law Enforcement Employees, by State and University or College, 2010—*Continued*

(Number)

State, University/College	Campus	Student enrollment[1]	Total law enforcement employees	Total officers	Total civilians
Murray State University		10,071	20	15	5
Northern Kentucky University		15,378	24	17	7
University of Kentucky		26,295	62	50	12
University of Louisville		21,016	76	41	35
Western Kentucky University		20,712	35	25	10
LOUISIANA					
Delgado Community College		16,758	37	25	12
Louisiana State University:	Baton Rouge[2]		65	62	3
	Health Sciences Center, New Orleans	2,644	28	28	0
	Health Sciences Center, Shreveport	823	61	45	16
	Shreveport	4,667	9	9	0
McNeese State University		8,638	18	12	6
Nicholls State University		7,169	15	10	5
Northwestern State University		9,247	24	18	6
Southeastern Louisiana University		15,151	33	23	10
Tulane University		11,464	56	43	13
University of New Orleans		11,724	24	24	0
MAINE					
University of Maine:	Farmington	2,361	6	5	1
	Orono	11,894	26	18	8
University of Southern Maine		9,655	18	9	9
MARYLAND					
Bowie State University		5,617	25	13	12
Coppin State University		3,801	49	24	25
Frostburg State University		5,385	19	15	4
Hagerstown Community College		4,452	2	1	1
Morgan State University		7,226	51	33	18
Salisbury University		8,204	30	17	13
St. Mary's College		2,060	12	1	11
Towson University		21,177	57	39	18
University of Baltimore		6,265	37	14	23
University of Maryland:	Baltimore City	6,382	145	56	89
	Baltimore County	12,870	37	25	12
	College Park	37,195	126	84	42
	Eastern Shore	4,433	19	16	3
MASSACHUSETTS					
Amherst College		1,744	17	12	5
Assumption College		2,794	28	16	12
Bentley College		5,628	32	23	9
Boston College		15,036	65	48	17
Boston University		31,960	63	51	12
Brandeis University		5,598	24	22	2
Bridgewater State College		10,774	36	20	16
Bristol Community College		8,767	8	5	3
Bunker Hill Community College		11,009	11	10	1
Clark University		3,416	16	12	4
Dean College		1,113	14	7	7
Emerson College		4,556	17	16	1
Fitchburg State College		7,043	19	16	3
Framingham State College		5,989	16	13	3
Hampshire College		1,463	14	9	5
Harvard University		27,651	104	84	20
Holyoke Community College		7,473	12	12	0
Lasell College		1,672	15	14	1
Massachusetts College of Art		2,422	23	8	15
Massachusetts College of Liberal Arts		1,962	12	9	3
Massachusetts Institute of Technology		10,384	52	49	3
Massasoit Community College		7,941	14	12	2
Merrimack College		2,090	19	13	6
Mount Holyoke College		2,304	23	16	7
Northeastern University		27,537	82	58	24
North Shore Community College		7,968	21	20	1
Quinsigamond Community College		8,349	13	13	0
Salem State College		10,125	26	22	4
Smith College		3,121	18	16	2
Springfield College		5,107	38	16	22
Tufts University:	Medford	10,252	67	38	29
University of Massachusetts:	Amherst	27,016	81	62	19
	Dartmouth	9,302	41	26	15
	Harbor Campus, Boston	14,912	29	23	6
	Medical Center, Worcester	1,091	33	23	10
Wellesley College		2,324	18	14	4
Wentworth Institute of Technology		3,808	19	13	6
Western New England College		3,710	28	17	11
Westfield State College		5,675	21	15	6
Worcester Polytechnic Institute		4,961	23	16	7

[1] The student enrollment figures provided by the United States Department of Education are for the 2009 school year, the most recent available. The enrollment figures include full-time and part-time students.

[2] Student enrollment figures were not available.

Table 79.   Full-Time Law Enforcement Employees, by State and University or College, 2010—*Continued*

(Number)

State, University/College	Campus	Student enrollment[1]	Total law enforcement employees	Total officers	Total civilians
MICHIGAN					
Central Michigan University		27,247	34	21	13
Delta College		11,354	11	8	3
Eastern Michigan University		22,893	44	33	11
Ferris State University		13,865	17	13	4
Grand Rapids Community College		16,944	16	12	4
Grand Valley State University		24,408	20	16	4
Kirtland Community College		1,972	1	1	0
Lansing Community College		21,123	15	12	3
Macomb Community College		24,376	36	30	6
Michigan State University		47,071	100	66	34
Michigan Technological University		7,136	15	11	4
Mott Community College		12,151	11	7	4
Northern Michigan University		9,428	24	20	4
Oakland Community College		28,042	28	26	2
Oakland University		18,918	25	21	4
Saginaw Valley State University		10,498	13	11	2
University of Michigan:	Ann Arbor	41,674	90	54	36
	Dearborn	8,379	18	6	12
	Flint	7,773	28	12	16
Western Michigan University		24,576	59	28	31
MINNESOTA					
University of Minnesota:	Duluth	11,664	11	10	1
	Morris	1,705	5	3	2
	Twin Cities	51,659	62	46	16
MISSISSIPPI					
Coahoma Community College		2,565	10	9	1
Itawamba Community College		7,596	13	12	1
Jackson State University		8,783	56	35	21
Mississippi State University		18,601	39	31	8
Northeast Mississippi Community College		3,633	7	5	2
University of Mississippi:	Medical Center	2,412	85	61	24
	Oxford	15,932	50	31	19
MISSOURI					
Lincoln University		3,314	16	13	3
Mineral Area College		3,671	8	7	1
Missouri Southern State University		5,701	9	6	3
Missouri University of Science and Technology		6,814	21	11	10
Missouri Western State University		5,703	12	10	2
Northwest Missouri State University		7,076	10	8	2
Southeast Missouri State University		10,801	26	17	9
St. Louis Community College:	Florissant Valley	7,210	11	9	2
	Meramec	11,186	12	9	3
Three Rivers Community College		3,527	4	3	1
Truman State University		5,781	11	10	1
University of Central Missouri		11,191	21	17	4
University of Missouri:	Columbia	31,237	49	34	15
	Kansas City	14,799	42	26	16
	St. Louis	16,534	26	20	6
Washington University		13,575	42	25	17
MONTANA					
Montana State University		12,348	33	17	16
University of Montana		14,921	25	13	12
NEBRASKA					
University of Nebraska:	Kearney	6,650	6	5	1
	Lincoln	24,100	58	32	26
NEVADA					
Truckee Meadows Community College		12,942	10	5	5
University of Nevada:	Las Vegas	29,080	55	35	20
	Reno	16,875	26	20	6
NEW HAMPSHIRE					
University of New Hampshire		15,253	32	17	15
NEW JERSEY					
Brookdale Community College		15,639	23	13	10
Essex County College		13,314	53	13	40
Kean University		15,051	52	28	24
Middlesex County College		13,356	17	12	5
Monmouth University		6,499	44	21	23
Montclair State University		18,171	44	33	11
New Jersey Institute of Technology		8,840	62	29	33
Richard Stockton College of New Jersey		7,559	30	22	8
Rowan University		11,006	62	23	39
Rutgers University:	Camden	5,781	38	19	19
	Newark	11,501	36	31	5
	New Brunswick	37,366	75	45	30

[1] The student enrollment figures provided by the United States Department of Education are for the 2009 school year, the most recent available. The enrollment figures include full-time and part-time students.

[2] Student enrollment figures were not available.

Table 79.   Full-Time Law Enforcement Employees, by State and University or College, 2010—*Continued*

(Number)

State, University/College	Campus	Student enrollment[1]	Total law enforcement employees	Total officers	Total civilians
Stevens Institute of Technology		5,757	20	16	4
The College of New Jersey		6,980	27	19	8
University of Medicine and Dentistry:	Camden[2]		19	12	7
	Newark	6,055	127	46	81
	New Brunswick[2]		39	24	15
	Piscataway[2]		39	24	15
William Paterson University		10,820	42	31	11
NEW MEXICO					
Eastern New Mexico University		4,679	9	8	1
New Mexico Highlands University		3,739	7	3	4
New Mexico State University		18,526	28	17	11
University of New Mexico		27,241	53	34	19
Western New Mexico University		3,370	5	4	1
NEW YORK					
Cornell University		20,633	66	49	17
Ithaca College		6,894	27	18	9
Rensselaer Polytechnic Institute		6,901	37	21	16
State University of New York:	Albany	18,020	66	42	24
	Binghamton	14,709	46	33	13
	Buffalo[2]		61	55	6
	Downstate Medical Center[2]		129	36	93
	Maritime College	1,756	11	6	5
	Stony Brook[2]		143	65	78
	Upstate Medical Center[2]		91	11	80
State University of New York Agricultural and Technical College:	Alfred	3,530	15	10	5
	Canton	3,320	9	8	1
	Cobleskill	2,692	11	10	1
	Farmingdale[2]		21	14	7
	Morrisville[2]		11	10	1
State University of New York College:	Brockport	8,490	19	17	2
	Buffalo	11,714	31	30	1
	Cortland	7,322	22	17	5
	Environmental Science and Forestry	2,642	12	11	1
	Fredonia[2]		16	15	1
	Geneseo[2]		16	12	4
	New Paltz	7,907	24	21	3
	Old Westbury	3,897	23	19	4
	Oneonta	5,893	27	17	10
	Optometry	301	17	6	11
	Oswego	8,119	26	19	7
	Plattsburgh	6,453	20	13	7
	Potsdam	4,299	13	11	2
	Purchase	4,192	27	23	4
	Technology[2]		13	11	2
	Utica-Rome[2]		15	10	5
NORTH CAROLINA					
Appalachian State University		16,968	41	26	15
Beaufort County Community College		1,966	3	3	0
Belmont Abbey College		1,638	10	8	2
Davidson College		1,743	9	8	1
Duke University		14,350	146	53	93
East Carolina University		27,654	71	52	19
Elizabeth City State University		3,264	18	10	8
Elon University		5,666	14	13	1
Fayetteville State University		6,283	33	16	17
Methodist College		2,183	10	7	3
North Carolina Agricultural and Technical State University		10,614	76	28	48
North Carolina Central University		8,587	50	25	25
North Carolina School of the Arts		872	18	13	5
North Carolina State University:	Raleigh	33,819	64	49	15
Queens University		2,568	8	6	2
Saint Augustine's College		1,529	23	9	14
University of North Carolina:	Asheville	3,897	18	11	7
	Chapel Hill	28,916	88	45	43
	Charlotte	24,701	44	37	7
	Greensboro	21,306	54	31	23
	Pembroke	6,661	22	17	5
	Wilmington	12,924	47	32	15
Wake Forest University		7,079	42	20	22
Western Carolina University		9,429	21	16	5
Winston-Salem State University		6,427	37	18	19
NORTH DAKOTA					
North Dakota State College of Science		2,650	3	3	0
North Dakota State University		14,189	26	17	9
University of North Dakota		13,172	14	12	2

[1] The student enrollment figures provided by the United States Department of Education are for the 2009 school year, the most recent available. The enrollment figures include full-time and part-time students.

[2] Student enrollment figures were not available.

Table 79.   Full-Time Law Enforcement Employees, by State and University or College, 2010—*Continued*

(Number)

State, University/College	Campus	Student enrollment[1]	Total law enforcement employees	Total officers	Total civilians
OHIO					
Bowling Green State University		17,309	26	21	5
Central State University		2,436	13	12	1
Cleveland State University		16,216	34	21	13
College of Mount St. Joseph		2,324	9	7	2
Columbus State Community College		28,539	44	20	24
Cuyahoga Community College		29,807	35	27	8
Hocking College		6,340	5	5	0
Kent State University		25,127	42	32	10
Lakeland Community College		9,406	13	9	4
Miami University		16,884	33	24	9
Muskingum University		2,207	5	5	0
Notre Dame College		1,872	4	4	0
Ohio State University:	Columbus	55,014	135	53	82
	Marion	1,828	1	1	0
	Wooster[2]		5	5	0
Ohio University		22,647	31	24	7
Sinclair Community College		21,561	27	22	5
University of Akron		25,959	45	39	6
University of Cincinnati		31,134	101	56	45
University of Rio Grande		2,096	7	6	1
University of Toledo		23,064	56	35	21
Wilberforce University		710	3	3	0
Wright State University		17,558	29	20	9
Youngstown State University		14,644	25	20	5
OKLAHOMA					
Cameron University		6,126	12	12	0
East Central University		4,612	5	5	0
Murray State College		2,604	2	1	1
Northeastern Oklahoma A&M College		2,191	8	7	1
Northeastern State University:	Broken Arrow[2]		5	5	0
	Tahlequah	9,239	16	15	1
Oklahoma City University		3,829	18	13	5
Oklahoma State University:	Main Campus	23,033	42	31	11
	Okmulgee	4,129	6	6	0
	Tulsa[2]		9	7	2
Rogers State University		4,235	4	4	0
Seminole State College		2,444	3	3	0
Southeastern Oklahoma State University		4,229	8	7	1
Southwestern Oklahoma State University		5,010	6	5	1
Tulsa Community College		19,730	16	10	6
University of Central Oklahoma		16,092	20	14	6
University of Oklahoma:	Health Sciences Center	3,934	54	38	16
	Norman	25,881	70	40	30
PENNSYLVANIA					
Bloomsburg University		9,512	21	16	5
California University		9,017	19	14	5
Cheyney University		1,488	14	11	3
Clarion University		7,346	13	9	4
Dickinson College		2,376	19	14	5
East Stroudsburg University		7,576	18	15	3
Edinboro University		8,286	15	14	1
Elizabethtown College		2,361	17	11	6
Indiana University		14,638	28	21	7
Kutztown University		10,634	24	18	6
Lehigh University		6,996	36	22	14
Lock Haven University		5,329	12	10	2
Mansfield University		3,569	12	9	3
Millersville University		8,427	16	13	3
Moravian College		2,057	15	8	7
Pennsylvania State University:	Altoona	4,182	11	9	2
	Beaver	855	5	5	0
	Behrend	4,400	10	6	4
	Berks	2,759	9	8	1
	Harrisburg	4,012	8	7	1
	Hazelton	1,245	5	5	0
	McKeesport[2]		5	5	0
	Mont Alto	1,182	5	5	0
	University Park	45,185	72	50	22
Shippensburg University		8,253	20	17	3
Slippery Rock University		8,648	19	15	4
University of Pittsburgh:	Bradford	1,657	7	6	1
	Pittsburgh	28,328	127	72	55
West Chester University		14,211	21	21	0

[1] The student enrollment figures provided by the United States Department of Education are for the 2009 school year, the most recent available. The enrollment figures include full-time and part-time students.

[2] Student enrollment figures were not available.

Table 79.   Full-Time Law Enforcement Employees, by State and University or College, 2010—*Continued*

(Number)

State, University/College	Campus	Student enrollment[1]	Total law enforcement employees	Total officers	Total civilians
RHODE ISLAND					
Brown University		8,574	79	42	37
University of Rhode Island		16,389	27	22	5
SOUTH CAROLINA					
Benedict College		2,983	28	23	5
Bob Jones University		3,956	4	4	0
Clemson University		19,111	35	26	9
Coastal Carolina University		8,360	79	30	49
College of Charleston		11,772	59	30	29
Columbia College		1,444	12	10	2
Erskine College		874	2	2	0
Francis Marion University		3,957	13	12	1
Lander University		2,838	14	12	2
South Carolina State University		4,538	32	21	11
Spartanburg Methodist College		808	5	5	0
The Citadel		3,339	16	15	1
Trident Technical College		14,834	25	17	8
University of South Carolina:	Columbia	28,482	80	56	24
	Upstate	5,403	12	12	0
Winthrop University		6,241	22	15	7
SOUTH DAKOTA					
South Dakota State University		11,995	20	15	5
TENNESSEE					
Austin Peay State University		10,188	25	14	11
Christian Brothers University		1,926	16	9	7
East Tennessee State University		14,421	26	19	7
Middle Tennessee State University		25,188	39	32	7
Northeast State Community College		6,270	5	5	0
Southwest Tennessee Community College		13,016	30	16	14
Tennessee State University		8,824	50	33	17
Tennessee Technological University		10,847	20	13	7
University of Memphis		21,424	37	32	5
University of Tennessee:	Chattanooga	10,526	16	11	5
	Health Science Center[2]		57	25	32
	Knoxville	29,934	93	50	43
	Martin	8,163	17	13	4
Vanderbilt University		12,506	134	93	41
Volunteer State Community College		8,430	6	5	1
Walters State Community College		6,853	10	9	1
TEXAS					
Abilene Christian University		4,813	16	15	1
Alamo Community College District[2]			81	61	20
Alvin Community College		5,240	13	11	2
Amarillo College		11,289	15	13	2
Angelo State University		6,387	18	12	6
Austin College		1,364	8	7	1
Baylor Health Care System[2]			185	64	121
Baylor University:	Waco	14,614	31	24	7
Blinn College		17,173	18	16	2
Brookhaven College		11,814	20	17	3
Central Texas College		24,133	9	8	1
College of the Mainland		3,916	8	7	1
Eastfield College		11,944	21	16	5
El Paso Community College		28,168	44	37	7
Grayson County College		4,856	4	3	1
Hardin-Simmons University		2,305	8	7	1
Houston Baptist University		2,710	15	12	3
Houston Community College		54,942	104	61	43
Lamar University:	Beaumont	13,992	33	20	13
Laredo Community College		9,361	23	21	2
McLennan Community College		9,128	17	8	9
Midwestern State University		6,341	14	9	5
Mountain View College		8,203	12	12	0
North Lake College		11,644	22	21	1
Paris Junior College		5,580	4	4	0
Rice University		5,576	47	30	17
Southern Methodist University		10,891	35	26	9
South Plains College		10,011	6	6	0
Southwestern University		1,301	7	6	1
Stephen F. Austin State University		12,845	45	28	17
St. Mary's University		3,893	20	17	3
Sul Ross State University		3,047	9	7	2
Tarleton State University		10,424	14	13	1
Texas A&M International University		6,419	25	17	8

[1] The student enrollment figures provided by the United States Department of Education are for the 2009 school year, the most recent available. The enrollment figures include full-time and part-time students.

[2] Student enrollment figures were not available.

Table 79.   Full-Time Law Enforcement Employees, by State and University or College, 2010—*Continued*

(Number)

State, University/College	Campus	Student enrollment[1]	Total law enforcement employees	Total officers	Total civilians
Texas A&M University:	College Station	48,702	131	61	70
	Commerce	9,021	24	16	8
	Corpus Christi	9,468	28	16	12
	Galveston	1,774	9	8	1
	Kingsville	8,194	18	12	6
Texas Christian University		8,853	45	29	16
Texas Southern University		9,394	66	37	29
Texas State Technical College:	Harlingen	5,988	12	8	4
	Marshall	963	5	5	0
	Waco	6,816	18	16	2
Texas State University:	San Marcos	30,803	37	31	6
Texas Tech University:	Lubbock	30,049	85	47	38
Texas Woman's University		13,338	37	16	21
Trinity University		2,693	25	14	11
Tyler Junior College		11,045	19	11	8
University of Houston:	Central Campus	37,000	145	43	102
	Clearlake	7,643	27	16	11
	Downtown Campus	12,742	31	17	14
University of Mary Hardin-Baylor		2,689	10	9	1
University of North Texas:	Denton	35,003	87	46	41
	Health Science Center	1,395	19	10	9
University of Texas:	Arlington	28,085	95	34	61
	Austin	50,995	145	62	83
	Brownsville	17,151	43	18	25
	Dallas	15,783	52	23	29
	El Paso	21,011	50	20	30
	Health Science Center, San Antonio	3,223	122	34	88
	Health Science Center, Tyler[2]		16	6	10
	Houston[2]		316	89	227
	Medical Branch	2,430	88	49	39
	Pan American	18,337	39	17	22
	Permian Basin	3,546	21	9	12
	San Antonio	28,955	112	49	63
	Southwestern Medical School	2,459	135	37	98
	Tyler	6,201	19	10	9
West Texas A&M University		7,634	14	11	3
UTAH					
Brigham Young University		34,130	38	27	11
College of Eastern Utah		2,419	1	1	0
Southern Utah University		8,066	6	5	1
University of Utah		29,284	92	31	61
Utah State University		15,612	17	11	6
Utah Valley University		28,765	10	8	2
Weber State University		23,001	10	9	1
VERMONT					
University of Vermont		13,391	33	21	12
VIRGINIA					
Christopher Newport University		4,952	24	17	7
College of William and Mary		7,874	23	18	5
Emory and Henry College		1,002	4	2	2
Ferrum College		1,425	8	7	1
George Mason University		32,067	67	48	19
Hampton University		5,402	47	29	18
James Madison University		18,971	38	30	8
J. Sargeant Reynolds Community College		12,729	31	17	14
Longwood University		4,832	21	15	6
Norfolk State University		6,993	37	24	13
Northern Virginia Community College		46,619	46	45	1
Old Dominion University		24,013	58	47	11
Radford University		8,878	27	21	6
Richard Bland College		1,579	7	7	0
Thomas Nelson Community College		10,606	11	9	2
University of Mary Washington		5,381	17	12	5
University of Richmond		4,344	32	19	13
University of Virginia		24,355	119	51	68
University of Virginia's College at Wise		2,015	9	8	1
Virginia Commonwealth University		32,172	190	82	108
Virginia Military Institute		1,500	10	10	0
Virginia Polytechnic Institute and State University		30,870	71	48	23
Virginia State University		5,366	35	21	14
Virginia Western Community College		8,927	8	8	0
WASHINGTON					
Central Washington University		11,357	14	13	1
Eastern Washington University		11,300	12	11	1
Evergreen State College		4,891	16	10	6

[1] The student enrollment figures provided by the United States Department of Education are for the 2009 school year, the most recent available. The enrollment figures include full-time and part-time students.

[2] Student enrollment figures were not available.

Table 79.   Full-Time Law Enforcement Employees, by State and University or College, 2010—*Continued*

(Number)

State, University/College	Campus	Student enrollment[1]	Total law enforcement employees	Total officers	Total civilians
University of Washington		45,943	72	46	26
Washington State University:	Pullman	26,101	24	17	7
	Vancouver[2]		6	3	3
Western Washington University		14,575	20	14	6
WEST VIRGINIA					
Bluefield State College		1,989	2	2	0
Concord University...		2,882	11	7	4
Fairmont State University		4,574	8	6	2
Glenville State College		1,721	6	3	3
Marshall University..		13,776	22	21	1
Potomac State College...		1,810	7	6	1
Shepherd University		4,256	11	9	2
West Liberty State College		2,651	5	5	0
West Virginia State University..		4,003	13	11	2
West Virginia Tech...		1,244	6	6	0
West Virginia University		28,898	55	45	10
WISCONSIN					
University of Wisconsin:	Eau Claire	11,216	10	9	1
	Green Bay	6,638	11	5	6
	La Crosse	10,009	10	8	2
	Madison	41,654	106	60	46
	Milwaukee	30,418	46	34	12
	Oshkosh	13,192	10	8	2
	Parkside	5,303	10	6	4
	Platteville	7,803	8	7	1
	Stevens Point	9,209	5	2	3
	Stout	9,017	8	7	1
	Superior	2,794	7	2	5
	Whitewater	11,139	13	12	1
WYOMING					
Sheridan College		3,899	2	2	0
University of Wyoming...		12,427	25	14	11

[1] The student enrollment figures provided by the United States Department of Education are for the 2009 school year, the most recent available. The enrollment figures include full-time and part-time students.

[2] Student enrollment figures were not available.

Table 80.   Full-Time Law Enforcement Employees, by State by Metropolitan and Nonmetropolitan Counties, 2010

(Number)

State/County	Total law enforcement employees	Total officers	Total civilians	State/County	Total law enforcement employees	Total officers	Total civilians
ALABAMA–Metropolitan Counties				Navajo	137	44	93
Autauga	64	26	38	Santa Cruz	96	38	58
Bibb	12	11	1	**ARKANSAS-Metropolitan Counties**			
Blount	49	45	4	Benton	206	132	74
Calhoun	57	52	5	Cleveland	13	8	5
Chilton	167	27	140	Craighead	105	27	78
Colbert	55	31	24	Crawford	60	27	33
Elmore	88	41	47	Crittenden	138	31	107
Etowah	156	65	91	Faulkner	151	68	83
Geneva	27	10	17	Franklin	19	9	10
Greene	29	11	18	Garland	122	44	78
Hale	11	8	3	Grant	17	15	2
Henry	15	10	5	Jefferson	164	47	117
Houston	95	61	34	Lincoln	20	9	11
Jefferson	655	506	149	Lonoke	45	26	19
Lauderdale	44	35	9	Madison	18	10	8
Lawrence	48	26	22	Miller	71	28	43
Lee	154	68	86	Perry	18	10	8
Limestone	102	41	61	Poinsett	41	12	29
Lowndes	39	15	24	Pulaski	468	126	342
Madison	342	109	233	Saline	84	40	44
Mobile	483	170	313	Sebastian	144	46	98
Montgomery	177	130	47	Washington	291	152	139
Morgan	185	53	132	**ARKANSAS-Nonmetropolitan Counties**			
Russell	91	35	56	Arkansas	48	10	38
Shelby	213	124	89	Ashley	43	19	24
St. Clair	49	43	6	Baxter	50	32	18
Tuscaloosa	199	98	101	Boone	51	25	26
Walker	81	35	46	Bradley	5	3	2
ALABAMA-Nonmetropolitan Counties				Calhoun	11	5	6
Baldwin	271	99	172	Carroll	20	17	3
Bullock	14	6	8	Chicot	8	7	1
Butler	12	10	2	Clark	26	12	14
Chambers	55	20	35	Clay	24	9	15
Cherokee	42	20	22	Cleburne	39	22	17
Clarke	39	14	25	Columbia	35	17	18
Clay	28	11	17	Conway	35	16	19
Cleburne	27	12	15	Cross	37	17	20
Coffee	43	19	24	Dallas	26	6	20
Coosa	22	11	11	Desha	7	6	1
Covington	27	24	3	Drew	11	10	1
Crenshaw	10	8	2	Fulton	13	6	7
Cullman	135	81	54	Greene	48	12	36
Dale	40	24	16	Hempstead	51	16	35
Dallas	50	25	25	Hot Spring	23	15	8
De Kalb	103	35	68	Howard	23	10	13
Escambia	64	54	10	Independence	72	48	24
Franklin	47	15	32	Izard	26	12	14
Jackson	81	32	49	Jackson	21	11	10
Lamar	20	8	12	Johnson	34	12	22
Macon	38	19	19	Lafayette	16	8	8
Marengo	24	10	14	Lawrence	25	14	11
Marshall	71	33	38	Lee	10	5	5
Monroe	53	19	34	Little River	17	8	9
Perry	17	7	10	Logan	26	13	13
Pickens	32	9	23	Marion	20	18	2
Pike	30	15	15	Mississippi	91	34	57
Randolph	43	13	30	Monroe	14	6	8
Sumter	22	6	16	Montgomery	19	10	9
Talladega	102	40	62	Nevada	17	6	11
Tallapoosa	54	23	31	Newton	11	7	4
Washington	13	8	5	Ouachita	37	15	22
Winston	22	9	13	Phillips	19	16	3
ARIZONA-Metropolitan Counties				Pike	20	7	13
Maricopa	3,323	715	2,608	Polk	22	11	11
Mohave	251	88	163	Pope	82	32	50
Pima	1,444	506	938	Prairie	17	7	10
Pinal	624	205	419	Randolph	19	10	9
Yavapai	167	120	47	Scott	18	8	10
Yuma	334	86	248	Searcy	13	6	7
ARIZONA-Nonmetropolitan Counties				Sevier	28	12	16
Apache	76	30	46	Sharp	30	12	18
Cochise	200	85	115	St. Francis	41	21	20
Gila	143	49	94	Stone	20	8	12
Graham	75	23	52	Union	57	25	32
La Paz	85	30	55	Van Buren	32	13	19

Table 80.   Full-Time Law Enforcement Employees, by State by Metropolitan and Nonmetropolitan Counties, 2010—*Continued*

(Number)

State/County	Total law enforcement employees	Total officers	Total civilians	State/County	Total law enforcement employees	Total officers	Total civilians
White	96	52	44	Pueblo	314	162	152
Woodruff	17	6	11	Teller	74	51	23
Yell	26	13	13	Weld	329	131	198
CALIFORNIA-Metropolitan Counties				**COLORADO-Nonmetropolitan Counties**			
Alameda	1,635	986	649	Alamosa	38	19	19
Butte	258	101	157	Archuleta	37	15	22
Contra Costa	952	637	315	Baca	11	4	7
El Dorado	346	173	173	Bent	18	8	10
Fresno	891	693	198	Chaffee	45	19	26
Imperial	271	180	91	Cheyenne	10	5	5
Kern	1,091	822	269	Conejos	23	8	15
Kings	214	76	138	Costilla	7	5	2
Los Angeles	16,990	9,501	7,489	Crowley	11	6	5
Madera	104	71	33	Custer	20	8	12
Marin	296	193	103	Delta	64	29	35
Merced	250	113	137	Dolores	7	5	2
Monterey	412	307	105	Eagle	79	47	32
Napa	129	99	30	Fremont	83	35	48
Orange	3,511	2,074	1,437	Garfield	136	48	88
Placer	403	214	189	Grand	48	20	28
Riverside	3,805	2,086	1,719	Gunnison	30	13	17
Sacramento	1,897	1,186	711	Hinsdale	4	3	1
San Benito	68	58	10	Huerfano	24	11	13
San Bernardino	3,310	1,767	1,543	Jackson	7	4	3
San Diego	3,675	2,201	1,474	Kiowa	7	6	1
San Francisco	1,065	896	169	Kit Carson	23	7	16
San Joaquin	699	292	407	Lake	20	9	11
San Luis Obispo	358	147	211	La Plata	129	99	30
San Mateo	603	320	283	Las Animas	32	13	19
Santa Barbara	605	436	169	Lincoln	20	8	12
Santa Clara	690	537	153	Logan	51	25	26
Santa Cruz	313	131	182	Mineral	4	3	1
Shasta	210	141	69	Moffat	38	16	22
Solano	394	107	287	Montezuma	76	30	46
Sonoma	655	469	186	Montrose	118	56	62
Stanislaus	557	402	155	Morgan	54	47	7
Sutter	137	108	29	Otero	22	10	12
Tulare	662	481	181	Ouray	7	7	0
Ventura	1,205	739	466	Phillips	4	4	0
Yolo	236	83	153	Pitkin	44	26	18
Yuba	168	130	38	Prowers	31	9	22
CALIFORNIA-Nonmetropolitan Counties				Rio Blanco	32	17	15
Alpine	18	15	3	Rio Grande	31	13	18
Amador	89	46	43	Routt	47	21	26
Calaveras	95	52	43	Saguache	19	8	11
Colusa	69	36	33	San Juan	4	3	1
Del Norte	63	30	33	San Miguel	31	27	4
Glenn	68	26	42	Sedgwick	9	6	3
Humboldt	227	177	50	Summit	58	51	7
Inyo	53	34	19	Washington	44	15	29
Lake	153	58	95	Yuma	20	8	12
Lassen	94	72	22	**DELAWARE-Metropolitan Counties**			
Mariposa	69	56	13	New Castle County Police Department	464	351	113
Mendocino	156	118	38	**FLORIDA-Metropolitan Counties**			
Modoc	26	18	8	Alachua	810	297	513
Mono	51	28	23	Baker	134	55	79
Nevada	185	72	113	Bay	276	211	65
Plumas	63	31	32	Brevard	1,176	809	367
Sierra	15	10	5	Broward	2,763	1,498	1,265
Siskiyou	99	76	23	Charlotte	391	277	114
Tehama	112	80	32	Clay	557	261	296
Trinity	31	15	16	Collier	928	579	349
Tuolumne	128	65	63	Escambia	655	413	242
COLORADO-Metropolitan Counties				Flagler	175	120	55
Adams	508	361	147	Gadsden	67	46	21
Arapahoe	531	254	277	Gilchrist	53	27	26
Boulder	361	211	150	Hernando	510	324	186
Clear Creek	72	28	44	Hillsborough	3,365	1,192	2,173
Douglas	425	282	143	Indian River	476	195	281
Elbert	33	27	6	Jefferson	52	21	31
El Paso	599	419	180	Lake	719	356	363
Gilpin	44	28	16	Lee	933	568	365
Jefferson	801	552	249	Leon	354	241	113
Larimer	370	161	209	Manatee	980	457	523
Mesa	220	96	124	Marion	830	530	300
Park	56	28	28	Martin	508	251	257

Table 80.   Full-Time Law Enforcement Employees, by State by Metropolitan and Nonmetropolitan Counties, 2010—*Continued*

(Number)

State/County	Total law enforce-ment employees	Total officers	Total civilians	State/County	Total law enforce-ment employees	Total officers	Total civilians
Miami-Dade	4,363	2,980	1,383	Gwinnett County Police Department	1,011	729	282
Nassau	220	155	65	Hall	474	306	168
Okaloosa	337	248	89	Harris	65	63	2
Orange	1,981	1,356	625	Heard	34	20	14
Osceola	591	380	211	Henry	277	263	14
Palm Beach	3,269	1,471	1,798	Henry County Police Department	271	231	40
Pasco	1,126	484	642	Jones	72	43	29
Pinellas	1,329	745	584	Lamar	56	31	25
Polk	1,572	636	936	Lanier	15	11	4
Santa Rosa	256	177	79	Lee	69	44	25
Sarasota	921	398	523	Liberty	115	62	53
Seminole	1,080	397	683	Lowndes	225	155	70
St. Johns	540	260	280	Madison	60	38	22
St. Lucie	618	254	364	McIntosh	65	62	3
Volusia	701	427	274	Meriwether	59	33	26
Wakulla	94	61	33	Monroe	97	55	42
FLORIDA-Nonmetropolitan Counties				Murray	65	38	27
Bradford	37	24	13	Newton	242	150	92
Calhoun	28	16	12	Oconee	89	57	32
Citrus	368	224	144	Paulding	267	232	35
Columbia	167	89	78	Pickens	94	73	21
DeSoto	81	54	27	Pike	52	29	23
Dixie	75	27	48	Rockdale	276	257	19
Franklin	74	35	39	Spalding	172	145	27
Glades	139	93	46	Twiggs	41	20	21
Gulf	41	27	14	Walton	180	159	21
Hamilton	56	18	38	Whitfield	197	125	72
Hardee	92	44	48	Worth	35	24	11
Hendry	150	73	77	**GEORGIA-Nonmetropolitan Counties**			
Highlands	321	130	191	Baldwin	119	56	63
Holmes	24	18	6	Ben Hill	54	49	5
Jackson	79	60	19	Bleckley	41	12	29
Lafayette	25	12	13	Bulloch	114	50	64
Levy	152	71	81	Calhoun	16	7	9
Liberty	20	14	6	Camden	133	64	69
Madison	46	32	14	Charlton	33	20	13
Monroe	492	208	284	Coffee	114	53	61
Okeechobee	112	79	33	Early	42	24	18
Putnam	222	119	103	Elbert	58	53	5
Sumter	152	98	54	Emanuel	31	15	16
Suwannee	103	57	46	Evans	19	11	8
Taylor	43	30	13	Fannin	43	41	2
Union	19	14	5	Franklin	52	25	27
Walton	235	162	73	Gilmer	99	56	43
Washington	78	55	23	Gordon	88	76	12
GEORGIA-Metropolitan Counties				Greene	52	35	17
Augusta-Richmond	702	631	71	Habersham	40	38	2
Barrow	190	125	65	Hancock	1	1	0
Bartow	231	224	7	Hart	37	22	15
Bibb	342	279	63	Irwin	19	11	8
Brantley	46	22	24	Jackson	151	98	53
Brooks	42	19	23	Jeff Davis	40	16	24
Butts	76	37	39	Jefferson	53	50	3
Catoosa	138	72	66	Jenkins	16	15	1
Chatham	409	339	70	Johnson	21	9	12
Cherokee	394	331	63	Laurens	105	62	43
Clarke	164	141	23	Lumpkin	69	60	9
Clayton	342	260	82	Macon	10	9	1
Clayton County Police Department	363	311	52	Miller	18	10	8
Cobb	748	478	270	Morgan	52	28	24
Cobb County Police Department	720	592	128	Peach	59	29	30
Columbia	361	302	59	Pierce	29	13	16
Coweta	219	143	76	Polk County Police Department	38	35	3
Dade	27	24	3	Quitman	9	7	2
Dawson	117	65	52	Schley	8	4	4
DeKalb County Police Department	1,331	1,017	314	Seminole	25	12	13
Douglas	314	278	36	Stephens	71	35	36
Echols	9	8	1	Stewart	8	4	4
Fayette	222	142	80	Sumter	105	48	57
Floyd	129	80	49	Tattnall	37	19	18
Floyd County Police Department	78	73	5	Taylor	28	19	9
Forsyth	363	282	81	Telfair	22	20	2
Fulton	1,066	829	237	Thomas	77	73	4
Fulton County Police Department	191	140	51	Tift	113	59	54
Glynn	135	33	102	Towns	26	23	3
Glynn County Police Department	128	115	13	Treutlen	19	8	11

Table 80. Full-Time Law Enforcement Employees, by State by Metropolitan and Nonmetropolitan Counties, 2010—*Continued*

(Number)

State/County	Total law enforce-ment employees	Total officers	Total civilians	State/County	Total law enforce-ment employees	Total officers	Total civilians
Troup	135	80	55	Kendall	117	55	62
Union	37	34	3	Lake	499	186	313
Upson	63	34	29	Macon	135	61	74
Ware	123	44	79	Macoupin	46	34	12
Washington	37	33	4	Madison	164	79	85
Wheeler	9	3	6	Marshall	18	8	10
White	63	42	21	McHenry	420	108	312
Wilcox	14	8	6	McLean	135	54	81
Wilkes	33	13	20	Menard	14	8	6
Wilkinson	27	16	11	Mercer	31	12	19
HAWAII-Nonmetropolitan Counties				Monroe	30	15	15
Hawaii Police Department	536	410	126	Peoria	193	70	123
Kauai Police Department	175	134	41	Piatt	32	10	22
Maui Police Department	460	337	123	Rock Island	145	61	84
IDAHO-Metropolitan Counties				Sangamon	209	68	141
Ada	396	134	262	Stark	13	5	8
Bannock	66	40	26	St. Clair	164	150	14
Boise	13	10	3	Tazewell	110	41	69
Bonneville	98	64	34	Vermilion	94	38	56
Canyon	249	123	126	Will	602	250	352
Franklin	15	12	3	Winnebago	342	102	240
Gem	24	13	11	Woodford	39	38	1
Jefferson	33	18	15	**ILLINOIS-Nonmetropolitan Counties**			
Kootenai	159	85	74	Adams	57	57	0
Nez Perce	40	23	17	Brown	6	6	0
Owyhee	20	11	9	Bureau	38	20	18
Power	17	9	8	Carroll	25	9	16
IDAHO-Nonmetropolitan Counties				Cass	8	7	1
Adams	18	11	7	Christian	35	17	18
Bear Lake	12	6	6	Clark	10	9	1
Benewah	18	9	9	Clay	17	11	6
Bingham	55	35	20	Coles	46	26	20
Blaine	24	19	5	Crawford	21	9	12
Bonner	55	38	17	Cumberland	14	5	9
Boundary	20	11	9	De Witt	25	14	11
Butte	10	4	6	Douglas	30	14	16
Camas	6	4	2	Edgar	19	8	11
Caribou	16	9	7	Edwards	7	4	3
Cassia	53	33	20	Effingham	48	20	28
Clark	7	3	4	Fayette	33	11	22
Clearwater	22	15	7	Franklin	42	17	25
Custer	14	8	6	Fulton	39	21	18
Elmore	43	22	21	Gallatin	4	4	0
Fremont	25	16	9	Greene	13	6	7
Gooding	18	12	6	Hamilton	9	5	4
Idaho	32	21	11	Hancock	21	9	12
Jerome	23	17	6	Hardin	6	3	3
Latah	38	26	12	Henderson	12	7	5
Lemhi	13	8	5	Iroquois	21	11	10
Lewis	10	5	5	Jackson	75	27	48
Lincoln	7	6	1	Jasper	11	6	5
Madison	33	23	10	Jefferson	68	19	49
Minidoka	26	17	9	Jo Daviess	37	19	18
Oneida	13	7	6	Johnson	13	8	5
Payette	31	17	14	Knox	60	21	39
Shoshone	28	17	11	La Salle	113	42	71
Teton	24	12	12	Lawrence	16	6	10
Twin Falls	69	47	22	Lee	39	21	18
Valley	30	15	15	Livingston	60	26	34
Washington	17	12	5	Logan	30	20	10
ILLINOIS-Metropolitan Counties				Marion	35	13	22
Alexander	5	5	0	Mason	21	9	12
Bond	19	11	8	Massac	27	10	17
Boone	96	38	58	McDonough	25	13	12
Calhoun	10	5	5	Montgomery	39	15	24
Champaign	59	53	6	Morgan	30	15	15
Clinton	35	16	19	Moultrie	11	10	1
Cook	6,729	2,155	4,574	Ogle	70	29	41
De Kalb	97	42	55	Perry	35	14	21
Du Page	541	417	124	Pike	27	12	15
Ford	24	7	17	Pope	6	3	3
Grundy	65	31	34	Pulaski	12	11	1
Henry	66	23	43	Putnam	13	8	5
Jersey	29	13	16	Randolph	35	14	21
Kane	114	85	29	Richland	23	8	15
Kankakee	200	60	140	Saline	47	12	35

Table 80.   Full-Time Law Enforcement Employees, by State by Metropolitan and Nonmetropolitan Counties, 2010—*Continued*

(Number)

State/County	Total law enforcement employees	Total officers	Total civilians	State/County	Total law enforcement employees	Total officers	Total civilians
Schuyler	8	3	5	Pike	27	10	17
Scott	7	3	4	Pulaski	42	13	29
Shelby	20	12	8	Randolph	41	15	26
Stephenson	60	26	34	Ripley	28	10	18
Union	17	16	1	Rush	26	11	15
Wabash	8	4	4	Scott	26	11	15
Warren	21	12	9	Spencer	15	14	1
Washington	25	10	15	Starke	26	11	15
Wayne	21	11	10	Steuben	58	21	37
White	7	5	2	Switzerland	31	11	20
Whiteside	49	21	28	Wabash	31	12	19
Williamson	74	36	38	Warren	20	7	13
INDIANA-Metropolitan Counties				Wayne	111	71	40
Bartholomew	91	38	53	White	33	13	20
Benton	19	7	12	**IOWA-Metropolitan Counties**			
Boone	60	28	32	Benton	23	12	11
Brown	38	13	25	Black Hawk	135	102	33
Carroll	22	9	13	Bremer	31	11	20
Clark	143	35	108	Dallas	47	22	25
Clay	41	13	28	Dubuque	80	68	12
Dearborn	85	31	54	Grundy	16	12	4
Elkhart	212	69	143	Guthrie	10	5	5
Floyd	102	32	70	Harrison	10	9	1
Gibson	43	17	26	Johnson	88	65	23
Greene	39	14	25	Jones	24	10	14
Hamilton	240	62	178	Linn	167	112	55
Hancock	71	39	32	Madison	16	7	9
Harrison	54	19	35	Mills	20	11	9
Hendricks	105	45	60	Polk	455	137	318
Jasper	53	21	32	Pottawattamie	187	50	137
Johnson	142	112	30	Scott	154	44	110
La Porte	159	60	99	Story	80	30	50
Madison	102	49	53	Warren	32	22	10
Monroe	110	34	76	Washington	49	18	31
Morgan	29	25	4	Woodbury	115	106	9
Newton	45	18	27	**IOWA-Nonmetropolitan Counties**			
Ohio	9	9	0	Adair	10	6	4
Owen	33	12	21	Adams	11	6	5
Porter	150	65	85	Allamakee	15	8	7
Posey	13	12	1	Appanoose	16	8	8
Putnam	36	18	18	Audubon	8	5	3
Shelby	85	29	56	Boone	27	11	16
St. Joseph	267	110	157	Buchanan	29	13	16
Sullivan	34	10	24	Buena Vista	29	11	18
Tippecanoe	142	46	96	Butler	20	11	9
Tipton	27	12	15	Calhoun	15	6	9
Vanderburgh	258	105	153	Carroll	15	9	6
Vermillion	23	8	15	Cass	10	7	3
Warrick	82	38	44	Cedar	37	10	27
Washington	34	12	22	Cerro Gordo	72	20	52
Wells	39	15	24	Cherokee	17	6	11
Whitley	48	15	33	Chickasaw	13	8	5
INDIANA-Nonmetropolitan Counties				Clarke	19	6	13
Blackford	30	9	21	Clay	18	10	8
Cass	54	17	37	Clayton	27	12	15
Clinton	70	22	48	Clinton	39	23	16
Crawford	14	7	7	Crawford	13	10	3
Daviess	64	19	45	Davis	6	5	1
Fulton	24	10	14	Decatur	11	6	5
Grant	114	46	68	Delaware	15	11	4
Henry	62	27	35	Des Moines	50	22	28
Huntington	39	14	25	Dickinson	19	9	10
Jackson	61	15	46	Emmet	17	8	9
Jay	43	11	32	Fayette	32	10	22
Jefferson	34	14	20	Floyd	18	11	7
Jennings	38	14	24	Franklin	11	8	3
Knox	38	13	25	Fremont	19	8	11
Kosciusko	70	36	34	Greene	15	7	8
LaGrange	63	18	45	Hamilton	29	10	19
Lawrence	64	25	39	Hancock	10	8	2
Marshall	58	21	37	Hardin	29	10	19
Martin	21	7	14	Henry	27	12	15
Montgomery	64	20	44	Howard	13	6	7
Noble	73	20	53	Humboldt	9	8	1
Orange	30	9	21	Ida	16	9	7
Parke	37	27	10	Iowa	25	11	14
Perry	17	7	10	Jackson	15	9	6

Table 80. Full-Time Law Enforcement Employees, by State by Metropolitan and Nonmetropolitan Counties, 2010—*Continued*

(Number)

State/County	Total law enforcement employees	Total officers	Total civilians	State/County	Total law enforcement employees	Total officers	Total civilians
Jasper	44	14	30	Elk	10	5	5
Jefferson	30	10	20	Ellis	29	18	11
Keokuk	8	5	3	Ellsworth	16	8	8
Kossuth	24	9	15	Finney	92	37	55
Lee	30	15	15	Ford	61	26	35
Louisa	30	9	21	Gove	5	4	1
Lucas	13	5	8	Graham	7	3	4
Lyon	23	9	14	Grant	16	7	9
Mahaska	25	9	16	Gray	17	10	7
Marion	32	12	20	Greeley	7	3	4
Marshall	55	18	37	Greenwood	23	13	10
Mitchell	15	6	9	Hamilton	9	3	6
Monona	17	7	10	Harper	11	6	5
Monroe	12	5	7	Haskell	15	10	5
Muscatine	58	22	36	Hodgeman	10	5	5
O'Brien	28	9	19	Kearny	16	9	7
Osceola	14	9	5	Kingman	18	7	11
Page	15	8	7	Kiowa	17	8	9
Palo Alto	15	8	7	Labette	35	18	17
Plymouth	28	10	18	Lane	10	5	5
Pocahontas	17	8	9	Lincoln	13	8	5
Poweshiek	25	11	14	Logan	4	3	1
Ringgold	11	7	4	Lyon	40	25	15
Sac	19	8	11	Marion	10	7	3
Shelby	9	8	1	Marshall	20	8	12
Sioux	38	14	24	McPherson	34	16	18
Tama	23	13	10	Meade	16	5	11
Taylor	9	5	4	Mitchell	14	7	7
Union	12	6	6	Morris	12	7	5
Van Buren	11	5	6	Morton	7	6	1
Wapello	39	10	29	Nemaha	17	8	9
Wayne	15	6	9	Neosho	27	14	13
Webster	32	15	17	Ness	11	5	6
Winnebago	10	6	4	Norton	10	5	5
Winneshiek	23	10	13	Osborne	14	8	6
Worth	20	8	12	Ottawa	18	5	13
Wright	20	8	12	Pawnee	15	8	7
KANSAS-Metropolitan Counties				Phillips	14	9	5
Butler	113	59	54	Pratt	14	8	6
Doniphan	14	4	10	Rawlins	4	3	1
Douglas	136	80	56	Reno	78	66	12
Franklin	62	27	35	Republic	13	7	6
Geary	82	29	53	Rice	8	6	2
Harvey	38	16	22	Rooks	10	5	5
Jackson	24	15	9	Rush	9	4	5
Jefferson	39	22	17	Russell	18	11	7
Johnson	595	474	121	Saline	105	47	58
Leavenworth	94	56	38	Scott	7	3	4
Linn	23	11	12	Seward	51	17	34
Miami	48	27	21	Sheridan	8	3	5
Osage	43	23	20	Sherman	13	6	7
Pottawatomie	44	26	18	Smith	5	5	0
Riley County Police Department	164	99	65	Stafford	10	4	6
Sedgwick	538	180	358	Stanton	13	5	8
Shawnee	204	113	91	Thomas	13	6	7
Sumner	42	20	22	Trego	3	2	1
Wabaunsee	20	8	12	Wallace	6	2	4
Wyandotte	197	64	133	Washington	15	7	8
KANSAS-Nonmetropolitan Counties				Wichita	8	4	4
Allen	27	10	17	Wilson	33	11	22
Anderson	28	21	7	Woodson	11	8	3
Barber	9	4	5	**KENTUCKY-Metropolitan Counties**			
Bourbon	9	7	2	Boone	139	131	8
Brown	23	8	15	Bourbon	9	8	1
Chase	9	5	4	Boyd	34	27	7
Cherokee	29	19	10	Bracken	5	4	1
Cheyenne	4	4	0	Bullitt	47	41	6
Clark	11	6	5	Campbell	12	9	3
Clay	19	8	11	Campbell County Police Department	31	30	1
Cloud	15	9	6	Christian	33	29	4
Coffey	32	13	19	Clark	17	13	4
Cowley	44	24	20	Daviess	45	40	5
Crawford	68	33	35	Edmonson	9	5	4
Decatur	3	3	0	Gallatin	10	9	1
Dickinson	28	16	12	Gallatin County Police Department	1	1	0
Edwards	10	6	4	Grant	7	6	1

Table 80. Full-Time Law Enforcement Employees, by State by Metropolitan and Nonmetropolitan Counties, 2010—*Continued*

(Number)

State/County	Total law enforce-ment employees	Total officers	Total civilians	State/County	Total law enforce-ment employees	Total officers	Total civilians
Greenup	18	14	4	Ohio	18	15	3
Hancock	7	6	1	Owen	7	5	2
Hardin	42	36	6	Owsley	3	2	1
Henderson	25	21	4	Perry	24	13	11
Henry	7	6	1	Pike	28	12	16
Jefferson	271	221	50	Pulaski	41	33	8
Jessamine	34	25	9	Robertson	1	1	0
Kenton	33	25	8	Rockcastle	5	4	1
Kenton County Police Department	36	34	2	Rowan	14	11	3
McLean	10	8	2	Russell	10	9	1
Meade	14	11	3	Simpson	17	15	2
Nelson	31	23	8	Taylor	14	12	2
Oldham	17	15	2	Todd	4	3	1
Oldham County Police Department	33	31	2	Union	8	7	1
Pendleton	8	7	1	Washington	8	6	2
Scott	32	30	2	Wayne	11	10	1
Shelby	25	24	1	Whitley	15	12	3
Spencer	6	5	1	Wolfe	4	3	1
Trimble	1	1	0	**LOUISIANA-Metropolitan Counties**			
Warren	74	53	21	Ascension	279	239	40
Webster	8	6	2	Bossier	370	293	77
Woodford	8	8	0	Caddo	650	446	204
KENTUCKY-Nonmetropolitan Counties				Calcasieu	842	428	414
Adair	8	6	2	Cameron	73	61	12
Anderson	17	15	2	De Soto	110	90	20
Ballard	13	13	0	East Baton Rouge	838	703	135
Barren	20	16	4	East Feliciana	59	59	0
Bath	5	3	2	Grant	67	49	18
Bell	21	8	13	Lafayette	643	464	179
Boyle	11	9	2	Livingston	240	240	0
Breathitt	4	2	2	Ouachita	391	290	101
Breckinridge	14	11	3	Rapides	458	360	98
Butler	6	5	1	St. Bernard	271	237	34
Caldwell	10	8	2	St. Charles	376	279	97
Calloway	23	16	7	St. Helena	53	24	29
Carroll	4	3	1	St. Martin	241	136	105
Carter	12	10	2	St. Tammany	682	413	269
Casey	8	6	2	Terrebonne	373	160	213
Clay	15	12	3	Union	52	36	16
Clinton	5	4	1	West Baton Rouge	191	153	38
Crittenden	4	3	1	West Feliciana	74	49	25
Cumberland	5	3	2	**LOUISIANA-Nonmetropolitan Counties**			
Fleming	18	15	3	Acadia	108	55	53
Floyd	14	11	3	Avoyelles	398	398	0
Franklin	21	18	3	Bienville	55	33	22
Fulton	4	3	1	Caldwell	27	26	1
Garrard	9	8	1	Catahoula	106	16	90
Graves	17	12	5	Claiborne	34	34	0
Green	4	4	0	Evangeline	62	23	39
Harlan	24	20	4	Franklin	134	109	25
Harrison	10	10	0	Jackson	169	34	135
Hart	11	8	3	Jefferson Davis	65	50	15
Hickman	3	3	0	La Salle	45	45	0
Hopkins	26	18	8	Lincoln	63	47	16
Jackson	7	5	2	Natchitoches	82	58	24
Johnson	15	11	4	Red River	44	44	0
Knox	13	10	3	Sabine	74	74	0
Laurel	35	22	13	St. James	99	77	22
Leslie	8	7	1	St. Landry	221	97	124
Letcher	14	12	2	St. Mary	204	203	1
Lewis	7	5	2	Tangipahoa	263	104	159
Lincoln	12	10	2	Tensas	124	30	94
Livingston	7	7	0	Vermilion	129	109	20
Lyon	6	6	0	Webster	146	47	99
Madison	38	24	14	West Carroll	18	18	0
Magoffin	5	4	1	**MAINE-Metropolitan Counties**			
Marion	6	4	2	Androscoggin	28	18	10
Marshall	27	25	2	Cumberland	61	52	9
Mason	16	14	2	Penobscot	31	26	5
McCracken	43	38	5	Sagadahoc	23	20	3
McCreary	8	6	2	York	29	26	3
Menifee	5	4	1	**MAINE-Nonmetropolitan Counties**			
Mercer	13	11	2	Aroostook	17	15	2
Montgomery	14	13	1	Franklin	25	15	10
Muhlenberg	11	11	0	Hancock	17	15	2
Nicholas	4	2	2	Kennebec	22	19	3

Table 80.　Full-Time Law Enforcement Employees, by State by Metropolitan and Nonmetropolitan Counties, 2010—*Continued*

(Number)

State/County	Total law enforcement employees	Total officers	Total civilians	State/County	Total law enforcement employees	Total officers	Total civilians
Knox	19	18	1	Chippewa	15	13	2
Lincoln	25	23	2	Clare	28	23	5
Oxford	22	21	1	Crawford	26	16	10
Piscataquis	18	7	11	Delta	29	15	14
Somerset	17	15	2	Dickinson	33	13	20
Waldo	19	17	2	Emmet	46	24	22
Washington	16	15	1	Gladwin	41	16	25
MARYLAND-Metropolitan Counties				Gogebic	22	16	6
Allegany	12	10	2	Grand Traverse	124	64	60
Allegany County Bureau of Police	19	19	0	Gratiot	35	19	16
Anne Arundel	100	70	30	Hillsdale	43	27	16
Anne Arundel County Police Department	840	634	206	Houghton	30	20	10
Baltimore County	98	83	15	Huron	36	20	16
Baltimore County Police Department	2,217	1,899	318	Iosco	20	4	16
Calvert	137	116	21	Iron	17	8	9
Carroll	97	69	28	Isabella	49	23	26
Cecil	95	83	12	Kalkaska	34	18	16
Charles	435	288	147	Keweenaw	7	6	1
Frederick	231	169	62	Lake	69	14	55
Harford	375	292	83	Leelanau	19	18	1
Howard	70	48	22	Lenawee	110	41	69
Howard County Police Department	604	438	166	Luce	5	4	1
Montgomery	166	141	25	Mackinac	26	13	13
Montgomery County Police Department	1,577	1,169	408	Manistee	30	14	16
Prince George's	319	226	93	Marquette	56	23	33
Prince George's County Police Department	1,804	1,562	242	Mason	40	20	20
Queen Anne's	54	50	4	Mecosta	47	22	25
Somerset	22	19	3	Menominee	30	30	0
Washington	243	95	148	Midland	56	33	23
Wicomico	107	84	23	Missaukee	27	12	15
MARYLAND-Nonmetropolitan Counties				Montcalm	58	29	29
Caroline	31	29	2	Montmorency	24	10	14
Dorchester	40	34	6	Oceana	35	19	16
Garrett	54	29	25	Ogemaw	27	16	11
Kent	28	23	5	Ontonagon	12	9	3
St. Mary's	248	132	116	Osceola	35	17	18
Talbot	31	28	3	Oscoda	17	11	6
Worcester	50	43	7	Otsego	24	11	13
MICHIGAN-Metropolitan Counties				Presque Isle	24	13	11
Barry	54	30	24	Roscommon	41	27	14
Bay	81	36	45	Sanilac	57	24	33
Berrien	160	71	89	Schoolcraft	12	4	8
Calhoun	172	77	95	Shiawassee	66	32	34
Cass	70	33	37	St. Joseph	48	22	26
Clinton	59	25	34	Tuscola	50	25	25
Eaton	139	71	68	Wexford	49	23	26
Genesee	233	133	100	**MINNESOTA-Metropolitan Counties**			
Ingham	176	102	74	Anoka	246	127	119
Ionia	53	22	31	Benton	74	27	47
Jackson	133	53	80	Blue Earth	59	26	33
Kalamazoo	206	146	60	Carlton	46	19	27
Kent	536	202	334	Carver	152	80	72
Lapeer	79	47	32	Chisago	77	38	39
Livingston	109	65	44	Clay	62	31	31
Macomb	486	248	238	Dakota	176	71	105
Monroe	173	84	89	Dodge	29	21	8
Muskegon	123	47	76	Hennepin	784	332	452
Newaygo	68	25	43	Houston	26	14	12
Oakland	973	778	195	Isanti	59	20	39
Ottawa	223	128	95	Nicollet	38	12	26
Saginaw	128	57	71	Olmsted	151	59	92
St. Clair	170	66	104	Polk	27	22	5
Van Buren	87	44	43	Ramsey	387	226	161
Wayne	1,022	928	94	Scott	125	38	87
MICHIGAN-Nonmetropolitan Counties				Sherburne	261	80	181
Alcona	25	14	11	Stearns	184	64	120
Alger	13	11	2	St. Louis	231	91	140
Allegan	66	57	9	Wabasha	31	18	13
Alpena	25	12	13	Washington	225	90	135
Antrim	48	20	28	Wright	214	137	77
Arenac	21	12	9	**MINNESOTA-Nonmetropolitan Counties**			
Baraga	13	6	7	Aitkin	46	19	27
Benzie	35	11	24	Becker	56	21	35
Branch	49	26	23	Beltrami	74	29	45
Charlevoix	39	18	21	Big Stone	8	5	3
Cheboygan	36	18	18	Brown	36	10	26

Table 80.   Full-Time Law Enforcement Employees, by State by Metropolitan and Nonmetropolitan Counties, 2010—*Continued*

(Number)

State/County	Total law enforcement employees	Total officers	Total civilians
Cass	54	36	18
Chippewa	18	8	10
Clearwater	22	9	13
Cook	18	11	7
Cottonwood	20	9	11
Crow Wing	118	36	82
Douglas	75	23	52
Faribault	25	8	17
Fillmore	31	19	12
Freeborn	66	23	43
Goodhue	102	39	63
Grant	11	6	5
Hubbard	41	15	26
Itasca	71	61	10
Jackson	19	8	11
Kanabec	48	19	29
Kandiyohi	109	33	76
Kittson	10	5	5
Koochiching	18	10	8
Lac Qui Parle	9	7	2
Lake	28	16	12
Lake of the Woods	9	5	4
Le Sueur	29	15	14
Lincoln	10	4	6
Lyon	47	14	33
Mahnomen	19	12	7
Marshall	17	11	6
Martin	30	11	19
McLeod	59	24	35
Meeker	45	20	25
Mille Lacs	65	25	40
Morrison	52	18	34
Mower	66	22	44
Murray	13	9	4
Nobles	33	11	22
Norman	8	5	3
Otter Tail	79	32	47
Pennington	29	8	21
Pine	74	28	46
Pipestone	22	12	10
Pope	14	7	7
Red Lake	10	6	4
Redwood	22	12	10
Renville	27	12	15
Rice	50	24	26
Rock	15	10	5
Roseau	22	12	10
Sibley	22	10	12
Steele	23	18	5
Stevens	13	6	7
Swift	14	8	6
Todd	31	14	17
Traverse	13	7	6
Wadena	21	8	13
Waseca	27	12	15
Watonwan	21	8	13
Wilkin	17	6	11
Winona	58	20	38
Yellow Medicine	19	8	11
MISSISSIPPI-Metropolitan Counties			
Copiah	42	22	20
DeSoto	241	101	140
Forrest	121	85	36
George	28	16	12
Hancock	75	50	25
Harrison	351	110	241
Hinds	504	126	378
Lamar	90	39	51
Madison	133	57	76
Marshall	55	28	27
Perry	17	7	10
Rankin	190	80	110
Simpson	42	16	26
Stone	20	18	2
Tate	53	24	29
Tunica	145	64	81

State/County	Total law enforcement employees	Total officers	Total civilians
MISSISSIPPI-Nonmetropolitan Counties			
Adams	66	56	10
Alcorn	36	17	19
Amite	13	5	8
Attala	13	8	5
Benton	15	5	10
Bolivar	113	18	95
Calhoun	10	5	5
Chickasaw	16	15	1
Choctaw	12	6	6
Claiborne	30	12	18
Clarke	14	10	4
Clay	32	10	22
Coahoma	23	20	3
Covington	18	12	6
Franklin	6	3	3
Greene	16	8	8
Grenada	16	13	3
Holmes	22	14	8
Humphreys	12	6	6
Issaquena	4	4	0
Itawamba	13	12	1
Jasper	28	15	13
Jefferson	16	9	7
Jones	37	32	5
Kemper	13	7	6
Lafayette	67	30	37
Lauderdale	122	53	69
Lawrence	27	11	16
Leake	16	14	2
Lee	127	46	81
Leflore	33	22	11
Lincoln	43	21	22
Lowndes	110	44	66
Marion	23	16	7
Monroe	61	27	34
Montgomery	8	6	2
Neshoba	18	18	0
Newton	18	10	8
Noxubee	11	5	6
Oktibbeha	53	29	24
Panola	68	28	40
Pearl River	97	39	58
Pike	55	27	28
Pontotoc	35	19	16
Prentiss	32	13	19
Quitman	10	6	4
Scott	60	24	36
Sharkey	10	6	4
Smith	16	11	5
Tallahatchie	30	13	17
Tippah	22	9	13
Tishomingo	27	13	14
Union	32	17	15
Walthall	16	9	7
Warren	66	37	29
Washington	66	37	29
Wayne	27	13	14
Webster	7	5	2
Wilkinson	16	8	8
Winston	10	9	1
Yalobusha	14	9	5
Yazoo	17	15	2
MISSOURI-Metropolitan Counties			
Andrew	14	10	4
Bates	41	15	26
Bollinger	10	8	2
Boone	78	62	16
Buchanan	103	76	27
Caldwell	38	8	30
Callaway	23	21	2
Cape Girardeau	71	44	27
Cass	92	73	19
Christian	78	38	40
Clay	186	113	73
Clinton	29	18	11

Table 80.   Full-Time Law Enforcement Employees, by State by Metropolitan and Nonmetropolitan Counties, 2010—*Continued*

(Number)

State/County	Total law enforcement employees	Total officers	Total civilians	State/County	Total law enforcement employees	Total officers	Total civilians
Cole	71	48	23	Pike	27	10	17
Dallas	22	16	6	Pulaski	37	16	21
De Kalb	11	5	6	Putnam	4	3	1
Franklin	136	114	22	Ralls	6	6	0
Greene	302	158	144	Randolph	37	18	19
Howard	11	7	4	Reynolds	16	8	8
Jackson	140	98	42	Ripley	9	7	2
Jasper	165	115	50	Saline	33	20	13
Jefferson	199	140	59	Schuyler	8	3	5
Lafayette	40	37	3	Scotland	6	2	4
Lincoln	86	46	40	Scott	39	22	17
McDonald	29	27	2	Shannon	8	4	4
Moniteau	9	4	5	Shelby	9	5	4
Newton	55	44	11	St. Clair	66	20	46
Osage	15	11	4	Ste. Genevieve	54	40	14
Platte	115	80	35	St. Francois	67	55	12
Polk	36	21	15	Stoddard	23	11	12
Ray	33	15	18	Stone	54	47	7
St. Charles	226	154	72	Sullivan	5	4	1
St. Louis County Police Department	1,028	786	242	Taney	61	45	16
Warren	62	35	27	Texas	13	8	5
Washington	32	21	11	Vernon	23	14	9
Webster	28	15	13	Wayne	16	7	9
MISSOURI-Nonmetropolitan Counties				Worth	4	3	1
Adair	38	14	24	Wright	13	6	7
Atchison	10	5	5	**MONTANA-Metropolitan Counties**			
Audrain	42	25	17	Carbon	13	8	5
Barry	35	21	14	Cascade	129	32	97
Barton	16	6	10	Missoula	160	48	112
Benton	23	15	8	Yellowstone	147	54	93
Butler	42	18	24	**MONTANA-Nonmetropolitan Counties**			
Camden	107	69	38	Beaverhead	21	6	15
Carroll	10	9	1	Big Horn	32	15	17
Carter	9	4	5	Blaine	13	8	5
Cedar	18	12	6	Broadwater	22	10	12
Clark	14	7	7	Carter	3	3	0
Cooper	9	8	1	Chouteau	18	9	9
Crawford	37	28	9	Custer	15	6	9
Dade	7	2	5	Daniels	4	3	1
Daviess	6	5	1	Dawson	6	5	1
Dent	17	13	4	Deer Lodge	18	18	0
Douglas	9	6	3	Fallon	9	3	6
Dunklin	11	9	2	Fergus	15	9	6
Gasconade	14	13	1	Flathead	105	53	52
Grundy	14	4	10	Gallatin	66	48	18
Harrison	11	5	6	Garfield	2	2	0
Henry	36	24	12	Glacier	19	12	7
Hickory	14	9	5	Golden Valley	2	2	0
Holt	9	4	5	Granite	9	5	4
Howell	34	24	10	Hill	28	13	15
Iron	12	7	5	Jefferson	23	13	10
Johnson	39	31	8	Judith Basin	5	4	1
Knox	5	3	2	Lake	56	25	31
Laclede	23	22	1	Lewis and Clark	75	44	31
Lawrence	39	29	10	Liberty	10	5	5
Lewis	11	5	6	Lincoln	36	20	16
Linn	6	5	1	Madison	19	10	9
Livingston	17	9	8	McCone	4	4	0
Macon	15	12	3	Meagher	8	4	4
Madison	10	8	2	Mineral	15	6	9
Maries	9	6	3	Musselshell	9	8	1
Marion	37	16	21	Park	22	13	9
Mercer	8	3	5	Petroleum	1	1	0
Miller	16	14	2	Phillips	11	7	4
Mississippi	41	10	31	Pondera	10	9	1
Monroe	8	7	1	Powder River	7	3	4
Montgomery	15	13	2	Powell	17	10	7
Morgan	42	21	21	Prairie	3	3	0
New Madrid	28	13	15	Ravalli	61	30	31
Nodaway	11	11	0	Richland	14	7	7
Oregon	10	6	4	Roosevelt	25	11	14
Ozark	14	8	6	Rosebud	25	13	12
Pemiscot	50	24	26	Sanders	21	8	13
Perry	25	16	9	Sheridan	8	7	1
Pettis	43	26	17	Silver Bow	98	49	49
Phelps	62	27	35	Stillwater	13	7	6

Table 80. Full-Time Law Enforcement Employees, by State by Metropolitan and Nonmetropolitan Counties, 2010—*Continued*

(Number)

State/County	Total law enforcement employees	Total officers	Total civilians	State/County	Total law enforcement employees	Total officers	Total civilians
Sweet Grass	12	6	6	Pierce	9	4	5
Teton	12	9	3	Platte	66	20	46
Toole	20	12	8	Polk	13	7	6
Treasure	2	2	0	Red Willow	8	6	2
Valley	13	8	5	Richardson	9	5	4
Wheatland	9	5	4	Rock	7	3	4
Wibaux	1	1	0	Saline	10	10	0
NEBRASKA-Metropolitan Counties				Scotts Bluff	26	18	8
Cass	74	53	21	Sheridan	7	6	1
Dakota	17	15	2	Sherman	6	5	1
Dixon	12	7	5	Sioux	1	1	0
Douglas	191	127	64	Stanton	8	7	1
Lancaster	98	81	17	Thayer	11	7	4
Sarpy	198	132	66	Thomas	1	1	0
Saunders	19	11	8	Wayne	6	5	1
Seward	23	12	11	Webster	9	6	3
NEBRASKA-Nonmetropolitan Counties				Wheeler	2	2	0
Adams	19	17	2	York	23	9	14
Antelope	12	6	6	**NEVADA-Metropolitan Counties**			
Arthur	1	1	0	Carson City	131	91	40
Banner	1	1	0	Storey	23	21	2
Blaine	1	1	0	Washoe	704	417	287
Boone	12	5	7	**NEVADA-Nonmetropolitan Counties**			
Box Butte	20	5	15	Churchill	48	40	8
Brown	9	5	4	Douglas	119	106	13
Buffalo	44	25	19	Elko	69	53	16
Burt	9	4	5	Esmeralda	16	12	4
Butler	8	7	1	Eureka	19	14	5
Cedar	10	4	6	Humboldt	49	36	13
Chase	8	4	4	Lander	31	19	12
Cherry	12	5	7	Lincoln	32	27	5
Cheyenne	8	6	2	Lyon	101	73	28
Colfax	9	7	2	Mineral	25	19	6
Cuming	6	5	1	Nye	141	101	40
Custer	7	6	1	Pershing	19	12	7
Dawes	9	3	6	White Pine	32	25	7
Dawson	60	30	30	**NEW HAMPSHIRE-Metropolitan Counties**			
Deuel	5	4	1	Rockingham	48	25	23
Dundy	8	4	4	**NEW HAMPSHIRE-Nonmetropolitan Counties**			
Fillmore	11	7	4	Carroll	24	12	12
Franklin	7	3	4	Cheshire	21	10	11
Frontier	8	5	3	Merrimack	33	16	17
Furnas	10	8	2	**NEW JERSEY-Metropolitan Counties**			
Gage	15	12	3	Atlantic	133	108	25
Garden	9	4	5	Bergen	524	439	85
Garfield	1	1	0	Bergen County Police Department	166	91	75
Gosper	5	4	1	Burlington	87	73	14
Grant	1	1	0	Camden	182	151	31
Greeley	3	2	1	Cape May	147	125	22
Hall	36	29	7	Cumberland	64	58	6
Hamilton	19	9	10	Essex	453	389	64
Harlan	8	4	4	Gloucester	102	88	14
Hayes	2	2	0	Hudson	340	226	114
Hitchcock	7	4	3	Hunterdon	26	22	4
Holt	11	5	6	Mercer	163	129	34
Hooker	2	2	0	Middlesex	224	182	42
Howard	11	5	6	Monmouth	562	411	151
Jefferson	14	7	7	Morris	322	251	71
Johnson	11	7	4	Ocean	238	132	106
Kearney	11	6	5	Passaic	721	572	149
Keya Paha	1	1	0	Salem	194	169	25
Kimball	9	4	5	Somerset	202	166	36
Knox	12	5	7	Sussex	154	130	24
Lincoln	51	24	27	Union	214	168	46
Logan	2	2	0	Warren	20	16	4
Loup	1	1	0	**NEW MEXICO-Metropolitan Counties**			
Madison	52	25	27	Bernalillo	336	272	64
McPherson	1	1	0	Dona Ana	231	137	94
Merrick	11	6	5	Sandoval	57	50	7
Morrill	8	3	5	San Juan	121	92	29
Nance	11	7	4	Santa Fe	101	73	28
Nemaha	5	5	0	Torrance	18	13	5
Nuckolls	7	4	3	Valencia	45	36	9
Otoe	26	16	10	**NEW MEXICO-Nonmetropolitan Counties**			
Pawnee	5	4	1	Catron	11	7	4
Perkins	8	4	4	Chaves	51	41	10
Phelps	27	6	21	Cibola	22	15	7

Table 80.   Full-Time Law Enforcement Employees, by State by Metropolitan and Nonmetropolitan Counties, 2010—*Continued*

(Number)

State/County	Total law enforce-ment employees	Total officers	Total civilians	State/County	Total law enforce-ment employees	Total officers	Total civilians
Colfax	13	11	2	St. Lawrence	34	33	1
Curry	28	18	10	Sullivan	47	46	1
De Baca	5	5	0	Wyoming	41	30	11
Eddy	55	46	9	Yates	45	26	19
Grant	41	38	3	**NORTH CAROLINA-Metropolitan Counties**			
Guadalupe	4	4	0	Alamance	270	123	147
Hidalgo	13	10	3	Alexander	46	27	19
Lea	66	45	21	Anson	60	30	30
Lincoln	25	16	9	Brunswick	200	135	65
Luna	33	30	3	Buncombe	376	232	144
McKinley	51	40	11	Burke	118	89	29
Mora	7	5	2	Cabarrus	238	195	43
Otero	58	40	18	Caldwell	120	67	53
Quay	8	7	1	Catawba	176	127	49
Rio Arriba	25	22	3	Chatham	99	77	22
Roosevelt	17	14	3	Cumberland	529	298	231
San Miguel	10	8	2	Currituck	99	63	36
Sierra	14	12	2	Davie	78	47	31
Socorro	15	12	3	Durham	421	157	264
Taos	27	20	7	Edgecombe	134	53	81
Union	6	5	1	Forsyth	527	228	299
NEW YORK-Metropolitan Counties				Franklin	106	65	41
Albany	168	122	46	Gaston	211	121	90
Broome	69	54	15	Gaston County Police Department	224	133	91
Chemung	53	44	9	Greene	46	25	21
Dutchess	138	105	33	Guilford	557	252	305
Erie	196	151	45	Haywood	82	48	34
Herkimer	15	6	9	Henderson	187	132	55
Livingston	74	50	24	Hoke	95	53	42
Madison	39	30	9	Johnston	181	104	77
Monroe	341	280	61	Madison	24	17	7
Nassau	3,223	2,429	794	Mecklenburg[1]	1,236	294	942
Niagara	143	110	33	Nash	134	76	58
Oneida	113	84	29	New Hanover	386	293	93
Onondaga	266	228	38	Onslow	117	104	13
Ontario	101	67	34	Orange	139	105	34
Orange	113	101	12	Pender	95	57	38
Orleans	41	25	16	Person	47	41	6
Oswego	83	68	15	Pitt	321	138	183
Putnam	100	82	18	Randolph	216	154	62
Rensselaer	38	33	5	Rockingham	140	96	44
Rockland	115	81	34	Stokes	64	42	22
Saratoga	150	112	38	Union	249	185	64
Schenectady	16	10	6	Wake	801	349	452
Schoharie	29	15	14	Wayne	152	86	66
Suffolk	413	281	132	Yadkin	45	33	12
Suffolk County Police Department	3,117	2,510	607	**NORTH CAROLINA-Nonmetropolitan Counties**			
Tioga	49	32	17	Alleghany	28	12	16
Tompkins	41	38	3	Ashe	54	24	30
Ulster	78	57	21	Avery	33	24	9
Warren	109	69	40	Beaufort	82	47	35
Washington	37	31	6	Bertie	33	25	8
Wayne	58	50	8	Bladen	66	40	26
Westchester Public Safety	330	257	73	Camden	18	17	1
NEW YORK-Nonmetropolitan Counties				Carteret	91	52	39
Allegany	47	28	19	Caswell	47	36	11
Cattaraugus	88	65	23	Cherokee	65	27	38
Cayuga	45	36	9	Chowan	35	15	20
Chautauqua	107	69	38	Clay	41	15	26
Chenango	38	23	15	Cleveland	126	84	42
Clinton	23	23	0	Columbus	109	64	45
Columbia	57	47	10	Craven	122	70	52
Cortland	52	33	19	Dare	138	61	77
Delaware	27	16	11	Davidson	191	125	66
Essex	6	5	1	Duplin	89	67	22
Franklin	7	3	4	Gates	13	12	1
Fulton	43	27	16	Graham	23	14	9
Genesee	79	49	30	Granville	88	49	39
Greene	31	29	2	Halifax	87	61	26
Hamilton	6	5	1	Harnett	199	110	89
Jefferson	53	44	9	Hertford	50	22	28
Lewis	30	19	11	Hyde	20	16	4
Montgomery	34	22	12	Iredell	219	162	57
Otsego	19	17	2	Jackson	72	47	25
Schuyler	19	17	2	Jones	22	13	9
Seneca	42	31	11	Lee	37	7	30
Steuben	55	43	12	Lenoir	102	64	38

[1] The employee data presented in this table for Mecklenburg represent only Mecklenburg County Sheriff's Office and exclude Charlotte-Mecklenburg Police Department.

Table 80.   Full-Time Law Enforcement Employees, by State by Metropolitan and Nonmetropolitan Counties, 2010—*Continued*

(Number)

State/County	Total law enforcement employees	Total officers	Total civilians	State/County	Total law enforcement employees	Total officers	Total civilians
Lincoln	158	108	50	Steele	3	3	0
Macon	65	46	19	Stutsman	10	8	2
Martin	36	34	2	Towner	3	2	1
McDowell	62	39	23	Traill	13	8	5
Mitchell	15	14	1	Walsh	16	10	6
Montgomery	52	31	21	Ward	48	22	26
Moore	114	74	40	Wells	3	3	0
Northampton	52	27	25	Williams	34	20	14
Pamlico	48	15	33	**OHIO-Metropolitan Counties**			
Pasquotank	46	41	5	Brown	43	24	19
Perquimans	14	11	3	Carroll	25	19	6
Polk	34	22	12	Clark	170	127	43
Richmond	56	50	6	Delaware	209	94	115
Robeson	228	128	100	Erie	67	36	31
Rowan	161	115	46	Fairfield	127	100	27
Rutherford	126	75	51	Fulton	31	20	11
Sampson	133	89	44	Geauga	117	48	69
Scotland	69	41	28	Greene	138	88	50
Stanly	88	51	37	Jefferson	61	29	32
Surry	97	58	39	Lake	196	54	142
Swain	41	18	23	Licking	182	124	58
Transylvania	78	58	20	Medina	85	56	29
Tyrrell	16	10	6	Miami	85	47	38
Vance	91	45	46	Montgomery	442	201	241
Warren	64	36	28	Morrow	48	19	29
Washington	40	21	19	Ottawa	58	20	38
Watauga	87	48	39	Pickaway	86	36	50
Wilkes	115	67	48	Portage	128	55	73
Wilson	141	92	49	Preble	45	11	34
Yancey	33	14	19	Richland	101	33	68
NORTH DAKOTA-Metropolitan Counties				Stark	220	127	93
Burleigh	81	41	40	Trumbull	138	52	86
Cass	138	72	66	Warren	182	94	88
Grand Forks	37	30	7	Washington	82	42	40
Morton	35	20	15	**OHIO-Nonmetropolitan Counties**			
NORTH DAKOTA-Nonmetropolitan Counties				Allen	145	67	78
Adams	4	4	0	Ashland	68	39	29
Barnes	7	6	1	Ashtabula	56	17	39
Benson	4	4	0	Auglaize	56	22	34
Billings	4	4	0	Belmont	61	50	11
Bottineau	14	10	4	Champaign	25	23	2
Bowman	3	3	0	Clermont	183	81	102
Burke	4	4	0	Clinton	67	36	31
Cavalier	11	5	6	Crawford	53	21	32
Dickey	5	4	1	Cuyahoga	1,075	163	912
Divide	4	4	0	Darke	63	39	24
Dunn	7	6	1	Defiance	36	20	16
Eddy	5	4	1	Fayette	32	21	11
Emmons	4	3	1	Franklin	869	663	206
Foster	3	3	0	Guernsey	41	19	22
Golden Valley	4	3	1	Hamilton	822	309	513
Grant	4	4	0	Hancock	82	33	49
Griggs	5	4	1	Harrison	18	15	3
Hettinger	3	3	0	Henry	20	18	2
Kidder	4	3	1	Highland	47	29	18
Lamoure	5	4	1	Hocking	25	20	5
Logan	2	2	0	Huron	69	23	46
McHenry	7	7	0	Logan	72	35	37
McIntosh	3	3	0	Marion	33	29	4
McKenzie	17	8	9	Meigs	15	13	2
McLean	31	17	14	Mercer	48	27	21
Mercer	23	14	9	Monroe	20	16	4
Mountrail	15	9	6	Morgan	13	8	5
Nelson	5	4	1	Muskingum	115	74	41
Oliver	5	4	1	Noble	15	7	8
Pembina	13	7	6	Paulding	21	14	7
Pierce	7	3	4	Perry	16	11	5
Ramsey	7	6	1	Putnam	54	31	23
Ransom	5	4	1	Sandusky	53	31	22
Renville	5	5	0	Scioto	71	40	31
Richland	25	13	12	Seneca	83	38	45
Rolette	16	8	8	Shelby	59	35	24
Sargent	5	4	1	Tuscarawas	98	27	71
Sheridan	2	2	0	Van Wert	35	19	16
Sioux	1	1	0	Vinton	15	10	5
Slope	1	1	0	Wayne	57	50	7
Stark	16	13	3	Williams	21	17	4
				Wyandot	24	12	12

Table 80.   Full-Time Law Enforcement Employees, by State by Metropolitan and Nonmetropolitan Counties, 2010—*Continued*

(Number)

State/County	Total law enforcement employees	Total officers	Total civilians	State/County	Total law enforcement employees	Total officers	Total civilians
OKLAHOMA-Metropolitan Counties				Washita	16	7	9
Canadian	59	37	22	Woods	10	5	5
Cleveland	122	59	63	Woodward	21	9	12
Comanche	40	29	11	**OREGON-Metropolitan Counties**			
Creek	69	34	35	Benton	75	62	13
Grady	21	14	7	Clackamas	450	223	227
Le Flore	18	13	5	Columbia	41	35	6
Lincoln	31	11	20	Deschutes	210	82	128
Logan	25	15	10	Jackson	163	117	46
McClain	26	15	11	Lane	374	70	304
Oklahoma	668	204	464	Marion	336	85	251
Okmulgee	13	12	1	Multnomah	750	95	655
Osage	76	40	36	Polk	64	47	17
Pawnee	18	8	10	Washington	539	240	299
Rogers	34	29	5	Yamhill	96	45	51
Sequoyah	46	15	31	**OREGON-Nonmetropolitan Counties**			
Tulsa	527	223	304	Baker	25	12	13
Wagoner	50	21	29	Clatsop	55	27	28
OKLAHOMA-Nonmetropolitan Counties				Coos	85	25	60
Adair	33	9	24	Crook	28	15	13
Alfalfa	9	4	5	Curry	37	14	23
Atoka	8	8	0	Douglas	144	112	32
Beaver	13	7	6	Gilliam	6	5	1
Beckham	33	11	22	Grant	16	5	11
Blaine	15	6	9	Harney	17	11	6
Bryan	17	14	3	Hood River	33	16	17
Caddo	31	17	14	Jefferson	46	14	32
Carter	57	18	39	Josephine	93	34	59
Cherokee	32	24	8	Klamath	67	34	33
Choctaw	14	5	9	Lake	20	7	13
Cimarron	10	3	7	Lincoln	87	27	60
Coal	10	6	4	Linn	189	79	110
Cotton	11	6	5	Malheur	51	20	31
Craig	25	10	15	Morrow	27	27	0
Custer	35	12	23	Sherman	7	6	1
Delaware	45	20	25	Tillamook	60	56	4
Dewey	11	4	7	Umatilla	74	49	25
Ellis	15	5	10	Union	11	9	2
Garfield	61	23	38	Wallowa	13	7	6
Garvin	28	13	15	Wasco	29	14	15
Grant	9	4	5	Wheeler	14	3	11
Greer	7	3	4	**PENNSYLVANIA-Metropolitan Counties**			
Harmon	4	3	1	Allegheny	187	156	31
Harper	8	4	4	Allegheny County Police Department	268	210	58
Haskell	16	5	11	Beaver	30	23	7
Hughes	12	6	6	Berks	109	95	14
Jackson	37	12	25	Blair	10	6	4
Jefferson	12	2	10	Butler	20	17	3
Johnston	27	8	19	Cumberland	33	27	6
Kay	20	12	8	Erie	42	37	5
Kingfisher	14	7	7	Luzerne	10	10	0
Kiowa	16	9	7	Mercer	16	13	3
Latimer	17	5	12	Northampton	54	50	4
Love	19	6	13	Pike	25	21	4
Major	9	4	5	Washington	30	27	3
Marshall	24	9	15	York	115	105	10
Mayes	48	20	28	**PENNSYLVANIA-Nonmetropolitan Counties**			
McCurtain	20	17	3	Adams	14	12	2
McIntosh	14	10	4	Bedford	12	10	2
Murray	12	6	6	Bradford	11	9	2
Muskogee	43	33	10	Clarion	8	5	3
Noble	19	5	14	Clearfield	11	8	3
Nowata	20	9	11	Elk	6	5	1
Okfuskee	17	8	9	Franklin	18	14	4
Ottawa	34	16	18	Greene	7	6	1
Payne	76	28	48	Huntingdon	9	8	1
Pittsburg	62	19	43	Jefferson	3	3	0
Pontotoc	36	12	24	Snyder	5	5	0
Pottawatomie	25	22	3	Tioga	7	5	2
Pushmataha	12	7	5	Union	9	8	1
Roger Mills	12	7	5	**SOUTH CAROLINA-Metropolitan Counties**			
Seminole	25	13	12	Aiken	168	127	41
Stephens	46	18	28	Berkeley	221	148	73
Texas	41	12	29	Calhoun	23	21	2
Tillman	27	7	20	Charleston	766	254	512
Washington	48	23	25	Darlington	80	71	9

Table 80.   Full-Time Law Enforcement Employees, by State by Metropolitan and Nonmetropolitan Counties, 2010—*Continued*

(Number)

State/County	Total law enforcement employees	Total officers	Total civilians	State/County	Total law enforcement employees	Total officers	Total civilians
Dorchester	162	119	43	Hughes	48	6	42
Edgefield	58	32	26	Hutchinson	3	3	0
Fairfield	51	45	6	Hyde	2	2	0
Florence	245	124	121	Jackson	2	2	0
Greenville	492	400	92	Jerauld	2	2	0
Horry	327	237	90	Jones	2	2	0
Horry County Police Department	273	249	24	Kingsbury	5	4	1
Kershaw	74	62	12	Lake	10	5	5
Lexington	389	253	136	Lawrence	44	14	30
Pickens	136	99	37	Lyman	4	3	1
Richland	670	457	213	Marshall	11	6	5
Saluda	53	20	33	McPherson	2	2	0
Spartanburg	331	302	29	Mellette	5	4	1
Sumter	133	122	11	Miner	4	3	1
York	188	154	34	Moody	8	4	4
SOUTH CAROLINA-Nonmetropolitan Counties				Perkins	4	3	1
Abbeville	54	29	25	Potter	2	1	1
Bamberg	16	13	3	Roberts	24	3	21
Barnwell	45	29	16	Sanborn	3	3	0
Beaufort	259	233	26	Shannon	1	1	0
Cherokee	94	47	47	Spink	12	7	5
Chester	99	45	54	Stanley	7	6	1
Clarendon	57	54	3	Sully	3	3	0
Colleton	126	62	64	Todd	1	1	0
Greenwood	117	75	42	Tripp	5	4	1
Jasper	40	34	6	Walworth	10	3	7
Lancaster	145	92	53	Yankton	12	10	2
Lee	25	25	0	Ziebach	2	2	0
Marion	39	36	3	**TENNESSEE-Metropolitan Counties**			
Marlboro	30	25	5	Anderson	165	59	106
McCormick	40	18	22	Blount	288	140	148
Newberry	94	46	48	Bradley	208	109	99
Oconee	143	82	61	Cannon	33	14	19
Orangeburg	117	87	30	Carter	83	49	34
Union	59	33	26	Cheatham	66	31	35
Williamsburg	40	37	3	Chester	38	13	25
SOUTH DAKOTA-Metropolitan Counties				Dickson	131	56	75
Lincoln	18	16	2	Fayette	89	39	50
McCook	7	6	1	Grainger	50	20	30
Meade	52	17	35	Hamblen	85	29	56
Minnehaha	204	88	116	Hamilton	316	161	155
Pennington	104	67	37	Hartsville-Trousdale	39	16	23
Turner	10	8	2	Hawkins	83	40	43
Union	23	7	16	Hickman	44	23	21
SOUTH DAKOTA-Nonmetropolitan Counties				Jefferson	88	44	44
Aurora	4	3	1	Knox	1,078	470	608
Beadle	21	5	16	Loudon	63	39	24
Bennett	4	4	0	Macon	62	26	36
Bon Homme	8	3	5	Madison	229	73	156
Brookings	21	13	8	Marion	47	19	28
Brown	50	16	34	Montgomery	309	78	231
Brule	9	4	5	Polk	50	19	31
Buffalo	1	1	0	Robertson	138	42	96
Butte	13	4	9	Rutherford	408	200	208
Campbell	2	2	0	Sequatchie	38	18	20
Charles Mix	11	4	7	Shelby	1,885	549	1,336
Clark	4	4	0	Smith	52	19	33
Clay	11	7	4	Stewart	41	18	23
Codington	24	8	16	Sullivan	256	108	148
Corson	4	3	1	Sumner	241	69	172
Custer	12	10	2	Tipton	87	47	40
Davison	8	6	2	Unicoi	44	23	21
Day	8	4	4	Union	36	22	14
Deuel	8	4	4	Washington	206	87	119
Dewey	4	3	1	Williamson	205	108	97
Douglas	2	2	0	Wilson	225	91	134
Edmunds	7	4	3	**TENNESSEE-Nonmetropolitan Counties**			
Fall River	15	5	10	Bedford	100	35	65
Faulk	10	4	6	Benton	39	17	22
Grant	8	3	5	Bledsoe	20	10	10
Gregory	3	2	1	Campbell	76	30	46
Haakon	1	1	0	Carroll	47	23	24
Hamlin	4	4	0	Claiborne	89	31	58
Hand	3	2	1	Clay	17	9	8
Hanson	2	2	0	Cocke	60	33	27
Harding	3	2	1	Coffee	81	43	38

Table 80. Full-Time Law Enforcement Employees, by State by Metropolitan and Nonmetropolitan Counties, 2010—*Continued*

(Number)

State/County	Total law enforcement employees	Total officers	Total civilians
Crockett	32	13	19
Cumberland	101	46	55
Decatur	33	14	19
DeKalb	42	21	21
Dyer	72	26	46
Fentress	29	11	18
Franklin	61	34	27
Gibson	73	29	44
Giles	62	29	33
Greene	150	59	91
Grundy	28	18	10
Hancock	20	11	9
Hardeman	47	24	23
Hardin	50	22	28
Haywood	45	21	24
Henderson	60	28	32
Henry	63	32	31
Houston	23	12	11
Humphreys	35	19	16
Jackson	41	14	27
Johnson	41	16	25
Lake	20	10	10
Lauderdale	65	20	45
Lawrence	84	42	42
Lewis	29	13	16
Lincoln	60	26	34
Marshall	49	24	25
Maury	150	80	70
McMinn	82	38	44
McNairy	36	17	19
Meigs	21	13	8
Monroe	69	39	30
Moore	26	13	13
Morgan	44	17	27
Obion	63	25	38
Overton	54	21	33
Perry	33	12	21
Pickett	17	11	6
Putnam	125	58	67
Rhea	54	54	0
Roane	71	39	32
Scott	66	21	45
Sevier	116	93	23
Van Buren	14	14	0
Warren	81	41	40
Wayne	37	12	25
Weakley	47	20	27
White	65	29	36
TEXAS-Metropolitan Counties			
Aransas	76	26	50
Archer	17	8	9
Armstrong	8	3	5
Atascosa	73	32	41
Austin	60	38	22
Bandera	60	27	33
Bastrop	205	76	129
Bell	256	89	167
Bexar	1,726	515	1,211
Bowie	47	40	7
Brazoria	341	162	179
Brazos	219	92	127
Burleson	33	11	22
Caldwell	101	24	77
Calhoun	66	26	40
Callahan	13	5	8
Cameron	418	115	303
Carson	14	6	8
Chambers	89	42	47
Clay	18	9	9
Collin	481	157	324
Comal	260	123	137
Coryell	66	28	38
Crosby	14	5	9
Dallas	2,263	445	1,818
Delta	19	8	11

State/County	Total law enforcement employees	Total officers	Total civilians
Denton	584	160	424
Ector	216	95	121
Ellis	223	80	143
El Paso	1,084	247	837
Fort Bend	716	497	219
Galveston	429	159	270
Goliad	26	11	15
Grayson	139	62	77
Gregg	237	99	138
Guadalupe	215	83	132
Hardin	65	32	33
Harris	3,816	2,307	1,509
Hays	283	124	159
Hidalgo	733	260	473
Hunt	146	43	103
Irion	7	3	4
Jefferson	386	133	253
Johnson	126	85	41
Jones	19	9	10
Kaufman	251	87	164
Kendall	74	48	26
Lampasas	33	19	14
Liberty	72	51	21
Lubbock	430	138	292
McLennan	353	115	238
Medina	65	26	39
Midland	177	76	101
Montgomery	646	373	273
Nueces	305	79	226
Orange	140	64	76
Parker	117	85	32
Potter	201	90	111
Randall	174	84	90
Robertson	34	14	20
Rockwall	119	38	81
Rusk	72	39	33
San Jacinto	59	28	31
San Patricio	109	47	62
Smith	331	161	170
Tarrant	1,377	1,241	136
Taylor	195	83	112
Tom Green	166	60	106
Travis	1,497	300	1,197
Upshur	76	45	31
Victoria	193	108	85
Waller	72	42	30
Wichita	171	58	113
Williamson	494	217	277
Wilson	69	26	43
Wise	138	56	82
TEXAS-Nonmetropolitan Counties			
Anderson	80	45	35
Andrews	34	12	22
Angelina	116	51	65
Bailey	21	5	16
Baylor	8	3	5
Bee	41	20	21
Blanco	19	9	10
Borden	3	2	1
Bosque	36	19	17
Brewster	29	15	14
Briscoe	2	2	0
Brooks	35	13	22
Brown	65	25	40
Burnet	58	43	15
Camp	18	7	11
Cass	44	20	24
Castro	18	8	10
Cherokee	74	32	42
Childress	24	5	19
Cochran	13	7	6
Coke	6	5	1
Coleman	6	6	0
Collingsworth	5	5	0
Colorado	48	20	28

Table 80.   Full-Time Law Enforcement Employees, by State by Metropolitan and Nonmetropolitan Counties, 2010—*Continued*

(Number)

State/County	Total law enforcement employees	Total officers	Total civilians	State/County	Total law enforcement employees	Total officers	Total civilians
Comanche	28	10	18	Madison	24	10	14
Concho	14	7	7	Marion	15	14	1
Cooke	74	22	52	Martin	8	4	4
Cottle	2	2	0	Mason	9	5	4
Crane	11	6	5	Matagorda	76	34	42
Culberson	12	6	6	Maverick	93	46	47
Dallam	5	5	0	McCulloch	12	6	6
Dawson	19	7	12	McMullen	5	4	1
Deaf Smith	36	12	24	Menard	10	5	5
Dewitt	41	11	30	Milam	58	16	42
Dickens	6	2	4	Mills	10	6	4
Dimmit	33	22	11	Mitchell	11	5	6
Donley	10	6	4	Montague	25	9	16
Eastland	27	10	17	Moore	49	17	32
Edwards	11	5	6	Morris	23	9	14
Erath	58	23	35	Motley	2	2	0
Falls	10	5	5	Nacogdoches	105	51	54
Fannin	107	20	87	Navarro	131	60	71
Fayette	44	21	23	Newton	23	12	11
Fisher	9	5	4	Nolan	29	11	18
Floyd	7	3	4	Ochiltree	19	8	11
Foard	3	2	1	Oldham	11	6	5
Franklin	20	10	10	Palo Pinto	55	25	30
Freestone	42	16	26	Panola	56	29	27
Frio	22	13	9	Parmer	19	6	13
Gaines	25	11	14	Pecos	36	22	14
Garza	32	10	22	Polk	96	55	41
Gillespie	42	28	14	Presidio	10	9	1
Glasscock	4	3	1	Rains	22	10	12
Gonzales	44	15	29	Reagan	20	9	11
Gray	44	15	29	Real	8	4	4
Grimes	51	25	26	Red River	29	13	16
Hale	71	29	42	Reeves	45	20	25
Hall	10	4	6	Refugio	42	14	28
Hamilton	27	15	12	Roberts	6	5	1
Hansford	9	8	1	Runnels	26	6	20
Hardeman	11	6	5	Sabine	16	7	9
Harrison	90	51	39	San Augustine	17	7	10
Hartley	5	5	0	San Saba	9	4	5
Haskell	6	3	3	Schleicher	11	5	6
Hemphill	17	10	7	Scurry	26	11	15
Henderson	153	76	77	Shackelford	15	5	10
Hill	73	31	42	Shelby	31	16	15
Hockley	25	15	10	Sherman	10	5	5
Hood	125	51	74	Somervell	41	20	21
Hopkins	56	25	31	Starr	106	54	52
Houston	38	19	19	Stephens	25	6	19
Howard	43	15	28	Sterling	4	3	1
Hudspeth	38	15	23	Stonewall	7	2	5
Hutchinson	35	12	23	Sutton	14	4	10
Jack	34	13	21	Swisher	11	4	7
Jackson	33	14	19	Terrell	13	7	6
Jasper	48	19	29	Terry	34	12	22
Jeff Davis	7	5	2	Throckmorton	7	2	5
Jim Hogg	38	20	18	Titus	59	27	32
Jim Wells	64	28	36	Trinity	18	11	7
Karnes	17	9	8	Tyler	30	15	15
Kenedy	18	11	7	Upton	21	10	11
Kent	6	3	3	Uvalde	34	19	15
Kerr	94	44	50	Val Verde	64	41	23
Kimble	15	10	5	Van Zandt	74	27	47
King	1	1	0	Walker	88	37	51
Kinney	15	7	8	Ward	31	13	18
Kleberg	76	27	49	Washington	55	32	23
Knox	10	4	6	Wharton	71	45	26
Lamar	75	26	49	Wheeler	9	4	5
Lamb	30	13	17	Wilbarger	18	7	11
La Salle	23	9	14	Willacy	38	14	24
Lavaca	29	14	15	Winkler	29	10	19
Lee	41	13	28	Wood	59	24	35
Leon	40	25	15	Yoakum	20	8	12
Limestone	63	23	40	Young	33	14	19
Lipscomb	10	6	4	Zapata	107	48	59
Live Oak	40	10	30	**UTAH-Metropolitan Counties**			
Llano	50	26	24	Cache	148	113	35
Loving	4	3	1	Davis	354	142	212
Lynn	20	7	13	Juab	21	9	12

Table 80. Full-Time Law Enforcement Employees, by State by Metropolitan and Nonmetropolitan Counties, 2010—*Continued*

(Number)

State/County	Total law enforcement employees	Total officers	Total civilians	State/County	Total law enforcement employees	Total officers	Total civilians
Morgan	13	11	2	Mathews	23	12	11
Salt Lake County Unified Police Department	435	305	130	Montgomery	115	101	14
Summit	106	77	29	Nelson	17	16	1
Tooele	105	35	70	New Kent	39	29	10
Utah	359	144	215	Pittsylvania	124	107	17
Washington	152	43	109	Powhatan	56	40	16
Weber	92	90	2	Prince George County Police Department	75	57	18
UTAH-Nonmetropolitan Counties				Prince William County Police Department	666	557	109
Beaver	78	23	55	Pulaski	52	42	10
Box Elder	84	74	10	Roanoke County Police Department	150	138	12
Carbon	46	39	7	Rockingham	66	51	15
Daggett	23	8	15	Scott	35	26	9
Duchesne	52	22	30	Spotsylvania	207	157	50
Emery	42	33	9	Stafford	224	163	61
Garfield	26	6	20	Surry	21	13	8
Grand	34	19	15	Sussex	44	39	5
Iron	78	39	39	Warren	92	46	46
Kane	30	15	15	Washington	73	51	22
Millard	47	24	23	York	112	103	9
Piute	3	3	0	**VIRGINIA-Nonmetropolitan Counties**			
Rich	10	4	6	Accomack	61	50	11
San Juan	32	27	5	Alleghany	61	43	18
Sanpete	55	39	16	Augusta	68	59	9
Sevier	65	53	12	Bath	16	16	0
Uintah	68	21	47	Bland	17	11	6
Wasatch	46	38	8	Brunswick	34	20	14
Wayne	6	5	1	Buchanan	46	32	14
VERMONT-Metropolitan Counties				Buckingham	25	17	8
Chittenden	18	16	2	Carroll	35	29	6
Franklin	21	15	6	Charlotte	34	32	2
VERMONT-Nonmetropolitan Counties				Culpeper	95	78	17
Addison	10	7	3	Dickenson	30	21	9
Bennington	11	10	1	Essex	24	18	6
Caledonia	4	3	1	Floyd	27	17	10
Essex	2	1	1	Grayson	28	21	7
Lamoille	23	13	10	Greensville	33	20	13
Orange	6	6	0	Halifax	40	36	4
Orleans	6	4	2	Henry	121	108	13
Rutland	21	16	5	Highland	12	7	5
Washington	13	11	2	King George	43	29	14
Windham	17	13	4	Lancaster	35	29	6
Windsor	15	12	3	Lee	35	35	0
VIRGINIA-Metropolitan Counties				Lunenburg	21	14	7
Albemarle County Police Department	138	112	26	Madison	32	19	13
Amelia	22	14	8	Mecklenburg	93	53	40
Amherst	66	61	5	Middlesex	23	18	5
Appomattox	32	29	3	Northampton	77	60	17
Arlington County Police Department	419	340	79	Northumberland	29	18	11
Bedford	83	77	6	Nottoway	23	13	10
Botetourt	111	89	22	Orange	46	37	9
Campbell	65	57	8	Page	65	50	15
Caroline	68	49	19	Patrick	38	24	14
Charles City	15	9	6	Prince Edward	30	30	0
Chesterfield County Police Department	573	474	99	Rappahannock	23	23	0
Clarke	29	17	12	Richmond	20	12	8
Craig	14	9	5	Rockbridge	38	29	9
Cumberland	22	15	7	Russell	50	34	16
Dinwiddie	42	39	3	Shenandoah	76	68	8
Fairfax County Police Department	1,777	1,401	376	Smyth	41	41	0
Fauquier	124	109	15	Southampton	78	64	14
Fluvanna	37	27	10	Tazewell	54	43	11
Franklin	90	72	18	Westmoreland	32	22	10
Frederick	126	109	17	Wise	62	49	13
Giles	35	25	10	Wythe	47	40	7
Gloucester	95	78	17	**WASHINGTON-Metropolitan Counties**			
Goochland	41	31	10	Asotin	14	12	2
Greene	38	22	16	Benton	67	56	11
Hanover	232	205	27	Chelan	66	55	11
Henrico County Police Department	770	586	184	Clark	213	137	76
Isle of Wight	48	41	7	Cowlitz	55	45	10
James City County Police Department	97	92	5	Douglas	34	27	7
King and Queen	21	13	8	Franklin	26	24	2
King William	32	20	12	King	324	229	95
Loudoun	587	488	99	Kitsap	149	119	30
Louisa	61	48	13	Pierce	359	301	58

Table 80.   Full-Time Law Enforcement Employees, by State by Metropolitan and Nonmetropolitan Counties, 2010—*Continued*

(Number)

State/County	Total law enforcement employees	Total officers	Total civilians	State/County	Total law enforcement employees	Total officers	Total civilians
Skagit	105	54	51	Randolph	12	10	2
Skamania	26	22	4	Ritchie	10	7	3
Snohomish	342	277	65	Roane	8	7	1
Spokane	187	133	54	Summers	7	6	1
Thurston	102	82	20	Taylor	14	7	7
Whatcom	102	83	19	Tucker	4	4	0
Yakima	93	66	27	Tyler	8	7	1
WASHINGTON-Nonmetropolitan Counties				Upshur	13	11	2
Adams	28	17	11	Webster	9	5	4
Clallam	43	35	8	Wetzel	15	10	5
Columbia	14	9	5	Wyoming	26	20	6
Ferry	22	7	15	**WISCONSIN-Metropolitan Counties**			
Garfield	14	7	7	Brown	320	151	169
Grant	62	48	14	Calumet	47	22	25
Grays Harbor	80	40	40	Chippewa	56	51	5
Island	58	33	25	Columbia	97	40	57
Jefferson	44	23	21	Dane	554	452	102
Kittitas	66	35	31	Douglas	87	80	7
Klickitat	49	18	31	Eau Claire	77	34	43
Lewis	56	39	17	Fond du Lac	119	56	63
Lincoln	22	13	9	Iowa	38	19	19
Mason	64	48	16	Kenosha	326	110	216
Okanogan	33	28	5	Kewaunee	37	35	2
Pacific	21	18	3	La Crosse	103	42	61
Pend Oreille	20	17	3	Marathon	172	66	106
San Juan	31	19	12	Milwaukee	1,278	416	862
Stevens	31	26	5	Oconto	61	26	35
Wahkiakum	16	7	9	Outagamie	195	74	121
Walla Walla	33	27	6	Ozaukee	102	79	23
Whitman	22	18	4	Pierce	50	46	4
WEST VIRGINIA-Metropolitan Counties				Racine	236	141	95
Berkeley	81	55	26	Rock	202	95	107
Boone	26	22	4	Sheboygan	177	77	100
Brooke	30	19	11	St. Croix	83	75	8
Cabell	48	41	7	Washington	174	72	102
Clay	6	5	1	Waukesha	335	160	175
Hampshire	18	15	3	Winnebago	189	127	62
Hancock	31	26	5	**WISCONSIN-Nonmetropolitan Counties**			
Jefferson	32	25	7	Adams	59	29	30
Kanawha	134	102	32	Ashland	36	18	18
Lincoln	9	9	0	Barron	71	35	36
Marshall	29	26	3	Bayfield	41	19	22
Mineral	15	13	2	Buffalo	22	13	9
Monongalia	60	36	24	Burnett	32	16	16
Morgan	12	11	1	Clark	49	46	3
Ohio	30	28	2	Crawford	31	30	1
Pleasants	7	6	1	Dodge	175	76	99
Preston	27	18	9	Door	66	51	15
Putnam	50	38	12	Dunn	56	25	31
Wayne	24	21	3	Florence	12	12	0
Wirt	3	3	0	Forest	38	18	20
Wood	71	36	35	Grant	47	26	21
WEST VIRGINIA-Nonmetropolitan Counties				Green	57	35	22
Barbour	8	7	1	Green Lake	44	17	27
Braxton	11	10	1	Iron	19	10	9
Calhoun	6	3	3	Jackson	44	20	24
Doddridge	6	6	0	Jefferson	125	98	27
Fayette	38	31	7	Juneau	56	44	12
Gilmer	5	5	0	Lafayette	25	13	12
Grant	7	7	0	Langlade	35	16	19
Greenbrier	32	28	4	Lincoln	59	28	31
Hardy	10	8	2	Manitowoc	105	59	46
Harrison	45	43	2	Marinette	61	29	32
Jackson	21	14	7	Marquette	38	36	2
Lewis	13	11	2	Menominee	20	11	9
Logan	28	20	8	Monroe	55	23	32
Marion	41	31	10	Oneida	86	38	48
Mason	24	17	7	Pepin	18	7	11
McDowell	17	15	2	Polk	75	29	46
Mercer	30	26	4	Portage	92	46	46
Mingo	22	19	3	Price	32	20	12
Monroe	8	8	0	Richland	30	17	13
Nicholas	30	27	3	Rusk	31	17	14
Pendleton	3	3	0	Sauk	164	58	106
Pocahontas	12	8	4	Sawyer	47	32	15
Raleigh	62	45	17	Shawano	108	38	70

Table 80.   Full-Time Law Enforcement Employees, by State by Metropolitan and Nonmetropolitan Counties, 2010—*Continued*

(Number)

State/County	Total law enforce-ment employees	Total officers	Total civilians	State/County	Total law enforce-ment employees	Total officers	Total civilians
Taylor	42	19	23	Converse	14	12	2
Trempealeau	51	25	26	Crook	21	9	12
Vernon	46	27	19	Fremont	39	35	4
Vilas	74	36	38	Goshen	14	11	3
Walworth	210	81	129	Hot Springs	9	7	2
Washburn	34	15	19	Johnson	13	12	1
Waupaca	102	42	60	Lincoln	19	19	0
Waushara	64	24	40	Niobrara	5	4	1
Wood	69	43	26	Park	27	18	9
WYOMING-Metropolitan Counties				Platte	12	10	2
Laramie	59	49	10	Sheridan	25	21	4
Natrona	56	44	12	Sublette	40	35	5
WYOMING-Nonmetropolitan Counties				Sweetwater	50	43	7
Albany	22	21	1	Teton	37	21	16
Big Horn	9	7	2	Uinta	38	24	14
Campbell	60	45	15	Washakie	9	8	1
Carbon	30	17	13	Weston	10	8	2

Table 81.   Full-Time Law Enforcement Employees, by State and Agency, 2010

(Number)

State, agency, unit/office	Total law enforcement employees	Total officers	Total civilians
ALABAMA—State Agencies			
Alabama Alcoholic Beverage Control Board	154	132	22
Alabama Conservation Department Marine Police	72	60	12
Alabama Department of Mental Health	5	4	1
Alabama Public Service Commission Enforcement Division	9	8	1
State Capitol Police	66	55	11
ALABAMA—Tribal Agencies			
Poarch Creek Tribal	48	42	6
ALABAMA—Other Agencies			
22nd Judicial Circuit Drug Task Force	6	5	1
24th Judicial Circuit Drug and Violent Crime Task Force	5	4	1
Marshall County Drug Enforcement Unit	7	5	2
Norfolk Southern Railway	6	6	0
ALASKA—Other Agencies			
Anchorage International Airport	64	56	8
Fairbanks International Airport	30	25	5
ARIZONA—State Agencies			
Arizona State Capitol	55	29	26
ARIZONA—Tribal Agencies			
Ak-Chin Tribal	34	14	20
Cocopah Tribal	29	22	7
Colorado River Tribal	30	18	12
Fort Apache Agency	6	5	1
Fort McDowell Tribal	27	21	6
Gila River Indian Community	124	97	27
Hualapai Tribal	18	15	3
Quechan Tribal	14	10	4
Yavapai-Prescott Tribal	12	9	3
ARIZONA—Other Agencies			
Tucson Airport Authority	48	23	25
ARKANSAS—State Agencies			
Camp Robinson	10	10	0
State Capitol Police	22	19	3
CALIFORNIA—State Agencies			
Atascadero State Hospital	123	111	12
California State Fair	7	3	4
Coalinga State Hospital	236	223	13
Department of Parks and Recreation: Capital	717	665	52
Napa State Hospital	100	97	3
Patton State Hospital	52	40	12
CALIFORNIA—Tribal Agencies			
Hoopa Valley Tribal	15	7	8
CALIFORNIA—Other Agencies			
East Bay Regional Parks: Alamaeda County	78	55	23
Fontana Unified School District	71	15	56
Monterey Peninsula Airport	6	6	0
Port of San Diego Harbor	157	135	22
San Bernardino Unified School District	80	24	56
San Francisco Bay Area Rapid Transit: Contra Costa County	266	190	76
Shasta County Marshal	27	23	4
Stockton Unified School District	24	19	5
Twin Rivers Unified School District	29	22	7
COLORADO—State Agencies			
Colorado Bureau of Investigation	203	89	114
Colorado Mental Health Institute	82	18	64
COLORADO—Other Agencies			
Two Rivers Drug Enforcement Team	7	6	1
CONNECTICUT—State Agencies			
State Capitol Police	36	27	9
CONNECTICUT—Tribal Agencies			
Mashantucket Pequot Tribal	12	11	1
CONNECTICUT—Other Agencies			
Metropolitan Transportation Authority	755	684	71
DELAWARE—State Agencies			
Attorney General:			
Kent County	60	35	25
New Castle County	288	143	145
Sussex County	50	23	27
Division of Alcohol and Tobacco Enforcement	16	14	2
Environmental Control	11	9	2
Fish and Wildlife	31	26	5
Park Rangers	19	19	0
River and Bay Authority	63	46	17
State Capitol Police	65	41	24
State Fire Marshal	53	20	33

Table 81. Full-Time Law Enforcement Employees, by State and Agency, 2010—*Continued*

(Number)

State, agency, unit/office	Total law enforcement employees	Total officers	Total civilians
DELAWARE—Other Agencies			
Amtrak Police	19	19	0
Drug Enforcement Administration: Wilmington Resident Office	23	18	5
Wilmington Fire Department	16	9	7
FLORIDA—State Agencies			
Capitol Police	102	78	24
Department of Environmental Protection, Division of Law Enforcement: Leon County	176	132	44
Department of Law Enforcement: Leon County, Tallahassee	1,640	414	1,226
Florida Game Commission: Leon County	836	663	173
State Treasurer's Office: Division of Insurance Fraud	179	135	44
FLORIDA—Tribal Agencies			
Miccosukee Tribal	56	36	20
Seminole Tribal	254	144	110
FLORIDA—Other Agencies			
Duval County Schools	57	47	10
Florida School for the Deaf and Blind	18	10	8
Jacksonville Airport Authority	30	27	3
Lee County Port Authority	64	40	24
Melbourne International Airport	12	11	1
Miami-Dade County Public Schools	180	155	25
Palm Beach County School District	223	144	79
Sarasota-Bradenton International Airport	12	11	1
Tampa International Airport	126	60	66
Volusia County Beach Management	54	50	4
GEORGIA—State Agencies			
Atlanta State Farmers Market	17	17	0
Georgia Bureau of Investigation: Headquarters	824	377	447
Georgia Department of Transportation: Office of Investigations	2	2	0
Georgia Forestry Commission	4	4	0
Georgia Public Safety Training Center	168	31	137
Georgia World Congress	74	24	50
Ports Authority: Savannah	120	74	46
GEORGIA—Other Agencies			
Augusta Board of Education	44	37	7
Bibb County Board of Education	33	28	5
Chatham County Board of Education	45	37	8
Dougherty County Board of Education	20	20	0
Fayette County Marshal	11	10	1
Fulton County Marshal	69	58	11
Fulton County School System	65	63	2
Glynn County School System	16	16	0
Gwinnett County Public Schools	27	23	4
Hartsfield-Jackson Atlanta International Airport	139	129	10
Metropolitan Atlanta Rapid Transit Authority	354	307	47
Muscogee City Marshal	26	19	7
Richmond County Marshal	45	40	5
Stone Mountain Park	24	20	4
IDAHO—Tribal Agencies			
Coeur d'Alene Tribal	16	15	1
Fort Hall Tribal	34	21	13
Nez Perce Tribal	17	12	5
ILLINOIS—State Agencies			
Illinois Commerce Commission	20	12	8
Illinois Department of Natural Resources	150	139	11
Secretary of State Police	244	130	114
State Fire Marshal	20	18	2
ILLINOIS—Other Agencies			
Burlington Northern Santa Fe Railroad	23	20	3
Canadian National Railway	13	13	0
Capitol Airport Authority	6	6	0
Chicago Fire Department: Arson Investigations	11	3	8
Cook County Forest Preserve	107	101	6
Crystal Lake Park District	3	3	0
CSX Transportation	24	24	0
Decatur Park District	5	5	0
Du Page County Forest Preserve	30	25	5
Indiana Harbor Belt Railroad	12	12	0
John H. Stroger Hospital	49	44	5
Kane County Forest Preserve	6	6	0
Lake County Forest Preserve	19	17	2
Norfolk Southern Railway	41	40	1
Pekin Park District	1	1	0
Rockford Park District	17	16	1
Springfield Park District	6	6	0
Will County Forest Preserve	13	11	2

Table 81.   Full-Time Law Enforcement Employees, by State and Agency, 2010—*Continued*

(Number)

State, agency, unit/office	Total law enforcement employees	Total officers	Total civilians
INDIANA—State Agencies			
Indiana State Excise Police	94	87	7
Northern Indiana Commuter Transportation District	8	7	1
INDIANA—Other Agencies			
Indianapolis International Airport	90	42	48
St. Joseph County Airport Authority	17	17	0
KANSAS—State Agencies			
Kansas Alcoholic Beverage Control	43	21	22
Kansas Bureau of Investigation	268	79	189
Kansas Department of Wildlife and Parks	181	179	2
Kansas Lottery Security Division	9	6	3
Kansas Racing Commission: Security Division	34	15	19
Securities Office: Investigation Section	6	6	0
State Fire Marshal	12	11	1
KANSAS—Tribal Agencies			
Iowa Tribal	8	8	0
Kickapoo Tribal	9	5	4
Potawatomi Tribal	23	12	11
Sac and Fox Tribal	7	6	1
KANSAS—Other Agencies			
Blue Valley School District	7	7	0
Johnson County Park	18	17	1
Metropolitan Topeka Airport Authority	22	18	4
Shawnee Mission Public Schools	8	8	0
Topeka Fire Department: Arson Investigation	3	3	0
Unified School District:			
Auburn-Washburn	1	1	0
Bluestem	1	1	0
Goddard	6	5	1
Maize	4	4	0
Seaman	3	3	0
KENTUCKY—State Agencies			
Alcohol Beverage Control	60	30	30
Fish and Wildlife Enforcement	145	137	8
Forestry Enforcement	146	132	14
Kentucky Horse Park	8	8	0
Park Security	50	50	0
Unlawful Narcotics Investigation: Treatament and Education	21	18	3
KENTUCKY—Other Agencies			
Adair County Constable: District 6	1	1	0
Barren County Drug Task Force	5	4	1
Buffalo Trace-Gateway Narcotics Task Force	4	4	0
Central Kentucky Area Drug Task Force	1	1	0
Cincinnati-Northern Kentucky International Airport	63	49	14
Clark County School System	2	2	0
Fayette County Schools	31	27	4
Graves County Schools	1	1	0
Greater Hardin County Narcotics Task Force	9	7	2
Jefferson County Board of Education	28	20	8
Lake Cumberland Area Drug Enforcement Task Force	5	4	1
Lexington Bluegrass Airport	28	19	9
Louisville Regional Airport Authority	47	42	5
McCracken County Public Schools	4	4	0
Montgomery County School District	2	2	0
Northern Kentucky Narcotics Enforcement Unit	2	1	1
Ohio County School System	1	1	0
Pennyrile Narcotics Task Force	12	9	3
Scott County Constable: District 6	1	1	0
South Central Kentucky Drug Task Force	1	1	0
LOUISIANA—State Agencies			
Department of Public Safety: State Capitol Detail	41	35	6
Tensas Basin Levee District	3	2	1
LOUISIANA—Tribal Agencies			
Chitimacha Tribal	14	9	5
Coushatta Tribal	20	18	2
MAINE—Tribal Agencies			
Passamaquoddy Indian Township	10	6	4
Penobscot Nation	9	5	4
MARYLAND—State Agencies			
Comptroller of the Treasury: Field Enforcement Division	54	25	29
Department of Public Safety and Correctional Services: Internal Investigations Unit	24	16	8
General Services:			
Annapolis, Anne Arundel County	62	27	35
Baltimore City	164	62	102
Natural Resources Police	501	245	256
Springfield Hospital	24	5	19

Table 81.   Full-Time Law Enforcement Employees, by State and Agency, 2010—*Continued*

(Number)

State, agency, unit/office	Total law enforcement employees	Total officers	Total civilians
State Fire Marshal	76	43	33
Transit Administration	171	154	17
Transportation Authority	619	448	171
MARYLAND—Other Agencies			
Maryland-National Capital Park Police:			
Montgomery County	94	76	18
Prince George's County	125	100	25
MASSACHUSETTS-State Agencies			
Massachusetts Bay Transportation Authority	277	267	10
MICHIGAN—Tribal Agencies			
Keweenaw Bay Tribal	14	13	1
Lac Vieux Desert Tribal	8	8	0
Little River Band of Ottawa Tribal	18	17	1
Little Traverse Bay Tribal	16	11	5
Nottawaseppi Huron Band of Potawatomi	5	4	1
Pokagon Tribal	18	16	2
Saginaw Chippewa Tribal	24	24	0
MICHIGAN—Other Agencies			
Bishop International Airport	8	7	1
Capitol Region Airport Authority	17	9	8
Gerald R. Ford International Airport	19	18	1
Huron-Clinton Metropolitan Authority:			
Hudson Mills Metropark	5	5	0
Kensington Metropark	8	8	0
Lower Huron Metropark	10	10	0
Stony Creek Metropark	9	9	0
Wayne County Airport	112	102	10
MINNESOTA—State Agencies			
Capitol Security: St. Paul	58	18	40
MINNESOTA—Tribal Agencies			
Lower Sioux Tribal	4	4	0
Mille Lacs Tribal	22	20	2
Nett Lake Tribal	5	4	1
Red Lake Agency	37	25	12
White Earth Tribal	29	22	7
MINNESOTA—Other Agencies			
Minneapolis-St. Paul International Airport	115	80	35
Three Rivers Park District	44	27	17
MISSISSIPPI—State Agencies			
State Capitol Police	74	61	13
MISSOURI—State Agencies			
Capitol Police	31	28	3
Department of Conservation	188	180	8
Department of Social Services: State Technical Assistance Team	13	9	4
Division of Alcohol and Tobacco Control	21	10	11
Gaming Commission: Enforcement Division	115	113	2
State Fire Marshal	22	21	1
State Park Rangers	40	39	1
State Water Patrol	86	83	3
MISSOURI—Other Agencies			
Bootheel Drug Task Force	4	4	0
Clay County Drug Task Force	5	5	0
Clay County Park Authority	7	7	0
Jackson County Drug Task Force	19	17	2
Jackson County Park Rangers	21	19	2
Lambert-St. Louis International Airport	95	82	13
Springfield-Branson Airport	10	10	0
St. Charles County Park Rangers	11	11	0
St. Peters Ranger Division	6	6	0
MONTANA—State Agencies			
Gambling Investigations Bureau	24	21	3
MONTANA—Tribal Agencies			
Blackfeet Agency	22	11	11
Crow Tribal	21	15	6
Flathead Tribal	31	24	7
Fort Belknap Tribal	19	13	6
Fort Peck Assiniboine and Sioux Tribes	20	18	2
Northern Cheyenne Tribal	22	15	7
Rocky Boys Tribal	17	7	10
NEVADA—State Agencies			
Taxicab Authority	55	27	28
NEVADA—Tribal Agencies			
Duckwater Tribal	2	2	0
Ely Shoshone Tribal	2	2	0
Moapa Tribal	8	5	3
Pyramid Lake Tribal	14	12	2

Table 81. Full-Time Law Enforcement Employees, by State and Agency, 2010—*Continued*

(Number)

State, agency, unit/office	Total law enforcement employees	Total officers	Total civilians
Walker River Tribal	5	5	0
Washoe Tribal	20	12	8
Yerington Paiute Tribal	4	4	0
NEVADA—Other Agencies			
Clark County School District	200	162	38
Washoe County School District	41	37	4
NEW HAMPSHIRE—State Agencies			
Liquor Commission	33	21	12
NEW JERSEY—State Agencies			
Department of Human Services	135	128	7
Division of Fish and Wildlife	54	49	5
New Jersey Transit Police	271	214	57
Palisades Interstate Parkway	26	26	0
State Park Police	80	78	2
NEW JERSEY—Other Agencies			
Park Police:			
Camden County	18	17	1
Morris County	31	30	1
Union County	83	72	11
Prosecutor:			
Atlantic County	167	77	90
Bergen County	251	110	141
Burlington County	136	77	59
Camden County	233	156	77
Cape May County	82	36	46
Cumberland County	109	38	71
Essex County	278	142	136
Gloucester County	90	33	57
Hudson County	223	96	127
Hunterdon County	50	23	27
Mercer County	166	51	115
Middlesex County	195	75	120
Monmouth County	280	79	201
Morris County	149	63	86
Ocean County	169	77	92
Passaic County	185	78	107
Salem County	50	21	29
Somerset County	119	53	66
Sussex County	49	29	20
Union County	246	75	171
Warren County	59	21	38
NEW MEXICO—Tribal Agencies			
Acoma Tribal	20	12	8
Isleta Tribal	38	22	16
Jemez Tribal	10	9	1
Northern Pueblos Tribal	12	10	2
Ramah Navajo Tribal	11	10	1
Santa Ana Tribal	21	20	1
Southern Pueblos Agency	18	13	5
Taos Pueblo Tribal	9	7	2
Tesuque Pueblo	17	9	8
Zuni Tribal	31	22	9
NEW YORK—State Agencies			
StatePark:			
Allegany Region	15	12	3
Central Region	21	17	4
Finger Lakes Region	18	16	2
Genesee Region	14	13	1
Long Island Region	66	63	3
New York City Region	20	16	4
Niagara Region	29	28	1
Palisades Region	43	36	7
Saratoga/Capital Region	23	23	0
Taconic Region	12	11	1
Thousand Island Region	15	14	1
NEW YORK—Tribal Agencies			
Oneida Indian Nation	42	36	6
St. Regis Tribal	28	23	5
NEW YORK—Other Agencies			
Board of Water: Ulster County	197	183	14
New York City Metropolitan Transportation Authority	755	684	71
Onondaga County Parks	1	1	0
Suffolk County Parks	49	48	1
NORTH CAROLINA—State Agencies			
Department of Human Resources	9	9	0
Department of Wildlife	234	213	21
Division of Alcohol Law Enforcement	128	108	20

Table 81.   Full-Time Law Enforcement Employees, by State and Agency, 2010—*Continued*

(Number)

State, agency, unit/office	Total law enforcement employees	Total officers	Total civilians
Division of Marine Fisheries	63	54	9
North Carolina Arboretum	3	3	0
State Capitol Police	83	54	29
State Fairgrounds	6	1	5
State Park Rangers:			
Carolina Beach	6	4	2
Cliffs of the Neuse	4	2	2
Crowders Mountain	7	6	1
Dismal Swamp	6	3	3
Elk Knob	2	2	0
Eno River	5	4	1
Falls Lake Recreation Area	16	14	2
Fort Fisher	4	4	0
Fort Macon	4	4	0
Goose Creek	8	2	6
Gorges	3	3	0
Hammocks Beach	5	5	0
Hanging Rock	11	6	5
Haw River	2	2	0
Jockey's Ridge	6	5	1
Jones Lake	5	4	1
Jordan Lake State Recreation Area	16	15	1
Kerr Lake	14	12	2
Lake James	5	4	1
Lake Norman	5	4	1
Lake Waccamaw	5	4	1
Lumber River	7	6	1
Mayo River	4	1	3
Medoc Mountain	6	3	3
Merchants Millpond	7	4	3
Morrow Mountain	9	4	5
Mount Mitchell	3	2	1
New River-Mount Jefferson	8	8	0
Pettigrew	4	3	1
Pilot Mountain	3	3	0
Raven Rock	4	3	1
Singletary Lake	5	2	3
South Mountains	8	7	1
Stone Mountain	8	6	2
Weymouth Woods/Sandhills Nature Preserve	3	2	1
NORTH CAROLINA—Tribal Agencies			
Cherokee Tribal	55	49	6
NORTH CAROLINA—Other Agencies			
Asheville Regional Airport	19	14	5
Beaufort County Alcohol Beverage Control Enforcement	1	1	0
Durham County Alcohol Beverage Control Law Enforcement Office	3	3	0
Nash County Alcohol Beverage Control Enforcement	2	2	0
Piedmont Triad International Airport	21	18	3
Raleigh-Durham International Airport	33	31	2
Triad Alcohol Beverage Control Law Enforcement	5	4	1
WakeMed Campus Police	76	44	32
Wilmington International Airport	13	9	4
NORTH DAKOTA—Tribal Agencies			
Fort Berthold Agency	25	15	10
Fort Totten Tribal	17	11	6
Standing Rock Agency	25	18	7
OHIO—State Agencies			
Ohio Department of Natural Resources	495	393	102
OHIO—Other Agencies			
Cedar Point	11	11	0
Cleveland Metropolitan Park District	77	67	10
Columbus and Franklin County Metropolitan Park District	43	41	2
Delaware County Preservation Parks	9	9	0
Erie MetroParks	4	4	0
Greater Cleveland Regional Transit Authority	113	101	12
Hamilton County Park District	38	34	4
Johnny Appleseed Metropolitan Park District	9	7	2
Lake Metroparks	15	13	2
Licking Park District	4	1	3
Lima Park Services: Ranger Division	4	4	0
Lorain County Metropolitan Park District	16	16	0
Port Columbus International Airport	58	41	17
Robinson Memorial Hospital	8	8	0
Toledo-Lucas County Port Authority	9	9	0
Toledo Metropolitan Park District	23	23	0
Wood County Park District	6	6	0

Table 81. Full-Time Law Enforcement Employees, by State and Agency, 2010—*Continued*

(Number)

State, agency, unit/office	Total law enforcement employees	Total officers	Total civilians
OKLAHOMA—State Agencies			
Capitol Park Police	55	25	30
Grand River Dam Authority: Lake Patrol	12	10	2
OKLAHOMA—Tribal Agencies			
Absentee Shawnee Tribal	12	9	3
Cherokee Nation	35	28	7
Choctaw Tribal	27	26	1
Citizen Potawatomi Nation	21	13	8
Comanche Tribal	25	19	6
Eastern Shawnee Tribal	12	11	1
Kaw Tribal	4	4	0
Kickapoo Tribal	12	11	1
Muscogee Nation Tribal	47	38	9
Osage Nation	19	18	1
Otoe-Missouria Tribal	10	9	1
Tonkawa Tribal	8	3	5
Wyandotte Nation	6	6	0
OKLAHOMA—Other Agencies			
Guymon Public Schools	1	1	0
Jenks Public Schools	8	7	1
Madill Public Schools	1	1	0
McAlester Public Schools	2	2	0
Norman Public Schools	4	4	0
Putnam City Campus	10	6	4
OREGON—State Agencies			
Liquor Commission:			
Benton County	1	1	0
Clatsop County	2	1	1
Columbia County	1	1	0
Coos County	2	1	1
Douglas County	2	1	1
Hood River County	1	1	0
Jackson County	5	4	1
Josephine County	2	2	0
Klamath County	1	1	0
Lane County	6	5	1
Lincoln County	1	1	0
Linn County	1	1	0
Malheur County	2	1	1
Marion County	6	5	1
Multnomah County	11	11	0
Umatilla County	2	2	0
Washington County	1	1	0
Yamhill County	1	1	0
OREGON—Tribal Agencies			
Burns Paiute Tribal	4	3	1
Coquille Tribal	4	4	0
OREGON—Other Agencies			
Port of Portland	69	52	17
PENNSYLVANIA—State Agencies			
Department of Environmental Resources	12	5	7
State Capitol Police	141	132	9
State Park Police:			
Pine Grove Furnace	2	2	0
Prince Gallitzin	16	7	9
Pymatuning	3	3	0
PENNSYLVANIA—Other Agencies			
Allegheny County District Attorney: Criminal Investigation Division	33	26	7
Allegheny County Housing Authority	9	8	1
Allegheny County Port Authority	56	40	16
Altoona Hospital	18	16	2
County Detective:			
Beaver County	8	8	0
Berks County	32	30	2
Bucks County	20	16	4
Butler County	4	4	0
Chester County	22	19	3
Dauphin County	15	12	3
Lackawanna County	13	13	0
Lebanon County	8	6	2
Lehigh County	19	16	3
Pike County	3	3	0
Schuylkill County	6	6	0
Westmoreland County	56	14	42
York County	11	9	2
Delaware County District Attorney: Criminal Investigation Division	39	32	7
Delaware County Park	56	55	1

Table 81. Full-Time Law Enforcement Employees, by State and Agency, 2010—*Continued*

(Number)

State, agency, unit/office	Total law enforcement employees	Total officers	Total civilians
Easton Area School District	7	6	1
Erie City School District	3	3	0
Fort Indiantown Gap	23	7	16
Harrisburg International Airport	15	7	8
Tyrone Area School District	1	1	0
Uniontown Hospital	14	14	0
Washington County Alternative Education	1	1	0
Westmoreland County Park	22	21	1
Wilkes-Barre Area School District	5	5	0
RHODE ISLAND—State Agencies			
Department of Environmental Management	42	33	9
Rhode Island State Airport	47	39	8
SOUTH CAROLINA—State Agencies			
Bureau of Protective Services	71	66	5
Department of Mental Health	127	80	47
Employment Security Commission	4	4	0
Forestry Commission:			
Aiken County	1	1	0
Anderson County	1	1	0
Barnwell County	1	1	0
Beaufort County	1	1	0
Berkeley County	1	1	0
Charleston County	1	1	0
Chesterfield County	5	5	0
Colleton County	2	2	0
Darlington County	2	2	0
Fairfield County	1	1	0
Florence County	1	1	0
Greenville County	1	1	0
Hampton County	1	1	0
Horry County	1	1	0
Kershaw County	2	2	0
Lancaster County	1	1	0
Lee County	1	1	0
Lexington County	2	2	0
Oconee County	1	1	0
Orangeburg County	1	1	0
Pickens County	1	1	0
Richland County	2	2	0
Sumter County	6	6	0
Williamsburg County	1	1	0
York County	1	1	0
South Carolina School for the Deaf and Blind	1	1	0
State Museum	1	1	0
State Ports Authority	72	31	41
State Transport Police:			
Abbeville County	11	11	0
Aiken County	55	28	27
Allendale County	12	12	0
Anderson County	19	17	2
Berkeley County	20	17	3
Cherokee County	9	9	0
Darlington County	12	12	0
United States Department of Energy: Savannah River Plant	63	50	13
SOUTH CAROLINA—Other Agencies			
Charleston County Aviation Authority	38	27	11
Greenville-Spartanburg International Airport	22	16	6
Whitten Center	1	1	0
SOUTH DAKOTA—State Agencies			
Division of Criminal Investigation	154	44	110
SOUTH DAKOTA—Tribal Agencies			
Rosebud Tribal	34	26	8
Sisseton-Wahpeton Tribal	16	7	9
TENNESSEE—State Agencies			
Alcoholic Beverage Commission	55	30	25
Department of Correction: Internal Affairs	12	8	4
State Fire Marshal	26	23	3
State Park Rangers:			
Bicentennial Capitol Mall	6	6	0
Big Hill Pond	2	2	0
Big Ridge	4	4	0
Bledsoe Creek	2	2	0
Booker T. Washington	3	3	0
Burgess Falls Natural Area	2	2	0
Cedars of Lebanon	4	4	0
Chickasaw	4	4	0
Cove Lake	4	4	0

Table 81.   Full-Time Law Enforcement Employees, by State and Agency, 2010—*Continued*

(Number)

State, agency, unit/office	Total law enforcement employees	Total officers	Total civilians
Cumberland Mountain	5	5	0
Cumberland Trail	6	6	0
David Crockett	4	4	0
Davy Crockett Birthplace	4	4	0
Dunbar Cave Natural Area	3	3	0
Edgar Evins	3	3	0
Fall Creek Falls	6	6	0
Fort Loudon State Historic Park	4	4	0
Fort Pillow State Historic Park	2	2	0
Frozen Head Natural Area	3	3	0
Harpeth Scenic Rivers	3	3	0
Harrison Bay	4	4	0
Henry Horton	4	4	0
Hiwassee/Ocoee State Scenic Rivers	5	5	0
Indian Mountain	2	2	0
Johnsonville State Historic Park	1	1	0
Long Hunter	3	3	0
Meeman-Shelby Forest	4	4	0
Montgomery Bell	5	5	0
Mousetail Landing	3	3	0
Natchez Trace	5	5	0
Nathan Bedford Forrest	3	3	0
Norris Dam	4	4	0
Old Stone Fort State Archaeological Park	3	3	0
Panther Creek	3	3	0
Paris Landing	3	3	0
Pickett	3	3	0
Pickwick Landing	5	5	0
Pinson Mounds State Archaeological Park	2	2	0
Radnor Lake Natural Area	5	5	0
Red Clay State Historic Park	2	2	0
Reelfoot Lake	5	5	0
Roan Mountain	4	4	0
Rock Island	3	3	0
Sgt. Alvin C. York	2	2	0
South Cumberland Recreation Area	5	5	0
Standing Stone	4	4	0
Sycamore Shoals State Historic Park	2	2	0
Tim's Ford	4	4	0
T.O. Fuller	3	3	0
Warrior's Path	4	4	0
TennCare Office of Inspector General	42	14	28
Tennessee Bureau of Investigation	463	178	285
Tennessee Department of Revenue: Special Investigations Unit	48	26	22
Wildlife Resources Agency:			
Region 1	43	40	3
Region 2	60	50	10
Region 3	46	43	3
Region 4	49	46	3
TENNESSEE—Other Agencies			
Chattanooga Housing Authority	5	4	1
Chattanooga Metropolitan Airport	10	10	0
Dickson Parks and Recreation	11	3	8
Drug Task Force:			
1st Judicial District	6	5	1
3rd Judicial District	6	5	1
4th Judicial District	3	2	1
5th Judicial District	12	9	3
8th Judicial District	3	3	0
9th Judicial District	2	2	0
10th Judicial District	15	14	1
12th Judicial District	2	2	0
13th Judicial District	2	2	0
14th Judicial District	3	3	0
15th Judicial District	2	1	1
17th Judicial District	3	2	1
18th Judicial District	8	7	1
19th Judicial District	3	2	1
21st Judicial District	14	11	3
22nd Judicial District	3	3	0
23rd Judicial District	10	7	3
24th Judicial District	3	2	1
25th Judicial District	2	2	0
27th Judicial District	2	1	1
Knoxville Metropolitan Airport	45	27	18
Memphis International Airport	60	48	12
Metropolitan Nashville Park Police	23	23	0

Table 81. Full-Time Law Enforcement Employees, by State and Agency, 2010—*Continued*

(Number)

State, agency, unit/office	Total law enforcement employees	Total officers	Total civilians
Nashville International Airport	76	60	16
Smyrna/Rutherford County Airport Authority	4	4	0
Tri-Cities Regional Airport	14	13	1
West Tennessee Violent Crime Task Force	8	7	1
TEXAS—Tribal Agencies			
Ysleta Del Sur Pueblo Tribal	9	7	2
TEXAS—Other Agencies			
Amarillo International Airport	14	14	0
Dallas-Fort Worth International Airport	396	263	133
Hospital District:			
Dallas County	79	52	27
Tarrant County	62	42	20
Houston Metropolitan Transit Authority	230	190	40
Independent School District:			
Aldine	50	44	6
Alvin	22	17	5
Austin	105	70	35
Barbers Hill	4	3	1
Bay City	6	5	1
Cedar Hill	23	5	18
Conroe	64	46	18
Corpus Christi	51	29	22
East Central	9	8	1
Ector County	30	28	2
Fort Bend	61	43	18
Hallsville	2	2	0
Humble	38	27	11
Judson	18	16	2
Katy	44	35	9
Kaufman	5	4	1
Killeen	14	14	0
Klein	50	31	19
Laredo	105	27	78
Mexia	4	4	0
Midland	17	11	6
Pasadena	38	31	7
Pflugerville	17	17	0
Spring	43	41	2
Spring Branch	39	32	7
Taft	1	1	0
United	166	53	113
Port of Houston Authority	75	50	25
UTAH—State Agencies			
Parks and Recreation	76	75	1
Wildlife Resources	82	73	9
UTAH—Other Agencies			
Granite School District	34	15	19
Utah County Attorney: Investigatiaons Division	7	5	2
Utah Transit Authority	35	33	2
VERMONT—State Agencies			
Attorney General	3	3	0
Department of Liquor Control: Division of Enforcement and Licensing	20	16	4
Department of Motor Vehicles	46	32	14
Fish and Wildlife Department: Law Enforcement Division	38	36	2
VIRGINIA—State Agencies			
Alcoholic Beverage Control Commission	139	107	32
Department of Conservation and Recreation	244	105	139
Department of Game and Inland Fisheries: Enforcement Division	186	167	19
Department of Motor Vehicles	88	72	16
Southside Virginia Training Center	17	16	1
Virginia State Capitol	80	68	12
VIRGINIA—Other Agencies			
Norfolk Airport Authority	44	37	7
Port Authority: Norfolk	80	73	7
Reagan National Airport	308	216	92
Richmond International Airport	34	26	8
WASHINGTON—State Agencies			
State Insurance Commissioner: Special Investigations Unit	6	4	2
WASHINGTON—Tribal Agencies			
Chehalis Tribal	10	9	1
Colville Tribal	43	31	12
Jamestown S'Klallam Tribal	10	3	7
Kalispel Tribal	13	12	1
La Push Tribal	4	4	0
Lummi Tribal	24	22	2
Makah Tribal	12	5	7
Nisqually Tribal	19	15	4

Table 81. Full-Time Law Enforcement Employees, by State and Agency, 2010—*Continued*

(Number)

State, agency, unit/office	Total law enforcement employees	Total officers	Total civilians
Nooksack Tribal	9	7	2
Port Gamble S'Klallam Tribal	8	7	1
Puyallup Tribal	42	30	12
Quinault Indian Nation	10	8	2
Sauk-Suiattle Tribal	5	4	1
Shoalwater Bay Tribal	3	3	0
Skokomish Tribal	7	5	2
Spokane Tribal	24	16	8
Squaxin Island Tribal	16	13	3
Stillaguamish Tribal	7	7	0
Suquamish Tribal	17	16	1
Swinomish Tribal	16	14	2
Tulalip Tribal	50	30	20
Upper Skagit Tribal	5	4	1
Yakima Tribal	48	22	26
WASHINGTON—Other Agencies			
Port of Seattle	124	95	29
WEST VIRGINIA—State Agencies			
Capitol Protective Services	35	19	16
Division of Natural Resources:			
Barbour County	1	1	0
Berkeley County	4	4	0
Boone County	1	1	0
Braxton County	2	2	0
Brooke County	1	1	0
Cabell County	2	2	0
Calhoun County	1	1	0
Clay County	2	2	0
Doddridge County	1	1	0
Fayette County	4	3	1
Gilmer County	2	2	0
Grant County	2	2	0
Greenbrier County	1	1	0
Hampshire County	5	4	1
Hancock County	1	1	0
Hardy County	1	1	0
Harrison County	3	3	0
Jackson County	2	2	0
Jefferson County	1	1	0
Kanawha County	3	3	0
Lewis County	1	1	0
Lincoln County	1	1	0
Logan County	2	2	0
Marion County	4	3	1
Marshall County	1	1	0
Mason County	1	1	0
McDowell County	1	1	0
Mercer County	3	3	0
Mineral County	2	2	0
Mingo County	1	1	0
Monongalia County	2	2	0
Monroe County	1	1	0
Morgan County	1	1	0
Nicholas County	4	4	0
Ohio County	1	1	0
Pendleton County	2	2	0
Pleasants County	2	1	1
Pocahontas County	2	2	0
Preston County	2	2	0
Putnam County	5	4	1
Raleigh County	4	4	0
Randolph County	4	3	1
Ritchie County	1	1	0
Roane County	1	1	0
Summers County	4	4	0
Taylor County	1	1	0
Tyler County	1	1	0
Upshur County	2	2	0
Wayne County	2	2	0
Webster County	3	3	0
Wetzel County	1	1	0
Wirt County	2	2	0
Wood County	3	3	0
Wyoming County	1	1	0
State Fire Marshal: Kanawha County	40	32	8

Table 81. Full-Time Law Enforcement Employees, by State and Agency, 2010—*Continued*

(Number)

State, agency, unit/office	Total law enforcement employees	Total officers	Total civilians
WEST VIRGINIA—Other Agencies			
Central West Virginia Drug Task Force	5	5	0
Eastern Panhandle Drug and Violent Crime Task Force	7	6	1
Greenbrier County Drug and Violent Crime Task Force	1	1	0
Hancock/Brooke/Weirton Drug Task Force	5	5	0
Huntington Drug and Violent Crime Task Force	14	13	1
Kanawha County Parks and Recreation	3	3	0
Logan County Drug and Violent Crime Task Force	7	6	1
Metropolitan Drug Enforcement Network Team	17	16	1
Ohio Valley Drug and Violent Crime Task Force	3	3	0
Potomac Highlands Drug and Violent Crime Task Force	4	4	0
WISCONSIN—State Agencies			
Capitol Police	45	36	9
Department of Natural Resources	465	427	38
WISCONSIN—Tribal Agencies			
Lac du Flambeau Tribal	12	10	2
Menominee Tribal	44	23	21
Oneida Tribal	28	20	8
St. Croix Tribal	18	12	6
OTHER OUTLYING AREAS			
Virgin Islands:			
St. Croix	291	217	74
St. Thomas	313	252	61
FEDERAL AGENCY			
National Institutes of Health	124	97	27

SECTION VI:
HATE CRIMES

HATE CRIMES

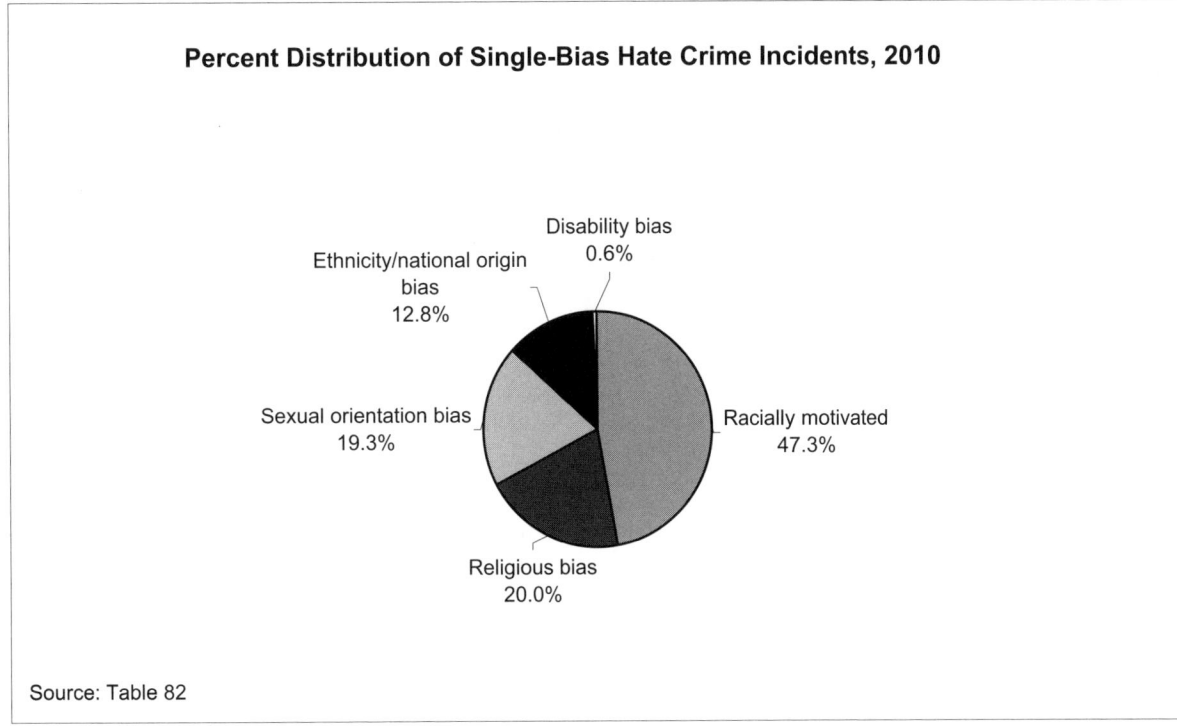

Percent Distribution of Single-Bias Hate Crime Incidents, 2010

Disability bias
0.6%

Ethnicity/national origin bias
12.8%

Sexual orientation bias
19.3%

Racially motivated
47.3%

Religious bias
20.0%

Source: Table 82

The Federal Bureau of Investigation (FBI) began the procedures for implementing, collecting, and managing hate crime data after Congress passed the Hate Crime Statistics Act in 1990 which required the collection of data "about crimes that manifest evidence of prejudice based on race, religion, sexual orientation, or ethnicity." In 1994, the Hate Crime Statistics Act was amended to include bias against persons with disabilities. The Church Arson Prevention Act, which was signed into law in July 1996, removed the sunset clause from the original statute and mandated that the collection of hate crime data become a permanent part of the UCR Program. In 2009, Congress further amended the Hate Crime Statistics Act by passing the Matthew Shepard and James Byrd, Jr. Hate Crime Prevention Act. The amendment includes the collection of data for crimes motivated by bias against a particular gender and gender identity, as well as for crimes committed by, and crimes directed against, juveniles. The FBI is currently making plans to implement changes to collect these data. (See www.fbi.gov/about-us/cjis/ucr/hate-crime/2010/resources/hate-crime-2010-hate-crime-statistics-act for referenced legislation, as amended.)

Definition

Hate crimes include any crime motivated by bias against race, religion, sexual orientation, ethnicity/national origin, and/or disability. Because motivation is subjective, it is sometimes difficult to know with certainty whether a crime resulted from the offender's bias. Moreover, the presence of bias alone does not necessarily mean that a crime can be considered a hate crime. Only when law enforcement inves-

tigation reveals sufficient evidence to lead a reasonable and prudent person to conclude that the offender's actions were motivated, in whole or in part, by his or her bias, should an incident be reported as a hate crime.

Data Collection

The UCR (Uniform Crime Reporting) Program collects data about both single-bias and multiple-bias hate crimes. A single-bias incident is defined as an incident in which one or more offense types are motivated by the same bias. A multiple-bias incident is defined as an incident in which more than one offense type occurs and at least two offense types are motivated by different biases.

Crimes against persons, property, or society

The UCR Program's data collection guidelines stipulate that a hate crime may involve multiple offenses, victims, and offenders within one incident; therefore, the Hate Crime Statistics Program is incident-based. According to UCR counting guidelines:

- One offense is counted for each victim in *crimes against persons*.

- One offense is counted for each offense type in *crimes against property*.

- One offense is counted for each offense type in *crimes against society*.

Victims

In the UCR Program, the victim of a hate crime may be an individual, a business, an institution, or society as a whole.

Offenders

According to the UCR Program, the term *known offender* does not imply that the suspect's identity is known; rather, the term indicates that some aspect of the suspect was identified, thus distinguishing the suspect from an unknown offender. Law enforcement agencies specify the number of offenders and, when possible, the race of the offender or offenders as a group.

Race/ethnicity

The UCR Program uses the following five racial designations in its Hate Crime Statistics Program: White; Black; American Indian/Alaskan Native; Asian/Pacific Islander; and Multiple Races, Group. In addition, the UCR Program uses the ethnic designations of Hispanic and Other Ethnicity/National Origin.

Agencies that participated in the Hate Crime Statistics Program in 2010 represented more than 285 million inhabitants, or 92.3 percent of the Nation's population, and their jurisdictions covered 49 states and the District of Columbia. The law enforcement agencies that voluntarily participate in the Hate Crime Statistics Program collect details about an offender's bias motivation associated with 11 offense types already being reported to the UCR Program: murder and nonnegligent manslaughter, forcible rape, aggravated assault, simple assault, and intimidation (crimes against persons); and robbery, burglary, larceny-theft, motor vehicle theft, arson, and destruction/damage/vandalism (crimes against property). The law enforcement agencies that participate in the UCR Program via the National Incident-Based Reporting System (NIBRS) collect data about additional offenses for *crimes against persons* and *crimes against property*. These data appear in the category of other. These agencies also collect hate crime data for the category called *crimes against society*, which includes drug or narcotic offenses, gambling offenses, prostitution offenses, and weapon law violations.

National Volume and Percent Distribution

In 2010, 1,949 law enforcement agencies reported 6,628 hate crime incidents involving 7,699 offenses. Of these, 6,624 were single-bias offenses. An analysis of the single-bias incidents revealed 47.3 percent were racially motivated, 20.0 percent were motivated by religious bias, 19.3 percent resulted from sexual-orientation bias, 12.8 percent were based on an ethnicity/national origin bias and 0.6 percent were prompted by a disability bias. (Table 82)

The majority of the hate crime offenses that were racially motivated resulted from an anti-Black bias (69.8 percent) followed by an anti-White basis (18.2 percent). Bias against people of more than one race accounted for 5.7 percent of offenses, while anti-Asian/Pacific Islander bias accounted for 5.1 percent of racially motivated offenses, and anti-American Indian bias accounted for 1.2 percent. (Table 82)

Hate crimes motivated by religious bias accounted for 1,409 offenses reported by law enforcement. A breakdown of these offenses revealed 65.4 percent were motivated by anti-Jewish bias, 13.2 percent by anti-Islamic bias, 3.8 percent were anti-multiple religions or groups, 4.3 percent an anti-Catholic bias, 3.3 percent were anti-Protestant, 0.5 percent were anti-Atheism, and the remainder, 9.5 percent, of offenses were based on a bias against other religions—those not specified. (Table 82)

In 2010, slightly more hate crimes were committed on the basis of sexual bias than on religious bias. Of the 1,470 offenses based on sexual orientation, 57.9 percent were classified as having an anti-male homosexual bias, 27.4 percent had an anti-homosexual bias, 11.4 percent had an anti-female homosexual basis, 1.9 percent had an anti-bisexual bias, and 1.4 percent had an anti-heterosexual bias. (Table 82)

The vast majority of 1,040 offenses that were committed on the perceived ethnicity or national origin of the victim had an anti-Hispanic basis (65.5 percent). The remaining 34.5 percent were based on bias against another ethnicity or national origin. (Table 82)

Other hate crime offenses were committed based on disability. The majority (55.8 percent) were classified as anti-mental disability, with the rest (44.2 Percent) were classified as anti-physical disability. (Table 82)

Crimes against Persons

Law enforcement agencies reported 4,824 hate crime offenses against persons in 2010. Nearly half of them (46.2 percent) involved intimidation, 34.8 percent involved simple assault, and 18.4 percent involved aggravated assault. In addition, there were 7 murders and 4 forcible rapes. (Table 83)

Crimes against Property

In 2010, hate crime offences against property totaled 2,861. Approximately 81.1 percent of offenses involved destruction/damage or vandalism. The remaining 18.9 percent of crimes against property consisted of robbery, burglary, larceny-theft, motor vehicle theft, arson, and other crimes. (Table 83)

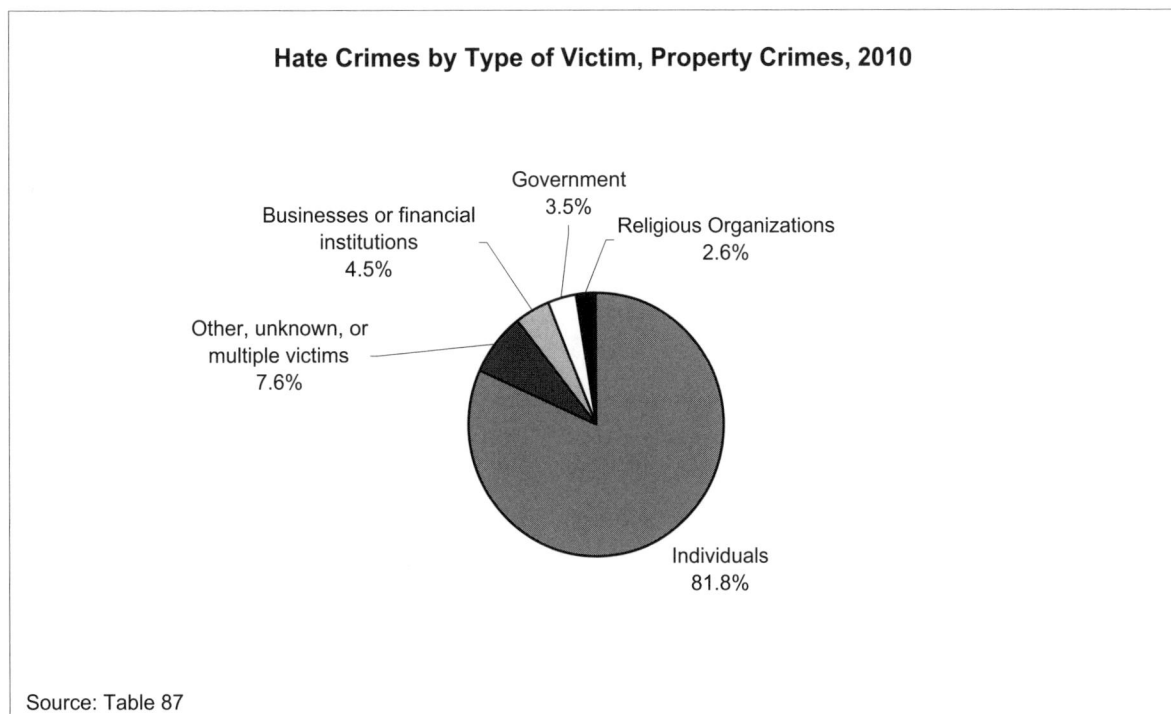

Hate Crimes by Type of Victim, Property Crimes, 2010

Government
3.5%

Businesses or financial
institutions
4.5%

Religious Organizations
2.6%

Other, unknown, or
multiple victims
7.6%

Individuals
81.8%

Source: Table 87

Table 82. Incidents, Offenses, Victims, and Known Offenders, by Bias Motivation, 2010

(Number)

Bias motivation	Incidents	Offenses	Victims[1]	Known offenders[2]
TOTAL	6,628	7,699	8,208	6,008
Single-Bias Incidents	6,624	7,690	8,199	6,001
Race:	3,135	3,725	3,949	2,934
Anti-White	575	679	697	649
Anti-Black	2,201	2,600	2,765	1,974
Anti-American Indian/Alaskan Native	44	45	47	43
Anti-Asian/Pacific Islander	150	190	203	156
Anti-Multiple Races, Group	165	211	237	112
Religion:	1,322	1,409	1,552	606
Anti-Jewish	887	922	1,040	346
Anti-Catholic	58	61	65	22
Anti-Protestant	41	46	47	6
Anti-Islamic	160	186	197	125
Anti-Other Religion	123	134	141	72
Anti-Multiple Religions, Group	48	53	55	30
Anti-Atheism/Agnosticism/etc.	5	7	7	5
Sexual Orientation:	1,277	1,470	1,528	1,516
Anti-Male Homosexual	739	851	876	904
Anti-Female Homosexual	144	167	181	152
Anti-Homosexual	347	403	420	412
Anti-Heterosexual	21	21	22	21
Anti-Bisexual	26	28	29	27
Ethnicity/National Origin:	847	1,040	1,122	887
Anti-Hispanic	534	681	747	593
Anti-Other Ethnicity/National Origin	313	359	375	294
Disability:	43	46	48	58
Anti-Physical	19	22	24	28
Anti-Mental	24	24	24	30
Multiple-Bias Incidents[3]	4	9	9	7

[1]The term *victim* may refer to a person, business, institution, or society as a whole.
[2]The term *known offender* does not imply that the identity of the suspect is known, but only that an attribute of the suspect has been identified, which distinguishes him/her from an unknown offender.
[3]In a *multiple-bias incident,* two conditions must be met: (a) more than one offense type must occur in the incident and (b) at least two offense types must be motivated by different biases.

Table 83. Incidents, Offenses, Victims, and Known Offenders, by Offense Type, 2010

(Number)

Offense type	Incidents[1]	Offenses	Victims[2]	Known offenders[3]
TOTAL	6,628	7,699	8,208	6,008
Crimes against persons:	3,978	4,824	4,824	4,873
Murder and nonnegligent manslaughter	6	7	7	9
Forcible rape	4	4	4	7
Aggravated assault	695	888	888	1,144
Simple assault	1,472	1,681	1,681	1,972
Intimidation	1,790	2,231	2,231	1,726
Other[4]	11	13	13	15
Crimes against property:	2,861	2,861	3,370	1,419
Robbery	146	146	168	290
Burglary	125	125	163	88
Larceny-theft	175	175	195	141
Motor vehicle theft	16	16	16	8
Arson	43	43	45	30
Destruction/damage/vandalism	2,321	2,321	2,747	831
Other[4]	35	35	36	31
Crimes against society[4]	14	14	14	18

[1]The actual number of incidents is 6,628. However, the column figures will not add to the total because incidents may include more than one offense type, and these are counted in each appropriate offense type category.
[2]The term *victim* may refer to a person, business, institution, or society as a whole.
[3]The term known offender does not imply that the identity of the suspect is known, but only that an attribute of the suspect has been identified, which distinguishes him/her from an unknown offender. The actual number of known offenders is 6,008. However, the column figures will not add to the total because some offenders are responsible for more than one offense type, and they are, therefore, counted more than once in this table.
[4] Includes additional offenses collected in the NIBRS.

Table 84.   Known Offender's Race, by Offense Type, 2010

(Number)

Offense type	Total offenses	Known offender's race						Unknown offender
		White	Black	American Indian/ Alaskan Native	Asian/Pacific Islander	Multiple races, group	Unknown race	
TOTAL..	7,699	3,176	905	52	61	238	597	2,670
Crimes against persons:...........................	4,824	2,751	767	44	52	189	305	716
Murder and nonnegligent manslaughter....................	7	4	3	0	0	0	0	0
Forcible rape..	4	2	2	0	0	0	0	0
Aggravated assault..	888	549	197	9	20	49	28	36
Simple assault..	1,681	955	340	26	18	113	82	147
Intimidation..	2,231	1,236	218	9	14	27	195	532
Other[1]..	13	5	7	0	0	0	0	1
Crimes against property:.........................	2,861	415	138	6	9	48	292	1,953
Robbery...	146	40	57	3	1	17	13	15
Burglary..	125	27	4	0	1	4	19	70
Larceny-theft...	175	40	17	1	0	3	23	91
Motor vehicle theft.......................................	16	1	4	0	0	0	2	9
Arson...	43	15	3	0	0	1	3	21
Destruction/damage/vandalism..............................	2,321	279	48	1	6	22	226	1,739
Other[1]..	35	13	5	1	1	1	6	8
Crimes against society[1]............................	14	10	0	2	0	1	0	1

[1]Includes additional offenses collected in the NIBRS.

SECTION VI: HATE CRIMES   531

Table 85.   Number of Offenses and Offense Type, by Bias Motivation, 2010

(Number)

Bias motivation	Total offenses	Crimes against persons					Other[1]
		Murder and nonnegligent manslaughter	Forcible rape	Aggravated assault	Simple assault	Intimidation	
TOTAL	7,699	7	4	888	1,681	2,231	13
Single-Bias Incidents	7,690	7	4	886	1,679	2,231	13
Race:	3,725	1	2	444	755	1,227	5
Anti-White	679	0	2	92	192	157	3
Anti-Black	2,600	1	0	315	486	933	2
Anti-American Indian/Alaskan Native	45	0	0	3	12	2	0
Anti-Asian/Pacific Islander	190	0	0	15	42	73	0
Anti-Multiple Races, Group	211	0	0	19	23	62	0
Religion:	1,409	3	0	35	133	321	1
Anti-Jewish	922	0	0	12	65	201	0
Anti-Catholic	61	0	0	0	5	7	0
Anti-Protestant	46	0	0	0	1	3	0
Anti-Islamic	186	0	0	17	46	69	0
Anti-Other Religion	134	3	0	4	11	25	1
Anti-Multiple Religions, Group	53	0	0	2	5	15	0
Anti-Atheism/Agnosticism/etc.	7	0	0	0	0	1	0
Sexual Orientation:	1,470	2	1	247	495	331	6
Anti-Male Homosexual	851	1	0	158	301	190	3
Anti-Female Homosexual	167	0	1	23	40	52	3
Anti-Homosexual	403	0	0	58	139	84	0
Anti-Heterosexual	21	0	0	3	7	1	0
Anti-Bisexual	28	1	0	5	8	4	0
Ethnicity/National Origin:	1,040	1	1	154	276	347	0
Anti-Hispanic	681	1	1	112	183	227	0
Anti-Other Ethnicity/National Origin	359	0	0	42	93	120	0
Disability:	46	0	0	6	20	5	1
Anti-Physical	22	0	0	4	8	5	1
Anti-Mental	24	0	0	2	12	0	0
Multiple-Bias Incidents[2]	9	0	0	2	2	0	0

Bias motivation	Crimes against property							Crimes against society[1]
	Robbery	Burglary	Larceny-theft	Motor vehicle theft	Arson	Destruction/ damage/ vandalism	Other[1]	
TOTAL	146	125	175	16	43	2,321	35	14
Single-Bias Incidents	146	125	173	16	43	2,318	35	14
Race:	53	61	84	7	12	1,045	18	11
Anti-White	32	22	49	6	0	111	10	3
Anti-Black	19	25	16	1	11	781	5	5
Anti-American Indian/Alaskan Native	1	1	17	0	0	5	3	1
Anti-Asian/Pacific Islander	0	7	1	0	0	52	0	0
Anti-Multiple Races, Group	1	6	1	0	1	96	0	2
Religion:	11	29	38	1	17	816	4	0
Anti-Jewish	9	6	8	0	2	619	0	0
Anti-Catholic	0	6	10	1	0	31	1	0
Anti-Protestant	0	5	3	0	1	33	0	0
Anti-Islamic	1	1	3	0	1	47	1	0
Anti-Other Religion	1	9	8	0	12	59	1	0
Anti-Multiple Religions, Group	0	1	5	0	1	23	1	0
Anti-Atheism/Agnosticism/etc.	0	1	1	0	0	4	0	0
Sexual Orientation:	56	19	24	4	7	273	5	0
Anti-Male Homosexual	39	6	12	1	5	134	1	0
Anti-Female Homosexual	2	4	2	1	0	39	0	0
Anti-Homosexual	15	8	3	1	2	92	1	0
Anti-Heterosexual	0	0	1	0	0	8	1	0
Anti-Bisexual	0	1	6	1	0	0	2	0
Ethnicity/National Origin:	23	15	20	4	7	183	7	2
Anti-Hispanic	16	9	11	3	5	105	7	1
Anti-Other Ethnicity/National Origin	7	6	9	1	2	78	0	1
Disability:	3	1	7	0	0	1	1	1
Anti-Physical	0	0	3	0	0	0	0	1
Anti-Mental	3	1	4	0	0	1	1	0
Multiple-Bias Incidents[2]	0	0	2	0	0	3	0	0

[1] Includes additional offenses collected in the NIBRS.

[2] In a *multiple-bias incident,* two conditions must be met: (a) more than one offense type must occur in the incident and (b) at least two offense types must be motivated by different biases.

Table 86.   Known Offender's Race, by Bias Motivation, 2010

(Number)

Bias motivation	Total offenses	Known offender's race						Unknown offender
		White	Black	American Indian/ Alaskan Native	Asian/Pacific Islander	Multiple races, group	Unknown race	
TOTAL	7,699	3,176	905	52	61	238	597	2,670
Single-Bias Incidents	7,690	3,173	905	52	61	236	597	2,666
Race:	3,725	1,700	383	36	30	97	298	1,181
Anti-White	679	112	303	18	5	23	67	151
Anti-Black	2,600	1,417	56	11	20	54	184	858
Anti-American Indian/Alaskan Native	45	19	2	5	2	1	2	14
Anti-Asian/Pacific Islander	190	83	13	0	3	13	17	61
Anti-Multiple Races, Group	211	69	9	2	0	6	28	97
Religion:	1,409	270	73	1	5	33	112	915
Anti-Jewish	922	134	25	0	3	23	62	675
Anti-Catholic	61	8	7	0	0	0	8	38
Anti-Protestant	46	2	1	0	0	0	3	40
Anti-Islamic	186	77	21	0	1	6	16	65
Anti-Other Religion	134	32	7	1	1	4	15	74
Anti-Multiple Religions, Group	53	14	11	0	0	0	5	23
Anti-Atheism/Agnosticism/etc.	7	3	1	0	0	0	3	0
Sexual Orientation:	1,470	638	310	5	12	56	121	328
Anti-Male Homosexual	851	357	199	1	6	45	64	179
Anti-Female Homosexual	167	78	32	0	1	3	12	41
Anti-Homosexual	403	178	76	4	5	5	38	97
Anti-Heterosexual	21	10	2	0	0	0	3	6
Anti-Bisexual	28	15	1	0	0	3	4	5
Ethnicity/National Origin:	1,040	540	129	10	14	45	66	236
Anti-Hispanic	681	367	100	8	2	30	41	133
Anti-Other Ethnicity/National Origin	359	173	29	2	12	15	25	103
Disability:	46	25	10	0	0	5	0	6
Anti-Physical	22	11	5	0	0	3	0	3
Anti-Mental	24	14	5	0	0	2	0	3
Multiple-Bias Incidents[1]	9	3	0	0	0	2	0	4

[1]In a *multiple-bias incident,* two conditions must be met: (a) more than one offense type must occur in the incident and (b) at least two offense types must be motivated by different biases.

Table 87.   Victim Type, by Offense Type, 2010

(Number)

Offense type	Total offenses	Victim type					Other/ unknown/ multiple
		Individual	Business/ financial institution	Government	Religious organization	Society/ public[1]	
TOTAL	7,699	6,283	343	271	201	14	587
Crimes against persons[2]	4,824	4,824	...	...	...	...	...
Crimes against property:	2,861	1,459	343	271	201	0	587
Robbery	146	114	1	0	0	0	31
Burglary	125	84	10	4	10	0	17
Larceny-theft	175	120	34	2	5	0	14
Motor vehicle theft	16	15	1	0	0	0	0
Arson	43	20	5	1	13	0	4
Destruction/damage/vandalism	2,321	1,077	287	263	173	0	521
Other[2]	35	29	5	1	0	0	0
Crimes against society[2]	14	...	...	...	...	14	...

[1]The victim type *society/public* is collected only in the NIBRS.
[2]Includes additional offenses collected in the NIBRS.

Table 88.   Number of Victims and Offense Type, by Bias Motivation, 2010

(Number)

Bias motivation	Total offenses	Crimes against persons					
		Murder and nonnegligent manslaughter	Forcible rape	Aggravated assault	Simple assault	Intimidation	Other[1]
TOTAL	8,208	7	4	888	1,681	2,231	13
Single-Bias Incidents	8,199	7	4	886	1,679	2,231	13
Race:	3,949	1	2	444	755	1,227	5
Anti-White	697	0	2	92	192	157	3
Anti-Black	2,765	1	0	315	486	933	2
Anti-American Indian/Alaskan Native	47	0	0	3	12	2	0
Anti-Asian/Pacific Islander	203	0	0	15	42	73	0
Anti-Multiple Races, Group	237	0	0	19	23	62	0
Religion:	1,552	3	0	35	133	321	1
Anti-Jewish	1,040	0	0	12	65	201	0
Anti-Catholic	65	0	0	0	5	7	0
Anti-Protestant	47	0	0	0	1	3	0
Anti-Islamic	197	0	0	17	46	69	0
Anti-Other Religion	141	3	0	4	11	25	1
Anti-Multiple Religions, Group	55	0	0	2	5	15	0
Anti-Atheism/Agnosticism/etc.	7	0	0	0	0	1	0
Sexual Orientation:	1,528	2	1	247	495	331	6
Anti-Male Homosexual	876	1	0	158	301	190	3
Anti-Female Homosexual	181	0	1	23	40	52	3
Anti-Homosexual	420	0	0	58	139	84	0
Anti-Heterosexual	22	0	0	3	7	1	0
Anti-Bisexual	29	1	0	5	8	4	0
Ethnicity/National Origin:	1,122	1	1	154	276	347	0
Anti-Hispanic	747	1	1	112	183	227	0
Anti-Other Ethnicity/National Origin	375	0	0	42	93	120	0
Disability:	48	0	0	6	20	5	1
Anti-Physical	24	0	0	4	8	5	1
Anti-Mental	24	0	0	2	12	0	0
Multiple-Bias Incidents[2]	9	0	0	2	2	0	0

Bias motivation	Crimes against property							Crimes against society[1]
	Robbery	Burglary	Larceny-theft	Motor vehicle theft	Arson	Destruction/ damage/ vandalism	Other[1]	
TOTAL	168	163	195	16	45	2,747	36	14
Single-Bias Incidents	168	163	193	16	45	2,744	36	14
Race:	63	70	84	7	12	1,250	18	11
Anti-White	39	22	49	6	0	122	10	3
Anti-Black	21	30	16	1	11	939	5	5
Anti-American Indian/Alaskan Native	2	1	17	0	0	6	3	1
Anti-Asian/Pacific Islander	0	11	1	0	0	61	0	0
Anti-Multiple Races, Group	1	6	1	0	1	122	0	2
Religion:	11	32	38	1	17	956	4	0
Anti-Jewish	9	7	8	0	2	736	0	0
Anti-Catholic	0	7	10	1	0	34	1	0
Anti-Protestant	0	5	3	0	1	34	0	0
Anti-Islamic	1	1	3	0	1	58	1	0
Anti-Other Religion	1	10	8	0	12	65	1	0
Anti-Multiple Religions, Group	0	1	5	0	1	25	1	0
Anti-Atheism/Agnosticism/etc.	0	1	1	0	0	4	0	0
Sexual Orientation:	68	23	26	4	8	311	6	0
Anti-Male Homosexual	42	7	14	1	5	153	1	0
Anti-Female Homosexual	4	4	2	1	0	51	0	0
Anti-Homosexual	22	10	3	1	3	99	1	0
Anti-Heterosexual	0	0	1	0	0	8	2	0
Anti-Bisexual	0	2	6	1	0	0	2	0
Ethnicity/National Origin:	23	37	36	4	8	226	7	2
Anti-Hispanic	16	29	26	3	6	135	7	1
Anti-Other Ethnicity/National Origin	7	8	10	1	2	91	0	1
Disability:	3	1	9	0	0	1	1	1
Anti-Physical	0	0	5	0	0	0	0	1
Anti-Mental	3	1	4	0	0	1	1	0
Multiple-Bias Incidents[2]	0	0	2	0	0	3	0	0

[1]Includes additional offenses collected in the NIBRS.

[2]In a *multiple-bias incident*, two conditions must be met: (a) more than one offense type must occur in the incident and (b) at least two offense types must be motivated by different biases.

Table 89.   Number of Incidents and Victim Type, by Bias Motivation, 2010

(Number)

Offense type	Total offenses	Victim type					
		Individual	Business/ financial institution	Government	Religious organization	Society/ public[1]	Other/ unknown/ multiple
TOTAL	6,628	5,236	331	267	188	9	597
Single-Bias Incidents	6,624	5,232	331	267	188	9	597
Race	3,135	2,574	167	162	20	7	205
Religion	1,322	678	112	74	163	0	295
Sexual Orientation	1,277	1,177	30	18	1	0	51
Ethnicity/National Origin	847	764	21	13	4	1	44
Disability	43	39	1	0	0	1	2
Multiple-Bias Incidents[2]	4	4	0	0	0	0	0

[1]The victim type *society/public* is collected only in the NIBRS.

[2]In a *multiple-bias incident,* two conditions must be met: (a) more than one offense type must occur in the incident and (b) at least two offense types must be motivated by different biases.

Table 90. Known Offender's Race, 2010[1]

(Number)

Race	Number
TOTAL	6,008
White	3,522
Black	1,104
American Indian/Alaskan Native	61
Asian/Pacific Islander	65
Multiple Races, Group[2]	534
Unknown Race	722

[1]The term *known offender* does not imply that the identity of the suspect is known, but only that an attribute of the suspect has been identified, which distinguishes him/her from an unknown offender.

[2]The term *multiple races, group* is used to describe a group of offenders of varying races.

Table 91. Number of Incidents and Bias Motivation, by Location, 2010

(Number)

Location	Total incidents	Bias motivation					Multiple-bias incidents[1]
		Race	Religion	Sexual orientation	Ethnicity/ national origin	Disability	
TOTAL	6,628	3,135	1,322	1,277	847	43	4
Air/bus/train terminal	70	31	8	21	9	1	0
Bank/savings and loan	12	7	1	2	2	0	0
Bar/nightclub	144	54	7	62	20	0	1
Camp/campground	1	0	0	0	1	0	0
Church/synagogue/temple	244	26	207	7	4	0	0
Commercial office building	123	63	20	16	23	1	0
Construction site	11	7	0	1	3	0	0
Convenience store	68	33	8	9	17	1	0
Department/discount store	72	34	15	14	9	0	0
Drug store/Doctor's office/hospital	55	24	22	5	3	1	0
Field/woods	65	34	9	14	8	0	0
Gambling facility/casino/race track	1	1	0	0	0	0	0
Government/public building	106	58	22	15	11	0	0
Grocery/supermarket	39	18	4	8	9	0	0
Highway/road/alley/street	1,127	593	109	268	148	9	0
Hotel/motel/etc.	38	21	3	7	6	1	0
Industrial site	1	0	1	0	0	0	0
Jail/prison	52	35	2	10	5	0	0
Lake/waterway	14	8	3	3	0	0	0
Liquor store	8	4	1	2	1	0	0
Parking lot/garage	385	188	45	88	63	1	0
Park/playground	2	2	0	0	0	0	0
Rental storage facility	5	1	2	1	1	0	0
Residence/home	2,079	1,052	352	399	261	14	1
Restaurant	107	54	8	21	23	1	0
School/college	724	368	168	107	71	9	1
Service/gas station	59	30	8	9	12	0	0
Shopping mall	2	1	0	1	0	0	0
Specialty store (TV, fur, etc.)	55	21	14	10	10	0	0
Other/unknown	950	361	283	177	125	4	0
Multiple locations	9	6	0	0	2	0	1

[1]In a *multiple-bias incident,* two conditions must be met: (a) more than one offense type must occur in the incident and (b) at least two offense types must be motivated by different biases.

Table 92. Offense Type, by Participating State, 2010

(Number)

| Participating state | Total offenses | Crimes against persons | | | | | Other[1] |
		Murder and nonnegligent manslaughter	Forcible rape	Aggravated assault	Simple assault	Intimidation	
TOTAL	7,699	7	4	888	1,681	2,231	13
Alabama	24	2	0	0	6	15	0
Alaska	9	0	0	3	4	2	0
Arizona	300	0	0	56	51	106	0
Arkansas	85	0	0	8	24	23	0
California	1,331	1	1	197	280	354	0
Colorado	196	0	0	39	37	78	0
Connecticut	168	0	0	10	29	54	1
Delaware	20	0	0	0	1	7	0
District of Columbia	66	0	1	16	21	12	0
Florida	146	0	0	32	24	37	0
Georgia	19	0	0	3	3	5	0
Idaho	34	0	0	6	12	4	0
Illinois	116	0	0	16	26	29	0
Indiana	116	0	0	8	22	52	0
Iowa	23	0	0	4	6	1	0
Kansas	73	0	0	17	19	17	0
Kentucky	205	1	0	21	38	44	4
Louisiana	17	0	0	0	5	0	0
Maine	76	0	0	3	15	40	0
Maryland	82	1	0	10	8	0	0
Massachusetts	360	0	0	31	53	156	2
Michigan	372	0	0	30	64	137	1
Minnesota	140	0	0	14	68	20	0
Mississippi	11	0	0	0	2	2	0
Missouri	167	0	0	29	31	50	0
Montana	37	0	0	11	11	0	0
Nebraska	62	0	0	3	25	16	0
Nevada	76	0	0	16	19	7	0
New Hampshire	35	0	0	2	6	17	0
New Jersey	557	0	0	7	26	277	0
New Mexico	25	0	0	14	6	3	0
New York	710	0	0	48	295	91	0
North Carolina	132	0	0	29	13	48	0
North Dakota	13	0	0	0	7	3	0
Ohio	295	0	0	9	60	115	0
Oklahoma	60	0	0	13	9	20	0
Oregon	161	0	0	15	25	52	3
Pennsylvania	69	0	0	8	8	40	0
Rhode Island	21	0	0	1	7	2	0
South Carolina	129	0	0	22	25	28	0
South Dakota	56	0	0	6	22	4	0
Tennessee	163	0	0	19	42	44	0
Texas	202	1	0	36	54	52	0
Utah	67	0	0	2	22	3	1
Vermont	22	0	0	6	4	2	0
Virginia	204	1	1	20	55	36	1
Washington	301	0	0	21	50	120	0
West Virginia	36	0	0	4	11	3	0
Wisconsin	108	0	1	23	30	3	0
Wyoming	2	0	0	0	0	0	0

[1]Includes additional offenses collected in the NIBRS.

Table 92. Offense Type, by Participating State, 2010—*Continued*

(Number)

Participating state	Crimes against property							Crimes against society[1]
	Robbery	Burglary	Larceny-theft	Motor vehicle theft	Arson	Destruction/ damage/ vandalism	Other[1]	
TOTAL	146	125	175	16	43	2,321	35	14
Alabama	0	0	0	0	0	1	0	0
Alaska	0	0	0	0	0	0	0	0
Arizona	2	0	0	0	4	81	0	0
Arkansas	0	5	10	0	1	12	2	0
California	35	19	6	1	8	429	0	0
Colorado	0	0	1	0	0	40	0	1
Connecticut	3	1	4	0	0	66	0	0
Delaware	0	0	0	0	1	11	0	0
District of Columbia	8	0	0	0	0	8	0	0
Florida	4	1	1	0	0	47	0	0
Georgia	0	0	0	0	1	7	0	0
Idaho	0	2	1	0	0	9	0	0
Illinois	0	1	2	0	0	42	0	0
Indiana	0	2	1	0	0	31	0	0
Iowa	0	1	1	0	0	9	0	1
Kansas	1	1	2	0	0	16	0	0
Kentucky	4	21	12	2	0	51	3	4
Louisiana	0	2	3	0	0	5	2	0
Maine	0	0	0	0	0	18	0	0
Maryland	2	1	0	0	0	60	0	0
Massachusetts	1	1	13	2	0	101	0	0
Michigan	3	9	19	4	3	100	2	0
Minnesota	5	0	0	0	1	32	0	0
Mississippi	0	0	2	1	0	1	3	0
Missouri	3	6	4	1	1	41	0	1
Montana	1	2	6	0	0	5	0	1
Nebraska	1	0	0	0	0	17	0	0
Nevada	3	1	1	0	2	27	0	0
New Hampshire	0	0	0	0	0	10	0	0
New Jersey	2	1	2	0	2	240	0	0
New Mexico	1	0	0	0	0	1	0	0
New York	34	9	7	0	2	224	0	0
North Carolina	0	1	4	0	1	36	0	0
North Dakota	0	0	1	0	0	2	0	0
Ohio	10	10	17	0	2	69	3	0
Oklahoma	0	2	0	0	0	16	0	0
Oregon	3	5	2	0	3	52	1	0
Pennsylvania	1	0	0	0	4	8	0	0
Rhode Island	0	0	0	0	0	10	1	0
South Carolina	1	2	6	2	0	37	3	3
South Dakota	1	1	4	1	1	11	5	0
Tennessee	2	5	3	0	1	46	1	0
Texas	4	1	2	1	1	50	0	0
Utah	1	3	9	0	1	22	2	1
Vermont	0	0	2	0	0	8	0	0
Virginia	3	0	7	0	3	76	1	0
Washington	1	1	7	0	0	98	1	2
West Virginia	0	2	3	1	0	7	5	0
Wisconsin	6	6	10	0	0	29	0	0
Wyoming	0	0	0	0	0	2	0	0

[1]Includes additional offenses collected in the NIBRS.

Table 93. Agency Hate Crime Reporting, by State, 2010

Participating state	Number of participating agencies	Population covered	Agencies submitting incident reports	Total number of incidents reported
TOTAL	14,977	285,001,266	1,949	6,628
Alabama	331	3,762,738	12	19
Alaska	1	290,334	1	7
Arizona	89	6,328,446	22	236
Arkansas	254	2,752,987	30	63
California	733	37,200,288	249	1,092
Colorado	217	4,908,638	44	154
Connecticut	102	3,574,097	43	147
Delaware	56	897,934	10	20
District of Columbia	2	601,723	1	57
Florida	505	18,705,419	65	136
Georgia	501	7,653,795	7	17
Idaho	104	1,554,255	11	28
Illinois	550	10,497,883	44	94
Indiana	138	3,720,793	17	94
Iowa	221	2,968,611	14	17
Kansas	350	2,230,776	23	58
Kentucky	360	3,202,734	91	173
Louisiana	90	2,617,664	9	13
Maine	148	1,328,361	26	61
Maryland	157	5,773,552	16	80
Massachusetts	313	6,296,379	84	316
Michigan	588	9,703,717	137	304
Minnesota	92	2,698,621	32	127
Mississippi	63	794,800	1	11
Missouri	633	5,987,789	29	142
Montana	99	981,587	14	31
Nebraska	187	1,534,659	4	61
Nevada	34	2,700,551	6	68
New Hampshire	151	1,155,769	22	31
New Jersey	509	8,790,283	172	543
New Mexico	46	1,130,803	3	24
New York	574	19,307,186	97	699
North Carolina	519	9,534,813	46	94
North Dakota	97	659,331	7	8
Ohio	591	9,667,899	83	247
Oklahoma	316	3,713,732	24	49
Oregon	216	3,286,084	30	134
Pennsylvania	1,347	12,659,293	31	57
Rhode Island	48	1,052,567	11	20
South Carolina	429	4,614,153	47	109
South Dakota	112	723,676	11	51
Tennessee	466	6,346,105	58	147
Texas	1,032	25,083,730	66	174
Utah	124	2,718,676	32	63
Vermont	83	614,990	9	17
Virginia	413	8,001,024	53	175
Washington	250	6,717,480	56	232
West Virginia	277	1,713,013	17	33
Wisconsin	395	5,682,402	30	93
Wyoming	64	559,126	2	2

Table 94.　Hate Crime Incidents per Bias Motivation and Quarter, by State and Agency, 2010

State	Agency type/Agency name	Number of incidents per bias motivation					Number of incidents per quarter[1]				Popu-lation[2]
		Race	Religion	Sexual orient-ation	Ethnicity	Disability	1st quarter	2nd quarter	3rd quarter	4th quarter	
ALABAMA	**Total**	12	2	2	3	0	...	...	...	...	...
	Cities	7	1	2	2	0	...	...	...	...	...
	Decatur	1	0	1	1	0	0	0	1	2	57,153
	Hoover	1	1	0	0	0	0	1	0	1	74,687
	Jasper	1	0	0	0	0	0	1	0	0	14,138
	Lanett	1	0	0	0	0	0	0	0	1	7,026
	Madison	1	0	0	0	0	0	0	1	0	41,426
	Oneonta	0	0	0	1	0	0	1	0	0	7,317
	Riverside	1	0	0	0	0	0	0	0	1	2,146
	Slocomb	1	0	0	0	0	1	0	0	0	2,065
	Talladega	0	0	1	0	0	0	1	0	0	16,826
	Metropolitan Counties	5	0	0	1	0	...	...	...	...	...
	Blount	0	0	0	1	0	...	1	0	0	...
	Tuscaloosa	5	0	0	0	0	...	4	1	...	...
	Nonmetropolitan Counties	0	1	0	0	0	...	...	...	...	...
	Clarke	0	1	0	0	0	1	0	0	0	
ALASKA	**Total**	3	1	1	1	1	...	...	...	...	...
	Cities	3	1	1	1	1	...	...	...	...	...
	Anchorage	3	1	1	1	1	1	1	4	1	290,334
ARIZONA	**Total**	98	48	51	37	2	...	...	...	...	...
	Cities	85	38	49	35	2	...	...	...	...	...
	Apache Junction	3	1	1	0	0	1	2	2	0	33,225
	Avondale	1	0	0	0	0	1	0	0	0	82,580
	Flagstaff	0	0	1	0	0	0	0	0	1	58,739
	Glendale	7	3	1	2	0	0	4	3	6	245,387
	Kingman	1	0	0	1	0	0	2	0	0	26,671
	Lake Havasu City	0	0	1	0	0	1	0	0	0	53,938
	Mammoth	0	1	0	0	0	0	0	1	0	2,618
	Maricopa	0	0	0	1	0	1	0	0	0	43,310
	Mesa	6	1	0	0	0	2	1	2	2	452,725
	Peoria	2	0	0	0	0	0	1	0	1	158,184
	Phoenix	50	19	37	27	2	24	35	48	28	1,544,427
	Prescott	1	0	0	0	0	0	1	0	0	41,428
	Scottsdale	7	5	2	2	0	4	5	4	3	230,496
	Show Low	1	0	0	1	0	1	0	0	1	11,965
	Springerville	0	0	1	0	0	0	1	0	0	1,943
	Tempe	1	1	2	0	0	2	1	1	0	173,004
	Tucson	3	7	3	1	0	9	2	3	0	527,107
	Yuma	2	0	0	0	0	0	1	0	1	88,291
	Universities and Colleges	2	1	0	2	0	...	...	...	...	...
	University of Arizona	2	1	0	2	0	1	1	0	3	38,767
	Metropolitan Counties	11	9	2	0	0	...	...	...	...	...
	Maricopa	6	2	0	0	0	1	1	1	5	...
	Pima	3	7	1	0	0	1	4	3	3	...
	Pinal	2	0	1	0	0	2	0	0	1	...
ARKANSAS	**Total**	41	6	10	6	0	...	...	...	...	...
	Cities	30	6	10	3	0	...	...	...	...	...
	Benton	1	0	0	1	0	0	2	0	0	30,692
	Bentonville	2	0	0	0	0	1	0	0	1	39,161
	Bryant	1	0	0	0	0	0	1	0	0	16,740
	Conway	1	1	0	0	0	0	0	0	2	61,425
	Crossett	2	0	0	0	0	2	0	0	0	5,349
	Elkins	1	0	0	0	0	0	1	0	0	2,703
	Hot Springs	1	0	0	0	0	1	0	0	0	40,081
	Jacksonville	3	0	1	0	0	0	0	1	3	31,833
	Jonesboro	1	0	0	0	0	1	0	0	0	67,382
	Marmaduke	1	0	0	0	0	0	1	0	0	1,177
	Marvell	1	0	0	0	0	0	0	1	0	1,065
	Morrilton	0	0	1	0	0	1	0	0	0	6,571
	North Little Rock	1	0	1	0	0	0	1	1	0	60,129
	Paragould	2	0	0	0	0	0	1	1	0	25,350
	Pine Bluff	1	2	0	0	0	2	0	0	1	49,971
	Rogers	3	3	2	1	0	1	2	4	2	61,417
	Searcy	1	0	0	0	0	1	0	0	0	23,791
	Sherwood	0	0	4	0	0	1	0	3	0	29,370
	Siloam Springs	1	0	1	0	0	0	0	1	1	15,337
	Springdale	3	0	0	1	0	0	0	4	0	71,047
	Texarkana	2	0	0	0	0	1	1	0	0	30,488
	Ward	1	0	0	0	0	0	0	1	0	4,311
	Universities and Colleges	1	0	0	0	0	...	...	...	...	...
	University of Arkansas, Pine Bluff	1	0	0	0	0	1	0	0	0	3,792

[1] Agencies published in this table indicated that at least one hate crime incident occurred in their respective jurisdictions during the quarter(s) for which they submitted a report to the Hate Crime Statistics Program. Elipses indicate quarters for which agencies did not submit reports.

[2] Population figures are published only for the cities. The figures listed for the universities and colleges are student enrollment and were provided by the United States Department of Education for the 2009 school year, the most recent available. The enrollment figures include full-time and part-time students.

Table 94.   Hate Crime Incidents per Bias Motivation and Quarter, by State and Agency, 2010—*Continued*

State	Agency type/Agency name	Number of incidents per bias motivation					Number of incidents per quarter[1]				Popu-lation[2]
		Race	Religion	Sexual orient-ation	Ethnicity	Disability	1st quarter	2nd quarter	3rd quarter	4th quarter	
ARKANSAS—*Continued*											
	Metropolitan Counties	6	0	0	3	0	...	...	...	...	...
	Benton	1	0	0	1	0	0	2	0	0	
	Garland	0	0	0	1	0	0	1	0	...	...
	Lonoke	0	0	0	1	0	1	0	0	0	...
	Perry	1	0	0	0	0	0	0	1	0	...
	Pulaski	4	0	0	0	0	2	1	0	1	...
	Nonmetropolitan Counties	4	0	0	0	0	...	...	...	...	...
	Independence	3	0	0	0	0	0	1	1	1	...
	White	1	0	0	0	0	1	0	0	0	...
CALIFORNIA	**Total**	436	198	277	176	5	...	...	...	...	...
	Cities	353	157	239	137	5	...	...	...	...	...
	Agoura Hills	1	0	1	0	0	0	1	1	0	22,318
	Alameda	1	1	0	0	0	2	0	0	0	71,016
	Albany	2	0	2	0	0	1	0	1	2	16,096
	Aliso Viejo	0	0	0	1	0	0	0	0	1	41,989
	Anaheim	1	0	0	0	0	1	0	0	0	338,492
	Antioch	4	0	0	1	0	2	1	2	0	102,125
	Apple Valley	2	0	0	0	0	0	2	0	0	71,834
	Arcata	0	1	2	0	0	1	1	0	1	17,172
	Azusa	4	0	0	0	0	0	3	1	0	46,824
	Bakersfield	3	0	1	0	0	0	0	2	2	333,458
	Baldwin Park	1	0	0	0	0	0	0	0	1	77,127
	Belmont	0	1	0	0	0	0	0	1	0	24,881
	Berkeley	0	0	1	0	0	1	0	0	0	102,700
	Beverly Hills	1	2	0	0	0	0	2	0	1	34,329
	Bishop	0	0	1	0	0	1	0	0	0	3,412
	Brentwood	1	0	0	1	0	0	0	2	0	53,312
	Buena Park	0	0	0	1	0	1	0	0	0	79,929
	Burbank	2	2	0	1	0	2	1	2	0	103,304
	Calabasas	0	2	0	0	0	1	1	0	0	22,223
	Camarillo	0	0	0	1	0	0	1	0	0	64,577
	Campbell	0	1	0	0	0	0	0	0	1	38,854
	Carlsbad	0	0	1	0	0	0	1	0	0	100,461
	Carmel	1	0	0	0	0	1	0	0	0	3,882
	Carson	1	0	0	0	0	1	0	0	0	92,409
	Cathedral City	0	1	0	1	0	0	2	0	0	53,449
	Cerritos	1	0	0	1	0	1	0	0	1	51,025
	Chico	3	1	2	1	0	1	3	2	1	85,630
	Chino	0	0	0	1	0	1	0	0	0	84,170
	Chula Vista	2	0	0	1	0	0	2	0	1	229,060
	Citrus Heights	0	0	1	0	0	0	0	0	1	84,476
	City of Angels	1	0	0	0	0	0	0	0	1	3,774
	Clearlake	1	0	0	1	0	0	1	0	1	15,352
	Clovis	1	3	2	0	0	0	0	5	1	95,901
	Commerce	1	0	0	1	0	0	0	2	0	13,466
	Compton	2	0	1	0	0	1	1	1	0	93,916
	Concord	3	0	1	1	0	0	2	2	1	122,119
	Corona	1	0	0	1	0	1	0	1	0	153,311
	Coronado	0	0	1	0	0	0	0	0	1	22,033
	Costa Mesa	1	2	1	1	0	2	1	2	0	110,424
	Covina	1	0	0	0	0	0	1	0	0	46,728
	Cypress	2	0	0	0	0	0	1	1	0	47,320
	Davis	5	3	3	0	0	2	2	4	3	63,292
	Delano	1	0	0	0	0	0	0	1	0	54,298
	Del Mar	1	0	0	0	0	0	0	0	1	4,554
	Downey	1	0	0	1	0	0	2	0	0	106,992
	Duarte	1	0	0	0	0	0	0	1	0	21,789
	Dublin	1	0	0	0	0	1	0	0	0	46,209
	East Palo Alto	0	0	0	1	0	0	1	0	0	34,294
	El Cajon	0	0	1	0	0	0	1	0	0	94,311
	El Cerrito	1	0	1	0	0	1	1	0	0	22,263
	El Monte	2	0	0	2	0	1	1	1	1	121,884
	Emeryville	0	0	1	0	0	1	0	0	0	10,207
	Encinitas	3	1	2	1	0	3	3	1	0	61,898
	Escalon	0	0	0	1	0	0	0	1	0	7,463
	Escondido	6	0	1	1	0	2	1	3	2	140,662
	Eureka	0	0	1	0	0	0	0	1	0	25,143
	Fontana	0	0	0	1	0	1	0	0	0	192,595
	Fort Bragg	0	0	1	2	0	0	1	0	2	6,550
	Foster City	0	1	0	0	0	0	0	0	1	29,283
	Fountain Valley	0	1	0	0	1	2	0	0	0	55,879
	Fremont	0	1	1	0	0	0	0	2	0	205,477

[1] Agencies published in this table indicated that at least one hate crime incident occurred in their respective jurisdictions during the quarter(s) for which they submitted a report to the Hate Crime Statistics Program. Elipses indicate quarters for which agencies did not submit reports.

[2] Population figures are published only for the cities. The figures listed for the universities and colleges are student enrollment and were provided by the United States Department of Education for the 2009 school year, the most recent available. The enrollment figures include full-time and part-time students.

Table 94. Hate Crime Incidents per Bias Motivation and Quarter, by State and Agency, 2010—*Continued*

State	Agency type/Agency name	Number of incidents per bias motivation					Number of incidents per quarter[1]				Popu-lation[2]
		Race	Religion	Sexual orient-ation	Ethnicity	Disability	1st quarter	2nd quarter	3rd quarter	4th quarter	
CALIFORNIA— *Continued*											
	Fresno	0	1	4	1	0	3	2	1	0	484,734
	Galt	0	1	0	0	0	1	0	0	0	24,517
	Garden Grove	2	0	0	1	0	0	2	1	0	166,287
	Glendale	0	2	0	2	0	3	0	1	0	196,877
	Grass Valley	1	0	0	0	0	0	1	0	0	12,330
	Greenfield	1	0	0	0	0	1	0	0	0	15,626
	Gridley	0	0	0	1	0	1	0	0	0	6,528
	Hawaiian Gardens	1	0	1	0	0	1	0	1	0	15,211
	Hercules	2	0	0	0	0	0	0	2	0	25,192
	Hermosa Beach	1	0	0	0	0	0	1	0	0	19,408
	Hesperia	2	0	0	0	0	1	0	1	0	88,876
	Huntington Beach	2	5	1	2	0	2	5	2	1	193,545
	Indio	1	0	2	0	0	1	1	0	1	89,621
	La Habra	3	0	0	0	0	1	1	1	0	59,355
	Lake Forest	0	0	1	0	0	0	0	1	0	75,780
	Lakewood	2	1	1	0	0	2	2	0	0	77,901
	La Mesa	1	0	1	0	0	1	1	0	0	55,580
	Lancaster	4	0	1	2	0	2	1	4	0	148,632
	La Quinta	1	1	1	3	0	2	1	1	2	47,441
	La Verne	0	0	1	0	0	1	0	0	0	34,066
	Lemoore	1	0	0	0	0	0	0	1	0	24,766
	Livermore	8	2	5	0	0	1	11	3	0	81,769
	Lodi	0	0	0	1	0	0	0	1	0	61,812
	Long Beach	2	1	7	0	0	1	3	2	4	462,267
	Los Alamitos	0	3	1	0	0	1	0	3	0	11,698
	Los Angeles	39	28	37	33	1	29	43	38	28	3,841,707
	Los Gatos	4	0	2	0	0	6	0	0	0	29,558
	Madera	0	0	3	0	0	0	0	3	0	58,147
	Malibu	0	1	2	0	0	0	1	2	0	13,078
	Manteca	0	0	1	0	0	0	1	0	0	67,344
	Marina	0	1	0	0	0	0	0	1	0	17,921
	Marysville	1	0	0	0	0	0	0	1	0	11,548
	Maywood	0	1	0	0	0	0	1	0	0	28,114
	Merced	1	0	1	0	0	1	0	1	0	77,484
	Millbrae	1	0	0	0	0	0	0	1	0	21,295
	Mission Viejo	1	1	0	1	0	2	0	1	0	94,679
	Modesto	5	1	0	0	0	1	2	2	1	203,890
	Monterey	2	0	1	0	0	1	0	1	1	27,619
	Moreno Valley	2	1	0	1	0	1	3	0	0	197,294
	Murrieta	1	0	0	0	0	0	0	0	1	104,343
	National City	1	0	0	0	0	1	0	0	0	56,270
	Newark	1	0	2	0	0	0	1	1	1	42,099
	Newport Beach	0	0	0	1	0	0	1	0	0	81,882
	Norwalk	2	0	1	0	0	2	1	0	0	102,221
	Novato	3	1	0	1	0	3	1	0	1	54,009
	Oakland	5	1	6	3	0	3	3	6	3	409,723
	Oakley	1	0	1	0	0	0	1	1	0	33,556
	Oceanside	4	2	0	0	0	0	1	5	0	173,901
	Ontario	1	0	1	0	0	0	1	1	0	172,814
	Oxnard	7	0	1	1	0	1	2	1	5	189,051
	Pacifica	1	1	0	0	0	0	2	0	0	37,917
	Pacific Grove	1	0	0	0	0	0	0	0	1	14,537
	Palmdale	4	1	0	1	0	1	3	1	1	146,819
	Palm Springs	2	0	14	0	0	2	8	3	3	48,696
	Palo Alto	2	0	0	0	0	0	1	1	0	60,288
	Paradise	1	0	0	0	0	0	0	0	1	26,424
	Paramount	1	0	0	0	0	1	0	0	0	54,914
	Parlier	0	0	1	0	0	0	1	0	0	13,532
	Pasadena	2	0	0	1	0	1	0	1	1	144,496
	Patterson	1	0	0	0	0	0	0	1	0	19,938
	Perris	2	0	0	0	0	1	1	0	0	58,622
	Petaluma	1	0	0	0	0	0	1	0	0	55,168
	Pico Rivera	0	0	0	1	0	0	0	0	1	62,783
	Placentia	1	0	0	0	0	0	1	0	0	50,237
	Pleasant Hill	1	0	0	0	0	0	1	0	0	33,048
	Pomona	1	0	3	1	0	0	1	2	2	152,673
	Poway	0	1	0	0	0	0	1	0	0	50,010
	Rancho Cucamonga	2	0	0	0	0	0	1	0	1	176,686
	Rancho Palos Verdes	3	0	0	0	0	0	0	3	0	40,905
	Rancho Santa Margarita	1	0	0	0	0	0	0	1	0	49,665
	Red Bluff	1	0	0	0	0	0	1	0	0	13,836
	Redding	4	1	0	0	0	3	1	1	0	91,414

[1] Agencies published in this table indicated that at least one hate crime incident occurred in their respective jurisdictions during the quarter(s) for which they submitted a report to the Hate Crime Statistics Program. Elipses indicate quarters for which agencies did not submit reports.

[2] Population figures are published only for the cities. The figures listed for the universities and colleges are student enrollment and were provided by the United States Department of Education for the 2009 school year, the most recent available. The enrollment figures include full-time and part-time students.

Table 94. Hate Crime Incidents per Bias Motivation and Quarter, by State and Agency, 2010—*Continued*

State	Agency type/Agency name	Number of incidents per bias motivation					Number of incidents per quarter[1]				Popu-lation[2]
		Race	Religion	Sexual orient-ation	Ethnicity	Disability	1st quarter	2nd quarter	3rd quarter	4th quarter	
CALIFORNIA— *Continued*											
	Redlands	0	0	0	1	0	1	0	0	0	70,552
	Redondo Beach	3	1	3	0	0	2	2	1	2	66,985
	Redwood City	0	0	1	0	0	0	1	0	0	74,355
	Richmond	2	0	1	2	0	0	3	1	1	103,442
	Ridgecrest	1	0	0	0	0	0	0	1	0	25,973
	Ripon	3	0	0	1	0	0	3	0	1	15,271
	Riverbank	2	0	0	0	0	2	0	0	0	21,241
	Riverside	8	5	4	4	0	6	2	6	7	301,859
	Rohnert Park	0	0	2	3	0	1	2	2	0	40,843
	Rolling Hills Estates	0	1	0	0	0	0	0	1	0	7,841
	Roseville	1	1	0	1	0	1	1	1	0	119,755
	Sacramento	6	7	8	3	1	5	7	8	5	472,469
	San Bernardino	1	0	1	0	0	0	2	0	0	199,214
	San Bruno	0	1	1	0	0	0	0	1	1	41,517
	San Diego	12	8	20	9	0	11	13	13	12	1,313,433
	San Francisco	28	7	24	4	0	18	10	18	17	818,594
	San Jacinto	1	0	0	0	0	0	1	0	0	39,703
	San Jose	7	8	6	3	0	4	4	9	7	970,252
	San Juan Capistrano	1	0	0	0	0	0	0	1	0	35,241
	San Leandro	6	2	3	0	0	0	1	5	5	78,447
	San Luis Obispo	0	2	0	1	0	1	2	0	0	44,008
	San Marcos	3	0	1	1	0	1	1	3	0	83,671
	San Mateo	0	1	0	0	0	0	0	1	0	92,724
	San Pablo	1	0	0	0	0	0	1	0	0	31,122
	San Rafael	5	0	0	0	0	1	1	1	2	55,832
	San Ramon	2	0	0	0	0	0	2	0	0	50,006
	Santa Ana	1	0	2	1	0	0	1	1	2	340,240
	Santa Barbara	0	0	1	2	0	1	0	2	0	85,967
	Santa Clarita	2	0	0	3	1	1	2	3	0	170,458
	Santa Cruz	1	4	6	0	0	4	3	3	1	56,860
	Santa Maria	0	1	1	0	0	0	0	1	1	87,803
	Santa Monica	1	0	0	0	0	0	0	1	0	87,817
	Santa Rosa	0	1	1	0	0	0	0	1	1	158,182
	Santee	2	1	0	1	0	3	0	0	1	55,533
	Scotts Valley	0	1	0	0	0	1	0	0	0	11,243
	Shafter	1	0	0	0	0	0	0	1	0	16,247
	Sierra Madre	1	0	0	1	0	1	0	0	1	10,796
	Simi Valley	1	3	0	0	0	0	2	0	2	121,755
	Soledad	1	0	0	1	0	0	2	0	0	28,655
	Sonoma	0	0	0	1	0	0	0	0	1	10,068
	Sonora	1	0	0	0	0	0	1	0	0	4,627
	South Gate	0	0	0	1	0	0	0	1	0	96,182
	South Lake Tahoe	4	0	0	0	0	0	1	0	3	23,540
	Stanton	1	1	0	0	0	2	0	0	0	37,912
	Stockton	2	0	0	0	0	2	0	0	0	292,047
	Sunnyvale	0	1	1	1	0	1	0	0	2	134,073
	Tehachapi	0	0	1	0	0	1	0	0	0	12,137
	Temecula	0	2	0	0	0	1	0	0	1	102,474
	Temple City	0	0	0	1	0	1	0	0	0	38,648
	Thousand Oaks	0	3	0	1	0	1	1	2	0	124,042
	Torrance	1	2	0	0	0	1	0	1	1	140,411
	Tracy	0	1	1	0	0	1	1	0	0	81,712
	Truckee	0	0	1	0	0	0	1	0	0	16,491
	Turlock	1	0	1	0	0	0	1	0	1	69,961
	Tustin	1	1	0	0	0	0	1	0	1	72,982
	Union City	2	0	0	0	0	0	0	1	1	73,356
	Upland	1	0	0	1	0	0	1	1	0	73,341
	Vacaville	1	1	0	0	0	0	0	1	1	92,177
	Vallejo	2	1	2	1	0	1	2	1	2	114,258
	Ventura	2	1	2	1	0	2	1	2	1	104,661
	Visalia	2	1	1	1	0	0	0	3	2	125,036
	Vista	1	1	1	0	0	1	0	1	1	92,765
	Walnut Creek	1	1	0	0	0	0	0	1	1	63,897
	Watsonville	1	0	0	2	0	0	0	3	0	51,488
	West Covina	1	0	1	0	0	1	0	1	0	105,395
	West Hollywood	1	0	7	0	1	1	3	3	2	35,885
	Westminster	6	1	0	0	0	2	2	2	1	89,604
	Whittier	1	0	0	0	0	0	0	1	0	81,611
	Yorba Linda	0	1	0	0	0	0	0	1	0	66,813
	Universities and Colleges	21	17	14	7	0	...	...	...	...	...
	Allan Hancock College	1	0	0	1	0	1	1	0	0	11,070
	California State Polytechnic University, Pomona	2	1	0	0	0	2	1	0	0	22,273
	California State University:	...	...	...	...	...	...	...	...	...	...

[1] Agencies published in this table indicated that at least one hate crime incident occurred in their respective jurisdictions during the quarter(s) for which they submitted a report to the Hate Crime Statistics Program. Ellipses indicate quarters for which agencies did not submit reports.

[2] Population figures are published only for the cities. The figures listed for the universities and colleges are student enrollment and were provided by the United States Department of Education for the 2009 school year, the most recent available. The enrollment figures include full-time and part-time students.

Table 94. Hate Crime Incidents per Bias Motivation and Quarter, by State and Agency, 2010—*Continued*

State	Agency type/Agency name	Number of incidents per bias motivation					Number of incidents per quarter[1]				Popu-lation[2]
		Race	Religion	Sexual orient-ation	Ethnicity	Disability	1st quarter	2nd quarter	3rd quarter	4th quarter	
CALIFORNIA— *Continued*											
	Channel Islands	1	0	0	0	0	0	0	0	1	3,862
	Dominguez Hills	0	0	1	0	0	0	1	0	0	14,477
	Fresno	1	0	0	0	0	0	0	1	0	21,500
	Fullerton	1	0	0	0	0	0	1	0	0	36,262
	Long Beach	0	0	1	0	0	0	1	0	0	35,557
	Northridge	1	1	0	1	0	0	0	2	1	35,198
	San Bernardino	1	0	0	0	0	1	0	0	0	17,852
	San Marcos	3	2	4	1	0	6	4	0	0	9,767
	Riverside Community College	1	0	0	0	0	0	0	0	1	36,586
	San Diego State University	1	0	0	0	0	0	1	0	0	32,817
	University of California:	...	...	...	...	...	...	...	...	...	...
	Berkeley	3	8	2	2	0	3	6	4	2	35,830
	Davis	0	2	3	0	0	2	1	0	2	31,247
	Los Angeles	0	2	1	0	0	1	1	0	1	38,550
	Riverside	0	0	0	2	0	1	0	0	1	19,384
	San Diego	5	0	0	0	0	3	1	1	0	28,418
	San Francisco	0	1	0	0	0	0	0	1	0	3,119
	Santa Cruz	0	0	2	0	0	0	0	2	0	16,775
	Metropolitan Counties	56	21	19	25	0	...	...	...	...	...
	Butte	1	0	0	0	0	0	0	1	0	...
	Contra Costa	1	0	1	0	0	0	0	0	2	...
	El Dorado	1	0	0	0	0	0	0	1	0	...
	Kern	2	0	0	3	0	1	1	1	2	...
	Los Angeles	18	8	9	6	0	9	7	12	13	...
	Madera	0	1	0	0	0	0	0	1	0	...
	Monterey	1	0	0	0	0	0	0	1	0	...
	Orange	0	1	0	2	0	1	0	1	1	...
	Riverside	5	2	1	2	0	5	2	2	1	...
	Sacramento	5	3	2	3	0	5	2	2	4	...
	San Bernardino	0	0	1	1	0	0	1	1	0	...
	San Diego	18	1	3	6	0	6	8	10	4	...
	San Joaquin	1	0	0	0	0	0	0	1	0	...
	San Mateo	0	1	0	0	0	1	0	0	0	...
	Santa Barbara	0	0	1	0	0	0	1	0	0	...
	Santa Clara	1	1	0	1	0	1	1	1	0	...
	Santa Cruz	0	1	0	0	0	0	0	0	1	...
	Shasta	1	0	0	0	0	1	0	0	0	...
	Sonoma	0	1	1	0	0	1	0	0	1	...
	Stanislaus	1	0	0	1	0	0	1	1	0	...
	Ventura	0	1	0	0	0	0	0	1	0	...
	Nonmetropolitan Counties	3	1	1	5	0	...	...	...	...	...
	Colusa	1	0	0	0	0	0	0	1	0	...
	Lake	1	1	1	1	0	1	1	2	0	...
	Mariposa	0	0	0	1	0	0	0	1	0	...
	Mendocino	1	0	0	3	0	2	0	1	1	...
	Other Agencies	3	2	4	2	0	...	...	...	...	...
	Los Angeles Transportation Services Bureau	2	0	3	1	0	0	1	2	3	...
	San Francisco Bay Area Rapid Transit, San Francisco County	0	1	0	0	0	0	0	0	1	...
	Santa Clara Transit District	1	1	1	1	0	0	1	2	1	...
COLORADO.............	**Total**	61	26	39	27	1	...	...	...	...	...
	Cities	52	20	34	18	1	...	...	...	...	...
	Arvada	0	1	0	0	0	0	0	1	0	107,227
	Aspen	2	1	0	0	0	1	1	0	1	6,012
	Aurora	2	1	0	2	0	1	3	1	0	323,483
	Boulder	2	0	0	0	1	0	0	2	1	99,255
	Breckenridge	0	0	0	1	0	0	0	0	1	3,557
	Centennial	2	1	0	0	0	1	1	1	0	98,902
	Colorado Springs	10	1	4	0	0	3	4	2	6	397,886
	Commerce City	1	1	1	0	0	0	1	1	1	46,771
	Denver	14	10	16	3	0	14	5	11	13	607,051
	Evans	0	0	0	1	0	0	0	0	1	20,440
	Florence	1	0	0	0	0	0	0	0	1	3,533
	Fort Collins	2	0	4	1	0	3	2	1	1	138,689
	Frederick	1	0	0	0	0	0	0	1	0	9,196
	Fruita	0	0	1	0	0	1	0	0	0	12,848
	Golden	0	1	0	1	0	2	0	0	0	17,226
	Grand Junction	2	0	1	0	0	0	0	3	0	59,029
	Greeley	1	1	1	0	0	2	1	0	0	92,804
	Greenwood Village	0	0	0	1	0	0	1	0	0	14,430
	Lafayette	1	0	1	0	0	0	1	1	0	26,055
	Lakewood	1	0	0	0	0	0	1	0	0	139,615

[1] Agencies published in this table indicated that at least one hate crime incident occurred in their respective jurisdictions during the quarter(s) for which they submitted a report to the Hate Crime Statistics Program. Elipses indicate quarters for which agencies did not submit reports.

[2] Population figures are published only for the cities. The figures listed for the universities and colleges are student enrollment and were provided by the United States Department of Education for the 2009 school year, the most recent available. The enrollment figures include full-time and part-time students.

Table 94. Hate Crime Incidents per Bias Motivation and Quarter, by State and Agency, 2010—*Continued*

State	Agency type/Agency name	Number of incidents per bias motivation					Number of incidents per quarter[1]				Popu-lation[2]
		Race	Religion	Sexual orient-ation	Ethnicity	Disability	1st quarter	2nd quarter	3rd quarter	4th quarter	
COLORADO— *Continued*											
	Littleton	0	0	1	0	0	1	0	0	0	40,544
	Longmont	1	0	0	2	0	0	0	3	0	88,913
	Louisville	0	0	1	0	0	0	1	0	0	19,429
	Loveland	3	0	0	1	0	1	1	2	0	66,857
	Montrose	1	0	0	0	0	0	0	1	0	18,758
	Monument	0	1	0	0	0	0	1	0	0	5,257
	Northglenn	0	0	1	0	0	1	0	0	0	34,467
	Pagosa Springs	0	1	0	0	0	1	0	0	0	1,814
	Pueblo	3	0	1	1	0	1	1	0	3	103,612
	Steamboat Springs	0	0	1	0	0	0	0	0	1	12,426
	Thornton	1	0	0	0	0	0	1	0	0	119,989
	Trinidad	1	0	0	0	0	0	0	1	0	8,933
	Wheat Ridge	0	0	0	3	0	1	0	2	0	30,400
	Yuma	0	0	0	1	0	0	0	1	0	3,240
	Universities and Colleges	0	0	1	0	0	…	…	…	…	…
	Colorado State University, Pueblo	0	0	1	0	0	1	0	0	0	6,443
	Metropolitan Counties	8	6	2	8	0	…	…	…	…	…
	Adams	1	0	1	0	0	1	0	1	0	…
	Arapahoe	2	2	1	1	0	1	3	2	0	…
	Douglas	4	4	0	5	0	3	4	5	1	…
	Jefferson	0	0	0	1	0	0	0	0	1	…
	Larimer	1	0	0	0	0	0	0	0	1	…
	Mesa	0	0	0	1	0	0	0	0	1	…
	Nonmetropolitan Counties	1	0	1	1	0	…	…	…	…	…
	Montezuma	1	0	1	0	0	1	0	0	1	…
	Summit	0	0	0	1	0	1	0	0	0	…
	State Police Agencies	0	0	1	0	0	…	…	…	…	…
	Colorado State Patrol	0	0	1	0	0	1	0	0	0	…
CONNECTICUT..........	**Total**	68	46	18	15	0	…	…	…	…	…
	Cities	64	39	15	15	0	…	…	…	…	…
	Bridgeport	3	0	2	0	0	2	0	2	1	138,810
	Coventry	2	3	1	0	0	3	2	1	0	12,546
	Cromwell	0	1	1	0	0	1	0	0	1	13,919
	Enfield	2	0	0	0	0	2	0	0	0	45,837
	Fairfield	0	1	0	0	0	0	0	0	1	58,331
	Glastonbury	3	0	0	0	0	0	2	1	0	33,921
	Greenwich	0	0	1	0	0	0	1	0	0	63,281
	Groton Town	0	1	0	1	0	0	0	1	1	29,842
	Hartford	6	0	4	2	0	2	6	1	3	125,626
	Manchester	10	6	1	1	0	5	4	4	5	57,271
	Middletown	2	0	1	0	0	1	1	1	0	49,281
	Milford	2	1	0	0	0	0	0	3	0	57,565
	Naugatuck	1	1	1	0	0	0	0	2	1	32,529
	New Britain	2	0	0	0	0	1	0	1	0	71,344
	New Canaan	0	3	0	0	0	0	2	1	0	20,312
	New Haven	2	0	0	2	0	1	1	0	2	124,856
	Newington	2	3	1	0	0	1	1	3	1	30,246
	New London	1	1	1	0	0	1	0	0	2	26,517
	Newtown	1	2	0	1	0	0	2	2	0	27,366
	Norwalk	8	3	0	1	0	1	6	3	2	84,944
	Norwich	1	0	0	0	0	0	0	1	0	37,157
	Old Saybrook	0	0	0	1	0	0	0	1		10,696
	Seymour	0	2	0	0	0	0	1	0	1	16,616
	Shelton	1	2	0	0	0	2	0	0	1	41,037
	Simsbury	1	0	0	0	0	1	0	0	0	23,988
	Southington	0	0	1	3	0	1	1	1	1	43,354
	South Windsor	1	0	0	1	0	0	2	0	0	26,781
	Stonington	1	0	0	0	0	0	0	0	1	18,807
	Torrington	3	1	0	1	0	2	1	1	1	35,876
	Trumbull	2	0	0	0	0	1	1	0	0	35,425
	Wallingford	1	0	0	0	0	0	0	1	0	45,636
	Waterford	0	1	0	0	0	0	0	0	1	19,161
	West Hartford	2	3	0	0	0	1	1	2	1	61,603
	West Haven	2	2	0	0	0	2	0	2	0	53,746
	Weston	0	0	0	1	0	0	0	1	0	10,344
	Windsor Locks	1	2	0	0	0	2	1	0	0	12,722
	Wolcott	1	0	0	0	0	0	0	1	0	16,799
	Universities and Colleges	2	5	1	0	0	…	…	…	…	…
	Eastern Connecticut State University	0	1	0	0	0	0	1	0	0	5,610
	Southern Connecticut State University	0	1	0	0	0	0	0	1	0	11,815
	University of Connecticut, Storrs, Avery Point, and Hartford[3]	1	3	1	0	0	1	2	0	2	…
	Western Connecticut State University	1	0	0	0	0	0	1	0	0	6,617

[1] Agencies published in this table indicated that at least one hate crime incident occurred in their respective jurisdictions during the quarter(s) for which they submitted a report to the Hate Crime Statistics Program. Elipses indicate quarters for which agencies did not submit reports.

[2] Population figures are published only for the cities. The figures listed for the universities and colleges are student enrollment and were provided by the United States Department of Education for the 2009 school year, the most recent available. The enrollment figures include full-time and part-time students.

[3] Student enrollment figures were not available.

[4] Includes one incident reported with more than one bias motivation.

Table 94. Hate Crime Incidents per Bias Motivation and Quarter, by State and Agency, 2010—*Continued*

State	Agency type/Agency name	Number of incidents per bias motivation					Number of incidents per quarter[1]				Population[2]
		Race	Religion	Sexual orient-ation	Ethnicity	Disability	1st quarter	2nd quarter	3rd quarter	4th quarter	
CONNECTICUT— *Continued*											
	State Police Agencies	2	1	2	0	0	...	...	...	...	...
	Connecticut State Police	2	1	2	0	0	2	1	1	1	...
	Other Agencies	0	1	0	0	0	...	...	...	...	...
	Metropolitan Transportation Authority	0	1	0	0	0	0	0	0	1	...
DELAWARE	**Total**	11	5	3	1	0	...	...	...	...	...
	Cities	6	1	1	0	0	...	...	...	...	...
	Bethany Beach	1	0	0	0	0	1	0	0	0	988
	Delmar	1	0	0	0	0	1	0	0	0	1,597
	Newark	3	0	0	0	0	1	2	0	0	30,543
	Rehoboth Beach	0	1	0	0	0	0	0	1	0	1,624
	Smyrna	1	0	0	0	0	0	1	0	0	9,322
	Wilmington	0	0	1	0	0	1	0	0	0	73,270
	Universities and Colleges	2	3	0	0	0	...	...	...	...	...
	University of Delaware	2	3	0	0	0	2	1	1	1	21,138
	State Police Agencies	3	1	2	1	0	...	...	...	...	...
	State Police:	...	...	...	...	...	...	...	...	...	...
	Kent County	1	0	0	0	0	0	0	1	0	...
	New Castle County	1	1	0	1	0	0	1	1	1	...
	Sussex County	1	0	2	0	0	0	1	2	0	...
DISTRICT OF COLUMBIA	**Total**	14	4	35	4	0	...	...	...	...	...
	Cities	14	4	35	4	0	...	...	...	...	...
	Washington	14	4	35	4	0	7	16	14	20	601,723
FLORIDA	**Total**	65	29	29	13	0	...	...	...	...	...
	Cities	36	19	19	7	0	...	...	...	...	...
	Boca Raton	1	3	0	0	0	2	1	1	0	86,707
	Cape Coral	0	0	1	0	0	0	1	0	0	160,432
	Clearwater	3	0	0	0	0	1	0	1	1	105,647
	Coconut Creek	0	1	0	0	0	0	1	0	0	51,184
	Coral Springs	0	1	0	0	0	1	0	0	0	127,113
	Davie	1	0	0	0	0	1	0	0	0	92,661
	Daytona Beach	0	0	1	0	0	0	0	0	1	63,736
	Deland	2	0	0	0	0	1	0	0	1	27,926
	Fort Lauderdale	0	0	2	0	0	1	0	0	1	186,170
	Fort Myers	1	0	0	0	0	0	0	1	0	66,053
	Fort Pierce	0	0	1	0	0	0	0	0	1	42,797
	Fort Walton Beach	0	0	1	0	0	0	0	1	0	18,432
	Gainesville	3	4	2	2	0	1	5	2	3	116,880
	Hallandale	1	1	1	0	0	0	1	2	0	39,359
	Homestead	1	0	0	0	0	0	0	0	1	63,761
	Indian Shores	0	0	1	0	0	1	0	0	0	4,213
	Key Biscayne	0	1	0	0	0	0	0	0	1	10,097
	Key West	0	0	1	0	0	0	0	1	0	22,167
	Kissimmee	1	0	0	0	0		0	0	1	64,122
	Lake Worth	0	1	0	0	0	1	0	0	0	35,977
	Melbourne	0	2	0	0	0	0	2	0	0	77,861
	Miami Beach	0	0	1	0	0	0	0	0	1	87,990
	Miami Gardens	1	0	0	1	0	0	1	0	1	110,130
	Miramar	0	0	1	0	0	0	0	1	0	113,385
	New Port Richey	1	0	0	0	0	0	1	0	0	17,634
	North Miami	1	1	0	0	0	0	1	0	1	57,796
	North Port	3	1	0	0	0	0	2	1	1	59,076
	Ocoee	1	0	0	1	0	0	0	1	1	33,650
	Orlando	4	0	2	1	0	1	2	3	1	240,222
	Palm Bay	2	0	0	0	0	0	0	2	0	103,350
	Palm Beach Gardens	0	1	0	0	0	0	1	0	0	51,458
	Panama City	2	0	0	0	0	0	1	1	0	36,593
	Pompano Beach	1	0	0	0	0	1	0	0	0	102,749
	Port Richey	0	0	0	1	0	0	0	0	1	3,426
	Port St. Lucie	0	1	0	0	0	0	0	0	1	163,089
	Seminole	1	0	0	0	0	0	0	1	0	19,055
	St. Cloud	0	0	0	1	0	0	0	0	1	30,245
	Surfside	1	0	0	0	0	1	0	0	0	4,684
	Tallahassee	1	0	1	0	0	0	1	1	0	174,516
	Temple Terrace	1	0	0	0	0	1	0	0	0	22,760
	Treasure Island	0	0	1	0	0	0	0	0	1	7,399
	Wilton Manors	0	1	2	0	0	1	1	1	0	12,873
	Winter Haven	2	0	0	0	0	0	1	1	0	33,981
	Metropolitan Counties	25	10	10	5	0	...	...	...	...	...
	Alachua	2	0	1	0	0	1	1	1	0	...
	Brevard	1	0	0	0	0	0	1	0	0	...
	Broward	1	1	2	0	0	1	1	2	0	...
	Clay	1	0	0	1	0	1	1	0	0	...

[1] Agencies published in this table indicated that at least one hate crime incident occurred in their respective jurisdictions during the quarter(s) for which they submitted a report to the Hate Crime Statistics Program. Elipses indicate quarters for which agencies did not submit reports.

[2] Population figures are published only for the cities. The figures listed for the universities and colleges are student enrollment and were provided by the United States Department of Education for the 2009 school year, the most recent available. The enrollment figures include full-time and part-time students.

Table 94.   Hate Crime Incidents per Bias Motivation and Quarter, by State and Agency, 2010—*Continued*

State	Agency type/Agency name	Number of incidents per bias motivation					Number of incidents per quarter[1]				Popu-lation[2]
		Race	Religion	Sexual orient-ation	Ethnicity	Disability	1st quarter	2nd quarter	3rd quarter	4th quarter	
FLORIDA— *Continued*											
	Collier	1	4	1	2	0	0	5	2	1	...
	Escambia	0	0	2	1	0	0	1	1	1	...
	Flagler	3	0	0	0	0	0	0	3	0	...
	Hillsborough	2	0	0	0	0	0	1	0	1	...
	Martin	1	1	1	0	0	0	3	0	0	...
	Miami-Dade	1	1	0	0	0	2	0	0	0	...
	Okaloosa	3	0	0	0	0	0	1	2	0	...
	Orange	2	0	2	0	0	1	0	1	2	...
	Osceola	1	0	0	0	0	0	1	0	0	...
	Palm Beach	0	2	0	0	0	1	0	1	0	...
	Pasco	0	0	1	0	0	0	1	0	0	...
	Pinellas	2	0	0	0	0	1	0	0	1	...
	Polk	1	0	0	0	0	1	0	0	0	...
	Santa Rosa	3	1	0	0	0	0	2	0	2	...
	Volusia	0	0	0	1	0	0	0	1	0	...
	Nonmetropolitan Counties	2	0	0	1	0	...	...	...	...	...
	Highlands	2	0	0	1	0	0	0	2	1	...
	Tribal Agencies	1	0	0	0	0	...	...	...	...	...
	Seminole Tribal	1	0	0	0	0	0	0	0	1	
	Other Agencies	1	0	0	0	0	...	...	...	...	
	Palm Beach County School District	1	0	0	0	0	0	1	0	0	
GEORGIA	**Total**	11	3	2	1	0	...	...	...	...	...
	Cities	5	0	1	0	0	...	...	...	...	
	Atlanta	3	0	1	0	0	0	0	1	3	536,472
	LaGrange	1	0	0	0	0	0	1	0	0	27,712
	Sylvania	1	0	0	0	0	1	0	0	0	2,610
	Universities and Colleges	1	2	0	1	0	...	...	...	...	
	Southern Polytechnic State University	0	0	0	1	0	1	0	0	0	5,183
	University of Georgia	1	2	0	0	0	3	0	0	0	34,885
	Metropolitan Counties	4	1	1	0	0	...	...	...	...	
	Henry County Police Department	4	1	1	0	0	1	2	2	1	...
	Nonmetropolitan Counties	1	0	0	0	0	...	...	...	...	
	White	1	0	0	0	0	0	0	1	0	...
IDAHO	**Total**	18	4	2	4	0	...	...	...	...	...
	Cities	16	3	0	4	0	...	...	...	...	
	Boise	4	1	0	1	0	1	2	2	1	205,902
	Coeur d'Alene[4]	5	1	0	0	0	3	0	3	0	44,626
	Hailey	0	0	0	1	0	0	0	1	0	8,242
	Idaho Falls	0	1	0	0	0	0	1	0	0	55,524
	Nampa	3	0	0	1	0	1	1	0	2	84,179
	Payette	3	0	0	0	0	1	1	1	0	7,688
	Twin Falls	1	0	0	1	0	1	0	0	1	43,434
	Metropolitan Counties	2	1	1	0	0	...	...	...	...	
	Ada	0	1	0	0	0	1	0	0	0	...
	Bonneville	0	0	1	0	0	0	1	0	0	...
	Kootenai	2	0	0	0	0	0	1	0	1	...
	Nonmetropolitan Counties	0	0	1	0	0	...	...	...	...	
	Elmore	0	0	1	0	0	0	0	1	0	...
ILLINOIS	**Total**	45	19	20	9	1	...	...	...	...	...
	Cities	32	17	13	8	1	...	...	...	...	
	Aurora	1	0	0	0	0	0	1	0	0	174,255
	Bradley	0	0	0	1	0	0	0	1	0	15,131
	Burbank	1	0	0	0	0	0	0	0	1	27,135
	Cahokia	1	0	0	0	0	0	1	0	0	14,826
	Carol Stream	0	0	0	1	0	0	0	0	1	39,577
	Casey	1	0	0	0	0	0	0	1	0	2,829
	Centralia	1	0	0	0	0	0	1	0	0	13,237
	Champaign	0	0	1	0	0	0	0	0	1	80,489
	Chicago	6	7	4	0	0	6	2	4	5	2,833,649
	Decatur	3	0	0	0	0	1	1	1	0	74,857
	Downers Grove	1	0	0	0	0	0	0	0	1	48,574
	East Peoria	1	0	0	0	0	1	0	0	0	22,638
	Evanston	0	5	0	0	0	1	2	0	2	77,418
	Evergreen Park	2	0	0	0	0	0	0	2	0	18,888
	Galesburg	1	0	0	0	0	0	0	0	1	30,424
	Grand Ridge	0	0	1	0	0	1	0	0	0	510
	Marion	0	0	1	0	0	1	...	...	...	17,405
	Minooka	0	0	1	0	0	0	0	1	0	11,652
	Moline	1	0	0	0	0	0	1	0	0	42,510
	Nauvoo	0	1	0	0	0	1	0	...	...	1,136
	Normal	0	0	2	0	1	1	0	0	2	53,014
	Oak Lawn	0	1	0	0	0	0	1	0	0	52,172
	Pekin	2	0	0	0	0	2	0	0	0	33,196

[1] Agencies published in this table indicated that at least one hate crime incident occurred in their respective jurisdictions during the quarter(s) for which they submitted a report to the Hate Crime Statistics Program. Elipses indicate quarters for which agencies did not submit reports.

[2] Population figures are published only for the cities. The figures listed for the universities and colleges are student enrollment and were provided by the United States Department of Education for the 2009 school year, the most recent available. The enrollment figures include full-time and part-time students.

Table 94.   Hate Crime Incidents per Bias Motivation and Quarter, by State and Agency, 2010—*Continued*

State	Agency type/Agency name	Number of incidents per bias motivation					Number of incidents per quarter[1]				Popu-lation[2]
		Race	Religion	Sexual orient-ation	Ethnicity	Disability	1st quarter	2nd quarter	3rd quarter	4th quarter	
ILLINOIS— *Continued*											
	Peoria	0	0	0	1	0	0	1	0	0	114,557
	Rockford	0	0	0	1	0	0	1	0	0	156,180
	Rock Island	0	0	1	0	0	0	0	0	1	37,534
	Salem	1	0	0	0	0	0	1	0	0	7,180
	Skokie	2	1	1	0	0	1	1	2	0	66,088
	Springfield	2	0	1	2	0	1	1	2	1	117,383
	Sycamore	1	0	0	0	0	0	1	0	0	18,283
	Tinley Park	1	1	0	1	0	2	1	0	0	59,607
	Urbana	2	1	0	1	0	0	2	1	1	39,784
	Wood River	1	0	0	0	0	1	0	0	0	10,787
	Universities and Colleges	2	0	4	0	0	...	...	...	...	...
	Illinois State University	0	0	2	0	0	0	0	2	0	21,184
	Northwestern University, Evanston[3]	0	0	1	0	0	...	...	...	1	...
	Oakton Community College	1	0	0	0	0	0	1			12,087
	Western Illinois University	1	0	1	0	0	2	0	0	0	12,679
	Metropolitan Counties	11	2	3	1	0	...	...	...	...	...
	Du Page	3	2	1	0	0	3	2	1	0	...
	Macon	1	0	0	0	0	0	0	0	1	...
	Madison	1	0	0	0	0	1	0	0	0	...
	Peoria	2	0	1	1	0	0	2	1	1	...
	Sangamon	1	0	0	0	0	1	0	0	0	...
	Will	3	0	0	0	0	2	0	0	1	...
	Woodford	0	0	1	0	0	0	0	0	1	...
INDIANA..............	**Total**	57	12	17	8	0	...	...	...	...	...
	Cities	42	9	15	8	0	...	...	...	...	...
	Bloomington	7	3	7	1	0	3	6	6	3	72,286
	Fort Wayne	0	4	0	1	0	1	4	0	0	257,009
	Frankfort	0	0	0	1	0	0	1	0	0	16,533
	Goshen	0	0	0	1	0	0	1	0	0	32,812
	Greenwood	1	0	0	0	0	1	0	0	0	49,847
	Hammond	0	0	1	0	0	1	0	0	0	76,216
	Highland	1	0	0	0	0	0	1	0	0	22,583
	Indianapolis	30	2	7	4	0	10	9	16	8	822,211
	La Porte	2	0	0	0	0	0	0	2	0	21,282
	West Lafayette	1	0	0	0	0	0	0	0	1	31,945
	Universities and Colleges	12	3	2	0	0	...	...	...	...	...
	Indiana State University	4	0	0	0	0	1	0	2	1	10,534
	Indiana University:	...	...	...	...	...	...	...	...	...	...
	Bloomington	0	1	0	0	0	0	0	0	1	42,347
	Indianapolis[3]	1	0	0	0	0	0	0	1	0	...
	Purdue University	7	2	2	0	0	6	3	1	1	41,052
	Metropolitan Counties	1	0	0	0	0	...	...	...	...	...
	Elkhart	1	0	0	0	0	0	1	0	0	...
	Nonmetropolitan Counties	1	0	0	0	0					...
	Noble	1	0	0	0	0	0	1	0	0	...
	State Police Agencies	1	0	0	0	0	...	...	...	...	...
	Indiana State Police	1	0	0	0	0	...	...	...	1	...
IOWA	**Total**	10	0	5	2	0	...	...	...	...	...
	Cities	8	0	5	2	0	...	...	...	...	...
	Altoona	0	0	1	0	0	0	0	1	0	15,012
	Bettendorf	1	0	1	0	0	0	0	1	1	33,690
	Clarinda	1	0	0	0	0	0	1	0	0	5,316
	Council Bluffs	1	0	0	0	0	0	0	0	1	61,181
	Davenport	1	0	0	1	0	0	0	1	1	102,628
	Des Moines	0	0	2	0	0	0	1	1	0	202,564
	Dubuque	1	0	0	0	0	0	0	0	1	57,744
	Fairfield	1	0	0	0	0	0	1	0	0	9,251
	Grinnell	0	0	1	0	0	0	1	0	0	9,147
	Iowa City	1	0	0	0	0	1	0	0	0	70,411
	Manchester	0	0	0	1	0	0	0	0	1	4,880
	Pleasant Hill	1	0	0	0	0	0	0	1	0	8,922
	Universities and Colleges	2	0	0	0	0	...	...	...	...	...
	Iowa State University	1	0	0	0	0	0	0	0	1	27,945
	University of Iowa	1	0	0	0	0	0	0	1	0	28,987
KANSAS..............	**Total**	32	2	16	8	0	...	...	...	...	...
	Cities	23	2	12	7	0	...	...	...	...	...
	Abilene	2	0	0	0	0	0	0	1	1	6,284
	Andover	1	0	0	0	0	0	1	0	0	11,091
	Atchison	1	0	0	0	0	0	0	0	1	10,483
	Bonner Springs	0	1	0	0	0	0	1	0	0	7,349
	Emporia	0	0	3	0	0	2	1	0	0	24,856
	Hays	2	0	1	0	0	0	0	1	2	20,537
	Hutchinson	1	0	0	0	0	0	1	0	0	40,981

[1] Agencies published in this table indicated that at least one hate crime incident occurred in their respective jurisdictions during the quarter(s) for which they submitted a report to the Hate Crime Statistics Program. Elipses indicate quarters for which agencies did not submit reports.

[2] Population figures are published only for the cities. The figures listed for the universities and colleges are student enrollment and were provided by the United States Department of Education for the 2009 school year, the most recent available. The enrollment figures include full-time and part-time students.

Table 94. Hate Crime Incidents per Bias Motivation and Quarter, by State and Agency, 2010—*Continued*

State	Agency type/Agency name	Number of incidents per bias motivation					Number of incidents per quarter[1]				Popu-lation[2]
		Race	Religion	Sexual orient-ation	Ethnicity	Disability	1st quarter	2nd quarter	3rd quarter	4th quarter	
KANSAS— *Continued*											
	Independence	1	0	0	0	0	0	1	0	0	9,203
	Iola	2	0	0	0	0	0	1	1	0	5,704
	Lawrence	2	0	0	0	0	0	2	0	0	93,945
	Leavenworth	0	0	1	0	0	0	0	0	1	35,290
	Maize	0	0	0	1	0	0	0	0	1	3,477
	Salina	2	0	0	1	0	0	1	2	0	46,547
	Shawnee	0	0	0	1	0	0	0	1	0	63,652
	Wichita	8	1	7	4	0	3	4	7	6	376,880
	Winfield	1	0	0	0	0	0	1	0	0	11,126
	Universities and Colleges	1	0	1	1	0	...	...	...	...	...
	Emporia State University	0	0	1	0	0	0	0	0	1	6,314
	Kansas State University	1	0	0	1	0	1	1	0	0	23,581
	Metropolitan Counties	8	0	3	0	0	...	...	...	...	...
	Johnson	3	0	1	0	0	0	2	2	0	...
	Riley County Police Department	0	0	1	0	0	0	0	0	1	...
	Sedgwick	1	0	0	0	0	0	0	1	0	...
	Shawnee	4	0	0	0	0	0	0	4	0	...
	Wyandotte	0	0	1	0	0	0	0	1	0	...
KENTUCKY...............	**Total**	121	13	18	19	2	...	...	...	...	...
	Cities	68	7	11	14	1	...	...	...	...	...
	Ashland	1	0	0	1	0	1	1	0	0	21,209
	Bardstown	4	0	0	1	0	0	1	3	1	11,339
	Beaver Dam	0	0	0	1	0	0	0	0	1	3,120
	Bellevue	1	0	0	0	0	0	0	1	0	5,822
	Bowling Green	3	1	0	2	0	1	2	0	3	57,308
	Calvert City	1	0	0	0	0	0	1	0	0	2,753
	Campbellsville	2	0	0	0	0	0	0	2	0	11,340
	Covington	5	3	4	0	0	2	1	8	1	43,054
	Danville	1	0	0	1	0	0	1	1	0	15,646
	Dayton	0	1	0	0	0	1	0	0	0	5,418
	Elizabethtown	2	0	0	1	0	0	1	2	0	24,712
	Elsmere	1	0	0	0	0	0	0	1	0	7,999
	Eminence	1	0	0	1	0	0	0	0	2	2,245
	Flatwoods	1	0	2	0	0	2	0	0	1	7,678
	Florence	4	0	0	1	0	2	0	2	1	28,869
	Fort Mitchell	1	0	0	0	0	0	0	0	1	7,539
	Fort Thomas	1	0	0	0	0	0	1	0	0	15,141
	Glasgow	1	0	0	0	0	0	1	0	0	14,381
	Grayson	1	0	0	0	0	0	0	0	1	3,871
	Harrodsburg	0	0	1	1	0	0	2	0	0	8,154
	Hopkinsville	3	0	0	0	0	0	0	1	2	32,265
	Horse Cave	1	0	0	0	0	1	0	0	0	2,292
	Independence	2	0	0	0	0	0	0	0	2	22,935
	Irvine	1	0	0	0	0	0	0	1	0	2,616
	Leitchfield	1	0	0	0	0	0	0	1	0	6,562
	Louisa	0	0	0	0	1	0	0	1	0	2,091
	Ludlow	2	0	0	0	0	0	2	0	0	4,845
	Mayfield	0	1	0	0	0	0	0	0	1	10,149
	Morehead	1	0	0	1	0	0	0	1	1	7,714
	Newport	4	0	0	0	0	1	2	1	0	15,738
	Nicholasville	1	0	0	0	0	0	0	0	1	27,686
	Oak Grove	2	0	0	0	0	1	0	1	0	9,673
	Owensboro	4	0	2	0	0	0	4	1	1	55,848
	Paducah	3	0	0	0	0	0	1	2	0	25,643
	Pikeville	2	0	0	0	0	1	0	0	1	6,407
	Princeton	1	0	0	0	0	1	0	0	0	6,366
	Radcliff	0	0	0	1	0	0	0	0	1	22,251
	Richmond	1	1	1	1	0	1	1	1	1	34,068
	Shelbyville	0	0	0	1	0	0	1	0	0	11,637
	Shepherdsville	2	0	0	0	0	0	0	1	1	9,424
	Shively	1	0	0	0	0	0	0	1	0	16,609
	Somerset	1	0	0	0	0	1	0	0	0	12,266
	St. Matthews	1	0	0	0	0	0	0	0	1	18,885
	Taylor Mill	1	0	0	0	0	0	0	0	1	7,123
	Versailles	1	0	0	0	0	0	1	0	0	7,924
	Vine Grove	0	0	1	0	0	0	0	0	1	4,558
	Winchester	1	0	0	0	0	1	0	0	0	16,754
	Universities and Colleges	10	1	1	0	0	...	...	...	...	...
	Eastern Kentucky University	1	0	0	0	0	1	0	0	0	16,268
	Morehead State University	2	0	0	0	0	1	0	0	1	8,822
	Murray State University	1	0	0	0	0	0	0	1	0	10,071
	Northern Kentucky University	4	0	0	0	0	0	0	4	0	15,378
	University of Kentucky	1	0	0	0	0	1	0	0	0	26,295

[1] Agencies published in this table indicated that at least one hate crime incident occurred in their respective jurisdictions during the quarter(s) for which they submitted a report to the Hate Crime Statistics Program. Elipses indicate quarters for which agencies did not submit reports.

[2] Population figures are published only for the cities. The figures listed for the universities and colleges are student enrollment and were provided by the United States Department of Education for the 2009 school year, the most recent available. The enrollment figures include full-time and part-time students.

Table 94.   Hate Crime Incidents per Bias Motivation and Quarter, by State and Agency, 2010—*Continued*

State	Agency type/Agency name	Number of incidents per bias motivation					Number of incidents per quarter[1]				Popu-lation[2]
		Race	Religion	Sexual orient-ation	Ethnicity	Disability	1st quarter	2nd quarter	3rd quarter	4th quarter	
KENTUCKY— *Continued*											
	University of Louisville	1	1	0	0	0	1	0	0	1	21,016
	Western Kentucky University	0	0	1	0	0	0	0	0	1	20,712
	Metropolitan Counties	15	2	3	2	0	...	...	...	...	...
	Boone	4	2	1	0	0	1	4	2	0	...
	Bourbon	1	0	0	0	0	1	0	0	0	...
	Boyd	1	0	0	0	0	0	0	1	0	...
	Bullitt	2	0	0	0	0	0	1	0	1	...
	Daviess	0	0	1	0	0	0	0	0	1	...
	Hardin	0	0	0	1	0	0	0	1	0	...
	Jessamine	1	0	0	0	0	0	0	0	1	...
	Kenton County Police Department	1	0	0	0	0	0	1	0	0	...
	Nelson	1	0	0	1	0	1	0	0	1	...
	Oldham	1	0	0	0	0	0	0	0	1	...
	Oldham County Police Department	2	0	0	0	0	0	0	2	0	...
	Shelby	1	0	0	0	0	1	0	0	0	...
	Warren	0	0	1	0	0	0	1	0	0	...
	Nonmetropolitan Counties	19	1	1	1	0	...	...	...	...	...
	Ballard	1	0	0	0	0	0	0	1	0	...
	Bell	1	0	0	0	0	0	0	0	1	...
	Calloway	2	0	0	0	0	0	1	1	0	...
	Franklin	1	0	1	0	0	1	0	0	1	...
	Fulton	1	0	0	0	0	1	0	0	0	...
	Hopkins	2	1	0	0	0	0	3	0	0	...
	Knox	1	0	0	0	0	0	1	0	0	...
	Lawrence	1	0	0	0	0	0	0	1	0	...
	Madison	2	0	0	0	0	2	0	0	0	...
	Marshall	1	0	0	0	0	0	1	0	0	...
	McCracken	2	0	0	0	0	0	2	0	0	...
	Menifee	1	0	0	0	0	0	1	0	0	...
	Rowan	1	0	0	1	0	0	2	0	0	...
	Simpson	1	0	0	0	0	0	1	0	0	...
	Washington	1	0	0	0	0	0	0	1	0	...
	State Police Agencies	4	2	1	2	0	...	...	...	...	...
	State Police:	...	...	...	...	...	...	...	...	...	...
	Bowling Green	1	0	1	0	0	1	1	0	0	...
	Dry Ridge	1	0	0	0	0	1	0	0	0	...
	Madisonville	1	2	0	1	0	2	1	1	0	...
	Mayfield	0	0	0	1	0	0	0	0	1	...
	Morehead	1	0	0	0	0	0	1	0	0	...
	Other Agencies	5	0	1	0	1	...	...	...	...	...
	Cincinnati-Northern Kentucky International Airport	1	0	0	0	0	0	0	1	0	...
	Fayette County Schools	1	0	0	0	0	0	0	1	0	...
	Jefferson County Board of Education	3	0	0	0	1	3	0	0	1	...
	McCracken County Public Schools	0	0	1	0	0	0	0	1	0	...
LOUISIANA	**Total**	4	7	2	0	0	...	...	...	...	...
	Cities	1	0	1	0	0	...	...	...	...	...
	Bossier City	1	0	0	0	0	0	0	1	0	64,232
	Plaquemine	0	0	1	0	0	0	0	0	1	6,646
	Metropolitan Counties	2	7	1	0	0	...	...	...	...	...
	Ascension	0	1	0	0	0	0	0	0	1	...
	Caddo	0	1	0	0	0	0	1	0	0	...
	Calcasieu	0	5	0	0	0	1	3	1	0	...
	Grant	1	0	0	0	0	...	...	...	1	...
	Lafayette	0	0	1	0	0		1	0	0	...
	Livingston	1	0	0	0	0	1	...	...	...	...
	Nonmetropolitan Counties	1	0	0	0	0	...	...	...	...	...
	Madison	1	0	0	0	0	1	0	0	0	...
MAINE	**Total**	30	7	18	5	1	...	...	...	...	...
	Cities	20	6	12	5	1	...	...	...	...	...
	Augusta	4	1	2	1	0	0	2	3	3	18,514
	Baileyville	0	0	1	0	0	0	1	0	0	1,524
	Bangor	0	1	0	0	0	1	0	0	0	31,587
	Bar Harbor	0	0	1	0	0	0	0	0	1	5,243
	Belfast	0	1	0	1	0	0	0	1	1	6,748
	Biddeford	3	0	0	0	0	0	0	2	1	21,511
	Bucksport	1	0	0	0	0	0	0	0	1	4,951
	Damariscotta	0	1	0	0	0	0	0	0	1	1,905
	Kittery	1	0	0	0	0	1	0	0	0	10,632
	Lewiston	0	0	1	0	0	1	0	0	0	35,153
	Livermore Falls	0	0	1	0	0	0	0	1	0	3,134
	Old Orchard Beach	1	0	1	0	0	0	0	2	0	9,494
	Paris	0	0	0	1	0	0	0	0	1	4,942
	Portland	3	0	2	1	1	1	4	2	0	63,166

[1] Agencies published in this table indicated that at least one hate crime incident occurred in their respective jurisdictions during the quarter(s) for which they submitted a report to the Hate Crime Statistics Program. Elipses indicate quarters for which agencies did not submit reports.

[2] Population figures are published only for the cities. The figures listed for the universities and colleges are student enrollment and were provided by the United States Department of Education for the 2009 school year, the most recent available. The enrollment figures include full-time and part-time students.

Table 94. Hate Crime Incidents per Bias Motivation and Quarter, by State and Agency, 2010—*Continued*

State	Agency type/Agency name	Number of incidents per bias motivation					Number of incidents per quarter[1]				Popu-lation[2]
		Race	Religion	Sexual orient-ation	Ethnicity	Disability	1st quarter	2nd quarter	3rd quarter	4th quarter	
MAINE— *Continued*											
	Rockland	0	0	1	0	0	0	0	0	1	7,458
	Saco	3	1	0	0	0	0	0	1	3	18,417
	Sanford	1	1	1	1	0	2	1	1	0	21,216
	South Portland	2	0	1	0	0	0	2	1	0	24,144
	Yarmouth	1	0	0	0	0	0	0	1	0	8,157
	Universities and Colleges	1	0	2	0	0	...	...	...	...	...
	University of Southern Maine	1	0	2	0	0	1	0	1	1	9,655
	Metropolitan Counties	3	0	2	0	0	...	...	...	...	...
	Androscoggin	0	0	1	0	0	0	0	1	0	...
	Cumberland	1	0	0	0	0	1	0	0	0	...
	Sagadahoc	2	0	1	0	0	1	1	1	0	...
	State Police Agencies	6	1	2	0	0	...	...	...	...	...
	State Police:	...	...	...	...		...	...	...	...	...
	Androscoggin County	0	0	1	0	0	1	0	0	0	...
	Somerset County	2	1	0	0	0	0	3	0	0	...
	York County	4	0	1	0	0	2	0	2	1	...
MARYLAND	**Total**	44	17	13	6	0	...	...	...	...	...
	Cities	5	2	5	2	0	...	...	...	...	...
	Annapolis	1	0	0	0	0	0	1	0	0	37,180
	Baltimore	3	2	4	2	0	4	2	3	2	639,929
	Laurel	1	0	0	0	0	0	0	1	0	22,960
	Takoma Park	0	0	1	0	0	0	0	1	0	18,200
	Universities and Colleges	0	0	2	1	0	...	...	...	...	...
	Salisbury University	0	0	0	1	0	0	1	0	0	8,204
	Towson University	0	0	1	0	0	0	0	0	1	21,177
	University of Maryland, College Park	0	0	1	0	0	1	0	0	0	37,195
	Metropolitan Counties	36	14	6	3	0	...	...	...	...	...
	Anne Arundel County Police Department	1	0	0	0	0	0	0	0	1	...
	Baltimore County Police Department	22	4	3	1	0	16	8	2	4	...
	Calvert	1	0	0	0	0	0	1	0	0	...
	Frederick	2	2	0	1	0	1	3	1	0	...
	Harford	4	0	0	0	0	0	3	0	1	...
	Montgomery County Police Department	4	8	1	1	0	5	1	3	5	...
	Prince George's County Police Department	1	0	2	0	0	0	0	1	2	...
	Wicomico	1	0	0	0	0	0	1	0	0	...
	State Police Agencies	3	1	0	0	0	...	...	...	...	...
	State Police, Carroll County	3	1	0	0	0	0	2	2	0	...
MASSACHUSETTS	**Total**	148	57	69	42	0	...	...	...	...	...
	Cities	139	50	61	41	0	...	...	...	...	...
	Acton	2	1	0	0	0	1	0	0	2	21,090
	Amherst	2	0	0	1	0	0	2	1	0	36,004
	Andover	0	0	0	1	0	0	1	0	0	33,505
	Arlington	0	1	1	0	0	0	1	1	0	41,212
	Barnstable	3	0	1	1	0	2	0	1	2	45,599
	Belmont	0	1	0	0	0	1	0	0	0	23,430
	Berlin	1	0	0	0	0	0	0	1	0	2,978
	Beverly	2	0	0	0	0	0	1	1	0	39,064
	Billerica	0	2	0	0	0	0	0	1	1	39,519
	Boston	75	15	43	15	0	30	30	46	42	644,064
	Bourne	1	0	0	0	0	1	0	0	0	19,239
	Boylston	2	1	0	0	0	0	2	1	0	4,384
	Braintree	0	0	1	0	0	0	0	0	1	35,298
	Brockton	1	0	0	0	0	0	1	0	0	92,383
	Cambridge	3	1	0	3	0	1	1	2	3	108,356
	Chelsea	0	0	1	0	0	1	0	0	0	37,335
	Chicopee	1	0	0	0	0	0	0	0	1	55,444
	Danvers	0	1	0	1	0	0	0	1	1	27,165
	Dedham	1	0	0	0	0	0	1	0	0	24,687
	Dennis	0	1	0	0	0	0	0	0	0	15,212
	Douglas	0	1	0	0	0	0	1	0	0	8,109
	Duxbury	2	0	0	0	0	1	0	1	0	14,222
	Easthampton	0	0	0	1	0	0	0	1	0	16,116
	East Longmeadow	0	1	0	0	0	0	0	0	1	15,916
	Egremont	2	0	2	0	0	...	3	1	...	1,329
	Everett	0	0	0	2	0	0	2	0	0	37,897
	Great Barrington	0	1	0	0	0	0	0	0	1	7,263
	Greenfield	0	0	2	0	0	1	1	0	0	17,625
	Hampden	1	0	0	0	0	0	1	0	0	5,346
	Hinsdale	0	1	0	0	0	...	...	1	...	1,890
	Hudson	1	0	0	0	0	0	1	0	0	19,985
	Hull	0	2	0	0	0	0	1	1	0	11,008
	Ipswich	2	0	0	1	0	0	3	0	0	13,307

[1] Agencies published in this table indicated that at least one hate crime incident occurred in their respective jurisdictions during the quarter(s) for which they submitted a report to the Hate Crime Statistics Program. Elipses indicate quarters for which agencies did not submit reports.

[2] Population figures are published only for the cities. The figures listed for the universities and colleges are student enrollment and were provided by the United States Department of Education for the 2009 school year, the most recent available. The enrollment figures include full-time and part-time students.

Table 94. Hate Crime Incidents per Bias Motivation and Quarter, by State and Agency, 2010—*Continued*

State	Agency type/Agency name	Number of incidents per bias motivation					Number of incidents per quarter[1]				Popu-lation[2]
		Race	Religion	Sexual orient-ation	Ethnicity	Disability	1st quarter	2nd quarter	3rd quarter	4th quarter	
MASSACHUSETTS— *Continued*											
	Kingston	0	0	1	0	0	0	0	1	0	12,419
	Lee	0	0	0	1	0	0	0	0	1	5,654
	Lincoln	0	2	0	0	0	0	0	0	2	8,622
	Lynn	1	0	0	0	0	0	0	0	1	86,340
	Malden	1	0	1	0	0	2	0	0	0	55,540
	Marblehead	0	2	0	0	0	1	0	1	0	19,705
	Mashpee	1	0	0	0	0	0	1	0	0	14,347
	Medfield	0	0	0	1	0	1	0	0	0	12,134
	Medway	1	0	0	0	0	0	1	0	0	12,820
	Methuen	0	1	0	0	0	0	0	1	0	43,938
	Natick	1	0	0	1	0	0	1	1	0	32,017
	New Bedford	1	0	0	0	0	0	1	0	0	89,613
	Newton	1	2	0	0	0	2	0	1	0	83,781
	North Adams	2	0	0	0	0	2	0	0	0	13,590
	North Attleboro	0	0	0	1	0	0	0	1	0	27,559
	Norton	2	0	0	0	0	0	0	0	2	19,217
	Pittsfield	1	1	0	0	0	0	0	0	2	41,666
	Plymouth	3	2	0	0	0	2	2	0	1	56,751
	Quincy	2	0	0	3	0	0	0	4	1	90,304
	Revere	5	1	1	3	0	2	4	2	2	51,597
	Salem	1	1	0	0	0	...	...	2		41,017
	Sharon	0	1	0	0	0	0	0	1	0	17,903
	Southampton	0	0	1	0	0	0	0	1	0	5,957
	Southbridge	1	0	0	1	0	0	0	2	0	17,305
	Spencer	1	0	0	0	0	0	0	1	0	11,909
	Springfield	3	0	5	3	0	1	5	0	5	154,314
	Stoneham	1	0	0	0	0	0	0	0	1	21,285
	Stoughton	0	1	0	0	0	0	1	0	0	26,866
	Waltham	0	1	0	0	0	0	1	0	0	60,106
	Webster	0	0	1	0	0	0	0	0	1	16,721
	Wellesley	1	0	0	0	0	0	0	1	0	27,143
	West Bridgewater	1	0	0	0	0	0	0	0	1	6,619
	Westfield	1	0	0	0	0	0	0	0	1	41,899
	Weymouth	0	0	0	1	0	1	0	0	0	53,400
	Williamsburg	1	0	0	0	0	0	0	0	1	2,491
	Wilmington	0	1	0	0	0	0	0	0	1	22,230
	Winthrop	0	1	0	0	0	0	1	0	0	19,127
	Worcester	3	3	0	0	0	0	5	1	0	181,908
	Wrentham	1	0	0	0	0	0	1	0	0	11,166
	Universities and Colleges	8	7	8	1	0	...	...	...	...	...
	Assumption College	0	0	1	0	0	0	0	0	1	2,794
	Bentley College	1	0	0	0	0	1	...	...	...	5,628
	Brandeis University	0	1	0	0	0	1	...	...	...	5,598
	Clark University	1	4	1	0	0	4	...	1	1	3,416
	Emerson College	0	0	1	0	0	...	...		1	4,556
	Harvard University	0	0	1	0	0	...	...	1	0	27,651
	Massachusetts Institute of Technology	1	0	0	0	0	1	0	0	0	10,384
	Merrimack College	1	0	0	0	0	...		1		2,090
	Northeastern University	2	1	3	1	0	3	1		3	27,537
	University of Massachusetts:	...	...	...	...	...	...	...	...	...	...
	Amherst	2	1	0	0	0	2	1	0	0	27,016
	Dartmouth	0	0	1	0	0	...	...	...	1	9,302
	Other Agencies	1	0	0	0	0	...	...	...		...
	Massachusetts Bay Transportation Authority, Suffolk County	1	0	0	0	0	...	...	...	1	...
MICHIGAN	**Total**	197	29	49	29	0	...	...	...	...	...
	Cities	145	23	32	21	0	...	...	...	...	...
	Adrian	1	0	0	0	0	0	1	0	...	20,997
	Alpena	1	2	0	0	0	0	2	1	0	10,184
	Ann Arbor	3	0	1	0	0	0	1	3	0	111,745
	Auburn Hills	0	1	0	0	0	1	0	0	0	20,870
	Battle Creek	1	0	0	0	0	1	0	0	0	60,386
	Bay City	3	0	0	0	0	1	0	0	2	33,200
	Belleville	2	0	0	0	0	2	0	0	0	3,392
	Berkley	1	0	0	0	0	0	0	1	0	14,609
	Beverly Hills	0	1	0	0	0	0	1	0	0	9,739
	Birmingham	2	1	1	0	0	0	0	0	4	18,823
	Blackman Township	1	0	0	0	0	0	0	0	1	37,751
	Bloomfield Hills	0	1	0	0	0	0	1	0	0	3,731
	Bloomfield Township	2	0	0	0	0	0	0	1	1	40,490
	Boyne City	0	0	1	0	0	0	1	0	0	3,049
	Brown City	1	0	0	0	0	0	0	1		1,203
	Cadillac	6	0	1	0	0	2	1	0	4	10,101

[1] Agencies published in this table indicated that at least one hate crime incident occurred in their respective jurisdictions during the quarter(s) for which they submitted a report to the Hate Crime Statistics Program. Elipses indicate quarters for which agencies did not submit reports.

[2] Population figures are published only for the cities. The figures listed for the universities and colleges are student enrollment and were provided by the United States Department of Education for the 2009 school year, the most recent available. The enrollment figures include full-time and part-time students.

Table 94. Hate Crime Incidents per Bias Motivation and Quarter, by State and Agency, 2010—*Continued*

State	Agency type/Agency name	Number of incidents per bias motivation					Number of incidents per quarter[1]				Popu-lation[2]
		Race	Religion	Sexual orient-ation	Ethnicity	Disability	1st quarter	2nd quarter	3rd quarter	4th quarter	
MICHIGAN— *Continued*											
	Canton Township	3	3	1	1	0	3	2	3	0	80,039
	Center Line	0	0	1	0	0	0	0	1	0	8,017
	Chelsea	0	1	0	0	0	1	0	0	0	5,051
	Chesterfield Township	7	0	0	0	0	0	0	3	4	45,027
	Clawson	1	0	0	0	0	0	0	0	1	12,025
	Clinton	1	0	0	0	0	0	0	1	0	2,358
	Clinton Township	6	0	0	0	0	0	2	3	1	95,167
	Clio	1	0	0	0	0	0	0	0	1	2,434
	Covert Township	0	0	1	0	0	0	0	1	0	3,047
	Davison Township	1	0	0	0	0	0	1	0	0	18,214
	Dearborn	4	2	0	2	0	1	4	1	2	82,612
	Dearborn Heights	2	0	0	0	0	0	0	2	0	49,674
	Decatur	0	0	1	0	0	0	1	0	0	1,806
	Detroit	1	0	3	0	0	0	1	1	2	899,447
	Dewitt Township	1	0	0	0	0	0	1	0	0	13,074
	East Lansing	1	0	0	0	0	0	1	0	0	45,058
	Eastpointe	5	0	0	1	0	1	1	3	1	32,016
	Elk Rapids	1	0	0	0	0	0	1	0	0	1,630
	Escanaba	2	0	1	0	0	1	0	2	0	11,918
	Ferndale	1	0	1	0	0	1	0	0	1	20,847
	Flint Township	1	0	0	0	0	0	0	0	1	30,778
	Flushing	1	0	0	0	0	0	0	0	1	7,584
	Fremont	0	0	1	0	0	0	1	...	...	4,077
	Genesee Township	1	0	0	0	0	0	0	1	0	22,571
	Grand Blanc Township	1	0	0	0	0	0	0	0	1	34,634
	Grand Rapids	2	0	2	3	0	3	0	1	3	191,566
	Greenville	1	0	0	0	0	0	1	0	0	7,957
	Hillsdale	1	0	0	0	0	0	1	0	0	7,574
	Holland	3	0	0	1	0	0	1	1	2	33,652
	Inkster	0	0	1	0	0	1	0	0	0	25,428
	Jackson	1	0	2	0	0	1	1	1	0	32,741
	Jonesville	2	0	0	0	0	0	1	1	0	2,164
	Kalamazoo	2	0	1	0	0	0	1	1	1	71,775
	Keego Harbor	0	0	1	0	0	0	0	0	1	2,828
	Laingsburg	1	0	0	0	0	0	1	0	0	1,220
	Lansing	3	1	0	0	0	2	1	0	1	112,254
	Lincoln Township	1	0	0	0	0	0	1	...	...	14,281
	Litchfield	1	0	0	0	0	1	0	0	0	1,351
	Livonia	4	1	0	0	0	0	4	1	0	87,434
	Madison Heights	2	1	1	0	0	2	2	0	0	29,174
	Manistee	1	0	0	0	0	0	0	1	0	5,985
	Manistique	0	0	0	1	0	0	1	0	0	2,969
	Marshall	1	0	0	0	0	0	0	1	0	7,005
	Mattawan	3	0	0	0	0	2	1	0	0	2,846
	Meridian Township	4	1	1	1	0	3	3	1	0	38,105
	Monroe	3	0	0	0	0	1	1	0	1	21,062
	Morenci	2	0	0	0	0	1	0	1		2,195
	Mount Morris Township	3	0	0	0	0	2	0	1	0	21,614
	Mundy Township	1	0	0	0	0	0	1	0	0	13,810
	Muskegon	0	0	1	1	0	0	1	0	1	38,829
	Muskegon Heights	1	0	0	0	0	0	0	1	0	11,420
	New Baltimore	1	0	0	0	0	0	0	0	1	11,701
	Niles	1	0	0	0	0	0	0	0	1	11,084
	Northville	1	0	0	0	0	1	0	0	0	5,839
	Oak Park	0	1	0	0	0	0	0	1	0	30,131
	Owosso	0	0	4	0	0	0	1	2	1	14,526
	Paw Paw	1	0	0	0	0	0	1	0	0	3,179
	Pentwater	1	0	0	0	0	1	0	0	0	928
	Pittsfield Township	0	1	0	1	0	0	0	1	1	34,681
	Pontiac	0	0	0	1	0	0	0	1	0	65,517
	Port Huron	2	0	0	0	0	0	1	0	1	30,132
	Richfield Township, Roscommon County	1	0	0	0	0	0	0	0	1	3,971
	Rochester	0	0	1	0	0	1	0	0	0	10,982
	Royal Oak	4	1	0	0	0	1	0	3	1	56,408
	Saginaw	2	0	0	0	0	0	0	1	1	54,155
	Saginaw Township	1	0	0	0	0	0	0	1	0	37,872
	Shelby Township	1	1	0	0	0	0	0	1	1	71,589
	Somerset Township	1	0	0	0	0	1	0	0	0	4,584
	Southfield	2	1	0	0	0	0	1	1	1	74,587
	St. Clair	1	0	0	0	0	0	0	1	0	5,646
	St. Clair Shores	0	0	1	0	0	0	0	1	0	59,522
	Sterling Heights	0	0	0	3	0	2	0	1	0	126,291
	Taylor	0	0	1	1	0	1	0	1	0	58,158

[1] Agencies published in this table indicated that at least one hate crime incident occurred in their respective jurisdictions during the quarter(s) for which they submitted a report to the Hate Crime Statistics Program. Elipses indicate quarters for which agencies did not submit reports.
[2] Population figures are published only for the cities. The figures listed for the universities and colleges are student enrollment and were provided by the United States Department of Education for the 2009 school year, the most recent available. The enrollment figures include full-time and part-time students.

Table 94.   Hate Crime Incidents per Bias Motivation and Quarter, by State and Agency, 2010—*Continued*

State	Agency type/Agency name	Number of incidents per bias motivation					Number of incidents per quarter[1]				Popu-lation[2]
		Race	Religion	Sexual orient-ation	Ethnicity	Disability	1st quarter	2nd quarter	3rd quarter	4th quarter	
MICHIGAN— *Continued*											
	Trenton	1	1	0	0	0	0	0	1	1	17,217
	Troy	0	0	0	1	0	0	1	0	0	79,794
	Van Buren Township	1	0	1	0	0	1	1	0	0	25,627
	Warren	6	0	0	1	0	1	1	4	1	132,266
	Waterford Township	1	0	0	0	0	0	0	0	1	70,013
	Wayne	1	0	0	0	0	1	0	0	0	16,454
	West Bloomfield Township	0	1	0	0	0	0	0	0	1	63,345
	Westland	1	0	0	1	0	0	1	0	1	75,726
	White Lake Township	2	0	0	0	0	0	0	1	1	29,890
	Wyandotte	1	0	0	0	0	1	0	0	0	23,607
	Wyoming	2	0	0	1	0	0	1	2	0	70,160
	Universities and Colleges	8	1	2	1	0	...	...	...	...	...
	Central Michigan University	0	0	0	1	0	1	0	0	0	27,247
	Eastern Michigan University	0	1	1	0	0	1	0	0	1	22,893
	Ferris State University	1	0	0	0	0	0	0	0	1	13,865
	Lansing Community College	2	0	0	0	0	2	0	0	0	21,123
	Michigan State University	1	0	0	0	0	0	1	0	0	47,071
	University of Michigan, Ann Arbor	4	0	1	0	0	0	1	1	3	41,674
	Metropolitan Counties	31	5	10	6	0	...	...	...	...	...
	Calhoun	1	0	1	0	0	2	0	0	0	...
	Eaton	0	0	0	1	0	0	0	1	0	...
	Genesee	1	0	0	0	0	0	0	0	1	...
	Jackson	2	1	0	0	0	0	1	1	1	...
	Kalamazoo	1	0	0	0	0	0	0	0	1	...
	Kent	4	1	1	0	0	1	3	1	1	...
	Livingston	0	1	0	2	0	2	1	0	0	...
	Macomb	4	0	1	0	0	1	2	0	2	...
	Monroe	2	0	0	0	0	1	0	1	0	...
	Oakland	10	1	4	2	0	7	4	3	3	...
	Ottawa	2	0	1	0	0	1	1	1	0	...
	Saginaw	0	0	0	1	0	0	0	1	0	...
	St. Clair	0	1	0	0	0	0	0	0	1	...
	Van Buren	2	0	0	0	0	0	0	1	1	...
	Washtenaw	2	0	2	0	0	1	1	2	0	...
	Nonmetropolitan Counties	10	0	4	1	0	...	...	...	...	...
	Alger	1	0	0	0	0	0	0	1	0	...
	Allegan	0	0	1	0	0	1	0	0	0	...
	Benzie	1	0	0	0	0	0	1	0	0	...
	Chippewa	1	0	0	0	0	0	0	0	1	...
	Grand Traverse	1	0	0	0	0	1	0	0	0	...
	Missaukee	0	0	0	1	0	0	0	1	0	...
	Montcalm	3	0	0	0	0	2	1	0	0	...
	Ogemaw	0	0	2	0	0	0	0	1	1	...
	Oscoda	1	0	0	0	0	0	1	0	0	...
	Presque Isle	0	0	1	0	0	0	0	1	0	...
	St. Joseph	1	0	0	0	0	0	0	0	1	...
	Tuscola	1	0	0	0	0	0	0	1	0	...
	State Police Agencies	2	0	1	0	0	...	...	...	...	...
	State Police:	...	...	...	...	...	...	...	...	...	...
	Ionia County	1	0	0	0	0	0	0	1	0	...
	Van Buren County	0	0	1	0	0	0	0	0	1	...
	Wayne County	1	0	0	0	0	1	0	0	0	...
	Other Agencies	1	0	0	0	0	...	...	...	...	...
	Wayne County Airport	1	0	0	0	0	0	0	0	1	...
MINNESOTA	**Total**	69	9	22	27	0	...	...	...	...	...
	Cities	61	6	20	26	0	...	...	...	...	...
	Bemidji	0	0	1	0	0	0	0	0	1	13,911
	Benson	0	0	1	0	0	0	0	1	0	2,930
	Blaine	2	0	0	0	0	1	1	0	...	57,561
	Bloomington	0	0	0	1	0			1	...	82,715
	Brooklyn Park	4	0	0	0	0	3	1	...	...	72,682
	Duluth	3	0	1	1	0	1	1	2	1	84,249
	Eagan	0	0	0	1	0			1	...	64,239
	Eden Prairie	1	0	0	1	0	0	1	1	...	63,159
	Elk River	3	0	0	1	0	1	2	1	...	24,025
	Fridley	1	0	0	0	0	...	1	...	...	25,857
	Jordan	1	0	0	0	0	...	...	1	...	5,731
	Lino Lakes	0	0	1	0	0	...	1	...	...	20,953
	Mankato	8	0	5	1	0	4	2	5	3	36,921
	Maplewood	0	0	0	1	0	...	...	...	1	36,907
	Mendota Heights	0	0	0	1	0	...	...	1	...	11,697
	Minneapolis	27	3	9	8	0	8	15	14	10	385,704
	Minnetonka	0	0	0	1	0	1	...	...	...	50,753

[1] Agencies published in this table indicated that at least one hate crime incident occurred in their respective jurisdictions during the quarter(s) for which they submitted a report to the Hate Crime Statistics Program. Elipses indicate quarters for which agencies did not submit reports.

[2] Population figures are published only for the cities. The figures listed for the universities and colleges are student enrollment and were provided by the United States Department of Education for the 2009 school year, the most recent available. The enrollment figures include full-time and part-time students.

Table 94.   Hate Crime Incidents per Bias Motivation and Quarter, by State and Agency, 2010—*Continued*

State	Agency type/Agency name	Number of incidents per bias motivation					Number of incidents per quarter[1]				Popu-lation[2]
		Race	Religion	Sexual orient-ation	Ethnicity	Disability	1st quarter	2nd quarter	3rd quarter	4th quarter	
MINNESOTA— *Continued*											
	New Brighton	1	0	0	0	0	0	0	1	0	21,689
	Plymouth	0	1	0	1	0	1	1	...	...	73,579
	Robbinsdale	0	0	1	0	0		1	...	...	13,822
	Rochester	3	0	0	2	0	0	2	1	2	105,027
	South St. Paul	1	0	0	0	0	0	1	0	0	19,434
	St. Louis Park	1	2	0	4	0		3	4		45,690
	St. Paul	5	0	1	2	0	2	2	1	3	281,166
	Universities and Colleges	2	0	1	0	0	...	...	...	...	
	University of Minnesota, Twin Cities	2	0	1	0	0	0	2	1	0	51,659
	Metropolitan Counties	4	3	1	1	0	...	...	...	...	...
	Chisago	1	0	0	0	0	0	1	0	...	...
	Dakota	0	0	1	0	0	...	1			...
	Olmsted	1	3	0	1	0	1	3	1	...	...
	Polk	1	0	0	0	0	0	0	1	0	...
	Washington	1	0	0	0	0	0	1	0	0	...
	Nonmetropolitan Counties	2	0	0	0	0	...	...	...	...	...
	Beltrami	1	0	0	0	0	0	...	1	0	...
	Mille Lacs	1	0	0	0	0	0	1	...	...	...
MISSISSIPPI...............	**Total**	2	0	0	9	0	...	...	...	...	...
	Cities	2	0	0	9	0	...	...	...	...	...
	Gulfport	2	0	0	9	0	3	5	2	1	70,806
MISSOURI..................	**Total**	91	16	22	13	0	...	...	...	...	...
	Cities	78	14	19	12	0	...	...	...	...	...
	Bolivar	1	0	0	0	0	0	0	0	1	11,308
	Bridgeton	1	0	0	0	0	0	0	1	0	14,900
	Byrnes Mill	1	0	0	0	0	0	0	0	1	2,977
	Canton	0	1	0	0	0	0	0	0	1	2,403
	Cape Girardeau	1	0	0	0	0	0	1	0	0	37,627
	Columbia	2	0	1	0	0	1	0	1	1	103,417
	Independence	1	1	1	1	0	0	1	2	1	121,141
	Joplin	0	0	0	1	0	1	0	0	0	50,346
	Kansas City	49	8	11	8	0	13	16	21	26	483,191
	Kirksville	1	0	0	0	0	0	1	0	0	17,406
	Lee's Summit	2	0	0	1	0	0	0	1	2	87,707
	O'Fallon	1	0	0	0	0	0	1	0	0	81,851
	Raytown	1	0	1	0	0	0	1	1	0	28,616
	Riverview	1	0	0	0	0	0	1	0	0	2,874
	Rolla	1	0	1	0	0	1	0	0	1	18,575
	Springfield	8	3	2	1	0	4	5	5	0	157,110
	St. Charles	1	0	0	0	0	0	0	1	0	65,729
	St. Joseph	0	1	0	0	0	0	0	1	0	75,922
	St. Louis	2	0	2	0	0	1	1	2	0	355,151
	St. Peters	3	0	0	0	0	0	2	0	1	56,518
	Town and Country	1	0	0	0	0	1	0	0	0	10,626
	Universities and Colleges	2	0	1	1	0	...	...	...	...	
	University of Missouri, Columbia	2	0	1	1	0	1	1	1	1	31,237
	Metropolitan Counties	9	2	1	0	0	...	...	...	...	...
	Franklin	0	1	0	0	0	0	1	0	0	...
	Jefferson	4	0	0	0	0	2	0	2	0	...
	St. Charles	2	0	0	0	0	2	0	0	0	...
	St. Louis County Police Department	3	1	1	0	0	1	3	1	0	...
	Nonmetropolitan Counties	1	0	1	0	0	...	...	...	...	...
	Laclede	1	0	0	0	0	0	1	0	0	...
	Ste. Genevieve	0	0	1	0	0	0	1	0	0	...
	State Police Agencies	1	0	0	0	0	...	...	...	...	...
	State Highway Patrol, St. Joseph	1	0	0	0	0	1	0	0	0	...
MONTANA..................	**Total**	15	3	11	1	1	...	...	...	...	...
	Cities	4	3	8	1	1	...	...	...	...	...
	Billings	1	0	0	0	0	1	0	0	0	108,039
	Helena	0	1	2	0	0	0	1	1	1	30,520
	Kalispell	0	0	0	0	1	0	0	1	0	22,568
	Miles City	0	0	1	0	0	0	1	0	0	8,141
	Missoula	2	2	4	1	0	1	4	3	1	70,559
	Red Lodge	0	0	1	0	0	0	0	1	0	2,531
	Troy	1	0	0	0	0	0	0	0	1	969
	Metropolitan Counties	0	0	1	0	0	...	...	...	...	...
	Missoula	0	0	1	0	0	0	0	1	0	...
	Nonmetropolitan Counties	11	0	2	0	0	...	...	...	...	...
	Big Horn	2	0	0	0	0	0	2	0	0	...
	Deer Lodge	0	0	1	0	0	0	1	0	0	...
	Lewis and Clark	3	0	0	0	0	0	2	1	0	...
	Phillips	1	0	0	0	0	0	1	0	0	...
	Ravalli	2	0	1	0	0	2	0	0	1	...
	Silver Bow	3	0	0	0	0	0	3	0	0	...

[1] Agencies published in this table indicated that at least one hate crime incident occurred in their respective jurisdictions during the quarter(s) for which they submitted a report to the Hate Crime Statistics Program. Elipses indicate quarters for which agencies did not submit reports.

[2] Population figures are published only for the cities. The figures listed for the universities and colleges are student enrollment and were provided by the United States Department of Education for the 2009 school year, the most recent available. The enrollment figures include full-time and part-time students.

Table 94.   Hate Crime Incidents per Bias Motivation and Quarter, by State and Agency, 2010—*Continued*

State	Agency type/Agency name	Number of incidents per bias motivation					Number of incidents per quarter[1]				Popu-lation[2]
		Race	Religion	Sexual orient-ation	Ethnicity	Disability	1st quarter	2nd quarter	3rd quarter	4th quarter	
NEBRASKA................	**Total**	37	7	7	10	0	...	...	...	...	...
	Cities	36	7	7	10	0	...	...	...	...	...
	Fremont	1	0	0	3	0	0	0	4	0	25,262
	Lincoln	27	4	4	5	0	8	5	19	8	259,672
	Omaha	8	3	3	2	0	7	6	0	3	464,628
	Nonmetropolitan Counties	1	0	0	0	0	...	...	...	...	...
	Adams	1	0	0	0	0	0	0	1	0	...
NEVADA	**Total**	23	20	15	10	0	...	...	...	...	...
	Cities	22	18	15	10	0	...	...	...	...	...
	Fallon	1	0	0	0	0	0	0	0	1	8,552
	Henderson	1	3	1	1	0	1	3	1	1	264,280
	Las Vegas Metropolitan Police Department	19	13	13	7	0	14	15	11	12	1,416,401
	North Las Vegas	1	2	1	2	0	0	4	1	1	238,004
	Universities and Colleges	0	2	0	0	0	...	...	...	...	...
	University of Nevada, Las Vegas	0	2	0	0	0	2	0	0	0	29,080
	Nonmetropolitan Counties	1	0	0	0	0	...	...	...	...	...
	Humboldt	1	0	0	0	0	1	0	0	0	...
NEW HAMPSHIRE....	**Total**	11	6	11	3	0	...	...	...	...	...
	Cities	11	6	11	3	0	...	...	...	...	...
	Bristol	1	0	0	0	0	0	0	1	0	3,110
	Concord	0	0	1	0	0	0	0	1	0	42,190
	Conway	2	0	0	0	0	0	2	0	0	9,195
	Danville	1	0	0	0	0	0	0	1	0	4,326
	Derry	0	1	1	0	0	1	0	1	0	34,075
	Durham	0	0	1	0	0	0	0	1	0	14,465
	Exeter	0	0	1	0	0	0	1	0	0	14,924
	Farmington	1	0	0	0	0	0	0	1	0	6,764
	Hampton	1	0	1	0	0	1	0	1	0	15,270
	Hinsdale	0	0	1	0	0	1	0	0	0	4,124
	Hooksett	0	1	0	0	0	0	0	1	0	14,075
	Laconia	1	0	0	0	0	0	0	1	0	16,973
	Lee	0	1	0	0	0	0	1	0	0	4,461
	Littleton	0	0	0	1	0	0	0	1	0	6,111
	Manchester	2	1	1	0	0	1	1	0	2	108,101
	Marlborough	1	0	0	0	0	0	0	0	1	2,052
	Merrimack	0	0	1	1	0	0	1	0	1	26,501
	Pelham	1	0	0	0	0	1	0	0	0	12,770
	Plymouth	0	2	1	0	0	0	0	1	2	6,647
	Sandown	0	0	1	0	0	0	1	0	0	5,907
	Seabrook	0	0	0	1	0	0	1	0	0	8,471
	Tilton	0	0	1	0	0	0	0	1	0	3,542
NEW JERSEY..............	**Total**	224	221	40	52	6	...	...	...	...	...
	Cities	223	220	40	52	6	...	...	...	...	...
	Aberdeen Township	2	2	0	1	0	1	1	2	1	18,575
	Asbury Park	4	0	2	1	0	0	4	1	2	16,625
	Atlantic City	2	2	1	2	0	2	2	1	2	39,787
	Avalon	0	1	0	0	0	0	0	1	0	2,094
	Barnegat Township	3	0	0	0	0	0	0	3	0	23,692
	Bayonne	0	1	0	1	0	0	1	1	0	58,393
	Beachwood	1	1	0	0	0	0	0	0	2	11,001
	Belleville	0	1	0	0	0	1	0	0	0	33,849
	Bergenfield	0	1	0	0	0	0	1	0	0	25,680
	Berkeley Township	0	0	2	0	0	0	0	1	1	43,531
	Blairstown Township	1	0	0	0	0	1	0	0	0	5,985
	Bogota	1	0	0	0	0	0	0	0	1	7,933
	Boonton	0	1	0	0	0	0	0	1	0	8,552
	Boonton Township	0	4	0	0	0	0	0	4	0	4,539
	Branchburg Township	1	0	0	0	0	1	0	0	0	15,263
	Brick Township	2	0	0	0	0	0	1	1	0	79,569
	Camden	0	1	0	0	0	0	0	1	0	79,081
	Carney's Point Township	1	0	0	0	0	0	0	1	0	8,076
	Chatham Township	0	1	0	0	0	0	0	0	1	10,302
	Chesterfield Township	1	0	0	0	0	0	0	1	0	7,860
	Cliffside Park	0	0	0	1	0	0	1	0	0	23,139
	Clifton	0	0	1	0	0	1	0	0	0	78,632
	Colts Neck Township	0	2	0	0	0	0	0	1	1	10,180
	Cranbury Township	1	0	0	0	0	0	0	0	1	4,023
	Delanco Township	2	0	0	0	0	2	0	0	0	5,000
	Eastampton Township	0	1	0	0	0	0	1	0	0	6,597
	East Brunswick Township	9	8	1	0	0	4	10	1	3	47,620
	East Newark	1	0	0	0	0	0	0	1	0	2,116
	East Windsor Township	1	1	1	0	0	2	1	0	0	27,424
	Eatontown	0	1	0	0	0	0	0	0	1	14,428

[1] Agencies published in this table indicated that at least one hate crime incident occurred in their respective jurisdictions during the quarter(s) for which they submitted a report to the Hate Crime Statistics Program. Elipses indicate quarters for which agencies did not submit reports.

[2] Population figures are published only for the cities. The figures listed for the universities and colleges are student enrollment and were provided by the United States Department of Education for the 2009 school year, the most recent available. The enrollment figures include full-time and part-time students.

Table 94. Hate Crime Incidents per Bias Motivation and Quarter, by State and Agency, 2010—*Continued*

State	Agency type/Agency name	Number of incidents per bias motivation					Number of incidents per quarter[1]				Popu-lation[2]
		Race	Religion	Sexual orient-ation	Ethnicity	Disability	1st quarter	2nd quarter	3rd quarter	4th quarter	
NEW JERSEY—*Continued*											
	Edison Township	4	3	1	0	0	1	0	7	0	100,395
	Elk Township	1	5	0	0	0	0	0	6	0	4,084
	Englewood	1	1	1	1	0	1	2	0	1	30,023
	Evesham Township	7	4	0	0	0	2	5	4	0	45,959
	Ewing Township	0	2	0	0	0	0	1	1	0	36,612
	Fort Lee	0	3	0	0	0	0	1	1	1	36,580
	Franklin Township, Gloucester County	0	0	0	1	0	0	0	0	1	17,679
	Freehold	1	0	0	1	0	0	0	1	1	11,548
	Freehold Township	1	1	0	0	0	0	2	0	0	35,117
	Galloway Township	1	1	0	0	0	1	1	0	0	37,367
	Gibbsboro	1	1	0	0	0	0	2	0	0	2,447
	Glassboro	2	3	0	0	1		0	2	4	20,047
	Glen Rock	1	0	0	0	0	0	0	1	0	11,158
	Gloucester Township	3	0	0	0	0	1	0	1	1	65,239
	Hackettstown	0	0	0	1	0	0	0	1	0	9,653
	Haddon Township	1	0	0	0	0	0	1	0	0	14,432
	Hamilton Township, Atlantic County	1	0	0	1	0	1	0	0	1	24,892
	Hammonton	1	1	0	0	0	0	0	1	1	13,603
	Hanover Township	0	1	0	0	0	0	1	0	0	13,905
	Harding Township	0	2	0	0	0	0	2	0	0	3,375
	Hardyston Township	1	1	0	1	0	1	1	0	1	8,621
	Harrison Township	1	0	0	0	0	0	0	1	0	13,122
	Hazlet Township	1	0	0	0	0	1	0	0	0	21,013
	High Bridge	1	0	0	0	0	1	0	0	0	3,712
	Highlands	1	0	0	0	0	1	0	0	0	5,299
	Hillsborough Township	0	1	0	2	0	0	1	1	1	40,011
	Hillsdale	1	0	0	0	0	0	1	0	0	9,884
	Hoboken	4	1	1	0	0	2	1	3	0	41,515
	Hopewell Township	0	1	0	0	0	0	0	1	0	18,060
	Howell Township	1	6	0	4	0	3	0	7	1	52,130
	Jackson Township	3	4	0	2	0	1	0	7	1	54,638
	Jersey City	0	2	1	1	1	0	1	1	3	244,201
	Keansburg	18	2	4	2	0	11	6	7	2	10,579
	Lacey Township	0	2	0	0	0	0	0	2	0	26,852
	Lakehurst	0	1	0	0	0	0	1	0	0	2,743
	Lakewood Township	4	20	1	1	1	2	10	10	5	72,960
	Lambertville	0	1	0	0	0	0	0	1	0	3,802
	Lawrence Township, Mercer County	1	1	0	0	0	1	1		0	32,104
	Linden	0	1	0	0	0	1	0	0	0	39,680
	Little Egg Harbor Township	5	2	0	2	0	0	2	4	3	21,508
	Little Falls Township	4	1	1	1	0	0	1	3	3	11,703
	Little Silver	1	1	0	0	0	1	1	0	0	6,175
	Livingston Township	1	0	0	0	0	0	0	1	0	27,775
	Lodi	2	3	0	0	0	2	1	1	1	23,895
	Long Beach Township	1	1	0	0	0	0	1	1	0	3,628
	Lopatcong Township	3	0	0	0	0	2	0	1	0	8,744
	Lower Township	2	1	0	0	0	0	3	0	0	20,114
	Lumberton Township	2	0	1	0	0	0	2	1	0	12,184
	Manalapan Township	2	5	0	0	0	0	3	3	1	40,301
	Manasquan	1	1	0	1	0	1	1	1	0	6,309
	Manchester Township	1	2	1	1	0	0	2	2	1	42,400
	Mansfield Township, Burlington County	1	1	0	0	0	0	1	1	0	8,405
	Mansfield Township, Warren County	1	0	0	1	0	1	0	1	0	8,139
	Maple Shade Township	1	0	0	1	0	1	0	1	0	19,297
	Marlboro Township	5	7	0	0	0	2	3	6	1	41,231
	Medford Township	1	4	2	1	0	3	2	0	3	22,914
	Merchantville	1	0	0	0	0	0	1	0	0	3,784
	Middlesex	1	0	0	1	0	0	0	2	0	13,732
	Middle Township	1	0	0	0	0	0	0	0	1	16,580
	Middletown Township	2	2	0	0	0	0	3	1	0	66,915
	Milltown	1	0	0	0	0	0	1	0	0	7,007
	Millville	0	1	0	0	0	0	0	1	0	29,497
	Monroe Township, Middlesex County	2	5	1	1	0	0	2	4	3	38,777
	Montclair	2	2	0	0	0	2	2	0	0	37,425
	Montville Township	0	8	0	0	0	0	1	0	7	21,253
	Moorestown Township	3	1	0	0	0	1	1	2	0	19,653
	Mount Holly Township	1	0	0	0	0	1	0	0	0	10,246
	Mount Laurel Township	1	1	0	1	0	0	1	1	1	39,696
	Mount Olive Township	2	0	0	1	0	0	0	2	1	26,431
	Mullica Township	1	0	0	0	0	0	1	0	0	6,104
	Neptune Township	11	2	4	2	1	2	6	4	8	28,586
	New Brunswick	2	2	0	0	0	1	1	1	1	52,245
	North Brunswick Township	0	3	0	0	0	1	0	2	0	40,123

[1] Agencies published in this table indicated that at least one hate crime incident occurred in their respective jurisdictions during the quarter(s) for which they submitted a report to the Hate Crime Statistics Program. Elipses indicate quarters for which agencies did not submit reports.

[2] Population figures are published only for the cities. The figures listed for the universities and colleges are student enrollment and were provided by the United States Department of Education for the 2009 school year, the most recent available. The enrollment figures include full-time and part-time students.

Table 94.   Hate Crime Incidents per Bias Motivation and Quarter, by State and Agency, 2010—*Continued*

State	Agency type/Agency name	Number of incidents per bias motivation					Number of incidents per quarter[1]				Popu-lation[2]
		Race	Religion	Sexual orient-ation	Ethnicity	Disability	1st quarter	2nd quarter	3rd quarter	4th quarter	
NEW JERSEY— *Continued*											
	North Caldwell	0	1	0	0	0	0	0	0	1	7,086
	North Haledon	0	1	0	0	0	1	0	0	0	9,058
	North Plainfield	0	4	0	0	0	0	0	0	4	21,373
	Norwood	0	1	0	0	0	0	1	0	0	6,290
	Oakland	0	0	0	1	0	1	0	0	0	13,454
	Oaklyn	0	0	1	0	0	1	0	0	0	4,047
	Ocean City	0	0	0	2	0	0	0	2	0	14,725
	Ocean Gate	0	0	0	1	0	0	0	1	0	2,171
	Old Bridge Township	3	2	1	0	0	1	1	0	4	66,913
	Oradell	0	1	0	0	0	1	0	0	0	7,811
	Palmyra	0	0	0	1	0	0	1	0	. . .	7,400
	Paramus	1	0	0	0	0	1	0	0	0	26,340
	Passaic	0	0	1	0	0	0	0	0	1	67,356
	Paterson	1	0	0	0	0	0	0	0	1	146,356
	Pine Hill	1	0	1	0	0	1	0	0	1	11,449
	Piscataway Township	3	0	1	0	0	0	0	3	1	52,897
	Pitman	2	0	0	0	0	0	0	2	0	9,271
	Plainfield	1	0	0	1	0	0	0	0	2	46,459
	Plainsboro Township	1	0	0	0	0	0	0	1	0	21,407
	Plumsted Township	2	0	0	0	0	2	0	0	0	8,446
	Pohatcong Township	0	1	0	0	0	0	0	0	1	3,331
	Point Pleasant	1	1	0	0	0	2	0	0	0	20,569
	Point Pleasant Beach	1	0	0	0	0	1	0	0	0	5,492
	Ramsey	0	3	0	0	0	0	2	0	1	14,846
	Randolph Township	2	0	0	0	0	0	2	0	0	25,391
	Ridgefield	0	1	0	0	0	1	0	0	0	10,953
	Ridgewood	0	1	0	1	0	0	1	0	1	24,260
	Ringwood	1	0	0	0	0	0	0	0	1	12,822
	River Edge	0	2	0	0	0	0	1	1	0	10,733
	River Vale Township	0	1	0	0	0	0	0	0	1	9,730
	Runnemede	1	0	1	0	0	1	1	0	0	8,449
	Scotch Plains Township	0	3	0	0	0	0	2	1	0	23,231
	Somerville	0	1	0	0	0	0	0	0	1	12,847
	South Brunswick Township	3	11	0	3	0	8	3	5	1	41,861
	South Plainfield	0	2	1	0	0	0	1	1	1	22,848
	South River	0	0	0	1	0	0	1	0	0	15,809
	South Toms River	1	0	2	0	0	0	1	2	0	3,759
	Sparta Township	0	0	0	0	1	0	0	1	0	19,466
	Spotswood	1	0	1	0	0	1	0	1	0	8,261
	Springfield	0	3	0	0	0	0	2	1	0	15,353
	Teaneck Township	1	5	0	0	0	1	1	4	0	38,666
	Tinton Falls	4	1	0	0	0	4	1	0	0	20,257
	Trenton	1	0	0	0	0	0	1	0	0	83,552
	Union City	0	0	0	0	1	0	0	0	1	61,855
	Union Township	2	1	0	0	0	2	1	0	0	53,945
	Vernon Township	0	0	1	0	0	0	1	0	0	24,993
	Verona	1	0	0	0	0	0	1	0	0	12,636
	Voorhees Township	0	1	0	0	0	0	0	1	0	32,441
	Waldwick	1	0	0	0	0	0	0	0	1	9,643
	Warren Township	0	1	0	0	0	0	0	0	1	16,356
	Washington Township, Gloucester County	6	2	0	1	0	3	4	1	1	52,251
	Washington Township, Warren County	1	0	0	0	0	1	0	0	0	6,949
	Watchung	0	1	0	0	0	1	0	0	0	6,752
	Waterford Township	0	0	1	0	0	1	0	0	0	10,774
	Weehawken Township	0	2	0	0	0	0	0	2	0	12,351
	Westampton Township	2	0	0	0	0	0	1	0	1	8,877
	West Deptford Township	3	2	1	0	0	0	2	4	0	22,482
	West Long Branch	1	2	0	0	0	0	2	1	0	8,482
	West New York	0	0	0	1	0	0	0	1	0	46,907
	West Orange	0	2	0	0	0	0	1	0	1	42,590
	Wildwood	0	1	0	0	0	0	1	0	0	5,222
	Willingboro Township	1	0	0	0	0	1	0	0	0	36,888
	Winslow Township	2	1	0	1	0	0	0	2	2	40,393
	Woodbridge Township	4	1	0	0	0	2	2	1	0	98,576
	Woodbury	2	0	0	0	0	0	0	1	1	10,527
	Woodbury Heights	1	0	0	0	0	0	0	0	1	3,079
	Woodstown	3	0	0	0	0	0	0	0	3	3,392
	State Police Agencies	1	1	0	0	0	. . .	. . .	. . .	. . .	. . .
	State Police:	. . .	. . .	. . .	. . .	. . .	. . .	. . .	. . .	. . .	. . .
	Hunterdon County	0	1	0	0	0	1	0	0	0	. . .
	Sussex County	1	0	0	0	0	1	0	0	0	. . .

[1] Agencies published in this table indicated that at least one hate crime incident occurred in their respective jurisdictions during the quarter(s) for which they submitted a report to the Hate Crime Statistics Program. Elipses indicate quarters for which agencies did not submit reports.

[2] Population figures are published only for the cities. The figures listed for the universities and colleges are student enrollment and were provided by the United States Department of Education for the 2009 school year, the most recent available. The enrollment figures include full-time and part-time students.

Table 94.   Hate Crime Incidents per Bias Motivation and Quarter, by State and Agency, 2010—*Continued*

State	Agency type/Agency name	Number of incidents per bias motivation					Number of incidents per quarter[1]				Popu-lation[2]
		Race	Religion	Sexual orient-ation	Ethnicity	Disability	1st quarter	2nd quarter	3rd quarter	4th quarter	
NEW MEXICO	**Total**	12	1	5	6	0	...	...	...	...	...
	Cities	9	1	5	6	0	...	...	...	...	...
	Albuquerque	9	1	5	6	0	10	4	6	1	545,389
	Metropolitan Counties	3	0	0	0	0	...	...	...	...	...
	Bernalillo	1	0	0	0	0	1	0	0	0	...
	San Juan	2	0	0	0	0	...	1	1	...	...
NEW YORK	**Total**	189	275	137	97	1	...	...	...	...	...
	Cities	142	208	102	74	0	...	...	...	...	...
	Albany	9	1	2	0	0	0	5	5	2	92,713
	Amherst Town	1	1	0	0	0	0	2	0	0	109,138
	Auburn	1	0	0	0	0	0	1	0	0	26,448
	Buchanan Village	1	0	0	0	0	0	1	0	0	2,223
	Buffalo	24	0	4	3	0	11	9	2	9	265,128
	Camden Village	1	0	0	0	0	0	1	0	0	2,219
	Canandaigua	1	0	0	0	0	1	0	0	0	11,054
	Cheektowaga Town	1	0	3	0	0	1	1	2	0	76,671
	Clarkstown Town	1	5	0	0	0	1	2	3	0	78,365
	Coeymans Town	0	0	1	0	0	0	0	0	1	7,939
	Cooperstown Village	1	0	0	0	0	0	1	0	0	1,849
	Cortland	2	0	0	0	0	1	1	0	0	17,930
	Crawford Town	2	0	0	0	0	1	0	0	1	9,492
	Deerpark Town	1	1	0	0	0	0	0	2	0	8,495
	Dewitt Town	0	1	0	0	0	0	1	0	0	21,202
	Dobbs Ferry Village	0	1	0	0	0	0	1	0	0	11,151
	East Greenbush Town	1	0	0	0	0	0	0	1	0	16,873
	Elmira Heights Village	0	0	1	0	0	1	0	0	0	3,849
	Evans Town	1	0	0	0	0	0	0	0	1	16,561
	Frankfort Village	1	0	0	0	0	1	...	...	...	2,308
	Geddes Town	0	1	0	0	0	1	0	0	0	10,269
	Goshen Village	1	0	0	0	0	0	1	0	0	5,553
	Greece Town	1	0	0	0	0	0	0	1	0	92,282
	Greenburgh Town	0	1	0	0	0	0	0	0	1	43,314
	Hamburg Town	0	0	0	2	0	2	0	0	0	43,642
	Hastings-on-Hudson Village	0	1	0	0	0	0	1	0	0	7,887
	Haverstraw Town	0	2	0	0	0	0	1	1	0	37,489
	Hempstead Village	0	0	0	1	0	1	0	0	0	53,443
	Hudson	0	1	1	0	0	0	1	1	0	6,691
	Hudson Falls Village	0	0	0	1	0	0	0	1	0	6,491
	Ithaca	3	0	1	0	0	2	0	0	2	29,791
	Jamestown	1	0	0	0	0	0	0	1	0	28,785
	Mechanicville	1	0	0	0	0	0	0	1	0	4,827
	Monticello Village	2	0	0	0	0	0	0	0	2	6,240
	Mount Vernon	1	0	0	0	0	0	0	1	0	68,081
	Newburgh	0	0	1	1	0	0	1	1	0	27,836
	New Rochelle	0	2	1	2	0	0	2	2	1	73,648
	New York	51	173	75	49	0	89	90	79	90	8,336,002
	Niagara Falls	1	0	1	0	0	0	0	2	0	50,321
	North Syracuse Village	0	0	0	1	0	0	0	1	0	6,477
	Norwich	2	0	0	0	0	1	0	1	0	6,778
	Oswego City	0	0	1	0	0	0	0	1	0	16,897
	Port Jervis	1	0	0	0	0	0	1	0	0	9,061
	Poughkeepsie	1	0	1	5	0	3	2	1	1	29,175
	Poughkeepsie Town	3	0	0	1	0	1	3	0	0	42,538
	Ramapo Town	1	6	0	0	0	1	2	1	3	77,482
	Rhinebeck Village	0	1	0	0	0	0	0	1	0	2,982
	Rochester	4	0	6	1	0	2	2	4	3	203,802
	Saranac Lake Village	1	0	0	0	0	0	1	0	0	4,689
	Saratoga Springs	2	0	0	0	0	0	1	0	1	29,080
	Saugerties Town	2	1	0	1	0	2	2	0	0	19,375
	Scarsdale Village	0	1	0	0	0	0	1	0	0	17,530
	Schenectady	4	0	0	0	0	0	2	1	1	60,751
	Shelter Island Town	0	0	0	1	0	0	1	0	0	2,555
	South Glens Falls Village	1	0	0	0	0	1	0	0	0	3,371
	South Nyack Village	0	1	0	0	0	0	0	1	0	3,306
	Spring Valley Village	1	2	1	3	0	0	2	1	4	24,965
	Suffern Village	0	0	1	0	0	0	1	0	0	10,917
	Ticonderoga Town	0	0	0	1	0	1	0	0	0	4,853
	Tonawanda	1	0	0	0	0	0	1	0	0	14,475
	Troy	1	0	0	0	0	0	0	1	0	46,861
	Washingtonville Village	1	0	0	0	0	1	0	0	0	6,122
	Waterloo Village	1	1	0	0	0	1	0	0	1	4,905
	West Seneca Town	1	0	0	1	0	0	1	0	1	43,061
	Yonkers	1	1	1	0	0	1	0	2	0	199,296
	Yorktown Town	2	3	0	0	0	1	1	1	2	37,684

[1] Agencies published in this table indicated that at least one hate crime incident occurred in their respective jurisdictions during the quarter(s) for which they submitted a report to the Hate Crime Statistics Program. Elipses indicate quarters for which agencies did not submit reports.

[2] Population figures are published only for the cities. The figures listed for the universities and colleges are student enrollment and were provided by the United States Department of Education for the 2009 school year, the most recent available. The enrollment figures include full-time and part-time students.

Table 94. Hate Crime Incidents per Bias Motivation and Quarter, by State and Agency, 2010—*Continued*

State	Agency type/Agency name	Number of incidents per bias motivation					Number of incidents per quarter[1]				Popu-lation[2]
		Race	Religion	Sexual orient-ation	Ethnicity	Disability	1st quarter	2nd quarter	3rd quarter	4th quarter	
NEW YORK— *Continued*											
	Universities and Colleges	5	11	11	2	0	...	...	...	...	...
	Cornell University	0	0	0	1	0	1	0	0	0	20,633
	State University of New York:	...	...	...	...	...	...	...	...	...	...
	Albany	0	1	0	0	0	0	0	0	1	18,020
	Stony Brook[3]	0	1	0	0	0	1	0	0	0	...
	State University of New York College:	...	...	...	...	...	...	...	...	...	...
	Buffalo	2	2	1	0	0	2	2	0	1	11,714
	Cortland	0	0	2	0	0	0	1	1	0	7,322
	New Paltz	0	0	1	0	0	0	0	0	1	7,907
	Oneonta	0	0	1	0	0	0	0	0	1	5,893
	Oswego	1	4	2	1	0	4	3	1	0	8,119
	Plattsburgh	1	2	2	0	0	0	1	0	4	6,453
	Potsdam	1	0	1	0	0	0	1	1	0	4,299
	Purchase	0	1	1	0	0	0	0	1	1	4,192
	Metropolitan Counties	30	51	23	17	1	...	...	...	...	...
	Broome	2	0	0	0	0	0	1	1	0	...
	Erie	2	0	0	0	0	0	1	1	0	...
	Monroe	2	0	0	0	0	0	2	0	0	...
	Nassau	11	39	8	3	0	10	22	18	11	...
	Orange	1	0	0	0	0	0	1	0	0	...
	Orleans	0	1	0	0	0	0	0	1	0	...
	Suffolk County Police Department	10	11	13	14	1	8	8	18	15	...
	Wayne	2	0	1	0	0	0	2	1	0	...
	Westchester Public Safety	0	0	1	0	0	0	0	0	1	...
	Nonmetropolitan Counties	0	1	0	1	0	...	...	...	...	...
	Chenango	0	0	0	1	0	0	0	1	0	...
	Sullivan	0	1	0	0	0	0	1	0	0	...
	State Police Agencies	4	0	1	2	0	...	...	...	...	...
	State Police:	...	...	...	...	...	...	...	...	...	...
	Broome County	0	0	1	0	0	0	1	0	0	...
	Clinton County	1	0	0	0	0	1	0	0	0	...
	Orange County	0	0	0	1	0	0	0	1	0	...
	Saratoga County	1	0	0	0	0	1	0	0	0	...
	Steuben County	1	0	0	1	0	0	2	0	0	...
	Westchester County	1	0	0	0	0	0	0	1	0	...
	Other Agencies	8	4	0	1	0	...	...	...	...	...
	New York City Metropolitan Transportation Authority	6	4	0	1	0	3	3	2	3	...
	State Park, Finger Lakes Region	1	0	0	0	0	0	0	1	0	...
	Suffolk County Parks	1	0	0	0	0	0	0	1	0	...
NORTH CAROLINA	**Total**	61	13	14	6	0	...	...	...	...	...
	Cities	42	10	10	3	0	...	...	...	...	...
	Albemarle	1	0	0	0	0	0	1	0	0	15,446
	Asheboro	1	0	0	0	0	1	0	0	0	25,017
	Asheville	5	3	0	0	0	0	2	1	5	77,067
	Black Mountain	3	0	0	0	0	0	1	0	2	7,953
	Carrboro	0	0	1	0	0	0	1	0	0	18,448
	Charlotte-Mecklenburg	6	5	2	1	0	1	4	8	1	797,733
	Creedmoor	2	0	0	0	0	1	0	1	0	3,898
	Durham	1	0	0	0	0	1	0	0	0	233,790
	Elkin	1	0	0	0	0	0	1	0	0	4,117
	Gastonia	3	0	0	0	0	0	2	1	0	73,533
	Greensboro	2	0	2	0	0	1	1	2	0	257,237
	Hickory	0	0	1	0	0	1	0	0	0	41,892
	High Point	2	0	0	0	0	0	0	2	0	105,278
	Jacksonville	1	0	0	0	0	0	1	0	0	82,254
	Kannapolis	0	0	1	0	0	0	1	0	0	44,084
	King	1	0	0	0	0	0	1	0	0	7,092
	Long View	1	0	0	0	0	0	1	0	0	5,005
	Matthews	0	0	1	0	0	0	0	0	1	27,989
	Mint Hill	1	0	0	0	0	0	1	0	0	21,032
	Mooresville	1	0	0	1	0	0	1	0	1	22,430
	Morganton	1	0	0	0	0	0	1	0	0	17,001
	New Bern	2	1	0	0	0	0	1	2	0	29,657
	Oxford	0	1	0	0	0	0	0	0	1	8,699
	Raleigh	1	0	0	0	0	0	0	0	1	419,700
	Roanoke Rapids	0	0	1	0	0	0	0	1	0	16,121
	Roxboro	1	0	0	0	0	0	0	1	0	8,683
	Salisbury	1	0	1	0	0	1	1	0	0	31,106
	Smithfield	1	0	0	0	0	0	0	0	1	13,448
	Sylva	1	0	0	1	0	1	1	0	0	2,460
	Wadesboro	1	0	0	0	0	0	0	0	1	5,145
	Wilson	1	0	0	0	0	0	0	1	0	49,134

[1] Agencies published in this table indicated that at least one hate crime incident occurred in their respective jurisdictions during the quarter(s) for which they submitted a report to the Hate Crime Statistics Program. Elipses indicate quarters for which agencies did not submit reports.

[2] Population figures are published only for the cities. The figures listed for the universities and colleges are student enrollment and were provided by the United States Department of Education for the 2009 school year, the most recent available. The enrollment figures include full-time and part-time students.

Table 94. Hate Crime Incidents per Bias Motivation and Quarter, by State and Agency, 2010—*Continued*

State	Agency type/Agency name	Number of incidents per bias motivation					Number of incidents per quarter[1]				Popu-lation[2]
		Race	Religion	Sexual orient-ation	Ethnicity	Disability	1st quarter	2nd quarter	3rd quarter	4th quarter	
NORTH CAROLINA— *Continued*											
	Universities and Colleges	1	0	0	1	0	...	...	...	...	...
	North Carolina State University, Raleigh	1	0	0	1	0	0	1	1	0	33,819
	Metropolitan Counties	14	3	3	1	0	...	...	...	...	...
	Buncombe	2	1	0	0	0	0	0	1	2	...
	Caldwell	2	0	0	0	0	0	0	1	1	...
	Catawba	1	0	0	0	0	0	0	1	0	...
	Chatham	0	1	0	0	0	0	1	0	0	...
	Davie	1	0	0	0	0	0	1	0	0	...
	Forsyth	1	1	2	0	0	1	1	1	1	...
	Gaston County Police Department	2	0	0	1	0	2	0	1	0	...
	Guilford	3	0	1	0	0	2	2	0	0	...
	Henderson	1	0	0	0	0	0	0	0	1	...
	Person	1	0	0	0	0	0	1	0	0	...
	Nonmetropolitan Counties	4	0	1	0	0	...	...	...	...	...
	Jackson	1	0	0	0	0	0	1	0	0	...
	Rutherford	1	0	1	0	0	0	0	0	2	...
	Transylvania	2	0	0	0	0	2	0	0	0	...
	Other Agencies	0	0	0	1	0	...	...	...	...	...
	Raleigh-Durham International Airport	0	0	0	1	0	0	1	0	0	
NORTH DAKOTA......	**Total**	3	1	3	1	0	...	...	...	...	...
	Cities	3	1	3	1	0	...	...	...	...	...
	Bismarck	0	0	1	0	0	0	0	1	0	64,142
	Devils Lake	1	0	1	0	0	0	1	1	0	6,917
	Dickinson	0	1	0	0	0	0	0	1	0	16,917
	Fargo	0	0	1	0	0	0	0	0	1	99,694
	Grand Forks	1	0	0	0	0	0	0	0	1	53,382
	Mandan	1	0	0	0	0	0	0	1	0	19,134
	Watford City	0	0	0	1	0	0	0	1	0	1,450
OHIO	**Total**	147	37	37	23	3	...	...	...	...	...
	Cities	129	33	27	20	2	...	...	...	...	...
	Akron	7	0	3	3	0	1	4	6	2	205,760
	Alliance	1	0	0	0	0	...	...	...	1	22,467
	Athens	1	0	0	1	0	2	0	0	0	22,161
	Bath Township, Summit County	1	0	0	0	0	0	0	1	0	10,214
	Boardman	0	3	1	0	0	0	4	0	0	38,524
	Bowling Green	0	2	0	0	0	1	0	0	1	28,617
	Brookfield Township	2	0	0	0	0	0	1	0	1	9,310
	Canal Fulton	1	0	0	0	0	0	0	1	0	5,037
	Chillicothe	2	0	0	0	0	1	0	0	1	22,143
	Cincinnati	8	0	1	1	0	1	1	4	4	332,365
	Cleveland	12	0	1	1	0	4	2	6	2	426,042
	Columbus	25	5	10	6	0	14	13	15	4	772,974
	Cortland	1	0	0	0	0	0	1	0	0	6,257
	Dayton	2	1	0	2	0	1	2	1	1	152,319
	Englewood	1	0	1	0	0	0	1	1	0	12,647
	Fairfield Township	0	1	0	0	0	0	0	0	1	17,538
	Findlay	2	1	0	0	0	0	3	0	0	36,324
	Fostoria	3	5	0	0	0	0	7	1	0	12,741
	Franklin	3	0	0	0	0	0	1	0	2	13,260
	Fremont	0	0	0	1	0	0	1	0	0	16,305
	Gahanna[4]	1	0	1	0	0	2	0	0	0	34,335
	Grove City	2	1	0	0	0	1	2	0	0	35,339
	Hamilton	1	0	0	0	0	0	0	0	1	62,805
	Heath	1	0	0	0	0	1	0	0	0	8,950
	Hubbard	0	0	1	0	0	0	0	0	1	7,549
	Huber Heights	0	0	0	1	0	1	0	0	0	36,736
	Hudson	1	0	0	0	0	0	0	0	1	23,023
	Jackson Township, Stark County	0	0	0	1	0	1	0	0	0	40,877
	Kettering	2	1	0	0	0	1	1	0	1	52,931
	Lakewood	2	0	0	0	0	1	0	0	1	49,526
	Lorain	5	0	1	0	0	0	3	2	1	70,242
	Madison Township, Lake County	0	1	0	0	0	0	1	0	0	17,187
	Mansfield	11	0	2	1	0	1	6	3	4	49,069
	Marion	1	0	0	0	0	1	0	0	0	35,540
	Mason	0	1	0	0	0	1	0	0	0	30,805
	Massillon	0	1	1	0	0	2	0	0	0	32,768
	Miamisburg	0	0	1	0	0	0	0	1	0	19,679
	Miami Township, Montgomery County	2	1	0	0	0	1	0	1	1	24,822
	Montgomery	1	1	0	0	0	0	1	0	1	10,606
	Montpelier	0	0	0	0	1	0	0	0	1	3,928
	New Albany	1	0	0	0	0	0	1	0	0	7,766
	Niles	0	3	0	0	1	2	2	0	0	18,906
	Norwood	0	1	0	0	0	0	0	0	1	20,240

[1] Agencies published in this table indicated that at least one hate crime incident occurred in their respective jurisdictions during the quarter(s) for which they submitted a report to the Hate Crime Statistics Program. Elipses indicate quarters for which agencies did not submit reports.

[2] Population figures are published only for the cities. The figures listed for the universities and colleges are student enrollment and were provided by the United States Department of Education for the 2009 school year, the most recent available. The enrollment figures include full-time and part-time students.

Table 94.   Hate Crime Incidents per Bias Motivation and Quarter, by State and Agency, 2010—*Continued*

State	Agency type/Agency name	Number of incidents per bias motivation					Number of incidents per quarter[1]				Popu-lation[2]
		Race	Religion	Sexual orient-ation	Ethnicity	Disability	1st quarter	2nd quarter	3rd quarter	4th quarter	
OHIO— *Continued*											
	Ottawa Hills	1	0	0	0	0	0	0	1	0	4,578
	Parma	1	0	0	0	0	0	1	0	0	76,303
	Perry Township, Stark County	1	0	0	0	0	0	1	0		27,930
	Pickerington	3	1	0	0	0	1	1	2	0	18,801
	Piqua	0	0	1	0	0	0	0	0	1	20,478
	Portsmouth	2	0	1	0	0	1	0	1	1	20,254
	Powell	0	1	0	0	0	0	1	0	0	14,121
	Reynoldsburg	2	1	0	0	0	0	0	3	0	34,208
	Salem	1	0	0	1	0	0	0	1	1	11,676
	Sharonville	2	0	0	0	0	0	1	1	0	13,337
	South Euclid	2	0	0	0	0	1	1	0	0	20,750
	Springdale	1	0	0	0	0	0	1	0	0	10,436
	Springfield Township, Hamilton County	2	0	0	0	0	0	1	1	0	39,931
	Stow	1	0	0	0	0	0	0	0	1	33,938
	Trotwood	0	1	0	0	0	0	0	0	1	25,685
	Washington Court House	1	0	0	0	0	0	0	0	1	13,468
	Weathersfield	1	0	0	0	0	0	0	1	0	8,071
	Westerville	0	0	1	1	0	1	0	0	1	36,966
	Whitehall	1	0	0	0	0	0	1	0	0	18,332
	Wilmington	2	0	0	0	0	0	1	0	1	12,578
	Youngstown	2	0	0	0	0	1	0	0	1	71,380
	Universities and Colleges	3	2	2	0	0	...	...	...	...	...
	Capital University	0	1	0	0	0	0	0	0	1	3,540
	Ohio State University, Columbus	1	0	0	0	0	0	1	0	0	55,014
	Wright State University	2	1	2	0	0	5	0	0	0	17,558
	Metropolitan Counties	8	1	5	2	0	...	...	...	...	...
	Butler	1	0	2	1	0	1	0	1	2	...
	Delaware	1	0	0	0	0	1	0	0	0	...
	Franklin	1	0	0	0	0	0	1	...	...	...
	Geauga	0	1	0	0	0	0	0	1	0	...
	Licking	0	0	1	0	0	0	1	0	0	...
	Montgomery	3	0	1	0	0	0	0	4	0	...
	Pickaway	0	0	0	1	0	0	0	1	0	...
	Stark	1	0	1	0	0	0	1	0	1	...
	Summit	1	0	0	0	0	1	0	0	0	...
	Nonmetropolitan Counties	7	1	3	1	1	...	...	...	...	...
	Ashland	0	1	0	0	0	0	0	1	0	...
	Clinton	1	0	0	0	0	0	1	0	0	...
	Coshocton	1	0	1	0	0	0	1	1	0	...
	Fayette	1	0	2	0	0	0	2	1	0	...
	Putnam	1	0	0	0	0	0	1	0	0	...
	Ross	3	0	0	0	1	2	0	2	0	...
	Shelby	0	0	0	1	0	...	0	0	1	...
OKLAHOMA.............	**Total**	32	3	10	4	0	...	...	...	...	...
	Cities	30	3	10	4	0	...	...	...	...	...
	Ada	2	0	0	0	0	2	0	0	0	17,298
	Apache	0	0	1	0	0	0	1	0	0	1,540
	Atoka	1	0	0	0	0	0	0	1	0	3,092
	Bixby	1	0	0	0	0	1	0	0	0	22,683
	Blackwell	1	0	0	0	0	1	0	0	0	7,238
	Chickasha	0	0	0	1	0	0	1	0	0	17,507
	Choctaw	2	0	0	0	0	1	0	1	0	11,942
	Coweta	0	0	2	0	0	1	0	1	0	9,248
	Edmond	1	1	0	0	0	2	0	0	0	83,337
	Heavener	0	0	0	1	0	0	0	0	1	3,254
	Hinton	1	0	0	0	0	1	0	0	0	3,746
	Moore	0	0	1	0	0	0	0	0	1	55,788
	Norman	4	1	2	0	0	0	2	3	2	111,534
	Oklahoma City	8	1	4	1	0	3	3	2	6	571,865
	Okmulgee	1	0	0	0	0	1	0	0	0	12,648
	Perkins	1	0	0	0	0	1	0	0	0	2,680
	Sallisaw	1	0	0	0	0	0	1	0	0	8,985
	The Village	1	0	0	0	0	1	0	0	0	9,923
	Tulsa	2	0	0	1	0	1	0	2	0	393,412
	Valliant	1	0	0	0	0	0	0	0	1	743
	Warr Acres	1	0	0	0	0	0	0	1	0	9,579
	Yukon	1	0	0	0	0	1	0	0	0	24,023
	Universities and Colleges	1	0	0	0	0	...	...	...	...	...
	Tulsa Community College	1	0	0	0	0	1	0	0	0	19,730
	Metropolitan Counties	1	0	0	0	0	...	...	...	...	...
	Tulsa	1	0	0	0	0	0	1	0	0	...

[1] Agencies published in this table indicated that at least one hate crime incident occurred in their respective jurisdictions during the quarter(s) for which they submitted a report to the Hate Crime Statistics Program. Elipses indicate quarters for which agencies did not submit reports.

[2] Population figures are published only for the cities. The figures listed for the universities and colleges are student enrollment and were provided by the United States Department of Education for the 2009 school year, the most recent available. The enrollment figures include full-time and part-time students.

Table 94.   Hate Crime Incidents per Bias Motivation and Quarter, by State and Agency, 2010—*Continued*

State	Agency type/Agency name	Number of incidents per bias motivation					Number of incidents per quarter[1]				Popu-lation[2]
		Race	Religion	Sexual orient-ation	Ethnicity	Disability	1st quarter	2nd quarter	3rd quarter	4th quarter	
OREGON......................	**Total**	57	18	33	25	1	...	...	...	...	...
	Cities	47	17	27	21	1	...	...	...	...	
	Albany	0	0	1	0	0	...	...	1	...	48,777
	Beaverton	8	0	0	0	0	2	3	1	2	93,993
	Bend	0	0	0	1	0	1	0	0	0	79,556
	Central Point	0	1	0	0	0	1	0	0	0	16,819
	Corvallis	2	0	0	3	0	4	0	0	1	51,276
	Eugene	8	9	8	4	1	14	8	8	...	153,269
	Lake Oswego	0	0	0	1	0	...	...	...	1	37,349
	Lebanon	1	1	1	0	0	0	1	2	0	16,084
	McMinnville	0	0	0	1	0	0	0	1	0	31,748
	Medford	1	0	0	0	0	1	0	0	0	73,525
	Newport	0	0	1	0	0	1	0	0	0	9,877
	Portland	11	2	13	3	0	6	10	10	3	564,392
	Redmond	0	0	1	1	0	0	1	0	1	25,480
	Roseburg	0	1	0	0	0	1	0	0	0	20,169
	Salem	2	1	2	1	0	3	1	1	1	155,820
	Seaside	1	0	0	0	0	...	...	1		6,157
	Springfield	6	2	0	4	0	2	6	0	4	57,081
	Sutherlin	1	0	0	0	0	0	0	0	1	7,064
	Tigard	6	0	0	1	0	1	2	2	2	49,466
	Woodburn	0	0	0	1	0	1	0	0	0	23,032
	Metropolitan Counties	6	0	2	2	0	...	...	...	...	...
	Benton	1	0	0	0	0	1	0	0	0	...
	Clackamas	3	0	0	0	0	3	...	...	...	...
	Deschutes	0	0	1	0	0	0	0	0	1	...
	Lane	1	0	1	2	0	4	...	...	...	...
	Yamhill	1	0	0	0	0	0	0	1	0	...
	Nonmetropolitan Counties	4	1	4	2	0	...	...	...	...	...
	Douglas	2	0	1	0	0	2	1	0	0	...
	Lincoln	2	1	0	0	0	2	1	0	0	...
	Tillamook	0	0	1	0	0	0	0	1	0	...
	Umatilla	0	0	1	2	0	0	1	2	0	...
	Union	0	0	1	0	0	0	1	0	0	...
PENNSYLVANIA	**Total**	33	8	10	6	0	...	...	...	...	...
	Cities	23	7	6	5	0	...	...	...	...	...
	Abington Township	0	1	0	0	0	0	0	0	1	54,235
	Ambler	1	0	0	0	0	1	0	0	0	6,228
	Avoca	0	0	0	1	0	1	0	0	0	2,659
	Chester	1	0	0	0	0	1	0	0	0	37,308
	Corry	1	0	0	0	0	1	0	0	0	6,315
	East Hempfield Township	0	2	0	0	0	0	1	1	0	24,035
	Harrisburg	1	1	1	0	0	1	0	0	2	47,509
	Hastings	1	0	0	0	0	0	0	1	0	1,285
	Johnstown	2	0	0	0	0	0	1	1	0	22,900
	Lancaster	1	0	0	0	0	...	1	0	0	55,582
	Lower Paxton Township	1	0	0	0	0	0	0	0	1	46,144
	Old Forge	1	0	0	0	0	0	1	0	0	8,525
	Paxtang	1	0	0	0	0	1	0	0	0	1,493
	Philadelphia	2	2	2	2	0	4	2	2	0	1,558,378
	Pine Grove	1	0	0	0	0	0	1	0		2,036
	Pittsburgh	6	1	2	0	0	0	2	3	4	312,737
	Reading	0	0	1	0	0	0	0	0	1	81,370
	Shenandoah	1	0	0	0	0	1	0	0	0	5,121
	South Park Township	1	0	0	0	0	0	0	0	1	14,057
	State College	0	0	0	2	0	0	0	1	1	54,649
	West Hills Regional	1	0	0	0	0	0	0	1	0	10,549
	Universities and Colleges	2	1	3	0	0	...	...	...	...	...
	Pennsylvania State University, University Park	1	1	2	0	0	0	1	2	1	45,185
	West Chester University	1	0	1	0	0	0	0	2	0	14,211
	State Police Agencies	8	0	1	1	0	...	...	...	...	...
	State Police:	...	...	...	...	...	...	...	...	...	...
	Adams County	0	0	0	1	0	0	0	0	1	...
	Chester County	1	0	0	0	0	0	0	0	1	...
	Elk County	2	0	0	0	0	0	0	2		...
	Juniata County	1	0	0	0	0	1	0	0	0	...
	Lawrence County	0	0	1	0	0	0	0	1	0	...
	Monroe County	1	0	0	0	0	0	0	1	0	...
	Potter County	1	0	0	0	0	0	0	0	1	...
	Washington County	2	0	0	0	0	0	1	1	0	...
RHODE ISLAND........	**Total**	10	5	3	1	1	...	...	...	...	...
	Cities	5	3	3	1	1	...	...	...	...	...
	Burrillville	0	0	0	0	1	0	0	0	1	16,637
	Charlestown	0	0	1	0	0	0	0	0	1	8,093

[1] Agencies published in this table indicated that at least one hate crime incident occurred in their respective jurisdictions during the quarter(s) for which they submitted a report to the Hate Crime Statistics Program. Elipses indicate quarters for which agencies did not submit reports.

[2] Population figures are published only for the cities. The figures listed for the universities and colleges are student enrollment and were provided by the United States Department of Education for the 2009 school year, the most recent available. The enrollment figures include full-time and part-time students.

Table 94. Hate Crime Incidents per Bias Motivation and Quarter, by State and Agency, 2010—*Continued*

State	Agency type/Agency name	Number of incidents per bias motivation					Number of incidents per quarter[1]				Popu-lation[2]
		Race	Religion	Sexual orient-ation	Ethnicity	Disability	1st quarter	2nd quarter	3rd quarter	4th quarter	
RHODE ISLAND— *Continued*											
	Coventry	1	0	0	0	0	1	0	0	0	35,021
	East Providence	1	0	0	1	0	1	0	0	1	48,507
	Hopkinton	0	0	1	0	0	1	0	0	0	8,021
	Newport	0	2	0	0	0	0	1	1	0	23,173
	Pawtucket	1	1	1	0	0	1	1	1	0	71,782
	Providence	1	0	0	0	0	0	0	0	1	171,565
	West Warwick	1	0	0	0	0	0	0	0	1	29,251
	Universities and Colleges	5	2	0	0	0	...	...	...	...	...
	Brown University	0	1	0	0	0	0	1	0	0	8,574
	University of Rhode Island	5	1	0	0	0	1	2	0	3	16,389
SOUTH CAROLINA...	**Total**	54	19	29	5	2	...	...	...	...	...
	Cities	22	16	23	1	1	...	...	...	...	...
	Aiken	0	0	1	0	0	0	0	1	0	29,875
	Anderson	0	0	1	0	0	0	0	0	1	27,325
	Andrews	0	0	3	0	0	2	1	0	0	2,965
	Batesburg-Leesville	0	0	1	0	0	0	0	1	0	5,670
	Beaufort	2	0	0	0	0	1	1	0	0	12,076
	Bennettsville	0	1	0	0	0	1	0	0	0	8,941
	Cayce	4	0	0	0	0	2	1	0	1	13,161
	Charleston	0	1	0	0	0	0	1	0	0	117,551
	Chester	2	0	0	0	0	0	0	0	2	5,915
	Columbia	4	0	4	0	0	1	2	2	3	130,498
	Florence	0	3	0	0	0	0	1	0	2	32,273
	Goose Creek	2	0	0	0	0	0	2	0	0	39,955
	Greeleyville	0	0	1	0	0	0	0	0	1	369
	Hardeeville	1	0	0	0	0	1	0	0	0	3,795
	Marion	2	0	0	0	0	0	0	2	0	6,649
	Mauldin	1	0	1	0	0	1	1	0	0	23,218
	Mount Pleasant	1	0	0	0	0	0	1	0	0	68,555
	Myrtle Beach	0	3	1	1	0	1	3	1	0	32,907
	Ninety Six	0	0	1	0	0	0	0	0	1	1,951
	North Charleston	0	0	1	0	0	0	0	1	0	99,447
	Pageland	0	0	2	0	0	0	0	2	0	2,508
	Prosperity	0	0	2	0	0	0	0	2	0	1,063
	Rock Hill	0	0	1	0	0	0	0	0	1	71,456
	Spartanburg	0	0	1	0	0	0	1	0	0	40,448
	St. George	1	0	0	0	0	0	1	0	0	2,156
	Sumter	0	0	0	0	1	1	0	0	0	38,228
	Walterboro	0	8	1	0	0	3	3	2	1	5,841
	Williston	0	0	1	0	0	0	0	0	1	3,121
	York	2	0	0	0	0	1	0	0	1	8,327
	Universities and Colleges	5	0	0	0	0	...	...	...	...	...
	Clemson University	1	0	0	0	0	0	1	0	0	19,111
	College of Charleston	4	0	0	0	0	4	0	0	0	11,772
	Metropolitan Counties	15	3	3	3	1	...	...	...	...	...
	Anderson	6	0	1	1	0	3	1	2	2	...
	Berkeley	1	0	0	0	0	1	0	0	0	...
	Charleston	2	0	0	0	0	0	1	0	1	...
	Horry County Police Department	4	1	0	1	0	2	4	0	0	...
	Laurens	0	1	0	0	0	0	1	0	0	...
	Pickens	0	0	0	1	0	0	0	1	0	...
	Richland	1	1	2	0	0	1	1	2	0	...
	Spartanburg	1	0	0	0	1	1	0	1	0	...
	Nonmetropolitan Counties	12	0	3	1	0	...	...	...	...	...
	Chesterfield	1	0	2	0	0	3	0	0	0	...
	Colleton	3	0	0	0	0	0	2	1	0	...
	Dillon	1	0	0	0	0	0	1	0	0	...
	Greenwood	1	0	0	0	0	0	0	1	0	...
	Hampton	4	0	0	0	0	1	2	1	0	...
	Oconee	0	0	0	1	0	0	0	0	1	...
	Union	1	0	1	0	0	0	1	1	0	...
	Williamsburg	1	0	0	0	0	0	0	0	1	...
SOUTH DAKOTA.......	**Total**	27	1	11	12	0	...	...	...	...	...
	Cities	26	1	11	12	0	...	...	...	...	...
	Belle Fourche	0	0	0	1	0	0	1	0	0	4,972
	Box Elder	0	0	1	0	0	0	0	0	1	4,340
	Flandreau	0	0	1	0	0	0	0	0	1	2,171
	Freeman	0	0	0	1	0	0	0	1	0	1,157
	Pierre	1	0	0	3	0	2	0	2	0	14,003
	Rapid City	3	0	2	0	0	1	1	1	2	67,436
	Sioux Falls	15	1	6	5	0	8	6	7	6	160,679
	Spearfish	0	0	1	0	0	0	1	0	0	10,057
	Tea	5	0	0	1	0	0	0	1	5	5,058
	Watertown	2	0	0	1	0	1	1	1	0	20,232

[1] Agencies published in this table indicated that at least one hate crime incident occurred in their respective jurisdictions during the quarter(s) for which they submitted a report to the Hate Crime Statistics Program. Elipses indicate quarters for which agencies did not submit reports.

[2] Population figures are published only for the cities. The figures listed for the universities and colleges are student enrollment and were provided by the United States Department of Education for the 2009 school year, the most recent available. The enrollment figures include full-time and part-time students.

Table 94.   Hate Crime Incidents per Bias Motivation and Quarter, by State and Agency, 2010—*Continued*

State	Agency type/Agency name	Number of incidents per bias motivation					Number of incidents per quarter[1]				Popu-lation[2]
		Race	Religion	Sexual orient-ation	Ethnicity	Disability	1st quarter	2nd quarter	3rd quarter	4th quarter	
SOUTH DAKOTA— *Continued*											
	Metropolitan Counties	1	0	0	0	0	...	...	...	...	...
	Minnehaha	1	0	0	0	0	0	1	0	0	...
TENNESSEE	**Total**	95	11	25	10	6	...	...	...	...	...
	Cities	70	5	23	10	6	...	...	...	...	...
	Alcoa	1	0	0	0	0	1	0	0	0	8,775
	Bolivar	2	0	0	0	0	0	2	0	0	5,516
	Brownsville	2	0	0	0	0	0	0	2	0	10,138
	Chattanooga	0	1	0	1	3	0	1	2	2	172,460
	Clarksville	1	0	0	0	0	0	0	1	0	126,548
	Cleveland	2	0	2	0	0	2	0	1	1	40,452
	Collierville	1	0	1	0	0	1	0	0	1	40,286
	Columbia	3	0	0	1	0	3	0	0	1	35,364
	Cookeville	3	0	1	1	0	1	0	3	1	30,179
	Covington	1	0	0	0	0	0	0	0	1	9,396
	Cross Plains	1	0	0	0	0	1	0	0	0	1,728
	Dickson	2	0	4	0	0	0	3	3	0	14,100
	Dyersburg	0	0	1	0	0	0	1	0	0	17,104
	Franklin	1	0	0	0	0	0	0	1	0	62,127
	Gallatin	1	0	0	0	0	0	1	0	0	31,229
	Germantown	0	0	0	0	1	1	0	0	0	41,347
	Greenbrier	0	0	3	0	0	0	0	3	0	6,899
	Hendersonville	1	0	1	0	0	0	1	1	0	49,010
	Jackson	0	1	0	0	0	0	0	1	0	63,969
	Johnson City	2	0	0	1	0	2	0	1	0	63,750
	Kingsport	2	0	1	0	0	0	1	0	2	44,587
	Lawrenceburg	1	0	0	0	0	1	0	0	0	10,877
	Lexington	9	0	0	0	0	7	1	0	1	7,876
	Madisonville	1	0	0	0	0	0	0	0	1	4,761
	Manchester	0	0	1	0	0	0	0	0	1	10,210
	Memphis	6	2	4	2	1	1	2	7	5	673,650
	Morristown	3	0	0	0	0	0	2	0	1	28,147
	Mount Carmel	0	0	1	0	0	0	0	0	1	5,525
	Murfreesboro	2	0	1	0	0	1	2	0	0	109,199
	Nashville	6	0	1	1	0	0	3	4	1	616,366
	Oakland	1	0	0	0	0	0	0	1	0	5,878
	Oak Ridge	0	1	0	0	0	0	0	1	0	27,728
	Pigeon Forge	0	0	1	0	0	0	0	1	0	6,532
	Red Bank	4	0	0	0	0	1	1	1	1	11,680
	Rockwood	0	0	0	0	1	0	1	0	0	5,536
	Shelbyville	1	0	0	0	0	1	0	0	0	20,527
	Smithville	1	0	0	0	0	0	0	0	1	4,465
	Smyrna	3	0	0	0	0	1	1	0	1	41,071
	Soddy-Daisy	2	0	0	0	0	0	1	0	1	12,967
	Spring Hill	3	0	0	1	0	0	3	1	0	30,829
	Union City	1	0	0	0	0	0	0	1	0	10,486
	Westmoreland	0	0	0	2	0	0	0	0	2	2,243
	Universities and Colleges	3	0	0	0	0	...	...	...	...	...
	Middle Tennessee State University	2	0	0	0	0	2	0	0	0	25,188
	Vanderbilt University	1	0	0	0	0	0	0	1	0	12,506
	Metropolitan Counties	16	5	2	0	0	...	...	...	...	...
	Anderson	1	0	0	0	0	0	0	0	1	...
	Bradley	0	0	1	0	0	0	0	0	1	...
	Cheatham	1	0	0	0	0	0	0	0	1	...
	Hamblen	0	0	1	0	0	0	1	0	0	...
	Hamilton	7	1	0	0	0	1	3	1	3	...
	Knox	0	1	0	0	0	1	0	0	0	...
	Rutherford	1	2	0	0	0	1	1	0	1	...
	Stewart	1	1	0	0	0	2	0	0	0	...
	Sumner	4	0	0	0	0	0	3	0	1	...
	Washington	1	0	0	0	0	0	0	1	0	...
	Nonmetropolitan Counties	5	1	0	0	0	...	...	...	...	...
	Decatur	4	0	0	0	0	0	0	0	4	...
	Lewis	0	1	0	0	0	0	0	1	0	...
	Maury	1	0	0	0	0	0	0	1	0	...
	Other Agencies	1	0	0	0	0	...	...	...	...	...
	Memphis International Airport	1	0	0	0	0	0	0	1	0	...
TEXAS	**Total**	85	19	39	30	1	...	...	...	...	...
	Cities	75	19	34	28	1	...	...	...	...	...
	Abilene	1	0	0	0	0	1	0	0	0	116,938
	Allen	0	0	0	1	0	0	1	0	0	89,459
	Arlington	0	1	0	2	0	0	2	1	0	383,715
	Austin	0	1	3	1	0	2	1	1	1	796,310
	Beaumont	2	1	0	0	0	1	1	1	0	109,430

[1] Agencies published in this table indicated that at least one hate crime incident occurred in their respective jurisdictions during the quarter(s) for which they submitted a report to the Hate Crime Statistics Program. Elipses indicate quarters for which agencies did not submit reports.

[2] Population figures are published only for the cities. The figures listed for the universities and colleges are student enrollment and were provided by the United States Department of Education for the 2009 school year, the most recent available. The enrollment figures include full-time and part-time students.

Table 94. Hate Crime Incidents per Bias Motivation and Quarter, by State and Agency, 2010—*Continued*

State	Agency type/Agency name	Number of incidents per bias motivation					Number of incidents per quarter[1]				Popu-lation[2]
		Race	Religion	Sexual orient-ation	Ethnicity	Disability	1st quarter	2nd quarter	3rd quarter	4th quarter	
TEXAS — *Continued*											
	Bedford	3	0	0	0	0	1	1	1	0	49,993
	Bryan	2	0	0	0	0	1	0	0	1	75,350
	Cedar Park	1	0	0	0	0	0	0	0	1	70,363
	Center	1	0	0	0	0	0	0	0	1	5,769
	Collinsville	0	0	0	1	0	0	1	0	0	1,539
	Corpus Christi	1	1	1	0	0	2	1	0	0	287,559
	Dallas	2	3	5	2	0	8	1	3	0	1,306,775
	Denton	1	0	1	0	0	1	0	1	0	127,251
	Edgewood	0	0	0	1	0	0	1	0	0	1,429
	Elgin	1	0	0	0	0	1	0	0	0	10,437
	El Paso	3	0	2	0	0	0	2	1	2	624,322
	Floydada	1	0	0	0	0	1	0	0	0	3,003
	Fort Worth	5	1	5	3	0	0	5	5	4	746,433
	Gainesville	1	0	0	0	0	0	1	0	0	16,558
	Galveston	3	0	0	1	0	1	0	2	1	55,835
	Garland	1	0	0	0	1	0	0	0	2	221,921
	Grapevine	2	0	0	2	0	0	3	1	0	51,869
	Henderson	1	0	0	0	0	0	0	0	1	11,652
	Houston	5	0	6	2	0	2	3	5	3	2,280,859
	Hurst	1	0	0	0	0	0	0	1	0	39,147
	Hutto	1	0	0	0	0	0	1	0	0	17,962
	Lake Jackson	0	0	1	0	0	1	0	0	0	29,037
	La Porte	0	0	1	0	0	1	0	0	0	34,304
	Lewisville	0	2	0	0	0	0	0	2	0	107,968
	Longview	1	0	0	0	0	0	0	0	1	78,319
	McKinney	3	0	1	3	0	2	2	0	3	138,306
	Missouri City	0	1	0	0	0	0	0	1	0	77,181
	New Braunfels	0	0	0	1	0	0	1	0	0	57,796
	North Richland Hills	2	0	1	0	0	1	0	0	2	66,897
	Orange	1	0	0	0	0	1	0	0	0	19,452
	Pearland	4	0	1	1	0	1	4	0	1	91,679
	Plano	0	3	0	1	0	0	4	0	0	278,244
	Richland Hills	1	0	0	0	0	0	1	0	0	8,196
	Round Rock	1	0	0	1	0	0	1	1	0	111,099
	Rowlett	1	1	1	1	0	0	1	2	1	57,852
	Sachse	0	1	0	0	0	0	1	0	0	20,548
	San Angelo	0	0	2	0	0	1	0	0	1	92,234
	San Antonio	2	0	2	1	0	3	2	0	0	1,392,198
	San Marcos	1	0	0	0	0	0	0	1	0	55,100
	Schertz	0	0	1	0	0	0	1	0	0	33,451
	Sherman	0	1	0	0	0	1	0	0	0	38,623
	Sweetwater	2	0	0	2	0	0	2	2	0	10,607
	Terrell	3	0	0	0	0	0	2	1	0	20,241
	Thorndale	1	0	0	0	0	0	0	0	1	1,308
	Tomball	2	0	0	0	0	2	0	0	0	10,272
	Tyler	2	0	0	0	0	0	0	2	0	100,125
	Universal City	0	0	0	1	0	0	0	0	1	18,511
	Victoria	0	1	0	0	0	1	0	0	0	63,215
	Vidor	3	0	0	0	0	2	0	1	0	10,611
	Wichita Falls	5	1	0	0	0	1	2	1	2	100,716
	Wylie	1	0	0	0	0	0	1	0	0	43,508
	Universities and Colleges	5	0	1	0	0	...	...	...	...	...
	Houston Community College	1	0	0	0	0	0	0	0	1	54,942
	Texas A&M University, College Station	3	0	0	0	0	0	2	1	0	48,702
	University of Texas:										
	Austin	1	0	0	0	0	0	0	0	1	50,995
	Permian Basin	0	0	1	0	0	0	1	0	0	3,546
	Metropolitan Counties	4	0	4	1	0	...	...	...	...	...
	Comal	0	0	1	0	0	0	0	1	0	...
	Harris	1	0	1	0	0	0	0	1	1	...
	Kaufman	2	0	2	0	0	0	2	2	0	...
	Travis	1	0	0	0	0	1	0	0	0	...
	Wise	0	0	0	1	0	1	0	0	0	...
	Other Agencies	1	0	0	1	0	...	...	...	...	...
	Dallas-Fort Worth International Airport	1	0	0	1	0	0	0	2	0	...
UTAH	**Total**	24	18	16	5	0	...	...	...	...	...
	Cities	19	15	11	5	0	...	...	...	...	...
	Bluffdale	0	1	1	0	0	...	0	1	1	8,246
	Bountiful	3	1	0	1	0	2	1	0	2	43,485
	Draper	2	1	0	0	0	1	1	1	0	44,259
	Farmington	0	0	0	1	0	0	1	0	0	17,977
	Layton	1	3	1	0	0	1	1	2	1	65,610
	Midvale	0	1	0	0	0	0	0	0	1	28,739

[1] Agencies published in this table indicated that at least one hate crime incident occurred in their respective jurisdictions during the quarter(s) for which they submitted a report to the Hate Crime Statistics Program. Elipses indicate quarters for which agencies did not submit reports.

[2] Population figures are published only for the cities. The figures listed for the universities and colleges are student enrollment and were provided by the United States Department of Education for the 2009 school year, the most recent available. The enrollment figures include full-time and part-time students.

Table 94.   Hate Crime Incidents per Bias Motivation and Quarter, by State and Agency, 2010—*Continued*

State	Agency type/Agency name	Number of incidents per bias motivation					Number of incidents per quarter[1]				Popu-lation[2]
		Race	Religion	Sexual orient-ation	Ethnicity	Disability	1st quarter	2nd quarter	3rd quarter	4th quarter	
UTAH— *Continued*											
	Murray	2	1	1	1	0	0	1	3	1	45,305
	Ogden	0	0	1	0	0	0	1	0	0	81,431
	Pleasant Grove	1	0	0	0	0	0	1	0	0	35,589
	Price	1	0	0	0	0	0	0	1	0	7,979
	Provo	0	1	1	0	0	1	1	0	0	117,734
	Salt Lake City	1	0	1	0	0	0	1	1	0	177,873
	Sandy	1	0	0	0	0	1	0	0	0	95,173
	Saratoga Springs	1	0	0	0	0	1	0	0	0	20,490
	South Jordan	0	1	0	0	0	0	1	0	0	56,502
	South Salt Lake	0	2	1	0	0	0	1	1	1	21,107
	St. George	1	0	0	0	0	0	0	1	0	73,086
	Syracuse	0	0	1	0	0	1	0	0	0	23,780
	Tooele	1	2	3	1	0	1	4	2	0	30,663
	Vernal	1	0	0	0	0	0	0	1	0	9,121
	West Jordan	1	1	0	0	0	0	1	1	0	104,783
	West Valley	1	0	0	1	0	0	2	0	0	123,089
	Woods Cross	1	0	0	0	0	0	1	0	0	8,899
	Universities and Colleges	0	1	2	0	0	...	...	...	...	...
	University of Utah	0	0	1	0	0	0	0	1	0	29,284
	Utah State University	0	1	1	0	0	0	0	2	0	15,612
	Metropolitan Counties	5	2	1	0	0	...	...	...	...	...
	Davis	0	0	1	0	0	0	0	0	1	...
	Salt Lake County Unified Police Department	0	1	0	0	0	1	0	0	0	...
	Summit	1	0	0	0	0	0	1	0	0	...
	Utah	0	1	0	0	0	0	1	0	0	...
	Washington	4	0	0	0	0	1	1	0	2	...
	Nonmetropolitan Counties	0	0	1	0	0	...	...	...	...	...
	Uintah	0	0	1	0	0	0	1	0	0	...
	Other Agencies	0	0	1	0	0	...	...	...	...	...
	Utah Transit Authority	0	0	1	0	0	1	0	0	0	...
VERMONT..............	**Total**	7	2	7	1	0	...	...	...	...	...
	Cities	7	1	7	0	0	...	...	...	...	...
	Bennington	3	0	0	0	0	0	1	1	1	15,086
	Brattleboro	2	0	0	0	0	0	0	0	2	11,573
	Burlington	2	0	3	0	0	3	1	0	1	38,699
	Middlebury	0	0	1	0	0	1	0	0	0	8,340
	Montpelier	0	0	1	0	0	0	1	0	0	7,708
	Rutland	0	1	0	0	0	0	0	0	1	16,643
	Vergennes	0	0	2	0	0	0	1	1	0	2,675
	Nonmetropolitan Counties	0	1	0	1	0	...	...	...	...	...
	Lamoille	0	0	0	1	0	0	1	0	0	...
	Orange	0	1	0	0	0	0	1	0	0	...
VIRGINIA	**Total**	107	25	15	24	4	...	...	...	...	...
	Cities	57	11	10	9	2	...	...	...	...	...
	Alexandria	2	1	1	0	0	0	3	1	0	152,801
	Bedford	1	0	0	0	0	0	1	0	0	6,377
	Charlottesville	2	0	0	0	0	1	0	0	1	42,590
	Chesapeake	4	0	3	1	0	3	2	0	3	225,627
	Christiansburg	1	0	0	0	0	0	0	0	1	19,997
	Danville	1	0	0	0	0	1	0	0	0	44,192
	Fredericksburg	2	0	0	0	0	1	0	1	0	23,704
	Front Royal	1	0	1	0	0	1	0	1	0	14,725
	Grottoes	1	0	0	0	0	1	0	0	0	2,212
	Hampton	5	0	0	1	0	1	3	2	0	144,545
	Harrisonburg	1	0	1	1	0	1	1	0	1	45,804
	Manassas	1	0	0	0	0	0	0	1	0	36,822
	Newport News	8	1	0	2	0	1	1	8	1	195,225
	Norfolk	2	0	1	0	0	1	0	1	1	234,100
	Portsmouth	6	1	0	1	0	4	1	1	2	99,576
	Purcellville	1	1	0	0	0	0	1	0	1	5,533
	Richmond	3	0	1	1	1	0	3	1	2	205,883
	Roanoke	1	0	1	0	0	0	0	1	1	94,795
	Smithfield	0	0	0	1	0	0	0	0	1	7,173
	Suffolk	1	0	0	1	0	1	1	0	0	86,226
	Vienna	1	0	0	0	0	0	0	0	1	15,343
	Vinton	1	0	0	0	0	0	0	0	1	7,851
	Virginia Beach	10	7	1	0	1	3	5	5	6	435,873
	Williamsburg	1	0	0	0	0	0	0	0	1	12,854
	Universities and Colleges	10	1	2	0	0	...	...	...	...	...
	Christopher Newport University	1	0	0	0	0	0	0	0	1	4,952
	College of William and Mary	4	0	0	0	0	2	2	0	0	7,874
	George Mason University	0	1	1	0	0	0	1	1	0	32,067
	Longwood University	0	0	1	0	0	1	0	0	0	4,832

[1] Agencies published in this table indicated that at least one hate crime incident occurred in their respective jurisdictions during the quarter(s) for which they submitted a report to the Hate Crime Statistics Program. Elipses indicate quarters for which agencies did not submit reports.

[2] Population figures are published only for the cities. The figures listed for the universities and colleges are student enrollment and were provided by the United States Department of Education for the 2009 school year, the most recent available. The enrollment figures include full-time and part-time students.

Table 94.　Hate Crime Incidents per Bias Motivation and Quarter, by State and Agency, 2010—*Continued*

State	Agency type/Agency name	Number of incidents per bias motivation					Number of incidents per quarter[1]				Popu-lation[2]
		Race	Religion	Sexual orient-ation	Ethnicity	Disability	1st quarter	2nd quarter	3rd quarter	4th quarter	
VIRGINIA— *Continued*											
	Old Dominion University	1	0	0	0	0	0	0	1	0	24,013
	Radford University	3	0	0	0	0	1	0	0	2	8,878
	University of Mary Washington	1	0	0	0	0	0	1	0	0	5,381
	Metropolitan Counties	37	13	2	13	0	...	...	...	...	...
	Albemarle County Police Department	7	0	0	1	0	2	3	3	0	...
	Amelia	2	0	0	0	0	0	1	1	0	...
	Arlington County Police Department	2	3	0	2	0	0	3	2	2	...
	Campbell	0	1	0	0	0	0	1	0	0	...
	Chesterfield County Police Department	6	1	0	2	0	1	3	3	2	...
	Fairfax County Police Department	10	3	2	5	0	4	6	8	2	...
	Fauquier	0	0	0	1	0	0	0	0	1	...
	Goochland	1	0	0	0	0	1	0	0	0	...
	Henrico County Police Department	3	3	0	0	0	0	2	3	1	...
	James City County Police Department	0	0	0	1	0	1	0	0	0	...
	Loudoun	1	1	0	0	0	0	0	0	2	...
	Montgomery	1	0	0	0	0	0	0	0	1	...
	Prince George County Police Department	2	0	0	0	0	1	0	1	0	...
	Rockingham	0	1	0	0	0	0	0	0	1	...
	Spotsylvania	1	0	0	1	0	0	0	1	1	...
	Warren	1	0	0	0	0	0	1	0	0	...
	Nonmetropolitan Counties	2	0	1	1	2	...	...	...	...	...
	Accomack	0	0	0	0	1	1	0	0	0	...
	King George	1	0	0	0	0	1	0	0	0	...
	Madison	0	0	1	0	0	0	1	0	0	...
	Page	1	0	0	1	1	2	1	0	0	...
	State Police Agencies	0	0	0	1	0	...	...	...	...	...
	State Police, Fauquier County	0	0	0	1	0	0	0	0	1	...
	Other Agencies	1	0	0	0	0	...	...	...	...	...
	Richmond International Airport	1	0	0	0	0	0	1	0	0	...
WASHINGTON	**Total**	127	34	28	41	2	...	...	...	...	...
	Cities	88	26	22	35	0	...	...	...	...	...
	Auburn	3	2	0	0	0	2	2	1	0	64,139
	Battle Ground	2	1	0	0	0	0	1	0	2	18,076
	Bellevue	3	2	1	1	0	0	1	3	3	127,735
	Bellingham	7	0	1	1	0	2	1	4	2	81,139
	Burien	1	0	1	0	0	0	0	2	0	31,831
	Camas	4	0	0	0	0	0	2	0	2	18,850
	Centralia	1	1	1	1	0	1	0	1	2	15,736
	Cheney	1	0	0	3	0	0	2	2	0	11,030
	Everett	0	0	0	2	0	1	0	1	0	99,387
	Federal Way	0	0	0	1	0	1	0	0	0	85,623
	Grand Coulee	0	0	0	1	0	1	0	0	0	1,969
	Issaquah	0	0	0	1	0	0	1	0	0	25,784
	Kennewick	0	0	0	2	0	0	2	0	0	68,501
	Lakewood	2	0	0	0	0	1	1	0	0	57,459
	Liberty Lake	1	0	0	0	0	0	1	0	0	8,300
	Longview	1	0	0	0	0	0	1	0	0	36,550
	Lynden	0	1	0	1	0	1	0	0	1	12,377
	Maple Valley	0	0	0	1	0	0	0	1	0	21,797
	Mercer Island	0	0	0	1	0	0	0	1	0	24,715
	Mount Vernon	1	1	0	1	0	1	1	0	1	32,630
	Oak Harbor	0	1	0	0	0	0	1	0	0	22,873
	Olympia	3	1	0	0	0	2	1	0	1	46,264
	Port Angeles	0	0	0	1	0	0	0	0	1	18,901
	Poulsbo	0	1	0	0	0	0	1	0	0	8,386
	Pullman	1	1	1	1	0	0	1	2	1	27,806
	Puyallup	6	0	0	1	0	2	0	3	2	37,964
	Redmond	0	1	0	0	0	0	0	0	1	52,972
	Richland	2	2	0	1	0	1	0	3	1	48,335
	Sammamish	1	0	0	0	0	0	0	1	0	43,048
	Seattle	7	0	5	3	0	5	4	3	3	620,195
	Sequim	1	1	0	0	0	1	0	0	1	5,978
	Shoreline	0	0	0	1	0	0	0	1	0	52,567
	Spokane	11	4	2	1	0	2	10	5	1	203,272
	Stanwood	1	0	0	0	0	0	0	1	0	5,519
	Tacoma	19	4	8	4	0	5	7	11	12	199,595
	Tukwila	0	1	0	0	0	0	0	0	1	17,337
	University Place	0	1	0	0	0	0	0	1	0	30,655
	Vancouver	6	0	1	5	0	3	0	4	5	167,264
	Walla Walla	1	0	1	0	0	2	0	0	0	31,265
	West Richland	1	0	0	0	0	0	0	1	0	11,840
	Yakima	1	0	0	0	0	0	1	0	0	85,802

[1] Agencies published in this table indicated that at least one hate crime incident occurred in their respective jurisdictions during the quarter(s) for which they submitted a report to the Hate Crime Statistics Program. Elipses indicate quarters for which agencies did not submit reports.

[2] Population figures are published only for the cities. The figures listed for the universities and colleges are student enrollment and were provided by the United States Department of Education for the 2009 school year, the most recent available. The enrollment figures include full-time and part-time students.

Table 94. Hate Crime Incidents per Bias Motivation and Quarter, by State and Agency, 2010—*Continued*

State	Agency type/Agency name	Number of incidents per bias motivation					Number of incidents per quarter[1]				Popu-lation[2]
		Race	Religion	Sexual orient-ation	Ethnicity	Disability	1st quarter	2nd quarter	3rd quarter	4th quarter	
WASHINGTON— *Continued*											
	Universities and Colleges	5	3	3	0	1	...	...	...	...	...
	Eastern Washington University	3	1	3	0	0	3	3	0	1	11,300
	Evergreen State College	1	1	0	0	0	0	1	0	1	4,891
	University of Washington	1	1	0	0	1	1	1	0	1	45,943
	Metropolitan Counties	33	4	2	5	0	...	...	...	...	...
	Chelan	2	0	0	0	0	1	0	1	0	...
	Clark	15	0	0	1	0	1	6	4	5	...
	King	5	3	2	2	0	5	3	1	3	...
	Kitsap	1	0	0	0	0	0	0	0	1	...
	Pierce	6	1	0	1	0	2	4	0	2	...
	Spokane	1	0	0	0	0	0	1	0	0	...
	Thurston	3	0	0	0	0	0	2	1	0	...
	Yakima	0	0	0	1	0	0	1	0	0	...
	Nonmetropolitan Counties	1	0	1	0	1	...	...	...	...	...
	Adams	0	0	0	0	1	0	0	0	1	...
	Clallam	1	0	0	0	0	0	1	0	0	...
	Walla Walla	0	0	1	0	0	0	0	1	0	...
	Other Agencies	0	1	0	1	0	...	...	...	...	...
	Port of Seattle	0	1	0	1	0	0	0	1	1	...
WEST VIRGINIA.......	**Total**	24	3	4	2	0	...	...	...	...	...
	Cities	11	3	3	2	0	...	...	...	...	...
	Beckley	0	0	1	1	0	0	0	2	0	16,990
	Buckhannon	1	0	0	0	0	1	0	0	0	5,601
	Ceredo	1	0	0	0	0	0	1	0	0	1,608
	Charleston	1	0	0	0	0	0	0	1	0	50,822
	Clarksburg	0	0	0	1	0	0	1	0	0	16,652
	Fairmont	2	0	0	0	0	0	0	2	0	19,332
	Huntington	2	0	2	0	0	2	0	1	1	49,703
	Martinsburg	0	1	0	0	0	0	1	0	0	17,654
	Nitro	1	0	0	0	0	0	1	0	0	6,836
	Parkersburg	2	0	0	0	0	0	0	1	1	32,001
	South Charleston	1	1	0	0	0	0	1	0	1	12,691
	Wheeling	0	1	0	0	0	1	0	0	0	29,054
	Universities and Colleges	1	0	0	0	0	...	...	...	...	...
	West Virginia University	1	0	0	0	0	0	0	0	1	28,898
	Metropolitan Counties	11	0	1	0	0	...	...	...	...	...
	Berkeley	1	0	0	0	0	0	0	0	1	...
	Brooke	6	0	0	0	0	1	1	0	4	...
	Kanawha	4	0	1	0	0	0	2	3	0	...
	Nonmetropolitan Counties	1	0	0	0	0	...	...	...	...	...
	Raleigh	1	0	0	0	0	0	0	1	0	...
WISCONSIN................	**Total**	42	13	28	8	2	...	...	...	...	...
	Cities	37	11	27	8	2	...	...	...	...	...
	Appleton	1	0	0	0	0	0	0	1	0	70,975
	Berlin	0	1	0	0	0	1	0	0	0	4,932
	Fond du Lac	0	1	0	0	0	0	0	1	0	42,369
	Green Bay	1	0	0	0	0	0	1	0	0	101,320
	Hudson	4	0	0	0	0	0	4	0	0	12,832
	Janesville	1	0	1	0	0	1	0	0	1	63,651
	Kaukauna	0	0	1	0	0	0	0	0	1	15,948
	Kenosha	0	0	0	1	0	1	0	0	0	98,961
	La Crosse	1	0	1	0	0	1	0	1	0	51,184
	Madison	8	0	5	3	2	1	4	7	6	238,224
	Merrill	1	0	0	0	0	0	1	0	0	9,433
	Milwaukee	16	6	12	1	0	8	10	9	8	605,921
	North Fond du Lac	0	1	0	0	0	0	1	0	0	5,108
	Oak Creek	1	0	1	1	0	1	0	0	2	34,572
	Rhinelander	0	0	1	0	0	0	0	0	1	7,471
	Ripon	0	1	0	0	0	0	0	1	0	7,481
	River Falls	0	0	1	0	0	0	0	0	1	14,745
	Seymour	0	0	2	1	0	1	1	0	1	3,396
	Sheboygan	0	1	1	0	0	0	2	0	0	47,516
	Shiocton	1	0	0	1	0	0	0	0	2	943
	Tomahawk	1	0	0	0	0	1	0	0	0	3,580
	Wausau	1	0	0	0	0	0	0	0	1	38,429
	Whitewater	0	0	1	0	0	0	0	1	0	14,211
	Universities and Colleges	1	0	0	0	0	...	...	...	...	...
	University of Wisconsin, Platteville	1	0	0	0	0	...	...	0	1	7,803
	Metropolitan Counties	3	1	0	0	0	...	...	...	...	...
	Dane	1	0	0	0	0	0	0	0	1	...
	Iowa	0	1	0	0	0	0	1	0	0	...
	Outagamie	1	0	0	0	0	1	0	0	0	...
	Racine	1	0	0	0	0	0	0	0	1	...

[1] Agencies published in this table indicated that at least one hate crime incident occurred in their respective jurisdictions during the quarter(s) for which they submitted a report to the Hate Crime Statistics Program. Elipses indicate quarters for which agencies did not submit reports.

[2] Population figures are published only for the cities. The figures listed for the universities and colleges are student enrollment and were provided by the United States Department of Education for the 2009 school year, the most recent available. The enrollment figures include full-time and part-time students.

Table 94. Hate Crime Incidents per Bias Motivation and Quarter, by State and Agency, 2010—*Continued*

State	Agency type/Agency name	Number of incidents per bias motivation					Number of incidents per quarter[1]				Popu-lation[2]
		Race	Religion	Sexual orient-ation	Ethnicity	Disability	1st quarter	2nd quarter	3rd quarter	4th quarter	
WISCONSIN—											
Continued											
	Nonmetropolitan Counties	1	1	1	0	0	...	...	...	...	...
	Clark	0	1	1	0	0	2	0	0	0	...
	Manitowoc	1	0	0	0	0	1	0	0	0	...
WYOMING..................	**Total**	2	0	0	0	0	...	...	...	...	...
	Metropolitan Counties	1	0	0	0	0	...	...	...	...	...
	Laramie	1	0	0	0	0	0	0	0	1	...
	Nonmetropolitan Counties	1	0	0	0	0	...	...	...	...	...
	Niobrara	1	0	0	0	0	1	0	0	0	...

[1] Agencies published in this table indicated that at least one hate crime incident occurred in their respective jurisdictions during the quarter(s) for which they submitted a report to the Hate Crime Statistics Program. Elipses indicate quarters for which agencies did not submit reports.

[2] Population figures are published only for the cities. The figures listed for the universities and colleges are student enrollment and were provided by the United States Department of Education for the 2009 school year, the most recent available. The enrollment figures include full-time and part-time students.

APPENDIXES

APPENDIX I. CRIME TRENDS

For the fist six months in 2011, preliminary figures indicate that, as a whole, law enforcement agencies reported a decrease of 6.4 percent in the number of violent crimes when compared with figures reported for the same time in 2010. The violent crime category includes murder, forcible rape, robbery, and aggravated assault. The number of property crimes for this same period decreased 3.7 percent when compared with data from the same time period in 2010. Property crimes include burglary, larceny-theft, and motor vehicle theft. Arson is also a property crime, but data for arson are not included in property crime totals. Figures for 2011 indicate that arson decreased 8.6 percent when compared to 2010 figures from the same time period. (See www.fbi.gov/about-us/cjis/ucr/crime-in-the-u.s/2011/pre-liminary-annual-ucr-jan-jun-2011.)

Types of Crimes in 2011

The trend and the types of crimes committed in the United States not only continues to cover the main categories of murder, forcible rape, robbery, aggravated assault, burglary, larceny-theft, motor vehicle theft, and arson described in our earlier chapters, but we are also facing a continuous increase in crimes committed through cyberspace and the Internet. These crimes are classified as scams or Internet fraud.

As Internet use has become a mainstay in our society and the world, the occurrence and development of Internet-based crimes has become widespread. As individuals, businesses, and organizations look for and implement efficient and effective ways to deter the ability of criminals to attack through cyberspace, new ways of victimizing Internet users continue to evolve.

Internet Fraud

The Internet Fraud Complaint Center—a partnership between the National White Collar Crime Center (NW3C), the Bureau of Justice Assistance (BJA), and the Federal Bureau of Investigation (FBI)—was established May 8, 2000, to address the ever-increasing incidence of online fraud. Just three years later, in response to the exponential increase in cyber crime of all types, the center changed its name to the Internet Crime Complaint Center (IC3®). With more than two million complaints received since its inception, IC3 serves as the nation's portal for reporting Internet crime and suspicious activity.

In 2011, the Internet Crime Complaint Center (IC3) actively pursued its mission to address crimes committed using the Internet, providing services to both victims of online crimes and to law enforcement. IC3 marked the third consecutive year of receiving more than 300,000 complaints, a 3.4 percent increase over 2010. The adjusted dollar loss of complaints was $485.3 million.[1]

The 2011 IC3 Internet Crime Report reveals both the scope of online crime and IC3's battle against it. The most common victim complaints included FBI-related scams, identity theft and advance fee fraud.[2] IC3 received and processed more than 26,000 complaints per month. Based on victim complaints, the top five states were California (34,169), Florida (20,034), Texas (18,477), New York (15,056) and Ohio (12,661). Victims in California reported the highest dollar losses with a total of $70.5 million. The average financial loss for reporting victims was $4,187.

IC3 serves as a powerful conduit for law enforcement to share information and pursue cases that often span jurisdictional boundaries. Collaboration within this partnership has produced a number of technological advancements to streamline the way complaints are processed and referred to investigators. Initially established as simply a convenient method for citizens to report Internet crime information, IC3 has evolved into a vital resource for both victims of online crime and for law enforcement across the country whom investigate and prosecute a wide range of cases.

Below are recent scams and cyber crimes reported by the IC3 and the FBI in recent FBI press releases, and tips on ways to avoid becoming a victim of these crimes. Any type of cyber attack should be immediately reported to the local FBI office as well as to the IC3's website at www.IC3.gov . The IC3's complaint database links complaints together to refer them to the appropriate law enforcement agency for case consideration. The complaint information is also used to identify emerging trends and patterns. Information about recent Internet and cyber crime can be found at http://www .fbi.gov/scams-safety/e-scams .

Mystery/Secret Shopper Schemes

The IC3 has been alerted to an increase in employment schemes pertaining to mystery/secret shopper positions. Many retail and service corporations hire evaluators to perform secret or random checks on themselves or their competitors, and fraudsters are capitalizing on this employment opportunity. Victims have reported to the IC3 that they were contacted via email message and U.S. mail to apply to be a mystery shopper. Applicants are asked to send a resumé and are purportedly subject to an extensive background check

1. IC3 Internet Crime Complaint Center, 2011 Internet Crime Report, www.ic3.gov/media/annualreport/2011_IC3Report.pdf .

Methodology of evaluating loss amounts: FBI IC3 Unit staff reviewed for validity all complaints that reported a loss of more than $100,000. Analysts also converted losses reported in foreign currencies to dollars. The final amounts of all reported losses above $100,000 for which the complaint information did not support the loss amount were excluded from the statistics.

2. Complaint category statistics that are based on the perceptions of the complaints are not typically accurate for statistical purposes. The statistics pulled from the complaints themselves, however, are considerably more accurate as they are categorized and grouped through the IC3 automated system. IC3 does not verify complaint data.

before being accepted as a mystery shopper. The employees are sent a check with instructions to shop at a specified retailer for a specific length of time and spend a specific amount on merchandise from the store. The employees receive instructions to take note of the store's environment, color, payment procedures, gift items, and shopping/carrier bags and report back to the employer. The second evaluation is the ease and accuracy of wiring money from the retail location. The money to be wired is also included in the check sent to the employee. The remaining balance is the employee's payment for the completion of the assignment. After merchandise is purchased and money is wired, the employees are advised by the bank the check cashed was counterfeit, and they are responsible for the money lost in addition to bank fees incurred.

In other versions of the scheme, applicants are requested to provide bank account information to have money directly deposited into their accounts. The fraudster then has acquired access to these victims' accounts and can withdraw money, which makes the applicant a victim of identity theft.

Tips

Here are some tips you can use to avoid becoming a victim of employment schemes associated with mystery/secret shopping:

- Do not respond to unsolicited (spam) email messages.

- Do not open links contained within an unsolicited email message.

- Be cautious of email messages claiming to contain pictures in attached files, as the files may contain viruses. Only open attachments from known senders. Scan all attachments for viruses, if possible.

- Avoid filling out forms contained in email messages that ask for personal information.

- Always compare the link in the email message to the link you are actually directed to and determine if they match and will lead you to a legitimate site.

- There are legitimate mystery/secret shopper programs available. Research the legitimacy on companies hiring mystery shoppers. Legitimate companies will not charge an application fee and will accept applications online.

- No legitimate mystery/secret shopper program will send payment in advance and ask the employee to send a portion of it back.

Work from Home Scams

Consumers continue to lose money from work-from-home scams that assist cyber criminals to move stolen funds.

Worse yet, due to their deliberate or unknowing participation in the scams, these individuals may face criminal charges. Work-from-home scam victims are often recruited by organized cyber criminals through newspaper ads, online employment services, unsolicited email messages or "spam," online and social networking sites advertising work-from-home opportunities. Once recruited, however, rather than becoming an employee of a legitimate business, the consumer is actually a "mule" for cyber criminals who use the consumer's or other victim's accounts to steal and launder money.

Fraudulent Classified Ads and Auction Sales

Internet criminals post classified ads and auctions for products they do not have and make the scam work by using stolen credit cards. Fraudsters receive an order from a victim, charge the victim's credit card for the amount of the order, then use a separate stolen credit card for the actual purchase. They pocket the purchase price obtained from the victim's credit card and have the merchant ship the item directly to the victim. Consequently, an item purchased from an online auction but received directly from the merchant is a strong indication of fraud. Victims of such a scam not only lose the money paid to the fraudster, but may be liable for receiving stolen goods.

Shoppers may help avoid these scams by using caution and not providing financial information directly to the seller, as fraudulent sellers will use this information to purchase items for their schemes. Always use a legitimate payment service to ensure a safe, legitimate purchase.

Diligently check each seller's rating and feedback along with their number of sales and the dates on which feedback was posted. Be wary of a seller with 100 percent positive feedback, with a low total number of feedback postings, or with all feedback posted around the same date and time.

Phishing and Smishing Schemes

In phishing schemes, the fraudster poses as a legitimate entity and uses email messages and scam websites to obtain victims' personal information, such as account numbers, user names, passwords, and so on. Smishing is the act of sending fraudulent text messages to bait a victim into revealing personal information.

Be leery of email messages or text messages that indicate a problem or question regarding your financial accounts. In this scam, fraudsters direct victims to follow a link or call a number to update an account or correct a purported problem. The link directs the victim to a fraudulent website or message that appears legitimate. Instead, the site allows the fraudster to steal any personal information the victim provides.

Smishing schemes involve fraudsters calling victims' cell phones and offering to lower the interest rates for credit cards the victims do not even possess. If a victim asserts that they do not own the credit card, the caller hangs up. These fraudsters call from TRAC cell phones that do not have voicemail, or the phone provides a constant busy signal when called, rendering these calls virtually untraceable.

Another scam involves fraudsters directing victims, via email, to a spoofed website. A spoofed website is a fake site that misleads the victim into providing personal information, which is routed to the scammer's computer.

Tips to avoid becoming a victim of cyber fraud:

- Do not respond to unsolicited (spam) email messages.

- Do not open links contained within an unsolicited email messages.

- Be cautious of email messages claiming to contain pictures in attached files, as the files may contain viruses. Only open attachments from known senders. Scan the attachments for viruses, if possible.

- Avoid filling out forms contained in email messages that ask for personal information.

- Always compare the link in the email message with the link to which you are directed and determine whether they match and will lead you to a legitimate site.

- Log directly onto the official website for the business identified in the email message, instead of "linking" to it from an unsolicited email message. If the email message appears to be from you bank, credit card issuer, or other company you deal with frequently, your statements or official correspondence from the business will provide the proper contact information.

- Contact the actual business that supposedly sent the email message to verify whether the email message is genuine.

- If you are asked to act quickly, or there is an emergency, it may be a scam. Fraudsters create a sense of urgency to get you to act quickly.

- Verify any requests for personal information from any business or financial institution by contacting them using the main contact information.

- Remember, if it looks too good to be true, it probably is.

Prize Sweepstakes or Lottery Schemes

Prize sweepstakes or lottery scheme perpetrators use counterfeit checks that bear legitimate-looking logos of various financial institutions to fool victims into sending money to the fraudsters.

Fraudsters tell victims they've won a sweepstakes or lottery, but to receive a lump sum payout, they must pay the taxes and processing fees up front. Fraudsters direct individuals to call a telephone number to initiate a letter of instructions. The letter alleges that the victim may elect to take an advance on the winnings to make the required up-front payment. The letter includes a check in the amount of the alleged taxes and fees along with processing instructions. Ultimately, victims believe they are using the advance to make the required up-front payment, but in reality they are falling prey to the scheme.

The victim deposits the check into their own bank, which credits the account for the amount of the check before the check clears. The victim immediately withdraws the money and wires it to the fraudsters. Afterwards, the check proves to be counterfeit and the bank pulls the respective funds from the victim's account, leaving the victim liable for the amount of the counterfeit check plus any additional fees the bank may charge.

Persons may fall victim to this scheme due to the allure of easy money and the apparent legitimacy of the check the fraudsters included in the letter of instruction. The alleged cash prizes and locations of the financial institutions vary.

Tips to avoid being scammed:

- A federal statute prohibits mailing lottery tickets, advertisements, or payments to purchase tickets in a foreign lottery.

- Be leery if you do not remember entering a lottery or sweepstakes.

- Beware of lotteries or sweepstakes that charge a fee prior to delivering your prize.

- Be wary of demands to send additional money as a requirement to be eligible for future winnings.

Charitable Contribution Schemes

Because of recent tornadoes that affected several Southern states and caused flooding and loss of life and property, the FBI warns the public to be aware of and report any instances of alleged fraudulent activity related to relief operations and funding for victims. Criminals exploit these tragedies by sending fraudulent email messages and creating phony websites designed to solicit contributions.

The National Center for Disaster Fraud was created by the Department of Justice to investigate, prosecute, and deter fraud in the wake of Hurricane Katrina, when billions of dollars in federal disaster relief poured into the Gulf Cost region. Its mission has expanded to include suspected fraud from any natural or manmade disaster. More than 20 federal agencies, including the FBI, participate in the National Center for Disaster Fraud, which allows the center to act as a centralized clearinghouse of information related to disaster relief fraud.

Use due diligence before giving contributions to anyone soliciting donations or individuals offering to provide assistance to those affected by the tornadoes. Solicitations can originate from email messages, websites, door-to-door collections, flyers, mailings, telephone calls, and other similar methods.

Before making a donation of any kind, consumers should adhere to the following guidelines.

- Do not respond to any unsolicited (spam) incoming email messages, including requests to open links contained within those messages, because they may contain computer viruses.

- Be skeptical of individuals representing themselves as members of charitable organizations or officials asking for donations via email messages or social networking sites.

- Beware of organizations with copy-cat names similar to but not exactly the same as those of reputable charities.

- Be cautious of email messages that claim to show pictures of the disaster areas in attached files because the files may contain viruses. Only open attachments from known senders.

- Ensure that contributions are received and used for intended purposes by making contributions directly to known organizations rather than relying on others to make the donation on your behalf.

- Do not be pressured into making contributions; reputable charities do not use such tactics.

- Be aware of whom you are dealing with when providing your personal and financial information. Providing such information may compromise your identity and make you vulnerable to identity theft.

- Avoid cash donations if possible. Pay by credit card or write a check directly to the charity. Do not make checks payable to individuals.

- Verify websites. Legitimate charities do not normally solicit donations via money transfer services. Most legitimate charities' websites end in .org rather than .com.

Scareware

Scareware is malicious software that poses as legitimate computer security software and purports to detect a variety of threats on the affected computer that do not actually exist. Users are then informed they must purchase what they are told is anti-virus software to repair their computers. The users are then barraged with aggressive and disruptive notifications until they supply their credit card number and pay for the worthless "anti-virus" product. The product is, in fact, fake.

The FBI has seized 22 computers and servers in the United States that were involved in facilitating and operating a scareware scheme. In addition, 25 computers and servers located abroad were taken down as part of the operation.

The scareware scheme used a variety of ruses to trick consumers into infecting their computers with the malicious scareware products, including web pages featuring fake computer scans. Once the scareware was downloaded, victims were notified that their computers were infected with a range of malicious software, such as viruses and Trojans, and badgered into purchasing the fake anti-virus software to resolve the non-existent problem at a cost of up to $129. An estimated 960,000 users were victimized by this scareware scheme, leading to $72 million in actual losses.

Online Vehicle Shopping Scams

Online vehicle shoppers are being victimized by fraudulent vehicle sales and false claims of vehicle protection programs (VPP). In fraudulent vehicle sales, criminals attempt to sell vehicles they do not own. They create an attractive deal by advertising vehicles for sale at prices below book value. Often the sellers purport they need to sell the vehicle because they are moving for work, to include military deployments.

Because of the alleged pending move, criminals refuse to meet the victim in person or allow a vehicle inspection, and they often attempt to rush the sale. To make the deal appear legitimate, the criminal instructs the victim to send full or partial payment to a third-party agent via a wire transfer payment service and to fax the payment receipt to the seller as proof of payment.

The criminal pockets the payment but does not deliver the vehicle. Criminals also attempt to make their scams appear valid by misusing the names of reputable companies and programs.

In a new twist, criminals use a live-chat feature in email correspondence and electronic invoices. As live-chat assistants, the criminals answer victims' questions and assure them the deals are safe, claiming that safeguards are in place to reimburse buyers for any loss. The criminals falsely assert that their sales are protected by liability insurance coverage up to $50,000.

Automotive shoppers should exercise due diligence before engaging in transactions to purchase vehicles advertised online. In particular, shoppers should be cautious of the following situations:

- Sellers who want to move the transaction from one platform to another (for example, from Craigslist to eBay Motors).

- Sellers who claim that a buyer protection program offered by a major Internet company covers an auto transaction conducted outside that company's site.

- Sellers who push for speedy completion of the transaction and request payments via quick wire transfer payment systems.

- Sellers who refuse to meet in person, or refuse to allow the buyer to physically inspect the vehicle before the purchase.

- Transactions in which the seller and vehicle are in different locations. Criminals often claim to have been transferred for work reasons, deployed by the military, or moved because of a family circumstance, and could not take the vehicle with them.

- Vehicles advertised at well below their market value. Remember, if it looks too good to be true, it probably is.

Timeshare Marketing Scams

Timeshare owners across the country are being scammed out of millions of dollars by unscrupulous companies that promise to sell or rent the unsuspecting victim; timeshares. In the typical scam, timeshare owners receive unexpected or uninvited telephone calls or email messages from criminals posing as sales representatives for a timeshare resale company. The representative promises a quick sale, often within 60 to 90 days. The sales representatives often use high-pressure sales tactics to add a sense of urgency to the deal. Some victims have reported that sales representatives pressured them by claiming there was a buyer waiting in the wings, either on the other line or present in the office.

Timeshare owners who agree to sell are told that they must pay an upfront fee to cover anything from listing and advertising fees to closing costs. Many victims have provided credit cards to pay the fees ranging from a few hundred to a few thousand dollars. Once the fee is paid, timeshare owners report that the company becomes evasive—calls go unanswered, numbers are disconnected, and websites are inaccessible.

In some cases, timeshare owners who have been defrauded by a timeshare sales scheme have been subsequently contacted by an unscrupulous timeshare fraud recovery company as well. The representative from the recovery company promises assistance in recovering money lost in the sales scam. Some recovery companies require an up-front fee for services rendered, while other promise no fees will be paid unless a refund is obtained for the timeshare owner. The IC3 has identified some instances where people involved with the recovery company also have a connection to the resale company, raising the possibility that timeshare owners are being scammed twice by the same people.

If you are contacted by someone offering to sell or rent your timeshare, the IC3 recommends using caution. Listed below are tips you can use to avoid becoming a victim of a timeshare scheme:

- Be wary if a company asks you for up-front fees to sell or rent your timeshare.

- Read the fine print of any sales contract or rental agreement provided.

- Check with the Better Business Bureau to ensure the company is reputable.

To obtain more information on Internet schemes, visit www.LooksTooGoodToBeTrue.com. Also, anyone who believes they have been a victim of this type of scam should promptly report it to the IC3's website at www.IC3.gov.

Payday Loan Telephone Collection Scams

The typical payday loan scam involves a caller who claims that the victim is delinquent on a payday loan and must make payment to avoid legal consequences. Callers pose as representatives of the FBI, "Federal Legislative Department," various law firms, or other legitimate-sounding agencies and claim to be collecting debt for companies such as United Cash Advance, U.S. Cash Advance, U.S. Cash Net, or other Internet check-cashing services. The fraudsters relentlessly call the victim's home, cell phone, and place of employment in attempts to obtain payment. The callers refuse to provide information regarding the alleged payday loan or any documentation and become verbally abusive when questioned.

One of the most insidious aspects of this scam is that the callers have accurate information about the victims, including Social Security numbers, dates of birth, addresses, employer information, bank account numbers, and names and telephone numbers of relatives and friends. The method by which the fraudsters obtained the personal information is unclear, but victims often relay that they had completed online applications for other loans or credit cards before the calls began.

The Internet Crime Complaint Center has observed variations of the scam in which the caller tells the victim that there are outstanding warrants for the victim's arrest. The caller claims that the basis of the warrants is non-payment of the underlying loan and/or hacking; if it's the latter, the caller tells the victim that he or she is wanted for hacking into a business" computer system to steal customer information. The caller will then demand payment via debit/credit card; in other cases, the caller further instructs victims to obtain a prepaid card to cover the payment.

The high-pressure collection tactics used by the fraudsters have also evolved. In one complaint, a person posed as a process server and appeared at the victim's job. In another instance, a phony process server came to a victim's home. In both cases, after claiming to be serving a court summons, the alleged process server said the victim could avoid going to court if he or she provided a debit card number for repayment of the loan.

If you are contacted by someone who is trying to collect a debt that you do not owe, you should take the following steps.

- Contact your local law enforcement agencies if you feel you are in immediate danger.

- Contact your bank(s) and credit card companies.

- Contact the three major credit bureaus and request an alert be put on your file.

- If you have received a legitimate loan and want to verify that you do not have any outstanding obligation, contact the loan company directly.

- File a complaint at www.IC3.gov.

Malware Installed on Travelers' Laptops through Software Updates on Hotel Internet Connections

Analysis from the FBI and other government agencies demonstrates that malicious actors are targeting travelers abroad through pop-up windows while they are establishing an Internet connection in their hotel rooms.

Travelers' laptops are being infected with malicious software when using hotel Internet connections abroad. In this attack, the traveler attempts to set up the hotel room Internet connection and is presented with a pop-up window notifying the traveler to update a widely used software product. If the traveler selects to accept and install the update, malicious software is installed on the laptop. The pop-up window appears to be offering a routine update to a legitimate software product for which updates are frequently available.

The FBI recommends that all government, private industry, and academic personnel who travel abroad take extra caution before updating software products through their hotel Internet connection. Checking the author or digital certificate of any prompted update to see if it corresponds to the software vendor may reveal an attempted attack. The FBI also recommends that travelers perform software updates on laptops immediately before traveling, and that they download software updates directly from the software vendor's website if updates are necessary while abroad.

Tips for Online Shopping

As more and more individuals purchase merchandise online via company web sties or auction sites, users need to take precautions to ensure safe and reliable transactions. Safeguard online purchases by following these general tips to protect you on auction sites and to avoid credit card fraud.

Tips to Avoid Internet Auction Fraud:

- Before you bid, understand how the auction works—what your obligation is as the buyer, and what the seller's obligations are.

- Find out what actions the website or company takes if a problem occurs.

- Consider insuring the transaction and shipment.

- Learn as much as possible about the seller. Check the Better Business Bureau, if the seller is a business.

- Check reviews and comments about the seller.

- Determine the method of payment the seller is asking from the buyer and where the payment is to be sent.

- Purchase items online using your credit card, if possible, because you often have protection if something goes wrong. (See tips on avoiding credit card fraud below.)

- Be cautious when dealing with sellers outside the United States. It could be difficult to rectify a problem internationally.

- Ensure that there are no unexpected costs associated with the sale, including shipping and handling.

- Find out when to expect delivery and whether the item(s) purchased are covered by a warranty or can be easily exchanged.

Tips to Avoid Credit Card Fraud

- Only submit your credit card number online on those sites that are secure and reputable. You can usually determine a secure site with the presence of a tiny icon of a padlock on the site, however the icon is not a guarantee of a secure site.

- Don't trust a site just because it claims to be secure.

- Make sure that you are purchasing merchandise from a reputable source.

- Determine the legitimacy of the individual or company.

- Be sure to get a physical address; not a post office box and a telephone number. Call the seller to determine that the telephone number is correct and working.

- Test the email address, by sending an email message to the seller to ensure that it is active; be wary of those that use free email services where a credit card was not required to open the account.

- Be careful when responding to special investment offers, especially through unsolicited email messages.

- Keep a list of all your credit cards and account information along with the card issuer's contact information. Contact the card issuer immediately if you lose your credit card or if anything looks suspicious.

The FBI warns to be cautious when making transactions over the Internet—making purchases, investments, doing business with unknown Internet companies, or doing business with foreign countries (419 fraud—a letter from a foreign country or government asking for your cooperation with moving large sums of money to overseas bank accounts). Some of these sites could be fraudulent or be scams to get access to your bank accounts and money. The FBI advises us to do our homework and confirm the legitimacy of any business or site that we contemplate transacting business with over the Internet.

APPENDIX II. METHODOLOGY

Submitting Uniform Crime Reporting (UCR) Program data to the Federal Bureau of Investigation (FBI) is a collective effort on the part of city, county, state, tribal, and federal law enforcement agencies to present a nationwide view of crime. Law enforcement agencies in 46 states and the District of Columbia voluntarily contribute crime data to the UCR Program through their respective state UCR Programs. For those states that do not have a state Program, local agencies submit crime statistics directly to the FBI. The state UCR Programs function as liaisons between local agencies and the FBI. Many states have mandatory reporting requirements, and many state Programs collect data beyond the scope of the UCR Program to address crime problems specific to their particular jurisdictions. In most cases, state Programs also provide direct and frequent service to participating law enforcement agencies, make information readily available for statewide use, and help streamline the national Program's operations.

Criteria for State UCR Programs

The criteria established for state Programs ensure consistency and comparability in the data submitted to the national Program, as well as regular and timely reporting. These criteria are:

1. The state Program must conform to the national UCR Program standards, definitions, and information required.
2. The state criminal justice agency must have a proven, effective, statewide Program and have instituted acceptable quality control procedures.
3. The state crime reporting must cover a percentage of the population at least equal to that covered by the national UCR Program through direct reporting.
4. The state Program must have adequate field staff assigned to conduct audits and to assist contributing agencies in record-keeping practices and crime-reporting procedures.
5. The state Program must furnish the FBI with all of the detailed data regularly collected by the FBI from individual agencies that report to the state Program in the form of duplicate returns, computer printouts, and/or appropriate electronic media.
6. The state Program must have the proven capability (tested over a period of time) to supply all the statistical data required in time to meet publication deadlines of the national UCR Program.

Data Completeness and Quality

National Program staff members contact the state UCR Program in connection with crime-reporting matters and, when necessary and approved by the state, they contact individual contributors within the state. To fulfill its responsibilities in connection with the UCR Program, the FBI reviews and edits individual agency reports for completeness and quality. Upon request, they conduct training pro-

grams within the state on law enforcement record-keeping and crime-reporting procedures. The FBI conducts an audit of each state's UCR data collection procedures once every three years, in accordance with audit standards established by the federal government. Should circumstances develop in which the state Program does not comply with the aforementioned requirements, the national Program may institute a direct collection of data from law enforcement agencies within the state.

Reporting Procedures

Offenses known and value of property—Law enforcement agencies tabulate the number of Part I offenses reported based on records of all reports of crime received from victims, officers who discover infractions, or other sources, and submit these reports each month to the FBI directly or through their state UCR Programs. Part I offenses include murder and nonnegligent manslaughter, forcible rape, robbery, aggravated assault, burglary, larceny-theft, motor vehicle theft, and arson. Each month, law enforcement agencies also submit to the FBI the value of property stolen and recovered in connection with the offenses and detailed information pertaining to criminal homicide.

Unfounded offenses and clearances—When, through investigation, an agency determines that complaints of crimes are unfounded or false, the agency eliminates that offense from its crime tally through an entry on the monthly report. The report also provides the total number of actual Part I offenses, the number of offenses cleared, and the number of clearances that involve only offenders under the age of 18. (Law enforcement can clear crimes in one of two ways: by the arrest of at least one person who is charged and turned over to the court for prosecution or by exceptional means—when some element beyond law enforcement's control precludes the arrest of a known offender.)

Persons arrested—In addition to reporting Part I offenses each month, law enforcement agencies also provide data on the age, sex, and race of persons arrested for Part I and Part II offenses. Part II offenses encompass all crimes, except traffic violations, that are not classified as Part I offenses.

Officers killed or assaulted—Each month, law enforcement agencies also report information to the UCR Program regarding law enforcement officers killed or assaulted, and each year they report the number of full-time sworn and civilian law enforcement personnel employed as of October 31.

Hate crimes—At the end of each quarter, law enforcement agencies report summarized data on hate crimes; that is specific offenses that were motivated by an offender's bias against the perceived race, religion, ethnic or national origin, sexual orientation, or physical or mental disability of the victim. Those agencies participating in the UCR Program's National Incident-Based Reporting System (NIBRS) submit hate crime data monthly.

Editing Procedures

The UCR Program thoroughly examines each report it receives for arithmetical accuracy and for deviations in crime data from month to month and from present to past years that may indicate errors. UCR staff members compare an agency's monthly reports with its previous submissions and with reports from similar agencies to identify any unusual fluctuations in the agency's crime count. Considerable variations in crime levels may indicate modified records procedures, incomplete reporting, or changes in the jurisdiction's geopolitical structure.

Evaluation of trends—Data reliability is a high priority of the FBI, which brings any deviations or arithmetical adjustments to the attention of state UCR Programs or the submitting agencies. Typically, FBI staff members study the monthly reports to evaluate periodic trends prepared for individual reporting units. Any significant increase or decrease becomes the subject of a special inquiry. Changes in crime reporting procedures or annexations that affect an agency's jurisdiction can influence the level of reported crime. When this occurs, the FBI excludes the figures for specific crime categories or totals, if necessary, from the trend tabulations.

Training for contributors—In addition to the evaluation of trends, the FBI provides training seminars and instructional materials on crime reporting procedures to assist contributors in complying with UCR standards. Throughout the country, representatives from the national Program coordinate with representatives of state Programs and law enforcement personnel and hold training sessions to explain the purpose of the Program, the rules of uniform classification and scoring, and the methods of assembling the information for reporting. When an individual agency has specific problems with compiling its crime statistics and its remedial efforts are unsuccessful, personnel from the FBI's Criminal Justice Information Services Division may visit the contributor to aid in resolving the problems.

UCR Handbook—The national UCR Program publishes the *Uniform Crime Reporting Handbook* (revised 2004), which details procedures for classifying and scoring offenses and serves as the contributing agencies' basic resource for preparing reports. The national staff also produces letters to UCR contributors, state Program bulletins, and UCR newsletters as needed. These publications provide policy updates and new information, as well as clarification of reporting issues.

The final responsibility for data submissions rests with the individual contributing law enforcement agency. Although the FBI makes every effort through its editing procedures, training practices, and correspondence to ensure the validity of the data it receives, the accuracy of the statistics depends primarily on the adherence of each contributor to the established standards of reporting. Deviations from these established standards that cannot be resolved by the national UCR Program may be brought to the attention of the Criminal Justice Information Systems Committees of the International Association of Chiefs of Police and the National Sheriffs' Association.

Population Estimation

For the 2010 population estimates used in this report, the FBI computed individual rates of growth from one year to the next for every city/town and county using 2000 decennial population counts and 2001 through 2009 population estimates from the U.S. Census Bureau. Each agency's rates of growth were averaged; that average was then applied and added to its 2009 Census population estimate to derive the agency's 2010 population estimate.

Population estimates for 2009 are based on the percent change in the state population from the U.S. Census Bureau's 2008 revised estimates and 2009 provisional estimates. Population estimates for 2006 are based on the percent change in the state population from the U.S. Census Bureau's 2005 revised estimates and 2006 provisional estimates. Population totals for 2000 are from the U.S. Census Bureau's 2000 decennial population counts.

NIBRS Conversion

Thirty-two state Programs are certified to provide their UCR data in the expanded National Incident-Based Reporting System (NIBRS) format. For presentation in this book, the NIBRS data were converted to the historical Summary Reporting System data. The UCR Program staff constructed the NIBRS database to allow for such conversion so that UCR's long-running time series could continue.

Crime Trends

By showing fluctuations from year to year, trend statistics offer the data user an added perspective from which to study crime. Percent change tabulations in this publication are computed only for reporting agencies that provided comparable data for the periods under consideration. The FBI excludes from the trend calculations all figures except those received for common months from common agencies. Also excluded are unusual fluctuations of data that the FBI determines are the result of such variables as improved records procedures, annexations, and so on.

Caution to Users

Data users should exercise care in making any direct comparison between data in this publication and those in prior issues of *Crime in the United States*. Because of differing levels of participation from year to year and reporting problems that require the FBI to estimate crime counts for certain contributors, some data may not be comparable.. In addition, this publication may contain updates to data provided in prior years' publications. For example, because of the receipt of additional data after the 2009 publication deadline, the 2009 Supplementary Homicide Report (SHR) data in last year's publication may not match the 2009 SHR data in this 2010 publication.

Arrest Data, 2010

- Limited arrest data were received from Illinois. Arrest counts were received for Chicago and Rockford only.

- Except for the cities of Minneapolis and St. Paul, the Minnesota State UCR Program's guidelines for reporting forcible rape arrest counts do not comply with the national UCR Program's guidelines; that is Minnesota data include arrests made for forcible rapes of male victims. Therefore, the state forcible rape counts that are published include only the totals received from Minneapolis and St. Paul.

- For 2010, only arrest totals (with no age or gender breakdowns) are available for Florida. Therefore, Florida arrest totals are included only in Table 69, "Arrests by State, 2010."

- No 2010 arrest data were received from the District of Columbia's Metropolitan Police Department. The two agencies in the District of Columbia for which 12 months of arrest data were received, Metro Transit Police and the National Zoological Park, have no attributable population.

- No 2010 arrest data were received from the New York City Police Department. However, arrest totals for this agency were estimated by the national UCR Program and were included in Table 29 "Estimated Number of Arrests, United States, 2010."

- Beginning in 2010, the national UCR Program no longer publishes data for runaways.

Offense Estimation

Tables 1 through 5 and Table 7 of this publication contain statistics for the entire United States. Because not all law enforcement agencies provide data for complete reporting periods, the FBI includes estimated crime numbers in these presentations. The FBI estimates data for three areas: Metropolitan Statistical Areas (MSAs), cities outside MSAs, and nonmetropolitan counties; and computes estimates for participating agencies that do not provide 12 months of complete data. For agencies supplying 3 to 11 months of data, the national UCR Program estimates for the missing data by following a standard estimation procedure using the data provided by the agency. If an agency has supplied less than 3 months of data, the FBI computes estimates by using the known crime figures of similar areas within a state and assigning the same proportion of crime volumes to nonreporting agencies. The estimation process considers the following: population size covered by the agency; type of jurisdiction; for example, police department versus sheriff's office; and geographic location.

Estimation of State-Level Data

In response to various circumstances, the FBI calculates estimated offense totals for certain states. For example, some states do not provide forcible rape figures in accordance with UCR guidelines. In addition, problems at the state level have, at times, resulted in no useable data. Also, the conversion of the National Incident-Based Reporting System (NIBRS) data to Summary data has contributed to the need for unique estimation procedures. A summary of state-specific and offense-specific estimation procedures can be found online at http://www.fbi.gov/about-us/cjis/ucr/crime-in-the.u.s/2010/crime-in-the-u.s.-2010/methodology

APPENDIX III. OFFENSE DEFINITIONS

The Uniform Crime Reporting (UCR) Program divides offenses into two groups. Contributing agencies submit information on the number of Part I offenses known to law enforcement; those offenses cleared by arrest or exceptional means; and the age, sex, and race of persons arrested for each of these offenses. Contributors provide only arrest data for Part II offenses. These are definitions of offenses set forth by the UCR.

The UCR Program collects data on Part I offenses to measure the level and scope of crime occurring throughout the Nation. The Program's founders chose these offenses because (1) they are serious crimes, (2) they occur with regularity in all areas of the country, and (3) they are likely to be reported to police.

Part I offenses include criminal homicide, forcible rape, robbery, aggravated assault, burglary, larceny-theft, motor vehicle theft, and arson.

Criminal homicide—a.) Murder and nonnegligent manslaughter: the willful (nonnegligent) killing of one human being by another. Deaths caused by negligence, attempts to kill, assaults to kill, suicides, and accidental deaths are excluded. The program classifies justifiable homicides separately and limits the definition to (1) the killing of a felon by a law enforcement officer in the line of duty; or (2) the killing of a felon, during the commission of a felony, by a private citizen. b. Manslaughter by negligence: the killing of another person through gross negligence. Deaths of persons due to their own negligence, accidental deaths not resulting from gross negligence, and traffic fatalities are excluded.

Forcible rape—The carnal knowledge of a female forcibly and against her will. Assaults and attempts to commit rape by force or threat of force are also included. Statutory rape (no force used—female victim is under the age of consent) and other sex offenses are excluded. Sexual attacks on males are counted as aggravated assaults or sex offenses, depending on the circumstances and the extent of any injuries.

Robbery—The taking or attempted taking of anything of value from the care, custody, or control of a person or persons by force or threat of force or violence and/or by putting the victim in fear.

Aggravated assault—An unlawful attack by one person upon another for the purpose of inflicting severe or aggravated bodily injury. This type of assault usually is accompanied by the use of a weapon or by means likely to produce death or great bodily harm. Simple assaults are excluded.

Burglary (breaking or entering)—The unlawful entry of a structure to commit a felony or a theft. Attempted forcible entry is included.

Larceny-theft (except motor vehicle theft)—The unlawful taking, carrying, leading, or riding away of property from the possession or constructive possession of another. Examples are thefts of bicycles or automobile parts and accessories, shoplifting, pocket-picking, or the stealing of any property or article that is not taken by force and violence or by fraud. Attempted larcenies are included. Embezzlement, confidence games, forgery, worthless checks, and the like, are excluded.

Motor vehicle theft—The theft or attempted theft of a motor vehicle. A motor vehicle is self-propelled and runs on land surface and not on rails. Motorboats, construction equipment, airplanes, and farming equipment are specifically excluded from this category.

Arson—Any willful or malicious burning or attempt to burn, with or without intent to defraud, a dwelling house, public building, motor vehicle, aircraft, personal property of another, and the like.

The **Part II** offenses for which only arrest data are collected, are:

Other assaults (simple)—Assaults and attempted assaults that are not of an aggravated nature and do not result in serious injury to the victim. Included in this category are stalking, intimidation, coercion, and hazing.

Forgery and counterfeiting—The altering, copying, or imitating of something, without authority or right, with the intent to deceive or defraud by passing the copy or thing altered or imitated as that which is original or genuine; or the selling, buying, or possession of an altered, copied, or imitated thing with the intent to deceive or defraud. Attempts are included.

Fraud—The intentional perversion of the truth for the purpose of inducing another person or other entity in reliance upon it to part with something of value or to surrender a legal right. Fraudulent conversion and obtaining of money or property by false pretenses. Confidence games and bad checks, except forgeries and counterfeiting, are included.

Embezzlement—The unlawful misappropriation or misapplication by an offender of money, property, or some other thing of value entrusted to that offender's care, custody, or control.

Stolen property; buying, receiving, possessing—Buying, receiving, possessing, selling, concealing, or transporting any property with the knowledge that it has been unlawfully taken, as by burglary, embezzlement, fraud, larceny, robbery, and the like. Attempts are included.

Vandalism—To willfully or maliciously destroy, injure, disfigure, or deface any public or private property, real or personal, without the consent of the owner or person having custody or control by cutting, tearing, breaking, marking, painting, drawing, covering with filth, or any other such means as may be specified by local law. Attempts are included.

Weapons; carrying, possessing, and the like—The violation of laws or ordinances prohibiting the manufacture, sale, purchase, transportation, possession, concealment, or use of firearms, cutting instruments, explosives, incendiary devices, or other deadly weapons. Attempts are included.

Prostitution and commercialized vice—The unlawful promotion of or participation in sexual activities for profit, including attempts. To solicit customers or transport persons for prostitution purposes; to own, manage, or operate a dwelling or other establishment for the purposes of providing a place where prostitution is performed; or to otherwise assist or promote prostitution.

Sex offenses (except forcible rape, prostitution, and commercialized vice)—Offenses against chastity, common decency, morals, and the like. Incest, indecent exposure, and statutory rape, as well as attempts are included.

Drug abuse violations—The violation of laws prohibiting the production, distribution, and/or use of certain controlled substances. The unlawful cultivation, manufacture, distribution, sale, purchase, use, possession, transportation, or importation of any controlled drug or narcotic substance. Arrests for violations of state and local laws, specifically those relating to the unlawful possession, sale, use, growing, manufacturing, and making of narcotic drugs. The following drug categories are specified: opium or cocaine and their derivatives (morphine, heroin, codeine); marijuana; synthetic narcotics—manufactured narcotics that can cause true addiction (demerol, methadone); and dangerous non-narcotic drugs (barbiturates, benzedrine).

Gambling—To unlawfully bet or wager money or something else of value; assist, promote, or operate a game of chance for money or some other stake; possess or transmit wagering information; manufacture, sell, purchase, possess, or transport gambling equipment, devices, or goods; or tamper with the outcome of a sporting event or contest to gain a gambling advantage.

Offenses against the family and children—Unlawful nonviolent acts by a family member (or legal guardian) that threaten the physical, mental, or economic well-being or morals of another family member and that are not classifiable as other offenses, such as assault or sex offenses. Attempts are included.

Driving under the influence—Driving or operating a motor vehicle or common carrier while mentally or physically impaired as the result of consuming an alcoholic beverage or using a drug or narcotic.

Liquor laws—The violation of state or local laws or ordinances prohibiting the manufacture, sale, purchase, transportation, possession, or use of alcoholic beverages, not including driving under the influence and drunkenness. Federal violations are excluded.

Drunkenness—To drink alcoholic beverages to the extent that one's mental faculties and physical coordination are substantially impaired. Excludes driving under the influence.

Disorderly conduct—Any behavior that tends to disturb the public peace or decorum, scandalize the community, or shock the public sense of morality.

Vagrancy—The violation of a court order, regulation, ordinance, or law requiring the withdrawal of persons from the streets or other specified areas; prohibiting persons from remaining in an area or place in an idle or aimless manner; or prohibiting persons from going from place to place without visible means of support.

All other offenses—All violations of state or local laws not specifically identified as Part I or Part II offenses, except traffic violations.

Suspicion—Arrested for no specific offense and released without formal charges being placed.

Curfew and loitering laws (persons under 18 years of age)—Violations by juveniles of local curfew or loitering ordinances.

APPENDIX IV. GEOGRAPHIC AREA DEFINITIONS

The UCR Program collects crime data and supplemental information that make it possible to generate a variety of statistical compilations, including data presented by reporting areas. These statistics enable data users to analyze local crime data in conjunction with those for areas of similar geographic location or population size. The reporting areas that the UCR Program uses in its data breakdowns include community types, population groups, and regions and divisions. For community types, the UCR Program considers proximity to metropolitan areas using the designations established by the U.S. Office of Management and Budget (OMB). (Generally, sheriffs, county police, and state police report crimes within counties but outside of cities; local police report crimes within city limits.) The number of inhabitants living in a locale (based on the U.S. Census Bureau's figures) determines the population group into which the program places it. For its geographic breakdowns, the UCR Program divides the United States into regions and divisions.

Regions and Divisions

The map below illustrates the nine divisions that make up the four regions of the United States. The UCR Program uses this widely recognized geographic organization when compiling the nation's crime data. The regions and divisions are as follows:

Northeast

New England—Connecticut, Maine, Massachusetts, New Hampshire, Rhode Island, and Vermont
Middle Atlantic—New York, New Jersey, and Pennsylvania

Midwest

East North Central—Illinois, Indiana, Michigan, Ohio, and Wisconsin

West North Central—Iowa, Kansas, Minnesota, Missouri, Nebraska, North Dakota, and South Dakota

South

South Atlantic—Delaware, District of Columbia, Florida, Georgia, Maryland, North Carolina, South Carolina, Virginia, and West Virginia

East South Central—Alabama, Kentucky, Mississippi, and Tennessee

West South Central—Arkansas, Louisiana, Oklahoma, and Texas

West

Mountain—Arizona, Colorado, Idaho, Montana, Nevada, New Mexico, Utah, and Wyoming

Pacific—Alaska, California, Hawaii, Oregon, and Washington

Community Types

To assist data users who wish to analyze and present uniform statistical data about metropolitan areas, the UCR Program uses reporting units that represent major population centers. The program compiles data for the following three types of communities:

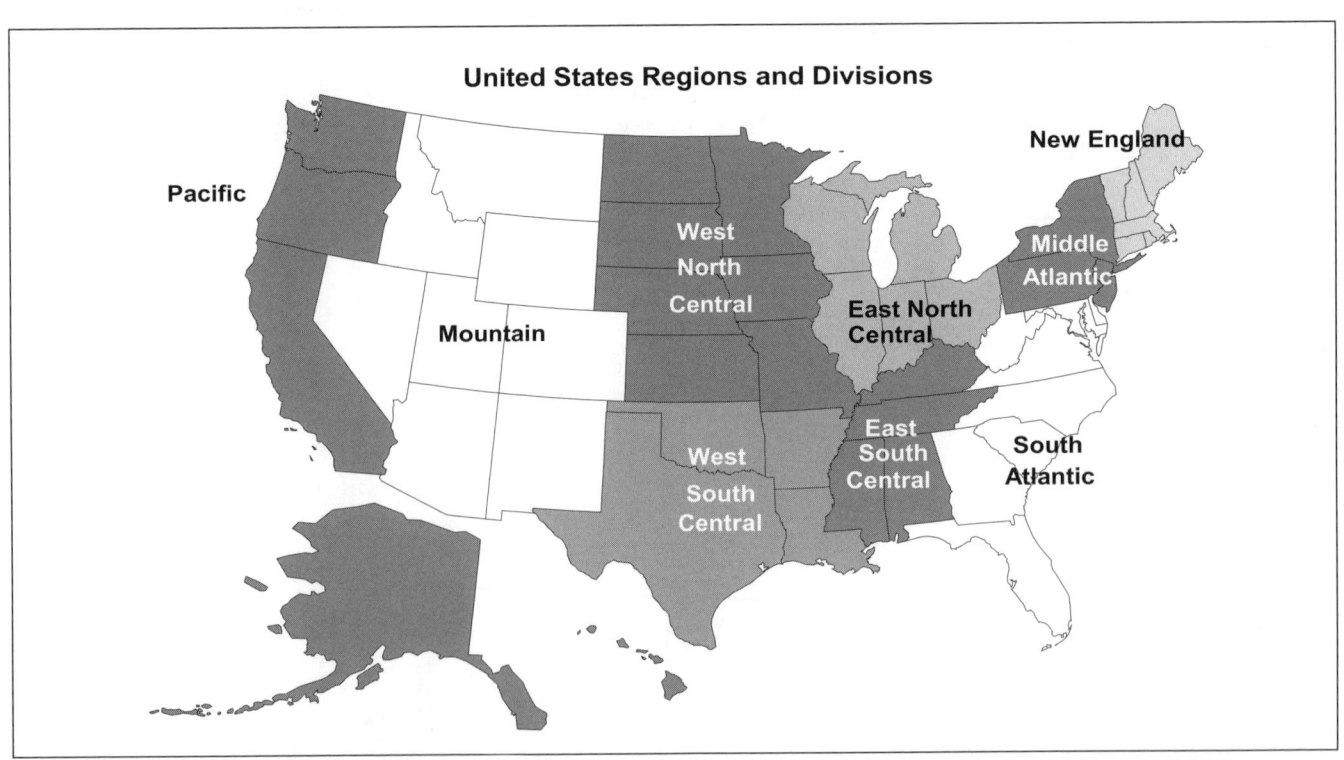

United States Regions and Divisions

Metropolitan Statistical Areas (MSAs)—Each MSA contains a principal city or urbanized area with a population of at least 50,000 inhabitants. MSAs include the principal city, the county in which the city is located, and other adjacent counties that have a high degree of economic and social integration with the principal city and county (as defined by the OMB), which is measured through commuting. In the UCR Program, counties within an MSA are considered metropolitan counties. In addition, MSAs may cross state boundaries.

In 2010, approximately 83.7 percent of the nation's population lived in MSAs. Some presentations in this publication refer to Metropolitan Divisions, which are subdivisions of an MSA that consists of a core with "a population of at least 2.5 million persons. A Metropolitan Division consists of one or more main/secondary counties that represent an employment center or centers, plus adjacent counties associated with the main county or counties through commuting ties," (*Federal Register* 65 [249]). Also, some tables reference suburban areas, which are subdivisions of MSAs that exclude the principal cities but include all the remaining cities (those having fewer than 50,000 inhabitants) and the unincorporated areas of the MSAs.

Because the elements that comprise MSAs, particularly the geographic compositions, are subject to change, the UCR Program discourages data users from making year-to-year comparisons of MSA data.

Cities Outside MSAs—Ordinarily, cities outside MSAs are incorporated areas. In 2010, cities outside MSAs made up 6.5 percent of the nation's population.

Nonmetropolitan Counties Outside MSAs—Most nonmetropolitan counties are composed of unincorporated areas. In 2010, 9.8 percent of the nation's population resided in nonmetropolitan counties.

Metropolitan and nonmetropolitan community types are further illustrated in the following table:

Metropolitan	Nonmetropolitan
Principal cities (50,000+ inhabitants) Suburban cities	Cities outside metropolitan areas
Metropolitan counties	Nonmetropolitan counties

Population Groups

The UCR Program uses the following population group designations:

Population Group	Political Label	Population Range
I	City	250,000 or more
II	City	100,000 to 249,999
III	City	50,000 to 99,999
IV	City	25,000 to 49,999
V	City	10,000 to 24,999
VI[1,2]	City	Fewer than 10,000
VIII (Nonmetropolitan county)[2]	County	N/A
IX (Metropolitan county)[2]	County	N/A

[1]Includes universities and colleges to which no population is attributed.
[2]Includes state police agencies to which no population is attributed.

Individual law enforcement agencies are the source of UCR data. The number of agencies included in each population group may vary from year to year because of population growth, geopolitical consolidation, municipal incorporation, and so on. In noncensus years, the UCR Program estimates population figures for individual jurisdictions. (A more comprehensive explanation of population estimations can be found in Appendix I.)

The categories below show the number of agencies contributing to the UCR Program within each population group for 2010:

Population Group	Number of Agencies	Population Covered
I	76	57,354,512
II	204	30,475,928
III	477	32,657,104
IV	867	29,867,508
V	1,928	30,605,315
VI[1,2]	9,434	26,499,453
VIII (Nonmetropolitan county)[2]	3,032	30,180,370
IX (Metropolitan county)[2]	2,091	70,105,348
Total	18,108	308,745,538

[1]Includes universities and colleges to which no population is attributed.
[2]Includes universities and colleges to which no population is attributed.

APPENDIX V. THE NATION'S TWO CRIME MEASURES

The Department of Justice administers two statistical programs to measure the magnitude, nature, and impact of crime in the nation: the Uniform Crime Reporting (UCR) Program and the National Crime Victimization Survey (NCVS). Each of these programs produces valuable information about aspects of the nation's crime problem. Because the UCR and NCVS programs are conducted for different purposes, use different methods, and focus on somewhat different aspects of crime, the information they produce together provides a more comprehensive panorama of the nation's crime problem than either could produce alone.

Uniform Crime Reporting (UCR) Program

The UCR Program, administered by the Federal Bureau of Investigation (FBI), was created in 1929 and collects information on the following crimes reported to law enforcement authorities: murder and nonnegligent manslaughter, forcible rape, robbery, aggravated assault, burglary, larceny-theft, motor vehicle theft, and arson. Law enforcement agencies also report arrest data for 20 additional crime categories.

The UCR Program compiles data from monthly law enforcement reports and from individual crime incident records transmitted directly to the FBI or to centralized state agencies that report to the FBI. The program thoroughly examines each report it receives for reasonableness, accuracy, and deviations that may indicate errors. Large variations in crime levels may indicate modified records procedures, incomplete reporting, or changes in a jurisdiction's boundaries. To identify any unusual fluctuations in an agency's crime counts, the program compares monthly reports to previous submissions of the agency and to those for similar agencies.

The FBI annually publishes its findings in a preliminary release in the spring of the following calendar year, followed by a detailed annual report, *Crime in the United States*, issued in the fall. (The printed copy of *Crime in the United States* is now published by Bernan Press.) In addition to crime counts and trends, this report includes data on crimes cleared, persons arrested (age, sex, and race), law enforcement personnel (including the number of sworn officers killed or assaulted), and the characteristics of homicides (including age, sex, and race of victims and offenders; victim-offender relationships; weapons used; and circumstances surrounding the homicides). Other periodic reports are also available from the UCR Program.

The state and local law enforcement agencies participating in the UCR Program are continually converting to the more comprehensive and detailed National Incident-Based Reporting System (NIBRS). The NIBRS provides detailed information about each criminal incident in 22 broad categories of offenses.

The UCR Program presents crime counts for the nation as a whole, as well as for regions, states, counties, cities, towns, tribal law enforcement areas, and colleges and universities. This allows for studies among neighboring jurisdictions and among those with similar populations and other common characteristics.

National Crime Victimization Survey

The NCVS, conducted by the Bureau of Justice Statistics (BJS), began in 1973. It provides a detailed picture of crime incidents, victims, and trends. After a substantial period of research, the BJS completed an intensive methodological redesign of the survey in 1993. It conducted this redesign to improve the questions used to uncover crime, update the survey methods, and broaden the scope of crimes measured. The redesigned survey collects detailed information on the frequency and nature of the crimes of rape, sexual assault, personal robbery, aggravated and simple assault, household burglary, theft, and motor vehicle theft. It does not measure homicide or commercial crimes (such as burglaries of stores).

Twice a year, Census Bureau personnel interview household members in a nationally representative sample of approximately 43,000 households (about 76,000 people). Approximately 150,000 interviews of individuals 12 years of age and over are conducted annually. Households stay in the sample for 3 years, and new households rotate into the sample on an ongoing basis.

The NCVS collects information on crimes suffered by individuals and households, whether or not those crimes were reported to law enforcement. It estimates the proportion of each crime type reported to law enforcement, and it summarizes the reasons that victims give for reporting or not reporting.

The survey provides information about victims (age, sex, race, ethnicity, marital status, income, and educational level); offenders (sex, race, approximate age, and victim-offender relationship); and crimes (time and place of occurrence, use of weapons, nature of injury, and economic consequences). Questions also cover victims' experiences with the criminal justice system, self-protective measures used by victims, and possible substance abuse by offenders. Supplements are added to the survey periodically to obtain detailed information on specific topics, such as school crime.

The BJS published the first data from the redesigned NCVS in a June 1995 bulletin. The publication of NCVS data includes *Criminal Victimization in the United States*, an annual report that covers the broad range of detailed information collected by the NCVS. The bureau also publishes detailed reports on topics such as crime against women, urban crime, and gun use in crime. The National Archive of

Criminal Justice Data at the University of Michigan archives the NCVS data files to help researchers perform independent analyses.

Comparing the UCR Program and the NCVS

Because the BJS designed the NCVS to complement the UCR Program, the two programs share many similarities. As much as their different collection methods permit, the two measure the same subset of serious crimes with the same definitions. Both programs cover rape, robbery, aggravated assault, burglary, theft, and motor vehicle theft; both define rape, robbery, theft, and motor vehicle theft virtually identically. (Although rape is defined analogously, the UCR Program measures the crime against women only, and the NCVS measures it against both sexes.)

There are also significant differences between the two programs. First, the two programs were created to serve different purposes. The UCR Program's primary objective is to provide a reliable set of criminal justice statistics for law enforcement administration, operation, and management. The BJS established the NCVS to provide previously unavailable information about crime (including crime not reported to police), victims, and offenders.

Second, the two programs measure an overlapping but nonidentical set of crimes. The NCVS includes crimes both reported and not reported to law enforcement. The NCVS excludes—but the UCR Program includes—homicide, arson, commercial crimes, and crimes committed against children under 12 years of age. The UCR Program captures crimes reported to law enforcement but collects only arrest data for simple assaults and sexual assaults other than forcible rape.

Third, because of methodology, the NCVS and UCR have different definitions of some crimes. For example, the UCR defines burglary as the unlawful entry or attempted entry of a structure to commit a felony or theft. The NCVS, not wanting to ask victims to ascertain offender motives, defines burglary as the entry or attempted entry of a residence by a person who had no right to be there.

Fourth, for property crimes (burglary, theft, and motor vehicle theft), the two programs calculate crime rates using different bases. The UCR Program rates for these crimes are per capita (number of crimes per 100,000 persons), whereas the NCVS rates for these crimes are per household (number of crimes per 1,000 households).

Because the number of households may not grow at the same annual rate as the total population, trend data for rates of property crimes measured by the two programs may not be comparable. In addition, some differences in the data from the two programs may result from sampling variation in the NCVS and from estimating for nonresponsiveness in the UCR Program.

The BJS derives the NCVS estimates from interviewing a sample and are, therefore, subject to a margin of error. The bureau uses rigorous statistical methods to calculate confidence intervals around all survey estimates, and describes trend data in the NCVS reports as genuine only if there is at least a 90-percent certainty that the measured changes are not the result of sampling variation. The UCR Program bases its data on the actual counts of offenses reported by law enforcement agencies. In some circumstances, the UCR Program estimates its data for nonparticipating agencies or those reporting partial data. Apparent discrepancies between statistics from the two programs can usually be accounted for by their definitional and procedural differences, or resolved by comparing NCVS sampling variations (confidence intervals) of crimes said to have been reported to police with UCR Program statistics.

For most types of crimes measured by both the UCR Program and the NCVS, analysts familiar with the programs can exclude those aspects of crime not common to both from analysis. Resulting long-term trend lines can be brought into close concordance. The impact of such adjustments is most striking for robbery, burglary, and motor vehicle theft, whose definitions most closely coincide.

With robbery, the BJS bases the NCVS victimization rates on only those robberies reported to the police. It is also possible to remove UCR Program robberies of commercial establishments, such as gas stations, convenience stores, and banks, from analysis. When users compare the resulting NCVS police-reported robbery rates and the UCR Program noncommercial robbery rates, the results reveal closely corresponding long-term trends.

Conclusion

Each program has unique strengths. The UCR Program provides a measure of the number of crimes reported to law enforcement agencies throughout the country. The program's Supplementary Homicide Reports provide the most reliable, timely data on the extent and nature of homicides in the nation. The NCVS is the primary source of information on the characteristics of criminal victimization and on the number and types of crimes not reported to law enforcement authorities.

By understanding the strengths and limitations of each program, it is possible to use the UCR Program and NCVS to achieve a greater understanding of crime trends and the nature of crime in the United States. For example, changes in police procedures, shifting attitudes towards crime and police, and other societal changes can affect the extent to which people report and law enforcement agencies record crime. NCVS and UCR Program data can be used in concert to explore why trends in reported and police-recorded crime may differ.

INDEX

INDEX